...and improve your grade in the process!

Web Connections - provide you with two or three relevant links to the internet for each of the boxes that appear within the textbook.

Internet Connections - offer direct access to the sites highlighted throughout each chapter in the Internet Connections feature. If a link in the textbook should break, this is where you would find the replacement link for that exercise.

Video Exercises - view videos that discuss the applications of sociology to everyday life and respond to what you see as the impact of that particular issue.

You can also personalize your view of the *Companion Website™* using our Browser Tune-up function, as well as communicate with other students using our Message Board and i-Chat features that are a vital part of the *Companion Website™*.

IN YOUR RESEARCH... DON'T SEARCH.... FIND!
USING ContentSelect!

As part of the **Sociology *Companion Website™*,** you now have free and unlimited access to a customized sociological database from **EBSCO**'s ContentSelect service. Whether you are looking for information for a paper or pursuing a personal interest in a topic within **Sociology**, you will have a great start to finding this information using ContentSelect.

This sociological database contains articles from over 75 leading sociological journals and publications that are known for their academic quality and their strong reputations. In an age of questionable sources, it's nice to know that you have this resource in your corner.

Use a keyword from the text to search **ContentSelect,** and watch the relevant articles come back with very little effort. Now, more time can be spent "researching" rather than searching. Plus, all articles can be downloaded and printed.

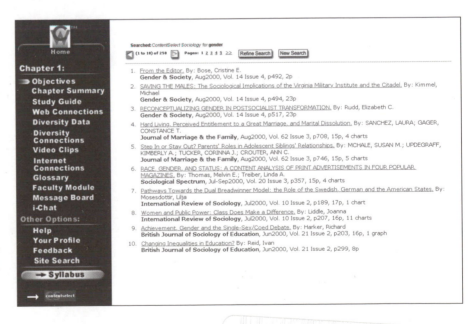

SOCIOLOGY

Second Edition

SOCIOLOGY

Linda L. Lindsey

Maryville University of St. Louis

Stephen Beach

Kentucky Wesleyan College

Prentice
Hall

Upper Saddle River, New Jersey 07458

Library of Congress Cataloging-in-Publication Data

Lindsey, Linda L.
    Sociology / Linda L. Lindsey, Stephen Beach.—2nd ed.
    p. cm.
    Includes bibliographical references and index.
    ISBN 0-13-041325-9
    1. Sociology.   I. Beach, Stephen.   II. Title

HM585.L56   2002
301—dc21   00-052412
                                                CIP

VP, Editorial director: Laura Pearson
AVP, Publisher: Nancy Roberts
Senior acquisitions editor: Christopher DeJohn
Developmental editor: Rochelle Diogenes
AVP, Editor-in-chief of development: Susanna Lesan
VP/Director of production and manufacturing:
    Barbara Kittle
Executive managing editor: Ann Marie McCarthy
Production liaison: Fran Russello
Editorial/production supervision: Bruce Hobart,
    Pine Tree Composition
Buyer: Mary Ann Gloriande
Prepress and manufacturing manager: Nick Sklitsis

Line art manager: Guy Ruggiero
Creative design director: Leslie Osher
Art director: Ximena Tamvakopoulos
Marketing manager: Beth Gillet Mejia
Editorial assistant: Christina Scalia
Interior image specialist: Beth Boyd
Manager, rights and permissions: Kay Dellosa
Director, image resource center: Melinda Reo
Photo researcher: Diana Gongora
Marketing assistant: Judie Lamb
Senior media editor: John J. Jordan
Media production manager: Maurice Murdock

This book was set in 10/12 Janson Text by Pine Tree Composition
and was printed and bound by World Color.
The cover was printed by The Lehigh Press, Inc.

Cover images: Boy playing baseball, Bill Hickey/Image Bank; young man sitting,
Color Day Production/Image Bank; two boys playing, Juan Silva/Image Bank;
senior couple, © Masterfile; couple outdoors, Larry Williams/Masterfile

 © 2002, 2000 by Prentice-Hall, Inc.
A Division of Pearson Education
Upper Saddle River, New Jersey 07458

Printed in the United States of America

10 9 8 7 6 5 4 3 2

ISBN 0-13-041325-9

PRENTICE-HALL INTERNATIONAL (UK) LIMITED, *London*
PRENTICE-HALL OF AUSTRALIA PTY. LIMITED, *Sydney*
PRENTICE-HALL CANADA INC., *Toronto*
PRENTICE-HALL HISPANOAMERICANA, S.A., *Mexico*
PRENTICE-HALL OF INDIA PRIVATE LIMITED, *New Delhi*
PRENTICE-HALL OF JAPAN, INC., *Tokyo*
PEARSON EDUCATION ASIA PTE. LTD., *Singapore*
EDITORA PRENTICE-HALL DO BRASIL, LTDA., *Rio de Janeiro*

BRIEF CONTENTS

To Joe Overton
—Linda L. Lindsey

To Edward A. Tiryakian
and John Wilson
—Stephen Beach

CONTENTS

10

ECONOMIC STRATIFICATION 238

11

SOCIAL CLASS IN MODERN
SOCIETIES   266

12

RACIAL AND ETHNIC
MINORITIES   292

EMERGING INSTITUTIONS: MEDIA AND SPORT   512

POPULATION, URBANIZATION, AND THE ENVIRONMENT   536

FORMAL ORGANIZATIONS AND THE SOCIOLOGY OF WORK   564

BOX FEATURES

Global Connections

Media Connections

Practicing Sociology

PREFACE

Sociology is about connections. The groups in which we live—our families, our peer groups, or our societies—connect us to one another in profound ways. We are also connected by the explosion of information technology and the Internet, still in its infancy, that has transformed the globe. At the same time, our membership in these groups creates a diversity that helps us explore and celebrate how and why we are different from people in other groups. We are diverse because we are female or male, African American or Native American, rich or poor, young or old, gay or straight. We are also diverse because we are Catholic or Muslim, urban or rural, born in the developed or developing world. Diversity is what's happening globally as well as in the United States. Groups are more diverse yet more connected to one another than at any other time in human history. The second edition of *Sociology* emphasizes this reality and encourages students to grasp the three-dimensional nature of these connections. The fundamental goal of the text is to take students on a sociological journey through the United States and across the globe that clearly shows how social diversity and social connections profoundly influence their lives.

TEXT FEATURES

Students become excited about sociology through the introductory course. We have developed a text that forges a partnership between professors who teach the course and their students, who are its ultimate beneficiaries. Through its distinctive approach to the field, its readability and its relevance to students' lives, the second edition of *Sociology* assists professors in developing the sociological imagination in their students by encouraging them to see all dimensions of sociology. Material is presented in ways that allow students to become active learners and help professors translate the sociological perspective to the classroom.

In telling sociology's story to students, each author brings over 20 years of teaching the introductory sociology course to a variety of students, in large and small classes, and at a variety of institutions. The text, therefore, is grounded in teaching. The following text features demonstrate this foundation.

New Features. *Sociology, Second Edition,* updates data in all content areas and reflects the most important trends currently affecting society.

- This edition enlarges the scope of global diversity. Sociology's message about diversity is contained in every chapter and easily discovered through many highlighted sections. These include discussing minority relations in Northern Ireland and Germany (Chapter 12), which emphasizes connections among religion, race, and nationality; profiling America's major religious groups according to gender, class, and race (Chapter 17); demonstrating the intersection of class and race in suburbia (Chapter 18); and understanding why linking race, class, and gender is a better way to explain health and mental illness (Chapter 19).
- There has been an explosion of research showing that sexuality is interwoven into the social fabric and that people experience sexuality according to the diverse groups to which they belong. To reflect this new research, a new chapter on sexuality is included in this edition. This chapter emphasizes material that is relevant to college students, such as the exploration of sexuality, the sexual double standard, date rape, and sexual violence.
- To highlight the emergence of the Internet as a major tool for teaching sociology, all chapters have a new Internet feature, Internet Connections, that can accompany lectures and serve as springboards for discussion.
- To focus on the applied side of sociology, new boxes on "Practicing Sociology" are featured.

Theoretical Applications. Theory is the core of sociology. The major sociological perspectives are introduced in Chapter 1 and are applied throughout the text. This edition reflects an expanded discussion of the feminist theoretical perspective and includes it throughout the text to extend coverage and explanations of diversity. Most chapters feature separate theory sections integrated with many research examples. Theoretical perspectives are applied repeatedly throughout the text. This approach helps students make connections between theory and their own lives, as reflected in the text's discussion of human sexuality (Chapter 7) and deviant behavior (Chapter 8). This text is thus both student friendly and sociologically rigorous.

Life Connections. Focusing on diversity, all chapters have a "Life Connections" section highlighting recent research on multicultural life in the United

States. This material was carefully chosen to reflect the latest trends in the various social institutions that are especially relevant for college students. Topics include American socialization through family, peers, and media; how gender, race, and class affect socialization (Chapters 5, 11, and 12); college life as an exploration of sexuality (Chapter 7); why crime rates are dropping (Chapter 9); how schools are preparing to educate America's new majority, students of color (Chapter 16); and how social movement activists are trained (Chapter 23).

Society Connections.   Students are also shown the relevance of the sociological perspective by connecting broader social issues to their personal lives, as found in the "Society Connections" sections in all chapters. Many of these sections also highlight the global context of personal lives, regardless of where we call home. Issues such as sexual harassment (Chapter 6), welfare reform (Chapter 10), the crisis in health care (Chapter 19), and population control (Chapter 21) are discussed. These sections remind students that they are connected to one another through social groups—whether members of the groups or not—and that groups often clash when they have different visions of diversity and social change.

Emerging Institutions.   Social change is transforming the globe. *Sociology, Second Edition*, highlights important trends that are engines for change through the creation of new social institutions. Chapter 18 shows government and the economy converging into a new and powerful social institution, the political economy. In Chapter 20, we witness the evolution of new institutions based on sports and media that serve leisure needs. Social change is also occurring on a social psychological level; examples include how girls and boys are socialized differently (Chapter 5) and how children interact with peers from the other gender (Chapter 6).

Focus on the Developing World.   The spotlight of global interdependence is now on the developing world. This text offers current information on social change and development derived from a variety of sources, including the World Bank, the United Nations, and non-governmental organizations throughout the world. This material provides insights into a host of issues, such as why crime rates vary cross-culturally (Chapter 9), how women are affected by economic development programs (Chapter 13), how population growth and urbanization affect the environment (Chapter 21), and why some nations choose to actively resist modernization (Chapter 24).

TEACHING TOOLS

Sociology, Second Edition, offers a variety of innovative teaching tools located throughout the text to help students see the relevance of course material to their own lives.

Boxed Features.   Every chapter includes features that provide in-depth views of relevant topics based on recent research. These features end with critical thinking questions that serve as springboards for class discussion. There are five types of features in this edition.

- *U.S. in Focus* features present data and issues relevant to the United States, many with a focus on diversity. Examples include: "The Sexualization of America," "Informal Social Control: Shunned at Berkeley," "African Americans Move Back South," "America's Violent Schools," and "Up in Smoke: The Cigar Craze."
- *Practicing Sociology* features show how sociological knowledge can be applied to a variety of settings, including the workplace. Examples include: "What Can I Do with a Degree in Sociology?"; schools, "Pygmalion in the Classroom"; and corporations, "The Business of Consumer Research."
- *Then & Now* features highlight historical facts to show students connections between social change and modern life. For example, the effect of diversity on contemporary sociology is discussed in "Rediscovering Sociology's Diverse Roots," "The Tuskegee Experiment" views changing research ethics, and "Childhood Innocence or a World of Little Adults?" discusses how the meaning of childhood has been transformed. Other features that college students will find especially interesting are "Changing Styles of Campus Deviance," "Women's Basketball: Before & After Title IX," and "Careers in the 21st Century."
- *Media Connections* features highlight the growing influence of the information age on our attitudes and behavior. Examples include how a traditional culture made use of the media to save itself from extinction, "The Kayapo Meet the Press"; the influence of media on our self-image and our views of others, "The Good, the Bad and the Ugly"; controversies about popular music, "Sex, Drugs, and Rock 'n' Roll"; and the increasing use of the Internet by the elderly in "Senior citizen.com."
- *Global Connections* features offer comparative perspectives on important issues that may affect us differently depending on our culture, such as euthanasia, "Planning for Death in the Netherlands"; the pressure to achieve, "Examination

Hell in Japan"; and the difference that social class makes, "Upper-Middle Class Culture in the U.S. and France." Global Connections boxes also allow students to use other cultures as mirrors to discover what they take for granted in their own cultures. Examples include women and religion, "Rediscovering the Feminine Face of God"; women as a commodity, "Dowry and the Worth of a New Bride"; and how religion impacts all parts of life, "Religious Law in Iran."

Diversity Data. All chapters include graphs illustrating current data from the National Opinion Research Center (NORC) General Social Survey. These graphs are strategically placed to complement and extend chapter material. Each graph is summarized and includes critical thinking questions allowing students to explore various sociological interpretations of the data. The diversity data feature emphasizes the ways in which race, class, and gender affect a person's attitudes. Graphs also show the interactive effects of multiple types of diversity. Examples include level of support for busing by race; the influence of age and gender on health; how age and race influence attitudes about urban spending; and whether belief in God varies by gender and race.

Internet Connections. In every chapter, placed to coincide with chapter content, students are offered creative Internet-based exercises. The Internet offers an amazing array of sociological material that both student and professor will find exciting, such as Web sites devoted to the exotic Nacireman culture, to the surprising habits of the baby boom generation, and to how colleges are ranked by quality.

Key Terms. Key terms are highlighted in each chapter, reviewed in other chapters, and defined in a glossary at the end of the book. The book also introduces a number of newer concepts and theories that are emerging in the sociological literature, such as end-point fallacy, classism, non-governmental organizations, gender schema theory, and rational choice theory.

Critical Thinking Questions. Found at the end of each chapter and in all boxes, Internet, and Diversity Data features, these thought-provoking questions move beyond description and allow students to apply their sociological imaginations in a variety of ways. For example, students may be asked to demonstrate how the same research can be explained by different theories. These questions can be easily adapted as the basis for class discussion and debating points for an entire chapter.

Sociology, Second Edition, interweaves a distinctive approach to sociology focusing on social connections and diversity with learning tools explicitly designed to engage students and make sociology relevant to their lives. As symbolized by the interwoven multicolored ribbons used as a design element, the text emphasizes sociology's central lesson: we are irrevocably connected to one another.

The ancillary materials that accompany *Sociology, Second Edition,* have been carefully created to enhance the topics being discussed. Please contact your school's Prentice Hall representative for more information or to order copies for your classroom use upon adoption.

FOR THE INSTRUCTOR

Instructor's Resource Manual. For each chapter in the text, this resource provides a detailed outline, list of objectives, discussion questions, and additional activities.

Test Item File. This carefully prepared resource, available in both print and computerized form, includes 2,400 questions—100 per chapter—in multiple choice, true/false, and essay formats. The answers to all questions are page-referenced to the text. Prentice Hall Custom Test is a computerized test generator designed to allow the creation of personalized exams. It is available in Windows and Macintosh formats. Prentice Hall also provides a test preparation service to users of this text that is as easy as one call to our toll-free 800 number.

Film/Video Guide, 6/E. This helpful guide describes films and videos appropriate for classroom viewing for each of the chapters in the text (more than 200 suggestions in all). The Guide also provides summaries, discussion questions, and rental sources for each film and video.

Prentice Hall Color Transparencies: Sociology Series VI. Full color illustrations, charts, other visual materials, including all of the Diversity Data graphs, from the text as well as outside sources have been selected to make up this useful in-class tool.

Prentice Hall Instructor's Guide to Transparencies, Series VI. This guide offers suggestions for using each transparency effectively in the classroom.

Prentice Hall Introductory Sociology Power Point Slides. Created by Roger J. Eich of Hawkeye Community College, this PowerPoint slide set combines graphics and text in a colorful format to help convey sociological principles in a new and exciting way. Created in PowerPoint, an easy-to-use widely available software program, this set contains over 300 content slides keyed to each chapter in the text.

ABCNEWS ABC News/Prentice Hall Video Library for Sociology.

Prentice Hall and ABC News are working together to bring you the best and most comprehensive video ancillaries available for your introductory course. Selected video segments from award-winning ABC News programs such as *Nightline, ABC World News Tonight,* and *20/20* accompany topics featured in each chapter. In addition, an instructor's guide to the videos includes a synopsis of video and discussion questions to help students focus on how concepts and theories apply to real-life situations.

Volume I: Social Stratification I (0-13-466228-8)
Volume II: Marriage/Families I (0-13-209537-8)
Volume III: Race/Ethnic Relations (0-13-458506-2)
Volume IV: Criminology (0-13-375163-5)
Volume V: Social Problems I (0-13-437823-7)
Volume VI: Intro to Sociology I (0-13-095066-1)
Volume VII: Intro to Sociology II (0-13-095060-2)
Volume VIII: Intro to Sociology III (0-13-095773-9)
Volume IX: Social Problems II (0-13-095774-7)
Volume X: Marriage/Families II (0-13-095775-5)
Volume XI: Social Stratification II (0-13-021134-6)
Volume XII: Institutions (0-13-021133-8)
Volume XIII: Introductory Sociology IV
    (0-13-018507-8)
Volume XIV: Introductory Sociology V
    (0-13-018509-4)

Distance Learning Solutions. Prentice Hall is committed to providing our leading content to the growing number of courses being delivered over the Internet by developing relationships with the leading platforms—Blackboard™ and Web CT™, as well as CourseCompass, Prentice Hall's own easy-to-use course management system powered by Blackboard™. Please visit our technology solutions website at http://www.prenhall.com/demo for more information or contact your local Prentice Hall representative.

FOR THE STUDENT

Study Guide. This complete guide helps students review and reflect on the material presented in the text. Each of the chapters in the study guide provides an overview of the corresponding chapter in the student text, summarizes its major topics and concepts,

offers relevant exercises, and features end-of-the-chapter quizzes with solutions.

Lindsey/Beach Premium *Companion Website*™. In tandem with the text, students and professors can take full advantage of the World Wide Web to enrich the learning process in sociology. Features of the Web site include chapter objectives, chapter summaries, quizzes, flash cards, animations, interactive exercises, as well as hundreds of links to interesting material and information from other sites on the Web that can reinforce and enhance the content of each chapter. The address is www.prenhall.com/lindsey and it can be visited using the access code packaged with this new textbook.

The New York Times/**Prentice Hall Themes of the Times for Introductory Sociology.** *The New York Times* and Prentice Hall are sponsoring *Themes of the Times*, a program designed to enhance student access to current information relevant to the classroom. Through this program, the core subject matter provided in this text is supplemented by a collection of timely articles from one of the world's most distinguished newspapers, *The New York Times.* These articles demonstrate the vital, ongoing connection between what is learned in the classroom and what is happening in the world around us.

To enjoy the wealth of information of *The New York Times* daily, a reduced subscription rate is available. For information, call toll-free: 1-800-631-1222.

Prentice Hall and *The New York Times* are proud to co-sponsor *Themes of the Times.* We hope it will make the reading of both textbooks and newspapers a more dynamic, involving process.

ContentSelect Research Database. Prentice Hall and EBSCO, the world leader in online journal subscription management, have developed a customized research database for students of sociology. The database provides free and unlimited access to the text of over 75 peer-reviewed sociology publications through this book's *Companion Website*™, which is accessed using the access code within this new textbook.

10 Ways to Fight Hate. This brochure is produced by the Southern Poverty Law Center, the leading hate-crime and crime-watch organization in the United States. It walks students through 10 steps that they can take on their own campus or within their own communities to fight hate on an everyday basis. It can be packaged for free with this textbook.

Sociology on the Internet: Evaluating Online Resources, 2001.

The guide provides a brief introduction to navigating the Internet, along with references related specifically to the discipline of sociology and information on how to use the *Companion Website™* for *Sociology, Second Edition*. This supplementary book is free to students when packaged with *Sociology, Second Edition*.

Critical Thinking Audiocassette Tape.

In keeping with the critical thinking coverage within the text, a sixty-minute audiotape is available to encourage students to think and to read more critically.

ACKNOWLEDGMENTS

Because of the monumental effort by the editors and staff of Prentice Hall, this edition was completed on time and continues to reflect the highest standards of textbook publishing in all its phases. Prentice Hall provided us with the peer reviews, editorial comments, and suggestions for reorganizing and updating material that nurtured our writing skills and creativity. We would particularly like to thank Chris DeJohn for overseeing the second edition from start to finish. Chris's continued support and enthusiasm for our work on this edition are sincerely appreciated. Publisher Nancy Roberts was always available to patiently listen and to offer encouraging words when time was short and deadlines loomed. Developmental editor Rochelle Diogenes provided insightful chapter reviews, recommendations for chapter organization, and suggestions for innovative content areas that certainly increased the quality of *Sociology, 2/E*. Editor-in-Chief of Development Susanna Lesan ensured that all the pieces fit together and that authors, editors, and staff remained partners in the production process. Editorial Assistant Christina Scalia juggled a myriad of production tasks, yet assured that material was sent and questions were promptly answered. Fran Russello, Prentice Hall's liaison, and Bruce Hobart, of Pine Tree Composition, expertly managed an extremely tight production schedule. Guy Ruggiero brought to life the Diversity Data graphs throughout the book. Ximena Tamvakopoulos created a design that reinforces and enhances the strengths of this book. We would also like to thank Beth Gillett Mejia and Judie Lamb for managing the marketing of the book. Finally, we would also like to thank the Prentice Hall folks who present the book to our colleagues.

Linda Lindsey would like to thank colleagues who reviewed portions of the manuscript for both editions, including Sarah Boggs (University of Missouri-St. Louis), Phil Loughlin and Larry Grieshaber (Maryville University), Walter Brumm (California University of Pennsylvania), Gerry James Jobes, and Glenn Walker. Faculty and administrative colleagues at Maryville also provided encouragement for the project and, along with those mentioned above, I would like to thank Kent Bausman, Tom Bratkowski, Sally Harris, Pat Thro, and Margie Wade. Other Maryville staff provided much assistance at various stages of the project, including Betty Bockhorst, Juanita Aycock, and Carol Trauth. A special thanks to friends and family who gave me needed and much appreciated ongoing support and advice for many months, including Marsha Balluff, Betty Buck, Cheryl Hazel, Nancy Hume, Morris Levin, Ruth Lindsey, Phil Loughlin, Jim Massey, Bill Nagel, and Wayne Spohr. The St. Louis Bread Company in Kirkwood continues as my place of refuge to reflect and re-energize, and I thank their staff, especially Amanda, Berlinda, Jen, and Stella for the wonderful setting they provide.

Steve Beach would like to thank a number of people who have contributed over the years to his professional and personal development. In particular, the following individuals played an important role in his evolution as a sociologist: Sanford Dornbusch, Gordon Craig, Edward A. Tiryakian, John Wilson, Joel Smith, Kurt Back, Alan Kerckhoff, John McKinney, Marian Kilson, Audie Blevins, Saul Feinman, Garth Massey, Marilyn and Tom Carroll, Margaret Britton, Linda Lindsey, and Bill Conroy. He would also like to acknowledge the personal support of the following true friends: Jim and Mike Beach, Laura Anderson, Mike Stoller, Larry and Ann Byler, John Forester, John and Eva Bacon, John Goodrich, Nancy Meyer, Elaine Bodurtha, Jeff and Jenny Skinner, Dorothy Ann Lynch, Joann Spillman, Cheryl Daniels, Paul and Jeannie McCarthy, Bob Powell, Paul Leonard, Corky Carrel, Dianne Echohawk, Ken Ayers, Mike Fagan, Billy Long, Shana Pack, Matt Schoenbachler, Jim Welch and all of the members of Stanford-in-Germany Group XIII.

William Aho	Rhode Island College
Robert Anwyl	Miami-Dade Community College
John Arthur	University of Minnesota
Robert Bausch	Cameron University
Jane Bock	University of Wisconsin–Green Bay
Jane A. Brown	Case Western Reserve University
Daniel Cervi	West Virginia University
Glenna Colclough	University of Alabama at Huntsville

Yvonne Downs	State University of New York at Fredonia	Gregory D. Squires	University of Wisconsin at Milwaukee
Lois Easterly	Onondaga Community College	Eric Swank	Morehead State University
Lynn England	Brigham Young University	Gail A. Thoen	University of Minnesota
Norman Goodman	State University of New York at Stony Brook	Tami Videon	Rutgers University
		J. Allen Williams, Jr.	University of Nebraska–Lincoln
C. Allen Haney	University of Houston	Ronald Wohlstein	Eastern Illinois University
Alexander Hicks	Emory University	Richard E. Yinger	Palm Beach Community College
Dwight Landua	Southeastern Oklahoma State University		
Richard Paulman	Frostburg State University		
Harland Prechel	Texas A&M University	L.L.L	
Ferris Ritchey	University of Alabama–Birmingham	St. Louis, Missouri	
Luis Salinas	Houston Community College	S.B. Owensboro, Kentucky	

ABOUT THE AUTHORS

Professor Linda L. Lindsey received her B.A. from the University of Missouri, St. Louis and her M.A. and Ph.D. from Case Western Reserve University. She is the author of *Gender Roles: Sociological Perspectives, Third Edition*, (Prentice Hall) and has also written various articles and conference papers on women in development, health and healthcare issues, refugees, internationalizing the sociology curriculum, and minority women in Asia, especially in China. Her major interest, both personally and professionally, is the developing world. She has traveled extensively in pursuing her research and teaching interests, especially in conjunction with the Asian Studies Development Program, a joint program of the East-West Center and University of Hawaii. While home in St. Louis she enjoys swimming and hiking and is active in community service groups focusing on advocacy concerning women and children. Dr. Lindsey is currently Professor of Sociology at Maryville University of St. Louis.

Professor Stephen Beach received his A.B. in history from Stanford University, where he participated in a six-month overseas study program in Germany. He received his M.A. and his Ph.D. in sociology from Duke University, having spent a year researching social movement dynamics in Belfast, Northern Ireland. His primary sociological specialties include the sociology of religion and social movements. His personal interests include film, folk and rock music, and progressive politics. He shares his apartment with a large grey cat named Murgatroyd. Professor Beach is an Associate Professor of Sociology at Kentucky Wesleyan College.

 **1** # THE SOCIOLOGICAL PERSPECTIVE

OUTLINE

Sociologists are men and women who are fascinated by human social life and who actively strive to understand why people behave as they do. The topics that sociologists study vary from the routines of everyday life to the great transformations that remake our world. Here are a few recent news items that any sociologist would probably find interesting:

Seattle, Washington

Tens of thousands of activists took to the streets in mid-December of 1999 to protest a meeting of the World Trade Organization, an international agency that they accused of working on behalf of powerful multinational corporations and against the interests of the world's poor people. Graying veterans of the social movements of the 1960s and 1970s were enthralled, convinced that the heady days of their youth had returned. But this was not your father's protest.

For one thing, the Seattle demonstrations were coordinated over the Internet, not by means of flyers run off on mimeograph machines. That meant that participants could be drawn from all over the country and the world, not just from the Seattle area. In addition, the crowds were far more diverse than they had been in the days of the civil rights movement and the Vietnam War protests. Teamsters and steelworkers mingled with environmentalists, feminists, animal rights activists, and anarchists. Tactics ranged from peaceful demonstrations to guerilla violence. In the end, the protesters succeeded in disrupting the WTO meetings, but at a cost of over $3 million in property damage (Elliott, 2000; Klee, 2000).

Sociologists wonder why large-scale protests have reappeared on the American scene after decades of relative quiet. How are they led? Who joins them? How do they differ from earlier waves of protest? Will the new century see a rebirth of political activism?

Tokyo, Japan

In most ways, Japan is a model post-industrial society, but it lags behind virtually every other modern nation in providing equal rights to women. Gender inequality is especially evident in the workplace. Only one out of every thousand corporate executives in Japan is female, and more than 95 percent of business managers are male. In 1990, the average salary earned by women in Japan was precisely half of that earned by men. The comparable figure for the United States was 74 percent. Ninety-seven percent of the workers on career tracks in Japanese businesses are male.

Discrimination against Japanese women is so pervasive that it has even affected the divorce rate, which is the lowest in the developed world. Women in Japan tend to stay married, even if their family life is deeply unsatisfying, because of a lack of decent employment opportunities for women, because very few men are willing to marry divorced women, and because welfare benefits for female-headed single parent families are extremely low (Kerbo & McKinstry, 1998: 66–68).

Sociologists wonder why Japanese society has been so slow to offer equal rights to women. Will the wage gap narrow in coming decades? What are the prospects for the growth of a Japanese feminist movement?

Springfield, Illinois

In September 1998, just two days before Anthony Porter was scheduled to die by lethal injection for a double homicide committed sixteen years earlier, the Illinois Supreme Court issued a stay of execution on the grounds that Porter, an African American man with an IQ of 51, might not have been mentally competent to stand trial. He was still on Death Row, awaiting retrial, when another man confessed to shooting the victims over a drug dispute. A joyful Porter exclaimed, "Nobody but God did this!"

Porter had been helped by a group of college students at Northwestern University. As a classroom assignment, several of them had analyzed the records of the case, reenacted the crime, and concluded that the evidence just didn't add up. With the aid of a private detective, they located witnesses who said the police had pressured them to give false testimony. Faced with the new evidence, the real murderer made a videotaped confession to the detective. Porter was the tenth man removed from Death Row since 1976 in Illinois alone (McCormick, 1999).

Sociologists wonder whether the death penalty is an effective deterrent. Is its application racially biased? How many innocent people have been executed? Will the United States eventually follow the lead of most European nations and abandon capital punishment?

As these accounts suggest, sociology is strongly oriented toward the study of social issues such as capital punishment, the growth of the world economy, and the gender gap in wages. It pays special attention to how women, minorities, the elderly, and the poor are treated in society. And it is increasingly global in its scope, recognizing the escalating interdependence of people everywhere in the world.

WHAT IS SOCIOLOGY?

Some disciplines are best defined by their subject matter: Botanists study plants; political scientists study government. But sociology is quite different. As a glance at the table of contents of this text will readily illustrate, sociologists study a very broad range of topics. What makes the field distinctive is primarily its *perspective*, its way of interpreting human behavior, rather than its specific subject matter. Sociology is, then, at its core, less a body of research findings than a type of consciousness (Berger, 1963).

Formally defined, **sociology** is the scientific study of human social behavior. Sociology begins with the observation that social life displays certain basic regularities. Further, it assumes that social factors—rather than biological or psychological ones—are especially useful in explaining these regularities. Thus, sociologists focus on how individual behavior is shaped by factors such as the influence of the groups to which we belong (such as families, juvenile gangs, or protest movements), the social categories in which we are located (such as race, gender, age, or social class), and how we are taught to behave by those with whom we interact. Sociologists also pay attention to how people actively create groups; collectively define the meaning of being Hispanic or white, old or young, rich or poor, male or female; and establish and communicate rules for behavior. In other words, sociology views individuals and society as mutually influencing each other. People create the society in which they live, and at the same time, they are shaped by it.

The sociological perspective does not focus on individuals in isolation, but rather on the impact of social forces on human behavior. Sociologists study *collectivities* such as groups, organizations, and whole societies. It is a fundamental theme of the sociological perspective that the characteristics of a social group cannot be directly predicted from the qualities of the individuals who make it up (Lemert, 1997). For example, people often become frustrated with bureaucracies and criticize individual employees for seeming cold and uninterested. In fact, on their own time these workers may well be warm and caring people, but they must act impersonally at work because they are part of an organization whose basic rules and structure require that they behave in a very formal fashion.

Many people tend to lose track of the importance of social forces and come to believe that they alone shape their lives (Bellah et al., 1985; Babbie, 1994).

These youthful demonstrators were among the thousands who took to the streets of Seattle in December of 1999 to protest against the World Trade Organization.

Such individuals would benefit by developing a *sociological imagination*, a term first used by C. Wright Mills (1959). He defined it as an understanding of the relationship between larger social factors and people's personal lives. Without employing the sociological imagination, we may fail to recognize the true origins and character of the problems we face and we may be unable to respond to them effectively.

Mills differentiates between *personal troubles*, which result from individual failings, and *social issues*, which are caused by larger social factors. For example, many years ago when divorce was quite uncommon, it was generally understood as a personal trouble caused by individualistic factors such as adultery; its remedy required that the particular individuals involved in a marriage change, perhaps through some form of counseling or therapy. Today divorce is widespread, and although personal factors and individualistic solutions remain relevant in specific cases, divorce in this country has become a social issue, influenced by social trends such as the increasing availability of jobs that pay well enough to allow women to support themselves if they choose to leave bad marriages and the greater acceptance of divorced individuals by society in general—two factors that, significantly, are *not* as common in low-divorce Japan as they are in the United States. From this perspective, it does not make sense to assume that the only way to lower the divorce rate is to concentrate on individuals' failings. If we wish to respond to such social issues as divorce, crime, pollution, or poverty, we must use the sociological imagination in order to identify and change the collective as well as the individual causes of these problems.

THE SOCIOLOGICAL PERSPECTIVE

The sociological perspective—the way sociologists view social life—has several important qualities: It employs the scientific method, it encourages people to *debunk* or be skeptical of conventional explanations of social life, it directs our attention to social diversity with a special emphasis on race and gender, and it displays a strong global orientation.

Sociology as a Science

When we say that sociology is a science, we mean that sociologists collect information about social reality following a rather specific set of research procedures (to be discussed in detail in Chapter 2) that are designed to ensure that their conclusions are as accurate as is humanly possible (Salkind, 2000). This does not

mean that sociologists are always right, but it does mean that, for example, if your roommate tells you that capital punishment is an effective deterrent to crime and you hear the opposite from your sociology professor, you would be wiser to believe your professor, because in most cases sociologists base their claims on systematic, scientific research, not on casual observation, stereotypes, hearsay, or tradition (Berrick, 1995).

Science is a way of seeking knowledge that relies on the careful, systematic, and repeated collection and analysis of **empirical evidence**—data that derive directly from observation and experience, not from conjecture, intuition, or hearsay. Thus, as scientists, sociologists do not study phenomena that are not subject to empirical observation, such as angels or demons. Sociologists also do not address questions such as "What is the best form of government?" because it is impossible for everyone to agree on what "the best" means. They do, however, study topics like why so many minorities have been successful in professional sports or whether the wage gap between Japanese men and women is declining, because

Early TV sitcoms like Father Knows Best *presented an idealized image of the American family that appeals to members of groups like the Promise Keepers. Sociologists doubt that many real families of the 1950s and early 1960s were as idyllic as TV programs made them appear.*

questions like these can be answered through empirical research.

Sociologists normally study a number of cases so that their findings can be extended or *generalized* fairly broadly. This process of generalization allows researchers to apply the same fundamental explanations to many different specific cases. Thus they would start an investigation of a topic such as minority involvement in big-time athletics by studying many different instances of minority participation in sports—if possible, in different places and at different times. Such studies do in fact demonstrate that minority athletes have been highly successful in recent decades (Coakley, 1998).

However, sociologists' ultimate goal in conducting research, as is always the case in science, is not just to find out the facts, but to go further and uncover the *causes* of the regular behavior patterns that have been identified. This is an important point. Sociologists are never content with just describing social life, and they are never satisfied with the claim that things just happen. They always assume that some causal factors, normally social ones, can be found to explain why things are as they are (Bourdeau et al., 1991).

This means that after careful empirical research has identified a pattern or regularity in social life, sociologists must develop a theory that explains this pattern (Collins, 1989; Cuzzort & King, 1995). In sociology, as in all science, a **theory** is an explanation of the relationship between specific facts.

Regarding the involvement of minorities in professional sports, sociologists might start constructing an explanatory theory by noting that performance in sports is subject to very precise measurement. If a

Sociologists are interested in identifying the social factors that help explain why minority athletes such as tennis champion Venus Williams have been exceptionally successful in college and professional sports.

baseball player hits .350, he or she is obviously successful. This is true regardless of the individual's race. Measures of success in other fields, like business or medicine, are much less objective. Even prejudiced people must acknowledge the talent of a .350 hitter, whereas their biased perceptions might lead them to ignore and devalue the skills of minorities in more subjective activities such as music or even medicine.

Given these realities, sociologists might go on to further theorize that minorities may put extra effort into sports because they know that their athletic talents are likely to be recognized. In addition, they can see many successful role models in professional athletics, whereas until recently there were relatively few successful minority businesspeople or doctors. These factors encourage minorities to participate in sport as a means of obtaining upward social mobility.

Theories in sociology are thus based on empirical research and aim to identify the underlying causes of social behavior. In addition, they must always be testable and subject to possible refutation. The ultimate aim of any sociological theory is to allow us to make accurate predictions about people's future behavior.

The classic example of the interplay of research and theory in sociology is a study of the causes of suicide conducted by the late-nineteenth-century French scholar Émile Durkheim (Durkheim, 1966). Writing in an era when sociology was just beginning to establish itself as a science, Durkheim chose to research suicide precisely because it was widely believed at the time that this act was caused entirely by nonsocial factors, especially psychological ones.

Durkheim did not deny that *individuals* who commit suicide may be suffering from psychological problems, but as a sociologist he directed his attention to seeking an explanation for how the *collective* suicide rate varied from group to group. He started by carefully obtaining factual information on the subject. The data showed, among other things, that there were markedly higher suicide rates in geographical areas that were primarily Protestant rather than Catholic; for single people as opposed to married people; and for city dwellers as opposed to people who lived in small towns.

Focusing in on the religious factor, he then asked what it was about being Catholic that might tend to lower the suicide rate; in other words, he sought to develop a theory. What is it, he asked, about the social reality of being Protestant that seems to lead to high suicide rates in heavily Protestant areas?

Both religions overtly discourage suicide. But Durkheim observed that, on the average, Catholics interacted more frequently with other Catholics than

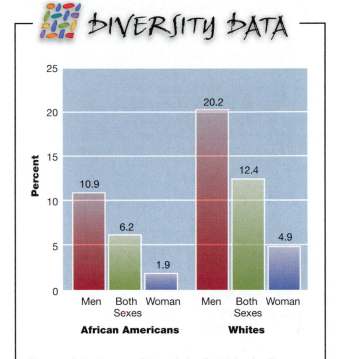

DIVERSITY DATA

FIGURE 1.1   Rates of Death by Suicide, by Race and Sex, for the United States. These figures for suicide in the United States show that fewer women than men commit suicide, and that fewer African Americans than whites of either sex commit suicide.
Source: U.S. National Center for Health Statistics (1999).

To view an interactive version of each of the Diversity Data graphs in this textbook, please visit the Companion Website for this book at http://:www.prenhall.com/lindsey and select the appropriate chapter.

Protestants interacted with other Protestants. In part this pattern resulted from the stronger emphasis within Catholicism on regular church attendance; in part it resulted from the larger number of church-related voluntary associations, like youth groups or the Knights of Columbus, that were available in his era to Catholics, and in part it simply reflected the typically larger size of the Catholic family. Together, these factors meant that, compared with Protestants, Catholics tended to display higher levels of sustained involvement with other people—a quality that Durkheim called *social integration*. He concluded that more frequent interaction with like-minded others—with people who can continually remind us that suicide is bad—provided a sociological explanation for the observed differences in suicide rates between Catholics and Protestants.

Durkheim and other researchers tested and extended his initial theory by comparing the suicide rates among other groups of Catholics and Protestants and by comparing rates among other highly socially integrated groups, like married people and those who live in small towns, with the rates that are typical of less well-integrated people, such as those who are single and live in large cities. The findings of such research have quite consistently supported the original theory. Suicide rates tend to vary with the level of social integration.

Note carefully that these findings refer to *collective* rather than individual behavior patterns. Durkheim's work shows that some groups are likely to have higher suicide rates than others, all other factors being equal, but we must not mechanically apply group-level findings to particular individuals—a logical error known as the **ecological fallacy.** The fact that Joan is a Protestant does have some effect on her individual chances of killing herself, but at the individual level this effect is limited. After all, most people, whatever their religion, do not commit suicide. If we commit the ecological fallacy—if we say that because, *as a group,* Asian Americans tend to do well in school, then Kevin, a Chinese American, *will* necessarily have high grades—we are simply stereotyping, not doing sociology.

What about free will? The logic of scientific sociology does suggest that human behavior is caused, or at least influenced, by social factors such as the level of social integration, but the effects are often indirect. Being Protestant or unmarried does increase the likelihood that one will choose to commit suicide, but each individual still makes a choice. That choice is not completely free—it is influenced by a multitude of factors—but it is still, ultimately, a choice. For this reason, all sociological theories are *probabilistic* or *conditional*: They predict future behavior, but they are always phrased in terms such as "given certain specified social conditions, a particular outcome is likely" rather than in claims such as "given certain specified social conditions, a particular outcome will occur." Human beings are not robots—but they are also not unaffected by those around them (Wrong, 1961).

Scientific, research-based theories are not the only way to explain why people act as they do. We can derive useful insights from poetry and drama, from philosophy and theology. But because sociological theories are based in careful empirical research, they are generally more precise and more useful than nonscientific paths to knowledge. We hear that "birds of a feather flock together" but also that "opposites attract." Both adages have some truth, but only scientific inquiry can tell us under exactly what circumstances one or the other is more correct.

Debunking

The term **debunking** refers to a habit of looking beyond the obvious or surface-level explanations that people provide for social behavior and of seeking out less obvious and deeper explanations (Berger, 1963). Durkheim was debunking when he showed that suicide stems not only from psychological problems but also from low levels of social integration. Debunking is not limited to sociology—it is a theme in all the social sciences—but sociologists put a particularly strong emphasis on it.

Debunking is a state of mind that is undeniably a little cynical. When sociologists debunk, they assume that "official" explanations are incomplete and often self-serving. They see old realities in new ways. They refuse to ignore inconvenient facts. Sociologists who have studied how the death penalty is being used have convincingly debunked the myths that it is applied without racial bias and that innocent people are never condemned to die.

As sociology has become more popular, debunking has become increasingly common among the general public. For example, when the United States waged the Gulf War against Iraq in the early 1990s, almost everyone recognized that the government's motive was not just to free Kuwait from Iraqi domination but also to keep cheap oil flowing to the developed world. Similarly, when neighborhood residents band together to fight the establishment of a halfway house for recovering drug addicts on their block, claiming that they are worried about the safety of their children, most people realize that, while the residents may indeed be genuinely concerned about their children, they are also motivated by fear that their property values might decline if a halfway house is built.

The sociological theme of debunking helps explain why the discipline thrives during times of social turmoil, when many conventional truths seem unconvincing, and is less popular in quiet eras (Mills, 1959). Thus sociology grew rapidly in the United States during the turbulent 1920s, the Great Depression, and the social upheaval of the 1960s, but was less widely accepted in more conformist decades like the 1950s and the 1980s. Events like the Seattle WTO protests suggest that a major upswing in the popularity of sociology may well be imminent.

By much the same logic, the individuals who are most likely to question the established truths and thus to be naturally most inclined to debunk are those who are not members of the more powerful groups in society. Such people display the quality of **social marginality;** they are to some extent excluded, through no fault of their own, from the mainstream of

These protestors against the Gulf War were skeptical of official explanations for American participation. Their mindset is similar in a sense to that of sociologists who make use of the debunking theme of the discipline.

society. It is no coincidence that most of the European founders of the discipline of sociology were Jewish, or that a great deal of the most important work now being conducted in sociology is being done by racial and ethnic minorities and women. As partial outsiders, marginal people are especially well situated to realize that the emperor may indeed be wearing no clothes.

Diversity

When sociologists debunk, they frequently find that the common-sense understandings many people embrace concerning social reality are systematically biased or distorted in ways that promote the interests of the more powerful members of society. These powerful people have the ability to strongly influence what we learn in school, from the media, and even in church. They often use their collective social power to more or less subtly encourage everyone to see society as they do, and this way of looking at life tends to legitimate their privileged positions.

As will be documented throughout this text, sociological research often reveals that widespread beliefs about the poor, racial and ethnic minorities, women, the young and the elderly, the physically and mentally disabled, and gays and lesbians are inaccurate, some-

times wildly so. As a result, many sociologists have chosen to focus their research on such groups.

When sociology first developed in Europe, some early scholars made a point of studying economic diversity with special reference to the problems of the poor. When the field became established in the United States early in the twentieth century, sociologists directed considerable attention to the problems of racial minorities; in fact, sociological research played an important role in the struggle for civil rights. Over the past thirty years, the discipline has closely studied the place of women in society (Smith, 1992). Note that two of the accounts that opened this chapter—those concerning the gender-based wage gap in Japan and the near-execution of an innocent African American man—reflect the sociological emphasis on diversity.

More recently, sociologists have begun to emphasize the combined effects of race, class, gender, age, and sexual orientation. This line of thought, which will be developed throughout the text, acknowledges the linkages between these social identities and reminds us that the experiences of people who are multiply disadvantaged—for example, elderly African American women—cannot be fully understood by studying the effects of each social factor separately.

Modern sociology also acknowledges the fact that many societies are moving toward **multiculturalism,** the idea that different groups of people should be able to live side by side without one dominating the others or any group having to abandon its heritage. This concept will be developed more fully in Chapter 3.

Globalization

A final important theme in modern sociology is a rapidly increasing emphasis on the numerous interconnections that link the world's societies together into a single global system (Wallerstein, 1990; Robertson, 1992). This world-system has been growing since the sixteenth century, but the pace of globalization has accelerated tremendously in recent decades.

In the economic sector, the wealth of the multinational corporations has come to exceed that of many small and medium-sized nations (Barnet & Cavanagh, 1994). Transnational trade agreements such as NAFTA and groups like the World Trade Organization are shaping many aspects of our daily lives. Eighty percent of new jobs in the United States rely in some way on foreign trade (Council on International Educa-

tional Exchange, 1988). New technologies are diffused around the world almost instantaneously, and more and more products are being constructed on a "global assembly line." And as environmental awareness increases, we are recognizing that only a regional or global perspective can allow us to reduce pollution and respond effectively to problems like global warming and resource depletion—one of the key demands of the Seattle protestors.

More generally, a global culture is beginning to emerge. Despite resistance, English is becoming a universal language, and American music, films, and television shows are viewed worldwide. At the same time, however, American popular culture is being more and more heavily influenced by developments in other nations. All of these changes have been greatly facilitated by modern means of transportation and by the new instantaneous media of communication, especially fax machines and the Internet.

This text will consistently emphasize this trend toward globalization. In particular, it will underscore an important theme in modern sociology: the contrasts—and the interconnections—between the

As culture globalizes, American films, television, sports, and music are marketed throughout the world. Many films earn more money abroad than they do at home.

wealthy nations of the *developed world* (North America, Europe, Australia, and Japan) and those in the much poorer *developing world* in which over three-quarters of the human population now lives.

MAJOR TOPICS OF SOCIOLOGICAL INTEREST

Although the field of sociology is extremely broad, most sociological studies may be categorized into one of four very general areas: socialization, structured social inequality, social institutions, and social change. A brief overview of these topics will expand your understanding of the sociological perspective as well as provide an overview of some of the subjects that will be covered in the remainder of this book.

Socialization

Recall that sociologists consistently emphasize the extent to which powerful social forces guide, limit, or constrain human behavior. In fact, some go so far as to describe society as a system in which people in effect agree to abandon much of their freedom in return for the advantages that result from joining with others in cooperative activities (Babbie, 1994). This implicit social contract requires that we learn and accept the rules that govern social behavior. The mechanism by which this learning is accomplished is called **social-ization.** In Chapter 5 socialization will be defined as the lifelong process by which we learn our culture, develop our sense of self, and become functioning members of society. Most socialization takes place through an ongoing process of social interaction—the topic of Chapter 6. When socialization efforts fail, or when people are socialized to act in ways that the authorities or other powerful figures in society regard as wrong, the result is deviant behavior, some of which takes the form of crime—issues that will be addressed in Chapters 8 and 9.

Structured Social Inequality

One of the phenomena found in virtually every society in the world is the division of people into several different social categories, some of which enjoy better opportunities than others to obtain valued resources including money, nice homes, attractive mates, prestige, power, and the ability to pass on these advantages to their children. As outlined in Chapters 10 through 14, these categories include, but are not limited to, economic classes, ethnic and racial minority groups, the male and female genders, and age groups such as teenagers and the elderly.

It is important to note that members of these categories obtain different levels of valued resources not solely because of their individual abilities or deficiencies, but also on the basis of their category membership—because they are upper class or lower class, male or female, African American or white, old or young. Of course, how well *particular* people do is affected by both their individual skills and by their category memberships, but sociologists concentrate primarily on the latter factor. Because the advantages and disadvantages enjoyed by members of different social categories are *built into* daily life, sociologists use the term **structured social inequality** or, somewhat more narrowly, *social stratification*, to refer to this characteristic of societies.

The primary means by which structured social inequality is maintained do not involve force or coercion. It is much easier and more reliable if the more advantaged people socialize everyone to accept a belief system or **ideology** that legitimates existing patterns of structured social inequality—that is, that defines them as just and proper. Racism, sexism, and ageism are good examples of such ideologies. They teach us that discrimination on the basis of race, gender, or age is appropriate. Uncovering the way these ideologies function is an excellent example of the debunking theme in sociology.

Social Institutions

People in every society must accomplish certain basic tasks. They must, among other things, produce and distribute goods and services, care for and socialize their children, protect themselves against invaders and criminals, make decisions to which the society as a whole is committed, heal the ill, and respond to the sacred.

A **social institution** is a predictable, established way to provide for one or more of society's basic needs. Chapters 15 through 20 will present sociological analyses of eight important institutions: the family, education, religion, the economy, the political institution, health and medicine, the media, and sports.

Every society must fulfill all of these major needs, but each does so in a somewhat different fashion. Over time, the existing institutional arrangements come to be seen by the people of a given society as the right and proper way to behave. As a result, institutions like the family or government tend to be quite stable and institutional change is often viewed as institutional collapse, as exemplified by current concerns over the supposed decline of the family. The sociological perspective often, but not always, suggests that changing institutional patterns are better understood as adaptations to new realities rather than as examples of degeneration.

America Through Foreign Eyes

Travel, they say, is broadening—even if you stay away from the pastry shops! In this context, "broadening" means that when we see people acting differently from the way our friends and neighbors act at home, we can use these observations to enhance our understanding of and appreciation for the tremendous diversity of human behavior. Open-minded travelers return home more enlightened as a result of their experiences, able to understand and empathize more effectively with people—not just those from other parts of the world, but also those individuals in their own communities who differ from them with regard to racial or ethnic identity, gender, age, or economic status.

By the same logic, we can learn a lot about our own society from the observations of visitors from other countries. Here are three short accounts that illustrate how daily life in America impressed newly arrived foreign scholars. First, a Philippine student comments on American informality:

> American children, I observe, are allowed to call older people by their first names.... [One] incident took place in the university cafeteria. To foster collegiality among the faculty and graduate students, professors and students usually ate lunch together. During one of these occasions, I heard a student greet a teacher, "Hey, Bob! That was a tough exam! You really gave us a hard time, buddy!" I was stunned. I couldn't believe what I heard. All I could say to myself was "My God!

How bold and disrespectful!" (Ojeda, 1993: 56)

Next, a French anthropologist reports that she was amazed to learn about some of the things that American women will openly discuss:

> I had an interesting conversation with a group of five women all roughly my age. I say "interesting" not because there were any overlapping interests, but because I felt so alien. Most of the discussion centered around their bodies. I was amazed to find them absolutely at ease discussing their weight, how much they were going to lose, and how they were going to lose it. . . . I wrote to a friend of mine in France about the discussion, and in the correspondence that followed we agreed that such intimacies would never be revealed in such a setting. Talk about the imperfections of one's body is limited to closest friends and mothers. (Dussart, 1993: 71)

Finally, a Polish professor discusses violence and death in America:

> The constant forced awareness—the information [in the news] on how and why someone was killed or raped—accustoms Americans to violence. They treat it as something natural, as just another case of a person killing or being killed. Violent death or abuse belongs to the profane, ordinary world of America.... On the other hand, death by natural causes is almost completely removed

from everyday lives. Old people die in nursing homes or hospitals. (Mucha, 1993: 23–24)

Comments like these remind us that whenever we view social reality, we do so through a kind of lens or filter that is the result of our own unique life experiences. In other words, we each have our own distinctive perspective on life. This is very natural, very human—but it can also be limiting. We can greatly benefit by learning to view the world through multiple perspectives, each one adding additional depth to our understanding. This broadening of one's perspective, much like that resulting from extensive travel, is precisely the promise and the appeal of sociology.

1. If you have traveled abroad or to other parts of the United States, what are some of the different patterns of social life that caught your attention during your travels? How did you interpret and respond to these differences?
2. All of the examples cited in this box concern aspects of American life that evoke negative reactions from foreign observers. What do you think people from other countries might *like* about the United States?
3. How does the concept of social marginality help you to understand why outsiders are often able to see things that people who have grown up in a society may not perceive?

Sources: Dussart, 1993; Mucha, 1993; Ojeda, 1993.

Social Change

Sociology is centrally concerned with the analysis of social change. As we shall see, the discipline initially emerged as a way of understanding and responding to the great transformations that created the modern world. All three of the accounts that opened this chapter implicitly or explicitly concerned efforts to

promote some sort of social change. Sociologists studying socialization, structured social inequality, and social institutions often explore how and why these phenomena change. However, several specialties have also developed within sociology to explore some of the dynamics of change in today's world.

Chapter 21 investigates population growth, urbanization, and the rapidly changing relationship between people and the physical environment. Chapter 22 introduces the concept of bureaucracy and explains how it has radically transformed the workplace. Chapter 23 discusses collective behavior with a special emphasis on social movements—one of the most effective means by which ordinary people can work for change. And the final chapter (Chapter 24) combines a general discussion of social change at the theoretical level with a detailed analysis of global change and its impact on the developing world.

THE DEVELOPMENT OF SOCIOLOGY

Sociology is among the newest of the sciences, having arisen in Europe during the latter half of the nineteenth century. However, it grew out of a long tradition of social philosophy that stretches all the way back to the ancient world. Thinkers as diverse as Plato, Aristotle, Saint Augustine, Thomas Aquinas, Niccolo Machiavelli, Thomas Hobbes, John Locke, Jean-Jacques Rousseau, Edmund Burke, and John Stuart Mill all wrote extensively about social issues. However, their approaches differ from that of modern sociologists because they did not base their work on scientific research, and because their primary concern tended to be identifying the character of what they regarded as an ideal society rather than describing social life as it really was and explaining why it took the forms that it did. Most scholars believe that sociology as we know it began around 1850 in an effort to understand and respond to a series of dramatic changes that had swept over Europe during the preceding two hundred years.

The Sociohistorical Context

For many centuries after the fall of the Roman Empire, almost all Europeans lived in small farming villages in which life changed very little from century to century. Most people were serfs, subject to the everyday control of a small group of feudal lords and to the ultimate, although rather abstract, power of a monarch whose authority was believed to stem directly from God. The Roman Catholic Church controlled many aspects of daily life, literacy was extremely uncommon, tradition was rarely challenged, and the family was enormously powerful. Most people were born, lived, and died without ever traveling more than a few dozen miles from their homes. No doubt they assumed that their children and their children's children would live almost exactly the same way they did (Volti, 1988).

Four key developments shattered this traditional way of life, leading ultimately to the birth of sociol-

ogy. First, growing out of the Renaissance and the work of thinkers such as Galileo, Newton, and Copernicus, scientific ways of investigating the natural world began to gain greater acceptance despite the hostility of the Church. The development of the scientific method and the gradual spread of early inventions like the printing press quickened the pace of social change.

Second, the thinkers of the Enlightenment, including Hobbes, Locke, and Rousseau, popularized radically new political ideas such as individual rights, liberty, equality, and democracy. These notions, in turn, inspired widespread demands for political reform culminating in the French and American revolutions. In both politics and science, the notion spread that the human condition could and should be improved through the application of reason (Nisbet, 1969).

Third, during the early nineteenth century, the spread of the steam engine led to the Industrial Revolution in the nations of northern Europe. Millions of peasants abandoned traditional village life and flooded into the rapidly growing cities in search of factory jobs (Ritzer, 1994). A host of new social problems emerged, especially in the industrial slums where workers, including young children, routinely toiled for twelve hours or more each day, only to return at night to crowded, disease-ridden tenements. Poverty and crime increased massively. Appalled by these conditions, the earliest sociologists began to apply scientific logic to the effort to understand their causes and attempted to develop rational solutions to social problems, which were now viewed as violations of basic human rights. In the process, the early sociologists thoroughly debunked traditional ways of understanding social life.

A final factor that influenced the early sociologists was the rapid expansion of colonialism, especially in the decades following 1880. By the time of World War I, most of Africa, Asia, and Oceania had been absorbed into the colonial empires of the major powers. Contact with non-European peoples increased sociologists' awareness of diversity, sensitized them to globalization, and provided them with alternate models of social life (Nisbet & Perrin, 1977; Lemert, 1997).

European Origins of Sociology

The founders of sociology attempted to use the logic and methods of science to identify what had gone wrong in European society and to explore how contemporary social problems might be ameliorated. Thus they combined an interest in objective analysis with a desire for social reform (Lazarsfeld & Reitz,

Wealth and poverty are not just the consequences of individual people's ability and efforts. They are actually built into the structure of society.

1989). Sociology first developed in France, Germany, and England.

France.   It should come as no surprise that sociology began in France. In the first place, Paris was the undisputed intellectual center of Europe during the seventeenth and eighteenth centuries. In addition, the French Revolution of 1789 initiated truly radical changes in that society, changes that dramatically altered relationships among different groups of people that had endured for centuries. The old aristocracy and monarchy were swept away, in some cases by the guillotine, only to be followed by successive waves of revolutionary governments, culminating in the military dictatorship of Napoleon.

Auguste Comte.   Best known among the first generation of French sociologists was Auguste Comte (1798–1857), who actually named the field (although he initially wanted to call it social physics). Comte took a generally negative view of post-revolutionary France. He favored responding to the fragmentation of society by rebuilding it along feudal lines but replacing the Church with a "priesthood" of sociologists who would use science to identify the proper way for people to live. Comte strongly advocated taking a scientific (he used the term *positivistic*) approach to the study of society, but in practice he did not conduct research, and his work is rarely read today.

Émile Durkheim.   In contrast, the other great nineteenth century French sociologist, Émile Durkheim (1858–1917), did empirical research (recall his study of suicide rates), and his work is still widely viewed as relevant. Durkheim was more optimistic than Comte regarding the direction in which society was moving, but he did note with concern a tendency, especially in the new industrial cities, toward the growth of what he called *anomie* or a general decline in the strength of the rules that guided people in deciding how they should behave in society. Durkheim linked anomie to low levels of social integration and regulation and established that it was a source of numerous social problems, including deviance and suicide. Most of his writings focus on the causes of this decline in moral solidarity and on the institutions of religion and education, which he believed had the potential to lessen anomie.

Germany.   Sociology spread rapidly to Germany, where two important nineteenth-century thinkers, Karl Marx and Max Weber, developed analyses of the crisis of early industrial society that remain relevant today.

Karl Marx.   Marx (1818–1883) is, of course, best known for his political philosophy. His work inspired the state socialist systems that controlled the Soviet Union and Eastern Europe until the late 1980s and that continue to rule China, North Korea, and Cuba today (although none of these societies closely resembles the economic and political system Marx advocated). He saw himself as an economist, a political scientist, and a historian as well as a sociologist. He identified the chief problem facing modern society not as anomie, but rather as the oppression of the workers by the capitalist factory owners. His primary contributions to sociology include the idea that social

Contact with non-European people helped spur the development of sociology. Today, sociologists celebrate the richness and diversity of the world's many cultures.

life can be fruitfully viewed as an arena of conflict between different groups, an emphasis on the importance of economics in shaping social life, and an orientation toward the study of structured social inequality, especially social class. His work will be discussed at greater length in Chapter 10.

Max Weber. Weber (pronounced *Vay-ber*) (1864–1920) ranks with Durkheim and Marx as a founding figure of sociology. His concerns centered on the increasing *rationalization* of the modern world, by which he meant that virtually all human activities were becoming more and more oriented toward the deliberate selection of the most efficient possible means to accomplish any particular task. Weber recognized that rationalization made society more productive, but he feared that it could eventually create a world full of people who acted like machines and who had lost much of the sometimes quirky individuality that made them fully human. He was less optimistic than Durkheim or Marx about the possibility that the negative aspects of modern life could be overcome. Weber's work continues to be relevant to many areas of sociology; it will be discussed at some length as part of the analysis of bureaucracy in Chapter 22.

Because the thought of Durkheim, Marx, and Weber continues to inspire modern sociologists, Chapter 24 will return to the notions of anomie, oppression, and rationalization and will explore some ways in which these concepts continue to be useful in interpreting social life at the beginning of the new century.

England.   If your sociological imagination is functioning properly, you will probably have noticed that all of the figures discussed to this point have been male. Until the 1960s, women met great resistance when they attempted to enter academic careers, and even when they overcame this opposition, their work was rarely taken very seriously (Kandal, 1988). Only in recent decades have sociologists begun to acknowledge the contributions of early female sociologists to the development of the field.

Harriet Martineau.   One such figure was Harriet Martineau (1802–1876), a British author who is probably best known for having translated Comte's works into English. A strong supporter of feminism and a passionate opponent of slavery, Martineau toured America in 1834 and, three years later, published a perceptive book called *Society in America* that was based on fieldwork at a time when empirical sociological research was uncommon. One year later, she wrote *How to Observe Manners and Morals*, one of the first books to address the issue of sociological methodology (Hoecker-Drysdale, 1992; Lengermann & Niebrugge-Brantley, 1998).

Herbert Spencer.   Far better known in the nineteenth century, though rarely read today, was Herbert

Spencer (1820–1903). In his era, Spencer's work was given more attention than that of Durkheim, Marx, or Weber. He was strongly influenced by the writings of Charles Darwin, and his sociology is principally intended to explain how human societies evolve through a series of stages from simple to ever-more-complex forms. Today he is probably best remembered for staunchly opposing aid to the poor on the grounds that such assistance interferes with natural selection or "the survival of the fittest," a phrase Spencer originated. This philosophy, which has enjoyed something of a revival in recent years, is called *social Darwinism*.

Sociology in the United States

Academic courses in sociology were offered in the United States as early as the 1880s, but the first American department of sociology was not founded until 1892, when Albion Small organized one at the newly established University of Chicago. The "Chicago School," as it was called, virtually dominated American sociology until the late 1930s (Mitchell, 1968; Faris, 1979; Collins & Makowsky, 1998).

Sociologists in this country shared the social concerns of the discipline's European founders. In fact, the Chicago School was probably more strongly oriented than the Europeans (aside from Marx) toward

trying to improve society, perhaps as a legacy of the fact that many early American sociologists were raised as liberal, reform-oriented Protestants (Lewis & Smith, 1980; Turner & Turner, 1990). Americans were also, from the start, more highly committed than most Europeans to large-scale empirical research.

In the early twentieth century, the city of Chicago was growing very rapidly and displayed all of the ills of the industrial era. The Chicago sociologists viewed their city as a kind of vast social laboratory. They undertook major research projects to study such topics as poverty, crime, and immigration, interpreting these problems in the context of the physical growth of the metropolis in an approach called *urban ecology*.

While the Chicago sociologists, virtually all of whom were male, favored reform, they still saw their primary task as uncovering the fundamental principles that guide social life, and they left the job of actually trying to improve society largely to the emerging, female-dominated discipline of social work. Some members of the Chicago School worked closely with Jane Addams (1860–1935), who founded a famous social agency called Hull House where she and her followers worked with Chicago slum-dwellers to improve their lives. Addams won the Nobel Peace Prize in 1931 for her efforts.

Like women, minorities were largely excluded from prestigious positions in academics until quite re-

Jane Addams was the founder of Hull House, a famous social agency that worked with Chicago's poor. She used her sociological expertise to improve others' lives in an era when women were largely excluded from the academic world.

cently. Just as Harriet Martineau has recently been rediscovered, sociologists of late have become increasingly familiar with the legacy of W. E. B. Du Bois (1868–1963), who was the first African American to earn a doctorate at Harvard and who taught at the then predominantly black Atlanta University (Zamir, 1995). Du Bois wrote extensively on minority-related issues; his activist orientation led him to become a founder of the National Association for the Advancement of Colored People (NAACP), a key organization in the civil rights struggle (Deegan, 1988). The careers of Addams and Du Bois are discussed at more length in the box entitled "Rediscovering Sociology's Diverse Roots."

During the 1940s and 1950s, American sociology turned away from its reformist orientation and concentrated heavily on empirical research, often on topics unconnected to social problems, with the intent of validating sociology's status as an objective empirical science (Laslett, 1990). The line dividing sociology from social work became sharper. The dominant figure in sociological theory in this era was Talcott Parsons (1902–1979), based at Harvard, whose work was highly abstract and largely removed from the real-world concerns of most earlier sociologists. The best-known activist of this era was C. Wright Mills (1916–1962), discussed earlier, whose writings concentrated mostly on the distribution of power in U.S. society.

The 1960s and 1970s brought tremendous changes. In the context of the war on poverty, the civil rights and feminist movements, the opposition to

INTERNET   CONNECTIONS

The text discusses four key theoretical perspectives: functionalism, conflict theory, symbolic interactionism, and the feminist approach. Your understanding of sociological theory will be enhanced by accessing the *Map of Sociological Theory*: http://www.hewett.norfolk.sch.uk/curric/soc/Theory.htm. From the opening page, click on "Brief Introduction to the Sociological Perspectives on Society." After doing this, you will note that the "map" is "clickable." Try clicking on "conflict/consensus," "functionalism," and "symbolic interactionism." Summarize what you've learned.

the war in Vietnam, and the substantial cultural changes initiated by the baby boom generation, sociology's orientation to debunking contributed to a massive increase in the discipline's popularity. The number of American sociologists rose from 3,000 to 25,000, and sociology became the largest single academic major in many colleges and universities. It was also during this era that the work of women and minorities began to have a major impact on the discipline.

A return to social conservatism in the 1980s, symbolized by the election of Ronald Reagan as president and the growth of post-Watergate skepticism about the possibility of meaningful social reform, led to a decline in interest in sociology. This trend has begun to reverse over the past decade, however, in part because sociology is well equipped to explore the increasing globalization of social life. The discipline today is probably as balanced as it has ever been between activist and pure science orientations, with most sociologists drawing on an eclectic mix of theoretical and empirical traditions (Huber, 1995). In addition to more emphasis on globalization, modern sociology has been greatly influenced by the continuing development of feminist scholarship. Also new is the fact that an increasing number of sociologists are working outside of academic settings.

THEORETICAL PERSPECTIVES IN SOCIOLOGY

Up to this point, we have been talking about *the* sociological perspective, but in fact there are several distinct theoretical orientations within the discipline. While virtually all sociologists agree on the scientific nature of the field and on the importance of social factors in explaining human behavior, there is less consensus regarding which theoretical perspectives are most useful.

Historically, most sociologists have tended to make use of one or more of three broad **theoretical perspectives** or general ways of understanding social reality: functionalism, conflict theory, and symbolic interactionism. Recent decades have witnessed the emergence of a fourth perspective—feminism—which is beginning to rival the other three in popularity. Each of these theoretical orientations begins by making different assumptions about the fundamental character of social life, and each directs its adherents to ask certain kinds of questions about the topics they are studying (Kuhn, 1970; Suppe, 1974; Wallace & Wolf, 1999). Sociologists using different theoretical perspectives are like optimists and pessimists, both

Rediscovering Sociology's Diverse Roots

Prior to the 1960s, virtually all senior academic positions in American sociology were held by white males, except for some of those located at traditionally female or black institutions. It is more than ironic that the discipline of sociology, which has extensively documented the consequences of discrimination against women and minorities, has a long history of ignoring the contributions of nonwhites and women to its own development.

As our understandings have changed over the past thirty years, historians of the discipline have made a conscious effort to seek out early figures who made strong contributions to sociology despite having been excluded from the inner circles of academe. Jane Addams and W. E. B. Du Bois are two of the most important of these rediscovered sociologists.

Addams was born in 1860 to a wealthy family in Massachusetts. She attended the Women's Medical College of Philadelphia but dropped out due to illness. While traveling in England she observed social workers struggling to

Despite the pervasive racism of his era, W.E.B. Du Bois was one of the outstanding pioneers of early American sociology.

improve the lives of the residents of London's Victorian slums and resolved to carry their message home. In 1899, Addams founded Hull House, a "settlement house" located on Chicago's

West Side, and for the next twenty years she and her followers worked with the city's poor, sick, and elderly.

Jane Addams was a charter member of the American Sociological Association and published eleven books and hundreds of articles, many in prestigious sociological journals. In 1931, she was honored with a Nobel Peace Prize for her work at Hull House. Yet Addams was never invited to join the sociology department at the University of Chicago, and she was even denied an honorary degree from the school.

William Edward Burghardt Du Bois was also a native of Massachusetts, born in modest circumstances eight years after Addams. His father was a Haitian of African and French ancestry; his mother's background was African and Dutch. Despite being poor and a minority, Du Bois became one of the leading scholars of his era, earning an undergraduate degree at Fisk University and becoming the first African American person to earn a doctorate at Harvard. His dissertation was in history, but while working on his degree

---

looking at the same glass of water, one seeing it as half full and the other seeing it as half empty. None of the major perspectives is better than the others in any absolute sense, although one may be more appropriate than another for the analysis of a given topic.

One important way in which theoretical perspectives vary concerns the level of analysis at which they operate. Functionalism and conflict theory are **macrosociological** perspectives because they direct attention to large-scale social phenomena: large groups, organizations, institutions, and whole societies. In contrast, symbolic interactionism is **microsociological** because it concentrates on the details of interaction between people, mostly in small group settings.

In the following discussion we will outline the assumptions of each theoretical perspective and we will

illustrate each with comments concerning how it might guide a sociological analysis of the prison, a topic that will be considered at greater length in Chapter 9. Study these sections carefully because the different issues addressed by each perspective will be a continuing theme throughout this text.

Functionalism

Functionalism, or as it is sometimes called, structural-functionalism, is a macrosociological theoretical perspective that grew out of the work of Émile Durkheim, Herbert Spencer, the Italian sociologist Vilfredo Pareto, and Talcott Parsons. It was very popular in American sociology around the middle of the twentieth century and it remains important today.

he attended sociological lessons by Max Weber at the University of Berlin, and as the new field began to emerge, he became an early convert, founding America's second department of sociology at Atlanta University.

Du Bois published a book on race every year between 1886 and 1914, receiving the most attention for *The Philadelphia Negro*, an important contribution to the social survey tradition, and *The Souls of Black Folk*, in which he proposed the notion of *double consciousness*. No doubt influenced by the fact that both of his parents shared African and European heritages, Du Bois observed that every African American maintained a duel identify, simultaneously American and black, thus experiencing what sociologists today would call social marginality.

Like Addams, Du Bois was largely ignored by the sociologists of his day; *The Philadelphia Negro* was not even reviewed in major sociological journals. In part, this was due to the fact that both Addams and Du Bois took an activist stance regarding the proper role of sociology: Addams founded Hull House and Du Bois was a central figure in the Niagara Movement, which grew into the National Association for the

Advancement of Colored People, a group Addams also joined.

For many years, Du Bois worked as a leader within the black elite to improve the conditions of his people, but eventually he became disgusted with the slow pace of racial progress and veered sharply to the left, embracing revolutionary socialism and emigrating at the age of ninety-three to the African nation of Ghana, where he died two years later in 1963.

Despite the contributions of pioneers such as Addams and Du Bois, American sociology remained overwhelmingly white and male far into the twentieth century. Today, however, the demographics of the field are changing. In 1999, 48 percent of the overall membership and 64 percent of the student members of the American Sociological Association (ASA) were women. Two-thirds of ASA members were white, 5 percent African American, 5 percent Asian or Pacific Islander, 2 percent Hispanic, and 3 percent Native American or "other." In addition, two caucuses have emerged within the ASA—Sociologists for Women in Society and the Association for Black Sociologists—that actively promote gender and racial/ethnic diversity in the discipline.

Primarily reflecting their relatively recent entry into the field, women made up just 22 percent of full professor, 51 percent of assistant professors, and 58 percent of students in departments that granted graduate degrees in 1997–1998. The movement of women and persons of color into sociology has already contributed to its growing emphasis on the intersection of race, class, and gender; to its support of multiculturalism; and to the emergence of the feminist theoretical perspective. As women and minorities continue to grow in numbers and to assume positions of greater influence within sociology, they will massively impact the directions in which the discipline moves in the twenty-first century.

1. How does being a female or a minority contribute to the development of an individual's sociological imagination?
2. Should sociologists follow the lead of Addams and Du Bois and become more involved in applying sociological findings in order to improve people's lives?

Sources: Du Bois, 1968; Addams, 1910/1981; Aptheker, 1990; Lewis, 1993; Spalter-Roth & Lee, 2000.

Functionalism interprets all social groups of whatever size, from a family to a whole society, as systems whose parts are interdependent so that a change in one element necessarily leads to changes in every other element. For example, note how every player on a basketball team must constantly change position in response to his or her teammates' motions. Similarly, consider how a change in one part of a prison—for example, a strike by the guards or the establishment of a new treatment program—will have some effect on the operation of virtually every other part of the organization.

The assumption that all social groups can be understood as interdependent systems reflects an underlying *organic analogy* that compares social groups to the organs in a body, with each organ carrying out a particular function necessary for the continued

smooth operation of the whole system (Turner & Maryanski, 1979). Thus, just as the heart pumps blood, the intestines digest food, and the kidneys filter out wastes, in a prison the guards try to maintain order, the cooks prepare meals, and the parole board decides who will be released. Each part exists for a reason, and if it fails to perform its appropriate function, the whole system works less effectively, much as the whole body is harmed if one organ fails. Similarly, if a part of a social system serves no function, then it is likely to eventually fade away—which is why you will have a great deal of trouble finding a store that can repair an eight-track cassette player or a mechanic who is qualified to work on a Model T.

Note that the *function* actually provided by a social system, or by one of its parts, is not necessarily the same as its *purpose*—what we intend for it to do.

In an era of rapid growth in the number of people behind bars, American correctional officers often find it very difficult to control the prison population.

Most people want prisons to reduce crime, but the very high rate of recidivism (repeat offending) strongly suggests that they frequently fail to perform this function effectively.

In this context, the American sociologist Robert Merton has suggested that we need to distinguish between the **manifest functions** of a social system—the obvious functions we openly intend it to perform—and the **latent functions**, or the unintended and often unrecognized functions it also provides (Merton, 1968). Thus a prison has a manifest function of crime reduction—which, as we have seen, it may or may not perform adequately. It also performs several latent functions, some of which (such as providing employment to prison guards) do not interfere with its ability to perform its manifest function and others of which definitely weaken its ability to function as intended (such as the fact that inmates often learn how to be better criminals from their fellow prisoners). The identification of such latent functions is an important part of the process of sociological debunking.

Classic functionalism also assumes that social systems tend to remain largely unchanged so long as all of their parts are functioning properly. This condition of stability is referred to as **equilibrium** or balance. It can be disrupted when elements of the system fail to perform their functions properly, often due to the intrusion of outside forces. These disruptions are referred to as **dysfunctions** because they keep the system from operating smoothly and efficiently (Merton, 1968). In the system of the human body, diseases or accidents can be seen as dysfunctional; in the family, incest is highly dysfunctional; in a prison, a sharp cut in funding or the introduction of large numbers of poorly trained guards or exceptionally violent prisoners will undermine the system's ability to function properly.

Since social systems inherently resist change, if dysfunctions arise, internal mechanisms will activate to restore equilibrium, much as a thermostat turns on the air conditioning when the temperature rises and turns it off once the air has cooled off enough. The human body has similar mechanisms that try to maintain a steady temperature and blood pressure despite the disequilibrating influences of diseases and other dysfunctional factors. Similarly, if the social system of a prison is thrown out of balance by dysfunctional changes that lead to resistance or rioting on the part of the inmates, then the authorities will take steps such as instituting a twenty-four-hour lockdown or firing incompetent guards—steps intended to restore proper functioning.

Finally, the functional perspective suggests that people in a normally functioning social system will share a number of values—understandings of what is good and desirable—that help hold the society together and maintain a state of equilibrium (Turner & Maryanski, 1979). A primary purpose of the socialization process is to ensure that there is a fairly high degree of consensus concerning values. When such consensus does not exist, systems are likely not to function very effectively—precisely the reason why there is so much dysfunctional conflict in prisons, where inmates and staff tend to have very different values.

Thirty-nine people were killed by authorities during a major riot at the Attica State Prison in upstate New York in September of 1971. Functionalists analyze the activities of control agents as intended to maintain or restore a state of equilibrium.

Critique. Functionalism correctly points out that changes in one part of society often lead to changes in other parts. In addition, we can all think of social situations in which stability has been maintained despite potentially disruptive or disequilibrating intrusions. However, some critics charge that the functional perspective overemphasizes the extent to which harmony and stability actually exist in society. By implying that order is more basic than change, and by maintaining that change is frequently dysfunctional, functionalists seem to be saying that the status quo is almost always desirable; yet we all know that sometimes (as in the case of slavery in the Old South) change is badly needed in order to create a new, more just, and ultimately more effectively functioning system. In short, although efforts are now being made to correct this failing (see Alexander, 1998), classic functionalism tended to overlook the positive consequences that can result from conflict and struggle (Coser, 1956; Merton, 1967).

Conflict Theory

Conflict theory is a macrosociological theoretical perspective that is in many ways the mirror image of functionalism. It is heavily based on the work of Karl Marx, but it also reflects insights developed in the twentieth century, most notably by Ralf Dahrendorf (born 1929), Pierre Bourdieu (born 1930), and Randall Collins (born 1941). It has dominated European sociology throughout most of this century and has been popular in the United States since the mid-sixties.

Instead of interpreting social life as normally cooperative and harmonious, conflict theorists view society as an arena in which different individuals and groups struggle with each other in order to obtain scarce and valued resources, especially property, prestige, and power. Thus, in a prison, inmates and staff are continually in conflict in order to get what each group wants—in the case of the prisoners, privileges that will allow them to do "easy time"; in the case of the staff, higher wages and enough control to make their jobs safe. Similarly, the ethnic gangs into which inmates in many prisons are divided—African American, Hispanic, and white—compete with each other for power. Shifting to a larger frame of reference, the prison system is constantly struggling with other governmental functions such as education or highway construction for limited tax dollars.

Sometimes these struggles can be more or less equitably resolved for all parties, but conflict theory tends to argue that many social struggles are zero-sum games in which, if one party wins, the other(s) lose.

Conflict theorists do not deny that certain types of social arrangements are functional, but they insist that we must always ask *for whom* they are functional. They view with great skepticism the functionalist assumption that many existing social arrangements can be interpreted as *generally* positive for an entire social system. For instance, new tax codes will be generally defended as "reforms" by their proponents, but they often benefit some people more than others. In the prison setting, strict rules often are functional for the guards but may work against the interests of the inmates. Similarly, what is dysfunctional for one person

Conflict theorists view prison life, with its clearly-cut distinction between powerless inmates and powerful guards, as fundamentally similar to many other aspects of everyday social life.

or group may be highly functional for another (Tumin, 1964). Cutbacks in prison funding, identified in the previous section as generally dysfunctional, may be very functional *from the standpoint of the inmates* because they weaken the ability of the warden and guards to control them.

The conflict perspective suggests that change, not stability, is normal. When a given social system—such as a prison—is stable, conflict theorists tend to interpret this not as a sign of harmony and shared values, but rather as evidence that one group—in this case, the prison staff—has enough power to force its preferences on everyone else (Dahrendorf, 1959; Gramsci, 1971; Collins, 1975; Duke, 1976). In other words, social order is more commonly the result of the exercise of elite power rather than a reflection of true consensus.

Critique. Conflict theory counterbalances the optimism of functionalism by emphasizing the significance of power and struggle in social life; issues such as child abuse, terrorism, sexism, and revolution seem naturally suited for a conflict analysis. However, the conflict approach does tend to ignore the many areas of social life in which most people really do arrive at an uncoerced consensus about important values such as the desirability of staying to the right when walking down a hallway. Struggles occur, but so does harmony. Conflict theorists also sometimes fail to emphasize the fact that much struggle is institutionalized through such consensus-building procedures as elections or collective bargaining between labor and management.

Sociologists who favor conflict theory tend, in contrast to most functionalists, to believe that they should become actively involved in society, usually on the side of people who lack substantial social power (Fay, 1987). Critics believe that such activism violates the principle of scientific objectivity and charge that the work of conflict theorists will be disregarded by those who disagree with their values. Conflict theorists respond that functionalists whose research uncovers what appear to be unfair social arrangements but who do not try to change them are no more moral than bystanders who do not try to help people who have been hurt in a traffic accident.

Symbolic Interactionism

The third major sociological theoretical perspective, symbolic interactionism, originated in the United States. It is based on the work of George Herbert Mead (1863–1931) and Charles Horton Cooley (1864–1929), although it was first named and systematized by Herbert Blumer (1969).

Symbolic interactionism differs from the other major perspectives above all in its microsociological orientation. Instead of focusing on groups, organizations, institutions, and societies, symbolic interactionists study specific cases of how individual people behave in particular face-to-face social settings (Stryker, 1990; Denzin, 1992).

Both functionalists and conflict theorists regard groups, organizations, institutions, and societies as objectively real and as exerting a strong, even coercive

We do have the ability to change the meanings we apply to people and their actions, and that can make a great difference in a person's life. The man shown here in a wheelchair taking part in the New York Marathon may have a physical handicap, but that is not limiting the ways in which he can participate in a physical sport such as running a marathon.

power over human behavior. On the other hand, symbolic interactionists emphasize that all these larger structures are ultimately nothing more than the creations of interacting people and that they can, therefore, be changed. While social structures may indeed appear to constrain our options, if we employ our sociological imagination and debunk them, we will discover that we have more freedom than we thought we did.

For symbolic interactionists, then, society is simply people interacting (Rock, 1985). Crucially, the *meaning* of various aspects of social reality is not predetermined but is established through human action. People do not respond directly to the world around them, but rather to the meaning they collectively apply to it (Blumer, 1969). For example, until recently, many Americans accepted stereotyped notions about racial minorities. But over the past few decades, activists have challenged these biased and inaccurate *definitions of the situation* (Thomas, 1923) and more and more people, whites and minorities alike, are adopting less restrictive understandings of what it means to be a member of a minority group. Furthermore, as socially accepted definitions change, so does people's behavior, which is an important reason why minorities are now enjoying greater opportunities.

This point of view was eloquently summed up early in the century by W. I. Thomas in what has come to be known as the **Thomas Theorem:** "If men [*sic*] define situations as real, they are real in their consequences" (Thomas & Thomas, 1928). In other words, if we collectively define prisons as brutal places where criminals are sent to suffer, and if we construct them with that definition in mind, then that is what they will be; if we think of them as places where peo-

ple can be rehabilitated and if our actions are guided by that definition, then *that* is what they will be.

Obviously, there are some practical limitations to our ability to alter social life by changing the meanings we apply to people and their actions—a physically handicapped athlete will never be a world champion runner—but symbolic interactionists maintain that much of reality is indeed *socially constructed*, a topic which will be discussed at some length in Chapter 6 (Berger & Luckmann, 1966). Whether we view someone as a hopeless cripple or as a successful Special Olympian can make a tremendous difference in his or her life.

Finally, since symbolic interactionists place so much emphasis on identifying the meanings people apply to social phenomena, they consider it especially important to explore how individuals subjectively interpret reality. This is an approach that Max Weber termed *verstehen*, which may be translated as "to understand." This means that, when conducting research, symbolic interactionists usually spend a great deal of time simply observing and listening to people with the objective of gaining an understanding of precisely how their subjects perceive the social world in which they live.

Critique.   Symbolic interactionism draws our attention to the importance of the way people define the social situations in which they find themselves, and it reminds us that social reality is, in the final analysis, a human construct. It liberates us by emphasizing that we can often change undesirable aspects of our lives. But macrosociologists, especially conflict theorists, argue that symbolic interactionists fail to acknowledge how difficult it is to change long-established social arrangements. The fact that a prison is ultimately a human creation is of very little relevance or comfort to an inmate serving a life term.

The Feminist Perspective

The feminist perspective directs our attention to the *androcentric* bias of both traditioinal sociology and contemporary culture (Lindsey, 1997). As we discuss in Chapter 13, an androcentric bias in sociology assumes that research conducted on males can explain patterns of social behavior for all people. For example, virtually all of the major theories of crime are based on research conducted on men and reflecting the distinctive realities of men's lives, yet they have historically been presented as explanations of crime *in general* rather than as theories of *men's crime* (Belknap, 1996; Naffine, 1996; Pollock, 1999). Even when conducting research on men, traditional sociologists have often ignored factors such as race and class, which might help account for differences among men. Feminist sociologists address this problem by making the links between gender, class, and race explicit in their research. For example, when looking at women's experiences in college, they would take into account how race, ethnicity, socioeconomic status, sexual orientation, and age might influence that experience.

Consistent with conflict theory, feminist sociologists argue that structured social inequality (discussed earlier in the chapter) is supported by ideologies accepted by both the privileged and the oppressed. The privileged are challenged only when oppressed groups gain the resources necessary to do so. As more women become sociologists, they are able to question traditional male-dominated sociological research and theories. Thus, the feminist perspective makes use of insights that occur naturally to people who have been personally disadvantaged by subordination (Handel, 1993; Lengermann & Niebrugge-Brantley, 2000). This is consistent with our earlier observation that individuals who are socially marginal, in this case, women, are often especially well prepared to embrace the sociological imagination.

Symbolic interactionism is also useful in building feminist theory, especially when it is linked to the conflict perspective. One promising direction is to focus on the unequal power relations between men and women from the point of view of the women who are "ruled." For example, corporate women who are continually passed over for promotion must manage their behavior in gender-appropriate ways that help them fight for promotion but also allow them to maintain a sense of personal integrity. Symbolic interactionists thus focus on how the label of "feminine" is important in how

these women are judged by their peers and by themselves.

Regarding prison, feminists have noted that juvenile females typically serve longer terms in institutions than male juveniles despite the fact that females generally have committed less serious crimes. In part this is because the primary reason why young women are brought to the attention of the courts is usually precocious sexuality, which the male-dominated legal system finds much more threatening in girls than in boys. It also results from the sexist image that women are weaker and thus more easily changed or reformed than men. Thus sexually active young women are locked away in the paternalistic hope of reforming them, while sexually active young men are often seen as simply "sowing their wild oats" (Chesney-Lind & Shelden, 1998).

Critique. The feminist perspective has had a tremendous impact on sociology over the past three decades, greatly enhancing our ability to understand society as a structure of domination. Criticisms of this perspective center around concerns regarding the possibility of bias. Can feminist sociology uphold the discipline's tradition of scientific objectivity? Some feminists respond by charging that the demand for objectivity is often a smokescreen hiding male bias: Androcentric research is frequently described as objective, while feminist work is decried as lacking objectivity.

Table 1.1 summarizes some of the most important characteristics of the major theoretical perspectives in sociology. As we said at the beginning of this section, none of these ways of interpreting social reality is inherently better than the others. Each has its own strengths and weaknesses, and we can gain the most insight by using more than one of them simultaneously (Emimbeyer & Goodwin, 1994). Most of the chapters in this text will employ multiple theoretical perspectives, and the current trend in sociology is definitely toward the synthesis of several perspectives (Levine, 1991; Lieberson, 1992).

THE USES OF SOCIOLOGY

At this point, you may well be asking: Why bother to study sociology? What's in it for me other than a few hours of college credit and a warm, dry classroom in which to sit when it's cold and wet outside? Sociologists believe that their discipline provides students with three general benefits: It can help them to address major social issues more effectively, it can improve their ability to make a living, and it can assist them in making more intelligent decisions about the course of their lives.

Table 1.1 Three Theoretical Perspectives in Sociology		
	Functionalism	Conflict Theory	Symbolic Interactionism
Level of Analysis	macrosociological	macrosociological	microsociological
Image of Society	objectively real social structure	objectively real social structure	subjective, a product of human interaction
How Order Is Maintained	voluntarily, through shared values	involuntarily, through exercise of power	through common definitions of reality
View of Change	usually disruptive	normal and often positive	results from alterations in subjective views of reality
Key Figures	Émile Durkheim Herbert Spencer Vilfredo Pareto Talcott Parsons Robert Merton	Karl Marx C. Wright Mills Ralf Dahrendorf Randall Collins	George Herbert Mead Charles Horton Cooley Herbert Blumer
Major Criticisms	too conservative; implies that which is must be	too radical; ignores cooperative aspects of social life	ignores coercive effects of social structure

Improving Society

We must have accurate information about present social conditions before we can develop practical plans to improve them. If, for example, we desire to create a more effective welfare system, we must know many things. We must find out how many people are currently receiving welfare, what their social characteristics are, and how they came to be on public assistance. We must also study both the strengths and the failings of the current system. If we want people to leave the welfare rolls as quickly as possible and earn a living on their own, we must explore what kinds of jobs are currently available, which skills they require, and how welfare recipients can most effectively be trained in these skills. As we will see in Chapter 11, there are many widely held myths about welfare; if we do not debunk these misunderstandings, then any effort to build a better system will fail because it will be based on a false foundation.

Sociology is well equipped to uncover the truth about social problems precisely because of its emphasis on careful, reliable empirical research. In addition, sociology's global orientation can familiarize us with how other societies have responded to their problems. Cross-cultural research can save us from wasting our time grappling with issues that others have addressed and in some cases solved.

Each of the following chapters will end with a "Life Connections" section, which will present a sampling of some important facts about everyday life that sociologists have uncovered, and a "Society Connections" section, which will explain how such information is related to the effort to solve major social problems.

Some sociologists believe that their efforts to address social problems should be limited to researching the facts and developing theories to explain them. These advocates of **pure sociology** believe that it is the responsibility of other disciplines—especially social work, urban planning, and public administration—to actually use sociological data in the effort to improve social life.

Others, and their numbers are increasing, believe that sociologists should put their knowledge and skills to work in the real world. This orientation is called **applied sociology** (Sullivan, 1992; Larson, 1995). Applied sociologists have been particularly active as advisors and consultants in evaluation research, in which they assess the effectiveness of programs designed to remedy various social problems. Others have gone further, actively developing and implementing plans to accomplish goals such as reducing racial and gender discrimination in the business world or helping neighborhood residents organize to demand needed changes from local governments. Today, over one-quarter of all sociology Ph.D.s are employed in applied roles in nonacademic settings (Lyson & Squires, 1993).

Making a Living

Some students choose to major in sociology as a way to prepare themselves to enter the field as academics or high-level applied sociologists. If you make this decision, you will need to plan on earning at least a master's degree and probably a doctorate. However, an undergraduate degree in sociology is also a useful job credential. The box on page 26 entitled "What Can I

What Can I Do with a Degree in Sociology?

A liberal arts degree in sociology (or in any other area) is a different sort of job credential than a preprofessional degree in a field like business, nursing, or medical technology. Students who major in these areas are relatively narrowly prepared for specific jobs, whereas liberal arts majors obtain a broader education with special emphasis on the development of such skills as critical thinking, oral, and written communication, and quantitative reasoning.

Many students find sociology fascinating but may not be in a position to enter graduate school; at the same time they are not sure what sorts of jobs are available to someone with an undergraduate major in sociology. According to the American Sociological Association, a

> well educated sociology BA graduate acquires a sense of history, other cultures and times; the interconnectedness of social life; and different frameworks of thought. He or she is proficient at gathering information and putting it into perspective. Sociological training helps students bring a breadth and depth of understanding to the workplace. A sociology graduate learns to think abstractly, formulate problems, ask appropriate questions, search for answers, analyze situations and data, organize material, write well, and make oral presentations that help others develop insight and make decisions. (*Careers in Sociology*, 1995: p. 7)

In the short run, students with preprofessional degrees sometimes find the job search easier, but over the long haul many people believe that liberal arts graduates are better prepared for career employment.

Some undergraduate majors do find employment in sociology, generally in support roles in research, policy analysis, and program evaluation. They find that their courses in research, methods, statistics, and computer applications provide them with their most important technical skills. Many eventually return to school to earn advanced degrees in sociology that open the doors to higher level employment.

However, most people who complete an undergraduate education in sociology begin working in entry-level positions such as these:

social services—in rehabilitation, case management, group work with youth or elderly, recreation, or administration.

community work—in fund-raising for social service organizations, nonprofit groups, child-care or community development agencies, or environmental groups.

corrections—in probation, parole, or other criminal justice work.

business—in advertising, marketing and consumer research, insurance, real estate, personnel work, training, or sales.

college settings—in admissions, alumni relations, or placement offices.

health services—in family planning, substance abuse, rehabilitation counseling, health planning, hospital admissions, and insurance companies.

publishing, journalism, and public relations—in writing, research, and editing.

government service—in federal, state, and local government jobs in such areas as transportation, housing, agriculture, and labor.

teaching—in elementary and secondary schools, in conjunction with appropriate teacher certification. (*Careers in Sociology*, 1995: pp. 9–10)

1. How do the four key qualities of the sociological imagination—scientific orientation, debunking, diversity, and global focus—help prepare students for today's job world?

2. How would undergraduate preparation in sociology benefit students who seek graduate degrees in fields such as law, medicine, and social work?

Do with a Degree in Sociology?" presents more information about this option.

Most students who take an introductory course in sociology will not become sociology majors. However, everyone who completes college will find some preparation in sociology valuable because sooner or later virtually all college graduates end up working closely with people. You will need an accurate understanding of why people behave as they do so that you can interact with them smoothly and inspire them to work collectively toward the accomplishment of shared objectives.

Sociology can also provide students with skills in applying scientific research methods, which can be helpful in careers as varied as education, marketing, law enforcement, or government service. These methods will be discussed in Chapter 2.

Making Life Choices

Beyond the world of work, we all face many important life decisions: Whether and when and whom to marry. Whether to divorce, or to remarry. How to

INTERNET ⟶ CONNECTIONS

Many people think that the only careers open to sociologists involve teaching and research. The text points out that there are a variety of *applications* of sociological knowledge and research. *Applied sociology* is a recognized content area within the discipline, and the **Society for Applied Sociology (SAS)** is the official representative organization. On the Internet, the SAS Web site may be accessed at: http://www.appliedsoc.org. Go to the site and on the opening page, click on "35 Things You Should Think About If You're Considering a Career in Sociology." Write a brief report on the types of career opportunities available to those who have applied sociological training.

vote. Where to live. How to relate to our parents as they age. How to raise our children. When and where to retire. Society provides us with "scripts" that guide us in these decisions, but in many cases, the standard scripts do not include all of the options that are really open to us.

The study of sociology has a unique capacity to make us aware of the full range of alternatives from which we may choose as well as to provide information that can help us make the decisions that are right for us. In the end, the authors of this text believe that sociology's greatest promise is simply this: It can help you to debunk your own life; to see that you have more freedom than you may have thought.

For example, some years ago, one of the authors had as a student a woman in her thirties who had recently been released from prison for killing her boyfriend, a man who had subjected her to severe mental and physical abuse. During a class discussion of family violence, she commented that she had grown up in an environment in which virtually every woman she knew had been beaten by a father, boyfriend, or husband. She had seen nonabusive families depicted on television, but never believed that people like that really existed. Through studying sociology, she began to realize that life held more options than she had thought possible. She learned that many people really do establish the kind of caring relationships that she had always believed to be nothing more than fantasies. She learned that she had the right to expect to be treated with respect.

By the time this student reached her senior year, she had also begun to debunk her career options. She had been socialized to believe that women ideally should not work or that, if they must, they should limit themselves to traditionally female "pink collar" jobs like secretaries, waitresses, and maids. Again, her knowledge of sociology broadened her horizons: She realized that women today have the freedom to enter virtually any occupation that interests them. Gifted with considerable artistic talent, she chose to pursue a fulfilling career as a sculptor.

A few decades ago, many businesses restricted the opportunities of women and minorities, but sociological debunking has encouraged millions of people to break through traditional barriers.

In both of these ways, this student was able to greatly improve her life by using the sociological imagination to debunk the narrow scripts that she had once thought she had to follow. The authors hope that you too may find sociology to be useful in helping you to live as fulfilling a life as possible.

SUMMARY

1. Sociology is a perspective or way of thinking that systematically addresses the impact of social forces on human behavior.

2. Sociologists employ scientific research procedures in order to collect empirical data and construct theories that explain social reality as accurately as possible.

3. Sociologists try to identify the hidden as well as the more obvious explanations for social behavior, a process called debunking.

4. The discipline of sociology emphasizes cultural diversity and the globalization process in explaining contemporary patterns of social life.

5. Sociologists pay particular attention to four general aspects of social life: socialization, structured social inequality, social institutions, and social change.

6. Sociology arose in Europe during the mid-nineteenth century; its development was encouraged by the expansion of science, the ideas of the Enlightenment, the Industrial Revolution, and the spread of colonialism.

7. Key figures in the growth of sociology include Auguste Comte and Émile Durkheim in France, Karl Marx and Max Weber in Germany, and Harriet Martineau and Herbert Spencer in England.

8. Women and minorities, largely excluded from the discipline until recently, are now making substantial contributions.

9. The functional theoretical perspective analyzes how the various components of social systems work to keep them operating smoothly and efficiently and to avoid dramatic changes.

10. Conflict theory maintains that social life is best understood as a struggle between competing individuals and groups for scarce and valued resources and that change in social life is constant.

11. The symbolic interactionist perspective focuses at the microsociological level on how the meanings that people construct through interaction shape human social behavior.

12. Feminism is an emerging perspective in sociology that draws heavily on the understandings of women and members of other groups that have experienced subordination.

13. Sociology may be useful in helping people solve social problems, earn a living, and make major life decisions.

KEY TERMS

applied sociology 25	latent functions 20	socialization 11
debunking 8	macrosociology 18	social marginality 8
dysfunction 20	manifest functions 20	sociology 4
ecological fallacy 8	microsociology 18	structured social inequality 11
empirical evidence 5	multiculturalism 9	theoretical perspective 17
equilibrium 20	pure sociology 25	theory 6
ideology 11	social institution 11	Thomas Theorem 23

CRITICAL THINKING QUESTIONS

1. Do you think that sociology can be as scientific in its approach to its subject matter as biology or chemistry are, or are there inherent limitations to the extent to which sociologists can be truly scientific?

2. Both sociology and psychology try to understand the causes of human social behavior. Why do you think some people tend to find one of these disciplines more useful or valid than the other?

3. Why do you think that sociology, and in particular its orientation to debunking, is more popular in some eras than in others? Do you think that the appeal of debunking is currently growing? Why?

4. What are some of the sorts of questions that sociologists using the four major theoretical perspectives might ask concerning the Seattle WTO protest?

THE RESEARCH PROCESS

OUTLINE

Class and Race in an Urban Neighborhood

Elijah Anderson, an African American sociologist, began his fourteen-year study of an urban neighborhood in an eastern U.S. city when he and his wife moved into the neighborhood, and he continued it after he moved away. He spent many hours on the street—talking, listening, interviewing, and getting to know all kinds of people, from small-time drug dealers to police officers, middle-class whites, and African American community activists. By day, according to his description of the neighborhood, it is a pleasant community of close friends and civil people. It has a reputation for being the most diverse and socially tolerant area of the city. But at night things change. People Anderson interviewed see the same streets as a jungle after dark—places of uncertainty at best and hostility at worst. Strangers are monitored, especially African American males who cross the invisible class boundary when they wander into the neighborhood. The research reveals that class and race are linked. Residents socialize with others they feel most comfortable with—people who are superficially similar to themselves in both social class and color. Class and race pieces fit together only because of the researcher's deep familiarity and personal experience with the neighborhood. (Adapted from Anderson, 1990)

Music and Mayhem

We turn on music to unwind at the end of a stressful day, or simply to enjoy ourselves with friends. Surely the lyrics of songs we listen to repeatedly do not prompt us to violent acts. Sociologists are not so certain. They have looked for links between listening to certain kinds of music and acts of violence like suicide, assault, rape, and even murder. Their findings have sometimes been disturbing. For instance, fans of country music, with its frequent lyrics of despair and unrequited love, have a higher risk of taking their own lives than do people who seldom listen to country songs. And it is not just country music that shows this connection. Other popular songs with a suicide message have also been linked to suicide among listeners. Some teenage suicide victims had reportedly listened to Ozzy Osbourne's popular "Suicide Solution," for example. Yet it isn't easy to say exactly what these connections mean. Are song lyrics "causing" violent behavior, or is the link between the two better explained in some other way? Answering such questions is one of the challenges in doing sociological research. (Binder, 1993; Snipes & Maguire, 1995; Stack & Gundlach, 1995)

Obeying Authority

At the end of World War II, Nazi leaders were put on trial for crimes against humanity, including murdering millions of Jews. The defense they gave was simple: "I was only following orders." Two decades later, researcher Stanley Milgram did a series of experiments to determine just how far people will go in obeying orders. Through newspaper ads he recruited men to participate in what he claimed was a study of how punishment affects learning. Participants thought they were being randomly assigned to one of two roles in the experiment, but in reality they were all made "teachers," and the "learners" were Milgram's confederates. The experimenter, played by a stern-looking man in a lab coat, ordered "teachers" to give "learners" an electric shock in increasing intensity with each wrong answer. The electric shock generator was fake and no real shocks were given, but the "teachers" did not know this. If they hesitated in delivering the shock, the experimenter firmly told them to continue. Although many were trembling with distress, the majority still obeyed the experimenter and many even administered shocks up to the highest level of 450 volts—even after a "learner," who was tied to a chair in the next room, stopped pounding on the wall and fell ominously silent. If a shock this strong had actually been given, the teacher would have killed the learner! (Milgram, 1963, 1974)

These vignettes illustrate three of the many ways that social scientists conduct research. Elijah Anderson did *field research*, collecting data in the natural setting of his neighborhood that allowed for a great deal of in-depth understanding of the neighborhood. Sociologists who explore the link between song lyrics and violence often conduct *survey research*. They ask people to fill out questionnaires or they interview them about the influence of music in their lives. They can explore the same topic using *secondary research*, analyzing documents, records and existing data on CD sales, amount of air time devoted to different types of music, suicide rates, assaults, and murder, looking for relationships between them. Stanley Milgram designed an *experiment* and directly observed subjects in a setting he could control. As we will see, although his work raises important ethical issues about deceiving research subjects, experiments are important tools of scientific research. This chapter will describe the research process by focusing on pioneering studies that have served as standards for research in sociology. It will also demonstrate how all stages of research are guided by sociological theory. Finally, it will highlight some of the ethical issues that are raised when any research is conducted.

RESEARCH AND THE SCIENCE OF SOCIOLOGY

We live in a world where research is a central element of modern life. The research results that are reported to us—especially through the media—impact our everyday lives in many ways. Research is used to determine how much we pay for car insurance, what kinds of TV programs we watch, and whether our tax dollars should be spent on a new jail or a new park. Reports on the latest research related to health and lifestyle aid in our choices of the foods we eat, the amount of exercise we get, and the medicines we take. Businesses rely heavily on consumer behavior research to determine the array of products and services offered to their customers.

Sociologists play key roles in both gathering and explaining research data. They are interested in *social research*—that is, research regarding people and their interactions with one another. But their main focus is on social *scientific* research—studying people for the purposes of testing and building theories to explain social behavior. The quest for these explanations is the most important reason to do scientific research.

Because sociology is a science, it is guided in its quest for knowledge by a set of standards designed to ensure that what we know is both accurate and useful. These standards are part of the **scientific method,** a systematic procedure for acquiring knowledge that relies on *empirical evidence*, defined in the first chapter as data derived from observation and experience. The scientific method is the basic blueprint for the work of sociologists.

In sociology, theory and research are always intertwined. Chapter 1 discussed how sociologists describe and explain human social behavior through a variety of theoretical perspectives, particularly functionalism, conflict theory, symbolic interactionism, and the feminist perspective. Sociological research tests, modifies, and develops specific theories that are based on these and other broad perspectives. In this way, sociologists gain better and better understandings of social behavior. The completion of any research project sets the stage for the next one, which builds on what has been learned so far to reach the next level of understanding. It is useful to think of the research process as the research *cycle*. Scientific knowledge is continually broadened, corrected, and refined.

Scientific research is expected to be *objective*—carried out in a neutral, unbiased way. Scientists try not to let personal beliefs or feelings interfere with the conduct of their research. Recognizing that sociology would be in peril if values or personal opinions biased research, Max Weber (1925/1946), one of the founders of sociology, called for sociologists to be *value-free* in their work. At the same time, Weber also believed that sociology would be well served by using methods that provide the researcher with an understanding of the people being studied. Can researchers ever be totally value-free? Contemporary sociologists think not. As scientists, for example, sociologists must make decisions based on ethical principles; otherwise, the people they study might be put at risk.

But the scientific method helps protect science as a whole from errors in human judgment in two important ways. First, the scientific method is basically a

---

Sociological research uncovers patterns of behavior. This crowded urban street with many white collar workers can be a laboratory to determine how race, gender, and social class may be linked.

a hypothesis to be tested is the most common one in sociology and is illustrated in Figure 2.1. It will be useful to refer to this figure as you move between the various research steps. We will examine the major steps in the research process using the topic of

self-correcting one. Not only is knowledge corrected through research, but different researchers investigating similar research questions should arrive at similar conclusions. If they do not, then flaws in the original research were likely discovered by later research. However, another reason for the discrepancy is that things have *actually* changed in the topic under investigation. The later research points out the changes and new knowledge is gained. In either case, when all scientists adhere to the scientific method, likely explanations for varying research results can be put forward. The second way science deals with errors in judgment is that research is carried out under fairly strict ethical guidelines, especially important to sociologists who use human subjects in research. As we will discuss later, scientists in every discipline are guided today by codes of ethics in conducting their research.

STEPS IN THE RESEARCH PROCESS

The scientific method provides a roadmap for the research process. This map designates different routes depending on whether the researcher's purpose is to start with a testable **hypothesis** (an expectation or prediction derived from a theory) or to explore a topic and end with a hypothesis. The route that starts with

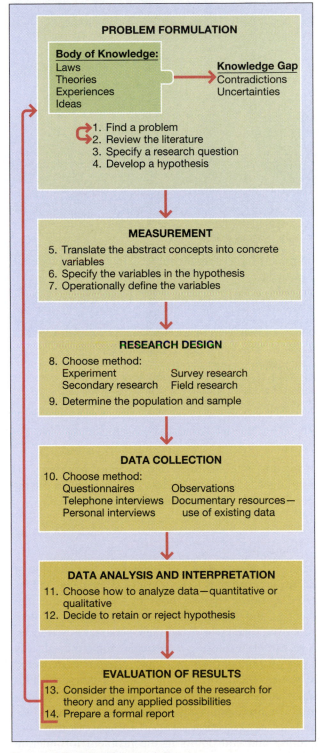

FIGURE 2.1   The Research Process

Sociologists study how the media influences behavior. Teens who listen to music containing violent messages—such as the lyrics and videos of rock musician Marilyn Manson—may be more antisocial or violence prone than those who listen to other types of music.

"romantic love"—a topic that has been of interest to sociologists for many decades. The first step in the research process is to formulate a problem.

Formulating the Problem

There are always gaps in knowledge. The key role of scientific research is to help bridge these gaps. As Figure 2.1 shows, the vast body of knowledge includes theories and scientific laws as well as people's ideas about the social world and their personal experiences. A researcher exploring a particular topic may already know of some of these gaps, but others are discovered in the problem formulation stage of research. This stage of research begins with identifying a general topic to study and ends with forming a specific hypothesis or prediction about it. In between these beginning and end points in the problem formulation stage come three other steps: reviewing the literature,

determining a research question, and developing a hypothesis.

The problem formulation stage is often the most difficult because many different options are usually examined before coming up with a final hypothesis. Finding a problem also requires that some exploration of past research occurs even before a detailed literature review takes place later, as shown by the arrow loop linking steps 1 and 2. This makes problem formulation very creative but also very time-consuming. Students frequently report putting in many "wasted" hours on this stage. But without this effort, a meaningful research question and hypothesis rarely materialize. Of all the steps in the process, problem formulation often takes the most time, but when done accurately, it can yield large research payoffs.

Reviewing the Literature.   Reviewing the literature involves thoroughly examining scientific journals and other reputable sources to become informed about the past research and theories related to a topic. The researcher compares this information, drawing conclusions from many separate studies that address similar questions. The literature review allows the researcher to build a *conceptual framework* that summarizes information about the research and integrates important concepts. The conceptual framework is essential for all scientific research because it is here that the theory on which the entire study is based is explored. The arrows in Figure 2.1 show that the research process is circular, suggesting that when the conclusions from the research are evaluated, they must be related back to the body of knowledge (theories) from which they originated.

For the topic of romantic love, a literature review shows that it is a concept that includes many components, such as altruism, sexual intimacy, compassion, sacrifice, and trust. The review also provides strong empirical evidence that these components are likely to be expressed differently by women compared with men. When the research on the components of romantic love is brought together with the research on how women and men express them, building a conceptual framework begins. Thus the literature review showed that the concepts of gender and romantic love are linked by empirical evidence. The path to new research on the topic begins.

Specifying the Research Question.   Since the literature review builds a conceptual framework that exposes gaps in the body of knowledge, the next step is to determine a research question that addresses the gaps. The research question usually asks about a relationship between concepts. For example, the researcher may notice that there is a gap in knowledge

In studying social interaction, research is often conducted in settings that are set up to be as natural as possible, but with some control over how the observations are recorded.

about the influence of gender on expression of romantic love. The logical question the researcher might then ask: "What is the relationship between gender and the expression of romantic love?"

Developing a Hypothesis.   By predicting an answer to this question, the researcher is forming a hypothesis. The concepts in a hypothesis are stated as **variables**—characteristics or traits that can be measured. Age is one example of a variable; it is a factor that differs from one person to the next. Age varies along a continuum such as people under or over a certain age, or whether they see themselves as young, middle age, or elderly. The variable age, then, is divided into categories called *attributes*. Researchers focus on whatever attributes are relevant to their study. In research on gender and romantic love, gender is a variable, and its attributes are male and female.

In forming a hypothesis, a researcher relates an independent to a dependent variable. An **independent variable** is one that is presumed to cause change in the dependent variable. It follows, then, that a **dependent variable** is one that is presumed to be changed or caused by the independent variable. In other words, changes in the dependent variable at least partially *depend* on changes in the independent variable. Through the literature review the researcher forms the hypothesis that "Men are likely to express romantic love sooner in a relationship than are women." Here "gender" is the independent variable and "expression of romantic love" is the dependent variable. As gender varies (that is, as the researcher looks at men versus women), the expression of love is predicted to change—gender is hypothesized to be a "cause" of when love is expressed. Explaining the change in the

dependent variable, in this case the timing of romantic love, is why the research is being conducted.

Hypotheses may also account for other variables as well. The most important of these are called control variables. **Control variables** are those that are held constant to clarify the influence of the independent variable on the dependent variable. For example, since the literature review determined that women in the lower social classes express love sooner than do women in the middle or upper social classes, researchers would have to make sure that social class (the control variable) was held constant in any study of how gender affects expression of love. If not, they would have trouble explaining why one person is declaring love sooner than another: Is it because of gender or because of social class? So when the control variable is added, additional hypotheses can be formed, such as: Regardless of social class, men express love earlier than women.

Measurement

In order to test the hypothesis that gender and love are related, the concepts of gender and love need to be translated into variables that can be measured. By assigning values, such as numbers, to variables, *measurement* moves research from the level of abstract concepts to the concrete, empirical level.

An operational definition is a key requirement for measuring any variable. An **operational definition** specifies how concepts and variables, in this case gender and romantic love, will be empirically measured. Gender is a given and needs only to be classified according to its two attributes, male and female. Love, on the other hand, is a very complex concept that

Romantic love can be studied many different ways. One way is to observe couples in public settings to determine if different couples show similar kinds of behaviors, such as kissing and hugging.

needs to be narrowed considerably for research purposes. The following example illustrates this important measurement procedure:

What Is Romantic Love?

Conceptual level: Love is the attraction to another person that is associated with intense feelings of joy, passion, and sexual attraction.

Empirical level: Love is a state of emotional well-being and physiological changes when thinking about or being with the target of one's affection.

Operational definition: Love is determined by the number of times one calls and thinks about the love target and shows certain psychological, behavioral, and physiological changes in his or her presence, such as heart pounding, pupil dilation, smiling, laughing, and forgetfulness.

Notice how the definition becomes more specific as it approaches the operational level.

Operational definitions are necessary to measure variables, but sometimes the measurement itself seems far removed from the original concept. This raises the issue of measurement quality. To condense the complexity of love into three simple indicators of joy, passion, and sexual attraction might not accurately represent what love is all about. If only one indicator, such as pupil dilation, is used, love may be reduced even more. This involves the issue of **validity**—whether you are measuring what you think you are measuring. The greater the distance from the conceptual level to the operational one, the more concern about validity. The gender variable poses no real validity problem, but the love variable does. Is the operational definition of love an accurate definition?

A second issue of measurement quality involves **reliability**—whether you would get the same results if you repeated the measurement. The key concern about reliability is the *consistency* of the measurement. Again, gender presents no problem. But a reliable tool to measure love may be more difficult to construct.

As for validity, researchers can never be completely certain that measurements are accurate. However, if researchers choose measurements that have successfully been used in past studies, they have reason to believe that those measurements have some validity. Sociologists have studied romantic love extensively, and a number of sound measurement tools have been developed.

Fortunately, science and the research process itself help deal with these measurement quality issues. As noted earlier, a major assumption about science is that it is self-correcting because the research on which it is based is continually improved upon. Although it is not foolproof, continual refinements in measurement quality help in the self-correction process.

The next two steps of the research process—research design and data collection—will now be overviewed. The specific elements making up each step will be discussed in detail later.

Choosing a Research Design

The research process is guided by a **research design,** an organized plan for collecting data. There are four major research designs—experiments, surveys, secondary research, and field research, which will be discussed more fully later in the chapter. The research question and its hypothesis help determine which

Global Connections

Doing Cross-Cultural Research

All research is influenced by culture, and problems arise when these influences are taken for granted. Problems are magnified in *cross-cultural research*—where data from several different cultures will be collected and compared. This form of research requires good political conditions and open access to the gathering of data inside a culture. If these conditions are not met, data may be unavailable or available data may be suspect. Another potential problem is translation. The same questionnaire items are often asked in different languages in order to compare responses across cultures, but it is sometimes impossible to translate items literally into another language. The following examples of printed signs translated into English illustrate the translation hazard:

In a dry cleaner's store in Thailand: Drop your trousers here for best results.

In the window of a Swedish furrier: Fur coats made for ladies from their own skins.

In a Romanian hotel: The lift is being fixed the next day; during this time we regret that you will be unbearable.

In a Greek hotel: Visitors are expected to complain at the office between the hours of 9 and 11 A.M. daily.

In a Hong Kong dentist's office: Teeth extracted by the latest Methodists.

Detour sign in Japan: Stop! Drive sideways.

Although there are cultural pitfalls in gathering and analyzing these data,

researchers working in other cultures will do a better job when they take the following suggestions seriously:

1. Work as closely as possible with people from the cultures to be compared, both as subjects and as collaborators. If you don't have a collaborator, get one.
2. Get as comprehensive a demographic and social picture as possible from all subjects in all cultures. Go beyond the usual age, gender, race, and occupation variables and seek out religion, ethnicity, sexual orientation, birth order, education, and family practices, to name a few. These are key variables that help in understanding cultural diversity. The multiple contexts of the lives of your subjects are also revealed.
3. Develop research tools that are appropriate to the cultures in question. Do not assume that a method that succeeds in Southeast Asia will also succeed in East Africa. Researchers in Vietnam and Thailand, for example, face a "courtesy bias" in which all household guests are treated with honor and politeness. Often the courtesy bias generates a cross-cultural Hawthorne effect. Subjects will give researchers any information they think the researcher—the household guest—desires, regardless of what they really believe about the topic under study. On the other hand, the Nuer of East Africa are suspicious of outsiders and expert at sabotaging inquiry at any level and either refuse to answer questions or give circular answers or meaningless responses to the simplest questions.
4. Collect the same data on yourself as you get from your subjects. This is not only a good way for the researcher to gain some insight on how subjects may be impacted by the topic, but it can reveal what the researcher takes for granted culturally. For instance, if you are from a secular state and want to compare religiosity in your culture with that of people living in a religious culture where the state and religion are one and the same, you will quickly discover the degree to which religion influences your own life.

Sociology as a discipline has much to gain from cross-cultural research and access to comparative data. This type of research is one of the best ways to enhance knowledge about the variety of human social diversity. Most important, cross-cultural research allows theories to be built that explain how cultures are both alike and different, a necessary ingredient for global sociology.

1. What opportunities and challenges are offered by doing research on people from different cultures who happen to live in the same city? Demonstrate how the principles of doing cross-cultural research apply.
2. How would you deal with language and other cultural barriers when doing research on sexuality with couples in cultures where women are restricted from interacting with strangers?

Sources: Nowak, 1989; Billson, 1991; Marin & Marin, 1991; Reinharz, 1992; Triandis, 1994:82; Matsumoto, 1994; Sjoberg & Nett, 1997.

---

plan to select. In addition to the research question, the selection of a research design is also determined by the population that the researcher wants to study. A **population** is the entire group of people who are the focus of the research and to whom the research results will be generalized. Since populations are usually too large to study as a whole, a **sample**—a subset or part of the larger population that is being studied—is drawn. The sample is supposed to represent the larger population. In answering the question concerning gender and expression of romantic love, for example, survey research would be a good research design to use. The survey could be done on a sample of students in selected colleges who are believed to

INTERNET ━━ CONNECTIONS

Observational research techniques, including participant observation, have many advantages. Go to "Collecting Data Through Observation": http://trochim.human.cornell.edu/tutorial/brown/LauraTP.htm. What are the major advantages of observational field research? What are this method's weaknesses? What are the two most commonly used types of *direct observation*? What are the main concerns in using this method?

represent the larger population of all college students. Once the sample is selected, data collection can begin.

Collecting Data

Armed with operational definitions of variables and a research design, a researcher is ready for data collection. Sociologists rely on four major methods of data collection: written questionnaires filled out by respondents, interviews conducted by the researcher or trained interviewers, observations of behavior, and documentary resources. These methods can be used singly, but when they are used in combination, the quality of measurement is enhanced. *Triangulation* is the use of multiple data collection methods. A questionnaire may assess attitudes on a topic, but when questionnaire responses are found to be consistent with observed behavior, validity increases. For example, on a questionnaire to measure attitudes toward romance, people may say they are not romantic, but

when interviewed about this topic they may reveal romantic behavior on a number of occasions. What people say and what they actually do may be different. As triangulation demonstrates, more valid data are obtained when questionnaires are supplemented by interviews. Questionnaires and interviews are data collection techniques that are widely used with survey research design.

Analyzing and Interpreting Data

With carefully collected data in hand, these data are ready to be analyzed. At this stage researchers summarize and interpret their findings, drawing conclusions about whether the findings support their hypothesis. In doing this, they answer four major questions (Bouma, 1993:178):

1. What did they ask?
2. What did they find?
3. What is concluded from the findings?
4. To whom do the conclusions apply?

Answering "What did they ask?" forces researchers back to the theoretical roots of their research question. They must address not only what they asked but also how they asked it, confronting the validity issue again. Did they measure concepts appropriately to link theory to data? In a study of romantic love, for example, is it valid to assess love by giving people questionnaires that ask how they respond to a loved one? If so, the study got off to a good start.

The second question ("What did they find?") involves coding and summarizing the data. *Coding* means transforming the raw data into numbers to make it suitable for analysis. There are many statistical tools

Face to face interviews are the best way to get answers to complex questions. Prearranged interviews in the home have much higher response rates and are enjoyed more by the respondents than interviews when respondents may feel intruded upon by the interviewer.

available for data analysis. Students often fear this stage of the research process because they are faced with a torrent of numbers that seems to demand a great deal of quantitative sophistication. The good news is that computers help process data efficiently. Once the researcher decides on the appropriate statistics, computers can do the calculations and generate tables quickly. The hard part is not actually "doing" the statistics, but understanding how to interpret them when they are presented in tables. Some of the most commonly used statistics in sociology are shown in Figure 2.2. Courses in research and statistics can teach you many other data analysis techniques. Such courses are beneficial because research and its interpretation are done in almost any work setting.

Good statistical analysis of data facilitates answering the third question: "What is concluded from the findings?" Was the hypothesis supported, partially supported, or not supported at all and under what circumstances? The degree the hypothesis is supported is critical for later evaluation of the results. Finally, researchers must determine to whom the results apply. Do they apply only to the people in the sample, to a broader population these people represent, or to others who may have been studied previously on the same topic? Can the college students who provided data on their attitudes about romantic love represent *all* college students? Again, appropriate statistics and sampling techniques can answer this question.

Evaluating the Results

Creativity is a hallmark of the last stage of research, evaluation of the research results. This is the stage where the researcher must consider two important issues: one theoretical and one applied. The theoretical issue involves whether the theory on which the research is based will be refined. If the hypothesis is partially supported or is not supported at all, the theory from which the hypothesis was derived may be in doubt. Researchers refine the theory to explain discrepancies, offering potential for future research. New gaps are created that should be explored further. The arrows in Figure 2.1 from the evaluation stage back to the problem formulation stage show the progression to future research. Even in studies where hypotheses are supported, theories are usually refined. For scientific knowledge on social behavior to advance, theories need to be modified and conclusions applied to wider and wider groups of people. The process of science, therefore, "continues continually."

The applied issue involves how the study results may be used in various settings. For example, if there are important differences between college men and women in expression of romantic love, do these differences impact their college lives? Chances are they do. Student service personnel may apply the results to better understand cycles of elation or depression that may interfere with study habits, academic performance, and interpersonal relationships. Researchers often provide reports of research results to people who participated in the study as well as others who may find the results useful. Because research benefits science, it must ultimately benefit people in general.

RESEARCH DESIGN

Some questions are better answered with one type of research design than another. Scientists can select from a variety of "standard" designs, as well as modify

Measures of Central Tendency—Statistics that summarize data by describing the typical or average score in a distribution of scores. These statistics can be demonstrated with a distribution of scores on a sociology exam, where seven students received the following scores:

55   68   73   79   88   88   95

1. *Mean*—The arithmetic average of a distribution. Add up the scores, then divide by the number of scores. The mean is 78 (546/7).
2. *Median*—The middle score in a distribution. List the scores from low to high (as shown above) and find the middle one. The median is 79.
3. *Mode*—The most frequently occurring score in a distribution. The mode is 88, the only score occurring more than once.

Measures of Variation

1. *Range*—The distance from the lowest score to the highest score in a distribution. The *range* can be stated as either 55 to 95, or as 40, found by subtracting the lowest from the highest score.
2. *Standard deviation*—Summarizes the distribution's spread around the mean. The standard deviation can be used to compare test scores over a semester. Tests with larger standard deviations, thus larger variability, may be redesigned since instructors may want student scores less spread out from the average score.

Correlation Coefficient—Measures the strength of a relationship between two variables. Pearson's product–moment correlation (r) is the most widely used statistic for correlation. The higher the correlation between two variables, the stronger the relationship. If data on test scores in college are highly correlated with income after graduation, we can say that test scores in college are good predictors of later income.

FIGURE 2.2   Commonly Used Measures in Sociological Research

or combine aspects of different designs to better facilitate answering the research question. We will concentrate on those most commonly used in sociological investigation, with special emphasis on survey research. However, one specific type of research design—the experiment—is the foundation for all science, regardless of discipline.

Experimental Design

The goal of science is to build sound theories for explaining topics important to the specific discipline. This goal is achieved through devising research to determine the effect one variable has on another. But it is only through a well-controlled experiment, probably in a laboratory setting, that scientists can legitimately use the word "cause" in explaining the connection between variables.

Experiments rely on the essential condition that the researcher can manipulate, and thus control, the independent variable in certain ways. This need to control the independent variable makes a laboratory setting the logical site for conducting experiments, since the researcher oversees the setting and can better deal with anything that may intrude on the research. "Classic" experimental design involves four steps:

1. The researcher divides subjects into two equivalent groups: an **experimental group** that is exposed to the independent variable and a **control group** that is not.
2. Division into these groups is accomplished according to *random assignment*—by flipping a coin, for example—so subjects do not self-select either group. Subjects are not told to which group they are assigned. This precaution ensures that the two groups are as much alike as possible except for the exposure of the experimental group to the independent variable. Random assignment of subjects to experimental and control groups is the principal way to rule out other variables that may affect the results. Causality can thus be inferred. If some subjects are more hungry, fatigued, bored, or more knowledgeable about the topic under study than other subjects—factors that may compromise the experiment—random assignment assumes that an equal number of hungry or knowledgeable subjects will be in each group. The researcher can therefore rule out potential influence of these factors on the dependent variable.
3. Before the experiment, the researcher measures the dependent variable in both groups by means of a *pretest*. After the experimental group is exposed to the independent variable, the researcher measures both groups again on the dependent variable by means of a *posttest*.
4. The researcher compares the pretest and posttest measurements. Any difference in the dependent variable between the two groups can be attributed to the influence of the independent variable. If the experiment was properly conducted, and all conditions met, it can be concluded that the independent variable *caused* the change in the dependent variable.

What Is a Cause?   Determining causality is the most important goal in doing research, but it is the most difficult goal to accomplish. There are four conditions that must be met before a researcher can say that an independent variable or variables caused the change in the dependent variable. We will look at the research question "What is the relationship between education and income?" to show how these conditions can be applied. Education is the independent variable and income is the dependent variable. The hypothesis—the probable answer to the research question—is that education "influences" income. To substitute the word "cause" for the word "influence," however, all four of the following conditions must be met.

1. *Time order*. The cause must come before the effect. Something in the future cannot cause something in the present or the past. A person will complete some schooling before getting a job. Education precedes income.
2. *Correlation*. The independent and dependent variables are linked in a patterned way so that a change in one variable corresponds to a change in the other. There is a systematic statistical link between them. This systematic relationship is called a **correlation.** As education increases, income increases.
3. *Elimination of spuriousness*. The observed correlation or relationship between the independent and dependent variables cannot be explained by a third variable. Thus, research must eliminate the possibility of a false or **spurious relationship** that is not a relationship at all because another variable is the true explanation for it. In our example, education must be the sole reason for any variation in income. However, since more than one cause can produce an effect, if researchers can identify all the independent variables (or causes), it is possible to rule out spuriousness. Education in combination with gender and job specialty, for example, may be all the likely independent variables needed to explain differences in income. The Life Connections section explores these links further.
4. *Theory*. If one variable causes another, there must be some logical link between them that explains

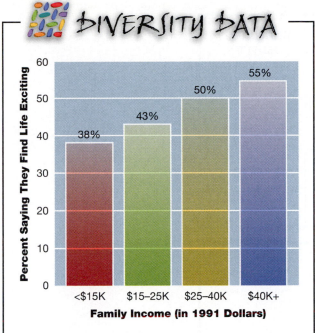

FIGURE 2.3   Percent Saying They Find Life Exciting, by Family Income. As family income increases, the number of people who find life exciting also increases. Although income level is one of the strongest variables in predicting quality of life overall, what other variables might also predict it? Would any additional variables make the relationship between income and quality of life a spurious one?

Source: NORC. General Social Surveys, 1972–1996. Chicago: National Opinion Research Center, 1996.

why the two are related. There is a logical fit between education (independent variable) and income (dependent variable). Higher-paying jobs require more education and expertise that goes along with it, so education produces a corresponding rise in income. Research must always be framed in a theory that explains empirical findings.

Meeting all four conditions is difficult for researchers. Even when a logical correlation exists, there may be no clear indication of which variable comes first. Education may precede higher income, but the reverse could also be true. As education increases, income increases. But those with higher income can afford more education in the first place. So education causes an increase in income and income causes an increase in education. The same problem arises when studying correlations between other attitudes and behavior. For example, consider the possi-

ble correlations in the music vignette: Do already violent people listen to violent music or does violent music precede violent behavior? Or for a correlation between depression and listening to country music, which comes first? Are depressive people drawn to country music or do country music fans become depressed? Plausible theories might explain either time order.

Eliminating spuriousness is extremely difficult to do in sociological research. The country music example is an excellent illustration of this. Although the relationship between air time devoted to country music and suicide risk is documented, data also show that fans of country music have higher levels of gun ownership and marital disruption than nonfans. When controlling for these variables, the original relationship becomes spurious. Other factors that are correlated to suicide among country music fans are poverty and living in the South (Snipes & Maguire, 1995; Stack & Gundlach, 1995). These are only a few of the many possible variables that still need to be studied. Thus it is impossible to say that listening to too much country music *causes* suicide.

Psychologists in controlled laboratory settings often use the technique of random assignment to rule out factors that may affect the dependent variable, thus eliminating spuriousness. But controlled laboratory settings are less suitable for large groups of people, the main concern of sociology. However, sociologists who do research on small groups of people may design experiments in natural settings that build in some control, even though spuriousness cannot be entirely eliminated.

Illustrating a Field Experiment. *Field experiments* are carried out in settings typical to the lives of the subjects who are being studied. An important set of field experiments conducted more than sixty years ago inadvertently encountered the problem of spuriousness. These experiments took place at the Western Electric Company's Hawthorne plant near Chicago, using as subjects employees who made telephone equipment (Mayo, 1933; Homans, 1951). The company had always been concerned about good working conditions and employee welfare. Managers wanted to learn how they could raise both worker productivity (the speed and efficiency of output) and worker satisfaction, the dependent variables. The independent variables included different working conditions, such as lighting changes, the number and duration of rests, total hours of work each day, degree of supervision, and type of equipment used. Although the researchers did not use a control group in these studies, they did take pretests of productivity and satisfaction before introducing each change in an

Can you spot the spurious relationship here? What is the independent variable? What is the dependent variable?
Source: DILBERT reprinted by permission of United Feature Syndicate, Inc.

independent variable. Then, after the change in that variable, they took posttests to gauge what, if any, effects had occurred. "Average" workers were chosen to participate in the research. These workers knew they were involved in important experiments and that the eyes of management were upon them. The experiments clearly showed that better working conditions improved productivity as well as employee satisfaction.

As the experiment continued, productivity increased. But it became apparent that something was puzzling about the experiment. Productivity rose regardless of how the experimental conditions were changed. If lighting was dimmer, breaks were shorter, and there was less supervision, output still increased. Changes taking place in productivity had no simple correlation to the experimental changes in the working conditions. If the working conditions did not cause the changes in productivity, what did?

The answer turned out to be the experiment itself. The workers were being influenced simply by the knowledge that they were part of an important study— a phenomenon now called the **Hawthorne effect.** Workers wanted to please the researchers and look good in the eyes of management. As a result, they worked harder no matter what conditions they encountered. Simply by conducting the experiment, the researchers caused a spurious relationship to occur.

The Hawthorne effect is most likely to occur in a field experiment like this one in which the subjects come to the study highly motivated to "shine" in their performance. The researchers could not eliminate the desire to please the employer that was so widespread at the Hawthorne plant. Difficulty in controlling such influences is one of the limitations of doing experiments in natural settings. However, if the Western Electric researchers had used an appropriate control group, they would have detected the Hawthorne effect sooner. Given your knowledge of control groups, you can probably explain why.

For experiments to be successful, the trade-off between naturalness of setting and control of setting must be resolved. Too much naturalness hurts control, and too much control hurts naturalness. If subjects act unnaturally because they are in an experiment, because they are being observed, or because the setting is too artificial, then results cannot be generalized to a wider population—even if causality can be inferred. Field experiments can only approximate the experimental ideal.

INTERNET ━━━●━━━ CONNECTIONS

The Polling Report publishes results from the latest opinion surveys by major polling organizations like Gallup and Harris. Using its site, www.poll-ingreport.com, write a short news article telling how the American public feels about some event or topic of current interest.

Surveys

In sociology, **survey research** is conducted far more often than experiments because surveys are well suited to studying large numbers of people. Studying people's attitudes is particularly suitable for surveys. Survey data can reveal what people think about almost anything—from their assessment of the president of the United States, to their confidence in the economy, to their concerns about global warming, to their degree of marital satisfaction, happiness during old age, or feelings of loneliness during adolescence. The increasing reliance on surveys makes knowledge of this tool a requirement for almost any career. Survey research typically provides information useful for **quantitative analysis**—data that are readily translated into numbers.

Like experiments, surveys can be used to test hypotheses, but correlations rather than causes are drawn from the data. It is impossible for surveys to build in every potential variable that may eliminate spuriousness. A literature review may reveal that education explains a great deal of the income variation between people, but the same review may also suggest numerous other explanations. Three of the four conditions of causality can usually be met through survey research, but it is almost impossible to eliminate spuriousness.

Sampling.   Surveys do have one major advantage over experiments: Their results can be generalized to a much larger population. To understand why requires a knowledge of sampling, particularly random sampling. A **random sample** is one in which subjects are selected so that every member of the population has an equal chance of being chosen. If a sample of people surveyed is randomly selected and sufficiently large, the results based on that sample can be generalized to the broader population from which the sample is drawn. A random sample of students from the same college represent the population of all students at the college so, in studying gender and love, for example, we can generalize the results and legitimately say that

male students express love sooner than female students at "Midwest University."

To say that a sample must be sufficiently large does not mean the larger the better—very large samples are not necessarily the best. This was shown in 1936 when *Literary Digest* magazine predicted that Republican Alf Landon would win the presidential election by a landslide over Democrat Franklin Roosevelt. The researchers used telephone directories and automobile registration lists to draw the sample. They sent out an astounding 10 million ballots, and over 2 million people returned the ballot. Yet this huge sample failed to predict Roosevelt's victory, even though he won by the largest margin in the nation's history. What went wrong?

Faulty sampling was the culprit. In the midst of the Great Depression, telephones and cars were luxuries that many could not afford, so the sample overrepresented higher income people, who were also more likely to be Republican. The sample virtually excluded poor and lower income people, who made up the majority of the population at the time. So even if the number of survey respondents is huge, without random sampling techniques, survey results cannot be generalized to the total population. With careful sampling, a random sample of no larger than 2,000 people can be used to accurately predict a national election.

This is not to say that the findings of surveys from nonrandom samples are not useful. Frequently survey researchers use *convenience samples* of people who are readily available to them. For instance, sociologists know a lot about college students—what they eat, what they wear, where they go for spring break, how they spend their money, whom they prefer to date, their attitudes and behavior on topics ranging from politics, sexuality, family life, and race relations—all this because college students are so readily available to researchers teaching at universities. But even though college students share some important characteristics with their peers throughout the country, because the samples are usually not random, caution is necessary in how the data are interpreted and generalized.

After the sample is determined, survey researchers generally select from the three most common techniques for data collection: self-administered questionnaires, personal interviews, or telephone interviews.

Questionnaires.   Questionnaires are data collection devices that are filled out by the respondent and returned directly or by mail. They contain items based on operational definitions of all the variables of interest to the researcher—independent, dependent, and control. In our gender and love example, social class is a control variable and can be operationally

The Business of Consumer Behavior

San Antonio, Texas has one of the largest Hispanic American communities in the United States. In the 1980s a telephone company designed a major campaign to increase long distance usage in San Antonio's Hispanic population. Ads in Spanish language newspapers and radio stations focused on the ease and low cost for calls between the United States and Mexico. The ad campaign was successful—there was a dramatic increase in both international and national long distance usage. Unfortunately, the highest usage was from the poorest customers. In addition, not enough Spanish-speaking operators were hired to deal with the problems that arose because existing phone lines could not handle the call volume. Results: Many poorer customers who could not afford to pay for the long distance calls had their phone service cut off. Many middle-class customers abandoned this phone company because services were severely disrupted. The ad campaign was "success-

ful" but the company lost money and customers.

Today business managers worldwide must be mindful of two fundamental business principles. The first principle is that they must have the best information available to control the destinies of their businesses. The second principle is that their businesses must be able to adjust to a rapidly changing competitive marketplace. The marketplace itself exists in a world of massive social change. Any business not accounting for these two principles is doomed. It simply cannot compete in an information-driven, rapidly changing global economy. However, businesses can use sociological tools to deal with the two principles of information and being attuned to social change.

Information
The first principle is based on *consumer behavior*—understanding the forces affecting the buying habits of consumers.

Although research on consumer behavior is guided by the same principles as sociological research in general, consumer research is much more likely to be exploratory and qualitative. For business, the end product of consumer research is often to develop specific research questions that are then turned over to marketing departments. Marketing begins with the idea of a product or service and ends only when the consumer buys the product or service. *Marketing research* gathers and analyzes information about the market for decision making. This information is usually obtained through survey research and analyzed quantitatively. It fits the typical research model in Figure 2.1. In the San Antonio case, the company knew about the increased Hispanic immigration but failed to recognize other socioeconomic characteristics of the targeted consumers such as lack of resources. Although sociologists do both consumer research and marketing research, sociological expertise is

defined as a combination of education, income, and occupation. Questionnaire items may ask respondents to check boxes on years of schooling, gross annual household income (in $10,000 increments), and whether they work in a white-collar or blue-collar job. These are called *closed-ended questions* because they offer fixed choices to issues the researcher already knows are important. Closed-ended items increase questionnaire return rate because they are easy to answer. The answers to these questions are also easy to summarize for analysis, and they tend to be reliable measures—people would give similar answers if asked the same questions again.

But the problem with closed-ended questions is the limited choices they offer, which can make it hard for researchers to learn all that respondents think about a subject. Sometimes the choices seem so limited that people refuse to answer the question, especially if it addresses an emotionally charged or controversial issue. The more knowledge researchers have about a topic, the better the closed-ended questions they can construct.

The most important rule in constructing closed-ended items for questionnaires is that the list of possible responses must be both *mutually exclusive* (there should be no overlap in the alternatives) and *exhaustive* (all possible alternatives should be listed). Each respondent should be able to mark only one appropriate item. A multiple-choice question on an exam is a good example of this rule. In asking about religious preference most Americans could comfortably respond to the categories of Protestant, Catholic, Jewish, and Muslim, since they represent the country's major religious groups. But the categories are not exhaustive, because there are also Hindus, Buddhists, and many other smaller religious groupings. And what about people who have no religious preference? Adding the categories of "other" and "none" makes the religious preference item both mutually exclusive and exhaustive.

Open-ended questions ask respondents to provide their own answers to a question, rather than having to choose from a list of answers. This makes them more flexible than closed-ended questions and allows the

particularly relevant to the consumer behavior side in three major areas:

1. Secondary research—Businesses rely heavily on secondary resources, especially census data and economic indicators. Sociologists are also informed about many other rich sources of secondary data such as national and international databases on public opinion that tap changes in cultural values. Details of consumer culture valuable to businesses may be uncovered when these and other sources are viewed sociologically.
2. Social variables—Sociologists focus on three key social variables in consumer behavior that help people form ideas about what they want to buy: their culture, providing values and customs; their social class, giving them the resources for buying; and their reference groups, the people they want to be like. By combining these three variables distinctive "lifestyle" groupings of consumers emerge. For example, the "light blue collar" are those who do not aspire to a higher social class but they want and will pay for better quality merchandise.
3. Diversity links—Businesses that link social variables will have the edge in understanding their customers and marketing to them. Sociologists know that diversity in all its forms must be accounted for in research. Consumer research is no exception. If the San Antonio phone company had explored the links between ethnicity and social class, for example, a disastrous marketing campaign could have been averted.

Social Change
Business managers are under constant pressure to predict changes in consumer behavior. At the same time they must deal with rapid and relentless social change also impacting all consumers. Those managers gaining maximum benefit from consumer research will understand how the research corresponds to shifting social trends. Social change may be rapid and relentless, but there are patterns to change that can be uncovered and explained. Although the phone company in San Antonio had data indicating a large increase in the Hispanic population, they neglected to monitor broader social trends. The surge in this population

was from new arrivals with fewer resources who immigrated at a time of economic recession—trends the company needed to know how to interpret to better serve the new arrivals. Sociologists, who may be business managers or consumer researchers themselves, can readily show benefits to their companies or their clients when research on consumer behavior is explained according to principles of social change. When businesses add new customers and keep existing customers satisfied, these benefits translate to company profit.

1. What research questions should have been asked before the phone company began its advertising campaign? What research techniques would best answer these questions?
2. How would you design a consumer research study exploring why some people at upscale supermarkets prefer fresh foods and others prefer frozen foods? What variables must be accounted for in your exploration?

Sources: Lindsey, 1979; Rapp & Collins, 1994; Goldman et al., 1995; Edmunds, 1996.

---

researcher to ask for a more or less complete response. In assessing marital satisfaction, for example, commonly asked open-ended questions include, "What do you believe is the major strength of your marriage?" and "What is the one issue about which you and your spouse disagree most strongly?" A more extensive response is called for when follow-up questions are asked, such as "Provide a specific example of how the issue you identified has affected your marriage." Because respondents bring their own understanding to such questions and are free to answer as they see fit, validity is enhanced. But this advantage leads to a disadvantage in terms of reliability. It is more difficult to code and summarize data from open-ended questions. In addition, people may not want to take the time to write out long or detailed responses.

The mail questionnaire is an excellent and effective way to survey a wide distribution of people. It can offer anonymity, efficiency, and low cost. A short questionnaire that contains a mixed format of open- and closed-ended questions serves both research and respondent needs fairly well. The major disadvantage

is that *response rate*—the percentage of people who return the completed questionnaire—is usually relatively low. A 30 percent initial response rate is typical, and a low response rate can compromise validity and bias a study (Bolstein, 1991). Follow-up letters to respondents offering them incentives, such as money or small gifts, increase response rates, but people who must be enticed to finally answer a questionnaire may be different from those who respond early without any tangible incentives.

Personal Interviews. The same principles used in constructing surveys apply to constructing guides for personal interviews. However, interviews eliminate some of the problems associated with self-administered questionnaires and are more flexible, for a number of reasons. First, some people, such as the visually impaired, may be able to respond verbally but not in written form. Second, if the respondent misunderstands a question, an interviewer can repeat and clarify it. An interviewer can also use probes to get respondents to expand on incomplete answers or to clarify answers that are inconsistent with the question.

Third, an interviewer can note any factors in the interview setting that may affect responses, such as noise or interference from another person. Ideally, the interviewer can maintain some control over the interview situation, scheduling the interview in the home or at another site where privacy can be assured. Fourth, by carefully matching the interviewer with the interviewees, researchers can obtain better quality results. For example, using an interviewer from the same culture as the interviewee makes the interview more comfortable for both parties and provides insights that may be lost to outsiders. But the chief advantage of a personal interview compared with a self-administered questionnaire is even simpler: People would rather talk than write. If the interview is set up in advance, this method produces response rates approaching 95 percent.

Interviews also have disadvantages. First, interviews cost more than questionnaires. The longer the interview and the more open-ended questions asked, the higher the cost, both in interviewer time and in summarizing the data later. Second, interviewers are expected to record all responses verbatim. Open-ended questions require fast and continuous writing, often resulting in inaccuracies even by the most competent interviewer. Third, interviewer bias can creep in when respondents need questions clarified. Interviewers are supposed to remain neutral, but they may inadvertently steer the respondent toward answering in a certain way.

The most difficult obstacle to resolve in personal interviews is that of anonymity. While confidentiality can be assured in interviews, anonymity is impossible, because the interviewer is face to face with the interviewee. The interviewer may not know the interviewee's name or address, but some type of relationship has been established between them. What if these two people meet again in another setting or even become friends as a result of the interview? Because there is no anonymity, interviewees may be reluctant to answer truthfully, especially when sensitive information is called for. If an adolescent is interviewed about unacceptable or illegal behavior, for instance, lack of anonymity could compromise the validity of the data.

Telephone Interviews.   When speed of data collection over a wide geographical area is essential, the best method is the telephone interview. Through *random digit dialing*, telephone numbers in desired exchanges can be randomly accessed, a procedure that permits calls to unlisted numbers, new numbers, and numbers for those who live in institutions, such as college dorms. Telephone research has become so efficient that within a few hours of any important event, researchers can survey public opinion worldwide, with results aired on the evening news or put on the Internet.

Certain procedures help ensure the success of a telephone interview. Length is one important factor. The best telephone interviews consist of a limited number of well-defined, usually closed-ended questions that can be answered in twenty minutes or less. However, successful thirty-minute to one-hour telephone interviews are possible when the topic is of particular interest to respondents. Conducting phone interviews from a single site also improves results. Supervisors are available to address any problems that arise and to oversee quality control. Reliability is therefore quite high. Identifying the sponsoring organization is important in surveys, but perhaps moreso in telephone surveys since sales gimmicks frequently come in the guise of research. When respondents are assured that the survey is legitimate and confidential, they are more likely to answer all questions.

Telephone interviews have several advantages in addition to efficiency. One is cost. Telephone interviews are more economical than personal interviews and mail-in questionnaires, which helps explain growing popularity of telephone research. Compared with personal interviews, telephone interviews are two to three times cheaper. When low cost is linked to high measurement quality, the advantages of telephone interviews increase. Telephone interviews also offer interviewer safety when access to respondents from potentially dangerous locations is desired.

There are also disadvantages to telephone interviews. One is that respondents can become impatient if interviewers ask too much. As a general rule, interviews by phone should be kept as simple as possible. Benefits taper off quickly as interview complexity and length increase. Two other disadvantages are that visual aids such as graphs or maps cannot be used over the phone and that the interviewer has no knowledge of or control over factors that could be distracting a respondent, such as an interesting television program or a demanding child.

Comparing Survey Data Collection Methods. In an ideal research world, where time and money are of no concern, personal interviews would often provide more meaningful data than phone interviews. But in the real research world, time and money are dominant concerns. Researchers conducting surveys must weigh these factors against whatever gains they might obtain. They inevitably make decisions that stray from the ideal research process. These decisions should be viewed as meeting the challenges of ensuring that the research is high quality rather than making compromises.

Secondary Research

In research designs using **secondary analysis,** data and information compiled for other purposes are accessed and reanalyzed. Secondary analysis relies heavily on the wealth of information available from documentary resources, including archives, newspapers, diaries, government and private records, public opinion polls, and any other materials that may be tapped for research purposes. For example, studies linking music to violence do secondary analysis of existing data on air time devoted to different types of music, poverty and divorce rates, and records of gun ownership.

Sociology has a long and prestigious heritage of secondary research using documentary resources. The best known is Émile Durkheim's (1897/1964) classic work *Suicide,* in which he used official records on suicide in some European countries to generate a theory of social cohesion, or social connectedness (see Chapter 1). Durkheim found a consistent pattern of higher suicide rates in Protestant areas than in Catholic ones. He also found lower suicide rates for women, for married people, and for those with children. Suicide rates that vary by religion, gender, and marital and family status became key determinants for building his theory. Durkheim suggested that the greater a person's degree of social connectedness, the lower the suicide rate. Despite a century of massive social change since Durkheim's study, essentially the same correlation between suicide and social connectedness exists today.

Secondary analysis is responsible for some of the most important theoretical work in sociology. For example, Karl Marx (1867/1975) used documentary resources—current economic indicators—to demonstrate his link between capitalism and class struggle. Max Weber (1905/1977) also used documentary resources to analyze capitalism. But Weber used historical documents to argue that religion is a dominant factor in determining the progression of capitalism. The perspectives of both Marx and Weber are discussed in Chapter 10. Durkheim, Marx, and Weber all analyzed available documentary resources to support their own theoretical approaches, generating a wealth of potential hypotheses for later study. Taking the lead from Weber, for example, Robert Bellah (1957) used original texts and documents from Japan to document the religious and philosophical roots of the development of a Japanese system of capitalism.

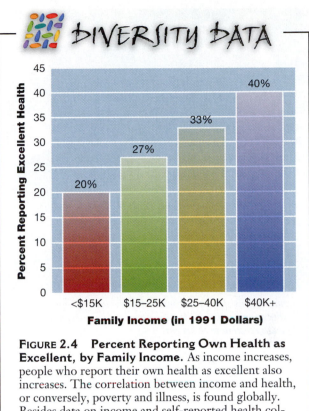

FIGURE 2.4   Percent Reporting Own Health as Excellent, by Family Income. As income increases, people who report their own health as excellent also increases. The correlation between income and health, or conversely, poverty and illness, is found globally. Besides data on income and self-reported health collected by the GSS on Americans, what other sources of data collected globally can be used to measure both poverty and health?
Source: NORC, General Social Surveys, 1972–1996. Chicago: National Opinion Research Center, 1996.

Contemporary research on social change continues to rely heavily on documentary resources, especially economic and social indicators generated by such organizations as the United Nations, the World Bank, and the World Health Organization. Another very valuable documentary resource is the General Social Survey, produced by the National Opinion Research Center. It is a collection of annual national surveys on a variety of topics conducted by personal interview on a random sample of the U.S. population. The General Social Survey (GSS) contains hundreds of items of interest to sociologists and is relied on extensively as a source of documentary data. The Diversity Data graphs in this text are from the General Social Survey.

Government data collected on a wide array of topics at particular points in time also offer valuable research materials. Sociologists routinely use government data to study change in the rates of divorce, illness, unemployment, immigration, and crime. At the same time, demographic or population characteris-

Content analysis of the print media before, during, and after the Bill Clinton impeachment trial is a good way to determine public and media reaction to the event.

tics—such as gender, age, race, birth and death rates, and marital status—provide necessary background information for almost any research. The census in particular offers a vital demographic database for secondary analysis. When linked with other available data used as dependent variables, demographic information can suggest many plausible independent variables. For instance, what is the relationship between poverty and illness? Documentary resources can help answer this question using government statistics on income and employment as operational measures of poverty, and disease and disability rates as measures of illness. Internet sources also allow for speedy global comparisons.

Documentary resources available through the Internet offer research opportunities that are limited only by a researcher's ingenuity and patience. Cross-cultural research is fueled by secondary analysis, especially when Internet sources are easily accessed. It usually begins with a *comparative approach*, allowing data to be collected and analyzed according to the similarities and differences between cultures or countries, making extensive use of large, national data archives (Lane, 1990).

Overall, secondary analysis of documentary resources is popular because it is probably the least expensive way to collect data. If carried out appropriately, it makes a meaningful contribution to sociology.

Content Analysis.   Researchers can examine documentary resources in a variety of ways. **Content analysis** is a technique in which researchers systemat-

ically examine and code the content of documents, such as magazines or newspapers, noting what they consider important to the research question. A researcher interested in political campaigns, for example, might look through newspapers and record the amount of coverage given to different aspects of political candidates, from their personal backgrounds to their views on education or the economy. Such analysis has revealed that much more coverage is given to the personal character of candidates than to their stands on political issues (Ansolabehere et al., 1991, 1993).

Progress for racial minorities and women has also been charted using content analysis. For example, content analysis has documented a long history of stereotyped portrayals of Asians in the movies and on television. Portrayals of African Americans, in contrast, have become more positive over the last thirty years (Chapter 6), although stereotypes of them still persist (Kitano & Daniels, 1995; Wilson, 1995). Betty Friedan's (1963) pioneering work, *The Feminine Mystique*, used content analysis to trace women's images in popular magazines. Friedan showed that fictional portrayals of women changed over time but that "happy housewife" themes dominated. Content

Calista Flockhart, who portrays lawyer Ally McBeal, is wildly popular among teen girls and young adult women. The mass media provide ideals for females that are based on appearance. In a show where the star often trips over her words (and her own feet) it's difficult for viewers to look past her short skirt to appreciate her achievements as a lawyer.

analysis of magazines over the next thirty years showed new themes emerging, such as educational opportunities, paid employment, and legal concerns of women. However, the themes of beauty and relationships with men still dominate (Chapter 13). As these examples demonstrate, content analysis is an excellent technique for analyzing important aspects of the media over time.

Unobtrusive Measures. Documentary resources are categorized as **unobtrusive measures** because the researcher who uses them is removed from what is being studied and so can have no influence on the data. One source of unobtrusive measures is a *physical trace*—evidence left from people's past behavior that can be examined for information about what those people valued, thought, or felt. An example of a physical trace is graffiti in public places, which can be analyzed for clues to social issues and social concerns. In repressive societies, where open protest is impossible, graffiti may function as an underground newspaper. Urban graffiti in the United States can be analyzed for insights into street gangs. It is a significant factor in the spread of gang violence and one that police monitor carefully.

There are many other kinds of physical traces available for sociological study. A researcher interested in assessing the degree of tension among fans at a baseball game can inspect the litter at the game's end and compare the number of beer containers with the number of popcorn or peanut bags. In a tense game with a close score, people crunch away their anxiety on popcorn or peanuts, but in a relaxed game with a foregone conclusion, fans sit back and drink beer. Other physical traces are not tangible objects, but rather signs of selective use such as wear on carpet, showing where people chose to walk. Selective wear on the floor of a museum, for instance, may indicate preferences in exhibits. It is even possible to count the fingerprints and nose prints on display cases for information about what people like. The cleaner the glass, the less popular the display (Webb et al., 1966). And to assess young children's interest in an exhibit, pay attention to the fingerprints and nose prints that are less than about three feet high!

Think of studying physical traces as similar to investigating a crime. What evidence does the criminal leave behind that will lead to an arrest? For sociologists, what material is left behind as people carry out their daily activities that can be used as evidence to test a hypothesis? A major specialty area for sociologists is criminology, which uses unobtrusive measures extensively. Careers in the criminal justice system provide excellent opportunities for students of sociology, enabling them to transfer the investigative principles of research methods to now investigate crime and criminal behavior.

Assessing Documentary Methods. For documentary resources to be used successfully in research, two major hurdles must be overcome. First, the researcher must gain access to these resources. This is no problem with government sources, but many other documents—such as a company's sales records or a person's letters and diaries—are private. If access to private documents is granted, a second hurdle must be overcome: making do with whatever data exist. Rarely will documentary data be perfect for a researcher's needs. For example, official records of household income may be broken down by larger increments than a researcher would like. Or a researcher studying crime may find that it is hard to compare crime statistics across states because a felony in Texas is defined differently from a felony in New York. There is even the problem of whether the accuracy of the document can be trusted. Famous people write letters and keep diaries with the knowledge that these documents may be published after their deaths, so they tend to present themselves in the most favorable light possible. For all these reasons, the validity and reliability of research based on documentary resources may be called into question. Generally, documentary resources should be triangulated—combined with data collected in other ways.

Field Research

Creativity is the hallmark of **field research.** As mentioned at the beginning of the chapter, it was the research design Elijah Anderson used to study an urban neighborhood. Field researchers collect data about the social behavior of people in natural settings. Sociologists conducting field research routinely triangulate data collection methods, especially observations and personal interviews. Often they do not begin with specific research questions, but rather do an exploratory study that ends with questions or hypotheses that will be tested later. In this way, field research is sometimes just the first phase of an ongoing research project.

Do not confuse field experiments with field research. The Hawthorne experiments, for example, were done in the "field"—the natural setting of a workplace rather than an artificially created environment—but their purpose was to study the effects of specific factors on worker productivity. The researchers tested hypotheses and quantitatively analyzed results. In contrast, field research typically uses **qualitative analysis,** summarizing data in nonnumerical ways in order to discover underlying meanings

To be successful field researchers on teenage dating behavior, sociologists need to first learn as much as possible about the places where social interaction occurs, such as the settings where teens congregate.

and build theory. Rather than *testing* hypotheses, qualitative analysis is commonly used to *develop* hypotheses.

Sometimes the goal of field research is to produce an **ethnography,** a description of customs, beliefs, and values of a particular culture compiled by researchers who spent prolonged periods actually living with the people they are studying. These researchers rely heavily on data collection methods that allow them to get an "insider" view. For field research to be effective, fairly close involvement between observer and those being observed is needed.

Participant Observation.   The best way to gain an insider's view is to actually become an insider through **participant observation,** where the researcher witnesses, experiences, and engages firsthand in the activities of the group being studied. This requires that the researcher take on some accepted status (position) within the group.

There are two typical roles for participant observers in field research. One is the role of *complete participant,* where the researcher becomes a member of the group being studied, interacting with subjects as naturally as possible, but does not inform them of the research being done. Judith Rollins (1985) chose to become a complete participant in order to investigate relationships between African American domestic workers and their white employers. Domestic work is one of the commonest occupations of low-income women worldwide, but there are major gaps in knowledge about how women adjust to this work.

Believing that this gap may be bridged with insider knowledge, Rollins obtained a job as a domestic worker for ten different families. She knew that her study would be severely compromised if her employers found out about the research, even if she assured them of confidentiality. Uncomfortable with the ethics of the complete participant role, Rollins asked herself whether the research gain was worth the deception. Ultimately she concluded that it was. She discovered, for example, that domestic workers used various strategies to maintain dignity when their domestic work roles were demeaned or scorned. Rollins' work contributes to the growing body of theory related to actions women use to resist victimization. She also considered the applied aspects of her research since her findings could help others understand the lives of these women and would perhaps benefit them in some way.

If it is not practical to become a complete participant, a researcher may choose the role of *participant-as-observer.* In this role, researchers inform subjects of the study being done and try to participate in the group as much as possible. Most field researchers prefer this role, largely because it is less deceptive. An example of participant-as-observer research is Elijah Anderson's study of a neighborhood in transition, highlighted in this chapter's opening vignette.

Another example of this research role is William Foote Whyte's *Street Corner Society*, a classic study of Italian American working-class men living in a slum area of Boston (Whyte, 1943/1981). Whyte's study hinged on his being accepted into the lives of these men. Realizing that gaining the support of a few key people was the best approach, he became friends with one of the group's leaders, "Doc," who introduced him to others until he gradually was accepted. He could never be a bona fide member of the group because he was a sociologist doing research, but he established a degree of intimacy and rapport that provided the necessary insider status. Doc and a few other group members served as informants, becoming partners in his research and giving him information about what the men said and did in his absence. Whyte's research showed that the city "slum" is an organized community of kinship, friendships, neighborhood associations, and distinctive values that serve as anchors to those who live there. This slum neighborhood was not the chaotic place most outsiders imagined it to be.

Whyte's field research established both a theoretical framework and a research model that many other sociologists have since used in studying urban areas. For instance, Herbert Gans's (1962/1982) research in another Boston Italian American community found patterns similar to those Whyte discovered. Gans focused on how neighborhoods are disrupted by urban change, but how some manage to maintain a sense of community. In another urban field study, *Tally's Corner*, Elliot Liebow (1967) entered the lives of African American men who congregated in front of a laundromat in Washington, DC. He informed them about his research, and like Whyte, he gradually became accepted. He visited their homes, participated in their activities, and gave them financial and legal advice. Contrary to the stereotype of the urban ghetto, Liebow found precarious but stable social relationships in this corner of the city. Again, in a seemingly chaotic environment, underlying stability was uncovered. For our purposes, the key point in all these studies is the research design used. The participant-as-observer role provided opportunities for ethically acceptable research on people and places otherwise inaccessible.

Another role for field researchers combines aspects of the complete participant and participant-as-observer roles. In this role the researcher does not have to become a member of the group under study because she or he *already* is a member. However, the people being studied may or may not be told that research is being conducted on them by another member of their group. This membership allows for an easier transition from outsider to insider. Elijah Anderson initially lived in the neighborhood he studied and told people in his neighborhood about the research he was conducting. Sociologists are creative in using their everyday roles and experiences to do research, and special access by way of membership provides extraordinary opportunities for research.

When Julius Roth (1963) found himself confined to a hospital as a long-term tuberculosis patient, he turned adversity into advantage and saw his hospital bed as a "good observation post" to learn about the social structure of the hospital. But unlike Anderson, his subjects—staff and fellow patients—were unaware of his study. Although his patient status made him a "legitimate" group member, since subjects did not know about the research, he took on the complete participant role. Tuberculosis patients at that time were often quarantined for up to several years. Roth's first impression was the concern with time. Almost as in a prison, the question on everyone's mind was "How long are you in for?" Using a symbolic interactionist framework, Roth showed how "timetables" were socially constructed. TB patients played "games" with hospital staff and with each other to discover their timetables and chart their progress. TB ran in unpredictable cycles, so timetables served as a way for patients to symbolically control their destiny. As his own "time" progressed, Roth's insider status permitted in-depth observations that gradually led to a theory about how patients and staff socially constructed time according to norms or informal rules. His participant observation study is a good example of both the theory and the method of field research. Qualitative research through participant observation allows for developing hypotheses that can be tested later with quantitative research.

On Leaving the Field. Because their work involves establishing relationships with subjects, often intensely emotional ones, field researchers confront two important questions. The investigator must first ask: "How much of an impact has this investigation had on the people being studied?" and second, "How much of an impact have the people being studied had on me?"

A famous study of a doomsday cult conducted by Leon Festinger and his colleagues (1956) illustrates issues surrounding the first of these two questions. Festinger and his co-workers, acting as complete participants, pretended to be converts to a cult predicting that the end of the world was near. The members of the cult believed that aliens would save them from destruction by taking them to another world in a spaceship. Festinger wondered how the cult members would react when the appointed time for the end of the world came and went. Festinger and his colleagues tried not to influence the cult members' thinking, but the cover stories they devised to explain why they joined the group backfired on them. The cult members concluded that the researchers were really messengers from the alien rescuers! (Indeed, they *were* messengers from another world, but not the one the group thought.) Since the world did not end, the cult members reduced their dissonance by deciding that the end was still near, just later than they thought. The researchers had influenced the group in a way that might not have occurred otherwise and were there to observe it. Festinger's study led to the development of a major social psychological theory known as *cognitive dissonance*. This theory explains how people reconcile what they believe to be true with their real-life observations, such as those the cult members experienced.

In Festinger's study, the researchers' influence on the group being studied was outside the awareness of group members. In contrast, Elliot Liebow influenced his subjects in ways they were well aware of because he gave them various kinds of support. When Liebow ended his study and left "Tally's Corner," his availability for support and advice—which some of the men had come to rely on—came to an end. Even when a researcher maintains contact with subjects after a study is over, it is impossible to continue in the same capacity. Lives change and people move on. The difficulty in making this break with subjects is an important ethical issue in doing field research.

The second question the researcher must ask on leaving the field is, "How much of an impact have the people being studied had on me?" Too much distance between researcher and subjects hinders relationship building, but too much closeness hurts objectivity. Field researchers have the difficult task of simultaneously being objective observers and involved, concerned participants. Sometimes fieldworkers are accused of romanticizing subjects and selecting data that paint positive portraits while ignoring the negative parts of their subjects' lives. At other times, they may feel disdain and disgust toward their subjects but attempt to transform these emotions into more favorable ones. There are also cases in which the research is so heartrending that it harms the investigator. Linda Dunn's (1991) research on battered women involved such emotionally draining interviews that she experienced sleep disorders and stomach ailments. In retrospect she realized that these physical responses, and the powerlessness and anger she felt while doing the research, paralleled the reactions expressed by her subjects.

Finally, fieldworkers can become so immersed in the lives of their subjects that they shed the researcher role and "go native," becoming converts to whatever group they are studying. This happens most often to the lone ethnographer in an isolated setting who has minimal contact with colleagues for long periods of time. But it is a risk all social scientists face when they begin to identify intensely with their subjects. Passion replaces sociological understanding and, unfortunately, the research story they intended to tell is lost. Sociological training for fieldwork is increasingly accounting for the critical impact that emotions have on participant observation—both during and after the research (Kleinman & Kopp, 1993).

Feminist Research Methods and Links to Diversity. Until fairly recently, sociologists routinely used white, male, middle-class samples in conducting research, particularly samples of college students. Entire theories were developed based on the attitudes and behavior of these subjects. But the world is not comprised of white, male, and middle-class people. Like many countries, for instance, the already strong multicultural heritage in the United States is fueled with immigration and the globalization of business. It is essential to consider race and ethnicity as variables in research. The variables of social class and gender

must also be considered in order to avoid a distorted view of society and social behavior.

Recent research on women is an excellent example of how sociological research has widened. Feminists have challenged the lack of diversity in research and their efforts have led to an explosion of feminist research methods. Although these methods single out *androcentrism*, the male-centered bias in research, and calls attention to the oppression of women, feminist methods can be applied to human diversity in all its forms. These methods are guided by feminist theory, which issues a challenge to the status quo that subordinates women and other minorities (Chapter 1). Thus feminist research uses a variety of techniques to hear the voices of formerly silenced women (Reinharz, 1992:240).

Medical research in particular has shown an androcentric bias. Some studies that use males as the medical norm are rather infamous, such as a major federally funded study examining the effects of diet on breast cancer. Only men were used as subjects (Travis, 1996). Or consider the widely publicized study on the effect of aspirin on heart attacks using a sample of over 35,000 men. The reduced heart attack risk was so spectacular that results were made public even before the study ended. But since the sample was made up only of men, results could not be generalized to women, despite the fact that heart disease is the number one killer of both genders (Steering Committee of the Physician's Health Study, 1989; Rosser, 1994). In challenging the male-as-norm bias, feminist research is helping close the gap that excludes women as research subjects.

Since feminist methods typically lead to studies in which special relationships are developed between researchers and subjects, field research, ethnographies, participant observation, and in-depth interviews are favored techniques. The voices of victims of rape and domestic violence are better portrayed using these methods. Feminist approaches have allowed new research topics to evolve and old ones to be viewed from a different angle. They have led to cross-cultural research focusing not only on women, but also on other marginalized groups—those that are disadvantaged or out of society's mainstream. Feminist research strengthens sociology's goal of more accurately representing human diversity in research.

Source: © 1999 by Nicole Hollander. Distributed by Los Angeles Times Syndicate.

≋ LIFE CONNECTIONS: Gender and the Wage Gap

Americans put a strong emphasis on achievement and talent, expecting these attributes to pay off in the workplace. Sociological research into the earnings gap between men and women in the United States has provided some fascinating data that may contradict this strongly held conviction. Table 2.1 shows a statistical relationship between gender and earnings. Gender is the independent variable and is divided into its two attributes, male and female. Weekly earnings in dollars is the dependent variable and is divided according to four time periods.

The table reveals that while income increased for both males and females, the increase for males was consistently higher. Only between 1990 and 1995 was the increase for women ($60) higher than for men ($57). This slight increase was not enough to enable women to catch up with men. In 1997 men earned $148 more per week on the average than women.

In order to determine whether gender is indeed a key variable in understanding the wage gap, other variables must also be taken into account. For example, sociological research shows that Americans strongly believe that education is *the* critical ingredient for economic success. Measuring the earnings of men and women at different educational levels can determine whether the original relationship between gender and earnings continues to hold true or if it is a spurious one. Table 2.2 shows what happens when education is added as a third variable. This table reveals that at all educational levels, males still outearn females and that the wage gap generally increases at the higher educational levels. Male college graduates on the average earn $21,788 more than female college graduates.

Are these figures convincing enough to say that a wage gap in gender exists? What about other variables that could still explain the gender differences in earnings? Overall, the gender gap in earnings holds true even when race, age, occupation, seniority, and region are also added to the picture. From all available records, the wage gap has been a persistent economic fact in the United States over time (Reskin, 1988; Kemp, 1994; Wendt & Slonaker, 1994). The original relationship between gender and income is not spurious. While we cannot say that gender is *the* cause of income differences between Americans, we can safely conclude that it is *a* cause—and a significant one.

Today a full-time female worker earns about 75 percent of what a full-time male worker earns.

The data are certainly clear. But the reason to do research is not simply to collect data but to *explain* them. Why do men earn more money than women? Different theoretical perspectives provide different answers. Functionalists suggest that women act as a reserve labor force to be called on when needed by their families or by society. Conflict theorists suggest that men make the rules that will maintain their economic advantage over women; hence, gender discrimination in the workplace remains a reality. Symbolic interactionists suggest that since the workplace is largely gender segregated, powerful social definitions assign a lesser value to the work women do compared with the work men do. Each of the three perspectives explains the same data on gender and the wage gap differently. The best explanations account for most of the data and for changes in the data over time.

≋ SOCIETY CONNECTIONS: The Ethics of Research

Like all scientists, sociologists routinely confront ethical issues in conducting their research. These ethical issues are more apparent in some studies than in others. As demonstrated by the infamous Tuskegee study (see box), research has sometimes been conducted under ethically deplorable conditions. Stanley Milgram's study of obedience to authority, described in an opening vignette, caused the subjects severe anxiety as they struggled with the choice of whether to follow orders and administer shocks. Milgram's findings certainly gave important insights into human behavior, but at what price to his subjects? The challenge in studying human beings is to conduct research that is both sociologically relevant and ethically acceptable. We can explore the difficulty of meeting this challenge by looking at two other studies often cited as ethically compromising to the human subjects who participated in them. The first is a study of prison life by social psychologist Philip Zimbardo (1972).

Losing Self-Identity

Philip Zimbardo was interested in the degree to which certain environments, such as prisons, could alter a person's sense of self-identity. This was (and is)

Table 2.1	Median Weekly Earnings in Dollars by Gender			
	1985	1990	1995	1997
Males	406	481	538	579
Females	277	346	406	431

Source: U.S. Bureau of the Census, 1998.

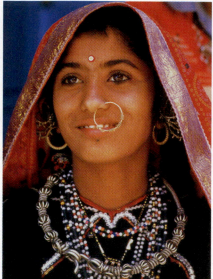

Feminist research methods focus on how women are different and how they are alike. The viewpoints of women from diverse backgrounds are highlighted through these methods.

an important question given the reality that for many convicts, prison life does not "rehabilitate" but instead stabilizes a prison identity that is difficult to dislodge once the prisoner is released. Do prisons brainwash people so that the nonprisoner identity is abolished? Since Zimbardo could not study this question in a real prison, he decided to construct a mock prison in the basement of a building on the Stanford University campus over summer break. He recruited and paid male college students to participate in his research and randomly assigned them to "play" the role of prisoners or guards. Then he observed what happened.

In only a few days, both groups shed their college identities and "became" prisoners and guards. The experiment became a reality. Guards progressively became more threatening and brutal; prisoners reacted with submissiveness and fear, becoming servile, dehumanized robots. Zimbardo decided to end the experiment prematurely because of the real danger that the guards could do physical harm to the prisoners, some of whom became emotionally impaired after the first few days of the experiment. As Zimbardo concludes, these abnormal personal and social reactions are best

seen as products of an environment that created, and then reinforced, behavior that would be pathological in other settings. In less than a week the experience of imprisonment undid a lifetime of learning.

Observing Very Private Behavior

In exploring deviant behavior, sociologist Laud Humphreys (1970) raised different ethical concerns about research than did Zimbardo. Humphreys was interested in studying "tearooms"—public restrooms frequented by men in search of "instant sex" from other men. The sex was quick, impersonal, and silent. Since this behavior was not only deviant but illegal, covert observation was the research method selected. It was actually participant observation because Humphreys served in the role of lookout for the tearoom, situating himself at the door or window and warning the men by a cough or nod if someone was approaching.

Humphreys discovered that more than half his subjects were married and living with their wives. Some of these men were heterosexual, except for the tearoom encounters. Others were active in a homo-

Table 2.2	Annual Earnings in Dollars of Full-Time Workers by Gender and Educational Level			
	Some High School	High School Graduate	Some College	BA degree+
Males	25,283	35,521	38,491	63,127
Females	17,313	21,893	25,889	41,339

Source: U.S. Bureau of the Census, 1998.

The Tuskegee Experiment

At the beginning of the twentieth century syphilis was a ravaging and incurable disease. Little was known about its progression in the human body. To learn more about the disease, in 1932 the U.S. Public Health Service (USPHS) worked with prestigious Tuskegee University to recruit as research subjects 399 African American men from Macon County, Alabama, one of the state's poorest rural areas. All of the men had syphilis, but were told they were being treated for "bad blood." On clinic days they ate, had a place to stay, and received free medical care—luxuries for poor people during the Depression. What they were told was a sham. What they were not told was the true research question: "What are the long-term effects of untreated syphilis on Negro males?" The study continued for the next three decades, even after penicillin became the standard remedy for syphilis. During World War II the subjects were

screened out of the armed forces for fear they would leave the study because their disease would be discovered. But the disease was left untreated. Some men became incapacitated, blind, and impotent. Others died. In 1972, when the study became public, the American Medical Association charged the USPHS with conducting genocide against the poor. The race factor in the experiment could not be denied. In 1997 President Bill Clinton apologized to those who survived the Tuskegee Experiment.

Today many legal, institutional, and professional pressures put researchers under continual scrutiny to ensure that scientific investigations are carried out ethically. Ethical guidelines are in place that ask an essential question: How has respect for the rights and welfare of the participants been demonstrated? Informed consent is one way to demonstrate this respect. But because there will always be research that can-

not provide complete information to subjects, the strategy of "reasonably informed consent" has been accepted as a model. If people are told what they can "reasonably" expect in terms of risk or discomfort, as well as potential benefits, and are given answers to their questions, then according to the model they should be able to make an informed decision about whether to participate as research subjects.

1. How could the Tuskegee experiment be redesigned so that it could be carried out ethically yet still provide important answers to the question of the impact of syphilis? What changes in the study question would have to be made?
2. Can the Tuskegee study legitimately be described as an experiment? Why or why not?

Sources: Allen, 1978; Reynolds, 1982:4; Jones, 1993.

sexual subculture and exhibited a strong gay identity. But how did Humphreys learn about the backgrounds of these men from only covert observations? He recorded license plate numbers, tracked down the owners' addresses, and six months later, with enough change in appearance to avoid recognition, he visited

their homes as a survey researcher. He *was* conducting a survey, but his subjects never suspected its true purpose.

At a time when knowledge about homosexual activities and lifestyles was limited, Humphreys' research was extremely valuable. But deceit was involved in gaining access to this group, and the research violated the privacy of people engaged in extremely private acts. Were the findings worth the methods used to gain them?

INTERNET ⸺ CONNECTIONS

The text discusses the ethical implications of social research. The Council of American Survey Research Organizations (CASRO) has assembled a code of standards and ethics for survey research. You may review these ethical standards at: http://www.casro.org/casro.htm. What are the researcher's responsibilities to respondents and clients? What are the responsibilities associated with reporting to clients and the public? How does the issue of *informed consent* fit in here?

Informed Consent and the Need to Know

No one disputes that the studies by Milgram, Zimbardo, and Humphreys provided valuable data on social behavior. But each also raised serious ethical concerns. Milgram's and Zimbardo's subjects were not the same after the experiment. They had undergone a very emotionally stressful experience, and many were ashamed of their behavior. In the Humphreys case, although subject confidentiality was maintained, these men were no longer anonymous once Humphreys had their names. Their lives could literally have been ruined if their identities had been divulged. On the other hand, Milgram and Humphreys could not have carried out the research if the subjects had been told its true purposes. And Zimbardo himself did not predict the risk to his subjects and perhaps continued the experiment too long even when it was clear that emotional harm had already occurred.

Today, ethical codes are designed to protect subjects from harm or risk that may result from participating in scientific research. It is doubtful that Milgram, Zimbardo, and Humphreys could have conducted their experiments in the same manner today. The American Sociological Association (ASA) sets ethical standards that underlie the professional conduct of sociologists. The guidelines on issues that sociologists may encounter in their activities are contained in the ASA Code of Ethics. The code has as its primary goal the welfare and protection of the individuals and groups with whom sociologists work. The basic principles established by the code call for sociologists to

1. Maintain the highest competence in their work.
2. Be honest, fair, and respectful of others in all professional activities.
3. Adhere to the highest scientific and professional standards.
4. Accept social responsibility for their work.
5. Respect the rights, dignity, and worth of all people.

The principle of respecting people's rights comes to the forefront every time sociologists conduct re-

search. **Informed consent** is a basic tenet of all scientific research and is found in the code of ethics of every professional association that uses human subjects. With informed consent, potential research subjects have enough knowledge about the research to determine whether they choose to participate. The well-being of research participants must be safeguarded at all times.

Sociologists see to it that confidentiality is protected. They do so to ensure the integrity of the research and to maintain open communication with research participants. The ASA Code of Ethics specifically calls for sociologists not to allow information gained in confidence to be used in ways that would unfairly compromise these participants (American Sociological Association, 1997).

Codes of ethics are general guidelines only and are always subject to interpretation. There are no easy answers to many ethical questions raised in doing scientific research. Ethical guidelines can be viewed not as constraints on research, but rather as enhancements to it. Science thrives in an atmosphere of free and open discussions, including discussions about ethical issues. A fundamental principle of science is that it gains headway not despite but because the research it is based on is carried out ethically and humanely. The future of all sociological research and the benefits that it provides depend on this principle.

SUMMARY

1. Sociologists use the scientific method as a blueprint for research. Key objectives for scientific research are to test, modify, and develop theories.
2. The research process allows researchers to either test or develop hypotheses. Methods to test hypotheses are the most frequently used in sociological research.
3. The first step in the research process is to find a problem to investigate. After reviewing the literature on work that has already been done on a topic, the researcher poses a research question and formulates a prediction or potential answer, called a hypothesis.
4. A hypothesis is also a prediction about the relationship between two variables: the independent variable, presumed to be the cause that reveals changes in the other, dependent variable. Both variables must be operationally defined in such a way that they can be measured.

5. Besides summarizing the results of their research and drawing conclusions, sociologists must deal with issues of measurement quality—validity (data accuracy) and reliability (data consistency). They must also decide whether results from a sample of people can apply legitimately to a broader population.
6. There are four major types of research design (a plan for collecting data): experiments, surveys, secondary research, and field research.
7. The research design for an experiment typically has four steps: (1) Establish two separate groups, an experimental group and a control group; (2) assign subjects to the two groups randomly; (3) measure the dependent variable both before and after the experiment; and (4) compare the two sets of measurements.
8. To establish a causal relationship between two variables, experimenters must satisfy four

conditions: (1) The cause must precede the effect; (2) the two variables must be correlated, or linked systematically; (3) the relationship between the two variables must not be explained by another variable; and (4) there must be a logical explanation for the relationship.

9. Sociological experiments may be conducted in the field (the natural settings where people live and work). Because experimental conditions cannot be controlled in this type of setting, field experiments cannot usually determine causality.

10. Surveys are a type of research well suited to studying the attitudes of large groups of people. Though surveys cannot establish a causal relationship between variables, they can quantify the relationship and, with random sampling, the results can often be applied to a broader population.

11. Sociologists collect survey data using questionnaires, personal interviews, and telephone interviews. Although personal interviews are the best for response rate and validity, they are more costly and time-consuming compared with questionnaires and telephone interviews.

12. Secondary research involves analyzing data drawn from existing sources—such as archives, newspapers, diaries, government records, or public opinion polls. Although it is the least expensive research to carry out, secondary research has problems with validity and is often triangulated (used in combination with other methods).

13. Field research involves in-depth study of groups of people in their natural environments by sociologists who may choose to participate in the groups. This method of research is suited to qualitative, or nonnumerical, analysis of data and is generally used to explore a topic or develop a hypothesis about a topic.

14. In the past most sociological research was done on white, middle-class males. Guided by feminist research strategies, sociologists now study more diverse samples of people, especially women and racial minorities.

15. Sociologists must take care to follow ethical guidelines in their research to protect the rights and dignity of those they study. Confidentiality and informed consent—the requirement that a sociologist first explain a study to participants and obtain their permission to be studied—are imperative.

KEY TERMS

content analysis   48

control group   40

control variable   35

correlation   40

dependent variable   35

ethnography   50

experimental group   40

field research   49

Hawthorne effect   42

hypothesis   33

independent variable   35

informed consent   56

operational definition   35

participant observation   50

population   37

qualitative analysis   49

quantitative analysis   43

random sample   43

reliability   36

research design   36

sample   37

scientific method   32

secondary analysis   47

spurious relationship   40

survey research   43

unobtrusive measures   49

validity   36

variable   35

CRITICAL THINKING QUESTIONS

1. Demonstrate how theory and research are linked in a cycle and why this linkage is necessary for the objectives of science.

2. Explain why identifying the causes for human social behavior is the most difficult task sociologists face in doing research. How can they design research to overcome this difficulty?

3. You have been assigned to do field research on the aged. Because you are much younger than the group you are to study and do not feel comfortable joining them in their activities, you decide to remain an outsider. Is your choice an ethical one? How might it affect the results of your study? What might be a better solution to your problem?

4. Why is informed consent necessary to conduct research but also compromising for the goals of research?

CULTURE

Initiating a Masai Warrior

"Circumcision will have to take place even if it means holding you down," my father explained to the teenage initiates. "The pain you feel is symbolic. There is deeper meaning because circumcision means a break between childhood and adulthood. For the first time you will be regarded as a grown-up. You will be expected to give and not just receive and no family affairs will be discussed without your being consulted. Coming into manhood is a heavy load. If you are ready for these responsibilities tell us now." After a prolonged silence, one of my half-brothers said awkwardly. "Face it . . . it's painful. I won't lie about it. We all went through it. Only blood will flow, not milk." There was laughter and my father left. Among the Masai of East Africa, the rite of circumcision swiftly transforms an adolescent boy to an adult man. (Adapted from Saitoti, 1994:159)

You Don't Love Me: The Remorseful Chinese Child

"My parents do not love me. They are cold, distant, and remote." This feeling is commonly voiced among children of Chinese immigrants to the United States. Many Chinese children long for the affection they see in American movies and television and read about in magazines. Their experiences with their parents and other members of their extended family are formal and distant, so they conclude that love is lacking. In China, where such behavior is the norm, children do not question it. The lack of open affection extends to spouse and friends. To the Chinese, physical intimacy and love are private matters. Even when it comes to handshaking, the traditional Chinese way is to clasp one's own hands in greeting. Kissing and hugging a friend is most inappropriate, and kissing a spouse in public is shameless and ill-mannered. In fact, until recently any kissing in China was considered so vulgar it was thought to suggest cannibalism! In America, Chinese children feel deprived because they see affection all around them but receive no outward expression of it themselves. It is an important example of bicultural conflict that confronts newcomers to America and several succeeding generations. (Hsu, 1981; Sung, 1994)

Americana

The Festival of American Folklife is a summer event held on the Mall in Washington, DC. Moving among the booths, one encounters midwestern farmers, rhythm-and-blues musicians, North and South American Indians, and Indonesians—all drumming, threshing, carving, singing, dancing, cooking, explaining, costuming, building, and generally going through the yearly ritual that showcases America as a nation of nations. E pluribus unum, hands across the water, black and white together. Up and down the Mall, real Indians are carving and real Indonesians are sitting cross-legged under thatched roofs making ornaments, although a folk purist would be shocked to learn that the Indonesian uses a stapler to fasten the ornaments. One Delta bluesman wore a New York Mets cap and was making weathervanes in the shape of Tweety Bird and Sylvester the Cat. Who is to say what is an "authentic" part of American culture? Everything at the festival is "authentic." One of the pleasures of the festival is that it turns everybody there into your own kind. Everybody is American. (Adapted from Allen, 1994:201–203)

Human behavior is immensely varied, and the variations are fundamentally determined by culture. **Culture** is a human society's total way of life; it is learned and shared and includes the society's values, customs, material objects, and symbols. Our culture provides our social heritage and tells us which behaviors are appropriate and which are not. Unlike the Masai, most Americans would regard circumcision at adolescence as cruel. Unlike the Chinese, Americans regard kissing as a typical and accepted pattern of showing affection. The Festival of American Folklife highlights the fact that America's cultural heritage is diverse, yet also binding—turning

INTERNET ⟡ CONNECTIONS

Like so many places around the world, the land of the noble Masai warrior has been taken over by tourism. Check site www.masai.com to sign up for your safari. How do you suppose today's Masai warriors regard tourists.

everybody into "your own kind." As these vignettes suggest, culture both unites and divides people—a theme we will explore in this chapter as we examine culture's powerful role in determining human social behavior.

CULTURE AND SOCIETY

Culture encompasses all that we have developed and acquired as human beings. Culture guides our choices of food and clothing, our reading material and art, and our dating partners and friends. Stop reading for a moment and quickly survey the area around you. If you are in your dorm, the library, sitting on a bench in the quad, or reading at the beach, everything that encircles you is culturally produced. Culture can be subdivided into two major segments: **material culture,** which includes tangible artifacts, physical objects, and items that are found in a society; and **nonmaterial culture,** which includes a society's intangible and abstract components such as values, beliefs, and traditions. The two are inextricably bound.

Each person is a unique individual with his or her own hopes and dreams, likes and dislikes, attitudes and opinions, habits and routines. Yet many of our feelings, beliefs, and customs are reflections of our culture. For example, selecting a marriage partner on the basis of romantic love seems like the natural thing to do in the United States. Yet in most of the world's cultures, selection of a spouse is in the hands of marriage brokers, parents, other relatives, or matchmakers. Culture is so much taken for granted that we rarely think about alternatives to what we usually think and do. Only when we compare our cultural beliefs and customs with those of other cultures do we discover what we take for granted in our own culture.

Ethnocentrism and Cultural Relativism

In the study of culture, the essential element that sociology shares with all other sciences is a neutral and unbiased approach to the subject. The scientific

method gives some protection against inaccurate reporting, but it does not tell us how to remain emotionally aloof from attitudes and behavior that we may find personally disturbing. Culture exerts such a powerful influence that most people exhibit **ethnocentrism,** the tendency to evaluate their own culture as superior to others. Being a citizen of a particular culture instills a sense of group loyalty and pride that is useful when cultural unity is necessary, such as when facing a common enemy in war. But for social scientists or those who simply want to study or understand another culture, ethnocentrism is inappropriate.

The opposite of ethnocentrism is **cultural relativism,** the view that all cultures have intrinsic worth and that each culture must be evaluated and understood according to its own standards. On one level, cultural relativism is an ethical principle: You should not judge another people's customs especially until you understand them. On another level it is pragmatic: You cannot do business with members of a different culture if you unknowingly behave in ways that offend them and if you misinterpret their polite behavior for stubbornness or backwardness. Equally important, cultural relativism is a scientific principle. In studying other cultures, as in all scientific endeavors, anthropologists and sociologists strive to be objective.

Cultural relativism is easier said than done. Scientists, tourists, students, or businesspeople who first encounter cultures vastly different from their own will likely experience a feeling of **culture shock**—they will tend to experience feelings of alienation, depression, and loneliness until they become acclimated to the new culture. Anthropologist Conrad Kottak describes his own culture shock on his first encounter with Bahia, Brazil:

> I could not know just how naked I would feel without the cloak of my own language and culture. . . . My first impressions of Bahia were of smells—alien odors of ripe and decaying mangoes . . . and of swatting ubiquitous fruit flies. . . . There were strange concoctions of rice, black beans, and gelatinous globs of meats and floating pieces of skin. I remember . . . a slimy stew of beef tongue in tomatoes. At one meal a disintegrating fish head, eyes still attached, but barely, stared up at me as the rest of its body floated in a bowl of bright orange palm oil. (Kottak, 1987:4)

Kottak eventually grew accustomed to this world. He not only learned to accept what he saw, he began to appreciate and enjoy its new wonders. Culture shock and ethnocentrism gave way to cultural relativism.

A college education in the United States represents an important cultural value related to achievement. Women and racial minorities now attend college in the highest numbers since the founding of the United States.

Values and Beliefs

Values are cultural ideals about what is considered moral and immoral, good and bad, or proper and improper. As shared beliefs about ideal goals and behavior, they serve as standards for social life. Values also serve as criteria for assessing your own behavior as well as that of others.

In small, traditional, relatively isolated societies, agreement on values may be close to universal. However, even larger, ethnically diverse cultures that experience ongoing and rapid social change have identifiable core values. These core values are embraced by most members of the culture and help distinguish it from other cultures. Over a half century of research continues to document a consistently held core value set that defines America's national character (Mead, 1942; Williams, 1951; Devine, 1972; Harris, 1981). The following list, although not inclusive, identifies some of the most important U.S. values. Some of these values are not only taken for granted, but may be viewed negatively by people from other cultures.

1. *Individualism*. The United States is a highly individualistic culture emphasizing personal independence and self-reliance. Individual self-interest rather than group goals is an acceptable guide to behavior.

2. *Achievement*. Talent, motivation, and work are the ingredients for success. Rewards are based on merit. Individuals whose hard work transforms their rags to riches are idealized models for Americans. A related value is competition, which maximizes both the merit and the reward. May the best person win.

3. *Material comfort*. The fruits of hard work and achievement are the financial rewards that can buy a desired lifestyle—what is wanted as well as what is needed.

4. *Democracy and equality of opportunity*. These values can be accomplished only in a political, educational, and economic climate that maximizes freedom of choice and equality of opportunity at all institutional levels. If the playing fields are equal—in school, the political system, and the economy—then the best person should succeed.

5. *Nationalism*. America is the world's role model for democracy, and Americans are proud of their political system and economic accomplishments. Regardless of their ethnic background, most people see themselves as Americans first.

6. *Group superiority*. Americans believe that their culture is superior to other cultures. Beliefs about superiority also extend to how Americans rank groups within their culture. Although Americans believe that all individuals are equal, they view

62   Chapter 3   Culture

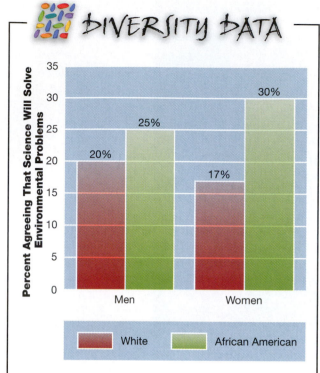

DIVERSITY DATA

FIGURE 3.1   Will Science Solve Environmental Problems?   For both men and women, and for whites and African Americans, only about one-fourth tend to agree science will solve environmental problems. Yet Americans also highly value science as a basis of action. What explains this apparent cultural contradiction? Why is the largest difference in level of agreement between African American and white women?
Source: NORC General Social Surveys. 1972–1996. Chicago: National Opinion Research Center, 1996.

some as "more equal"—more deserving of respect—than others because of their race, ethnicity, gender, age, wealth, achievements, or other social markers.

7. *Science and efficiency.* Americans use scientific principles as a basis for action. They favor logical ways of doing things that save time and money. Emotion and intuition are out; practicality and rationality are in.

8. *Humanitarianism.* Despite their highly individualistic culture, Americans are concerned for the welfare of others. They believe assistance should be offered to people who both need it and deserve it.

Some of these core values (for example, individualism and achievement) are functionally integrated: They support and reinforce one another. But the list

also contains obvious contradictions. For example, belief in the superiority of certain groups is at odds with values relating to democracy, freedom, and equality of opportunity. To include group superiority on a list of core values is offensive to many Americans since it may suggest that racism and sexism, for instance, are intrinsic to American culture. However, the core values, even group superiority, are not disappearing, but their rank shifts or emphasis on one or the other changes over time.

At the same time, other values are emerging that may eventually become part of this core set. For example, the value to pursue material comfort and financial success has increased sharply (Astin et al., 1989). People expect to work hard to succeed, but they want to work less, retire earlier, and have more leisure time. Leisure itself is becoming so important to Americans that it is emerging as another core value. In other cultures, such as Germany, leisure has long been a priority (Glouchevitch, 1992). Americans "take" vacations; Germans feel entitled to time off for recreation.

In some cases, contradictions in values are so obvious that public debate is open and contentious. Often these debates revolve around moral dilemmas created by the contradictions. For example, most Americans now disdain public expressions about the superiority of certain groups, especially regarding race and ethnicity. In fact, condemnations of racism are routine. However, many Americans are also uncomfortable with the very programs that mandate equal opportunity for people of color, such as affirmative action. Ethnocentrism is a fact of group life, and one that can translate into feelings of superiority, both between and within cultures. Thus some groups may still be defined as better or more worthy than others. The value of maintaining cultural identity in a diverse society is rapidly increasing, and as we shall see, has produced much social tension.

Another example is the American reliance on science as the key to social progress. Science is, by definition, secular. Science demands that assertions be questioned, tested, and proved or disproved. But Americans also express very high degrees of faith, as indicated by religious affiliation, beliefs, and practices. Regardless of the particular religion with which they may identify, almost all Americans believe in the existence of God or a universal spirit, and the majority attend religious services on a regular basis (Chapter 17). Faith and science represent opposite viewpoints in debates related to teaching evolution in the schools, scientific experimentation on animals and humans, euthanasia and prolonging life, and research on fertility and cloning, to name a few issues.

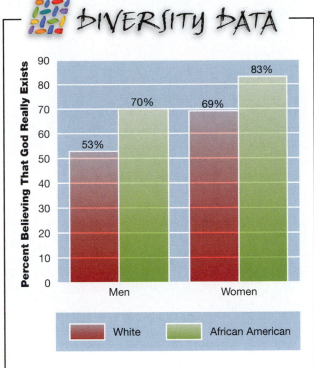

DIVERSITY DATA

FIGURE 3.2   Percent Believing that God Really Exists, by Gender and Race. The majority of whites and African Americans as well as both genders firmly believe in God. However, while a large majority of African American women have the firmest beliefs, only a slight majority of white men do. How can American cultural values be used to explain this difference?

Source: NORC General Social Surveys. 1972–1996. Chicago: National Opinion Research Center, 1996.

Norms and Sanctions

Values help define the character of a culture, but they do not provide specific courses of action. Values generally tell us what we should do, but not how to actually do it. They express *ideal culture* in guidelines and standards accepted in principle, embraced by the public, and extolled by politicians. Even with contradictions, values remain more or less consistent over time. **Norms** are rules of conduct that guide people's behavior in specific situations. They express *real culture* in that they are practiced on an ongoing basis in one's daily life.

The values of ideal culture tell us that honesty is the best policy. The norms of real culture tell us when it is permissible to tell "white lies" (to explain why we are late for work or a date, to reject an invitation po-

litely, to save face, to embellish a story we're telling to friends, and so on). Norms also help us to decide which value takes precedence in a given situation. Unlike values, norms change much more rapidly and are modified or discarded as *conditions* change.

Norms are maintained through **sanctions,** penalties for violating norms as well as approval or reward for adhering to norms. As children we learn our culture's norms not only through explicit instruction by our parents and others, but also by observing how other people react to our behavior. Without verbalizing specific rules, we learn what makes our parents smile or scold us, our playmates seek or shun us. As adults, abiding by norms becomes almost second nature. Most of the time we play by the rules. We know that deliberate and even unintentional violations have consequences. Agreement on norms smooths social interaction. Hence we try both to abide by norms ourselves and to correct people who violate our own codes—whether by avoiding these people, talking with them, or bringing a lawsuit. When our values are threatened, however, we may attempt to restore order or ideals by deliberately violating norms.

There are two categories of norms, based on the degree of importance we attach to a norm as well as the degree we are sanctioned when we violate it. The first category is made up of norms called **folkways,** which are informal norms regulating customary ways of behaving. Our daily lives are organized around folkways that tell us how to act in a classroom, on a bus, or in a restaurant. They consist of thousands of conventional forms of behavior taught by our culture that allow us to move freely within it. Without folkways, we would have to treat each social encounter as a unique event. For the most part, we conform to folkways automatically. In diverse cultures we are likely to encounter groups that practice different folkways, but we learn quickly what is expected of us. For example, students who transfer from one college to another generally adapt their behavior to the different folkways they encounter, such as forms of dress and customs related to acceptable study and party times.

There are so many folkways that help guide our interaction, it is impossible to behave "properly" according to all of them all the time. Therefore, it is likely that some folkways will be violated and that people will generally accept these as unintentional and forgivable lapses of proper human conduct.

Violations of mores, the second category of norms, are not as easily forgiven. **Mores** are norms that members of a society or culture consider vitally important, necessary, and inviolable. Violation invokes strong disapproval and often severe sanctions, ranging from expulsion to execution. A college transfer student may find tattered jeans and music after midnight acceptable in the new school (folkways), but neither the old nor the new school will tolerate cheating, plagiarism, or sexual violence (mores).

The American cultural value of achievement is demonstrated in mores against plagiarizing another person's work. In college the sanctions against plagiarizing are failing the course or expulsion. Outside of college, laws punish individuals and corporations for copyright violations, theft of company secrets and property, and insider trading of stocks. Because cultural components, especially values, are so interdependent, if deceit replaces merit as a measure of success, the entire social fabric is weakened. For this reason, violations of mores rarely go unsanctioned. Mores usually provide the basis for **laws,** formal norms codified and enforced by the legal power of the state.

CULTURE AS A SYMBOL SYSTEM

In any society, guidelines for behavior can be transmitted only if people share a common symbol system. A **symbol** is something that stands for or represents something else and is given meaning by those who use it. Agreed-upon meanings shared by a culture are, in essence, what distinguishes one culture from another. As mentioned in Chapter 1, the major principle of symbolic interactionism is that society (or culture) is "socially constructed." This principle suggests that every time we interact, we interpret the interaction according to the subjective meaning we bring to the interaction. Although the cultural symbols we share in common allow us to interact more smoothly, each of us may bring to any interaction differing interpretations of the symbols. Thus our perception of the "reality" of social interaction is constructed. This principle will guide our discussion of culture as symbolic.

The Emotional Impact of Symbols

A flag is a symbol of a nation and evokes powerful emotional reactions in its people. Wars have started because an enemy desecrated a flag. Flag burning during the anti–Vietnam War movement of the 1960s and 1970s was severely sanctioned, both informally and legally. The American flag as a national symbol is so powerful that Congress regularly debates passing a federal law that would make flag desecration a crime. This debate reflects a conflict between the cultural values of nationalism and democracy: Is the flag sacred? Or will freedom of expression in a democracy be compromised if there are legal restrictions on how the flag is displayed or used,

Symbols, such as the swastika on this father's arm, evoke powerful emotions. Many of us viewing this scene would have a very different reaction to this symbol than the child in the photo will (or will when he grows up).

even as a form of artistic expression? The flag of the Southern Confederacy also remains a powerful symbol. Some people associate it with a heritage of southern pride and tradition that should be preserved and respected. Others find it a reminder of an appalling era in United States history during which slavery flourished and a civil war tore the nation apart. To them, flying the Confederate flag today evokes images of bigotry and racism.

Within a culture, groups may use different symbols to represent themselves. Symbols that evoke nationalistic, religious, political, and regional sentiments are usually invested with a great deal of emotion, both positive and negative. A symbol of an enemy elicits as much hostility from you as your symbol does from the enemy.

Language

All cultures are represented through language. A **language** is a shared symbol system of rules and meanings that govern the production and interpretation of speech. Language exerts such a strong influence on culture that it is often used as a key marker for determining the number of world cultures. If the criterion for culture is a distinct language, the speakers of which cannot understand the speakers of another language, then there are several thousand cultures in the world (Triandis, 1994). Although social scientists use a combination of factors to distinguish between cultures, most people consider language the marker of a distinct culture and identity. Research supports this popular view, indicating that when a language is "lost," the culture loses its most important survival mechanism (Linden, 1994; Rappaport, 1994). For this reason, language and all it represents is a highly controversial issue. If language is a key cultural marker, then learning a language means learning the culture.

Language and Thought. One of the most important but controversial views of language and culture was put forward by the linguists Edward Sapir (1949) and Benjamin Lee Whorf (1956). According to the **Sapir-Whorf hypothesis,** language determines thought. Different languages have different grammars and vocabulary, and these in turn affect what people notice, label, and think about as well as how they organize and categorize what they perceive. Language tells us to notice some things and to ignore others and thus shapes the ways in which its speakers habitually think about and actually "see" the world. For example, the Inuit of the northwest coast of Canada have many different words for snow because snow is a major influence in their everyday lives. Speakers of English have only one word and hence see only "snow." If snow becomes important to English speakers—as in the case of skiers, for example—then they develop new words for what they need to see.

Whorf used Hopi, a Pueblo Indian language spoken in the American Southwest, to support his case. The English language separates experiences into distinct "things," such as "sky" and "hill." Hopi uses words that flow together into whole experiences. It is an unusually rich language for defining repetitive occurrences. Time is an exceedingly valuable cultural commodity for speakers of English, who divide time into discrete, separate categories of past, present, and future. By focusing attention on specifics, the English language leads speakers to think about "this" or "that" storm and how it differs from other storms. In contrast, by merging past and present, wind and rain, cause and consequences, the Hopi language leads speakers to think about storms as a single phenomenon, wherever and whenever they occur. As a result, speakers of Hopi and English are said to have different perceptions of time and reality. Although later research shows that Whorf somewhat misinterpreted Hopi (Edgerton, 1992), it still illustrates his argument.

Subsequent research has shown, however, that although language and culture are intertwined, there is little evidence that language actually *determines* thought. Research clearly documents that concepts can and do exist independently of language (Bloch, 1994; Strauss & Quinn, 1994). Prelinguistic children have concepts such as "house" before they learn the word "house." Research with color shows that even when people do not have a word to name a color, they can readily identify the color or shade itself. In English, a woman might describe a certain color as "ecru" or "ivory," whereas a man might describe it as "tan." They both *see* the same color, but cultural conditioning related to gender makes women likely to have names for a wider range of color gradations than do men. Speakers of other languages, who may have no words for the colors, also see the same shades, but may name them differently or add modifiers to existing color designations of their language. Research shows, therefore, that the Sapir-Whorf hypothesis is not particularly strong (Kay & Kempton, 1984; Triandis, 1994).

However, research does show that language can bias cognition to the extent that when we hear certain words we conjure up images related to the words (Hamilton, 1988). Language may not be the sole determinant of thought, but it certainly provides directions for our perception, and thus our attention. When words are used habitually, they may take on a reality of their own.

Americans are becoming more sensitized to the power of words when the words are associated with negative labeling. Yet when alternative word options are offered, people often express annoyance that they are being forced into "political correctness." This term represents a backlash against language changes that are thought to be unnecessary and artificial. However, according to symbolic interactionism, labels can change behavior. For example, labeling children as retarded, slow learners, or underachievers may become a self-fulfilling prophecy because teachers and parents offer them less challenging activities and pay more attention to their failures than to their achievements. A frequent result is that the children do not fulfill their potential and may come to see themselves as unintelligent. For this reason, derogatory labels are being replaced by neutral, less stigmatizing terms or words of the groups' own choosing. Homosexuals who have endured labels of contempt such as "fag" or "fruit" are now routinely referred to in the media as "gay" and "lesbian." Children previously labeled "retarded" are now identified as "special needs children" in school settings. People feel more comfortable in seeking psychiatric therapy when they are referred to as "clients" rather than as "patients." Not

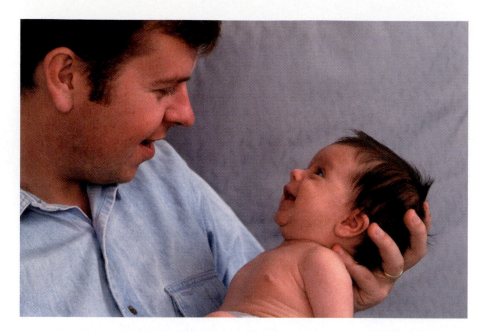

Children learn culture through language. Even at infancy they are learning appropriate behaviors during social interaction.

all the negative connotations that are culturally associated with such groups are removed by changing the labels, but the effort is a step in the right direction. The Sapir-Whorf hypothesis has not been completely abandoned. Consistent with symbolic interactionism, language *influences* interpretations of social reality.

Nonverbal Communication.   Less obvious than sounds or words, but equally significant sociologically, is the nonverbal dimension of language, such as how people use space in their social interaction. Cul-

INTERNET   CONNECTIONS

The text discusses the relationship between language and *gender*. Deborah Tannen is a well-known authority on communication differences between men and women and her "genderlect styles" have become widely quoted in the gender studies literature. You may review these "genderlect styles" at: http://www.usm.maine.edu/com/genderlect/index.htm. Why does Tannen refer to male-female conversation as *cross-cultural communication*? Explain how the film "When Harry Met Sally" is an illustration of gender communication differences?

tures collide when such variations are misunderstood. In his classic work on the cultural differences in physical distance and space, Edward Hall (1959, 1966) states that how we distance ourselves from each other sends subtle nonverbal messages. In American culture, *intimate* distance, which extends to about 18 inches, is reserved for loved ones. *Personal* distance extends from about 1 1/2 to 4 feet and is reserved for friends and acquaintances. In other words, standing within touching distance symbolizes intimacy, and standing farther apart symbolizes familiarity but with a degree of formality. Most Latin American, Hispanic American, and Arab cultures use closer personal spaces for interaction. An American conversing with a Brazilian might be uncomfortable when the Brazilian "invades" his or her personal space, so might unconsciously retreat a step—in turn causing the Brazilian to close the distance by moving forward a step. Research shows that Arabs tend to interact at closer distances, but also to talk louder and touch each other more than do Americans (Watson, 1970). What an American interprets as pushy or aggressive, a Brazilian or Saudi Arabian interprets as cold or unfriendly. In Middle Eastern cultures, it is easy to spot Americans in crowded rooms. They are the ones backed into walls and corners by their friendly hosts.

Germans and Japanese have wider personal space zones than do Americans, as shown in their architecture. Traditional German homes have lockable solid doors separating most rooms, in contrast to American homes, where rooms are connected by halls and open doorways. Japan is a geographically small country

Some minority males may learn masculinity through the language of "cool pose." Gang signs are often a part of that language and serve to cement ties to peers.

with a relatively large population. Space is limited, so people must deal with privacy a different way. Although small by American standards, the rooms in Japanese homes can be divided with thin paper and bamboo sliding doors. A paper door cannot provide silence or invisibility, but it offers symbolic privacy. Use of physical space is one of many areas of nonverbal communication, or, as Hall (1959) called it, the "silent language" of any culture. Nonverbal communication will be explored in Chapter 6.

Language and Gender. Although the strong distinction between men's and women's places in society has somewhat decreased, traditional gender roles are still embedded in language. Beginning with the pioneering work of Robin Lakoff (1975), research has shown that women and men who speak the same language, such as English, have different styles of communicating—a pattern found in all cultures. Some of these differences include the following:

1. Women use more qualifiers and tag questions than men. Rather than describing a person as "shy," a woman is apt to add a modifier, such as "kind of" or "somewhat." Adjectives provide other modifiers,

so that a woman may describe a party as "divine" and a croissant as "absolutely wonderful." She may end a sentence with a tag question, as if she were asking the other person's permission to express her opinion: "It's a beautiful day, isn't it?" "I really liked the movie, didn't you?" (Lakoff, 1975, 1991; McMillan et al., 1977).

2. In specialized role areas, women's vocabulary is more complex and descriptive than men's. Women use a greater range of words for colors, textures, food, clothing, cooking, and most relevant, parenting. They describe themselves and others in terms of complex interpersonal characteristics, using a greater variety of words and communication styles. When talking to their children about emotional aspects of events, they use a greater number of "emotion" words with daughters than with sons (Kuebli & Fivish, 1992; Flannagan et al., 1995).

3. Men use speech that is less polite and more direct than women. Men issue commands (the imperative form): "Close the door"; women make polite requests: "Please close the door." Both genders use expletives, but women do so less frequently and less explicitly: "Damn," "hell," and "shit" become "darn," "heck," and "shoot" (Kemper, 1984; Selnow, 1985).

4. Women converse in open, free-flowing ways and appreciate self-disclosure, whereas men feel uncomfortable in this regard. Women tend to like both men and women who confide information about their private lives and inner feelings, but men do not. Men converse on "safe" topics, such as sports and politics, that do not require them to reveal personal details to each other. When men want to encourage or cement friendships with other men, they engage in activities like poker, sports, and watching television, which allow time together but discourage lengthy conversations (Arliss, 1991; Inman, 1996). Male locker-room talk often involves joking, bragging, and competition. In the "ladies' room" at a theater or restaurant, women share experiences and seek common ground.

5. At the beginning of a male–female relationship, men talk more than women, but once the relationship "takes hold," communication decreases. Women would like to talk more, men would like to talk less. As she attempts to draw him out, he silently resists. Wives are more likely than their husbands to identify communication as a problem (Tannen, 1990; Bruess & Pearson, 1996).

Cultural norms and the roles that men and women play explain these patterns. Just as language reflects what is culturally important, specialized

Men learn about masculinity through sports, as partipants and as observers. Sports offer avenues for competition and aggression as part of masculinity norms.

language patterns emerge with specialized roles. For example, men more than woman are likely to be in workplace roles that are associated with giving orders, making speedy decisions, maintaining emotional distance between themselves and co-workers, and communicating by phone and e-mail rather than in person. Men are therefore encouraged to talk less, use imperatives more and refrain from emotional displays. On the other hand, women more than men are likely to be in domestic, home-based roles that are associated with nurturing, resolving conflicts between family members and relationship issues. The tag questions and intensifiers women use more often than men may not suggest that women are equivocal or tentative but rather that their nurturing roles make them more attuned to the feelings of other people. As Deborah Tannen (1990:83) notes, a woman has had practice all her life "in verbalizing her thoughts and feelings with people she is close to; all his life he has had practice in dismissing and keeping them to himself."

Men and women are rewarded for the speech patterns that are culturally prescribed. As gender roles change, language changes accordingly. Gender differences in conversation topics are decreasing over time, and in many verbal and nonverbal behaviors, girls and boys are more alike than different (Bischoping, 1993; Kolaric & Galambos, 1995). As more women enter the boardroom as executives and more men enter the classroom as elementary school teachers or assume more equal parenting responsibilities in the home, language choice and style will change.

The Language of Laughter.   On a plane from New York City to Chicago, people were politely helping each other stow luggage and letting each other pass through the narrow aisles when a man with an unmistakable New York accent said: "What's everybody being so nice for? We're still in New York" (Norrick, 1993:3).

Laughter is social glue. A recent study showed that people are thirty times more likely to laugh when in groups than when alone, with talkers chuckling almost 50 percent more than listeners (cited in Angier, 1997). Studying laughter and the jokes that elicit it are excellent ways to demonstrate the taken-for-granted role of culture on our behavior. Strangers can exchange and enjoy jokes because they share common cultural symbols, stereotypes, habits, and assumptions about who jokes about whom, when, and where, and what subjects are joked about (Norrick, 1993). If a joke must be explained, it loses its spontaneity and is therefore not funny. To understand the culture's humor requires an understanding of its stereotypes. To appreciate the airplane joke, the stereotype of New Yorkers being gruff must be recognized. And for it to be "funny" to everyone present, the New Yorker must be the one poking fun at himself and his city; otherwise it would be insulting. The following examples (Davis, 1993; Metcalf, 1993) demonstrate the need to know the cultural context to understand the joke:

How many Californians does it take to change a light bulb? Four. One to screw in the light bulb and three to share the experience.

I'm Korean. Childhood games were always traumatic for me. I hated playing cowboys and Indians. I was always the cook.

Hell is where the Italians are the bureaucrats, the French are the engineers, the British are the cooks, the Germans are the police, the Russians are the historians, and the Americans are the lovers.

Studying what a culture regards as funny also provides insight into the major theoretical perspectives in sociology. Symbolic interactionism emphasizes that jokes allow us to present a version of "self" in the way we would most like to be thought of, both as the joke giver and as the listener (Goffman, 1959). Thus in the following joke, a man presents himself as "one of the boys," even though he's about to marry: "I'm getting married, but it's not going to work out. My wife expects to move in with me."

Functionalism emphasizes that joking binds a culture together. The subtleties that speakers of a common language are aware of allow for wordplay and puns that are mysterious to linguistic outsiders. Knowledge of American English can elicit a chuckle at the following pun: "I said to my dentist, 'Do you promise to pull the tooth, the whole tooth, and nothing but the tooth?'" More significantly, humor has a function in cultural preservation. The comedy of Bali, part of the Indonesian archipelago, is shaped by the island's ongoing conflict between modernity and tradition. Troupes of clowns travel from village to village enacting the roles of legendary heroes in fifteenth century battles who are interrupted by souvenir-hunting tourists and government bureaucrats. Tourists and bureaucrats are outwitted by the Balinese clowns, who represent the resilience of the traditional culture (Jenkins, 1994b).

Conflict theory emphasizes how humor is used as a political tool, whether to support the status quo or to oppose it. Commenting on football during the protest movement of the 1970s, African American comedian Dick Gregory noted: "It's the only sport in the world where a black man can chase a white man and forty thousand people stand up and cheer." Jokes about food shortages in Eastern Europe both before and after the transition to capitalism continue to abound: "Why are meat shops in Russia (or Poland, or Bulgaria, or Albania) all built five miles apart? So the lines don't get tangled."

Racial and ethnic jokes have long been a mainstay of American humor. From a conflict perspective, such jokes reinforce the tellers' feelings of superiority ("we" are smarter, braver, and more honorable than are "they"). At the same time they serve to divert attention from the true sources of inequality and also to quell fears that the group in question might become serious competitors in the struggle for wealth and power. For this reason, many jokes contain a great deal of masked aggression (Berger & Wildavsky, 1994). What is most relevant for sociology is that the general script for these jokes remains constant over time, but the target of the jokes changes. The following jokes about mythical Lobodomians are benign examples:

A Lobodomian won his country's first gold medal. He was so proud of it he had it bronzed.
There are no more ice cubes in Lobodomia. The inventor died and the recipe was lost forever.

Over time, Scandinavians, Germans, Italians, Irish, Chinese, Japanese, Jews, Catholics, African Americans, and Native Americans have been plugged into the same basic formula, with slight variations as to their supposed deficiencies. This suggests that when a racial or ethnic group mobilizes the resources to challenge how they are portrayed, the "old style" humor is no longer humorous. Stereotypes about the group are abandoned, at least in polite company, and new scapegoats found (Davies, 1990; Davis, 1993; Metcalf, 1993). Overall, there are some cultural "in-

sights that one can obtain only while laughing" (Berger, 1963:165):

How many sociologists does it take to change a light bulb? It isn't the light bulb that needs changing, it's the system.

Culturally Speaking: What Separates Humans from Other Animals?

In 1960, the famed British scientist Jane Goodall was just beginning her research in the Gombe National Park in Tanzania, East Africa, observing and documenting the behavior of chimpanzees in their natural environment. The Gombe chimps, she discovered, used blades of grass and sticks to fish out termites from their hills. Even more significant, they reshaped these objects to conform to the particular termite hill to make them more efficient for enticing the tasty insects. Making and using tools, however rudimentary, had long been considered one of the distinguishing traits of humankind. Goodall wired the news to her mentor, the late anthropologist Louis Leakey, who wired back: "Either we will have to change our definition of mankind, or admit chimpanzees into the human family."

Most nonhuman animals communicate. Chimps and dolphins in particular have complex forms of communication that combine instinctive and learned behavior. Communication that is innate occurs through *signs* to which a meaning is attached and does not vary. The vast majority of animal communication is based on these signs. However, chimps and gorillas who have been taught hand gestures to convey their desires can eventually learn to put certain gestures together to form simple sentences. They can even teach many of the gestures to their offspring (Patterson, 1978; Fouts et al., 1984; Gardner & Gardner, 1985).

A wealth of evidence from research in both natural and laboratory environments suggests that animals—in particular chimps and the higher primates—have many characteristics we associate with culture. But to say that animals possess culture requires a giant and untenable leap, for two reasons. First, there are biological differences, especially in the capacity to develop language, that separate people from the higher primates. Only the human brain has the potential for learning any cultural tradition to which it is exposed.

The second and more important reason animals do not have culture is because humanity's outstanding feature is its symbolic basis. Instincts or other unlearned patterns of behavior are not cultural precisely because they have no symbolic referent. Humans live according to meanings that they create, accept, or

Some elements of culture may be identified in studying the behavior of chimps, but using symbols to convey ideas is not one of them.

discard at will. No other animal has Tuesdays, for example. Nonhuman animals fully depend on their physical environment and live in the here and now, not in the symbolic world of Tuesdays and Sundays. "Ducks and beavers cannot even recognize Tuesday, let alone organize their lives around them" (Barrett, 1991:55). Although many animals can vocalize and even socialize, they cannot symbolize. Culture is the sole possession of humanity.

CULTURAL CHANGE

Culture is not a random assortment of beliefs, practices, and symbols; to serve as a way of life, the different elements of culture must reinforce one another to some extent. At the same time, culture is never fixed or static. Culture is always changing, always "on the move"—whether because of innovations within a cultural group, changes in the physical environment, or contact with other cultures. **Cultural integration** describes the process by which cultural elements become closely connected and mutually interdependent. Inevitably, a change in one part of the culture will produce change in other areas. When new cultural elements fit with existing beliefs and practices, cultural integration is strengthened and cohesiveness and harmony maintained. When too many conflicting elements are introduced to be easily absorbed, cultural integration is threatened.

Both cultural change and cultural integration are influenced by two very important elements. These elements are bridges between material and nonmaterial culture. The first is **technology,** tools and the body of knowledge pertaining to their use that help accomplish social tasks. The second is **popular culture,** cultural patterns that are produced and spread through the mass media, especially television. The American popular culture industry dominates the world and, as we shall see, has fueled the emergence of a global culture. Clearly technology and popular culture are major ingredients for cultural change, but also major impediments for cultural integration.

Even what we might see as a trivial element of technology can have a major impact on a culture. When the Mekranoti Indians of central Brazil were introduced to metal pots in the 1950s, they switched from roasting to boiling their food. This allowed nursing mothers to feed supplemental food to their infants earlier and in turn steadily decreased the average nursing period by almost three months (Milton, 1994). Because nursing provides a form of natural birth control, a metal cooking pot led to an increase in fertility, and this in turn impacted the entire social and economic life of the village. A simple cooking pot created major cultural upheaval for a tiny, relatively isolated society. Think what one personal computer connected to a modem could do in another culture that was artificially isolated because of political repression.

As you might expect, material culture changes faster than nonmaterial culture. Because different parts of the culture change at different rates, a gap often exists between the time an artifact is introduced and the time it is integrated into a culture's value system. This gap is an example of **cultural lag.** Scientific technology related to health and medicine provides numerous examples of cultural lag. Technology is available to create and prolong life as well as end it through euthanasia. Successful animal cloning has generated research related to human cloning. There have been remarkable advances in organ transplants from human to human and from animal to human. Research has allowed the egg and sperm of a formerly infertile couple to be incubated outside the womb and later implanted safely in the woman or in another woman who carries the fetus to birth. In the latter case a woman literally "rents" her womb to the couple. Sperm banks now provide options for infertile couples, as well as for those women who desire children but do not want to be married. Men may want to be genetic fathers for the same reason.

Although these procedures are subject to rigorous guidelines, the ethical implications cannot be dismissed. The new technology raises fundamental questions: What is life? When does life end? Who is a parent? Do children have the right to know their biological (or genetic) parents? and Who "owns" a child?

Each culture must decide how to answer these questions. But clearly, technological change—whether in the form of animal cloning, sperm banks, or a cooking pot—will continue to outpace value change in any society. Cultural lag in this regard works against cultural integration.

Processes of Cultural Change

The spread of cultural elements, both material and nonmaterial, from one society to another is called cultural **diffusion.** It can be *direct*, such as when two cultures intermarry or wage war against one another and seize territory and prisoners, or when missionaries or tourists from one culture "invade" another. It can be *indirect*, when cultural patterns and products move into a culture without firsthand contact with members of the culture that originated them. The first trading centers and ports became the havens for indirect cultural exchange. Traders, sailors, and entrepreneurs met at these ports, then met at other ports, and eventually took back with them not only new products but different attitudes and behaviors. Today, indirect cultural diffusion occurs daily via the Internet. Any time you forward an e-mail message that was forwarded to you from someone in a different society, indirect cultural diffusion occurs.

Cultural integration is enhanced when both direct and indirect diffusion allow for cultural elements to be modified to suit the norms and material culture of the receiving culture. Through e-mail and the Internet, this author has received over fifty variations of

The media provide opportunities for cultural contact (even indirectly) and diffusion. When Madonna accepted an MTV music award wearing clothing typical of women from India, women in other countries watching the awards began to purchase similar clothing. Cultural diffusion of Indian fashion occurred.

chocolate cookie recipes that evolved from recipes unique to cultural conditions—use of cocoa when cold storage is a problem, from metric to nonmetric instructions, from gas to propane to cow dung as fuel. Recipes have made the rounds from a tiny village in the West African nation of Mali, to Calcutta, India, Sydney, Australia, and Omaha, Nebraska. This form of indirect cultural diffusion is functional for satisfying a global sweet tooth.

Cultural change also occurs through *invention*, when existing cultural elements are combined to form new ones, and through *discovery*, the creation of new cultural elements or the reinterpretation of existing ones. The innovations that result from both invention and discovery illustrate the power of cultural suggestibility. Scientists operate according to traditions and share a common framework or outlook for research (Kuhn, 1970). Thus scientists who share the same traditions are likely to make parallel innovations (inventions and discoveries). This explains why so many important innovations of Western civilization were discovered by several people at the same time. Examples of simultaneous invention include the discovery of oxygen, the principles of genetics, the cellular basis of life, elements of calculus, rocketry, and the invention of the steamboat, telegraph, television, and telephone (Barrett, 1991).

THEORETICAL PERSPECTIVES ON CULTURE

In explaining human social behavior, sociologists must always take into account the processes of change. Indeed, the strength of all sociological theories rests on how well they can explain changes in culture and society.

Functionalism

The functionalist theoretical perspective stresses that all societies must meet basic needs, such as food and shelter, in order to survive. We will see in the next chapter how all societies develop basic social structures organized around these requirements. All known prehistoric and historic societies are thought to have common features, called **cultural universals,** that aided in their survival. More than a half century ago anthropologist George Murdock (1945) compiled a list of more than seventy cultural universals, including family patterns, food taboos, religious rituals, adornment and decorative arts, ethics, folklore, food habits, and healing techniques. One of the most important cultural universals is the *incest taboo*, which restricts sexual relations or marriage between people who are closely related to one another. Although this taboo is universal, precisely whom it applies to—parents and siblings, first and second cousins, or an entire clan—varies. So it is with other cultural universals.

While all societies share broad cultural universals, the specifics are incredibly varied. Cultural habits surrounding food illustrate the variety. Roast dog is a culinary delight in some provinces in China, in Vietnam, and in many other parts of Asia. Grubs, beetles, iguanas, and lizards are relished throughout South America and in Australia. In Colombia, toasted ants are consumed daily. While shellfish are plentiful in many countries, the French consume snails in great quantity, but Americans prefer oysters and clams. Jews and Muslims share a taboo against eating pork. Catholics eat pork and other meat, but on specified religious holidays consume only fish. Hindus do not eat meat, but their Muslim neighbors in India do—often a cause for violent clashes. Beef is widely consumed in America, but some cuts of beef are preferred over others. Those who can afford it eat filet mignon and prime rib, and almost everyone eats hamburgers. Americans generally do not like animal organs, but tripe (beef stomach) and sweetbreads (the thymus or pancreas) are considered delicacies in continental Europe, and kidney pie is a favorite in Great Britain. Lungs, tonsils, and thyroids are consumed readily in many African cultures. Many East African pastoralists, including the Masai, butcher cattle only on ceremonial occasions; their everyday staple is cattle blood (taken from live animals) mixed with milk.

According to the functionalist perspective, unique customs develop and persist because they are adaptive: They improve a people's chances of survival and reproduction. **Adaptation** specifically refers to the process whereby a culture maintains equilibrium despite fluctuations and change. Customs that reduce the survival chances of a culture are unlikely to persist.

The sacred cows of India are a good example. They remain a functional necessity for much of the culture. They give milk, pull plows, and provide dung for fuel and fertilizer for crops, and when they die a natural death, every inch of the animal is used in some product, from its hide for leather sandals to its bone for polished jewelry. Tanning leather is the job of the lowest caste people, those at the very bottom of the social hierarchy, who depend on the job, hence the cow, to survive. In the midst of starvation a naive outsider might look at a healthy cow and ask why the cow is not eaten to survive. However, cows are more valuable and they contribute more to human survival alive than if they were butchered, cooked, and consumed. Religious values and mythology develop or are adapted in support of such cultural practices. The relationship between people and cow enhances adaptation and cultural integration (Harris, 1994).

Functionalism suggests that such culturally variable habits emerged because they filled a purpose. They were integrated into the value system and may persist even if the original usefulness becomes obsolete.

Conflict Theory

Conflict theory holds that whichever group controls a culture's *ideology*, the value system defining social inequality as just and proper, also determines how power and resources are allocated. According to Karl Marx, the dominant ideology eventually becomes part of the value system of an oppressed group. The group may view its own culture as inferior and attempt to improve its position by adopting the ways of the dominant culture. One way in which an elite controls subordinate groups is through language.

During the nineteenth and early twentieth centuries, the Pacific islands (Polynesia, Micronesia, and Melanesia) were colonized by Europeans. One of the supposed benefits of colonization was education:

Global Connections

Culture as Cure

The impact of culture on health is enormous. Culture-bound syndromes exist worldwide and are associated with unique symptoms that people within the culture classify as disease. Among Aboriginal Australians, "fear of sorcery syndrome" is linked to voodoo and causes a range of ailments. Death can occur by "bone-pointing," in which a sharp stick is ritually cast into the victim's body. In Japan, men who are otherwise healthy drop dead from karoshi, the disease of overwork. The United States has its share of culture-bound syndromes: Type A behavior, eating disorders like anorexia nervosa, and "petism," excessive devotion to pets. Petism may explain the American aversion to having a cat, dog, or canary as a dinner course.

Cultural practices can work against disease or transmit it. Malaria in Nigeria occurs when water in clay pots is left at shrines that then become breeding grounds for mosquitoes. Cement foot-baths in mosques in Muslim countries produce skin fungus. Resistance to using condoms is found throughout Africa and Asia because of strong cultural beliefs that they compromise a man's sexual potency. Surely these be-liefs hasten the spread of AIDS. Blood transfusions in these same cultures are resisted because of the belief that the donor's sins will be transferred to the recipient.

Many cultures explain disease as a result of the imbalance between the physical, social, and spiritual worlds of the patient. A belief that good health is a process of balancing the forces of good and evil is found throughout Africa and Latin America. Diseases are divided between those that are caused by gods, spirits, or the evil intent of others and those that are not. People choose their practitioner according to the cause of the disease. A shaman can only remove a curse. A physician can only remove a tumor. If the curse caused the tumor, both can be con-sulted.

In much of the world, health care is provided by traditional or "folk" heal-ers. The ethnocentric notion long prevalent in the Western world that tra-ditional healing would be replaced by scientific medicine is now questioned. Folk healers are successful because they understand patient concerns from the viewpoint of the patient's culture. China's "barefoot doctors" are recruited from the villages they eventually serve. They understand village culture and combine techniques from both tradi-tional and scientific medicine.

Rather than dying out, traditional healers are adapting to cultural change. Herbal remedies, understanding the role of emotion in disease, and acupuncture are used successfully by folk healers but have only recently been considered important enough for scien-tific research. Science is skeptical about why or how the healing occurs. The eyes of culture may blind scientists to other methods of healing.

1. What traditional practices and be-liefs in your own culture may pro-mote illness or health and well-being?
2. What suggestions would you offer to health-care practitioners whose pa-tients adopt practices that are med-ically harmful by scientific standards but are also strongly supported by cultural traditions?

Sources: Crandon, 1983; Simons & Hughes, 1985; Henderson, 1989; Basch, 1990; Gesler, 1991; Plotkin, 1993; Chi, 1994; Santiago-Irizarry, 1996.

Indigenous people were given the opportunity to go to school and learn to read, not in their own language but in that of their colonizers. In fact, schools and lit-eracy were tools for implanting the dominant colonial ideology in local children; they eroded the values and the leadership of the traditional, orally transmitted culture (Topping, 1992). Literacy brings power but at the expense of vital aspects of traditional culture (Graff, 1987). When young people see the world through "literate culture" eyes, their elders often see them as betraying traditional, oral culture values. Youth think and act differently from their oral culture counterparts, a scenario being played out with indige-nous peoples worldwide. Oral culture and its tradi-tional values struggle to survive in a literate culture environment (Eggington, 1992). It is estimated that of the world's 6,000 languages, 3,000 are doomed and only about 300 have a reasonably secure future (Lin-den, 1994).

The conflict perspective shows that language and literacy also can be tools for reclaiming autonomy and fighting against cultural subordination. Such is the case with the Aborigines in Australia's Northern Ter-ritory. For a long time, Aborigines were denied all but a minimal education. They wanted their children to gain access to all English—not just the kind they learned in the first missionary schools or in the later government-supported schools. This "secret" English helped the Aborigines gain control over their com-munity's education program, which in turn helped them fight racism (Eggington, 1992). Literacy al-lowed access to an entire system of documents and

In America and many places in Europe, cultural beliefs about attractiveness propel people to sit in the direct sunlight for hours to obtain a bronze body. This cultural practice persists in spite of widespread knowledge that premature aging and skin cancer are common results.

colonial history that had formerly been denied to them (Martin, 1990). Once they mastered the language, they could interpret documents and write books consistent with their own ideology.

Similarly, native Hawaiians are working toward cultural revitalization, specifically aimed at preserving their language and the cultural traditions associated with it. The flourishing of hula schools since the early 1970s, for example, is associated with the "Hawaiian renaissance." The dance and chants in all their different and subtle forms are imbued with powerful religious symbolism and speak to ancient traditions. Today both haoles (whites) and native Hawaiians recognize that the thriving interest in hula also symbolizes an increase in the power of Hawaii's indigenous peoples. In line with a democratic value system, they can more readily reinstate native languages in schools, teach children about their own cultural heritage, and gain access to the technology necessary to preserve an oral heritage (Buck, 1993).

This analysis indicates that conflict theory faces the same basic dilemma as functionalism in its expla-

nation of cultural change. It is supportive of indigenous people's efforts at cultural preservation but at the same time recognizes that this very preservation serves to isolate and marginalize them, especially if they are denied access to technology and education. Overall, the conflict approach favors the notion that cultural change rather than cultural continuity is more beneficial to oppressed people. For functionalism, the principle of adaptation assumes that cultures must change in order to survive, but too much change is detrimental to social order. The question is how much to emphasize cultural similarities, which functionalism does, and how much to emphasize cultural differences, which conflict theory does. Cultures continue to change because people are creative and inventive; they can adapt to natural and social forces, and they can adapt these same forces to their benefit.

Symbolic Interactionism

Not all sociologists and anthropologists agree that culture and its customs can be explained solely or even mainly in terms of adaptation (Sahlins, 1976; Murphy, 1994). A large number of inefficient, disadvantageous, and even dangerous customs persist in most cultures. In cultures where malnutrition is common, taboos against eating certain foods put children at risk for illness and death. Eggs are regarded as a cause of late speech development in Korea and of mental retardation in East Africa. In some tropical areas the belief persists that the plentiful papaya causes worms in children (Lambrecht, 1985). Similarly, Western conceptions of beauty propel Caucasians to spend hours in the sun or in salons in search of a perfect tan, a practice that has dramatically increased rates of skin cancer.

Members of the same culture often disagree about their own culture. Symbolic interactionists emphasize that informants present views of their own culture that are flexible and pragmatic and that vary according to their personal situation. Their definitions about how and why they do things change as their cultural circumstances change. The Tsimihety people of Madagascar represent this view:

> Some villages irrigated their rice fields while others relied upon rain. Some organized cooperatives that exchanged labor; others worked on their own. Some men performed a certain ritual using a prayer; others omitted the prayer or used a different one. (Cited in Vayda, 1994:321)

Symbolic interactionists also point out that a people may consciously and deliberately reject an innovation that they recognize as adaptive. The Rwala Bedouins of Saudi Arabia retain ancient camel herding practices that require long training in difficult environmental conditions. Lifestyle pressures make camel herding an arduous occupation, both physically and economically. Sheepherding now offers these people a less strenuous existence and future economic advantages that they clearly recognize. Then why do so many Rwalas still herd camels? The answer seems to be that they like camels and don't much like sheep. Their reason is an emotional one and not an economic one. Camel herding also helps them retain a greater sense of independence and cultural integrity (Lancaster, 1997).

Functionalists might view the Tsimihety culture as disintegrated and Rwala camel herding as maladaptive. Symbolic interactionists would disagree. In their view, what matters is that people attach particular meanings to what they do and why they do it. These meanings are social constructions and should be researched in order to understand these, or any other, cultures.

CULTURAL DIVERSITY

Immigration, technology, media-based popular culture, tourism, the uprooting of people due to war and politics or disaster and famine, and most important, the requirements of a global economy, affirm that cultural diversity is rapidly becoming a fact of life in even the most remote areas of the world. Traditional cultures, which have been patterned primarily according to gender and age, are now incorporating other factors as part of their cultural mix. And in some cases, groups within a society maintain or develop a distinctive cultural identity.

Subcultures: The Significance of Being Different

A **subculture** is a segment of a culture sharing characteristics that distinguish it from the broader culture. Subcultures often have distinct values and norms, folkways and mores setting them apart from mainstream culture. Ethnic subcultures are a clear example; immigrants often settle in the same areas and neighborhoods and maintain many elements of their native culture in their new setting, at least among themselves. These characteristics can include dress, food, style of language (or even a different language), economic activity, dating patterns, and child-rearing practices. Many immigrant groups adapt to the broader culture in their work lives but effectively return to their original culture in their homes and neighborhoods.

Subcultures are typically based on race, ethnicity, age, religion, gender, or occupation. But subcultures will also evolve when attitudes and patterns of behavior are distinctive enough, or important enough, to unite people. There are subcultures based on sexual orientation, art and music, sports, and physical disability. Your college functions as a strong subculture—a lifestyle shared with college students across the country, even around the globe. You dress, speak, and act a bit differently in the college subculture than in any other subcultures to which you belong. Like culture, subcultures provide guidelines for effective interaction in diverse societies.

Yet subcultures are also found in smaller, homogeneous societies that are uniform in terms of race and religion and whose members may not differ significantly in terms of social class and economic functions. In such societies, age and gender usually form the most important criteria in which subcultures evolve. The Masai are a pastoral people of cattle herders living in Kenya and Tanzania who remain culturally distinctive despite years of colonial rule, political upheaval, and tourist invasions (Spencer, 1988). Masai legends trace their culture back three hundred years, although anthropologists believe they migrated

American college campuses represent an amazing degree of subcultural diversity. Colleges are struggling with the issue of celebrating diversity but also valuing unity among their students, whether they are American students or international students.

Like the Masai of East Africa, many cultures have strong norms about gender and age segregation. Traditional Masai culture is being eroded by the forces of modernization.

to the region about a thousand years ago. They exist as a traditional subculture in the rapidly developing political states in which they are legally contained. But within Masai subculture, another powerful age- and gender-based subculture also thrives. The life of Masai males, especially, follows a prescribed progression based on culturally determined age grades (Bernardi, 1985). As in the circumcision rite described in the opening vignette, a male's life is distinguished by elaborate ceremonies, or rites of passage, that mark the transition from one life stage to another—from childhood to boyhood, to warriorhood, to elderhood. The tribe is structured around these rituals, because from birth boys grow up with their peers in an age-set to which they belong throughout their lives. Although not as formally restricted to interaction with their age-mates as boys, Masai girls are socialized into their roles as lover, wife, and childbearer, and in all instances are subservient to boys and men (Blauer, 1994). For both males and females, the subculture they inhabit is mysterious to members of the other gender.

Countercultures: Different but Opposed

Sometimes the distinctiveness of a subculture puts it in such sharp contrast with the broader culture that it becomes a **counterculture,** with values and norms in opposition to the dominant culture. The term was popularized by Theodore Roszak (1969) during the student protest movement against the war in Viet-

nam. This movement was also associated with rock music, sexual experimentation, and illegal drug use, particularly marijuana—all of which parents and society as a whole viewed as subversive, dangerous, and wrong. Most important, the protest movement generally gained its recruits from white, middle-class families that were the supposed standard-bearers for the American Dream. Resistance to fighting a war many considered unjust coincided with the emergence of a radically different vision of "the good life." Members of the counterculture questioned traditional values such as nationalism and patriotism. They questioned the belief that science and technology represented progress. And they rejected materialism as a guideline for living, and valued individualism—"Do your own thing"—over conformity and traditional measures of success. Some pursued alternative lifestyles based on interdependence and affection in rural communes or in large cities such as San Francisco. The critical factor, however, was that large numbers of young people rejected conventional lifestyles and the "work ethic" that held that the primary goal of life was to work hard in the present to secure material benefits for oneself and one's children in the future. Many literally "dropped out" in rejection of the American cultural standard for achievement. The counterculture was born. The power of sheer numbers in mass protest played a key role in America's eventual pullout from Vietnam.

The youth countercultures that have since evolved are still made up mostly of teenagers and young adults who strive for immediate gratification of goals. But the similarity stops there. Contemporary youth countercultures are smaller, more homogeneous, and more organized. They are not interested in broad-scale social reform and are likely to be racist, anti-Semitic, or overtly intolerant and suspicious of any ethnic or racial group different from their own. They do embrace important American goals, such as material comfort and power through competition, at least for their specific group, but they achieve these goals through illegal and often violent means. Tattoos, graffiti, group identity, secret signs, specialized language, and dangerous rites of passage are associated with countercultures across the globe.

Gangs and gang violence are not new. What is new, however, is that the violence is less contained and more lethal with easy access to guns and recruiting increasingly younger members. Some countercultures may not be engaged in illegal activities but operate on the fringes of the law. Skinheads, the Ku Klux Klan, and antigovernment militia groups have been implicated in many violent activities but manage to survive as distinct groups. Like other subcultures and the broader culture in which they exist, countercultures provide values and guidelines for behavior. However, contemporary countercultures ultimately socialize members into a set of values that is usually dysfunctional for counterculture members as well as society as a whole.

≋ LIFE CONNECTIONS: Who Is an American?

Culturally diverse since its founding, the United States has always struggled with the question, Who is an American? For most of the twentieth century, the dominant image was of America as a melting pot—a giant cauldron where people of diverse backgrounds would be submerged and then reemerge as a unified group known as "Americans." In this hypothetical melting pot, immigrants would shed previous cultural identities and embrace the culture and values of their new homeland. This ideal held sway, although it was never fully achieved in practice. Some ethnic groups were not considered 100 percent American—whether they were deliberately and forcibly excluded from mainstream society (especially African Americans and Native Americans), or chose to maintain their distinctive ethnic identity (Latinos, to some degree Italian Americans, as well as groups such as the Mormons and Amish), or a combination of the two. Chinese Americans, for example, encountered strong prejudice and discrimination and also chose to "keep to themselves." Immigrant children such as the Chinese American girl in the vignette at the beginning of the chapter are often caught between what broader American values tell them they should do and be and

what their cultural heritage tells them they should do and be. How much is she culturally "American," culturally "Chinese," or culturally "Chinese American?"

In recent decades, the question of who is American—and of maintaining some degree of cultural integrity in an increasingly heterogeneous society—has taken on new meaning. Over the last fifteen years, not only has the United States experienced one of the highest rates of immigration in its history, but these immigrants are from countries that are culturally less similar to America than immigrants of the past (see Chapter 12). At the same time, established groups such as African Americans, Native Americans, and other formerly excluded peoples are reclaiming their heritages and reasserting their distinctive cultural identities. Always "a nation of nations," America today is more multicultural than ever before. Like the Chinese American girl of the vignette, the struggle of immigrant children to adjust traditional values to modern society is one of the stories that multiculturalism has uncovered.

The term *multiculturalism* has two levels of meaning. First, multiculturalism means that different cultural groups exist side by side in the same culture. These different groups are basically subcultures. Second, multiculturalism refers to the emerging value of cultural identity. Multiculturalism is associated with a belief that the ethnic heritage of all groups should be understood and respected—whether in the folkways of food and dress, or the mores of religion and morality. However, the equal respect owed to other subcultures does not mean that critical judgment of these subcultures should be suspended. If different cultures are to be equally respected, then they must also be "worthy" of critiques by outsiders. All practices of all subcultures do not have to be accepted as right and proper by everyone for multiculturalism to flourish in America. Multiculturalism does not imply relativism. While the value of cultural identity is an emergent one, the challenge of incorporating it into America's core value set is as old as the nation itself. How can unity be maintained in the face of increasing cultural diversity?

The unity–diversity issue is highlighted in regard to language. Which groups of Americans speak which language? Many believe that if all Americans spoke the same language, then cultural unity would be easier to accomplish, regardless of a person's cultural heritage. Sixteen states have passed laws making English their official language (Auerbach, 1992). California recently made English the standard language in schools despite the growing Asian and Latino populations who retain and speak their native tongues (see Table 3.1). The issue is especially important for the estimated 25 million Spanish speakers in America,

Global Connections

The Exotic Nacirema

In studying cultures throughout the globe, social scientists encounter an extraordinary array of exotic customs, superstitious beliefs, and magical behaviors. A half century ago, anthropologist Horace Miner encountered a culture so remarkable that his description of it remains one of the most significant contributions to cultural understanding. As described by rituals involving the body, we provide Miner's portrait of the Nacirema, a people still inhabiting the territory between the Canadian Cree and the Yaqui Indians of Mexico in North America.

The Nacirema believe that the human body is ugly and that its natural tendency is to debility and disease. The only way to avert these characteristics is to use powerful rituals and ceremonies in special shrine rooms all households have devoted solely to this purpose. The rituals carried out in the shrine room are not family ceremonies but are private and secret. The focal point of the shrine is a box that is built into the wall. The box contains many charms and magical potions that the natives believe they cannot live without. These preparations are obtained from powerful healers who must be rewarded with expensive gifts. The healers do not provide the potions directly to their clients but decide on what the ingredients should be. They write them down in an ancient and secret language and then send their clients to herbalists, the only ones who can interpret the language and, for another gift, will provide the required potion. After the potion serves its purposes, it is placed in the charm box in the wall. These magical materials are specific for certain ills. Since the real or imagined maladies of the Nacirema are many, the charm box is usually full to overflowing. The magical packets are so numerous that people forget what their purposes are and fear to use them again. The natives are very vague on why they retain all the old magical materials in the charm box, before which the body rituals are conducted. In some way they must protect the worshiper.

Beneath the charm box is a small font. Every day family members separately enter the shrine room, bow their heads before the charm box and mingle different sorts of holy waters secured from the Water Temple of the community, where priests conduct elaborate ceremonies that make the liquid ritually pure. Another daily ritual performed in the shrine room font is the mouth-rite. The rite involves a practice that strikes the uninitiated stranger as a revolting. The ritual consists of inserting a small bundle of hog hairs into the mouth, along with certain magical powders, and then moving the bundle in a highly formalized series of gestures. In addition to the daily mouth-rite, the natives seek out special holy-mouth-practitioners once or twice a year for the exorcism of the evils of the mouth.

---

half of whom regularly speak Spanish at home. English fluency is associated with educational achievement and higher paying jobs and bilingualism increases opportunities for advancement (Bean & Tienda, 1987; McGroarty, 1996). For Latinos, the Spanish language is the distinguishing cultural marker. While cultural identity is maintained through Spanish, Latinos are clearly aware that fluency in English is vital for success in America. Latinos are similar to other groups who wish to preserve some cultural distinctiveness within a society as diverse as the United States. Although the language issue is far from resolved, multicultural appreciation is now a significant part of all levels of education, a topic we will discuss further in Chapter 16.

Chinese immigrants to the United States, and their patterns of adjustment, are good examples of how a subculture has maintained a visible presence but, until recently, an obscure one. Tourists flock to the Chinatowns of New York, Chicago, Honolulu, and San Francisco for food and souvenirs but have little knowledge about how and why such communities developed. Multiculturalism fuels an appreciation of ethnic diversity, and is taking hold in places beyond classrooms. The result is that increased knowledge about various subcultures is gradually being introduced to American culture as a whole. Popular culture, for example, is a major vehicle for all Americans

INTERNET — CONNECTIONS

Can you believe that Nacirema has a Web site? After you explore www.beadsland.com/nacirema, write your own short essay on the exotic habits of Nacirema culture.

Holy-mouth practitioners use an impressive set of paraphernalia that involve almost unbelievable ritual torture of the client, especially when magical material is put in the holes of clients' teeth. Clients endure the torture because they believe it will arrest decay and draw friends. It is suspected that the mouth practitioners have a certain amount of sadism as they watch the tortured faces of their clients. In turn, most of the Nacirema population show definite masochistic tendencies. The theoretically interesting point is that what seems to be a preponderantly masochistic people have developed sadistic specialists.

The exotic behavior of the Nacirema described by Miner fifty years ago has intrigued sociologists so much that there has been continuous research on this culture. For example, a Portuguese anthropologist studied their complex and contradictory cultural traits, including language use. The Nacirema delight in using the word "nice," as in: "Nice to meet you"; "Have a nice day"; "How do you like Nacirema? Oh that's nice!" "Have a nice stay." Their abuse of the word

"nice" shocks the hearing of a visitor. Either their language doesn't have the richness to avoid repetitions, or the Nacirema have a mental laziness that keeps conversation very simplistic. Perhaps the Nacirema are so anxious to please newcomers and be friendly that words such as "nice" are overly used. A Polish sociologist living among these people notes that they do exhibit much friendship and kindness. "Everyone wants to help me, to thank me for calling or for stopping by. They become my friends very quickly." The Nacirema call one another by their first names and commonly avoid distinctions and titles based on rank and age. Teachers are often addressed by their first names, and nicknames are given to foreign visitors to show informality and cement friendship.

But closer examination of the Nacirema reveals many contradictions. The use of first names does not necessarily indicate a close relationship. In Nacirema, quality friendships that are lasting, intimate, and emotionally involving are difficult to develop. Nacirema say they have many friends. But for both the Polish sociologist and

a sociolinguist from central Africa who lived in Nacirema for many years, the word "acquaintance" would probably be a better term to describe these relationships.

As Miner suggested, "the ritual life of the Nacirema has certainly showed them to be a magic-ridden people." Later research on the contradictions in Nacirema culture may agree with his conclusion that it is difficult to understand how they have managed to last so long under the burdens they impose on themselves. As you have probably already figured out, Nacirema is American spelled backwards.

1. For both Americans and those from other nations, does this portrait arouse any emotions about your own culture?
2. How can sociologists studying other cultures remain objective in their reporting when they encounter cultural traits vastly different from their own?

Sources: Adapted from Miner, 1956; Mucha, 1998; Mufwene, 1998; Ramos, 1998.

---

to learn the stories of subcultural groups, such as Chinese Americans, with whom they have coexisted for centuries. Amy Tan's novel the *Kitchen God's Wife* and the movie adapted from another of her novels, *The Joy Luck Club*, offer complex and touching portrayals of three generations of Chinese families in their struggle to adjust and succeed in America. Coupled with very successful movies like *The Last Emperor*, documenting important events in China, these movies lay the historical groundwork for understanding the traditions and lifestyles of contemporary Chinese Americans.

Movies spotlighting multiculturalism are not only increasing in number, but many of the newer images of cultural diversity are undoubtedly offering challenges to once prevalent but demeaning stereotypes. The acclaimed 1970s television movie *Roots* portrayed the slavery-to-freedom existence of one African American family. *The Color Purple* in the 1980s showed the misery and triumph of an African American girl growing up in the rural South during the De-

pression. *Amistad*, filmed in the 1990s, traced the legal battle of shipwrecked slaves in America in their attempt to be defined first as human beings and only secondly as slaves. Kevin Costner's performance in *Dances with Wolves* provides a glimpse of nineteenth-century Native America—both brutal and humane—that was largely unknown to most Americans. A movie popular in the southwestern United States is *La Familia*, tracing how several generations of a Mexican American family adapted to a new culture while also preserving traditions from the old culture.

Although stereotypes of America's subcultural groups still abound in movies and other parts of popular culture, the new value of multiculturalism has fueled portrayals that are more accurate and positive. More important, these portrayals highlight the fact that cultural differences can be appreciated rather than scorned. Who is an American can only be understood in the context of America's extraordinary multicultural heritage.

Language Spoken at Home	Number of People	Percent Speaking English Less Than "Very Well"
Speak only English	198,601	—
Speak other language	31,845	43.9
Speak Spanish or Spanish Creole	17,345	46.9
Speak an Asian or Pacific Islander language	4,473	54.1
Speak other language	10,028	32.4

Table 3.1   People Age Five and Older in the United States Speaking a Language Other Than English at Home (in thousands)

Selected Language	People Who Speak Language
Spanish	17,339
French	1,702
German	1,547
Italian	1,309
Chinese	1,249
Polish	723
Korean	626
Vietnamese	507
Japanese	428
Greek	388
Arabic	355
Hindu (Urdu)	331
Russian	242
Yiddish	213
Navaho	149
Hungarian	148

Source: Adapted from U.S. Census of Population and Housing Data Paper Listing (CPH-L-133), 1990.

SOCIETY CONNECTIONS: Cultural Change and Cultural Survival

Through the lens of sociology, a picture of culture emerges that focuses on two central images: cultural diversity and cultural change. These features represent contemporary cultures at all levels and at all stages of development. Although the degree of cultural contact varies from society to society, it is virtually impossible for even the smallest culture in the most remote areas of the world to remain immune to outside influences. The globe is already economically and environmentally interdependent, a trend that can only increase in the future. Some cultures may be on the verge of extinction because their way of life and cultural identity cannot be preserved.

A major cultural transition is occurring among the !Kung (the exclamation point is pronounced as a click in their language), hunter-gatherers of the Kalahari Desert region of southern Africa, one of the few known remaining hunter-gatherer societies on earth. In recent years the !Kung have begun settling down, adopting the horticultural way of life of neighboring Bantu tribes and now intermarrying with them. With no written language, the !Kung transmit their culture orally. With !Kung assimilation into Bantu society on the horizon, an entire way of life—the way our ancestors lived for millions of years—is disappearing (Kent, 1989; Yellen, 1994; Shostak, 1994). Around the globe, traditional indigenous cultures are disappearing. The Masai of East Africa, the Kalam of New Guinea, and the Souma in the Central African Republic may also be losing the battle (Blauer, 1994; Linden, 1994). Neither coercion through war, forced migration, nor starvation are responsible for this transformation. It is part of a peaceful process of gradual but accelerating cultural change. It is also a largely voluntary process. With no apparent effort by these groups to work against the process, it appears to be inevitable.

The extinction of a culture through conquest and often deliberate genocide is called *ethnocide* by anthropologists. The first culture conquered by the Europeans was probably the Guanache, the native people of the Canary Islands of Africa's northwest coast. After resisting numerous waves from invaders, the Guanache succumbed to full Spanish control by 1496 and fifty years later virtually disappeared (Crosby,

1986). Although deliberate ethnocide is frequently attempted today, it rarely succeeds for two main reasons. First, geographical isolation no longer assures communication isolation. Global culture, by definition, is a connected one. Second, there is global consensus on **human rights,** those rights inherent to human beings in any culture, including, but not limited to, the right to dignity, personal integrity, inviolability of body and mind, and those civil and political rights associated with basic democratic freedoms. Torture, state-supported terrorism, forced labor, and rape of refugees are human rights violations. The global media commonly spotlight human rights violations, as we have recently witnessed in Bosnia, Somalia, Cambodia, and Congo. Safeguarding minority subcultures is a human rights concern.

The global culture, like any other culture, has a core value set associated with it. In addition to the value of human rights, the global culture has economic values related to free trade based on capitalistic models. Another value affirms every culture's right to make its own decisions regarding how to operate in the global economy. This value certainly endorses cultural relativism. Respect for all cultures leads, in turn, to the principle that one society should not interfere with the rights of another society.

Yet the very concept of global interdependence means that it is impossible to separate what goes on inside a culture from what goes on outside it—today's world has many borders but fewer boundaries (Lopez et al., 1997). As we have already seen, core values in any culture, including the global one, are not necessarily consistent and can be contradictory.

Cultural relativism is often used to the disadvantage of minorities within a culture. People throughout the world are denied education, food, and opportunities for livelihood because they are affiliated with certain subcultures. And to reinforce the most important point: These subcultures are usually minority ones. Yet the state tells the rest of the world that there should be no "interference" in their internal affairs. A good example is the use of religion to deny women access to education or employment—in Afghanistan under the authority of the Taliban, but also in Sudan, Pakistan, Iran, and Saudi Arabia. From the viewpoint of these cultures, religion is interpreted according to their own standards and enables them to maintain cultural identity in the face of frightening globalization, while still participating fully in the lucrative global economy.

The tide appears to be turning against those who raise the charge of cultural interference in the face of obvious human rights violations. The weight of international public opinion is against religion, for example, when it is used to restrict human rights. Religion can be reinterpreted so that it becomes liberating rather than restricting and becomes a weapon *for* empowerment of both women and men (Lindsey, 1995b). With women as the catalyst and advocates such as the United Nations supporting them, the theme that human rights are also women's rights has struck a resonant chord worldwide. The ideal of human rights now gains a place in the core value set of the dawning global culture.

SUMMARY

1. Culture is a shared way of life that includes material objects—food, clothing, furniture—to intangibles like values, customs, and symbols. Culture is learned and, because of its symbolic basis, is possessed only by humans.

2. Most people consider their own culture as superior to other cultures, a view known as ethnocentrism. But as a science, sociology is based on cultural relativism, the principle that all cultures must be understood and respected on their own terms.

3. Values are the ideals that underlie a culture's moral standards. American have a core value set that includes individualism, achievement, equality of opportunity, and humanitarianism. They

   also believe in group superiority, showing that core values may be contradictory.

4. Values are expressed through rules of conduct, called norms, and penalties for violating those rules, called sanctions. Norms include both the folkways that regulate daily life and stronger mores on which a society's laws are based.

5. Shared symbols, such as a flag or a language, distinguish one culture from another. Language is a key marker that provides distinctive cultural identity. If a language is lost, the culture it represents may die with it.

6. Though language does not determine thought, as the Sapir-Whorf hypothesis suggests, it can bias one's perceptions and behavior. The undesirable

effects of negative labeling serve as one example of the power of language to bias thought.

7. Language use varies with gender, based on cultural norms and roles prescribed for men and women. American men are more assertive, more direct, and less revealing in their speech, while women are more polite, open, and descriptive in their conversation.

8. Humor is based on a shared knowledge of cultural stereotypes. While functionalists see humor as a kind of social glue, conflict theorists see jokes based on ethnic and racial slurs as masked aggression.

9. Culture is always changing due to contact with other cultures, environmental change and innovation. Cultural integration is the process where cultural elements become interdependent when culture changes.

10. Technology and popular culture are cultural elements spread through the media that fuel both cultural integration and cultural change. Both elements are integrated more quickly than the values associated with them, creating cultural lag.

11. The spread of culture from one society to another, called diffusion, occurs directly through contact between people or indirectly, where goods and ideas are exchanged without firsthand contact. Culture changes through invention—the novel use of existing cultural elements—or discovery—the creation of new cultural elements.

12. Functionalism suggests that cultural universals shared by all cultures, such as the incest taboo and religious rituals, aid in cultural survival; each culture expresses universals in uniquely adaptive ways. Conflict theorists suggest that the ideology of the dominant group in a culture controls its value system.

13. Symbolic interactionists point out cultures often retain dangerous or disadvantageous customs because of emotional attachments. Meanings attached to customs are social constructions.

14. A subculture is a group whose values, norms, and mores set it apart from mainstream culture. Subcultures may be based on race, ethnicity, religion, age, gender, occupation, sexual orientation, disability, or some special interest.

15. A counterculture is a subculture in which the values and norms are opposed to those of the dominant culture. Past student protest movements and contemporary gangs are examples of countercultures.

16. America is becoming more diverse, both culturally and linguistically, creating a highly multicultural society. An emergent value of respect for cultural identity is entering America's set of core values.

17. Globalization as well as human rights violations are threatening the survival of indigenous and minority cultures. However, there is global consensus that human rights violations should not be tolerated and that minority cultures must be protected.

KEY TERMS

adaptation 72	ethnocentrism 60	norms 63
counterculture 76	folkways 63	popular culture 70
cultural integration 70	human rights 81	sanction 63
cultural lag 70	language 64	Sapir-Whorf hypothesis 65
cultural relativism 60	laws 64	subculture 75
cultural universals 72	material culture 60	symbol 64
culture 59	mores 63	technology 70
culture shock 60	nonmaterial culture 60	values 61
diffusion 71		

CRITICAL THINKING QUESTIONS

1. Based on your understanding of the role of culture in attitudes, language, and behavior, argue for or against the idea that "we are all prisoners of our own culture."

2. How do sociologists explain cultural change from the perspectives of functionalism, symbolic interactionism, and conflict theory?

3. How does cultural diversity both fuel and slow down cultural change? In the United States, how can cultural unity be strengthened when multicultural diversity is also valued?

4. How do sociologists as scientists deal with violations of human rights that continue in the name of "noninterference" in another culture? How does the general public view the same issue?

 SOCIAL STRUCTURE

OUTLINE

Joining the Crips

I never saw the blow to my head come from Huck. Bam! And I was on all fours, struggling for my equilibrium. Kicked in the stomach, I was on my back counting stars in the darkness. Grabbed by the collar, I was made to stand again. A solid blow to my chest exploded pain in bold red letters on the blank screen that had now become my mind. Bam! . . .

In the heat of desperation I struck out, hitting Fly full in the chest, knocking him back. Then I just started swinging, with no style or finesse, just anger and the instinct to survive. Of course, this did little to help my physical situation, but it showed the others that I had a will to live. And this in turn reflected my ability to represent the set in hand-to-hand combat. (Shakur, 1993: 8–9)

These are the words of Kody Scott, a former member of a Los Angeles street gang. Kody is describing part of the initiation ritual he endured in order to join a local branch (or "set") of the Crips. First, he stole an automobile to demonstrate his "street smarts" and willingness to break the law. Then he allowed himself to be beaten, showing both that he was tough and that he was ready to do whatever the gang required of him. He completed the process by participating in a "military action"—killing a member of a rival gang. Initiations like this are by no means rare in today's street gangs (Curry & Decker, 1998). Kody, by the way, was just eleven years old.

Learning to Be a Freshman

At the small residential college in the South where one of the authors teaches, all entering freshmen participate in a three-day orientation period called the Foundations program. The new students are divided into groups of fifteen headed by a faculty member and two upper-class students. Foundation groups eat their meals together, bowl and play miniature golf as a group, go to a college-wide swim party, put in four hours of community service, and attend sessions about their college's traditions. Throughout the three days, students are encouraged to wear their Foundations group's tee shirt—a modern version of the freshman "beanies" seen on college campuses early in the century.

As these accounts suggest, people who are joining groups like street gangs or entering new social environments such as colleges are often required to participate in initiation ceremonies. In Chapter 3, these ceremonies were called *rites of passage*. The main purpose of such rituals is to teach new members the culture of the group they are joining—to pass on to them the norms, values, and styles of behavior they will be expected to display as members.

This process of learning could be accomplished more simply by merely requiring recruits to become familiar with a written list of rules, but it is generally more effective to teach new members what is expected of them within the context of ongoing group interaction. This is true because culture becomes meaningful in people's lives only when it is enacted. It is one thing to simply tell a new gangbanger that he is expected to be physically aggressive and quite another to require him to actually take part in collective violence. Similarly, freshmen could learn about their school's traditions by reading about them, but the learning process is much more vivid and longer-lasting if it occurs within a group or some other type of *social structure*.

Sociologists use the term **social structure** to refer to the relatively stable patterns of social interaction that characterize human social life (Smelser, 1988; Mark, 1998). Culture and social structure are intimately interconnected. Culture provides the blueprint or programming for the ways people behave. Social structure provides the setting in which culture is acted out.

We will begin our analysis at the microsociological level by discussing how people participate in social structure as individuals. Then we will gradually expand our scope to examine social groups and larger elements of social structure including institutions and entire societies. The chapter will conclude with a consideration of how social life changes as societies evolve from relatively simple systems to the complex patterns typical of the developed world and a brief discussion of some new forms of social structure that may develop in the coming decades.

STATUS AND ROLE

The smallest elements of social structure are statuses and roles, two closely related concepts that form the basic building blocks of all social life.

Status

Undeniably, a group (or any other element of social structure) is made up of interacting people. However, sociologists tend to initially analyze social structures as composed of a number of interrelated positions and only later to factor in the personal characteristics of the individuals who happen to be occupying those positions at any given time. Thus a Foundations group might be made up of Steve, Antonio, Jami, and fifteen freshmen, but sociologists would analyze it as composed of the *positions* of faculty leader (currently occupied by Steve), student leaders (Antonio and Jami) and freshmen (the fifteen new students).

Sociologists adopt this approach because they are more interested in knowing about groups in general than in knowing about the specifics of any particular group. After all, there will be orientation groups next year and every year that will be made up of the same positions and will therefore be very much like this year's groups, although the positions will be occupied by different individuals.

Sociologists use the term **status** to refer to a social position that an individual occupies (Linton,

1936). Your statuses largely define who you are in relation to other people, especially when you do not know the others intimately. At home, an individual is usually treated as a unique person, but at work that same individual interacts with others mostly in terms of his or her occupational status—clerk, police officer, nurse, or CEO. Note that from this perspective, a group, or any larger element of social structure, is simply a set of interrelated statuses.

This usage of the term status is somewhat different from the meaning it has in everyday speech, where it usually refers to an individual's level of prestige. Thus people may say that a physician is high in status and a sewer worker is low. Sociologists recognize that many social statuses are ranked—generals over privates, seniors over freshmen—but this comparative aspect of status is secondary to its core meaning—a social position that people occupy. After all, some important social statuses are not ranked—basketball players are not generally seen as superior to football players, or Methodists as inferior to Presbyterians.

All of the statuses which an individual occupies make up that person's **status set.** Thus, every member of a Foundation orientation group also has a gender status (male or female), an ethnic or racial status (African American, white, Latino), an age status (teenager, middle-aged), a religious status (Mormon, Catholic), a class status (middle or working class), a sexual orientation status (straight or gay), various family statuses (mother, cousin, brother), perhaps an occupational status (lifeguard, part-time burger flipper), and many others. Note also that not all of the statuses an individual occupies are necessarily relevant to any given interaction—for example, the fact that someone is red-haired or left-handed is unlikely to influence his or her behavior in a street gang.

Sometimes the different statuses that make up an individual's status set do not fit together smoothly because they are ranked at different levels, a condition called **status inconsistency.** Examples include a 10-year-old college student or a Ph.D. working behind the counter of a Baskin-Robbins. Such situations can be quite uncomfortable for the individuals involved.

We often interact with others on the basis of the statuses they occupy rather than who they are, especially in the modern impersonal world. When you renew your driver's license, the clerk does not know you personally and you do not know him or her, yet the interaction usually goes smoothly because it is based on the statuses of clerk and applicant. Because so much interaction is status specific, people frequently display *status symbols* that identify the statuses they are occupying and thus tell others how to behave towards them. Again, note that contrary to everyday

INTERNET — CONNECTIONS

To learn more about Los Angeles street gangs, including the Crips, check site www.street-gangs.com. What is the appeal of gangs for the people who join them?

The military may be viewed as a complex system of ranked statuses. Individuals occupying the status of drill sergeant command more power and prestige than those occupying the position of boot camp trainee.

usage, status symbols may denote either prestigious positions (a wealthy person's sports car) or those that others look down on (a street person's tattered clothes).

Achieved and Ascribed Status.   Some of our social statuses are **ascribed statuses,** those into which we are born and that we cannot change, or that we ac-

People experience status inconsistency if they simultaneously hold two or more statuses that are differently evaluated. One example would be an individual whose achieved occupational status is higher than his or her ascribed racial status.

quire involuntarily over the life course. Gender, race or ethnicity, certain family statuses (eldest sister, son), and life cycle statuses such as adolescent or senior citizen are all ascribed statuses. Although we cannot change our ascribed statuses, we can work with others to try to increase the esteem with which they are viewed. This has been a primary objective of the feminist and minority liberation movements of recent decades.

We also occupy **achieved statuses,** positions we acquire over time as a result of our own actions. Examples of achieved statuses include one's occupation, educational status (college graduate or high school dropout), some family statuses (wife or father), and political affiliation (Democrat or Independent). Note that achieved statuses that are ranked may be high (physician) or low (convict) in prestige. The important point is that we are not locked into them at birth, although in some cases we may inherit an initial status placement that may or may not change later, as is the case with religion and social class.

Master Status.   Not all statuses are equally important. A **master status** is a social position that is exceptionally powerful in determining an individual's identity, often to the point where other statuses are virtually ignored (Hughes, 1945). For example, someone who is a Catholic priest or the president of the United States is likely to be treated as a priest or president in almost all interactions. Master statuses may also be negative, in which case they are called **stigmas** (Goffman, 1963b). Thus blemishes of character, such as conviction for a serious crime, often function as master statuses (Gove, 1980; Fine & Asch, 1988; Charmaz, 1991).

Status Symbols

Most sociologists tend to favor a relatively broad definition of the concept of status symbol. In this view, anything that identifies any position or status that an individual is occupying to those with whom that person is interacting, thereby facilitating interaction, is a status symbol. It doesn't matter how that status is evaluated. Thus diamond jewelry is a status symbol, but so is a prisoner's uniform. Status symbols may be physical objects, people (servants, "trophy wives"), or even accents (a key symbol of class position in Britain).

In everyday usage, however, most people use the term primarily to refer to symbols that are *high* in prestige. It is this meaning that captured the attention of Thorsten Veblen (1857–1929), a noted economist and sociologist who developed an incisive analysis of American social behavior in the early decades of the twentieth century.

Veblen was especially interested in the status symbols employed by the wealthy of his era. Of course, then as now, large homes, expensive clothing, and fine furniture were obvious marks of the social elite. Veblen coined the phrase *conspicuous consumption* to refer to the ostentatious and public display of luxury goods as a claim to high status. Beyond that, he noted that the wealthy of his day also demonstrated their status by *conspicuous waste*. Although the father of the family generally had to work, his status and that of his dependents would be raised if his wife did not work, even in the home (that was what servants were for!); if he could afford to allow his children to study obscure subjects like medieval poetry that were unlikely to be of much value to them in the marketplace; and if he could throw lavish parties and employ workers to do frivolous things such as trim shrubbery into elaborate topiary sculptures. It is no surprise that Veblen used the term "the leisure class" to refer to the elite.

How have status symbols changed since Veblen wrote? Here are some recent trends, each of which may provide some insight into how society has changed over the past few generations.

Status symbols seem to have become even more conspicuous and less subtle. For example, in Veblen's day, you often had to know just what to look for to evaluate the social meaning of clothes. Today, after almost a century of the growth of the mobility-oriented *Gesellschaft* model of society, class lines are less clearly drawn and higher status people seem to need to assert and defend their rank more aggressively and unambiguously by such means as displaying highly visible brand-name labels on their clothes, shoes, and automobiles. Two generations ago, this overt a display of status symbols would almost certainly have been regarded as vulgar or uncouth.

This trend toward the overt display of brand names may also suggest that, perhaps as a result of a gradual increase in the prestige of business in society since the 1970s, more people seem comfortable displaying a level of commercialization that might well have struck previous generations as crass. Few in Veblen's day would have been willing to become "walking billboards" advertising high-status brand names.

Conspicuous waste is still with us, but in a somewhat different form. Reflecting the greater egalitarianism, individualism, and competitiveness of the modern era, spouses and children of upper crust families are no longer expected to publically display their idleness. But early retirement after a productive career has become an increasingly potent status symbol. Hundreds of thousands of people, some as young as their thirties, have made their fortunes (especially in sports, entertainment, or high-tech industries) and then simply quit working. What more powerful and visible statement could you make to others of having "made it" than to say that not only do my spouse and children not have to work (unless they want to), but neither do I?

Another observation: Previously, status symbols always seemed to "trickle down" over time. For example, the clothing styles worn last season by the elite were often adopted this year by the middle classes—forcing the upper strata to find some new way of dressing to display their rank. Today, however, we occasionally see exactly the opposite pattern: clothing styles (like blue jeans or "grunge" fashions) or music that was previously identified with the lower classes (folk, jazz, blues) suddenly become "cool"—it "trickles up" and becomes accepted by and even symbolic of the elite. This may reflect our current emphasis on egalitarianism and the more negative connotations of snobbery that have resulted from the successes of the women's and minority liberation movements.

The more frequent use of "ethnic identifiers" as positive status symbols has been another consequence of the continuing empowerment of minorities and other groups. Examples include the spread of braided or natural "Afro" hairstyles among African Americans or the resurgent popularity of distinctively ethnic names among a number of ethnic minorities.

1. What are some of the symbols used by your friends and family to announce their social status? Speculate on the underlying social meanings of these particular symbols.
2. Some elite symbols are easily imitated. Examples include knock-off designer clothing and fragrances or Chevrolets that look a lot like last year's Cadillacs. What problems are created for the elite by this? Can you think of some elite status symbols that cannot be so easily copied?

Sources: Lerner, 1948; Ridgeway, 1991; Davis, 1992; Lipovetsky, 1994.

The ascribed statuses of race and gender have commonly functioned as master statuses, especially when most members of the group an individual is joining are of a different race or the other gender. Thus the first female executive in a firm is often dealt with more on the basis of her gender status than as an executive; such an individual is sometimes described as a *token*. Male nurses or the first few African Americans who join a previously all-white fraternity may experience similar treatment. However, as more women and minorities enter positions from which they were previously excluded, these identities are gradually becoming less likely to function as master statuses.

Other master statuses are somewhat less pervasive but still important. Occupation is frequently a master status; it tends to be the first thing we ask about when we meet someone, and its significance often lingers after we have left our jobs: People are commonly introduced as former teachers or ex-military officers.

Role

The concept of role is closely related to that of status. A **role** consists of the norms associated with a particular status—norms that specify the behavior required of an individual occupying that position. Thus the role of a gang member consists of all the expectations that people have about how such an individual ought to act. Role is the dynamic dimension of status. Roles are learned, as all norms are, through socialization. They represent the intersection between culture and social structure. The concepts of status and role are easy to confuse, but you can keep them straight by always remembering that we *occupy* a status but we *play* or *enact* a role (Linton, 1936).

Most important statuses are accompanied by a cluster of related but somewhat distinct roles or what may be called a **role set** (Merton, 1968). Thus, for example, someone who occupies the status of college professor may be simply said to play the role of professor, or we may dig deeper and identify the several elements of this person's role set, which will include distinct norms guiding such activities as preparing lectures, teaching classes, advising students, conducting research, doing committee work, and perhaps leading a freshman orientation group. Similarly, the role set of parent includes components such as teacher, nurse, cook, disciplinarian, and chauffeur.

The notion of role is obviously based on an analogy between social life and the theater. This is the basic insight behind the *dramaturgical* perspective that was pioneered by Erving Goffman and will be discussed in Chapter 6. As on the stage, there is often a difference between what is formally expected of a social actor (*role expectations*) and how the role is actually played (*role performance*). However, social actors have considerably more freedom than actors on a stage because the "scripts" for social roles nearly always allow a good deal of room for improvisation. In fact, as the symbolic interactionist perspective would emphasize, people are constantly engaged in the process of *role making*, negotiating with other role players how they will perform their parts (Turner, 1962; Strauss, 1977; Wasserman & Faust, 1994).

Thus, for example, an individual occupying the status and playing the role of student is expected to take school seriously. Actual performance varies, however: Some students never miss a class, some barely show up for exams, and most negotiate a position somewhere between these two extremes.

As mentioned in Chapter 1, one of the advantages of acquiring the sociological imagination is learning to debunk. Role expectations do not always have to be rigidly obeyed. In fact, role making and negotiation are especially common when role definitions are in flux (as is the case with contemporary gender roles, a central topic of Chapter 13), or when a new role is emerging, such as holistic health counselor or "partner" in a committed gay relationship.

Role Strain. Sometimes people experience **role strain**, difficulty adequately performing all the elements of the role set connected to a single status (Goode, 1960). For example, a police internal affairs agent is expected to be a loyal member of the police and also to root out corruption on the force (Mulcahy, 1995). Foremen and military chaplains may experience similar problems. Role strain is especially likely to arise when role sets are relatively complex (Coser, 1991).

Role Conflict. In contrast to role strain, **role conflict** arises when the expectations for the roles connected to one status clash with those associated with one or several entirely separate statuses coincidentally occupied by the same person (Lang, 1992; Giglotti & Huff, 1995). This is sometimes a problem of a lack of time, as anyone knows well who has ever tried to work, go to school, and raise children.

Role conflict may also result from status inconsistency, as previously discussed, or from direct clashes between the requirements of two role sets. This type of role conflict may arise, for example, if a college basketball coach is also the mother of one of the players, because a coach is required to treat her players evenhandedly, whereas a mother is generally expected to favor her own children.

There are a number of ways to resolve role strain and role conflict (Goode, 1960). Determining which roles (or elements of the role set) are most important and which are secondary allows a person to concen-

A physician who treats young children must modify his or her role perform- ance in order to emphasize warmth and caring as well as professional expertise.

trate on only the most important role demands; par- ents who decide to reduce their involvement at work in order to spend more time with their children are adopting this strategy. *Compartmentalization* or *role segregation*, playing your different and conflicting roles at different places and in front of different audi- ences, also can help. Thus an individual who is a street gang member and an A student is unlikely to play both roles in front of the same audience.

People who are having role problems sometimes experience *role embracement*, the feeling that they are nothing more than the roles they are expected to play (Goffman, 1961b). A good antidote is provided by *role distance*, a process by which an individual deliberately communicates, either in words or in body language, that he or she is indeed much more than a simple role player: "I may be waiting on tables, but I'm really an actress."

The topics of roles and role playing will be more fully explored in Chapter 6.

SOCIAL GROUPS

Groups are essential to human life. They shape our goals, our values, our behavior, and our self-concepts. In a very real sense, we are different people in differ- ent groups: Compare what you are like at home with how you behave as a member of a team or among your close friends. The differences result from the fact that we occupy different statuses and play differ- ent roles in different groups.

As sociologists use the term, a **social group** con- sists of two or more people who regularly interact and feel some sense of solidarity or common identity. People in groups normally share some values and

norms and often work to achieve common goals. Families, sports teams, religious congregations, col- lege orientation groups, and street gangs are all exam- ples of social groups.

We should differentiate between social groups and two other closely related concepts, aggregates and categories. **Aggregates** are collections of people who are physically at the same place at the same time, but do not interact in any meaningful way, like people in an elevator or those standing on a street corner waiting for a bus. Aggregates lack not only interaction but also appreciable feelings of solidarity. However, if they are given a common focus of attention—if the el- evator jams or the bus fails to arrive on time—the members of an aggregate may start to interact and be- come a group.

Categories are collections of individuals who share a social status, such as people with red hair, Asian Americans, Bruce Springsteen fans, college freshmen, or sociologists. Members of a category may share some vague sense of solidarity, but because they are not physically in each other's presence, they do not interact and accordingly are not a group.

Types of Groups

People join social groups for two principal reasons: (a) to relate to others in order to enjoy a measure of intimacy and combat loneliness and (b) to accomplish goals they would have difficulty achieving on their own—editing a newspaper, raising a barn, or robbing a bank. Groups tend to specialize to some extent in one or the other of these functions, as the next section explains.

Primary and Secondary Groups.   Charles Horton Cooley (1909) used the term **primary group** to refer to small groups characterized by warm, informal, and long-lasting interaction. People in primary groups know each other well and interact on the basis of their entire identities and personalities rather than just as role players; members of primary groups are not easily replaced. Primary groups generate high levels of solidarity and loyalty. They are ends in themselves, not means to an end. The most common examples are families and groups of friends, but many work groups, sports teams, small classes, and military units also may be primary groups. Figure 4.1 illustrates data concerning how gender affects participation in various types of primary groups.

Cooley called such groups "primary" for two reasons: They are the *first* kind of group we experience, and they are *central* to our lives. The people who make up our primary groups are, by definition, important to us: For this reason they are often called *significant others*. Our membership in these groups is a cornerstone of our identity and absolutely vital to our mental health (Messeri et al., 1993; Egolf et al., 1993).

Obviously, not all families and other primary groups are equally warm and caring and supportive. Actual groups and the relationships that comprise them fall along a scale or continuum (see Figure 4.2). Relationships that closely fit the definition of primary groups, like those between close friends, would fall toward the top of the scale. Those that lack some but not all primary characteristics would be located toward the center. Street gangs probably belong here. Groups and relationships at the bottom end of the continuum are secondary in character.

Secondary groups tend to be formal, emotionally cool, and often temporary. Interaction in secondary groups is typically role specific, and individual members are easily replaced. People's involvement in secondary groups is rational and calculative; they value these groups chiefly as a means to accomplish a particular task or end. Examples include most classrooms, offices, and voluntary associations such as

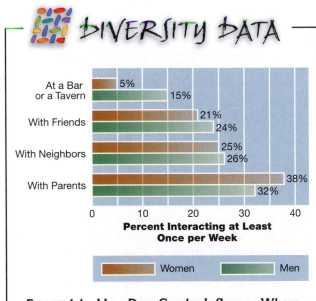

FIGURE 4.1   How Does Gender Influence Where and With Whom People Interact? Women are more likely than men to spend their leisure time with their parents. Men tend to interact more frequently than women in bars or with friends. Both genders are about equally likely to spend time with neighbors. What does this data suggest about the relative strength of the ties of women and men to their parents?
Source: NORC. General Social Surveys, 1972-1996. Chicago: National Opinion Research Center, 1996.

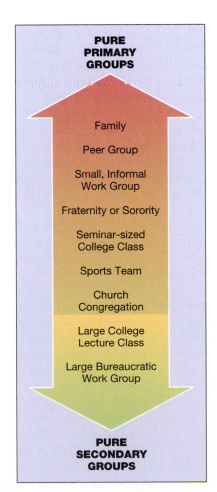

FIGURE 4.2   The Continuum from Primary to Secondary Groups.

PTAs or church congregations. Bureaucratic formal organizations, one of the principal topics of Chapter 22, are also secondary groups.

While the emotional tone of secondary groups is cool, members may be strongly committed to the group—not so much because of their personal interest in their fellow members, but rather because they strongly desire the goals toward which the group is working.

Secondary groups may be either large or small, although they are most characteristically large. Some small secondary groups may become increasingly primary over time as the members get to know each other better (S. Marks, 1994). Furthermore, primary groups are often embedded in or emerge from secondary groups. Thus large classes are secondary groups, but smaller more primary groups of friends, study partners, and students working together on a class project are normally present within them.

One of the most important patterns of change in today's world is a gradual but substantial decline in the time most people spend in primary groups and a corresponding rise in their secondary involvements. This change accompanies the shift from farming to industry and the growth of the modern city. Closely connected with the shift towards more secondary group memberships is a move away from ascribed and toward achieved statuses. The result is that people today are much freer to be individuals, but they are often left feeling more lonely and isolated.

Voluntary associations such as social clubs, service organizations, and youth groups, although essentially secondary, can provide some primary interaction for their members, helping to counter contemporary trends toward isolation. Figure 4.3 documents how gender affects membership in such associations.

In addition to primary and secondary groups, sociologists identify several other important types of social groups. The most important are in-groups, out-groups, and reference groups.

In-Groups and Out-Groups. As you might expect, **in-groups** are the groups to which individuals belong and toward which they feel pride and loyalty, while **out-groups** are groups to which they do not belong and toward which they feel disdain and perhaps hostility (Sumner, 1960). Of course, the distinction between in-groups and out-groups is entirely relative. A Texan may normally view a New Yorker as a member of an out-group, but when traveling abroad everyone from the United States is likely to be seen as part of one's in-group.

Group membership tends to bias our judgments and perceptions: In-group virtues are often seen as out-group vices (Merton, 1968; Tajfel, 1982). *We* are

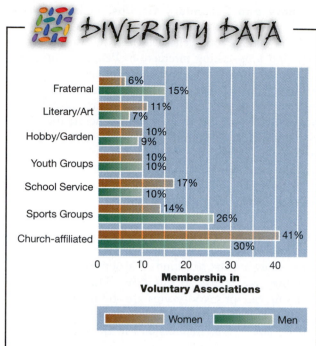

FIGURE 4.3   Membership in Voluntary Associations, by Gender. Women are more likely than men to participate in literary and artistic, school-related, and religious organizations. Men tend to be more active in fraternal and sports groups. These patterns are clearly in line with traditional gender roles. Do you think they may change if gender roles continue to become less rigid and more egalitarian?
Source: NORC. General Social Surveys, 1972-1996. Chicago: National Opinion Research Center, 1996.

intelligent, dedicated, and consistent; *they* are cunning, fanatical, and rigid.

Commitment to in-groups tends to be strengthened by conflict with out-groups (Lamont & Fournier, 1992) and by the presence of visible "markers" that identify members of the two groups to each other and to outsiders. Almost anything can serve as a marker: skin color, gang "colors," a distinctive T-shirt, or even sitting at a particular table in the school dining hall.

In-groups, whether primary or secondary, provide positive feelings of solidarity and self-worth (Coser, 1956). Membership in them is frequently an important element of our social identity. But they have a dark side as well. Especially if in-groups are competing for scarce resources, conflict between them can be bitter and violent, promoting extreme forms of ethnocentrism (see Chapter 3), as is evident in the contemporary Arab–Israeli struggle over the occupation of the West Bank or in conflicts between street gangs (Blackwell, 1982; Noel, 1991).

A church choir is a good example of a small group. Choir members interact regularly, feel a sense of solidarity, share common values and norms, and cooperate to achieve mutual goals.

Reference Groups.   **Reference groups** are composed of people we look to in order to evaluate our own behavior (Hyman, 1942). Actually, they serve two closely related but distinct functions: a *normative* function of providing guidance concerning how to act and a *comparative* function whereby we can assess ourselves in relation to others (Merton & Kitt, 1950). When these functions are provided by a single person, we call that individual a *role model*.

At any given point in time, most people are guided by several different reference groups, with the result that they may sometimes receive contradictory messages. For example, law students who have a big exam the next day may be torn between following the lead of friends who are settling in for a long night of studying and the model of another group of friends who are heading out to the bars.

Sometimes we are actually members of our reference groups, as in the case of a nurse who has just joined the staff of a hospital and who looks to his or her fellow nurses for reference group functions. Or we may choose reference groups to which we do not belong, as when a young basketball player copies the behavior of NBA stars. Some reference groups are even fictional—"What would Captain Kirk do in this situation?"

Group Dynamics

Social psychologists have devoted a great deal of attention to the study of *group dynamics*—the reciprocal influence between the individual and the small group (Homans, 1950; Hare et al., 1994). *Small groups* are those in which each member can interact regularly and directly with all of the other members—a situation that becomes difficult once the group is larger than about twelve. Among the major topics studied by students of group dynamics, four are especially important: the impact of group size, leadership, conformity, and decision making (Levine & Moreland, 1998).

Group Size.   Any sociological consideration of the effects of group size must begin with the work of the German sociologist Georg Simmel (1858–1918) (pronounced *Zim-mel*). Simmel identified several crucial differences between *dyads* (two-person groups) and *triads* (three-member groups) (Simmel, 1950).

The dyad is simultaneously the most intimate group experience possible and the most fragile one. Think of a husband and wife or two very close friends. Members of a committed dyad may give themselves to the other more completely and fully than ever occurs in a larger group. It is in the dyad that individuals can experience the most intense primary relationship possible (Palazzolo, 1981; Solano & Dunnam, 1985). But if the relationship sours and one member leaves, the group disintegrates. This fragility is why virtually all societies back up the dyadic marriage bond with legal and religious injunctions against leaving the marriage except under extreme circumstances.

If we add a third member to a dyad, the group becomes less intimate but also less fragile; no longer does the loss of one person end it. There are now three relationships in the group where before there was only one (see Figure 4.4 on page 111). The third member may play several different roles. He or she

A family becomes a triad after the first child is born. The addition of a third member to a group may either strengthen or weaken its cohesiveness.

may further unify the group, as sometimes occurs within a family after the first child is born. Or the new member may form a coalition with one of the others, usually the weaker of the two, against the third. Or the third member may try to "divide and rule," forming and breaking alliances in a way that works to his or her advantage.

When groups grow beyond three, the basic principle that intimacy and intensity decline and stability increases continues to hold true. Also, as group size increases, the number of relationships in the group increases geometrically. There is only one relationship in a dyad and there are only three in a triad, but there are six in a four-person group and ten in a group with five members (see Figure 4.4) (Palazzolo, 1981).

When groups exceed five or six members, they become more formal. People *address* larger groups rather than talking to them conversationally (Bales, 1951). Furthermore, as group size increases, more formal rules develop and the group's leaders may become more powerful because it becomes easier for them to simply ignore dissenting members.

Leadership. Are leaders born or made? Many people, perhaps most, would probably choose the former option, especially if they are thinking about great historical leaders such as Abraham Lincoln, Nelson Mandela, or Mahatma Ghandi, but a large body of classic sociological research strongly suggests that group leadership is less a quality of a particular individual than a two-way relationship between leaders and followers that rests heavily on the leader's effectiveness in interacting with the members and the extent to which he or she is seen as committed to the group's goals and values

(Stogdill, 1974). Someone who is an excellent leader in one context may be utterly ineffective in another. In other words, leadership is best understood as a characteristic of social structure rather than as an attribute of particular individuals.

Nevertheless, leaders do often share certain characteristics. Leaders tend to be original problem solvers who are comfortable acting on their own initiative and they tend to be self-confident and good at living with a certain amount of frustration (Stogdill, 1974). They are more talkative than followers. They also tend to be taller and to be perceived as more attractive (Crosbie, 1975; Kalick, 1988).

Every small group tends to develop not one but two distinct leaders. One, the **instrumental** (or task) **leader,** is primarily concerned with making the decisions that will help the group achieve its goals; the other, the **expressive** (or socioemotional) **leader,** concentrates on keeping the group's morale high (Bales, 1950, 1953; Fiedler, 1981). Both types are crucial if the group is to function effectively. Occasionally, one person may fill both roles, but this is rare because an instrumental leader must sometimes ruffle people's feathers in order to keep the group moving in the right direction—a responsibility that makes it difficult to be well-liked enough to be an effective expressive leader (Olmstead & Hare, 1978). Good instrumental leaders earn the respect of their followers; good expressive leaders receive their affection.

Group dynamics researchers have identified three types of instrumental leaders based on how directive they are (White & Lippitt, 1960). An **authoritarian leader** assigns tasks, makes the major decisions for the group, pays relatively little attention to the con-

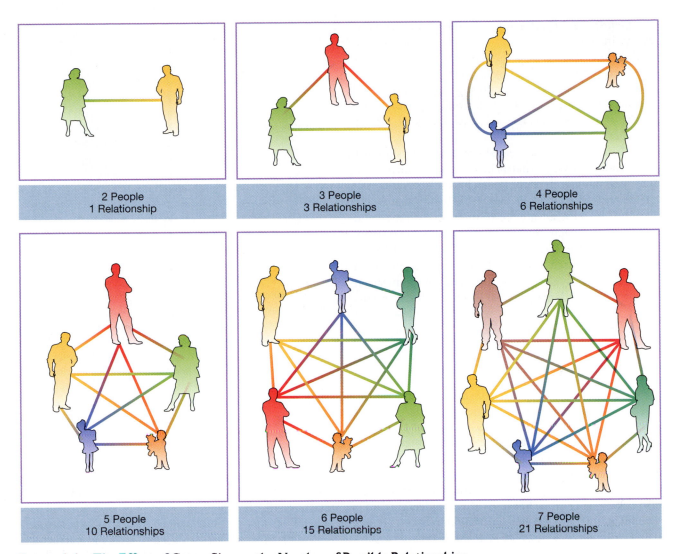

FIGURE 4.4   The Effect of Group Size on the Number of Possible Relationships.

cerns of the followers, and praises or criticizes group members without adequately explaining the criteria on which they are being judged. In contrast, a **democratic leader** encourages group discussion and input, works to build group consensus, and tries to explain why members are being rewarded or punished. A **laissez-faire leader** (from the French term for "let it be") is highly nondirective, letting group members make their own decisions without much help or input.

As you might expect, laissez-faire leaders are the least effective and sometimes the least popular (Fiedler, 1967), but the relative advantages of authoritarian and democratic leadership are more difficult to determine (Fiedler, 1981). Authoritarian leaders are generally not well liked, and members of groups under their direction usually report lower morale. At the same time, authoritarian leaders are good in a cri-

sis, when decisions must be made quickly and obeyed without question. Democratic leaders do not fare well in emergencies. On the other hand, when there is time for discussion and when a certain amount of dissent can be tolerated, democratic leadership creates groups that are more satisfied, work better without direct supervision, and, in many cases, are more productive (Tjosvold et al., 1992).

It should be noted, however, that these findings are primarily based on research conducted in societies like the United States, where there is a strong cultural bias toward democratic leadership (Olmstead & Hare, 1978). It may be that in nations with weaker democratic traditions, authoritarian leadership is more popular and effective. The key point is that leaders must be seen to accept the group's values, whatever they are.

Gender and Leadership. In the traditional family, as in many other types of groups, instrumental leaders have historically tended to be male and expressive leaders, female. This pattern persists to some extent today because of enduring expectations and socialization patterns, but it is gradually weakening as the importance of the ascribed status of gender declines.

Most research into small-group leadership has been androcentric in that it has focused primarily on males. Traditionally, Americans have displayed a cultural bias toward male leadership, a reality that works very much to the advantage of men. In fact, men and women have been repeatedly shown to be roughly equally effective as leaders (Eagly & Johnson, 1990).

Early research suggested that women and men tended to display somewhat different communication patterns and leadership styles. In line with the instrumental/expressive distinction, male leaders were found to be relatively directive or authoritarian, whereas women were more democratic, collaborative, and participatory (Eagly & Karau, 1991). Women were described as seeking leadership roles out of a desire to be helpful, whereas men were more commonly driven by the need to achieve and dominate (Bridges, 1989). However, newer research suggests that such distinctions are fading as more women enter leadership positions (Klenke, 1996).

Interestingly, women who adopt a directive approach are commonly judged by their subordinates as too harsh, perhaps because this leadership style clashes with their stereotypical gender role. But the same principle does not seem to hold for men: Supportive male leaders, whose leadership style violates traditional male role expectations, are more likely to be appreciated than are more authoritarian male leaders (Butler & Geis, 1990).

Conformity. The way in which individuals interact in a group is determined not only by the size of the group and its leadership, but also by group pressures toward conformity. A classic study by social psychologist Solomon Asch (1952) illustrates this fact.

Imagine that you are a participant in Asch's experiment. You arrive at a social science laboratory and are told to sit at the end of a row of six other people whom you assume to be fellow research subjects. In fact, however, they are working with Asch: You are the only person being tested.

You are told—falsely—that you are participating in a study of perception. You are then shown a sample card (see Figure 4.5) and told that your task will be to decide which of the three lines on the bottom (X, Y, or Z) is the same length as the one on the top (A). As it happens, the correct answer is obvious. During the first "trial run," everyone announces the correct an-

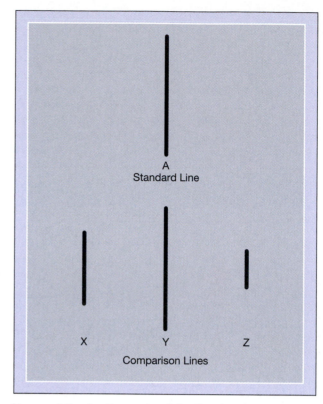

FIGURE 4.5   An Example of the Cards Used in the Asch Experiment.

swer, one at a time. You give your answer next to last because of where you are sitting in the row.

Then the real experiment starts. You are shown a total of eighteen cards. In every case the correct answer is obvious. But on the third card, and eleven times thereafter, everyone in the group gives the wrong answer and then they all look at you to see what you will say.

What do you think you would do in this situation? Asch found that about one-third of his subjects went along with the group—giving an answer they *knew* was wrong—at least half the time. Another 40 percent conformed less frequently, and just 25 percent gave the correct answer throughout the experiment. Through interviews, he found that almost all the conformers knew they were answering incorrectly but were not willing to openly defy the expressed opinion of the rest of the group.

The real significance of this research is evident if we reflect on the fact that this was a very artificial situation. The experimental subject did not even know the other people in the group. Consider what happens when we are in real groups that are important to us, like our families and peer groups, and you will get a sense of how easily groups can affect behavior.

Decision Making. Do groups make better decisions than individuals? With several people working

*Groupthink may occur when confor-
mity pressures in highly cohesive
groups prevent members from questioning an emerging group consensus.*

on a problem, you have a larger pool of knowledge
to draw on, and the chances increase that someone
will detect errors in the group's collective thought
process. However, these advantages may be short-
circuited by groupthink (Phillips & Wood, 1984;
Watson et al., 1991).

Groupthink, a phenomenon first identified by
Irving Janis (1972), refers to the tendency of highly
cohesive groups to make poor decisions because the
members are unwilling to threaten the group's solidarity. As a consensus emerges, dissent is stifled because of conformity pressures similar to those studied
by Asch (Hart, 1991; Kameda & Sugimori, 1993).
Self-appointed "mindguards" arise who pounce on
anyone who disagrees with the collective mind-set of
the group and label dissenters disloyal.

Janis and other researchers have identified groupthink as a key factor in a number of disastrous governmental decisions, including the failure to prepare
Pearl Harbor for a Japanese sneak attack, the
Kennedy administration's decision to invade Cuba
that led to the Bay of Pigs fiasco (McCauley, 1989),
Watergate (Hart, 1991), and the *Challenger* tragedy.

Now that sociologists have identified the symptoms of groupthink, steps can be taken to prevent it.
Future leaders in business, politics, and the military
are being formally taught to solicit and reward well-
considered opposition to an emerging consensus
(Aldag & Fuller, 1993). This is another example of
how applying the sociological imagination can improve people's lives.

LARGER ELEMENTS OF SOCIAL STRUCTURE

Many of our most important social interactions take
place within small groups, but these groups are located within the context of various larger units of
social structure. The most important of these larger
units are networks, formal organizations, communities, strata, institutions, and, finally, entire societies.

Networks

A **network** is a broad web of social ties that radiates
out from a given individual, linking him or her to a
large number of other people. Networks are person-
specific; that is, they are different for each individual.
They include our primary and secondary group memberships but also connect us with large numbers of
people whom we know more or less well but with
whom we only occasionally interact. Networks are
looser and less coherent than groups, lacking clear
boundaries or any appreciable sense of collective
identity. They tend to be quite large, typically varying
from 500 to perhaps 2,500 people (Milgram, 1967).

The study of networks is a relatively new but
rapidly expanding topic in sociology. Stanley Milgram's (1967) "small world" study was one of the first
major research projects concerning networks. Milgram randomly selected individuals from all across
the United States and designated them as either
"starters" or "targets." The starters were given a letter
that was addressed to one of the targets. However, the
starters could not simply mail the letter to the target,
but instead were required to send it on to someone
they knew on a first-name basis and who might personally know the designated target. Successive members of the chain followed the same instructions. Most
of the letters did eventually reach their final destina-
tions and it typically took only between five and seven
links for them to do so.

Networks include both *strong* links, connecting
people who know each other well (Fischer, 1982) and
weak links, between individuals who know each other
less intimately (Granovetter, 1973). Highly educated

people usually have more strong ties and a larger number of ties to non-kin—both factors that increase their ability to accomplish their ends. Older people and individuals living outside of urban areas have fewer strong ties (Marsden, 1987). People with smaller and weaker networks tend to be more vulnerable to physical and mental health problems (Seeman et al., 1985).

When people use the term "networking" in everyday speech, they are usually talking about business and professional networks (Granovetter, 1995). People with extensive work-related networks are at a distinct advantage in advancing their careers (Marsden, 1992). Studies show that up to 60 percent of all job seekers find their positions through networking rather than by responding to printed advertisements (Lin et al., 1981). Thus, the cynical saying "It's who you know, not what you know" is frequently quite true (Marsden & Lin, 1982; Knoke, 1990).

Historically, men have been better connected than women, hence the term the *old boys' network* (Montgomery, 1992). Men's networks tend to be stronger and to include more powerful and higher status individuals. But this is changing as more and more women are forming "old girls' networks" to help them advance in their business and professional lives (Moore, 1991; Ferguson & Dunphy, 1992; Wright, 1995).

It's not just American professionals who network, either. Research shows that networking is important among such diverse groups of people as organized criminals (Block, 1983; Chambliss, 1988), top civic and political leaders (Domhoff, 1974; Useem, 1984), maids (Hondagneu-Sotelo, 1994), and Asian businessmen (Gerlach, 1992; Kotkin, 1993).

Since the next four larger elements of social structure are discussed at length later in the text, we will only briefly introduce them here.

Formal Organizations

A **formal** (or complex) **organization** is a large secondary group that is explicitly designed to accomplish specific tasks by means of an elaborate internal division of labor (Etzioni, 1964). Examples include General Motors, the University of Kentucky, the World Health Organization, or the government of the state of Missouri. Most modern formal organizations are structured as bureaucracies. Chapter 22 examines bureaucratic formal organizations in depth, with special attention to the workplace.

Communities

Traditionally, the term *community* has been used to refer to a relatively large number of people who live in one geographic area and are connected to each other by a variety of social bonds (Poplin, 1979; Lowery, 1993). More recently some sociologists have dropped the requirement that members of a community must share a territorial base, as reflected in the fact that we often use expressions like "the business community" to describe people who do not necessarily live anywhere near one another but who regularly communicate and share various concerns. More conventional examples of communities includes cities, towns, villages, and neighborhoods. Chapter 21 will develop a sociological analysis of this topic.

Strata

Strata or "layers" (singular: stratum) are segments within a large population that receive different amounts of scarce and valued resources (property, prestige, and power) by virtue of their position in a ranked system of structural inequality. Examples include social classes, castes, genders, racial and ethnic groups, and different age categories. Chapters 8 through 14 examine these different types of strata.

Institutions

Social institutions were defined in Chapter 1 as predictable, established ways to provide for one or more of a society's basic needs. They are composed of interrelated statuses, roles, norms, values, and groups. Most sociologists identify five core institutions—the family, religion, the economy, the political institution (or polity), and education.

These institutions must fulfill five critical needs, which are present in all societies and are sometimes called *functional requisites* (Aberle et al., 1950; Mack & Bradford, 1979). They are:

1. Replacing members. This is a primary responsibility of the family.
2. Socializing new members. The family, education, and religion accomplish this function.
3. Producing and distributing goods and services—the principal task of the economy.
4. Preserving order. This is accomplished by the polity, in particular by the specialized institutions of law, the criminal justice system, and the military.
5. Providing a sense of meaning and purpose, a traditional function of religion.

A number of additional institutions, including medicine, science, law and the criminal justice system, sport, the media, and the military, have emerged as distinct systems separate from the five core institutions in the modern era. Eight major social institutions are explored in detail in Chapters 15 through 20.

Societies

Societies are the largest elements of social structure. A **society** is defined as a sizable number of people who interact, share a culture, and usually live in a single geographic territory. A society is, at least in principle, self-perpetuating and independent of all other societies, although in the modern world virtually all but the most isolated societies are highly interdependent. Many societies are equivalent to nation-states—France and Japan are good examples—but in some instances one nation-state incorporates two or more distinct societies. For example, the former Yugoslavia encompassed Croatians, Bosnian Muslims, Serbs, and Montenegrans; both Tutsis and Hutus live in the nation-state of Rwanda. In other instances, members of a single society may be spread out among several nation-states, as is the case with the Kurds, who live as a minority group in Iraq, Pakistan, and several other countries.

The study of how societies change is one of sociology's most important objectives. Chapter 24 will be devoted exclusively to this topic. In the next section we will introduce three classic theories of societal change that will prove useful at several points later in the text.

THE EVOLUTION OF SOCIETIES

Early sociologists Émile Durkheim and Ferdinand Tönnies developed theories of societal change that continue to be useful today. After introducing their work, we will turn to Gerhard and Jean Lenski's more recent theory of sociocultural evolution.

Émile Durkheim: Mechanical and Organic Solidarity

Durkheim (1933), one of the founders of the functionalist perspective, observed that most societies throughout history have been characterized by high levels of **mechanical solidarity,** a form of internal cohesion that results from people being very much like each other. In societies with a limited economic division of labor, almost everyone of the same gender and approximately the same age does pretty much the same sort of work. For example, in most agrarian cultures, nearly all adult men work in the fields and most adult women stay at home, cook, tend to other household tasks, and look after the children. Durkheim maintains that people who play the same economic role tend to share very similar values and general understandings of the world, and these similarities directly bond them. We experience a degree of mechanical solidarity when we are a part of a crowd cheering for the home team. Think about how much stronger our feelings of solidarity would be if these other people were similar to us in almost every way.

As societies grow, economic competition combined with larger population size leads to an increase in the division of labor and the emergence of different occupational specialties. Shoe salespeople and nurses and farmers and college professors live in different social worlds and have relatively little in common with one another. Consequently, mechanical solidarity weakens, although it does not disappear.

Instead, a new type of social bond, called **organic solidarity,** arises in order to keep the society functioning. Organic solidarity is based, not on similarity but rather on difference and interdependence. Unlike

In traditional cultures, people of the same gender and age generally share the same values, norms, and worldview. These similarities strengthen the social bond between them, a phenomenon that Durkheim calls mechanical solidarity.

The Amish are a subculture that has preserved its distinctive way of life by withdrawing into an isolated community and minimizing interaction with those around them.

the era of mechanical solidarity when each family was substantially economically independent, in modern times we must directly or indirectly rely on thousands of other people to provide the goods and services we need. The organic solidarity that results from economic interdependence may not leave us feeling warm and emotionally bonded to our fellows, but it does oblige us to maintain close connections with them simply because we need them.

Ferdinand Tönnies: *Gemeinschaft* and *Gesellschaft*

The German sociologist Ferdinand Tönnies (1855–1937) studied the same broad processes of societal change as Durkheim, but he took a slightly different approach (Tönnies, 1963). Tönnies started at the micro level by comparing social interaction in traditional and modern societies. He argued that most relationships in premodern societies displayed a high level of *natural will,* by which he meant that they were generally considered to be ends in themselves rather than as means to an end. Cooley would have thought of them as primary relationships.

Tönnies called a society constructed primarily on the basis of natural will relationships a *Gemeinschaft.* A *Gemeinschaft* is typically small, rural, strongly committed to custom and tradition, and centered on kinship and other ascribed statuses. Most relationships are personal and long-term. Because everyone knows everyone else, there is little privacy, and conformity is promoted largely by gossip. The community is more important than the individual. Everyone sees the world the same way, and each individual's first responsibility is to be like everyone else.

There are still some true *Gemeinschafts* left in the United States—the Amish, for example (Hostetler, 1980)—but most of us no longer live that way. Today, most social interactions reflect *rational will,* meaning that relationships are chiefly means of obtaining what we want. Business transactions are rational will relationships, and of course this style of interaction is especially characteristic of secondary groups.

Tönnies used the word *Gesellschaft* to designate a society based largely on rational will. A *Gesellschaft* such as the contemporary United States is normally large, urban, strongly oriented toward change, and centered on achieved statuses. Many relationships are impersonal and short-term. Since people are always trying to maximize their personal advantage and there are few widely accepted moral values, conformity is generally enforced by formal agencies such as the police and the courts. The individual is more important than the community and people's primary responsibility is to look out for themselves.

Gerhard and Jean Lenski: Sociocultural Evolution

Contemporary American theorists Gerhard and Jean Lenski provide a third, more detailed perspective on the historical transition from mechanical to organic solidarity or from *Gemeinschaft* to *Gesellschaft* (Nolan & Lenski, 1999). They divide the process of sociocultural evolution into five stages, with each stage reflecting a fundamentally different subsistence strategy, or method of obtaining food.

Hunting and Gathering Societies.   From the beginning of human life on earth until about twelve thousand years ago, every society employed a subsistence strategy called *hunting and gathering;* in other words, their sole sources of food were wild animals and plants (Service, 1966; Nolan & Lenski, 1999). This economic base limited the size of these cultures to small bands of twenty-five to fifty people. Also, because food resources became depleted over time in any particular area, almost all hunter-gatherers were nomadic.

Hunting and gathering societies have a very simple division of labor, with men normally responsible for hunting and women for most domestic tasks and gathering wild plants. Anthropologists believe that many early hunter-gatherers lived in very fertile environments and thus probably devoted less time and energy to food production and the other necessities of daily life than members of any other type of society (Sahlins, 1972). Still, everyone except very small children had to spend a certain amount of time every day finding food. This meant that these societies could not develop any full-time specialists such as toolmakers, and in consequence their level of technological development was very low.

At this stage of societal evolution, all of the needs met in modern societies by specialized institutions are provided by the family. For example, children do not go to school; they learn everything they need to know from their relatives. Although the dominant males within each family hold a certain amount of political power, their ability to compel obedience is very limited. For the most part, they can do little more than encourage people to follow long-established traditions. As in any *Gemeinschaft,* deviance is controlled informally. Food and craft goods are produced and distributed within the family; there is no concept of money or of profit. There are no full-time religious specialists, although some individuals, called *shamans,* do claim special knowledge of the supernatural, which they use to heal the sick.

Because hunter-gatherers are nomadic, they do not accumulate much property. Consequently, these societies are highly egalitarian, with no social classes and hence no wealthy or poor people. Gender relations also tend to be quite equal, in part because women make substantial contributions to economic subsistence—usually more than the men (O'Kelly & Carney, 1986; Lorber, 1994). Finally, collective violence is limited to occasional feuds and raids; there is no war as we know it (Sahlins, 1960).

If this description makes hunting and gathering life sound idyllic, bear in mind that these cultures had little medical knowledge and virtually no ability to control nature. As a result, over half the people in hunting and gathering societies of the past died before reaching the age of twenty (Nolan & Lenski, 1999).

Today only a handful of hunting and gathering societies survive. The best known include the !Kung and the Mbuti in southern Africa, the Australian Aborigines, and the Semai of Malaysia. It is very doubtful that this style of life can endure anywhere for more than another generation because of the constant incursion on their territories by the rapidly growing, technologically advanced societies that have come to dominate the planet (Wolf, 1983).

Horticultural Societies. Between ten and twelve thousand years ago, hunter-gatherers in the Near East and later in several other parts of the world learned to domesticate various species of animals and plants. This development led to the emergence of *horticultural society.*

Horticulturalists supplement hunting and gathering by raising crops in small garden plots using simple hand tools such as digging sticks and hoes. These people generally stay put for several years until the fertility of the ground is exhausted, at which time they move to another site. They often return to areas where they lived previously when the soil there has become productive again. Many horticulturists use a "slash and burn" technology, cutting down ground cover and burning it to increase the soil's fertility.

This technology may sound primitive, but it leads to some truly dramatic changes in social life. Most significantly, horticultural societies produce substantially larger amounts of food than is possible by hunting and gathering. This surplus allows small bands to grow into tribes of up to several thousand people.

Shamans play an important role in traditional societies, using their special connections to the spirit world to perform a variety of healing rituals.

Worlds Apart: Gopalpur and Walnut Grove

As members of a postindustrial, future-oriented, urban society, or *Gesellschaft*, Americans take for granted numerous impersonal, short-term relationships and encounters with strangers, the existence of diverse lifestyles and occupations, and the pursuit of individual achievement. In much of the world, however, *Gemeinschaft* is (or was until recently) the norm. Most people live in small, traditional, rural villages where little changes from one generation to the next.

The village of Gopalpur in southern India is good example of a *Gemeinschaft* (Beals, 1980). The same families have lived in Gopalpur for as long as anyone can remember. Few people travel as far as the nearest town, only fifteen miles away. Men live and die in the village in which they were born; women, often betrothed in childhood, spend their adult lives in their husband's family's village.

Except for a few specialists (such as the village carpenter and the blacksmith, who inherited their trades), all the men in Gopalpur are farmers. Families grow their own sorghum, rice, and vegetables. Most also plant fruit trees and keep at least one water buffalo for milk plus a few sheep, goats, and chickens for feasts and sacrifices. The pace of life is slow and the work hard.

While the men are working, the women go about their chores: hauling water from the river, carrying rubbish and cow manure to a compost heap outside the village, tending the cooking fire, grinding grain and mixing dough for flatbread, and preparing pots of beans, chili, and vegetables for the family's main meals. This routine is broken only during harvest time, when, in addition to these chores, women work in the fields alongside men, and on special occasions such as weddings.

Each extended family has its own house—typically a windowless 30-by-40-foot stone and mud structure with holes in the roof for light and air and a raised veranda across the front. The entrance is a set of carved, heavy wooden double doors that open onto a courtyard. Beyond, in the darkness, is a raised platform with millstones and mortars for processing grain. A door on the left leads to a washing and cooking area. Not homes in the Western sense, Gopalpur houses are more like storehouses or small forts. There are no living rooms or bedrooms. The family eats on the front veranda and, at night, sets up cots outside.

Privacy is nonexistent in Gopalpur. Social life takes place on the streets under the watchful eyes of men gathered under shade trees and women working and chatting on verandas as their babies doze in hammocks and small children play nearby. During the hottest months, villagers sleep by day and socialize at night. This is the season for visits by elders from another village to discuss marriage arrangements with the father of a village girl; wrestling matches and drama competitions; feasts and festivals; and predawn expeditions to collect firewood.

The rules of life in Gopalpur are

Furthermore, horticulture is productive enough so that a few individuals in every community are freed from daily subsistence work and can focus all their attention on crafts and making more sophisticated tools.

The process of institutional differentiation begins at the horticultural stage (Parsons, 1966). A few full-time religious specialists emerge and, while the power of political leaders remains limited, some men become chiefs. However, the extended family continues to be the primary setting for social life.

The semisedentary lifestyle typical of horticulturalists permits the accumulation of personal property, as does the existence of a predictable food surplus. These developments, in turn, lead to greater social inequality. Wealthier and poorer families start to appear. However, women continue to enjoy substantial equality in most societies at this level, again because they usually assume the primary responsibility for raising crops once the men have done the heavy work of clearing the land.

The existence of a surplus also allows horticulturists to trade with other societies, which in turn stimulates the more rapid diffusion of new ideas and technologies. It is also at this stage that warfare and slavery appear (Harris, 1977). In societies that are particularly warlike, women's status starts to erode (O'Kelly & Carney, 1986).

Like hunting and gathering cultures, horticulturalists are becoming increasingly rare in the modern world. Among the most extensively studied are the Yanomamo of Brazil and Venezuela and the Truk of the Caroline Islands in the western Pacific.

Pastoral Societies. At about the same time that horticultural societies were appearing in the more fertile parts of the world, people living in arid regions of North Africa, the Middle East, and parts of Central Asia were domesticating herd animals such as cattle, sheep, goats, and camels and developing a style of life known as *pastoralism*. Pastoral societies are thus an

so well known that they are rarely discussed. A man must find a bride, father children (especially sons), accumulate enough wealth to arrange proper marriages for them, and make more friends than enemies so that his funeral will be well attended. A woman's duty is to obey her father, then her husband and mother-in-law, and to bear and raise children. To be sure, individuals stray—but not for long.

Men keep daggers in their house for protection against roving bandits, but violence toward neighbors is rare. Crops sometimes fail, but no one is homeless or hungry. "[P]eople do not regard Gopalpur's pattern as something to be changed, improved, or fought. Things, both good and bad, are as they always have been and as they always will be" (Beals, 1980: 11).

Walnut Grove, an [hypothetical] apartment complex in the San Francisco Bay area, has about the same number of residents as Gopalpur—but the similarity ends there. Residents of Walnut Grove have little in common beyond their address. None grew up in the complex, though some are native Californians. Most will move again as their job opportunities and family lives change. Tenants include families with young children; singles of various ages living alone, with roommates, or with a partner; middle-aged couples in first or second marriages; and retirees. Unlike the extended families of Gopalpur, each household is independent. Some residents phone family members every week and visit on holidays; others rarely do. Also unlike the villagers of Gopalpur, they practice different religions; work at different jobs; and have different tastes in clothes, music, and books.

Privacy and anonymity are as highly valued in Walnut Grove as sociability and familiarity are in Gopalpur. Residents do not view one another as part of a community. Indeed, most prefer to remain strangers. Neighbors observe a polite distance, not inquiring into the personal details of one another's lives. Mothers with children the same age or singles who enjoy hiking may become friends, but they are the exception. For the most part, residents lead separate lives; many do not know their next-door neighbor's name. Printed rules posted in the mail room and hired security guards relieve tenants of the need to resolve conflicts face to face.

Furthermore, at Walnut Grove different elements of each person's life are compartmentalized. On weekdays individual family members go their separate ways: children to day care or school, each parent to his or her job. The roles individuals play at work are distinct from the roles they play at home. Weekends are set apart as a time to relax, pursue hobbies, entertain friends, do chores, and go shopping. Individuals are expected to have unique needs, interests, and goals.

Gopalpur and Walnut Grove are worlds apart—socially and culturally as well as geographically.

1. Would it be easier for an Indian villager to adapt to life in Walnut Grove or for a modern American to learn to live in Gopalpur? Explain your answer.
2. Do you think the residents of Gopalpur feel confined and constrained by their lack of privacy?
3. What is gained and what is lost as societies evolve from the traditional agrarian pattern to modern postindustrial structures?

Source: Beals, 1980.

environmentally mandated alternative to horticulture rather than an advancement over it.

Pastoralists are mostly nomads, following their herds as they migrate with the seasons, although they may be sedentary at certain times of the year. They frequently establish ongoing trade relations with more settled peoples. Pastoral societies have roughly the same level of institutional differentiation as horticultural ones. They, too, generate a regular surplus and can support some full-time specialists (Evans-Pritchard, 1940). Social inequality increases as wealthy families accumulate larger herds than their poorer fellows. Gender inequality is usually moderate.

One of the most interesting historical developments at this stage concerns religion. Three of the great world religions—Judaism, Christianity, and Islam—developed in pastoral societies. This helps explain many passages in the Bible, such as "the Lord is my shepherd," and why the word "pastor" is used to refer to certain religious leaders.

Pastoral societies endure, often in the places where they first developed, in large part because the land they occupy has not until recently been seen as worth very much. But this is changing. As the world population has soared in recent decades, pastoralists have found their lifestyles increasingly constrained by the outside world (Bacon, 1980). Contemporary examples of pastoral societies include the Basseri of Southern Iran and the Karimojong, who live in Uganda.

Agrarian Societies.   In the valleys of the Tigris and Euphrates Rivers, in what is now Iraq, the invention of the plow and the refinement of metallurgical technology about six thousand years ago led to the agrarian revolution (Childe, 1951). Similar developments took place in Egypt, in India, along the Yangtze River in China, and, much later, in Peru. *Agrarian societies* use animal power to produce levels of surplus food, especially grains, far beyond anything

In pastoral societies, life is organized around the daily and seasonal needs of the animals. Pastoralists around the world keep a number of different species of herd animals, including oxen, goats, sheep, llamas, and camels.

previously possible. In a relatively short period of time, society changed beyond recognition.

Perhaps most obviously, the agrarian revolution led to unprecedented increases in the size of the population, with the largest societies swelling to several million people. The first cities arose at this time. In them, substantial numbers of people, freed from the requirement that they contribute to the production of food, became full-time specialists in fields such as metallurgy, woodworking, and pottery. Human knowledge expanded rapidly, leading to the invention of writing and mathematics and ultimately to "high culture" in the form of philosophy, theology, literature, art, architecture, and science (Jacobs, 1970). Trade grew, further quickening the pace of social change, and money was developed as a universal medium of exchange.

In agrarian societies, religious and political institutions became substantially differentiated, although they were often intermingled in the form of a *divine kingship* in which the leader of the society was not only a king but was also viewed by his subjects as a god. The state grew in power, sometimes basing its legitimacy on the control of the elaborate irrigation systems that were often needed for large-scale agrarian production (Wittfogel, 1957). The first universal legal codes were written. The scale of war expanded as great empires like Rome rose and fell. The family continued to be important, but more aspects of daily life were becoming increasingly independent of kinship.

The immense productivity of agrarian society accelerated the trend toward social inequality; most societies became divided into a small, extremely wealthy elite and a great majority of poor peasants (Pirenne, 1937). Removed from the core productive process by

male-dominated agriculture, women saw their status decline sharply (Boulding, 1976; Fisher, 1979).

Many nations of the world today remain heavily agrarian, but none has escaped the impact of the next great societal revolution, which began in England in the middle of the eighteenth century.

Industrial and Postindustrial Societies. *Industrial society* is based on the use of non-animate sources of energy for economic production. Its origin a little over 150 years ago transformed human society even more radically than the agrarian revolution six thousand years earlier.

Once again, the scale of society changed. Science led the way to a dramatic expansion of life expectancy and an unprecedented population explosion. Cities mushroomed. Mechanical solidarity and *Gemeinschaft* waned. The five major institutions became fully differentiated from each other. The importance of the economy, the government, and education greatly increased, while the family and, to a lesser extent, religion declined. New institutions such as medicine and criminal justice emerged.

As populations grew and physical mobility increased, many societies became far more culturally and racially diverse. During the early phases of industrialization, social inequality continued to grow, but this trend seems to have reversed itself and the extremes of early industrial-era poverty have been substantially reduced (Critchlow & Hawley, 1989). The importance of ascribed status is gradually declining in industrial societies as women, ethnic and racial minorities, and other previously devalued groups have demanded and often received more equal treatment.

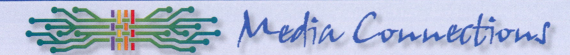

The Kayapo Meet the Press

The idea that traditional cultures are doomed to extinction has become part of the conventional wisdom. In the early 1980s, the Kayapo, a society of about 2,500 Ge-speaking Indians who occupy an area the size of Scotland in the Amazon rain forest, appeared to be on the verge of fulfilling this prophecy. Divided into fourteen independent villages, the Kayapo depended for subsistence on a combination of slash-and-burn horticulture, fishing, hunting, and foraging with tools they made themselves. The concept of progress had little meaning for the Kayapo, who lived as their ancestors had lived for hundreds, perhaps thousands of years. But their world was under assault.

In principle, the Kayapo Indigenous Area was protected by the Brazilian government, but in practice Indian rights were seldom respected. In 1971, the government built a highway through the reserve and declared the land on one side of the road "open territory," attracting land speculators and timber companies. The subsequent discovery of gold led to the opening in 1983 of two large illegal mines employing more than 3,000 Brazilian workers. Rumors began to circulate that the government was planning to construct a series of hydroelectric dams that would flood much of Kayapo country. The Kayapo's future looked utterly hopeless. But they did not quietly fade away, the hapless victims of "progress."

The Kayapo resistance began as a campaign of relentless, armed attacks on Brazilian intruders. After fifteen years and some fifty Brazilian (but no Kayapo) deaths, the government officially returned the "open" territory to the Kayapo. Unappeased, a force of two hundred Kayapo, armed with a mix of traditional weapons and firearms, attacked the gold mines and occupied the landing strip that provided the only access to the largest mine. After a ten-day standoff, the government gave in to their demands, granting the Kayapo title and administrative authority over the mines plus a significant share of the profits. A few village leaders pocketed the proceeds and moved away. But others established a communal bank account, opened a tribal office in the nearest town, purchased a small airplane, and hired a pilot. This enabled them to carry goods and medical assistance to their scattered, otherwise inaccessible villages and, equally important, to create a communications network among villages.

When the government announced plans to dump radioactive waste on their land, the Kayapo sent a hundred men to the national capital, Brasilia, where—decorated in tribal paint and feathers—they staged a sit-in. Government officials were shocked, angry, and bewildered. The dumping plan was canceled. But the matter of the hydroelectric dams remained unresolved.

The Kayapo demonstrations in Brasilia attracted international attention and, in 1988, two tribal leaders were invited to the United States for a conference on tropical forest ecology. The Kayapo leaders were impressed by the amount of interest in environmental issues in general, and in the Amazon rain forest in particular, in the outside world, and also by the power of the mass media.

Building on their experiences in the United States and the contacts they had made with nongovernmental organizations (NGOs) such as the Friends of the Earth and the World Wildlife Federation, the Kayapo decided to convene a congress of Amazonian peoples in the small town of Altamira, the site of the first proposed dam. In February, 1989, six hundred Amazonian Indians and an almost equal number of journalists, politicians, and representatives of various NGOs gathered for five days of meetings, speeches, press conferences, and ritual performances. The pope sent a telegram, and the rock star Sting made an appearance. The congress issued a statement condemning the dam project on behalf of native Amazonian peoples. Two weeks later, the World Bank withdrew funding for the project. Under continued pressure, the government declared the area around Altamira a Kayapo reserve in 1991.

Since then the Kayapo have remained active, supporting programs to promote sustainable, noninvasive use of the rain forest (such as collecting nuts, honey, and natural resins) as well as defending the rights of other indigenous peoples.

The Kayapo resistance set a precedent. What was new was a traditional society using advanced transportation and communications systems to defend its way of life—in effect, using modern technology to fight modernization. Through skillful public relations, the Kayapo were able to bypass the government of Brazil and appeal directly to the peoples, governments, and NGOs of the world.

Equally significantly, the Kayapo demonstrated to a global audience that indigenous peoples are not just passive victims of unstoppable environmental destruction, but can be active participants in the solution. The Kayapo who visited the United States were surprised to find human rights and environmental groups divided into separate factions devoted to isolated issues and competing against one another for public attention and funds rather than working together toward common goals. They also objected to the condescending view that "we" (members of advanced societies) can save "them" (indigenous peoples) but that "they" have nothing to teach "us."

1. What are the long-term prospects for the survival of the Kayapo and similar premodern societies?
2. What sorts of things can people in modern postindustrial societies learn from the Kayapo?

Source: Turner, 1993.

Table 4.1	Stages of Sociocultural Evolution		
	When First Appeared	Economic Basis	Settlement Size
Hunting and Gathering	250,000 years ago or more	Hunting wild game, gathering wild plants, fishing	25–100
Horticultural	12,000–10,000 years ago	Gardens tended with hand tools	100–2,000
Pastoral	12,000–10,000 years ago	Domesticated herd animals	100–2,000
Agrarian	6,000 years ago	Fields plowed by draft animals	Up to 1 million
Industrial	200 years ago	Factories powered by non-animate energy sources	Millions
Postindustrial	Now emerging	Services and information, computers	Millions

Source: Nolan & Lenski, 1999.

Today we are on the threshold of yet another dramatic transformation. Advanced industrial societies are rapidly moving toward a *postindustrial* model, where the economy is based more on services than on manufacturing and knowledge-based economic activities predominate (Kumar, 1995). Whereas in industrial societies most people worked with relatively simple machines to produce physical goods like automobiles or toasters, in the postindustrial economy workers use computers and other advanced electronic technologies to provide information and services.

Table 4.1 summarizes the main points of the Lenskis' theory of sociocultural evolution.

The transition to a fully postindustrial society will likely be as wrenching—and at least as radical—as the Industrial Revolution. It will be a primary task of sociology in the twenty-first century to analyze the character of the new computer-mediated society that has begun to take shape in the last few decades. The final sections of this chapter briefly examine some of the ways in which the Internet is changing both social structure and culture as we enter the postindustrial era.

LIFE CONNECTIONS: Social Structure and Technology

Through most of history, nearly all social interaction took place on a face-to-face basis. This began to change only with the invention of the movable type printing press in the fifteenth century. Communication by means of the written word allowed a sort of slow-motion, long-distance interaction, but it lacked the instantaneous give and take that is possible in more personal contexts.

Subsequent technological developments—first the telegraph, then the telephone, and now the Internet—have made long-distance interaction much faster

and easier and have greatly altered the character of social life. With about half of American households owning personal computers, *diffuse interaction* (as opposed to face-to-face interaction) has become increasingly common.

These developments have led sociologists to start to rethink the concepts of groups and more generally of social structure (Meyrowitz, 1984; Hafner, 1994). Some maintain that online multiuser domains like chat rooms meet all the traditional defining criteria of social groups: They sustain continuous two-way interaction, they foster a sense of solidarity, their members share norms and values, and they work toward shared goals (Turkle, 1995; Casalego, 1996).

Virtual interaction and computer-mediated diffuse social structure are emerging as critically important sociological research topics in the post-industrial era. Here are some of the issues that will need to be explored:

• How does interaction change when people cannot physically observe each other? The fact that women, minorities, the physically disabled, and occupants of other traditionally stigmatized statuses can conceal most aspects of their identities online is often experienced as liberating (Donath, 1997). In addition, diffuse interaction allows us to experiment by trying on new identities (Waskul, 1997). A 45-year-old white male can present himself online as a 12-year-old Latino girl if he wishes to do so. However, the very anonymity of cyberspace makes it difficult to evaluate the authenticity of an individual's presentation of self, a process that is much easier when the social cues provided by people's social statuses, expressions, gestures, and other forms of nonverbal behavior can be directly observed (Rhinegold, 1994; Schellenberg, 1996).

Mobility	Institutional Differentiation	Structured Inequality	Status of Women
Nomadic	All institutions contained within the family	Egalitarian except for gender and age distinctions	Substantial gender equality
Semisedentary	Polity and religion begin to emerge as specilized institutions	Substantial inequalities emerge	Women beginning to lose status
Mostly nomadic	Similar to horticultural	Similar to horticultural	Similar to horticultural
Sedentary	Family losing some importance; most institutions distinct	Great extremes of wealth and poverty; estates and castes; little mobility	Women occupy clearly subordinate role
Sedentary	Family loses many roles; full institutional differentiation	Reduced inequality; social classes; substantial mobility	Movement toward increasing equality of the sexes
Sedentary	Full institutional differentiation	Too early to determine	Probably highly egalitarian

- People communicating online can be amazingly open about revealing personal details of their lives (Marriot, 1998). One source describes diffuse interaction as "a moderately strong, intimate secondary relationship" (Wellman et al., 1996). Sociologists wonder whether online groups can ever be truly primary in character. Is the sense of closeness that many participants experience genuine or illusory? (Cerulo et al., 1992; Gabriel, 1996; Parks, 1996) Can a truly intimate relationship develop when each party can end the interaction with the click of a mouse?

- Today, entire "virtual communities" are coming into existence. At many colleges, students can now access library materials, chat with fellow students, ask professors questions, download music, and order pizza, all without ever leaving their dorm rooms. Is it possible that a new form of social solidarity, neither mechanical nor organic, may emerge from this sort of online interaction? (Hornsby, 1998) If so, what would it look like?

SOCIETY CONNECTIONS:
Inequality, Globalization, and the Internet

The dramatic growth of the Internet has created a number of important social issues. Two of them concern equality of access to the "information superhighway" and the possibility that a single world society may eventually develop.

Access to the Internet

Conflict theorists are concerned that the computer revolution may be intensifying the division between the haves and the have-nots in a world in which economic success is increasingly linked to the ability to use computers effectively. As of the late 1990s, U.S. Internet users were 95 percent white and 60 percent male (Edmondson, 1997). Just one-quarter of those lacking high school degrees use computers regularly compared with 82 percent of people with graduate degrees. Regarding gender, computer games, which often get youth hooked on cyberspace, are generally designed to appeal to boys, and males dominate most college computer science departments.

Globally, many of the nations of the developing world are lagging behind in computer technology. Currently about 26.3 percent of Americans use the Internet compared with 0.1 percent of people in sub-Saharan Africa and just 0.04 percent of those in South Asia. In addition, only 7 percent of computer users in China and 4 percent in the Arab world are women (United Nations Development Programme, 1999:

INTERNET **CONNECTIONS**

The "Society Connections" feature in this chapter deals with the relationship between globalization, the Internet, and social inequality. The gap between people who have access to the Internet and those who do not has been referred to as the *digital divide*. The Clinton Administration has established a Digital Divide Web site: http://www.digitaldivide.gov (and it is likely that the next administration will continue this site). From the opening page, click on "About the Digital Divide." What are your thoughts about this "new" form of social inequality?

New electronic technologies allow sustained interaction between people located in different parts of the world. Sociologists are exploring how these new patterns of interaction vary from those typical of traditional face-to-face groups.

63). If something is not done soon to change these patterns, billions of people may be left behind.

Toward a Global Society?

There can be no doubt that the Internet has promoted the emergence of a global culture, a trend that has been labeled *cultural leveling*. Many observers are concerned because so much of this global culture originates in the United States. English is well on its way to becoming a universal second language: Worldwide, about 90 percent of the messages posted on the Internet are in English. Some describe this trend as a sort of worldwide *cultural imperialism* in which diverse lifestyles are being lost beneath a numbing tide of CNN, Disney, and Hollywood (Kuisel, 1993; Pollack, 1996).

While there is some truth to these charges, the cultural influence does not flow in only one direction. Virtual groups, like La Francophonie in France, have been formed to resist the dominance of English online. More generally, increasing numbers of Americans are eating sushi and Thai food, listening to "world music," and watching Hong Kong action movies (Lyotard, 1993).

Globalization and the Internet are reshaping social structure as well as culture. A world economy is emerging, dominated by a handful of immense multinational corporations. Regional trade agreements such as the European Union and the North American Free Trade Agreement (NAFTA) are reducing the economic significance of the nation-state. Military interventions are increasingly conducted under the banner of the United Nations or other multinational consortiums. Hundreds of international nongovernmental organizations (NGOs) have been established to work for change in areas such as women's rights, the environment, and the refugee crisis. Regular global conferences link key government and NGO decision makers all around the world, connections easily maintained through the Internet.

Will a world society ever emerge? Some observers believe that such a development is quite possible at some point in the future as the full potential of the computer revolution manifests itself. Others, however, point to the resurgence of ethnic nationalism and regionalism in the former Soviet Union, Yugoslavia, and elsewhere as evidence that globalization has clear limits.

The most likely prediction is that global culture will continue to evolve but that regional cultures will also survive. Regarding social structure, both the local and the transnational levels will gain in importance while the traditional nation-state may weaken (Kennedy, 1993).

SUMMARY

1. Social structure consists of the relatively stable patterns of social interaction that characterize human social life; it is within the context of social structure that people enact culture.

2. Statuses are the key components from which larger units of social structure are constructed.

3. Statuses may be ascribed or achieved. When a status is especially important in determining

an individual's identity, it is called a master status.

4. Roles are the dynamic aspect of statuses—we occupy a status but we play a role.

5. Role strain and role conflict can result when people play several roles at the same time.

6. Social groups consist of several people who regularly interact and feel some sense of solidarity or common identity.

7. Primary groups provide warmth and intimacy, whereas secondary groups are important for accomplishing specific objectives.

8. In-groups, out-groups, and reference groups are other important types of social groups.

9. The size of a group is crucial in determining how it functions.

10. All groups have two types of leaders: instrumental leaders, who concentrate on achieving group goals, and expressive leaders, who maintain group morale.

11. People in small groups feel strong pressure to conform to the expectations of others and to obey group leaders.

12. Groupthink can interfere with the ability of a cohesive group to make wise decisions.

13. Networks are an increasingly important type of relatively diffuse social structure.

14. Larger elements of social structure include formal organizations, communities, strata, institutions, and societies.

15. Durkheim identified an historical transition from mechanical to organic solidarity; Tönnies analyzed the same shift using the terms *Gemeinschaft* and *Gesellschaft*.

16. Gerhard and Jean Lenski argue that sociohistorical evolution proceeds through several stages: hunting and gathering, horticultural or pastoral, agrarian, industrial, and postindustrial.

17. Today new forms of computer-mediated diffuse social structure are emerging that will be a major research topic for sociologists in the future.

18. Structural issues raised by the computer revolution include the problem of differential access to cyberspace and the possibility of the emergence of a single world society.

KEY TERMS

achieved status 87	instrumental leader 94	role set 89
aggregate 90	laissez-faire leader 95	role strain 89
ascribed status 87	master status 87	secondary group 91
authoritarian leader 94	mechanical solidarity 99	social group 90
category 90	network 97	social structure 85
democratic leader 95	organic solidarity 99	society 99
expressive leader 94	out-group 92	status 86
formal organization 98	primary group 91	status inconsistency 86
Gemeinschaft 100	reference group 93	status set 86
Gesellschaft 100	role 89	stigma 87
groupthink 97	role conflict 89	strata 98
in-group 92		

CRITICAL THINKING QUESTIONS

1. The general trend in modern societies is toward an increase in the importance of achieved statuses and a decrease in the importance of ascribed ones. Why do you think this change is taking place? Who stands to lose and who stands to gain as a result of this transformation?

2. The Asch experiment shows that people are strongly inclined to conform to the expectations of others. Does this tendency contribute to social problems as well as to social order? Should we try to make people less willing to conform? How might we go about such a task?

3. Is the balance between primary and secondary interaction about right in most people's lives, or have we swung too far toward the latter type? Explain your view.

4. How do diffuse, computer-mediated groups differ from conventional face-to-face groups? What is gained and what is lost as we move toward a society in which more and more interaction is diffuse?

 **SOCIALIZATION**

OUTLINE

Extreme Human Isolation

Anna lived with her mother and her grandfather, a widowed farmer. She was born out of wedlock and kept in an attic room because her grandfather severely disapproved of this "evidence" of her mother's indiscretion. When Anna was finally removed from the home just before her sixth birthday, she was emaciated and undernourished, with skeleton-like legs and a bloated abdomen. Deprived of normal human contact and receiving only a minimal amount of care to keep her physically alive, she could not talk, walk, or do anything that showed intelligence. Two years after being discovered, she had learned to walk, understand simple commands, and feed herself. After two more years she formed toilet habits, could feed herself with a spoon and could dress herself. But by age nine she was less than four feet tall and weighed only sixty pounds. When she died at age ten, she had progressed to about the mental level of a two-and-a-half-year-old. She could talk in phrases but never developed a true language capability. Her extreme isolation at an early age prevented the mental development that was undoubtedly part of her capacity. (Adapted from Davis, 1947)

Cases of Monkey Isolation

Like humans, monkeys live in family social groupings and depend on each other for learning in order to survive. In a series of famous experiments, psychologist Harry Harlow and his associates showed that when monkeys are raised in complete isolation, they do not develop normal monkey behavior. They are withdrawn, fearful, or aggressive. Female monkeys raised in isolation abuse or neglect their offspring. They never learn from other monkeys how monkeys are "supposed" to behave. A later study by Gordon Gallup demonstrated a similar pattern with chimpanzees. Chimps raised in isolation did not react to their own reflection in a mirror and did not even recognize themselves. The socially experienced chimps immediately used the mirror to explore areas of their head that had been painted with red dye. These experiments also demonstrated that the longer the isolation, the more difficult it is for animals to develop normal behavior. Indeed, full recovery from the effects of early isolation may be impossible. (Harlow, 1958; Harlow & Harlow, 1970; Gallup, 1977)

In both humans and social animals, social interaction is needed to learn about ourselves and about others. How do we learn to become human? Since we are born as human beings we do not have to learn to become what we already are, so the question at first seems contradictory. But sociology approaches it from a different view. The Harlow and Gallup experiments with primates and the tragic case of Anna clearly demonstrate that social contact is necessary for learning and the development of the self.

Socialization is the lifelong process whereby we learn our culture, develop our sense of self, and become functioning members of society. Until we are socialized we have not "learned" humanness. Socialization shows why children reared with little human contact, such as Anna, cannot seem to grasp the meaning of acceptable human behavior. The biological being who emerges from the womb possesses the physiological readiness to learn, but only through sustained, structured interaction with a culture and a social environment will an individual be able to demonstrate his or her humanness.

To represent these issues, the theme of gender socialization will be applied throughout this chapter. **Gender socialization** is the process by which individuals learn the cultural behavior of feminine or masculine that is associated with the biological sex of female or male. As we individually progress through life, socialization becomes the key factor that determines the directions we take. Sociology provides a critical lens for viewing this remarkable process.

THEORETICAL PERSPECTIVES ON SOCIALIZATION

All theories of socialization begin with the notion that social interaction is necessary for the development of our human potential and sense of self. In addition to social interaction, there are other important elements, such as biology, personality, and various social structures—family, school, media, and so on—through which socialization is mediated. Different theories give different weight to each element. These theories also demonstrate the importance of interdisciplinary work. In the area of socialization, significant bridges have been built between the social and behavioral sciences.

Nature Versus Nurture

How much of our behavior is determined by genetic inheritance and how much is determined by the environment or culture in which we live and learn? The discipline of sociology is rooted in the nurture (environment) side of this question. Social interaction is the essential element for "nature"—the trigger for developing *human* potential. As explained in Chapter 3, animals are unlike humans because they cannot symbolize and therefore do not possess culture. Soci-

During the first school experiences children are socialized into new roles and learn to interact and cooperate with peers who may be different than themselves.

ologists do recognize that nature (heredity) plays an important part in explaining key aspects of human social behavior, such as intelligence and sports ability. Other scientists, however, believe that humans and animals are much more alike than sociologists claim.

The field of **sociobiology** addresses the question of how human behavior is determined, but it is rooted in the "nature" side of the question by examining the biological roots of social behavior. Originally developing out of research based on insects, (Wilson, 1975), sociobiologists argue that the theory of evolution can be used to draw conclusions about humans from studies of social animals. According to sociobiological reasoning, human behavior is largely determined by genes because humans, like other animals, are structured by nature (biology) with an innate drive to ensure that their individual genes are passed on to the next generation. It is as adaptive for a mother to care for her children in order to continue her genes as it is for men to be promiscuous, and thus have as many chances to continue their genes as possible. Each sex evolved attributes to increase its reproductive success (Dovidio et al., 1991). As a natural result, the separate worlds of male and female emerged.

Sociobiologists have been successful in applying evolutionary theory to animal behavior, but empirical support for their arguments about human behavior are weak and have not had much following in the social sciences. Sociobiologists themselves generally prefer to keep their work in the area of animal research. Social scientists suggest that extending the theory of sociobiology to humans makes faulty assumptions about human behavior and disregards well-documented research about animals. For example, it ignores the fact that the female chimp is notoriously promiscuous. Sexual selection in sociobiology emphasizes competition and aggression in male chimps, but neglects the other half of the process, in which female chimps make choices among males. Female chimps can be sexually aggressive and competitive just as male chimps can be nurturing and passive (Hrdy, 1986; Hubbard, 1994).

As we will revisit in Chapter 13, the nature versus nurture debate is perhaps a false one since scientists in all disciplines recognize that both ingredients are needed to explain human social behavior. Each discipline has a different emphasis for these explanations. Sociologists emphasize that social interaction makes us human, or, stated another way, it humanizes us. Biology (nature) makes us ready for socialization. But the process of social interaction (nurture) activates it. The theoretical perspective of symbolic interactionism clearly illustrates this activation process.

INTERNET CONNECTIONS

The text discusses the "nature vs. nurture" issue. One very interesting example of the nature-nurture debate involves the cause(s) of *alcoholism.* Do people "learn" to be alcoholics, or are they biologically predisposed to become alcoholic? Christa Gerrish's web site, "Alcoholism: Nature or Nurture" offers evidence on both sides of this debate:

http://www.umm.maine.edu/BEX/students/ChristaGerrish/cg320.html. After you have read the contents of her discussion, write a brief position paper summarizing both sides of the nature-nurture debate concerning alcoholism.

Sociology: Symbolic Interactionism and the Development of the Self

Sociologists and psychologists agree that the **self** is the unique sense of identity that distinguishes each individual from all other individuals. The self is a key element of **personality,** the distinctive complex of attitudes, beliefs, behaviors, and values that makes up an individual. Personality and self come together to form *personal identity*, which gives each individual a sense of separateness *and* uniqueness. No one else is quite like you.

Whereas psychology highlights the role of personal identity in explaining attitudes and behavior, sociology emphasizes *social identity*, the part of the self that is built up over time through participation in social life. We derive pleasure from a sense of community, the feeling of belonging and having things in common with others. Your social identity as a college student is celebrated when your school wins a football game. Your social identity as a fraternity member is celebrated when your chapter is recognized for its efforts at raising money for charity.

Social identity is linked to what biologists and psychologists say is a human need for affiliation, the desire to seek relationships with others. We suffer great psychological anguish if this need is denied for an extended period. For this reason, solitary confinement is considered the harshest possible punishment for prisoners.

What We Think Others Think of Us. The emergence of the self over time in interaction with others is an active process. As children we quickly learn that what others think of us has major consequences on our lives. As a pioneer of the symbolic interactionist perspective, Charles Horton Cooley (1864–1929) provided a major tool for sociology with his concept of the **looking-glass self.** Cooley explained this as the idea that we use other people as a mirror to ourselves. We imagine how others see us and we imagine their judgment of that appearance. Our image of ourselves then develops based on that imagination (Cooley, 1902/1983).

Having fun with others is a way of building social identity and a sense of community. People feel most connected to those who share similar interests and values.

If in class you imagine that your professor sees you as bright, attentive, and interested and gives you positive signs that reflect that perception, you begin to develop a positive self-view in regard to the academic side of your college life. From the professor's viewpoint, when students stifle yawns or appear bored and disinterested, the professor may question his or her ability to teach effectively and may develop a negative self-view in regard to the academic side of his or her life. This reality highlights symbolic interactionists' idea that only through interaction can we learn about ourselves and make social comparisons necessary to acquire a sense of self-esteem.

The Importance of Role-Taking. Perhaps the most influential player in forging symbolic interactionism and its connection to socialization is George Herbert Mead (1863–1961), who was responsible for a rather simple but important assertion. He maintained that the self is made up of two components. The first he called the **I,** that aspect of self that is spontaneous, creative, and impulsive and sometimes unpredictable. It shows itself when feelings of emotion arise—excitement, anger, joy—and you want to express yourself openly. Imagine that you have just received an A in a difficult course and want to share your triumph with others. Yet, in line with the looking-glass self, symbolic interactionists argue that your behavior is influenced by how you imagine others view you, so you reconsider how to share the accomplishment. Mead called this second aspect of self the **me,** which is the socialized self, and the one that makes you concerned about how others view and judge you. So as not to appear too boastful, you decide to express your elation over the good grade by bringing it up over coffee in the student center with a close friend. Even in cultures where bragging about accomplishments is more acceptable, there are limits to how much bragging is tolerated. The *me* helps us control our impulses and allows us to choose our behavior rationally (Mead, 1934). The socialized self means that we think before we act.

Both the *I* and the *me* continually interact to help guide behavior. There are links among all the concepts discussed so far. Mead's *I* is similar to personal identity, and the *me* is similar to social identity. Cooley's idea of the looking-glass self is more closely linked with social identity because it focuses on the development of self based on imagining how others view us—part of being connected rather than being separate. Even if we misinterpret another person's view of us, it does not diminish the power of this process. As discussed in Chapter 6, we continually reevaluate and alter our behavior based on social interaction. We determine reality subjectively.

The looking-glass self reminds us of what others think of us. But this process is a complex one in several ways. First, all of these "others" are not the same. We pay more attention to how some people judge us than to how all others judge us. Those people whose approval and affection we desire the most and who are therefore most important to the development of our self-concept are called **significant others.** Parents, for example, are a child's first significant others. Second, not only do we imagine what others think of us, but we imagine what it is like to be in their shoes as well. When we engage in such **role-taking** we begin to develop empathy for others as well as to increase our social connectedness (role-taking inevitably draws us closer to other people). Another practical benefit of role-taking is that mental rehearsals allow us to anticipate others' behavior. Suppose you want to ask a classmate out on a date. You imagine several possible responses and are therefore prepared to modify your own response according to the one that occurs.

Third, as we mature we recognize that all the separate impressions we have of others and the world we live in eventually form a pattern. By age twelve most children have developed an awareness of the **generalized other**—the ability to understand broader cultural norms and judge what a typical person might think or do. After asking a number of people out on dates, gaining information from friends on their dating successes, and learning about dating norms, you will probably be more successful in predicting who will go out with you and whether it is likely to be a satisfying experience. The next potential dating partner becomes a generalized other.

Mead believed that children learn these abilities in stages as they mature and expand their social world. As described below, these stages can also be viewed in relation to other components of socialization.

1. *Preparatory Stage (to about age 3).* Children interact through imitation but do not understand the meaning of the interaction. They identify significant others, usually their parents, and seek their approval. Rewards and punishment nurture the development of the *I,* but the *me* is forming in the background and with it the grains of a sense of self. All these ingredients are necessary to prepare a child for later role-taking.

2. *Play Stage (about ages 3 to 5).* Children model others in their play ("I'll be the mommy and you be the daddy"), so they are now moving beyond simple imitation of others to acting out imagined roles, but only one at a time. Significant others become the most important models to imitate. The *me* grows stronger because children are concerned about the judgment of significant others. Language is used more accurately at this stage; it must be

mastered in order for a stable sense of self to emerge.

3. *Game Stage (early school years)*. The ability to take on the roles of several people at once emerges along with the generalized other. Complex games such as team sports require this ability. The game stage is developed in school, but its abilities are readily transferred to other real-life situations. Thus children develop the me and a relatively stable sense of self (Mead, 1934).

The game stage does not end the process of socialization or the continued development of the self. **Primary socialization,** in which language is learned and the first sense of self is gained, occurs mostly during the early years of life. Later experiences can modify this sense of self. Continuing socialization is thus a lifelong process and provides a basis for the later, varied roles individuals are expected to fulfill. Nonetheless, primary socialization puts an indelible mark on a person. Symbolic interactionism emphasizes the social construction of reality and how individuals continually create and re-create it. An illustration is **anticipatory socialization,** in which we practice what we want to achieve, such as excelling in college, being invited to pledge the best fraternity, or landing a good job.

Because socialization is an ongoing process that occurs in an ever-changing social world, other forces are at work that make the process uneven both for individuals and for the categories to which they belong. For example, some evidence suggests that boys advance to the game stage more quickly than girls. At an earlier age boys play games such as kickball that have more participants and are more complex, competitive, and rule-governed than games played by girls (Lever, 1978; Corsaro & Eder, 1990). Girls play ordered games, like hopscotch and jump-rope, in groups of two or three, with a minimum of competitiveness. Through the games they play, boys may learn role-taking associated with a generalized other sooner than girls. This learning process may have negative effects on girls. Compared with the games of young girls, the games of young boys provide earlier guidelines that are helpful for success later in life, such as the importance of striving for individual excellence through competition as emphasized in American culture.

Psychology: Socialization as Crisis

Psychology contributes a great deal to our understanding of socialization, and certain psychological theories help clarify sociological thought on the topic. Symbolic interactionism views socialization as a normal process that is not particularly stressful. People may move through its various stages at different rates and still end up as fully functioning members of society. But most psychological theories acknowledge that while people eventually learn what they need to learn, the process itself creates inner conflict. Socialization is marked by a series of predictable crises that must be resolved in order for people to have a productive and successful life.

Psychosexual Development. The work of Sigmund Freud (1856–1939) has had a profound impact on the social sciences. According to Freud, humans have basic biological needs or drives that conflict with one another. Biology is an important part of human behavior, but, unlike animals who exist solely on inborn traits, humans have only a few general (but powerful) instinctive forces. Freud's model of personality is built around this clash of forces (Freud, 1961, 1963).

The model has three parts. The **id** is Freud's term for an individual's biological drives and impulses; the id is selfish, irrational, ever-striving for pleasure and gratification, and it is unconscious. The id is not necessarily antisocial as much as it is nonsocial; it has no regard for anyone or anything but pleasure and gratification. Newborns are totally id-driven, as are some adults who were isolated or abused as children or who are developmentally disabled. Others may have the capacity for learning but may not have developed a capacity for language. Helen Keller, for example, blind and deaf from infancy, could be said to be id-driven until she was able to grasp the idea of language. Until then she lived in a world of wordless sensation, made up only of attempts to remove any feelings of discomfort.

Since parents must inevitably begin to say no to young children, the unsocialized drives propelled by the id come into conflict with another part of the personality, the **superego.** This is Freud's term for all the norms, values, and morals that are learned through socialization. Essentially, these form the demands of society and are internalized as a person's conscience. For successful socialization, the id must be controlled, and it is the task of the superego to do so. Since pleasure and gratification are always lurking in the unconscious, the road to the socialized personality is not an easy one. It is the third part of the personality, the **ego,** that acts as a mediator between the biological drives and the society that would deny them. The ego is largely conscious and reality-based, which means it provides rational plans to get what the individual wants, but in a socially acceptable way (Freud, 1961).

Freud was particularly concerned about the impact of the sex drive on the mediation process. His five stages of psychosexual development (see Table 5.1) revolve around attempts to satisfy id-driven

Freud believed that biological drives related to sexual attraction are kept in check by social norms. Dancing is an activity that allows some sexual expression but in a socially acceptable way.

sexual needs. He believed that even very young children experience sex-related pleasure, an idea that was quite scandalous in the Victorian era when he lived.

Of Freud's five stages of psychosexual development, the one that has received the most attention is the *phallic stage*, especially as it relates to gender socialization. At age 3 to 5, children focus gratification on the genitals (the clitoris for the girl and the penis for the boy), and masturbation and sexual curiosity increase for both sexes. According to Freud, girls come to believe that the penis, unlike the barely noticeable clitoris, is a symbol of power denied to them. Freud argued that the result is penis envy, which culminates in a girl's wish that she could be a boy (Freud, 1962). She views her mother as inferior because she, too, does not have a penis. The girl's *libido*, or sexual energy, is transferred to the father, who becomes the love-object. Later writers called this experience the *Electra complex*. The resolution occurs when the girl's wish for a penis is replaced by the wish for a child. A male child is even more desirable than a female because he brings the longed-for penis with him.

A boy also experiences conflict during the phallic stage, when his libido is focused on his mother, and his father is the rival for his mother's affections. Freud called this experience the *Oedipus complex*. When a boy discovers that a girl does not have a penis, he develops castration anxiety, according to Freud. The

psychic turmoil a boy experiences during this stage leads to the development of a strong superego. Freud believed that girls have weaker superegos, since the resolution of the Electra complex occurs with envy rather than fear.

The sexism in Freudian theory is obvious, even though its unfortunate effects concerning the idea of female inferiority far exceeded the intentions of Freud himself (Millett, 1995:61). He wrote during a period that embraced strict gender differentiation based on traditional roles for men and women in a patriarchal world. Freud was severely criticized for his ideas about infantile sexuality and the psychosexual stages of development but gained quiet acceptance for his comments on the biologically inferior design of females. However, feminist scholars do recognize that Freud's ideas give some insight into the way in which gender role socialization is also a power process. Freud offers a way of viewing domination not so much as a problem of human nature, but one of human relationships (Benjamin, 1988:5).

Many of Freud's concepts are so well-known that even though most remain as untestable assumptions, people typically use Freudian terms in describing others. How many times have you heard someone described as having a big ego, being anal-retentive, or being stuck in the oral stage? These expressions are examples of "pop-Freud." Even with Freud's insis-

| Table 5.1 | Sigmund Freud's Stages of Psychosexual Development | | |
Stage	Age	Description	Crisis to Resolve
Oral	0–1	Infants gain pleasure through the mouth. Feeding and sucking are key activities. Dependency and trust begin.	Weaning must not occur too early or too late or child may become a hostile, mistrustful, or gullible dependent adult.
Anal	2–3	Toilet training occurs. Child tests independence and is developing a sense of self.	Child must learn to control a biological urge. Either too much anxiety or not enough parental control can create a compulsively clean or overly messy adult.
Phallic	3–5	Feeling of sexual attraction toward same-sex parent occurs. Pleasure is transferred to genitals. Masturbation is common. Superego develops.	Boys must resolve castration anxiety and girls must resolve penis envy.
Latency	6–11	Gender identity develops. Boys and girls seem to ignore one another and sexual needs. Biological urges are lurking in the background.	Child focuses on learning skills and confronting issues to become a productive member of society.
Genital	Adolescence	Puberty occurs, focus is again on genitals. Normal interest in other sex develops.	Need to control sexual stirrings. Search for love and a marriage partner.

tence that social interaction is necessary for socialization, the "nature" side of the nature–nurture debate is given more weight than scientific evidence suggests.

Social Learning Theory. Unlike Freud's psychoanalytic approach, which focuses on powerful biological drives and internal conflict, social learning theory focuses on observable behavior. The key idea is that behavior is shaped by early experiences. Once behavior is learned, it becomes habitual. Socialization is considered in terms of reinforcing appropriate behavior or extinguishing inappropriate behavior according to how rewards and punishments are used. Specifically, social learning theory is concerned with the ways children model the behaviors they view in others, such as cooperation and sharing or selfishness and aggression. At first, imitation and modeling are spontaneous in children, but patterns of behavior develop through reinforcement.

As with other behaviors, gender roles are learned directly, through reprimands and rewards, and indirectly, through observation and imitation (Bandura & Walters, 1963; Mischel, 1966). The logic is simple. In gender role socialization, there is differential reinforcement for doing either "boy" or "girl" things. For example, a boy is praised by his peers for changing a flat tire but laughed at for playing with dolls. A girl is praised by her peers for knitting a sweater but laughed at for playing with toy soldiers in the mud.

Children associate the label of boy or girl with the rewards that come with the appropriate behavior. This association is the basis for gender identity. Chil-

dren develop **gender identity** when they become aware that the two sexes (male and female) behave differently and that two different gender roles (masculine and feminine) are proper. Once we develop our gender identity, we perceive ourselves as either male or female. We then act out gender roles, according to that perception. As parents and teachers model gender roles during the critical primary socialization years, children imitate accordingly. Continued reinforcement of the valued gender identity results.

According to social learning theory, gender-appropriate behavior is strongly associated with social approval for both genders. For males, masculine gender roles are more inflexible than those offered to females. Social learning theorists suggest that gender role inflexibility is a critical factor that makes male socialization difficult. For females, the socialization path is also difficult, but for a different reason. Even young children are bombarded by messages indicating that higher worth, prestige, and rewards are accorded to males than to females. Gender expectations lead to a preference for characteristic male behavior. Girls are offered subordinate roles that encourage deference and dependence (Geis, 1993). If modeling and reinforcement are as compelling enticements to behavior as social learning theory suggests, a girl could understandably become quite anxious when she must perform roles held in lower esteem. For socialization overall, girls have the advantage in gender role flexibility but boys have the advantage in higher prestige associated with their gender role.

Social learning theory provides a foundation for explaining much research on socialization, especially when it is combined with a symbolic interactionist perspective emphasizing the importance of role-taking. Role-taking allows opportunities for behavior to be rewarded or punished; it also allows behavior to be imitated. But reinforcement and modeling are more complex than social learning theory proposes for two important reasons. First, children may not model same-gender parents or may choose other-gender models outside the family (Lott & Maluso, 1993). Second, children model their parents, but parents also model their children. Parents often use their children as barometers of changing gender roles. Social learning theory minimizes the importance of social change as well as a child's ability to choose behavior. And regardless of the differences, both girls and boys learn to prefer their own sex and the gender roles associated with it. Other theoretical views help explain why.

Cognitive Development. Jean Piaget (1896–1980) was interested in how children gradually develop intelligence, thinking, and reasoning. His work is consistent with symbolic interactionism in two important ways. First, he starts with the idea that cognitive abilities are developed in stages through ongoing social interaction. Second, behavior depends on how a person perceives a social situation. Social learning theory suggests that children are passive learners who behave according to the stimuli presented to them. Cognitive

theory stresses a child's active role in structuring and interpreting the world.

The child's level of understanding of the world varies with the stage of cognitive development (see Table 5.2). In the first, *sensorimotor stage*, infants learn their world through sight, sound, and touch. They begin to form attachments to parents or other caretakers. **Schema,** cognitive structures used to understand the world and process new information, begin to be formed. By the time children reach age 2, Piaget's *preoperational stage*, they begin to use pretending and imaginary play. Since the preoperational stage occurs during early childhood, most children are not yet capable of creating many new schema, so they tend to rely on those schema they have already developed.

Sociologists are particularly interested in the latter two stages of cognitive development, when new schema are developed more rapidly. From age 7 to 11, a time Piaget refers to as the *concrete operational stage*, children have developed a range of schema to classify material. They begin to use logic and reasoning to solve problems, and their mental images of the world become more complex. According to Piaget, the capacity for abstract reasoning develops at around age 12, a time he calls the *formal operational stage*. Adolescents at this stage can consider several alternative solutions to problems and can imagine a number of abstract possibilities. Since the mind matures through interaction with the environment, each stage of

Social learning theory suggests that children model the behavior of others. The way parents act out aggression according to gender roles will be acted out similarly by their children.

INTERNET CONNECTIONS

Freud's theories led to a treatment for emotional problems called "psychoanalysis." The patient would lie on a couch and simply talk with Freud, allowing him—so Freud claimed—to learn the root of his or her problem. A later psychotherapist named Carl Rogers modified this technique, still encouraging patients to talk but responding only with empty comments. Indeed, there was so little substance to Rogers' responses that a computer scientist, Joseph Weizenbaum, wrote a famous program called ELIZA to simulate a Rogerian psychotherapist. Remarkably, people "conversing" with ELIZA often forgot that "she" was a machine, not a person. Try ELIZA yourself at www.-ai.ijs.si/eliza/eliza.html. See if you can trick ELIZA into making "non-human" responses.

Table 5.2   Stages of Cognitive and Moral Development

Jean Piaget: Cognitive Development	Lawrence Kohlberg: Moral Development
Sensorimotor (0–2 years) Infants explore their world through their senses and motor activities: They touch, hear, smell, grasp, suck, and shake objects. Object permanence and emotional attachment to a few important people form. *Preoperational* (2–7 years) Children learn language to represent objects and begin to use pretending and thinking about things they cannot see. They are egocentric (self-centered) at this stage, seeing things only from their own perspective. *Concrete operational* (7–11) Logical reasoning develops, but is very concrete and linked to objects they can see. They learn to add and subtract and figure out the principle of conservation—physical properties of objects (weight, volume) are the same (conserved) even if appearance (form, shape) changes. *Formal operational* (12 years to adult) Abstract thinking develops. Concepts are manipulated and problem solving is thought out in advance. Historical time can be fully understood. Adolescents are cognitively *capable* of such thinking, but some adults do not become fully formally operational.	*Preconventional* (beginning at about age 7) Moral reasoning develops based on meeting personal motives to obtain rewards or avoid punishment. *Conventional* (about age 10 to adolescence) Moral dilemmas are resolved by established social convention, the law, or other sources of authority. Social approval for moral behavior is sought. *Postconventional* (adulthood) Morality is linked to universal ethical principles—equality, justice, reciprocal rights and responsibilities—that may transcend authority. Conscience may override law. Some adults do not advance to the postconventional level.

cognitive development provides necessary tools for proceeding to the next stage (Piaget, 1950; Piaget & Inhelder, 1969).

Building on the work of Piaget, Lawrence Kohlberg (1969, 1981) surveyed the responses of people who were confronted with moral dilemmas they were asked to resolve. Kohlberg suggests that, like cognitive ability, moral development also occurs in stages (Table 5.2). To determine which stage of moral development a person is in, a scenario is presented to subjects involving a dying woman whose husband cannot afford a life-saving drug and a pharmacist who refuses to sell it at lower cost or let the husband pay for it later. The husband breaks into the pharmacy and steals the drug. According to Kohlberg, adolescents are at the conventional stage of moral development. They are likely to take a "law and order" view of the world, condemn the husband's actions, and believe that moral behavior is what is approved and necessary for the broader social good. Kohlberg's conventional stage of moral development corresponds to the start of Piaget's formal operational stage of cognitive development. Individuals need to achieve a certain level of cognitive development before they reach an advanced level of moral development.

A good example of the application of cognitive development theory to gender socialization comes from Kohlberg (1966) himself. According to Kohlberg, children also learn their gender roles according to their level of cognitive development. One of the first ways a child organizes reality is through the self, a highly valued part of the child's existence. Anything associated with the self becomes highly valued as well. By age 3, children begin to self-identify by gender and accurately apply gender-related labels to themselves and often to others (Kessler & McKenna, 1978). By age 6 a girl knows she is a girl and will remain one. Only then, Kohlberg asserts, is gender identity said to be developed. Gender identity becomes a central part of self, invested with strong emotional attachment.

Once gender identity is developed, much behavior is organized around it. Children seek models that are labeled as girl or boy and female or male. While children base much of their behavior on reinforcement, cognitive theorists see a different sequence in gender socialization than do social learning theorists. This sequence is: "I am a boy, therefore I want to do boy things, therefore the opportunity to do boy things (and to gain approval for doing them) is rewarding" (Kohlberg, 1966:89). Reinforcements are important, but the child is directed by the need to perform roles according to the sense of self (Serbin et al., 1993).

Gender schema theory, an important offshoot of cognitive development theory, suggests that once the child learns cultural definitions of gender, these schema become the core around which all other information is organized (Bem, 1981, 1983). The schema tell children what they can and cannot do according to their gender. They affect their behavior and influence their self-esteem. An individual's adequacy as a person is tied to the adequacy of matching behavior to gender schema. The influence of gender schema may help explain why it is so difficult to dislodge gender stereotypical thinking.

There is fairly wide support for the cognitive development approach to gender role socialization. Research consistently finds that as age increases, there is an increasing agreement with adult gender role stereotypes, suggesting that children develop the ability to classify characteristics by gender (Leahy & Shirk, 1984:289). By early childhood, boys especially value their gender highly, prefer same-gender friends, and give gender-related reasons for these preferences (Cann & Palmer, 1986; Etaugh & Duits, 1990). However, the cognitive development model has been criticized on several grounds. First, it cannot account for all of gender role socialization. Second, it is difficult to test what comes first, gender identity or the child's understanding of gender constancy (that he or she will remain either a boy or girl) (Intons-Peterson, 1988:44). For the model to fit neatly with the stages outlined in cognitive development, gender identity must come first. To date research has been unable to confirm this sequence.

More damaging to the legitimacy of Kohlberg's work is the fact that he used exclusively male subjects; generalizing the results to females is not warranted. Carol Gilligan (1982) presented the moral dilemma scenario in a modified form to girls and boys of the same age and social class. Gilligan found that when informed choices must be made and no clear-cut answers are suggested, moral reasoning differs by gender: Boys are more likely to choose on the basis of the norm of justice (people meet the needs of others because they deserve it) and girls are more likely to choose according to the norm of social responsibility (people should help those who are dependent on them, regardless of how the needs came about). Both norms are activated at the final stage, which Kohlberg calls the *post-conventional stage* of moral development, where morality is linked to ethical principles that may supersede the law.

Gender socialization explains these moral choices. Girls exist in a more intimate web of relationships that is less hierarchal than that of boys. Boys depend more on impersonal rules for reaching consensus (Walker, 1994; Johnson, 1996). Females have more expressive and emotion-centered friendships, while males have more instrumental and goal-oriented friendships (Duck & Wright, 1993). Different moral choices may be traced to these influences; although different, they are "equal" in terms of level of moral superiority.

Gender schema theory may provide the best way to explain how people develop gender identities. It also bridges the gap between psychological and sociological approaches, because it assumes that as people interact with their environments they actively construct mental structures (schema) to represent their awareness of the events around them (Intons-Peterson, 1988:48). Other schema can also be identified, such as those based on age, ethnicity, or religion. These ideas are at the core of symbolic interactionism and provide a point of departure for interdisciplinary work on socialization.

Gender schema theory suggests that children match their behavior to their gender identity, such as boys choosing trucks and girls choosing dolls for toys.

Childhood as Innocence or as a World of Little Adults

A legislator in Texas recently proposed that the death penalty be extended to 11-year-olds. According to this view, as seen in school shootings during recent years in Arkansas, Kentucky, Mississippi, and Colorado, young children have advanced from being schoolyard bullies to being murderers. If they act like adults, they should be treated like adults. Childhood, after all, is a modern invention.

For centuries children around the world were treated as little adults by the time they reached age 7 or 8. In medieval times childhood was not viewed as a separate stage of life. A close look at medieval paintings shows children depicted as little adults in costume and expression. The art, language, and literature of the times gave little thought to children. Toys and games were not designed for children, but to be used by people of all ages. Age as an indicator of personal identity did not exist. Age was not even recorded in family and civil records. Through the nineteenth century, children were expected to participate in the economic life of their families, whether it was working in the field, the home, or the factory. Children emerged from infancy to become miniature adults.

The idea that children have a unique nature separate and different from that of adults was ushered in with the Enlightenment in the seventeenth century. A century later, the belief that childhood should be a period of innocence, and that children should be spared as long as possible from the turmoil faced by adults, became entrenched in the Western world. In the United States the belief in childhood innocence probably reached its peak at the beginning of the twentieth century. It was during this period that child labor laws, universal education, and juvenile justice systems were put into place. With new theories of childhood development to draw on, families and schools would guide the innocent child into adolescence and productive adulthood. Since a child is different from an adult, socialization must take this into account.

Certainly children are different from adults. But at the beginning of the new century, the clock may be turning backwards. Children today are under tremendous pressure to show off their accomplishments as soon as possible. Childhood is associated with day care, preschool, and latchkey homes where peers rather than adults exert powerful influences. The medieval portraits of children as little adults are showing up again as sexualized images of younger and younger children in ads for cologne and underwear. We are haunted by the image of murdered 6-year-old JonBenet Ramsey in her showgirl costume and resplendent makeup. As far as crime is concerned, virtually every state now has laws allowing 14-year-olds to be tried and sentenced as adults. For the death penalty to be carried out, some states do suggest waiting until the felon reaches age 18 or 21.

Throughout history, children were included in the world of adults in both knowledge and practice. Fueled by media, today they are excluded from adult practices but not adult knowledge. Children know about violence, sex, drugs, and AIDS. The television shows most popular with children, such as *South Park* and *The Simpsons* are replete with wisecracking and foul-mouthed elementary and high school students. Third graders worry about attractiveness and dating. Seventh graders worry about getting into medical school. Youthful innocence, if it occurred at all, is a hallmark only of the twentieth century. The problem faced by families and schools is that socialization practices often do not keep pace with what children are experiencing in other areas of their lives. Experts in child development suggest that a rich sense of adulthood depends on the play of childhood. Sometimes referred to as "kidult culture" (kid+adult), the question will be how socialization can be balanced to account for the blurring of childhood and adulthood. By viewing the history of childhood, symbolic interactionists point out that childhood is as much a social construction as it is a biological one. Childhood is not destined to end, but a different kind of childhood is on the horizon.

1. How can parents help their children prepare for adult roles that are now demanded at an earlier age, but still allow them to experience the freedom associated with childhood?
2. What childhood experiences did you have and at what age(s) did you realize that adulthood was looming? Do you believe your own childhood socialization adequately set the stage for your current roles?

Sources: Aries, 1962; Borstelmann, 1983; Asher, 1994; Coontz, 1997; Applebome, 1998.

SOCIALIZATION AND THE LIFE COURSE: CONNECTING SOCIOLOGY AND PSYCHOLOGY

The **life course** perspective of socialization is another strong link between psychology and sociology for several reasons. First, this view considers the roles people play over a lifetime and the ages associated with those roles. It stresses the importance of continuing socialization and the varied paths individuals take due to individual experiences as well as to broader social change. Whereas both Freud and Mead focused on primary socialization, the life course view argues that all stages of life are equally important (Hetherington & Baltes, 1988). Second, because the life course is broken down into a number of separate stages, a range of research can be incorporated into the various stages using age as the key variable.

Third, along with age, the life course view accounts for attitudes and behavior influenced by one's **birth cohort,** all the people born at a given period of time who age together and experience events in history as a group. When people live through events or time periods that become significant historically, their perception of the world is affected. Those born during the 1920s focus on the Great Depression and World War II. For Americans, those who were born during the 1950s vividly recall President John F. Kennedy's assassination, Woodstock, hippies, and the Vietnam War protests.

Finally, while psychology provides the springboard into life course explanations, sociology provides the link between micro and macro perspectives. In this way, then, a new *sociological* psychology emerges. It is through such interdisciplinary links that the best theories of human social behavior are built.

Psychosocial Development

Freud's work is the foundation of Erik Erikson's (1902–1994) view of development. Like Freud, Erikson believed that early childhood experiences are important for personality development and that socialization is marked by crises in which conflict between the individual and society must be resolved. Unlike Freud, Erikson argued that culture rather than biology plays the biggest part in socialization. Also unlike Freud, Erikson argued that later life experiences that come with continuing socialization can significantly alter personality (Erikson, 1963).

Erikson proposed eight life stages that all people must go through from infancy to old age. The stages are called "psychosocial" by Erikson because they reflect both the psychological and social challenges everyone faces during the life course. Each stage is

marked by a crisis (see Table 5.3). For example, during the first year of life, the crisis of *trust versus mistrust* occurs. This is the stage where infants depend on others for basic physical and emotional needs. When parents are warm, nurturing, and responsive, infants develop confidence or trust that their needs will be met—a trust that is extended throughout their lives. While these crises imply that stresspoints are normal throughout life, they are not necessarily filled with turmoil. They represent turning points where different roads may be taken. And since they do not occur suddenly, people can use anticipatory socialization to help them in their choices. Erikson's theory of socialization is similar to symbolic interactionism in that behavior is influenced by significant others and consciously chosen.

If children learn to trust others during infancy, and that sense of trust is nurtured throughout the next life stages, by puberty they should be better prepared to deal with one of the most stressful times in their lives—the adolescent identity crisis. Between about ages 13 and 19, Erikson believed, adolescents must confront the challenge of creating a sense of personal identity. Referred to as *identity versus role confusion*, much of the focus of Erikson's work has been on this stage.

Puberty transforms the child into an adult in the sexual sense, but social roles during this stage are not so transformed. As explained in Chapter 4, all roles include both privileges and obligations. Regardless of biological maturity, these "new adults" find that childhood obligations far outweigh adult privileges. This realization results in role confusion until a stable ego-identity can be formed. The following account of a 16-year-old's memories of this time of life illustrates the turmoil:

> I was losing myself. The ground, once so firm beneath my feet, quivered.... And then I met the abyss, where my own name and possessions became strangers, unfamiliar baggage in this formless place. But this very abyss, where all was lost, somehow, somewhere gave rise to what I now dare call "me." (Kroger, 1996:174)

There is no road map to matters of maturing (Kroger, 1996). Yet social resistance is high when teens experiment with new roles, especially if the roles are associated with rebellion against established norms and a focus on peers rather than parents or teachers as confidants and role models. If parents and teens can maintain close emotional ties during this time, adolescent self-esteem is bolstered. Research shows that enhanced self-esteem during adolescence carries through to adulthood (Roberts & Bengston, 1996). This finding supports Erikson's idea that a successful

Table 5.3	Erik Erikson's Stages of Psychosocial Development	
Stage	**Age**	**Crisis to Resolve**
Infancy	0–1	*Trust vs. Mistrust* Infants depend on others and learn to trust that their needs will be met; otherwise they become fearful, mistrusting their environment.
Toddler	2–3	*Autonomy vs. Shame or Doubt* Children learn to do things on their own and control their behavior. Encouragement and consistent discipline builds self-esteem and protects them from shame and humiliation.
Early childhood	3–5	*Initiative vs. Guilt* Exploration, role-playing, and inquisitiveness are invited by parents; if not, children feel guilty when they initiate new behaviors.
Elementary school	6–12	*Industry vs. Inferiority* Children need recognition in school and at home for achievements and support for failures; otherwise feelings of inadequacy result.
Adolescence	13–19	*Identity vs. Role Confusion* Young people deal with sexual maturity and impending adult roles. They must integrate previous experiences to develop a sense of personal identity. Without an identity compatible with who they believe they are, role confusion occurs. They act in ways to please others but not themselves.
Young adulthood	20–40	*Intimacy vs. Isolation* A strong personal identity helps develop the intimacy needed for commitment to others, such as a spouse; otherwise a person can become lonely and isolated.
Middle adulthood	40–65	*Generativity vs. Stagnation* Career, marriage, and children are central. Contributions to the next generation occur. Value is placed on what he/she is doing for others; otherwise, a person is resigned, unproductive, and may feel worthless.
Late adulthood/ old age	65 and over	*Integrity vs. Despair* A life review finds meaning or lack of it in accomplishments. Was life worthwhile or full of disappointments and failure?

resolution of the identity crisis has long-term positive effects.

Today sociologists have turned attention to applying Erikson's model to later life. Adulthood ushers in *maturity*, not simply in terms of age but in terms of emotional readiness to deal with the next stages of life. Maturity is an honest appraisal of one's own experience and the ability to use that knowledge caringly in relationship to one's self and others (Colarusso, 1994). For sociology, although maturity is a necessary component, social roles and social institutions take center stage in explaining transitions throughout the life course. As people move through the life course, continuing socialization occurs. Erikson's work serves as a vital sociological link in understanding continuing socialization.

The Sociology of Adult Development and Aging

Life is a ongoing process of development, socialization, and adaptation. Personality is important in determining how we adapt to the different stages of life.

Our personality gives us an overall direction when choices for behavior arise. People do not undergo sudden personality shifts in confronting new or stressful situations. They do not lose their capacity to learn or change; this capacity is at the core of adult development (Atchley, 2000). The sociology of adult development looks at how people adapt to ongoing role changes, especially those associated with age roles and age norms.

Early and Middle Adulthood. Young adults, those who are between the ages of about 18 and 22 and who are also in college, confront a later version of role confusion than that occurring in adolescence. Sometimes referred to as boys and girls, at other times as men and women, even among themselves, the confusion associated with the status of college student underscores the fact that in the United States there is no single identified marker between being a minor and being an adult. Being able to vote at age 18 and consume alcohol legally at age 21 suggest adulthood. But college is also a semiprotected world shielding students from the responsibilities as well as

Birth cohorts experience historical events as a group. The movement against the Vietnam War in the late 1960s and early 1970s was led by the baby boomers and influenced the way their generation viewed the world.

the privileges of full adulthood. First-year students are honored for being on their own, and professors confirm adult status. But these same messages can be experienced as abandonment and a refusal to care. A modified personality based on the subculture of college life has not yet formed, but the old personality has been lost (Kegan, 1982:186). Clearly these young adults are not children, but they do not yet fit various criteria for defining adulthood, such as financial independence or emotional readiness for marriage and family (McCandless & Coop, 1979).

Beginning at about age 20, the phases of adulthood can be marked according to age-related norms. This assumes that there is an accepted sequence of events and life activities appropriate for each age. The cultural pattern in the United States is for early adulthood to include the completion of formal schooling, marriage, raising children, and becoming established in a career. Because the career commitment of women is severely compromised by their roles as wife and mother, they are often caught in an age and gender norm dilemma: Early adulthood is a time when raising a family and establishing a career occur simultaneously, and both are desired. A typical resolution of this dilemma—or crisis, in Erikson's words—is that the woman ends her career, puts it on hold, or changes directions (Silver & Goldscheider, 1994; Wharton, 1994). Whether the resolution is successful depends on the woman's long-term self-esteem and the marital satisfaction level of the couple.

Middle adulthood, ages 40 to 60, is marked by the last children leaving home and the birth of the first grandchildren, increased career commitment, and planning for retirement. This phase also heightens one's concern for maintaining health when the first signs of physical aging, such as gray hair and the need for reading glasses, become noticeable.

Gender role–related crises that occur during middle adulthood may affect men and women differently. For women, the moderate to severe depression that supposedly occurs when the last child is launched, or moves away from home, is referred to as the *empty nest syndrome*. Research shows, however, that the empty nest syndrome is largely a myth. Contrary to the stereotype, most women experience an upturn in life satisfaction and psychological well-being when children are launched (Harris et al., 1986). Most women look to the "empty nest" stage of life as offering opportunities to engage in activities that might have been put on hold during child raising. They generally seek expanded roles in a society increasingly receptive to women like themselves, who are venturing outside the traditional confines of the home. Reduced work and parental responsibilities help explain increased marital satisfaction in later life for both men and women (Orbuch et al., 1996).

Professionals have debated the idea that men experience a midlife crisis with physical and emotional symptoms, such as night fears, drenching sweat and chills, and depression. The psychological and social turmoil associated with these symptoms are often linked to hormonal changes, such as a drop in testosterone level. Gender scripts linking masculinity to sexual performance create a fear of impotence, which may come true not because of hormones but because of the fear itself (the massive sales of Viagra, the new drug that enhances the sexual performance of men, may be linked to this fear). Thus biological changes must be seen in the light of social and psychological factors.

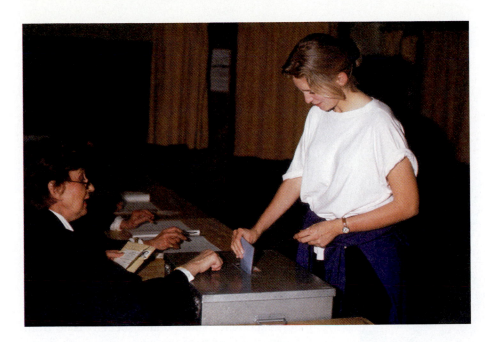

Adulthood is marked differently in different cultures. In the United States, voting is one marker.

Family changes may heighten the difficulties. For men, launching of their children may be accompanied by regrets that they have had limited contact with them due to career priorities. Evidence suggests that some men may have greater difficulty in this regard than women (Wink & Helson, 1993). To recapture the parenting experience, these men may turn to grandparenting. Grandfathers are often the soft spots in man-to-man relationships (grandfather-to-grandson) where men are free of power struggles and competitiveness (Garfinkel, 1985).

The differing views of midlife as an unsettling transition that people fear or as a normal and even healthy stage of life, allowing people the opportunity to make choices and life changes, is still debated. According to Daniel Levinson (1978, 1986), a wide variety of issues confront adults at this stage, with career and family taking precedence. For both men and women, the relationships that emerge inside and outside the family and the changes that occur shape every aspect of a person's life. Socialization continues, and self-concept is being reestablished or renewed (Sheehy, 1976). Decisions made at this stage strongly influence the time that is left.

Later Adulthood and Old Age. Later adulthood marks the beginning of the last stage of life, that of old age. In the developed world, 60 to 65 is usually the age marker of this stage. Of course, old age is as much personal and cultural as it is biological. For example, when people in England were asked when old age is thought to start, the older they were, the older the marker they chose. Those in the 16-to-24 range said it began at 63. Those age 75 and over said it

started at 76 (*Age Concern*, 1992). Unlike other phases of adulthood, transition to old age is often noted by formal **rites of passage**—a retirement dinner, a gold watch, a special birthday celebration to mark an important life transition.

As with other stages of life, adaptations to old age are based on earlier patterns, but there are some important differences. First, old age for most people is now the longest part of life, with an average of thirty years of life still ahead. These years can be subdivided into phases with certain features in common. Research on the "young" elderly (age 65–75), for example, shows high levels of life satisfaction and activity. The "middle" elderly (age 75–85) experience more physical slowdown and loss of some activities. But the majority of both these groups live independently. Only about 5 percent of those over age 65 live permanently in long-term care facilities. As would be expected, the oldest old, 85+, are the most likely to require such care.

These phases highlight another important difference compared with earlier life: The path of old age needs much more exploration. We know a lot about children and teenagers, less about adults at middle age, and the least about the elderly. As expressed by one person:

> I could never imagine getting old. I still can't, although I'm old. I still don't realize I've got to 73 because I don't feel 73, I don't feel what I imagine 73 to be like. (Slater, 1995:1)

The exploding field of *gerontology*, the scientific study of aging with a focus on the elderly population, is remedying this situation (see Chapter 14). "Travel

Although there is some slowdown, most elderly people have active lifestyles and high levels of life satisfaction.

guides" are now available for this phase of life, written by explorers of new terrains for the elderly. The media are also focusing on active, interesting, and innovative old people, including ordinary people who cannot be dismissed as exceptions that prove the rule (Slater, 1995).

Finally, sociological interest focuses on a key feature that distinguishes this stage from previous ones: role loss rather than role entry. Although mental decline is not the rule, loss of physical strength, especially among the oldest old, means that fundamental lifestyle changes are on the horizon. The preview of things to come is different from a review of what has occurred. Life is stretching out behind rather than in front.

Socialization into Death.   The stage of dying is mostly associated with the final stage of old age. But according to psychiatrist and author Robert Lifton (1979:5), there is no ongoing connection between life and death in American culture. Lifton believes that death as presented in the media is absurd and people do not know how to deal with the new evolutionary fact that they have the ability, whether through a virus like HIV (AIDS) or through an atomic bomb, to exterminate themselves as a species. Coupled with a

youth-oriented culture, death denial is the norm. With medical technology keeping people physically alive for extended periods of time, America is both a death-denying and death-defying society.

At middle age people experience the first real physical declines associated with aging. It is also the time when most confront the loss of parents. These become the personally significant ways in which people are socialized into death. Among the elderly, the reality of death becomes a fact of life.

The dying process itself has been extensively studied through the pioneering research of Elisabeth Kübler-Ross (1969). Through interviews with many terminally ill people, she determined a pattern, or series of stages, that people go through. Like a life course, there is a death course. The sequence of stages is as follows:

1. *Denial.* People who are told they have a terminal illness experience shock and disbelief. Aside from the personal horror of the news, in a death-denying society this is clearly a logical response.
2. *Anger.* Individuals express hostility and resentment, often toward others who will live on. "Why me?" they ask, with a strong sense of injustice.
3. *Bargaining.* Bargains are made, usually with God. "I will be a better person if only I can live, so please spare me."
4. *Depression.* The realization comes that they cannot negotiate their way out of the situation, depression occurs. Sorrow, guilt, and shame are linked with this stage.
5. *Acceptance.* By discussing these feelings openly, the person moves into a final stage in which death is accepted. Kübler-Ross believes that only with acceptance can inner peace be reached.

Kübler-Ross established the idea of *dying trajectories*, the courses dying takes in the social or psychological sense. Her model has been used to describe not only the sequence of dying, but also to suggest a set of therapeutic recommendations for how dying "should" take place (Kamerman, 1988). Hospital staff are taught to interpret terminally ill patients' behavior according to the stage theory and to work with them so that they will eventually move into stage five and accept their inevitable death. Symbolic interactionists suggest that such therapeutic recommendations socially construct the process of death—a description *of* the reality of dying according to stage theory becomes a prescription *for* reality—how dying is supposed to occur (Charmaz, 1980). As with other roles, a cultural standard for dying gradually emerges.

But research also shows that while there are categories of behavior that dying people exhibit, they do not occur in any predictable stages. Denial, for example, occurs at all points in the dying process

Planning for Death in the Netherlands

It appears from the results of the study that intravenous administration of thiopental followed by a muscle relaxant is the most reliable route for producing euthanasia.

The quote above is from a study conducted by the Royal Dutch Society for the Advancement of Pharmacy that determined the best drugs to administer to a dying patient so that death is painless and quick. The common practice is an injection to put the patient into a coma, followed by a second injection to stop the heart. The patient often administers the first injection. The Netherlands (Holland) is the only country in the world where euthanasia, assisted suicide by a doctor, is openly practiced. Dutch law does not specifically allow euthanasia, but it protects doctors practicing euthanasia who follow official guidelines. Doctors will not be prosecuted if they meet the requirements for euthanasia set by the Royal Dutch Medical Association. The requirements are:

1. The patient makes a repeated, voluntary request to die.
2. The request must be explicit, well informed, strong, and enduring.
3. The patient is in unacceptable suffering with no prospect for relief.
4. All other options for care have been exhausted or refused by the patient.
5. Euthanasia is administered by a physician.
6. The physician has consulted a colleague who agrees with the proposed euthanasia.

How many people choose euthanasia in the Netherlands? The answer depends on how euthanasia is defined and how the death is reported. Assisted suicide is called *active euthanasia*. When life support or extraordinary forms of treatment are withdrawn, *passive euthanasia* occurs. Death from euthanasia is commonly reported as "cardiac arrest." Most deaths from euthanasia are probably unreported. Estimates of the extent of euthanasia, therefore, vary widely, but between 5 and 10 percent of Holland's population are thought to end their lives by this practice.

Most people do not choose death by euthanasia in the Netherlands. But for those who do, the choice is viewed as an acceptable one. Since death by euthanasia is culturally permissible and guided by standard medical procedures, planning for the end stage of life is common. Although some Dutch religious groups and other organizations are appalled by the practice of euthanasia, they appear to be fighting a losing battle. Public opinion is that euthanasia can be the last dignified act in the health-care process. Socialization for death in the Netherlands includes euthanasia as a legitimate alternative.

The Netherlands is often cited as a role model for other countries looking for ways to introduce euthanasia to their own medical practices. The first Dutch physicians violated the ban on euthanasia over forty years ago to draw attention to the plight of dying patients, and now physicians in other countries are doing the same thing. In the United States, the infamous Dr. Jack Kevorkian, inventor of the "suicide machine," has been convicted of murder after innumerable arrests for assisted suicide. His sentence of ten to twenty-five years in prison has been called harsh and unjust by assisted suicide advocates. Several states have issued challenges to the constitutionality of laws against assisted suicide. Australia passed a law allowing euthanasia, but the law lasted only six months before angry opponents had it rescinded. Scotland is doing major research on euthanasia and testing public opinion on the subject.

Death socialization via euthanasia may be common in the Netherlands. There are other factors, however, that may make the Netherlands a less compatible role model for other countries struggling with the issue. For example, Holland has one of the highest standards of medical care in the world. Over 95 percent of the population is covered by private medical insurance. Care for those in extreme pain is highly advanced, and pain centers are attached to all hospitals. Very few such centers are found in other countries. In addition, the level of trust between doctor and patient is very high. During the Nazi occupation, Dutch doctors went to concentration camps rather than divulge the names of their patients. Patients often keep the same doctor over a lifetime. Most important, Holland is among the five countries with the highest life expectancies. These specific characteristics of Dutch culture show that countries need to find their own solutions to the euthanasia issue rather than trying to import the Dutch system wholesale.

1. Given that euthanasia is widely accepted in the Netherlands, do you think that the choice for euthanasia could become a prescription for it? What will prevent abuses in the system?
2. How does your own culture socialize its people into death? Could euthanasia become an acceptable alternative for dying patients?

Sources: Horgan, 1991; Brock, 1992; Euthanasia, 1993; Kimsa & Leeuwen, 1993; Royal Dutch Society, 1994; Wal & Dillman, 1994; Associated Press, 1999; Willing, 1999; http://www.euthanasia.org/dutch.html, 1999.

(Kastenbaum, 1985; Cassem, 1988). Socialization into even our own death is similar to other socialization experiences during the life course. The right to choose the way we want to die is compromised by the social roles we take on and the way others define these roles during the dying process. An "appropriate" death becomes a negotiation between these roles.

Coming to terms with death could be a ninth category in Erikson's model. At the end of life, there is the struggle (crisis) to affirm both individual choice (dying the way we want to) and social constraints (dying the way society tells us we ought to). Our funeral, another rite of passage, provides a socialization experience for those left behind.

The Life Course: A Critical Review

A sociological view of an age-based life course adds to an understanding of the process of socialization. All cultures have some type of an age-based sequence. However, cautions must be noted. Sociology recognizes that any society constructs stages according to what is important to that society. The identity crisis, for example, has attracted a great deal of research and popular attention. Parents and teachers routinely lament to sympathetic listeners about the unrest of the teenagers in their lives and the toll extracted on everyone concerned. Teenagers in turmoil become the accepted norm.

Furthermore, while all people in all places must be socialized, contrary to Erikson's assertion the stages are not culturally universal. The identity crisis for America's adolescents is particularly stressful. College continues the struggle to define adult status. In some African cultures, however, there is no time to have an identity crisis. One afternoon a 13-year-old boy is defined as a child. That evening he undergoes a circumcision rite of passage and is an adult. On the same day a 13-year-old girl is betrothed in another rite of passage. Two hours later she is an adult. Period.

Moreover, massive social change has altered the notion that people should accomplish certain developmental tasks at certain ages. In a study of college students between the ages of 17 and 22, for example, those whose parents were divorced during their adolescent years were at a higher level of moral development than comparably aged students whose parents were not divorced. According to this research, heightened moral judgment comes earlier because during adolescence they take on the perspective of their parents in the divorce process (Kogos & Snarey, 1995). By this reasoning, compared to just a few decades ago, divorce has produced a generation of more "mature" adolescents. Children are growing up faster than in the past.

In addition, social change has radically altered age-related norms. Examples of emerging norms are divorce and remarriage, adult children moving back with parents after divorce or job loss, women of all ages entering the paid labor force, and people changing careers several times in their lives. The social circumstances under which many children live have changed dramatically (Shehan & Seccombe, 1996). For the elderly, more and are exhibiting characteristics that were previously hallmarks of middle adulthood and even young adulthood. Does this mean they

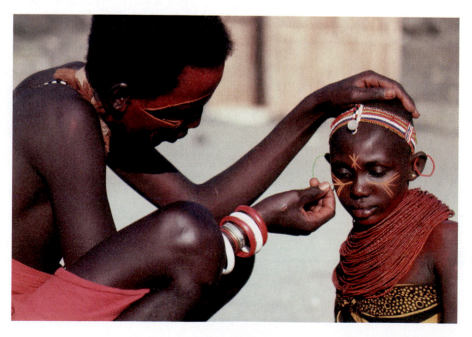

The identity crisis may be a Western invention. Among the Masai of East Africa, a young girl's betrothal marks her as an adult. She has no time for an identity crisis.

must go through the crises associated with these stages over again? Probably not. Age is only one way to monitor time-related changes and the developmental tasks involved. It is likely that, along with age, new criteria will emerge that will also define the life course.

This section has demonstrated that individuals must complete certain tasks in order to become functioning members of society. Principles consistent with symbolic interactionism provide the foundation for this discussion. But these tasks are embedded in broader social structures that also serve as socialization agents. Like the theories of socialization, most life course research is based on samples made up of white, middle-class males. However, research on primary socialization linking race, gender, and class is rapidly emerging.

AGENTS OF SOCIALIZATION: RACE, CLASS, AND GENDER DIVERSITY

Agents of socialization are the people, groups, and social institutions that provide the critical information needed for children to become fully functioning members of society. If these agents do not carry out their socialization tasks properly, the individual and social integration may be compromised. These agents do not exist independently of one another. What happens at school affects the child and family in the home. Loss of a job and a paycheck has repercussions for both the individual and society. Functionalist theorists are particularly concerned about these agents. They emphasize how the various agents should work together so that society operates smoothly and social equilibrium is not jeopardized. From the viewpoint of conflict theory, the various agents may work to the benefit of one group but against another.

The Family

The family plays the pivotal role in primary socialization. In the first years of life the family is largely responsible for the emerging identity, self-esteem, and personality of the child. The first values and attitudes you embrace as a child are from your family. Language learning and cognitive development reinforce these elements. In addition, families bestow race, ethnicity, religion, and socioeconomic status on their children. These are all forms of *cultural capital* that provide for the child's first social placement.

Cultural capital has been accounted for in examining racial differences in socialization as well as opportunities that affect the races differently. For example, while the majority of both African American

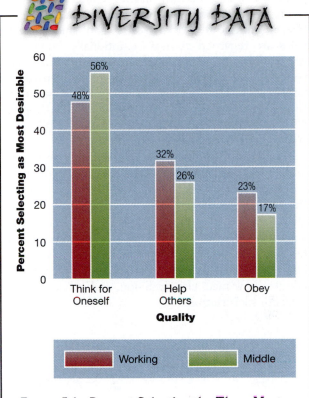

FIGURE 5.1 Percent Selecting the Three Most Desirable Qualities for a Child to Have, by Social Class. Both working and middle class people select thinking for oneself as a child's *most* desirable quality, followed by helping others and obeying. However, thinking for oneself is selected significantly more by the middle class, as are helping others and obeying by the working class. What do these differences suggest about a child's socialization for independence and autonomy in these two social classes?
Source: NORC. General Social Surveys, 1972–1996. Chicago National Opinion Research Center, 1996.

and white adolescents live in relatively advantaged homes, whites are much more advantaged. For African Americans, family advantages in social class may not make up for disadvantages in the larger society (Cutright, 1995; Cornwell et al., 1996). For Chinese American children, there are strong influences from traditional beliefs related to respect for parents and older people, as well as about family and kinship networks in the Chinese American community (Fong & Wu, 1996).

The first socialization into attitudes related to gender also occurs in families. Gender roles are more flexible in middle-class families than in working- and lower-class families (Brooks-Gunn, 1986; Lackey, 1989). In terms of race, African Americans are less stereotyped than whites in role expectations regarding gender. African American married couples are more egalitarian than families in other racial groups. African American working-class and middle-class males are regarded as more emotionally expressive than comparable white males and African American working- and middle-class females are regarded as more independent and less yielding than comparable white females (Bardwell et al., 1986; Penha-Lopes, 1993; Dill, 1999). Socialization for role flexibility in childhood carries through to adulthood.

Data from Puerto Rican and Mexican American samples show stronger support for a female role that is deferential and subordinate than is the case with African Americans or whites (Garcia, 1991; Lips, 1995). Female roles are bolstered by powerful religious socialization within some Latino subcultures that promote women's subservience to men (Anzaldua, 1995). This pattern among Latinos specifically indicates how race, class, religion, and gender all intersect in socialization.

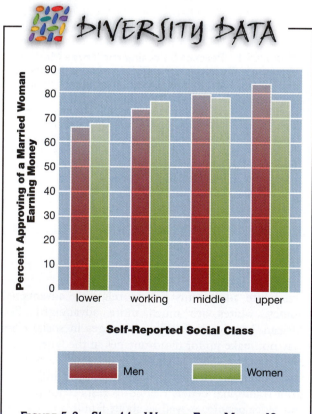

FIGURE 5.2 **Should a Woman Earn Money If Her Husband Can Support Her?** As self-reported social class increases, both men and women's approval of a married woman earning money increases. The lowest approval is from lower and working class men. Do you think children in these households will be socialized into these expectations more by their mothers or their fathers?

Although the media have popularized the belief that the American family is on the verge of collapse, the family is still *the* critical socialization agent. While other institutions may be extending the work originally done in the family, sociological studies clearly show that the family still oversees the socialization process. Family socialization enhances a child's life prospects—both psychologically and socially. This finding is illustrated by research showing that when parents have high degrees of involvement with their children, they can buffer the emotional stress children experience when moving to a new community (Hagan et al., 1996). On the social side, children draw on cultural capital in the years ahead (Mohr & DiMaggio, 1995). Socialization experienced in the family is never erased.

Education

The family paves the way for the next major agent of socialization, the school. In contrast to the intimacy of the family, the school evaluates children on the basis of what they do rather than who they are. Children acquire necessary knowledge and skills, but also learn new social roles by interacting with teachers and peers. In U.S. culture, the socialization function of education emphasizes that children learn academic content, social skills, and important cultural values. Core cultural values help prepare children for life in a democratic society that stresses free enterprise and capitalism. These core U.S. values include the three "Is"—initiative, independence, and individualism. Schools are also expected to play a major role in *assimilation*, bringing together children from diverse cultures and subcultures and transforming them into committed Americans. For twelve to twenty years, school plays a dominant role in socialization.

Besides the formal academic curriculum, schools also have a powerful *hidden curriculum*, which includes all the informal, unwritten norms that exist both inside and outside the classroom. This hidden curriculum plays an important part in gender role socialization. Teachers who care deeply about their students, and who honestly believe that they are treating girls and boys the same, are often unaware that they transmit gender-based stereotypes (see Chapter 16).

Although research shows that schools can unintentionally socialize children into ways that may perpetuate stereotypes, schools genuinely strive to use their socialization function to the benefit of children and society. Sociology recognizes that schools today are shouldering a bigger share of the socialization function in America than at any point in history.

Peers

As children are gradually introduced to the world outside the family, peers take on a major role in socialization. **Peer groups** are made up of people who are the same age and generally share the same interests and positions. Schools provide the setting for hierarchies of peer groups to form quickly. As early as third grade children identify with particular groups (Adler, 1996). While parents and teachers mold identity and self-esteem, peer groups are also leading players in the process.

Parents initiate the first peer relationships, and school allows for children to select friends from a wider range of peers. Parents both encourage and fear this prospect, especially during the middle school and high school years. As life course research suggests, the pull of the peer group during adolescence can be stressful for everyone. Patterns of early peer relations continue into the later school years. Students with unstable friendships or those who have had many negative interactions with friends suffer in their self-esteem (Keefe & Berndt, 1996). Adolescents with friends who are disruptive in school increase their own disruptiveness (Berndt & Keefe, 1995). Less attachment to parents and greater attachment to friends may predict antisocial behavior in middle school students (Marcus & Betzer, 1996). These findings support the wealth of research suggesting that peer involvement is the key ingredient in adolescent drug use and other forms of delinquent behavior. However, as we will see shortly, parents' fear of peers is probably more stereotyped than real.

"How is it gendered?"

Peer groups are usually segregated by gender. Boys interact in larger groups and have more extensive peer relationships. Girls have more intensive ones. Female peer groups have higher levels of self-disclosure, intimacy, and trust (Moore & Boldero, 1991; O'Connor, 1992). Once same-gender relationships are formed, gender boundaries are monitored and enforced by peers (Maccoby, 1994). One consequence of this process is that having learned different styles of interaction, girls and boys may meet in adolescence virtually as strangers (Fagot, 1994:62).

Media

Like the schools, the media have gradually taken on a stronger role in socialization. But in the media, the socialization function is more subtle, much of it occurring without conscious awareness.

Television is by far the most influential of the media. Television establishes standards of behavior, provides role models, and communicates expectations about all of social life. Note how these are the very terms used in describing all theories of socialization. We rely more and more on the mass media, especially television, to filter the enormous amount of information we receive. When television images are reinforced by other mass media, the impact on socialization is substantial.

In the United States, 98 percent of households have at least one TV and 40 percent have two or more, one of which is turned on an average of seven hours per day. Although people over age 55 are the heaviest viewers, preschoolers and young children may spend up to one-third of the day watching television. Children from poor homes watch television more than those from affluent homes, nonwhites more than whites, and working- and lower-class children more than those whose parents have higher education and income (Nielsen Media Research, 1994). Television does provide models of prosocial behavior, in which people help others out of unselfish motives. It also offers programming designed to help children learn to read or to fuel their interest in current events, nature, or the arts. However, when considering all the options television offers, such programming is extremely limited.

Overall, those who watch TV the most also have more stereotyped views of the world. As expected, young children are the most vulnerable to TV images since they may not be able to distinguish fantasy from reality, are still in the formative stages of their identity, and use television more for role-modeling. These are the facts that critics of the media use when considering the relationship between television and aggression. Over two thousand studies have documented a clear and consistent correlation between the two, a pattern supported cross-culturally as well (Huston et al., 1992).

Even those who continue searching for irrefutable causal links cannot dismiss the following facts:

- Two out of three TV programs contain violence that threatens or actualizes hurt and killing.
- By sixth grade the average child has witnessed at least 8,000 TV murders and 100,000 other violent acts.
- A Saturday morning and prime-time television world of crime and violence exists, with violent acts ten times as frequent as in the real world (Signorielli, 1990; Gerbner, 1994).

Viewing violence increases violence, and the more violent the content, the more aggressive the child (National Institute of Mental Health, 1982; American Psychological Association, 1993). From what we have learned about socialization, it is easy to understand how we can become desensitized to violent images, especially when the media glamorizes dehumanization. Much research concludes that media messages are internalized and frequently acted on (Burk & Shaw, 1995). While television is not *the* cause of violence, it is certainly *a* cause.

Socialization into gender roles is also media influenced. Much of the media violence is directed toward women. White adult males are more likely to be involved in violence and to get away with it. For every ten male perpetrators of violence on television there are eleven who are victimized by it; for every ten female perpetrators, there are sixteen victims, with women of color, older women, and foreign women the most likely targets. Men in general kill more than twice as often as they are killed. Overall, men kill and women get killed (Signorielli, 1991; Gerbner, 1993a). Boys identify with characters possessing physical strength and girls with those who are physically attractive (Reeves & Miller, 1978; Evans, 1993). As will be explained in Chapter 13, even young children learn the gendered media messages that men are aggressive and women are vulnerable.

Other Agents

Socialization continues throughout life and on multiple fronts. While the family and the school are held most accountable for socialization, other agents contribute to the process. Religious institutions reinforce earlier moral development. People also join a variety of organizations through schools and workplaces. In high school they play on sports teams and learn the rules of cooperation and competition. College students join fraternities and sororities that emphasize

family-like relationships. They join professional associations that help them network with colleagues and that provide mentoring opportunities to help them achieve on the job. These agents provide opportunities for continuing to mold identity and self-esteem well into adulthood. However, all socialization experiences at any point in the life course will be directly influenced by peers.

≡ LIFE CONNECTIONS: The Fear of Peers in American Socialization

Age segregation is a fact of life in America. Most people spend most of their time outside their families with those who belong to the same age groups. Since schools organize childhood and adolescence according to age, peer influences in socialization are very powerful. When parents realize they no longer have control over who their children interact with or become friends with, the dreaded "fear of peers" phase of parenthood begins. Parents worry that their children will get involved with the "wrong" crowd, who can be defined as unsavory, untalented, unimaginative, or simply poor. Parents may see peer groups propelling children to engage in all kinds of antisocial acts, from talking back to teachers and cheating on exams to shoplifting or gang violence. Fueled by media images, the distinction between a peer group and a gang is a blurry one in the minds of many parents.

Peer groups are the first ways children learn to exert some control over their lives. Adolescents say they can be themselves only when with their friends; they do not have to show deference to adults and can use the peer group to mock adult authority, particularly as represented by school. By joining forces, children learn they can often get what they want from otherwise reluctant adults (Cahill, 1987). Adolescents realize their potential power when they congregate in front of a movie theater, at a fast-food restaurant, or in a mall, which prompts a call to security to disperse them.

But the fear of peers cuts both ways. Parents worry when their children spend more time with their peers than with their families. Young people worry that they will become social outcasts if they do not spend enough time with their friends. Codes of conduct in peer groups are rigid, and the threat of exclusion is usually enough to enforce peer-approved behavior (Adler & Adler, 1995). To be "themselves" in the peer group, young people must dress and speak a certain way and possess what the group defines as important—whether in appearance, material possessions, sexual prowess, or sports talent.

For children in the United States, peers set standards of physical attractiveness that are strongly related to popularity. If you look good, people like you and want to be around you. If you do not look good in the eyes of your peers, you can be shunned. Peers assign many negative traits to unattractive children. Often a self-fulfilling prophecy occurs: Children actually display some of the negative behaviors peers attribute to them. Discipline from parents—having allowance withheld or being grounded—is exchanged for discipline from peers—name-calling, ridicule, or, at worst, social isolation (Langois & Downs, 1979; Howes, 1988). Even young children have an accurate notion about peer acceptance and will passionately work to protect it. Peer acceptance is a major factor in a child's self-esteem and can predict adjustment and well-being later in life (Parker & Asher, 1987).

However, data also show the positive impact of peers on adolescent self-esteem and prosocial behavior, particularly when adolescents are close to parents (Roberts & Bengston, 1996). African American and Latino adolescents who demonstrate high levels of commitment to others describe themselves in terms of moral personality traits and goals and think of themselves as melding their own ideals with positive images provided by their parents (Hart & Fegley, 1995).

These adolescents are applauded for their prosocial behavior by their community and their peers.

We have seen that children the world over are socialized by a number of agents, but peer groups in America are becoming more and more important. Teenage recreation in America is now focused outside the home—in malls, video arcades, and movie theaters. Within the home, middle-class teens and their friends can retreat to rooms that are replete with color televisions, VCRs, phones, stereos, and personal computers with Internet access. As in America as a whole, the media and electronic gadgetry children and adolescents use for recreation are also age-based. The childhood and teenage niche in media and electronics is a multimillion-dollar industry.

Since socialization in America hinges more on peer groups than ever before, the fear of peers may be justified. But peers come later in a child's life. The family is not only the first socialization agent, it is by far the most important. Both parents and their children may worry about peer influences; in the long run, however, sociological research shows that it is highly unlikely that peer group values replace parental values.

Peer groups in school strongly influence identity. Children usually form gender-segregated peer groups.

≋ SOCIETY CONNECTIONS: When Socialization Fails

Some people cannot make their way through the socialization process or are thwarted at some stage. This may be caused by biological limitations, such as severe birth defects that compromise a child both physically and mentally, or by social factors, such as the extreme isolation experienced by Anna. People may have accidents or experience medical problems such as strokes where mental and physical capacities are so compromised that they must relearn simple patterns of behavior. In all these cases socialization failed because of circumstances beyond their control. In other cases, however, socialization can be regarded as a failure because people choose behavior that is destructive to themselves or to society. Since the key role of socialization is to make a person a fully functioning member of society, behavior that goes against this process cannot be ignored.

Resocialization: Voluntary or Involuntary

When socialization fails, most people must go through the process of **resocialization** in order to remedy patterns of behavior that society finds destructive or to alter behavior to make it fit with other personal or social goals. For destructive behavior, this process may mean entering a drug rehabilitation program for heroin addiction or going to jail for theft. For changing behavior to fit with other goals, the military resocializes recruits to act according to rigid group-oriented rules necessary for war and other emergency situations.

Gender role resocialization may occur when a woman enters a culture that offers severely restricted roles for women. When Betty Mahmoody (1991) moved with her husband to Iran, she had to learn totally new patterns of behavior expected of Iranian women. Completely veiled when outside the home and restricted by extended family inside as well, she was effectively shut off from her old friends and prevented from establishing new ones other than through family links. Social disapproval and legal sanctions literally made her a prisoner in her new culture. Only after a dangerous journey was she able to escape from what she experienced as an intolerable life. Resocialization into her new culture was unsuccessful.

In most cases of resocialization, people are stripped of their old identity so that it can be rebuilt according to other standards. Much resocialization takes place in what Erving Goffman (1961a) termed **total institutions.** These are places of residence and work that are "total" because they exert complete control over the people they contain. Life is enclosed and supervised, and residents, or inmates, learn that it is easier to adjust than to rebel against the restrictive round of life. People may enter total institutions for voluntary resocialization, as in a religious community or in the military in countries without a draft. They may also voluntarily enter a mental hospital when they judge themselves as needing psychiatric therapy because they cannot cope with daily life.

However, although people may enter total institutions voluntarily, numerous barriers exist to keep them confined in these places until administrators grant approval to leave. A request for discharge from a mental hospital, the army, or even a convent is not automatically granted. A mental hospital may house people who are seen as a threat to themselves or others but who have not committed any crime. Regardless of whether they chose to enter the mental hospital, until they display "acceptable" behavior they may not be released. In some instances, people become stripped of their freedom because others judge them to be mentally ill. Their freedom rests on being "cured" of mental illness (Szasz, 1994b). Even a college campus has some qualities of a total institution, such as restricting activities on campus that could occur off campus or by putting up hurdles making it difficult to transfer credits or change schools altogether. Total institutions are by definition restrictive and people simply do not enter or leave them arbitrarily.

Although there are many unresolved questions related to voluntary resocialization, there is not a great deal of public concern about them. As you would expect, this is certainly not true for issues related to involuntary resocialization due to criminal behavior. Prisons are total institutions where retribution rather than rehabilitation is the norm. As discussed in Chapter 9, criminals are not only punished, but incarceration keeps them from committing more crimes, at least outside of the prison. High rates of *recidivism*—returning to prison—imply that total institutions may not radically change behavior and that resocialization has failed. The public generally supports the punishment orientation, so longer sentences and increased security become hallmarks of criminal justice in the United States (Cullen & Gilbert, 1982).

The Insanity Defense

Controversy over the "insanity defense" is a good example of issues surrounding failed socialization—such as criminal behavior (voluntary choices) and mental illness (involuntary choices). In the United States, insanity can be used as a defense against criminal prosecution because the person was not judged to be in his or her right mind at the time the crime was committed. If successfully employed, the verdict is that the person is "not guilty by reason of insanity." Although insanity is a legal term and not a psychiatric one, psychiatrists are routinely called as expert witnesses to determine the state of the mind of the accused. The insanity defense skyrocketed in public awareness in 1982 after John Hinckley attempted to assassinate Ronald Reagan. Hinckley was found not guilty by reason of insanity—he was diagnosed with schizophrenia—and sent to a mental hospital rather than a prison. The verdict and sentencing caused such public outrage that many states either modified or abolished the insanity defense altogether.

The public may believe that John Hinckley "got away with attempted murder." But contrary to public belief, the insanity defense is rarely used (less than 1 percent of all cases use it) and when it is used it is rarely successful. When it is "successful," a person can be confined to a mental institution for the criminally insane or in a psychiatric ward of a prison indefinitely—for as long as it takes until the person is considered "cured." The insanity defense can backfire. Not only is it more likely to be used by nonviolent offenders, but people are often locked up in hospitals longer than if convicted and they served their sentence (Walker, 1985).

Sociologists offer two important messages about the insanity defense. First, in the Hinckley case, he may or may not have realized he was doing something wrong at the time he shot the President. If Hinckley represented failed socialization, he is either not capable of understanding his actions, or capable of understanding but still willing to carry out the act, regardless of consequences. Whether as a criminal, a mentally ill person, or both, socialization was a still a failure. Second, what are the appropriate interventions for failed socialization? Should rehabilitation occur in a mental hospital or a prison? Should the person be released if "cured" of the illness, released because a sentence was served, or not released at all? How does the state know if resocialization (rehabilitation?) is indeed successful? Should punishment and retribution rather than rehabilitation be the goal for all criminals, regardless of their level of mental competency? In dealing with such questions, some states have established a "guilty but insane" plea where the defendant serves the first part of the sentence in a hospital and then is sent to a prison after being "cured."

Resocialization of juvenile offenders works best when they upgrade their education and receive job training.

The important point is that when socialization fails for reasons of criminal behavior, the state has a responsibility to intervene. Total institutions such as prisons and mental hospitals are set up for these interventions. The public is in favor of stiffer sentences for repeat offenders who commit violent crimes and of separating those who commit violent crimes, including the criminally insane, from other offenders (Roberts, 1996). But there is a great deal of disagreement over what constitutes punishment and what constitutes rehabilitation, especially when mental illness is involved. Punishment and rehabilitation exist side by side in total institutions. Symbolic interactionists argue that total institutions such as prisons and mental hospitals must resocialize patients and inmates into a radically altered view of themselves that extends after release. Whether such resocialization can be successful in reducing crime will be addressed in Chapter 9.

SUMMARY

1. Socialization is the lifelong process through which individuals acquire culture, develop their sense of self, and become functioning members of society.

2. Sociobiologists believe that human behavior is determined genetically, according to evolutionary principles. There is little evidence for this view.

3. Symbolic interactionists stress the importance of role-playing and the looking-glass self—imagining what others think of us—in developing social identity.

4. According to Freud, socialization is a multistage process in which the child struggles to reconcile basic biological drives with conflicting social norms and values.

5. Social learning theorists hold that children are socialized both directly, through rewards and punishments for specific behaviors and indirectly, through observation and imitation of others.

6. Jean Piaget proposed a multistage theory of cognitive development that became the foundation for several studies of moral development. Best known are Lawrence Kohlberg's work, which suggested that boys reach a higher stage of moral development than girls, and Carol Gilligan's critique, which indicated that girls use different but equally valid norms in their moral reasoning.

7. The life course perspective on socialization is an interdisciplinary approach that stresses adult as well as child development. Life course theorists are particularly interested in the attitudes and behaviors of birth cohorts, those who age together and experience events in history as a generation.

8. Erik Erikson proposed that human development occurs through eight life stages, each marked by special challenges and a central developmental crisis that must be resolved.

9. Compared with early and middle adulthood, later adulthood and old age are a time of role loss, although new roles may be substituted.

10. Elisabeth Kübler-Ross identified five stages people go through in coming to terms with death. Research suggests, however, that the dying do not necessarily progress through those stages in a set sequence.

11. Though life activities and gender role norms are associated with specific ages, life course theories do not apply to all cultures. In the United States, social change has altered the age at which many adults marry, have children, and enter and leave the labor force.

12. The family is the primary agent of socialization especially in the first years of life, nurturing self-esteem, providing language learning and cognitive development, and conferring cultural capital on the child, such as class, race, ethnicity, and religion.

13. Schools become influential socialization agents, teaching social skills and communicating core cultural values and gender role expectations to students. Gender-segregated peer groups formed at school are another means of socialization during these years.

14. The mass media, especially television, may socialize young viewers negatively through their portrayal of violence and gender stereotyped role models.

15. American parents often fear that their children will be unduly harmed by peer groups. However, peer values rarely replace parental values.

16. Resocialization, a process designed to eliminate destructive behaviors or alter behavior to fit new goals, is often pursued in total institutions such as mental hospitals and prisons that exert control over people's lives. People judged to be criminally insane can be confined longer than if given a prison sentence.

KEY TERMS

agents of socialization   129
anticipatory socialization   115
birth cohort   122
ego   115
gender identity   117
gender schema theory   120
gender socialization   111
generalized other   114
I   114

id   115
life course   122
looking-glass self   113
me   114
peer groups   131
personality   113
primary socialization   115
resocialization   134

rites of passage   125
role-taking   114
schema   118
self   113
significant others   114
sociobiology   112
superego   115
total institutions   134

CRITICAL THINKING QUESTIONS

1. Explain the following statement: Socialization requires group experience and social isolates fail to develop a normal personality.
2. Demonstrate how the life course is a continuous process of development, socialization, and adaptation.
3. Identify the similarities and differences in the sociological and psychological approaches to socialization.
4. Considering the different agents of socialization and how they are interdependent, which *one* agent do you believe is the most important for both the individual and society?
5. Based on your understanding of childhood socialization, do you think that the fear of peers by parents is justified? Do you think your own childhood and adolescent peer groups had more positive or negative effects on your current stage of life?

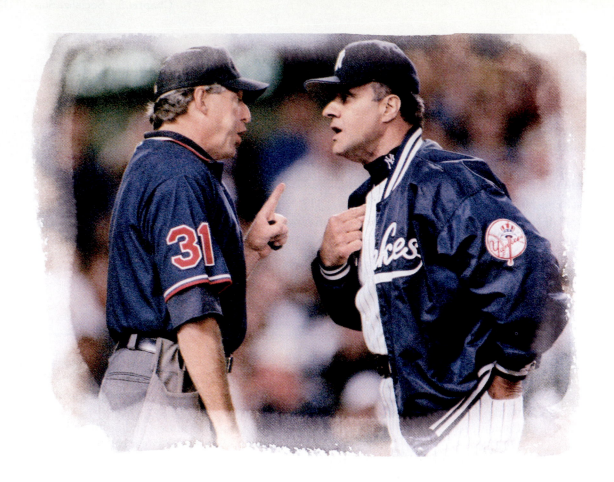

 # SOCIAL INTERACTION: CONSTRUCTING THE MEANING OF EVERYDAY LIFE

OUTLINE

It Really Isn't Work at All

On a weekend afternoon Tom Sawyer has been given the job of painting a very long fence when his friend Ben comes by and begins to taunt him:

"Say—I'm going in a-swimming, I am. Don't you wish you could? . . . But of course you'd druther work."

Tom contemplates the boy a bit, and says: "What do you call work?"

Ben replies, "Why, ain't that work?"

"Well maybe it is, and maybe it ain't. All I know is, it suits Tom Sawyer. . . . Does a boy get a chance to whitewash a fence every day?"

That put the thing in a new light. Tom sweeps his brush daintily back and forth. . . adding a touch here and there… Ben watching every move and getting more and more interested. . . . Presently he says "Say, Tom, let me whitewash a little." (Adapted from Mark Twain (1875/1946), *The Adventures of Tom Sawyer*)

Pygmalion: Transforming Eliza Doolittle

You see, really and truly, . . . the difference between a lady and a flower girl is not how she behaves but how she's treated. I shall always be a flower girl to Professor Higgins, because he treats me as a flower girl . . . but I know I can be a lady to you because you treat me as a lady.

Eliza Doolittle speaks these words in the play *Pygmalion*, by George Bernard Shaw. Eliza tells us that the expectations about how she is perceived make a difference in how she is treated.

She also tells us that she changes her own expectations about herself when she is treated differently. A "Pygmalion effect" occurs—she is transformed from a flower girl into a lady.

And We are Not Seen: Homelessness in America

Mass homelessness is now an accepted feature of American life. Where once there was a reservoir of compassion and concern about meeting the needs of homeless people, there now seems to be only frustration and hostility. Not that there is a failure of compassion or even moral failure, but a failure of "seeing" homelessness clearly. The failure of seeing is in part due to shifting constructions about homelessness in the media—from denial, to horror, to empathy, to futility, and today, to backlash. The homeless are often lumped together as panhandlers, mentally disordered, and substance abusers. When people are constructed as undeserving of help, help is rarely, or begrudgingly, given. (Adapted from Blasi, 1994)

These vignettes suggest that when people interact, either directly or through institutions such as the media, they bring their own definitions about what is considered appropriate behavior. They also suggest that not only can definitions change during the course of the interaction but that the definitions themselves influence the outcome of the interaction. Tom Sawyer convinced Ben that work was pleasure. Eliza Doolittle was gradually transformed from a flower girl into a lady when people treated her like a lady. And as portrayed in media, the homeless have become less deserving over time. In each instance, reality was constructed by the participants in the interaction. This chapter will explain how people construct social reality whenever interaction occurs. It will also show that these constructions are based not just on what we say and do, but also on *how* we say it, that is, through nonverbal communication. Finally, we will show that if social reality is constructed, it can also be reconstructed, as in the case of sexual harassment. Our discussion will be guided by symbolic interactionism, the most widely used theoretical perspective in sociology for explaining social interaction.

SOCIAL INTERACTION

As we saw in Chapter 5, the process of socialization explains how individual and group life are linked. We now explore these linkages further by describing how sociologists view social interaction in everyday life. **Social interaction** refers to how people behave toward one another when they meet. Social interaction occurs directly, such as in face-to-face encounters and indirectly, such as by telephone or e-mail. Another indirect way is by observing the interactions of others, such as watching television or viewing the actions of people in various social settings. All social interaction, by whatever means, helps us gain a better understanding of what is considered appropriate social behavior. Understanding social interaction is a goal of both sociology and psychology, but the goal is approached differently by each discipline.

Social Psychology

When sociologists examine social interaction from a *microlevel* perspective, they concentrate on the details of interaction that usually occurs between two people or in other small groups.

The analysis of social interaction is an area, like socialization, where sociology and psychology intersect. The field of social psychology reflects that intersection. Social psychology from the *psychological* view is interested in how the thoughts, feelings, and behaviors of individuals are influenced by other people. The individual is the focus of analysis. Social psychology from the *sociological* view is more interested in ongoing social interaction in social situations—where individuals are also changing because of the interaction.

For a psychologist, the social interaction between Tom Sawyer and Ben could be a study in persuasion, how Ben's behavior is changed to fit Tom's needs. For a sociologist, the same social interaction is a study in negotiating social reality. Tom and Ben came up with a definition that painting a fence isn't really work at all, but a pleasurable experience. Ben did not simply respond to Tom. The social reality that emerged was through altering definitions of "work" and "pleasure" and then agreeing on the new definitions. Reality became socially constructed. *Sociological psychology* offers a distinctly sociological understanding of social interaction, where participants are active and dynamic rather than actors who merely respond to others in the environment (Cahill, 1995a; Charon, 1995).

The Social Construction of Reality

Social interaction is a process governed by norms that are largely determined by our culture. But because people are not robots, they may act out the norms in various ways. Although cultural norms may tell us how we are *supposed* to behave we have many choices from a range of appropriate behavior. In addition, what is appropriate behavior at one point in time may not be appropriate at another point. Cultural norms are modified whenever social interaction occurs because, as the vignettes suggest, we also bring our own definitions about appropriate behavior to the interaction. These definitions shape the way we see and experience the world. Symbolic interactionists refer to this shaping process as the **social construction of reality**—our perception of reality is shaped by the subjective meanings we bring to any experience or social interaction.

A simple illustration of the social construction of reality is to think about how two students in the same class may view the actions of a professor quite differently depending on the grade each student received on the last exam. The student who received an "A" on the test sees the professor's smile to him or her as an affirmation of a good grade. The student who received a "D" may interpret the smile as a sign of pity or disgrace. The professor's "real" intentions remain unknown, but the A student smiles back and the D student turns away in apparent embarrassment. In turn, the professor's interpretation of the behavior of the A student as positive and the D student as negative may influence how the professor will later interact with both of them. Every time social interaction occurs, people creatively construct their own understanding of it—whether "real" or not—and behave accordingly.

Since the social construction of reality is considered a part of all social interaction, it is a key feature of the symbolic interactionist perspective and cannot be separated from the perspective as a whole. The principle that society is socially constructed will be applied throughout the chapter.

Symbolic Interactionism

Symbolic interactionism is at the heart of the sociological view of social interaction. With its focus on people's behavior, particularly in face-to-face social settings, symbolic interactionists explain social interaction as a dynamic process. People continually modify their behavior as a result of the interaction itself. Herbert Blumer (1900–1987), who originated the term symbolic interactionism, emphasized that people do not respond directly to the world around them, but to the meaning they bring to it—such as the encounters between Tom Sawyer and Ben and the students and professor. For Blumer and symbolic interactionists, society, its institutions, and its social structure exist—that is, social reality is bestowed—only through human interaction (Blumer, 1969).

Practicing Sociology

Pygmalion in the Classroom

Sociologists are keenly aware that since things are not always as they seem to be, it is often difficult for us to paint an accurate portrait of even the small portion of the social world we occupy. The portraits that we do paint, however, are largely based on expectations we have about other people's behavior. Like Eliza Doolittle's transformation from flower girl to lady, these expectations can alter the way we treat one another. A self-fulfilling prophecy can result—a positive one in Eliza's case. Although Eliza Doolittle is a fictional character, by understanding how her transformation occurred, the positive results accrued to Eliza might be reproduced in real-world settings. As documented in the following experiment, a typical elementary school classroom offers one such setting to study self-fulfilling prophecies.

During the spring semester all the children of grades one through six at Oak School in San Francisco were administered a test that was supposed to predict those students who were on the verge of an intellectual growth spurt. In each of the eighteen classrooms, 20 percent of the children were designated academic "spurters," and their names were given to their new teachers the following fall. At least this is what the teachers were told. The test was really a standardized IQ test and a table of random numbers—not any kind of test

score or student grades was used to designate the "spurters." Four months after the teachers had the names of the "special" children, students took the same form of the test again; a third test occurred another four months later.

The results were amazing. Almost half the children in the experimental group, the spurters, gained 20 or more IQ points, compared to about 20 percent in the control group making such gains (all the other children at the school). The greatest gains of spurters were made by first and second graders. Compared to the other children, teachers described the spurters as having a better chance for success in the future and as being significantly more curious and happy. Spurters were described as better adjusted, affectionate, and with lower needs for social approval. The results were clear. In both IQ test scores and social behavior, children from whom intellectual growth was expected became more intellectually alive. Teachers who defined children as bright acted toward them on the basis of that definition. Their expectations clearly had a powerful influence on student performance in this experiment, and more important, the experiment has been replicated many times in many different schools. Positive outcomes from guided self-fulfilling prophecies are both common *and* expected.

Sociologists who study social interaction are often called upon to provide guidelines for encouraging positive classroom outcomes. Their task is to provide teachers tools for discovering the hidden dimensions of social interaction that profoundly impact their students. As this chapter suggests, symbolic interactionism in particular provides many such tools, including understanding the dynamics of impression management and nonverbal communication. Teachers can also use ethnomethodology to discover what they and their students take for granted in classroom interaction. Some teachers may have lower expectations for disadvantaged or minority students so they demand less and do not push them to take challenging classes. Students in turn demand less of themselves.

The Pygmalion effect occurs all the time in classrooms, sometimes to the detriment rather than the benefit of students. When sociological insight is applied to social interaction in schools, teachers may paint a more accurate portrait of the classroom world they and their students inhabit.

1. As a sociological consultant, you have been hired by a suburban school district to help determine why fifth graders are performing lower than the state average in math and reading. As a specialist in symbolic interactionism, what suggestions would you offer to these fifth grade teachers to increase math and reading proficiency?
2. Provide an example of a guided self-fulfilling prophecy that can be used to enhance the self esteem of people who must move from welfare to meaningful work roles. Justify your approach by applying principles based on the social construction of reality.

Sources: Rosenthal & Jacobson, 1968; Rosenthal, 1995; Hacker, 2000.

Teacher Expectations Can Affect Student Performance   Holding a positive or negative expectation about a student can actually bring about student behavior consistent with the expectation.

According to the dramaturgical approach, throughout the world people perform expected roles on different stages, such as an elder teaching a child about preparing meat after a hunting expedition. In turn this elder's role-playing will shift to another stage when he offers the meat for his wife to cook.

Since people interact according to how they interpret situations, if the interpretation changes, so does the social reality. This principle accounts for complex social interaction. It also accounts for social cohesion. Symbolic interactionists are concerned with explaining how human interpretation not only makes social life possible, but how social life is organized and constructed, and how it changes over time.

To illustrate these important principles of symbolic interactionism, let's take the notion of the social construction of reality a step further. We have seen that people interact according to how they perceive a situation. Their perception is based on how they understand the social encounter and the meanings they bring to it. But there is an additional step in the process: how they *think* other people who are part of the interaction also understand the encounter. Each person's *definition of the situation* (Chapter 1) influences others' definitions, so the negotiation of social reality is ongoing. The advice a columnist gave to a 17-year-old gay male who asked if he should "come out" (admit his homosexuality) reflects how the definition of the situation can be used to negotiate and change social reality:

If you decide to come out, I'd suggest going first to the family member who you believe loves you the most—usually Mom. Tell her the news with warmth and good spirit. That is, present yourself in a light in which you want others to see you. Ask her to allow you to tell her the news in the best way—then go to the person you believe loves you the second most, and so on. (Savant, 1999:8)

The columnist's advice is for him to be positive so that in turn his mother will be positive. Although we do not know what her reaction will be, it is expected that the negotiation process will result in a favorable perception of his coming out.

Although the social construction of reality is a negotiated process that changes as it proceeds, symbolic interactionists assert that it is a rational one. People choose their behavior very carefully. We saw in Chapter 5 that socialization is necessary for a person to develop a sense of *self*, the identity that distinguishes each individual from all other individuals. Social interaction allows us to learn about ourselves and make the social comparisons that are necessary to acquire a self-concept. A person will invest a great deal of effort to protect his or her self-concept and maximize self-esteem.

Making Social Life Possible: Links to Gender, Race, and Class.   Starting with the everyday interactions between people in small groups, symbolic interactionists tell us that society as a whole is constructed through the subjective meanings brought to all social interactions. They assert that we are not born with the social statuses of gender, race, social class, or sexual orientation, for example, but they are given meaning only through social interaction. If you have the ability to define reality a certain way and then convince everyone else that your definition is the best or proper one, then it reflects your power or the power of a group to which you belong. The social construction of reality assumes that the power men have over women, whites have over people of color, and the middle class has over the lower class is reflected in the ability of those with power to control and shape the definitions of reality.

This point is well illustrated in the vignette about homeless people. Society is defining them as "less deserving" than in the past. They have neither the resources nor the power to challenge the definitions. Patterns of gender and ethnicity among the homeless further reinforce this lack of power. Over 80 percent of the homeless are men, but in many cites, over half are African American men, and in this half, some form of disability is usually evident. When women are counted among the homeless, they are likely to be younger than homeless men and even more likely to be members of a racial or ethnic minority. Single mothers with children are most likely to be African American. The concentration of African Americans among homeless women parallels their concentration in the ranks of the extremely poor (Baker, 1994). The intersection of key social statuses—young, female, African American, single mother, and most important, extreme poverty and homelessness—is clearly linked to those who have the least amount of power in broader society.

The meaning attached to important statuses, therefore, invades all social interaction. Besides the broader society, people's social statuses make a difference in how we, as individuals, choose to interact with them. We may take into account their gender, race, age, social class, religion, or ethnicity before we act. We may consider how our culture ranks the statuses. Whereas females hold less power than males in almost every culture, in some cultures a woman's wealth may be more important than her gender in the degree of power she has. In those cultures the choice may be to interact with her as a wealthy person rather than as a female who happens to be wealthy. Symbolic interactionists recognize that it is necessary

to account for such elements of social structure (macrolevel perspective) to understand social interaction between a few people (microlevel perspective). Both conflict theorists and symbolic interactionists agree, for example, that without the necessary power behind them, homeless people as a group cannot seriously challenge how they are defined by individuals or by broader society. The key point is that the reality of everyday life at both the macrolevel and microlevel is continually shaped, modified, constructed, and reconstructed.

Everyday life may always be changing, but the changes are not haphazard—there is a structure to them. A fundamental task of symbolic interactionism is to determine the rules that people use when they select their behavior and under what conditions the rules are accepted, modified, or broken. Ethnomethodology has developed as a subfield of symbolic interactionism to help uncover the rules of social interaction.

Ethnomethodology

How do people socially construct their everyday world and give meaning to their experiences and interactions? **Ethnomethodology** seeks to answer this question by understanding social interaction from the person's own frame of reference. An outsider's view of the social interaction is not as valid. Ethnomethodologists also want to discover the hidden rules in social interaction, what is taken for granted. Over time many of our actions become routine. Only when these habitual behaviors are challenged or when expectations are shattered do they resurface in our consciousness. When this happens, we need to regain a sense of control, a rule governed process that ethnomethodology seeks to uncover.

Harold Garfinkel (1967), a pioneer in ethnomethodology, asked his students to break some taken-for-granted rules of communication in social interaction. The following was reported by one student:

My friend and I were talking about a man whose overbearing attitude annoyed us. My friend expressed his feeling:

Him: I'm sick of him.
Me: Would you explain what is wrong with you that you are sick?
Him: Are you kidding me? You know what I mean.
Me: Please explain your ailment.
Him: (With a puzzled look). What's come over you? We never talk like this. (Adapted from Garfinkel, 1997:398)

In asking the friend what he meant by "I'm sick of him," Garfinkel's student challenged the usual definition of the situation, causing uneasiness and bewilderment. In seeking to regain control and figure out what was going on between them, the question by the friend is, "What's come over you?" Ethnomethodology shows that we are often unaware of the rules, or their power, until the rules are violated. If rules break down, new rules need to be negotiated and agreed upon and a new social reality built before communication can be successful.

Life-as-Theater

Another way to understand social interaction is to look at it as a play being acted out on a stage. This **dramaturgical approach** describes Erving Goffman's (1922–1982) view of social interaction. Like other symbolic interactionists, Goffman was searching for the rules that govern social interaction. By considering social life as a staged drama or performance, in which people act out certain roles, Goffman believed that the underlying structure and process of social interaction could be found (Goffman, 1959, 1974). Perhaps Goffman took his lead from Shakespeare: "All the world's a stage and all its men and women merely players."

Symbolic interactionists maintain that there are a number of competing "realities" in our lives, and we are constantly moving from one to the other. Using the life-as-theater metaphor, these transitions are marked by the rising and falling of symbolic curtains. In a "real" theater we are spectators transported to another world with its own meaning and order (Berger & Luckmann, 1966:25). When we return to our "real everyday" world, another set of meaning and order takes over. Just as in the theater, we construct our social realities through role playing. To test these ideas, think about your social status as a college student and the roles you play that confirm that status. The curtain rises when you enter the classroom, and you adjust your behavior to the audience of professor and classmates. The curtain falls as you leave that class and it rises again when you enter another "social reality," such as sports practice, part-time job, or coffee with friends. Roles are added or discarded in a neverending process as you move on and off various social stages.

The dramaturgical approach to social interaction in everyday life is expanded by Goffman through his model of *interaction ritual*—all the "small behaviors" that make up encounters, such as glances, gestures, positionings, and verbal statements. As social actors, we perform such rituals in deference to others and in light of cultural expectations and social norms. Interaction ritual determines what is needed to help make social

order possible. As a result, social interaction is cooperative. A good demonstration of interaction ritual are the two taken-for-granted rules of elevator riding:

1. When you get on a small elevator with one other person you each retreat to different sides of the car. A third person goes to the middle. Additional riders fill up middle space.
2. All elevator occupants must gaze at the floor numbers flashing by.

Modern society increasingly puts us in the company of strangers, and interaction rituals are performed to deal with any resulting discomfort. People find themselves in crowded elevators and subways with strangers, or in locker rooms waiting for others to vacate showers. Parents deal with unmanageable children in the candy aisles of grocery stores. To stare at each other in these situations is considered rude, embarrassing, or even threatening. We practice what Goffman calls *civil inattention*, by a quick glance to acknowledge another's presence and a glance away just as quickly. In this instance, interaction ritual keeps discomfort at a minimum, even when acknowledging the presence of strangers. However, what if a homeless person carrying all his or her possessions in plastic bags stares fixedly at passersby who will not return the eye contact? In this case, the homeless person breaks the ritual, perhaps intentionally, and creates discomfort.

In interaction rituals, there are no "empty" or random gestures—all have subtle meanings and patterns. These everyday rituals and social encounters give meaning to our social lives and allow us to coordinate our behavior with people we do not know (O'Brien & Kollock, 1997:170).

Impression Management

Interaction rituals and the life-as-theater view of social interaction describe what we do. Symbolic interactionists offer explanations of why we do it. They believe that how we behave in social interaction is determined a great deal by efforts to protect our self-esteem. In social encounters we use strategies of **impression management** where we provide information and cues to others to present ourselves in a favorable light. We design a "self" that we present to others to give them what we consider to be the most desired impression of us.

Impression management is practiced routinely in the classroom. Students who usually come to class in tattered jeans and t-shirts will put on "nicer" clothes for a class presentation. In Goffman's theatrical terms this "frontstage" behavior is performed in a manner others expect (Goffman, 1959). By altering clothing and grooming, students send messages that the pre-

Social interaction is in part based on how we perceive social statuses, such as age, gender, race, and social class, as well as nonverbal cues of others. Which person would you ask direction from?

sentation is an important event. "Backstage" behavior refers to actions that are hidden from others, where people can just "be themselves" and where the audience is restricted, such as having pizza with a close friend in the dorm or chatting on the phone while your roommate is watching television. But even during these backstage performances, people are still playing roles. The concern for impression management follows people to whatever stage they are on.

Another side to impression management involves presenting ourselves in ways others *want* us to be—not just what they expect us to be. And not only do we perform for others, we are the audiences for their performances as well (Cahill, 1995b:188). When you are introducing your girlfriend to your parents for the first time, you, your date, and your parents are all practicing impression management. Each person is evaluating the performance of the others. Your date's performance takes center stage—she wants to present herself according to the way both you and your parents want her to be. All the roles we play come together to form a negotiated self. Through processes like impression management, "selves" are crafted and we gain a sense of control in social interaction. The ideal result is that we get what we want, and in doing so our self-esteem is elevated.

Symbolic interactionism's principle of the *definition of the situation* can also be applied to impression management. If you believe the person sitting next to

you in your sociology class is attracted to you, and you believe yourself to be attractive, you may decide to ask him or her out for coffee. Your definition of the situation suggests that this perception will result in a successful date. In contrast, shyness, averting eye contact, or displaying behaviors that suggest you are ill at ease can be interpreted as disinterest at best or hostility at worst. If you believe you lack self-confidence, it in turn increases the risk that the person you are asking out will decline the offer. A **self-fulfilling prophecy** occurs: Your expectations about others lead them to behave in ways that confirm the expectations. In other words, predictions shape actions. In the dating example, you have verified your own sense of inadequacy by your original definition of the situation. The result is that the other person doesn't go out with you. First impressions of others toward you, as well as how you think you are coming across to them, shape all later social interaction. This process is also a likely reason, for example, for the strong correlation between low self-esteem and loneliness in adults (Olmstead et al., 1991).

The concept of a self-fulfilling prophecy can also be applied to specific expectations you have of yourself, such as your expectation that you will fail a difficult exam. Acting on the expectation of failure, you do not study and hence fail the exam. However, symbolic interactionists use the concept basically to explain social interaction rather than individual behavior.

Impression Management in the Global Workplace

When Fred Bailey was offered the position of managing director of his firm's Japan office he saw it as an unbelievable opportunity. It meant moving from Boston to Tokyo, but it was a career opportunity too good to pass up. The benefit package for overseas employees—"expatriates"—was generous. Fred and his family had about three weeks to prepare for the move.

The first week on the job, Fred and his management team met with a team from a Japanese firm, an important prospective client. Not wanting to waste time and to show how well prepared they were, Fred's team immediately laid out the proposal and asked for a reaction from the Japanese. When the Japanese did not respond, Fred summarized the proposal again, thinking that the translation was insufficient. Again there were only vague responses.

Fred decided that the problem was lack of knowledge about the prospective client. The proposal would have to be repackaged. They chose a promising young research associate, Tashiro, to prepare the report, which was needed in a week. "Can you do it?" Fred asked Tashiro. Tashiro hesitated, and then responded, "I am not sure what to say." Fred smiled, walked over to Tashiro, extended his hand and said "Hey, there. Nothing to it. We're just giving you the opportunity you deserve." A week passed with no word from Tashiro on his progress. Tashiro did not complete the report on time. He was chewed out because at the outset he knew he couldn't do it but did not tell his supervisors.

Fred could not understand why Tashiro didn't speak up. No one, including the other Japanese employees, offered any answers, and the incident left everyone suspicious and uncomfortable with one another. Other incidents, big and small, occurred. Fred felt that working with the Japanese was like working with people on another planet. Fred had intended to stay three years in Japan but left within a few months.

Fred Bailey's problem of adjustment is typical of expatriates who enter settings where new behaviors are expected but the expatriate does not understand the culture enough to properly interact with host nationals. Fred applied American business rules to the Japanese firm—getting to the point, making decisions quickly, asking direct questions while expecting immediate answers, and showing confidence in employees. For American business, these are sound management practices. For the Japanese, however, they are counterproductive. Not only are the Japanese much more indirect in questions and answers, they take time to discuss proposals and come up with consensus before a decision is made. A Japanese manager would have found out how much time Tashiro needed for the report, but in a manner that would allow Tashiro to "save face" if it would take longer than expected. Japanese do not single out employees for either special opportunities (Tashiro deserved it) or punishment (Tashiro was chewed out), especially in front of other employees.

Critiquing the Social Construction of Reality

There are several criticisms of symbolic interactionism's approach to social interaction. First, since reality is socially constructed, it assumes that undesirable behavior can be changed by simply altering the construction, our perceptions about others as well as about ourselves. By this reasoning, if a mental patient is believed to be sane, and then is treated as sane, the behaviors that created the diagnosis of mental illness should disappear. Research suggests, however, that trained interviewers can accurately spot people with serious mental disorders, regardless of the labels used to diagnose the disorder (Regier et al., 1993).

Second, symbolic interactionists minimize the impact of broader social structure on behavior choices. Blumer himself must have recognized this very criticism since he called social structure a "straitjacket" that intrudes on behavior (Blumer, 1969). Social statuses such as race, class, and gender are central features of this structure. The very fact that we take into account the social statuses of others in social interactions show that they are key determinants of our behavior. Social institutions are also part of social structure and regulate behavior choices. As pointed out in Chapter 4, society is organized according to long-established social institutions that macrolevel sociologists say are difficult to change. For example, there are newer perceptions about women entering high-powered careers such as law or medicine. Even though women define themselves as talented, confident, and assertive and others accept that definition, women must still contend with law firms and hospitals that still perceive women according to roles of wife or potential wife and mother. And as we will see, the perception of women as sex objects still haunts many work settings, where sexual harassment remains widespread. Workplaces developed around these definitions and have not changed significantly to account for the newer perception that women can be talented physicians and attorneys as well as talented mothers

When people from different cultures come together in the workplace, new rules of impression management need to be learned. Fred Bailey may have wanted to create a favorable impression, but his lack of understanding about Japan and its management style did just the opposite.

Multinational firms are aware of cultural barriers within their organizations. But research shows that these firms are not very successful in coming up with procedures that are satisfactory to employees from all the cultures represented in the firm. For example, Japanese typically want more participative management techniques than American managers. Too much participation makes Americans dissatisfied because decisions are too slow. Too little participation makes the Japanese dissatisfied because decisions are too fast. Hungarians who work in Japanese firms find the emphasis on teamwork problematic; they are even more individualistic than Americans, preferring to make decisions without consulting anyone.

Language barriers, both verbal and nonverbal, are ranked the number one problem among employees in multinational firms. Other issues routinely reported as causing problems are differences in work method, differences in how employees are ranked, and differences in perspectives on time. Employees also frequently report that they cannot convince upper level management that cultural differences are important!

The workplace is rapidly becoming more diverse. Over half of the United States' labor force is made up of women, racial minorities, and immigrants. A similar trend is occurring in countries throughout the world. Training employees in impression management benefits both employees and the firms they represent:

1. Employees on all parts of the globe can learn to respect, understand, and appreciate the values and traditions of each other's cultures.
2. The negative effects of culture shock for expatriates can be overcome or reduced.
3. Feelings of confusion, surprise, or indignation, such as in Fred Bailey's case, when people are trying to adapt to new environments may also be reduced.
4. Communication is helped by creating a healthy work setting for collaboration between expatriates and host nationals.

For firms to be economically successful, employees must be interculturally successful. Culturally appropriate impression management is now recognized as a key to this success.

1. From your knowledge of impression management, what advice would you give to an American employee who has been hired by a Japanese firm, with headquarters in London, to market its products in Germany, Brazil, and Indonesia?
2. What can businesses do to transfer positive social interaction between employees of different cultures in the workplace to outside the workplace? What would be an incentive for business to do this?

Sources: Child & Markoczy, 1993; Lichtenberger & Naulleau, 1993; Giacalone & Beard, 1994; Mendenhall & Wiley, 1994; Lindsey, 1997.

(Hoffnung, 1995). Most mothers do work outside the home, and the workplace may be more mother-friendly than it was in the past. But the family and the economy are established social institutions that are resistant to change. It may take decades before competing perceptions of women's talents outside the home change the practices of social institutions.

Third, behavior is supposed to be selected from a continuous stream of choices. We think before we act in ways that are supposed to protect our sense of self-esteem. However, our actions often reinforce inaccurate perceptions. Impression management inevitably masks who we "truly" are, and role performances ultimately seek to deceive others. And even Goffman (1959) pointed out that people can be so caught up in their own performances that in seeking to deceive others they deceive themselves. They may end up with "negotiated" selves that alienate them from their "true" selves. Rather than promoting self-esteem, these very behaviors can lead to anxiety, uncertainty, and depression.

Overall, interaction as socially constructed can be viewed in two competing ways: one in a cynical way, suggesting that social interaction is inaccurate, deceptive, and self-defeating, the other in a liberating way, suggesting that social interaction celebrates human creativity, choice, and freedom. The choice of one view over another is a philosophical one that sociologists cannot address. However, sociologists can address the usefulness of the social construction of reality in assessing other research on social interaction, including nonverbal communication.

NONVERBAL COMMUNICATION

In Chapter 3 we saw how language is the symbol system that enables even diverse subcultures in one culture to be bound together. Language also creates barriers between cultures. Learning a language means learning a culture. In foreign language classes you probably first concentrated on vocabulary, grammar,

Impression management during a job interview is a key factor in its success. The interviewer will notice not only what is said, but how the candidate acts nonverbally.

and phonology (sound or dialect). These are the key elements of spoken language and provide the necessary tools for formal language learning. However, to truly understand how a culture is reflected in its language, it is also necessary to understand the complexity of the other part of the symbol system—its nonverbal element. What we say is often interpreted according to how we say it. Socialization into your culture and those subcultures of which you are a member assumes you learn how to communicate both verbally and nonverbally.

Nonverbal communication includes the ways people communicate without words—using body movements such as gestures, facial expressions, eye contact, use of personal space, and touching. It also includes use of *paralanguage*, such as length and rate of speaking, tone of voice, loudness, hesitation, and

amount of interruption. If you can communicate appropriately using both verbal and nonverbal elements, you have made a giant leap in learning the culture.

Nonverbal communication offers a good resource for understanding the process of impression management. Too much discrepancy between verbal and nonverbal language can generate mistrust and suspicion. For American couples, when a romantic relationship is fading, nonverbal signals are the first to show the decline, especially by the person who would like to pull back or out of the relationship. There is less touch and more physical distance between the couple, eye contact is averted, posture is more rigid, and speaking is slower, with less fluency (Arliss, 1991; Wood, 1994). Such nonverbal cues eventually become so obvious that the inevitable "What's wrong?" question occurs, most often initiated by the person who wants the relationship to continue. This question allows for verbal communication to begin. It also serves as a face-saving device for the person who wants out of the relationship. You can probably predict the next sentence: "Well, since you brought it up, we need to talk about our relationship."

INTERNET ➤ CONNECTIONS

Sociologist Erving Goffman wrote extensively about the process of *impression management*, including his distinction between "front-stage" and back-stage" behavior. Drawn from his book, *The Presentation of Self in Everyday Life* (1959), a description of the process of impression management in Goffman's own words may be found at: http://wizard.ucr.edu/~bkaplan/soc/lib/goffmpr.html. After you have reviewed this material, give three examples of what Goffman refers to as *faux pas* interactions with others.

Nonverbal Communication as a Polygraph

As mentioned earlier, there is some controversy as to whether role performances are meant to deceive others. Since nonverbal communication may be unintentional, it provides a good test for how well we can manage our impressions and detect the emotions of others. In this way it can be used as a polygraph, or lie detector. For example, enlargement or dilation of eye pupils is a sign of being attracted to someone or something. Once we learn from our culture what is considered attractive, our response is a physiological process that is almost impossible to disguise. People who are romantically attracted to each other have dilated pupils. When women see pictures of babies and infants their pupils dilate; men's pupils get smaller. Even the best poker players cannot conceal a good hand, because their pupils tend to dilate (Kleinke, 1986; Stiff et al., 1989). When an emotion cannot be masked completely, *leakage* occurs and the hidden emotion "drips" out (Goffman, 1961b; 1967).

Expressions of genuine happiness or devastating grief are betrayed by leakage through facial characteristics. A true smile or one intentionally designed to conceal negative emotion is demonstrated by a particular facial pattern (Ekman et al., 1988). Unlike smiling, laughter is more spontaneous; because it reflects emotion more than a rational act, it is difficult to fake. As an indication of leakage, a great deal of evidence shows that lying is revealed nonverbally rather than verbally. And it is detected more easily in people who are the most motivated to get away with their lies (DePaulo et al., 1991)!

Cultural Variations in Nonverbal Communication

Research suggests that there are some emotional expressions, such as fear and joy, that are similar cross-culturally in facial patterns. But because nonverbal communication is largely learned through socialization and results in successful impression management, only an observer who knows the culture very well is able to detect leakage and uncover deception. Among many Asian cultures, including Japan and Thailand, displays of emotions such as broad grins or angry outbursts are considered impolite. It is also rude to show disagreement with another person's behavior in these cultures. Middle Eastern and Latin cultures expect such displays as signs of interpersonal closeness.

In the United States, smiling is associated with friendliness and happiness, but not so in Korea. Korean retailers in the United States are viewed as hostile by non-Korean customers because they do not smile (Dresser, 1994). Smiling is a taken-for-granted cultural norm in most parts of the United States, especially by a shopkeeper hoping to make a sale. Yet there are consequences of breaking nonverbal norms that are more unsettling. People may be considered mentally ill because they do not show emotions—referred to as "flat affect" by psychologists—in situations that call for emotional expression. They violate taken-for-granted cultural rules of nonverbal communication. Since some cultures may view flat affect as the appropriate response in the same situations, other measures may be necessary to diagnose mental illness.

There are other practical purposes for becoming knowledgeable about nonverbal behavior, especially in the context of a culture different from your own. In the United States, a thumb's up sign indicates victory and the circular a-ok sign means affirmation or giving the go-ahead. In much of the Middle East and South Asia these same two signs would be nonverbally translated as extremely insulting, similar to Americans "giving the finger." These gestures could be responsible for provoking a physical fight. The way to hail a taxi in the United States is to wave your hand above your head, usually with your index finger pointing up. In Greece this same gesture is extremely offensive. So if you hail a taxi in Greece the way you hail a taxi in the United States, the cab driver or passersby might decide to punch you out.

Understanding sexual implications in nonverbal behavior is crucial throughout the world. A man's steady gaze at a woman is interpreted as threatening in many cultures. Even a man's glance at a completely veiled woman in North Africa can be seen as sexually provocative and could make him the target of a physical attack by the woman's male companions. Modestly dressed Western women traveling in South Asia and the Middle East report that men routinely pinch, touch, and fondle them as they walk through crowded streets. Media stereotypes in those regions reinforce the belief that any adult female who is unveiled and not in the company of a male relative is either a prostitute or "loose" woman and therefore fair game for curious men. These examples illustrate how people in one culture can misinterpret the nonverbal communication of those from other cultures. Unless there is a way to correct the problem, the *misinterpreted* nonverbal patterns in turn become part of a communication system. All these cases indicate the potential dire consequences of nonverbal misunderstanding.

Gendered Nonverbal Communication

Understanding nonverbal communication is important to sociological analysis because it also serves as an excellent mirror of *social stratification*—that is, how people are ranked according to the various social statuses they hold. Nonverbal behavior can show which groups wield power and which groups are subject to it. In all cultures differences in power between females and males are clearly reflected in nonverbal communication. The following list summarizes some of the important differences in nonverbal communication between the genders in the United States. Although there are nonverbal patterns that are typical to the culture as a whole, a narrower pattern is revealed indicating that a gender subculture exists. There are distinct patterns of behavior between females and males, including communication, which are different

In Korea, people don't usually smile in public, so this man may be viewed as unfriendly in North America, where smiling is more the norm.

from the broader culture. Some of this list is likely to surprise you, because of prevalent but inaccurate gender role stereotypes.

1. Men interrupt women more than women interrupt men, especially to change topics. When women interrupt conversations they do so to indicate interest in the topic, to respond, or to show support (West & Zimmerman, 1983; Stewart et al., 1990).

2. Men dominate women in arguments verbally. Structured conversations where there is an explicit agenda, such as at a meeting or in a work-related brainstorming session, are dominated by men. Women have more control over free discussion, where there is no agenda, such as colleagues having lunch together (Kimble et al., 1981; Kimble & Musgrove, 1988). Domination of conversations and amount and rate of talk are other examples of paralanguage.

3. Women engage in more eye contact than men. In both same-gender and other-gender conversational pairs, women will look at the other person more and retain longer eye contact, a pattern found in children as young as age 2 (Podrouzek & Furrow, 1988; Tannen, 1994).

4. Men are more talkative than women in mixed-gender groups, a consistent research finding on paralanguage. In classroom interaction at all educational levels, male students talk more and for longer periods than female students. In arguments men talk more than female opponents. When expertise is an ingredient, male "experts" talk more than female "experts" (Brooks, 1982; Kimble & Musgrove, 1988).

    Even when men speak two to three times longer than women, the men believe they do not have their fair share of conversation. As the research notes, "If a woman is expected to be quiet, then any woman who opens her mouth can be accused of being talkative" (Spender, 1989:9). Within same-gender groups, women talk for longer periods, enjoy it more, and converse on a wider variety of topics. For women, talk is a preferred social activity (Coates, 1988; Johnson, 1996).

5. In decoding nonverbal cues, not only do women rely more on facial expressions, they also show a greater variety of them, including more open expression of emotions (Halberstadt & Saitta, 1987; Ekman & O'Sullivan, 1991). For example, women smile more than men. As a test of this, take a look at your high school yearbook.

    The notable exception to male lack of emotional expression is anger. It is more acceptable for males and less acceptable for females to display anger. For females, anger may be masked by another emotion, such as crying, which may be more acceptable in some situations. Women are much better than men at successfully decoding nonverbal cues.

6. Men touch women more than women touch men. Since touch can suggest a range of motives, such as affection, dominance, aggression, or sexual interest, the context of the touching is important. Superiors touch subordinates with a hand on the shoulder or a pat on the back. But when passengers poke and pinch flight attendants or when a man fondles a status equal in the office, sexual overtones cannot be easily dismissed. Women tend to view touch as harassing when men use it to establish power, but when women touch men, the men are viewed as passive by both men and women (Forden, 1981; Poire et al., 1992).

    Men rarely touch each other. Even intimate displays of physical contact during sports events have limits. Soccer players were told by the International Soccer Federation in Zurich that their outbursts of jumping on top of one another, kissing, and embracing were excessive and inappropriate. They were reminded to "behave like adults" (cited in Parlee, 1989:14); they were actually being told to behave like males.

7. Men are more protective of their personal space and guard against territorial invasions. Men invade intimate and personal space of women more than the reverse, with the invasion more tolerated by women. The space privilege by males is taken for granted. The next time you are on an airplane or in a theater, note the gender differences in who gets access to the armrests. In walking or standing, women yield their space more readily than men, especially if the approacher is a man. Men retreat when women come as close to them as they do to women and feel provoked if other men come as close to them as they do to women (Arliss, 1991).

Theoretical Perspectives on Nonverbal Communication

The various sociological theories can explain these and other patterns of nonverbal communication. Knowledge about culture and social stratification, especially related to gender and race, is important in these explanations.

Functionalists maintain that nonverbal communication serves to bind people to their culture. Social equilibrium is helped when one language, including its nonverbal elements, is used and accepted by everyone. Functionalists would suggest, therefore, that any gender differences in nonverbal communication are useful for maintenance of this equilibrium. When men and women in the United States communicate nonverbally in ways that reinforce traditional gender roles, there is less possibility for disrupting social patterns.

Conflict theory looks at gendered nonverbal communication patterns quite differently. A conflict perspective argues that men's interruption of women indicates the right of a superior to interrupt a subordinate, in the same way that children (subordinates) are interrupted by parents (their superiors). Space invasion offers another example. Subordinates are expected to give up space to superiors. Eye contact can indicate a similar model of superior-subordinate relations, in which the gazer is subordinate to the gazee. An employee must be anxiously watchful of the employer to determine what comes next in the interaction, such as a secretary waiting for directives from the boss. The boss, on the other hand, does not need to look at the secretary while issuing these directives. Direct eye contact by employer and employee can serve to diminish the employer's superior status. A rigid posture of the subordinate and a relaxed posture of the superior reinforce this. Superiors expect subordinates to be prepared. Because women are more likely than men to be employee-subordinates, they are also more adept in adjusting their nonverbal behavior.

Linking Gender and Race: Symbolic Interactionism.   Symbolic interactionism interprets nonverbal communication patterns by focusing on the setting of the conversation and on impression management. For all races, nonverbal behavior enhances interpersonal intimacy and friendship; this is especially true for women. For both genders, interpersonal intimacy is enhanced in contexts when power and domination are less important. Nonverbal behaviors between people who are equal in status tend to affirm and cement relationships.

In contexts in which statuses are unequal, the situation is different. For example, higher amount of direct eye contact may be interpreted as assertive, with strength rather than meekness being communicated. A female executive in the boardroom regulates her nonverbals to the situation. Status equals look directly at one another. Status unequals do not. Women who want career advancement can adjust their eye contact so that they appear not quite as watchful, but still deferential, to their superior. Subordinates thus practice impression management through type of eye contact.

When different races are present in the nonverbal situation, the gender pattern varies. A common testimonial from African American men is that white women plant broad grins on their faces when passing them, supposedly as a sign of trust. The men see it as fear and deference. As reported by a young African American man in New York City:

> They give you the eye. You can see 'em lookin' right at you. They look at you and turn back this way, and keep on walkin'. Like you don't exist, but they be paranoid as hell. Won't say hello. But some of 'em do. Some of 'em say hi. Some of 'em smile. But they always look scared. . . . (Anderson, 1995:153)

Another example is from an African American male who came across a white woman late one evening on a deserted street in Chicago.

> As I swung onto the avenue behind her, there seemed to be a discreet, uninflammatory distance between us. Not so. She cast back a worried glance. To her, the youngish black man . . . seemed menacingly close. After a few more quick glimpses she picked up her pace and was soon running in earnest. (Staples, 1997:228)

These nonverbal exchanges reflect the idea that race is a more important variable than gender, since the supposedly "higher" social category of white defers to the "lower" social category of black. The exchanges also reinforce the stereotypes associated with the danger of African American men to white women. Finally, but contrary to symbolic interactionism, such nonverbal exchanges correlate with research suggesting that the harmful effects of stereotypes cannot be

INTERNET ← CONNECTIONS

Social interaction often consists of *nonverbal communication*. How much do think you know about this phenomenon? Try testing your knowledge of nonverbal communication by taking the "Quiz" that may be found at: http://www.quia.com/pop/1704.html. Were you surprised by your knowledge or lack thereof? Why or why not?

completely overcome with individual attempts at impression management (Riordan et al., 1994). In both instances the women reinforced stereotypes by their failure to convince the African American men—or themselves—that they were unafraid. To effectively attack such stereotypes, all social institutions at all levels must be part of the effort. The definition of the situation must change. The mass media is one institution where definitions about race and race stereotypes appear to be changing.

≋ LIFE CONNECTIONS: Constructing Social Class on Television

The mass media have an extraordinary influence in social constructions of everyday life. Television, for example, is the main vehicle by which children gain first views of the world outside their immediate families and neighborhoods. Symbolic interactionists point out that media classify people according to various cultural categories, such as those based on race, gender and social class. These categories are constructed so that differences rather than similarities between people are highlighted. By emphasizing differences between various cultural categories, the media send messages about the value or importance of the people contained in them. The media, therefore, construct and then reinforce beliefs about difference as well as beliefs about inequality in society. The intersection of the cultural categories of social class and race as presented in prime time television provides an excellent demonstration of how everyday life in America is socially constructed.

The Race and Class Television Intersection

Until the mid-1960s prime time television was mainly inhabited by white middle-class professional and managerial men of generic northern European back-

ground. They were married to women of similar backgrounds who were depicted as full-time homemakers. When people of color were seen, they usually fell into three categories: African American chauffeurs and maids, Asian cooks and gardeners, and Latino desperados and druglords. However, the next two decades saw a marked shift for people of color in both numbers as well as type of roles, a pattern that continues today. Not only have the number of nonwhite characters jumped to well over 10 percent, a wider range of roles—including more positive portrayals—accompanied the increases. African Americans are the biggest beneficiaries, with a fourteen-fold increase. Asians come in second in both numbers and positive portrayals. Latinos, however, remain a distant third. Some increase in numbers is noted but Latinos are largely supporting players and background figures and are much more likely to be portrayed as poor or criminal compared to all other racial and ethnic groups (Castleman & Podrazik, 1982; Lichter & Amundson, 2000).

With Latinos as the notable exception, a gradual but steady blurring of racial differences is occurring on prime time television. However, as racial differences steadily decrease, a corresponding increase in class differences is occurring. Gone are the struggling working-class African American families of earlier television. The laborers, servants, and junk collectors of the Evans family (*Good Times*) and *Sanford and Son* were replaced by business owners, ministers, teachers, nurses, and attorneys in shows such as (*Julia, The Jeffersons, Martin, and The Cosby Show*. Adventure and science fiction shows gave us leading roles for African American secret agents, detectives, police officers, and military commanders (*I Spy, Mission Impossible, Miami Vice,* and *Deep Space Nine*). For the white working class, a similar pattern occurred, especially for women. Struggling waitresses (*Alice* and *Flo*) and assembly line workers (*Laverne and Shirley*) disappeared and in their place came professionals (*Mary Tyler Moore, Family Ties,* and *Murphy Brown,*).

As people from all races moved up in social class, they left their working class counterparts behind. By the 1990s, television became a virtual haven for the middle class (*Judging Amy, ER, Spin City, Diagnosis Murder,* and *Allie McBeal*). The middle class of prime television are college-educated men and women who lead interesting and productive lives and have disposable income to travel and buy expensive artifacts for their tastefully decorated homes. Many have servants and household helpers. They attend art shows and concerts and sit in box seats at sporting events. Since advertisers may dictate program content to producers, their desires to show a full range of products used by glamorous people are often catered to. The result is television shows built around affluent characters (Butsch, 2000). The psychiatrist brothers of *Frasier* represent the middle-class standard of prime time television. Racial stereotypes are still very apparent, but class stereotypes appear to be on the fast track in overtaking them.

Television's Working Class

Middle-class roles offer a great deal of diversity and less negative portrayals overall. The same cannot be said for television's portrayal of America's working class. In the real world, people in the working class are those who lift, bend, drive, keyboard, clean, load, unload, provide physical care for others, cook, and serve (Ehrenreich, 1998). They are likely to be high school graduates working for a wage rather than a salary and employed in blue-collar positions, retail sales, and lower level white-collar clerical occupations. Although they represent over two-thirds of employed Americans (Chapter 11), the working-class of prime time television is mostly invisible. A study of 262 situation comedies from 1946 to 1990 found working-class household heads at only 11 percent of the total. Blue-collar families were the most underrepresented at 4 percent (Butsch, 2000).

For the small group of working-class families who *are* seen, prime time television's construction of them is presented as a vastly different reality than that of the middle class. Blue-collar workers especially are depicted as needing supervision, and it is up to middle-class professionals to provide it. Working-class characters have few starring roles and are usually depicted as friends of the main characters or as unsavory characters lurking in the background of police precincts and hospital waiting rooms. They are often called as witnesses to crimes, but are easy targets for more logical cross-examining attorneys who find holes and inaccuracies in their stories. The testimony of working-class witnesses is, therefore, untrustworthy.

Unlike racial portraits, working-class portraits have remained virtually the same throughout television's relatively young history. Ralph Cramden, Fred Flintstone, and Archie Bunker have been replaced by Homer Simpson, Al Bundy (*Married With Children*), and Drew Carey's semiliterate friends. The few shows that portray working-class people in lead roles have prototype characters: They are white males depicted as lovable but incompetent, as clowns but losers. They are parochial, redneck, inarticulate, vaguely or openly racist, and have poor or questionable taste in all things. These middle-aged men are "addicted to cigarettes, Budweiser, polyester, and network television" (Ehrenreich, 1998:148). The men are basically insecure but hide it beneath a thin veil of exaggerated masculinity that is easily unwoven by their ever-suffering wives. Wives hold the family together as their husbands bumble their way through get rich schemes

that inevitably fail and keep them trapped in their working-class existence. The significant holdout to this pattern was *Roseanne*, which for a decade was one of most popular shows on television. Roseanne's family deviated from the working-class norm by showing them in diverse roles dealing sensitively with a range of difficult issues all families face. Comedy was not sacrificed for such diverse portrayals.

As you would expect, producers defend portrayals of social class in the name of profit. Advertisers desire to spotlight a wide range of products, so series revolving around working-class families who have less disposable income are not encouraged. A typical television term applied to the working-class or to middle-class people accused of lowering their class standards is "tacky"—meaning they have poor taste. If one is tacky, one also cannot be middle class, and the middle class are supposed to know better. Even if the working class know how *not* to be tacky, they cannot afford to do so. Prospects for television's less stereotypical

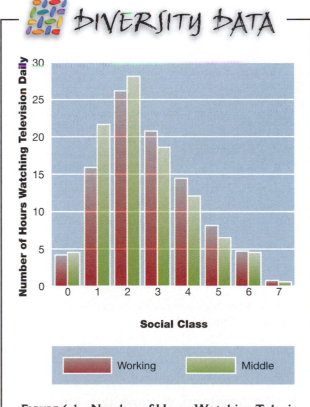

FIGURE 6.1   Number of Hours Watching Television on an Average Day, by Social Class. People in the working class watch significantly more television than those in the middle class. However, the working class is portrayed less and stereotyped more in social interaction. By watching television, are working class people showing agreement with these portrayals?

The Good, the Bad, and the Ugly

"Beauty is only skin deep." "You can't judge a book by its cover." "The worth of people is not in their faces and figures but in their hearts and minds." Parents and teachers use such messages to guide children in humane ways of social interaction (see Figure). But children also receive messages that counter good intentions. Throughout life, media bombard us with messages that beauty *does* count and we *are* judged by our looks and the looks of our friends—and woe to those of us who are not at least "minimally" attractive. Fortunately, there are ways to remedy our physical misfortunes. We can buy cosmetics, wrinkle-removing cream, hair-regrowth salve, diet pills, and exercise equipment. If these are not enough, there is always plastic surgery.

Television portrays attractive and unattractive people quite differently. Unattractive people are used as contrasts to other, more attractive characters. The unattractive are often cast as friends of the beautiful. They are likable, but bumbling and socially inept. They have intellectual flaws and often fail to see that others make fun of them. Examples include

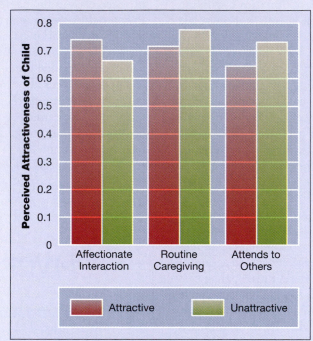

Attractive Children Can Even Affect Their Parents. Mothers of more attractive infants show them more affection and are more playful with them, whereas mothers of less attractive children are more likely to pay greater attention to people other than their infants.
Source: J. H. Langlois, J. M. Ritter, R. J. Casey, & D. B. Sawin, 1995. Infant attractiveness predicts maternal behaviors and attitudes. *Developmental Psychology, 31,* 464–472. Reprinted by permission of American Psychological Association. All rights reserved.

George Costanza and Kramer in *Seinfeld*, Bulldog in *Frasier*, and Norm and Carla in *Cheers*. The unattractive are also cast in bad guy (mostly male) roles. The murderers, drug addicts, and robbers who inhabit the wards of *ER* and *Chicago Hope* and the precincts of *Law and Order* and *NYPD: Blue* can be described as "unattractive." "Ugly" may be a better word.

Research suggests that standards of attractiveness are strongly media based. After years of watching television and movies and viewing thousands of ads in magazines and on billboards, people gradually learn which types of faces and figures are considered to be the most attractive. These features may change over time, but people within a culture agree on what the beauty standards are. Standards of beauty have powerful influences on how we perceive ourselves and others and how we socially interact. Research on the influence of attractiveness in social behavior centers on the "beautiful-is-good" (BIG) stereotype. BIG means that people asso-

images of the working classes remain dim (Blumler & Spicer, 1990; Butsch, 1992).

Class as Socially Constructed

Television perpetuates the myth that America is a classless society—everyone is middle class. The few portrayals that are not so middle class are the exceptions, different from the norm. A small, closed community made up of Hollywood executives and creative personnel make up an elite media subculture who determine television programming. They are responsi-

ble for what we see or do not see on television. Most television messages are openly and explicitly delivered—audiences have little trouble deciding, for instance, whether a television character is positive or negative. But some messages are delivered much more subtly—audiences do not have enough information about characters to make a reasonable judgment about who they are and whether they are to be liked or disliked. Invisibility sends such a subtle message: Those who are not seen are less important than those who are seen. And seldomly seen groups, such as Latinos and working-class people, are much more likely to be portrayed stereotypically and unfavorably.

ciate beauty with an amazing variety of positive characteristics. As reinforced in the media, what is beautiful is also good. The "good" characteristics of the physically attractive compared to the less attractive include the following:

1. Throughout their lives, people who are physically attractive are liked better. They are often held to a different standard of judgment. When attractive people do negative things, their behavior is often excused with "they had a bad day." When unattractive people do the same things, their behavior is viewed in terms of "who they are," symptoms of larger personality problems. "Mimi" of the *Drew Carey Show* is obese and has outrageous hair, clothing, and makeup. She is bizarre, even psychotic, in her behavior. What she does is who she is—and who she is, is ugly.

2. Attractive people are rated higher on kindness, strength, sexual responsiveness, social skills, and intelligence. The strongest ratings come from teens. The popularity of shows such as *Friends* among college students and *Beverly Hills: 90210* among high schoolers—with casts of exceptionally beautiful people— reflect such ratings. Vanity is the major variation to these beliefs. Beautiful people are rated as more conceited, such as Nina, the ex-model in *Just Shoot Me*.

3. Higher ratings sometimes translate to advantages for the physically attractive. They are more popular, get more dates, and are more favorably treated in school and work. In the long-running show *The Wonder Years*, cute Kevin attracted many girls throughout elementary and high school, while Paul, his kind but "nerdy" friend, rarely had a date. *Happy Days* had virile and handsome Fonzi, with women falling all over him, in contrast to physically plain Ralph Malph, who strived, but was usually unsuccessful, in finding women to date.

BIG may be unfair and unkind, but is it accurate? Remember that stereotypes are largely inaccurate but persist because they also contain some grains of truth. BIG is no exception. Emotional stability and dominance are unrelated to attractiveness, as are intelligence and academic ability. Attractiveness has no influence on ratings of concern for others or level of integrity. The physically attractive have better social skills and experience less loneliness than the less attractive, but these differences are small. The grains of truth in BIG include higher popularity and higher work evaluations for the attractive compared to the unattractive. The most important finding about BIG, however, is that the more we get to know others through social interaction, concern for physical attractiveness, both theirs and others, fades. BIG oversimplifies rat-

ings on others when information about them is limited.

Symbolic interactionism can explain why BIG is inaccurate but persistent. When first meeting an attractive person, we have a positive definition of the situation that may have been media inspired. People who are comparably as handsome as Tom Cruise or as beautiful as Gwyneth Paltrow are also seen to possess the heroic (good) behaviors we associate with them. This definition creates favorable circumstances for beautiful to "become" good. The good traits we first associate with beauty are reinforced in our social interaction and may create a self-fulfilling prophecy. Media may be the most powerful socialization factor for the BIG stereotype. Positive portrayals of people with less-than-perfect faces and figures will help break down BIG.

1. Do you think that two equally qualified people, one who is attractive and the other who is not, who apply for the same job, will be on an equal playing field for hiring?

2. Media portrayals of women and racial minorities are becoming more positive. Do media have any responsibility in altering the portrayal of people based on how attractive they are?

Sources: Eagly et al., 1991; Frieze et al., 1991; Feingold, 1992; Larose et al., 1993; Jackson et al., 1995; Langlois & Musselman, 1995.

Symbolic interactionists would argue that the elite media subculture is made up of middle-class people who reproduce class stereotypes in the shows they create, write, and produce. News and talk shows also bolster a middle-class programming bias. The counterparts to the Hollywood media subculture in other mass media are the owners, publishers, and editors of major channels of information and opinion, such as the *New York Times* and *Wall Street Journal* (Blasi, 1994). Both subcultures are effectively shielded from other views, since they only hear the opinions of their own members and look to the very media created by their middle-class predecessors to get these opinions

reinforced. As mentioned earlier, the media construction of homelessness has shifted over time. The homeless are the nameless and faceless murder victims on television, whether in "true" news stories or in fictionalized accounts. Rarely are they called upon by the media to comment on decisions others make that will profoundly impact their lives. The working class and everyone below them in the stratification system are judged through the experiences of middle-class people who socially construct them for the American viewing public.

These constructions are not likely to change unless social reality becomes profitable and society overcomes its fears of those who are different from "us" (Nardi, 2000).

≡ SOCIETY CONNECTIONS:
Reconstructing Social Reality

Symbolic interactionists explain that social issues arise through a process of collective definition. Only when enough people become aware that a condition is harmful and should be remedied can we say that a social problem actually exists. Social problems are socially constructed. Poverty, for example, is a long-standing social condition. When poverty is elevated from a social condition to a social problem, there is a consensus that poverty is not only harmful to some members of society but is also harmful to the society as a whole. Poverty is discovered and rediscovered as a social problem over time as the public shifts its attention from one issue to another. Collective definitions shift with the attention span of the public.

Often an important individual's definition of the situation can help shape the collective definition. Ac-

tivists in the areas of animal rights, food and nutrition, and health and environmental concerns have succeeded in getting their causes into the public consciousness because celebrities, politicians, or other notables have embraced the causes. For example, Americans expect that the First Lady will take on a "cause" during her White House stay. Her high public profile allows for a swift transformation of an individual definition of the situation to a collective one. First ladies thus promote a view that a social condition is serious enough for it to become a social problem. Lady Bird Johnson raised the nation's collective consciousness regarding littering and the environment, Jacqueline Kennedy did the same for mental retardation, as did Barbara Bush for child welfare and Hillary Clinton for women in poverty. Symbolic interactionists point out that even though such conditions may have caused suffering and deprivation before they gained public attention, until they became defined as *social threats* they did not emerge as *social problems*. There is no objective reality; social problems are matters of collective definitions.

AIDS was first identified as an individual illness. It was redefined as a social problem when it was seen as harmful to society as a whole.

Sexual Harassment

We conclude with a topic that illustrates well sociology's approach to social interaction and draws together many of the concepts discussed in this chapter. The process of redefining behavior from acceptable to unacceptable—or more forcefully, to deviant (see Chapter 8)—can be considered in the issue of sexual harassment. Compared to other social problems such as the health consequences of smoking, there is less agreement about what constitutes sexual harassment. This disagreement was made abundantly clear in 1991 during the confirmation hearings for Supreme Court Justice Clarence Thomas, when Professor Anita Hill said that she had been a target of sexual harassment by him when he was her superior. The public furor over the hearings showed that a virtual chasm existed between women's experiences of sexual harassment and

The confirmation hearings for Supreme Court Justice Clarence Thomas, and the testimony of Anita Hill, brought the issue of sexual harassment to the public forefront, helping to redefine it as a social problem.

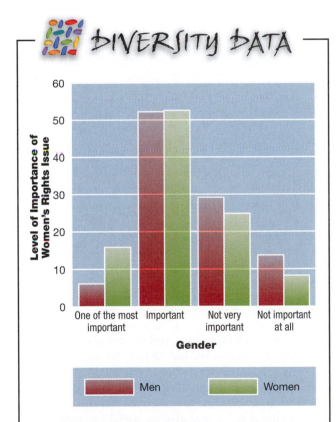

FIGURE 6.2   Percent of Respondents Stating Level of Importance for Women's Rights by Gender. Women are more likely to say that women's rights is one of their most important or important issues. Men are more likely to say the issue is not very important or not important at all to them. The specific women's rights issue of sexual harassment has an even wider difference in attitudes between men and women. On which women's rights issues do you think men and women have the least amount of difference?

how it was understood by the wider society (Sheffield, 1995).

Sexual harassment is a form of sex discrimination that is prohibited under Title VII of the 1964 Civil Rights Act. According to the Equal Opportunity Employment Commission's (EEOC) definition, **sexual harassment** consists of "unwelcome sexual advances, requests for sexual favors, and other verbal or physical conduct of a sexual nature" that are used as a condition of employment or a basis for employment decisions. Such conditions can also create an intimidating, hostile, or offensive work environment.

The Thomas confirmation hearings allowed a firsthand view of the behavior sexual harassment can encompass. A poll conducted immediately after the hearings found that 70 percent of military women, 50 percent of women who work in congressional offices, and 40 percent who work in federal agencies had experienced it (*Parade Magazine*, 1991). Many men who were polled said they were sympathetic but bewildered by the claims made by women.

The EEOC regulations were approved in 1980, but until the Thomas hearings they were routinely ignored by both those being harassed and their employers. Sexual harassment is associated with emotional problems, compromised work productivity, and a deterioration in morale that has serious impact on a person's work and private lives. Fear of retaliation by employers and co-workers that can amount to career suicide is a commonly cited reason for the failure to report it (Gehry et al., 1994; Martin, 1995). But sexual harassment is hard to identify and resolve because of accepted definitions of sexuality that disguise and dismiss sexual domination and exploitation in the workplace.

Sexual harassment in schools is also widespread. Surveys of female high school students report that over one-third had observed or experienced it (Sauerwein, 1996). Examples from these students included: "talking about people with large chests," "pinching butts on the bus," and "half of everything said on the Commons." On college campuses, between 30 and 70 percent of female faculty and female students have experienced it (Paludi & Barickman, 1991; Dziech & Weiner, 1993). Sexually suggestive comments are often heard in college classrooms, including referring to women by parts of their body, portraying them as teases, and showing them as part of a "decoration" on a slide (Sandler, 1987:1150). Sexual harassment of males is infrequent, but numbers are growing. Although fear of reprisal makes women reluctant to report it, males are even less likely to report sexual harassment by females. Norms about masculinity make it difficult for men to admit that they may be intimidated by women (American Association of University Women, 1993).

The Hill-Thomas confrontation resulted in a large increase in sexual harassment lawsuits, prompting companies to adopt more rigorous policies to protect employees (Solomon, 1991). It challenged the taken-for-granted belief that women in school or workplace roles could expect to be sexually harassed. Times have changed, at least legally. In a straightforward and unanimous Supreme Court ruling, Justice Sandra Day O'Connor stated that targets of sexual harassment do not need to show they suffered psychological damage to win their suits. The court upheld the notion that sexual harassment violates workplace equality.

Compared to the public outrage against the tobacco industry, there has been less public enthusiasm for policies designed to deal with sexual harassment. Confusion still exists about what the public identifies as sexual harassment. People do not support sexual harassment, but the definition of a woman first as a sexual being and then as a person is pervasive. Such social definitions are reinforced by *institutional sexism*, the subordination of women that is embedded in social institutions. The women's movement will continue to challenge definitions suggesting that sexual harassment is acceptable.

For successful assaults on sexual harassment and other social problems, definitions of social reality need to be reconstructed at both the individual and societal levels. Women in particular can then gain a sense of *empowerment*, acting as agents to first redefine and then to realize their own power. They become social actors who are in control of their destiny. These new definitions help women gain resources to wage a challenge to institutional sexism. In Chapter 13 we will consider the success of such challenges.

SUMMARY

1. Social interaction is an active, dynamic process in which participants may choose from a range of appropriate behaviors. In doing so, people construct social reality and modify existing cultural norms.

2. The field of social psychology reflects the intersection of psychology and sociology. However, sociologists in this field are interested more in ongoing social interaction than in individual behavior.

3. According to symbolic interactionism, people interact on the basis of their own definitions of a situation and their assumptions about others' definitions.

4. Symbolic interactionists believe that the broader statuses of race, class, and gender also intrude on social interaction but that behavior is still selected based on subjective meanings given to people in those statuses.

5. Ethnomethodology is the study of the taken-for-granted rules that govern social interaction. By uncovering the rules, we better understand how communication occurs and how social reality is constructed.

6. According to Erving Goffman's dramaturgical approach, social interactions are similar to theatrical performances and are culturally and socially prescribed. People play roles conferred on them by their social status.

7. Symbolic interactionists suggest that people try

to manage the impressions they give others, to protect their self-esteem, and to please others.

8. Self-fulfilling prophecies can result when people are led to behave in ways that confirm your expectations about them. Symbolic interactionists believe that predictions about behavior shape behavior.

9. The social construction of reality approach has been criticized for minimizing the importance of social structure, such as institutions, in interaction. The approach may be viewed as one that is inaccurate and deceitful or one that is creative and liberating.

10. Nonverbal communication—gestures, facial expressions, eye contact, touching, tone of voice, speed and volume of speech—is socially constructed and varies between cultures. Nonverbal messages are often more important than verbal ones in social interaction.

11. Studies of Americans reveal important gender differences in the use of nonverbal communication. Functionalists suggest that gender differences in nonverbal communication help to maintain social equilibrium by reinforcing differences in gender roles. But conflict theorists see such differences as evidence of differences in power between men and women.

12. Symbolic interactionists focus on the setting of interaction, impression management, and the definitions people bring to all social interaction.

13. American television portrays people according to race, class, and gender stereotypes. Although racial stereotypes are declining, class stereotypes are not, especially for the working class. Shows about the middle class dominate television.

14. According to symbolic interactionists, social problems like poverty, child abuse, and environmental degradation are socially constructed. Only when they are defined as social threats by large numbers of people do they become problems.

15. Sexual harassment has been redefined as a social problem, but there is disagreement about what it constitutes. The Supreme Court has ruled that sexual harassment violates workplace equality. Definitions that sexual harassment is acceptable have been challenged by the women's movement.

KEY TERMS

dramaturgical approach   144
ethnomethodology   143
impression management   144

nonverbal communication   148
self-fulfilling prophecy   145
sexual harassment   157

social construction
   of reality   140
social interaction   140

CRITICAL THINKING QUESTIONS

1. From a symbolic interactionist view, explain how social interaction is characterized by cooperation. Bring in the definition of the situation and impression management in your answer.

2. Demonstrate how social interaction forms our identities as individuals and also creates society.

3. Children voluntarily segregate themselves by gender, a pattern that increases as children get older. How is this fact explained by a social psychologist who adopts a psychological perspective and by a social psychologist who adopts a sociological perspective?

4. Describe a college classroom according to the dramaturgical approach. Provide examples of role playing, frontstage and backstage behavior, and impression management.

5. From a symbolic interactionist perspective, what suggestions would you offer to make American television less stereotyped in terms of race, class, and gender, but still entertaining and provocative?

 SEXUALITY

OUTLINE

What Sexual Revolution?

Baby boomers supposedly started the sexual revolution to give in to their appetites for sex, drugs, and rock and roll—especially sex. Compared to world of the pre-1960s, men and women, married and single, younger and older, have more sex, more sex partners, more sexual variety, and more sexual satisfaction. But does this mean there has been a sexual revolution? Humorist Garrison Keillor puts it this way:

> Despite what you have read lately, there is an incredible amount of normality going on in America these days. America is not so obsessed with sex. To the contrary, we wear ourselves out with work, we are surrounded with distraction and all manner of entertainment. Considering what the American couple is up against, it's astounding to think that maybe once a week or month or on holidays or whenever the coast is clear they actually have sex. It's worth growing up and becoming middle-aged to be able to enjoy it utterly.

Sex makes people happy but it is doubtful if they have been revolutionized by it. (Adapted from Keillor, 1994; Grant, 1993; McClaren, 1999)

What Is Sexually Attractive?

Cultural differences abound when considering what is sexually attractive and erotic. A twelfth-century Chinese emperor was said to have been erotically aroused by tiny feet in women, and so the practice of footbinding ensued. Thus, for centuries Chinese men have been socialized to believe that tiny feet are sexually attractive and Chinese women have undergone this painful and crippling procedure. Although footbinding has been banned only recently, tiny feet are still seen as erotic by Chinese men. For the Abkhasians of Russia, the female armpit is just as arousing, and viewing it is forbidden except for a women's husband (Kammeyer et al., 1990). Kissing is the norm in the United States, but unknown in some cultures. It has only recently been practiced in Japan due mainly to Western influence. As a form of sexual foreplay, kissing occurs less often than genital manipulation in many cultures. (Frayser, 1985; Dworkin, 1989; Kammeyer et al., 1990)

When people talk about sexuality and the sex act itself, they often accept the idea that sex and the pleasure it brings come "naturally"—that it is completely driven by biological makeup and physiological urges. As the vignettes demonstrate, however, sexuality is not as "natural" as people believe. **Sexuality** is a type of social interaction where we perceive, experience, and express ourselves as sexual beings. As the vignettes suggest, it is through culture where we are taught how to experience sexual pleasure, who is sexually attractive, and how sexual intercourse should be conducted. We also need to have enough time for sex and cultural constraints may keep us from it. Therefore, although sexual intimacy is intensely private, our sexual lives are encroached upon by society in part because sexual expression is organized and governed by social rules and cultural stereotypes.

In this chapter we expose common beliefs about human sexuality to the lens of sociology. Sociological data and explanations for the data will allow us to accept or thoughtfully reject preconceived notions about sexuality. Such data are most often based on the sexual interaction and intimate activities of couples, so a microlevel perspective is very useful in explaining sexuality. Symbolic interactionism is by far the most

Global Connections

Female Genital Mutilation

It looked as though thieves broke into my room and kidnapped me from my bed. My thighs were pulled wide apart, gripped by steel fingers. A knife dropped between my thighs and a piece of flesh was cut off from my body. I screamed with pain despite the tight hand held over my mouth and saw a pool of blood around my hips. I wept and called to my mother for help. But the worst shock was when I saw her at my side surrounded by strangers, talking to them and smiling to them, as though she had not participated in slaughtering her daughter just a few moments ago. They carried me to my bed. They caught hold of my sister sleeping next to me, who was two years younger.

A 6-year-old Egyptian girl has just been "circumcised." It was about to happen to her 4-year-old sister as well.

Do people have a right to sexual pleasure? Westerners believe that not only is sexual pleasure a right, but that both men and women are entitled to it

with a consenting partner they freely choose. In many parts of the world, however, sexual pleasure—if seen as a right at all—is reserved for men. For millions of the world's women, sexual pleasure is effectively eliminated by the procedure now commonly referred to as "female genital mutilation" (FGM). FGM is justified in many cultures by the belief that women are more promiscuous and sexual than men. A girl's virginity must be protected. The "protection" takes two forms. One is by purdah—secluding women in their homes or veiling them when they venture outside. The second is by FGM—a variety of genital operations designed to reduce or eliminate a woman's sexual pleasure and ensure her virginity. If virginity is safeguarded, then she is marriageable. Otherwise, she can be condemned and live the life of an outcast. Sometimes she is murdered.

FGM is routinely performed without anesthetic and in unsanitary conditions. Referred to incorrectly as female circumcision, FGM is not at all equivalent to the far less radical procedure of

male circumcision. FGM may range from a partial clitoridectomy to full removal of the clitoris, a woman's most erotically sensitive organ. In its more extreme form, FGM removes the clitoris and then the vagina is sewn almost completely shut, leaving an opening just large enough to release urine and menstrual blood. The vagina is cut open again on the woman's wedding night. FGM is believed to make childbirth easier and enhance male sexual pleasure. Whether men actually experience greater sexual pleasure is debatable, but many women die in childbirth as a direct result of botched FGM when they were younger.

FGM is practiced in parts of the Middle East, throughout North Africa, and in some sub-Saharan regions. The total number of living females who have undergone FGM range from 80 to 100 million, including 4 or 5 million children as young as age 4. It is practiced by Muslims and Christians, by the wealthy and the poor, and in rural and urban areas. FGM's past is untraceable. It pre-dates Islam, although some Is-

important microlevel theoretical perspective in this explanation and will guide much of this chapter's discussion of the topic.

SEXUALITY IN A DIVERSE WORLD

Research reveals remarkable variability in human sexuality. As emphasized by symbolic interactionists, what one culture views as erotic or sexually stimulating might be disdained or even forbidden in another culture. For example, human females are born with the capacity to experience the sexual pleasure that comes with orgasm. However, research reviewing sexuality in 186 cultures in the developing world concludes that female sexual pleasure is correlated more with the culture's beliefs about the purposes of sexual intercourse and whether sexual pleasure should even be experienced by women (Reiss, 1986). The So peo-

ple of Uganda believe that only males experience orgasm (the climax of sexual arousal). Genital touching is forbidden. These So women do not enjoy sex, but they tolerate it in order to conceive. On the other hand, among the Mangaian people of Polynesia, children are socialized about giving and receiving the pleasures of sexual intimacy. Girls in particular are sexually active early in life and encouraged to have intercourse with a number of boys until they find the best match for a spouse who gives the most sexual enjoyment. Unlike So women, who believe female orgasm is impossible, Mangaian women are thought to have triple the number of orgasms as Mangaian men (Allgeier & Allgeier, 2000).

Throughout the developing world, particularly in North and Sub-Saharan Africa and the Middle East, heavier people are considered the most attractive. In the Tonga Islands of the South Pacific, the most attractive men are built like football linebackers and the

Waris Dirie, from Somalia, was recently named special ambassador on female genital mutilation by the U.N. Population Fund. Dirie, currently a model for Revlon, underwent the surgical removal of her clitoris when she was 4 years old in Somalia. Until she left home years later, she said, she did not even know that there existed places in the world where female genital mutilation did not occur.

lamic cultures justify it today on religious grounds. As brutal as the practice is, FGM continues because it forms the core cultural identity of many traditional people. Like the mother of the Egyptian girl, women who themselves were forced to undergo the painful procedure are often its strongest advocates.

Three United Nations Conferences on Women took up the FGM issue. In 1980 African delegates argued that FGM was essential to guarantee a girl's marriageability. Delegates from Western culture, appalled by FGM, thought it should be eliminated and were accused of interfering with hallowed cultural traditions. Dialogue remained open and five years later the issue was discussed with much less confrontation. A decade later the conference reached consensus that FGM was a human rights violation. Egypt, Nigeria, and Ghana have banned the practice. The United States may grant asylum to keep a girl from returning to a country where FGM is practiced.

With the first consensus reached at the United Nations conferences, global opinion is starting to mirror this consensus—that FGM is a human rights violation. How this consensus was reached illustrates symbolic interac-

tionism's "definition of the situation" in two ways. First, what used to be named female circumcision has been renamed female genital mutilation. The former name suggests something mild or benign. The latter name clearly does not. Second, the movement against FGM has been redefined as a defense of human rights rather than as cultural interference. The new definition of the situation is fast becoming the reality and, FGM is declining and in some cultures has been eliminated.

1. How does the FGM case apply to the movement to eliminate male circumcision in the United States, one of the few countries that still practices it? Why does it continue when it is no longer justified on medical grounds?
2. Is sexual pleasure a human right? If so, what culturally acceptable changes must occur to ensure it in the United States and in North Africa?

Sources: El Saadawi, 1980; Kouba & Muasher, 1985; Zenie-Ziegler, 1988; Rushwan, 1995; Gruenbaum, 1997; Burstyn, 1996; AAASHRAN, 1998 .

women are expected to be round and chunky (Cobb, 1997:8T). Weight is associated with wealth in many of these societies. Stouter people are those who can afford to eat more. In the West, the reverse is true. Both men and women subscribe to the "you can never be too rich or too thin" standard. The result has been a dramatic increase in eating disorders such as anorexia nervosa, a disease of self-induced severe weight loss, primarily affecting young women. A thin woman with large breasts is sexually idealized in the West. Obsession with thinness is definitely media based. Evidence for Western media influence on other cultures is suggested by a global increase in eating disorders in societies where they were previously unknown (Katzman & Wooley, 1994; Kelly, 1997).

Attitudes and behavior regarding sexuality change gradually. It took nine centuries before footbinding was banned in China. Since change is gradual, the idea of a sexual revolution is misleading—an idea con-

firmed by the opening vignette asking about "what sexual revolution?" A revolution assumes an abrupt, complete, and often reversed change of behavior. In the United States, changes in patterns of sexuality became evident in the 1920s, when women from all social classes began entering the labor force in greater numbers. Higher rates of premarital sex and out-of-wedlock births were reported. The divorce rates began to increase. Small but noticeable increases in tolerance related to attitudes on unmarried couples living together, sex education, and homosexuality occurred (Harriss, 1991; Cherlin, 1992; National Center for Health Statistics, 1999). As the opening vignette noted, baby boomers accelerated the patterns. But the earlier patterns were not demolished. Change as well as continuity related to sexuality characterized this period. Sociologists accept the notion that sexual *evolution* rather than sexual *revolution* is perhaps a better way to describe patterns of

For Better or For Worse®   **by Lynn Johnston**

Due mainly to media images showing ultra thin models and actresses, teenage girls usually want to be thinner than they are—even when they are of normal weight. Weight obsessed adolescents and young women are at risk for eating disorders such as anorexia.
Source: "For Better or For Worse" copyright 1992 Lynn Johnston Productions, Inc. Reprinted with permission of Universal Press Syndicate. All rights reserved.

human sexuality over the last century (Eshleman, 2000).

Chapter 3 showed us that there are important cultural universals related to sexuality, especially regarding its regulation. However, as we will continue to document, both within and between cultures, sexual attitudes and behaviors vary widely, but our humanness unfolds only by culture and socialization.

SEXUALITY AS SOCIALLY CONSTRUCTED

Symbolic interactionists maintain that the variety of human sexual expression found throughout the globe is largely socially constructed. As discussed in Chapter 5, we interact on the basis of how we perceive the interaction, including the expectations we perceive others have of us. Since sexual interaction is no exception to this rule, sexual beliefs and behaviors are built up (constructed) over time. Culture is the major influence in providing the meanings people use to distinguish their sexual feelings, identities, and practices (Levine, 1998). For symbolic interactionists, the sexual excitement that appears to be naturally driven by biology is a learned process (Gagnon & Simon, 1973). A great deal of research suggests that biological facts do not have direct effects on human sexual experiences.

Defining Sex, Gender, and Sexual Orientation

With symbolic interactionism as a framework, sex and gender are now regarded by scientists in all disciplines as two different realities. **Sex** is described as those biological characteristics distinguishing male and female. Males and females are biologically distinguished, for example, by differences in chromosomes and hormone levels. **Gender** is described as those social, cultural, and psychological characteristics linked to male and female that define people as masculine and feminine.

Two other areas of human sexuality are particularly important to symbolic interactionists. The first is *gender identity*, discussed in Chapter 5 as a person's awareness that the two sexes behave differently and that two *gender roles*—one emphasizing masculinity and the other emphasizing femininity—are proper. The second is **sexual orientation,** a person's preference for sexual partners, usually of one gender. We will see, however, that all these categories are not totally separate and overlap much more than most people realize. Many of the vast differences in human sexuality can be traced to how gender identity and sexual orientation are socially constructed.

Gender Identity

The overlap of sex and gender identity is one good way to show how symbolic interactionists discuss human sexuality. By age 6 children have developed gender identity, a general pattern found throughout the globe. Gender identity is a central part of self and is invested with strong emotional attachment. Biological sex does not automatically grant gender identity. It is something that must be learned through socialization. You become aware that you are a girl or boy (gender identity), then you construct your behavior, including sexual behavior, around that awareness (gender role). Males and females have many ready opportunities for the social construction of gender roles, such as through their own families, peer interaction, schools, and the media (see Chapter 13). Information from these and other social sources is also selected for the sexual component of their gender roles.

Data on **hermaphrodites,** children born with both male and female sexual organs or ambiguous genitals (such as a clitoris that looks like a penis), tend to support the social construction of gender identity. Assigned one sex at birth, the child's genetic sex is often discovered later. These studies point out that

Since much behavior is constructed around gender identity, children are offered many opportunities to learn appropriate gender roles. In constructing a bow and arrow, this Kaiapo boy from Brazil is learning about hunting—an important aspect of a masculine gender role in his society.

nected with different sexual scripts—one considered more appropriate for males, and the other considered more appropriate for females. Although the world has supposedly witnessed a sexual revolution, sexual scripts continue to be based on beliefs that for men sex is for orgasm and physical pleasure, and for women sex is for love and the pleasure that comes from intimacy. While people may desire more latitude in their sexual scripts—such as more emotional intimacy for men and more sexual pleasure for women—they often feel constrained by the traditional scripting of their sexuality. When both men and women accept such scripts and carry scripted expectations into the bedroom, *gendered* sexuality is being socially constructed. Beliefs about gendered sexuality have contributed to increased sexual violence toward women. But such beliefs also hold disadvantages for both men and women and constrain their sexual pleasure. Gendered scripting illustrates that biology alone cannot explain human sexuality. Indeed, compatible with symbolic interactionism, the evidence is overwhelming that biology is a player in the sexuality game, "but it is not the only player or even captain of the team" (Schwartz & Rutter, 1998:28). Sexuality is much less spontaneous than we think.

Sexual scripts may provide the paths to sexuality, but symbolic interactionists also assert that over time new paths offering new directions for sexuality can be built. It is unlikely that gendered sexuality will be eliminated. However, it *is* likely that as gender roles become more egalitarian, both men and women will find that their sexual lives are enhanced.

hermaphrodites are likely to take on the gender identity of whichever sex is assigned, regardless of the genetic sex.

The age of the child is the crucial factor in adjustment if sex reassignment surgery (SRS) is an option. In SRS, genitals are surgically altered so that a person changes from one biological sex to the other. By age 4 a child acquires both language and a sense of self. Gender identity is developing. Even by 4 years of age, powerful social definitions related to appropriate gender role behavior have already occurred. In a case of sex reassignment, not only must the child change his or her gender identity, but others who know the child as one sex must now start treating him or her as the other sex (Money & Ehrhardt, 1972).

Sexual Scripts. **Sexual scripts** are shared beliefs concerning what society defines as acceptable sexual thoughts, feelings, and behaviors for each gender (Gagnon, 1990). For example, gender roles are con-

SEXUAL ORIENTATION

Like gender identity, sexual orientation is not automatically granted by biological sex. Humans share the same anatomy and have the same capacity for sexual pleasure, but there is a great deal of variation in how and with whom people experience sexual pleasure. According to symbolic interactionists, comparable to gender identity, sexual orientation is a social construction built during social interaction. Like heterosexuals, both men and women who see themselves as homosexual maintain a gender identity consistent with their biological sex. They are socialized into prevailing gender roles except for their sexual orientation. (Peplau & Gordon, 1983; Viss & Burn, 1992). However, since gender identity is accompanied by gender roles that are defined as masculine or feminine, it is much more susceptible to change over time than is sexual orientation. In the middle of the nineteenth century a masculine gender role was associated with employment roles that included elementary

Then & Now

Does Nature Rule? A Case of Sex Reassignment

On August 22, 1965, Janet and Ron Reimer of Winnipeg Canada became the parents of identical twin sons named Bruce and Brian. Eight months later, to correct a minor urination problem, the babies were to be circumcised. Circumcision is not routinely performed in Canada. Baby Bruce was picked up first by the nurse. A few minutes later Ron and Janet were informed that an accident occurred—an electric current was set too high and Bruce's penis was burned off. When Janet looked at what was left of his penis, she described it as "blackened, a little string." It could never come back to life. Baby Brian was whisked away without the circumcision. The teams of Canadian and U.S. physicians who examined Bruce came to the same discouraging conclusion: Constructing an artificial penis was possible but not promising.

Ten months after the accident Janet Reimer happened to watch a talk show where Dr. John Money, one of the world's foremost experts on gender identity, spoke of encouraging results with sex reassignment surgery (SRS) for children born with ambiguous genitalia. According to Money, gender identity was solely shaped by parents and environment. The topic of sexuality is now standard fare for the talk show circuit, but imagine Janet Reimer's discovery thirty years ago about a technique that might change the life of her son. Dr. Money agreed to take on Bruce's case. Just before his second birthday, Bruce underwent surgery to remove the remaining penile tissue. Bruce became Brenda.

The transformation from Bruce to Brenda was not an easy one. She rebelled almost from the start, tearing off dresses, preferring boy toys, and fighting with her brother and others. There was nothing feminine about Brenda. She had a masculine gait and was teased in school. At age 8 she had a nervous breakdown. But with strong support from Money, the Reimers were convinced that Brenda could be "taught to want to be a girl." Vaginal surgery was the next step. But any time the topic was broached, she would adamantly refuse to accept the possibility. Mere mention of the word "penis" or "vagina" induced explosive panic. In most therapy sessions she was sullen, angry, and unresponsive. At times she would "play the game" and give them the answers they wanted to hear: "I want to be pretty; I'm a girl, not a boy." At age 12 she began estrogen therapy and breasts formed. She binged ate and gained weight to cover them up. In the meantime, Brenda's case became famous in scientific circles as proof that a child could be taught the gender identity corresponding to a new sex. All reports said she was adjusting nicely and acting out typical female roles—that she accepted her gender identity as a female.

When did Brenda learn that she was born Bruce? At age 10, in an embarrassed and fumbled attempt, her

school teaching and clerical work. Today these same roles are associated with femininity.

Problems with Definitions

Public interest on the topic of sexual orientation is reflected in its coverage in the mass media. Terminology to describe the topic, once familiar mainly to scientists, has made its way into public usage. Scientific nomenclature about "sexual orientation," including this very term, is offensive to some in the homosexual community. Terms and definitions remain contested (Kahn, 1997). Generally accepted usages, however, are included in this chapter.

Sexual orientation is divided into the categories of heterosexual and homosexual in most Western cultures. **Heterosexual** is the category for people who have sexual preference and erotic attraction for those of the other gender. Heterosexuals are also referred to as *straight*. **Homosexual** is the category for people who have sexual preference and erotic attraction with those of their own gender. Homosexual males are also referred to as *gay men* and homosexual females as *lesbians*. The term *gay* is often used to include both gay men and lesbians. **Bisexual** is the category for people with shifting sexual orientations; they are sexually responsive to either gender. Experts disagree as to whether bisexuality represents a distinct sexual orientation or is simply "homosexuality in disguise" (Weinberg et al., 1994; Garber, 1995).

The last point about bisexuality highlights an important problem when identifying categories of sexual orientation. Science requires such categories for accurate reporting of research, but there is a major pitfall: They overlap a great deal. Is it accurate to say that heterosexuals *only* have sexual relations (behavior) with, and sexual fantasies (attitudes) about, the other sex? Most people in Western cultures categorize anyone who does not as homosexual (Katz, 1995). Whether experts agree, the public tends to put bisexuals in the homosexual category.

father told her that she needed surgery because a doctor "made a mistake down there." Brenda's sole response: "Did you beat him up?" Although Brenda did not understand what her father was saying, some believe that at this point Brenda subconsciously knew she was a boy. At age 14 she was finally told the truth. Her response this time was anger, doubt, and amazement—but mostly relief. She vowed to change back to a boy. His new name would be David, since he felt the name Bruce was too "geeky." At age 18 at a relative's wedding, he made his public debut as a boy. He married in 1990.

In 1952 when George Jorgenson was surgically transformed in Denmark to become Christine Jorgenson, the world's most well-known transsexual was "born." The first complete transsexual surgery performed in the United States was not until 1965. David Reimer had a rudimentary penis and testicles constructed in 1981, requiring eighteen hospital visits. Just before his 22nd birthday, new techniques for microvascular reconstruction were used with much better results.

Most children who have SRS are born with ambiguous genitals, so David's case is very rare. The current advice for such children is to assign a firm sex at birth—the child must be raised either a boy or girl. Any irreversible surgery must wait until children are old enough to know and say which gender they feel closer to. "Rear the child in a consistent gender—but keep away the knife." While not a perfect solution, it does consider biological, psychological, and social forces at work on the child.

In the media frenzy that followed David's "coming out" as a boy, the public heard only that gender identity is a natural, inborn process. The role of nurture is given little credit in the process. For many, the case seemed to "prove" that if nurture plays a role in shaping masculinity and femininity, nature is by far stronger.

Sociologists never discount biology as a key factor in explaining human behavior, especially related to sexuality. Although David's case questions the belief that gender identity is learned, it cannot be totally rejected. Symbolic interactionists focus on the critical role of socialization in learning gender identity. Consider, for example, that Bruce became a girl nearly two years after everyone, including twin brother Brian, treated her like a boy. Interviews with Brian showed him confused as well. He was also embarrassed by Brenda's tomboy behavior, which no one accepted. Two years of gender socialization cannot be easily erased—if at all. At one point the Reimers moved to get away from "ghosts and doubters." The media also never questioned the ability of a host of players to carry out a giant pretense. There are good arguments for biological and cultural factors on gender identity. Both need to be considered. Everybody may have been playing a game of science fiction—but the game of social reality was largely ignored.

1. Do you think the Reimers made the correct decision when they agreed to have Bruce undergo SRS? If not, what advice would you have offered to them?
2. What does "real gender" mean to you? Even if people can change biological sex, can they ever change gender identity?

Sources: Money & Ehrhardt, 1972; Money & Tucker, 1975; Diamond & Sigmundson, 1997; Colapinto, 2000.

So Who Is Gay? A Continuum of Sexual Orientation

The pioneering work of Alfred Kinsey and his associates (1948; 1953) led to a scientific assault on the view that sexual orientation is *either* heterosexual *or* homosexual. According to Kinsey's research, sexual orientation can be measured by degrees on a continuum of sexual behavior involving one's own or the other gender (Figure 7.1). Later research added a psychological dimension to the continuum. People could be rated according to level of erotic attraction and fantasies for their own or the other gender, regardless of actual sexual behavior. As you would expect, this addition decreases the numbers of people who may be exclusively heterosexual. There are many roadblocks in determining prevalence rates of gay men and lesbians.

The original Kinsey data on sexual behavior showed that 37 percent of men and 13 percent of women said they achieved orgasm with a person from their own gender after puberty. Correcting for sampling bias (he overrecruited gay men, for instance) later research in 1970 showed about 20 percent for men (Fay et al., 1989). When erotic attraction to own gender is added to sexual behavior, some data show about one-fifth of both men and women reporting homosexual activities (Sell et al., 1995). Data consistently report that gay men are likely to be exclusively homosexual in behavior but less than half say they are exclusively homosexual in feelings. In contrast, lesbians report significantly more heterosexual feelings *and* behavior. However, of the men and women who give homosexuality a try, very few decide to repeat the experience and even fewer identify themselves as exclusively homosexual (Bell & Weinberg, 1978; Troiden, 1988).

Instead of asking about sexual behavior and attitudes, some surveys simply ask people to state their sexual preference. A recent such poll in 1996 showed 5 percent of respondents self-identifying as gay, lesbian, or bisexual, more than triple the number who

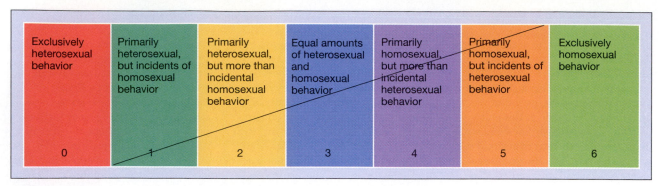

FIGURE 7.1   The Kinsey Continuum of Sexual Orientation

Source: "Kinsey's Sexual Behavior Continuum" from *Sexual Behavior in the Human Male*, The Kinsey Institute. William B. Saunders, 1948. Reprinted by permission of The Kinsey Institute for Research in Sex, Gender, and Reproduction, Inc.

self-identified when a similar poll was conducted in 1994 (Riggle & Tadlock, 1999). Results also change when surveys ask when people had their first same-gender sexual experiences, if experiences continued and for how long, and type and frequency of erotic attraction without sexual experiences (Diamond, 1993; Laumann et al., 1994). Since Kinsey's study, surveys on sexuality have become much more sophisticated in both sampling and types of questions asked. Overall, it is safe to conclude that in Western cultures, more or less exclusive homosexuality ranges from 5 percent to 10 percent for men and 3 percent to 5 percent for women (Fay et al., 1989; Laumann et al., 1994; Weston, 1998).

So do these numbers tell us who is gay? Symbolic interactionists think not for one major reason. For symbolic interactionists, what you are is what you think you are—both in identity and way of life. Even when polls ask people to "self-identify" their sexual orientation, how the identity is translated into way of life is the very dimension that is largely absent in surveys on sexual orientation. The term homosexual refers to people who define themselves as gay men or lesbians and who adopt behavior corresponding to this identity.

Global Patterns

Historical and cross-cultural research support Kinsey's contention that sexual orientation, like other forms of human sexuality, is extremely varied. Research also shows that the conceptual distinction between gender identity and sexual orientation is a blurry one. The ancient Greeks, for instance, accepted both homosexuality and heterosexuality as "natural" relationships, with no moral overtones. Although a man's preference for males or females was seen as a matter of taste and desire, the enjoy-

ment of one over the other did not categorize men according to a gender preference for sexual interaction. A man who pursued males, therefore, did not see himself as any different from one who pursued females. Greek society associated masculinity and femininity with certain types of gendered behavior. For males at least, Greek society agreed. It was common for a man to change his sexual preference to women after spending his youth loving boys (Foucault, 1990). Even after marriage to women, large numbers of upper-class youth continued sexual relations with boys and men (O'Kelley & Carney, 1986). For the Greeks, gender identity existed but sexual orientation did not.

Another example of the gender identity–sexual orientation blurring comes from India, where men known as "hijras" dress up in women's clothing and are called upon to bless newborn infants. In order to become a hijra and perform this important cultural role, most of these men by choice have been emasculated—their testicles have been removed. Hijra are not homosexual. They think of themselves more as females and thus prefer heterosexual men as sexual partners. They generally live and dress as females, often in a separate subculture. In the rural areas of India where hijras practice their trade, sexual orientation and gender identity do not appear to be concerns either for their society or for themselves. Making a living as a "true" hijra is a more important concern. This sentiment is expressed by one hijra:

> There are other people who imitate us, who dress up in woman's clothes and go where a baby is born, but only we have the power to give it a blessing. This is because we are neither men nor women. . . . A hijra is born from the stomach of a woman, but can be counted neither among the men nor the women. . . . The other people who imitate us, they are real men, with wives and

INTERNET ✦ CONNECTIONS

As pointed out in your text ("Problems with Definitions"), there is a great deal of misinformation surrounding human sexuality. After reading this chapter, are you clear on how to distinguish between a homosexual and a transsexual? Even if you think you are well informed, go to the site: http://www.transsexual.org/. Click on "What Exactly Is Transsexuality?" After you have read the contents, write a brief report on why definitions relating to sexual orientation are problematic.

children. They come to join us only for making a living. (Adapted from Nanda, 1990:11–12)

Hijras are ambivalent figures in India. They are teased and mocked but also valued and esteemed (Ward, 1999). The hijras have a gender role that legitimizes their function as ritual performers. This role forms the core of their self-definition and the basis of their positive, collective self-image.

Unlike hijras, who live openly as females, some people move freely with "mixed" gender identities. A number of Native American tribes believe sex and gender are not always the same. Until they were colonized by whites, some Native American tribes accepted the cross-gender role of biological female who performed male duties (Blackwood, 1984). The role of *berdache*, a title conferred on males who do not exhibit masculine traits, still exists today in some tribes. In tribal mythology, berdache may act as mediators between men and women and between the physical and spiritual worlds (Roscoe, 1992). Native Americans refer to those who act out cross-gender roles as having "two spirits." Over 130 two-spirited cultures existed in Native North America before colonization (Callender & Kochems, 1983; Williams, 1996).

The *xanith* of the Arab state of Oman are also biological males. They work as homosexual prostitutes and skilled domestic servants. Described as a "third" gender, they have male names but distinctive dress and hair styles, unlike that of either men or women. Xanith are not men because they can interact with women and are not women because they are not restricted by purdah, the system of veiling and secluding women (Lips, 1997).

The berdache and xanith are roles associated with approval, and sometimes honor, rather than disdain and immorality. These people violate the principle of **sexual dimorphism,** the separation of the sexes into two distinct groups, and show that what is socially defined as sexually unacceptable in one culture can be defined as sexually acceptable in another. Symbolic interactionists emphasize that these roles attest to the powerful impact of culture on both gender identity and sexual orientation.

Transsexuals

Unlike hermaphrodites, *transsexuals* are genetic males or females who psychologically believe they are members of the other gender. They feel "trapped" in the wrong bodies and may undergo sex reassignment surgery (SRS) to "correct" the problem. Only then can their gender identity and their biological sex be consistent. By this reasoning, transsexuals are not homosexuals. They are newly minted males or females who desire sexual intimacy with the other gender. Their ideal lover would be a heterosexual man or woman. The reality, however, is that most heterosexuals would not choose transsexuals as lovers. *Transvestites*, mostly males who are sexually aroused when they dress in women's clothing, are not transsexuals. Transsexuals are rare in society. The numbers worldwide are thought to be 1 in 100,000 males and 1 in 130,000 females (Allgeier & Allgeier, 2000).

Psychotherapy aimed at acceptance of a transsexual's biological sex instead of sex reassignment surgery is generally unsuccessful. The outcomes of SRS are mixed. Research from the United States in the 1970s showed overall negative results. Some transsexuals believed the surgery was a mistake and others reported no better adjustment after than before surgery. Later research describes more positive outcomes. International data indicate that the majority of transsexuals report satisfaction with their choice of sex reassignment (Lindermalm et al., 1986; Blanchard et al., 1985; Lief & Hubschman, 1993). Most people are puzzled by transsexuals because they do not see any contradictions between biological sex and gender identity. But as one researcher concludes:

> When you see a transsexual . . . it's no use asking "Is she really still a man?" or "Was she really a woman all those years?" The question is meaningless. All you can say is that this is a person whose sex organs (were) male and whose gender identity (is) female (Money & Tucker, 1975).

Discrimination and Diversity

Western societies, including the United States, are primarily *heterosexist*—people tend to view the world only in heterosexual terms. In doing so, other sexual orientations are devalued. At various times in history homosexuality was a sin, a disease, a crime, a mental illness,

Demonstrating the end point of homophobia, during World War II the Nazis routinely arrested and executed gay men. Homosexuals were forced to wear a pink triangle as a symbol of their homosexuality, such as these concentration camp survivors who appeared at a 1947 rally in their camp uniforms.

an immoral choice, an alternative lifestyle, and today, a health threat (Troiden, 1988). **Homophobia,** negative attitudes and overall intolerance toward homosexuals and homosexuality, is expressed by a wide spectrum of the U.S. public. However, people in some demographic categories are more homophobic than others. Higher levels of homophobia are associated with the following characteristics: Practitioners are more likely to be male, heterosexual, elderly, have not gone to college, live in the South, and are religiously, sexually, and politically conservative. They tend to be more authoritarian and believe in rigid gender roles. Negative attitudes are also associated with having few or any gay friends or acquaintances. Research shows that knowing gay people personally increases positive attitudes toward homosexuals as a group (Yang, 1997).

Race and Ethnicity.   Racial and ethnic minorities in the United States are subject to prejudice and discrimination (Chapter 12). When the minority status of "homosexual" is added, their already disadvantaged position gets worse. Those disadvantages may be higher *within* their own ethnic subcultures as well. Among Latinos, for example, men are expected to be dominant, tough, and fiercely competitive with other males. This exaggerated masculinity, often referred to as *machismo*, is an acceptable part of these subcultures. Women are expected to be submissive to men and remain virgins until marriage. This pattern frees men to at times engage in male-male sexual encounters. These may be accepted as transitory until marriage. A gay identity, however, is not acceptable. While some people believe that the machismo tradition makes it more disgraceful in Latino communities for men to be gay than women, others disagree. Latino women

who take on a lesbian identity are doubly denounced—not only are they lesbians but that status challenges the machismo of male dominance (Trujillo, 1991; Greene, 1994; Kahn, 1997).

We saw earlier that many Native American tribes accepted those with mixed-gender identities. During the colonial period Catholicism prevailed and eventually eliminated many of these traditions. It remains to be seen if acceptance levels will be higher for gay men and lesbians living on reservations where ancient traditions are being revitalized. Among Asian Americans, especially in Chinese communities, gender roles are extremely rigid. Since a women's fundamental role is to ensure the family line through conceiving sons, gay men and lesbians pose major threats. They are likely to be isolated from their families unless they give up their "gayness" and return to traditional roles. Thus, gay Chinese Americans express high levels of anguish because they were socialized for strong family ties, but are now rejected by their families. For some, the gay subcultures cannot offer the sense of family and community they desire (Chan, 1992; Kahn, 1997). Evidence is mixed for African Americans. Some studies find whites having more homophobic attitudes than African Americans and others find no significant differences (Simon, 1998; Lewis & Rogers, 1999). Though it is difficult to generalize about levels of homophobia within different racial and ethnic groups, it is clear that gay men and lesbians must contend with another layer of minority status that will undoubtedly impact their lives.

Gender.   Over time homophobia has declined significantly for most demographic categories, especially in the areas of support for rights related to employment

Although many churches offer marriage ceremonies to celebrate and publicly acknowledge unions between gay men and lesbians, to date marriage between homosexuals is not legally recognized in the United States.

and military service (Haeberle, 1999). Some states are now allowing gay couples to adopt children under the same rules as unmarried couples (Havemann, 1997). Less change toward tolerance is reported in the belief that sexual relations between adult gays should be legalized. Nonetheless, even with widespread homophobia, today over half of the United States population of young adults can be described as somewhere between "tolerant" and "accepting" of homosexuals (Gallup, 1997; NORC, 1999).

Gender is the single most important category where this trend is not evident. Males may be less homophobic than in the past, but they have been slower to change than other groups. In fact, the "homophobic gap" between men and women is actually widening, specifically in attitudes toward gay men (Kite & Whitley, 1996; Lewis & Rogers, 1999). Both genders appear to hold similar views about lesbians—with men generally as accepting of them as women. Sociol-

ogists explain this trend by highlighting contemporary notions about U.S. masculinity.

Men and Masculinity. Sociological research linking homophobia to a masculine gender role supports the following conclusion: Homophobia is such an integral part of heterosexual masculinity that being a man means *not* being a homosexual (Badinter, 1995:115). One example is the "antifeminine standard"—the male rejection of any behavior that has a feminine quality. Homophobia endorses antifemininity. Devastating labels boys use against other boys are *sissy*, *queer*, or simply *girl*. Homophobia is learned early. A large majority of teenage males express disgust and intolerance concerning images of homosexual men (Marsiglio, 1993). As adults, men still fear the labels of gay, faggot, or homosexual. The norm of homophobia is used by men to control other men in their male roles (Lehne, 1992:389).

The traditional male gender role encourages homophobia for several reasons. First, women and anything perceived as feminine are less valued than men and anything perceived as masculine. Second, men generally accept stereotypes about gays and homosexuality. These stereotypes are negative but also very powerful. Men see little need to seek out facts because, just by doing so, they may be threatened with a homosexual label. Finally, early socialization offers few alternative models for boys (Chapter 5). An often rigid standard of masculinity is upheld. Boys learn quickly from their peers that gestures of intimacy with other males are discouraged and that expressions of femininity, verbally or nonverbally, are not tolerated. Male role models—fathers, teachers, and brothers—provide the cues and the sanctions to ensure compliance on the part of the young boy (Strikwerda & May, 1992; Plummer, 1999).

In school, for example, boys strictly segregate themselves from girls. Intimacy with boys must be achieved in culturally acceptable ways. Throughout childhood and into adult life, male camaraderie occurs in male-only secret clubs, fraternal organizations, the military, sports teams, or the neighborhood bar. Even though men are taught that intimacy among males is taboo, they still want informal interaction with other men. These are approved havens, otherwise society could be suspicious of such close male interaction. Homophobia blocks the expression of the deepest feelings of affection between men (Letich, 1991).

Gay Rights. The emergence of a gay rights movement has helped gays to affirm positive identities and the right to sexual self-determination (Kinsman, 1992:491). Patterned somewhat after the women's movement, one faction of the movement is working to

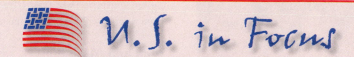

The Sexualization of America

America has a message about sex. The message says that almost everyone but you is having endless, fascinating, varied sex.

This message opens one of the most important studies on sex in the United States since Kinsey—the 1990s' version, rather than the 1950s' version. This study and other recent ones provide data that test what we call the "sexualization thesis"—that Americans are preoccupied with sex; they eagerly engage in frequent sex with a variety of interesting partners. The media are seen as fueling this belief. Does the sexualization thesis have merit? Review some of the latest data on U.S. sexuality to determine if the thesis is, indeed, correct.

Sex is for pleasure: Virtually all surveys report that Americans have sex mainly for erotic pleasure. Sex for reproduction takes a distant second place. U.S. Catholic couples, for example, typically use contraceptives even though the rhythm method is the only form of birth control sanctioned by the Catholic church. The sex that Americans have is also more frequent and more varied than in the past. They experiment with different sexual techniques more than their parents and certainly more than their grandparents. Masturbation and oral sex are common

and accepted. *BUT*: Over three-quarters of adults say that media concentrate too much on sex. Advertising, movies, videos, and television overdo the showing of breasts and buttocks, nudity and near-nudity. Americans are used to these images but would prefer fewer of them. And even if people are personally more open to sexual experimentation, traditional vaginal intercourse tops the list of the most appealing sexual practice for the vast majority of adults—regardless of gender, race, class, or age.

First sex: Age for first intercourse has steadily declined. The average age of lost virginity for people born in the 1930s and 1940s was 19. Today it is 16. Women who were either virgins when they turned 20 or had sexual intercourse with only one person declines from 84 percent for those born before 1953 to 50 percent for those born after. About four-fifths of U.S. teens have their first intercourse before they turn 20. *BUT*: More teens in the 1990s report that they intend to abstain from sex before marriage than those in the 1980s. Data are still incomplete to determine if they "do not practice" what they preach.

Sex partners: Americans have more sex partners than just two decades ago. About a third of people over age 50 say they had at least five partners in

their lifetimes, but about half of people between age 30 and 50 report this. The highly educated have more partners over their lifetime than the least educated. About one-third of those who did not finish high school report having five-plus partners, compared to about half of those finishing college. Does this pattern mean that "smarter" people are more sexually active? Probably not. A better explanation is that people with more education postpone marriage to finish school, so they have more time and chances to meet and date a variety of people, many of whom become sex partners. *BUT*: For data on number of sex partners the past year, 70 percent say they had one and 12 percent say none.

Sex frequency: About two-thirds of all people have sex from a few times per month to several times per week. Sex is probably with the same partner and with a spouse if they are married. *BUT*: About 20 percent of married Americans report that they had an affair, showing a steady increase over the last two decades. While the large majority of married couples (80%) do not cheat on their spouses, it is clear that affairs are becoming more acceptable.

Sex knowledge: Compared to past generations, U.S. teenagers know more about sex and understand what they know. Beginning at about age 12

escape the bonds of a sexist culture. This faction recognizes the common oppression they share with women. They seek to abandon restrictive role playing with women and cast aside crippling straitjackets that keep them emotionally distant from men (Kleinberg, 1992).

On the other hand, some gay men recognize that since women and gay men are both subordinate in society, it may be better to capitalize on their advantage of being male—regardless of how it undermines women. From this "male advantage" view, a gay male executive moving up the corporate ladder can wield power over any competing female. As conflict theory suggests, males are higher in the stratification system than females. Males are socialized into accepting masculinity norms—whether they are gay or not. As we

will see in the next section, these standards show up in all forms of sexuality.

SEXUALITY: ATTITUDES AND BEHAVIORS

Until fairly recently, beliefs about human sexuality have been shrouded in myth and superstition. Just as Sigmund Freud stunned the scientific world and then the general public with his pronouncements on sexuality, the original Kinsey data at mid-century sent similar shockwaves when he interviewed Americans about their sexual behaviors. Not only were Americans much more sexually active than most

Sexuality in advertisements is a taken for granted fact of life in American society.

use them, even during anal intercourse. Women often report that their boyfriends do not like condoms, so they go along with these preferences. They do, however, take oral contraceptives. Safe sex to them means not getting pregnant.

Clearly, there is a great deal of evidence supporting the sexualization thesis. But the data also show that Americans are much less "sexualized" than people believe. The sexual lives of ordinary men and women revolve around sex with a spouse or in a committed relationship, which provides them with erotic pleasure and excitement. The sexualization of the United States is associated with erotic pleasure but also moral panic. It is associated with fascination of sexual things but also disdain when these very things surround them too much, especially through the media. As this chapter shows, cultural beliefs explain much of the inconsistency.

1. From these patterns of sexuality here, do you think the United States will become more or less sexualized? What factors prevent or promote sexualization?
2. From conflict and functionalist perspectives, explain why many do *not* act on their sex knowledge, even when health is risked.

Sources: Janus & Janus, 1993; Laumann et al., 1994; Michael et al., 1994; Coleman & Rocker, 1998; McClaren, 1999; Pearson, 1999.

through age 17, their levels of sexual understanding increase dramatically. At every age, girls know more than boys, and know more on every topic. For both genders, their bodies are physically changing and they talk about these changes to their friends and families. Adolescents report good communication with their parents on sexual matters. Sex education is moving to lower grades, so knowledge and communication are reinforced. In the 1950s, 15-year-olds may have had basic sex education. Today it is taught in more depth to 11-year-olds. *BUT*: The majority of all teens believe that boys can't

control their sex urges and girls can. They also believe that a girl cannot get pregnant unless a boy has an orgasm and ejaculates directly into her vagina.

Sex and disease: Not only do teens have more formal sex education, the sex and health link is clearer for them. For example, most high school students understand how HIV is transmitted and what they need to do to protect themselves and their partners from the disease. *BUT*: Regardless of age, risky sexual behavior is common. Some studies show only 20 percent of nonmarried couples use condoms. Those under age 19 are less likely to

people realized, but those activities strayed far from what people thought were sexually appropriate norms. A half century later another major sex survey showed a rather startling twist. In the century of sexuality, Americans were less sexual then previously thought (Laumann et al., 1994). This section explores changes and continuities in sexual behaviors and attitudes.

Gendered Sexuality

The original Kinsey data revealed that 92 percent of males and 58 percent of females masturbated (sexual self-stimulation) to orgasm. Males begin to mastur-

bate during early adolescence. Females begin to masturbate later than men, often in their twenties and thirties. These patterns have not changed significantly since Kinsey's original research (Hunt, 1974; Laumann et al., 1994; Hyde, 1996).

During intercourse men are more likely to have an orgasm than women. Kinsey found that over one-third of married women never had an orgasm prior to marriage and that one-third of married women never had an orgasm. Later data show that almost 90 percent of all women experience orgasm, whether married or not, and virtually all married women (98 percent) do reach orgasm, although not with every sexual intercourse. Husbands generally would like more frequent intercourse than their wives, especially early in the marriage. Later in their married life this trend may reverse. An interesting fact about gender differences in orgasm for heterosexual couples is that women are very close in their estimates of male orgasm, but the proportion of men who claimed that their partners *always* had an orgasm was 15 percent higher than what women report. The percentage jumps to 20 percent for men with less than a college education, and to 27 percent for men who are in cohabitational relationships (Hunt, 1974; Michael et al., 1994).

Premarital Sex. Kinsey's (1953) data reported that one-fourth of unmarried women born before 1900 had experienced coitus (sexual intercourse). Overall, Kinsey found that one-third of young women reported premarital sex by age 25. For unmarried college women today, almost 90 percent are sexually experienced (DeBuono et al., 1990; Miller et al., 1993). For males, premarital sex remains high, 77 percent in the Kinsey data to 95 percent twenty years later, a pattern that persists today (Fig. 7.2). Females not only have fewer sex partners than men, but they will plan for their first intercourse. Girls whose first intercourse occurred before age 16 are more likely to report that it was not voluntary. A male's first experience is likely to be with a pickup or a casual date. The average age of first intercourse for girls today is 16 and for boys 15.5. The girl's first sexual partner is several years older than she; the boy's first sexual partner is within a year of his age (Miller & Heaton, 1991; Centers for Disease Control, 1997).

But throughout life, women have fewer sex partners than men. For men, African Americans and whites have more sex partners than Asian Americans and Hispanic Americans (Carroll et al., 1985; Michael et al., 1994). Unlike in the Kinsey era, today premarital sex is the norm. Actually, a more accurate term to describe today's norm is *nonmarital* sex, since most people have several sexual experiences with people whom they will not likely marry.

Extramarital Relationships.   Once called adultery but now commonly called affairs, another form of nonmarital sex is the extramarital relationship. These take on many forms. They involve different degrees of openness and include married as well as single people. They may or may not include sexual involvement. The emotional involvement with a partner other than one's spouse can be more threatening to the marriage even without sexual involvement. Most people disapprove of affairs in any form, but Kinsey's data indicated that 50 percent of males and 26 percent of females engaged in extramarital sex by age 40 (see Fig. 7.3). The best estimates with the most representative data are that about 25 percent of men and 16 percent of women report

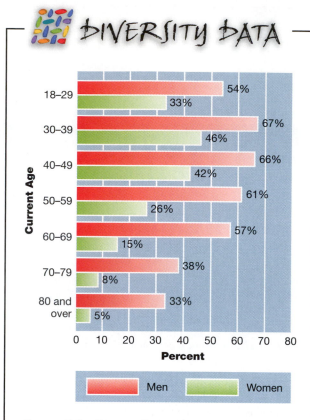

FIGURE 7.2   Percent Reporting Four or More Other-Sex Partners Since Age 18, by Age and Gender, Reported in 1990s GSS Samples. In the 1990s, at all age levels, men are significantly more likely than women to report having four or more other-sex partners. However, earlier data do show that women are gradually increasing their number of sex partners. Do you think that the double standard in number of sex partners will eventually be eliminated for men and women?
Source: NORC. General Social Surveys, 1972-1996. Chicago: National Opinion Research Center, 1996. Reprinted by permission of NORC, Chicago, IL.

having had an extramarital affair (Atwater, 1982; Lawson, 1988; Laumann et al., 1994). It is clear that while most people disapprove of affairs, a significant number of these same people engage in them.

But there are problems with these data for a number of reasons. First, although extramarital relationships are likely to be discreet, they vary in degrees of openness. Sometimes the spouse and other friends are aware of the relationship. Sometimes the awareness translates to either tolerance or acceptance, especially if physical abuse, mental illness, or alcoholism are evident in the marriage. In this sense, the label of "affair" is a false one since it implies secrecy. Second, single women and men are involved with married women and men, but figures usually only give the married

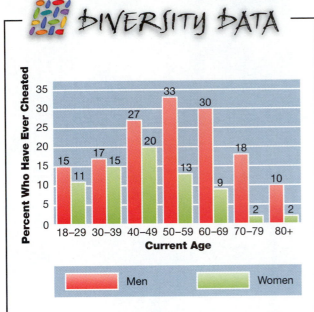

DIVERSITY DATA

FIGURE 7.3 Percent Who, While Married, Ever Had Sex with Someone Other than Spouse, by Age and Gender. At all age levels, but especially during middle age, men show significantly higher rates of extramarital sex than women. Considering the difficulty of collecting accurate data, do you think these figures may be either higher or lower for both genders?

Source: NORC. General Social Surveys, 1972-1996. Chicago: National Opinion Research Center, 1996. Reprinted by permission of NORC, Chicago, IL.

INTERNET CONNECTIONS

The text discusses the issues surrounding *homophobia*. You may wish to explore these issues further by accessing: http://hcqsa.virtualave.net/phobia.html. After you have examined this web site, answer the question, "Am I homophobic?" as honestly as you can. If your answer is "yes," do you think what you have learned in your sociology class has been instrumental in changing your point of view about homosexuality and homosexuals? Why or why not?

ficult to arouse sexually, and became aroused less frequently. These assumptions have all been proven false (Hoyenga & Hoyenga, 1993). The clitoris, not the vagina, as Freud insisted, is responsible for women having multiple orgasms.

When considering sexual attitudes, however, major gender differences persist. For women more than men, emotional closeness is a prerequisite for sexual intercourse. Men say sexual pleasure and conquest are the main motives (Leigh, 1989; Moore et al., 1989; Centers for Disease Control, 1997). Women adopt more of a person-centered approach to sex, and men adopt more of a body-centered approach. Most important, males are less likely to be criticized or to feel guilty about their sexual activities compared to females (Williams & Jaccoby, 1989; Davidson & Moore, 1994).

Such gendered attitudes are especially clear for extramarital relationships. Both genders act on their desire to have affairs, but men express a greater willingness to pursue them compared to women (Seal et al., 1994). There is less of a gap between what men say and actually do compared to what women say and actually do. Sexual excitement is a stronger motivator for men to have affairs than it is for women. Married women report that their affairs are less for sexual fulfillment and more for emotional support and companionship. Men report the reverse.

Symbolic interactionists highlight the fact that pleasurable sexual activities are gendered—conditioned by sexual scripts defined as acceptable for men or women. A double standard remains that reinforces a woman's passivity during the heterosexual sex act. The data on female sexuality are still viewed in light of male dominance in sexuality. Women and men both believe that her orgasm is a sign of his success as a lover. The idea that women are sexual beings who can and should experience sexual pleasure is relatively recent.

estimates. Third, depending on how an extramarital relationship is defined, sex may or may not be part of it. Fourth, reporting on these kinds of relationships is often threatening to respondents who are engaging in them. Although later research validated Kinsey's data, the high percentage of affairs he reported was suspect. It is also clear that when respondents report their knowledge of affairs *others* are having, the numbers increase. Finally, the fact that divorce is less stigmatized is also associated with more married people being open to extramarital relationships. Thus, it is probable that reported figures for extramarital relationships are lower than the actual.

The Double Standard. A *double standard* that men are allowed to express themselves sexually and women are not has traditionally existed in society. Since nonmarital sexual behavior for males and females is now similar, does a double standard still exist? The answer is yes when considering biological sex—but no when considering gender. Data on sexual behavior has changed dramatically. It was assumed that, compared to men, women had weaker sex drives, were more dif-

Ironically, the disappearance of a sexual double standard may not be desirable. No significant gender differences in frequency of nonmarital sexual activities, number of partners, or degree of emotional involvement with partners could trigger a lifetime of more sex with not only more people, but more people who are less known to their partners. Given the risks to both genders related to health and sexually transmitted diseases, sexual violence, and unplanned pregnancy, the disappearance of a sexual double standard may be ominous.

Sexuality in Later Life

The cultural barriers, gender norms, and the behavior-attitude discrepancy in sexuality also applies to later life. For the elderly, an already difficult situation is made worse by a combination of age and gender-related stereotypes. Because sexuality is associated with youth and virility, among the elderly it has been ignored or demeaned. The elderly are perceived to be sexless. If elderly males show sexual interest, they are labeled as "dirty old men." Once childbearing and mothering are completed for women, they are expected to retreat to a sexless existence. The situation is worsened since women and men also age differently in their sexuality, but in this case to the advantage of the woman. Women experience more comfort and less anxiety about sex as they age, thereby increasing their desire for intercourse. On the other hand, widows significantly outnumber widowers, so options for sexual activity decline for women, despite the fact that sexual desire remains strong.

Research by two other pioneers of sexuality, William Masters and Virginia Johnson (1966, 1970), shows that when advancing age and physiological changes influence sexual ability for men, performance anxiety increases. A man's wife may believe his "failure" is a rejection of her. Men are socialized early in life that they will be judged by their sexual potency and talents. As suggested earlier, when a couple accepts such beliefs, a cycle of less sex, less interest in sex, and increased emotional distance between them is perpetuated. The irony is that it is easier to cope with these incorrect beliefs if society assumes the elderly are not supposed to be sexually active anyway.

Research clearly illustrates that men and women of all age groups are far less sexually different from each other than once thought. Consistent with symbolic interactionism, they differ more in how they negotiate sexual activities and in the kinds of sexual relationships they seek. The social construction of women as passive sexual beings and men as sexual conquerors can be reconstructed to make them partners in a mutually pleasurable experience.

Despite the popular belief that elderly people are "sexless," the vast majority of older couples remain sexually active and sexually responsive to their partners throughout their lifetimes.

MACROLEVEL PERSPECTIVES: FUNCTIONALISM AND CONFLICT THEORY

Although the microlevel perspective of symbolic interactionism provides an excellent framework for understanding human sexuality, macrolevel perspectives also have much to offer on the subject. The macrolevel perspectives of functionalism and conflict theory emphasize how sexuality is located and arranged in large-scale social structures, such as social institutions. Both perspectives also emphasize that sexuality is a legitimate area of public debate, since it is associated with a host of social issues, including nonmarital pregnancy, sex education, prostitution, sexual victimization, the rights of homosexuals, and the spread of AIDS. Because social structures are interdependent, the sexual attitudes and practices occurring at one level in society will eventually influence other levels. The increased pregnancy rate for unmarried teens, for example, has major economic consequences for the families of the young couple if the child is not put up for adoption. Welfare and health benefits may be necessary, especially if the couple remains unmarried. High schools may offer babysitting for mothers so a diploma can be earned. All social institutions are impacted. Functionalism and conflict theory focus on different elements of this impact.

Functionalism

Functionalists maintain that society experiences the least disruption when sexuality is regulated by custom and law. Social equilibrium is maintained when people know the normative rules of sexuality and follow these rules. Problems that can arise when sexual norms are violated include unwanted pregnancy, family disruption, sexual violence, and the spread of sexually transmitted diseases such as AIDS. Functionalists suggest that sexual relationships occurring between adult, heterosexual married couples offer the best opportunities for social equilibrium. Other types of sexual relationships, from heterosexual cohabitation to homosexual liaisons, are potentially disruptive of this equilibrium.

An illustration of the functionalist approach to explaining social disruption when sexual norms are violated is child sexual victimization, especially incest. Cases of sexual victimization of children in families are not only increasing, but much higher than would be predicted by a culturally universal incest taboo (Chapter 3). For the United States, estimates of incestuous relationships run as high as 17 percent (Thornton, 1984; Gorey & Leslie, 1997). Given the profound personal and social results, it follows from functionalist theory that perpetrators of childhood sexual victimization need to be dealt with harshly. When perpetrators are publicly condemned, models for positive adult-child intimate standards are reinforced. Public consensus denouncing childhood sexual victimization is built voluntarily. Sexual order—therefore social order—is maintained.

Conflict Theory

Conflict theory also explains sexuality in terms of social location, arrangement, and the impact of sexuality on all the social institutions. But conflict theory focuses on how this arrangement is based on a hierarchy—how sexuality is stratified by degree of power. According to conflict theory, sexuality is embedded in larger social structures in which some groups wield more power over others. Inequality between groups is the inevitable result of these arrangements. The inequality existing in other social structures intrudes into the sexual lives of all members of society. Thus, sexuality is defined more by degree of power rather than degree of cooperation.

To return to the child victimization example, conflict theorists focus on the adult as wielding power over the child. Age is one form of accepted inequality that obviously puts children under the authority of parents and other adults. The most common form of child victimization involves younger females as victims and older males (including father, stepfather, and brother) as perpetrators. For incest, father-adolescent daughter/stepdaughter is the most common form (Russell, 1984; Finkelhor et al., 1990; Gelles & Harop, 1991). In larger society, females are subordinate to males. The more *patriarchal*—male-dominated—the society, the higher the level of female subordination. Thus, conflict theorists suggest that when a father engages in incest with his daughter, he expresses the right of access to any female. All types of sexual terrorism, whether incest, rape, the threat of violence, or even nonviolent sexual intimidation against women, are reinforced by patriarchal attitudes.

Although conflict theorists focus on the power of some to oppress others, they also suggest that power is a shifting resource. When powerless people join forces, they begin to amass resources to challenge existing power relationships, sexual or otherwise. Incest survivors speak out, rape victims bring rapists to trial, and sexual intimidation in school or workplace is reported. Conflict theorists point out that when men and women share sexual power more equally, sexual terrorism is reduced and joy of sexual intimacy is enhanced (Yllo, 1994; Sheffield, 1995).

≋ LIFE CONNECTIONS:
Sex and the College Student

College students are no exception to the now-expected U.S. pattern of nonmarital sex. Nonmarital sex among college students is also based on decades of data suggesting that college functions as the key marriage market for middle-class Americans. A number of important factors—such as romantic love, commitment, emotional attachment, physical attractiveness, and demographic similarity of partners—connect with sexuality when the marriage market is navigated. These factors will be explored in detail in Chapter 15. For now, however, the focus is on sexuality. As reflected in a major study of college students by Michael Moffatt, sexual chastity for the unmarried is "almost as dead as the dodo" (Moffatt, 1989).

Exploring Sexuality

Moffatt says that there is an undergraduate version of U.S. sexual standards that students embrace and celebrate. The major influence on the sexuality of the students he studied was U.S. popular culture. They located their sexual ideas almost entirely in the mass consumer culture of movies, popular music, advertising and television—from Dr. Ruth and sex manuals, to *Playboy* and *Penthouse* for men and Harlequin romance pulp fiction for women. Even sex education and popular psychology are filtered through these mass media sources.

Sex is important for college students, even if they are not very sexually active—the shy worry about not having it and those who opt for limited sex often give up the battle. These ideas are reflected in the following comments:

> From a male junior: I have never had sexual contact of any kind . . . and I am not proud of this fact. I just haven't been fortunate enough to have any. I consider sex a basic need in life, comparable to food and shelter.

> From a female sophomore: I personally prefer sex not too often. My boyfriend is just the opposite . . . I think (it might be) . . . that I am not ready to handle being sexually active. Don't get me wrong. I do enjoy sex and I do need it.

Both women and men celebrate sexual pleasure, but women promoted the value of sexual pleasure more than men. Moffatt suggests that these women may be making a deliberate effort to deny what they view as the outmoded "nice girls don't" stereotype. On the other hand, some women were afraid to talk about sexual pleasure or sexual experiences because as one woman stated, "I am basically afraid of what people might think of me if they knew about my sexual experiences." For women, celebrating the value of sexual pleasure did not make it easier for them to achieve it. Orgasm through intercourse was especially troublesome. Half of women reported they were still "failing" in achieving orgasm. For males, sexual pleasure was discussed less often either as an actuality or a problem. Moffatt believes that the male unspoken view on sexual pleasure is "Of course I enjoy sex. I'm a normal guy. It goes without saying!"

The celebration of sexual pleasure is backed by other data showing that college students are increasing the number of their sex partners and have sex with or without emotional involvement. However, females still report fewer partners and more emotional involvement in their sexual partners than men (Lottes, 1993). Male college students engage in riskier sexual behavior more often than females and have less knowledge about their sex partners. College males masturbate more fre-

Because of ads like this one, college students have a great deal of knowledge about sexually transmitted diseases, especially AIDS. However, college students are less likely to use condoms and rely more on birth control pills for "safe sex"—which may prevent pregnancy but not AIDS.

quently than college females (Oliver & Hyde, 1993; Poppen, 1995). Overall, these findings reflect that the celebration of sex as well as the sexual double standard are alive and well on college campuses.

One caution needs to be addressed here. These data reflect the sexual attitudes and behaviors of a large and growing segment of U.S. college students. They may not be representative of students attending colleges that are more conservative or religiously oriented. However, the broader generalization that college life typically includes an exploration of sexual life cannot be dismissed.

Nonconsensual Sex

The exploration and the celebration of sexuality expressed by the students in Moffatt's study are in stark contrast to the dark side of sexuality also existing on contemporary college campuses. Both in the United States and Canada, almost 30 percent of college

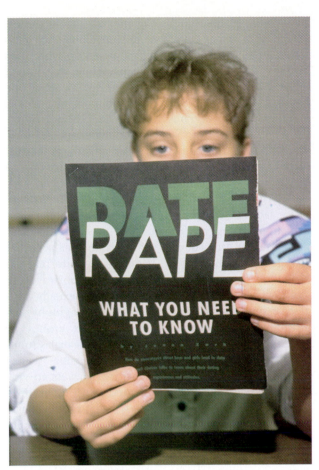

Date rape is common on college campuses but most women do not report the offense to either the police or to campus authorities. College personnel now routinely offer information to all students about the causes and consequences of date rape.

women report a rape or attempted rape (Barnes et al., 1991; Koss et al., 1994). Nonconsensual or pressured intercourse by physical force, drugs, alcohol, and psychological intimidation is the typical pattern reported by college women. A number of surveys of college males asking them if there was any chance they would rape a woman if they could be assured they would not be punished show that about one-third admit to it as at least a slim possibility.

Date or acquaintance rape is a fact of life on college campuses, with data indicating that half of college men have engaged in some form of sexual aggression on a date and between one-fourth and one-half of college women reporting being sexually victimized (Herman, 1989; Koss et al., 1994). Despite these high numbers, when victim and offender know one another and alcohol is involved, it is less likely to be reported and even less likely to gain a criminal conviction. It is estimated that only 1 in 100 acquaintance rapes gets reported to the police (Bohmer & Parrott, 1993; Finley & Corty, 1995).

Date rape is also associated with alcohol, the belief that men are entitled to sex after initiating and paying for the date, fraternity parties, and length of time the couple has been dating (Hirsch, 1990; Richardson & Hammock, 1991; Martin & Hummer, 1993). And despite substantial empirical evidence to the contrary, rape myths (Table 7.1) are more likely to be accepted by male college students than female.

According to the feminist perspective, increasing sexual violence and rape are spurred by a number of elements in society. Media representations often legitimize male aggression and reinforce gender stereotypes, especially in college life. Movies such as the classic "Animal House" seem to legitimate men's engaging in sexual "antics" that are hurtful to women and may even be criminal offenses. U.S. culture in general condones relationships that put men in dominant and aggressive roles and women in passive and submissive ones. Also, feminists believe that women continue to be treated as property owned by men.

Table 7.1	Myths of Rape
Myth	Reality
1. Rape is a sexual act.	Rape is an act of violence to show dominance of the rapist and achieve submission by the victim.
2. Rapes are committed by strangers.	Rape is more likely to occur between acquaintances. Date rape is an example.
3. Most rapes are spontaneous, with the rapist taking advantage of the opportunity to rape.	Rape is likely to be pre-planned. If spontaneity occurs, it may be part of another crime, such as robbery.
4. Women wear provocative clothing or flirt with men.	This is the classic blaming the victim myth. Since most rapes are preplanned, the rapist will strike regardless of appearance.
5. Women enjoy being raped.	The pain, violence, degradation, and psychological devastation experienced by the victim are overwhelming.
6. Most rapists are psychopathic or sexually abnormal.	It is difficult to distinguish the rapist from other men in terms of personality or ideas about sexuality.
7. When she says no to sex she really means yes.	When she says no she really means no.

Source: Table on p. 237 of *Gender Roles: A Sociological Perspective,* 3e by Linda L. Lindsey. Copyright © 1997 by Prentice-Hall, Inc. Reprinted by permission of Prentice-Hall, Inc. Upper Saddle River, NJ.

Some states do not have laws against marital rape. Sex is seen as part of the marriage agreement, whether the wife wants it or not. Both genders are socialized with these standards in mind—specifically the belief that women want to be dominated. This view allows the victim to be blamed and justifies the crime.

College men and women bring their socialization experiences with them to campus life. Their sexual behavior is shaped by these prior experiences as well as ongoing cultural influences. By studying sexual interactions on campus, sociologists help debunk long-held beliefs and hope to give students a sharper awareness of their social environment.

≋ SOCIETY CONNECTIONS: Sex for Profit

Catering to the sexual tastes and desires of people around the world has turned into a multibillion dollar industry. The two most profitable enterprises related to sexuality are *pornography*, selling sexually explicit material designed to enhance sexual arousal, and *prostitution*, engaging in sex acts for money. Because sexual expression is always regulated, what the sex industry finds as profitable and acceptable for its customers broader society may find unacceptable and illegal.

Pornography

Since ideas about sexual attractiveness are so diverse, a large variety of products and sexually stimulating material are produced for entertainment for adults across the globe. These include magazines, films, books, and sexual toys that are developed for customers who form distinct niches based on what they find sexually appealing or arousing. About one-fourth of men and one-tenth of women see at least one X-rated movie per year (Laumann et al., 1994). Pornography is big business. In the United States alone, it takes in over $6 billion dollars a year (Flowers, 1998). Pornography has come under a great deal of scientific and legal scrutiny because of its link to sexual aggression.

Pornography can be categorized according to two major factors—degree of depiction of sexual acts and depictions of aggression in these acts. "Hard-core" pornography often depicts genitalia and sex acts that are aggressive and violent. Women are uniformly the objects of the violence. Rarely are men portrayed in this manner. In experimental research, sexually suggestive but nonviolent "soft-core" pornography appears to have no direct effect on sex crimes or attitudes to rape. However, aggressive sexual stimuli or hard-core pornography showing rape scenes heightens sexual arousal, desensitizes viewers to violent sexual acts, and sees rape victims as less injured and less worthy (Silbert & Pines, 1984; U.S. Department of Justice, 1986). Whether the arousal actually leads to later aggression has not been fully determined. What is known, however, is that pornography is most dangerous for men who cannot effectively distinguish between aggression, control of women, and sexual arousal. Convicted rapists are as aroused by rape scenes as they are by portrayals of sex between consenting partners (Abel et al., 1977; Gray, 1990).

Men are often allies with women in believing that commercial sex—such as prostitution and pornography— is degrading to women.

The issue of what actually constitutes pornography and whether it should be illegal is hotly debated. One side of the debate focuses on pornography as implicitly condoning the victimization of women. This side argues that sexual violence against women is increasing and pornography fuels the desensitization to the violence. The longer the exposure, the greater the desensitization. They point to serial killer Ted Bundy's final statement about violent pornography the day before he was executed for killing at least twenty-three young women:

> . . . there is no way that killing me is going to restore those beautiful children . . . but there are lots of other kids playing on the streets who are going to be dead tomorrow . . . because other young people are reading the kinds of things that are available in the media today. (Mind of a killer, 1990)

The other side contends that pornography may actually reduce sex crimes by providing a nonharmful release of sexual tension. This side does not deny the association of pornography with women's degradation, but asserts that campaigns against it obscure more urgent needs of women. For instance, making pornography illegal denies income for women who are pornographic models and actresses. There is concern in both camps that constitutional issues are involved and that banning pornography amounts to censorship in a free society. All factions do agree, however, that child pornography should be censored. There is also some consensus on distinguishing pornography according to its degree of violent imagery. Both sides rely on social scientific research to support their contentions. The battle lines are clearly drawn, but to date neither side has been victorious.

Prostitution

Since sexuality is so diverse, prostitutes cater to that diversity. Some work occasionally as prostitutes in their roles as hostesses and adult entertainers. Others derive their total income from prostitution. Male prostitutes representing all sexual orientations cater to specific clienteles. Heterosexual men usually offer services as escorts and sex partners for wealthy women. Some of these men are referred to as *gigolos* and are the male counterparts to mistresses who are "kept" by wealthy men. More common among male prostitutes are those homosexual or bisexual men who frequent gay bars to ply their trade. They engage in prostitution for money as well as for sexual pleasure.

Children, especially young girls, are also recruited, or forced, into prostitution. Between 300,000 and 600,000 girls under the age of 18 are estimated to be working as prostitutes in the United States

INTERNET CONNECTIONS

What are your attitudes toward sex for profit? Do you think prostitution should be legalized? Are you aware that in many counties within the state of Nevada, prostitution is legal? Some houses of prostitution have their own web sites. With the disclaimer that some may find the contents offensive, you may wish to access the web site for the *Hacienda Ranch*, located in Wells, Nevada: http://haciendaranch.com/. If you choose to explore this site, what are your reactions?

(Goodall, 1995). In some parts of the developing world, girls are often abducted from their villages by owners of brothels dotting the sprawling urban slums. The more common pattern is that these girls are sold into sexual slavery by impoverished parents (Atlink, 1995). Sex tourism flourishes across the globe and many young prostitutes are paid for specific sex acts requested by men from Western Europe, the United States, and Japan (Oppermann, 1998). A key reason behind the increased demand for child prostitutes is the AIDS scare—there is a false sense of security that minors are less likely to be infected. Girls as well as boys are being marketed as "virgins, free of AIDS," so an even higher price is paid for their virginity (Flowers, 1998).

Historically, poverty-stricken women turned to prostitution as a survival means, a pattern that continues today. Attitudes toward these women have shifted between acceptance and toleration to outright condemnation. Prostitution flourished throughout the Roman Empire and declined when Christianity enveloped Europe and stamped the practice as irrevocably immoral for both prostitute and customer. But morality had a practical side as well. In nineteenth century Europe, an alarming rise in sexually transmitted diseases was traced to prostitutes whose clients were sailors returning from the New World (Bullough & Bullough, 1987). Today the global AIDS epidemic has fueled public urgency to deal with the "problem" of prostitution.

Prostitution is fundamentally a female occupation. Two-thirds of the white males in Kinsey's sample said they had seen a (female) prostitute at least once and almost one-fifth said they did so regularly. Greater sexual freedom combined with AIDS fear have dramatically decreased these percentages. Men who came of age in the 1950s were far more likely to

These teens have been arrested for prostitution. Did they engage in prostitution out of absolute economic deprivation—they had no choice— or did they freely choose to sell their services to willing clients?

have lost their virginity with a prostitute than men who came of age in the 1980s. Do these women offer their services because of financial desperation or as a freely chosen occupation? Feminists disagree on the answer to this question.

One faction argues that prostitution exists due to male demand, a need to subordinate women to male sexuality. If a woman chooses prostitution because of economic needs, then it is not a free choice. Therefore, sex traffickers and buyers should be criminalized and prostitution eliminated (MacKinnon, 1989; Barry, 1979, 1995). The other faction argues that sex workers are free agents who choose the best job they can of the gendered work available. The sexism in

prostitution is no different than sexism in the rest of society. Although the feminization of poverty may be a factor in a woman's choice to become a prostitute, women should not be further impoverished by denying them income from prostitution. Like other service industries, prostitution and its traffickers and buyers can be regulated, but laws against prostitution oppress sex workers the most. Prostitution, therefore should be decriminalized (Jenness, 1993; Doezema, 1998; Simmons, 1999).

For both pornography and prostitution, it is important to recognize macrolevel and microlevel perspectives. Social structure and sexual identity influence how they exist in society.

SUMMARY

1. Sexuality is social interaction where we perceive, experience and express ourselves as sexual beings. Most data on sexuality comes from intimate activities of couples, so the microlevel perspective of symbolic interactionism is most useful in explaining the data.

2. Sexuality is very diverse around the world—what one culture views as erotic, attractive, or sexually stimulating, another culture may disdain or even forbid.

3. Symbolic interactionists state that sexuality is socially constructed; sexual excitement that appears to be naturally driven by biology is a learned process.

4. Sex describes the biological characteristics distinguishing males and females) while gender is the social, cultural, and psychological characteristics defining masculinity and femininity. Sexual orientation is the preference for sexual partners, usually of one gender. All these categories overlap more than most people realize.

5. People construct their gender roles around their gender identity. Hermaphrodites, those born with both male and female or ambiguous genitals, often construct their gender identity on whichever sex is assigned to them at birth.

6. Sexual scripts are beliefs about acceptable sexual behavior for both genders. These beliefs con-

tribute to "gendered" sexuality and may serve to undermine options for different kinds of sexual expression for men and women.

7. Heterosexuals have sexual preferences for the other gender; homosexuals have sexual preferences for their own gender. Bisexuals are sexually responsive to either gender. There are problems with these definitions especially since the categories overlap a great deal. Because sexual orientation is so varied, Kinsey as well as contemporary researchers now suggest that it is better viewed as a continuum between exclusive heterosexuality and homosexuality.

8. Sexual dimorphism, separating the sexes into two distinct groups, is violated by groups such as the Native American berdache and Arab xanath. Transsexuals and transvestites may also violate the principle.

9. Homophobia—negative attitudes to homosexuals—is widespread. While the evidence is mixed for race and homophobia, it is clear that males are more homophobic than females because masculinity norms support homophobia. However, tolerance and acceptance of homosexuals is increasing, especially with young adults.

10. Kinsey's original data found relatively high rates of masturbation, orgasm, and premarital sex for both genders, patterns that persist and have increased since. Extramarital sex is disapproved but a high percentage of people engage in it. It is likely that the numbers for extramarital sex are higher than reported.

11. Both men and women have similar rates of nonmarital sex, but the double standard discouraging sexuality for women and encouraging it for men persists. The elderly are particularly vulnerable to gendered stereotypes about sexuality.

12. Functionalists and conflict theorists view sexuality in terms of how it is located in large-scale institutions. Functionalists believe custom and law must regulate sexuality to keep society from the least disruption. Conflict theorists look at people's location in the social structure, which puts some at risk more for sexual violence than others.

13. College life comes with the expectation to explore and even celebrate sexuality, but men and women do so differently and the double standard persists. College life may also be sexually violent, with almost 30 percent of college women reporting a rape or attempted rape.

14. According to feminist sociologists, the media and U.S. culture condone relationships in which men are aggressive and women are submissive. This reinforcement contributes to sexual violence.

15. Pornography and prostitution profit through sex. Defining what constitutes pornography and what types should be illegal is hotly debated. The legalization of prostitution hinges on beliefs about whether prostitutes freely choose their occupation.

KEY TERMS

bisexual   166

gender   164

hermaphrodites   164

heterosexual   166

homophobia   170

homosexual   166

sex   164

sexual dimorphism   169

sexual orientation   164

sexual scripts   165

sexuality   161

CRITICAL THINKING QUESTIONS

1. Explain how research on sexuality can be used to claim that there *has* been a sexual revolution as well as that there *has not* been one. What research would you focus on to justify one or the other claim? How do the media influence the beliefs about sexuality?

2. Speaking as a sociologist who is also a symbolic interactionist, what would you say to a person who states that sexuality is solely a biological fact?

3. From the research on hermaphrodites, gender identity and sexual orientation, demonstrate how the principle sexual dimorphism may be violated.

4. Show how sexuality is "gendered" with reference to sexuality inside and outside of marriage and issues surrounding "sex for profit."

 **8** DEVIANT BEHAVIOR

OUTLINE

Peyote on the Reservation

Joseph, an 18-year-old Navajo boy, recently joined a 125-year old Christian sect called the Native American Church that uses the bud of the peyote cactus in its sacred rituals. Although considered a dangerous drug by many people because of the vivid hallucinations it produces, peyote has long been familiar to Native Americans as a traditional means of promoting healing and self-knowledge (Aberle, 1982). Similarly, before the reservation era, it was expected that young members of a number of different Western tribes would engage in "vision quests," periods of prolonged fasting and self-mutilation that eventually led to hallucinations much like those Joseph is now seeking through peyote. Indeed, in some traditional Native American cultures, youths who were not successful in evoking visions of ancestor spirits were considered deviant, or at least less than full adults. (Lame Deer & Erdoes, 1972)

Marijuana in the Netherlands

Pieter, a young resident of Amsterdam, is on his way to pick up his girlfriend for a Friday night date. He stops at a local coffee shop and purchases a small bag of marijuana and several grams of hashish. This is, for all practical purposes, a legal transaction. The Netherlands treats "soft" drugs much as the United States attempts to control alcohol and tobacco (Perrine, 1994). Contrary to what one might think, the Dutch policy, in force for several decades, has apparently led to a substantial *decrease* in the use of marijuana and hashish. (Trebach, 1989)

Coca Cola® in Utah

As a Mormon living in a small town in Utah, Susan knows that her spiritual well-being depends on, among other things, following her church's teachings requiring abstinence from drugs—including not only alcohol and tobacco (to say nothing of peyote and hashish!), but also caffeine-laden drinks such as tea, coffee, and some soft drinks (Whalen, 1964). But sometimes it's hard to live up to these ideals. Earlier today Susan drank a Coca Cola, and now she can't stop worrying about her lapse into "drug abuse."

Each of these three young people has used a mood-altering drug, and in each case, some people would consider the behavior wrong while others would see it as perfectly acceptable. This chapter examines how behaviors such as drug taking come to be socially defined as unacceptable. We will also explore a number of different explanations for why people engage in such activity.

WHAT IS DEVIANCE?

Deviance may be defined as behavior, beliefs, or conditions that are viewed by relatively powerful segments of society as serious violations of important norms. Let's look at each element of this definition more closely.

When most Americans think of deviants, they visualize drug addicts, rapists, and child molesters. This view emphasizes behaviors that involve *major* violations of *important* norms. People are not generally defined as deviant for such minor violations as not applauding at the end of a play or wearing mismatched clothes.

But note that by the sociological definition, deviance may consist not only of *behaviors*, but also of *beliefs*—atheism and communism come to mind—and *conditions*, such as being physically handicapped, mentally ill, HIV-positive, or morbidly obese (Degher & Hughes, 1991).

Students are frequently uncomfortable with the fact that sociologists commonly characterize people who are physically disabled or mentally ill as deviants. Such an interpretation seems unjust: These people did not choose to be different. Yet it is clear that they are frequently denied full acceptance in society, just as

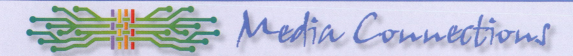

Sex, Drugs, and Rock 'N' Roll

Popular culture—and especially popular music—has always been controversial. Almost 2400 years ago, the Greek philosopher Plato wrote the following words of warning:

Forms and rhythms in music are never changed without producing changes in the most important political forms and ways...The new style quickly insinuates itself into manners and customs and from there it issues a greater force [and] goes on to attack laws and constitutions, displaying the utmost impudence, until it ends by overthrowing everything, both in public and in private.

The immediacy and pervasiveness of the modern means of mass communication have greatly intensified such concerns. Since the birth of rock music in the 1950s, critics have repeatedly charged it with being responsible for promoting deviance and moral decay among teenagers. A few historical highlights:

- In the mid-1950s a congressional subcommittee investigated the purported link between juvenile delinquency and rock. Major concerns centered around sexuality and race: The music and hip-swiveling performances of Elvis and his imitators were (correctly) charged with openly celebrating adolescent sexuality and with bringing elements of African-American music into the mainstream culture.
- The controversy escalated further during the rebellious 1960s and 1970s. Lyrics became more sexually explicit and some very popular songs deliberately encouraged drug use and political protest. Beatle John Lennon casually claimed that his group was "bigger than Jesus." The odor of burning vinyl wafted over church parking lots as conservative ministers and their flocks registered their outrage by burning Beatles records.
- In the 1980s the center of attention shifted to heavy metal: Artists like Ozzy Osborne and Alice Cooper

were charged with promoting every form of deviance up to and including Satanism. In May 1985, a group of prominent Washington wives headed by Tipper Gore founded the Parents' Music Resource Center (PMRC) to promote, among other things, advisory warning stickers on albums whose lyrics they found offensive. Again, congressional hearings were held. South Carolina Senator Fritz Hollings orated, "We must rescue the tender young ears of this nation from this rock porn." Rock musician Frank Zappa responded by suggesting that the PMRC's solution was like treating dandruff with decapitation.

- More recently, rap has become the prime target. In 1990 a judge in Fort Lauderdale, Florida, ruled that the lyrics of some of 2 Live Crew's songs were legally obscene. An article in *Newsweek* criticized the emerging "gangsta rap" subgenre for its violent, racist, and misogynistic (anti-female) themes and described the

---

bank robbers and bigamists—people who are generally thought to have chosen to violate norms—are looked down upon. The extent to which an individual's behavior is voluntary may affect how negatively he or she is viewed, but it is not necessary that nonconformity or difference be freely chosen for it to be classified as deviance (Link et al., 1987; Gortmaker et al, 1993; Crandall, 1995).

Along the same lines, note that an individual need not cause harm to anyone in order to be regarded as deviant. Most mental patients, many drug users, and the vast majority of members of unconventional religious groups harm no one except, arguably, themselves, yet they are clearly deviants in most people's eyes.

Deviance should be differentiated from the related concept of crime, which we will discuss in the next chapter. A **crime** is a violation of a formal statute enacted by a legitimate government. Acts such as homicide, arson, or rape are clearly both criminal and deviant. However, some criminals are not treated as deviants, including most traffic offenders and people

who cheat on their income taxes. Furthermore, many types of deviance, such as mental illness or not bathing regularly, are not covered by the criminal statutes (see Figure 8.1).

The Nature of Deviance

The three vignettes that opened this chapter illustrate an important point: *Deviance is relative*. What is regarded as deviant in one society may be accepted or even honored in another (Goode, 1997). Smoking marijuana is likely to be seen as deviant in the United States, but not in the Netherlands; drinking Coca Cola is deviant for a Mormon, but not for a Catholic or Jew. And, as we have said, in many Native American cultures, *not* experiencing hallucinations during a vision quest meant that a young man was not a full adult.

Some of the most striking examples of the relative nature of deviance concern sexuality, the topic of Chapter 7. Some cultures are extremely repressed by American standards, regarding as seriously de-

music as savage, ugly, sullen, appalling, vile, revolting, and repulsive. Public Enemy came under attack for "By The Time I Get to Arizona," which depicted members of the group assassinating Arizona state officials who refused to endorse a state holiday honoring Martin Luther King, Jr. Ice T's speed metal song "Cop Killer," which openly condoned the killing of police officers, was even more controversial. President Bush denounced "Cop Killer" and sixty members of Congress asked Time-Warner to stop distributing the album on which it appeared.

And the beat goes on. The fastest selling hip-hop record of all time, Eminem's *The Marshall Mathers LP*, released early in 2000, featured the song "Criminal," which included the following deeply homophobic lyric:

I'll stab you in the head / Whether you're a fag or a les / Or a homosex / A hermaph or a trans-a-ves / ... Hate fags? The answer's yes.

Why do themes of deviance recur generation after generation in popular music? The simplest answer is because such themes are popular among the young people who buy tapes and discs. In a capitalist society, businesses provide what their customers will buy. If refined melodies and inoffensive lyrics sold well, the entertainment industry would be only too happy to supply them.

At a deeper level, we might ask why many adolescents are attracted to images of violence and deviance. Sociologists note that modern teenagers are engaged in a difficult process of identity construction. Precisely because the process of becoming an adult involves suppressing their more hedonistic inclinations, youth are often attracted to music that is overtly rebellious. This is no different from a bored office worker rushing to watch the latest Mel Gibson action flick. We live out vicariously that which we have learned we cannot do in the real world.

The vast majority of youths who listen to gangsta rap will not grow up to become cop-killing outlaws, but the fact that such a possibility is given a measure of legitimacy in rap lyrics deeply disturbs many adults.

With this said, we still need to ask whether popular music actually does promote deviance. If people absorbed media imagery directly, a view we will call the *hypodermic model* in Chapter 20, then some concern would seem reasonable. But sociologists who have studied the effects of the media are generally in agreement that media messages are filtered through the values and norms we learn during the process of primary socialization and are further interpreted through conversations with our family and peers. So long as most youth are socialized into generally pro-social attitudes, images of deviance in popular music will have little effect on them. If most people were no longer socialized to be pro-social, we would be facing much more serious problems than the occasional offensive song lyric!

1. Do parental advisory labels on tapes and CDs keep youths from buying offensive music or do they actually encourage sales by making the music seem like "forbidden fruit"?
2. What is a more serious social problem, offensive lyrical content or the threat of censorship?

Sources: Gates, 1990; Leland, 1993; Epstein, 1994; Rose, 1994; Wekesser, 1995; De Curtis, 2000.

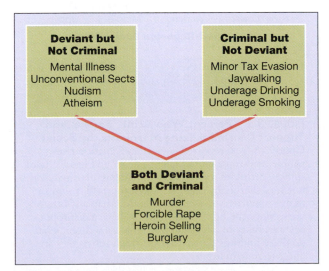

FIGURE 8.1   The Relationship Between Deviance and Criminality

viant many behaviors that we consider normal. Among the traditional Cheyenne, for example, a girl who lost her virginity was permanently dishonored and considered unmarriageable (Hoebel, 1978). Residents of Inis Beag, an island off the west coast of Ireland, were even more conservative, traditionally disapproving of nudity even in the marital bed (Messenger, 1971).

On the other hand, about 25 percent of all societies fully accept premarital sex by both genders (Broude & Greene, 1976). In the developed world, the Scandinavian cultures are widely known for their sexual openness. The least sexually repressed people in the world may well be the Polynesians of Mangaia in the Cook Islands; early field work among these people reported intense sexual activity among both women and men, largely devoid of romantic attachment and beginning well before puberty (Marshall, 1971; see Harris, 1995, for a more skeptical account).

What is regarded as deviant also changes over time within any particular society. A hundred years

Less than fifty years ago, the stigma of homosexuality was so severe that the vast majority of gays and lesbians chose to keep their sexual orientation carefully hidden. Today, same-sex couples are a familiar sight in America's larger cities, especially in the less conservative parts of the country.

ago, child-rearing practices that would be seen as abusive today were not only accepted but encouraged. Parents were told, "Spare the rod and spoil the child." Racial discrimination, far from being condemned, was legal and widely endorsed from church pulpits. And millions of respectable Americans routinely used drugs that are illegal today. Opium was a common ingredient in over-the-counter medications, and Coca Cola originally contained a small dose of cocaine.

On the other hand, many practices that most Americans now take for granted were once regarded as deviant, including participating in lotteries, women smoking and wearing pants in public, and unmarried couples cohabiting.

Deviance is relative in other ways as well. Behavior that is generally acceptable for one gender—such as asking a friend to accompany you to a public restroom—is unacceptable for the other. Behavior that is strongly encouraged in one subculture may be equally strongly rejected by another. For example, members of street gangs are expected to fight—but the Amish are characterized by strict norms against physical combat.

Deviance also varies by place—language heard in a football locker room would be most unseemly at a church social. Class also matters. Although standards are currently changing, bearing children out of wedlock continues to be more acceptable in the lower class than in the middle and upper strata of U.S. society. Figure 8.2 illustrates how class affects drinking, smoking, and attitudes concerning whether marijuana ought to be decriminalized.

The great variation in what is considered deviant in various contexts strongly suggests that *no behavior is inherently deviant*. While some actions, such as incest within the nuclear family, are widely condemned, researchers have not been able to identify any universally deviant behaviors.

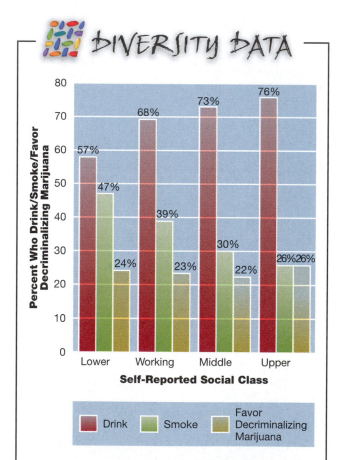

FIGURE 8.2   Percent Who Drink, Smoke, and Support Decriminalizing Marijuana, by Social Class   As self-reported social class position rises, people tend to be more likely to drink and less likely to smoke. Attitudes toward decriminalizing marijuana do not vary sharply by class, although the elite is slightly more supportive of decriminalization than any other class. Since the upper class tends to have a disproportionate ability to affect the way laws are written, what do these findings suggest about which substances are likely to remain legal?

Source: NORC. General Social Surveys, 1972–1996. Chicago: National Opinion Research Center, 1996.

Since deviance is a relative concept, the question of *who decides* what will and will not be considered deviant is a crucial one. In small, traditional societies with a very high level of consensus regarding norms and values, it may be reasonable to say that the society as a whole makes this decision. However, in modern societies where disagreement about norms is widespread, deviance is primarily defined by individuals and groups with high levels of power and prestige. In these societies, the definition of deviance is therefore a political process (Schur, 1971).

There is widespread agreement in modern societies that certain types of behaviors, especially predatory crimes like robbery and forcible rape, are seriously deviant. But in other areas, such as attitudes toward recreational drug use, soft-core pornography, and homosexuality, where value-consensus is lacking, the preferences of the powerful usually dominate. Thus, for example, the primary reason why one drug—say, marijuana—is generally considered deviant, whereas another drug—say, whiskey—is widely accepted, is not because of the relative dangerousness of these substances but rather because the most pow-

Interracial couples or those in which one partner is substantially older than the other frequently encounter negative informal social control in the form of critical comments from family and friends.

erful members of society—typically older, middle- and upper-class white males—are much more likely to relax after work with a few drinks than with a joint.

Finally, *deviance is a cultural universal*. In other words, deviance can be found in every society (Durkheim, 1897/1964). Even in a culture with a high degree of normative consensus and virtually no serious crime, there is occasional misbehavior. However, as the story of Susan (the Mormon girl who indulged in a forbidden soft drink) suggests, in a strongly moralistic society, what outsiders might consider to be a minor type of deviance will likely be viewed as a relatively major violation.

Deviance and Social Control

As the previous section noted, deviance consists of the violation of important social norms, the expectations that guide people's behaviors. Sociologists use the term **social control** to refer to measures taken by members of society intended to encourage conformity to norms. In other words, the purpose of social control is to reduce, if not eliminate, deviance (Gibbs, 1989). This can be done in three general ways: through formal social control, informal social control, or internalized normative standards.

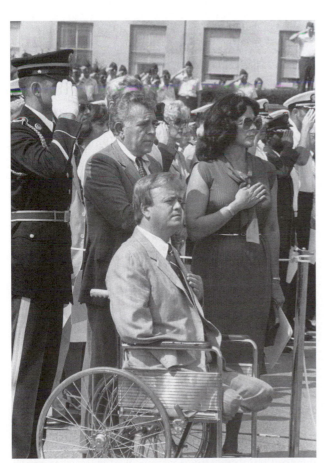

People with serious physical disabilities are often treated as deviants. However, a record of outstanding personal achievement can help to overcome the stigma. Senator Max Cleland of Georgia is an excellent example, as is former presidential candidate Bob Dole.

Formal social control consists of efforts to discourage deviance made by people such as police officers and college deans whose jobs involve, in whole or in part, punishing nonconformity and rewarding obedience.

Punishments, referred to as **negative sanctions,** are especially important at the formal level. Negative sanctions range from a parking fine or academic probation to the total ostracism of a deviant by an entire community (Hostetler & Huntington, 1971). The ultimate negative formal sanction is, of course, execution.

Formal social control may also involve **positive sanctions** or rewards, such as a good conduct medal or an A on an examination. In either case, the purpose of the sanction is the same: to promote conformity and to discourage deviance.

While formal social control is necessary to restrain the most serious deviants, no society could survive if people conformed only to avoid formal sanctioning. A far more effective way to reduce deviance is through **informal social control**—positive and negative sanctions applied by friends and family. The desire for approval from significant others can be a far stronger motive for conformity than the fear of negative formal sanctions. After all, while the authorities may have a great deal of power over us, it is usually the opinions of those who are closest to us that really matter. Gossip is an excellent means of informal social control (Cohen, 1985).

However, neither formal nor informal social control is society's main line of defense against deviance. Most conformity results from the *internalization of norms* during the process of moral socialization. Fear of externally imposed sanctions is often far less powerful than the desire to avoid feelings of guilt. Similarly, the pleasure obtained from positive sanctions can't compare with the sense of self-esteem that comes from living up to internalized normative expectations (Berger, 1963: 93).

FOUR QUESTIONS ABOUT DEVIANCE

Sociologists who study deviance are generally interested in answering one or more of four important theoretical questions:

1. Who decides what behaviors, beliefs, and conditions will be defined as deviant?
2. What are the social functions of deviance?
3. Why do people deviate?
4. How do people react to deviants—and how do these reactions in turn affect the behavior of the deviants?

Later in this chapter, we will explore each of these issues in some depth. However, before we proceed further, it will be instructive to introduce one of the most widely read research studies in the sociology of deviance, William Chambliss's (1973) analysis of two groups of juveniles whom he called the "Saints" and the "Roughnecks." Despite the fact that this study was carried out a generation ago, its central findings remain as valid and relevant as they were when the study was first published. We will use this research to illustrate a number of important theoretical points.

The Saints and the Roughnecks were two groups of boys who attended the same high school. The Saints grew up in middle-class families. The other clique, the Roughnecks, came from lower-class backgrounds.

Both groups of boys were fairly seriously delinquent. The Saints cut school regularly, drank excessively, drove recklessly, and committed various acts of petty and not-so-petty vandalism. The Roughnecks, too, were often truant and stole from local stores, got drunk, and fought with other youths. But despite these similarities, the two groups were regarded very differently by social control agents, in particular by the police and school authorities.

The middle-class Saints were perceived as basically good boys. This image was partly a direct reflection of the respectability of their parents, but it was also influenced by other class-based factors. The Saints had learned during primary socialization to treat authority figures with the appearance of respect: When they cut school, they arranged for fake excuses; when stopped by the police, they were always polite and deferential. Further, since they could afford cars, their deviance was generally carried out in other towns or at least well away from the eyes of their neighbors. When the Saints were caught misbehaving, social control agents consistently made excuses for them.

In contrast, the Roughnecks were viewed as no-good punks heading for trouble. Again, this label was both a direct and an indirect consequence of their class status. Their socialization had not prepared them to sweet-talk the authorities; instead, they tended to be insolent and aggressive when confronted. Lacking the means to own cars, they hung out on a centrally located street corner where everyone in the community could see them. When they were caught in some criminal or deviant act, nobody was inclined to go easy on them.

Which group was more deviant? In the eyes of the community, clearly the Roughnecks. Yet, according to Chambliss, the Saints caused at least as much harm as the Roughnecks, and they probably committed more criminal acts. But the fact that the Roughnecks were labeled as deviant had devastating

Informal Social Control: Shunned at Berkeley

Informal means of controlling deviance are far more common and often much more effective than the formal controls applied by the police, courts and prisons. Small, traditional societies, or *Gemeinschafts* (see Chapter 4), rely especially heavily on informal social control. The Amish custom of *meidung*, or shunning, is a classic example (Wasilchick, 1992). When an individual violates important religious rules, the faithful—including the person's immediate family—are forbidden to speak to that person, eat at the same table with him or her, or even, in the case of a spouse, engage in marital relations. Shunning is the ultimate penalty: Imagine living in a community where everyone behaved as if you no longer existed.

Even in modern *Gesellschaft* societies in which elaborate formal social control mechanisms are present, informal social control remains important. On Memorial Day weekend, 1997, University of California student David Cash and his best friend Jeremy Strohmeyer visited a casino outside Las Vegas. Around 3:30 AM, Strohmeyer lured a 7-year-old girl into a ladies room. Cash followed, watched as his friend forced the child into a stall, then walked outside. Not long afterward, Strohmeyer rejoined Cash and confessed that he had raped and murdered the girl. Cash had made no effort to stop the assault; nor did he report the crime—out of loyalty to his friend, he

later claimed. Strohmeyer was arrested a few days later. To avoid the death penalty, he pleaded guilty and was sentenced to life without parole. But prosecutors could not bring charges against Cash because he had not broken any law (Hammer, 1998).

During his freshman year at Berkeley, Cash went unnoticed. That August, however, he appeared on a popular radio talk show, defended his behavior, and proclaimed, "the university officials are behind me, baby." And they were. Because he had not committed a crime or violated campus codes, university officials (agents of formal social control) had no grounds for expelling him or even reviewing his case. In the chancellor's words, "We cannot set aside due process based upon our outrage over a particular instance." But Berkeley students who learned about the case disagreed. Soon after the talk show, a large demonstration alerted other students to Cash's presence on campus. He was thrown out of a fraternity party and chased to his dormitory room by an angry mob. Overnight, spray-painted graffiti reading EXPEL DAVID CASH appeared all over the campus. The Berkeley student senate passed a bill asking Cash to withdraw voluntarily. Invoking due process, the president of the senate vetoed the bill. In his words, "David Cash is morally repugnant. But if you don't like him, don't talk to him. That's all you can do."

Cash continued to attend classes at Berkeley, but as an outcast, shunned (in Amish tradition) by fellow students. No one spoke to him, though some students muttered obscenities when he passed by. Everywhere he went, he confronted graffiti calling for his expulsion. He avoided major gatherings. When he walked into a nearby 7-Eleven store, a stranger spat in his face. Thus when formal social controls failed to satisfy public outrage, Berkeley students applied informal controls.

The shunning of David Cash shows that even in a modern, heterogeneous society, there is a high level of consensus on certain issues, such as child molestation. Berkeley has a reputation as an exceptionally tolerant campus where widely different points of view are respected. But even there, Cash found few defenders. Just as prisons isolate child molesters from other inmates for their own protection, so Cash was accompanied everywhere by a plain-clothes police officer.

1. Do you think Cash would have been more likely to have come to understand the seriousness of his failure to act had he simply been expelled from Berkeley rather than being shunned?
2. Can you think of examples from your own experience of informal social control? Were they effective?

Sources: Wasilchick, 1992; Hammer, 1998.

consequences. Seven of the eight Saints finished college and most established themselves in careers as doctors, politicians, and businessmen. Two of the seven Roughnecks never graduated from high school, three became heavily involved in criminal activities, and only two achieved stable, respectable community roles.

Now we will return to the four questions that opened this section and explore how sociologists respond to them, making reference to the Saints and Roughnecks as appropriate. This discussion will also

illustrate how many sociological explanations of deviance are linked to the major theoretical perspectives that were introduced in Chapter 1.

WHO DEFINES WHAT IS DEVIANT?

The first question sociologists must consider in explaining deviance is how—and by whom—certain behaviors, beliefs, and characteristics come to be understood in a given society as deviant. We touched briefly on this issue earlier in the chapter; here we go into greater detail.

The question of who defines deviance has principally been addressed by conflict theorists (Lynch, 1994). Their answer, in short, is that societal elites control the definition process (Turk, 1977; Chasin, 1997).

You will recall that conflict theory is based on principles first developed by Karl Marx, who maintained that the ruling class in a capitalist society controls all the major institutions and uses them to protect its interests (Lynch & Groves, 1989). Their control of the political institution is especially significant. The legal statutes that define what will be considered criminal deviance clearly reflect the values and interests of the ruling class (Quinney, 1970; Greenberg, 1981). Crimes committed mostly by the poor—robbery, burglary, larceny, aggravated assault—carry heavy penalties, while offenses most commonly committed by elites, such as price-fixing, dumping hazardous wastes, or maintaining unsafe working conditions, carry lesser penalties (Reiman, 1995). Conflict theorists also charge that the police and courts routinely discriminate in the application of the law, a problem we will take up in Chapter 9 (Smith et al., 1984; Arvanites, 1992).

The elite also control the schools and the mass media, two additional important social institutions, and use them to shape people's understandings of what sorts of behaviors and ideas ought to be considered deviant. Again, these definitions are biased in favor of the capitalists' interests and emphasize the seriousness of types of deviance that are especially common among the poor and minorities (Quinney, 1970). Note that these insights concerning how deviance is

defined reflect a synthesis of the conflict and symbolic interactionist perspectives.

Richard Quinney is a contemporary American conflict theorist who has addressed these issues. Quinney accepts the basic Marxist view that the ruling class defines deviance and enforces the laws in a biased and self-serving fashion. He goes on to note that this state of affairs actually promotes norm violation among both the wealthy and the poor (Quinney, 1977). The elite commit what Quinney calls "crimes of domination and repression," which are designed to increase their wealth and power and to control the middle and lower classes, with relative impunity. After all, writes Quinney (1972), "... those in power, those who control the legal system, are not likely to prosecute themselves and define their official policies as crime."

At the same time, the poor have little choice but to engage in predatory deviance in order to survive. Most of their acts are property crimes such as larceny and burglary. The lower classes also engage in a great deal of violent personal crime, which Quinney sees as an expression of their anger and frustration. Crime, then, is a rational choice for both the upper class—because they can get away with it—and the poor—because they have few other options (Gordon, 1973).

Conflict theorists believe that most sociologists are too willing to accept elites' definitions of deviance. Mainstream sociologists, they say, effectively allow the dominant class to define their research agenda. As a result, many sociologists do not devote sufficient attention to the great harm that results from the misbehavior of elites and from the inequities of the criminal law (Liazos, 1972).

For example, America's current drug laws mandate much more severe penalties for the possession or

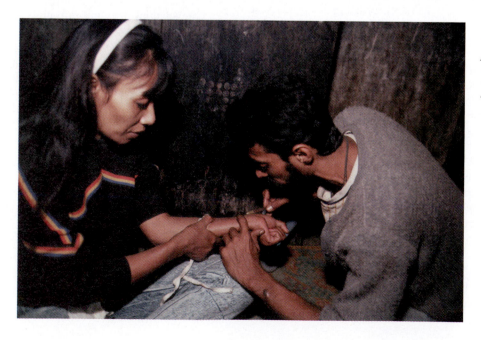

Conflict theorists maintain that the high rate of drug abuse among the poor results from the same frustrations and anomie that help explain their heavy involvement in violent and property crime.

On February 4, 1999, New York City police fired 41 shots into the home of unarmed African immigrant Amadou Diallo, killing him instantly. Shared opposition to this act of apparent police brutality unites the members of this protest crowd.

sale of crack cocaine than for the powdered form of the drug (Smolowe, 1995). The average prison sentence for crack is three to eight times longer, yet the two forms of the drug are, in essence, chemically identical (Kappler et al., 1996). Crack, however, is used primarily by lower-class African Americans, while the majority of powdered cocaine offenders are white. Similarly, the police are much more likely to arrest streetwalkers, who are heavily minority, than to go after call girls, who are mostly white. They also rarely arrest female prostitutes' male customers.

Conflict theory can be easily applied to the Saints and the Roughnecks. The middle-class Saints misbehaved extensively, yet they suffered no lasting consequences because the authorities identified them as "our kind" and accordingly treated them with a presumption of innocence. Conversely, the lower-class Roughnecks were defined as members of the "dangerous classes" and treated accordingly. No conflict theorist would be at all surprised by the different paths these two groups traveled after high school.

The primary policy implication of conflict theory is that economic inequality must be substantially reduced in order to prevent the dominant class from distorting the process of deviance definition to its own advantage. Most conflict theorists believe that this reduction can only be achieved by a fundamental shift in the American political economy away from

capitalism and toward some form of democratic socialism (Pepinsky & Quinney, 1993; Milovanovic, 1996).

Conflict theory's great strength is that it directs our attention to the importance of power in shaping social definitions of deviance. It has also highlighted the biases present in our criminal justice system. Yet the conflict approach enjoys only limited acceptance among sociologists and has had little effect on the general public's attitude. In a sense, this lack of acceptance may validate a central tenet of conflict analysis: Most Americans, perhaps including many sociologists, have internalized elite definitions of deviance and, therefore, consider the conflict perspective too "radical" to merit serious consideration.

Nonetheless, there are some real problems with conflict theory (Toby, 1979; Inciardi, 1980; Sparks, 1980; Gibbs, 1987; Wilbanks, 1987). First, its claim that the elite control the process whereby deviance is defined makes the most sense with regard to acts such as insider trading or drug use. It is hard to support when applied to predatory crimes such as murder, forcible rape, or robbery, which almost everyone, regardless of class, regards as seriously harmful. Furthermore, the primary solution that conflict theory proposes—socialism—is not only unlikely to be achieved (Owomero, 1988), but also did not appear to be effective in reducing deviance and crime in the old Soviet bloc nations.

WHAT ARE THE FUNCTIONS OF DEVIANCE?

The conflict perspective, as we have just seen, is useful for answering the first of our key questions: Who decides what is deviant? The second question, however, is best addressed by the functionalist perspective.

Functionalists maintain that any aspect of a society that fails to contribute to its stability tends eventually to fade away. Since deviance is a cultural universal, it follows that, although it is socially devalued, it must serve some functions (Erickson, 1966). There are three critical positive functions of deviance:

1. *The Boundary Setting Function.* In complex modern societies, it is often unclear what the *real* rules are. How frequently and how extensively can students cheat before they are expelled? How fast can you really drive on the interstate without getting a ticket? How much can you drink before people will start thinking of you as an alcoholic? In some cases, there are no official rules; in others, there are formal rules but they are enforced with a degree of tolerance, which means that there is a difference between the *formal* and the *actual* boundaries of tolerated behavior.

From Getting High to Getting Drunk: Changing Styles of Campus Deviance

The marijuana "epidemic," as some called it, peaked in the mid-1970s (Akers, 1992). Study after study in this era found that two out of three college students had used pot, up from a mere 5 percent in the mid-1960s. At the time, marijuana was widely considered a "gateway drug": Someone who used it was believed to be likely to progress to more powerful and addictive "hard" drugs, such as cocaine or heroin. Simply put, smoking pot was seen as the first step toward becoming a junkie. Prior to the 1960s, marijuana use had been largely confined to "outsiders," especially Mexican American laborers and jazz musicians, whom respectable people did not consider "one of us." Use of the drug by these groups merely confirmed their otherness; it was not a cause for public alarm.

When middle-class college students—presumably the best and the brightest American youth and the nation's future leaders—began using marijuana, it was a different story. As part of the hippie rebellion, college students were also experimenting with cocaine, LSD, amphetamines, and other illicit substances. Clearly, the nation's youth were at risk. And so campaigns like DARE and Just Say No were born.

Over time, the use of marijuana and other illicit drugs by college students declined. But a new epidemic was on the horizon. In 1994 the Harvard School of Public Health issued a report on the use of alcohol on college campuses. A survey of 140 campuses found that almost half of all students engaged in "binge drinking" (consuming five or more drinks at one sitting for men, four or more for women). Even more alarming, half of students who binge do so regularly. First-year students are most likely to describe their weekend plans as "drink, dance, scream, puke, pass out." Binge drinkers are far more likely than other students to engage in unprotected sex, drive while intoxicated, miss classes, and experience memory lapses. They are also more likely to commit acts of vandalism, get into fights, and injure themselves.

Indeed, drinking too much too fast can be deadly. Each year an estimated fifty students die from bingeing, either because they pass out and choke to death on their own vomit or because their blood becomes so thick that oxygen can't reach their brain (alcohol poisoning). The effects of binge drinking are not limited to participants. At schools with high binge rates, a majority of students who don't drink report such second-hand effects as not being able to sleep or study, enduring insults or unwanted sexual advances, and having to care for drunken friends. A recent study found that despite campaigns publicizing the dangers of alcohol abuse, the percentage of binge drinkers on college campuses has declined only slightly while the proportion of students who admit they drink specifically to get drunk (not because they enjoy the taste of beer, wine, or whiskey) has increased.

The shift from getting high to getting drunk lends support to the functional view that although patterns of deviance change over time, the overall level of deviance remains more or less constant. When frequent use of marijuana on college campuses declined, heavy drinking replaced it. This pattern also suggests that public perception of deviance remains steady. During the marijuana years, alcohol did not disappear on campuses, but most people did not consider college drinking a problem. After all, alcohol wasn't a "drug" in the social sense of being an illicit substance. Beer bashes on football weekends were considered a normal, even traditional, part of the college experience. Likewise, marijuana hasn't disappeared from college campuses, but the public is now less likely to view cannabis as dangerously addictive and morally subversive. To the contrary, possession of small quantities of marijuana has been decriminalized in a number of states and reduced from a felony to a misdemeanor in others. Many groups are now calling for the legalization of pot for medicinal purposes. At the same time, attitudes toward alcohol, and particularly toward drunken drivers, have changed. Once viewed as a matter of personal choice, heavy drinking has been redefined as a public health issue.

Why do college students engage in high levels of deviance? From the functionalist perspective, societies need a certain level of nonconforming behavior in order to test and reaffirm the boundaries of acceptable behavior. College students are well situated to perform this function. As young adults, they are no longer expected to accept their parents' authority without question; nor do they have as many responsibilities as they will when they embark on careers, marry, and become parents. In effect, the college years are a "time out" when the penalties for nonconformity are reduced. Students are expected to question ideas and engage in critical thinking; that some question society's norms and values should not be a surprise. Most people who frequently smoked pot in college do not become life-long drug users; nor do most college binge drinkers continue to abuse alcohol. Having tested the boundaries of acceptable behavior, most choose respectability. But the next generation of college students, and the next, reenact the cycle.

1. Is binge drinking widespread on your campus? How do participants explain and excuse their behavior? What additional interpretations might be suggested by a sociologist?
2. Do you believe that programs like DARE and groups like MADD and SADD are effective in combating alcohol abuse? Discuss.
3. What should be the goals of a sociologically informed campus-based campaign to oppose binge drinking? How would you structure such an effort?

Sources: Akers, 1992.

We learn the real boundaries by observing what happens to people who deviate; we know that we cannot go as far as they do unless we are willing to risk punishment ourselves. In other words, publicly labeled deviants define the range of acceptable behaviors by exceeding that range, and they encourage conformity by showing what happens to people who fail to conform.

It can be argued that one reason there are so many portrayals of deviance in the mass media is to spread public awareness of the true limits of tolerance. Thus, in an ironic way, one of the principal functions of deviance is to encourage conformity!

2. *The Solidarity Function*. Nothing unites a group of people better than their shared opposition to an enemy; this phenomenon is especially evident in societies engaged in warfare. For example, many Americans felt a great surge of patriotism during the war in the Persian Gulf against Saddam Hussein's Iraq. Deviants provide a domestic equivalent of Hussein.

3. *The Warning Function*. When any type of deviance becomes more common, it sends a signal that something is wrong in society. Sometimes this warning is intentional, as when radical pro-lifers bomb abortion clinics. More often it is not deliberate, as when there is a sharp increase in the use of illegal drugs by teens. In either case, the authorities may respond to the warning in one of two ways: They may modify the rules or laws to fit changing circumstances, or they may simply step up their social control efforts. Either way, deviance has served a warning function.

The fact that deviance serves positive functions implies that societies may take covert steps to ensure that they do not "run out" of deviants (Erickson, 1962). Thus, for example, we claim that prisons are designed to reduce crime. Yet, since there is little emphasis on rehabilitation in modern prisons, what inmates actually learn while incarcerated often consists largely of tips picked up from fellow inmates about how to become better—more effective—offenders. And then, after they are released, ex-prisoners often find it extremely difficult to find honest employment, strongly pushing them toward illicit sources of income. In light of these facts, it seems possible that prison is really less about reducing crime levels than about maintaining them (Reiman, 1995).

Chambliss's study of the Saints and the Roughnecks nicely illustrates the boundary setting and solidarity functions of deviance. The official response to the misdeeds of the Roughnecks clarified for other youths the actual limits of toleration, and the community clearly was united in condemning the gang's deviance.

Of course, deviance also is dysfunctional for society. In addition to the numerous physical and economic injuries that result from acts such as robbery, arson, manufacturing hazardous products, or domestic violence, deviance has at least three important general dysfunctions. First, it makes social life problematic because it reduces our certainty that others will obey the norms. Much like someone driving in the wrong lane of a highway, the presence of criminals and deviants makes our lives less predictable.

Second, if deviance is seen to be rewarded, it reduces people's willingness to play by the rules. If your neighbor gets away with cheating on her income tax, why should you report every penny? If your friends get A's by cheating, why study?

Finally, deviance is dysfunctional because it is very costly. The United States loses as much as $450 billion annually due to crime, including both direct and indirect costs (Mandel & Magnusson, 1993). These resources could be used for other, more constructive purposes, such as reducing poverty or funding higher education.

The most important policy implication of the functional approach to deviance is to remind the authorities that it is not possible, or even desirable, to attempt to eradicate all deviation. Certainly, we should try to reduce serious predatory crime as much as possible, but at the same time we need to recognize that a certain amount of relatively harmless nonconformity has positive social value. In fact, there is some evidence that if one sort of deviance is sharply reduced, whether by effective social control or by redefinition, some other type of deviance is likely to become more common (Erickson, 1966). Attempts by extremely repressive states such as Singapore to stamp out deviance are, therefore, unlikely to meet with long-term success (Wilkinson, 1988).

WHY DO PEOPLE DEVIATE?

Through most of history, the usual answer to the question of why people violated important norms was a moralistic one. Thus, deviance might be explained by demonic possession or by a simple declaration that deviants and criminals were "evil" or "sinful" or "bad" people.

But in the late eighteenth century, Enlightenment thinkers such as Caesare Beccaria and Jeremy Bentham challenged these early explanations by asserting that deviance could best be understood as a consequence of the exercise of free will (Bentham, 1967; Devine, 1982). Deviants, they maintained, consciously assessed the costs and benefits of conformity and nonconformity and chose the latter only when it seemed advantageous to do so. This perspective, known as *classical theory*, was dominant in the early nineteenth century and has enjoyed renewed popularity in the past two decades under the name **rational choice theory** (Cornish & Clarke, 1986). Classical theory led to more humane social control efforts than moralistic theories, but it fell into disfavor late in the nineteenth century with the rise of positivistic thinking in the social sciences.

Positivism is an approach to understanding human behavior based on the scientific method. Positivistic theories are research-based, concentrate on measurable aspects of empirical reality, and aim to identify the precise causes of behavior. They are strongly oriented toward reducing deviance in that if we can identify the cause of a behavior pattern, we can use that knowledge to change the behavior. Classical theory simply states that people choose crime because they think such a choice will benefit them. Positivistic theories, in contrast, explore the *reasons* for that choice, therefore allowing us to develop more effective techniques of social control.

It is important to recognize that, in contrast to classical theory, positivism does *marginally* reduce the degree to which deviants are considered responsible for their behavior. If deviance is *purely* a result of free will, then deviants are entirely responsible for their actions. If, on the other hand, the decision to deviate is shaped by biological, psychological, or social factors—which are, to some extent, beyond the deviant's ability to control—then individual responsibility is somewhat lessened. But this does *not* mean that, in practice, positivists regard most criminals as personally blameless.

Positivists therefore see punishment as part of an appropriate response to misbehavior, but they insist that society needs to go beyond punishment and consider causal factors in order to reduce deviance effectively. Failing to consider factors that shape the decision to deviate places too much weight on the shoulders of the individual; it is a form of victim-blaming (Ryan, 1971).

Biological Positivism

The first positivistic theories of deviance were heavily grounded in biology, arising as they did when Darwin's theory of evolution was having a profound influence on European and American intellectual thought. The most popular of these approaches was that proposed by Italian criminologist Caesare Lombroso, who maintained that many criminals were born rather than made (Lombroso-Ferreo, 1972). Without altogether denying the importance of other factors, Lombroso argued that some lawbreakers were genetically inferior throwbacks to an earlier, more brutal type of humanity. Defective in reasoning power and physically distinctive, sometimes deformed, these individuals could not be reformed or even reasoned with.

A child with learning disorders may become frustrated and even hostile at school. This in turn may promote deviance by alienating the child and cutting off the path to economic success that would be open through educational achievement.

Some early twentieth century theorists continued to search for a general genetic cause of deviation that would allow them to put deviants and nondeviants into two distinct categories. However, most of this early work was marred by serious methodological weaknesses, and biological positivism lost popularity early in this century, only to be revived in a more sophisticated form during the last thirty years (Wilson, 1975).

Recent biological theories have more modest goals than did their predecessors. Instead of arguing that misbehavior is directly caused by biology, they generally maintain that certain physical traits, acting in concert with psychological and social factors, increase the chances that an individual will engage in deviance (Ellis & Hoffman, 1990). The key factor is often aggressiveness. Among the physical factors that may contribute to a violent temperament are dietary deficiencies, hypoglycemia (low blood sugar), allergies, hormonal abnormalities, environmental pollution, abnormal brain wave patterns, and tumors (Siegel, 1995: 138–150).

Other biological research posits a connection between deviance and physiologically based difficulties in learning. There is convincing evidence that offenders are disproportionately likely to exhibit various forms of learning disorders, often linked to minimal brain dysfunction or to attention deficit disorder (Monroe, 1978; Farone et al., 1993; Hart et al., 1994). Researchers maintain that children who have difficulty learning will become frustrated and, consequently, hostile in the classroom. This, in turn, may promote deviance by alienating the child from the conformist world and closing the doors to economic success attained through educational achievement (Patterson et al., 1989).

In sum, research strongly suggests some linkage between genetics and deviance, but this does not mean that any significant amount of violent crime is caused exclusively by physiological factors. Sociological critics say that biologically oriented theorists overstate the importance of genetics. They also argue convincingly that there are serious methodological problems in many biological studies, including very small samples and a tendency to study only incarcerated male offenders, a nonrandom subset of the larger category of all offenders (Walters & White, 1989).

The policy implications of biological theories are potentially disturbing. While some biological problems can be remedied with improved diet and medical treatment, others cannot. Moreover, we are not even close to being able to accurately predict people's future behavior on the basis of inborn physiological variables. If we treat someone like a potential deviant, aren't we running a risk of creating a *self-fulfilling prophecy*? And even if we could accurately identify at-risk individuals, what should we do with them? Psychological therapy or social reform will be, by definition, inadequate. Should we sterilize them? And who decides?

Psychological Positivism

Unlike biological positivism, psychological positivism does not consider deviance inborn. Rather, the tendency toward deviance is seen as developing in infancy or early childhood as a result of abnormal or inadequate socialization by parents and other care givers (Andrews & Bonta, 1994). Each of the several branches of psychology takes this fundamental insight in a different direction.

Thus the *psychoanalytic* approach, based on the work of Sigmund Freud, holds that criminals typically suffer from weak or damaged egos or from inadequate superegos that are unable to restrain the aggressive and often antisocial drives of the id (Byrne & Kelly, 1981). The *cognitive* school assumes that deviants have failed to reach more advanced stages of moral reasoning (Kohlberg, 1969; Veneziano & Veneziano, 1992) or that they have difficulty properly processing the information they receive. *Social learning* theorists maintain that children learn how to act by observing the kinds of behaviors that are rewarded. If deviance is positively reinforced, whether in real life or in the media, it is likely to be imitated (Bandura, 1973). Finally, *personality* theorists search for personality traits that are disproportionately present among deviants, such as aggressiveness or inability to defer gratification (Andrews & Warmith, 1989).

The policy implications of psychological positivism appear humane. Instead of punishing deviants in order to deter them, as classical theory mandates, or subjecting them to surgical intervention, as the biological school may suggest, psychologists recommend various forms of therapies, often combined with tranquilizers and antidepressants. Their goal is to reform or rehabilitate deviants. (This approach may not be as progressive as it seems, however; this is a controversial issue that we address toward the end of this chapter.) Yet the idea of rehabilitating deviants, widely endorsed by social control agencies through most of this century, is perceived by the general public as not just humane but indeed "soft." Most people think the therapeutic approach to criminality has been ineffective, which partially explains the renewed popularity in recent decades of harsher crime-control policies based on biological and free will understandings (Von Hirsch, 1976).

All children act out their aggressive impulses from time to time, but social psychologists have found that those with sociopathic tendencies are unusually prone to violent behavior.

Sociologists generally acknowledge the value of psychological positivism, especially in analyzing the origins of some of the more extreme types of deviance. Serial killers, for example, are often diagnosed as *sociopaths*, individuals with highly antisocial personalities lacking any appreciable conscience (McCord & Tremblay, 1992).

However, critics note some serious problems with the psychological approach. The worst may be that there is no one-to-one correspondence between any particular personality pattern and a given type of deviance. Thus some people who are impulsive, immature, defiant, and destructive as youths may grow up to be career deviants, but others with the same characteristics as youths become normal conforming citizens. Conversely, some thieves or drug addicts may display certain distinctive personality patterns,

but others do not. As a result, psychologically oriented researchers are rarely able to accurately predict which youths will become seriously deviant, missing some and mislabeling others (Tennenbaum, 1977).

There are other problems as well. Like biological theory, traditional psychological positivism tends to ignore the social context in which deviance occurs. Both approaches also accept the definition of crime and deviance as given, meaning that—as conflict theorists are quick to point out—they devote little attention to elite deviance. In sum, both biological and psychological positivism provide useful but incomplete paths to understanding why some people deviate.

Sociological Positivism

Whereas biological and psychological positivism locate the cause of deviation *inside* the individual, sociological approaches focus on the influence of the *external* social environment.

There are two major types of sociological explanations. *Social structure theories* explore the reasons why different rates of deviance and criminality are found in different sectors of society. *Social process theories* examine how particular people learn to think about and evaluate deviance within a given social setting (Akers, 1997).

Social Structure Theories.   Observers have long noted the heavier involvement in deviance among persons occupying certain social statuses. In our society, the highest rates of officially recorded crime occur among young, lower-income, minority males. Conflict theorists argue that this pattern is primarily a result of the inability of the relatively powerless segments of society to influence the deviance definition process or the actions of the criminal justice system. Without necessarily denying the value of this insight, social structural theorists think it is still well worth investigating why so many young, poor, minority males break the law.

The connection between social structure and individual behavior was first explored by the early functionalist Émile Durkheim. As discussed in Chapter 1, Durkheim's study of suicide rates emphasized that people who are strongly integrated into social groupings that disapprove of suicide are unlikely to take their own lives (Durkheim, 1897/1964). But when people become less involved in such groups or when the group's commitment to a particular normative position weakens, the suicide rate rises. In Durkheim's terms, a weakened collective conscience leads to the dysfunctional state of *anomie* or normative uncertainty. In such a situation, society no longer offers adequate guidelines for behavior and, naturally, deviance increases (Durkheim, 1897/1964).

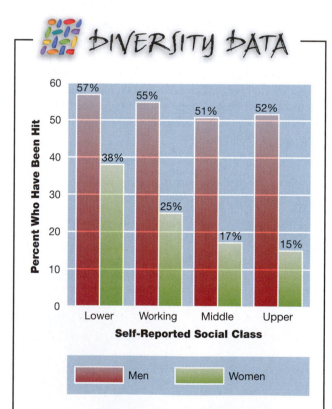

DIVERSITY DATA

FIGURE 8.3   How Do Gender and Class Affect the Chances That Someone Has Ever Been Hit? As the self-reported social class position of women rises, the likelihood that they have been hit declines sharply. A similar pattern is apparent among men, but the differences between the classes are much less substantial. At all class levels, men are considerably more likely than women to have experienced interpersonal violence. What social factors explain why violence seems to be more common among men and the lower classes?
Source: NORC. General Social Surveys, 1972–1996. Chicago: National Opinion Research Center, 1996.

Anomie is generally low in traditional cultures, but industrialization and urbanization break down normative consensus and promote nonconformity. Deviance is particularly likely to occur among young people, the poor, and minorities precisely because these groups tend to experience significant levels of anomie in modern societies (Menard, 1995).

Strain Theory.   In the late 1930s, Robert Merton extended Durkheim's functionalist observations into the best-known sociological theory of deviance (Merton, 1938). He started with the observation that virtually all Americans accept the desirability of attaining certain "success goals," especially wealth. While some may have stronger needs to succeed than others, almost everyone is socialized in the family, at school, and through the mass media to desire material success. We also learn that only some means are appropriate or legitimate ways to seek this goal. In America, one can properly obtain wealth by inheriting it, working hard, going to school, or perhaps by winning the lottery, but not by selling drugs, holding up banks, or printing hundred dollar bills in the basement.

However, according to Merton, social structural factors limit the ability of many people—especially the poor and minorities—to effectively seek wealth using only the approved means. Merton refers to such a situation as a *blocked opportunity structure*. Lack of equal opportunity is dysfunctional and it throws society out of balance or equilibrium. People who are blocked experience anomie because they are not sure how to behave; Merton refers to their feeling a sense of *strain*.

Such people may try to reduce their strain in five different ways (see Table 8.1). First, they may continue to slog away in pursuit of success using only the legitimate means despite the fact that their opportunities to succeed are severely limited. Merton terms this response *conformity* and notes that, fortunately, it is the most common pattern among members of at-risk groups.

Second, individuals experiencing strain may become *innovators*, meaning that they continue to desire to attain the success goals but they reject the established ways of doing so and substitute illegitimate means—they embezzle, they kidnap the children of the rich and hold them for ransom, they join an organized crime family. This response is clearly deviant.

Third, people trapped in a blocked opportunity situation may become what Merton calls *retreatists*—they drop out and stop seeking any goals beyond immediate self-indulgence. Retreatists often are heavily involved in drugs and alcohol. They are generally regarded as deviants.

Ritualism is a fourth way of responding to a blocked opportunity structure. Ritualists abandon the idea of achieving economic success but they still go through the motions of striving for it. They are not seriously deviant, though we may consider them a little eccentric. A graduate student toiling away for a Ph.D. in an obscure discipline with very limited employment possibilities would be a ritualist.

Finally, people may respond to strain by becoming what Merton terms *rebels*. Like retreatists, rebels turn their backs on established goals and the legitimate means to reach them. But, unlike retreatists, they substitute new goals and new ways of attaining these new goals, often in the company of like-minded others. Individuals who channel their energies heavily into the pro-choice or pro-life movements are a good example of what Merton means by rebellion, as are political revolutionaries.

Merton's theory can be applied to the Roughnecks, but, strictly speaking, not to the Saints, since the latter group did not have to deal with the strain of blocked opportunities. The Roughnecks, raised in the lower classes, responded to structural strain through innovation, in the form of theft, and retreatism, in their continual truancy from school and frequent indulgence in alcohol.

Table 8.1   Robert Merton's Strain Theory of Deviance

Form of Adaptation	Attitude Toward Conventional Success Goals	Attitude Toward Legitimate Means to Achieve Success Goals	Deviant?	Examples
Conformity	desire	accept	no	work hard; earn a college degree
Innovation	desire	replace	yes	drug dealer; counterfeiter
Retreatism	reject	reject	yes	crack addict; dropout
Ritualism	reject	accept	maybe	PhD in unmarketable discipline; bureaucrat mired in red tape
Rebellion	replace	replace	yes	political revolutionary; full-time environmental activist

The primary policy implication of Merton's theory is that the structural factors that contribute to deviance by blocking opportunity must be opened up. At a minimum, this means expanding educational opportunities for the lower classes and attacking racist and sexist discrimination (Kobrin, 1959).

Merton's theory highlights the importance of social factors and is supported by a good deal of empirical research (Cohen, 1965; Passas & Agnew, 1997). In particular, the finding that deviance thrives where there is a great disparity between rich and the poor is in line with his work. This relationship holds both within the United States (D. Jacobs, 1989; Simons & Gray, 1989) and globally (Archer & Gartner, 1984).

However, Merton's work can also be criticized. First, it is not clear that everyone is equally committed to striving for material success; some argue that the working and lower classes aspire to a somewhat different and more realistic set of goals—not to become fabulously wealthy, but simply to own a home and make enough money to live fairly comfortably (Matza, 1969; Messner & Rosenfeld, 1994). Others question whether Merton's theory can be applied to women without substantial modification (Pollock, 1999). In addition, Merton does not adequately specify the conditions under which people who are experiencing strain come to choose one or another of the five resolutions. Neither does he explain why most people abandon deviance as they become older. Finally, Merton does not address the deviance that occurs among societal elites; he seems to uncritically accept the view that only lower-class deviation needs explanation.

Lower-Class Focal Value Theory. Another influential variation of social structure theory has been developed by Walter Miller (1958). Miller agrees with Merton that deviance is concentrated in the lower classes, but he denies that it results from a socially imposed inability to live up to internalized cultural values. Rather, Miller thinks deviance reflects the acceptance by poor young males of a lower-class subculture. The content of this subculture is not entirely distinct from the norms and values of the mainstream culture, but the lower class tends to wholeheartedly accept certain orientations that are less important to members of the higher classes. Miller identifies several "focal concerns" as particularly relevant to the lower-class subculture. Accepting these subcultural values does not necessarily lead directly to deviance, but it can promote such an outcome. They include:

- *Trouble* and *Excitement*—Both getting into trouble and dealing with it effectively are highly valued.
- *Smartness*—The lower class does not necessarily disparage book learning, but it emphasizes "street smartness," the ability to manipulate others and not be taken advantage of.
- *Fate* and *Autonomy*—Members of this subculture believe that much of what happens in life is due to factors beyond their control; at the same time, they attempt to emphasize as much as possible their independence from external authority figures.
- *Toughness*—Frequently raised in female-dominated families, lower-class boys struggle to affirm their masculinity; this effort often leads to an exaggerated "macho" emphasis on fighting and physical strength.

Both the Saints and the Roughnecks valued excitement, street smartness, trouble, and autonomy. However, the middle-class Saints placed less emphasis on physical toughness and fate than the Roughnecks. As a result, the Saints generally avoided physical confrontations, which reduced their chances of coming into contact with formal agents of social control. Furthermore, believing they were in control of their own destiny, they did a much better job of planning their misbehavior so as to not be apprehended.

The most obvious policy implication of Miller's focal-value theory is that if the value system of the lower class could be changed, deviance would decline. However, in order to do this, it would probably be necessary to institute the sorts of reforms implied by Merton's theory. Thus all varieties of social structure theory ultimately lead to the same conclusion: We must reduce inequality and lower the barriers to social mobility in order to combat deviance.

The key issue in assessing Miller's theory is whether the subculture of the poor is guided by its own relatively distinct set of norms and values. Research on this issue is inconclusive. Some scholars find solid evidence of different norms and values in the lower class (Banfield, 1974; Gaines, 1991), while others reach the opposite conclusion (Cernovich, 1978). Critics have also pointed out that Miller's work is focused exclusively on the values of lower-class males; women are again left out of the picture (Pollock, 1999).

INTERNET — CONNECTIONS

Should suicide be permitted for seriously ill people who want to end their lives? Dr. Jack Kevorkian, a proponent of this position, is discussed at www.pbs.org/wgbh/pages/frontline/kevorkian. What do you think?

Social Process Theories.   Social structure theories help explain the higher rates of deviance in some sectors of society, but they do not explore the micro-level question of why some individuals growing up in high-crime areas resist temptation and, conversely, why some of the privileged go astray. To answer such questions, we must consider how individuals learn attitudes regarding deviance and conformity from the people around them. Social process theories thus incorporate aspects of psychological learning theory, but they also include elements of the symbolic interactionist perspective. They are sometimes called *cultural transmission theories*. We will introduce two representative social process theories.

Differential Association Theory.   Writing around the same time as Merton, criminologist Edwin Sutherland addressed the question of how particular individuals, regardless of their place in the social structure, acquire positive attitudes toward crime and learn the skills they need in order to be successful criminals (Sutherland, 1940).

The result was the theory of differential association, which is ultimately based on the common observation that deviants and conformists tend to hang around mostly with other people like themselves. Expanding on that point, Sutherland argued that

- Deviance is learned, not inherited.
- Deviance is learned primarily through interaction in small, intimate groups. Media influence is indirect or filtered through the attitudes of the members of the group.

- A person becomes deviant because he or she encounters an excess of definitions favorable to violation of norms over definitions unfavorable to violation of norms.
- The relationships in which these definitions are transmitted may vary in *frequency* (how regularly a person interacts with a particular individual), *duration* (how long each interaction lasts), *priority* (how early in life the relationship begins), and *intensity* (how important the relationship is to the individual).

Differential association theory clearly applies to the Saints and the Roughnecks. Both groups absorbed definitions favorable to deviance from their peers, but the Saints also learned effective techniques for avoiding social control agents, which the Roughnecks did not acquire.

The primary policy implication of Sutherland's theory is that potentially wayward youth need to be encouraged to spend more time with conformist peers. For example, offering recreational programs like basketball leagues potentially weakens the hold of the deviant peer group or gang.

Differential association theory makes strong intuitive sense. Moreover, unlike social structure theory, it explains both conformity and deviance and applies equally well to both men and women and to members of all social classes. In fact, one of the reasons Sutherland developed it was to explain white-collar crime, which he believed was more likely when cohesive peer groups arose within corporations that endorsed unethical business practices (Sutherland, 1940).

According to differential association theory, after-school programs like this one, which expose at-risk children to extensive contacts with conformist peers, are often an effective way of reducing juvenile delinquency.

The idea that deviants generally associate with and learn from other deviants has been widely supported by research both in the United States (Short, 1960; Smith et al., 1991; Kandel & Davies, 1991; Heimer, 1997) and abroad (Cheung & Ng, 1988). The major criticism of this theory is that the terms frequency, duration, priority, and intensity are imprecise. For example, how could the intensity of a relationship be objectively measured? Differential association theory also fails to account for solitary deviants, such as check forgers and embezzlers.

Control Theory. A second school of thought within the social process tradition addresses the issue of the causes of deviance by turning the question upside down. Instead of assuming that obeying the rules is normal and that deviance is what must be explained, control theorists think it is *conformity* that must be explained. This perspective is congruent with many nonsociological views of human nature, especially that of Sigmund Freud, but is relatively uncommon within sociology. According to control theory, we all experience strong pushes toward nonconformity. Deviants are people who lack adequate internal or external controls (or containments) against norm violation (Reckless, 1969).

The most widely cited social control theory was developed in the late 1960s by Travis Hirschi (1969) and revised by Hirschi and Michael Gottfredson (Gottfredson & Hirschi, 1990). The original theory suggested that people were more or less successfully insulated from deviance by four types of social bonds:

- Perhaps the most important was *attachment*, a feeling of emotional connection with parents, teachers, and conformist peers. The desire not to disappoint people one cares about provides a good reason to avoid deviance.
- Also critical is what Hirschi called *commitment*, a strong interest in achieving goals—for example, attending a good college or becoming a police officer—that might be blocked by a criminal record or a reputation as a deviant.
- Hirschi also stressed the importance of *involvement*: People who are caught up in the busy routines of everyday life may not have enough time to become deviants.
- Finally, Hirschi cited the *belief* factor, which simply means that conformists accept conventional values.

Hirschi and Gottfredson's revised theory retains the emphasis on social bonds but adds a more extensive consideration of underlying personality and socialization factors. In particular, the theory suggests that social bonds will be less effective in restraining people whose parents failed to develop in them an adequate level of *self-control*.

The key insight that control theory provides regarding the Saints and the Roughnecks concerns the variable of commitment. While neither group accepted very many conformist beliefs or was tightly bonded to parents or teachers, and both seemed to find time to misbehave, the Saints' middle-class background gave them a reasonable expectation of attending college, a career path that might have been closed off if they had been tagged as serious deviants. In fact, all but one of the Saints completed college, while only two of the Roughnecks were able to do so, both of them on football scholarships.

Hirschi and Gottfredson's work suggests that in order to reduce crime we need to strengthen social bonds with conformist others and improve the quality of child socialization so as to increase people's self-control. Required parenting classes in high school might be a step in this direction.

Researchers have found substantial support for control theory (Grasmick et al., 1993; Nagin & Paternoster, 1993; Free, 1994). It has the virtue of explaining why criminality tends to decline as people move past their teenage years: Unlike adolescents, most adults acquire high levels of attachment, commitment, and involvement as they marry, take full-time jobs, and start raising families. Furthermore, like differential association theory, control theory explains both conformity and deviance and potentially applies to everyone regardless of class or gender.

SOCIAL REACTION TO DEVIANCE

A new approach to deviance, called **labeling theory,** emerged in the 1960s. This perspective explores how the label of "deviant" is applied to particular people and the ways in which this devalued identity influences their subsequent behavior—a way of thinking that is deeply grounded in the symbolic interactionist perspective as discussed at length in Chapter 6.

Labeling theorists emphasize the difference between *deviant acts* and a *deviant role* or *deviant identity* (Becker, 1963; Schur, 1971). All of us commit acts that could be defined as deviant from time to time, but most people do not become publicly known as deviant role players. Thus most students cheat on occasion but only a few acquire the identity of cheaters; many youths experiment with illegal drugs but only some come to be labeled "dopers."

The purpose of labeling is to apply a *stigma*, a powerfully negative public identity, to an individual who is believed to have violated important norms (Goffman, 1963b). The stigma dramatically influences the way others view the labeled individual. Instead of being seen as someone who occasionally has a few drinks, engages in casual sex, or drives too fast on the interstate, the stigmatized individual becomes an "alcoholic," a "libertine," or a "chronic speeder."

A label may be acquired in three ways. First, some people voluntarily engage in *self-labeling*. Often, they take this step because concealing their true identity requires a great deal of time, energy, and hypocrisy. Gays and lesbians who "come out" or openly announce their sexual orientation often find that it is easier to bear others' negative comments than to remain "in the closet." Others self-label because they have fully rejected the conventional point of view and actively embrace their deviance; examples include many atheists and motorcycle outlaws like the Hell's Angels (Thompson, 1966; Watson, 1988).

Second, people acquire labels *informally*, from family and friends. For example, many prostitutes are labeled as such by people around them long before they come into contact with the criminal justice system. This form of labeling can have a tremendous influence on an individual since almost everyone cares about the opinions of the people they are close to and with whom they regularly interact (Matsueda, 1992).

Labeling theory has traditionally put the strongest emphasis on the third way that people acquire labels—*formally* (Lerman, 1996). This type of labeling involves a type of public ritual called a **degradation ceremony** (Garfinkel, 1956). Degradation ceremonies, such as criminal trials, sanity hearings, and court martials officially devalue a deviant's identity, imposing a stigma that may be difficult or impossible to escape. Consider, for example, these words from the prosecution's closing argument in the trial of Oklahoma City bomber Timothy McVeigh:

> Take a moment and look at Timothy McVeigh. Look into the eyes of a coward and tell him you will have the courage. Tell him you will speak with one unified voice, as the moral conscience of the community, and tell him he is no patriot. He is a traitor, and he deserves to die. (Annin & Morganthau, 1997:41)

What influences the chances that someone will acquire a deviant label? Because we all prefer to believe that we live in a just world, we like to think that people who acquire a stigma have repeatedly committed serious and harmful deviant acts. Though there is certainly a good deal of truth to this claim, other factors also enter in, principally social power.

Blending themes from the conflict, feminist, and symbolic interactionist perspectives, labeling theorists note that in U.S. society, wealthy, white, male, middle-aged, heterosexual individuals are better able to resist stigmatizing labels than are the less socially em-

powered (Schur, 1984; Adams et al., 1998). Erving Goffman (1963b) goes so far as to consider minority or female status as a kind of "tribal stigma," an observation that emphasizes the severity of the multiple stigmatization of an individual who is not only defined as some sort of criminal or deviant but is also female, minority, and perhaps poor as well.

Other important factors influencing whether a stigmatizing label is applied include (a) how closely a person matches the popular, often media-generated, stereotype of a particular kind of deviant (Surette, 1998; Bailey & Hale, 1998); (b) how concerned formal social control agents currently are about any given type of norm violation (Margolin, 1992); and (c) how experienced the deviant is—beginners are more likely to be caught, all other factors being equal.

Edwin Lemert (1951) introduced the terms primary and secondary deviance to convey the importance of labeling. **Primary deviance** refers to any deviant act that is *not* followed by some form of labeling. Lemert's point is that primary deviance, even if engaged in for a very long time, rarely affects a person's life very much. You may shoplift, vacuum your apartment naked, smoke crack, or worship the devil for years, but so long as nobody knows about it—or at least nobody who is inclined to publicize this knowledge—it won't have much effect on your life.

On the other hand, once your norm violation is known, you enter into **secondary deviance,** that period of time in which you are compelled to reorganize your life around your devalued identity. Now everything changes. First of all, you may discover that many of your old friends are uncomfortable around you. They may engage in *retrospective reinterpretation* of their past interactions with you: "Last week she fell asleep in class; I thought she was just tired but now that I know she's an addict, I realize she was high" (Scheff, 1984).

Such reinterpretations may or may not be factually accurate, but once labeled you have little ability to correct them. You will probably find yourself in the market for new friends, and you are particularly likely to recruit them from fellow deviants who tend not to judge you negatively. Note, however, that in line with Sutherland's differential association theory, deviant friends are likely to propel you toward increased involvement in deviance.

Secondary deviance also requires changes in your major life roles. Labeled deviants frequently lose their jobs, are forced to move, drop out of school, and may become estranged from their families. Such changes then combine with the direct effects of stigmatization to lower one's chances of obtaining legitimate success (Schwartz & Skolnick, 1962). In Merton's terms, your opportunity structure becomes blocked and, again, you are pushed toward deviance.

An informal label like "class clown" or "troublemaker," which is acquired in small peer groups like this one, can be an important factor pushing a youth toward criminal or deviant activity.

Finally, secondary deviance also tends to change your self-image, even if you initially resist thinking of yourself as a deviant. A damaged self-image yet again increases the chances that you will move farther into deviance. As a symbolic interactionist would say, the deviant label becomes a self-fulfilling prophecy. The ultimate consequence of secondary deviance is *role engulfment*—deviance becomes your master status (Schur, 1980).

Chambliss's study of the Saints and the Roughnecks is a classic example of the power of labeling. The lower-class Roughnecks were probably no more delinquent than their middle-class counterparts. But, in part because they lacked the social power that would allow them to own cars and hence escape the relentless observation of the police and townspeople, they became known as no-good delinquent punks. This label then affected virtually everything that happened to them. The Saints were also labeled—as basically good kids who occasionally sowed a wild oat or two—a label that also had a great impact on their lives, but in quite the opposite direction.

If one accepts the labeling perspective, it leads to the conclusion that in order to avoid role engulfment, we should minimize the number of people who are publicly labeled, a policy termed *radical nonintervention* (Schur, 1973). In particular, while we must label and punish predatory criminals, we must not create a self-fulfilling prophecy by tagging young people who are not yet committed to crime as juvenile delinquents. In fact, not revealing the names of juvenile offenders, a practice now under vigorous attack, was originally intended to minimize destructive labeling (Kratcoski & Kratcoski, 1996).

Perhaps the most serious criticism of labeling theory is that research has not clearly demonstrated that formal labeling necessarily promotes greater commitment to deviance (Wellford, 1975; Sherman & Smith, 1992; Cavender, 1995). While some studies strongly support the role engulfment thesis (Ageton & Elliott, 1973; Ray & Downs, 1986), others refute it (Tittle, 1975). It may be that people who have a strong attachment to conformist others and to conformist goals, as Hirschi would argue, respond to the threat of labeling by reaffirming their commitment to

INTERNET ⬥ CONNECTIONS

Students sometimes have difficulty understanding the sociological approach to deviant behavior. In addition to your readings in the text, you may wish to experience a PowerPoint presentation that will serve as another useful "Introduction to Deviance." Go to: http://www.nwmissouri.edu/nwcourses/martin/deviance/introdev/index.htm. When you want to see the next "slide" click on the "Forward" button. After you have completed this "tour," write a brief report on the sociological meaning of **deviance.** If you have the time, go to: http://www.nwmissouri.edu/nwcourses/martin/deviance/devpoint.html and select another presentation on a different topic pertaining to deviant behavior.

Table 8.2	Theories of Deviance			
Type of Theory	Questions Addressed	Major Observations	Policy Implications	Representative Theorists
Classical Theory/ Rational Choice Theory	Why do individuals deviate?	People calculate the costs and benefits and rationally decide whether or not to deviate. Deviance is freely chosen.	Increase negative sanctions for deviance.	Caesare Beccaria, Jeremy Bentham, Marcus Felson, James Q. Wilson
Conflict Theory	In whose interests is deviance defined?	The rich and powerful define deviance to benefit themselves.	Reduce the power of elites.	Willem Bonger, Richard Quinney, Steven Spitzer
Biological Positivism	Why do individuals deviate?	Deviants are physically different than conformists.	Medical treatment, drugs, perhaps sterilization.	Caesare Lombroso, William Sheldon, Hans Eysenck
Psychological Positivism	Why do individuals deviate?	Deviants are psychologically different from conformists.	Better child rearing; psychological therapy.	Sigmund Freud, Lawrence Kohlberg, Stanton Samenow
Sociological Positivism (Social Structure Theory)	Why are some categories of people more deviant than others?	Certain social environments encourage deviance.	Change the social environment; offer more opportunity.	Robert Merton, William Miller, Albert Cohen
Sociological Positivism (Social Process Theory)	Why do individuals deviate?	People learn from others around them whether or not to deviate.	Provide more chances to learn from and bond with conformist others.	Edwin Sutherland, Travis Hirschi, Walter Reckless
Labeling Theory	What are the consequences of the ways in which members of society react to deviance?	Labeling people as deviants can reinforce their deviant identity and become a self-fulfilling prophecy.	Minimize labeling; radical nonintervention.	Edwin Lemert, Howard Becker, Harold Garfinkel

conventional norms, whereas people lacking such controls are pushed toward deviance by labeling.

Critics also charge that labeling theory's heavy emphasis on the relative nature of deviance and on the philosophy of radical nonintervention seem out of step with the law and order, "lock 'em up" mentality of the current era in the United States. Certainly the notion that a rapist or murderer whose crime goes undetected is in any meaningful sense not a deviant seems, at the very least, a little strange.

Table 8.2 summarizes the principal theories of deviance that have been discussed in this chapter.

≋ LIFE CONNECTIONS: Mental Illness as Deviant Behavior

What is the difference between a mentally healthy person and one who is mentally ill? This is not an easy question to answer, in large part because our understandings of what is and is not normal are heavily influenced by the social and cultural context in which a particular act takes place. For example, members of some religious groups are expected to enter trancelike states in which speaking in tongues is encouraged. So long as such behavior is defined in religious terms, most people in the United States would probably regard it as a little strange but basically normal. If, however, the same behavior were observed in a poorly dressed person standing on a street corner, many of us would have little difficulty defining that individual as "crazy."

The media also shape our understandings of mental disorders, sometimes in unfortunate ways. Media imagery of the mentally ill tends to stereotype them as violent and dangerous. In fact, the vast majority are neither.

Mental illness is widespread in modern societies. If it is defined as exhibiting severe enough symptoms to require ongoing treatment, then about 15 percent of all Americans are suffering from mental illness. If it consists of having some difficulty coping with every-day life due to stress, anxiety, or depression, then as much as 80 percent of the population may be affected (Dohrenwend & Dohrenwend, 1974; Coleman & Cressey, 1999; Gallagher, 1987; Regier, 1991). However it is defined, most people go untreated (Mechanic, 1989; Barker et al., 1992).

Most Americans understand mental illness in terms of the *medical model*, that is, as a disease with biological or genetic causes that is best treated by a psychiatrist or psychologist. While there is clear evidence that some forms of mental illness, especially the more serious ones such as schizophrenia, are indeed partly biologically caused, it is equally clear that many other types do not result from organic defect (Gatchel et al., 1989).

Many sociologists find labeling theory a more useful way to understand psychological disorders. This perspective interprets mental illness as a status with attached role requirements that are first internalized and then acted out. Although most norm violations evoke labels such as strange, eccentric, or criminal, if people violate certain basic and taken-for-granted expectations, they are likely to be labeled as mentally ill and that label is typically very difficult to remove. Examples include people who fail to observe basic principles of personal hygiene or who carry on animated conversations in public with individuals who are not present. Thomas Scheff (1963) refers to such violations of basic social conventions as *residual deviance*.

Some labeling theorists go even further, claiming that the very idea of mental illness is a myth. Thomas Szasz (1961, 1994b) embraces this view, maintaining that the people we call mentally ill are in fact simply experiencing what he calls unresolved "problems in living." He strongly criticizes psychiatrists, who he claims "know little about medicine and less about science," for labeling people as mentally ill and then taking away their freedom in the name of curing them (Szasz, 1994b: 36).

D. L. Rosenhan (1973) conducted a classic study that supports the conclusions of labeling theory. Rosenhan and seven of his colleagues presented themselves at a number of different mental hospitals claiming to hear voices. In fact, none of the "pseudopatients" had any history whatsoever of mental disorder. All were admitted with a diagnosis of schizophrenia; all stopped claiming to hear voices or displaying any other psychiatric symptom immediately upon entering the hospital.

Rosenhan suggested that, if psychiatric diagnoses were objective, the pseudopatients would soon be detected by the staff. This did not occur. The researchers' stays in the hospitals varied from seven to fifty-two

days; all were released with the diagnosis "schizophrenia in remission." The doctors and nurses never detected the deception, although some of the "real" patients did, an outcome Rosenhan attributed to the power of the label of "mental illness" to frame virtually all perceptions of the patients by the medical staff.

In a second stage of the study, Rosenhan told staff members at a prestigious mental hospital who were skeptical of the results of the initial research that he would be sending them more pseudopatients and asked them to identify any they detected. Over the next three months, 41 of 193 new patients were identified as fakes with a high degree of confidence by at least one staff member; in fact, Rosenhan sent *no* pseudopatients!

Sociologists have consistently found an inverse relationship between mental illness and social class. This is true for both treated and untreated populations and has also been found in other Western societies, including Britain and Canada (Turner & Marino, 1994; Armstrong, 1995; Cook & Wright, 1995). Although the connection between class and diagnosed mental disorder is firmly established, there is some disagreement as to whether mental illness is a cause or a consequence of being relatively low in class. The drift hypothesis suggests that people move downward on the class ladder because they are mentally ill. They are unable to function normally, and in particular to hold a job, because of their psychological problems. A number of research studies support this view (Turner & Wagonfeld, 1967; Harkey et al., 1976; Eaton, 1980). On the other hand, it is also clear that the strain of living in or near poverty directly contributes to poor mental health. There is probably a good deal of truth to both interpretations.

With regard to gender, there appear to be no significant differences in overall *rates* of mental disorder, but there are consistent differences in *type*. Women are more likely to suffer from affective and anxiety disorders, while men are more likely to be diagnosed with personality disorders (Rothblum, 1982; Chino & Funabiki, 1984; Darnton, 1985; Carson et al., 1988). Most sociologists suspect that these differences result more from the ways that therapists perceive men and women than from innate differences between the genders.

Employment and marital status are linked with gender. It is better for your mental health to be married, especially if you are male. Never-married, divorced, and single men have higher rates of mental illness than those who are married (American Psychological Association, 1985; Steil, 1995). But married women suffer more mental health problems than married men (Gove & Tudor, 1973; Steil &

Turetsky, 1987; Rosenfield, 1989; Simon, 1995). For both married men and women, however, working outside the home contributes to better mental health (Campbell, 1981; Sloan, 1985; Thoits, 1986). Female single parents, especially those who are living in poverty, are particularly likely to suffer from mental illness.

≡ SOCIETY CONNECTIONS: The Repression-Medicalization-Acceptance Cycle

There is a high level of agreement in modern societies concerning most forms of serious, harmful deviance. We may debate exactly how we should respond to acts like murder, forcible rape, treason, and child abuse, but almost everyone agrees that these behaviors are thoroughly despicable. However, there is much less consensus regarding many other acts that were once almost universally condemned, such as alcoholism and homosexuality.

How is it that some behaviors once considered deviant become acceptable? There appears to be a pattern in the way members of modern societies change their attitudes. This process is an excellent ex-

Alcoholics Anonymous has played an important role in redefining alcoholism as a disease rather than as a moral failing.

ample of a changing *definition of the situation*, a symbolic interactionist concept that was introduced toward the end of Chapter 6 in reference to the issue of sexual harassment. Initially, people *condemn and repress* deviant behaviors, frequently with religious justification. Deviants are seen as evil, sinful people unfit to enjoy normal status in society.

As the values of society become more diverse, however, commitment to traditional forms of religion weakens and a few voices are heard calling for change. Gradually, as moral consensus declines, repression is replaced by medicalization (Conrad & Schneider, 1980). The **medicalization of deviance** involves a redefinition of the character of the deviant from "evil" to "sick." Note that the behavior has not changed—only the label. Instead of punishing alcoholics and gays, we try to help them "get well." Alcoholics Anonymous has been especially effective in promoting the "disease theory" of alcoholism.

This shift in labels has several consequences (Macionis, 1999). It relocates social control efforts from the criminal justice system to the medical establishment, replacing punishment with therapeutic intervention. Medicalization promotes more humane treatment of deviants, but it also redefines the deviant as less morally responsible for her or his behavior and less personally competent to make decisions about the future. Some critics charge that the medicalization of deviance has simply replaced cops in blue coats with cops in white coats. Furthermore, these critics claim, our society protects the civil rights of "evil" criminals better than the rights of "sick" deviants (Szasz, 1961). In this sense, the medicalization of deviance may be less of a humane advance than it seems at first.

In response to such concerns, some organized groups of deviants have campaigned for yet another redefinition, this time from medicalization to acceptance. John Kitsuse (1980) calls such group efforts to achieve acceptance **tertiary deviance.** This shift has not occurred with alcoholism, but it has regarding homosexuality. In 1974 the American Psychiatric Association formally voted to redefine homosexuality as a variant type of sexual behavior, not a form of mental illness. Public attitudes toward homosexuality remain rather negative, but they are clearly moving toward toleration if not full acceptance. Figure 8.4 summarizes the repression-medicalization-acceptance cycle.

It is important to note that not all forms of deviance shift smoothly from repression to medicalization and then on to acceptance. Some, like pedophilia, remain in the repression stage despite the best efforts of groups like the North American Man-Boy Love Association. Others, like alcoholism, move only to

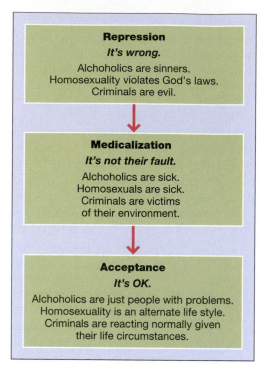

FIGURE 8.4   The Repression-Medicalization-Acceptance Cycle

medicalization. Substantial percentages of the population continue to endorse repression of abortion despite its legalization in the 1973 *Roe v. Wade* decision; as a result, its future status is uncertain at this time. And the popular reaction to a few types of behavior—as we will document shortly—is moving in the opposite direction, toward repression.

The point is not that movement toward acceptance is in any way inevitable, but rather that in modern societies shifting norms make it difficult to define deviance. We conclude this chapter with a brief discussion of some contemporary efforts to reverse the direction of the repression-medicalization-acceptance cycle.

Reversing the Cycle

While the dominant trend in modern society is away from defining various forms of deviance as evil and toward seeing them as signs of sickness (alcoholism) or as acceptable alternatives (homosexuality and possibly suicide), some behaviors that were accepted in the past are being redefined as more seriously deviant.

For example, campaigns by groups like MADD (Mothers Against Drunk Driving) have had a considerable effect on public attitudes toward driving under the influence of alcohol. While there has been no dramatic reduction in the incidence of drinking and driving (J. B. Jacobs, 1989; Mastrofski & Ritti, 1996), some jurisdictions have made taverns legally liable if

they continue to serve obviously intoxicated customers who later have auto accidents. Similarly, naming a "designated driver" who abstains from alcohol in order to drive others home safely is now a widely accepted practice.

Perhaps the most interesting example of the increasing stigmatization of behavior in American society concerns smoking. For centuries, using tobacco has been regarded as acceptable, at least for adult men; since the 1920s it has been generally allowed for women as well. In fact, during much of the twentieth century, smoking has been widely viewed as a sign of maturity and sophistication. However, this pattern is now changing.

The public's increased willingness to view cigarette smoking as deviant has a number of causes. Chief among them is the great emphasis that an aging America puts on good health combined with an ever-increasing body of research substantiating the damaging effects of smoking. A National Institute of Drug Abuse study found that there were 300 tobacco-related deaths among Americans for each death caused by cocaine (Reinarman & Levine, 1989). Americans have historically resisted seeing tobacco as an addictive drug, but many people are coming to realize that it is in fact just that. Thus, the current "war on drugs" campaign may well be having an anti-tobacco spillover effect.

The signs of this shift in the public temper toward smoking are everywhere. Laws now ban the practice in offices, airplanes, restaurants, and many other public places. A decade or two ago, asking someone to extinguish her or his cigarette in a public place would have been considered pushy and ill-mannered; now it is the smoker who is considered rude. The Clinton administration placed a high priority on trying to keep cigarettes out of the hands of children and adolescents and attempted to give the FDA the freedom to regulate tobacco as a drug. Spokespersons for the tobacco industry express fears that we may be moving toward some form of legal prohibition of their product.

The bottom line is that smoking is being redefined by many Americans as at least mildly deviant behavior. The small clusters of people huddled together just outside the doors of smoke-free buildings are visible proof of this redefinition. It is not clear at present how far this trend will go. The fact that many respectable middle-class people still smoke suggests that tobacco users probably do not face full criminalization of their habit, as does the substantial political clout of the tobacco lobby. Smokers may, however, be faced with trying to convince the majority that they ought to be regarded as nicotine addicts—sick—rather than as immoral devotees of the demon weed.

SUMMARY

1. Sociologists consider deviance a relative concept; therefore no behavior is seen as inherently deviant. Deviance is found in all societies.
2. Deviance may be interpreted as a negative label established and applied by the socially powerful. Actions, beliefs, and conditions may all be labeled deviant.
3. Social control is intended to encourage conformity and discourage deviance. It may consist of either punishments or rewards. Social control may be exercised by formal or informal agents and is also a consequence of moral socialization.
4. Conflict theory emphasizes the ability of social elites to define what is regarded as deviant in line with their own interests.
5. Although deviance makes social life problematic, erodes trust, and is very costly to control, it also serves several positive functions. It sets the boundaries of what is regarded as acceptable behavior, encourages solidarity, and warns that change is needed.
6. Biological and psychological positivism explain the origins of deviance in terms of internal factors; sociological positivism emphasizes the importance of external factors located in the social environment.
7. Social structure theories, such as Merton's strain theory or Miller's lower-class focal value theory, explain the high rates of deviance among the poor and minorities by reference to broad structural factors such as blocked opportunity or distinctive subcultural values.
8. Social process theories, such as Sutherland's differential association theory or Hirschi's control theory, explain individual decisions to deviate by reference to factors such as social learning or bonds to conventional society.
9. Labeling theory explores the consequences of applying deviant labels to individuals. It assumes that a stigma is likely to become a self-fulfilling prophecy.
10. In modern societies, which are characterized by considerable normative ambiguity, many forms of behavior once considered severely deviant and repressed come to be redefined as illness rather than sin. In some cases, these behaviors are later further reinterpreted as nondeviant and hence worthy of acceptance.
11. However, sometimes the repression-medicalization-acceptance cycle reverses, and previously accepted behaviors such as drunk driving or tobacco smoking come to be seen as deviant.

KEY TERMS

crime   186
degradation ceremony   203
deviance   185
formal social control   190
informal social control   190

labeling theory   202
medicalization of deviance   207
negative sanction   190
positive sanction   190
positivism   196

primary deviance   203
rational choice theory   196
secondary deviance   203
social control   189
tertiary deviance   207

CRITICAL THINKING QUESTIONS

1. Why do many people have trouble accepting the idea that all deviance is relative? Can a person be a good sociologist and at the same time be personally committed to an absolute moral standard?
2. What sort of social control is usually most effective—formal, informal, or internalized? Similarly, do you think positive or negative sanctions normally work better to reduce deviance?
3. Rational choice and biological theories of deviance seem to be more widely accepted by Americans than psychological and especially sociological theories. Why do you think this is the case? How do these preferences affect our social-control efforts?
4. Which of the theoretical approaches to deviance strikes you as most useful in interpreting the case of the Saints and the Roughnecks? Explain your choice.
5. What types of behavior, other than those discussed in this chapter, are either becoming more or less accepted in contemporary society? How do you account for these trends?

9
CRIME AND CRIMINAL JUSTICE

OUTLINE

Caned in Singapore

The case of 18-year-old Ohio native Michael Fay, a student at the Singapore American School, received worldwide attention in 1994. After being found guilty of vandalizing over fifty cars, Fay was held in custody for three months, fined $2200, and beaten on his bare buttocks with a cane hard enough to draw blood and leave permanent scars.

Severe punishment is not unusual in Singapore, a small Asian city-state famous for its harsh criminal justice system. Offenses such as chewing gum, spitting in public, feeding birds, or failing to flush a public toilet are punished by sizable fines. Less predictable was the substantial level of support in the United States for the caning: One survey showed that 38 percent of the general public approved of Fay's sentence while just 52 percent felt it was too harsh. (Elliott, 1994)

America's Toughest Sheriff

In 1996, opinion polls showed Maricopa County, Arizona, Sheriff Joseph Arpaio to be the most popular elected official in the state after he housed inmates in tents without air-conditioning during the searing Phoenix summer. Arapio also banned cigarettes, coffee, videos, and most television programs, and cut the cost of jail meals to 30¢ each by providing only food such as moldy bologna. In addition, he issued pink underwear to male inmates. (In a patriarchal culture, forcing men to wear a color traditionally identified with women is a tactic designed to further demean them). ("Arizona Sheriff...," 1996)

Getting Soft on Crime

The Mutter-Kind-Heim (Home for Mothers and Children) in Frankfurt, Germany, is a halfway house built to accommodate a maximum of twenty-three nonviolent female offenders together with their children under the age of 3. The facility is pleasant and homelike, with its own play yard, kitchen, and flower garden.

This arrangement prevents the traumatic separation of mothers and children that so often occurs in American prisons. Allowing the inmates to continue to nurture their babies appears to increase their self-respect and confidence. The mothers also receive educational, medical, and psychological assistance, learn work skills, and accumulate earnings that will help them adjust after they leave the institution. Upon release, they receive a welfare grant and free rent. Recidivism rates for this program are extremely low (Douglas, 1993).

In Chapter 8, *crime* was defined as a type of deviance involving the violation of formal statutes enacted by a legitimate government. Virtually every poll taken in recent decades has shown crime at or near the top of the public's list of concerns. As Figure 9.1 illustrates, in recent years between 40 and 45 percent of Americans have reported that there is at least one neighborhood within a mile of their homes where they are afraid to walk at night for fear of being victimized (Ferraro, 1995; Blakely & Snyder, 1998).

Is this level of concern justified? Official data suggest that violent street crime has actually been declining since 1991. However, this downturn follows a long period during which the crime rate was soaring. Between 1960 and 1994, while the American population grew 39 percent, reported crime increased roughly five-fold even though law-enforcement spending quadrupled.

Despite recent declines, the magnitude of the crime problem remains staggering. In 1997, for example, about 18,200 people were murdered and almost 13.2 million major crimes were reported to the police (U.S. Bureau of the Census, 1999). The total annual cost of street crime is estimated at roughly $18 billion, an enormous figure that is dwarfed in turn by the cost of white-collar crime, which may be as high as $472 billion per year (Donziger, 1996).

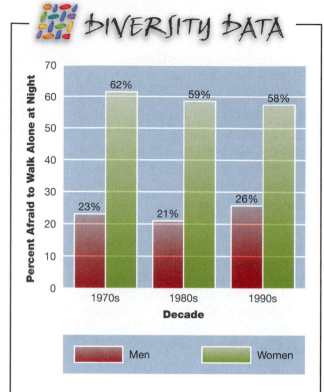

DIVERSITY DATA

FIGURE 9.1   Percent Afraid to Walk Alone at Night, by Gender. Women are consistently more likely than men to say that there are some places within a mile of their homes where they would be afraid to walk alone at night. Levels of fear appear to have declined slightly among women over the past thirty years while they have increased marginally among men. Will the sharp decreases in the crime rate which began in the early 1990s result in declines in public fear of crime?

Source: NORC. General Social Surveys, 1972–1996. Chicago: National Opinion Research Center, 1996.

Many Americans believe that such figures demonstrate the need for a larger and more punitive criminal justice system. Support for hard-line policies such as those of Sheriff Arpaio or the authorities in Singapore has boomed. Such sentiments have fueled unprecedented increases in the prison population, measures such as mandatory sentencing provisions for habitual criminals, and the 1994 federal Omnibus Crime Bill, which established fifty-two new capital crimes (crimes punishable by the death penalty) and increased spending by $30 billion, mostly to hire more policemen and build more prisons.

At the same time, as the account of the Mutter-Kind-Heim suggests, some societies have been moving in the opposite direction. They base their policies on the view that crime can best be reduced by treating

offenders with dignity, which will, in turn, increase their chances of being rehabilitated.

Which approach makes the most sense? This chapter will explore a number of topics that may help to answer this critical question. We will open with a brief discussion of the relationship between crime and the law. Next, the chapter will turn to an analysis of the extent of crime in the United States and other societies, followed by discussions of some of the major types of crime and of the criminal justice system. After presenting an analysis of the sociological characteristics of criminals and their victims, the chapter will conclude by outlining contemporary policy debates concerning capital punishment and how the law should respond to drug abuse.

CRIME AND THE CRIMINAL LAW

The definition of crime used in this text reflects a *legalistic approach* because it takes the common-sense view that a crime is whatever the law defines as a crime at a given time and in a particular place. As with deviance, a wide variety of acts have been considered to be criminal at some place or at some time.

Some people, however, prefer a less relative definition and endorse a *natural law approach*. In the past, most natural law definitions interpreted crime as a violation of divinely inspired guidelines. Today, advocates of this approach are more likely to see crimes as acts in opposition to universal secular principles of human rights. The Nuremburg trials following the end of the Second World War, during which many leading Nazis were found guilty of war crimes, were based on the natural law approach. Had the judges used a legalistic definition, they could not have found these men guilty, as their acts did not violate the laws of Nazi Germany.

Three Families of Criminal Law

The legal system of the United States is grounded in the English **common law** tradition. In this arrangement, the law develops gradually over time through the accumulation of many cases. Legal principles are based on precedent. Thus, in applying common law, a judge is guided by rulings made by other judges concerning similar cases in the past.

Such a system seems natural to us, but it is by no means universal. There are, in fact, three distinct families of criminal law in the modern world (Fairchild, 1993; Reichel, 1994). Most of the world's societies follow the **civil law** tradition, which is code-based rather than case-based. Instead of developing gradually from the bottom up, case by case, in the civil law tradition the law or code is written by the ruler, a legislature, or a judicial panel and imposed on society from the top down. For example, most European nations derive their law from the Code Napoleon, which was drawn up in France in 1804.

The world's third major legal family is **religious law.** Like the civil law tradition, it is constructed mostly from the top down. However, the source of the law is believed to be divine will rather than custom or human reason. Iran, where criminal law is based on the Shari'a ("the way") as revealed by Allah to the prophet Mohammed in the Qur'an (Koran) and other sacred writings, is a good example. The Iranian legal system will be discussed in a Global Connections box later in this chapter.

CRIME RATES

After briefly introducing some of the problems sociologists encounter in determining how much crime occurs, this section will examine the current rate of crime in the United States and then compare the U.S. crime rate with those of other similar societies.

Measuring Crime

American sociologists who wish to study crime rely heavily on two sources of official statistical information. Unfortunately, both have serious limitations (Biderman & Lynch, 1991). The most widely used source is the *Uniform Crime Reports* (UCR), which have been compiled and published annually by the FBI since 1930. These reports are based on information provided by roughly 15,000 local police agencies.

Eight street crimes, called **index crimes,** are given special attention in the UCR. They include four personal or violent index crimes: homicide, robbery, aggravated assault, and forcible rape (as opposed to statutory rape—intercourse between an adult and a minor); and four property crimes: burglary, larceny-theft, auto theft, and arson. Data recorded for these crimes include the number of offenses reported, the number of people arrested, the number of cases sent to trial, and selected demographic information concerning individuals who have been arrested and convicted.

There are serious problems with the UCR. We know that most crimes are never reported to the police, principally because many people don't think their victimization is important enough to be worth reporting or because they doubt the police can help them. Additionally, changes in police recording procedures, such as those resulting from the introduction of computers, can significantly influence crime rates. And, finally, only about one-fifth of all crimes reported to the police are actually solved by arrest. In sum, the UCR figures are not very reliable (Kempf, 1990).

The FBI is in the process of developing a National Incident-Based Reporting System that should correct some of the UCR's failings. However, no police-derived database will ever provide information about crimes that are not reported—the so-called "dark figure of crime." To investigate unreported crime, researchers use the *National Crime Victimization Survey* (NCVS), which is based on interviews conducted with a random sample of Americans aged 12 and over.

The NCVS began in 1972. The adult members of 43,000 households—about 80,000 individuals—are

Concern over the high crime rates in the United States clearly helps explain the widespread support in this country for a Singapore court's decision to subject American youth Michael Fay to corporal punishment for vandalizing dozens of automobiles.

Rape is one of the crimes that is least likely to be reported to the police. Victims may be willing to discuss what happened to them with friends, but they often hesitate to lodge an official complaint, in part because they may dread testifying in public about their traumatic experience.

asked about their experiences with crime victimization over the past six months. Six of the eight index crimes are covered; the exceptions being arson and homicide. The NCVS is probably a more useful source of information than the UCR, but it is not without its problems. For example, people often have difficulty applying official definitions to their experiences and may be hesitant to report particularly embarrassing victimizations.

Crime Rates in the United States

Table 9.1 summarizes trends for UCR index crimes between 1987 and 1997. Two points stand out:

- About 89 percent of all index crimes are property offenses; statistically speaking, violent crime is relatively uncommon.
- All crime categories have declined dramatically since 1991. A comparison between UCR data for 1995 and 1997 shows that violent index crime declined 9.3 percent. Homicide and robbery declined 17.1 percent and 15.7 percent, respectively. Index property crime dropped 6.1 percent during this same period. Furthermore, recent research shows these trends continuing, with both violent and property crime down 7 percent in 1999.

These decreases are unprecedented in modern times. What has caused them? Criminologists argue that the reduced crime rate is partly a result of changing demographics. Since most street crimes are committed by people in their teens and early twenties, in an era such as 1960–1975, when the baby boom generation was young, the crime rate naturally rose (Steffensmeier & Streifel, 1991). Today the youth population is relatively small, leading to lower crime rates (Steffensmeier & Harer, 1991).

But demography is only part of the story. The recent drop in crime may also be attributed to increasing rates of imprisonment. With almost exactly two million people behind bars as of early 2000, the criminal justice system may have finally managed—although at enormous cost—to incarcerate a large enough percentage of America's career criminals to start affecting the national crime rate. The economic boom of the past decade also may have played a role in reducing the crime rate.

This is encouraging news, but projected demographic trends for the next two decades suggest trouble ahead. There are presently about 39 million American children under the age of 10—an unusually high number. Soon these children will start moving into their teens. Between 1996 and 2006, America's adolescent population is expected to grow by 17 percent (Morganthau, 1995). Although juvenile homicide arrests declined 56 percent between 1993 and 1998, they had risen over 135 percent between 1980 and 1993 (U.S. Bureau of the Census, 1998). Many sociologists expect crime rates to rise in the next few years, perhaps despite anything we may do to try and keep them down.

Crime Rates in Cross-Cultural Perspective

Cross-cultural comparisons of crime rates are always difficult, in part because different nations define particular crimes quite differently and also because the

Table 9.1 Changes in Official Crime Rates for Selected Index Offenses, 1987–1997 (Arrest Rates per 100,000 People)				
Offense	1987	1991	1995	1997
Homicide	8.3	9.8	8.2	6.8
Forcible Rape	37.4	42.3	37.1	35.9
Robbery	212.7	272.7	220.9	186.1
Aggravated Assault	351.3	433.3	418.3	382.0
Violent Crime	**609.7**	**758.1**	**684.6**	**610.8**
Burglary	1329.6	1252.0	987.1	919.6
Larceny/Theft	3081.3	3228.8	3043.8	2886.5
Auto Theft	582.9	659.0	560.4	508.8
Property Crime	**4940.3**	**5139.7**	**4591.3**	**4311.9**

Source: U.S. Bureau of the Census, 1999, Table 242

accuracy of data collection varies sharply around the world. Comparisons are probably easiest concerning homicide because most nations take special pains to investigate murders and to accurately record their findings, although certain murders—such as the "honor killings" of women and female infanticide—may not be reflected in the official statistics.

As Figure 9.2 shows, a few nations report higher homicide rates than the United States, but the American rate substantially exceeds those of most other industrialized societies (Ellis & Walsh, 2000). The most dramatic comparison is with Japan, where despite recent increases the murder rate is still between six and eight times lower than the U.S. figure. In 1987, Tokyo, a city of 12 million, experienced 133 murders; in the same year, New York, with 7 million people, recorded 1672 homicides (Yanagishita & MacKellar, 1995). Note that the homicide rate is also very low in punishment-oriented Singapore.

More generally, in recent decades American violent crime rates have commonly been three to four times higher than those of other modern societies. However, cross-cultural differences in the rates of major property crimes are much less substantial, and a number of European nations have seen marked increases in both violent and property crime during the same years that crime declined in the United States.

Why are the U.S. rates as high as they are? Many sociologists are convinced that the single most important factor underlying our violent crime statistics is the American fascination with guns (Wright et al., 1983; Davidson, 1993). Between 60 and 70 million handguns and automatic weapons are currently in circulation in this country, and about 15,000 people die each year as a result of gun homicides—well over 400,000 since John Kennedy was assassinated in 1963 (Fingerhut, 1993). Homicide is now the number one

cause of death among African American youths, and close to 90 percent of these murders involve guns.

But the proliferation of guns is not the whole story. Several nations, including Switzerland, have high rates of gun ownership and low levels of personal crime. Could the pervasive violence in our media be a contributing factor? Possibly, but low-crime Japan is also known for its violent popular culture. The high levels of drug use in the United States doubtless contribute to the problem. So does frustration resulting from our extensive economic inequality (see Chapter 11). America's high level of cultural heterogeneity also plays a part (Hansmann & Quigley, 1982).

Many researchers have studied Japan in order to understand how a modern society can keep its crime rate low. The most important factors retarding crime in Japan appear to be (1) a high level of ethnic and cultural homogeneity; (2) a strong cultural emphasis on conformity, which is reinforced in the family, in the schools, at work, and through religion; (3) a relatively strong economy and a moderately generous welfare state that together have greatly reduced poverty; (4) strict gun control laws; and (5) an innova-

INTERNET ——→ CONNECTIONS

The FBI has an interesting Web site at www.fbi.gov/ucr.htm. From the most recent "Uniform Crime Reports," find how much crime there was in your city. (If you need to download Acrobat Reader, simply follow the instructions on your screen.)

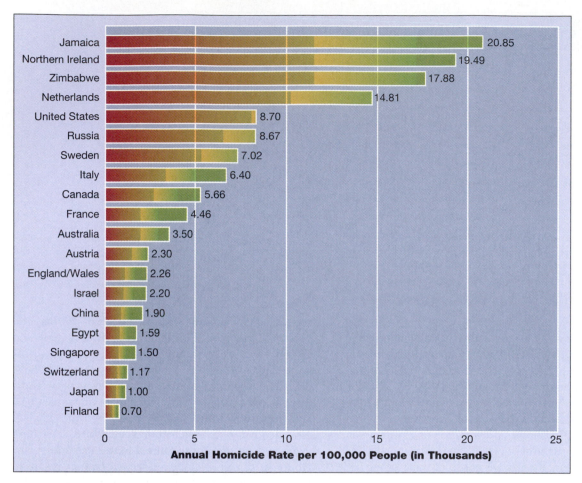

FIGURE 9.2   Homicide Rates Per 100,000 People for the United States and Selected Additional Countries, 1996

Source: Lee Ellis and Anthony Walsh. 2000. *Criminology: A Global Perspective.* Boston: Allyn and Bacon: p. 59.

tive criminal justice system that is strongly supported by the populace and that solves a very high percentage of its cases (Westerman & Burfeind, 1991; Miyazawa, 1992).

MAJOR TYPES OF CRIME

This section will examine some of the important characteristics of violent street crime, elite crime, and victimless crime.

Violent Street Crime

Only about 12.5 percent of all index offenses are violent crimes, but this is the type of offense that arouses the deepest fear among the public and is most frequently reported in the mass media (Warr, 1995). Vi-

olent crime also creates the most serious and lasting trauma for its victims (Parker, 1995).

Homicide.   15,839 Americans were murdered in 1997, an average of 305 per week. Although the percentage of murders committed by strangers is on the rise, most homicides still take place between people who know each other—family members, friends, neighbors, and drinking buddies (Wilson, 1993). What some sociologists call "the common homicide" occurs as a result of everyday interpersonal conflict between two or more young men that gets out of hand, typically late on Friday or Saturday night and after heavy use of alcohol by both participants.

Almost all homicides committed by women are defensive attacks against abusive husbands or boyfriends rather than drunken barroom brawls. Many stranger murders are committed accidentally in the course of other crimes such as robbery or burglary.

Many people look to Japan for new and innovative ideas in criminal justice. Despite the fact that life in Japan is fast-paced and modern, its crime rate is among the world's lowest.

Others, such as "drive-by" shootings, are related to turf conflicts between rival drug-distribution syndicates. A few—a very few, despite what Hollywood tells us—are carried out by professional hit men or by serial or mass murderers.

Rape.   Forcible rape, almost certainly the most feared of all crimes, was discussed in Chapter 8. It is undoubtedly the index offense for which the official data are least reliable. Several decades ago, it was thought that as many as 90 percent of all rapes were not brought to the attention of the authorities. Today, a comparison between UCR and victimization figures indicates that perhaps half of all rapes are reported. This increase is primarily a consequence of changes in the way the criminal justice system processes rape complaints. All-female police rape squads, reductions in requirements for corroborating evidence, and *shield laws*, which prohibit attorneys from probing into victims' private lives, have all increased rape survivors' willingness to report (Allison & Wrightman, 1993).

In searching for the causes of rape, many sociologists have been struck by research that shows many offenders are not severely psychologically disturbed. There are no significant personality traits that distinguish the rapist from the non-rapist. This strongly suggests that aspects of mainstream American culture may promote rape. From this perspective, both men and women are, in a sense, socialized for rape: women learn to be passive and agreeable while men are taught to be aggressive and to look at women as sex objects to be conquered. Rape is not, in this view, about passion but rather about power. This interpre-

tation is further supported by the observation that the primary function of homosexual rape in prison is clearly the establishment of a hierarchy of dominance, not the provision of sexual gratification.

The legal penalties for rape are severe; in fact, it is one of a rather small number of crimes for which offenders have, in the past, occasionally been sentenced to death. This strikes some observers as odd. Why would a man, an occupant of the more highly ranked gender status, be severely punished for a crime against a woman, an occupant of a less valued gender status? The feminist perspective provides a chilling explanation for this apparent contradiction. The law historically has treated rape not as a *personal* crime but rather as a *property* offense in which one man, the rapist, despoils a valuable possession of another man, the victim's father or husband. This may be the ultimate expression of how sexist culture treats women as objects rather than as people.

Elite Crime

Up to this point, we have focused on acts that are typically committed by lower-status individuals. However, criminal acts perpetrated by the well-to-do, which some have called "crime in the suites" (Nader & Green, 1972), cause far more financial harm and take far more lives than do the crimes that show up in the UCR. We will briefly consider two types of elite crime: organized crime and corporate crime.

Organized Crime.   **Organized crime** is criminal activity conducted by relatively large-scale and highly

Global Connections

Religious Law in Iran

At the heart of the Iranian criminal justice system is a blurring of the distinction between government and religion (Entessar, 1988). The leaders of the Iranian Revolution of 1978–1979 believed that secular governments, which rely on humanly made laws, inevitably fall victim to corruption and degeneration. Only by rejecting foreign influences and adhering to the God-given laws, or *Shari'a*, spelled out in the Koran, could their nation become whole again.

Islamic law has remained virtually unchanged for centuries. Muslim "fundamentalists" hold that when conflicts arise between Islamic law and the needs of a changing society, society must change to conform with the law, not the reverse. A key principle of the Islamic government of Iran is that legislative and judicial bodies exist not to create laws, but solely to enforce them. In most cases the punishment for a category of crimes is specified in the Koran and is nonnegotiable. Iran's Revolutionary Court, led by the supreme *faaih* or "just jurist," has the authority to issue *fatwahs* (or edicts) and to decide cases deemed a threat to the Islamic Republic; its decisions are final, with no right of appeal. Most of the executions carried out in Iran since 1979 have been ordered by the Revolutionary Court. More routine cases are heard and decided by *ulema*, religious scholars, or in some cases, by self-appointed neighborhood tribunals.

The Islamic penal code followed in the Republic of Iran recognizes three general categories of crimes. The first, *hudud* offenses, are acts including theft, adultery, heresy, and drinking alcoholic beverages prohibited by God and carrying mandatory penalties. If the accused is found guilty, the judge has no discretion regarding punishment. Theft is punishable by amputation of the hands; adultery, by stoning to death. Other *hudud* offenses, such as *mofsed-e fil arz* (Earthly corruption) and *mohareuh ba Khoda* (hostility to God)—both of which carry a mandatory death penalty—are largely undefined, allowing judges to exercise vast and arbitrary power with no semblance of impartiality.

The second category of crimes, *qisas*, includes murder, manslaughter, battery, and mutilation. Under Islamic law, such acts are considered crimes against the victim *and his or her family*, not solely against the individual or society. The family has the right to personally enact vengeance, inflicting injury or death on the culprit equal to that experienced by the victim. Although the Koran urges forgiveness, the victim is entitled to retribution in kind or "an eye for an eye."

The third category, *ta'zir* offenses, are roughly equivalent to misdemeanors: They include immoral behavior, wearing immodest clothing, and the like. Here, judges do have options. Depending on how disruptive they consider a transgression, they may issue a rebuke or a warning, impose a fine, seize property, or order a public flogging (the most common form of punishment in Iran today).

Divat refers not to a type of crime but to a form of punishment. If the victim of a *qisas* offense (or the victim's family) chooses not to exact retribution, he or she is entitled to compensation or "blood money." The Iranian government has established clear rules for the amount of *divat* due for various crimes as well as schedules for its payment.

The first *fatwah*, issued by the late revolutionary leader Ayatollah Khomeni in 1979, declared all prerevolutionary laws null and void. Since then Iranian authorities have consistently asserted that divine law overrides international law and widely shared western standards of human rights and just procedure. To outsiders, the Islamic penal code may seem barbaric. To Iranians, strict penalties are just, not only to the victim but also to the criminal, who, having paid for his or her sins, is more likely to ultimately receive mercy from God.

1. What are the advantages and disadvantages of explicitly grounding a legal system in a particular religious tradition? Should the United States attempt to integrate Christianity into its criminal justice system, as some conservatives recommend?
2. The Iranian legal system is more focused on protecting the rights of crime victims (and their relatives) than is American law. Should our courts move in this direction?

Source: Entessar, 1988.

---

structured gangs or syndicates that routinely use corruption and violence to maximize their profits. Most, but not all, organized crime groups are involved in providing illegal goods and services to the public (Abadinsky, 1990; Block, 1991). Popular understandings of organized crime tend to reflect the "Godfather" image or the *alien conspiracy model*, which suggests that most local criminal gangs are controlled by a single national organization of Sicilians called the *Mafia* or *La Cosa Nostra*. Whether American organized crime was ever this highly centralized is debatable, but there is no doubt that the alien conspiracy model is no longer accurate.

Organized crime arose in the United States long before the immigration of large numbers of Italians. Early in the nineteenth century, Irish and later Jewish gangs functioned as criminal syndicates in many large cities. They were displaced early in this century by Sicilian groups, but the era of Italian control over organized crime has ended (Block & Chambliss, 1981; Albanese, 1989). The gangs are increasingly run by members of ethnic groups such as African Americans (Ianni, 1974), Chinese (Chin, 1990), Cubans, Colombians, Jamaicans, and many others (Elliott, 1993). Some of these groups are strictly local, while others have national and international connections (Delattre, 1990).

The general process whereby different national origin groups assume control of criminal syndicates is termed *ethnic succession* (Bell, 1953). It occurs as groups migrate to this country only to find their opportunities for upward mobility limited. Refusing to abandon their dreams, many respond by innovating; in Robert Merton's terms, they find illegitimate ways of achieving success goals (O'Kane, 1992) (see Chapter 8). Over time, as legitimate opportunities gradually open up for each ethnic group, newer immigrants take their place in the syndicates.

Syndicated crime is by no means an exclusively American problem. It thrives throughout Europe (Fijnaut, 1990), in Russia (Bartos, 1995), and in Japan, where about one-third of all prison inmates are believed to be members of a syndicate called the *Yakuza* (Bryjak & Soroka, 1994: 274). Latin American and Southeast Asian syndicates are heavily involved in exporting drugs to America.

U.S. efforts to control syndicated crime are hampered by these groups' very deep leadership hierarchy, which makes it extremely hard to convict the top bosses. Systematic and widespread corruption of local, state, and federal officials is another barrier to effective prosecution (Newfield & Dubrul, 1979). However, in the past two decades, federal prosecutors have successfully gone on the offensive against the leaders of the old-line Sicilian groups. Armed with the witness-immunity program and the Racketeer Influenced and Corrupt Organizations Act (RICO), officials have substantially weakened the Cosa Nostra, but they have not prevented new ethnic gangs from taking its place.

Corporate Crime. Over fifty years ago, Edwin Sutherland directed sociologists' attention to a problem he called **white-collar crime,** criminal acts committed by high-status people in the course of their occupations (Sutherland, 1949). Sutherland's concept lumps together several very different types of crime. The most fundamental distinction is between **occupational crimes,** acts like embezzlement committed by individuals against their employers, and **corporate crimes,** criminal acts committed by businesses against

their employees, customers, or the general public (Clinard & Quinney, 1973).

We will briefly discuss four types of corporate crime. First, *financial offenses* involve acts such as insider trading, price fixing (Baker & Faulkner, 1993), bribery, kickbacks, and corporate tax evasion. The savings and loan scandal of the 1980s is the most widely publicized recent example of such crimes (Waldman & Thomas, 1990; Weisburd et al., 1991). During the Reagan era, the government relaxed regulations on the savings and loan industry, and some 500 executives began an orgy of what has been termed "collective embezzlement" (Calavita & Pontell, 1991). They paid themselves exorbitant salaries, made bad loans to friends and relatives that were covered by federal insurance programs, falsified records, and in some cases simply absconded with depositors' funds.

It is impossible to know how much the S&L scandal will ultimately cost the taxpayers; estimates vary between $300 billion and $1 trillion (Newdorf, 1991; Kettl, 1991). Using a relatively conservative figure of $500 billion, each man, woman, and child in the United States will eventually pay $2000 in taxes to make good the stolen funds. In contrast, the annual cost of all conventional property crime is about $5 billion (Michalowski, 1985).

A second type of corporate crime involves *hazardous working conditions* (Frank & Lynch, 1992). Although aware of the health dangers of asbestos since the 1930s, the Johns Manville corporation refused to make the modifications in its plants that would have protected workers. The consequence: Many thousands of painful and premature deaths from preventable lung diseases (Brodeur, 1985; Mokhiber, 1988). Not one Johns Manville executive went to jail for these crimes, and the corporation avoided full financial responsibility by declaring strategic bankruptcy and reorganizing itself (Calhoun & Hiller, 1988; Delaney, 1992).

Third, many corporations have been found guilty of *manufacturing unsafe products*. In the classic case, Ford executives rushed the Pinto into production in

INTERNET ⟶ CONNECTIONS

For one New York journalist's description of the Mafia, go to www.ganglandnews.com. In what ways does this criminal organization look like an association of legitimate businessmen?

Employees in the garment industry, both in this country and abroad, are frequently subjected to substandard working conditions in sweatshops like this one.

1970, even though they knew that when the car was struck from behind, the doors jammed and the fuel tank exploded. Ford calculated that it would cost $137 million to repair the problem, but only $49.5 million to settle claims resulting from the design flaw. In the end, 500 people died, but Ford's profits were not affected (Downie, 1977).

Finally, corporations have been heavily implicated in air and water pollution, toxic waste dumping, and other *environmental crimes*. The poisoning of the Love Canal district in upstate New York by the Hooker Chemical Company is one well-known example (Simon & Eitzen, 1986). Another is the release of poisonous gas from a Union Carbide plant in Bhopal, India, that killed over 2,000 people.

The overall cost of corporate crime is enormous (Moore & Mills, 1990). Some years ago the Justice Department estimated financial loss due to corporate crime at $200 billion per year, eighteen times the cost of all street crime (Gest & Schersel, 1985). Avoidable workplace hazards are responsible for one-third of all work-related deaths (Hills, 1987).

Corporate crime is extremely widespread. In a study of 600 of America's largest manufacturing companies, researchers found that, over a two-year period, 60 percent were charged with some sort of violation and 43 percent with more than one offense. Just 13 percent of the companies—concentrated in the oil, automobile, and pharmacy industries—were responsible for over half of the violations, suggesting that, like some street criminals, some corporations are, in effect, hardened and habitual offenders (Clinard & Yeager, 1980; Friedrichs, 1996).

Can corporate crime be controlled? There has been some movement in the direction of stiffer penalties in recent years, but, overall, the powerful are still punished less severely than the poor (Braithwaite, 1985; Pearce & Tombs, 1997). Many harmful business practices are controlled by regulatory agencies whose sanctioning power is largely limited to fines (Hawkins & Thomas, 1984; Gray & Scholz, 1993). Furthermore, these fines, while sometimes substantial, are minimal compared to the profits that result from corporate crime. Executives often regard them as part of the cost of doing business; some fines are even tax-deductible!

When corporate offenders *do* end up in criminal court, the penalties tend to be mild. In part this is because they can easily afford top-flight legal representation and in part it is because the law is more easily applied to individuals than to corporate entities (Reiman, 1995). Most cases are settled out of court, and fines (often paid by the firm), probation, or at the worst short prison sentences served in minimum-security facilities are the usual punishments.

Why such easy treatment? For one thing, corporate offenders simply don't fit our stereotypes of criminals: They are mostly otherwise respectable, church-going, middle-aged white suburban homeowners. Judges seem to find it difficult to send people much like themselves to jail for long terms—almost no matter how serious their offenses (Galanter, 1974; Mann, 1985; Wheeler et al., 1988). Moreover, the victims of corporate crimes are usually, though not always, difficult to identify. Industrial pollution kills far more people than muggers, but no one can point to a single polluter as specifically responsible for a given death, a fact that reduces public outrage against corporate criminals.

Victimless Crime

A third major type of crime consists of acts such as drug sales and possession, prostitution, pornography, and illicit gambling. **Victimless crimes** are created when we use the criminal law to attempt to prohibit the exchange of strongly desired goods and services between willing adults (Schur, 1979).

Some say victimless crimes are efforts to "legislate morality" (Jenness, 1990). Of course, most laws have a moral dimension, but those against other types of crimes are generally based on a strong level of social consensus. In contrast, there is substantial disagreement in modern societies concerning whether drug use, prostitution, and gambling are acceptable.

Because neither party in the exchange of outlawed goods and services feels victimized, there is generally no one to complain to the police. This makes victimless crime laws extremely difficult and costly to enforce. Not only must the authorities apprehend the offenders, they must also investigate in order to find that an offense has taken place. Although between 25 and 30 percent of all arrests are for victimless crimes, the overwhelming majority of all instances of drug use, prostitution, and illegal gambling do not come to the attention of the authorities. In practice, the police and courts generally realize that they can never substantially reduce these outlawed practices. Their periodic crackdowns are primarily intended to demonstrate to moralists that the law is still on their side.

The sexually oriented victimless crimes of prostitution and pornography are discussed in Chapter 7.

THE CRIMINAL JUSTICE SYSTEM

All modern societies have developed elaborate institutional structures to identify suspected offenders, determine their guilt or innocence, and punish the guilty. A structure of this sort, consisting of the police, the courts, and correctional institutions, is called a *criminal justice system*. This section will examine selected aspects of the criminal justice systems of the United States and of other nations around the world.

The Police

Because the public sees the police as front-line troops in the "war against crime," hiring more police officers is one of the most politically popular anti-crime measures. The number of police in the United States has roughly doubled over the past twenty years (Maguire et al., 1992). There are presently over 660,000 full-time sworn officers in this country, or about 25 police per 10,000 people (U.S. Bureau of the Census, 1999).

But some sociologists wonder whether increasing the number of police is the most effective way to spend our crime-prevention dollars. Research shows that police rarely spend more than 20 percent of their time in crime control; most of their day is devoted to routine public order activity—directing traffic, dealing with public nuisances, controlling crowds—and

Neighborhood watch programs have been instituted all across the country in the past few decades. They are based on the simple fact that the people who actually live in a neighborhood are far more likely to detect criminal activity than are the police.

completing routine departmental paperwork (Siegel, 2000). Police officers rarely witness crimes, and unless they do, they must depend on the testimony of victims and witnesses in identifying suspects.

The fact that so much is expected of them, yet they have surprisingly little ability to actually reduce crime, contributes to the heavy stress many officers experience. Rates of marital violence, divorce, suicide, and alcoholism are all high among the police. Although the public by-and-large supports the police, officers spend much of their time in contact with young poor minority males who, as a category, are especially prone to anti-police attitudes; such constantly negative interactions add to the strain police feel (Wilson, 1983). This strain promotes the development of a strong, isolated police subculture that is extremely suspicious of outsiders (Crank, 1997).

In the past two decades, many American police departments have moved towards *community policing*, a new model of police functioning that is based on the idea that crime control ultimately depends on people exercising informal social control because there will never be enough police to serve as more than a backup to the community's own internal control mechanisms (Wilson & Kelling, 1982). In community policing, officers institute neighborhood watch programs and walk beats rather than stay in their patrol cars as they drive through the streets of urban neighborhoods (L. Brown, 1990).

Community policing is, in fact, an international movement found, among other places, in Canada (Normandeau, 1993) and Germany (Brown, 1983). It is especially popular in low-crime Japan (Westerman & Burfeind, 1991). Most urban Japanese police are assigned to mini-stations called *kobans*, which are scattered throughout the nation's cities. Officers in these neighborhood police stations become intimately familiar with the people in their districts. They work 56 hours per week and may stay in the same *koban* for several years. Their duties include not just crime control but also helping people with everyday problems like finding addresses and locating misplaced property. If an American police officer is like a firefighter, who appears only when there is a problem, a Japanese officer is more like a letter carrier, part of the daily life of the community. As a result, the Japanese readily cooperate with the police rather than see them as outsiders.

We cannot solve our crime problems by simply copying the Japanese. Our culture is not prepared to allow police to enter unlocked homes at will, stop and question citizens on the street without cause, or conduct highly personal crime surveys of neighborhood residents. Few Americans would feel comfortable allowing the police to hold suspects up to twenty-three days and deny them food, sleep, and toilet privileges during interrogation, even though such practices help the Japanese achieve a better than 99 percent conviction rate. We are simply too individualistic and too culturally heterogeneous to trust the police as much as the Japanese do. But certain aspects of Japanese community policing have been accepted by U.S. departments and have improved the quality of American policing.

The Courts

Common law societies, including the United States, structure their courts according to the **adversarial principle.** That is, defendants are, in theory, considered innocent until proven guilty, and their guilt or innocence is determined through a contest between the defense and the prosecution with a neutral judge making the final decision (Eitzen & Zinn, 1992).

Of course, this is a very idealized image of how the American system functions. Criminologists Lawrence Friedman and Robert Percival use the concept of the *criminal justice wedding cake* to describe how the American courts *really* work (Friedman & Percival, 1981; Gottfredson & Gottfredson, 1988; Walker, 1994). As depicted in Figure 9.3, this model suggests that there are four fundamentally different types of crimes, each of which is treated somewhat differently in the courts. At the top are the highly publicized "celebrated cases" like the O.J. Simpson trial, which are processed in a fully adversarial fashion. Next come the serious felonies, like murder, forcible rape, and burglary, especially those committed by strangers; they also are handled adversarially, though somewhat less so.

The vast majority of criminal cases are minor felonies or misdemeanors—crimes like simple assault, theft, or vandalism—often occurring between people who know each other. They are resolved in an assembly-line fashion with the judge, prosecutor, and defense attorney working together rather than as opponents. Their goal is to ensure that defendants, who are in practice assumed to be guilty, receive a "going rate" sentence, neither harsher nor less severe than sentences given to similar defendants.

The primary means by which this assembly-line justice is accomplished is **plea bargaining,** a system by which defendants plead guilty to a lesser charge rather than go to full trial (Schulhofer, 1984). There is little doubt that if it weren't for plea bargaining, the overloaded American court system would simply grind to a halt. But it is equally clear that innocent defendants have sometimes been pressured to accept a

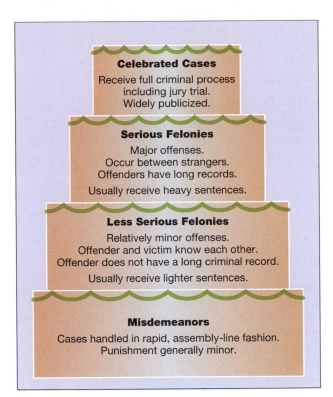

FIGURE 9.3 The Criminal Justice Wedding Cake
Source: Figure 2.2, p. 31 from *Sense and Nonsense About Crime and Drugs.* 4th edition by S. Walker. Copyright © 1998 by S. Walker. Reprinted by permission of Wadsworth, an imprint of the Wadsworth Group, a division of Thomas Learning. Fax 800-730-2215.

plea bargain, which amounts to a denial of due-process rights guaranteed by the Constitution.

Unlike common law societies, civil law nations such as France and Germany are based on the **inquisitorial principle** rather than the adversarial one. In this tradition, the judge's role is a greatly expanded one. Both before and during the trial, a civil law judge determines the truth of the matter at hand rather than simply mediating between two contesting sides. It is, therefore, the judge who calls and questions witnesses. Trials in the inquisitorial system avoid the long delays and courtroom dramatics that often occur in the adversarial system, but they do reduce the defendant's presumption of innocence.

The Purposes of Punishment

Why do we have prisons? This is a surprisingly difficult question, one for which there are at least four distinct answers: retribution, deterrence, rehabilitation, and incapacitation (Conrad, 1983; Siegel, 2000).

Retribution. The purpose of retribution is to restore the moral balance of society. Because a criminal has caused innocent victims to suffer, proponents of

retribution believe it is morally necessary that the offender suffer in turn. Thus, retribution is based on the ancient principle of *lex talionis,* "an eye for an eye."

Note that punishment as retribution is not a means of reducing crime. If our motive in executing a murderer is purely retributive, then it does not matter whether the murder rate decreases after the execution. What is important is that people are reminded that murder is immoral.

Retribution is the oldest of the four rationales for punishment. Over the past two centuries, though, it has lost substantial popularity. As modern societies sought ways to reduce crime, simple retribution came to be seen as bloody-minded and barbaric. But recent increases in the crime rate have eroded many people's faith in the efficacy of crime-control measures and led to a resurgence of retributive thinking.

Deterrence. The logic of deterrence rests squarely on the classical theory of criminality introduced in Chapter 8. If potential offenders think carefully and rationally about the risks and benefits of their actions and only decide to violate the law if the positives outweigh the negatives, then strengthening the penalties will change this "mental calculus" and reduce the crime rate (Gibbs, 1975).

There are two kinds of deterrence: **Specific deterrence** is punishment of a particular individual intended to keep him or her from violating the law in the future. **General deterrence** shows people who have yet to commit crimes what is done to offenders in the hope that they will decide not to break the law.

Does deterrence work? Will Michael Fay's caning and Sheriff Arpaio's moldy bologna eventually reduce the crime rate? This question has aroused passionate debate. Supporters point to research that shows criminals generally avoid victimizing individuals who they know to be armed, which implies that they are rational enough to avoid crime if the price

INTERNET CONNECTIONS

Many of us think of O. J. Simpson when we hear "the trial of the century," but another leading candidate concerned the kidnapping of aviator Charles Lindbergh's infant. Check www.lindberghtrial.com and then discuss how these two cases are similar and different.

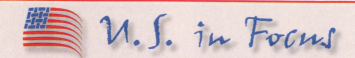

How Effective Is Specific Deterrence?

It is very difficult to research how well general deterrence works because there is no way to count the number of people who have not committed crimes for fear of punishment. Specific deterrence can, however, be studied by interviewing offenders. Unfortunately, most of this research is not very encouraging. For example, Kenneth Tunnell (1992) interviewed sixty men imprisoned for repeated property offenses. These were career criminals who had collectively committed almost 50,000 crimes. Tunnel investigated the process by which they decided to commit the crime for which they were currently incarcerated. He reached the following conclusions:

• Because most of these men had limited education, few conventional job skills, and lengthy criminal records, there was no legitimate way they could have earned even a minimally adequate living in today's economy. Only four of them even briefly considered working rather than committing crimes.

• Many of them were addicted to expensive drugs, making legitimate low-wage employment an even less viable alternative to crime.

• Most of these career criminals underestimated their chances of getting caught, did not know how long their sentences were likely to be if apprehended and convicted, and had not found their previous prison experiences intolerable.

• Finally, virtually all of them deliberately avoided thinking about the possible risks of crime by numbing themselves with drugs and alcohol or building up their confidence by talking with more experienced criminals. Just as a tightrope walker doesn't obsess over the pain of a possible fall, these men, having no real alternative to crime, did everything they could to put the possibility of failure out of their minds.

1. Name some social factors that might make the threat of a prison sentence more or less of a deterrent for a particular individual.
2. Why do many people persist in thinking that offenders like those studied by Tunnell can be deterred by the threat of prison?

Source: Tunnell, 1992.

---

tag is high enough (Greenberg & Kessler, 1982; Pontell, 1984; Hook, 1989). Opponents note that the United States already has extremely severe criminal penalties yet it also has a very high crime rate (Savelsberg, 1994). They argue that deterrence theorists overestimate the rationality of criminals (Aday, 1989; Pepinsky & Quinney, 1993; Chambliss, 1994). The U.S. in Focus box in this chapter reports on the results of an important study of the effectiveness of specific deterrence.

It seems clear that some crimes—and criminals—are more deterrable than others (Smith & Gartin, 1989). Much of the popular support for deterrence theory is based on the fact that most of us can remember times when the threat of punishment kept us from shoplifting, trying drugs, or committing some other minor criminal act. There is a good deal of evidence suggesting that basically law-abiding people who would lose a lot if they were labeled criminals are deterred by the threat of punishment (Parker & Grasmick, 1979; Klepper & Nagin, 1989b). But skeptics ask how much most career criminals have to lose if punished; for them, prison is simply an occupational hazard (Piliavin et al., 1986). Furthermore, many of the violent street crimes we fear the most are committed in the heat of passion, when rational calculation is largely or entirely blocked by emotion (Bouffard et al., 2000).

Five conditions must be met for a sanction to effectively promote deterrence. First, punishment must be *certain*. It should also be *swift*, *public* (so that general deterrence can operate), and perceived as *just*. Finally, deterrence theory holds that punishment should be *severe enough* to outweigh the rewards of crime (Sherman & Berk, 1984; Paternoster, 1989; Klepper & Nagin, 1989b).

Unfortunately, none of the first four conditions can be easily met in today's criminal justice system. Since most crimes are never even reported to the police, certainty of punishment is obviously impossible. The sheer volume of crimes that are reported slows down the system, making swiftness unlikely and reducing the chances that the punishment given for any particular crime will be publicized. And, finally, class- and race-based differences in how the law is applied—an issue that will be discussed toward the end of this chapter—reduce the chances that a given sentence will be seen as just.

Rehabilitation.   The growth of positivism in the social sciences (see Chapter 8) led directly to the concept of rehabilitation: If the decision to commit crime is caused by some combination of biological, psychological, and sociological variables, then therapeutic intervention should be able to "cure" the criminal. This optimistic philosophy has played an important role in criminal justice for most of the past two centuries, as is suggested by the use of words like "reformatory" and "correctional institution." It underlay the development of a system of juvenile justice in the late nineteenth century. It is clearly the guiding philosophy of Frankfurt's Mutter-Kind-Heim. Only in the past thirty years, because of the very high levels of public concern over crime, has the rehabilitative ideal become less popular (McCorkle, 1993).

Critics charge that the fact that between 60 and 75 percent of all offenders commit new crimes within three years after they are released from correctional institutions proves that efforts at rehabilitation are usually futile (Wilson, 1983). Some go farther, claiming that the very idea of rehabilitation excuses criminals from full responsibility for their acts (Methvin, 1997).

Do prisons as they are now run rehabilitate? Almost certainly not. As Sutherland's theory of differential association (see Chapter 8) suggests, if prisoners associate primarily with other unreformed offenders, then the only thing they are likely to learn is how to become better criminals. *Could* prisons rehabilitate? Perhaps. We do know that inmates who participate in well-constructed vocational and educational programs are substantially less likely to return to prison (Keller & Sbarbaro, 1994).

Incapacitation.   In the 1970s, many observers began to doubt whether prisons could either deter or rehabilitate; some skeptics began to argue that "nothing works" (Martinson, 1974). But even if we cannot reform offenders or frighten them into conforming, prisons can at least perform the function of incapacitation. We can keep the most dangerous criminals locked away where they cannot hurt anyone except each other.

It is this bottom-line rationale that currently dominates correctional thinking in the United States. As noted criminologist James Q. Wilson wrote, "Wicked people exist. Nothing avails except to set them apart from innocent people" (Wilson, 1983). And that is exactly what the United States has been doing, in unprecedented numbers and at unprecedented cost.

Group therapy sessions like this one are among the methods used by the juvenile justice system to try to rehabilitate wayward youths before they become committed to a long criminal career.

Corrections

As of 1997, nearly 5.7 million Americans were living under some sort of correctional supervision—prison, jail, probation, or parole. This amounted to one in every 150 citizens. Of these 5.7 million people, 3.26 million were on probation, 685,000 on parole, 1.19 million in federal and state prisons, and 558,000 in local jails (U.S. Bureau of the Census, 1999). This figure was over three times the 1980 total, reflecting an average annual growth rate of 7.4 percent over the fifteen-year period (see Figure 9.4). Only in the past two years has this growth begun to slow, with just a 4.8 percent increase between 1997 and 1998, the lowest figure since 1979.

One major consequence of this rapid expansion of corrections has been serious overcrowding, since prison construction has failed to keep pace with the growth in the number of inmates. State prison systems were operating about 25 percent over capacity in 1997; in some states, cells constructed for a single occupant were housing two or even three inmates. Such conditions not only violate basic constitutional guarantees of humane treatment, they also encourage inmate violence (Gaes & McGuire, 1985). In some cases, the courts have taken control of the prisons and reduced overcrowding, usually by giving relatively minor criminals early releases.

The expansion of the prison population has also caused financial havoc. The total cost of building and maintaining our correctional system is now about $30 billion annually—$4 billion in California alone. At an average cost of $17,000 per inmate per year, a 25-year-old given a life sentence without parole will ultimately cost taxpayers over $1 million (Mandel & Magnusson, 1993).

Why has this unprecedented expansion occurred? Not, as we have already seen, because crime is increasing rapidly. Nor is it because sentences are longer or because convicts are serving a higher proportion of their terms. The key is that several changes in the criminal justice system have sharply increased the chances that an individual who is convicted of a crime will actually be sent to prison (Langan, 1991). In particular, mandatory sentencing for drug offenses and, secondarily, for violent index crimes has swollen the population behind bars. In 1980, 19 of every thousand persons arrested on drug charges were eventually imprisoned; by 1993, the comparable figure was 104 per thousand. Laws that mandate long prison terms for persons convicted of three felonies over their lifetimes have also contributed to the enormous growth of the prison population (Irwin & Austin, 1994).

Who actually ends up in prison? Inmates are 95 percent male, most have not completed high school, and 80 percent have previously been incarcerated. Over half are serving time for offenses the public considers minor, such as petty theft or the possession of marijuana (Austin & Irwin, 1989). Although African Americans only make up 12 percent of the U.S. population, 41 percent of all prison inmates are black. Over 7 percent of all African American males are in prison compared with less than 1 percent of white males. About 25 percent of all black males in their twenties are under some form of correctional supervision compared with just 6 percent of young white men (Mauer, 1994).

If we look to European prisons for alternatives, we find vastly less punitive correctional institutions. For example, in the Netherlands there is an absolute prohibition against putting more than one inmate in a cell; consequently, minor offenders frequently wait to serve their time. Most Dutch prisons are small, sentences are short, and correctional officers are highly trained and well paid. Extensive therapeutic services and educational opportunities are available, and inmates are allowed regular conjugal visits. Prisoners even wear their own clothes and earn decent pay for their labor (Downes, 1992). Most Americans would

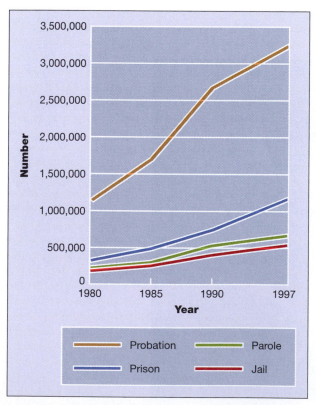

FIGURE 9.4 Adults Under Correctional Supervision, 1980–1997

Source: US Bureau of the Census, 1997.

probably reject the Dutch model as insufficiently retributive, even though it costs less, is less violent, and achieves a somewhat lower recidivism rate than does our system.

The Fundamental Dilemma of Criminal Justice

The most important underlying policy issue in the sociology of crime is balancing short-term and long-run solutions. Short-term approaches tend to be "hard-line" strategies, using the criminal justice system to incapacitate and (perhaps) deter: more cops, more prisons, longer sentences. These steps are popular with the public, and no one can deny that some career offenders simply must be locked away. For example, Inciardi (1992) studied 254 juvenile cocaine users in Miami and found that each had committed an average of 880 crimes, including 37 major felonies, in the past year. Obviously, some people must be confined to protect the public.

But if we devote nearly all our energies to hard-line responses, most sociologists believe that we will continue to be plagued by high levels of crime as far into the future as we can see. Perhaps we should direct more attention to remedying the underlying causes of crime. For example, a study conducted by the RAND Institute found that, dollar for dollar, programs that encourage at-risk youth to stay in school and avoid trouble prevent five times as many crimes as mandatory sentencing laws. Similarly, teaching parents of aggressive youth how to control their children is three times more cost effective (Montgomery, 1996).

Everything we know about deviance suggests that informal social control is more effective than formal control (Anderson et al., 1977; Paternoster et al., 1983). In particular, we need to help integrate at-risk individuals into small groups that oppose criminality (Heckathorn, 1990). Informal control through small groups is the cornerstone of the Chinese criminal justice system. Workplace and neighborhood-based "study groups" teach their members about the law and routinely intervene to censure even rather minor attitudinal or behavioral deviance. Formal authorities are used only as a last recourse. Can we learn anything from this?

More generally, many sociologists feel that reducing economic inequality is the best long-term solution to the crime problem (Messner & Rosenfeld, 1994). Conflict theorist Elliott Currie (1989) recommends fighting crime through large-scale government programs that reduce poverty, improve the wages and stability of low-skill jobs, strengthen community ties, and restore the vitality of the family.

☰ LIFE CONNECTIONS: Who Are the Offenders, Who Are the Victims?

Crime is not a random phenomenon. Some people are far more likely than others to commit offenses and, similarly, some people are more likely than others to be victims. In this section we will investigate the demographic characteristics of criminals and of crime victims.

Who Are the Offenders?

Certain sociological variables strongly influence the chances that particular individuals will commit crimes. Table 9.2 presents UCR data on the age, gender, and race of persons arrested for index crimes. It is apparent that offenders are predominantly young males and that minorities are heavily overrepresented. The UCR does not collect information on social class, but a walk through any prison will confirm that most inmates are drawn from the bottom of the economic ladder.

Age. With the exception of white-collar offenders, most criminals are young people, often only a few years past childhood. In 1996, 30.8 percent of all persons arrested for index crimes were under 18; 56 percent were under 25. These figures are congruent with a point made earlier in this chapter, that the surge in crime between 1960–1975 occurred largely because the enormous baby boom generation was passing through its teenage and young adult years. In fact, the generalization that most criminals are young appears to be broadly true in all historical eras and societies (Hirschi & Gottfredson, 1983; Land et al., 1990). Why should this be so?

The vigor and physical strength associated with youth is doubtless one factor, especially with regard to index street crime. However, two sociological theories also help explain this pattern. One is Travis Hirschi's control theory of deviance that was discussed in Chapter 8. Recall that Hirschi believed criminal impulses are restrained by an individual's social bonds. But note that these bonds are typically weaker for teenagers than for adults. In this context, consider Michael Fay, whose misbehavior resulted in violent punishment by the authorities in Singapore. Adolescents often seek to establish their independence from their parents; they normally lack the obligations associated with having spouses or children; they often do not realistically consider that they may be caught and stigmatized as criminals; and they tend to have plenty of spare time. In short, they are

Table 9.2   Percentage of Persons Arrested for Index Crimes By Age, Race, and Gender, 1996–1997

By Age (1996)	under 18	18–24	25–44	45–54	55–64	65+
Murder	15.0	41.0	36.7	4.8	1.6	1.0
Forcible Rape	17.0	26.6	48.1	5.7	1.8	0.7
Robbery	32.1	32.7	33.0	2.0	0.3	0.1
Aggravated Assault	14.7	25.4	50.6	6.6	1.8	0.8
Burglary	37.0	27.3	32.5	2.6	0.4	0.1
Larceny-Theft	33.8	23.2	36.2	4.8	1.3	0.8
Auto Theft	41.5	28.6	27.5	2.0	0.3	0.1
Percent of total population	26.0	9.3	31.2	12.6	8.2	12.7

By Gender (1997)	male	female
Murder	90.0	10.0
Forcible Rape	98.8	1.2
Robbery	90.2	9.8
Aggravated Assault	81.0	19.0
Burglary	88.2	11.8
Larceny-Theft	65.6	34.4
Auto Theft	85.5	14.5
Percent of total population	48.9	51.1

By Race (1997)	white	black	other
Murder	41.5	56.3	2.2
Forcible Rape	56.8	39.8	3.4
Robbery	39.4	58.7	1.9
Aggravated Assault	59.8	37.8	3.4
Burglary	67.2	30.4	2.4
Larceny-Theft	64.0	32.8	3.2
Auto Theft	57.0	40.0	3.0
Percent of total population	82.7	12.9	4.4

Source: US Bureau of the Census, 1999.

much less restrained than adults and are correspondingly more likely to gravitate toward crime.

Edwin Sutherland's differential association theory, also presented in Chapter 8, provides further insight into why most criminals are young. Sutherland emphasizes the importance of significant others' attitudes toward crime in shaping our own feelings and behaviors. In line with their desire to break away from their parents, teenagers often spend a great deal of time in the company of their peers; they also care deeply about what their friends think of them. But peers frequently propel youths toward deviance (Agnew & Petersen, 1989). As a result, while many adult crimes are committed in groups, adolescent crime—especially that committed by juvenile gangs—is strongly peer oriented.

The significance of age is underscored by the fact that crime declines sharply after the mid-30s, a phe-

nomenon known as **aging-out** (Hirschi & Gottfredson, 1983; Wilson & Herrnstein, 1985). Only 6.3 percent of all persons arrested for index crimes in 1996 were over 44. As people acquire adult responsibilities, spend more time with their families and less with peers, and obtain the means to get what they want legitimately, they are less likely to turn to crime.

Gender.   Most crime is heavily, and in some cases overwhelmingly, male. This generalization applies to all major crimes except prostitution. In 1997, 74.8 percent of all arrests for index crimes were of males. As with the tendency for criminals to be young, this overrepresentation of males is apparent worldwide (Heidensohn, 1991).

Furthermore, most females who *are* criminals are guilty of relatively minor crimes. For example, women who commit larceny-theft, the only index

While women continue to be substantially less likely than men to commit virtually every crime other than prostitution and shoplifting, the rate at which women offend has been rising much faster than the equivalent rate for men. The women shown here are inmates at a prison in Russia.

crime with substantial female involvement, are mostly small-time shoplifters. Female crime rates are gradually rising, but they remain much lower than male rates, and women's crimes continue to be primarily nonviolent (Pollock, 1999).

How do we account for women's lesser involvement in crime? Early explanations emphasized what were believed to be innate psychological and biological differences between the sexes. These theories have generally been abandoned for lack of empirical support (Klein, 1995), although men's larger physical size and higher levels of testosterone may contribute to their violence.

Sociological explanations for women's lower crime rates are more compelling. Traditional female gender role socialization, as discussed in Chapter 5, emphasizes conformity and passivity while discouraging aggressiveness. Drawing again on the work of Hirschi and Sutherland, women tend to be more tightly bonded to parents and less involved in potentially delinquent peer groups (Hagan et al., 1985). They also may have more to lose if they acquire a criminal identity: Our culture considers criminality more compatible with the male role, so female criminals are particularly likely to be viewed as seriously deviant.

Feminist theorists have emphasized the importance of studying how gender influences criminality because women very rarely become involved in serious crime (Naffine, 1996). Can we learn something from this that can be applied to both men and women? Feminists also maintain that the success of rehabilitation-oriented women's facilities such as the Mutter-Kind-Heim may indicate some ways in which the American system might be improved.

It has also been suggested that women, particularly white, working- and middle-class minor offenders, have historically been treated gently by the courts because of their gender, a view known as the **chivalry hypothesis** (Feinman, 1994). However, recent sharp increases in the number of incarcerated females suggest that this hypothesis is no longer valid (if indeed it ever was). These increases may in part reflect the criminal justice system's acceptance of the feminist movement's demand for equal treatment. But they are also the result of new mandatory sentencing laws for repeated and drug-related crimes.

Social Class. Official statistics strongly support the popular image of criminals as not only young and male but also disproportionately poor. This is true in the United States (Braithwaite, 1981; Wolfgang et al., 1987; Hsieh & Pugh, 1993) and also in virtually every other country (Nettler, 1984).

Such findings fit well with Robert Merton's anomie theory of deviance. Like everyone else, members of the lower classes desire material success. But, opportunities to achieve success goals are often blocked. Along these lines, a good deal of research suggests that when employment declines, crime usually rises (Thornberry & Christensen, 1984; Cantor & Land, 1985). Some people respond to a blocked opportunity structure by innovation—adopting alternative, illegitimate, and often criminal ways of obtaining desired goals. While most poor people remain

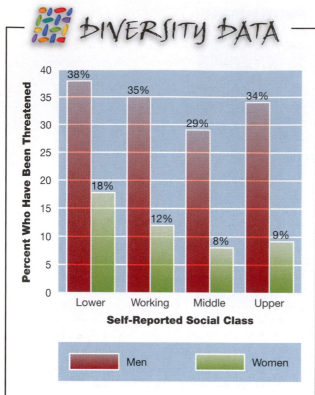

FIGURE 9.5   Percent Who Have Been Threatened by a Gun, by Gender and Class   As the self-reported social class position of women rises, the chance that they have been threatened with a gun tends to decrease. Class makes less difference among men, with the middle-class least likely to have been threatened. At all class levels, men are much more likely than women to have confronted firearm violence. Why do women generally report greater fear of violent crime despite the fact that they are at less risk of experiencing it?

Source: NORC. General Social Surveys, 1972–1996. Chicago: National Opinion Research Center, 1996. Reprinted by permission of NORC, Chicago, IL.

basically honest (Harries, 1990), a substantial percentage are drawn to crime, and many of these people show up in the UCR. The class–crime connection is particularly obvious among adults: While youth of all classes commit some acts of minor delinquency, class differences in official criminality are pronounced among people over 18 (Thornberry & Farnsworth, 1982).

But if we broaden our inquiry into the relationship between class and crime, the situation becomes more complex. Self-report studies show that serious street crimes are indeed concentrated among the poor, but lawbreaking occurs much more frequently among the privileged classes than UCR data suggest.

In fact, there may be very little overall correlation between class and criminality (Hirschi, 1969; Tittle et al., 1978; Tittle & Meier, 1990). Some researchers have even suggested that crime may be more common among the elite (Reiman, 1995).

In part, the disagreement over the extent of criminality in different classes reflects the use of different definitions of crime by different observers. Scholars who do not question the UCR's bias toward street crimes come up with strikingly different conclusions than do those who also take into account violations of trust such as embezzlement, price fixing, environmental crime, and the manufacture of substandard or hazardous products (Williams & Drake, 1990). Thus, if we broaden our conception of crime, we find criminals at all class levels, although members of different classes commit quite different crimes.

But even if we focus primarily on traditional predatory crimes, there is good reason to believe that the criminal justice system is more likely to apprehend and process the poor (Chambliss, 1969; Forer, 1984; C. E. Smith, 1991). All other factors being equal, lower-class offenders are more likely than the non-poor to be arrested (Smith, 1987), prosecuted (Sampson, 1986), and convicted.

Race.   Probably the single most prominent element in the popular stereotype of street criminals is race: Many Americans, both African American and white, tend to visualize criminals as minorities, particularly African Americans. Both UCR and victimization data lend some support to this stereotype. As Table 9.2 suggests, although only 12.9 percent of the U.S. population is African American, 35.6 percent of all persons arrested for index crimes in 1997 were blacks. In the same year, 56.3 percent of those arrested for murder and 58.7 percent of those arrested for robbery were African Americans. Latinos, who make up about 10 percent of the population, are apprehended for 10 to 15 percent of all serious violent crimes.

To a considerable extent, the high African American crime rate reflects the great number of blacks in the poorer classes, whose members are, as we have just indicated, particularly likely to be apprehended by the criminal justice system (Sampson, 1987). But poverty among African Americans is especially strongly associated with crime, principally because black poverty tends to be more severe than it is among other segments of the population. There are several reasons for this:

- The declining availability of low-skill, decent-paying jobs, a problem throughout America but a particularly severe one for minorities who still sometimes experience racist discrimination.

- The large numbers of single-parent, female-headed families in poor African American communities—largely due in turn to the lack of decent jobs that would allow young men to support their families. These single-parent families are less able to supervise their children or to provide positive male role models for them. Furthermore, single-parent families are very likely to fall below the poverty line, especially if headed by a female (Wilson, 1987).
- The out-migration of nearly all working- and middle-class African Americans from the highly segregated inner-city neighborhoods where crime is at its worst. This exodus of individuals who have achieved success legitimately means that youth growing up in these neighborhoods may see crime, especially drug dealing, as the only viable route out of poverty. As Sutherland's differential association theory would predict, when there is nobody to hang out with except criminals, crime becomes normative (Matsueda & Heimer, 1987).

These factors work in concert to intensify poverty and promote crime. Furthermore, although some sociologists deny that the criminal justice system is biased against minorities (Wilbanks, 1987), substantial evidence suggests that, above and beyond issues of class, the system stacks the deck against persons of color. Research shows, for example, that African American youth are more likely to be arrested than whites for the same crime (Krisberg et al., 1987). Young African Americans are also between five and thirteen times more likely than whites to be killed by the police on the street (Brown, 1993). African American youth are also more likely than whites to be tried as adults (Mauer, 1994).

While some studies have found that race has no effect on sentencing (Dannefer & Schutt, 1982; Miethe & Moore, 1986), others show clear evidence of bias, especially in the case of juveniles (Fagan et al., 1987). Furthermore, research confirms that, even if sentences do not differ substantially by race, African Americans actually end up serving more time for the same crimes (Huizinga & Elliott, 1987; Klein et al., 1988; Bridges & Crutchfield, 1988). Our prisons are now 41 percent black and over 25 percent of all African Americans in their twenties are either in prison or under some form of correctional supervision. In 1998, blacks were six times more likely than whites to be incarcerated ("Nation of Jailbirds," 1999). African Americans are also disproportionately likely to be sentenced to—and receive—the death penalty.

A careful evaluation of all evidence suggests that racial bias in the criminal justice system has diminished in recent decades and that most of the reason for the large number of minorities in the courts and prisons is due to their greater criminality (Balkwell, 1990). At the same time, some bias persists, at least at some times and in some places. Worse, perhaps, many minorities perceive the system to be unfair, a view that can easily become a self-fulfilling prophecy.

Who Are the Victims?

Historically, criminologists have focused almost exclusively on offenders. But the last twenty-five years have seen the birth of **victimology**, a subfield of criminology devoted to the study of the victims of crime (Karmen, 1995). National Crime Victimization Survey data, as summarized in Table 9.3, allow us to compare the demographic characteristics of crime victims with those of offenders for selected crimes as reported in Table 9.2.

The similarity between these two populations is striking: Both victims and offenders are predominantly young, lower-income males, with minorities strongly overrepresented. The similarities are greatest for violent personal crimes, which is not surprising since most homicides and many rapes and assaults grow out of ongoing relationships. It is less obvious, and certainly ironic, that victims of property crime frequently turn out to be as disadvantaged as the people who prey upon them. Robbers, thieves, and burglars tend to find it easier to victimize people who live near them, which generally means in poor neighborhoods. Wealthy people may have more property, but they also have a much greater ability to safeguard their possessions.

Crime victimization figures strongly illustrate the combined effects of minority status, poverty, and gender. For example, African American men experience an exceptionally high risk of homicide—six to eight times that of young white men. Young African American women are between three and four times as likely to be murdered as are their white counterparts (Karmen, 1996). And while female victimization rates remain well below those of males for all index crimes except rape and some types of larceny-theft, their level of fear of crime is much higher (Kennedy & Sacco, 1998). In part, this is due to their greater physical vulnerability, but it also reflects the fact that the patriarchal logic of the criminal justice system has tended to deemphasize the seriousness of domestic violence, a crime that disproportionately impacts women.

Table 9.3	Victimization Rates per 1,000 People by Age, Race, Gender, and Household Income for Selected Crimes, 1997						
By Age	12–15	16–19	20–24	25–34	35–49	50–64	65+
Rape	2.5	5.6	2.4	2.3	0.6	0.2	0.2
Robbery	8.2	10.2	7.4	4.7	3.7	2.2	0.9
Aggravated Assault	15.1	24.6	17.0	9.5	7.4	2.8	0.6
By Gender	male	female					
Rape	0.3	2.5					
Robbery	6.1	2.6					
Aggravated Assault	10.9	6.4					
By Race	white	black	other				
Rape	1.4	1.6	1.1				
Robbery	3.8	7.4	5.0				
Aggravated Assault	8.2	12.2	6.1				
Burglary*	42.3	62.5	36.2				
Theft*	188.1	205.3	177.9				
Auto Theft	11.9	24.1	23.3				
By Household Income	less than $7500	7500–14,999	15k–24,999	25k–34,999	35k–49,999	50k–74,999	over 75,000
Rape	5.2	2.2	1.5	1.5	0.6	0.7	1.1
Robbery	10.1	7.0	4.6	4.2	2.9	3.1	3.7
Aggravated Assault	13.6	11.8	10.4	8.2	8.6	7.2	4.7
Burglary*	79.5	53.9	47.2	42.4	39.8	35.0	42.4
Theft*	169.3	173.3	181.2	202.0	214.6	224.2	234.1
Auto Theft*	10.0	9.1	14.1	15.8	17.2	11.7	16.3

*per 1000 households
Source: U.S. Bureau of the Census, 1999. Tables 354 & 356

Victims' assistance programs have expanded dramatically over the past twenty years. Here a counselor helps prepare a crime victim to testify in court.

≡ SOCIETY CONNECTIONS: Capital Punishment and Drug Decriminalization

Of all the subfields of sociology, criminology is probably the most strongly oriented toward finding practical solutions to social problems. Two of the most intensely debated crime control issues concern capital punishment and decriminalizing drugs.

Capital Punishment

America's continuing support of the death penalty stands in stark contrast to virtually every other modern Western nation, where capital punishment has either been abolished outright or is, in practice, never used (Wood, 1996). The only nations that currently excecute more offenders than the United States are China, Iran, Saudi Arabia, and the Congo. International criticism of the United States has been particularly intense regarding this nation's willingness to execute people who are mentally retarded or who committed their crimes as juveniles.

Most of this concern is expressed in moral terms, but from a social science perspective, the most important issue is whether the death penalty is an effective deterrent. The evidence is mixed. Some research does support a deterrent effect, especially shortly after widely publicized executions (Phillips, 1980; Stack, 1990). But the clear majority of the evidence leads to the opposite conclusion (Paternoster, 1991; Bohm, 1991; Bayles, 1991; Peterson & Bailey, 1991). States with the death penalty tend to have higher murder rates. Furthermore, internationally,

the abolition of capital punishment has generally been followed by a drop in homicide rates (Archer & Gartner, 1984).

Why does capital punishment apparently fail to deter? Partly because most murders are crimes of passion and the offender is not thinking rationally. But also because the death penalty is neither swift—it commonly takes at least ten years to exhaust a prisoner's appeals—nor certain—if we execute 100 murderers annually, then the odds of any particular offender actually being killed are about 250 to 1.

There are several arguments in favor of the death penalty. It certainly provides both incapacitation and retribution. Relatives of homicide victims frequently, but not always, report a sense of relief after an execution. It also is supported by public opinion, never irrelevant in a democratic society.

On the other hand, in addition to the weak evidence for deterrence, there are other problems with capital punishment. It is irreversible, and, as discussed in the Then and Now box in this chapter, in this century alone, about 400 Americans have been sentenced to death and at least eighteen executed who were later found to be innocent (Radelet & Bedau, 1992). Furthermore, it is actually more expensive to provide full rights to appeal a capital conviction than it is to keep an offender locked up for a lifetime.

Finally, evidence of class and racial bias continues to be a concern. Between 1977 and 1997, 37.5 percent of all executed offenders were African Americans. But research suggests that the key variable is not so much the race of the offender as the race of victim: People who kill whites are 4.3 times more likely to be executed than those who kill African Americans (Baldus et al., 1990). However, the current Supreme

People on both sides of the capital punishment debate often express their feelings with great passion. Currently, a sizable majority of Americans support the death penalty, and the number of executions is rising each year.

Changing Views on Capital Punishment

The death penalty has been used in this country since colonial days. A total of 3,859 prisoners were executed between 1930 and 1966 alone. However, increasing concern over both the morality and the effectiveness of capital punishment as a deterrent led to a marked decline in its popularity in the years after World War II. Opinion polls showed that just 42 percent of the public backed the death penalty in 1966.

In 1972, the Supreme Court voted 5–4 in the case of *Furman v. Georgia* that capital punishment as it was being applied was both cruel and unusual. The Court's rationale was heavily based on sociological research that showed African Americans were disproportionately likely to be given the death penalty. For example, between 1945 and 1965, 13 percent of blacks but only 2 percent of whites convicted of rape were sentenced to die. This ruling voided capital punishment in thirty-nine states and permanently blocked the execution of over 600 convicts, including Sirhan Sirhan and Charles Manson.

After *Furman*, most states rewrote their capital punishment statutes to increase the court's ability to take aggravating or mitigating circumstances into account. In 1976, the Supreme Court determined in *Gregg v. Georgia* that these rewritten laws passed constitutional muster. Over the next two decades, fueled by a rising crime rate, public opinion swung sharply in favor of the death penalty. As of the beginning of 2000, thirty-eight states had reinstated capital punishment, 632 people had been executed (214 in Texas alone), and 3,652 inmates were housed on death rows around the country.

However, between 1976 and early 2000, eighty-seven condemned inmates were released from prison because it was determined that they did not commit the crimes of which they had been convicted. In Chapter 1, we introduced the case of Anthony Porter, who was freed from Death Row after his case was investigated by a group of Northwestern University students. How many other convicts awaiting execution are innocent? No one knows, but research making use of advances in forensic science (especially DNA tests) suggests that quite a few probably are.

For example, in 1988, Dennis Fritz and Ronald Williamson were convicted of the brutal rape and murder of a 21-year-old barmaid in a small town in Oklahoma. Fritz was sentenced to life imprisonment and Williamson received the death penalty. Scientific evidence helped to convict them: Experts testified that body hair and semen found on the victim could only have come from these men. However, in April 1999, both were exonerated on the basis of DNA tests that were not available at the time of their trial.

Why have so many people been wrongfully condemned to death? The main reason appears to lie within the legal system itself. Most people accused of capital crimes cannot afford to hire their own lawyer, much less a "defense team." The states that rarely hand down death sentences, such as New Jersey and New Hampshire, have strong public defenders' offices with sufficient financial resources to attract experienced lawyers and to allow them to follow a case from the initial trial through appeals and even up to the Supreme Court. And two-thirds of the 4,578 capital cases that were appealed between 1973 and 1995 were overturned.

In other states, such as Texas and Alabama, public defense is not coordinated or funded at the state level, but rather a county judge appoints a lawyer who is paid according to a fixed scale that does not cover federal appeals. As a result, accused murderers often are represented by inexperienced lawyers who lack the resources and incentive to mount a vigorous defense. Whether verdicts are rechecked and new evidence is uncovered is largely a matter of luck.

In response to such concerns, public opinion is beginning to change once again. Once backed by as much as 80 percent of the public, capital punishment today is favored by about a two to one margin. Significantly, in January of 2000, Illinois Governor George Ryan suspended all executions in his state pending a careful reappraisal of the procedures by which the death penalty is applied. As of June 2000, only two states (Illinois and New York) guaranteed inmates DNA testing, but the overwhelming majority of the public supported this safeguard.

1. Why do you think the United States is the only remaining postmodern nation that retains the death penalty?
2. If you support capital punishment, would you be willing to abandon it if convicted murderers could be sentenced to life imprisonment with absolutely no chance of parole? Similarly, if you oppose the death penalty, would you change your opinion if evidence emerged that proved that it really was an effective deterrent?

Sources: Wolfgang & Reidel, 1973; Johnson, 1990; Bell, 1992; Snell, 1996; McCormick, 1998, 1999; Dedman, 1999; Alter, 2000; Alter & Miller, 2000.

Court refuses to consider such statistical evidence as proof of injustice.

Drug Decriminalization

The war on drugs has had a major impact on America's criminal justice system. Court dockets and prisons are overflowing with drug cases. About 60 percent of all federal prisoners and 22 percent of the inmates in jails and state prisons—a total of over 400,000 people—are classified as drug offenders, most of them nonviolent. Arrests of adults for the sale and possession of illegal drugs doubled in the late 1980s and early 1990s, even though drug use was declining.

People who question the wisdom of using the criminal justice system to attempt to reduce drug use offer Prohibition as an example of the ineffectiveness of this strategy. Outlawing alcohol apparently did somewhat reduce consumption, since cirrhosis of the liver declined during the 1920s (Goode, 1989). But Prohibition did not end alcohol use in this country, and it ate up a tremendous amount of the criminal justice system's time and resources (Musto, 1987). The current anti-drug crusade faces similar criticisms. For example, between 1985 and 1988, despite the fact that federal anti-drug expenditures tripled, cocaine use is believed to have increased by over 30 percent (Vacon, 1990). More recently, despite 25 years of Just Say No programs, adolescent drug use was increasing in the late 1990s.

No one disputes the desirability of reducing drug abuse. The question is whether the criminal law is the best means of achieving this end. One alternative is **decriminalization,** a policy whereby currently illegal drugs would be treated much as alcohol and tobacco are now: prohibited to children but available to adults under certain conditions. Decriminalization is based on reducing *demand*, not cutting off *supplies*. Thus, under this policy, much of the money currently used by the criminal justice system for the drug wars would go to expanding educational and therapeutic programs, which have been found to be seven times more cost-effective in reducing drug use than law enforcement strategies (Rydell & Everingham, 1994).

Several nations have experimented with partial decriminalization. We mentioned Holland's nonpunitive approach to marijuana control in Chapter 8. The United Kingdom has been substantially more successful than the United States in controlling opiate abuse by allowing physicians to prescribe heroin to registered addicts. And in this country, voters in five states approved measures in 1998 to allow the medical use of marijuana by persons suffering from glaucoma, the side effects of chemotherapy for cancer, and several other conditions.

Does decriminalization make sense? In discussing this issue, it is important to focus on the positive and negative consequences of the *law* rather than on the negatives of the drug. The issue is not are drugs harmful—they are. It is whether criminalization is a rational way of trying to reduce drug use.

Opponents of decriminalization argue that existing laws reduce drug use even if they do not come close to ending it. Decriminalization, they claim, would open the floodgates to an unprecedented increase in addiction because drugs would be cheaper and easier to obtain and because drug use would be less stigmatizing. It would send precisely the wrong moral message, especially to impressionable youth.

Supporters of decriminalization doubt that drug use would sharply increase if the laws were changed. They point to the example of Denmark, which decriminalized pornography and saw usage decline. Certainly, most people who currently wish to purchase drugs are able to obtain them easily enough. And the simple fact that drugs are illegal makes them "forbidden fruit" and thus even more attractive to some youth.

Decriminalization would greatly reduce the amount of police time currently devoted to trying to track down drug sellers and users, leaving the criminal justice system far more able to deal with predatory crime. It would come close to eliminating police corruption, which almost always occurs in the context of victimless crime laws. It would have the potential of dealing a death-blow to organized crime, since the current laws create a black market, which amounts to an operating subsidy to the syndicates. The end of Prohibition led to dramatically reduced profits for the Mafia. Decriminalization would also cut down on theft to obtain money to buy drugs, and, if drugs were taxed, those revenues could be used to fight abuse. Decriminalization would also save the lives of users who buy impure drugs or share needles thereby risking AIDS. The key question is how much use would increase if drugs were decriminalized. If the upswing were moderate, then the advantages would seem to outweigh the costs; on the other hand, America certainly cannot afford to triple or quadruple its drug-dependent population. We won't know which side of this debate is right and which is wrong any time in the near future since only about 15 percent of the public currently approves of across-the-board decriminalization.

SUMMARY

1. The legalistic approach defines crime as any violation of a law enacted by a legitimate government. In contrast, the natural law approach sees crime as a violation of an absolute principle.

2. The United States follows the common law tradition in which numerous cases accumulate to form a coherent set of legal principles based on precedent. Most other societies embrace civil law or religious law traditions.

3. Most sociologists rely on information from the Uniform Crime Reports (UCR) or from the National Crime Victimization Survey (NCVS), although both sources have serious weaknesses.

4. Street crime has been declining in the United States since the early 1990s. Demographic changes and sharp increases in imprisonment help explain this trend.

5. Rates of violent crime are much higher in the United States than in other developed countries, especially Japan.

6. Homicides typically occur between people who know each other, often arising out of ongoing conflicts.

7. Organized crime is often a means by which immigrants and minorities can succeed when legal opportunities are blocked.

8. The four major types of corporate crime are financial offenses, maintaining hazardous working conditions, manufacturing unsafe products, and environmental crimes.

9. Victimless crimes, created when the law attempts to prohibit the exchange between willing adults of strongly desired goods and services, are extremely difficult to control.

10. Many nations, including the United States, are currently experimenting with community policing.

11. American courts operate according to the adversarial principle, but in practice most cases are plea bargained. In contrast, many European societies use the inquisitorial model.

12. Punishment is based on one or more of four rationales: retribution, deterrence, rehabilitation, or incapacitation.

13. The U.S. prison system has become enormously overcrowded over the past decade.

14. Societies must choose an appropriate balance between short-run solutions to crime and long-run solutions that address crime's underlying causes.

15. Persons who commit major street crimes tend to be young, lower-class males; a disproportionate number are members of minority groups. Most victims of street crimes come from the same demographic categories as do the offenders.

16. The United States is virtually alone among the highly developed nations in using capital punishment.

17. Some observers believe that the decriminalization of drug use would allow the criminal justice system to concentrate its energies and resources on more serious crimes.

KEY TERMS

adversarial principle   222

aging-out   228

chivalry hypothesis   229

civil law   212

common law   212

corporate crime   219

decriminalization   235

general deterrence   223

index crimes   213

inquisitorial principle   223

occupational crime   219

organized crime   217

plea bargaining   222

religious law   213

specific deterrence   223

victimless crime   221

victimology   231

white-collar crime   219

CRITICAL THINKING QUESTIONS

1. How do you think the United States should balance the public's pressure for short-term solutions to the crime problem with the need to also address the underlying causes of crime?

2. How much emphasis do you think the criminal justice system ought to put on each of the four possible rationales for punishment: retribution, deterrence, rehabilitation, and incapacitation?
3. Can you think of factors other than those mentioned in this chapter that help explain why the U.S. crime rate is so high?
4. Are the policy debates about the death penalty and the decriminalization of drugs primarily moral or practical?

❖10❖ ECONOMIC STRATIFICATION

OUTLINE

The Time Machine

One of H. G. Wells's best known novels is entitled *The Time Machine*. On one level it is a simple science fiction story, but on another, it is a cautionary tale about the widening of class inequality in late nineteenth century England (Wells, 1969). In the novel, a time traveler finds himself in a future populated by two cultures, the beautiful, delicate Eloi, who live on the surface of the Earth, and the brutish Morlocks, who dwell in subterranean caverns. At first the traveler cannot imagine how this arrangement could have come about, but when he observes that the Morlocks do all the work to support both communities, he realizes that the explanation lies in

. . . the gradual widening of the present . . . difference of the capitalist from the laborer. . . . The exclusive tendency of richer people . . . is already leading to the closing of considerable portions of the surface of the country against these latter. . . . So, in the end, you would have above ground the Haves, pursuing health, comfort and beauty, and below ground the Have-nots, the workers. . . . (Wells, 1969: 55–56)

The Morlocks, denied the opportunity to live in the sunlight, regularly kidnap and consume the Eloi—a uniquely vivid expression of class hostility!

Clothing and Class

The Victorian society in which Wells lived was one in which people were very aware of the differences between the social classes. In other cultures, including the United States, class distinctions are less immediately obvious. But anyone who thinks class is unimportant should study the history of fashion. Most cultures have used clothing style as a highly visible symbol of class position because people need to identify each other's class on sight in order to know how to interact with them.

For example, in many traditional cultures, slaves and serfs wore little more than loincloths, while aristocrats and members of the royal family favored much more extensive and elaborate garb. Laws commonly restricted certain clothing styles to the higher classes and prescribed substantial punishments for people who dressed inappropriately for their station.

Similarly, for centuries wealthy Europeans publicly identified themselves as such by wearing clothes made of damasked satins, patterned brocades, and handwoven velvets—expensive fabrics that the middle or lower classes could never afford to purchase. Today, inexpensive copies of designer clothes are readily available in any Wal-Mart. In response, many designers prominently display their "elite" brand name labels on the outside of their clothing rather than hiding them inside. You may like knowing that you're wearing Nike athletic shoes and a Tommy Hilfiger sweater—but it's essential that everyone else knows that you're wearing them! (Lurie, 1981)

These two brief accounts demonstrate the significance of class inequality, one of the most important varieties of **social stratification,** the division of a large group or society into ranked categories of people, each of which enjoys different levels of access to scarce and valued resources, chiefly property, prestige, and power. A **social class,** in turn, may be defined as a category of people who share a common position in a vertical hierarchy of differential social reward.

Social stratification may be based on any number of different social statuses. Besides class, the most important of these are age, gender, and race or ethnicity. The study of stratification is an investigation into the social factors determining who gets what, when, and why (Lenski, 1966). Why, for instance, should the Eloi in Wells's novel enjoy such a privileged existence and not the Morlocks?

Social stratification is sometimes also called *structured social inequality* in order to emphasize that the differential rewards allocated to occupants of different statuses are built into society. That is, they are supported by widely accepted norms and values, and they endure from generation to generation. By and large, stratification has very little to do with individual differences in ability. High-ranking persons, even those lacking substantial intelligence or ability, generally find it far easier to obtain property, prestige, and power than do even the most capable individuals who hold lower-ranking statuses.

Let's look a little more closely at the main types of stratification. *Gender* and *age stratification* are cultural universals (Rossides, 1990; Nolan & Lenski, 1999). In every known society, men and women and people in different age categories—at a minimum, children, adults, and the elderly—have different levels of access to scarce and valued resources. We will discuss gender and age inequalities in Chapters 13 and 14, respectively.

Americans may be particularly aware of *racial* and *ethnic stratification* because of the unusual diversity of the society in which they live. This form of social stratification—widespread in the modern world but uncommon in earlier eras when people were less geographically mobile—is the subject of Chapter 12.

This chapter and the one that follows are devoted to the topic of *economic stratification*, which involves the division of society into two or more social classes. This chapter concentrates on theories of economic stratification. Chapter 11 will discuss the class structure of postindustrial societies like the United States.

This chapter will also overview **global stratification,** the division of the nations of the world into richer and poorer categories. Just as the people in any particular society belong to wealthier and less-advantaged social classes, countries may be ranked by their differential access to valued resources.

LEGITIMATING STRATIFICATION

One of the first questions that arises in the study of social stratification is: "Why does structured inequality persist?" Many—usually most—people in society do not seem to benefit very much from it. Tens of millions of Americans are children, elderly, or racial and ethnic minorities; *most* are female and middle, working, or lower class. Yet society continues to be structured in a way that confers substantial advantages on males, whites, adults, and members of the upper class.

The elite in most societies do not maintain their position through force. While the upper classes do occasionally resort to the military to protect their privilege, it is generally as a last resort and extremely costly. A far more efficient method is to convince the lower-ranking categories of people that their lack of rewards is just and proper. This is the role of ideology.

Ideology

An *ideology*, in this context, is a belief that legitimates existing patterns of structured social inequality (Lipset, 1963; Kerbo, 1991; Tilly, 1994). It is easy to see why elites would accept ideology, but why would other members of society do so?

The answer is that the groups at the top of stratification systems generally enjoy a tremendous ability to shape how people think. They exercise *ideological hegemony* (Gramsci, 1959; Robertson, 1988; Abercrombie et al., 1990). People are consistently socialized—in school, in church, in the media, and even by their parents—to accept a worldview that leads them to see their relative lack of success as natural and proper.

Ideology comes in many varieties. Historically, most ideologies have been religious. The traditional Indian caste system (Lannoy, 1971; Kolenda, 1985) and the very rigid class structure of ancient China were considered expressions of divine will. Modern ideologies are more often supported by science, or pseudoscience, like the "scientific" proofs of racial inferiority that were widely believed earlier in this century.

In recent decades, most Americans have become aware of the bias inherent in the ideologies that have traditionally supported racial, gender, and age inequality. Later chapters will introduce the terms racism, sexism, and ageism for these ideologies. Interestingly, though, there is no generally accepted equivalent term to identify the ideology that legitimates economic inequality. We will call it **classism.**

Classism

Classism has been given many names over the years. It has been called "the ideology of competitive individualism" (Lewis, 1978). Others refer to it as the "Horatio Alger myth," after a nineteenth-century American author whose heroes invariably rose from poverty to wealth by virtue of unrelentingly hard work. Some simply define classism as excessive faith in the American Dream.

Clothing is often a useful symbol of an individual's class position. Uniforms, like those worn by these domestic workers, usually—but not always— indicate relatively low status.

Classism begins with accepting the idea that the United States offers, if not completely equal opportunity to achieve success, at least sufficiently equal opportunity so that everyone who works hard has an excellent chance of acquiring wealth (Ritzman & Tomaskovic-Devey, 1992). Most sociologists think this claim is greatly exaggerated. However, right or wrong, if it is accepted, classism leads to two important conclusions: first, that the wealthy deserve their privileges, and second, that the poor are largely responsible for their plight.

Classism thus promotes a narrow and stereotyped way of thinking. It suggests the poor are lazy, stupid, immoral, and without ambition (Huber & Form, 1973; Mead, 1992). It largely ignores structural barriers to upward mobility, and it implies that success or failure depends almost entirely on what individuals do—or fail to do. (See Figure 10.1) For this reason many sociologists see classism as a form of victim blaming (Ryan, 1971).

Like other ideologies, this way of thinking about wealth and poverty is first learned in childhood (Cummings & Taebel, 1978; MacLeod, 1987). And it is continually reinforced in media imagery, especially concerning the poor (Herman & Chomsky, 1988; Mantsios, 1995).

In addition to socialization, there is another reason why many Americans accept classism. As with all ideologies, there is a kernel of truth buried within its distortions. Some poor people who work hard *do* get ahead, and some poor people *are* held back by their own personal limitations. Unfortunately, such instances are more likely to be publicized in the media

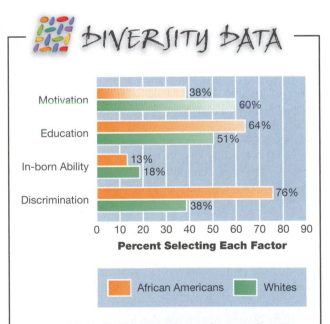

FIGURE 10.1   How Does Race Influence Opinions About Why African Americans Generally Have Lower Incomes and Poorer Jobs and Housing Than Whites? Whites emphasize the individual attributes of motivation and innate ability as factors that contribute to African Americans' lower income and poorer jobs and housing. In contrast, African Americans stress the impact of discrimination and quality of education. Given these findings, is it likely that most whites will enthusiastically support social programs designed to reduce discrimination?
Source: NORC. General Social Surveys, 1972–1996. Chicago: National Opinion Research Center, 1996. Reprinted by permission of NORC, Chicago, IL.

College Students and Structured Social Inequality: Resistance, Paralysis, and Rage

Sociologists commonly find that teaching about topics such as economic stratification, gender relations, or racial and minority groups—that is, the various forms of structured social inequality—is one of the most difficult tasks they confront. "As sociologists our message that structural sources . . . create and maintain inequality is, in many ways, fundamentally at odds with the beliefs of the larger culture in which students live" (Davis, 1992, p. 233). Students do not leave their ideologies and "isms" in lockers outside the classroom door. In many ways, college courses in social stratification are laboratories in analyzing and criticizing classist ideology.

Sociologist Nancy Davis identifies three basic ways students respond when they are first exposed to the realities of social stratification: resistance, denial, and rage. The most common is *resistance*. Many students simply deny the existence or at least the importance of structured social inequality in today's America. They tend to see racism and

sexism as history: problems that existed in the past but are no longer significant. They view classism as foreign. After all, the United States has never had a royal family or a titled aristocracy as England has; therefore, all Americans must be equal. Other students recognize inequalities in our society, but attribute them exclusively to individuals' personal weaknesses (in the case of poverty) or personal strengths (in the case of wealth). Few see the American emphasis on individualism—and the belief that anyone who works hard can get ahead—as components of an ideology that legitimizes inequality.

Davis points out that the cultural and political climate of the 1980s and 1990s, in which most of today's students grew up, glorified self-sufficiency, the pursuit of personal wealth, and private charity—as opposed to government intervention and collective action. Our heroes and heroines have been self-made multimillionaires, especially in sports, entertainment, and computer technology. The poor have been stereo-

typed as perpetrators of welfare fraud. In debates over affirmative action, African Americans, Native Americans, women, gays, and others are frequently portrayed as "special interest groups" seeking unfair advantage. Sympathy for the homeless has declined; people in line at soup kitchens are often seen as misfits and freeloaders.

The media reinforce classism with TV sitcoms that focus almost exclusively on middle- and upper-middle-class individuals whose problems are largely interpersonal, self-inflicted, and resolved within a half-hour. By implication, this is what America is about: being middle-class and taking care of your own problems. Popular magazines headline articles about how, with the right "packaging," anyone can be a success. Self-help books dominate best-seller lists, implying widespread discontent on the one hand, and on the other the belief that the solutions to most problems lie with the individual.

Students may resist the concept of structured inequality for various rea-

than are the counterexamples—the many capable individuals who work hard yet still fail. In consequence, people use the media's selective presentation to validate their classist worldview and lose track of how uncommon dramatic upward mobility really is.

Finally, the idea that hard work is sure to be rewarded appeals to people who want to believe they live in a just world, that if they simply apply themselves with enough diligence, they need not worry about falling behind (Kluegel & Smith, 1986; Ritzman & Tomaskovic-Devey, 1992).

After a lifetime of exposure to classist thinking, most Americans, not surprisingly, are not interested in changing the rules of the game. Instead of seeking structural changes that would make competition fairer, they simply want their share of the economic pie. Not only the advantaged, but also many poor

people accept this view. Those who question it tend to be viewed as radicals (Bobo, 1991).

What are the consequences of accepting classism? First, most Americans underestimate the importance of class in shaping people's lives. They also resist identifying themselves by their class position (Langston, 1992). In addition, classism often leads people to reject policies that would help the disadvantaged overcome the structural factors that limit their opportunities for upward mobility. Examples include proposals for universal health care, extensive job-training programs, or marked increases in the progressivity of the income tax.

Some trends suggest that classism is being challenged more frequently today. Awareness of class, while muted, is by no means absent in the United States (Vanneman & Cannon, 1987; Simpson et al.,

sons. One is that the picture sociologists paint is often gloomier than the images that students see in the media. Why wouldn't a young woman prefer to hear about women who "have it all" (career, marriage, and family) rather than learning that half of all marriages end in divorce or that even women with advanced educations soon fall behind their male peers in pay and prestige? Students from advantaged backgrounds may feel that members of the group from which they come, or perhaps even they themselves, are being cast in the role of exploiters. But less advantaged students are often equally resistant to discussions of prejudice, discrimination, and other structural barriers to success, as if acknowledging their problems would be admitting their own failure.

Another reason for resistance is inexperience. Many students come from homogeneous communities where they have rarely encountered stark inequalities. Accustomed to testing the validity of an argument or research finding against their own experience, they are skeptical. Comments like "I'm a woman and I've never been discriminated against" or "the president of my class was African American" are common. Moreover, students tend to take many aspects of modern life for granted, such as the right of every adult to vote, un-

employment insurance, racially integrated classrooms, and female physicians and lawyers—all of which were seen as radical ideas at one time. The women's, labor, and civil rights movements that won these "privileges" are not part of most contemporary students' living memory.

Not all of the students Davis has taught were resistant. She describes some as *paralyzed*. Aware that the deck is stacked against certain categories of people, they tend to see the current system of stratification as inevitable and themselves as powerless. In some cases, these students have been victims of, or witnesses to, incidents of racial taunting or gay bashing; they or someone they know may have been raped or battered; they may have seen a parent who was laid off slip into depression and alcohol abuse. Having kept these "guilty secrets" to themselves, they may withdraw when what they have thought of as their personal problems become the subjects of analysis in a sociology class.

The opposite of paralysis is *rage*. Some students enter stratification courses already nursing powerful feelings of injustice and indignation. They tend to blame everything that is wrong in the world on sexism, racism, or a capitalist conspiracy, and to see the world (and even members of their soci-

ology class) as divided into exploiters and the exploited, victimizers and victims. Their anger is both global and personal. For example, a self-proclaimed feminist may falsely see all men as sexist by virtue of their gender and all women as blameless in maintaining gender stratification.

Rage, paralysis, and resistance are not unique to students, but reflect attitudes held by the public at large. By addressing issues of power and privilege, advantage and disadvantage, and the ideologies that support social inequality, sociology students have the opportunity to examine their own biases and assumptions.

1. Did your high school classes fully explore the realities of structured social inequality or did they gloss over them? Would a teacher at your school have been allowed to critically discuss these issues?
2. If resistance, paralysis, and rage are all ultimately inappropriate responses to learning about the inequalities of class, gender, race, and age, then how should students be encouraged to respond when they learn about these issues?

Source: Davis, 1992.

1988). Educational levels are rising, and the information revolution makes it easier for disenfranchised groups of poor people and minorities to spread counterideologies. Finally, the poor are more likely than members of other classes to view the class system as unfair. They commonly understand that hard work often is not enough to ensure success (Kluegel & Smith, 1986; Polakow, 1993).

SYSTEMS OF ECONOMIC STRATIFICATION

Historically, patterns of structured economic inequality have varied greatly. Sociologists do, however, distinguish between two major types. *Closed systems* are based on ascribed statuses and permit very little social

mobility. Relatively *open systems*, on the other hand, focus more on achievement and permit substantial upward and downward mobility (Tumin, 1985). While some societies have been almost completely closed, none has ever been anywhere near fully open. In part, this is because elite parents use their wealth and power to send their children to expensive, prestigious universities and secure advantageous marriages for them, thereby greatly increasing their chances of future success. The United States is generally classed among the more open societies in the world today (Grusky & Hauser, 1984).

In addition to being more or less closed or open, societies also vary over time in the extent of inequality they display, that is, in the size of the gap between the rich and the poor. Economist Simon Kuznets (1955) developed an influential theory concerning how inequality changes as societies evolve. Referred to as the **Kuznets curve** (see Figure 10.2), the theory suggests that inequality mounts steadily as societies develop until they pass through the early phases of the industrial revolution, after which it tends to decline.

Gerhard and Jean Lenski's evolutionary theory of social development, which was discussed in Chapter 4, can help illustrate the dynamics of the Kuznets curve (Nolan & Lenski, 1999). *Hunting and gathering societies* were very open and nearly classless, although structured differences based on age and gender did exist in them (van den Berge, 1973; Harris, 1979). Some people may have had somewhat more power, property, and prestige than others, but these differences were relatively minor, were based chiefly on talent, and could not be easily passed on to the next generation.

It was in *horticultural societies* that significant social stratification first emerged. At this stage of social development, enough food could be produced in intensively cultivated garden plots to yield a fairly predictable surplus. Particular kinship groups came to

control the surplus and used it to elevate themselves over their fellows and ensure a head start for their children (Nolan & Lenski, 1999). Horticultural societies were thus much less open and more sharply stratified than the hunting and gathering cultures they replaced. The first distinct political systems—hereditary chiefdoms—arose in part to help the new horticultural elites safeguard their advantages.

Horticultural societies also saw the rise of *slavery*, a distinctive system of stratification based on the ownership of one group of individuals by another (Patterson, 1982). Slavery was common throughout the ancient world—including Greece, Rome, and Israel—and continued to be legal in some nations until the late nineteenth century. It persists even today in remote parts of Brazil and in some north African countries, including Mauritania and the Sudan (Jacobs & Athie, 1994). Some estimate that as many as three million people may be slaves today.

Agrarian societies are characterized by very high levels of structured social inequality (Dalton, 1967; Nolan & Lenski, 1999). At this stage, new technologies greatly expanded food production, which allowed elites to accumulate a massive surplus. At the same time, new agricultural technologies freed many people from working in food production. These people flocked to the newly founded cities to become specialized workers such as tool makers, weavers, and potters. Greatly expanded governments and new religion-based ideologies emerged to protect the privileges of the dominant strata. The elites, who often made up less than 2 percent of the population, typically held as much as half of the society's wealth.

Slavery persisted in agrarian societies; in fact, it reached its greatest extent in them. In addition, several new types of stratification developed. Most notable were **caste systems,** which are made up of a number of sharply distinct groups or *castes,* whose membership is based entirely on ascription (Berreman, 1987).

By definition, caste systems allow virtually no social mobility. Because of the tremendous gap between the castes, these systems emphasize accepting a legitimating ideology, nearly always religious in character. The very idea of social mobility is foreign in such a society. An individual's caste is absolutely central to her or his identity; it determines much of everyday behavior, from clothes to marriage patterns.

The best known example of caste in the world today is found in India. As early as 350 B.C.E., Indian society was divided into four great castes or *varnas*: Brahman, Kshiatriya, Vaishya, and Shudra. Each caste is loosely associated with a general type of work—priests and scholars, nobles and warriors, merchants and artisans, and cultivators and laborers, respec-

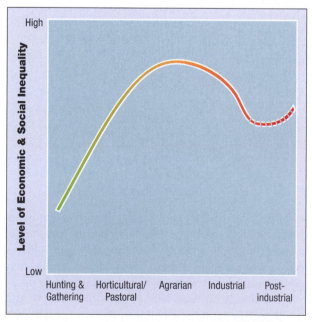

FIGURE 10.2　The Kuznets Curve. The Kuznets curve allows us to visualize the relationship between societal complexity and overall level of economic inequality. Hunting and gathering societies are highly egalitarian, but as horticulture and then agriculture emerge, a chasm opens up between the wealthy elite and the impoverished masses. This gap substantially narrows with the emergence of industrial society due to a dramatic expansion of education and the greatly increased productivity of the economy. However, some evidence suggests that inequality may be increasing once again as we move into the postindustrial era. *Source:* Atkinson et al., 1995: 40.

tively. A fifth group, the Harijan or "untouchables," technically not even part of the caste system, occupy the lowest rung on the ladder. The Harijan were traditionally responsible for sweeping streets, removing the corpses of dead animals, and other types of labor considered degrading. Each varna is subdivided into many hundreds of subcastes or *jati*, whose members are expected to specialize in a specific occupation.

Caste membership is hereditary and, although individuals within a given group may become richer or poorer, they can never change their *varna* or *jati* identity except through rebirth at a higher or lower level in the next life. Furthermore, each caste possesses a certain level of prestige or ritual purity, and an extremely elaborate set of rules dictates how the different caste groups must act toward each other. These rules cover virtually every aspect of life, but are especially detailed concerning food preparation and service (Wolpert, 1991). For example, a high-caste Brahman may receive an unpeeled banana from a Harijan, but not one from which the rind has been removed. Violating these rules creates "ritual pollution" and requires a sacred cleansing ceremony (Lannoy, 1975).

Although the Indian caste system was formally abolished half a century ago, it continues to thrive in traditional villages and also influences the modern sectors of the society. Legislation cannot easily erase thousands of years of tradition, especially when customs are legitimated by the Hindu religion. However, urbanization and industrialization have greatly increased geographic mobility, making it increasingly difficult to maintain traditional caste relations. Expanding educational opportunities encourage members of low-ranking castes to challenge age-old restrictions in the political arena. The Indian government has even sponsored affirmative-action plans on behalf of the untouchables, now referred to as the scheduled castes. And yet caste endures in Indian culture, most visibly in the context of marriage, which is still largely occurs only within castes.

Modern Japanese society includes a caste-like group of 1 to 3 million people. Known as the Burakumin, they resemble India's untouchables in many ways (Rowly, 1990; Guest, 1992). Until the mid-nineteenth century, the Burakumin were legally restricted from all but the least desirable occupations; they were confined to squalid ghettos, banned from marrying outside of their caste, and required to wear distinguishing clothing. The Burakumin now receive special governmental attention designed to compensate for prior mistreatment. Nevertheless, they suffer from negative stereotyping and, as a group, are still markedly less economically and educationally successful than most Japanese. Chapter 12 discusses the Burakumin at greater length.

INTERNET ◆ CONNECTIONS

The *Life Connections* feature in this chapter deals with America's homeless. After reading the text's discussion of this topic, go to the official Web site for the National Coalition for the Homeless: http://nch.ari.net/. From the opening page, click on "Facts About Homelessness." Then, one by one, click on "Why Are People Homeless?"; "How Many People Experience Homelessness?"; and "Who Is Homeless?" After you have read the contents of these installments, summarize what you now know about the homeless in America.

Other examples of caste in the modern world tend to be linked with race. Until recently, South Africa was characterized by a racial caste system called *apartheid* that divided the population into four distinct groups—whites, (Asian) Indians, Coloureds (whose ancestry was mixed European and African), and blacks. Apartheid required that the four groups remain almost completely separate from each other (Frederickson, 1981; Wilson & Ramphele, 1989). The system strongly favored the whites. After decades of protest, apartheid was finally abandoned in the early 1990s.

Many sociologists believe America's racial division has a distinctly castelike quality. This was certainly true in the post-Reconstruction South. Each race married only within itself, ascribed identity shaped virtually all aspects of life, and an elaborate etiquette defined relations between the two groups. For example, African Americans were expected to step aside to allow whites to pass them on the street, and they were required to address all whites formally ("Yes, Mrs. Jones"). Meanwhile, whites were free to call all African Americans, regardless of age or occupation, by their first names. As in India, these behavioral rules both reflected and reinforced the caste system.

Industrial and *postindustrial societies* typically grow increasingly open to social mobility, and the gap between elites and the rest of society narrows. However, the increased economic inequalities in many postindustrial nations since the early 1970s suggest that Kuznets's hypothesis may need revision.

Why does economic inequality decline in industrial societies? The primary reason is that a modern economy requires more highly educated workers to operate its increasingly sophisticated machinery (Lipset & Bendix, 1959; Drucker, 1969). With

In traditional India, the caste into which people were born shaped almost every aspect of their lives. The caste system has been formally abandoned for half a century, but it continues to have a powerful effect on the lives of hundreds of millions of Indians. Both of the photos show members of the Brahmin caste; the woman on the left is from India, the family above is from Nepal.

expanded education comes a better understanding of the inequities of class. At the same time, people become more aware of how to use an increasingly democratic political system to seek more equality.

In addition, industrialization is linked to a dramatic rise in urbanization. As workers become geographically concentrated in cities, they can more easily organize to demand reforms. The legalization of unions, unemployment compensation, welfare programs, and other political changes, taken together, tend to reduce economic inequality.

Finally, the tremendously increased productivity of the industrial system yields so much wealth that elites can permit an improved standard of living in the classes below them without making appreciable sacrifices themselves. As a result, even the poor in modern societies are generally much better off than much of the population in earlier eras.

With slavery virtually eliminated and caste systems fading, industrial societies are characterized by *class systems*, which are based principally on achievement rather than ascription and, hence, are relatively open, especially in the middle ranges (Berger, 1986). However, downward mobility from the extreme upper class and upward mobility from the very bot-

tom remain uncommon. In addition, the lines between the classes in the middle become blurred and awareness of class distinctions tends to decline.

Table 10.1 summarizes the characteristic changes in stratification systems which occur as societies develop.

EXPLAINING STRATIFICATION

Sociologists who study social stratification are principally interested in two questions: First, *is structured social inequality inevitable?* And second, *are its effects on society basically positive or negative?* These questions are of more than academic interest. If stratification is

INTERNET   CONNECTIONS

Incredibly, slavery still exists in the world today, as you can see in site http://www.anti-slavery.org/. What can be done to finally bring this ages-old institution to an end?

The racial caste system called apartheid was abandoned in the early 1990s. In 1994, these voters took part in the first election open to people of all races, ending centuries of white minority rule. Social stratification is still based on race in South Africa, but at least all people have an opportunity to vote.

inevitable, then efforts to eliminate or greatly reduce inequality are pointless. If it is not inevitable, but its consequences are primarily beneficial, then movements toward equality may succeed but are misguided. Finally, if structured inequality is not inevitable and also harmful, then efforts to reduce it are not only possible but badly needed.

Keep these questions in mind as we examine four theories of social stratification. We begin with deficiency theory. Then we will look at sociological explanations based on the functionalist, conflict, and symbolic interactionist perspectives.

Deficiency Theory

Deficiency theories of stratification explain differences in property, power, and prestige as the direct consequence of individual variations in ability. As such,

they are not really sociological in character, since they focus on the biology or psychology of particular people rather than on the social origins of structured inequality. Elites obtain and retain their advantages because they are better—smarter, harder working, more moral—than everyone else. Clearly this point of view is highly compatible with the interests of the upper classes. It also fits well with the ideology of classism. It suggests that social inequality is not only inevitable, but also desirable, since inherently inferior people obviously do not deserve equal rewards.

Deficiency theory was immensely popular in the later nineteenth century. Its principal spokesman was the British theorist Herbert Spencer, who was for a time the world's best-known sociologist. Spencer's philosophy came to be known as **social Darwinism**; in fact, it was he, not Darwin, who coined the phrase "the survival of the fittest."

Table 10.1	Societal Development and Structured Economic Inequality
Stage	**Patterns of Inequality**
Hunting and Gathering	Very little economic inequality. That which exists is based on personal talent with little if any inherited advantage or disadvantage.
Horticultural	Some kinship groups secure control over surplus production, producing substantial structured inequality. Slavery emerges in some societies.
Agrarian	Very high levels of structured inequality with an enormous gap between a small, highly privileged elite and the masses. Strong religious ideologies justify unequal arrangements. Slavery endures; caste systems dominate.
Industrial	Expansion of education spurs discontent among the masses; tremendous increases in economic productivity allow genuine improvement in the living standard of all groups. Gap between rich and poor narrows. Class systems replace castes.
Postindustrial	Some indication that economic inequality may increase; emerging patterns remain unclear.

Source: Table adapted from *Human Societies: An Introduction to Macrosociology*, 8th edition by Patrick Nolan and Gerhard E Lenski. Copyright © 1999 by McGraw-Hill Book Company. Reprinted by permission.

The policy implication of social Darwinism is clear. Just as weaker animals must die in order to keep a species' genetic stock strong, the poor must be allowed to suffer and expire. Keeping them alive may seem humane, but in the end, it will only weaken civilization and decrease the human race's chances for survival. In Spencer's own words, poverty is nature's way ". . . of excreting . . . unhealthy, imbecile, slow, vacillating, faithless . . ." people. Governments and other institutions must maintain a *laissez-faire* (hands off) attitude to the lower classes. And the same goes for individuals: People should resist the impulse to help the poor, with the possible exception of aiding "blameless" widows and orphans (Sumner, 1883).

Social Darwinism fell into disfavor early in the twentieth century as sociological interpretations grew in popularity. However, during the past two decades deficiency theory has become more widely accepted, although in a slightly different guise. In 1969, educational psychologist Arthur Jensen published an intensely controversial article that claimed about 80 percent of the variation in IQ scores is explained by genetic differences. A generation later, Richard Herrnstein and Charles Murray (1994) presented a broadly similar argument in their book, *The Bell Curve*.

Critics of deficiency theories are particularly concerned because minorities are disproportionately represented in the "inherently inferior" lower class. They point out that the IQ tests that Jensen and his followers take as accurate measures of ability are in fact biased against persons not raised in a white, middle-class environment.

If deficiency theorists are right, then helping the disadvantaged is a waste of money. If they are wrong, then their primary policy recommendation—to abandon programs like Head Start and affirmative action—amounts to kicking people who have already fallen due to factors that are largely beyond their control.

Most sociologists believe that deficiency theory is fundamentally off-track. If society does not aid the poor and they fail, does this prove that deficiency theory is right, or does it simply amount to a self-fulfilling prophecy? Deficiency theories are a classic example of blaming the victim. And they ignore the critical role of structural factors that strongly influence, if not determine, an individual's success or failure.

Unlike deficiency theory, all sociological interpretations of social inequality emphasize its structural character. That is, they view stratification as a characteristic of society rather than of individuals. Or, put yet another way, people in different classes receive different levels of reward as a result of the way society is organized, not because of differences in individual ability or effort. This way of thinking does not deny that individuals may have different talents, but it suggests that conditions of the social structure determine which abilities are considered important and how much opportunity different groups of people may have to develop their special skills. The first sociological theory we will discuss is based in the functionalist perspective.

Functionalism

The most influential functionalist theory of stratification was developed by Kingsley Davis and Wilbert Moore (1945). The **Davis-Moore thesis** maintains that inequality serves two vital functions: It motivates people to work hard, and it ensures that key statuses in society are occupied by highly capable people. Davis and Moore assume that certain occupational positions in society are critically important. Some of these positions, such as garbage collector, must be filled (lest we end up hip deep in orange peels), but they need not be filled by highly qualified people. Other positions, such as surgeons, corporate executives, or generals, absolutely must be staffed with highly capable individuals. The key is replaceability— garbage collectors are much easier to replace than brain surgeons (Weslowski, 1966).

Furthermore, these critical positions typically require not only considerable talent but also years of preparation and hard work. How can we ensure that highly capable people are recruited into these demanding statuses? Davis and Moore reply that we accomplish this by giving the people who occupy these important positions more rewards—more possessions, more prestige, and more power. The rewards compensate for the difficulty of preparing for and working in these jobs.

This argument is compelling, but it has been widely criticized (Tumin, 1953, 1963; Simpson, 1956; Wrong, 1959). First, according to Davis-Moore, inequality is beneficial only when it ensures that the most capable people occupy the most important positions. However, one of the rewards elites receive is the ability to help their offspring attain the good life. The problem is that the children of highly capable people are not necessarily highly capable themselves. The result is a situation in which many people enjoy upper-class status, not because of their merit, but because of that of their ancestors. Heavy inheritance or estate taxes might correct this problem, but the wealthy generally have enough political clout to keep their taxes low.

Second, the fact that modern societies continue to allow ascriptive factors such as gender and race to substantially limit access to elite positions, even for highly talented people, also challenges the logic of

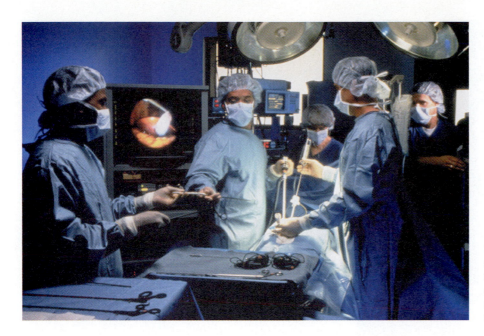

The Davis-Moore functional theory suggests that the medical professions are well paid and carry high prestige so that highly capable people will be attracted to these important and demanding occupations.

Davis-Moore. The relatively low salaries of such socially critical occupations as social workers, teachers, or child-care providers clearly demonstrate the extent to which gender bias rather than functional importance often determines salary levels.

Third, there are serious questions about which positions ought to be highly rewarded. In a capitalist economy, a given occupation's pay is chiefly determined by the market, not by a rational assessment of its worth to society. The result has been extremely high salaries for rock stars, athletes, and movie actors whose contribution to society is debatable.

Fourth, Davis and Moore ignore the role that power plays in determining how well various occupations will be rewarded. Professional associations, such as the American Medical Association and labor unions, have artificially driven up the wages of their members by restricting the supply of workers.

A final criticism concerns the *extent* of social inequality. Even granting the basic Davis-Moore argument, are the extremes of wealth and poverty that characterize the United States really functional? Major film stars can earn as much as $20 million per movie. Physicians' annual salaries commonly exceed $200,000. Presidents of major corporations routinely make at least 100 times more money than their entry-level employees. At the same time, 36 million people are living below the poverty line, and hundreds of thousands are homeless. Perhaps society needs inequality—but *this much*?

The Davis-Moore thesis does make some good points. The relatively low wages paid to scientists and engineers in the former Soviet Union did seem to

make them less willing to work hard (Aganbegyan, 1989). And survey research has found that 75 percent of Americans agree that "no one could be expected to study for years to become a doctor or lawyer unless they expected to earn a lot more than ordinary workers" (Stark, 1996a). However, the theory is at best one-sided in that it ignores the negative impact of structured inequality on the working and lower classes (Grimes, 1991). To balance the picture, we need to consider the conflict approach to stratification.

Conflict Theory

The conflict perspective is based on the assumption that all social life is a struggle for scarce resources. Applied to social stratification, this interpretation suggests that the social classes actively compete against each other in a battle that will inevitably produce winners and losers. Conflict theorists generally believe class inequality is harmful, but they disagree as to whether it is inevitable.

Karl Marx. Karl Marx (1818–1883) is the most important figure in the conflict analysis of social stratification. He believed class inequality was neither desirable nor inevitable. Writing in an era of extreme inequality and class conflict, Marx argued that sociologists must not only study society as it is, but must also work actively to end any injustices they uncover. This commitment to activism led him to become

Critics argue that the relatively low salaries of teachers, especially in comparison to the astronomical earnings of film stars and other entertainment figures, keep many capable people from entering fields like education.

closely involved with the political revolutionaries of his day.

For Marx, all of social life was shaped, and in some cases determined, by the relations people establish between each other in the process of economic production. Class was no exception to this general principle. Marx suggested that stratification originated in the struggle to control the surplus that accumulated when society moved beyond a subsistence economy. The groups involved in this struggle are social classes, which Marx defines as people who share a common relationship to a society's *means of production*, that is, to whatever is used in that society to create wealth. The nature of a society's means of production changes as its technology advances. In the Middle Ages, land was the most important form of productive property; in Marx's day, it was factories; today it is computers and communications systems. But the basic definition of social class remains the same.

Because individuals may be related to the means of production in a number of ways, there are a number of different social classes. But the most crucial distinction is always between those who *own* the means of production, the dominant or ruling class, and all of the classes that *do not own* productive resources and are therefore subordinate to the owners.

In Marx's day, the ruling class, called the **bourgeoisie** or capitalists, were the owners of large factories. The other major class, the **proletariat,** were industrial workers who had to sell their labor power to the bourgeoisie, generally on very disadvantageous terms, in order to survive. Other minor classes existed, including a remnant of the old feudal nobility, the *petit bourgeoisie,* who owned shops but did not employ workers (Robinson & Kelley, 1979), and the *lumpenproletariat* or urban underclass. But Marx considered their roles in history secondary to those of the bourgeoisie and the proletariat.

It is important to note that, for Marx, the interests of the social classes are, by definition, incompatible. The dominant class benefits from maintaining its position of control and extracting as much profit as possible from the workers. The subordinate classes can only improve their lot by overthrowing the ruling class and taking its place at the top of the stratification ladder. Without real power, they will never get more than the crumbs from the tables of the rich.

Marx saw all of history as a series of revolutions in which ruling classes were overthrown and absorbed into newly ascendent elite groups. These conflicts were generally violent because elites will not willingly give up their position of advantage. In order for a revolution to take place, the subordinate class must gain **class consciousness.** For Marx, this meant not only knowing what class you are in but also becoming aware of the true implications of your class position. In the case of a subordinate class, class consciousness meant realizing that you will never prosper so long as

Karl Marx's Cloudy Crystal Ball

The fact that the United States and other postindustrial societies have not, at least until recently, experienced a widening gap between the rich and the poor—or a communist revolution—as Marx predicted would occur, is not a valid reason for rejecting all of his insights. However, it is nevertheless instructive to briefly consider what happened in the United States that confounded Marx's expectations.

For one thing, since Marx's day governments have learned to actively intervene in the economy in order to smooth out the cycles of boom and bust that contributed heavily to the miseries of the nineteenth-century working class. Even more important, capitalist economies have become vastly more productive than Marx thought possible. Part of this has been the result of globalization, which has opened up vast new markets for exploitation, and part of it has been a consequence of the rapid development of new technologies.

These stable and highly productive economies have, until recently, allowed the real incomes of the workers to rise rather than fall and even, during some parts of the past century, have somewhat narrowed the economic gap between the classes. Individual upward mobility has been a real possibility for many workers, especially union members, a factor that greatly weakens the development of class consciousness. Furthermore, the growth of the welfare state, made possible by escalating economic productivity, has smoothed out the rough edges of capitalism by providing such benefits as unemployment insurance, worker's compensation, and expanded aid to the poor. Marx would argue, no doubt correctly, that government's motivation in providing such programs is less humanitarian and more an effort to prevent the growth of class consciousness; but the fact remains that government aid has been extremely effective in minimizing discontent among the lower classes, a reality that seems to have escaped the attention of the conservative politicians who are leading

an attack on the welfare state in the Western democracies.

Finally, Marx did not foresee the emergence of an enormous middle class of managers, professionals, and technical workers—often called the *new class*—who are structurally proletariat in that they do not own the means of production, but who identify more with the interests of the bourgeoisie than with those of the industrial workers. This new class has been a particular focus of attention among modern conflict theorists who have attempted to adapt Marx's analysis to the present era.

1. Do you think that a class-oriented revolution is possible in the United States? Explain your position.
2. Why do members of the new class strongly resist seeing their class position in Marxist terms?

Sources: Gurley, 1984; Edwards, 1985; Rubin, 1986; Wright & Martin, 1987; Wright, 1989; Kelley & Evans, 1995; Parenti, 1995.

you are under the heel of the ruling class, that revolution is essential (Ossowski, 1983). For the ruling class, it meant understanding that you must never lift your heel.

Obviously, it is not in the interests of the ruling class for members of other classes to gain class consciousness. The bourgeoisie work against this possibility in many ways. For one thing, they try to lock up the agitators. They are greatly aided in this effort by their control of the state and of the "state machinery"—police, prisons, the military—which they use to protect their class interests.

But it is always easier to head off dissent before it arises. The bourgeoisie do this by promoting false consciousness, narrowly defined as anything that retards the growth of class consciousness. More generally, **false consciousness** refers to any belief or social practice that convinces subordinate groups that their lack of property, prestige, and power is proper. Marx particularly stressed how religion strengthens false consciousness by encouraging poor people to focus on

the supposed rewards of the next life instead of trying to change things in the here-and-now.

Some modern conflict theorists argue that unions and democratic politics play a similar role, giving subordinate classes the illusion of real power in their relations with the elite. Above all, the fact that the ruling class controls the means of socialization—the schools, churches, and mass media—allows it to convince others to accept ways of thinking, classist ideologies, that defend its class advantages (Marger, 1993).

In opposition to false consciousness, Marxist revolutionaries like Lenin developed and popularized their own ideas or counterideologies which were designed to challenge classism. Thus, one of Marx's most important contributions is his insight that ideas are rarely neutral; they are weapons used to promote the interests of particular classes.

Evaluation.   Marx's work led directly to the development of the conflict perspective in sociology.

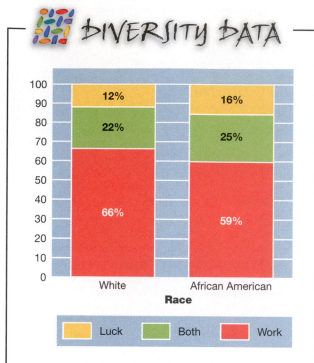

DIVERSITY DATA

Luck | Both | Work

FIGURE 10.3   How Does Race Influence Opinions About Whether People Mostly Get Ahead Due to Hard Work or Good Luck? While whites put slightly more emphasis than African Americans on hard work and African Americans consider luck slightly more important than whites do, the differences are small. Most people of both races consider hard work to be the most important factor explaining success. Would conflict theorists consider this an example of false consciousness among African Americans? Do you agree?

Source: NORC. General Social Surveys, 1972–1996. Chicago: National Opinion Research Center, 1996. Reprinted by permission of NORC, Chicago, IL.

Leaders of traditional societies may own no more property than anyone else, but they generally enjoy high levels of prestige and power, two important dimensions of stratification according to Max Weber.

His emphasis on the economic basis of society and on the importance of social class in history has been immensely influential (Gilbert & Kahl, 1993). His interpretation of the state as the agent of the ruling class is widely accepted by conflict theorists. The notion of false consciousness has been applied in many different contexts, perhaps most usefully in regard to gender and racial/ethnic oppression (Parenti, 1995).

Max Weber.   Weber believed that Marx's exclusive emphasis on people's relationship to the means of economic production resulted in a limited and simplistic theory. He also argued that Marx's passion for abolishing class inequality led him to confuse his own value preferences with objective social analysis. Thus, for Weber, Marx's dream of achieving a classless utopia was far from inevitable. In fact, Weber thought

that social stratification was, at least implicitly, unavoidable.

The central point in Weber's (1947) analysis is that social stratification is *multidimensional*. Societies, he maintained, are indeed divided into economic classes, much as Marx believed, but they also have separate and distinct stratification systems based on two factors other than property: prestige and power. In addition, for Weber, the lines separating the different strata were less sharply drawn than Marx believed. Most American sociologists have found Weber's analysis more useful than Marx's work in understanding our society, although Marx's influence remains substantial. Let's briefly examine each of the three systems of structured inequality Weber identified.

Property.   Weber's understanding of economic class was loosely similar to Marx's. However, he placed less emphasis on people's structural relationship to the means of production and more on the characteristics that allow different groups to participate more or less successfully in the market. Thus, for example, he distinguished between *entrepreneurs*, such as bankers, merchants, and factory owners, and *rentiers*, who live off the return from their investments. Marx would have classified both groups as bourgeoisie.

Weber thought economic class was relatively unimportant because most people do not consciously think of themselves in terms of their class identity. That is, they lack class consciousness, which Weber saw as simply the way things were rather than as Marx saw it—as a problem in need of correction.

Prestige. People may rarely think of themselves in class terms, but most are very much aware of their membership in what Weber called **status groups.** Status groups are ranked strata based on different lifestyles or patterns of consumption that are accorded different levels of honor, esteem or prestige.

Examples of status groups abound. Some are based on ethnicity: African Americans, WASPs, Hispanics. Some are religious: Jews, Southern Baptists, Catholics. Some reflect recreational lifestyle choices: skydivers, fitness buffs, dopers. Some are based on subcultural occupational groupings: manual laborers, academics, professionals. Note that members of a single class are typically drawn from many different status groups and, similarly, that several classes are typically represented in any given status group.

People frequently act collectively on the basis of their status group membership, something that rarely occurs with economic classes (Turner, 1986). Furthermore, members of status groups regularly interact with each other and, in the process, build up a shared culture (Beeghley, 1989). Some of these subcultural patterns are accorded more prestige than others. For example, the lifestyles of motorcycle gangs are generally considered less honorable than the lifestyles of, say, stockbrokers or school teachers. According to the contemporary French sociologist Pierre Bourdieu (1984, 1987), the shared subcultures of high-ranking status groups constitute valuable **cultural capital,** defined as those aspects of people's lifestyles—including values, attitudes, language patterns, and consumption preferences—that help to define their class location.

The Global Connections feature summarizes some of the results of a study concerning the different sorts of cultural capital valued by upper-middle-class men in France and in the United States.

Power. Finally, Weber noted that different groups of people could be ranked not only on the basis of economics and honor, but also in terms of how much power they had over others. For Weber, **power** was the ability of one social actor to compel a second social actor to behave in a way in which the latter would not otherwise have acted. Weber used the term "party" to refer to the various strata within society that were determined by different levels of power. But a "party" may also be called simply a "power group." Just as status group membership often crosscuts economic class, membership in Weber's power groups does not necessarily correspond to membership in either social classes or status groups.

The importance of power groups in modern society is most clearly seen in the context of bureaucratic organizations (see Chapter 22). The top managers in government, corporations, and other large bureaucracies may or may not earn enormous salaries and may occasionally be members of devalued status groups. But the power they derive from their bureaucratic status requires that we acknowledge their high ranking on at least this dimension of stratification. Similarly, the elites who ruled the Soviet Union did not occupy a class position that was, in Marx's terms, different from anyone else's, yet they derived enormous power from their authority within the state bureaucracy. The Soviet Union, then, although relatively classless, was in no sense unstratified, a fact that Weber's theory can easily explain but that Marx did not foresee (Hurst, 1992).

The fact that Weber identifies three distinct systems of stratification—property, prestige, and power—opens up the possibility of *status inconsistency*, a situation in which an individual occupies several ranked statuses, some of which are evaluated more positively than others. For example, most ministers are high in prestige but fairly low in economic class. Many high-status professionals are members of devalued minority groups. A mortician may be wealthy, but the job is not highly esteemed because it requires close contact with the dead. Or, as we have just noted, government bureaucrats may have great power but enjoy only limited economic rewards.

Most people display a reasonably high level of status consistency, especially at the top and bottom of society (Gilbert & Kahl, 1993). However, many others are seriously inconsistent. Generally, people who are caught in this sort of situation wish to be seen overall in terms of their most highly valued status. Thus college professors expect to be treated as highly educated professionals, not as people who earn only middling salaries. But people who come into contact with status inconsistents commonly emphasize these people's lower status identity, probably in order to feel as good as possible about themselves (Lenski, 1954, 1956).

Toward a Synthesis. Can the functionalist and conflict perspectives be combined? Macrosociologist Gerhard Lenski (Nolan & Lenski, 1999) thinks so. He suggests that in simple societies with little or no

Upper-Middle Class Culture in the United States and France

Possessing the right kind of what Pierre Bourdieu calls *cultural capital* is a critical resource for anyone hoping to achieve upward social mobility. This is because people commonly look at an individual's cultural capital to determine if he or she is "one of us." If you display the right lifestyle, it will be far easier to be accepted into the right social circles.

However, the specific content of what is seen as the appropriate cultural capital to validate membership in a given social class varies greatly from society to society. Sociologist Michael Lamont interviewed members of the upper-middle class in the United States and in France and discovered sharp variations in the sort of cultural capital that validated an individual's membership in that class in the two societies. He focused on three general categories of cultural capital: moral character, images of success, and cultural sophistication.

Moral character. Americans place a high value on honesty—or more precisely they look down on people whom they consider dishonest. They particularly dislike phonies (who pretend to be something they are not), social climbers (who are blatantly ambitious, show little courtesy to their colleagues or concern for their families, and forget or drop people who helped them in their scramble to the top), and "low types" (who lie, cheat, and steal in their personal lives as well as in their business dealings).

The French share their American counterparts' dislike of insincerity and social climbing. But they view other American moral standards, especially those regarding sex, as puritanical and outdated. In the words of one interviewee, a literature professor:

. . . I am completely indifferent to whether or not the president of the United States has one, two, three, or ten mistresses, whether he likes little boys, or is homosexual or bisexual. I would simply ask that he not spend too much time at it. . . .

He went on to explain that the French value honor, a complex concept involving being true to oneself, sincere in relations with others, and trustworthy in financial dealings.

Success. Both the Americans and French tend to judge other people's worth in terms of such external status symbols as what they do for a living, where they live, where they vacation, and the like. But Americans place more emphasis on financial success. To upper-middle-class American men, wealth—measured in terms of the items an individual can afford, including cars, homes, trips, electronic equipment, and, not least of all, advantages for one's children (from piano lessons and tennis or computer camp to an Ivy League education)—is both the symbol of, and the reward for, achievement.

In contrast, many French respondents considered questions about whether they themselves or their friends are "successful" to be uncouth. They view the pursuit of money—taking a job because it pays well, rather than because it offers opportunities to exercise creativity or to make a contribution to society—as debasing. Success, said one French entrepreneur, "is the full realization of oneself." Others value money not so much as a symbol of success, but as a means of maintaining their social identity and supporting a comfortable lifestyle, by which they mean being able to eat out regularly, go to the theater and other cultural events, and offer hospitality to friends and kin. They value inherited wealth and homes, art, and furniture that have been in the family for generations above "earned" money and recent purchases. Upwardly mobile, *nouveau riche* individuals who indulge in conspicuous consumption do not quite belong; they are "too American."

Cultural Sophistication. Both the Americans and the French see educational level and intelligence as impor-

tant. But here again, their criteria differ. Upper-middle-class U.S. men respect people who have a wealth of information—not only about their particular area of expertise, but also about the world at large—and the competence to translate this knowledge into action. They enjoy the company of people who, in the words of a real estate developer, have "the ability to recognize opportunities, to seize opportunities, to capitalize on them, and to make them work." They tend to see people with only "book learning" as lacking in common sense; their heroes are individuals like real estate magnate Donald Trump or Microsoft founder Bill Gates.

Upper-middle-class French are more likely to cite intellectuals like Raymond Aron and Jean-Paul Sartre as their heroes. They value *un sens critique* (a critical approach), combining intellectual playfulness, a capacity for abstraction and eloquence, and a distinct personal style above factual or practical knowledge. The French accept—and even brag about—a degree of ineptitude in mundane, everyday matters. Whereas Americans often say they feel inferior in the company of individuals who are more financially successful or more politically powerful than they, the French are awed by "people who strictly at the intellectual level make me feel very small . . . because I think they have succeeded at what I am trying to achieve."

In short, Lamont found that the heroes and models of upper-middle-class life in America would be considered vulgar and even mildly offensive by the equivalent French social circles.

1. What are some of the sociohistorical differences between the United States and France that might help to explain Lamont's findings?
2. What kinds of cultural capital are important in achieving entry into your campus's elite social circles?

Source: Lamont, 1997.

surplus, where most valued resources are necessities, the distribution of these resources will be reasonably egalitarian. This is necessary to keep everyone adequately fed, clothed, and sheltered. However, just as Davis and Moore argued, individuals who contribute more to the common good will be given extra shares as a reward for their contributions. Thus, functionalism provides a good explanation for the *origins* of structured inequality.

At later stages in sociocultural evolution, a surplus becomes available. There is no particular societal need for an egalitarian distribution of this surplus, so under these circumstances power determines who will enjoy society's luxuries. Thus, according to Lenski, conflict theory provides the most convincing explanation for the *persistence and intensification* of social stratification.

Symbolic Interactionism

Symbolic interactionism does not ask the same questions as functionalism and conflict theory. Instead of speculating about the inevitability of stratification, interactionists are principally interested in how class af-

fects patterns of everyday social life. They pay special attention to *status symbols* (Berger et al., 1992). Of course, not all status symbols accurately indicate an individual's class position, but many of the most important ones do.

Status symbols are especially important in the modern urban environment. In rural areas and small towns, most people's class position is well known within the community. This is not true in large anonymous cities. Urban life also allows greater freedom to present a false front by concealing symbols of lower status and appropriating those denoting a class position higher than one's own. All of us are familiar with people who drive cars they can't afford or wear imitation designer clothes. Consequently, people are somewhat skeptical concerning displays of the more readily obtained symbols of elite class status.

Nevertheless, some physical objects remain quite effective as cues to people's class position, especially at the extremes of the stratification ladder. A person's home is a good example. People who live in mansions located in gated communities with a private security force are making an unambiguous statement about their class position, as are people who live in shacks or public housing projects. As noted at the beginning of

Many urban residents in low-income nations make their homes in shacks and makeshift shelters like this one, which people in the developed world would find entirely unlivable.

this chapter, clothing is another good example (Mazur, 1993), especially clothes worn on the job. There is a good deal of truth to the old line that in the working class, your name goes on your shirt; in the middle class, on the door of your office; and in the upper class, on your company.

Some important symbols of class position are nonmaterial. In England, where the class lines are more sharply drawn than in the United States, accent is a reliable cue to class position. The popular 1950's musical "My Fair Lady" is about a gentleman named Henry Higgins who sets out to teach Eliza Doolittle, a woman from the lower classes, to speak with a "proper" accent in order to "pass" in genteel society.

Generally, lower-status people coming into contact with their "betters" are expected to respond with deference, another non-material symbolic representation of status differences. We have already mentioned examples of deference in relations between castes in traditional India and between the races in the old South. A good contemporary example concerns waiting: The lower your status compared to the person you are waiting to see, the longer you usually have to wait (Schwartz, 1975; Henley, 1977; Levine, 1987). In fact, the long waits in welfare and unemployment offices and Medicaid clinics are among the most stigmatizing aspects of poverty status.

Here's another good example of class-linked deference: In many languages, speakers use different terms to address persons higher in status than they use with class equals and inferiors. In German, for example, the equivalent of the English "you" when addressing someone who is higher in rank is "Sie." "Du" is a less formal term that is used only with intimates. The equivalents in Spanish are "usted" and "tu." Does

the fact that English lacks such constructions suggest that we are really a more egalitarian society, or is this simply another reflection of Americans' wholehearted acceptance of classist ideology?

Table 10.2 below summarizes the various theoretical perspectives on social stratification.

GLOBAL STRATIFICATION

The study of social stratification is not limited to consideration of the divisions between categories of people within a single society. It also encompasses *global stratification*, the separation of nations into ranked categories of wealth and power.

For many years, sociologists used the terms first, second, and third worlds to identify three broad "classes" of nations. In this scheme, the *First World* referred to the industrial and postindustrial "advanced" societies including the United States, most of Western Europe, Canada, Australia, New Zealand, and Japan. All of these nations industrialized early and are characterized by technologically sophisticated, capitalist economies. All have high standards of living and democratic governments, and all but Japan reflect European cultural patterns. In a global context, these nations made up the world's upper class.

The *Second World* consisted of the Soviet Union and its satellites in Eastern Europe. These nations featured state socialist economies, intermediate levels of industrialization, moderate standards of living, and authoritarian governments. The Second World was equivalent to a global lower-middle class.

The rest of the world's societies were lumped together as the *Third World*, equivalent to the working and lower classes. Located principally in South

Table 10.2	Theories of Stratification Compared		
Type of Theory	**Origins of Inequality**	**Policy Implications**	**Representative Theorists**
Deficiency	Differences in individual ability	Social Darwinism; efforts to lessen the distress of the poor are misguided and socially harmful	Herbert Spencer Richard Herrnstein and Charles Murray
Functionalism	Necessary in order to promote efficient functioning of society	Reducing extreme poverty is desirable but society needs substantial inequality	Émile Durkheim Talcott Parsons Kingsley Davis and Wilbert Moore
Conflict	Imposed by the powerful to promote their own interests	Dramatically reducing or even eliminating economic inequality is essential	Karl Marx Max Weber Ralf Dahrendorf
Symbolic Interactionism	Symbolic representations of inequality influence everyday interaction	None	Thorsten Veblen

America, Africa, Asia, and Oceania, the Third World included most of the world's people. These nations have low levels of industrialization and concentrate on subsistence production, their governments tend to be nondemocratic, and most of their citizens live in extreme poverty, although there usually is a small, highly privileged indigenous elite.

In recent decades, this typology has become outdated (Harris, 1987). This is partly a result of the Soviet system's collapse. But it is also because scholars came to feel that the Third World was an excessively broad and rather ethnocentric category. It lumped together all the following: rapidly developing nations such as South Korea and Singapore, which appear well on their way to First World status; oil-rich states such as Saudi Arabia and Kuwait whose citizens enjoy high incomes but that are structurally far from modern; relatively poor but economically developing nations such as Brazil and India; and the poorest of the poor, nations such as Somalia and Rwanda that cannot even feed their own people. The old scheme was also clearly value driven, implying that the First World was superior and the Third World backward.

No equally widely accepted typology has yet emerged. One alternative scheme, generally used in this text, divides nations into *developed* (or postindustrial), *developing*, and *underdeveloped* categories. The middle group includes most of the old Second World, the rapidly expanding economies of the Pacific Rim nations, and intermediate states such as Argentina and Turkey.

This model reflects contemporary geopolitical realities, but it does implicitly suggest that all societies are following the same general path that will eventually lead every nation to resemble the industrial West. Its terminology is, therefore, arguably ethnocentric. Moreover, there are solid reasons to doubt that full industrialization is possible for many of the world's poorer societies.

Another option simply divides nations into *high*, *medium*, and *low* income categories on the basis of their citizens' wealth (World Bank, 1995). Figure 10.4 shows how the world's societies may be classified according to this scheme. Like all such typologies, this model is ultimately arbitrary. It is, however, relatively value-neutral (Sklar, 1995).

Sociologists have developed three different theoretical explanations of global stratification: modernization theory, dependency theory, and world systems theory.

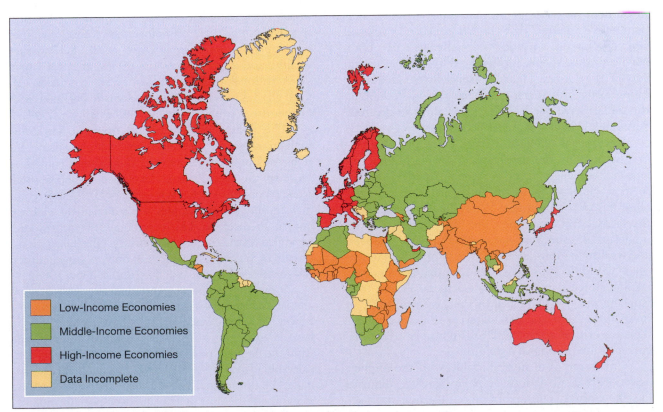

FIGURE 10.4   Global Stratification: Low-, Middle-, and High-Income Countries, 1995

Source: World Bank (1995).

Modernization Theory

Modernization theory originated in the United States during the 1950s. Its central argument is that the less-developed nations may be placed somewhere along an evolutionary path moving toward full modernization and that all will eventually come to closely resemble the United States and other "advanced" nations.

In this model, modernization is seen as not only inevitable, but also desirable and irreversible. Low-income nations are believed to be slow in developing because of internal problems: inadequate infrastructure, lack of investment capital, inefficient governments, and, above all, a traditional culture that is fatalistic and highly skeptical of new technologies and institutional arrangements (Eisenstadt, 1973; Inkeles, 1983; McCord & McCord, 1986; Rostow, 1978, 1990). High-income nations can, it is believed, help developing countries by producing capital and knowledge needed to expand their manufacturing sectors (Chodak, 1973; Rau & Roncek, 1987). Equally important, contact with developed nations will help overcome cultural inertia.

Evaluation. Modernization theory is accepted by many scholars in the developed world (Moore, 1979; Berger, 1986; Firebaugh & Beck, 1994). It is often used to justify the foreign policies and cross-national investment practices of the developed nations. This perspective assumes that contact between developed and developing societies normally benefits both. Modernization theory is often used to explain the success of the "Asian Tigers"—especially South Korea, Hong Kong, and Singapore. Their rapidly developing economies have particularly strong links to the fully developed U.S. and Japanese economies.

But not all scholars endorse modernization theory. Some point out that many of the world's poorest nations, especially those in Latin America, do not seem to be moving toward prosperity despite their close ties to the industrial West. The theory ignores the crucial fact that when the high-income nations modernized, they were not competing with powerful and wealthy nations, as is the case with today's developing world (Walton, 1987). In addition, the modernization process in countries such as France and England was greatly helped by the easy availability of inexpensive labor and raw materials in their colonies. This is a critical advantage that is not open to nations currently attempting to develop.

Critics are also uncomfortable with the implicit assertion that all nations *ought to* emulate countries like the United States, pointing out the numerous serious problems in our society. Neither are the critics comfortable with the notion that the problems keeping low- and middle-income nations undeveloped are all internal. They say this is a form of cross-national victim-blaming. Modernization theorists, they argue, ignore the role that the high-income nations play in holding back development in the rest of the world. In addition, there is considerable evidence that some traditional values, including a religiously motivated work ethic and a tradition of obeying paternalistic authority, may actually promote modernization (So, 1990).

Dependency Theory

Dependency theory emerged in the 1960s. Its leading exponent is Andre Gundar Frank (1966, 1967, 1980), but a number of other scholars, many working in Latin America and Africa, contributed to its development (Emmanuel, 1972; Amin, 1974). Dependency theory amounts to a fairly direct translation of conflict theory into the global arena. High-income nations play the role of the ruling class and the middle- and especially the low-income nations serve as the equivalent of the proletariat.

According to dependency theorists, the relationship between these two groups of societies is far from mutually beneficial; in fact, it is very one-sided, with the wealthy countries reaping almost all of the advantages. The continued prosperity of the industrialized world comes from exploiting the lower-income nations. These countries were, according to this perspective, often better off before they were drawn into ongoing economic interaction with the world's wealthy societies. During the 1980s, the per capita gross national product of forty-nine countries—almost all of them already poor—actually declined, with further drops predicted in the future (Brown, 1994).

This pattern of dependency originated in **colonialism**, a system whereby certain high-income nations took political, economic, and cultural control of most of the world's less developed societies (Bell, 1981; Worsley, 1984; Harrison, 1993). Under colonialism, indigenous peoples were denied the right to govern themselves. The economies of the colonies were also restructured to benefit the "mother nation," usually by serving as a source of minerals, agricultural raw materials, and cheap labor (Gill & Law, 1988).

Sometimes colonial economies became focused almost exclusively on the production of cash crops for export. In these cases, foodstuffs that could otherwise have been grown in the colony had to be imported from the colonial power and purchased, often at considerable expense, by the locals. Coffee in Brazil, bananas in Nicaragua, and rubber in the Congo are examples of this sort of extreme overspecialization.

Colonial powers also encouraged the growth of a small, indigenous elite with strong cultural connections to the "mother country." These people handled most of the day-to-day job of running the colony in the interests of the colonizers.

In the decades following World War II, almost all colonial societies gained political independence. But they continued to be economically and technologically dependent upon the old colonial powers. Today the colonial powers have been partially supplanted by vast multinational corporations (Webster, 1990). This pattern of continued dependency is known as **neocolonialism** (Harrington, 1977). Local governments, often controlled by the indigenous elite created by the colonizers, continue to let their countries' economies primarily serve foreign interests.

According to dependency theory, the high-income nations benefit greatly from their relationship with low-income countries. They obtain raw materials and cheap labor (Clinard, 1990). They can unload products they cannot sell at home, including flammable sleepwear, hazardous pesticides, and tobacco. They can relocate manufacturing plants that create pollution because low-income nations lack both the political will and the ability to enforce even minimal environmental regulations (Ehrenreich & Fuentes, 1981). In some cases, hazardous wastes are shipped to these countries and simply dumped (La Dou, 1991). The only negative effect on the high-income societies is unemployment, as manufacturing jobs move to developing countries.

From the perspective of the poor nations, the relationship looks much less positive (Brecher & Costello, 1994). In addition to distorting local economies by concentrating on a single cash crop, paying low wages, and polluting the environment, other problems commonly arise:

One of the most obvious signs of the global reach of modern corporation is the appearance in recent decades of fast food franchises all around the world. Kentucky Fried Chicken is becoming as popular in Beijing as it is in Louisville.

- It is difficult for a large, stable middle class to develop. In part, this is because the multinational corporations pay low wages and oppose organizing by unions (Moran, 1978; Bornschier et al., 1978; Evans, 1979). Poor countries therefore tend to remain divided between a very large lower and working class and a small, highly privileged elite. Further, the ruling elite tend to become corrupt in defense of their advantages (Lipton, 1979; Lappe et al., 1981; Bradshaw, 1988).
- When high-income nations, often acting through international organizations such as the International Monetary Fund or the World Bank, extend development loans to poorer nations, they often do more harm than good. The problem is that the recipients frequently are unable to repay the loans. The debt crisis worsens as interest charges spiral upward. By the early 1990s, the accumulated debt of the poor nations exceeded $1.5 trillion; interest payments alone ate up over $50 billion annually (Tordoff, 1992).

- The continuing influence of high-income countries keeps the cultures of their former colonies from developing, a situation termed **cultural imperialism.** The language, religion, and customs of the high-income countries are considered, at least by local elites, to be superior to their own (Harrison, 1993; Sklar, 1995; Barnet & Cavanagh, 1994).

Evaluation.   Dependency theory corrects some of the excessive optimism of modernization theorists. It is also particularly useful when applied to Latin America (Kahl, 1988). However, the theory has limitations. In particular, it assumes that all low-income countries face similar problems as a result of their unequal relationships with the developed world. It cannot therefore explain the rapid progress of former colonies such as the previously mentioned "Asian Tigers" (Berger, 1986).

Many scholars today maintain that if poorer nations proceed intelligently, neocolonialism is not necessarily a fatal obstacle to modernization (Cardoso & Faletto, 1979). Recent studies strongly suggest that foreign investments can promote growth, not dependency (Vogel, 1991; Firebaugh, 1992; Firebaugh & Beck, 1994). Thus, it is possible for both wealthy and poorer nations to benefit from economic interactions in some cases.

World Systems Theory

International economist Immanuel Wallerstein (1974, 1979, 1990, 1991) has developed a third theory of global stratification. His world systems theory combines the functionalist theme of the interdependence of the components of a social system with several elements of the conflict perspective. His purpose is to explain the *origins* of the present international economic order.

World systems theory proposes that, over the past 450 years, all the world's nations have become integrated into a single system of capitalistic economic interdependency, with different nations and multinational corporations playing different roles in a global division of labor. In effect, world systems theory visualizes the global economy as a kind of gigantic assembly line where workers in many different nations contribute in different ways to the productive process.

Wallerstein identifies three distinct groups of nations in the world system—the core, semiperiphery, and periphery—each playing a different role in the global division of labor. Over time, some nations have moved from one group to another, but the basic distinctions remain (Arrighi, 1994). Within each of these three categories, there is a tendency for nations to gradually become more like each other (Peacock et al., 1988).

The *core* is world systems theory's term for the high-income nations located mainly in Europe and North America. They control the global economy (Chase-Dunn, 1990), were the first to industrialize, and retain technological and managerial superiority. Most of the profits generated by the world system flow back to the core, and especially to the huge multinational corporations headquartered there. Less than 25 percent of the world's population lives in the core, but they consume up to three-fourths of the planet's resources (Mingione & Pugliese, 1994).

At the other extreme, the *periphery* consists mostly of former colonial nations whose primary role in the world economic system is to supply raw materials and labor for the global assembly line (Shannon, 1989). The periphery participates in the world economic system only on the terms set by and favorable to the core. The problems faced by the nations of the periphery are essentially the same as those that dependency theorists have identified as plaguing the world's poorer societies: unbalanced economies, low wages, pollution, rule by a small and unrepresentative elite, the lack of a stable middle class, high levels of foreign debt, and rampant cultural imperialism.

The nations of the *semiperiphery* stand in an intermediate position. This category includes, among others, Mexico, Argentina, Brazil, Russia, most of Eastern Europe, Ireland, Portugal, Greece, Spain, South Africa, the industrializing Pacific Rim nations, and the oil-producing states of the Middle East. Some, such as South Korea, are moving toward core status; others, such as Portugal, have been downwardly mobile. The semiperiphery is actively involved in the global economy but does not significantly shape it. Wallerstein views these nations as a kind of "buffer" between the core and the periphery.

Evaluation. World systems theory is a good middle ground between modernization and dependency theories. One of its strengths is its emphasis on the *structure* of global economic relations. Another is its extended time frame, which takes into account the centuries-long changes in the international economy that other theories tend to miss. Its weaknesses are that it ignores the positive aspects of contacts with the core for the economies of the periphery and the semiperiphery and that it downplays the importance of factors internal to the low-income nations that retard development (Cockerham, 1995b).

Table 10.3 summarizes key features of the three major perspectives on global stratification.

LIFE CONNECTIONS: America's Homeless

This chapter has presented a discussion of selected theoretical interpretations of economic stratification; Chapter 11 will put a more human face on the topic of wealth and poverty by exploring the everyday realities of class in the contemporary United States. While theory is important, we need to always bear in mind that sociologists study economic inequality largely because it has such enormous consequences on the lives of real people. In this section we will illustrate the impact of social class by exploring the life circumstances of the poorest of the poor, America's homeless.

No one really knows how many homeless people there are; the fact that they have no fixed place of residence makes it very difficult to count them accurately, although a number of attempts have been made to do so, both by sociological researchers and

Table 10.3 Theories of Global Stratification Compared				
Type of Theory	Theoretical Orientation	Explanation for Poverty of Some Nations	Solution for Poverty	Representative Theorists
Modernization	Functionalist	Failure to modernize, mostly due to internal cultural and structural inadequacies	Emulate fully industrialized nations	Walt Rostow
Dependency	Conflict	Colonial and neocolonial domination by the developed nations	Resist neocolonial domination	Andre Gunder Frank
World Systems	Blends functionalist and conflict themes	Disadvantageous location in the periphery of the world system	Attempt to relocate to semiperiphery or core	Immanuel Wallerstein

by the Census Bureau (Jencks, 1994). Conservative estimates suggest that perhaps 250,000 people are homeless on any given day, whereas poverty advocates have proposed numbers as high as three million. In the late 1980s, a group of researchers carefully enumerated Chicago's homeless and then extrapolated their findings to the national level, yielding an estimate of about 350,000 homeless people in the entire country, a figure that seems roughly accurate (Rossi et al., 1987). But the number of people who are homeless at some point during any given year is much higher, almost certainly exceeding one million, and the total number of people who have ever been homeless is estimated at 13.5 million, 1.75 million of whom have lived on the streets for longer than one year (Link et al., 1994).

There have always been homeless people in the United States, but prior to the mid-1970s they were principally unmarried elderly men, often with serious alcohol problems. Most spent their time working sporadically as laborers and living in the skid row districts of the nation's larger cities.

These men remain as a component of the homeless, but they have been joined by several other groups. A 1995 survey found that 46 percent of the urban homeless were single men; 14 percent were single women; 36.5 percent were families, almost all female-headed; and 3.5 percent were runaway and throwaway children (Worsnop, 1996). Families are the fastest growing part of the homeless population: One-third of the homeless are women and 25 percent are children.

Women and children suffer disproportionately from homelessness. One study found 89 percent of homeless mothers come from backgrounds of family violence and sexual abuse (Bassuk, 1991). Many leave

home to escape these problems (Browne & Bassuk, 1997). Once on the street, they are highly vulnerable to rape and other forms of criminal victimization (Liebow, 1995). Their children often suffer serious health problems and have great difficulty concentrating on schoolwork.

Another recent study found that 56 percent of the homeless are African American, 30 percent are white, and 10 percent are Hispanic (U.S. Conference of Mayors, 1996). The average age of homeless adults is in the mid-thirties. About one-quarter are seriously mentally ill and another 25 percent show some mental impairment (Tessler & Dennis, 1992). Most estimates suggest that over one-third of the homeless have major substance abuse problems. These are often the same people who are suffering from mental problems. Most of the homeless are high school graduates and some have attended college. A quarter are veterans (Edmonds, 1993). As many as 25 percent work, mostly part-time at minimum wage jobs.

When the homelessness problem first began to be publicized in the 1980s, the public was generally sympathetic, but in more recent years we have seen a great deal of what some have termed "compassion fatigue" (Smolowe, 1993). Cities around the nation have strengthened anti-loitering laws, closed shelters, and passed new ordinances against panhandling (National Law Center on Homelessness & Poverty, 1996).

These harsh measures doubtless reflect the fact that most people explain homelessness by reference to the personal failings of the homeless (Lee, 1992), who are widely believed to be lazy, mentally ill, addicts, or drunks. In contrast, sociologists put much more emphasis on structural factors (Burt, 1992). While a minority of the homeless are indeed mentally ill or substance abusers, most are not, and the vast majority of Americans who suffer from serious personal problems do not end up on the streets. Some of the mental problems of the homeless are better viewed as consequences rather than causes of their extreme poverty (Golden, 1992). The following social factors seem central in explaining the growth of the homeless population over the past three decades (Elliott & Krivo, 1991):

- *Persistent and severe unemployment.* The homeless are the poorest of the poor. The kinds of low-skill, decent-paying jobs that they might have been able to find in the past have largely disappeared due to globalization and the rise of a postindustrial economy (Katz, 1995). Many live with family or friends, typically for four years after they lose work, but eventually their safety net collapses and they find themselves on the street (Snow & Anderson, 1993).
- *Loss of affordable housing.* America's stock of low-cost rental housing has been declining for decades due to abandonment, arson, demolition, and *gentrification* (the upgrading of units so that they can be rented or sold to middle-class people). At the same time, the number of very poor families and individuals has been increasing. As of 1995, there were 4.4 million more needy families than available low-rent housing units (Janofsky, 1998). People living below the poverty line usually pay between 50 and 75 percent of their after-tax income for housing—when they can find a home at all (Dolbeare, 1995).
- *Cutbacks in government aid.* Direct federal aid for low-income housing dropped from $30 billion in 1980 to $8 billion in 1988 under the Reagan administration (Morganthau, 1988). Few of these cuts have been restored. Fifteen million families currently qualify for federal housing aid; fewer than one-third of them actually receive any (De-Parle, 1998).
- *Deinstitutionalization of the mentally ill.* A movement to reduce the number of people in mental hospitals began in the late 1950s, but it was not until the mid-1970s that substantial numbers of patients who could not care for themselves were released. Many ended up homeless (Patterson, 1994; Jencks, 1994).

The theoretical approaches to economic stratification introduced in this chapter may help explain homelessness. The widespread belief that the homeless are responsible for their own plight is a classic example of a victim-blaming ideology and very much in line with deficiency theories. Functionalists might

point out that believing the homeless to be exclusively responsible for their plight allows those opposed to aiding the poor to successfully oppose welfare initiatives that would raise their taxes (White, 1992). Conflict theorists see the homeless as the ultimate losers in the struggle to get ahead; Marx would define them as *lumpenproletariat*, and Weber would note that they were on the bottom of the class, status, and power rankings. Symbolic interactionists would emphasize the consequences of the heavy stigma they bear (Phelan et al., 1997).

The homeless are part of the fabric of social life in the United States and at the same time they constitute an important social issue, both in the United States and, as we shall see in the next section, in other countries as well.

SOCIETY CONNECTIONS: Wealth, Poverty, and Class Conflict in Brazil

Brazil, a nation of 161 million people, is an excellent example of a developing nation located in what world systems theory would call the semiperiphery. Earlier in this century, its economy was slow-growing and largely agricultural. But in recent decades it has been industrializing rapidly (Evans, 1979). In fact, the value of Brazilian manufactured goods has increased over a hundred-fold since 1965. The government has attracted foreign investment by improving transportation and communication systems, outlawing labor unions, and offering tax credits and low export fees to investors.

Development has not come without problems, however. The annual inflation rate ran as high as 2700 percent in the late 1980s, and the Brazilian foreign debt currently exceeds $130 billion, the highest figure worldwide outside of the core nations. As a result, in the early 1990s, the government was forced to privatize many public services and lay off some 250,000 civil service workers (Brooke, 1990). Nevertheless, the overall economic picture is quite encouraging for some Brazilians, although not for everyone.

Like many developing countries, Brazil has a wider gap between the rich and the poor than most Americans would find acceptable (Soares, 1996). According to the 1991 census, the top 10 percent of Brazilian society controls 49 percent of the nation's wealth and the bottom 10 percent less than 1 percent. Collectively, the upper 20 percent of the population owns thirty-two times as much as the bottom fifth. The average annual income is $5,370, but people in the bottom 10 percent earn an average of only $564.

The Brazilian upper class, about 1 percent of the total population, enjoys tremendous power and

Children like these who grow up in the slums of Brazil's large cities face a perilous, hand-to-mouth existence.

privilege. The middle classes—the next 26 percent of the population—are well educated, travel widely, and lead comfortable lives by American standards. But for the remaining 73 percent of the population—and especially for the 47 percent who are classified as poor—living conditions are dreadful (Fiechter, 1975; Wood & deCarvalho, 1988; Harrison, 1992).

Some of the worst conditions are found in the *favelas*, shantytowns housing hundreds of thousands of recent arrivals from the countryside who are seeking a better life (Perlman, 1976). Large families and limited job skills doom most of the poor to a marginal existence. One-fourth of Brazil's people go to sleep hungry every night.

Instead of clamoring for policies to reduce this misery, the middle and upper classes seem utterly un-

moved by it. In fact, they appear far less concerned about the suffering of the poor than about the possibility that they might be inconvenienced by efforts to help the lower classes. This is especially evident in the way many elite Brazilians respond to the millions of street children living in the nation's large cities (Sanders, 1987). Armed guards patrol municipal dumps lest children make off with scraps of edible garbage. And despite ongoing protests by international human rights organizations, thousands of poor Brazilian children have been murdered since 1985 by police and vigilante death squads hired by shopkeepers who don't want the sight of a begging child to scare off their middle-class customers (Larmer, 1992; Michaels, 1993).

SUMMARY

1. All but the most traditional societies are characterized by social stratification based on variables such as gender, age, race or ethnicity, and economic status.

2. Systems of social stratification are commonly legitimated by widely accepted belief systems termed ideologies.

3. The ideology that legitimates economic inequal-

ity in modern societies may be called classism. It suggests that because there is widespread equal opportunity, both the wealthy and the poor deserve their fates.

4. Structured economic inequality generally increases as societies develop until they reach the industrial stage, when this trend starts to reverse.

5. Historic patterns of social stratification include slave and caste systems; contemporary developed societies emphasize class rather than more ascriptive patterns of structured economic inequality.

6. Deficiency theories, generally regarded by sociologists as inaccurate and misleading, explain social stratification in terms of differences in individual ability.

7. Functionalist theory as developed in the Davis-Moore thesis argues that economic stratification is inevitable and that it serves the positive function of ensuring that the most important statuses in society are filled by the most capable people.

8. Conflict theorists disagree with the functional view that the effects of stratification are generally positive.

9. Karl Marx believed social classes, composed of people who share a common relationship to the means of production, are locked in irreconcilable conflict with each other. In order to win this struggle, subordinate classes must attain class consciousness; the dominant class attempts to retard class consciousness by encouraging various forms of false consciousness.

10. Max Weber identified three overlapping systems of stratification in modern societies: economic classes, status groups, and parties or power groups.

11. Symbolic interactionists emphasize the importance of status symbols and other ways that class differences influence everyday patterns of social life.

12. The modern world displays a pattern of global stratification into several distinct groups of nations: fully developed, developing, and underdeveloped, or high-, medium-, and low-income.

13. Modernization theory suggests that all of the world's societies will eventually become fully developed.

14. Dependency theory explains the poverty of many nations as a consequence of their economic domination by the developed world.

15. World systems theory divides the world's nations into three categories—core, semiperiphery, and periphery—with each group playing a different role in a sort of global assembly line.

16. While the homeless make up a relatively small percentage of the U.S. population, they illustrate the human consequences of living at the bottom of the stratification hierarchy. Sociologists generally see homelessness as more the result of structural rather than individual causes.

17. Extreme poverty is a very serious social problem worldwide, as illustrated by the condition of Brazil's underclass.

KEY TERMS

bourgeoisie 250
caste system 244
class consciousness 250
classism 240
colonialism 258
cultural capital 253
cultural imperialism 259
Davis-Moore thesis 248
deficiency theory 247
false consciousness 251
global stratification 240
Kuznets curve 244
neocolonialism 259
power 253
proletariat 250
social class 239
social Darwinism 247
social stratification 239
status groups 253

CRITICAL THINKING QUESTIONS

1. How deep is the average American's support for classist ideology? Do you think support for classism is currently increasing or weakening in this country? Why?

2. Functionalists and conflict theorists disagree regarding whether economic stratification is inevitable and also regarding whether its consequences are primarily positive or harmful. What is your view? Do you think you would have given the same answer if you had been born into a different social class?

3. What are the implications of the three global stratification theories for U.S. policy toward the world's poorer societies? Which view do you find most convincing? Defend your choice.

✤11✤ SOCIAL CLASS IN MODERN SOCIETIES

OUTLINE

Three Social Classes—Three Different Worlds

Susan Williams was born into an upper-class family in a North Shore suburb of Chicago. After attending an excellent and very expensive preschool, she was enrolled in a private elementary school and, upon graduation, entered an exclusive Connecticut prep school that had only recently began admitting women. The elite language patterns and lifestyle preferences that Susan had learned at home were reinforced by her school's curriculum. Although she maintained only a B average, she was accepted at Cornell, the same university her parents had attended and to which they had made substantial donations. After completing college, Susan entered Yale Law School; when she graduated she secured a position in a major law firm whose controlling partner was a good friend of the family.

Juan Gonzales was born in Chicago on the same day as Susan but to a middle-class family. He attended public schools and graduated in the upper 15 percent of his high school class. In order to save money, he went to a local community college for two years before transferring to the University of Illinois, where he majored in secondary education. After graduation, he married and taught in a high school in a Chicago suburb.

Vanessa Smith was born to an impoverished Chicago family on the same day that Susan and Juan came into the world. Unable to support his family, her father left home six months later. When Vanessa turned 4, a social worker helped enroll her in a Head Start program. She developed important preschool skills and seemed to be off to a good start, but in second and third grade she began falling behind. She completed middle school and two years of high school, but her grades grew worse, in part because she worked 30 hours a week at a local grocery store in order to help her mother pay the bills. She dropped out early in her junior year to go to work as a full-time stock clerk at a supermarket.

Susan, Juan, and Vanessa are not real people; they are fictional composites reflecting some fairly typical—but by no means universal—life experiences of young people in the upper, middle, and lower classes. The reason we have begun this chapter with their stories is to emphasize a key point: *Class matters.* Your class location affects almost every aspect of your daily life—not just your school experience and career opportunities, but also such things as your political leanings, the way you socialize your children, which church you attend, and the likelihood that you will be victimized by crime.

Gender and race or ethnicity also profoundly affect our lives, especially as they interact with the effects of class. These aspects of structured social inequality will be the topics of Chapters 12 and 13; however, in this chapter we will concentrate on social class in modern societies. We will begin by considering how sociologists determine an individual's class position. Next, we examine the U.S. class system, discuss social mobility, and explore how class affects life chances and lifestyles. The chapter concludes with a critical look at the welfare system in the United States.

MEASURING CLASS

Many sociological variables, including race, age, gender, and religion, are relatively easy to study because most people have a good idea of how to categorize themselves in relation to them. Fewer Americans are sure of their class position. Thus, how to identify someone's class is a significant issue. Researchers may use one or more of three distinct means of *operationalizing* the variable of class—that is, of defining class in such a way that it can be used in empirical research. These means may be termed the subjective, reputational, and objective approaches (Runciman, 1990).

The Subjective Approach

The **subjective approach** to identifying class—also called the self-placement approach—is the simplest of the three. It amounts to simply asking people to which class they think they belong. The data in Figure 11.1 reflect the use of the subjective approach.

In some cases, this methodology can be quite effective (Jackman & Jackman, 1983). If researchers provide respondents with a set of possible answers, then most people can manage to sort themselves out into classes. For example, in a recent national survey, 5 percent of males and 4 percent of females identified themselves as upper class, 45 percent of both genders called themselves middle class, 46 percent of men and 44 percent of women described themselves as working class, and 4 percent of men and 7 percent of women chose the label lower class (NORC, 1996). These findings suggest that Americans *are* aware of the fact that there are different classes and also that they have some idea of how they should be classified.

The problem with this approach is that many people do not have a *clear* understanding of particular class labels. Researchers, therefore, are not sure whether what one respondent means by, say, "working class," is identical to what other respondents or sociologists might mean by that label. Another problem is that some people may identify with a class to which they *aspire* rather than with the one in which they are actually located.

Furthermore, when no structured responses are provided, up to 94 percent of respondents identify themselves as middle class. (Vanneman & Cannon, 1987; Simpson, et al., 1988). Some wealthy people may call themselves middle class to avoid appearing arrogant. Working- and lower-class individuals may choose this label because, given the widespread acceptance of classism (see Chapter 10) in American society, to admit being less than middle class is to acknowledge a personal failing. Similar results have been found in contemporary Western European societies (Kelley & Evans, 1993).

Clearly, for many people "middle class" is a catchall category that applies to all Americans except those at the extreme top and bottom of society. This suggests that there is a relatively low level of class awareness in the United States; it also means that the

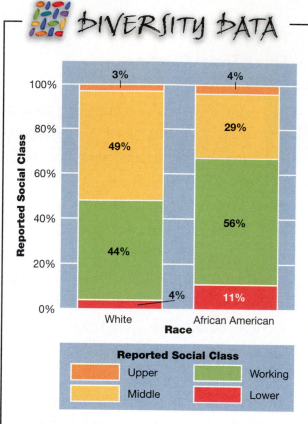

FIGURE 11.1   Percent Reporting Own Social Class, by Race. White people are substantially more likely than African Americans to describe themselves as middle-class, while African Americans are more likely than whites to report that they are either working or lower class. Why might respondents of either race resist seeing themselves as lower class?
Source: NORC. General Social Surveys, 1972–1996. Chicago: National Opinion Research Center, 1996. Reprinted by permission of NORC, Chicago, IL.

subjective approach is only of limited value to researchers studying this society.

The Reputational Approach

Some twentieth-century American sociologists studied class in smaller communities by asking well-informed local "judges" to classify their fellow citizens into such classes as "people who are doing very well" or "hard-working regular folks" or "trailer-park residents." The best-known research using this **reputational approach** was carried out in the 1930s by W. Lloyd Warner and his associates in a New England town he called "Yankee City." Warner identified six "prestige classes" ranging from the upper upper to the lower lower (Warner et al., 1941, 1949).

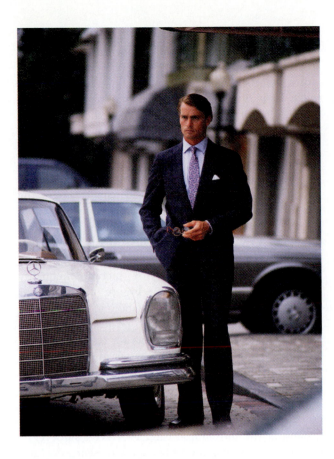

The lifestyles of people belonging to different social classes are so distinct that it is sometimes possible to get a fairly accurate idea of what class someone is in on the basis of his or her physical appearance alone.

The reputational approach remains useful in small communities with little population turnover where most residents know each other. However, fewer and fewer such communities exist in the modern world. Most contemporary sociologists reject both the subjective and the reputational approaches in favor of the objective method.

The Objective Approach

In the **objective approach,** sociologists ask their respondents for several facts about themselves and then use this information to place them into social classes. The most commonly used objective definition of class is called **SES** or **socioeconomic status** (Gilbert & Kahl, 1993). It is made up of three loosely related *indicators* (or measures): income, occupational prestige, and education.

All three indicators are necessary because any one may be misleading. For example, most people without a high school diploma are low in class, but there are some individuals who become millionaires even though they never graduated from high school. And money is not the whole story either: Drug lords may make vastly more money each year than priests do, but drug lords have much lower occupational prestige.

Dual Earner Households

As married women have flooded into the job market in recent decades, the task of measuring social class position has become more complicated (Beeghley, 2000). Researchers who use the objective measure to determine a family's class have developed new methodologies that not only take into account the income contributed by both earners but also factor in both the husband's and the wife's occupational prestige and educational attainment. Regarding the subjective approach, wives traditionally tended to classify themselves solely in terms of their husband's job and education, but now they are more likely to consider both their own qualifications and those of their husbands (Davis & Robinson, 1998).

PROPERTY AND PRESTIGE: TWO DIMENSIONS OF CLASS

The popularity of the objective approach has led many sociologists to focus on three dimensions of class in modern societies: property, occupational prestige, and, to a lesser extent, power. Chapter 18 addresses the distribution of power in America; here we will discuss property and prestige.

Property

Property is a critical indicator of class position. Sociologists divide it into two general categories: **income**, consisting of salaries, rents, and interest and dividends received from stocks and bonds; and **wealth**, net accumulated assets, including homes, land, automobiles, jewelry, factories, and stocks and bonds. The distribution of both income and wealth is markedly unequal in modern U.S. society.

Income. Figure 11.2 helps us to visualize the extent of income inequality in the United States. The top 20 percent of families received nearly half, 47.2 percent, of all income in 1997, while the bottom 20 percent earned just 4.2 percent. The top 5 percent of American families received 20.7 percent of all income; the minimum family income in this group was $137,080, compared with an average for all families of $44,570. The top 5 percent collectively received substantially more income than the entire bottom 40 percent.

Looking even higher up, in 1998 the average annual compensation package for the top two executives of the 365 largest public corporations was $10.6 million. AOL CEO Steve Case was paid over $117 million in 1999. In contrast, the average salary for factory workers was $29,270 in 1998 (Love, 1999). In the words of noted economist Paul Samuelson, "If we make an income pyramid out of a child's blocks, with each layer portraying $500 of income, the peak would be far higher than Mount Everest, but most people would be within a few feet of the ground" (Samuelson & Nordhaus, 1989: 644).

The United States has the most extreme income inequality in the developed world: Americans in the top 20 percent earn an average of eleven times more than the typical individual in the bottom 20 percent. In contrast, Sweden's ratio is less than four to one (Beeghley, 2000)

How have patterns of U.S. income inequality changed over recent decades? Figure 11.3 contrasts changes in average per capita income by quintiles (fifths of the population) in two periods, 1947–1973 and 1973–1993. During the earlier era, which included the post–World War II economic boom and a period of dramatic increases in social welfare spending, the average income of all Americans, rich and poor, grew at a roughly similar pace. In fact, the poorest 20 percent of the population actually gained ground at the most rapid rate. However, since 1973 the picture has changed radically, with sharp declines toward the bottom and increases at the top. The wealthiest 1 percent received 70 percent of all income gains made between 1977 and 1989, while the bottom quintile lost 9 percent of its income (Krugman, 1992).

The most extreme increases in income inequality occurred during the Reagan presidency (1981–1989) (Greenstein & Barancik, 1990; Phillips, 1991; Morris et al., 1994). In these years, the average income of the top 20 percent increased by 30 percent and that of the top 1 percent by 75 percent. Between 1989 and 1994 every group except the top 20 percent lost ground ("The widening gap," 1993). The gap continued to grow in the 1990s. The real earnings of the poorest fifth of the population rose less than 1 percent between 1988 and 1998 while those of top 20 percent increased fifteen percent.

The reasons for these trends are complex, including changes in the structure and health of the economy, in tax laws, and in welfare spending. We will discuss these factors later in the chapter when we analyze the shrinking of the U.S. middle class.

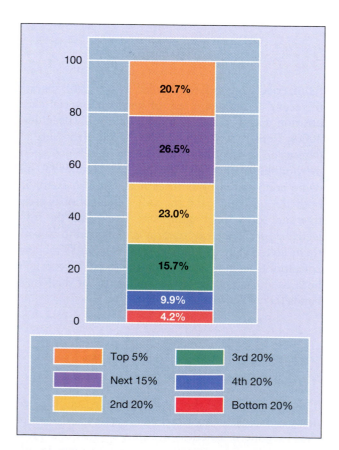

100

80

60

40

20

0

20.7%

26.5%

23.0%

15.7%

9.9%

4.2%

Top 5%   3rd 20%

Next 15%   4th 20%

2nd 20%   Bottom 20%

FIGURE 11.2 Distribution of Aggregate Family Income in the United States, 1997.
Source: 1999 Statistical Abstract, Table 751.

Wealth. The distribution of wealth in the United States is much less equal than that of income. The top 20 percent controls about 80 percent of all wealth. Another 15 percent is in the hands of the second 20 percent; the rest own virtually nothing. In fact, if we consider debts as well as assets, the lowest two-fifths

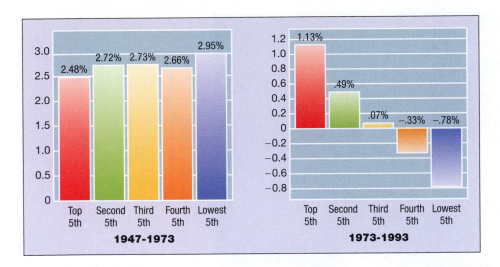

FIGURE 11.3 **Average Annual Growth in Individual Income in the United States by Fifths, 1947–1973 and 1973–1993**
Source: U.S. Bureau of the Census.

of the population owe more than their total wealth (Beeghley, 2000).

The concentration of wealth at the extreme top is staggering. 40-year-old Microsoft CEO Bill Gates headed the *Forbes* list of America's wealthiest people in 2000 with estimated holdings of $63 billion. In 1998 the top 0.5 percent of all households owned 25 percent of all wealth, an average of $15 million each. The top 1 percent have an average net worth of $5 million (McFeatters, 1999).

The wealth of the top 1 percent of U.S. households was estimated in the early 1990s at $5.7 trillion, more than the total assets of the bottom 90 percent (Nasar, 1992). Members of this group hold at least twenty-two times more wealth than the average individual in the bottom 99 percent (Oliver & Shapiro, 1990). The top 0.5 percent—430,000 people—own about 40 percent of all stocks, bonds, and similar assets (Rothchild, 1995).

As with income, the distribution of wealth in America is more unequal than it is in any other comparable country (Wolff, 1995). For example, in the United Kingdom, historically one of Europe's least egalitarian nations, the top 1 percent held about 18 percent of private wealth in the early 1990s compared with a U.S. figure of 34 percent.

Also as with income, the distribution of wealth has become even less equal in the United States over the past two decades. Between 1992 and 1998 the richest 1 percent of all households increased their share of the nation's wealth from 30 to 34 percent. In contrast, the wealth held by the bottom 90 percent declined from 33 percent to 31 percent.

How should we interpret these income and wealth trends? In line with the Davis-Moore theory discussed in Chapter 10, some functionalists see increases in economic inequality as a spur to ambition: The rewards of getting to the top are greater than ever. Others, especially conflict theorists, are uneasy about the concentration of power that accompanies increasing inequality in income and wealth. They fear that tens of millions of people at the bottom have become so poor that, whatever their talents and motivation, they will have great difficulty getting ahead.

Occupational Prestige

In everyday life, we usually ask what someone does for a living in order to identify his or her class position. We do this, in part, because it is considered impolite to ask people about their income and wealth, while it is socially acceptable to show interest in a person's work. But this is also a reflection of the fact that people generally agree about how much prestige accompanies various occupations. Table 11.1 summarizes the findings of recent research into occupational prestige rankings.

Take a few minutes to study this table. What seems to influence how Americans evaluate different jobs? Certainly money is part of the equation—most of the occupations toward the top of the list pay more than those near the bottom—but there are a number of exceptions to this rule—for example, truck drivers and carpenters may earn more than social workers or grade school teachers, two occupations whose wages are affected by the fact that they are predominantly female (Nakao & Treas, 1994). Jobs that are primarily held by minorities also tend to be less well paid and prestigious (Xu & Leffler, 1992; Carlson, 1992).

High-status occupations normally involve substantial autonomy and authority; being closely supervised and taking orders lowers occupational prestige (Vallas, 1987). Most highly ranked jobs also require extensive education (MacKinnon & Langford, 1994) and are usually "clean" in that they involve working

Computer entrepreneur Bill Gates, America's wealthiest individual, achieved an elite class position by virtue of the success of the Microsoft corporation, which he founded.

with people or ideas rather than with things. Interestingly, research shows that occupational prestige rankings have changed very little during the past century (Nakao & Treas, 1994). These rankings are also quite similar around the globe (Lin & Xie, 1988).

THE CLASS SYSTEM IN THE UNITED STATES

Sociologists take several different approaches in describing the U.S. class system (Lucal, 1994). Some follow the lead of Erik Olin Wright (1979, 1985; Wright et al., 1982), who identifies four classes based on the four possible combinations of two key factors: (a) whether the members of a class *own* means of creating significant wealth and (b) whether they exercise substantial *authority* over others. Figure 11.4 summarizes Wright's model.

At the top, like Marx (see Chapter 10), Wright identifies a powerful *capitalist class* that owns productive property and exercises extensive authority. At the bottom, there is a class of proletarian *workers* who neither own productive property nor exercise authority. The most interesting elements of Wright's model are the two classes that occupy what he calls "contradictory class locations" because they have some characteristics in common with the capitalists and in other ways resemble the workers. The *petite bourgeoisie* are the small shopowners and other entrepreneurs who own capital but employ few if any workers and so exercise little authority. This group makes up about 5 percent of the population. The fourth class, *managers*, work in firms owned by the capitalists but have au-

thority over a large number of workers. Most members of this managerial group identify with the capitalists, and yet ultimately they are as expendable as any other employees. This fact has become a bitter reality to large numbers of middle managers during the current era of corporate downsizing (Uchitelle & Kleinfeld, 1996).

Concerning the three individuals introduced at the beginning of this chapter, Wright would classify Susan Williams, the lawyer, as a manager. Juan

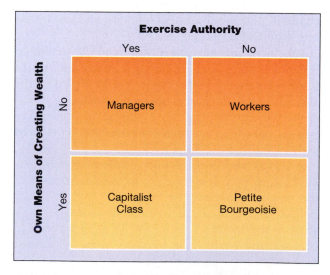

FIGURE 11.4   Erik Olin Wright's Model of the U.S. Class Structure. Wright identifies four classes based on the intersection of two factors: ownership of the means of creating wealth and exercising authority over others.
Source: Wright (1979, 1985); Wright et al. (1982).

Table 11.1	Prestige Rankings of Selected Occupations
Physician	86
Lawyer	75
University professor	74
Architect	73
Dentist	72
Pharmacist	68
Registered nurse	66
High school teacher	66
Accountant	65
Elementary school teacher	64
Computer programmer	61
Police officer	60
Librarian	54
Firefighter	53
Social worker	52
Realtor	49
Mail carrier	47
Secretary	46
Welder	42
Farmer	40
Carpenter	39
Child-care worker	36
Truck driver	30
Cashier	29
Garbage collector	28
Bartender	25
Farm laborer	23
Janitor	22
Shoe shiner	9

Source: NORC. General Social Surveys, 1972–1996: Cumulative Codebook. Chicago: NORC, 1996. Reprinted by permission of NORC, Chicago, IL.

of their money (Thurow, 1987); about 40 percent inherited all of it (Allen, 1987; Queenan, 1989). Susan Williams, the successful lawyer discussed at the opening of this chapter, clearly is a member of the upper class. In recent decades, the elite has used its political power to reshape the tax code so that most pay at lower rates than the rest of the population; a few take advantage of so many loopholes that they pay no federal taxes at all (Barlett & Steele, 1994).

Members of the upper class distinguish between two groups within it (Allen, 1987). At the extreme top are the "old rich," families like the Rockefellers, Fords, and duPonts, who have been wealthy for generations (Aldrich, 1988). Below them are people like Bill Gates or Steven Spielberg who earned their wealth more recently. This group also includes a few highly paid athletes and actors as well as top professionals.

Male members of the old rich may work, but many simply manage their investments, while many "new rich" men occupy top executive positions in the largest corporations. For this reason, the latter group is sometimes called the "corporate class." The women in both groups sometimes pursue careers but more commonly do civic and charitable work (Ostrander, 1984). In many cases, the new rich actually are wealthier than the old, but members of both groups generally acknowledge the higher status of the old rich.

Members of the upper class generally feel a strong sense of class consciousness (Baltzell, 1990). Traditionally, they were almost entirely white Protes-

Gonzales, who teaches high school, and Vanessa Smith, who works in a supermarket, are both workers.

Though Wright's model has much to recommend it, most sociologists prefer to analyze the U.S. class system in terms of a somewhat simpler scheme represented by the work of Dennis Gilbert and Joseph Kahl (1993) among others. The following discussion of the U.S. class system is based on this interpretation.

The Upper Class

Although only about 1 percent of all Americans are in the upper class, their influence is hard to overestimate, as is implied by the income and wealth data presented previously (Domhoff, 1990). Though members of this class earn at least several hundred thousand dollars a year, their chief economic resource is accumulated wealth rather than income. More than half of all upper-class families were born into the bulk

Members of the upper class are able to accumulate vast estates that allow them to live lives the rest of us can only dream about.

INTERNET ✦ CONNECTIONS

Bill Gates, chairman of the Microsoft Corporation, is often regarded as the wealthiest man in the world. To see his $64 million home, check out Web site http://www.goehner.com/gates.htm, and while you're there, be sure to take the US News interactive tour of his home. After you've looked around, answer the following questions.

- How could you modify the Gates home if you wanted to spend even more money?
- Imagine you lived there with your family and describe your typical day at home.

tants of British descent; now at least their lower ranks are opening to Catholics and some European ethnics but there are still very few African Americans or Hispanics among them. They tend to live in a small number of elite communities, marry other members of the upper class, send their children to the same prep schools and top private colleges, join the same clubs, and vacation in the same exclusive spots (Baltzell, 1990; Domhoff, 1998). More than any other class, members of the elite form distinct social networks.

Historically, many members of the old rich felt a strong sense of *noblesse oblige*, a belief that in return for being born to privilege, they ought to support charitable organizations and the arts (Lapham, 1988). However, according to some critics, this orientation seems to be diminishing among members of the modern corporate class (Dye, 1995).

The Upper-Middle Class

Most people have little contact with the upper class; the very rich tend to use their wealth to protect their privacy (Fussell, 1992). Not so the upper-middle class, whose members tend to be highly visible. Lacking significant power at the national level, these are the movers and shakers of the local community (Trounstine & Christensen, 1982).

Making up about 14 percent of the population, this class consists of high-level professionals and managers earning between $100,000 and $300,000 per year. Upper-middle class women typically work, although often more from choice than necessity. These families do not hold enormous wealth, but they are financially secure, drive new cars, and live in impressive homes. Their class position depends heavily on their education: Virtually all hold degrees and many have completed graduate work at high-quality colleges and universities. Most live in the suburbs, where they play a central role in groups such as the Chamber of Commerce and the local country club and often in local government as well. Although mostly white, they are more ethnically diverse than the upper class (Marger, 1998).

The Lower-Middle Class

About 30 percent of the American population falls in the lower-middle class. These are the lower managers, small-business operators, nonretail sales workers, upper clerical workers, and minor professionals such as teachers. Most people at this level have at least some postsecondary education, but many have not completed their degrees. Their family incomes range from about $30,000 annually to perhaps $70,000 or a little more (Marger, 1998). Juan Gonzales, the Chicago high school teacher, belongs here.

Normally, both husband and wife must work in order to maintain a moderately comfortable lifestyle, although one that is relatively insecure since people at this level do not have substantial investments or savings. Most can take occasional vacations, eat out fairly regularly, drive inexpensive late-model cars, and send their children to public universities or at least to community colleges. Historically, most have owned (or been buying) their own homes, although this goal is becoming increasingly difficult today (Cassidy, 1995).

Members of the lower-middle class typically encourage their children to complete their education in hopes of moving up; they are also deeply concerned about the possibility of sliding back into the working class. The vast majority of the members of this class are essentially powerless at the local and national levels, as well as in their jobs, where they follow rules established by their upper-middle class superiors.

The Working Class

Roughly 30 percent of the American people are in the working class. However, the line between the lower-middle and working classes is very indistinct. Most of the members of this class earn between $20,000 and $35,000 annually, but some, especially unionized production workers and skilled craft workers such as carpenters and electricians, earn substantially more. Those with higher incomes are characterized as working class mainly because their lifestyle is similar to that of others in this group (Beeghley, 2000)

Most members of the working class are skilled and semiskilled manual workers. The working class also includes low-level clericals, sales workers, and

Members of the petit bourgeoisie resemble the bourgeoisie in that they are not compelled to sell their labor to others in order to survive, but they differ from them because they employ few workers and accumulate little capital.

many female *pink-collar workers* such as waitresses and cooks. Most working-class jobs are highly routine and closely supervised. The large majority of wives in this class must work outside the home in order to help pay household bills (Rubin, 1994).

Working-class people usually complete high school, but few go on to college. Perhaps half of them own their own homes, but they have no other significant assets and are vulnerable to a financial crisis resulting from illness or unexpected unemployment (Rubin, 1994). The real (inflation-adjusted) income from most blue-collar jobs has been declining in recent years (Freeman, 1994). Most working-class peo-

ple drive used cars, live in modest neighborhoods, and must sacrifice in order to eat out or take a vacation.

While upward mobility is encouraged in the working class, many people in this stratum emphasize the importance of conventional respectability in order to underscore their superiority over the lower classes.

The Working Poor

Perhaps 22 percent of the population is in this class. They work, sometimes full-time and sometimes part-time, but receive such low wages that they live in or near poverty. In 1997, over 3 percent of all full-time

Unlike people farther down the class ladder, those in the upper-middle class can easily afford the lessons, clubs, and greens fees needed in order to become successful golfers.

workers actually fell below the poverty line. So much for the bumper sticker that reads "I fight poverty—I work!" (Bane & Ellwood, 1989).

How can this be? Doesn't the American Dream promise a decent life to anyone who is willing to work hard? Part of the problem is that the minimum wage has failed to keep pace with inflation. If it had been automatically adjusted to reflect increases in the cost of living, as Social Security is, then in order to give workers the same purchasing power in 1994 that they had in 1968, the minimum wage would have been $6.29 per hour. In fact, it was $4.25, where it stayed until 1996, when Congress approved an increase in two stages to $5.15, where it remains today, although ten states have raised their minimum wages above this level.

Lacking any accumulated wealth whatsoever, the working poor exist from paycheck to paycheck. Vanessa Smith, the supermarket stock clerk, is a member of this group. Most of the working poor hold low-pay, dead-end service jobs, often on a temporary basis, that rarely offer health insurance, pension plans, or other benefits. In fact, about 80 percent of the 44.3 million people who lacked health insurance in 1998 were full-time workers or their dependents (Westphal, 1999).

When families are intact, both parents work, but female-headed single-parent families are common among the working poor, a fact that worsens their economic dilemma since wages received by women are generally lower than those earned by men (Levitan & Shapiro, 1987). Members of this class have sometimes completed high school, but they lack job skills. Though the majority of the working poor are white, minorities are disproportionately represented, which further depresses their wages. They live in rental units in undesirable neighborhoods, drive old, unreliable cars if any, and cannot really afford any luxuries (Marger, 1998).

The "Underclass"

About 3 percent of the population is locked into long-term, chronic poverty. Sociologists disagree about what to call this group (Bagguley & Mann, 1992). Some use the term "underclass" (Myrdal, 1962; Glasgow, 1981; Auletta, 1982), but others argue that this word is stigmatizing, a real concern given the classist attitudes of most Americans (Gans, 1990). Similar criticisms apply to the terms "welfare class" and "lower lower class." William Julius Wilson proposes the term "ghetto underclass," but this phrase falsely implies that everyone in this group is African American (Wilson, 1987, 1991).

Some members of the underclass are so poor that they cannot even afford a place to live. In recent years, homeless individuals have become a common sight in large American cities.

Whatever we call them, the members of this class lack employable skills and have little or no experience in the job market. Unless given extensive training, many are virtually unemployable. Their household income is typically below $10,000 per year; the only legitimate source of support for most of them is public assistance. Many survive only through an elaborate network of sharing based largely on kinship ties (Stack, 1975).

The underclass is primarily, but not entirely, minority (Jencks & Peterson, 1991). Most of its members are women and children living in single-parent households. The combined effects of gender, race, and family status have a devastating effect on the incomes of underclass families. Many experience a wide range of social problems, including crime, drug abuse, malnutrition, violence, gangs, and disease.

The dilemma of the underclass may be the most serious social problem facing America. Only about half of the people born into chronic poverty ever get out of it (Gilbert & Kahl, 1993; Wacquant, 1994). For this reason, we turn next to a more detailed consideration of their plight.

INTERNET ✺ CONNECTIONS

Social critics charge that it is very difficult for the affluent to appreciate the plight of the *underclass* in America. It has been said that "a picture is worth a thousand words" and "seeing is believing." In order to develop a better appreciation of the *underclass*, take a look at "American Pictures: A Danish Vagabond's Personal Journey Through the Underclass": http://www.american-pictures.com/english/index.html. After you have examined the photographs, click on "Racism" and read the author's personal commentary about the underclass in American society. Do people who are part of the underclass have the same "life chances" in comparison with their more socioeconomically fortunate counterparts? The text points out that "class makes a difference." This exercise should help you to understand why.

POVERTY

How needy must people be before they are considered poor? This is by no means a trivial question because the way we define poverty determines who will be eligible for government assistance (Katz, 1989; Ruggles, 1990). There are two ways to define poverty—absolute and relative.

Absolute poverty refers to a life-threatening lack of food, shelter, and clothing. This definition has been used by the government since 1955. The official *poverty line* was originally computed by estimating the bare minimum cost of food necessary to keep people alive—a "short-term emergency diet"—and then tripling this figure, based on the assumption that poor people spend about one-third of their income on food (Orshansky, 1969). This figure is adjusted annually for inflation and has been modified in line with recent research that suggests food expenses make up only one-fourth of poor people's total budget. In 1999, the poverty line for a nonfarm family of four was $17,029. Remember that virtually all officially poor people make less than this; about 40 percent of the poor earn under $8,000, less than half of the poverty threshold.

This absolute approach to poverty has generated considerable controversy (Walker & Walker, 1995). Conservatives argue that the official definition is faulty because it does not consider food stamps, rent subsidies, and the cash value of Medicaid and Medicare benefits as income (Whiteman, 1994). If it did, the number of poor might drop by some 5 million people.

On the other hand, advocates for the poor maintain that the official figure is, in fact, set too low (Michael, 1995; Schwartz & Volgy, 1993; Ruggles, 1990). They cite recent research that suggests poor families typically spend only about one-sixth of their income on food because the rapidly escalating cost of housing consumes between 50 and 70 percent of their total budget (Dolbeare, 1995). Furthermore, the current scheme does not allow for child-care expenses, which is especially unreasonable given the large number of women with young children among the poor.

These critics believe **relative poverty** is a more realistic approach. By this definition, individuals who make substantially less than most of the people around them and who cannot afford purchases that most people take for granted are poor, even if they can afford the necessities of life (Ropers, 1991). Supporters of this method of defining poverty sometimes suggest that people who earn less than half the national median family income are poor.

The official poverty line in the 1960s was indeed about half the national median income. However, since then it has dropped to about 38 percent. By the relative standard, about 25 percent of the population would be considered as poor today, an unacceptably high figure for national policymakers.

How Many Poor?

The highest rate of poverty in the twentieth century occurred during the Great Depression of the 1930s when almost half of the American population was needy. By 1960, the year John Kennedy became president, the rate was slightly over 22 percent. In 1978, the figure had dropped to just 11.4 percent of the population, or 24.5 million people. This improvement was partly due to a very strong economy, which created the sorts of jobs that help poor people become self-sufficient. It was also partly a result of substantially increased government spending for social welfare (Gilbert & Kahl, 1993).

But in the 1980s the numbers turned upward until by 1993 the United States was experiencing a poverty rate of 15.1 percent and had the largest absolute poverty population (39.3 million) since the 1950s. These figures reflected a worsening economy combined with dramatic cuts in social services under Presidents Reagan and Bush. Since 1993 the economy has performed well and the poverty rate declined to 11.8 percent in 1999, its lowest rate in twenty-one years (Armas, 2000). However, the U.S. rate remained high compared to that typical of the other Western postindustrial societies. For example, America has roughly three times more poverty than Sweden and Norway (Smeeding et al., 1990).

Who Are the Poor?

Sociologically, the most important characteristics of the poor are their gender, family status, race, and age. Table 11.2 provides current data concerning the impact of these variables on poverty.

Gender. Sociologists use the phrase the **feminization of poverty** to refer to the growing percentage of the poverty population that is made up of women. Other societies as well as the United States are experiencing this trend, but it is especially serious here. Recent research shows that in the United States women are 41 percent more likely to be poor than men; the equivalent figures for other industrial nations range from 34 percent in Australia to 2 percent in the Netherlands (although in Sweden, men are 10 percent more likely to be poor than women) (Casper et al., 1994). In the United States today, two-thirds of all poor adults and 62.3 percent of all poor people are women.

Family Status. The best single predictors of poverty are gender combined with family status. In 1997, 35.1 percent of single-parent, female-headed families were poor compared with just 11.6 percent of all families. In fact, half of the increases in poverty in the 1980s can be explained by the growing number of these families (Eggebeen & Lichter, 1991).

Young unmarried lower-income women who become mothers are in a particularly difficult situation. Most lack the job skills to earn enough money to pay for day care as well as maintain a minimally adequate standard of living. The problem is intensified by the low wages typically paid to women. Marriage is often not a viable option; even if the father is willing, he is usually unable to earn enough to keep the family out of poverty. Many of these women end up on welfare, not because of some character flaw—unless wanting a family is a character flaw—but because welfare is the only way they can avoid destitution.

Race. About two-thirds of all poor people are white, but minorities are disproportionately likely to be poor. Specifically, in 1997, 11 percent of whites, 26.5 percent of African Americans, and 27.1 percent of Hispanics were below the poverty line. If we factor in the effects of gender and family status, we find that in 1996 49.9 percent of African American female-headed single-parent families and 51.6 percent of Hispanic female-headed single-parent families lived below the poverty line. The comparable figure for whites was 29.2 percent. Chapters 12 and 13 will further examine the impact of the combined variables of gender and race on class position.

Age. As late as 1967, almost 30 percent of the elderly were poor, but the indexing of Social Security to the inflation rate and the expansion of Medicare have reduced this figure to 10.5 percent. In fact, although many older people live just above the poverty line, today the elderly are actually less likely to be poor than the average member of the general population.

On the other hand, the United States has the worst child poverty problem in the developed world (Smeeding et al., 1988). Poverty among children grew tremendously in the 1980s (Lichter & Eggebeen, 1993). In 1997, 16.1 percent of all white children, 36.8 percent of all Hispanic children, and 37.2 percent of all African American children lived below the poverty line. About half of all poor children live in families with incomes below 50 percent of the poverty line.

Table 11.2	Selected Characteristics of the Poverty Population 1997
Category	Percent below the Official Poverty Line
Race	
All Races	13.3%
Whites	11.0
African-Americans	26.5
Hispanics	27.1
Age	
Under 18	19.9%
18 to 24	17.5
25 to 34	12.1
35 to 44	9.6
45 to 54	7.2
55 to 59	9.0
60 to 64	11.2
65 up	10.5
Household Composition	
All Families	11.6%
Single-parent, Female-headed Families	35.1

Source: Statistical Abstract, 1999, Tables 763 and 766

Explaining Poverty

There are two general approaches to explaining the causes of poverty (Harris, 1993). The first, widely accepted by the general public, looks to factors within poor individuals themselves. These theories are sometimes called *kinds-of-people* explanations; in Chapter 10 we discussed them under the heading of deficiency theories. The second approach, more in line with sociological understandings and research findings, directs attention to conditions of the larger social structure. These are *system-blaming* perspectives.

The crudest version of the kinds-of-people approach simply claims that poor people are poor because they are lazy and immoral (Mead, 1992). Since

The military has often been a way for men (and now women) to achieve upward mobility.

this is the land of opportunity, anyone who doesn't get ahead must have some serious character flaw. Exceptions are made for certain traditional categories of people—widows, orphans, the handicapped—who are defined as "the deserving poor"; but most poor people are considered "undeserving" (Katz, 1989). This point of view is a consequence of classist ideology, and people who accept it tend to perceive programs designed to aid the poor as "handouts" to the unworthy.

Sociologists have found little or no evidence to support this interpretation and commonly see it as a classic example of **victim blaming** (Ryan, 1971). If it were generally valid, then how could the size of the poverty population change as rapidly as it has in recent decades? Did half of all poor Americans move out of poverty in the 1960s because they suddenly became more virtuous? Or did structural factors change—with more good jobs created and more government aid available—allowing millions to work their way up out of poverty? Certainly some poor people are lazy; there are lazy people at all economic levels. But personality flaws are not the primary cause of poverty.

A substantially more sophisticated version of the kinds-of-people approach focuses on certain subcultural values that are said to be common among the poor. The **culture of poverty** perspective suggests that the poor are socialized in childhood by their parents and peers to accept a distinctive way of looking at the world. In particular, they do not learn deferred gratification, the ability to forego immediate pleasure in order to work toward long-range goals (Lewis, 1966; Banfield, 1974). Middle-class people, the argument goes, learn to save money, study, and work hard in order to attain future success. None of these activities is much fun, but in the end, they pay off. On the other hand, the culture of poverty is radically present oriented. Thus short-run hedonism locks the poor into poverty.

This thesis seems less biased against the poor than the view that they are simply lazy, but it still sees poverty as a personal rather than structural problem. Considerable evidence does suggest that many of the long-term poor—a small minority within the poverty population—do indeed have difficulty deferring gratification (Mayer, 1997). But is this a cause or a consequence of poverty? Life has taught the persistently poor that the future is unpredictable. Even if they try to save for the future, something beyond their control—sudden unemployment, illness, car problems—nearly always ruins their plans. Their experiences teach them over and over that gratification deferred is gratification lost (Liebow, 1967).

There *is* a culture of poverty and it *can* trap people, but this culture is best understood as a consequence of and a reaction to life at the bottom of the class ladder; values are not the primary cause of poverty (Beeghley, 1983; Harvey, 1993). Change the structural realities and in time the culture will change. But it is unrealistic to try to change the culture first. In fact, to take such an approach is a subtle form of victim blaming.

The second general explanation for poverty focuses on economic and social conditions. People who support this position acknowledge that personal and subcultural factors may be relevant at times, but overall, poverty is primarily the result of structural factors (Wilson, 1989).

One key structural variable promoting poverty is the loss in recent decades of millions of well-paying factory jobs as a result of *deindustrialization*, an issue that will be discussed in some detail in the next section (Burton, 1992). The poor lack the skills to compete for the new high-skill technical jobs, leaving

As in many developing societies, the distinction between the small elite class and the very large lower class is extremely sharp in Brazil.

them only the dead-end service jobs. But, as we have seen, minimum-wage jobs cannot lift families out of poverty, especially since so many of the poor are mothers and minorities who tend to receive lower wages than whites and males. Furthermore, even low wage jobs can be hard to find in poverty neighborhoods, and many poor people do not have reliable transportation that would allow them to work miles away from their homes.

A comprehensive antipoverty program would help compensate for structural factors that cause poverty, but most Americans oppose such programs (Shapiro & Greenstein, 1991; Phillips, 1991). Recall that poverty declined during the 1960s, the decade of the Great Society programs, and soared when social-welfare spending was sharply reduced in the 1980s. Many people believe that welfare spending encourages dependency and poverty, but research suggests otherwise. One major study found that the poor would have almost doubled to some 27 percent of the population if the relatively meager safety net provided in the 1980s had not been in place (Coder et al., 1989).

SOCIAL MOBILITY

Social mobility is a change in an individual or group's position in a stratification hierarchy, most commonly a class system (Sorokin, 1959). **Intergen-**

erational social mobility refers to an individual's class position compared to that achieved by his or her parents or grandparents. In contrast, **intragenerational social mobility** refers to changes in people's social standing over their lifetimes.

Sociologists who analyze social mobility usually study people who have moved up or down, such as an individual whose father was a bricklayer but who has become a corporate executive, or the daughter of a doctor who is clerking in a convenience store. These are intergenerational examples of **vertical mobility.** Sociologists also sometimes study **horizontal mobility,** which occurs when someone moves from one status to another that is roughly equal in rank—for example, if a carpenter's son or daughter becomes a plumber.

Most Americans assume that people get ahead mainly because of their own ability, dedication, and hard work. Sociologists, however, see most mobility as structural (Levy, 1988). **Structural mobility** is most often a consequence of a change in the range of occupations that are available in a given society (Lipset, 1982; Gilbert & Kahl, 1993: 145–156).

To better understand the concept of structural mobility, look at Figure 11.5. Note that over the course of the last century there was a major shift in the *kinds of jobs* provided by the U.S. economy. In 1900, only 17.5 percent of all jobs were classified as white collar, whereas by 1998 that figure had risen to 59 percent. A shift like this means that many people

Global Connections

How Do Other Nations Fight Poverty?

What would an effective anti-poverty program look like? Successful programs in European social democracies such as Sweden, Norway, or the Netherlands generally incorporate most of the following features:

1. A universal children's allowance paid by the government to all families regardless of income.
2. National health care.
3. Government-subsidized child care.
4. Extensive low-income housing subsidies.
5. High-quality public education for all.

6. Ongoing efforts to reduce discrimination against women and minorities.
7. Job creation programs in both the public and the private sectors.
8. Minimum wage adequate to allow a decent existence.
9. Progressive taxation at all levels, with the wealthy paying at a much higher rate than the poor.
10. A centralized, federal welfare system that eliminates inequities between states.
11. Welfare benefits that at least bring recipients up to the poverty line.
12. Training programs to prepare people for jobs that pay better than

poverty-level wages (Sidel, 1996: Chapter 7).

1. Do you think a real antipoverty program would make people dependent on the state? Or would it provide enough stability so that they could work to improve their futures? Explain your position.
2. Why do you think most of these reforms have been accepted in nations like Denmark, Germany, and Sweden while they remain politically unpopular in the United States?

---

will experience upward social mobility simply because there are *more good jobs* and *fewer bad jobs* than there used to be.

Does this mean that hard work and ability are irrelevant? Not at all. At the individual level, which people are able to take advantage of structural changes in society and move up is determined in large part by talent and drive. But if the structure of society had not changed, then all the individual hard work and ability in the world would not have produced the massive upward mobility that has characterized most of U.S. history (Archer & Blau, 1994).

Overall, then, upward social mobility in the United States was substantial until the early 1970s. Before that decade, about half of all Americans experienced some degree of upward intergenerational social mobility, about one-third stayed at about the same level as their parents, and perhaps one in six moved downward (Blau & Duncan, 1967). Almost half of all men in the middle class today had working-class fathers (Gilbert & Kahl, 1993: 147).

Most social mobility is incremental; dramatic leaps in one lifetime from rags to riches—or from riches to rags—occur, but they are rare (Solon, 1992). In addition, most social mobility does not involve the extreme top or the extreme bottom (Kurz & Muller, 1987). A very high percentage of people born into the upper class stay there, or at worst move down into the top levels of the upper-middle class (Boone et al., 1988). Similarly, about half of the people born in the underclass escape it, but few rise farther than the lower rungs of the working class (Marger, 1998).

Rates of upward social mobility among African Americans remain generally lower than those among whites (Featherman & Hauser, 1978; Pomer, 1986; Davis, 1995; Fosu, 1997). Patterns of intergenerational mobility among women are broadly similar to those of men, although women continue to experience substantial levels of occupational discrimination, as discussed in Chapter 13 (Hout, 1988; Biblarz et al., 1996).

Americans like to believe their nation offers unparalleled opportunity, but research shows that U.S. mobility patterns are broadly similar to those of the other Western democracies (Erikson & Goldthorpe, 1992). However, there is one important exception to this generalization: Americans born in blue-collar families have traditionally had an exceptionally good chance of climbing into the upper managerial or professional classes. Specifically, research by Blau and Duncan (1967) found that one out of every 10 sons of manual workers was able to make such a leap in the United States compared with one in 67 in France, one in 100 in Denmark, and one in 300 in Italy.

Structural factors in the United States thus allowed a good deal of upward mobility prior to the early 1970s (Archer & Blau, 1994). Since then, however, the trend has been generally downward (Levy, 1988; Blumberg, 1989; Krymkowski & Krauze, 1992; Gilbert & Kahl, 1993). In particular, the middle class has been shrinking, a pattern some have called the "middle-class slide" (Duncan et al., 1992).

In the decade of the 1980s, for every seven families who moved from the middle class to the upper class, ten fell from the middle class into poverty

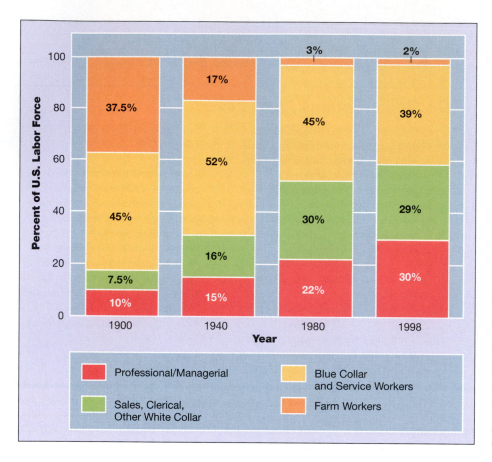

FIGURE 11.5 **The Changing U.S. Occupational Structure, 1900–1998.** Between 1990 and 1998, there was a major shift in the kinds of jobs available in the American economy.

Source: U.S. Bureau of the Census, *Historical Studies of the United States*, Vol. 1, 1975; U.S. Bureau of Labor Statistics, *Employment & Earnings*, 1993, Statistical Abstract, 1999, Table 675.

(Krugman, 1992). Income growth has stalled; between 1958 and 1973 the real (inflation-adjusted) income of a typical fifty-year-old man increased 50 percent; over the next twenty-one years, it did not grow at all (Russell, 1995). These trends have hit the young especially hard. Moreover, they have occurred even though an increasing number of families have more than one earner, and the average number of hours worked per week has steadily increased (Burtless, 1990). In fact, in 1997 wives in dual earner families worked an average of 223 hours more than they did in 1983, with a comparable figure for men of 158 hours (Sklar, 1999).

There are many individual exceptions to this pattern of downward mobility, of course. But many observers foresee an end to the easy assumption that unending upward mobility is the natural order of things in the United States. Between 1990 and 1993, median real income declined 7 percent. Even the exceptionally strong economy of the late 1990s produced only a modest reversal of the downward trend.

Today's youth may be the first generation in U.S. history that will not do as well on the average as their parents. Remember too that these patterns of substantial downward mobility are taking place at the same time that the upper class is becoming more wealthy. If this trend continues, the class structure of the United States could end up much like Brazil's, with a small but very wealthy elite group and a large majority of the population living in poverty or, at best, barely making ends meet.

Why has social mobility stalled out over the past three decades? This is a complex question, but three factors seem especially relevant. Above all, the decline of the middle class is a consequence of the globalization of the economy that has led to **deindustrialization** (Barnet, 1993), a process in which the manufacturing sector of the economies of the developed nations declines while the service sector expands (Myles & Turgeon, 1994).

This transformation has substantially reversed the patterns of upward structural mobility characteristic of the United States prior to about 1973. Millions of good-paying, mostly unionized, jobs have been lost, in large part because corporations have been shipping them to less-developed nations in order to take advantage of inexpensive foreign labor (Thurow, 1987; Reich, 1991). These are the jobs that traditionally allowed working-class people to move up the ladder.

In their place, two very different kinds of jobs are now being created in large numbers. First, the number of well-paid, highly technical service jobs is increasing. Most of these positions are taken by children of the middle and upper-middle classes, who can obtain the necessary skills and education. Unfortunately, not enough of these jobs are being created to replace the desirable manufacturing jobs that have been exported. The people who have lost these jobs

The children of the upper and upper-middle classes typically attend schools that offer far better facilities and teachers than those that are available to children from less elite class backgrounds.

and their children often end up in the second type of position that is now being created in the American economy—low-skill service jobs. These "McJobs" pay barely enough—or not enough—to keep workers out of poverty. Moreover, they offer no benefits or possibility of upward mobility. Of course, some individuals still manage to move into the middle class because of luck or outstanding ability, but they are swimming against the structural tide.

A second factor explaining the decline of the middle class is also linked, although less directly, to the globalization and deindustrialization of the American economy: corporate downsizing (Uchitelle & Kleinfeld, 1996). Since 1980 about 25 percent of all executive positions have been eliminated. Not only do these reductions further restrict upward mobility from the working class, they also force large numbers of formerly middle-class managers downward. Middle-class workers who lose their jobs tend to stay unemployed even longer than their working-class counterparts, and when they do find work, it is usually at lower pay. Many downsized workers are rehired by the same firms that fired them, but as part-timers or consultants, at lower salaries than they earned previously and with few benefits, if any.

A final factor contributing to the decline of the middle class is the revised federal tax code. Under the Reagan administration (1981–1989), the top tax rate was cut from 70 percent to 28 percent while federal taxes overall rose for the bottom 90 percent of the population (Phillips, 1991). These changes, which have been partially reversed by later administrations, were supposed to spur the American economy by giving the rich more money to invest so that new jobs could be created. The economy has indeed thrived, but as we have seen, the mix of jobs that has resulted has contributed to the middle-class slide. The tax policies were supposed to create a rising tide that

would lift all boats, but in reality, the people in yachts are doing well while a lot of those in rowboats are scraping the bottom.

≣ LIFE CONNECTIONS: The Difference Class Makes

Class matters because it affects so many aspects of our lives. Along with gender, race, and age, it strongly influences *life chances,* the likelihood that an individual will lead a successful and rewarding life (Gerth & Mills, 1958: 181), and also *lifestyles,* the subcultural patterns that characterize the different classes.

Life Chances

Susan, Juan, and Vanessa—the subjects of the vignettes that opened this chapter—experienced different life chances because they were born into different social classes. Not only was their schooling different, so were many other aspects of their lives. In this section, we'll briefly overview research on the effects of class on life chances.

Physical Health and Mortality.   Poverty is easily the number one social factor associated with ill health (Navarro, 1991; World Health Organization, 1995). At any given time, about 12 percent of the general population is sick; among the poor, that figure rises to 32 percent; among the homeless, 44 percent. Figure 11.6 illustrates how education, a key indicator of social class position, influences smoking and subjective assessment of health.

Not only does class affect physical health, it also influences how long people live: On the average, the poor die seven years earlier than the rest of the population as a result of inadequate medical care, poor

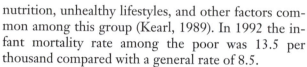

The contrast between the typical leisure-time activities of members of different classes is often quite dramatic.

nutrition, unhealthy lifestyles, and other factors common among this group (Kearl, 1989). In 1992 the infant mortality rate among the poor was 13.5 per thousand compared with a general rate of 8.5.

The relationship between social class and health is discussed in greater detail in Chapter 19.

Mental Health.   Extensive research shows that the poor are substantially more likely to suffer from mental problems (Faris & Dunham, 1939; Srole et al., 1962; Mirowski & Ross, 1989; Lynch et al., 1997). The best explanation seems to be that the stress associated with living in poverty contributes directly to mental illness. In addition, poor people who do develop mental problems are more likely to be treated with drugs or even surgery than with less intrusive approaches such as counseling and psychotherapy (Goldman et al., 1994).

Self-Esteem.   In a classic study, Richard Sennett and Jonathan Cobb (1973) conducted in-depth interviews with 150 working-class men and women in Boston and found a strong sense of inferiority among them. They were beaten down by the daily difficulties of making ends meet, but the main source of their low self-esteem came from internalizing classist ideology. They were convinced, on at least some levels, that their failure to succeed was their own fault. These attitudes, which are even more common among the poor than the working class, can create a fatalistic hopelessness that can lead to a self-fulfilling prophecy.

Education.   Life chances in education vary sharply by class. Because public education is supported primarily by local property taxes, the schools attended by middle-class children generally provide better prepared teachers and more extensive and up-to-date educational technologies than schools in lower-class neighborhoods (Kozol, 1991). Furthermore, *tracking*, or ability grouping in schools, tends to be strongly influenced by class, with lower and working-class students disproportionately channeled into noncollege tracks (Wheelock, 1992). As a result of such factors, educational attainment is markedly lower among poor children (Mortenson, 1992). Figure 11.7 demonstrates that the children of well-educated fathers tend to go much farther in school. All in all, the facts show that, contrary to popular opinion, schools are more important as a means of reproducing the existing class structure than as a way of allowing individuals to achieve upward mobility (Bowles, 1977).

Crime Victimization.   Poor people are substantially more likely to become victims of crime. This is particularly true for violent offenses, but it is also the case for property crime, despite the fact that the poor have far less to steal than the middle and upper classes (Karmen, 2000)

Lifestyles

Different behavioral patterns are associated with each class. In this section, we'll look at research concerning some of the main areas, starting with socialization and the family.

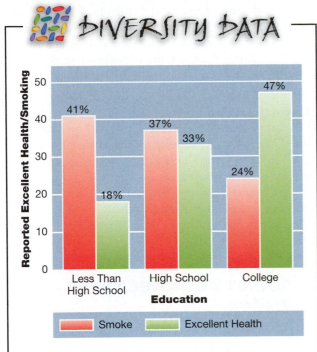

DIVERSITY DATA

FIGURE 11.6   How Does Education Affect Smoking and Assessment of Health? As education—a rough measure of social class—increases, the percentage of people who smoke goes down and the percentage who say that they are in excellent health increases. Why are better educated people less likely to be tobacco users?
Source: NORC. General Social Surveys, 1972–1996. Chicago: National Opinion Research Center, 1996. Reprinted by permission of NORC, Chicago, IL.

Child Socialization. Research by Melvin Kohn (1977) shows marked differences in childrearing patterns among classes. Compared to those in the middle class, working-class parents tend to stress obedience over self-direction and intellectual curiosity in their children. Working-class gender roles are relatively inflexible, and parents in this class are less likely to consider children's motivations when determining how to punish them. Working-class parents are also somewhat more likely to spank their children than middle-class parents.

Kohn notes that these socialization patterns make sense in light of the jobs children will probably enter. Whereas middle-class jobs typically demand originality and creativity, working-class employment more often requires reliability and obedience to authority. The implication is that working-class children may be virtually locked out of more prestigious and rewarding occupations.

Family. In general, the farther down the class ladder, the earlier couples marry and the larger their families (Collins, 1988). Middle- and upper-class

women are typically more knowledgeable about birth control and more consistent in using it, factors that reduce family size.

Style of marital interaction also varies by class. Men and women in working-class families live rather separate lives compared to couples in the middle and upper classes, who interact more with each other and typically have both male and female friends (Rubin, 1976). Working-class men are also more likely to assume patriarchal authority in the family. This fact, along with the stress of trying to survive on a limited income, may help explain the substantially higher divorce rate in the lower classes (Martin & Bumpass, 1989).

Politics. The Republican party has long been more closely associated with the interests of the wealthy and the Democrats with those of the less affluent. These orientations are reflected in class-based voting

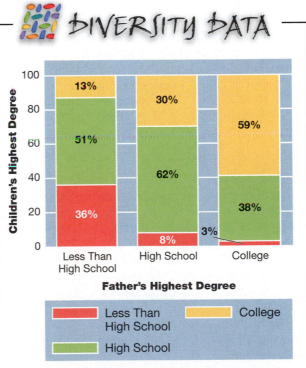

DIVERSITY DATA

FIGURE 11.7   How Does a Father's Level of Education Affect His Children's Education? Well over half of all children with college-educated fathers finish college compared with just 13 percent of those whose fathers did not graduate from high school. On the other hand, only 3 percent of the children of college graduates lack high school diplomas compared to over a third of the children of high school dropouts. Do these figures challenge Americans' belief that every child has a good chance to get ahead in life?
Source: NORC. General Social Surveys, 1972–1996. Chicago: National Opinion Research Center, 1996. Reprinted by permission of NORC, Chicago, IL.

INTERNET ● CONNECTIONS

Compare your high school to one of the nation's most exclusive prep schools, Choate Rosemary Hall, seen at Web site http://www.choate.edu/Default.htm. You may especially enjoy the scenes of the beautiful campus in the Photo Gallery. In case anyone you know would like to apply, check the Admissions procedures, where you will find the tuition.

After Choate, you might want to head to Princeton for college. Go to http://www.princeton.edu/Siteware/CampusLife.shtml for a description of campus life. Click on "Pictures" under the heading, "About Princeton."

- How do you suppose your social life in high school and college would have been different if you had gone to Choate Rosemary Hall and Princeton? (In case you're one of the few who did, then how would your social life have been different if you hadn't?)
- How do you think the quality of your education might have been different?
- How do you think your life after college graduation would be different?

preferences. More specifically, wealthier people tend to be conservative on economic issues, opposing such measures as government regulation of business and increases in the minimum wage. On the other hand, the higher classes are usually more liberal on social issues such as free speech, abortion, and separation between church and state (Lipset, 1959; Gilbert & Kahl, 1993). As for political participation, the lower classes are less likely to vote or become involved in community political life, which only intensifies their powerlessness (Conway, 1991).

Voluntary Associations. The lower classes are not just less likely to be politically involved, they are less likely to join any organizations other than unions and churches (Hyman & Wright, 1971). This reluctance to join groups is significant because only by working together with others can people safeguard their rights and achieve social change.

Religion. Different denominations appeal more to some classes than to others (Roof, 1979; Johnstone, 1997). Episcopalians and Presbyterians generally come from higher-class backgrounds than Methodists, Lutherans, and Catholics, who are, in turn, typically

better off than Baptists and members of religious sects. The church services of the poor tend to be more emotional and more focused on the rewards of the next world than are the services of middle-class congregations.

Communication Styles. People in different classes learn to express themselves differently as they grow up. Some research suggests that working-class people are less direct and self-assured than people in the middle class (Schatzman & Strauss, 1972). But even if the communication styles of all classes were equally effective, to middle-class audiences the speech patterns typical of the lower classes would still carry a stigma.

SOCIETY CONNECTIONS: Welfare

In discussing the welfare system, it is important to keep two points in mind. First, the vast majority of government spending for social needs is relatively noncontroversial because it is not **means-tested.** This means that people do not have to fall below a particular specified income level in order to be eligible for the program. The amount of money the government spends on Social Security, Medicare, unemployment compensation, public education, mortgage subsidies through tax deductions, and other similar social programs dwarfs what most people think of as "welfare" (Goodgame, 1993). Public debate becomes intense primarily when programs are proposed to assist the poor.

Second, we must distinguish between two kinds of means-tested welfare efforts: *antidestitution programs*, which simply supply poor people with enough money to make ends meet, and *antipoverty programs*, which, in addition to meeting people's immediate needs, also help them obtain job skills and address the structural factors which promote poverty.

Large-scale means-tested welfare programs began only after tens of millions of hard working Americans became impoverished in the early 1930s. Only then did many people begin to acknowledge that poverty does indeed have structural causes. Some of the earliest welfare programs consisted of simple cash grants to the poor, in particular the Aid to Dependent Children (ADC) program, which began in 1935. But others, such as the Civilian Conservation Corps and the Works Project Administration, provided both jobs and training and were, therefore, true antipoverty programs.

When the Depression ended, most of the work-training programs were phased out. ADC, however, was retained and, in 1950, it was renamed Aid to Families with Dependent Children (AFDC) to reflect the

Well-constructed welfare programs can help children to overcome the disadvantage of being born in poverty, but the stigma attached to public assistance sometimes keeps poor families from accepting assistance from the government.

fact that caregivers, usually mothers, could now also receive government assistance. In time, AFDC became the cornerstone of the nation's welfare system.

Again in the 1960s, a number of innovative antipoverty programs were developed. However, they weren't fully funded, at least in the eyes of their supporters, and most, with the exception of Head Start, were dismantled as the country swung to the right in the 1970s. The 1960s also saw the startup of food stamps, another major antidestitution program.

By the early 1990s, hard economic times had increased welfare rolls by about 20 percent (DeParle, 1992). AFDC was supporting over 13 million individuals in 5 million families, two-thirds of them children. In 1994, 27.5 million people received food stamps. Although the benefits of both programs had already been sharply reduced by the Reagan and Bush administrations—the real cash value of the average AFDC award had declined by 40 percent since 1972—the public supported even broader changes in the welfare system.

How may we explain the political popularity of President Clinton's promise to "end welfare as we know it"? Widespread misunderstandings concerning AFDC and other welfare programs contributed heavily to this political mood. Here are some of these misunderstandings—and the facts that refute them:

1. *Most poor people get welfare.* In 1994, just 27 percent of the people living under the poverty line received AFDC, which is what most people mean by "welfare." Forty-three percent received food stamps, 41 percent were enrolled in Medicaid, and 19 percent were helped with housing expenses. Twenty-seven percent of the poor received no government aid at all (1995 Statistical Abstract).

2. *Most welfare recipients are black.* In fact, fewer than half of the people on AFDC were African Americans.

3. *Welfare is a very expensive program.* In the mid-1990s, AFDC expenditures made up about 2 percent of the federal budget and between 3 and 4 percent of most state budgets. The total cost of the program at both levels was about $25 billion per year. This was roughly half the cost of the federal home mortgage tax deduction (which overwhelmingly benefits the more affluent) and less than 10 percent of either the defense budget or the cost of Social Security. AFDC expenditures accounted for just 4 percent of all welfare spending by the government and were equivalent to 0.4 percent of the nation's gross national product.

It is worth noting that the nations that provide the most generous welfare benefits—Sweden, Norway, and Germany—are the best both at moving the poor into jobs and at keeping overall poverty rates low, often below 6 percent.

4. *Life on welfare is easy.* Welfare benefits vary by state. In 1994 the median national monthly benefit was $381. In Mississippi, the average was just $122. In no state did AFDC plus food stamps bring recipients up to the poverty line (Sidel, 1996). Furthermore, the real value of welfare has been declining for decades. Measured in constant dollars, the typical family enrolled in both AFDC and food stamp programs received $10,133 in 1970 and $7,657 in 1992.

5. *Welfare promotes poverty because most recipients become dependent on it.* The truth is, the sizable majority of recipients do not stay on the welfare rolls very long

Getting Off Welfare

Shari Pharr, a 28-year-old mother of two, was angry and scared. Two weeks earlier, the state of Wisconsin had begun requiring welfare recipients to earn their monthly checks by attending job-training classes or performing community service while they looked for work.

Shari came from a "welfare family." Her mother, who had six children with five different men, had been on disability since her last husband shoved her out of a moving car. Shari only met her father once, when she was 5 years old. Following her mother's pattern, she became pregnant before her junior year of high school. Her boyfriend denied he was the father of their son, yet berated her for being on welfare. When she criticized him for losing one job after another because of his drinking, he abandoned her. For a short time, Shari worked for a company that made decorative candles for K-Mart, walking 40 minutes to and from work to save the cost of bus fare. When the company moved and Shari, who was pregnant again, lost her job, she went back on welfare. The father of her second child became addicted to crack and increasingly abusive. Shari later recalled, "I kept asking, what's wrong with me? Why is my life not working out?" She and her mother often cried about the bad men they had known. She hated the stereotype of the "welfare queen," collecting checks and spending all day in a bathrobe watching TV. Shari got up at 7:00 each morning, got dressed, and went out with her children, even if she had nowhere particular to go.

When the state of Wisconsin initiated welfare reform, Shari began attending job-training classes at the Milwaukee Job Center North, which emphasized speaking proper English and dressing properly. Like many others in the class, she found the experience patronizing. "They called us lazy," she said. Told that until she got a real job, she would have to sort and fold old clothes donated to Goodwill, Shari demanded to see her caseworker.

Preston White had grown up in the same neighborhood in which Shari now lived. He had been a case manager for five years, an easy but boring job that entailed little more than adding up benefits for poor women on the dole, or "the grant" as welfare was known in Wisconsin. At first, White was opposed to welfare reform: He was afraid that he couldn't make himself cut benefits for poor women and "throw their kids into the street" and afraid that he would lose his job if he didn't. But his attitude slowly changed. Many of his clients saw themselves as victimized by racism, the men in their lives, and the system, and therefore as entitled to welfare. They viewed getting an entry-level, "Mc-Work" job as giving into "the Man." And this attitude was a main obstacle to finding employment. White began to see welfare as an addiction and himself as "an enabler."

When Shari entered his office in March 1997, White recognized the resentment in her folded arms and hunched shoulders. He also noted that she was neatly dressed and had a small scar above her eye (inflicted by a former boyfriend). When she declared that she would not fold laundry, he challenged her to organize his office. In two weeks, she put his files in order, cleared the clutter on his desk, and began doing the same for other caseworkers. Soon after, Shari applied for a job at a warehouse sorting and packing chemicals for shipment. The interviewer found her bright and eager. A supervisor passing through his office asked, in jest, "Hey, I need another truck driver. Can you do that?" Without hesitation Shari responded, "No, but I can learn if that's what it takes." She was hired on the spot.

Shari now earns almost $10 an hour—enough to save for the house she hopes to buy one day. She is seeing a man she met at work who respects her as a working mom. Shari knows that if she loses this job or if her 10-year-old son, Charlie, gets into trouble, she could fall back "into that bad life." But her eyes sparkle when she describes a planned trip to a lake over Memorial Day weekend—her first real vacation in many years.

Her caseworker, White, has also changed. Welfare reform forced him to get involved and made him feel that he could change lives. Instead of just pushing papers, he was actually using his training as a social worker. About three-quarters of White's clients have found at least part-time work, but he worries about those who have serious drug or alcohol problems, do not show up for appointments or job training, and will soon lose all their benefits.

1. Were there any factors that made it easier for Shari Pharr to get off welfare than it might have been for some of Preston White's other clients? What were they?
2. What widely believed myths about welfare are challenged by Shari's story?

Source: McKormick Thomas, 1997.

(Corcoran et al., 1985; Sawhill, 1988). Most become eligible for assistance because of some sort of life crisis—unemployment, illness, divorce—and get off it as soon as they are back on their feet again (Bane & Ellwood, 1994). Seventy percent of all AFDC recipients left the program within two years, and 85 percent did so within four years (Bane & Ellwood, 1994). Seventy-one percent of adult recipients have recent work experience (Sidel, 1996: 12). Some of these people will need help again when another crisis comes along, but the vast majority of recipients do not become dependent upon government aid.

The benefits are too low, staying eligible is a bureaucratic hassle, and the stigma of being on welfare is too great.

It is true that some people *are* long-term welfare dependent. About 2.5 million people, 1 percent of the population, are locked into persistent poverty. Seven percent of the welfare population in the mid-1990s had received aid for at least eight straight years. Studies of these "hard-core" poor show that most are unmarried African American women with children, many of whom were raised in welfare families and became eligible for aid when they became pregnant as teenagers. They typically have low levels of education and few job skills (Devine et al., 1992).

However, 80 percent of daughters whose mothers received AFDC for at least eight consecutive years become self-supporting as adults (Ruggles, 1989). So, it is true there are people for whom welfare becomes a way of life and they are a genuine challenge to public policy. But they are a relatively small and quite atypical group compared to most welfare recipients. To remake public policy on the assumption that most AFDC families are like them is irrational.

6. *Welfare promotes poverty because it encourages single-parent families.* Until the 1990s, state laws generally denied AFDC to families in which an adult male was present. These policies were based on the assumption—far more valid in the past than today, given the nation's changing occupational structure—that any man could find work that would keep his family out of poverty. Under these circumstances, welfare did encourage family breakup. But this situation was the result of an ill-conceived policy; it was not an inevitable consequence of giving aid to the poor.

More generally, the trend toward single parenting is by no means limited to the poor. Female-headed single-parent families are becoming increasingly common at all class levels. The fact that they are especially prevalent among poor people is due to the lack of decent jobs in the U.S. economy. Men who are unable to adequately support their families do not make attractive potential husbands. Thus, single-parent families are not a major cause of poverty; they are mostly the result of larger structural factors (Sidel, 1996).

7. *Welfare promotes poverty because it encourages out-of-wedlock births.* A final popular myth is that unmarried poor women deliberately have large families in order to bring in larger benefit checks. In fact, the average size of welfare families has been shrinking since the early 1970s. In 1993, 71 percent of the families receiving AFDC included only one or two children; only 10 percent had four or more (see Figure 11.8).

Research shows no connection between the amount of welfare grants and the size of families among the poor. In fact, states whose payment levels are low tend to have higher rates of illegitimacy. Furthermore, women are less likely to have another child while on AFDC than are other low-income mothers (Rank, 1989). This should not be surprising: Welfare payments are far from generous (Edin, 1991; Jarret, 1994), and recipients know well that the cost of raising another child exceeds any increase in AFDC benefits.

Despite the facts, many people believe some or all of these myths. Only about 30 percent of the public realizes that most recipients truly need the welfare benefits they are receiving ("Welfare mistrust," 1996). Quite simply, the popular definition of the problem has shifted: Until recently, the problem was *poverty*; now it is *welfare* (Bray, 1992).

The mid-1990s saw substantial changes in welfare programs. The 1995 federal budget cut spending for means-tested welfare programs by $54 billion over the following six years, while leaving other entitlement programs, such as Social Security, Medicare, and unemployment compensation, largely untouched. The food-stamp program was especially deeply cut. And, in 1996, President Clinton signed into law a bill ending the federal government's sixty-year formal commitment to aiding all poor people.

This legislation terminated the AFDC program and restructured remaining federal welfare funds as bloc grants to the states in a program called TANF (Temporary Assistance to Needy Families). It lifted most previous restrictions and allowed states to develop new approaches to fighting poverty. It required states to move 25 percent of their welfare recipients into jobs or work activities (including job training) by the end of 1997 and 50 percent by 2002.

The 1996 bill also denies welfare aid to legal immigrants and establishes a lifetime limit of five years of federal funding for any particular individual, although states can exempt up to 20 percent of their clients from this requirement if they wish. It allows states to reduce benefits to the children of single mothers who refuse to name the fathers and to deny unmarried teenaged mothers assistance unless they stay at home and in school (Alter, 1996). It does not explicitly allocate federal money for job training, job creation, health insurance, or child care, although individual states can fund such programs if they wish.

What are we to make of these changes? They seem unlikely to result in a stronger antidestitution program, since the overall level of federal funding has been reduced. Nor is TANF at the federal level in and of itself an antipoverty program; it does nothing to directly address the structural causes of poverty. It can easily be argued that TANF is less an antidestitu-

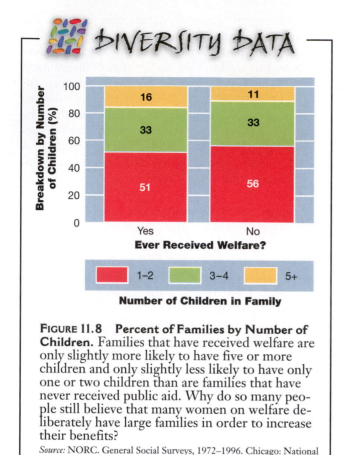

DIVERSITY DATA

FIGURE 11.8   Percent of Families by Number of Children. Families that have received welfare are only slightly more likely to have five or more children and only slightly less likely to have only one or two children than are families that have never received public aid. Why do so many people still believe that many women on welfare deliberately have large families in order to increase their benefits?

Source: NORC. General Social Surveys, 1972–1996. Chicago: National Opinion Research Center, 1996. Reprinted by permission of NORC, Chicago, IL.

tion or an antipoverty program than an antiwelfare program.

Many states have chosen to go beyond what the federal government requires and adopted true antipoverty strategies, but history suggests that only the more progressive ones are likely to fund such programs adequately. For example, Wisconsin and Illinois, among the national leaders in the antipoverty effort, have spent many millions of dollars on job training, child care, and expanded health benefits. Research clearly shows that these provisions work (Sack, 1992; Alter, 1996). But how many states will make such an effort?

The 1996 welfare bill clearly assumes that the primary cause of poverty is individual, not structural. This interpretation suggests that what is mostly needed is a "big stick"—a threat of utter destitution—

to motivate welfare recipients to get a job, any job. This approach is succeeding in that between 1994 and 2000 the number of people receiving welfare dropped from 14.2 million to 6.3 million, a decline of 56 percent (Hopper, 2000).

But the long-term prospects are unclear, especially when the current high rate of economic growth falters as it inevitably must (Samuelson, 1997). Each state will respond somewhat differently. Fortunately, there are enough loopholes built into the law so that many of the harshest provisions are likely to be moderated in practice (Kaus, 1997).

The old AFDC program certainly had its weaknesses, and the new rules have moved more poor mothers off welfare and into the labor force. However, most of the people who are cut off from welfare take low-paying jobs, often with few benefits and offering limited career opportunities. More specifically, between 50 and 65 percent of the adults who have lost their welfare benefits are in the work force, earning an average of between $5.50 and $7.50 per hour ("Life after welfare," 1999).

Without adequate job training and having to pay for child care, health insurance, work clothes, and transportation from their meager paychecks, many of these women—and their children—will remain poor. Moreover, because they will be working full time and also raising children, they are unlikely to attend school—their best hope of improving future job prospects (Harris, 1993). And what of those who simply are not employable? The people who are still receiving TANF are, in general, very poorly prepared to successfully enter the job market. Most have no work experience and little education; many have criminal records and drug habits.

Today, poverty is not a major item on the national agenda. If we ask why not, the answer is evident: Political priorities are determined by the upper and upper-middle classes, the classes that have power to shape the political process. The situation is not hopeless; the lower classes have successfully affected political decision making at times in the past. The Global Connections box, "How Do Other Nations Fight Poverty," discusses some experiences of other societies from which Americans might learn. But, in the end, we come back to where we began this chapter, with the observation that in the battle against poverty—or welfare—as in every other aspect of social life, *class matters!*

SUMMARY

1. Most sociologists use the objective approach to operationalize the variable of class, although some prefer the subjective or reputational methods.

2. Property—both income and wealth—is an important objective dimension of class. The gap between the rich and the poor, especially with regard to wealth, is greater in the United States than in other modern societies, and it is currently increasing.
3. Occupational prestige is a second important objective factor separating social classes.
4. Erik Olin Wright identifies four classes in U.S. society: capitalists, managers, the petit bourgeoisie, and workers.
5. Theorists such as Gilbert and Kahl divide U.S. society into ranked groups: the upper, upper-middle, lower-middle, and working classes, the working poor, and the "underclass."
6. Poverty is usually defined in absolute terms, but some sociologists believe that a relative definition presents a more accurate image.
7. The percentage of people living in poverty declined in the 1960s and early 1970s, but since then it has fluctuated at a somewhat higher level than previously. Currently, it is at very low levels due to the strong economy.
8. Poverty is concentrated among children, minorities, and women; it is an especially serious problem in single-parent female-headed families.
9. Sociologists find more support for system-blaming explanations of poverty than for kinds-of-people approaches such as the culture of poverty theory.
10. Most social mobility in modern societies is structural mobility.
11. The United States has historically offered substantial opportunities for upward social mobility, but recent trends suggest that downward mobility, especially out of the middle class, may be increasingly common in the immediate future.
12. Social class strongly influences people's life chances regarding such matters as physical health and mortality, mental health, self-esteem, education, and crime victimization.
13. Class also affects lifestyle patterns of child socialization, family life, politics, voluntary association membership, religion, and communication styles.
14. Public policies concerning poverty can be categorized as antidestitution, antipoverty, or antiwelfare approaches.
15. Research has found that many widely held beliefs about poverty are inaccurate. Nevertheless, these beliefs strongly influence public responses to the problem.
16. TANF has substantially reduced welfare rolls, but it is unclear whether it will be effective in actually fighting poverty.

KEY TERMS

absolute poverty 277
culture of poverty 279
deindustrialization 280
feminization of poverty 278
horizontal mobility 280
income 270
intergenerational social mobility 280

intragenerational social mobility 280
means-tested 286
objective approach 269
relative poverty 277
reputational approach 268
social mobility 280

socioeconomic status (SES) 269
structural mobility 280
subjective approach 268
vertical mobility 280
victim blaming 279
wealth 270

CRITICAL THINKING QUESTIONS

1. If current predictions about increasing rates of downward social mobility are borne out, how do you think most Americans will react?
2. Can you think of any aspects of social life that are not affected by social class?
3. What are some reasons many Americans believe some or all of the welfare myths discussed in this chapter?
4. Why do you think the United States is characterized by more inequality and fewer public efforts to reduce inequality than almost all other developed nations?

12 RACIAL AND ETHNIC MINORITIES

OUTLINE

Racial Profiling

In the late 1990s a new name—*racial profiling*—emerged to describe a familiar practice. Police were being accused of disproportionately stopping minority drivers and searching them for illegal drugs. Victims sometimes complained that they had been "pulled over for a DWB" (Driving While Black—or Brown). The language was ironic but the problem was real.

For example, Dr. Elmo Randolph, a 42-year-old African American dentist from New Jersey, complained that his gold BMW had been stopped at least fifty times over the past eight years yet the police had never issued him a ticket. Research by Temple University psychologist John Lamberth revealed that while 85 percent of the motorists on one section of I-95 were white, 35 percent of those pulled over and three-fourths of those arrested were African Americans.

From the perspective of blameless minority drivers who found themselves hassled by the police, racial profiling was just the latest indignity in a long history of oppression. On the other hand, although few law enforcement officers openly defended the practice, the fact that African Americans and Hispanics are arrested and convicted for drug offenses at much higher rates than whites seemed to justify giving special attention to minority drivers. Critics responded by noting that racial profiling sets up a self-fulfilling prophecy: If the police mainly investigate African American or Hispanic suspects, then they will primarily apprehend minority offenders, thus distorting the racial composition of the official crime data, which they in turn use to justify their biased practices. (Cannon, 1999; Hosenball, 1999)

America's New Wave of Immigration

Immigrants have been remaking the face of America for centuries. Today about 23 million residents of this country—8.4 percent of the population—were born somewhere else. Vietnam is one of the most important sources of contemporary migration into the United States. Only a handful of Vietnamese lived here when the war in Indochina ended in 1975, but the 1990 census showed a rapidly growing population already at 615,000. Current estimates suggest that there are over a million Vietnamese Americans. (Parrillo, 2000: 303)

Unlike earlier immigrant groups, many of which settled in ethnic communities in large cities, the Vietnamese are more widely dispersed. They live not only on the West Coast but also in such places as the gulf shore of Texas, Atlanta, and the suburbs of Washington, DC. Eden Center in Falls Church, Virginia, has become the largest Vietnamese shopping center in the country, boasting ethnic restaurants, travel agents specializing in flights across the Pacific, and nightclubs featuring the latest hits direct from Ho Chi Minh City. The center—70 percent of whose customers are Asian—flies both the U.S. and the Vietnamese flags and is decorated with traditional Oriental arches and a replica of a famous clock tower from old Saigon. (Clark, 1997)

Much more than most of the world's societies, the United States is a complex mosaic of racial and ethnic minority groups. Some, like Native Americans, African Americans, and Hispanics, have lived here for centuries or even millennia; others, like Vietnamese Americans, are much more recent arrivals. All have experienced some measure of discrimination, such as racial profiling. All have had to strike a balance between trying to fit into the dominant culture and, like the Vietnamese of Falls Church, maintaining their own distinctive lifestyles.

Most of the Vietnamese who immigrated to the United States in the 1970s arrived with few possessions. However, the strong work ethic and emphasis on education characteristic of their culture have helped many Vietnamese-American children to excel in school and achieve substantial upward social mobility.

We will begin this chapter by discussing a series of key concepts including race, ethnicity, minority groups, prejudice, discrimination, and racism. Next, we will consider the various ways that dominant and minority groups interact and we will take a brief look at the history and present circumstances of selected minority groups. The chapter concludes with a discussion of the emergence of multiracialism in America and a critical assessment of the policy of affirmative action.

RACE, ETHNICITY, AND MINORITY GROUPS

The peoples whom sociologists have traditionally regarded as minorities may be somewhat arbitrarily divided into races and ethnic groups.

Race: A Social Concept

Although nineteenth century scientists devoted a great deal of time to investigating what they believed to be the inherent characteristics of different races, we now know that what most people call races are nothing more than the result of the historic geographic isolation of human populations in very different environments (Smedley, 1999). Over the millennia, adaptation to environmental factors produced localized groupings of people with different skin colors, facial features, and so forth. There was never any set number of races; nor was there ever such a thing as a "pure" race (Montagu, 1964; Cavalli-Sforza et al., 1994).

The variations within any one race are generally greater than those that exist between different races. For example, Caucasians range from the blond hair and very light skin of Scandinavians to the dark skin and black hair of Asian Indians. Moreover, in the modern world, geographic mobility combined with increasing rates of intermarriage are gradually eroding the racial differences that do exist (Smedley, 1999).

Even more significant, the biological differences between groups identified as races are trivial. There is

INTERNET **CONNECTIONS**

Chapter 12 begins with a discussion of *racial profiling* and the predicament faced by some African Americans known as "DWB" (Driving While Black). The American Civil Liberties Union (ACLU) hosts a Web site that deals exclusively with the phenomenon of racial profiling, instructively entitled, *Arrest the Racism: Racial Profiling in America:* http://www.aclu.org/profiling/. When you access the opening page, click on one or more news articles within the "What's New" section. These installments illustrate racial profiling in action and highlight some of the legal and constitutional issues involved. Do you agree or disagree with the practice of racial profiling and why? What do you think the long-term implications of this practice will be?

Conflict between the Protestant and Catholic communities in Northern Ireland has continued for over 350 years. Outdoor murals cover the walls of many working-class homes throughout the province, proudly and aggressively identifying the ethnicity—in this case, Protestant—of the area's inhabitants.

no credible evidence that people of different races are innately different from each other in any significant way, either in temperament or in mental or physical abilities (Shanklin, 1993).

But the fact that race is biologically meaningless does not mean that it is sociologically insignificant. As we discussed in Chapter 6, the Thomas Theorem holds that what people believe to be real is real in its consequences.

The view that race is an important determinant of human behavior and, in particular, the ideology of white superiority emerged in the late 1700s as part of the Europeans' justification of their colonial domination of nonwhite people around the world (Reynolds, 1992). In the United States, this way of thinking became a cornerstone of the intellectual defense of slavery (J. Marks, 1994). Even after slavery ended, whites treated people of color differently, refusing them opportunities that members of the dominant group took for granted.

Today, sociologists are agreed that race is a sociological, not a biological, concept (Omi & Winant, 1994). We may define a **race** as a category of people who *are believed* to have significant biological differences that *are believed* to affect their character and ability to function in society.

Ethnic Groups

If race is—or, at least, is believed to be—about biology, ethnicity is a matter of culture. An **ethnic group** is a category of people who are seen by themselves and others as sharing a distinct subculture, somewhat different from the culture of the dominant group (Alba, 1992; Feagin & Feagin, 1999).

Of course, most racial groups also have somewhat distinctive cultures, but because race is so visible, racial identity usually overshadows ethnicity. Most people who are classified as ethnics in the United States are whites identified by their country of origin: Irish Americans, Italian Americans, Mexican Americans, and so forth. As these terms suggest, ethnicity is closely linked to migration (Handlin, 1992). When culturally distinct immigrants arrive in a new society, they commonly share a strong sense of ethnic identity or peoplehood. This is especially true if they come in large numbers, are quite different culturally from the dominant group, and experience substantial prejudice and discrimination (Doane, 1993).

If, however, succeeding generations adapt the dominant culture and start climbing the social class ladder, ethnic identity usually starts to fade (Gordon, 1964). This has already occurred with most European ethnic groups. In fact, children of the third and fourth generations often consciously seek to recapture the ethnic identity their grandparents and great-grandparents abandoned, an activity sociologists refer to as *ethnic work.*

Minority Groups

A **minority group,** whether racial or ethnic, is defined above all by its lack of power—economic power, political power, or simply the power to define what it means to be a member of the group. For this reason, sociologists often refer to minority groups as *subordinate groups* (Feagin & Feagin, 1999).

Most minority groups are smaller in number than the groups that hold the majority of the power, known as dominant groups. In the United States, the

Disability Culture: The Making of a Minority Group

Until quite recently, many disabled Americans were assigned to special classes in school, if they attended school at all; confined to hospitals and institutions; and refused advanced education or jobs. They were denied the right to make decisions regarding their own lives, even as adults. The disabled had no groups of their own to lobby for their rights.

However, disabled Americans have become increasingly well-organized and outspoken in recent years. After decades of fighting for access to everything from buses to colleges, groups such as Disabled in Action are putting forward ideas that shock many Americans. They disapprove of telethons to help the disabled, which they see as patronizing. They laugh at such politically correct labels as "physically challenged" and, perhaps most surprising to the nondisabled, many oppose the search for cures. "I would not trade my disability for anything," says Nadia LaSpina, a professor at the New School for Social Research in New York City who had polio as a child. LaSpina and others hold that disabled Americans have developed a distinct subculture and shared identity based on their minority group status.

Do disabled Americans qualify as a minority group? In sociological terms, the most important defining characteristic of minority groups is their lack of power—not just economic and political power, but also the power to define their own identity. A second defining characteristic of minority groups is that they are subject to prejudice and discrimination. At least publicly, most people are sympathetic—not hostile—toward disabled people. But pity can be a mask for revulsion, and it can accompany the unspoken belief that someone who does not meet our standards of "normal" appearance and behavior should keep out of sight.

Disabled Americans have been subjected to both direct and indirect institutional discrimination. Activists point out that Hitler murdered 200,000 handicapped people before launching his campaign of extermination against the Jews. In this country, disabled people have historically been scorned and incarcerated. Consider an individual example: Sherry Lampert has cerebral palsy. Although she is above average in intelligence, her parents placed her in a hospital ward for the mentally retarded. At 16, she tried to kill herself. Sherry recalls, "I felt like I wasn't part of the human race." Now 49, Lambert lives in her own apartment, with the assistance of round-the-clock attendants, and is a disability rights activist.

Indirect institutional discrimination took the form of unintentional exclusion. Public buildings, housing, transportation, and communication systems generally were designed for the able-bodied. As a result, many disabled Americans could not attend school; use public transportation; visit museums, stadiums, and the like; or shop for or live by themselves.

A third characteristic of minorities is in-group solidarity. As recently as 1990, few social scientists would have felt that disabled Americans met this criterion. But this is changing. Group consciousness among the disabled dates back at least to 1962, when quadriplegic Edward V. Roberts won his suit to be admitted to the University of California. After graduating, Roberts founded the Center for Independent Living (CID) in Berkeley, an organization dedicated to providing disabled people with the social, psychological, and technical means to lead autonomous lives.

In April 1977, CID joined other activist groups to protest the government's failure to enforce the 1973 Rehabilitation Act, which requires businesses that accept federal contracts to practice affirmative action in employing disabled people and to make "reasonable accommodations" to their needs. In San Francisco, 150 disabled people organized by CID occupied City Hall for more than three weeks, sent representatives to Washington, and attracted media attention. The San Francisco sit-in marked the beginning of the disability rights movement.

New legislation and court decisions provide disabled people the same rights given to other minority groups by the civil rights legislation of the 1960s. Federal law now guarantees mentally or physically disabled children "free appropriate public education" regardless of the severity of their condition. The landmark 1990 American with Disabilities Act prohibits discrimination against people with physical or mental disability in employment, public accommodations, transportation, and telecommunications. Carol Gill, the psychologist who coined the term "disability culture," herself a quadriplegic, has identified the basic characteristics of this emerging subculture: tolerance for differences, highly developed skills for managing multiple problems, and dark humor (as in the bumper sticker, "Not Dead Yet"). To be sure, only a small percentage of the estimated 48 million disabled Americans are part of this community, but their numbers are growing.

1. This essay has emphasized the ways in which the disabled are similar to members of other minority groups. In what ways are they different? How do these differences affect the way they are treated?

2. Do you believe the disabled should strive for full assimilation, pluralism, or separatism?

3. Businesses sometimes complain that the costs of complying with the ADA are prohibitive, especially since few of their customers are disabled. How would you respond to these charges?

Source: Text excerpts from "Eager to Bite the Hands That Would Feed Them" by Douglas Martin from *The New York Times,* June 1, 1997, Section 4, pp. 1, 6. Copyright © 1977 by The New York Times Company. Reprinted by permission of The New York Times Company.

dominant group—whites, especially those of Northern European heritage—has historically outnumbered African Americans, Hispanics, and other minorities. However, there are some exceptions to this rule. Blacks in apartheid-era South Africa provide a good example.

Because of their powerlessness, minorities experience both prejudice and discrimination—concepts we will explore more fully shortly. Members of a minority group are, by definition, stigmatized in the eyes of the dominant group. They are often treated not as individuals, but as members of a category. Further, most minority groups are based on ascribed statuses and tend to be *endogamous*, that is, members usually marry within their own group. Most minorities also develop a strong sense of in-group solidarity (Wirth, 1945; Wagley & Harris, 1958).

Around the world, minority groups are defined by various physical and cultural characteristics. Differences in skin color are particularly familiar to Americans, while Canadians usually think first of language (French versus English) and North Irish of religion (Catholic versus Protestant). For the most part, the more visible the defining characteristic, the more sharply minority and dominant groups are separated from each other and the more harsh the *stigma*—or negative social label—borne by the minority.

Double Jeopardy: The Additive Effects of Multiple Minority Group Membership. People who are members of more than one minority group—such as Jewish African Americans—tend to encounter increased levels of prejudice and discrimination based on the sum of their devalued identities. The signifi-

cance of multiple minority status becomes especially apparent when note that gender (Chapter 13) and other statuses such as age (Chapter 14) and sexual orientation (Chapter 7) commonly disadvantage people in much the same way as race and ethnicity do. Thus, for example, the median individual income in 1997 for white males was $26,115; for African American males, $18,096; but African American females earned only $13,038 (U.S. 1999: Bureau of the Census, Table 756).

PREJUDICE, DISCRIMINATION, AND RACISM

Both race and ethnicity are frequently *master statuses*—that is, they are often the primary determinants of how people are thought of and treated. Accordingly, we turn now to the dynamics of prejudice and discrimination.

Prejudice

A prejudice is, literally, a pre-judgment. Sociologists define **prejudice** as a negative attitude toward an entire category of people (Allport, 1958). Prejudice involves two components: a negative emotional reaction toward a group and a cognitive or intellectual element, usually called a stereotype.

Stereotypes are overgeneralizations about a category of people that are applied to all members of that category. Stereotypes may be accurate descriptions of some members within a group, but assuming that everyone in a certain group displays a particular trait

The members of many ethnic groups, even those who have lived in this country for several generations, keep the traditions of their homeland alive through street festivals such as this fiesta in Los Angeles, which features Mexican clothing, dances, and foods.

limits our ability to understand social reality. Even positive stereotypes, like the common belief that Asian Americans are highly intelligent, force people into pigeonholes and distort our perceptions of them (MacRae et al., 1996).

People who think in stereotypes tend to ignore evidence that contradicts their assumptions. Presented with an individual whose behavior does not fit the stereotype—for example, a Rhodes scholar who is a member of a minority group thought to lack intelligence—prejudiced people generally respond in one of two ways. They may say that the person is "the exception that proves the rule" (a truly absurd notion when you think about it), or they may redefine the behavior so that it fits their prejudgment: "It's amazing how cunning some of them are" (Jenkins, 1994a).

Is prejudice declining in the United States? There is no doubt that the *public* expression of stereotypes and prejudiced attitudes is less acceptable in many circles today than it was a generation or two ago. Research suggests that younger and better-educated people are especially likely to reject prejudice (Firebaugh & Davis, 1988; Bobo & Kluegel, 1991; Ransford & Palisi, 1992). But do these findings accurately reflect people's real feelings (Bakanic, 1995)? Quite a bit of evidence suggests that they do not: Hate crimes have apparently been increasing, and researchers continue to find high levels of prejudice on college campuses (Muir, 1991).

Prejudices are, by definition, attitudes, not actions. But insofar as they confirm dominant group members' assumptions of superiority, they can lead to unequal treatment of minorities, a type of behavior sociologists call discrimination.

Discrimination

Discrimination consists of treating individuals unequally and unjustly on the basis of their group memberships (Feagin & Feagin, 1996). In modern societies, widespread norms mandate equal treatment of all people. Teachers and employers, for example, must not let ascribed factors such as race, ethnicity, and gender influence how they treat their students and employees. Anyone who violates these norms is guilty of discrimination.

Until quite recently, however, most Americans openly accepted and, indeed, encouraged discrimination (Rose, 1990). For example, the Constitution denied African Americans the right to vote until 1865. Well into the 1960s, courts allowed restrictive covenants in real estate, which stipulated that house buyers would not resell to African Americans, Jews, or other "undesirables."

A given act of discrimination may be classified as individual, direct institutional, or indirect institu-

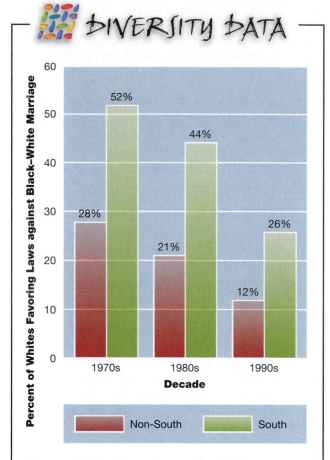

DIVERSITY DATA

FIGURE 12.1 Opposition among Whites to Racially Mixed Marriages, by Decade and Region. Over the past thirty years, racially mixed marriages have become more acceptable to all white Americans. However, Southerners remain consistently less tolerant of such marriages than people from other parts of the country. What factors would influence an increasing acceptance of racially mixed marriages?
Source: NORC. General Social Surveys, 1972–1996. Chicago: National Opinion Research Center, 1996.

tional. **Individual discrimination** is familiar to everyone (Carmichael & Hamilton, 1967). If your uncle refuses to hire an accountant to do his taxes because she is Hispanic or female, his behavior is clearly discriminatory. Today, few Americans publicly condone individual discrimination, although many still practice it.

Direct institutional discrimination (Davis, 1978; Feagin & Feagin, 1999) refers to openly biased practices of an institution. A bank that refuses to hire someone because he or she is African American or a university that won't admit a disabled student because its buildings are not handicapped accessible is guilty of institutional discrimination.

However, contrary to what most people believe, even if we could abolish all individual and direct

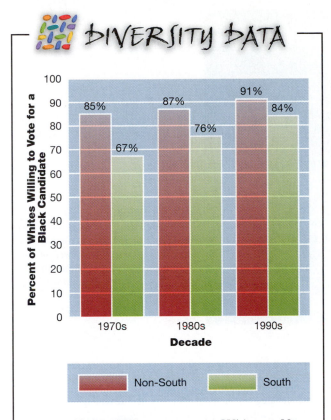

DIVERSITY DATA

FIGURE 12.2 **Willingness among Whites to Vote for an African American Candidate for President, by Decade and Region.** Over the past thirty years, white people throughout the country have indicated greater willingness to vote for a qualified African American candidate for president. However, opposition to an African American candidate remains strongest in the South. Southerners in the 1990s were about as willing to support a black for president as non-Southerners were in the 1970s. Do you think that the people answering this question were all being honest, or might some of them have just been trying to appear unprejudiced?

Source: NORC. General Social Surveys, 1972–1996. Chicago: National Opinion Research Center, 1996.

with the law. But if, instead, they announce that the layoffs are based on the "last hired, first fired" principle, then they do not appear to be discriminating, but the result is exactly the same: The minorities lose their jobs. Note that it is perfectly possible that the bank directors do not intend to be unfair—but, again, the result is the same.

Consider another example. Suppose that a law school announces that it will admit any student, white or black, whose grades and law board scores meet a given standard. This sounds non-discriminatory, doesn't it? But it fails to take into account the consequences of prior deliberate discrimination against African Americans. Compelled for generations to attend underfunded, segregated schools, until very recently few blacks had a realistic opportunity to prepare for college or do well on the law boards. Tremendous progress has been made in correcting these injustices, but to assume that the legacy of four hundred years of discrimination can be entirely undone in two generations is wildly optimistic. Given these realities, colorblind treatment is in fact frequently discriminatory against African Americans and other minorities.

The Relationship Between Prejudice and Discrimination. Is someone who discriminates necessarily prejudiced? Most of us assume that people's actions accurately reflect their inner feelings, but this is not necessarily true. Suppose, for example, that you were a totally unprejudiced white person living in the Deep South early in this century. If you owned a restaurant, would you serve African Americans? Not if you wanted to stay in business! If the Klan didn't shut you down, the local government would, since de jure segregation was in effect at the time. Similarly, suppose that you are a restaurant owner today in Madison, Wisconsin, and you just hate members of some ethnic group—say, the French. Are you going to post a big sign on your door saying "No French people admitted"? Again, not if you want to stay in business, because such a sign would offend many people's sensibilities and might also get you in trouble with the law.

The point is that you cannot always infer behavior from attitudes or vice versa. Sociologists have long known that what people think, say, and do often do not coincide (LaPierre, 1934; Kutner et al., 1952). As Robert Merton (1948) pointed out, people can be not only prejudiced discriminators and unprejudiced nondiscriminators, but they may also be, as suggested above, prejudiced nondiscriminators or nonprejudiced discriminators (see Figure 12.3). In fact, there is considerable evidence that prejudice is not the main cause of discrimination.

institutional discrimination, discriminatory behavior would persist. This is because of **indirect institutional discrimination**—policies that appear to be neutral or colorblind, but in practice discriminate against minority groups (Carmichael & Hamilton, 1967).

Here's how indirect institutional discrimination works: Suppose, for example, that a bank has recently hired a number of minority accountants, perhaps in response to pressure from civil rights groups. But now it must downsize its staff. If the bank directors simply fire the minorities overtly, they are guilty of direct institutional discrimination and might well be in trouble

The legally required racial segregation that was universal in the American Deep South prior to the late 1960s is an excellent example of direct institutional discrimination. While institutional discrimination against minorities endures in the United States, it is no longer this blatant.

Racism

In recent decades, the term "racism" has been tossed around so freely that some sociologists now hesitate to use the word at all (Wilson, 1987). However, it does have a core meaning that continues to be of value. In sociology, **racism** is understood to be an *ideology*, a way of thinking that justifies unequal treatment. More formally, racism is an ideology that maintains that one race is inherently superior to another (Miles, 1989).

Racist thought assumes that the concept of race is biologically meaningful and that race is directly related to ability. It has been used to defend virtually every form of discrimination from genocide to casual social exclusion (Doob, 1999).

EXPLAINING PREJUDICE AND DISCRIMINATION

Sociologists and social psychologists have proposed several theories to explain prejudice and discrimination.

Social Psychological Approaches

One of the earliest attempts to understand the origins of prejudice suggests that people who are frustrated, whether by a difficult home life, a boring job, poverty, or some other factor, and who are unable to strike back at the real cause of their frustration, often seek out **scapegoats,** people who are unfairly blamed for other people's problems (Dollard et al., 1939).

Minorities are convenient targets for scapegoating. They are relatively powerless, and there are often widely held beliefs among dominant group members that can be used to justify blaming them (Blackwell, 1982). A classic example is Hitler's scapegoating of the Jews for the ills that Germany experienced after its defeat in World War I. Another would be the wave of Japan-bashing that took place in the United States during the bad economic times of the late 1970s and early 1980s (Chan, 1991).

A second social-psychological perspective is based on the concept of the *authoritarian personality* (Adorno et al., 1950). According to this view, harsh child-rearing practices tend to produce people who are attracted to prejudiced patterns of thought. Uncomfortable with moral and ethical ambiguity, authoritarians tend to perceive people as either good or bad and to evaluate others as either their superiors or their inferiors. Minorities, of course, tend to fall in the latter category.

The reason we know that authoritarianism is a personality trait, not just a matter of learned bias, is that authoritarians tend to be willing to declare themselves opposed to all out-groups: African Americans, Latinos, gays, Jews, and so on (Hartley, 1946).

What are the policy implications of using social psychological perspectives to understand prejudice? They are twofold: We need to help people find less harmful ways of coping with daily frustrations and we need to improve our child-rearing practices.

Does the Person Discriminate?	
Yes	**No**

Is the Person Prejudiced?

Yes

Consistent Bigot
Prejudiced person who discriminates

Timid Bigot
Prejudiced person who does not discriminate

No

Fair-Weather Liberal
Nonprejudiced person who discriminates

Consistent Liberal
Nonprejudiced person who does not discriminate

FIGURE 12.3   The Relationship Between Prejudice and Discrimination.
Source: Merton, 1948.

Symbolic Interactionism

Symbolic interactionists, like all sociologists, take the social environment into account in constructing theories of prejudice and discrimination. In particular, they point out that attitudes toward minorities are *learned.* Research shows that by age 4 or 5, children have acquired attitudes concerning racial minorities from the people around them (Fishbein, 1996).

If prejudiced attitudes and discriminatory behavior are consistently reinforced, people learn to limit their perceptions of minorities in such a way that they never have to confront realities that might challenge their preexisting assumptions (Ehrlich, 1973). Learning theories take on particular significance when people grow up in cultures that embrace deeply racist worldviews, like the historic Deep South and South Africa.

Some symbolic interactionists go further and point out that the English language itself covertly supports racism. Suppose you were growing up as a person of color and learned that white was generally taken as a symbol of virtue ("as pure as the new driven snow") whereas darkness carries negative connotations ("a black mark on his character"). Could you ignore the implications of such symbolic expressions?

The primary policy implication of learning theory is that if prejudice is learned, it can be unlearned. According to the **contact hypothesis,** intergroup contact can reduce prejudice. However, members of each group must have equal status, be working together toward a common goal, and receive positive reinforcement for appropriate attitudes and behaviors (Sigelman & Welch, 1993).

Functionalism

Functionalists believe racist ideologies persist because they promote social stability. Minorities who have been socialized into accepting racist belief systems are

The Ku Klux Klan has long been America's best-known openly racist group. Today, the Klan is widely regarded as extremist and most people reject its views. However, more subtle forms of racism are widespread throughout American culture.

INTERNET ——— CONNECTIONS

The Ku Klux Klan is one of the most controversial groups in American history. Its point of view is on display at www.kukluxklan.com. Warning: Be aware that the openly racist content of this Web site will be highly offensive to most people. Do you believe that the First Amendment guarantee of free speech ought to apply even to groups like the Klan?

unlikely to challenge the existing arrangements (Levin & Levin, 1982). Furthermore, discrimination is clearly functional for dominant groups. Would you rather be a member of a group whose rights and opportunities are restricted or a member of the group doing the restricting? Who is likely to enjoy greater material rewards and prestige? The answers are self-evident.

However, functionalists also note that discrimination has several dysfunctions (Rose, 1951). It keeps society from making full use of the abilities of all of its citizens, and it aggravates social problems like poverty, crime, and family instability. Discrimination also requires substantial social control expenditures to keep down those discontent minorities who do not accept the dominant ideology.

The primary policy implication of the functionalist approach is that we must recognize the dysfunctions of racism and find less destructive ways of fulfilling the functions now served by prejudice and discrimination.

Conflict Theory

Conflict interpretations assume that conditions of unequal power and competition generate discrimination and emphasize the structural arrangements that create such conditions. There are several schools of thought within conflict theory.

For example, according to the *split labor market* perspective, modern societies are characterized by two distinct types of jobs. *Primary labor market* jobs generally pay well and offer fringe benefits and a chance of advancement. *Secondary labor market* jobs offer none of these advantages. Minorities are disproportionately channeled toward the secondary labor market, a pattern that benefits the entire dominant group, but particularly workers (Bonacich, 1972; Hodson & Kaufman, 1982). White workers defend

their advantage by keeping minorities out of their unions and opposing most civil rights initiatives.

In contrast, *Marxist exploitation theory* sees an economic elite benefiting from discrimination rather than the entire dominant group (Cox, 1948). Exploitation theory maintains that the ruling class deliberately promotes racism in order to divide the workers. Whites and minorities are taught to see each other rather than the owners as the enemy. As a result, workers are unlikely to join unions and similar organizations to demand fair treatment (Olzak & Nagel, 1986), and wages remain low. If dominant group workers unionize, African Americans and other minorities can be hired as strikebreakers because they are desperate for any kind of work (Bonacich, 1976). The big winners are the wealthy owners of the means of production. Workers—all workers—lose.

The policy implications of the conflict perspective are clear: The power differential between the elite and the masses must be sharply reduced. In such a restructured society, prejudice and discrimination would greatly diminish.

Table 12.1 summarizes and compares the major schools of thought concerning prejudice and discrimination.

PATTERNS OF MINORITY–DOMINANT GROUP RELATIONS

Dominant and minority groups can interact in many different ways. According to Simpson and Yinger (1985), most historical cases can be classified into one of six general categories: genocide, expulsion or population transfer, open subjugation, legal protection, assimilation, and pluralism.

Genocide

Genocide is the extermination of all or most of the members of a minority group. It is most likely to occur when the dominant group is much larger than the minority, when the minority is of little or no economic value to the dominant group, and when the dominant group needs a scapegoat to blame for economic or military setbacks (duPreez, 1994).

The best known modern example is doubtless the Holocaust, Hitler's "final solution" to the "Jewish problem." Six million Jews as well as hundreds of thousands of Roms (Gypsies), homosexuals, and other groups died in Nazi Germany's concentration camps (Baumann, 1991). Unfortunately, this was by no means the only instance of genocide in the twentieth century.

Table 12.1 Theoretical Explanations of Prejudice and Discrimination

	Specific Theories	Basic Logic	Policy Implications
Social Psychological Approaches	Scapegoat theory, authoritarian personality theory	Prejudice satisfies distinctive personality-level needs	Improve child-rearing practices and help people find more appropriate ways of dealing with everyday frustrations
Symbolic Interactionism	Learning theory	People learn prejudice and discrimination from those around them	Increase contacts with members of different groups; work to reduce biases inherent in culture
Functionalism	Functionalism	Prejudice and discrimination provide positive functions for some people	Find less harmful functional alternatives to prejudice and discrimination
Conflict Theory	Split labor market theory, Exploitation theory	Prejudice and discrimination help powerful groups maintain their advantages	Reduce power inequalities in society

For example, in 1915 the new Islamic government of Turkey ordered the forced deportation of the Christian Armenian minority, which led to the death of about 1 million people, more than half the total Armenian population. In the late 1970s, the Khmer Rouge in Cambodia killed at least 2 million people in an effort to wipe out all Western influences—even attempting to exterminate everyone who could read and write (Shawcross, 1979). The "ethnic cleansing" of Muslims and Croats by Serbian forces in Bosnia in the early 1990s cost thousands of lives (Watson, 1992). In 1994, the dominant group in the African nation of Rwanda, the Hutu, massacred almost a million Tutsi (Block, 1994; Gourevitch, 1995).

The principal victims of genocide in North America were the Native Americans. By 1890, the Indian population had been reduced by more than 90 percent (Garbarino & Sasso, 1994; Oswalt & Neely, 1999). Most of these deaths were caused by diseases such as smallpox, to which Native Americans had no resistance. Sometimes, however, the killings were deliberate. The view that "the only good Indian is a dead Indian" was widely endorsed in the nineteenth century (Dudley, 1998).

Expulsion and Population Transfer

Sometimes, under much the same circumstances that can lead to genocide, the dominant group forces a minority to emigrate or confines it to a limited territory. The decision to favor expulsion or population transfer instead of genocide may be due to some mix of morality and practicality, but the goal is essentially the same: to remove the minority group from society.

Forced migration is responsible for the millions of refugees who wander the globe today, from the former Yugoslavia to Central Asia, the Middle East, and sub-Saharan Africa. In the nineteenth century the United States government forced hundreds of thousands of Native Americans onto isolated and barren reservations, while whites grabbed the valuable land the Indians had abandoned.

During the Second World War over 110,000 men, women, and children of Japanese ancestry, most of whom were U.S. citizens, were forced to sell their homes and most of their possessions and move to detention camps in remote areas of the West (Kitano, 1980). None of these people had been found guilty of disloyal activities, and white-skinned Germans and Italians, some of whom were known to be Axis sympathizers, were never subjected to similar treatment. This forced relocation was declared unconstitutional by the Supreme Court in 1944, but it was not until 1989 that Congress voted reparations to the victims.

The most recent example of large-scale forced migration occurred in 1999. The government of Serbia used extreme means to compel thousands of Islamic ethnic Albanians to leave Kosovo—despite the fact that they constituted roughly 90 percent of the population of the province.

Open Subjugation

When the dominant group views the minority as economically valuable, it is unlikely to kill or expel them. Instead, it commonly forces them into a situation called *open subjugation* wherein no pretense is made that the minority is in any way equal to the dominant group.

Slavery in the American South and *apartheid* in South Africa before 1993 are historic examples of open subjugation. Labor was needed to work the

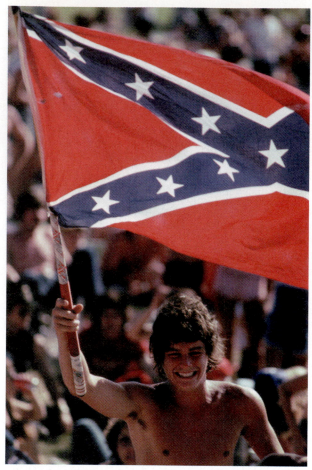

The Confederate flag is an intensely controversial symbol. Most blacks and liberal whites see it as a holdover from the days of slavery, but many Southern whites insist that it evokes only regional pride, not racism.

plantations of Virginia and Georgia and the mines and factories of the Transvaal. Prior to 1865, African Americans were subjected to the ultimate degradation of being owned; similarly, blacks under apartheid were technically free but their rights to live, work, and travel where they wished were greatly limited (Fredrickson, 1981; Sparks, 1990). In both cases the workers were regarded as less than fully human, denied most or all civil rights, and frequently treated with great brutality.

Legal Protection—Continued Discrimination

In the fourth pattern of dominant-minority relations, the government claims to grant basic civil rights to all of its citizens, but *de facto* discrimination continues. African Americans entered this phase at the end of the

Civil War and it continued until at least the passage of the 1964 Civil Rights bill.

It is under these circumstances that segregation is most visible. **Segregation** is the physical and social separation of dominant and minority groups. Under open subjugation, it is convenient for minorities to live with or near dominant group members so that they can serve them day and night, as during slavery. But once the state endorses the legal equality of all citizens, dominant groups tend to force—or at least encourage—minorities to keep to themselves in order to symbolically protect their higher status.

Assimilation

As dominant-minority relations improve, a real possibility arises of **assimilation,** the process by which minorities shed their differences and blend in with the dominant group. Assimilation is generally easier and more rapid under certain conditions: (1) if minority group members migrated voluntarily (Blauner, 1972), (2) if they are not sharply distinct physically from the dominant group, (3) if they are relatively small in number, (4) if they arrive when the economy is doing well, and (5) if they are culturally similar to the dominant group (Yinger, 1985).

There are two competing images of assimilation (Gordon, 1978). Most Americans are more comfortable with the *melting pot model*, which suggests that various racial and ethnic groups come to this country and then lose their distinctiveness and "melt" into a single American category. This view is represented in Figure 12.4 by the equation A + B + C = D, in which A represents the British-descended or Anglo settlers, B and C represent other immigrant groups, and D represents generalized Americans (Newman, 1973).

In contrast, the *Anglo-conformity model*—A + B + C = A'—suggests that immigrants lose most of their ethnic identity and learn to act and think like the Anglos who have always dominated U.S. society. Thus, Italian immigrants, for example, became fluent in English and abandoned nearly all of their own culture while the British learned to like pizza—hardly an even trade!

The melting pot model is in line with egalitarian U.S. values and is widely endorsed in the media (Parrillo, 1999). Most sociologists, however, think that melting pot assimilation is more myth than reality. After all, in the United States an "American" is generally assumed to be someone who speaks English and whose lifestyle is distinctly British—even if his or her last name is Cohen, Gonzales, or Furukawa.

Sociologists further distinguish between three levels of assimilation—cultural, structural, and bio-

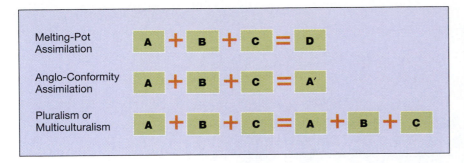

FIGURE 12.4   Three Models of Minority-Dominant Group Relations.
Source: Figure, "Three Models of Minority-Dominant Group Relations" from *American Pluralism: A Study of Minority Groups and Social Theory* by William M. Newman. Copyright © 1973 by William M. Newman. Reprinted by permission of Addison-Wesley Educational Publishers, Inc.

logical (Gordon, 1964). *Cultural assimilation*, sometimes also called *acculturation*, comes first: The minority accepts the dominant group's language, clothing styles, food preferences, many of its values and norms, and sometimes even its religion. This process initially creates people who are marginal—not fully accepted by either group (Weisberger, 1992)—but over time marginality declines as the dominant culture is more fully assimilated.

Cultural assimilation often leads to *structural assimilation*, whereby minorities live in the same neighborhoods, worship at the same churches, and work for the same firms as members of the dominant group.

The final step is intermarriage, referred to as *biological assimilation* or *amalgamation* (Spickard, 1991). As will be discussed later in this chapter, sociologists expect rates of amalgamation to increase in future decades.

Pluralism

The final pattern of minority-dominant relations is **pluralism**, sometimes also called *multiculturalism*. In this model, minority groups maintain much of their cultural identity, yet do not experience significant discrimination and participate in common economic and political institutions (Kuper & Smith, 1969; Taylor, 1995). Pluralism is summed up in Figure 12.4 by the formula A + B + C = A + B + C (Newman, 1973). Rather than a melting pot, the multicultural ideal visualizes America as a salad bowl where various elements mix together without losing their distinctiveness.

Pluralism is widely endorsed in U.S. society today (Glazer, 1997). The Vietnamese shopping center in Virginia discussed at the beginning of this chapter is a good example of contemporary pluralism. Pluralism is easiest to achieve when there are no sharp economic differences between the groups. Switzerland is a substantially multicultural society. Each of Switzerland's three major ethnic groups—German, French, and Italian—maintains its own language and traditions. None of the three constitutes a numerical majority,

and none is much better off than the others. Each lives mostly in its own part of the nation, but all Swiss interact regularly with each other on a basis of rough equality.

Minority Responses

When the dominant group insists on population transfer, open subjugation, or legal protection, minorities have few options. Some individuals, unfortunately, accept the ideology, which defines them as inferior; they do not actively resist oppression. A few are able to hide their minority-group membership and "pass," although often at great psychological cost. Some choose to emigrate. Others accept their devalued status publicly but not in private; for example, some slaves appeared resigned to their condition yet nurtured hope for eventual freedom while occasionally resisting through sabotage and work slowdowns. And still others actively work to change their status through social movements.

After dominant-minority relations improve, however, minorities may choose between three principal alternatives: assimilation, pluralism, and separatism.

Assimilation.   Assimilation holds forth the promise of full acceptance, and for this reason, it is generally the most widely embraced option among American minorities (Hirschman, 1983). However, there are serious doubts about whether racial minorities in the United States will be allowed to assimilate. Will most whites ever believe that people of color are just as good as they are (Zweigenhaft & Domhoff, 1991)? Furthermore, many minorities question whether they should abandon a culture that their ancestors treasured (Carmichael & Hamilton, 1967; Nagel, 1994).

Pluralism.   This option responds to some of these concerns. But the question arises, as it does regarding assimilation, whether whites can transcend racism and allow pluralism (Shorris, 1992). Skeptics point out that white commitment to multiculturalism is rela-

Since the end of the Cold War, ethnic conflicts have broken out in many parts of the former Soviet bloc. Some of the most intense struggles took place in 1999 in the province of Kosovo, when Serbian forces compelled hundreds of thousands of ethnic Albanians to flee their homes.

tively weak, as suggested by California's recent efforts to dismantle its bilingual education programs.

Even if pluralism can be achieved, some people question the ultimate wisdom of the policy. In a multicultural society, will dominant groups maintain their power by "playing off" other groups against each other, as predicted by Marxist exploitation theory (Marden et al., 1992)? Furthermore, in a truly pluralistic culture will there be enough common values to hold the society together, or will it fall apart, as has happened in the former Yugoslavia or as threatens to occur in Canada?

Separatism. Today many minorities, especially racial minorities, do not believe the dominant group will ever allow them to assimilate or to construct a truly pluralistic society. This view has led many to embrace **separatism,** also sometimes called *ethnic nationalism*, a policy of voluntary structural and cultural isolation from the dominant group. Superficially similar to segregation imposed by the majority, separatism is initiated by the minority group in defense of its own cultural integrity.

Separatism has been a fairly popular option among African Americans ever since Marcus Garvey's "back to Africa" movement of the 1920s (Cronin, 1969). Today, Louis Farrakhan's Nation of Islam advocates this model. Separatists generally recognize that they must remain enough in the mainstream culture so that they don't disadvantage themselves economically, but otherwise they try to distance themselves as much as possible from the dominant group. The widespread self-segregation of minority groups on many U.S. college campuses is a good example of separatism (Jordon, 1996).

IMMIGRATION

Most minority groups in the United States and worldwide occupy that status as a result of immigration. Many migrated to new countries in search of freedom and economic opportunity. Others, like Native Americans or Catholics in Northern Ireland, became minorities when outsiders came to their land and settled.

Not even the Native Americans originated here; their ancestors came to the Western Hemisphere from Siberia at least 14,000 years ago (Oswalt & Neely, 1999). European settlers from Spain, France, Holland, and England arrived in the sixteenth and seventeenth centuries, subdued the indigenous peoples, and established themselves on these shores. Africans were brought to the Americas by slave traders beginning in the early 1600s. Over the past two centuries, numerous additional waves of immigrants have arrived (Jacobson, 1998). Figure 12.5 shows the historic changes in immigration patterns since 1820.

In 1965 a new immigration act was passed that allowed far greater numbers of non-Europeans to enter the United States than had previously been permitted. In the 1980s, about 10 million people came to this country, legally or illegally—the greatest number in a single decade up to this point in U.S. history (Frey & Tilove, 1995). Almost 7 million more immigrants arrived in the first seven years of the 1990s.

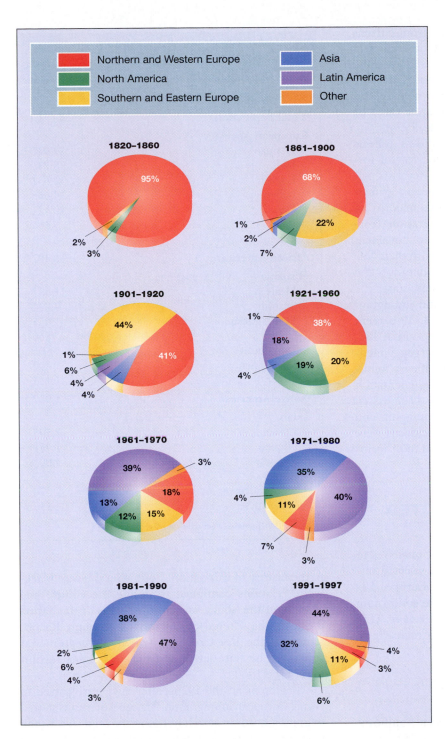

FIGURE 12.5   National Origins of Legal Immigrants Admitted to the United States, 1820–1997.

Source: Bouvier, Leon F. and Robert W. Gardner. 1986. "Immigration to the U.S.: An Unfinished Story." *Population Bulletin* 41 (November). 1999 *U.S. Statistical Abstract,* Table 8.

Even if immigration were drastically cut back tomorrow, the high fertility of most of the newly arrived groups guarantees their increased representation in the U.S. population. The Census Bureau predicts that non-Hispanic whites, who made up 72.3 percent of the population in 1998, will barely be a majority in 2050. While the African American population will grow slightly, from 12 percent to 14.4 percent of the total, Hispanics will increase from 10.3 percent to 22.5 percent; they will become the United States' largest minority group early in this century. The Asian American population will also grow rapidly, roughly tripling to perhaps 10 percent of the total by 2050.

Quite simply, the United States is very close to the end of the era in which most Americans could trace their roots to Europe (O'Hare, 1992). Shortly after the midpoint of this century, most Americans will be ethnic or racial minorities.

As you might expect, immigration has become very controversial in recent years. Some observers charge that immigrants take jobs away from citizens and that they use more than their share of public services such as education and welfare. Research on these issues is inconclusive. It is clear, however, that many immigrants hold jobs that few others would accept, and many thousands of additional jobs are created by immigrant entrepreneurs each year (Cole, 1994).

Some anti-immigrant feeling doubtless reflects little more than *xenophobia*, an irrational fear of foreigners (Portes & Rumbaut, 1990). Whatever its origin, anti-immigrant sentiment has been very evident in recent years. Polls show that a sizable majority of Americans support restrictions on immigration (Cornelius, 1996). A nationwide English Only movement has led over twenty states to declare English their "official language," endangering bilingual education and other immigrant-friendly programs in these states.

One of the clearest signs of this anti-immigrant backlash occurred in California: In 1994, 59 percent of the voters in that state approved Proposition 187, which denied public education, non-emergency medical services, and welfare assistance to illegal immigrants. Although the courts blocked implementation of Proposition 187, similar legislation has been passed at the federal level. In 1996, all illegal immigrants and most legal immigrants who are not yet citizens were barred from receiving Social Security and most forms of public assistance.

A CLOSER LOOK AT SELECTED MINORITY GROUPS

In the following discussion, we will limit ourselves to highlighting a few key points regarding selected minority groups in the United States and Europe. Tables 12.2 and 12.3 present important data concerning the size and social circumstances of the major U.S. minority groups and will be referred to regularly in the following pages.

African Americans

The first Africans to arrive in America in significant numbers landed at Jamestown, Virginia, in 1619, centuries before the ancestors of most white Americans came to these shores. These earliest immigrants were indentured servants, but by 1661 slavery was legally established in the colonies (Sowell, 1981). Of all American minorities, Africans were the only group to be enslaved in large numbers, the only group forced to entirely abandon its traditional culture, and the only group whose families were deliberately broken up (Franklin, 1967).

African American slavery was an important factor in the U.S. Civil War, certainly the most pivotal event

Table 12.2 Selected Racial and Ethnic Groups in the United States, 1990

Populations (in thousands)	
Total Population	248,710
European Ancestry	
German	57,947
Irish	38,736
English	32,652
Italian	14,665
French	10,321
Polish	9,366
Other	36,313
African American	30,392
Hispanic	
Mexican	11,587
Spanish	2,024
Puerto Rican	1,955
Cuban	860
Dominican	506
Salvadorian	499
Other	1,113
Native American	1,937
Asian	
Chinese	1,505
Filipino	1,451
Japanese	1,005
Korean	837
Asian Indian	570
Vietnamese	536

Source: 1998 *Statistical Abstract*, Tables 51, 54 and 58.

in the history of this nation. Following the war, black-white relations continued to define the culture and identity of the South, and in some ways of the nation itself, as the United States moved through Reconstruction, the Jim Crow era (when segregation was supported by state laws), and the civil rights revolution of the 1960s.

Beginning in the 1920s, after laws were passed to curtail European immigration, African Americans started migrating north in search of economic opportunity and in order to escape the pervasive segregation of the Deep South. In the fifty years between 1920 and 1970, the black population was transformed: Once overwhelmingly Southern and rural, it became urban and widely distributed throughout the nation (Lemann, 1991).

During the civil rights era, Dr. Martin Luther King, Jr. worked to establish a society in which race was no longer a stigma. In sociological terms, he envisioned a multicultural America with a good measure of assimilation. But as early as 1968, it was apparent that his dream was imperiled. In that year, the Kerner Commission, established to investigate the urban riots

Table 12.3	Social Characteristics of Selected Racial and Ethnic Groups				
	Median Family Income	Percentage of Individuals Below the Poverty Line	Percentage of Two-Parent Family Groups	Percent of Persons 25 and Over Completing High School	Percent of Persons 25 and Over Completing College
Non-Hispanic whites	$46,754 (1997)	11.0 (1997)	73.0 (1998)	83.7 (1998)	25.0 (1998)
African Americans	28,602 (1998)	26.5 (1998)	38.0 (1998)	76.0 (1998)	14.7 (1998)
Hispanics	28,141 (1998)	27.1 (1998)	64.0 (1998)	55.5 (1998)	11.0 (1998)
Native Americans	21,619 (1989)	31.2 (1989)	n. a.	65.6 (1990)	9.4 (1990)

Source: 1999 Statistical Abstract, Tables 51, 54, 55, 76, 260, 749 and 763.

that were sweeping America, concluded that America was rapidly becoming " . . . two societies, one black, one white—separate and unequal" (National Advisory Commission on Civil Disorders, 1968). Twenty-five years later, another national commission, once again organized in response to urban rioting, concluded that the Kerner Commission's analysis remained highly accurate (Milton S. Eisenhower Foundation, 1993). While real progress has been made, discrimination, such as the racial profiling discussed at the beginning of this chapter, endures.

A glance at Table 12.3 provides a starting point for understanding the current situation of black Americans. In 1998, the median family income for African Americans ($28,602) was just 61 percent of the figure for non-Hispanic whites. Only about 30 percent of all African American men and 60 percent of black women are currently employed in professional, technical, managerial, and administrative jobs, compared with roughly 50 percent of white males and 75 percent of white females. Over 28 percent of African Americans—and about 66 percent of those in single-parent families—live below the poverty line. Black unemployment figures are consistently more than twice the white figures, and the teenage unemployment rate tops 40 percent in some cities.

These problems have endured and in some cases worsened, despite rapid improvements in median levels of education. In 1980, about 50 percent of all African Americans had completed high school; by 1998, 76 percent had graduated. College enrollments have also substantially increased, although a dropout rate of almost 70 percent (compared with 40 percent for whites) lowers the percentage of African Americans who earn their degrees (Allen & Jewell, 1995; Leslie, 1995). Unfortunately, education often has less payoff for blacks: White male high school dropouts earn almost as much as black high school graduates, and white high school graduates earn only slightly less than African Americans who have attended (but not completed) college (Schaefer, 2000).

Saddest of all, African Americans continue to lag behind whites in vital statistics. In 1997, 13.7 out of every 1000 African American children died in their first year of life; the figure for whites was 6.0. In that same year, black men could expect to live, on the average, 67.3 years compared with 74.3 years for white men. The figures for females were 74.7 and 79.8, respectively.

Remember also that the negative effects of race and ethnicity are amplified in complex ways when we consider the combined impact of the variables of race, gender, class, age, and sexual orientation on the ways in which individuals are treated in society, a reality that has shaped a great deal of contemporary sociological research and theory construction (Anderson & Collins, 1998; Rothenberg, 1998).

A closer look at the African American population reveals a critical point that is not apparent from aggregate statistical data: Major changes have occurred in the African American class structure over the past forty years. Before the 1960s, the black middle class was small and composed largely of marginally well-paid government employees and free professionals. Today, about 40 percent of African Americans are middle class (Landry, 1988; Takaki, 1993) and, although they hold only about 15 percent of the wealth that the average white middle-class family controls (Oliver & Shapiro, 1995), they are otherwise beginning to approach parity with the dominant group.

On the other hand, the African American lower class has also expanded, and, by almost any measure, its life circumstances have worsened. The black poverty rate has increased by almost 50 percent since 1988, and roughly half of all African American children are now born into poverty (Pollard, 1992; Pinkney, 2000).

William Julius Wilson, a prominent African American sociologist, suggests that the key to understanding the plight of the inner-city poor lies in two factors: deindustrialization and the exodus of the black middle class (Wilson, 1987, 1996).

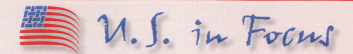

U. S. in Focus

African Americans Move Back South

Seventy-one-year-old Bennie Rayford, whose parents were sharecroppers, grew up in a county in rural Mississippi where black children didn't go to school until all the cotton was picked. Beating the odds, he finished high school, earned a college degree in education, and became the principal of a run-down, segregated school in his home state. In 1957, when Rayford organized his students' parents to petition for a new school bus in 1957, the county superintendent fired him. "You're too smart a nigger," his termination letter read. "We no longer need your services" (Smith & Pedersen, 1997, p. 36). He and his wife Hilda, also a teacher, decided then and there to head north and settled in Toledo, Ohio. When they retired, however, they moved back to Tchula, the small town in rural Mississippi where they both grew up; three of their adult children have now joined them there.

When the Rayfords moved to Ohio, they were participating in the largest internal migration in U.S. history. Between 1940 and 1970, more than 5 million African Americans left the rural South for cities in the North in the hope of finding better jobs and less discrimination. In the mid-1970s, however, this trend began to reverse. By 1990, half a million blacks had moved back to the South. If this trend continues, 2.7 million—more than half the number who fled—will have returned between 1975 and 2010. For hundreds of years the South humiliated African Americans—first through slavery, then through sharecropping and Jim Crow. For most of this century Southern blacks were not allowed to vote, forced to attend segregated schools, and systematically denied good jobs and housing. Why would anyone return to the scene of so much misery?

Young, middle-class African Americans are moving to the South for the same reasons other people are: bet-

ter jobs, affordable housing, cleaner air, and a more laid-back lifestyle. Atlanta, a magnet for both whites and blacks, is today the fastest-growing metropolitan region in the country. Beth Griffen visited Atlanta out of curiosity and decided to stay; so did her fiancé, Rick. They stayed because they felt there were better career opportunities for black men and women in Atlanta than in the North. Today Beth is a senior financial analyst for Coca-Cola and Rick works as a computer-software consultant. The Griffens believe they enjoy a better life here than they could elsewhere. Equally important, they want to raise their child in a city where there are a significant number of African American professionals, business owners, and other successful role models.

The Rayfords returned to Mississippi for much the same reason they left: Life in Toledo had become intolerable. Both taught in inner-city schools, where students brought guns into the classroom; the schools had become almost as dangerous as the streets at night. In some ways, Tchula hasn't changed much since they left more than forty-five years ago. People still sit on their porches, go for strolls, or visit neighbors at night without fear of being mugged. As before, the town is 80 percent black; also as before, most of the residents are poor and undereducated. In other ways, however, Tchula has changed: Both the local police force and the county board, once all white, are now largely African American. Equally important, the Rayfords have changed: Both have the experience and contacts needed to get things done. Hilda has started a learning center for adults as well as for young people. Bennie, who chaired Jesse Jackson's presidential campaign in Ohio in 1984, is the head of a local health center and vice chair of the Holmes County Republican Party.

Not all participants in the reverse migration South are as financially secure or sophisticated as the Griffens and the Rayfords. In her book *Call to Home* (1996) anthropologist Carol Stack tells the stories of African Americans who left crowded inner-city apartments for trailers, cabins, and small brick houses on dusty roads in rural North and South Carolina. Many had spent their childhood or their summers with relatives in the South, sent their children to be raised in the South, and on some level had never left the region. Second-generation migrants to the North, they found that the "promised land, the land of freedom and opportunity, had become the Rustbelt" (Stack, 1996: 48). The only jobs available to them didn't pay living wages; their marriages weren't holding together; their children were out of control; their lives weren't working out.

The migrants Stack got to know did not romanticize the rural South as a "paradise lost"; they knew that life there was as hard as ever. Certainly, they did not want to turn back the clock to the days of segregation and humiliation. But they missed the network of kin and neighbors who come to one another's aid in hard times. In Stack's view, "What people are seeking is not so much the home they left behind as a place they feel they can change, a place in which their lives and strivings will make a difference—a place in which to create a home" (1996, p. 199).

1. What, if anything, do these reverse migrants lose by returning to the South?
2. How much change do you believe has taken place in the racial attitudes of white Southerners in recent decades? What are the primary factors that have produced this change?

Sources: Stack, 1996; Smith & Pedersen, 1997.

Pluralism is an arrangement in which members of ethnic and racial minorities are encouraged to retain their distinctive patterns regarding matters such as food and dress while participating as full equals in the larger economic and political system.

By deindustrialization, Wilson means the steep decline in recent decades in the availability of decent jobs to inner-city black men. Two or three generations ago, capable and ambitious young African American men could find work near where they lived on assembly lines or operating machines. These jobs were far from ideal, but they provided a decent level of support, adequate to allow them to marry and father families, adequate to allow them to seek further education for themselves and their children. But over the years, most of these jobs vanished, moving abroad or to the suburbs, out of the reach of people lacking access to reliable transportation (Kasarda, 1989; Massey & Denton, 1993).

Recent generations have turned to drug sales and property crime or taken marginal service jobs that simply do not pay enough to support a family. At the same time, the percentage of two-parent families in the ghetto has declined precipitously (Jaynes & Williams, 1989; Mare & Winship, 1991; Pinkney, 2000). Today, most lower-class African Americans simply do not make enough money to support a family. Welfare policies, which traditionally denied benefits to intact families, only intensified the problem. Single-parent families are undoubtedly associated with problems of the inner city, but Wilson insists that family structure is more a *consequence* rather than the *cause* of African American poverty.

According to Wilson, a second factor complicating the problems of the ghetto poor is the out-migration of the African American middle class. Since desegregation opened up much of the housing market in American cities, black families with adequate incomes have streamed out of the inner city. In the process, poor neighborhoods have lost the mainstays of local institutions, from PTAs to political organizations to churches. These moderately affluent African Americans were also the people who helped finance local businesses and community projects. Once there were hard-working, conventional role models living on almost every block in the inner city; today drug dealers and professional athletes are often the only economically successful black people who are visible (Crane, 1991).

The implications of Wilson's analysis are clear. Programs preaching against drugs, crime, and pregnancy outside of marriage are not the answer because they focus on symptoms, not causes. The recent dramatic cuts in welfare (see Chapter 11) are also unlikely to reduce poverty. We need to provide decent jobs for the inner city poor, jobs that allow for the formation of stable families.

Hispanic Americans

America's Hispanic population is both large and diverse (Shorris, 1992). The 1990 census classified 9 percent of the U.S. population as Hispanic, but this count missed large numbers of undocumented immigrants. The true total is probably higher by about 6 million. The Hispanic population is young and growing so rapidly that it will overtake African Americans early in the twenty-first century (Exter, 1987).

Figure 12.6 shows the national origins of the Hispanic population in the United States. While over 60 percent of all Hispanic Americans trace their roots to Mexico, substantial numbers come from Puerto Rico,

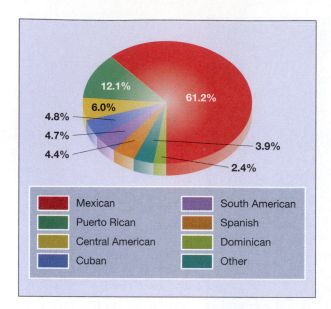

FIGURE 12.6   National Origins of the Hispanic Population, 1990.

Source: U.S. Census Bureau. 1993. *We The Americans: Hispanics.* Washington, DC: GPO.

Cuba, and many other Central and South American nations. There are many social and cultural differences between these groups; in fact, most Hispanics refer to themselves by their country of origin, not as Hispanics (Heyck, 1994). However, certain common patterns can be identified.

Most obviously, the fact that Hispanics are Spanish-speaking people has affected their experiences in the United States. Many Hispanic students enter school poorly prepared in English, contributing to high school dropout rates of about 30 percent and relatively low levels of educational attainment. As shown in Table 12.3, only 11 percent of Hispanics over 25 hold college degrees.

Because Latin America is so close to the United States, Hispanics, especially Mexican Americans and Puerto Ricans, often return home, sometimes temporarily, sometimes permanently. This, along with the language factor, often makes it more difficult for Hispanics to assimilate sufficiently to allow upward economic mobility. Thus, overall, Hispanics earn just 60 percent of the median white family income, although the Cuban figure is much higher and the Puerto Rican much lower. Roughly 27 percent of all Hispanics live below the poverty line.

Religion is another common factor among Hispanics. Protestant denominations are making inroads into the Hispanic population, but about 85 percent remain Catholic. The church has helped immigrants settle in their new land, but Catholic doctrine opposes all forms of artificial birth control, materially con-

tributing to the larger family size and resulting relatively low economic standing of most Hispanic groups. On the other hand, religious beliefs have doubtless helped strengthen the family; according to Table 12.3, 64 percent of all Hispanic families are intact.

Native Americans

Although they were not subjected to large-scale slavery, the trauma inflicted on the Native American population is not dissimilar to that experienced by African Americans. In at least one regard, their experience was worse. Slaves were economically valuable and their population increased in America, whereas the vast majority of the Native American population died as a result of contact with whites: Between 1500 and 1900 their numbers declined from between 2 and 3 million to about 240,000 (Brown, 1991).

White-Indian relations can be divided into three broad historic periods (Nichols, 1992; Hoxie & Iverson, 1998). Until 1871, the U.S. government made treaties with tribes as if they were conventional foreign nations, though it never fully honored those treaties and relentlessly pushed the Native Americans westward across the Mississippi. Between 1871 and 1934, official policy shifted to forced assimilation. The government gave individual families plots of reservation land in the hope of turning Native Americans into small farmers, and many thousands of children were sent away to boarding schools where they were taught white culture and punished if they did not abandon their traditional ways (Noley, 1990). Since 1934, government policy has gradually shifted toward pluralism, with the aim of incorporating Native Americans into national life as *Native Americans.* Tribal governments have been established, and today most Native American groups enjoy considerable autonomy.

Native Americans are generally considered the most disadvantaged of all minority groups. Overall, 31.2 percent of all Indians lived below the poverty line in 1990, the last year for which accurate data are available (see Table 12.3). But on the reservations, where about one-third of all Native Americans live, the poverty rate often exceeds 50 percent. School achievement, although increasing, remains low (Cage, 1993). Unemployment and infant mortality are exceptionally high, and the life expectancy of men on the reservation is just 45 years; for women, the average is 48 years (Churchill, 1994). Mental illness, suicide, and alcoholism are all too common (Bachman, 1992).

One of the most serious issues confronting Native Americans today is the choice between the reservation and the city (Dudley, 1998). On the one hand,

Despite the growth of a large black middle-class, about half of all African American children are still born into families living below the poverty line.

city life promises much greater economic opportunity, but it is difficult for small, isolated groups of urban Indians to maintain their cultural heritage. On the other hand, the reservation offers a more sheltered and nurturing environment but few decent jobs. Many young Native Americans shuttle back and forth between city and reservation, never fully committed to either.

Asian Americans

Like Hispanics, Asian Americans are entering the United States in great numbers, and they are a tremendously diverse group. Figure 12.7 identifies the principal countries from which Asians have immigrated. The number of Asians living in the United States increased by over 100 percent in the 1980s alone, it is expected to quadruple by 2050 (O'Hare & Felt, 1991). Each group has had unique experiences; yet, as with Hispanics, there are certain common themes.

Most Asian Americans, especially those who arrived on the West Coast in the nineteenth century, met substantial hostility (Kitano & Daniels, 1988). For example, the first major wave of Chinese immigrants came to build the railroads and to participate in the 1849 California gold rush, but they were so hardworking that many whites came to consider them dangerous economic competitors. These fears, intensified by the marked physical and cultural differences between whites and Chinese, led to the 1882 Chinese Exclusion Act that ended Chinese immigration until the early 1940s (Chan, 1991).

Japanese Americans, who arrived somewhat later than the Chinese, fared marginally better until they were forced into internment camps during World War II. More recent arrivals, especially refugees from the Vietnam War era, have continued to face opposition from time to time and, as the account that opened this chapter suggests, tend to resist complete assimilation.

From a sociological perspective, the remarkable fact about Asian Americans is how many of them have become economically successful and how quickly this success has come. Remember, this is a highly visible racial minority whose culture of origin is very different from mainstream American culture. Yet the median family income of Asian Americans is 113 percent of that of white families; they have the lowest unemployment rate of any group; and 52 percent of them own their own homes—a higher percentage than any group other than non-Hispanic whites and Cubans.

How can we explain these statistics? The key seems to be a very strong family structure. Nearly 80 percent of Asian American families are intact—a very high rate. Divorce and teenage pregnancy are uncommon. Socialization within the family tends to stress a very strong work ethic and the importance of education (Caplan et al., 1992).

Not all Asian Americans excel in school, of course, but so many do that they are disproportionately represented at the top of high school and college classes (Gibson & Ogbu, 1991; Rong & Grant, 1992). Almost 42 percent of Asian Americans over the age of 25 have college degrees, far more than the 25 percent of non-Hispanic whites in this age range.

Furthermore, most Asian American groups initially settled in strong, supportive communities that provided a base for developing new businesses (Light & Bonacich, 1988). As we enter the new century,

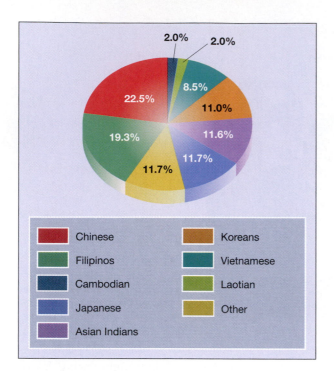

FIGURE 12.7   National Origins of the Asian American Population, 1990.
Source: 1999 *Statistical Abstract*, Table 32.

many Asian Americans have become highly assimilated—culturally, structurally, and, given their high intermarriage rate, biologically (Nee et al., 1994).

Because of their successes, Asian Americans are sometimes called "model minorities" (Winnick, 1990). Although there is considerable truth to this label, it is an oversimplification (Woo, 1985; Tyson, 1994). For one thing, many of the more recent arrivals from Asia are still living in Chinatowns or Little Saigons, experiencing considerable discrimination, and earning modest incomes or barely surviving on welfare (Ong, 1989). The Asian American poverty rate (15.2 percent in 1997) is still well above the white figure of 11 percent. In addition, the high median family income of Asian Americans reflects a larger number of wage earners per family than is typical of whites (Barringer et al., 1993; Takaki, 1993).

We conclude this section with brief discussions of minority groups in Northern Ireland and in Germany.

Catholics in Northern Ireland

For hundreds of years, Northern Ireland has been—and to a considerable extent it remains—a segregated society, even more so than the U.S. South before the civil rights era (Harris, 1972). Working-class Catholics and Protestants normally grow up in separate

neighborhoods, attend different elementary and secondary schools, play different sports, support different political parties, work for different employers (although this is gradually changing), and even use different names for the province: Protestants call it Ulster, while Catholics prefer Northern Ireland.

The Catholic population of Ireland has lived there over a millennium. Most of the ancestors of the present-day Protestant community emigrated to the northern coast of the island from Scotland in the early seventeenth century, displacing thousands of Catholic families from their land. Relations between the two groups have generally been hostile ever since, with the Protestants occupying the dominant role and the Catholics the subordinate one (Stewart, 1977).

The conflict in Northern Ireland is not really about religion. Rather, it is a struggle for political and economic power between two ethnic groups that happen to be identified by their faiths (Beach, 1977). Structurally, the North Irish situation resembles white-Indian relations in the United States in that, in both cases, the minority group has been subjugated in its own land by foreign invaders. The critical difference is that Native Americans constitute less than 1 percent of the population of the United States, whereas North Irish Catholics make up about 46 percent of the province (Darby, 1995).

The present configuration of interethnic relations was established in 1922 when the overwhelmingly Catholic southern 26 counties of Ireland (out of a total of 32) won political independence from Britain. Because the Protestants of the North feared discrimination in an independent, all-Ireland Catholic state, they established a six-county province that remained part of the United Kingdom where they currently enjoy a 54 percent majority (O'Malley, 1990).

In the fifty years between 1922 and the dissolution of the North Irish parliament in 1972, Protestants held complete control over Northern Ireland. They gerrymandered electoral boundaries and manipulated the franchise in order to maintain political control even over heavily Catholic areas. Catholics were openly discriminated against in employment and housing. The police were overwhelmingly Protestant, recruited in some cases directly from the ranks of the aggressively anti-Catholic Orange Order (Rose, 1971; Arthur, 1984).

The tenacity and longevity of this conflict has few parallels worldwide. For over eighty years, a Catholic-based group called the Irish Republican Army has employed force to attempt to oust the British from the island and end Protestant domination. A majority of the voters in the North approved a historic restructuring of the government in May 1998, but it remains to be seen whether it will be embraced by extremists on both sides.

Minorities in Japan

While virtually every modern society is characterized by minority groups, some include far more than others. The United States, Canada, and Australia, nations that have historically encouraged immigration, lie toward one end of this continuum. On the other hand, Japan is the most homogeneous of all developed societies. No more than 4 million Japanese—three percent of the population—are considered to be racial or ethnic minorities. However, their small numbers do not seem to have lessened the extent to which these people have experienced discrimination at the hands of Japan's collectivistic and strongly conformist dominant culture.

The Burukumin are Japan's largest and most severely stigmatized minority, despite being physically indistinguishable from other Japanese. Members of this group, who make up about 2 percent of the population, are believed to be the descendants of ancient outcastes who were looked down upon because they did "unclean" jobs like butchering or leatherworking.

The Burukumin were granted legal equality in 1871, but this did not end their minority status. To this day they are widely regarded as unsuitable marriage partners and continue to experience discrimination in employment. Burukumin are relatively less educated, more than twice as likely to be on welfare, and three times as likely to be arrested as other Japanese. They even score substantially lower on IQ tests.

The fact that the Burukumin are physically identical to everyone else creates problems for prospective employers and in-laws, who sometimes violate the law by hiring private detectives to check out the backgrounds of job applicants and the would-be spouses of their children. In the modern era, Burukumin liberation movements have successfully campaigned for government-sponsored scholarship programs and affirmative action initiatives, and today both college attendance and intermarriage rates are increasing rapidly.

Additional Japanese minority groups include:

- The Ainu, a racially distinct group of some 20,000 individuals descended from the original aboriginal inhabitants of Japan, most of whom live in the remote northern islands.
- Korean immigrants, numbering a little less than 1 million. Most came to Japan in the decades before World War II. Although most Koreans have adopted Japanese names and some conceal their ancestry, members of this ethnic group experience substantial discrimination. Only about half of all Korean boys in Japan finish high school (compared with 97 percent of other Japanese), Koreans are rarely welcomed as prospective spouses, and they tend to work in marginal blue-collar occupations.
- There are also some 150,000 persons of mainstream Japanese heritage whose ancestors emigrated to Peru and other parts of South America but who have returned to Japan in recent decades in search of employment. Like the Burukumin, they are physically indistinguishable from the general population, but they are ethnically distinct, speaking loudly in public, openly embracing each other, and holding street festivals featuring Latin music.

In addition to these racial and ethnic groups, Japanese women may also be analyzed as a minority. Women, in Japan and elsewhere, meet many defining criteria of a minority group: They occupy an ascribed status, are relatively powerless, experience prejudice and discrimination, and have some degree of solidarity.

Japanese women have enjoyed formal equality under the law since 1947 but they continue to be limited by a strong cultural separation of spheres that allows them control over the household while defining the outside world as the man's arena. Half of all Japanese women work, but employment discrimination is rampant. Women earn only about one-third of all wages and are very rarely found in prestigious jobs, especially in business. They are socialized to see themselves as mothers and wives, not as workers, and to subordinate themselves to the needs and desires of their families. The Japanese feminist movement is probably the weakest of any in the developed world, and the prospects for significant improvement in the treatment of women in Japan in the near future are quite dim.

1. Reflect on the case studies presented in this box and elsewhere in this chapter and see if you can develop some general principles about how the relative size of a minority group seems to affect how it is treated.
2. Is it fruitful to analyze women as a minority group or does this improperly blur the lines between gender, race, and ethnicity?

Sources: Lindsey, 1997; Kerbo & McKinstry, 1998; Schneider & Silverman, 2000.

Native Americans are the poorest minority group in the United States. Few economic opportunities are available on the reservation, but when Indians move to the cities, they find themselves isolated from their people and traditions.

Guest Workers in Germany

Beginning in the 1950s, *gastarbeiters*—guest workers—have flooded into Germany by the millions (Castles, 1986; Herbert, 1995). At the end of 1994, a total of 6,990,000 foreigners were living and working in Germany, 8.5 percent of the total population. Almost 2 million come from Turkey, 930,000 from the former Yugoslavia, half a million from Italy, 350,000 from Greece, and 261,000 from Poland (Thomas, 1996).

These workers are needed in Germany because of its expanding economy and low birthrate, yet they have met both formal and informal resistance. Officially, Germany is a "nonimmigration" country. This means that foreigners—even those who speak German and have lived in Germany for decades, even children of immigrants who were born in Germany—have traditionally not been eligible for citizenship (Jopke, 1996; Faist & Haubermann, 1996).

At the informal level, most Germans support anti-discrimination policies, but there is also a large and very vocal movement in opposition to the guest workers. The radical fringe of this movement openly employs Hitler-era tactics, including poisonous rhetoric, physical attacks, and even murder (Kramer, 1993). These neo-Nazi skinheads are small in num-

bers, but millions of Germans, especially in the economically strapped East, support right-wing political parties that scapegoat foreigners for Germany's problems (Echikson, 1992).

LIFE CONNECTIONS: Toward Multiracial America

Americans have traditionally believed that there were only a small (and fixed) number of races, that everyone could be unambiguously defined as a member of *one* of these races, and that anyone who had virtually any nonwhite ancestry was nonwhite—the uniquely American "fatal drop" principle (F. J. Davis, 1991; Wright, 1994; Feagin & Feagin, 1999). As recently as 1983 a Louisiana court ruled that a woman who was the great-great-great-great-granddaughter of a slave, but all of whose other ancestors were white, was officially an African American (Marger, 2000: 434).

However, since race is a social rather than a biological concept, racial labels are not fixed but are rather constantly changing, a process called *racial formation* (Omi & Winant, 1994). There appears to be increasing support in the United States today for a new "multiracial" category (Cose, 2000).

The key factor promoting this change is doubtless the increasing number of marriages across racial lines (Root, 1992). In 1980 1.3 percent of all married couples were interracial; by 1998 the percentage had risen to 2.4 (U.S. Bureau of the Census, 1999: Table 65). In 1970, only one out of every 100 children was bi- or multiracial; today one in nineteen is—one in ten in California and Washington (Clemetson, 2000).

Another important reason for this change is the immense popularity of multiracial golfer Tiger Woods, whose ancestry is 1/8 white, 1/8 Native American, 1/4 African American, 1/4 Thai, and 1/4 Chinese. Although the press often still follows the "fatal drop" rule and refers to him as black, Woods prefers to call himself "Cablinasian"—Caucasian, black, Indian, and Asian (White, 1997).

As the numbers and visibility of mixed race individuals increase, they are beginning to form a distinct subculture with their own magazines, web sites, and chat rooms. Over thirty universities now sponsor mixed-race student organizations. (Clemetson, 2000).

While most Americans still resist changing their understanding of race (Cross, 1991), a substantial and increasing minority is unhappy with the traditional rules. About 10 million people refused to check a racial/ethnic category on the 1990 census (Feagin & Feagin, 1999), leading to the demand that the option "multiracial" be included in 2000 (Della Piana, 1995; Kalish, 1995). Instead, the government compromised by allowing respondents to check as many categories as they felt applied. Although this change may make it more difficult for researchers to compare the results

News reports of the rebirth of Nazism in modern Germany have become commonplace in recent years. Are these demonstrators isolated extremists or are they the tip of an iceberg of resurgent racism?

of different censuses, it does seem to reflect the beginnings of a shift in the way Americans think about race.

Symbolic interactionists in particular would argue that this is not a trivial matter. As has been emphasized throughout this text, the linguistic categories that people use shape the way they think. If race is conceptualized as a matter of degree and choice, not as an absolute biological category—if we start thinking as Tiger Woods does rather than in terms of black-OR-white dichotomies—then the social meaning of race will be gradually transformed.

Perhaps the United States will eventually come to resemble societies like Brazil, in which innumerable intermediate statuses are recognized between white (*branco*) and black (*preto*) (Page, 1995; Marx, 1998). This does not mean that Brazil is a society without racial discrimination—it is well understood there that it is better to be light skinned—but it does mean that the boundaries between the races are less rigid, that the impact of race on people's lives is less dramatic, and even that race becomes to a certain extent an achieved status: Brazilians often say that "money whitens" and that "a rich Negro is a white man (sic)." (Marger, 2000: 434). Of course, skin color does not

actually change with wealth, but people's perceptions do, and that makes all the difference.

SOCIETY CONNECTIONS: Affirmative Action

For several decades, the United States has been engaged in efforts to increase the opportunities available to minorities. The most controversial of these programs is **affirmative action,** public and private efforts to recruit minorities and women into educational programs and jobs in which they have traditionally been underrepresented. At a minimum, affirmative action involves no more than being sure that minorities and women are made aware of the opportunities available to them. But many programs go further and give preferences to members of certain groups.

Through the later 1960s and 1970s, every president and both major political parties supported the principles of preferential hiring and admissions. By the early 1970s, the use of quotas had become fairly common in affirmative action programs. However, in the 1978 Bakke case, the Supreme Court ruled by a 5–4 vote that quotas were generally—but not always—inappropriate; at the same time the court reaffirmed that race could properly be taken into account in admissions and hiring.

The picture changed in 1980 with the election of Ronald Reagan, a dedicated opponent of preferential hiring and admissions. As the courts became more conservative during the 1980s, successive rulings began to erode affirmative action. In the 1970s, a lack of minority or female employees or students was generally enough to justify affirmative action (Commission on Civil Rights, 1981). More recently, the courts have generally required evidence of *intent* to discriminate, evidence that is often difficult to obtain.

In 1995, the Supreme Court further narrowed affirmative action by ruling that federal programs may include racial preferences only if they are "narrowly tailored" to accomplish ends that are of "compelling government interest" (Greenhouse, 1995). Also in 1995, California's governor banned all affirmative action in admissions to the state's public colleges and universities.

One year later, in 1996, a federal appeals court ruled that racial preference in admissions at the University of Texas Law School was unconstitutional. This ruling applied only to Texas, Louisiana, and Mississippi, but similar cases are working their way through the courts in other districts (Morganthau & Carroll, 1996; Schrag, 1996). Also in 1996, 54 percent of the voters in California approved Proposition 209, which prohibits all affirmative action programs (Ayres, 1996).

Affirmative action is, by definition, a temporary policy, to be used until the playing field is truly level. But have we reached that point? Can we abandon affirmative action programs without unduly harming minorities and women? Opponents of affirmative action raise the following points (Sowell, 1972; Glaser, 1976; Puddington, 1995):

- Affirmative action is reverse discrimination. The white males who lose opportunities have done nothing personally to merit not being hired, promoted, or admitted (Glaser, 1976).
- It is demeaning to minorities and women. Saying that they need extra consideration is tantamount to saying that they are incapable. Women and minorities who are hired under affirmative action programs never escape a cloud of suspicion about their abilities (Sowell, 1990; Steele, 1990; Carter, 1991).
- Affirmative action can result in hiring marginally less qualified people (Belz, 1991).
- Finally, affirmative action helps only people who are qualified for hiring or admission, mostly educated upper-working- and middle-class minorities and women. But these groups have made significant progress in the past several decades and may not need additional help. Meanwhile, affirmative action does little or nothing to help the poor and uneducated.

Advocates of continuing affirmative action respond as follows (Ezorsky, 1991; Wilkins, 1995):

- Reverse discrimination, if it occurs at all, is very rare (Burstein, 1991). Of some 3,000 affirmative action cases heard in the courts between 1990 and 1994, only 100 involved claims of reverse discrimination, and only six of these charges were upheld ("Reverse Discrimination . . .", 1995).
- Claiming that affirmative action is no longer necessary assumes that individual and direct institutional discrimination no longer exist in such areas as employment and housing. This is a widespread view among whites (Blauner, 1989; Kluegel, 1990; Hoschschild, 1995). But many research studies demonstrate that both individual and direct institutional discrimination most definitely endure (Galster, 1990; Canner et al., 1991; Mathews, 1992).
- Given the existence of indirect institutional discrimination, colorblind and gender-neutral policies are actually discriminatory in favor of white males. As Lyndon Johnson said, "You do not take a person who for years has been hobbled by chains, and liberate him [sic], bring him up to the starting line, and then say 'You are free to compete with all the others'" (Hacker, 1992). In other words, to get past race, we must first take race into account. Affirmative action makes up for the lingering consequences of earlier deliberate discrimination.
- Finally, much evidence shows that affirmative action works, especially for college graduates (Son et al., 1989; Beggs, 1995). Institutions that have followed affirmative action guidelines have hired or admitted minorities and women in larger numbers and more rapidly than similar institutions without such policies. When the law schools at the University of California and the University of Texas stopped following affirmative action guidelines, the percentage of minorities enrolling dropped sharply (Torry, 1997).

The debate continues, but the future of affirmative action looks dim given current political and legal trends. If it is, in the end, abolished, supporters say the most promising alternative approach would be either some form of class-based affirmative action program or a substantial strengthening of educational opportunities for the poor. Both schemes are colorblind, which is probably necessary to gain public acceptance (W. J. Wilson, 1990). Still, some observers doubt if either would help minorities as much as traditional affirmative action programs have (Lively et al., 1995).

SUMMARY

1. Although most people think of race as a biological concept, it is a social construct. Ethnic groups share a common subculture, somewhat distinct from the culture of the dominant group.
2. Minority groups lack power compared to dominant groups. They also experience prejudice and discrimination, feel a sense of solidarity or peoplehood, are defined by ascription, and are usually endogamous.
3. Prejudice is a negative attitude toward an entire category of people. There are two components of prejudice: an emotional reaction and a cognitive stereotype.
4. Discrimination consists of treating people differently on the basis of their category membership. It may be *de facto* or *de jure*; it may also be individual, direct institutional, or indirect institutional.
5. Prejudice and discrimination often occur independently of each other.
6. Racism is a widespread ideology that maintains one group is inherently superior to another.
7. Prejudice and discrimination may result from personality-level processes, social learning, or economic conflict; they serve a number of functions as well as dysfunctions.
8. Harmful patterns of dominant-minority group relations include genocide, expulsion, population transfer, open subjugation, and legal protection combined with *de facto* discrimination.
9. Assimilation is a process whereby minorities shed their differences and adopt the characteristics of the dominant group. There are three levels of assimilation: cultural, structural, and biological.
10. Under pluralism or multiculturalism, minorities retain their cultural identity yet peacefully coexist with other minorities and the dominant group.
11. Some minority group members seek assimilation, some prefer pluralism, and others advocate separatism.
12. Most Americans entered this country as immigrants. Since 1965, immigration from Latin America and Asia has been very substantial. By the middle of the new century, only a numerical minority of Americans will be able to trace their ancestry back to Europe.
13. As a result of rising intermarriage rates and changing social definitions, multiracial identity has become more widely accepted in the United States in recent years.
14. Affirmative action is a controversial policy designed to remedy the consequences of prior discrimination, generally through some sort of minority preferences.

KEY TERMS

affirmative action   317
assimilation   304
contact hypothesis   301
direct institutional discrimination   298
discrimination   298
ethnic group   295
genocide   302
indirect institutional discrimination   299
individual discrimination   298
minority group   295
pluralism   305
prejudice   297
race   295
racism   300
scapegoat   300
segregation   304
separatism   306
stereotype   297

CRITICAL THINKING QUESTIONS

1. Can the unequal treatment of minority groups be adequately addressed without responding to indirect institutional discrimination? Why do so many people—especially members of the dominant group—resist accepting the reality of this type of discrimination?
2. Which of the various theories of prejudice and discrimination offers the most promise for reducing the inequities experienced by minorities?
3. Do you believe that assimilation, pluralism, or separatism is the most appropriate policy for the various minority groups discussed in this chapter?
4. Should the United States continue to offer affirmative action programs for minority groups?

❖ 13 ❖ GENDER

Remember the Ladies

In 1776 Abigail Adams wrote the following letter to her husband John who was attending the Second Continental Congress:

In the new Code of Laws. . . . I desire you to remember the ladies and be more generous and favorable to them than your ancestors . . . That your sex is naturally tyrannical is a truth so thoroughly established as to admit of no dispute... so whilst you are proclaiming peace and good will to men, emancipation for all nations, you insist on retaining an absolute power over wives. But you must remember that arbitrary power is like most other things which are hard, very liable to be broken.

John Adams, who became the nation's second president, dismissed these warnings as he wrote back to Abigail:

As to your new Code of Laws, I cannot but laugh. . . . We know better than to repeal our masculine system. (Adapted from Norton & Alexander, 1996)

Nature Versus Nurture Revisited

Famed anthropologist Margaret Mead journeyed to New Guinea in the 1930s to learn about the different tribal groups comprising the nation. She lived with three different tribes. Among the gentle, peace-loving Arapesh, both men and women were nurturant and compliant, spending time gardening, hunting, and child rearing. The Arapesh gained immense satisfaction from these tasks,

which were eagerly shared by both men and women. Arapesh children grew up to mirror these patterns and became cooperative and responsive parents themselves. By contrast, the fierce Mundugumor barely tolerated children; they left them to their own devices as early in life as possible and taught them to be as hostile, competitive, and as suspicious to others as their elders were. Both mothers and fathers showed little tenderness to their children, commonly using harsh physical punishment. The Tchumbuli exhibited still a different pattern. Their women were practical and unadorned. Their men were passive, vain, and vindictive. Women's weaving, fishing, and trading activities provided the economic mainstay for the community; men remained close to the village and practiced dancing and art. Women enjoyed the company of other women. Men strived to gain the women's attention and affection, a situation women took with tolerance and humor, viewing men more as boys than peers. Contrary to her original belief that there were "natural" sex differences, Mead concluded after visiting these tribes that masculine and feminine are culturally, rather than biologically, determined. (Adapted from Mead, 1935)

Girls and Boys Together . . . But Mostly Apart

In elementary school, eating and walking are not sex-typed activities, but in forming groups in lunchrooms and hallways children often separate by gender. On the playground similar patterns show up. Boys control the large fixed areas for team sports such as soccer and football. Girls play closer to the building, using cement areas for jumprope and hopscotch. When children use gender to exclude others from play, they draw upon beliefs connecting boys to some activities and girls to others. A first-grade boy watching girls playing jumprope offered to swing the rope. The girls responded with, "No way, you don't know how to do it. You gotta be a girl." Boys who moved into female-marked space, such as the cafeteria line or female lunch table, are teased by other boys: "Look, Mike's in the girl's line" and pointing to a boy at an all-female table "That's a girl over there." Relaxed interactions between girls and boys often depend on adults, such as teachers, to set up and legitimize contact. But children are strongly oriented to segregation by gender and often resist adult interference into their segregated activities. (Adapted from Thorne, 1997:179)

321

These vignettes highlight several key themes we will view in this chapter. First, attitudes and behavior regarding gender are taken-for-granted assumptions about human social life. Second, when such assumptions are challenged, people have a variety of responses, ranging from puzzlement and disbelief to scorn and ridicule. Third, challenges calling for a change in gender roles are often resisted not only by those who hold power (mostly men), but also by those who have the lesser amount of power (mostly women). Abigail Adams issued a challenge to men's power and was laughed at by her husband. Margaret Mead's original challenge to the assumed biological (natural) basis of male and female behavior created skepticism in the scientific community. And those elementary school children who challenge the gender segregation of their activities are laughed at or ridiculed by their peers; attempts at gender desegregation are stubbornly resisted by both the girls and the boys. Finally, we will show other patterns of behavior that develop when gender intersects with race, class, ethnicity, and other categories of social life. Sociologists provide a number of explanations for all these patterns.

The study of gender has emerged as one of the most important trends in sociology in the twentieth century. Once a marginal concept, it is now a central feature of the discipline. Although all social relationships are ordered in some manner, gender is a key component of that ordering. Gender exerts a powerful influence on our lives because social institutions, as the key agents of socialization, are structured significantly according to attitudes and behaviors regarding gender.

considerably. People such as hermaphrodites, who are born with ambiguous sex characteristics, may be assigned one sex at birth but develop a different gender identity. And many cultures allow some people to move freely between genders. Sociology emphasizes how gender is learned, changes over time as cultural definitions change, and varies considerably in different cultures. Margaret Mead's work in New Guinea undeniably supports such an emphasis. **Gender roles,** then, are the expected attitudes and behaviors a society associates with each sex. This definition puts gender squarely in the sociocultural context.

Some biological differences must be accepted as given. But equally problematic is a model with too strong a focus on biological differences and insufficient attention to the institutionalized sexism that transforms male-female differences into male advantage and female disadvantage (Bem, 1996:11). As detailed in Chapter 5, although sociology certainly does not dismiss biology, the strength of its perspective on gender rests with the social side. Sociologists favor theories that account for a range of variables that are rooted in sociocultural factors and imply that female or male physiology does not limit achievement.

Scientists in all disciplines now agree that both biology and culture are necessary variables in explaining human social behavior. However, the biological differences between the sexes continue to be used to justify gender inequality. One major result of such a justification is **sexism,** the belief that one sex, female, is inferior to the other sex, male. Sexism is most prevalent in societies that are **patriarchal,** in which male-dominated social structures lead to the oppression of women. Patriarchy goes hand in hand with

SEX AND GENDER

In sociology, the terms sex and gender refer to two different content areas. As defined in Chapter 7, *sex* refers to the biological characteristics distinguishing male and female. This definition emphasizes male and female differences in chromosomes, anatomy, hormones, reproductive systems, and other physiological components. *Gender* refers to those social, cultural, and psychological traits linked to males and females through particular social contexts. Sex makes us male or female; gender makes us masculine or feminine. Sex is an ascribed status because a person is born with it. Gender is an achieved status because it has to be learned.

This relatively simple distinction is nonetheless loaded with problems because it implies unambiguous "either-or" categories. Recall from Chapter 7 that sexuality itself is culturally conditioned. *Sexual orientation,* how people experience sexual pleasure, varies

In many cultures women are likely to work outside the home but they still have responsibility for household tasks associated with traditional gender roles.

androcentrism, in which male-centered norms operate throughout all social institutions and become the standard to which all persons adhere. Sexism is reinforced by both patriarchy and androcentrism. The sociological perspective will show how sexism is maintained even when the majority of both men and women wish to eliminate it.

THEORETICAL PERSPECTIVES ON GENDER ROLES

Early sociological explanations related to gender roles evolved from work on the sociology of the family. These explanations centered on why men and women hold different roles in the family that in turn impact the roles they perform outside the family. To a large extent, this early work on the family has continued to inform current sociological thinking on gender roles.

Functionalism

The functionalist theoretical perspective, in keeping with its emphasis on society as made up of interdependent parts that are expected to work together smoothly, suggests that separate gender roles for women and men are beneficial. In preindustrial soci-

Functionalists suggest that families can be disrupted when men and women do not adhere to traditional gender roles, such as when a husband is the homemaker and a wife is the breadwinner.

eties, the most useful way to maintain order is to assign different tasks to men and women. In hunting and gathering societies, men were hunters, were away from home more, and were expected to bring food to their families and to protect them from harm. It was functional for women, more limited in mobility by pregnancy and nursing, to be assigned tasks related to child rearing and household maintenance. Women also obtained food by gathering or through subsistence agricultural activities. Children were needed to help with agricultural and domestic activities. Similar principles apply to families in contemporary societies, according to the functionalist perspective. Disruption is minimized and harmony is maximized when spouses assume complementary and specialized roles, such as breadwinner and homemaker (Parsons & Bales, 1955). If there is too much overlap in these roles, competition between spouses increases and the family system can be disrupted.

Functionalism offers a reasonably sound explanation for the origin of gender roles and demonstrates the functional utility of assigning tasks on the basis of gender, specifically in societies where children are needed for agricultural work. Overall, however, functionalist views of gender and the family have not kept pace with rapid social change and the move toward more egalitarian attitudes. It is based on a traditional white middle-class family structure in which women are in the home or, if outside the home, only as part of a reserve labor force, and where men are separated from their families. Contemporary families, especially in the developed world, simply do not fit this pattern.

Conflict Theory

Conflict theory reflects Marxian ideas about class conflict and the relationship between the exploiter and the exploited. Marx's collaborator, Frederich Engels (1884–1942), extended this idea to the family. According to Engels, after the introduction of private property and capitalism, a woman's domestic labor was no longer valued when compared to the basic necessities of life provided by the man. Women, therefore, are subordinate to men in the autocracy of the household and can never be emancipated until they can take part in paid production, with domestic work taking an insignificant amount of their time. Contemporary conflict theory concurs that men's economic advantage provides the basis for gender inequality both inside and outside the home. The conflict perspective is evident in research suggesting that household responsibilities have an effect on occupational location, work experience, and number of hours worked per week, all of which are linked to the gender gap in earnings (Shelton & Firestone, 1989).

Undesirable work will be performed disproportionately by those lacking resources to demand sharing the burden or purchasing substitutes (Spitze, 1986). Since household labor is unpaid, and thus associated with lack of power, the homemaker (wife) takes on virtually all domestic chores (Coverman, 1989; Lindsey, 1996a). The more powerful spouse performs the least amount of household work.

Conflict theory has been criticized for its overemphasis on the economic basis of inequality and its assumption that there is inevitable competition between family members. It tends to dismiss the consensus many wives and husbands have on how tasks are allocated. In addition, paid employment is clearly not the panacea envisioned by Engels in overcoming male dominance. In the old Soviet Union women had the highest levels of paid employment in the world, retained more household responsibilities than comparable women in other countries, and earned two-thirds of the average male income. In post-Communist Russia, there is no change in women's domestic work but women now earn less than half of men's average earnings (Gray, 1990; Hockstader, 1995). Research unanimously concludes that despite growing equity in the workplace, women employed full time take on a "second shift" of domestic work after returning home (Hochschild, 1989; Perkins & DeMeis, 1996).

Symbolic Interactionism

Consistent with the view that reality is what people agree it is, symbolic interactionism asserts that gender is a social construction and that people called "females" or "males" are endowed with certain traits defined as feminine or masculine. Concepts like gender must be found in the meanings people bring to them (Denzin, 1993). Gender emerges "not merely as an individual attribute but something that is accomplished in interaction with others." People "do" gender (West & Fenstermaker, 1995:21). In "doing" gender, symbolic interactionism takes its lead from Erving Goffman (1959a, 1963a), who maintains that when we want to create certain impressions we act out various roles, similar to what would occur in a theatrical performance. Research on singles bars typifies this approach. Both men and women "stalk" for partners, but they do it according to agreed-upon rules. A man, who usually comes to the bar alone, operates from a script in which he makes the first move. A woman, who is more likely to be with a female friend, must disengage herself from that friend if she is "selected" by the man. A process of unspoken negotiation and choice based primarily on gender roles is operating (Laws & Schwartz, 1977).

Gender roles are highly structured by one set of scripts designed for males and another designed for females. Although each script permits a range of behavior options, the usual result is that gender roles promote a pattern of between-sex competition, rejection, and emotional segregation. This pattern is reinforced when we routinely refer to those of the other sex (gender) as the "opposite" sex. Men and women label each other as opposite to who *they* are, then behave according to that label. The behavior serves to separate rather than connect the sexes.

Feminist Sociological Theory: Linking Race, Class, and Gender

Sociological theory must account for human social behavior in all its varieties. The most useful theories take into account the ways people are alike, and the ways they are different. Feminist sociologists were

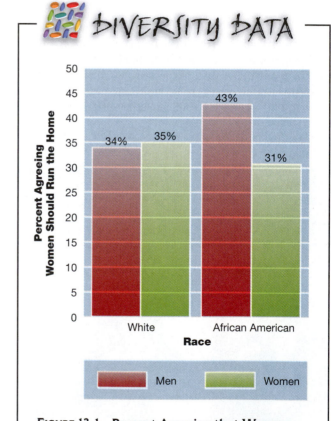

FIGURE 13.1 **Percent Agreeing that Women Should Run the Home While Men Run the Country.** About one-third of white men, white women, and African American women believe women should run the home and men should run the country. However, 43% of African American men believe this. how do gender and race link to account for this important difference?

Source: NORC. General Social Surveys, 1972–1996. Chicago National Opinion Research Center, 1996. Reprinted by permission of NORC, Chicago, IL.

among the first people in the discipline to account for these similarities and differences, specifically as related to race, social class, and gender. Along with linking these categories, the feminist perspective is also based on **feminism,** an inclusive world-wide movement to end sexism and sexist oppression by empowering women. Empowerment allows women to have a measure of control over their own destinies.

The race–class–gender linkage originated with African American feminists in the 1960s. These women recognized that analyzing social behavior by this linkage is necessary not only for scientific understanding, but also to determine how women are alike and how they are different. If the real differences between women in terms of race and class are ignored, feminism will falter. For example, when the issue of poverty becomes "feminized," the issue is defined primarily by gender—women are at a higher risk of being poor than men. A focus on the feminization of poverty ignores the links between race, social class, and marital status that puts at higher risk certain *categories* of women such as single parents, women of color, and elderly women living alone (Dressel, 1994). To explain poverty, racial and class oppression must be considered as well as gender. When white, middle-class feminists focus on oppression of women they sometimes have difficulty recognizing the privileges that come with their own race and class (Collins, 1996).

Thirty years ago the women's movement did not recognize that these intersecting categories can divide women. An African American woman living in poverty, for instance, might be more concerned about the disadvantages associated with her social class and race than the disadvantages associated with gender. Today the movement specifically addresses the concerns of women interconnected to various subcul-

tures, but it is still struggling to overcome the earlier legacy that overlooked these connections. As a result, the movement is less unified today (Almquist, 1995; Terrelonge, 1995).

Branches of Feminism.   The feminist movement is not completely unified in part because it *is* inclusive, and that very inclusiveness makes it difficult for agreement on some issues. As a result, the movement has several different branches that are divided according to general philosophical differences. Women and men do not generally "join" a branch of feminism, but different formal and informal groups are regarded as under the general umbrella of one branch or another. The following are the main branches of feminism.

Liberal Feminism.   Also called egalitarian or mainstream feminism, the philosophy of this branch is based on the simple idea that all people are created equal and should not be denied equality of opportunity because of gender. Since both genders benefit from eliminating sexism, numerous men also identify with this branch. The work of this branch is largely based on eliminating sexism in the overall social structure. The National Organization of Women is the formal group that represents this branch.

Socialist Feminism.   Also called Marxist feminism, this branch believes that the inferior position of women is linked to class based capitalism and the structure of the family in capitalistic societies. Capitalism is supported by women's unpaid household work and underpaid work in the labor force. Male supporters agree that the privileges they receive in the home are unjust to women. This branch works to adapt socialist principles to both workplace and home to increase gender equity.

Feminism has prompted sociological theory to account for the ways race, class and gender are linked and challenges the white, middle-class male norm for explaining social behavior.

The United Nations Conferences on Women: The Legacy of Beijing—A Personal Perspective

"Development, if not engendered, is endangered."
United Nations Development Program, 1995

In its Charter of 1945, the United Nations announced its commitment to the equality of women and men. The year 1975 was declared as International Women's Year and the years 1976 to 1985 were recognized by the United Nations (UN) General Assembly as the United Nations Decade for Women. Official conferences to mark the decade and work on a global agenda of women's issues were held in Mexico City in 1975; Copenhagen, Denmark, in 1980; and Nairobi, Kenya, in 1985. Under the banner of "equality, development, and peace," each conference assessed the progress of commitments made on behalf of women by various nations.

Alongside each official UN conference ran a parallel one, a forum consisting of hundreds of nongovernmental organizations (NGOs) that brought together women from all over the world and all walks of life representing a wide diversity of opinions and agendas. Inclusiveness brings dissent, and the conferences were marked by political,

religious, and economic factionalism, which, unfortunately, became media highlights. Efforts by conservative groups to discredit and interrupt the proceedings also occurred. Many women who attended the NGO Forum in Copenhagen were discouraged by the amount of friction that appeared to separate rather than unify women. Some women felt that the Copenhagen conference did not focus enough on the intersection of class and race with gender. They wanted to address issues relevant to all groups of women, especially women in the developing world. By Nairobi, then, friction was reduced and dialogue was opened. A fundamental change from Copenhagen was the recognition that the woman's movement is fundamentally a political movement.

Gains in political astuteness were clearly evident a decade later. In 1995, the international women's movement took center stage when Beijing, China, hosted the largest UN conference in history. With an attendance estimated at 50,000, Beijing was historic not only in terms of numbers, but because the women's agenda moved to the center of global debate. Beijing served as a watershed for the women's movement worldwide.

International media attention again focused on controversy and conflict—rather than on the more pervasive atmosphere of unity and support. Yet the truly remarkable events in Beijing finally managed to alter this trend. Even while attending the conference, many of us were acutely aware that the international media were dwelling on issues that generated the most controversy, especially religious fundamentalism. Demonstrations by those representing conservative groups were frequently staged. The Iranian delegation of fully veiled women and their male "escorts" provided the media with much camera time. Their efforts were met by what many women there described as "bemused toleration." But television crews would willingly follow behind them and report on the nightly news that religious fundamentalism was tearing the conference apart.

This could not have been further from the truth. While religious fundamentalism was certainly one of many controversial topics, the NGO Forum was remarkable in its ability to bring together women of all faiths to engage in dialogue over matters that affected their daily lives, such as reproduction, parenting, family violence, and health,

Radical Feminism. This branch believes that sexism is at the core of patriarchal society and all social institutions reflect that sexism. Women's oppression is from male domination so if men are the problem, neither capitalism nor socialism will solve it. Radical feminists desire to create separate institutions that are women centered—those that rely on other women rather than men.

Multicultural and Global Feminism. This branch of feminism explicitly acknowledges that gender intersects with race, class, issues of colonization, and the exploitation of women worldwide. Gender, however, is the overarching concern that unites the

men and women in this branch. They seek to work together across national boundaries to change patriarchy. They contend that no woman is free until the conditions that oppress women worldwide are eliminated. The people who came together for the United Nations Conferences on Women represent this branch.

Despite the philosophical differences, clearly these branches overlap a great deal. Feminists say that despite many different and often opposing "feminisms," feminists can agree to disagree. As psychologist Judith Worrell (1996:361) points out, "although we have joined a common parade, we do not all march to the same music."

In 1995, the UN Conference on Women in Beijing brought together 50,000 of all races, classes, and nations and adopted a platform of action calling for gender equality, development and peace.

cial delegations. While the Beijing conference was marked by negative international media attention, Chinese obstructionism, logistical nightmares, and inadequate facilities, the ability and perseverance of the women who attended and worked to get the Platform of Action adopted was nothing short of spectacular. As Hillary Clinton stated in her address to the Forum, "NGOs are where the action is." With thousands of NGOs as watchdogs, governments will be held accountable for the pledges made to women and their families throughout the world. In just five short years important elements of the platform have been put in place worldwide. Bolstered by NGO advocacy, more girls are in school, more women receive development funds, and more families are intact as direct results of the conference. This gathering of women in Beijing attests to the recognition that women's empowerment is beneficial to everyone.

1. What international events might alter the positive directions women's rights took after the Beijing conference?
2. Demonstrate how sociological knowledge of level of power between men and women and between the developed and the developing world can be helpful in predicting the future course of the women's movement.

Sources: Cagatay et al., 1989; Mann, 1996; U.N. Development Program, 1997.

all of which have religious overtones. When politics, religion, and cultural tradition were met head on, as between Palestinian and Israeli women or between African and other women who did and did not accept female genital mutilation, toleration and understanding emerged in an atmosphere of open dialogue. What became clear, however, is that the die is cast against religious fundamentalism when religion is used to deny women's human rights. Religion may be recast to become liberating and be used as a weapon against sexism and for empowerment.

The norm of the NGO Forum sessions was to ensure that everyone had the opportunity to voice opinions; thus, complete unity was rare. However, when people "agree to disagree," the stage is set for a better understanding of the issues and more toleration of dissenting opinion.

What is the legacy of Beijing? I speak from the perspective of attending the gatherings in Copenhagen and Nairobi as well as Beijing. The previous conferences were more divisive, but also smaller, less inclusive, and with fewer women on the organizing bodies or offi-

GLOBAL PERSPECTIVES: WOMEN AND DEVELOPMENT

The United Nations has spearheaded major efforts to reduce the gender gap in human capability—areas such as literacy, access to health care, job training, and family planning. Women in the developing world are the most restricted in almost all important areas of human capability. The good news is that since 1985 the gap in education and health has been cut in half. The bad news, however, is that data on the world's women continue to document patterns of gender inequality that have dire consequences on the lives of women and girls (United Na-

tions Development Program, 1997). These include the following:

1. Seventy percent of the 1.3 billion people worldwide who live in poverty are women and girls.
2. If women's unpaid work in the household was given economic value, it would add an estimated one-third ($4 trillion) to the world's economic product. When wage discrimination is factored in, the figure rises to $11 trillion.
3. More than two-thirds of the 960 million illiterate adults worldwide are women.

Females are less likely than males to attend school in developing societies when they are needed for domestic tasks, such as girls gathering cow dung patties for fuel in India.

4. Women grow half the world's food but are rarely land owners. Eighty percent of Africa's food is grown and processed by women.
5. Most of the world's 20 million refugees are women and their dependent children.
6. Ninety percent of all countries have organizations that promote the advancement of women, but women make up only 10 percent of the world's legislative seats.

Overall, the underlying cause of the inequality of women is that their roles are primarily domestic (mother, wife, homemaker), and although these are vital to the well-being of society, they are undervalued and unpaid (Lindsey, 1997). Other social institutions, especially the economy, reinforce the existing inequality.

Women's Economic Activities

In the developing world, the role and status of women in the process of economic development has emerged as a major issue that now advises many development assistance programs. From Ester Boserup's (1970) pioneering study on women in development, the argument that development has an adverse effect on women, often leading to further impoverishment and exploitation, is well documented (Afshar, 1991; Scott, 1995; Lindsey, 1996b). The path leading to negative development outcomes for women is a deceptively simple one: "As development proceeds, women are denied access to productive sources and new technologies," which then "serves to lower their relative, if not absolute, productivity" (Norris, 1992:183). In societies characterized by powerful patriarchal institutions, men and women rarely share equally the limited resources available to families, a situation that deteriorates with development. And when the development strategies are based on capitalism, the situation is worsened for women (Lockwood, 1997).

The hardest hit are rural women whose nondomestic work consists of subsistence farming. Even though they were not land owners, before cash crop farming, Latin American and African women for centuries managed farms and retained control over their produce. Colonialism and subsequent agricultural development projects introduced technology and cash-crop farming, which undermined farming practices and virtually eliminated the traditional economic resources available to women. Subsistence farming is vital to the livelihood of a family. But because subsistence agriculture is defined as domestic work and there is no cash exchanged and no surplus for profit in the marketplace, it is not considered "productive" in traditional economic definitions of labor (Waring, 1988). Development programs typically rely on the standard international economic definitions that exclude the majority of work women perform, such as child care, domestic labor, and subsistence farming.

In addition to farming, development policies have also ignored the gender implications of other labor-force activities. At the family level, the "trickle-down model" is supposed to operate. Policies are designed to upgrade the economic standards of families by concentrating on the assumed male head of household, who is the breadwinner, with his dependent wife in the homemaker role. It is reasoned that by improving employment of men, the whole family would benefit. By failing to acknowledge the varied productive roles of women, especially rural women, critics charge that this is a "ridiculous," urban middle-class model that is designed to advance women and their families but does just the opposite (Ahmad & Loutfi, 1985). Men often migrate to cities in search of paid work, leaving women with loss of help in remaining subsistence activities. Paid employment available to rural women usually consists of low-paid domestic work or work on commercial farms. Another option is the assembling and light-manufacturing plants that multinational

Women in the developing world have similar roles worldwide. Among subsistence farmers in Nepal and Kenya, women are responsible for both agricultural production and household work.

corporations are building on the fringes of urban areas in less-developed countries. Multinational corporations favor young women, most between ages 13 and 25, for their willingness to work for low wages in substandard conditions and their presumed docility that keeps them from unionizing (Moore, 1988; Ferraro, 1992).

On the positive side, the data that development is correlated with women's impoverishment is no longer ignored. Propelled by the international women's movement, strong women-oriented nongovernmental organizations (NGOs), and the Platform of Action adopted at the United Nations Conference on Women in Beijing, gender analysis in development planning has moved from the fringes to the center (Rao et al., 1991; Kusterer, 1993; United Nations Development Program, 1997).

GENDERED SOCIAL INSTITUTIONS

Like all socialization, gender socialization must be transmitted in a manner that allows people to learn what is expected of them. Since social institutions

provide that transmittal, they are important vehicles for demonstrating gendered social behavior. In Chapters 5 and 6 we learned how primary socialization and social interaction are significantly influenced by gender, especially in language and early sibling and peer relationships. Learned first in the family and then reinforced by other social institutions, gender is a fundamental shaper of all social life.

Family Life

The infant's first artifacts are clothes and toys. If the sex of a baby is not known in advance, friends and relatives choose gender-neutral gifts to avoid giving clothes or toys suggesting the "wrong" gender. Teddy bears and clothing in colors other than pink and blue are safe bets. But within weeks after the baby's arrival, the infant's room is easily recognizable as belonging to a girl or a boy. Color-coded and gender-typed clothing of infants and children is universal (Shakin et al., 1985). If she is not readily identifiable by her clothing, an infant girl of 3 months will often have a velcro bow attached to her bald head, in case onlookers mistakenly think she is a boy. A gendered

Multinational corporations typically build small plants near urban areas and employ young women who work for lower wages than men would receive. This work brings money to the family but girls are also kept from additional schooling.

clothing-toy link starts early in the family and is especially powerful for girls who buy "fashions" for their dolls. For example, in the last twenty-five years, over 250 million Barbie dolls have been sold, and every year over 20 million outfits are bought for Barbie, a pattern some suggest sows the seeds for a clothing addiction in girls (Freedman, 1995).

Toys for girls encourage domesticity, interpersonal closeness, and a social orientation. Boys receive more categories of toys, their toys are more complex and expensive, and they foster self-reliance and problem solving (Rheingold & Cook, 1975; Hughes, 1991). Both parents and children express clear preferences for gender-typed toys. These preferences reinforce the persistent gender-related messages that are sent to children through the toys. The gender-related messages, in turn, show up in differences between girls and boys in cognitive and social development in childhood as well as differences in gender roles as adults (Miller, 1987; Caldera et al., 1989; Etaugh & Liss, 1992). On your next outing to a toy store, note how shelves are categorized according to gender and how pictures on the boxes suggest how boys and girls should use the toys. Little Jane uses her tea set to give parties for her dolls in her room, while same-age Dick is experimenting with sports or racing trucks outside in the mud.

Toys encourage different levels of physical activity, and children stage their activities according to the toy. In early childhood girls are more imaginative in their play compared to boys, but the situation reverses after about age 7. Girls later script their play around role-taking in realistic settings, such as playing house, while boys script play around fantastic scenarios involving superheroes (Leaper, 1994). Children as young as age 2 have already developed a strong sense of gender roles, and older children expect their parents to respond to them accordingly (Dino et al., 1984). The development of gender-role identity is linked to the child's perception of his or her parents' behavior. Likewise parents perceive competencies in areas such as math, language, and sports in terms of the gender of their children, even when no real differences in competency exist (Eccles et al., 1990).

Gender is also a predictor of how parents will behave toward their children. Children of all ages are seen more frequently with mothers compared to fathers. Mothers talk to their children more and stay closer to them than fathers. Both parents are responsive to their infants, but as expected, as children get older, fathers are more involved with their sons. Mothers show more expressive and emotional support regardless of the child's gender. This pattern of gender intensification increases as children get older (Fagot, 1984; Hoffman & Teyber, 1985; Crouter et al., 1995).

Education

When children enter the classroom, earlier gender-role patterns follow them. Americans wholeheartedly embrace the belief that education is the key to success and the vehicle for social mobility. Gender equality in education is assumed. Yet when the female kindergarten teacher first removes Dick's mittens and helps Jane off with her coat, by virtue of gender alone, their long educational journey will contain essential differences.

Children the world over are socialized for future roles according to their gender. This girl from Mali is playing "house" with a baby on her back and her tunic pulled over her breasts like the adult woman.

Kindergarten. In kindergarten Jane gains approval from peers, parents, and teachers for her quiet demeanor and studiousness. Toys in kindergarten are likely to be a familiar extension of those at home. They encourage quiet play, especially the doll corner and minikitchen. Jane can pretend to cook, set the table, and clean with miniature household artifacts constructed for small hands. Girls may envy the boys as they display more power and freedom in their play behavior, but that envy is tempered by the teacher's obvious disapproval of the boys' boisterous classroom behavior. Jane rarely plays with the boys and prefers playing house or jump rope with a few friends. Kindergarten continues a process of self-selected gender segregation that increases during the school years (Paley, 1984; Davies, 1989).

Meanwhile, Dick enters the classroom more unprepared for the experience than Jane. His higher level of physical activity is incompatible with the sedate nature of school. Dick soon becomes aware that the teacher approves of the quieter children—and the quieter children are usually the girls. But the teacher pays attention to the children who are more disrup-

tive—and the more disruptive children are usually the boys. Dick may believe it is better to be reprimanded than ignored. When boys wander into the doll corner, they use the area for nondomestic games, mainly based on fighting and destruction. They invent "warrior narratives" to structure their play—games involving good and bad, pirates and police—and they alter the domestic artifacts to fit their needs (Jordan & Cowan, 1995). Although teachers maintain that they do not treat girls and boys differently, studies show that aggressive boys and dependent girls gain teachers' attention (Thorne, 1993; Sadker & Sadker, 1994).

Elementary School. For girls, elementary school is a vehicle for achievement. They receive higher grades than boys, and they exceed boys in most areas of verbal ability, reading, and mathematics. With a premium on being good and being tidy, high achievement coupled with low criticism should be an ideal learning environment. Yet the message that is communicated to girls very early in their education is that they are less important than boys. In curricular materials, for instance, over thirty years of research demonstrates that girls are virtually invisible, or at best, play insignificant roles. Boys do interesting and exciting things; girls do not (Best, 1983; Grossman & Grossman, 1994; Orenstein, 1997). Although curricular material is more egalitarian today, stereotyped gender portrayals are prevalent. For example, children's books show girls as brave, but still needing rescue. They show boys babysitting, but unable to express a full range of emotions. Boys see active and resourceful males who build, create, discover, and protect and rescue girls (Weitzman, 1984; P. Cooper, 1989; Purcell & Stewart, 1990).

Teacher behavior reinforces such messages. Girls are called on less frequently than boys; they receive less criticism but also less instruction. When teachers criticize boys for inadequate academic work, they suggest it is because of lack of effort rather than intellectual flaw, a point girls are less likely to hear (Acker, 1994; Mincer, 1994). Girls who do poorly in math, for instance, are less likely than boys to believe more effort will produce success (Stipek & Gralinski, 1991). Research demonstrates that elementary school teaches boys that problems are challenges to overcome; it often teaches girls that failure is beyond their control.

High School. Intellectual achievement and superior grades in elementary school do not predict academic success in high school. As might be expected, girls' standardized test scores decrease (Burton et al., 1988; Sadker & Sadker, 1994). Whereas in elementary school girls are confident and assertive, they leave adolescence with a poor self-image, with the sharpest drop in self-esteem occurring between elementary and middle school. It is even more pronounced for Hispanic girls who start out with the highest levels of self-esteem for all races. Compared to white girls, African American girls retain higher levels of self-esteem, but positive feelings about their teachers and their academic work drop significantly (American Association of University Women, 1992; Valenzuela, 1993; Orenstein, 1994). On the other hand, boys experience consistent gains in self-confidence and believe they are good at a lot of things. They are able to demonstrate their talents in courses and sports specifically designed for them (Eder & Kinney, 1995). By high school, scholastic achievement for girls begins to decline in reading and writing, but especially in mathematics, where boys are beginning to excel.

The finding that girls do not do as well in math as boys has led some to conclude that girls have a lower, biologically based analytic ability. The biology argument in explaining gender differences in math and science has used everything from chromosomes, hormones, brain organization, to genetic codes to explain the slight male edge (Christen, 1991; Peters, 1991; Casey et al., 1992). In terms of spatial ability, no gene has been identified that traces the ability from mother to son, and researchers are skeptical that such a "complex ability as spatial reasoning could possibly rest in a single gene" (McLoughlin, 1988:55). Biology cannot be completely discounted, since mathematics and spatial tests are related, and there are gender differences in rate of development. However, since even the small gender differences in mathematics have been steadily decreasing, researchers lean toward the counterargument that sociocultural factors propel boys but deter girls in mathematics. When verbal processes are used in math questions, girls outperform boys. When spatial-visual processes are used, boys outperform girls

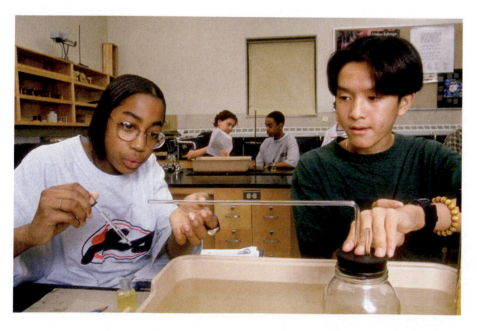

When girls take more math and science courses in high school, they are better prepared for entering certain high-paying research, engineering, and medical careers.

(Doyle & Paludi, 1995). When the number of math courses taken is controlled for, there are no real gender differences in spatial perception or mathematical capability (Fox, 1981; Chipman et al., 1985). Only 1 to 5 percent of male-female math difference can be explained by gender (Freidman, 1989; Tartre, 1990). The gender-math link is a critical one. In addition to preparation for high-paying careers, academic success in math and science is one of the strongest predictors of self-esteem for high school girls (American Association of University Women, 1992; Orenstein, 1994).

In summarizing the research, the major importance is that "sex differences can be manipulated, magnified, minimized, or even reversed" by relevant environmental factors and developmental experiences (Hoyenga & Hoyenga, 1993:400). Claiming that male superiority in math is innate is unjustified (Caplan & Caplan, 1994:43).

Higher Education. If high school has done its job well, the best and the brightest students will pursue a college education. Since World War II there has been a steady increase of both men and women attending college. Women are now enrolled in greater numbers than men, in part because of women over age 35, who attend part time. Ideally, college should be the one educational institution that evaluates students solely on criteria related to academic achievement and the potential for success. But the gender lessons of elementary school and high school are not easily forgotten.

In college as in high school, for girls, popularity is associated with how popular they are with boys. In tracing the experiences of even high-achieving college women, research suggests it is difficult to resist the "culture of romance." The ultimate effect is lowered ambition and a subversion of academic achievement (Holland & Eisenhart, 1990). College men are also not immune to gender-role changes regarding love and romance, which put some men in a double bind. Men value intelligence and originality in their female classmates more than in the past, yet many are unable to relinquish the internalized norm of male superiority. Tantalizing egalitarian ideals are held out to college men, who want to accept them, but these ideals represent the "lure and the threat" of the articulate, educated woman (Komarovsky, 1987).

College women may find it easier to choose the well-traveled road of majoring in the arts and humanities. Almost half of women who enter college with science-related interests switch to other majors. Pre-college preparation in math and science and lack of peers in the field are key factors in explaining this switch. Today women receive just over half of all undergraduate degrees and one-third of all doctorates. They earn slightly more than half of all doctorates in fields other than science and engineering. Gains in professional degrees have been steady; almost one-half of law degrees and one-third of medical degrees are awarded to women (Fox, 1995; U.S. Bureau of the Census, 1999). Considering that opportunities for women to pursue higher education are relatively recent, these numbers are impressive. But gender-specific patterns, which find women in areas that are more competitive and less financially rewarding, emerge. Compared to women, men are distributed in a wider variety of majors, and these majors lead to jobs in expanding, more lucrative technical fields such as engineering and computer science. Men dominate the most influential fields where graduate work is required and are at the top of the prestige hierarchy within them (Chapter 16). In medicine, men are surgeons and women are pediatricians. Men practice international law and women practice family law. The culmination of college or graduate school, whether as holder of B.A., M.D., or Ph.D., is also the culmination of a lifetime of attitudes and behaviors regarding gender.

The Lessons of Title IX. Title IX of the Educational Amendment Act of 1973 addresses many of the educational patterns described here. It prohibits sex (gender) discrimination in schools receiving federal funds. Title IX has helped alter blatant gender discrimination related to areas such as school admissions, financial aid, promotion and tenure of faculty, dress codes, counseling, and housing. Despite political compromises, it has had a large impact on college athletic programs. Instead of equal redistribution of financial resources—which would hurt "big ticket" men's sports such as football and basketball—Title IX calls for "reasonable opportunities" for financial assistance for each sex in proportion to the numbers participating in intercollegiate sports (Stetson, 1991). Before Title IX, few colleges offered female athletes adequate facilities, and no college gave women athletic scholarships. Budgetary allotments have improved, which may account for the impressive 600 percent increase in girls' participation in athletics in secondary schools. Today 40 percent of women students participate in college sports (Fox, 1995; Gavora, 1995). Title IX is unquestionably responsible for the dramatic success of women athletics in worldwide competitions such as the Olympics. Title IX is a major effort in dealing with gender equity in education.

Gender and the Workplace

Throughout history women have made major economic contributions to society, doing unpaid domestic work, producing goods or services at home for sale or exchange (cottage industry), and providing food for their families and villages (subsistence farming) (Christie & Lindsey, 1997). The Industrial Revolution opened up the world of paid work outside the home or farm for both men and women. Globally, the ratio of women to men in paid labor has jumped over 25 percent since 1970. In the United States, 60 percent of all women 16 years of age and over are in the labor force (Table 13.1). The participation rate of married women with very young children has doubled since 1975 (Table 13.2). There is a steady increase of labor-force participation of all working mothers with children under 1 year of age (Table 13.3). This entry has had profound consequences for all social institutions, especially family and school. Sociologists are interested in examining the type of paid work men and women do and why the work is differentially valued. For this reason, the workplace has become the strategic location in the battle for gender equality (Dunn, 1997).

The Wage Gap. Research consistently shows that even when controlling for education and work experience, and as measured by median annual earnings of full-time employees, women earn less than men, a global pattern that holds across all racial and ethnic groups and throughout occupations (Charles, 1992; Thornborrow & Sheldon, 1995; U.S. Bureau of the Census, 1999).

In the developed world, the United States and Canada have the highest wage gap (about 75 percent) and the Scandinavian countries the lowest (between

80 and 90 percent, with Iceland the lowest, at a remarkable 94 percent) (United Nations Development Program, 1997). A sociological perspective on gender roles helps explain why men are paid more than women.

As expected, the genders are not evenly distributed across occupations (see Table 13.4). When the majority of a particular occupation is made up of one gender, it becomes a normative expectation. This **gender-typing** of the occupation reinforces the segregation of the occupation by gender. If women are the majority of an occupation, the job is associated with fewer rewards. In the professions, accountants, architects, and engineers are predominantly male; teachers, nurses, and social workers are predominantly female. Males in female-dominated occupations have more advantages than women doing the same jobs. Referred to as the "glass escalator effect,"

Table 13.2 Married Women Employment (%) by Child Age, Selected Years

Child Age	1975	1985	1997
Under 3	32.7	50.5	61.3
3–5	42.2	58.4	67.0
6–13	51.8	68.2	76.5
14–17	53.5	67.0	80.1

Source: U.S. Department of Commerce, *Statistical Abstract of the United States*, 1998; adapted from Table No. 655.

Table 13.1 Characteristics of Women in the Labor Force, Selected Years

Status	1970	1975	1980	1985	1990	1995	1997
Total employed women 16+	43.3	46.3	51.5	54.5	57.5	58.9	59.8
Total unemployed women 16+	5.9	9.3	7.4	7.4	6.4	5.6	5.0
Total employed men 16+	79.7	77.9	77.4	76.3	76.1	76.7	75.0
Total unemployed men 16+	4.4	7.9	6.9	7.0	5.6	5.6	4.9
Female employment by age							
16 to 19	44.0	49.1	52.9	52.1	51.8	52.2	51.0
20 to 24	57.5	64.1	68.9	71.8	71.6	70.3	72.7
25 to 34	45.0	54.9	65.5	70.9	73.6	74.9	76.0
35 to 44	51.1	55.8	65.5	71.8	76.5	77.2	77.7
45 to 54	54.4	54.6	59.9	64.4	71.2	74.4	76.0
55 to 64	43.0	40.9	41.3	42.0	45.3	49.2	50.9
65+	9.7	8.2	8.1	7.3	8.7	8.8	8.6
Female employment by marital status							
Single	56.8	59.8	64.4	66.6	66.9	66.7[a]	67.9
Married with spouse	40.5	44.3	49.8	52.8	58.4	60.7[a]	61.6
Other	40.3	40.1	43.6	45.1	47.2	47.5[a]	48.6

[a] 1994 data

Source: U.S. Bureau of the Census, *Statistical Abstract of the United States*, 1991, 1995, 1998, *Employment and Earnings*, U.S. Bureau of Labor Statistics, Vol. 43(1), January 1998.

Table 13.3	Employed Mothers with Children Under 1 Year of Age
March of	Participation rate (%)
1990	49.5
1991	51.9
1992	52.2
1993	52.6
1994	54.6
1995	56.9
1996	55.4

Source: Howard V. Hayghe, "Developments in Women's Labor Force Participation," *Monthly Labor Review,* vol. 120, no. 9, September 1997.

Table 13.4 Occupational Distribution of Labor Force by Percent Female in Selected Occupations for 1983 and 1997		
Occupational Category	1983	1997
Executive, administrative, and managerial	32.4	48.9
Officials and public administrators	38.5	49.5
Personnel managers	43.9	63.4
Professional specialty	48.1	53.3
Engineers	5.8	9.6
Dentists	6.7	17.3
Nurses (RNs)	95.8	98.5
Physicians	15.8	26.2
University teachers	36.3	45.7
Elementary school teachers	83.3	83.9
Secondary school teachers	51.8	58.4
Clergy	5.6	13.6
Lawyers	15.3	26.6
Technicians and related support	64.6	64.1
Health technicians	84.3	80.2
Science technicians	29.1	39.5
Sales occupations	47.5	50.2
Real estate sales	48.9	50.0
Cashiers	84.4	78.4
Administrative support, including clerical	79.9	78.8
Secretaries	99.0	97.9
Computer operators	63.7	58.4
Service occupations	60.1	59.4
Child-care workers	96.9	96.8
Cleaners and servants	95.8	94.0
Police and detectives	9.4	16.4
Firefighting, fire prevention	1.0	3.4
Precision production, craft, and repair	8.1	8.9
Construction trades	1.8	2.4
Carpenters	1.4	1.6
Operators, fabricators, and laborers	26.6	24.7
Textile furnishing machine operators	82.1	72.1
Truck drivers	3.1	5.7
Farming, forestry, and fishing	16.0	19.8
Farm operators and managers	12.1	23.0
Farm workers	24.8	19.0

Source: U.S. Bureau of the Census, *Statistical Abstract of the United States,* 1995, 1998. Adapted from Table No. 649 (1995) and No. 672 (1998).

this pattern means men take their gender privileges with them and experience upward mobility as a result (Williams, 1992). Women are clustered in overcrowded, less-prestigious specialties (Bellas, 1993; Kaufman, 1995; Thornborrow & Sheldon, 1995). The result for women: less pay, less prestige, and less authority.

Race and ethnicity add double or triple jeopardy. Occupational distribution of minority women reflects changes in the labor force as well as gender inequality. After World War II, large numbers of African American women moved into government white-collar and clerical jobs and the lowest level private sector jobs, such as data entry or filing clerks (Glenn & Feldberg, 1995). Wage levels of minority women are unequal compared to men of the same group. African American, Asian American, and white women earn two-thirds to four-fifths of what men earn, with the greatest disparity occurring between white men and women (Marini, 1989; Xu & Leffler, 1992). Rooted in a tradition valuing economic opportunities for women, African American middle-class women moved into the professions earlier than white women. Like white women, they are steered into traditionally female occupations, but they have an added race liability. Concentrated in the public sector, such as teaching and social work, there is less discrimination but also less pay (Higginbotham, 2000). Although white women are also segregated in female-dominated professions, they are represented throughout the private sector where pay is higher.

The wage gap is also associated with the *human capital model.* According to this view, if there is inequality in wages, it is due to individual choices in matters of education and occupation. If women choose to interrupt schooling or careers for marriage and family reasons, experience and productivity are compromised and wages are lower (Blau & Ferber, 1992; Fermlee, 1995). In addition, the human capital model is consistent with the law of supply and demand. Women can be paid less because they choose occupations that make fewer demands on their family responsibilities. These are the very jobs that have an abundance of workers. The result is lower pay. If there is artificial intervention to make jobs equitable in terms of wages, such as setting quotas for certain jobs for men and women, the law of supply and demand will be compromised. To intervene will do more harm than good (Becker, 1994).

On the other hand, the wage gap can be explained according to the power relationships between men and women. This view of the wage gap suggests that men exercise power in a way that maintains their wage advantage. A good example is a protégé system, in which an already powerful member serves as a sponsor for entry and upward movement of a novice. An effective "old boy system" keeps power in the hands of a few men. Until women's networks include people of high rank, the corporate advancement of women will be stalled.

Regardless of how the wage gap is explained, its persistence is clearly linked to three factors:

1. The work women do, regardless of content, skill, or functional necessity, is less valued overall than the work men do.
2. The higher the number of women in the occupation, the lower the wages; the converse is true for male-dominated occupations. One-third of the wage gap is correlated with gender segregation.
3. Regardless of the law, gender discrimination in the workplace endures.

Overall, research points out that men are paid more than women for what they do simply because they are men (Fuchs, 1988; Kemp, 1994). Women's patterns of employment are different from men's, but for equal work there is not equal pay.

Women in Business.   An important economic trend of the last two decades is the rise of female-owned businesses, triple the rate of the increase in male-owned businesses (Noble, 1994; Walsh, 1995). Most increases are in traditional areas of female work, such as services and the retail trades. Although concentrated in peripheral economic niches that often lack access to capital, government contracts, and management expertise, women view their businesses as ways to gain autonomy, job mobility, and flexibility in balancing career and family (Committee on Small Business, 1988; Loscocco & Robinson, 1991). These women find small businesses a practical, financial, and psychologically rewarding alternative to management positions in large organizations.

What is clear, however, is that although women have made strides in middle management, they are deserting the ranks of larger organizations because they continue to be denied access to upper management (Fryxell & Lerner, 1989; Rosener, 1995). The **glass ceiling** is a term that describes women's failure to rise to senior level positions because of invisible and artificial barriers constructed by male management. Recruits into upper management are imaged, although unintentionally, according to a "white-male model," which excludes all women and men of color (Stuart, 1992). As long as sameness is valued, "women will continue to be disadvantaged merely because they are women" (Rosener, 1991:147). Many studies conclude that barriers to upward mobility are almost insurmountable and include career immobility, role

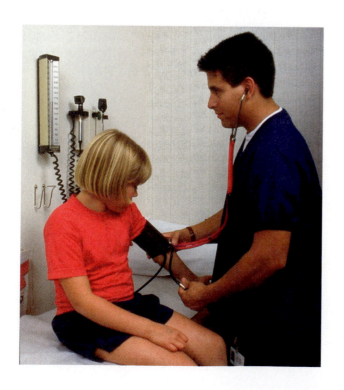

We associate certain jobs with one or the other gender and are often surprised when gender does not "match" the job, such as a male nurse or female engineer.

conflict, and lack of feedback and training (Morrison et al., 1992; Gregory, 1990). "Old style" gender bias also thwarts a woman's move up the corporate ladder (Antilla, 1995).

In cooperation with private enterprise, the federal government has begun a series of initiatives to counter the glass ceiling. The message the government is sending is that companies will ultimately lose if they continue to limit the talent and ambition of their female employees. If women leave a company to start their own businesses, former employees will be competitors. Another thrust of the government initiatives is to provide incentives for businesses to be more flexible with women who are juggling career and family responsibilities (U.S. Department of Labor, 1991; Federal Glass Ceiling Commission, 1997). Research continues to confirm that the loss of female talent is bad for business (Schwartz, 1989, 1994; Rosener, 1995).

Gendered Management Styles: The Partnership Alternative.   Despite past barriers to success, some research now suggests that a woman's socialization pattern may offer an advantage to modern corporations. In sharp contrast to the traditional corporate hierarchy, women tend to develop "weblike" leadership structures, relying on skills and attitudes valuable to a workplace in which innovation and creativity are demanded but where an authoritarian chain of command is obsolete (Helgesen, 1990:37). The woman's web extends to roles outside the corporation. Women bring interpersonal skills gained outside the organization back into the organization. They tend to form friendships in their workplace that extend outside the workplace and endure even after leaving a job. In contrast, male executives give up significant parts of their private lives for success in traditional business hierarchies, a situation emotionally detrimental to them as individuals and as employees (Halper, 1988).

For companies more receptive to alternative visions of corporate life, the distinctive management styles of women are encouraged. Women managers adopt styles compatible with overall female gender-socialization patterns, such as encouraging participation, mentoring, sharing power and information, interacting with all levels of employees, and connecting their on-job and off-job identities (Loden, 1985; Helgesen, 1990; Rosener, 1990).

These are the very patterns that are the hallmark of Japanese Style Management (JSM). JSM encourages a sense of community in the firms in which employees work, an interest in employees' lives outside of the office, consensus building, socioemotional bonding between employees and between management and labor, and a flattened management structure that is more egalitarian than hierarchical (Ouchi,

1982; Sasaki, 1990; Miwa, 1996). Principles of JSM are compatible with American gender role socialization patterns for females (Lindsey, 1992, 1998). JSM also fits with partnership models emerging in innovative corporations that emphasize linking rather than ranking, interactive and participative leadership styles, teamwork, and sharing (Eisler & Loye, 1990). Although Japanese executives in no way perceive their management styles as "feminine" and Japanese women are virtually excluded from top management positions, JSM is still compatible with gender role socialization practices in both the United States and Japan.

A problem may arise when the "celebration" of the female advantage in the workplace leads to increased stereotyping and a reaffirmation of the differences between women and men. If the workplace needs to be humanized, an emphasis on women being the ones to do it may widen the chasm between the genders (Faludi, 1991). The image of the nurturing women who smooth over problems is as stereotypical as the image of men who create the problems. On the positive side, virtually everyone in business today recognizes that difference does not imply better or worse or stronger or weaker (Segal, 1991:117).

REDUCING GENDER STRATIFICATION: POLITICS AND THE LAW

The political institution is responsible for enforcing laws designed to reduce gender inequality. Americans have no desire to eliminate social stratification. However, Americans believe that any inequality that exists should be traced to talent, ability, and motivation and not to ascribed statuses such as gender, race, or ethnicity (Chapters 11 and 12). The United States is firmly committed to the principle of gender equality in its legal structure.

Employment

Title VII of the 1964 Civil Rights Act makes it unlawful for an employer to refuse to hire, discharge, or discriminate against a person because of race, color, religion, sex, or national origin. The *Equal Employment Opportunity Commission* (EEOC) is the federal agency overseeing the enforcement of Title VII. EEOC was primarily aimed at protecting minority men. Through efforts of groups like the National Organization of Women (NOW), EEOC now protects women as well. Besides NOW's strategies, the mushrooming of sexual harassment cases has increased EEOC's responsibility considerably. As discussed in Chapter 6, the 1990s were the decade of sexual harassment notoriety, starting with the testimony given by Anita Hill during the hearings for Clarence Thomas's confirmation to the United States Supreme Court and culminating with allegations against President Clinton.

In employment, the only way that Title VII can be legally circumvented is through the *Bonafide Occupational Qualification* (BFOQ), which, for gender, means that one or the other sex is necessary for carrying out a job. A movie calling for a male actor or a female model for clothing are BFOQ examples. The courts have ruled that "customer preference" is not a BFOQ exemption; for example, men who were denied jobs as flight attendants. BFOQ is very narrowly interpreted and is seldom used as a defense for charges of sex discrimination in hiring.

The *Equal Pay Act* (EPA) of 1963 requires that females and males receive the same pay for the same work. Yet inconsistent with EPA, the wage gap has only slightly improved in the last two decades. Interpreted through Title VII provisions, **comparable worth** is the idea that male and female jobs should be assessed according to skill level, effort, and responsibility. Equal pay should be judged according to equal worth. In an early comparable worth suit in 1983, a federal court in Washington ruled that the state had to raise the wages of 15,500 employees in predominantly female occupations. Two years later a higher court overturned the decision, stating that market forces created the inequity and that the government had no responsibility to correct it. The later decision is based on the presumed gender neutrality of the human capital model, so that if women get paid less, they either prefer less demanding jobs or are less productive in the jobs they have (Rhoads, 1993). Research in the United States and Canada based on economic modeling that measures the impact of gender on jobs refutes the market-driven, human capital model. This research shows that wage discrimination exists because employers use gender to assign people to jobs, a technique limiting a woman's financial and career success (Sorensen, 1994; Ranson & Reeves, 1996). Overall, comparable worth has had positive effects on women's wages but negligible effects on employment (Figart, 1995).

Another cornerstone of federal law concerning gender and employment is *affirmative action* (see Chapter 12). With media attention focusing on quotas (*not* a provision of affirmative action), preferential hiring, and government control of private businesses, the policy has come under attack. Polls suggest that the public supports government objectives, but not quotas, to increase employment opportunities for women and minorities to get hired (Horner, 1996; Puddington, 1996). Data show that nonwhite women and women in management have benefited directly from affirmative action, but all women may benefit indirectly in its call for a fairer distribution of social benefits, a principle that has been constitutionally accepted and applied throughout U.S. history (Johnson, 1993).

The issue of self-esteem for the women who are hired through affirmative action should also be a factor in its evaluation. There may be psychological pain at being a "twofer," or a token employee on two counts, for example, a woman of color accepted into a male-dominated field. Despite outstanding credentials, her status is still defined by race and gender (Cruz, 1996). Stigma is a double-edged sword: When former Assistant Attorney General Barbara Babcock was asked how she felt about gaining a position because she was a woman, she answered, "It feels better than being denied the position because you're a woman" (Rhode, 1993:263).

Domestic Relations

Domestic law, more than any other area, demonstrates glaring gender inequity. Legal statutes regarding wife-husband roles are based on three general models (Stetson, 1991:132):

1. Unity: The husband is dominant, and the wife has few rights and responsibilities.
2. Separate but equal: The husband is the breadwinner and the wife is companion and nurturer of children, but they share similar legal rights. This is also referred to as the *reciprocity model*.
3. Shared partnership: The husband and wife have equal rights and overlapping responsibility.

The third notion (shared partnership) is the most equitable, but contemporary law is a mixture of all three, with separate but equal dominating.

Divorce. Property division in divorce is a good example. In a *community property* state, all property acquired during the marriage is jointly owned by the spouses. In a divorce, each partner is entitled to half the property. Community property implicitly recognizes the unpaid homemaker role. In a divorce, however, a woman is often forced to sell her share of the home, the only real property she has, while still maintaining responsibility for children. Other states are *common law*, with property belonging to the spouse in whose name it is held. Common law severely penalizes women economically, since men are more likely to have property in their name both before and during a marriage. To remedy the problem, "equitable distribution laws" are required. According to these laws, courts consider other factors, such as length of marriage, contributions of both partners to child care,

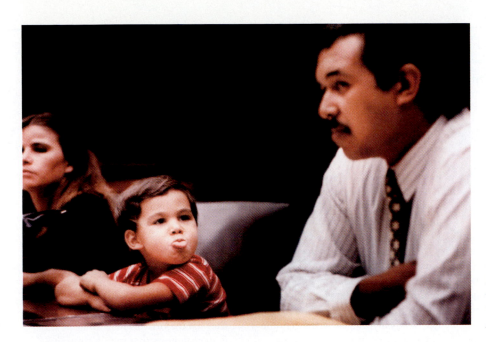

In uncontested divorces a mother usually gains custody, regardless of whether a child appears to dislike one parent over another.

earning capability, and health (Thorkelson, 1985). Unpaid homemaking roles are also considered. The problem, nonetheless, is that since the separate but equal doctrine still underlies much domestic law, the way couples determined how they distributed household assets during the marriage makes a difference in how assets will be divided in a divorce. In families where the husband is the wage earner, he may give "his" paycheck to his wife for household expenses, or he may give her an allowance for household or personal needs. The result is that women rarely receive half of the assets.

Confusion reigns in divorce law because of legislation that is both punitive and sexually biased. When a divorce involves children, the mother usually gains custody, the preferred pattern for both mothers and fathers. As we will see in Chapter 15, there is immense gender disparity in terms of child custody and support, and the economic consequences of a divorce on a woman and her children are often disastrous.

Considering the reciprocity (separate but equal) model, it is understandable that the courts have also been inconsistent in efforts to prosecute cases of wife abuse. Much of U.S. law is based on English common law and still reflects certain of these patterns. Until the middle of the nineteenth century, in the United States men had the right to beat their wives. This was a legally sanctioned practice dating back to feudal times under the infamous "rule of thumb" allowing a man to beat his wife as long as the stick was no bigger than his thumb. For rape, by 1990 all but eight states adopted laws allowing for charges to be brought by spouses. The notion of marital rape is so recent because historically sexual intercourse has been viewed

as "his right and her duty," again traced to English common law. For other cases of domestic abuse, which may or may not involve rape, judges have been reluctant to temporarily bar a husband from his home because his due process rights may be violated. Judges may accept the stereotype that her behavior was responsible for his abuse (Freeman, 1995; Sheffield, 1995). An Ohio judge told a woman who was testifying in court about her husband's attacks on her to study the Bible and "try harder to be a good wife" (Crites, 1987:50).

GENDERED MESSAGES IN MEDIA

The social institutions are powerful influences on gender roles. Although families provide the earliest gender messages, the mass media, especially television, quickly follow. A consistent research finding is that, among all ages and both genders, heavy television viewing is strongly associated with traditional and stereotyped gender views (Bryant, 1990; Signorielli, 1989, 1991). Children are especially vulnerable in believing that television images represent truth and reality. Television is strengthened by magazines, books, and music that present the genders in stereotyped ways.

Magazines and Advertising

Advertising is a powerful force in all the media, but particularly in magazines. Advertisers exert much control over article content in magazines (Steinem,

Men's Images in the Media

Compared to men, women have not fared well in the media. Men star in more television series, sell more records, make more movies, and are paid more than female media counterparts. But men, too, must pay a price for that popularity. From the media's standpoint, a man is a breadwinner who cheats on his wife, is manipulated by his children, has no idea how to use a washing machine or vacuum cleaner, and uses force to solve his problems. Men, like women, are increasingly used as sex objects in the media. On the other hand, a man is the voice of authority to be admired and respected. How do the various media contribute to these images?

Advertising

Advertisers divide products according to masculine and feminine. Cars, life insurance, and beer are masculine so men do the selling to other men. Men also sell products to women, even cosmetics and pantyhose. In fact, men do most of the selling on television, as evidenced by voice-overs, which are almost 90 percent male. Television beer commercials, especially during sports events, are almost exclusively male oriented. More than all other types of advertising they portray men as "good old boys" who are adventurous, play hard at sports, and have a country spirit. For other products and for both print ads and television commercials, men are portrayed as mature, successful, and strong. Although women are increasingly shown in activities outside the home, advertisers do not often show men in family roles and prefer instead to associate them with entertainment and sports. One result is that sex object portrayals are increasing.

Movies

Films routinely portray men in two thematic ways. The first is the hero theme. They are hard living and adventurous tough guys who quickly move in and out of relationships with women—but all the time righting wrongs and saving the day. John Wayne and Gary Cooper of the past have been replaced by Mel Gibson, Tom Cruise, and Jean-Claude Van Damme. Often men are linked in "buddy" movies. The plot calls for them to be competitive on the surface and then gradually move toward genuine—if begrudging—respect and camaraderie. If romance enters in, it is short-lived or not enough to keep the men from their carefree escapades. They learn to admire one another for traits they see lacking in their own personalities. *Blues Brothers, Batman and Robin*, and *Men in Black* suggest this theme.

Second is the violence theme. Both heroes and villains are violent and violence is needed to end violence as in *Star Wars*, and the Jackie Chan movies, as well as the kill and maim plots of films like *I Know What You Did Last Summer, Halloween* and *Friday the Thirteenth* show that revenge and violence in the name of a "good" cause are acceptable to men.

Television

Men on primetime dramas are portrayed as in control of most situations. These men recognize that power may bring adversity but they are willing to accept the consequences in shows such as *Walker—Texas Ranger, Law and Order*, and *Nash Bridges*. Television men are active, independent, and can solve their own problems. The major exception to this image is the situation comedy where men may take on a childlike dependence on their wives in household functioning, as in *Everybody Loves Raymond*. Some shows are now depicting men in loving and nurturing relationships with their children, but historically men are rarely shown as competent dads who can raise children without the help of women. Even single dad Andy Griffith had Aunt Bea.

Overall, the media may allow men to display a greater range of roles than women, but stereotypes still account for the vast majority of male images. Evidence suggests that men want to be portrayed differently—they are especially angered about increased images as both sex objects and "success objects" tied to money and status. These hopes, however, are apparently not in the intent of the media. The sensitive man image popularized a decade ago is retreating fast and as one researcher notes, "cradling a newborn is out and guy stuff is back." Until men are consistently portrayed as loving fathers, compassionate husbands, and household experts, stereotypes about rigid masculinity will not be significantly altered.

1. How do these themes about male roles appear in the television and movies you watch? What messages do these themes provide for men and women about masculinity and femininity?

2. How would a symbolic interactionist respond to television and music producers and who say that they are only giving the public what the public wants?

Sources: Condry, 1989; Binder, 1993; White & Gillett, 1994; Kanne, 1995.

1995). In women's magazines, an article about beauty will appear next to an ad selling makeup, and it is highly unlikely that any psychological or medical downside to makeup would appear anywhere in the magazine. Consistent with symbolic interactionism's view of the self-fulfilling prophecy, the advertising-article connection promotes almost narcissistic self-absorption, particularly to teenage girls who read magazines such as *Seventeen*, *Elle*, *Sassy*, and *Vogue*. Print ads and television commercials have actually increased their view of women as sex objects, dependent on men, and interested only in physical beauty. For a woman to be acceptable, she must be attractive. The dominant themes in both magazine ads and magazine fiction are how to become more beautiful and relationships with men—getting and keeping them (Lazier-Smith, 1989; Wolf, 1991; Saltzberg & Chrisler, 1995). When males are shown in ads, they reflect "face-isms," in that their faces are photographed more than their bodies. Females represent "body-isms" or "partialisms," in that parts of their body are shown, often without a face (Archer et al., 1983; Hall & Crum, 1994). Studies of news magazines, women's magazines, and newspapers continue to document that men are much less likely to be shown as "partials" and receive much more facial prominence than women (Nigro et al., 1988; Zuckerman & Kieffer, 1994). A body part without a face is the classic example of a sex object. A face identifies a person as a subject, a real person.

Television

The average American watches television almost 35 hours each week; children and those over age 55 are the heaviest viewers (Chapter 20). Viewers find some characters personally meaningful. Women are more likely to identify with less-than-perfect rather than glamorous characters; the women of *Friends* are less likely to be role models than the women of *The Practice* or *Family Law*. Television talk shows seem to have an influence on *misogyny*, defined as the dislike, disdain, or hatred of women. Misogyny may be demonstrated by a typical week of talk show topics (cited in *Parade Magazine*, 1995:12):

Maury Povich—Mothers who dislike their daughters.
Ricki Lake—Women who are dependent on men.
Gordon Elliott—Women who spy on their husbands.
Richard Bey—Criminals who blame their mothers.
Jenny Jones—Women who stick with cheating men.

More disturbing is the research suggesting that television can glamorize dehumanization and physical abuse (Gerbner, 1990; Burk & Shaw, 1995). As dis-

cussed in Chapter 5, much of this violence is directed toward women.

Television primetime revolves around men, with male characters outnumbering female over two to one. Males dominate dramatic shows, playing tough and emotionally reserved characters who remain unmarried but have beautiful female companions (Signorielli, 1989; Davis, 1990). In many shows, such as *Baywatch*, female characters are simply bystanders who add sex appeal. When race is added as a variable, some research suggests that African American women are shown more favorably and positively than their white counterparts. However, their roles are not represented in terms of variety (Goodwin, 1996). In comedies and soap operas, women appear in about equal frequency with men. Soap-opera women are likely to be portrayed as schemers, victims, bedhoppers, and starry-eyed romantics. But they are also shown as intelligent, self-reliant, and articulate. Soaps appear to both engage and distance their primarily female viewers and at the same time keep them entertained. The strong soap-opera women who question patriarchy may hint at progressive change regarding gender roles on television (Nochimson, 1992; Geraghty, 1993).

Music

Overall, music is the most stereotyped of all media in its gender portrayals. In the last four decades, popular music of all types and serving all age categories of listeners sings to the sex appeal of women who use it to control men or who are victimized by men. It is rock music, however, that has emerged as music's major artistic force and has promoted the restructuring of all music (Regev, 1995). Since the 1950s, views of women in rock music have become increasingly associated with sexual violence. The misogyny in many rock lyrics is unconcealed. Rock videos provide a visual extension and support a gender ideology of male power and dominance reinforcing misogyny (Lewis, 1990; Sommers-Flanagan et al., 1993). In general,

INTERNET — CONNECTIONS

The text points out that, overall, *music* is the most stereotyped of all media in its gender portrayals: In the last four decades, popular music of all types and serving all age categories of listeners sings to the sex appeal of women who use it to control men or who are victimized by men. Go to http://www.wfubmc.edu/newsdesk/archives/gender.shtml: "Music Videos Reinforce False Stereotypes." Read the contents of this site. After doing this, provide answers to these questions: Why do you think there are so many music videos that appeal to traditional conceptualizations of gender roles? Do you think that music videos have a negative effect on young people's perceptions of male-female relationships? Why or why not?

rock videos depict women as emotional, illogical, deceitful, fearful, dependent, and passive, while it depicts men as adventuresome, domineering, aggressive, and violent. Most rock videos combine sexual images with acts of violence (Hansen & Hansen, 1988; Seidman, 1992). Heavy metal and rap display the most violent lyrics and images. Women are routinely depicted as sex objects on whom violence is perpetrated, with increasing numbers of rape scenes being enacted (Vincent et al., 1987; Binder, 1993).

Research shows that men and women receive these messages differently. Women read the female images in rock videos as powerful and suggestive of control or as vulnerable and weak. Men read the same images as teasing and hard-to-get or as submissive and indecisive. Yet for male images there are no significant gender differences in interpretations (Kalof, 1993). Consistent with the symbolic interactionist theoretical perspective, this research suggests that gender is a social construction shaped by social myths articulated in popular culture (Denzin, 1992). The gender role effects are negative for both men and women.

A number of rock bands either led by women or with female and male lead singers and musicians have emerged. The names of Madonna, Gloria Estafan, Paula Abdul, Mariah Carey, k.d. laing, and Britney Spears are recognizable as leading women in the rock charts. It cannot be said, however, that many of their songs portray women in nonstereotyped ways. They, too, sing of love and pain, but also about vulnerable women being abandoned by men. A woman's revenge is to taunt the man she loves. One study of women in local rock groups finds that women would like to

change the sexist material of their bands but are compelled to both sing and dress in sexually provocative ways (Groce & Cooper, 1990). They are often not taken seriously as musicians for these very actions but cannot break out of the mold the rock subculture requires for popularity. They find themselves in a no-win situation. Thus there are few female rock musicians who can seriously challenge rock's misogynous lyrics.

LIFE CONNECTIONS: The Men's Movement in America

The first men's movement originated on college campuses in the 1970s as a reaction to the feminist movement—a positive reaction. Their support for feminist causes encouraged their reflection on how ideals about masculinity influenced their own self-image and their behavior toward other men. An individual man who rejects, for example, sexual bravado and oppressive behavior toward women is a target for ridicule and exclusion by other men (Hernandez, 1996). Research shows that definitions of masculinity that deny men expressions of vulnerability, nurturing, and caring serve to undermine psychological and physical well-being (Chapter 19). Since the 1970s, the National Organization of Changing Men (NOCM) has spearheaded conferences on themes related to parenting, sexism, violence against women, sexuality, sexual orientation, and friendship. Although feminist in stance, these conferences focus more on personal or social rather than political change. This men's movement works on male liberation by consciousness-raising related to the negative effects of striving for power and the disabling effects of rigid masculinity. Overall, only a minority of men have been attracted to the goals of NOCM.

The lack of public awareness for the first men's movement is revealed in how the media have publicized later men's "movements." In 1990 media attention focused on poet Robert Bly's belief that men are caught in a toxic masculinity that demands efficiency, competition, and an emotional distance that separates them from one another (Bliss, 1990; Kimbrell, 1993). In Bly's (1990) view, rooted in a competitive work environment that keeps fathers absent from their families, boys turn to women to meet emotional needs. According to Bly, men must unearth and celebrate their lost natural birthright of righteous anger and primordial masculinity, which can be regained *only* in communion with men (Gurian, 1992; Meade, 1993). Communication between men is encouraged, but the "sensitive man" who is out of touch with his masculinity and turns to women as authority figures is denounced. According to Bly, these men have surrendered their birthright of "righteous anger" that

Although there is no one Men's Movement, men have come together to highlight their roles in society, such as the "Million Man March," made up primarily of African American men.

makes them less whole and less masculine than they are naturally destined to be (Adler, 1991). Unlike the first movement, which is profeminist and argues against men's privilege, Bly's movement is promasculinist and seeks to heal men's pain by distancing them from women. Bly has attracted powerful men to his ranks, including corporate executives, political leaders, and those representing the elite professions. Both movements are made up mostly of white men, with working-class men and men of color virtually nonexistent.

Another men's movement focuses on the African American male experience. Research shows that African American males tend to construct definitions of masculinity in direct opposition to Euro-American male models (Franklin, 1994; Harris et al., 1994). Feeling blocked in achieving masculine goals offered by mainstream society, these men may initially adopt views of masculinity similar to Euro-American males. Their values change, however, as they get older (Hunter & Davis, 1994; Roberts, 1994). The 1997 "Million Man March" in Washington, DC was an effort to bring together African American men in support of one another and to offer role models to young people and their communities. The effort was largely successful, although the luster was tarnished by its antiwoman thrust. While all the national and international women's conferences welcomed men, the Million Man March explicitly did not invite women to join. And its organizer, controversial Black Muslim leader Louis Farakhan, later applauded Iran for setting a shining example to the world on behalf of democratic principles. Iran's unquestionably brutal record regarding both women and democracy intensified any existing schism between men and women.

The most recent men's movement, Promise Keepers, is by far the largest. Founded by Bill Mc-Cartney, former head football coach of the University of Colorado, Promise Keepers is an evangelical Christian organization dedicated to reestablishing male responsibility in the family and overcoming racial and sectarian divisions. Similar to both Bly and Farakhan, the Promise Keepers movement sees America's problems stemming from the fatherless home. It is different, however, in that its foundation appears to resonate with many more men. To become Promise Keepers, men must pledge their commitment to seven "promises," including honoring Jesus Christ, practicing spiritual and sexual purity, and building strong marriages and families.

Of the men's movements, Promise Keepers is the most diverse in class, race, and ethnicity. All the movements share a promasculinist stance that generally excludes women except as volunteers. In general, the media have given high approval rating to Promise Keepers but have tended to dismiss criticisms that the ultimate effect will be to subjugate women (Hetherly, 1997; Leeuwen, 1997). Promise Keepers leaders say that women need not be threatened, because in the kingdom "there is no male or female." Feminists point out, however, that when a man "returns" to the family to assume his "rightful" place as household head, patriarchy and not partnership is the logical outcome.

Feminism is supportive for men coming together in exclusive male groups for healing and sharing, but the promasculinist themes in all but the first men's movement (National Organization for Changing Men) suggests that women are responsible for the problems of men. Blaming serves to undermine

Opponents of pro-choice describe themselves as pro-life and typically use religious symbols in their activities. Men are often leaders of the pro-life group.

dialogue, reinforce sexism, and distance men and women from one another.

Do these gatherings of men suggest that a mass-based men's movement, whether promasculinist or profeminist, has occurred? Three decades of evidence suggest that it has not occurred. Although the media called Bly, Farakhan, and Bill McCartney leaders of men's "movements," none of the three have been shown the ability to maintain the continued commitment of large groups of men. As of this writing, Promise Keepers is in both a leadership and financial crisis. Its existence as a viable organization is in jeopardy.

NOCM has not received the publicity or attracted the numbers of the other three groups, but it is still convening conferences and drawing together men who are supportive of partnering roles with women. They have lasted thirty years. It remains to be seen if the other three groups will be as successful over the long run. The women's movement has touched the lives of millions of women; the same cannot be said for the men's movement.

SOCIETY CONNECTIONS:
The Gender Politics of Biology and Religion

A newspaper columnist advocating the belief that women should not be in the military supported her claim with the statement, "Men are physically stronger than women and if women object to that reality their complaint is with God" (Charon, 1997). God and biology are consistently used to support sexism, just as they were used to support racism. The biology-God link is a recurrent theme used in political agendas. The controversy surrounding reproductive rights clearly demonstrates this link.

Until the nineteenth century a woman's right to an abortion in the United States was legal as long as the procedure was prior to "quickening" of the fetus, when the mother felt the first movements. By 1900 abortion was banned in every state, except to save the mother's life. This changed on January 22, 1973 with two landmark Supreme Court decisions. In *Roe v. Wade* and *Doe v. Bolton*, a seven-to-two vote supported a woman's right to privacy, which allowed for a (now) legal abortion. Women did not have the absolute constitutional right to abortion on demand, but a broadening of the legal right to abortion was established. This right has been challenged ever since.

Bolstered by the reaffirmation of divinely ordained sex *and* gender differences, the New Christian Right, headed by conservative political leaders and aligned with fundamentalist churches, has been effective in challenging abortion rights. The association of their moral stance with religion is clear by the term "pro-life," adopted as a label for their group. In a study of Canadians who identified themselves as pro-life, a higher religiosity was the single most important element that separated these people from the general public in Canada (Rauhala, 1987). And for both the United States and Canada, a higher degree of religious fundamentalism is clearly associated with lower support for reproductive rights (Muraskin, 1993; Welch et al., 1995).

With religion as the factor that distinguishes pro-life activists from others, it is understandable that their antiabortion work is viewed as "God's work." As one pro-life activist said after her arrest for illegally blocking entrance to a clinic that performed abortions, "I know murder is against God's commandments. . . . These children we "rescue" are the children of God. It's God's will" (cited in Ruth, 1998: 253). Pro-life activists have succeeded in lobbying for legislation restricting government-funded abortion services to poor women. However, they were less successful in the 1992 watered-down Roe Supreme Court decision of *Planned Parenthood v. Casey*, which said that a state cannot place substantial obstacles in the path of a woman's right to choose an abortion before fetal viability—the fetus could survive outside the womb—is reached. States can still restrict previability abortions as long as the health of the mother and fetus are promoted (Tribe, 1992:243).

Antiabortion activists tirelessly lobby against funding for any national or international agencies offering abortion counseling, even if such counseling is only a small part of a broader program of family planning. Tactics to limit or eliminate abortion rights have ranged from gruesome antiabortion films and commercials on television and boycotting facilities where abor-

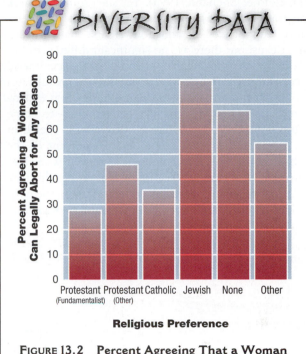

DIVERSITY DATA

FIGURE 13.2   **Percent Agreeing That a Woman Should be Able to Obtain a Legal Abortion if She Wants It for Any Reason.** Catholics and Fundamentalist Protestants have the lowest approval rates for abortion for any reason. Jewish and those stating no religious preference have the highest approval, with Other Protestants falling in between. What accounts for both the similarity between Catholics and Fundamentalists Protestants and the differences between them and other religious groups on the abortion issue?

tions are performed to death threats and bombing of abortion clinics. After the murder of a Florida physician, antiabortion activists were quick to point out that these tactics are neither advocated nor supported, although a small number of extremists in their ranks condoned the killing and publicly stated that it was justifiable homicide (Warner, 1993; Russo & Horn, 1995; Poppema, 1999). Public opinion is against any tactic that promotes violence in achieving its goals.

On the other side, and just as tireless, are "pro-choice" activists who cite public support for abortion rights. In 1995, the percentage of people who identified themselves as pro-choice hit an all time high of 74 percent, a 15 percent increase since 1991 (Lake & Breglio, 1992; Women's Equality Poll, 1995). The majority of both men and women describe themselves as pro-choice, but the percentage for men is higher than for women. Among all age groups of men, adolescents are the highest percentage of pro-choice supporters. For state legislators the reverse is true: 74 percent of the females and 61 percent of the males call themselves pro-choice (Mandel & Dodson, 1992;

Marsiglio & Shehand, 1993). Yet such numbers mask the complexity of the issue. For example, whites are more supportive of abortion rights than African Americans, but there are no significant differences between the races for females of childbearing age. For all races and even among fundamentalists, approval rates for abortion increase when the mother's life is endangered or when pregnancy occurs due to rape (Muraskin, 1993; Lynxwiler & Gay, 1994; Welch et al., 1995). Other polls show only 14 percent of the public wants abortion completely outlawed (U.S. Department of Justice, 1993). Feminists argue that the abortion question is actually a referendum on the control of women and the importance of motherhood (Luker, 1978, 1984; Tribe, 1992).

The abortion issue has been presented to the public as representing two intractable sides. This is not necessarily the case. There is at least tentative agreement that preventing unwanted pregnancy is a desirable option to abortion. People on both sides of the issue are beginning to discuss positive alternatives to abortion, such as sex education and better financial support for parents (Rosenblatt, 1992; Russo et al., 1992). But how these goals are to be achieved again relates to the gender intersection of religion and politics. Since antiabortion activists argue that life begins at conception, they promote abstinence for the unmarried and only certain types of contraception for the married (Tribe, 1992). The feminist view is that sex education and availability of contraception should be expanded for young people, married or not. However, at least by beginning with the idea that abortion is not in anyone's best interests, there is a glimmer of hope for consensus.

SUMMARY

1. For sociologists, sex is a biological category and gender is a social and cultural category that is learned, varies between cultures, and changes over time as cultural definitions change. Gender roles are socially defined masculine and feminine behaviors associated with each sex.

2. According to functionalism, gender roles developed as a practical way of dividing labor in preindustrial societies. Conflict theorists assert that in capitalist societies, gender inequality is largely explained by women's unpaid work in the home and men's economic advantage both inside and outside the home. Symbolic interactionists view gender roles as social constructions based on agreed definitions of masculinity and femininity.

3. The new feminist sociological theoretical perspective accounts for the links between race, class, and gender and how women are both alike and different. The branches of feminism—liberal, socialist, radical, and multicultural/global—demonstrate these similarities and differences.

4. Women in the developing world have been adversely affected by development strategies that were supposed to help them, often increasing rather than reducing poverty. However, with support by nongovernmental organizations (NGO's), gender analysis in development planning is helping women and families worldwide.

5. The family is an early and powerful source of gender socialization. Children as young as 2 years display gender roles learned through differences in ways parents interact with boys and girls and in toy and clothing selection.

6. Gender stereotypes are reinforced at all educational levels, through interaction with teachers, curricular material, and choice of majors. Title IX has helped reduce gender discrimination in education.

7. A wage gap where men earn significantly more than women persists despite women's education and work experience. Sociologists focus on gender-typing of occupations, the lower value placed on women's occupations, and gender discrimination in explaining the gap.

8. Gender inequality has been addressed with a number of laws and programs, including the Equal Employment Opportunity Commission, the Equal Pay Act, (comparable worth, and affirmative action. These programs, however, have only been partly successful.

9. The large amount of gender inequity in domestic law is based on models where the husband is dominant, where spouses have reciprocal rights, or where there is a shared partnership between spouses. Divorce law especially is punitive and sexually biased.

10. Mass media, from magazines to television to popular music, send gendered messages that suggest women are defined mainly by their appearance and that violence toward women by men is pervasive. Music is the most gender stereotyped of the mass media. Many women rock artists are emerging but to date have not been able to challenge gender stereotypes.

11. The first men's movement in America was accepting of feminism and worked for male liberation against rigid masculinity. Later and much

larger men's movements organized around Robert Bly, the Million Man March, and Promise Keepers tend to exclude women or blame women for men's problems.

12. The abortion rights debate involves two major groups—pro-life, supported by fundamentalist religious groups that advocate traditional gender roles, and pro-choice, supported by feminists and those who want to keep the right to abortion legal. There is some agreement between both sides that preventing unwanted pregnancy is a desirable option to abortion.

KEY TERMS

androcentrism 323	gender roles 322	patriarchal (patriarchy) 322
comparable worth 338	gender-typing 334	sexism 322
feminism 325	glass ceiling 336	

CRITICAL THINKING QUESTIONS

1. Demonstrate how the development process has an adverse affect on women. What suggestions would you offer to make this process beneficial rather than detrimental to women, but at the same time not make it detrimental to men?

2. How do functionalism, symbolic interactionism, and conflict theory explain the persistence of the wage gap in light of laws that require equal pay for equal work? Compare these explanations with the feminist theoretical perspective.

3. Of the various social institutions discussed in this chapter, which one institution do you believe has the most impact on gender-role socialization? Which one institution do you believe is the most amenable to change for gender equity?

4. How can gender roles explain the difference between the men's and women's movements and the successes or failures of each? What elements of masculinity are emphasized by promasculinists and profeminists in the men's movement? Do you think that these elements draw men together or keep them apart?

5. Describe how the law is gender biased and how this gender bias is disadvantageous to both men and women.

+14+ THE AGED AND SOCIETY

Live Long and Prosper?

Leah is a 71-year-old widow living with her two dogs in a large trailer home in Florida. She moved to Florida when she was unable to continue her job as a dietician because of arthritis. Her disability benefits ended when she turned 65 and became eligible for Social Security. She supplements her $440 Social Security check with her job as a hostess at Burger King. She needs knee and hip replacement surgery but fears she cannot pay the medical bills and will lose her job if she takes time off for surgery.

Also living in Florida, in a pleasant condominium community, are Nate and Selma Fiske. They spend summers in their hometown of Springfield, Massachusetts. The Fiskes live comfortably on two pensions, investment income, and Social Security. They play golf and bridge with their many friends, catch "early bird" specials at local restaurants, and enjoy visits from their children and grandchildren. (Adapted from Quadagno, 1999: 62–63)

Aging in Native America

"People come to him and ask him things—how to do things in the old way."

Among two rural nonreservation Oklahoma Indian tribes, the Oto-Missouri and Ioway, attitudes toward elders reflect respect, power, and prestige. These tribes define being old by roles and functions, not chronological age. Knowledge about tribal ways and customs, the role of grandparent, or the head of a family line bring honor and prestige. The elderly are the religious and ritual specialists of their culture and teach the language to anyone willing to learn. They preserve a vital oral history, passing down songs and legends to the younger generation. As one grandmother said, "Old people are useful in many ways. Grandparents are very useful to patch clothes, sew on buttons, be there to look after the children when the mother and father have to go somewhere." To be seen as old means you cannot take care of yourself, whether you are 40 or 85. The elderly are not reluctant to be dependent on family members if necessary and, even with dependence, they retain the right to make their own decisions. (Adapted from Schweitzer, 1983)

The Fear of Growing Old: The !Kung of South Central Africa

"I have gone far and killed lots of meat. My bones are hurting me and I am almost old." "Now I am too old. Who will give me food to eat?"

What does it mean to become old in a culture in which physical strength is essential for survival? The middle-aged !Kung men quoted above are already worried about old age. The !Kung live in small, kin-based villages, subsisting on the food and using the tools they produce themselves. In the struggle for survival, they continually face obstacles having to do with physical strength. They have nothing good to say about old age. The !Kung value independence and see children and old people as not fully "whole" persons because they must rely on the physical capabilities of others. As one older woman says, "Life is with me. I can get up and do the things I need to do. I can take care of myself. I can cook and sew and still have strength." She is still a "whole" person.

Although the !Kung fear old age, they do not resent helping others, especially elderly kin. It is considered good to take care of elders and for the old to benefit from the work of the young and middle-aged. Your hard work is returned at old age. As expressed by a !Kung man, "If they have a mother, they love her. They love to be with and take care of relatives." Older people live with their kin and participate fully in village activities. While the !Kung fear the loss of physical independence, they do not see reliance on others as either unusual or problematic. (Adapted from Keith et al., 1994)

There are many faces to the aged and the aging process. In Oklahoma Native America, the aged are valued. Among the !Kung of Botswana, aging itself is feared. Leah and the Fiskes represent the potential for either the liability or the leisure that are associated with being old in the United States. Although aging is neither uniformly positive nor uniformly negative, there are patterns to the process of aging that sociological research has uncovered and sociological theories can explain. In describing these patterns, this chapter will focus on the key factors of family, money, and health that help explain why there are so many faces to aging and the aged worldwide. As discussed in the first chapter, sociology is a "debunking" science. Our analysis of the aged and society will also debunk the widely held stereotype that the elderly are "all alike."

THE PROCESS OF AGING

There is a shared cultural universal in regard to the process of aging—every society marks the stages of the aging process in some manner. For example, some cultures mark the transition to old age simply in terms of whether the person has the physical capability to work on a subsistence farm. If a person does not have the physical stamina to continue such work, he or she is considered "old" and must be cared for by the family or community. But since the process of aging also involves biological, psychological, and social factors, different societies put more or less emphasis on different factors. We will now explore these factors through both the sociological perspective as well as through explanations from other disciplines. We will also show how these factors relate to the process of aging throughout the world.

Defining Old Age

We all age—but our society tells us when we reach old age. Western opinions of old age are chronologically based. This kind of classification is important in bureaucratic societies that must determine eligibility for a variety of services. In the United States, 65 is the standard for old age simply because the Social Security Act of 1935 set it as the basis for mandatory retirement and the original age when benefits could begin. But the norm of 65 had already been established in parts of Europe in the nineteenth century so that most of the developed world is now accustomed to using it as a classification for old age. However, as life expectancy continues to increase throughout the world and as people begin to retire earlier, the "age 65" standard is likely to change. In the United States,

for example, some people may now draw Social Security as early as age 62.

In addition to chronological age, old age may be defined by certain life passages or events. Recall from Chapter 5 that from the life course perspective, as we age we progress through a sequence of statuses that require certain kinds of role behavior. These include *rites of passage* to formally mark the transition from one status to another. These generational events, such as high school graduation or a retirement dinner, help us understand how our own individual histories are also linked to the larger groups to which we belong.

The scientific study of aging is called **gerontology;** it focuses on that population referred to as "aged" or "elderly." These terms will be used interchangeably throughout this chapter. Researchers generally use age 65 to put a person in those categories. The label "oldest old" describes people who are over age 80. If life expectancy rates continue to increase, this group may become the "young old" or the "middle old." Sociologists are also interested in how others in the population define and label old age. Terms range from very negative to more positive—coot, geezer, old-timer, elder, and senior citizen. Even the terms selected for use in this book, elderly and the aged, are rated somewhat negatively and may imply infirmity (Barbato & Feezel, 1987; Friedan, 1993). The key point is that there is confusion between being old chronologically and "old in the sense of worn out, outmoded, obsolete or discarded" (Palmore, 1990:41).

Throughout the world, old age is associated with role transitions that may occur at different chronological ages. Many of the indigenous peoples in Mexico, for instance, use age 52 as the beginning of old age. This age is marked as the "binding of years," followed by the period before death called "fulfillment of old age" (De Lehr, 1992). In some Native American tribes, a person cannot participate in certain rituals until designated an elder. In the age-graded systems of East Africa and the Amazon Basin, young people cannot become adults and adults cannot become elders until the existing elders as a group ritually give up their leadership roles (Keith, 1992). Seniority has its advantages.

Views from Other Disciplines

Aging is a multidimensional process. The best way to understand the process is to integrate material from a variety of disciplines. **Primary aging** involves the physical changes that accompany our body's biological processes. Changes such as decreased bone density, thinning hair, and hearing loss are included here. **Secondary aging** involves the lifetime of stresses our

Depending on a person's culture and his or her place in it, aging may be associated with uncertainty, fear, power, or contentment.

tempt to explain the aging process, but some offer better explanations than others. Genetic theories focus on inherited characteristics that program an individual to a specific aging pathway. Like a biological clock that is ticking, this genetic pathway will determine how long you can expect to live and what you are likely to die of. A pattern of heart disease in your family may have a genetic basis, increasing your risk of developing heart problems.

Other biological theories focus on aging as an outcome of all the external stresses on our bodies. The "wear and tear theory" points out that any living organism is like a machine, and after extended usage its parts inevitably wear out. "Free radical theory" assumes the culprit in aging can be traced to the damaging effects of unstable atoms in the cells. "Cross-linkage theory" concentrates on connective tissues such as collagen and elastin. As we age, changes occur in these tissues that result in wrinkled skin, sagging muscles, loss of elasticity in blood vessels, and slower healing of wounds. The "autoimmune theory" emphasizes breakdowns in the body's immune system so it can no longer produce the antibodies needed to protect against invading microorganisms and the body's own mutant cells (Whitbourne, 1985; Birren & Schaie, 1990). Each of these theories offers some help in explaining the mysteries surrounding the physical process of aging. Probably no single biological theory will be able to explain the entire process.

Although biologists still cannot agree on *why* we age, the physical patterns of *how* we age are very clear. We are all aware of the external signs of moving into middle and old age—gray hair, stiffening joints, wrinkled and blotchy skin, increase in weight, and decrease in height. More subtle changes such as

bodies are subjected to. These include everything from childhood diseases and emotional trauma to lack of exercise and cigarette smoking. From a sociological point of view, secondary aging includes how our bodies and minds react to social consequences, such as age prejudice, of growing old.

Biological View of Aging. Biologists and physiologists have developed a number of theories that at-

Gerontologists demonstrate that the aged exhibit a wide range of behavior patterns and lifestyles often associated more with race and social class than with age per se.

decreased need for sleep, higher frequency of urination, and lessening visual and hearing acuity are also likely. And depending on the habits developed over a lifetime, changes in physical energy, mobility, and coordination may be noticeable.

The important point to remember, however, is that while these changes are associated with aging, they are not necessarily associated with either illness or debilitation. Most elderly people are not in poor health. The onset of physical problems is probably due more to secondary aging, which is dependent on the habits we have developed over a lifetime. We can predict that age-related physiological changes will occur, although considerable variation exists in rates of aging and changes in physiological functioning (Riley & Bond, 1983). Many age-related pathological changes are not directly tied to the aging process itself (Manton & Soldo, 1992). So we cannot reliably predict which of us will experience poor health or disability in old age.

Psychological View of Aging.   The psychology of aging emphasizes age-related changes in cognitive functioning, creativity, and personality. One of the most important elements of cognitive functioning is intelligence. Research on changes in intelligence over the life course concludes that intelligence is generally stable and predictable throughout adult life, peaking in late middle age. Declines after age 60 occur on timed tests, word fluency tests, and tests of spatial abilities. But tests related to primary mental abilities, such as verbal reasoning and learning performance, show no decline in most people until advanced old age (Hertzog & Schaie, 1988; Schaie, 1990). Unless they are connected to physical problems, the declines

that do occur are not major disrupters of daily activities. Overall age-related changes in intelligence occur gradually, the degree varies from person to person, and changes are associated with both long plateaus and declines.

Like intelligence, creativity is also difficult to understand. While psychologists debate the meaning of creativity, most agree that its expression varies with age, increasing gradually and then declining. The age at which this happens varies by individual and by discipline. Scientists and artists tend to peak in their thirties and early forties. Scholars, novelists, and other writers tend to peak later, many into their seventies (Dennis, 1966; Simonton, 1990a).

Whether a peak time also produces the most significant work of one's career is also debatable. Grandma Moses, Benjamin Franklin, Leonardo DiVinci, and Irving Berlin continued high-quality work well into old age, making some of the most valuable contributions in their fields at this stage of life. Young creative people become old creative people. Even with some decline, the creative urges remain strong and can even resurge at old age (Simonton, 1990b). If poor health and age prejudice do not interfere, the creativity of the elderly may not be significantly hampered.

The Convergence of Biology and Psychology: Alzheimer's Disease. The fields of biology and psychology converge in discussing the impact of age on personality. Old age is not associated with personality discontinuity. Once personality traits are developed, they remain remarkably consistent (McCrae & Costa, 1982; Caspi & Bem, 1990). The emergence of psychiatric symptoms and noticeable personality change that may occur in old age can be a form of psychopathology. Alzheimer's disease is one such form. Since all studies show that Alzheimer's disease increases with age, people with the disease are likely to be in the "oldest old" category, age 80 and above. With increased longevity, the projection is that by 2050 13 to 17 percent of the population of over age 65 in the United States will experience some Alzheimer's related symptoms (Evans et al., 1992). Keep in mind, however, that while this disease is unique to older people, it is *not* part of normal aging.

Alzheimer's disease is a type of organic brain syndrome (OBS): It is a progressive and irreversible decay of brain tissue that significantly impairs mental functioning. It is characterized by short-term memory loss, confusion, impaired judgment, inability to concentrate, and personality change. As the disease progresses, memory loss can be complete and the patient becomes totally dependent, both physically and psychologically. The effects are devastating. The patient may forget how to urinate or open a door. The deterioration of the brain eventually leads to death. But since the disease is usually one of gradual onset, people can live up to twenty years after diagnosis (Heston & White, 1991). Thus in most cases, the patient is well aware that the mind as well as the body will succumb to the disease. Given the dependency that accompanies the disease, Alzheimer's patients are the people already likely to be institutionalized. The financial and psychological costs of caregiving to the Alzheimer's patient are formidable.

Global Graying

The world is experiencing enormous growth in the population over age 65 (Figure 14.1). This growth is one of the greatest success stories of all times. It attests to tremendous global gains in providing healthier and more secure living conditions. The technological change and advances in health and medicine that are associated with modernization have set the stage for this increase. As discussed in detail in Chapter 21, countries with the highest proportion of the elderly are also in the last phase of the *demographic transition*. This means that low birthrates and death rates are replacing high ones.

In addition to the global increase in the over 65 population, the percent of the oldest old is dramatically increasing as well (Figure 14.2). By the year 2025, *as a percentage of all elderly,* the United States will have the highest share of the oldest old in the world, followed closely by Germany and Japan (Myers et al., 1992). Even the poorest regions in the world are witnessing a similar, but slower, rate of growth in the population over age 65. By 2025, Africa is projected to have 4 percent of its population over age 65. Almost 12 percent of that elderly population will be age 80 and older (Meyers, 1992). While the

Caregiving for Alzheimer's patients is made more demanding because of impairment in both the mind and the body. Caregivers are usually the spouse or the female children of the patient.

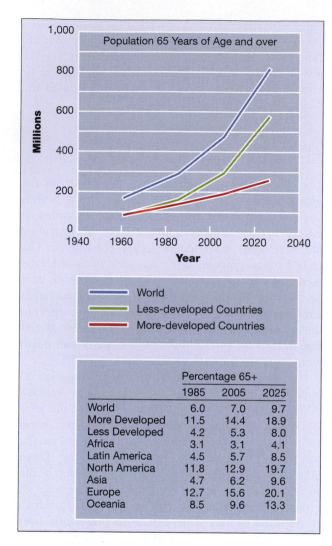

FIGURE 14.1   A Global View of the Growth
of the Elderly Population

Source: Adapted from Myers, 1992, pp. 33, 39 (based on UN population estimates).

growth may appear small, even a 1 percent jump over a twenty-year period profoundly effects a country's infrastructure. As we shall see, the impact on the family and health care systems is significant.

Gender.   When gender is added to the profile, the graying world becomes a female world. The current elderly population throughout the world is predominantly female, and it is projected to become even more so (Table 14.1). In less than a decade, many countries will have only 5 men to every 10 women over the age of 80. In the developed world the gender gap in mortality is declining slightly. Compared to women, men are making some gains in living longer. But the gap widens again at the oldest age. As the demographic transition proceeds, the developing world should also experience the same pattern. However,

the gap may remain wider in those places of the world where the sex ratio is artificially altered through such methods as sex selective abortion and abandonment of both infant and elderly females.

The Developed World.   For the developed world, a rapidly growing elderly population represents opportunities as well as challenges. The overall picture of the aged is one of health, adequate economic resources, and connectedness with family but independence in lifestyle (Suzman et al., 1992; Wenger, 1992). Families are still the key providers of health and support when needed, but these are supplemented by an array of public services to the elderly, particularly for those who live alone (Kendig et al., 1992, Habib et al., 1993). The elderly receive help, but also return it. Mutual help is a historical pattern and continues today. The United States, Britain, Sweden, and Denmark represent this pattern (Tornstam, 1992). In countries where independence is a strongly held cultural value, intergenerational helping assures that neither group becomes totally dependent on the other.

The welfare systems of Western Europe were first to help the poor. Today they have broadened their mission to deal with other issues of social and economic inequality, including those that occur when family and society are in a state of flux. The aged have been beneficiaries of such policies. Sweden, for example, provides the elderly with a network of publicly funded home and community services that are coordinated with the health and welfare system. Informal care by families and friends is bolstered by government help (Tornstam, 1992).

These opportunities for the elderly in the developed world—to enjoy an enhanced quality of life—are not without liability. The good news is that people are living longer and healthier lives. The bad news is that as they near the end of those lives they are likely to require an enormous output of resources—financial, social, and psychological. As discussed in Chapter 19, expensive health care options, whether home-based or not, are consuming vast amounts of public funds and contribute to the fiscal crisis facing all the nations in the developed world (Hashimoto & Kendig, 1992).

The Developing World.   Most countries in the developing world have no real infrastructure that formally supports services to their growing elderly population. Families are the indispensable caregivers, yet those families are changing. Among Asian immigrants to Israel, the rise of the nuclear family has undermined respect and power formerly held by the aged (Stahl, 1993). Evidence from India suggests that the elderly parental role in urban areas is minimized, and that old people experience loneliness and alienation (Gore, 1992). Throughout Africa, massive migration

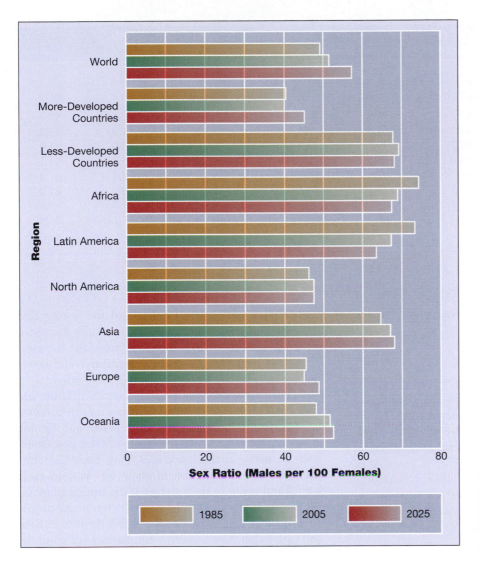

FIGURE 14.2   The Oldest Old: Projected Sex Ratios (Males per 100 Females) for Populations 80 Years of Age and Over in the World and in Major Regions

Source: Adapted from Myers (1992), p. 42.

of young people to urban areas in search of jobs has left the elderly behind in rural areas with little remaining family support. When the elderly themselves join their families in the cities, they relinquish community ties and are displaced at perhaps the most vulnerable times in their lives (Gibson, 1992).

In subsistence cultures, the elderly are at risk for abandonment or even killing when physical limitations make them a burden on the community (Glascock & Feinman, 1986). It is interesting that these practices do not necessarily mean that the elderly are held in low esteem but that they simply can no longer pull their weight in communities with scarce resources. In many cultures, the elderly person usually decides that death is necessary and a close relative is chosen to do the killing. High prestige coexists with killing or abandonment (Keith, 1992). On the other hand, the !Kung in the vignette are a subsistence culture where aging is feared but there is no resentment when caring for elderly kin.

Overall, elderly people in the developing world who live in extended families in rural areas have high prestige and respect. This prestige is preserved through ownership of land, continued productivity, and norms that reinforce reciprocity. A proverb from Ghana captures this reciprocity: "If your elders take care of you while cutting your teeth, you must in turn take care of them while they are losing theirs" (Apt, 1992:206). As we will see later, attitudes to the aged in the United States show some important similarities to those in the developing world.

SOCIOLOGICAL THEORIES OF AGING

With global graying on the horizon, sociological interest in the field of gerontology increased. While the major sociological theories had implications for the study of the life course and aging, it was not until

Table 14.1	Sex Ratios (Males per 100 Females) for Populations 65 and Over and 85 and Over in Selected Countries (Developed World)					
	1990			2025		
Country	All ages	65+	85+	All ages	65+	85+
Canada	97.2	71.9	52.4	95.7	77.4	59.4
France	95.1	64.4	44.3	95.6	74.0	55.0
Germany	92.7	50.5	39.0	96.5	76.0	52.9
Italy	94.4	67.1	49.5	95.4	75.3	56.1
Japan	96.7	67.6	55.1	96.1	78.5	61.6
Sweden	97.3	74.1	53.7	97.3	79.6	61.2
United Kingdom	95.3	66.3	42.4	97.1	77.7	57.8
United States	95.4	68.7	47.1	95.5	77.1	53.3

Source: Darnay, 1994: 71.

the early 1960s that the first formal theories related to a sociology of aging emerged.

Disengagement Theory

With sociological functionalism as its foundation, disengagement theory became an influential view of the aging process. **Disengagement theory** views aging as the gradual, beneficial, and mutual withdrawal of the aged and society from one another (Cumming & Henry, 1961). As older people inevitably give up some of the roles they have filled—as paid workers, for example—society replaces them with younger, more energetic people. Both groups benefit: The aged shed

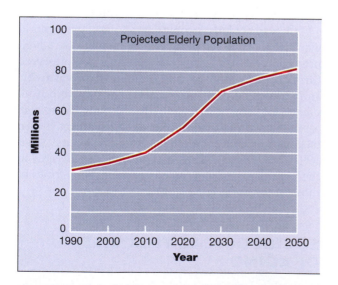

FIGURE 14.3   The Growth of the Elderly Population in the United States
Source: U.S. Department of Commerce, 1998 (Census Bureau, Population Projections).

the pressures of stressful roles, and the young find their own places in society. Society is less disrupted since the elderly relinquish these roles for the next generation. Ideally, the process is adaptive and benefits the elderly, the young, and society as a whole.

Disengagement theory also assumes that the life course follows a normative sequence of *age synchronization* that determines the appropriate age for life activities (Cox, 2000). In the United States people expect to marry in their twenties, have their last children in their thirties, be in their top jobs in their forties and retire in their sixties. If the timing of major life events is modified too quickly by too many people who make other choices, the stability, integration, and order that functionalism emphasizes are compromised.

Role loss is emphasized by disengagement theorists, but they do suggest that temporary role substitutions may serve as buffers until complete disengagement from previous roles occur. For example, a teacher who formally retires may decide to tutor on a self-determined schedule that is more flexible and less demanding. However, even when some role substitutions are suggested by disengagement theorists, the major thrust of the theory is that disengagement from previous roles must occur. Role loss is inevitable and even positive.

The theory has major criticisms. Often called the "rocking chair" approach to aging because withdrawal is the key to "successful" aging, disengagement theory is also seen as a blueprint for the elderly to follow to their deaths. This blueprint may not be beneficial to the aged. What happens to the people who do not want to give up—voluntarily disengage from—their roles or find that role substitutions are not satisfying? Are they aging "unsuccessfully"? Should they be forced out of paid work or community roles they wish to keep? Should the needs and desires of the elderly

Theories of aging have focused on whether the aged disengage or re-engage in productive and satisfying roles.

be abandoned to satisfy the needs and desires of younger people? To satisfy the assumed needs of society? Would the social order be compromised even when the aged work to keep themselves or their families out of poverty?

These questions point to another issue: They demonstrate how a theory, which is supposed to be a neutral, objective explanation of a social phenomenon, can become a philosophical justification for behavior. For example, older people who want to retain their jobs may be under pressure from their companies to retire early. Disengagement theory offers a justification for a retirement policy that does not serve the interests of some older workers. In Chapter 5 we saw how an influential theory of "dying in stages" became an accepted standard for "successful" dying. Disengagement theory has been criticized for doing the same thing: offering an accepted standard for "successful" aging. The problem is that theories can become cultural prescriptions about what people are supposed to do when they turn the magic age of 65 or when they are faced with dying.

Another criticism of disengagement theory is that the theory assumes there is an age-based orderly progression through the life course. Research does not support this assumption. There is such a great deal of individual variation presently that age patterns are tentative at best (Hogan, 1985). Given the massive changes occurring in economic and family institutions, it is even less likely in the future. Although disengagement theory offers a reasonably sound rationale for why people select certain roles at old age, sociologists are looking to other theories for more convincing interpretations of the aging process.

Activity Theory

In direct contrast to disengagement theory's assumption that it is the best for everybody that the elderly inevitably experience role withdrawal, **activity theory** suggests that successful aging means not only that role performance and involvements continue, but that new ones—not simply substitutions for old ones—are also developed (Havighurst, 1963; Havighurst et al., 1968). According to this theory, successful aging is linked to substantial levels of interpersonal, physical, and mental activity that help resist a potentially shrinking social world. The choices made at this stage of life will depend in part on opportunities for continued involvement in work or leisure activities that are not regulated by law or limited by cultural beliefs about the aged.

The elderly are assumed to have the same social and psychological needs as middle-aged persons, so these norms become the guideposts for behavior. In the United States, for example, consistent with a value system that supports keeping busy and staying young, activity theory is widely advocated among gerontologists. The late science fiction writer Isaac Asimov would be an excellent representative of the thrust of activity theory. In reflecting on more than a half century of writing with over 365 published books and additional volumes on the horizon, he stated that "naturally there's got to be some limit for I don't expect to live forever, but I do intend to hang on as long as possible" (Asimov, 1988:x). Isaac Asimov died at age 72 in 1992.

Is this activity-oriented view justified by research? There is a strong correlation between activity level,

The Elderly of China

Respect, honor, reverence. These words describe the view of the elderly in traditional Chinese culture. Yet Zhao Chunlan, a 73-year-old widow, had her son and daughter-in-law sign a formal support agreement assuring that they would provide for her needs—from cooking special meals and giving her a color television and the largest room in the house to never making her angry. If respect for the elderly is so much a part of Chinese culture, why is a formal agreement needed that *requires* family members to take care of their elders? To answer this question, we need to understand how tradition and change are colliding in China.

Respect for the elderly is based on two principles: *filial piety*, which is the duty and subordination of the son to the father and *xiao*, showing one's parents respect and obeying them without question. Dating from 800 B.C.E., these principles give the oldest men the most respect. In practice, all elderly—both men and women—gained. In traditional Chinese families, a woman's life is severely restricted. However, an elderly woman obeys her husband, but commands respect from her children. In traditional Chinese families, old age is the best way for a woman to gain some limited authority.

The family is the key institution around which support for the elderly is organized. Each generation rears the one behind it, which then becomes responsible for support of the preceding generation. The elderly remain in the family until death and provide valuable feedback in how the next two generations are reared. Violations of filial piety, such as failure to support the elderly, are illegal, but in rural areas public opinion, which denounces the violator to the community, carries more weight.

Traditions of filial piety and xiao are being eroded by a massive increase in China's elderly population. By the year 2025 this age group in China will double. When China's baby boomers reach old age, the social and economic burden will be enormous, quadrupling for urban families and doubling for rural families. With the Communist Revolution in 1949, the basic principle of filial piety was upheld. The communist government did enact new marriage laws to upgrade the position of women in their extended families. However, the traditional pattern of family support for the elderly was officially accepted by the new regime. China's economic resources are limited; it is the family that is still expected to be the major source of support for the elderly.

But the contemporary Chinese family is changing. It varies from smaller, nuclear families in urban areas to larger, extended families in rural areas. In rural areas the government appears satisfied with the expectation that elderly parents should live with adult children, primarily their married sons. Many rural areas and those regions

happiness, morale, and life satisfaction in late middle age and old age; (Sheehy, 1995). Both the men and women who emerge in old age as psychologically healthiest use activities to shape a "new" self, as their expectations and goals change. When disengagement occurs, it is most often due to poor health rather than any desire to limit activities or withdraw from social interaction. While involuntary role loss may occur, such as compulsory retirement, activity theory offers a variety of mechanisms to offset role loss. For example, roles may be consolidated. Rather than searching for new roles, time and energy may be redistributed to remaining roles (Atchley, 2000). Retirement may be an opportunity to expand time on enjoyable activities, such as cooking, reading, or volunteering, that before were minimized due to paid work and family obligations. Role consolidation can result in an activity level equal to the preretirement norm.

While activity theory is certainly appealing, it has its critics. Some elderly prefer to give up the pressures and high levels of activity of middle age, especially if they felt overinvolved during this time. Type of activity is also important. Informal activities are associated with higher levels of life satisfaction, whereas formal activities have a negative impact (Longino & Kart, 1982). Self-esteem may be compromised if problems related to health, income, or family limit desired activities. A feeling of controlling one's life and destiny may be considered a measure of self-esteem. Compared to their younger counterparts, older Americans who have increasing physical impairment and low levels of education report a substantial reduction in sense of control (Mirowsky, 1995). Activity theory cannot easily explain the intentional isolation that becomes the preferred lifestyle of some elderly.

Continuity Theory

Continuity theory offers more of a social psychological perspective in explaining the aging process. **Continuity theory** suggests that individual personality is important in adjusting to aging, with previously

with a high percentage of indigenous minority people are allowed to have more than one child. Since these areas produce their own food, they can also support larger extended families. In urban areas, China's one-child policy is more strictly enforced, so there will be fewer children available to care for the next generation of elderly.

On the other hand, elderly Chinese contribute to their children and their community. Extended family life in rural areas allows opportunities for elderly men and women to engage in agricultural work as long as they are physically capable. In urban areas, a retired man may be allowed to work on neighborhood committees and in cultural organizations. Women withdraw earlier from the work force after the birth of the first grandchild to focus their time and energy on household tasks and child care. In fact, elderly women perform most housework. Women continue economic activities longer than men and seem to willingly accept a life of "ceaseless toil." A lifestyle of leisure is neither available nor desired.

China has gained economically from the unpaid productive work of the

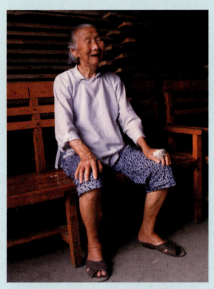

In China, old age brings honor and respect. It enhances the status of women who throughout their lives are subordinate to men.

elderly. When their "ceaseless toil" must finally cease, the government provides only limited help. Any public assistance to the elderly will also mean bolstering the family in their caregiving roles. Zhao Chunlan knows that her

son loves her and is bound by traditions of filial piety and *xiao*. But she is well aware that the formal support agreement will make him "conscious of his commitment" to her, as well as legally responsible. The system of support that evolves in China will be filtered through the family and shaped by an ancient tradition of respect for the elderly. It will also be shaped by the economic realities of one nation caring for the earth's largest percentage of elderly population.

1. Do you think that the tradition of honor and respect for the elderly in China will be eroded? What works for and against changes in this tradition?
2. Given the increase of the elderly population and the decrease in the birthrate, what policies related to support for the elderly could China adopt that would serve the needs of families and communities?

Sources: Fei, 1985; Martin, 1988; Sun, 1990; Davis-Friedmann, 1991; Fang et al., 1992; Hare-Mustin, 1992; Jiang, 1995; Lindsey, 1999.

---

developed personality patterns guiding the individual's thinking and acting (Neugarten et al., 1968; Bengston et al., 1985). More recent versions of the theory emphasize the evolution of adult development and our capacity to always learn from ourselves and our environments (Atchley, 1989). We adapt to change based on these patterns as well as on factors in the social structure, such as race, gender, and class. In other words, while we do not become different people simply because we are growing old, we have an overall developmental direction that we call upon when the opportunities for role choices arise. For instance, how do you spend your leisure time? Proponents of continuity theory would argue that if bicycling or hiking is your preference now, you are beginning to establish patterns of selection that will become stabilized by middle age. How do you deal with interpersonal problems? Talking things over with close friends may become the guideline.

At the core of adult development is the ability to preserve our adaptive capacity (Atchley, 2000). By

middle age we know our strengths and weaknesses and make our choices accordingly. The loving behavior of a grandparent to a grandchild suggests to continuity theorists that the loving older person was also a loving younger person. When the grandchildren are grown, the loving grandparent may turn to volunteer work with children. Consistent with activity theory, the continuity model suggests that when roles are lost, similar roles are substituted.

The strength of continuity theory as an explanation for adult aging lies in its interdisciplinary scope. It allows for the linking of individual personality and social structure in determining the attitudes and behaviors of the elderly. By adding the notion of ongoing adaptation to new situations, it overcomes the criticism that it is too deterministic and that we are caught in particular patterns of behavior that may be more detrimental than beneficial. The problem is that it is difficult to test empirically. We need longitudinal data to fully understand the internal and external adaptive mechanisms of adults (Atchley, 2000). This means studying those entering middle age now and following them through the rest of their life course. The premise of continuity theory is evident in these lines from Maya Angelou's (1978) poem, "On Aging":

I'm the same person I was back then,
A little less hair, a little less chin,
A lot less lungs and much less wind.
But ain't I lucky I can still breathe in.[1]

Age Stratification Theory

Using the wealth of sociological work on class stratification as a foundation, gerontologists have begun to develop newer models of stratification based on age (Riley, 1971, 1985, 1987; Riley et al., 1988). We have seen how stratification systems are cultural universals that emerge when societies use certain characteristics such as social class, race, age, and gender to rank members and determine their roles and statuses. Chronological and biological age are associated with a set of behavioral expectations or **age grades** that change as we get older. When a child is told to "act her age," it is in relation to what is expected for the age grade in her culture. She is part of a *birth cohort* of people born at a given period who age together and experience events in history as an age group.

The explosion of interest in gerontology, for example, is a direct result of the large cohort of "baby boomers"—those born between 1946 and 1964—who will be reaching retirement age within the next two decades. A cohort's "societal significance" is judged by the extent of influence one cohort exerts over others (Uhlenberg, 1988). As illustrated by the protest movements of the 1960s and 1970s, baby boomers have had a major impact on social institutions and public policy, not only in the United States but with their age partners throughout the world.

Using cohort analysis as a basis, **age stratification theory** seeks an understanding of how society makes distinctions based on age, with gerontologists interested in that period of life referred to as old age. As social change continues to alter patterns of aging, age cohorts exhibit both similarities and differences (Riley, 1987). People are not only living longer and healthier, they are more affluent, with age norms modified accordingly. Marketing strategies target the affluent aged, offering them a tantalizing array of consumer goods and services, from luxurious condominium living to adventure-oriented vacations. What is age-typical for you at age 75 will be different from that of your parents, just as it was for them from their parents.

The cohort analysis approach of age stratification theory offers a valuable tool for understanding the aging process. When tied to the broader conflict perspective in sociology, age stratification theory provides a more complete picture. All forms of social stratification produce social inequality. Even in small, technologically less sophisticated societies where rule by consensus is the norm, age in itself can bestow power. We saw how the !Kung associated old age with infirmity. But they also ensure that older men and women control limited resources. While their experience is essential for surviving in an adverse environment, they also retain their culture's accumulated knowledge, which must be passed on orally (Biesele & Howell, 1981).

When age and gender are combined so that the most powerful positions are assigned to the oldest men, a **gerontocracy** exists. This is the case in some East African cultures where reaching a certain age means automatically becoming part of the ruling elite (Keith, 1990). When age and social class are combined so that property remains in the hands of the oldest males, they can use it both to control other family members, especially their sons, and as leverage against being abandoned or mistreated if they become infirm.

Although the elderly may benefit from age stratification and the inequality that elevates their position in some cultures, conflict theory suggests several factors why this situation rarely exists. First, modernization has transformed much of the world and weakened those economic and kinship structures where the elderly have been accorded power and prestige. With modernization come industrialization, urbanization, mass education, scientific technology, highly individual roles, migration to urban areas, and increased mobility. Such processes literally can leave the elderly behind with fewer resources to compete effectively with younger age cohorts.

Second, age stratification leads to age segregation and greater social distance between age cohorts. Whether it is a retirement community for the more affluent or a transient hotel in an inner city slum for the poor, isolation and separation from younger people can occur. Third, compulsory retirement and the lack of skills to maintain a current job or successfully compete for another one put the elderly at financial risk. This problem is particularly acute considering that the current generation of elderly relies on Social Security as the most important source of income (Figure 14.4). Social Security accounts for almost 80 percent of income of the poor elderly (U.S. Senate Special Committee on Aging, 1991:69). Finally, age-based social inequality poses the potential for tension between the aged, who have lost valued roles and the associated resources, and the younger persons who gained them (Foner, 1984).

---

[1]From Maya Angelou, *And Still I Rise*. New York: Random House, 1978.

In some Pacific Islands, the village chief and the power associated with it resides with the oldest male.

Thus conflict theory focuses on the elderly's loss of resources and the inability to either retain or retrieve them. Power is transferred to another group, in this case a younger age cohort. A modified stratification system based in part on age discrimination is institutionalized. Once in place, this discrimination is difficult to eradicate. This cycle leads to **ageism**, the devaluation and negative stereotyping of the elderly.

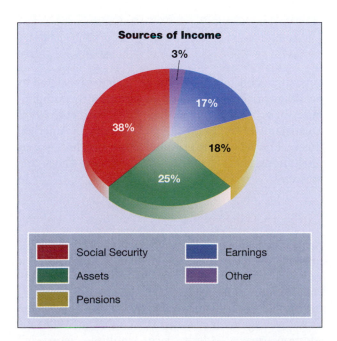

Sources of Income

3%
17%
38%
18%
25%

- Social Security
- Assets
- Pensions
- Earnings
- Other

FIGURE 14.4   Income for Americans Age 65 and Over
Sources: U.S. Special Senate Committee on Aging, 1991, p. 63; Darney, 1994: 332.

One problem with age stratification theory is that it is based on the assumption that age stratification is the dominant force in how resources are distributed in a society. The variation within cohorts may be as important as the variation between them (Passuth & Bengston, 1988). Age is one of many social divisions, but gender, race, class, and even health are other variables that reap social rewards and liabilities. Another problem is that there is contradictory evidence that modernization ushers in devaluation of the elderly. As societies continue to modernize, the quality of life improves for the aged. Higher prestige for the elderly is now associated with the most modern societies. Social policies have been adapted to the benefit of the aged (Cowgill, 1986). In the United States, for example, there is widespread consensus that public funds should be used for those who are prohibited from working or are no longer able to work because of age. There is a tradition of respect for the elderly, so mechanisms have been put in place to allow them some freedom from the stigma that may come from dependency. One such mechanism is Medicare. By bolstering income and health support, retirement becomes a time for self-fulfillment and self-sufficiency.

Symbolic Interactionism

Similar to continuity theory, symbolic interactionism takes a more social psychological perspective on aging. It resonates with that part of continuity theory that emphasizes adaptation and the ability to choose behavior. If we are constrained by our environment, then we modify it. If we are constrained by our individual needs, then we adjust them. A retired elementary school teacher, for example, may start a preschool, which sustains her or his individual need to help children. These choices are not made in a vacuum. As discussed throughout the text, symbolic interactionism argues that behavior is for the most part rationally chosen, based on our interpretations of others and the symbolic meanings we share in common.

Symbolic interactionism also capitalizes on the work of conflict and age stratification theory by focusing on the impact of ageism and how it can force the elderly into devalued age strata. As an offshoot of symbolic interactionism, labeling theory asserts that when the elderly are stereotyped through ageism, they may internalize the negative labels and learn to act in the manner the stereotypes suggest. By being labeled as incompetent, the elderly begin to question their ability to learn new skills or hone old ones. If the cycle continues, complete disengagement may occur, compromising the elderly person's capacity to take care of himself or herself. Labeling can usher in a self-fulfilling prophecy and lead to *social breakdown syndrome* (Kuypers & Bengston, 1973). This means that when we tell the elderly they are incompetent to do anything but "relax" in the rocking chair, they may never again be able to leave it. In this way, labeling and disengagement theory go hand in hand.

Overall, symbolic interactionism can adequately deal with how we perceive the elderly and how the labeling process can be detrimental or beneficial. And like continuity theory, it helps explain individual variations in behavior, from the aged person's point of view as well as that of other age cohorts. But as micro-level analysis, symbolic interactionism minimizes the impact of the broader social structure on behavior. Once ageism becomes institutionalized, it is difficult to dislodge it without a concerted attack on all social institutions. As a better model to explain social change as related to the elderly, elements from symbolic interactionism and conflict theory can be integrated. As we will see, ageism can be reversed and positive labeling can occur when the elderly build their resources and form a power base to challenge age-discriminatory practices.

A PROFILE OF THE AGED IN THE UNITED STATES

When profiling the aged in the United States, the portrait that emerges is a positive one. Most elderly people are married, are relatively secure financially, and live in their own homes or apartments. They have frequent contact with other family members and regularly see their children. They describe their health as

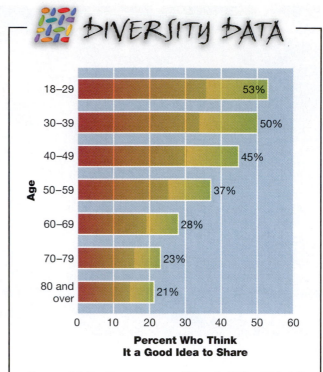

FIGURE 14.5   Percentage of People Who Think It a Good Idea for Older People to Share a Home with Their Grown Children, by Age As people get older, they are less likely to think that sharing a home with their grown children is a good idea—especially for those age 70 and older. How does this pattern challenge stereotypes regarding the dependent elderly and uncaring younger adults regarding their parents?
Source: NORC. General Social Surveys, 1972-1996. Chicago: National Opinion Research Center, 1996. Reprinted by permission of NORC, Chicago, IL.

generally good, and they view any problems related to health as not severe enough to significantly compromise their lifestyle (Rosenthal, 1997; Nemeth, 1998; Quadagno, 1999). In profiling the elderly in America, this section will focus on the diversity in those social institutions that have important consequences for lifestyle.

Links to Diversity

Age is only one of many categories of social structure in which people may be placed. The United States is a very diverse society, and there are many possible outcomes for the aged related to that diversity. Considering all age groups, financial inequality is highest for those over age 65 (Calisanti, 1996; O'Rand, 1996). In addition, many elderly face "multiple jeopardy" because, combined with their age, they fall into other categories that are associated with financial risk. The *theory of cumulative disadvantage* takes into account the social categories that increase inequality throughout the life course. (Quadagno, 1999). Advantages or disadvantages based on social class, gender, and race early in life carry through to old age.

Social Class.   Opportunities for an enhanced quality of life are offered for those elderly who are financially secure. Financial security is a key factor in maintaining a healthy and independent lifestyle during old age. As a group, the elderly have experienced a major decline in poverty since the 1960s. Coupled with economic growth and better pension plans, this decline is primarily due to the expansion of federal programs such as Medicare. Medicare is available to virtually all United States citizens age 65 and over as a health insurance program that covers significant health care costs (Chapter 19). Before Medicare, health care costs propelled many of the elderly into poverty. Since 1960, poverty among the elderly has declined from 30 percent to 10.8 percent in 1997 (see Table 14.2). Despite this success story, the figures mask a number of factors that not only keep many elderly in poverty but put certain groups at risk for poverty when they reach old age.

Age and Gender.   Income declines with age among the elderly. The younger elderly, age 65–80, have more resources than the oldest old, age 80 and above, the latter being the fastest growing age population in the United States. This decline is associated with changes in sources of income and, more important, with marital status (Atkins, 1992). The oldest old are also likely to be widows who experience severe economic consequences at the loss of their spouse. Spouse benefits provide some help for older widows, but they are at best precarious (Meyer et al., 1994). Women age 85 and above, who are living alone and are functionally impaired, have reduced financial resources (Barer, 1994). And a lifetime of employment does not protect women from poverty at old age.

The Minority Aged.   The minority elderly face multiple jeopardy for poverty. As with the elderly population as a whole, older African Americans have improved economically since the 1960s. But the poverty rate for this group is triple the poverty rate for older whites, and it is most pervasive for older African American women who head multigenerational households or who live alone (Watson, 1990; U.S. Senate Special Committee on Aging, 1991; U.S. Bureau of the Census, 1998). Research suggests that African Americans are forced from paid employment earlier in their careers than whites, often because of poor health. Unemployment reduces pension and Social Security benefits and puts them in a precarious economic position because they are likely to have more dependents than whites. Compounding this situation is the fact that their jobs often provided little in the way of economic security (Farley & Allen, 1987; Markides & Mindel, 1987). Retirement in the conventional sense is less applicable.

Interestingly, these economic disadvantages do not necessarily mean that African Americans face old age with misery. Although the oldest old African Americans are in poorer health and have lower incomes than comparably aged whites, they have significantly better morale (Johnson, 1994). Objectively, they are in ill health and poverty. Subjectively, they believe their situation is better than what they expected. As suggested by symbolic interactionism, it is the perception between expectation and reality that determines their attitudes.

Elderly Latino Americans of Mexican origin fall between African Americans and whites in poverty. Like the elderly of all races, these Latino have experienced a steady decline in poverty, but their poverty rate is still twice as high as that of the white elderly. Gender again increases risk for poverty. When compared to African American and white women, census figures show that elderly Latino women have the lowest median incomes.

The high poverty rate of elderly Latino is affected by unique cultural influences. Mexican American culture is described as extremely family oriented, with an expectation that kin will be available for support. Despite a strong belief that these families must care for the needs of their elderly, the intent to help varies with the financial ability to do so (Garcia, 1988). Even when formal sources of help are available, elderly Latino still prefer to rely on family (Markides et al., 1986). The elderly themselves perceive that such services are insensitive to their individual needs and ignore the cultural and language issues they face (Sotomayor & Randolph, 1988).

Native American elderly also see kinship as central to their economic and social lives, but they readily seek and use formal support services and any financial

Table 14.2	Poverty Rate of Elderly Adults, 65 and over, Selected Years		
Year	Poverty Rate	Year	Poverty Rate
1960	30.0	1982	14.6
1966	28.5	1986	12.4
1970	25.3	1990	12.2
1974	14.6	1994	10.5
1978	14.0	1997	10.8

Sources: Adapted from Weicher, 1989; Darnay, 1994: 254-55; U.S. Bureau of the Census, 1998.

Although African American elderly are likely to have low incomes, they express relatively high levels of life satisfaction and well-being.

help provided through such services (Markides & Mindel, 1987). The Native American population remains the poorest of all ethnic and racial minorities, and this poverty carries over into old age. Most elderly can still be found on reservations. Those who migrated to urban areas often return to spend their old age closer to kin. Reservation living is also associated with higher poverty. An interesting pattern of financial support has occurred among those elderly who qualify for some pension and welfare benefits. Many have voluntarily shared even these meager incomes with younger family members who come to rely on this steady support. In doing so, they uphold ancient traditions of sharing and interdependence, and the prestige of the elderly is enhanced (Foner, 1984; Markides & Mindel, 1987).

Retirement

The prospect of retirement presents a dilemma. Americans subscribe to a strong work ethic from which they gain a sense of identity and self-esteem. The transition to retirement requires major adjustments in all segments of life. It restructures daily living and alters family relationships and spending patterns. Retirement produces psychological stress and contributes to economic and social inequality (Pampel & Hardy, 1994). With senior citizens leading the way, the 1978 Amendments to Age Discrimination in Employment Act (ADEA) made mandatory retirement illegal until age 70. Amendments to ADEA in 1986 ended it entirely. Comparative data on mandatory retirement in the United States, Germany, Australia, and Great Britain show that Americans are

the most strongly opposed and the British the most accepting (Hayes & Vandenheuvel, 1994). Americans seem to be captivated with the prospect of work.

Other evidence suggests that captivation with work has changed to captivity. Retirement has become part of life's expectations, and norms for early retirement are rapidly being established. The stressful transition between work and retirement is eased by retirement seminars and financial counseling. Companies are offering benefit packages to encourage early retirement, and workers are receptive toward accepting them. If financial security is ensured, they prefer early retirement (Hooyman & Kiyak, 1996). For postindustrial nations, retirement has emerged as a basic right that is embraced by most workers (Ekerdt, 1998).

Although retirement is something most workers now look forward to, several factors are important in adjustment to, and satisfaction with, this life stage. Despite the role loss involved, a large majority of retirees do not experience a great deal of difficulty when they exit their jobs. Retirement correlates positively with self-esteem and negatively with depression (Reitzes et al., 1996). As predicted by activity theory, many find substitute roles that offer alternative sources of productivity, such as becoming entrepreneurs in home-based businesses (Quinn & Burkhauser, 1990; Kean et al., 1993). When social contacts are maintained or expanded, satisfaction with retirement and leisure activities also increases (Reeves & Darville, 1994). Higher levels of education and occupation offer more flexibility and variety in pursuing retirement opportunities and contribute to better adjustment (Calasanti, 1988).

Gender and Retirement. Gender is another variable that affects the retirement picture. Gender role differences predict that men would have a more difficult time with retirement than women, since men are expected to be the primary breadwinners in a household. Paid work, therefore, provides not only the practical benefit of income but also a sense of purpose and intrinsic satisfaction. Using such a male model of retirement may be biased, but the available data suggest that retirement satisfaction is based on the same factors for women and men (Seccombe & Lee, 1986; Calasanti, 1993). Like men, career women anticipate retiring at an earlier age (Feuerbach & Erdwins, 1994), but they use the resulting free time differently. Women look forward to retirement to allow them opportunities to restructure their domestic lives that were constrained because of work. Working-class women who would like to retire early have little choice but to stay in the labor force for as long as possible. Low earnings in gender-segregated jobs throughout their work lives take their toll in retirement. Poverty at retirement is a likely result (Perkins, 1993a, 1993b). Retirement needs to be more widely viewed from a model that incorporates the experiences of both men and women.

However, research consistently demonstrates that the two critical factors in retirement satisfaction are health status and financial situation. Workers are less satisfied if poor health forced them to retire or if deficient economic resources forced them to remain on the job (Atchley & Miller, 1983; Cavanaugh, 1993). While it is a myth that retirement harms health (Ekerdt, 1987), poor health obviously will impact what one does in retirement, just as it impacts the lifestyle of younger people. Must they return to the world of paid employment for economic survival? And are they physically fit enough to return? Acceptable options in health and wealth profoundly impact retirement adjustment and the lifestyle that results.

Living Arrangements

Our living environments at any age have a major impact on our lives. How we use and share our physical space make a difference in our behavior, quality of life, and sense of well-being (Saegert & Winkler, 1990). For the elderly in America, such issues are perhaps more important because at the last stages of life their choices for living arrangements may be severely curtailed (see Figure 14.6). Two questions need to be addressed in this regard: Is it better for the elderly to live independently but alone? Is it better to live with people their own age? Sociological research provides some answers to these questions.

The vast majority of the elderly—both couples and widow(ers)—not only live in their own homes and apartments, they are also likely to own them free of any mortgage (Hooyman & Kiyak, 1996). They are fully capable of functioning independently, even when living alone, and they strongly prefer to remain in their own homes. This preference is tied to a "loss continuum" that reduces social participation and increases social isolation (Pastalan, 1982). Elderly persons experience losses through widowhood, retirement, and the death of friends and siblings. A move from a home and community where they spent major

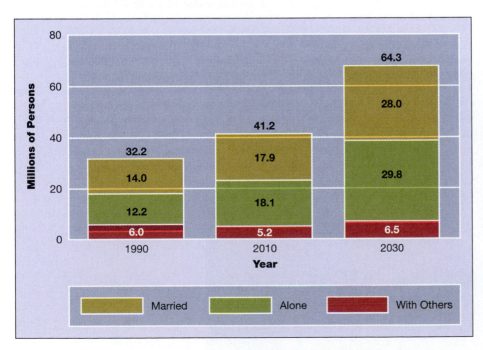

FIGURE 14.6   Living Arrangements of Elderly Persons Over Age 65, 1990–2030

Source: Adapted from Figure (p. 131) in *The Needs of the Elderly in the 21st Century* by Sheila R. Zedlewski, Roberta O. Barnes, Martha R. Burt, Timothy D. McBride and Jack A. Meyer. Copyright © 1990. Reprinted by permission of The Urban Institute Press, Washington, DC.

portions of their lives represents another loss. On the death of a spouse, the attachment to familiar surroundings becomes even more important (O'Bryant & Nocera, 1985).

Residential segregation of the elderly has received a great deal of research attention. Age-segregated housing offers both psychosocial benefits and costs. It can be attractive to those of the same birth cohort who share similar interests and lifestyles. Residences designed specifically for the elderly are usually safer, accessible to public transportation, and offer a range of services and recreational activities. After the move, residents report higher levels of social participation, an improved sense of well-being, and satisfaction with housing (Lawton et al., 1984; Cavanaugh, 1993). On the down side, the elderly may be *more* subject to isolation because they are separated from the larger society, caught in a narrow corridor where they interact only with other age peers. When younger people are deprived of contact with elders, ageism and negative stereotypes are heightened between both groups (Palmore, 1990). Residential segregation can be viewed in relation to both age stratification and conflict theory since it produces social inequality.

A Range of Housing Alternatives. The last two decades have witnessed a boom in housing alternatives for senior citizens. A range of housing options is shown in Figure 14.7. This classification indicates that the elderly represent a diverse population. The options are based on the degree of physical and psychological impairment—the critical factor in determining which services need to be provided within each alternative (Lindsey, 2000).

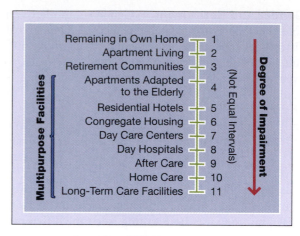

FIGURE 14.7 Housing Options for the Elderly
Source: Adapted from Lindsey, 2001: 91.

Many of the facilities are multipurpose in that they offer a variety of assistance, such as food and cleaning services, health and security checks, recreational activities, and volunteer opportunities. An example is congregate housing that serves the elderly who are impaired but not ill (Curry & Shroyer, 1989). For the elderly who are less capable and live with their working children, day-care centers can provide for their maintenance and supervisory needs for portions of the day (Lindsey, 2000). In all cases, maximizing independence is critical.

Too often, those who plan living arrangements for the aged, and with the best of intentions, do not recognize the diversity of their elderly clientele. The pervasive myth that the elderly are all alike still persists, even among some of those who work in geron-

Residential options for the elderly include apartment complexes and "leisure villages" where activities are offered with age peers that are associated with enhanced life satisfaction.

INTERNET ——— CONNECTIONS

Site www.netwalk.com/~duchapl/ lists some of the trivia of the Baby Boomer generation. Which ones do you think are the most ridiculous? What are the most inane habits of your own generation?

is their perception of how much control they have over their lives. It is clear that LTCFs can offer residents a great deal of this control (Langer, 1985; Diamond, 1992).

LIFE CONNECTIONS: Later Life in American Families

As mentioned above, most elderly are married. This translates to about two-thirds of elderly men and two-fifths of elderly women. (U.S. Bureau of the Census, 1999). Indeed, of today's elderly, less than 5 percent have never married. With increased longevity, and after the departure of the last child from the home, couples can expect to spend about one-fourth of their married life together.

The Marriage Relationship

For the married elderly, marital quality is high. Research spanning three decades demonstrates the same overall conclusion: that marital satisfaction is as high or higher in later life as it was at the beginning of the marriage (Rollins & Cannon, 1974; Berry & Williams, 1987; Brown, 1990). When combined with good health and financial security, retirement and the

tology. For those who do require support, individual wants and needs should be carefully considered when determining living arrangements.

Institutionalization. Most people routinely overestimate the percent of the elderly population who reside in long-term care facilities (LTCFs) or nursing homes. Only 5 percent of the elderly are in continuous long-term care. Some data suggest that if more noninstitutional options and social support networks were available, this number could be significantly reduced (Ham, 1980; Rivlin & Wiener, 1988). But for those elderly who are fully dependent, with extensive physical and psychological impairment and who required 24-hour support, admission to an LTCF may be the only realistic alternative.

An LTCF is another example of a *total institution* (Chapter 5). It is "total" because, like a prison, it exerts complete control over the individual. Can an LTCF institution be a "total" one, where administrative functions are carried out efficiently but where individual wants and needs are taken into account? Research suggests the answer is yes. For example, most nursing homes now have resident councils with some decision-making authority. Residents of LTCFs are also protected by federal legislation, such as the Older American Act passed in 1965, which established the Administration on Aging and allowed grants for planning, training, and coordination of services to the elderly. Most important, the 1975 amendments to this legislation established an ombudsman program designed to serve as a liaison between LTCF administration and residents. Ombudsmen are both paid and volunteer staff from outside the LTCF who serve as advocates and investigate complaints, bringing in legal counsel if necessary.

Although most elderly desperately wish to maintain at least a semi-independent existence in their own homes, some do prefer an LTCF where social isolation is reduced and they can live among peers. It is also difficult to rely completely on outside caretakers for all basic needs. Patient-centered approaches can make life better for those who reside in LTCFs. The key factor in the well-being of nursing home residents

Most elderly are married and exhibit high levels of marital satisfaction, which may actually increase at this stage of life.

last child leaving home allow the older couple more opportunities for shared activities and a reexploration of the marriage.

At that point, the marriage relationship itself again becomes the focus of life, another "honeymoon stage" when the couple can finally do the things they always wanted to do (Gilford, 1984). When asked what contributes to marital stability and satisfaction, both older men and women suggest similar things, including seeing your spouse as your best friend, sharing the same goals, having a sense of humor, viewing marriage as a long-term commitment, and wanting the relationship to succeed (Lauer & Lauer, 1986; Lauer et al., 1990). There is consensus on what is important for a good marriage with factors such as these suggested by all age groups (Chapter 15).

Remarriage.   While most elderly couples express a reasonably high degree of marital satisfaction, there is a small but growing percentage of divorces within this age group. In 1980 3.5 percent of people over age 65 were divorced; by 1998 the rate almost doubled, to 6.8 percent (U.S. Bureau of the Census, 1999). Age itself is probably less of a factor than the fact that people of all age groups are now more likely to see divorce as an acceptable option. This suggests that the elderly of today may not be subscribing to traditional values that would make divorce out of the question. Another factor is that the next generation of elderly will consist of a majority of women who have not only worked outside the home but may have retired from successful careers that offered retirement benefits. Their financial security may allow them more choice to end a marriage, particularly when "staying together for the sake of the children" may have kept the marriage intact.

Given the satisfying marital relationships that typify older couples, it is not surprising that many choose to remarry. Not only do later life remarriages have a better chance of success after a divorce, but couples also report that their marriages are happier (Campbell, 1981). Remarriage rates are higher for those who have divorced compared to those who are widowed, with age and gender explaining most of the differences (Ward, 1984). Women are at a disadvantage both as widows and if divorced because men marry younger women and women outlive men on the average of about 7.5 years. On the other hand, a woman may be reluctant to remarry if she must again take on a significant caretaking role, whether it means attending to the domestic daily needs of a husband or caring for him if he becomes debilitated. For men the opposite is true. Men who are inexperienced in looking after themselves want to remarry in part because their wives can provide these domestic services (Hayslip & Panek, 1993).

The most important reason for remarriage, however, is that couplehood is perceived as vital to life and happiness. Whereas the intense emotion associated with romantic love impels younger couples to marry, older couples express a simple desire for companionship and affection (Bengston et al., 1990). Sexuality, however, is still expressed as an important desire and is not necessarily compromised by old age (Chapter 7). Successful remarriages are associated with similarity of background, long-term prior friendship, often including the former spouse, and approval of family and friends (Vinick, 1979; Bengston et al., 1990). For all ages, marriage is associated with companionship, affection, and interdependency (Fig. 14.8). These characteristics appear to be even more important to those who remarry in later life.

Cohabitation

Just as higher divorce rates in the overall population are showing up among the elderly, so are rates of cohabitation, or living together without marriage. This may be surprising to those who believe that such a lifestyle is attractive only to younger people and college students. Although younger cohabitants are people who eventually get married (though not necessarily to those who they are living with), this is generally not true for the elderly. Other incentives propel elderly people to choose cohabitation rather than marriage. Many originally chose this lifestyle to avoid a reduction of Social Security benefits that, until the law changed in 1984, penalized those who remarried after age 60. However, widows and widowers may lose rights to their former spouses' pensions and health benefits, and inheritance of assets within a family may be jeopardized in the event of remarriage. Other older couples may simply want companionship and a sense of security without the legal entanglements of marriage.

The children of these couples face a dilemma. Do they sanction the cohabitant arrangement or encourage their parents to marry? It is difficult for adult children to envision a parent in such a relationship. And for older couples who grew up at a time when such liaisons were frowned upon, they may feel compelled to hide the arrangement from their peers, whom they believe would disapprove. Yet as norms are relaxed and cohabitation becomes more of an acceptable lifestyle among younger people, acceptance will probably increase among the elderly as well.

Grandparenting

Families in later life are also shaped by both the delights and burdens associated with grandparenting in America. The role of grandparent is ambiguous, but research has identified a number of important patterns. Three grandparenting styles are perhaps the most common (Neugarten & Weinstein, 1964; Bengston & Robertson, 1985). First, a "formal" grandparenting

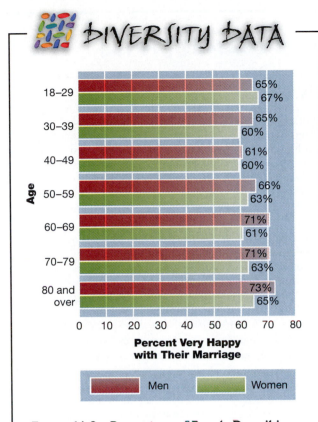

DIVERSITY DATA

Age	
18–29	Men 65% / Women 67%
30–39	Men 65% / Women 60%
40–49	Men 61% / Women 60%
50–59	Men 66% / Women 63%
60–69	Men 71% / Women 61%
70–79	Men 71% / Women 63%
80 and over	Men 73% / Women 65%

0 10 20 30 40 50 60 70 80

**Percent Very Happy
with Their Marriage**

■ Men   ■ Women

**FIGURE 14.8 Percentage of People Describing
Their Marriage as Very Happy, by Age and
Gender.** Although the majority of both men and
women at all age levels describe their marriages as very
happy, the elderly have the highest ratings for very
happy marriages. Although the factors for a happy
marriage are the same for the young and the old, why
do people believe that elderly married couples are "different" than their younger counterparts?
Source: NORC. General Social Surveys, 1972-1996. Chicago: National
Opinion Research Center, 1996. Reprinted by permission of NORC,
Chicago, IL.

style exists throughout America. This style stresses independence for grandparents but lots of love companionship between grandparents and grandchildren.
Grandparents may care for their grandchildren but do
not interfere with the parents' authority. They clearly
keep parenting separate from grandparenting. Second,
in sharp contrast to the formal style, is the "surrogate-
parent," where grandmothers usually care for grandchildren and exert a great deal of control over their
grandchildren (Minkler & Roe, 1991). Third, the "distant figure" style of grandparenting occurs when
grandparents have limited contact with their grandchildren, usually on holidays or special occasions only.
Giftgiving and kindness are common, but the grandparent vanishes until the next family event.

These styles are not mutually exclusive and are altered as family circumstances change. With its emphasis on companionship, the formal style is the ideal in
American society—loving grandparents who may indulge their grandchildren and help out their children
when necessary but who leave parenting to the parents. However, much research is now focusing on
the rapidly increasing surrogate-parent style. Divorce,
death, out-of-wedlock births, safety, and escalating
day-care costs often result in grandparenting becoming a full-time job. When their parents are not financially or emotionally capable of caring for their
children, grandparents are frequently gaining custody.
Only a decade ago 13 percent of African American
children, 3 percent Latino children, and 2 percent of
white children had grandparents as *sole* caregivers
(Shore & Hayslip, 1992; Jendrek, 1996). When grandparents become the parents of their grandchildren,
role strain, depression, lack of privacy, and heightened
physical and emotional problems are frequent byproducts. And there is every indication that the surrogate-
parent-grandparent trend is increasing.

*Grandparents are likely to be central
to the lives of their grandchildren,
although they leave the parenting
up to their children.*

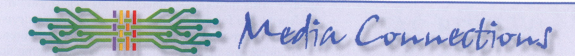

Seniorcitizen.Com

When grandmother Betty Fox began exploring the Web in search of sites dedicated to senior citizens, she discovered *thousands* of sites on an amazing array of topics—everything from supplemental medical insurance, Alzheimer's disease, and retirement relocation to investments, Elderhostel adventure travel, and Scrabble clubs. However, she also realized that the sites were in such a chaotic state that frustration rather than enlightenment often resulted from her Web surfing. She decided to set up her own Website to help older people navigate the Internet—www.grandmabetty.com. Today she not only offers links to other sites of interest to seniors, she peppers her senior-friendly website with lifestyle tips, jokes, and news of senior activities throughout the globe. Her site has certainly paid off—she gets over 30,000 hits a day.

Betty Fox's successful foray into the Internet on behalf of senior citizens underscores an important point highlighted in this chapter—the elderly are an extremely diverse group of people who continue to learn and are enhanced by that learning. For example, most colleges now offer programs for *lifelong education* designed to enhance knowledge and update existing knowledge. In college classrooms, particularly in sociology classes, older adults offer insights about career experiences and raising children that are valued by their younger classmates. Outside the classroom, the elderly can log on to Senior-Net, a national nonprofit organization offering courses to help older adults learn computer and Internet skills. Keeping in touch with family and friends who do not live close by is the most cited reason for seniors' going online. Courses fill quickly, and keeping up with the demand for new courses attests to SeniorNet's popularity. Nearly 80 percent of its students are over 65; as of 1998, SeniorNet had a membership of over 27,000.

The homebound, disabled, and elderly in long-term care facilities also benefit from the wired world, especially if non-profit organizations provide the necessary technology. Research indicates that the elderly can be successfully introduced to what computers can do, particularly when conducted in a safe, supportive setting, allowing any problems with memory or new learning to be handled in a nonintimidating manner. People who may feel outmoded are brought to the present and eagerly anticipate the future. The image of the elderly as disinterested, fearful, and disengaged from the computerized world is simply not supported.

Consider the following facts related to computers and the elderly:

1. Age is one of the best predictors of computer and online technology use. Baby boomers and young adults dominate use. However, over one-fourth of adults over age 50 use the Internet regularly and spend more online time than any other group. These are the baby boomers on the cusp of changing careers and early retirement. As early as 1996, another survey reported that one-third of seniors already use a computer, 9 percent use a modem, 4 percent use

Widowhood

As age increases so does the number of elderly living alone. The majority of elderly widows (approximately 80 percent) reside alone, and like married couples, they live independently in their own homes or apartments (U.S. Bureau of the Census, 1999). Social isolation and loneliness are frequent outcomes of widowhood, which in turn can produce such emotional distress that the surviving spouse is at higher risk for physical illness and even death (Ferraro, 1985; Silverstein & Bengston, 1991). If a caregiver-spouse dies, the already debilitated surviving spouse is left in an even more dependent and vulnerable position. Suicide rates among the elderly have increased since the 1980s, and they remain the highest for all age groups. White males between the ages of 80 and 84 have the highest suicide rates of all races and both genders (U.S. Bureau of the Census, 1998). Suicide attempts by younger people (those under age 35) are likely to fail; suicide attempts rarely fail for the elderly (Hendin, 1995).

Although the death of a spouse has a profound and devastating effect on the surviving partner, becoming a widow is a qualitatively different experience than becoming a widower. Older women are more likely to form their identity around marriage, so losing a spouse literally means loss of a central life role. Widows are likely to experience a sudden decrease in standard of living, and for working-class women, widowhood can quickly result in poverty. Isolation and support networks decrease, usually among in-laws (Barer, 1994; Meyer, 1996). These are worsened if the couple has moved away from her family for his career advancement. Finally, if a widow feels emotionally secure enough to venture into dating, prospects for male companionship and remarriage are limited.

Conversely, besides family members, the widow may be guided by the many others with whom she

the Internet, and 11 percent say they intend to buy or upgrade a computer. There is every reason to predict even higher computer usage as these groups age.

2. The Internet has been used by senior citizens long enough to show distinct patterns about the sites they visit. As Betty Fox discovered earlier, these marketers are developing senior-friendly messages and sites easing the burden for seniors to smoothly navigate their sites.

3. Senior citizens are overrepresented in visiting sites related to health care, pharmaceuticals, comparison shopping for older adult-based goods and services, and products designed to help with disabilities associated with aging, such as arthritis-friendly thermostats and home appliances, smoke alarms with lower frequency sounds for the hearing impaired, and voice-activated electronic memory devices to help older patients take medications on time and in proper dosage. Funeral-related sites are also extremely popular. Online wakes for the cremated, or for the more traditional, live video feeds from the chapel, are being marketed to well-heeled and savvy older consumers.

Although many elderly are the beneficiaries of computer technology, there still exists a "digital divide" between the "well-healed and savvy" group and a significant number of their age-mates who are left out of the wired world. First, those over age 65 are the most underrepresented of all age groups in significant computer use. Of the one-third of senior citizens mentioned above who regularly use computers, most of them are financially secure and learned computer basics during middle age. Second, for the financially strapped elderly, a home computer with Internet access is considered an unaffordable luxury. Nonprofit groups providing computer hardware to the homebound can only service a small percentage of those who could benefit from the technology. When coupled with other disabilities such as visual impairment, arthritis, or paralysis of the upper body, even free services offered at senior centers and libraries are out of reach. The computer world remains a graphically intense world and, even with visual improvements on the horizon, reasonable eyesight, for example, is vital to computer usage.

Internet access is increasingly necessary to fully participate in today's society—and it will be even more important in the future. Elderly who have been bypassed due to disadvantages related to education, finances, health, and age discrimination may not have enough time left to glimpse, much less access, the phenomenon known as the Internet. The good news is that the digital divide is narrowing as the most well-educated population in American history—the current baby boomers—makes its way to senior citizen status.

1. Based on your current computer and Internet knowledge, predict your own use and capability when you reach the golden age of 65. What do sociologists suggest that will enhance or deter your computer literacy at that stage of life?

2. What suggestions would you offer to bridge the digital divide that separates some seniors from others in computer usage? Consider enterprises that are both profit and nonprofit in your suggestions.

Sources: Arbuckle, 1996; Lustbader, 1997; Henderson, 1998; Russell, 1998; Whelan, 1998; Cleaver, 1999; *People*, 1999; Goldsborough, 2000; Perry, 2000.

---

can share her experiences, memories, and activities (DeSpelder & Strickland, 1996). Due to their numbers alone, a variety of roles have been carved out for widows (Lopata, 1973). These role choices may not be completely clear, may depend upon previous interaction with their husbands, family members, and friends, and how they have coped with crises in the past. But some expectations can help map out the road ahead. One role may allow for a widow's desire to keep the memory of her husband alive, particularly if the family supports this endeavor. Another can call for volunteer or even paid work. Anticipatory socialization, which plans for the role of widow, is offered as well. Since married women know that widowhood is probable, they may begin to actually mentally rehearse it. As indicated by continuity theory, this pattern shows how adjustment is related to both social and psychological factors.

The role of widower is much more vague than that of widow. At first glance, it would seem that adjustment is more difficult because men lose their most important source of emotional support and probably their major, if not their only, confidant. Wives typically take responsibility for maintaining the couple's social calendar and network of friendships. Lacking the strategies for either preserving or reestablishing intimate relationships, widowers have reduced social contracts (Norris, 1994). Retirement increases social isolation. Widowhood intensifies it. The net result is a loss of significant personal relationships. Older men are also less likely to be prepared for the everyday domestic responsibilities necessary for taking care of themselves. When ongoing relationships and customary responsibilities are shattered, anomie or normlessness can follow. This pattern helps explain the high suicide rate of elderly males.

Widowhood, especially for women, increases social isolation and decreases prestige and financial security in many cultures, such as among the Mendi of Papua, New Guinea.

On the other hand, marriage prospects remain bright for widowers, with many embarrassed by all the attention they receive from widows who want to "do" things for them. In addition to the numbers of women of their own age or younger who are available to widowers as potential dating and mating partners, men are better off financially to actually support another spouse. Finally, men may have a stronger need to be remarried, so they quickly move through the dating stage to make remarriage a reality (Hess & Soldo, 1985). Overall, adjustment to widowhood may be different for men and women, but it remains unclear as to which gender fares better.

≋ SOCIETY CONNECTIONS: Later Life as Risk or Opportunity

We have seen that throughout the world people are living longer and healthier lives. But opportunities for reaping the benefits of longevity are weakened when the elderly require more and more assistance as they age. Whether they live independently or in a group setting such as a nursing home, they must rely on caregivers to provide for their basic needs. Caregiving

has emerged as a major issue in the demographic revolution that is producing global graying.

Caregiving

When care for the elderly is necessary, the spouse is the first to provide it. The next level of responsibility falls to adult children. For the poor elderly, the next level is the network of extended family and kin.

While type of care and patterns of caregiving in families vary greatly, women are the primary caregivers to elderly parents, whether they are daughters or daughters-in-law (McGrew, 1991; Coward et al., 1992; Himes, 1994). They have been called the **sandwich generation** because they are caught between caring for the older and younger generations at the same time (Greenberg, 1994). Many of these women are middle-aged, in the work force, and still have children at home. Caregiving may provide opportunities to grow together to explore reciprocal relationship needs of elderly parents and their adult children in their final years together (Greenberg, 1994).

Love, commitment, and responsibility can describe caregivers. Other words to describe caregiving are guilt, burden, depression, and strain. Assistance to the elderly produces higher levels of caregiver strain and work interference than when providing assistance to adults 18 to 64 (Scharlach & Fredriksen 1994). The stress of the elder-care role for women is associated with compromises in both emotional health and psychological well-being (Moen et al., 1995). Time away from spouse and children can negatively affect their marriages, and guilt is produced when caregiving results in less affection to the parent (Hoyert & Seltzer, 1992).

Elder Abuse and Neglect.   While investigations of elder abuse and neglect occurring in long-term care facilities have resulted in a decline of the most glaring offenses, such as hitting or slapping residents, about 4 percent of all elderly people are abused each year in all settings. This abuse most commonly takes place as passive neglect, verbal and psychological abuse, and financial exploitation (Goldstein & Blank, 1988; Watson et al., 1993). Unfortunately, today's elderly are likely to be abused by their own spouses and other caregivers in the home.

Physical abuse of the elderly by adult children caregivers is common and is correlated with caring for mentally confused elderly, especially Alzheimer's patients (Steinmetz & Amsden, 1983; George & Gwyther, 1986). Alzheimer's disease is associated with uncontrolled outbursts of anger and unpredictable behavior that creates the most stress for the caregiver. Caregivers may counter with violence (Steinmetz, 1988).

INTERNET CONNECTIONS

The text discusses some of the issues surrounding *elder abuse and neglect*. There are public service organizations in many American communities that specialize in disseminating information related to this topic. One of these organizations is located in the East Bay region in California (Richmond). Go to their Web site: "Elder Abuse Prevention: Information and Resources Guide" - http://www.oaktrees.org/elder/. Click on "What is Elder Abuse"; "How Is It Recognized"; and "What Should I Do." After you have reviewed the contents of this Web site, respond to these questions:

1. As the baby boom generation becomes elderly, do you think that elder abuse will become a more serious and recognizable problem? If this happens, do you think that more resources will be devoted to preventing elder abuse?
2. Try to imagine that you are an elderly citizen who is dependent on others for your care. Would you want your care givers to be monitored or evaluated in any way? Why or why not?

Caregivers may be puzzled when charged with abuse. In one of the first systematic studies of elderly abuse in the home from the eyes of the caregivers, some reasons for this puzzlement surface (Steinmetz & Amsden, 1983). In-depth interviews of caregivers and their definition of the situation reveal the difficulties in separating victims from perpetrators. A daughter who had been caring for her 72-year-old mother for eight years exclaimed:

> I ripped her dress off when she refused to get ready to go out. I was sorry right after to think that I let her get to me . . . (Steinmetz, 1988:180).

The daughter is sorry for her behavior not because of what she did to her mother, but that she let her mother "get to me," to provoke the aggression. The daughter sees herself as the victim. While it may seem contradictory, the vast majority of interviewees were caring and loving children who were doing everything to ensure the best care for their parents. This interpretation of the data supports symbolic interaction theory's idea that the definition of the situation in understanding elder abuse is critical.

It is clear that as life expectancy increases, caregiving responsibilities for family members will also increase, raising the question: How will we care for the caregivers? More than at any other time in history, adult children are providing not only more care, but more humane care, but we cannot assume this will persist without adequate resources (Steinmetz, 1988). The caregiving role needs to be assessed in this light.

Advocacy and the Elderly: Senior Power

This chapter has demonstrated that throughout the world there are many contradictory attitudes associated with being old. Respect for the wisdom of the aged is countered by disdain for the burdens they may create for others. Positive labels to describe the elderly (independent, capable, strong, senior citizen) appear alongside negative ones (disabled, decrepit, frail, old fogy). The sociological perspective helps explain these apparent contradictions. Research demonstrates that many of the beliefs about old age are false, especially the myth that old people are abandoned by their families. Applied sociology shows how such findings can be used to benefit the aged.

Combatting ageism in our social institutions requires both scientific data and organizational strength. In general, older people are more interested in politics, are better informed, and have higher voting rates than younger people (Engelter, 1988; U.S. Senate Special Committee on Aging, 1991). However, this profile has not translated into a voting bloc that is exercised on behalf of their age peers.

This lack of a voting bloc does not mean that the elderly cannot or will not come together as an age-specific political group or that age alone is not salient in how political issues are debated. Their numbers are growing. They are becoming better educated. They are an informed citizenry. Politicians recognize the potential for senior power. Recent debates over changes in Medicare and health policy have been geared to senior citizens. If an age-based consciousness is lacking, politics will help create one.

But the real nurturers of a shared consciousness based on old age are the strong advocacy groups that have brought to the public's attention issues that impact senior citizens. Voluntary associations allow people to come together to work for morally worthwhile goals (Chapter 4). On an international level, these associations are referred to as nongovernmental organizations (NGOs). There are a number of such associations working to advance the cause of older people, including the National Council of Senior Citizens, National Council of Retired Federal Employees, National Caucus and Center on the Black Aged, and National Senior Citizen's Law Center. Except for some religious denominations, the largest voluntary association in the United States is the American

As founder of the Gray Panthers, the late Maggie Kuhn worked to change negative portraits of the elderly and to increase public awareness for the needs and the potential of the elderly worldwide.

Association of Retired Persons (AARP), which boasts a membership of over 33 million (Jacobs, 1990). Representing a very heterogeneous group, it has served to keep issues related to the aged in the public eye, especially in terms of health care.

An advocacy group more focused on fighting ageism is the Gray Panthers, with its motto of "age and youth in action." Founded by the late charismatic Maggie Kuhn, and with the assistance of thousands of volunteers, the Gray Panthers have been responsible for exposing scandalous conditions in nursing homes, monitoring the media on stereotypical portrayals of the elderly, fighting for housing suitable for older people and those who are physically challenged, and ensuring the political and economic rights of the aged. The Older Women's League (OWL) targets issues that perpetuate the double discrimination of gender and age, such as differential Social Security and pension plans, health insurance, and caregiving.

Both the Gray Panthers and OWL are action-oriented organizations working to promote an age-based consciousness. A number of national senior organizations have banded together to form the Advocated Senior Alert Process, an information and action network for political advocacy. They are not only mobilizing resources to challenge the current system, they want a new system. Thus they are in line with a conflict-theoretical perspective. For example, the Gray Panthers argue for a universal health care system, asserting such a system as a *right*, not a privilege. The term "productive aging" has emerged as a rallying cry for elder advocates, policymakers, and academicians across disciplines who are challenging stereotypes of the aged. Focusing on old age as a time of life for personal growth and exploration, the idea of productive aging has attracted people representing many different views. It emphasizes positive thinking about aging and the aged and the role older people can play in society (Caro et al., 1993).

These advocacy groups represent various constituencies for the aged. The productive-aging theme is one that they all likely share. They demonstrate that the possibility for a stronger social movement based on senior power exists. Many U.S. voluntary associations have joined with their international counterparts to raise a global consciousness about old age. As activists in their own countries and with their allies abroad, they have the potential to become formidable NGOs. This chapter has shown that the elderly are not all alike. However, by capitalizing on their increasing numbers they can gain improvements that will be beneficial for their age-mates in all social categories.

SUMMARY

1. Old age is defined differently in various cultures. In Western cultures old age is usually defined chronologically, but all cultures mark the aging process with role transitions.

2. Aging is a natural process that is influenced by stresses such as emotions and health habits. Primary aging refers to the physical changes that accompany aging; secondary aging refers to the life stresses that involve how our bodies and minds react to the social effects of growing old, such as age prejudice.

3. In general, old age is not associated with a significant decline in intelligence nor with changes in personality. Psychological impairment is associated more with poor health and age prejudice.

4. Alzheimer's disease is an organic brain syndrome characterized by progressively deteriorating mental functions. It is not a normal part of

aging. Most people who suffer from Alzheimer's disease are in the oldest old category, age 85 and above.

5. The elderly population is growing worldwide. Women outlive men all over the world. People are living longer and healthier, but care for the elderly toward the end of life strains resources of the developed world, which often relies on public funds for support.

6. Disengagement theory sees successful aging as the voluntary, mutual withdrawal of the aged and society from each other. In contrast, activity theory sees successful aging as continuing the usual roles and substituting new ones if role loss occurs.

7. Continuity theory, a social psychological perspective, suggests that adjustment to old age is an extension of earlier personality development. Race, gender, and SES affect the aging process more than personality.

8. Age stratification theory emphasizes generational differences such as birth cohort in the aging process and the effects of separating the young and the old. Symbolic interactionism emphasizes adaptation and choices of behavior in old age. It also focuses on ageism and the effects of labels on these choices.

9. Most elderly people in the United States are married, live in their own homes, report good health, and are not isolated from their families.

10. The poverty of the aged was cut in half by the advent of Medicare. However, widows, racial minorities, and the oldest old are most likely to be poor. Many elderly are in multiple jeopardy because of several minority statuses.

11. Most Americans look forward to retirement. The most important determinants of satisfaction with retirement are health and financial status.

12. The majority of elderly live in their own homes; only 5 percent are in long-term care facilities. The loss of a spouse produces such emotional distress that the surviving spouse is more susceptible to illness and death, especially suicide among widowers.

13. Later life in U.S. families shows high marital satisfaction for elderly couples. However, divorce and cohabitation are becoming more common. The remarriage rate is higher for elderly men; for both genders, remarriage is higher for the divorced compared to the widowed. Grandparenting roles for the elderly are expanding so that many are now primary caregivers for their grandchildren.

14. Women tend to be the primary caregivers for elderly parents and relatives. Because many are juggling responsibilities of parenthood and elder care, they have been dubbed the "sandwich generation." About 4 percent of the elderly are abused or neglected by spouses or caregivers in all settings.

15. Many advocacy groups such as the Gray Panthers have been formed to combat ageism and promote positive thinking about the aged and the roles they can play in society.

KEY TERMS

activity theory 357	**continuity theory** 358	**primary aging** 350
age grades 360	**disengagement theory** 356	**sandwich generation** 372
ageism 361	**gerontocracy** 360	**secondary aging** 350
age stratification theory 360	**gerontology** 350	

CRITICAL THINKING QUESTIONS

1. Demonstrate how biology, psychology, and sociology can work together to provide the best explanations for the process of aging. What theory from each discipline offers the best approach for interdisciplinary work?

2. Which social categories put people at most risk for social and individual problems when they become elderly? What social policies can be developed to reduce these risks to the benefit of all age groups?

3. What information can sociologists offer to the sandwich generation that can be helpful in dealing with caregiving? What information can be offered to those elderly who face dependence on caregivers, whether these caregivers are family members or not?

4. Given your knowledge of family patterns in later life, how would you respond to an elderly relative, perhaps your own widowed parent, who reports to you that he or she wants to cohabit or remarry?

 THE FAMILY

OUTLINE

Growing up in New Guinea

At first glimpse, the family of a New Guinea Manus child looks like the same kind of happy and intimate family Americans prefer. After the evening meal children are laid on mats to sleep, or they fall asleep in their elders' arms. Manus children live in a happy state of irresponsibility. The family is a place where the people who love each other best are closeted together around the fire, and everyone else is excluded. The tie between children and parents is close, but the relationship between husband and wife is usually strained and cold. To the children, father and mother seem two disparate people, playing with them, but against one another. Parents' blood ties to their children are stronger than their relationship to each other, and there are more factors to pull them apart than to draw them together. Husband and wife did not choose each other, and the sense that they will always belong to different groups will never vanish entirely, even after the marriage has endured for many years. (Adapted from Margaret Mead, 1953:39–47)

A Daughter's Story

I am a Chinese Korean American young woman. I was born two days before International Woman's Day, always a hectic time because my mother was busy going to meetings and organizing IWD programs. We weren't always close. As a young child I was resentful that she didn't spend more time with me. I felt closer to my father; he did things with me. My parents were probably gone the same amount of time but I blamed my mother more. She was sup-posed to be around. Looking back, I realize my mother made sure we had quality time together, while my father and I were content to bum around the house. I am a feminist by my own interpretation. Activism is definitely part of me. I would like to have the kind of relationship my parents have. They love, respect, and support each other but are not joined at the hip. They have learned, changed, and grown both as individuals and "together as one." (Adapted from Miriam Ching Yoon Louie and Nguyen Louie, 1998)

Still Around After All These Years

The family. We are a strange little band of characters trudging through life sharing diseases and toothpaste, coveting one another's desserts, inflicting pain and kissing to heal it in the same instant, loving, laughing, defending, and trying to figure out the common thread that binds us all together. The years have challenged families in ways no one would have thought it possible to survive. They've weathered combinations of step, foster, single, adoptive, surrogate, frozen embryo, and sperm bank. They've multiplied, divided, extended, and banded into communes. They've been assaulted by technology, battered by sexual revolutions, and confused by role reversals. But they're still here—playing to a full house. (Adapted from Erma Bombeck, 1987:11–12)

The family is not only a cultural universal (Chapter 3), it is the oldest and most conservative of the social institutions, the basic unit around which all social organization is built, and fundamental to the process of meeting social needs. In cultures that have relatively undifferentiated social organization, the family *is* society. As the vignettes suggest, expectations about how married couples should treat each other and how parents should treat children are learned in the family. This chapter will examine the remarkable diversity of the family and how social change accelerates it. It will also shed light on why such diversity is viewed as either a threat to social stability or an opportunity for family enhancement and individual growth.

WHAT IS A FAMILY?

Families continue to maintain primary responsibility for accomplishing critical social tasks. In fact, sociologists who study families find it easier to first describe what families *do* than what they *are*. We take that approach here since identifying the functions of the family gives us a good springboard for assessing how families are doing in accomplishing the tasks as well as the impact of social change in this process.

Family Functions

Almost a century of data suggests near consensus in both sociology and anthropology that the family carries out vital functions (Ogburn, 1938; Parsons & Bales, 1955; Aldous, 1991).

A review of these functions demonstrates key terms sociology applies to the social organization of the family.

1. *Reproduction*. In a fundamental sense, the future of the society is in the hands of the family. Families ensure that dying members of society will be replaced in an orderly fashion so there is a new generation to carry on. In most societies, the **family of procreation** is established at marriage and is the culturally approved sexual union that legitimizes childbearing.

2. *Regulation of sexual behavior*. All societies restrict sexual relations and reproduction among certain family members. The incest taboo is a powerful cultural universal (Chapter 3). **Exogamy** is a cultural norm in which people marry outside a particular group. For the family, exogamy is a mandate forbidding marriage between close kin. In the United States, for example, most states do not allow first cousins to marry, and third-cousin marriages are often restricted. Children learn early that the intimacy of the family does not extend to sexual relations.

3. *Socialization*. The **family of orientation** is the family in which children grow up; it is the vehicle for primary socialization, providing both social and individual benefits. In the family of orientation, children learn basic competencies, such as language, sexual rules, gender roles, and other behavioral norms that allow them to become fully functioning members of society. In the process, they also develop a sense of self. As we saw in Chapter 5, the self-esteem that is fostered in the family becomes a defining characteristic of people as they move into adulthood.

Although form has changed considerably, family and kinship remain powerful sources of personal and social identity.

4. *Protection, affection, and companionship.* The family provides the essential economic and emotional support to its members during all the events and inevitable crises in a typical family life cycle. To augment support for family members, roles are assigned. In traditional families, the husband-father usually takes the **instrumental role** and is expected to maintain the physical integrity of the family by providing food and shelter and linking the family to the world outside the home. The wife-mother takes the **expressive role** and is expected to cement relationships and provide emotional support.

5. *Social placement.* Families provide ascribed status, which places children at birth in various social hierarchies. This social location is related to **endogamy,** a cultural norm in which people marry within certain groups, with social class, race, and religion among the most important elements. Patterns of descent and inheritance are tied to social placement. In societies that use **patrilineal descent,** common throughout Asia, Africa, and the Middle East, the family name is traced through the father's line, and sons and male kin usually inherit family property. In **matrilineal descent,** least common today as well as historically, the family name is traced through the mother's line, and daughters of female kin usually inherit family property. **Bilateral** (or **bilineal**) **descent** uses both parents to trace family lines and is most common in Western societies. Even though in this pattern women at marriage typically assume their husband's surname, family connections are recognized between children and the kin of both parents. Bilateral systems do not ensure that females can inherit property, but they are the least restrictive in this regard. The critical point is that family name is significant in social placement and can enhance a child's prospects for upward mobility. This is clear, for example, when a Smith or a Jones marries a Rockefeller or a Roosevelt.

Family Structure

Families carry out these social functions but do so with a variety of family structures. In the developed world, the family has been transformed from a unit of production to one of consumption, a pattern that is being repeated in the developing world. In many regions of the developing world, large families are functional for subsistence agriculture, to produce goods for family use or for sale or exchange when surpluses are available. When it can feed itself, a larger family provides an economic advantage. Typical in rural areas globally are **extended families,** consisting of parents, dependent children, and other relatives, usually of at least three generations, living in the same household. In urban areas, larger families are an economic disadvantage since families consume but do not produce goods. **Nuclear families,** consisting of wife, husband, and their dependent children who live apart from other relatives in their own residence, are more typical globally in urban areas.

The "traditional" family has taken several forms, such as the 1930s extended family of The Waltons and the two parent–two child model today. However, neither form was or is the American norm.

The increased number of "latchkey" children—who are old enough to stay by themselves after school until their parents come home from work—reflects a change in traditional family structure (they may be from single-parent homes) and function (they may have two parents working outside the home).

Family structure has been profoundly altered by the twin processes of industrialization and its accompanying urbanization (Chapter 21). Evidence shows that nuclear family structure was normative in Western Europe as early as the seventeenth century and that social policies such as mandatory schooling were designed to shift some family responsibilities to the state (Lasch, 1979, Laslett; 1979; Berger & Berger, 1991). We can draw several implications from this pattern:

1. Modernization processes continue to modify a nuclear family model that is at least three hundred years old.
2. Modifications show up as changes in the roles of husband and wife in nuclear families. Nuclear families with dual-earner couples in more egalitarian gender roles are normative.
3. Modifications show up as changes in the structure of nuclear families. Increased numbers of single-parent families, cohabiting couples with children,

gay and lesbian families, and blended families due to remarriage are examples.

The contemporary reality is that "traditional" nuclear families coexist with other varieties. Since the conventional definition of *nuclear family* is too limited to encompass the structural diversity of U.S. households (Table 15.1), especially those without marriage partners, a more inclusive definition may be needed. A *modified-nuclear family* is a group of two or more persons related by blood, marriage, or adoption who reside together. The U.S. Bureau of the Census uses this description to define a "family" (Ahlburg & De-Vita, 1995).

THEORETICAL PERSPECTIVES

All theoretical perspectives in sociology recognize that the family is pivotal in carrying out the functions described above. There is also general agreement that the functions can be carried out within a variety of family structures found throughout the globe. However, sociologists disagree about the benefits and liabilities associated with social change on the family.

Functionalism

The functionalist perspective highlights the tasks as vital for social stability. If the institution of the family is ineffective in carrying out requisite social "duties," and other institutions have not picked up the slack, social equilibrium will be compromised. This is the core of the debate we will discuss later that relates to "family values," an issue on which sociology provides valuable input.

From the functionalist perspective, the socialization of children into accepted social roles is central to social stability, and role change is disruptive to family harmony and also to broader social harmony. For functionalists, families must somehow be immune to social change. Traditional family arrangements become the ideal to which all families should adhere. The problem with this view is that change is inevitable, so that what is "traditional" also changes over time. For example, functionalism tends to favor a family unit with nonoverlapping instrumental and expressive gender roles, where the husband-father has ultimate decision-making power.

Feminist and Conflict Theory Critiques of Functionalism

From a feminist view of the family, the functionalist ideal ignores the social changes that have occurred over the last half century, particularly the rise of

Table 15.1	Percentage Distribution of U.S. Households by Family Type	
	1990	1997
Family Households	71	70
Two-Parent Family	72	68
One-Parent Family	28	32
Single-parent mother	24	27
Single-parent father	4	5
Married Couple Family	56	53
With Children	26	25
Without children	30	28
Single-Person Households	23	25
Female	15	15
Male	10	10

Source: Adapted from Tables 71 and 79, U.S. Bureau of the Census, 1998

idealized fiction. Throughout the nineteenth century, poor women, especially immigrants and their children, worked in sweatshops or at home doing piecework. Victorian norms viewed middle-class women as physically frail and emotionally incapable of working in factories (Daniels, 1993). Nostalgia is expressed for a family unit typifying only a minority of Americans (Goode, 1984; Coontz, 1992).

Conflict theory focuses on the social placement function of the family in preserving existing inequality and power relations in the broader society. According to this perspective, social class endogamy and inheritance patterns ensure that property and wealth are kept in the hands of a few powerful families who safeguard these arrangements. This inequality is institutionalized through socialization that transmits the value that ability and motivation are keys to social mobility, but also perpetuates the notion that family wealth is deserved—and that those born into poor families remain poor because they lack talent and a work ethic. The structural conditions that sustain poverty are ignored. According to conflict theory, when social placement operates through patriarchal and patrilineal systems, wealth is further concentrated in the hands of males, which promotes female subservience, neglect, and poverty.

The functionalist emphasis on family harmony and the conflict emphasis on family problems are good examples of how sociologists can interpret data according to very different frameworks. Sociological research shows that family patterns change over time. The strength of any particular interpretation rests in the extent to which it documents both the changes and the regularities.

GLOBAL PERSPECTIVES

By viewing the diversity of family forms common to Western cultures, it is easier to grasp the extraordinary variations globally. This section will provide examples of marriage and family forms that typify many non-Western societies.

Marriage Forms and Residence Patterns

Cultural norms (exogamy and endogamy) and legal requirements determine who is allowed to marry whom. Most Western societies enforce **monogamy,** marriage to one spouse at a time. **Polygamy** means marriage to more than one spouse at a time. Although most societies allow for polygamy, compared with those that require monogamy, plural marriages are infrequent (Murdock, 1965; Lee & Whitbeck, 1993). Polygamy is usually associated with extended families and with either **patrilocal residence**—the couple

egalitarian families. Feminists express concern that when the patriarchal family is viewed as beneficial to social stability, it hampers the movement into egalitarian roles desired by both men and women. At the extreme, for instance, is Phyllis Schlafly (1981), who maintains that women who work outside the home take away jobs from men, sabotage family and social order, and undermine motherhood. Her view disregards the one-third of American households consisting of separated, single, and widowed people who do not have the luxury to decide whether to work outside the home.

Functionalist snapshots of families taken at different times in history show that families have varied considerably, but depending on when the snapshot was taken, the model for the "traditional" family looks different. At one time, the three-generation family living in the same household was believed to be the U.S. norm. Perpetuated by television, this was the model of *The Waltons*, a farm family surviving the Depression by hard work, faith, and devotion to family. However, a "new" traditional family that emerged in the 1950s has served as the idealized model ever since. At that time television gave us *Leave It to Beaver* and *Father Knows Best*. These shows portrayed a patriarchal family model with a bread-earning husband, a homemaker mother, and their at-home children—in which problems are solved in thirty minutes and virtual happiness is restored (Benokraitis, 1999). Although this model is believed to be the historical and contemporary U.S. norm, it emerged only a century ago, was associated with white, middle- and upper-class families, was never the norm, and is far from the norm today (Coontz, 1992, 1997; Roberts, 1993). Also, the values associated with the model are mostly

Polygamy still exists in the United States even though it is illegal. Here, Alex Joseph sits surrounded by his nine wives.

moves into the husband's home at marriage—or **matrilocal residence**—the couple moves into the wife's home at marriage. The most common form of plural marriage is **polygyny**, in which a man can marry more than one woman at a time. Although illegal in the United States, polygyny still exists, found primarily in Utah and Idaho. It is practiced by the descendants of those Mormon dissidents who broke away from the larger church in the mid-1800s (*Polygamy in Utah*, 1998). A classic historical case of a polygynous, patrilocal pattern was found among the upper classes in Chinese families for almost two thousand years. Because one man could have many wives and concubines, families became so large they occupied an entire village in such a complex set of household arrangements that it was often impossible to distinguish the village from the family (Lee, 1953; Baker, 1979).

A rare form of plural marriage found in a fraction of 1 percent of the world's societies is **polyandry**, in which a woman can marry more than one man at a time, usually brothers. It exists today among the remaining few hundred Toda tribe in south India, among some isolated Tibetan peoples, and among the Marquesan Islanders. To maintain a surplus of males, polyandry is associated with female infanticide and such a high degree of female subordination that an insurmountable chasm separates the genders in status (Cassidy & Lee, 1989; Queen et al., 1985).

Communal Families

Both globally and in the United States, communes have existed throughout history; like families overall, they vary considerably in structure and function.

Communes are collective households where people who may or may not be related share roles typically associated with families. Examples are the Oneida community and the Shakers of nineteenth-century America—communities that were religiously oriented and economically successful but radically different from the nuclear family, especially in their rejection of monogamy. The Shakers practiced celibacy and the Oneida community practiced complex group marriage (Matarese & Salmon, 1993). America became familiar with communes during the turbulent 1960s when many young people deserted conventional marriage and family practices and opted for different styles of cooperative living. Perhaps because of utopian visions and beliefs about family relationships at odds with the rest of society, most communes are short-lived, and even at their 1960s peak, represented less than one-half of 1 percent of the population (Goode, 1963; Zablocki, 1980).

In Denmark and Sweden, on the other hand, communes are institutionalized as alternatives to nuclear families. For many young people communes represent a normative stage in marriage and family formation that allows them to live cooperatively and intimately with others who may become marriage partners. When children are present, parents take more responsibility for their own children than other adults do, but agree to hand over important child-rearing functions to others in the commune. It is the child-centered approach to cooperative living that distinguishes the kibbutz from other communes worldwide. The *kibbutz* is an Israeli agricultural collective where children are raised together in an arrangement that allows their parents to become full participants in the economic life of the community.

Global Connections

Dowry and the Worth of a New Bride

Marriage and family customs usually reveal the position of women in society. In many cultures a woman's value is determined by what she can bring to the family in the form of a dowry, a payment from the bride's family to her husband's family to compensate them for her support. Dowry systems dominate in cultures where arranged marriages are normative, women's status is low, and the bride takes up residence in the groom's household. Dowries are also a means of social mobility whereby men use rights over women to compete for status. They existed in colonial America and are found throughout contemporary Asia and the South Pacific, the Middle East, and Eastern Europe. In almost all cultures, marriage unites families as well as couples. Dowries are critical in determining how well the bride will fare in her new extended family and the degree to which the families will cooperate with one another.

A family's economic survival is dependent on the number of sons and control of the numbers of daughters, who are regarded as financial liabilities. Families with more daughters than sons may be caught in an economic nightmare. It is easier to marry daughters off if they have large dowries. But an already poor family risks further impoverishment. If they have no sons, a daughter's "lost" dowry is never replaced by the dowry of a new bride brought into the family.

India is a case in point. When dowries are considered too paltry, the torture or death of the bride can occur. After a long dormant period, dowry abuse is increasing among all castes. In many cases the bride is doused with kerosene and set on fire so that the death looks like a cooking accident. Official figures from cities like Bombay show that one in four deaths of young women are due to so-called "accidental" incineration. Unreported dowry deaths, plus cases of abuse, neglect, and female infanticide, are included in the 22 million Indian females who are simply "missing."

Dowry systems remain strong in the developing world, especially in rural areas. Dowry abuses are clearly tied to women's subservience and persist in those societies that severely restrict women's roles. At this point in time, practices related to dowry systems suggest dire consequences for the well-being of daughters in many parts of the world.

1. What suggestions would you offer that would maintain dowry customs but minimize the abuses associated with them?
2. How do dowry systems reflect the link between gender inequality and economic patterns in families and in communities?

Sources: Schlegel & Eloul, 1988; Black, 1991; Teays, 1991; Watson & Ebrey, 1991; McCreery, 1993; Miller, 1993; *Breakaway*, 1995.

The kibbutz is a haven for meeting like-minded marriage partners. Between one and two months after birth, infants are moved to a children's house, where they will spend the next twelve years of their lives living with their peers. They spend several hours a day and most of the Sabbath with their parents.

The early kibbutzim were characterized by collectivization in family and work life that minimized gender role differences and maximized instrumental and expressive role sharing. Today, however, financial stability, economic productivity, and numbers sufficient for survival have accelerated gender stratification (Agassi, 1989; Neuman, 1991). Women function almost exclusively as child-care workers, teachers, and kitchen laborers, and their dissatisfaction with communal child-rearing has increased. This may explain why women are more likely than men to leave the kibbutz (Jacobsen, 1994). Despite obvious social stratification, kibbutzim remain ideologically committed to gender emancipation and allow some women to choose non–gender-related roles (Anson et al., 1990). Today the communal kibbutz family is neither extended nor completely nuclear, but is increasingly taking on more "nuclearlike" structural traits.

LOVE, MARRIAGE, AND DIVORCE—AMERICAN STYLE

We are so accustomed to viewing love and marriage as inseparable that it is rather startling to realize that in America they have been paired only recently. Romantic love as an ideal existed in Europe centuries ago, but it was not seen as a basis for marriage. Marriage was an economic obligation that affected power, property, and privilege and could not be based on something as transitory or volatile as romantic love. Marriage was the mundane but necessary alternative to the enchantment of feudal romance and courtly love games, which were reserved for the aristocracy. For the vast majority of people, personal fulfillment and compatibility of the couple were irrelevant. The decision to marry was rational rather than romantic.

The Puritan era in America ushered in the revolutionary idea that love and marriage should be tied together. This was a radical departure from early church teachings, which warned men that even looking on their wives with lust made them sinners. In the new ideal, if love was not the reason for marriage, it was expected to flourish later. Theories of family development from a functionalist perspective would support this expectation (Jamieson, 1994). Parental control over approval of marriage partners remained the norm, but the belief that love should play a part in the process became etched into the fledgling American consciousness. Today the idea of love as a factor in assessing a marriage partner is gaining worldwide popularity, but initially it was a phenomenon uniquely associated with the United States.

Mate Selection

I fell in love with him at first sight.
Then why didn't you marry him?
Oh, I saw him again afterwards. (Anonymous)

Since love is one of the most complicated emotions, beliefs about love have produced many myths (Table 15.2). Our attitudes and behaviors about gender roles, marriage, and the family are impacted by romantic ideals that are not enough to sustain couples for the adaptability and long-term commitment necessary for marriage. Although romantic love is idealistic, it is also very structured. Sociology documents the impact of **homogamy,** becoming attracted to and marrying someone similar to yourself. Unlike what would be predicted if romantic love were the sole basis for mate selection, homogamy results in **assortive mating,** where coupling occurs based on similarity rather than chance. Think about college, for example, as a powerful marriage market where people meet, date, fall in love, and marry. As a simple test of this, count the number of classmates who are engaged by their senior year. Parents send children to certain colleges with the expectation that they will not only receive an excellent education but they will meet potential partners from similar backgrounds. Brigham Young, Principia, Wittenberg, and Notre Dame attract Mormon, Christian Science, Lutheran, and Catholic youth respectively, to the relief of parents who want to enhance the prospect of an intrafaith marriage for their children.

Age and Race. The critical variable influencing mate selection is age. Most people marry others within a few years of their own ages. If there is an age difference, the man is usually older than the woman. Traditional gender expectations dictate that men must gain the requisite education and job skills necessary to support a family, thus keeping them out of marriage longer than women, who are socialized primarily for domestic roles. Since the 1950s there has been a gradual increase in the marriage age for both genders (Table 15.3 on page 387). With women now representing half of all college students and half of the labor force (see Chapter 13), traditional gender roles are being significantly altered so that women's age at first marriage should eventually approach that of men.

Of all demographic variables, homogamy is strongest for race. Between 1970 and 1995, interracial

---

Table 15.2 How Do I Love Thee? Myths of Romantic Love

Sociological research shows that what we often believe to be true about love is in reality romantic myth.

Myth	Reality
1. Love conquers all.	1. A person's partner cannot fulfill all needs and make all problems disappear.
2. Women are the romantic gender.	2. Men fall in love sooner and express love earlier in the relationship than do women.
3. Women are more emotional when they fall in love.	3. Related to #2, men are more idealistic; women are more pragmatic about love.
4. Love is blind.	4. The process of falling in love is highly patterned.
5. Opposites attract.	5. We fall in love with people similar to ourselves.
6. Love and marriage are prerequisites for sex.	6. Sex is likely in a relationship regardless of love, and premarital or nonmarital sex is now normative.
7. Absence makes the heart grow fonder.	7. Out of sight, out of mind. This is the problem with high school romances and leaving for different colleges. It is also the problem with commuter marriages.
8. The opposite of love is hate.	8. The "opposite" of love is more likely to be indifference—emotions are neutralized.

Table 15.3	Median Age at First Marriage of Bride and Groom for Selected Years	
	Women	Men
1890	22.0	26.1
1900	21.9	25.9
1910	21.6	25.1
1920	21.2	24.6
1930	24.3	24.3
1940	21.5	24.3
1950	20.3	22.8
1960	20.3	22.8
1970	20.6	22.5
1975	20.8	22.7
1980	21.8	23.6
1985	23.0	24.8
1990	24.0	26.0
1994	24.5	26.7

Source: Adapted from Table 159, U.S. Bureau of the Census, 1998.

SES is usually lower than the man's, a pattern that cuts across all races. When African Americans and whites are attracted to one another, the reasons are the same as in racially homogeneous couples (Murstein, 1986). As one white man married to an African American woman said, "From the beginning I was surprised less by how important race was than by how important it wasn't" (Tartakov & Tartakov, 1994:148).

The Marriage Squeeze. For both genders, age at marriage is also affected by the proportion of women and men who are available. When there is an unbalanced ratio of marriage-age women to marriage-age men, a *marriage squeeze* exists, in which one gender has a more limited pool of potential marriage partners. Table 15.3 shows that most people marry in their mid-twenties, and men marry women who are a few years younger than themselves. After World War II the birthrate increased considerably (the "baby boom" era). There were more women born in 1950 than men born in 1940. By the 1980s women faced a shortage of men. Given the sharp decline in birthrates in the 1960s and 1970s, men now in their mid-twenties face a shortage of women (Eshleman, 2000).

Gender. Whereas homogamy is the mate selection norm, it is filtered by the process of **hypergamy,** in which women tend to marry men of higher socioeconomic status, the conventional method women have used for upward mobility. Hypergamy is functional for women who prefer well-educated men who have the earnings capacity necessary to support a family (Hatfield & Sprecher, 1986; Murstein, 1991; Ganong & Coleman, 1992). Women place greater value than men on the instrumental qualities of a prospective mate. This is true even for college-educated women pursuing high-paying professions who say they want to combine career and marriage (Melton & Lindsey, 1987). Men, on the other hand, value physical attractiveness more than women do. For a quick confirmation of this fact, pick up any newspaper devoted to ads for dating partners. Women most sought after by men are "beautiful and slender," or at the very least exhibit proper "weight in proportion to height." Females most often seek "interpersonal understanding" while males seek physical attractiveness and thinness (Murstein, 1986; Smith et al., 1990). Male preoccupation with physical attractiveness cuts across race and social class and is associated with reasons why men fall in love sooner than women (Lott, 1994:134).

Macrolevel theoretical perspectives explain hypergamy. Reflecting functionalism, traditional gender socialization instills role-appropriate behavior in men and women that contributes to social equilibrium. Reflecting conflict theory, men do not need to be as

marriages doubled, but they still account for less than 3 percent of all marriages. Of these, about one-half of 1 percent are African American–white marriages, with 70 percent of these consisting of a white wife and an African American husband (Table 15.4 below). The remainder of interracial marriages are between whites and nonblacks, the typical pattern being an Asian woman and a white man. When comparing race and class in these marriages, the data generally support homogamy in socioeconomic status (Gadberry & Dodder, 1993; Kalmijn, 1993). However, when differences in socioeconomic status do occur, the woman's

Table 15.4	Interracial Marriages for Selected Years (in thousands)		
	1980	1990	1997
Same race couples	48,264	50,889	51,489
Interracial couples	651	964	1,264
Black/white	167	211	311
Black husband/white wife	122	150	201
White husband/black wife	45	61	110
White/other race*	450	720	896
Black/other race*	34	33	57
Hispanic/non-Hispanic origin	891	1,193	1,662

*Excludes white and black.
Source: Adapted from Table 67, U.S. Department of Commerce, 1998.

DIVERSITY DATA

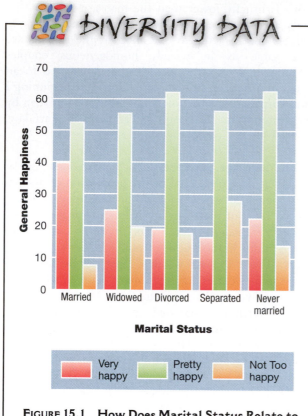

FIGURE 15.1   How Does Marital Status Relate to Happiness? Married people report higher levels of happiness than all other categories of marital status, but especially in comparison to divorced people. What are "happiness" benefits offered by marriage? Do you think that these divorced respondents would have reported lower levels of general happiness *during* their marriage?

attractive because they possess greater economic power and prestige in society than women. When excluded from power, women view themselves as they are viewed by men—as objects of exchange (Wolf, 1991).

Successful Marriages and Families

Marriage is satisfying for most couples, with both wives and husbands expressing happiness with their spouses (Michael et al., 1994). Satisfaction shows up in better physical and emotional health of the married compared with the unmarried, particularly for men (Gove et al., 1990; Ross et al., 1991; Wickrama et al., 1997). For marriages based on romantic love, the happiest families are those with high levels of caring, sharing, cohesion, open communication, trust, loyalty, sacrifice, and emotional support (Lauer & Lauer, 1991; Klagsbrun, 1995). Children bring joy to a couple but also increased marital tension. The easygoing

B.C. (Before Children) couple in the first years of marriage can decide on an hour's notice to go to the mountains for the weekend. Children change everything. Work, commitment, time, and energy are needed to keep the marital relationship healthy and strong. Focusing on couplehood in turn allows for better parenting. The B.C. life is gone forever, even after children leave home (Baldwin, 1988). While more energy is expended on children-related issues than on marriage-related ones, tension is balanced by the gratification that comes from being parents (Neal et al., 1989; Belsky & Kelly, 1995). There is life after parenthood, and the couple will be together long after the children are gone. The successful couple does not take their relationship for granted even when riding out the storms of raising children (Baldwin, 1988). Contrary to media stereotypes, sociologists consistently document that marriage and family are what most people want and that they are happy with their choices (Michael et al., 1994).

Divorce

An enduring marriage is not necessarily a successful one. People often stay together in conflict-ridden or devitalized marriages for the sake of children or because of other obligations (Furstenberg & Cherlin, 1991; Amato, 1993). Emotional divorce precedes a legal one. Since Americans say romantic love is the reason for marriage, "falling out of love" is also a reason for divorce. Global patterns of arranged marriages based on factors such as economics or family alliances rarely end in divorce. Though subject to historical anomalies like the Depression and World War II, the divorce rate has steadily increased throughout the last century, rapidly during the 1970s, peaking in the early 1980s, and plateauing or with modest decreases since (Table 15.5). There is evidence that the increase is leveling off so that if the divorce trend continues, it will do so at a slower rate (National Center for Health Statistics, 1997).

Depending on which standard for calculating divorce rates is used, the future of marriage for society as well as for individual couples may be more or less ominous. When comparing number of divorces to number of new marriages, it is fair to say that half will end in divorce. The problem with this number is that it does not account for how long a couple was married, so it may inflate the failure rate of new marriages. But when looking at annual divorces per 1000 married women (half of a married couple), the number is about 21. This indicates a less discouraging four-in-ten marriage failure rate. Nonetheless, by any measure, the United States has the highest divorce rate in the world (Goode, 1993).

The number of interracial marriages is increasing in the United States, the most common between Asian women and white men.

Predicting Divorce.   Research has identified several key variables of a couple's vulnerability to divorce. The two that in combination most consistently predict divorce are age and social class. Teenage marriages among couples from lower socioeconomic groups are the most likely to dissolve, probably within the first five years (Castro-Martin & Bumpass, 1989; Kurdek, 1993b). For teenage couples who start out with less education, fewer economic resources, and less emotional maturity, the idealization of love quickly fades with the stark reality of married life. Sociology suggests other important predictors of divorce. First, we have seen that homogamy structures what most of us think of as romantic love. When couples are demographically parallel in age, race, and religion and are comparable in attitudes and values, their chances for marital satisfaction and marital permanence are enhanced. Similarity breeds stability; dissimilarity breeds divorce. The major exception is for those occupying a low socioeconomic status, where economic disadvantage translates to the highest divorce rates. Higher education and income have beneficial effects on marital quality and stability (Conger et al., 1990; White, 1991). Second, since women are likely to be employed, they may have the financial latitude to end unhappy marriages. This situation combines with changes in patterns of authority in families. The most dissatisfied couples are those in which wives want joint decision making and household task sharing by husbands while husbands prefer a more traditional, patriarchal style of family functioning. Shifts in gender roles help explain why today's women are now more likely than their mothers and grandmothers to initiate divorce (Duxbury et al., 1994; Kincaid & Caldwell, 1995). Third, legal barriers to end marriage have eased considerably with *no-fault divorce*, which allows one spouse to divorce the other without placing blame on either, so there is no "aggrieved party" (Cherlin, 1992). Divorce is readily available to those who want it, such as women in abusive marriages and young couples who married quickly and confronted marital conflict just as quickly (Glenn, 1997; Rodgers et al., 1997).

When parents divorce, their offspring face increased risk of divorce. Children of divorced parents learn behaviors that may actually prevent mutually rewarding intimate relationships, which in turn contribute to an even higher divorce rate for remarried couples (Jacobson, 1995; Amato, 1996). The very

Table 15.5	Marriages and Divorces, Selected Years (Rates per Thousand Population)	
	Marriage	Divorce
1960	8.6	2.2
1970	10.6	3.5
1975	10.0	4.8
1980	10.6	5.2
1984	10.5	4.9
1990	9.8	4.7
1992	9.3	4.6
1994	9.1	4.4
1996	8.8	4.3
1998*	9.0	4.3

*Estimated.
Sources: Monthly Vital Statistics Reports, Vol. 42–44, 1993–1995, U.S. Public Health Service; Adapted from Table 156, U.S. Bureau of the Census, 1998.

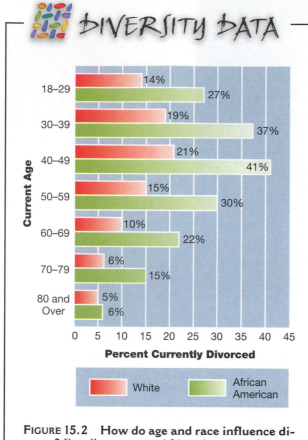

DIVERSITY DATA

FIGURE 15.2   How do age and race influence divorce? For all age groups, African Americans have higher divorce than whites. However, for both races, people who are 40–49 are most likely to be currently divorced. What family factors make people more vulnerable for divorce during middle adulthood?
Source: NORC. General Social Surveys, 1972–1996. Chicago: National Opinion Research Center, 1996. Reprinted by permission of NORC, Chicago, IL.

visibility of divorce contributes to its intergenerational transmission, reduces its stigma, and sets the stage for the next divorce wave.

Gender, Divorce, and the Feminization of Poverty.   Divorce has profound effects for the divorcing couple and their families. Research also shows that it has differential consequences for women and men. After the immediate trauma, women appear to adjust emotionally better than men. This is specifically true for certain categories of women: those under age 40, those with higher self-esteem, and those who opt out of unsatisfactory marriages (Grossman, 1986; Esterberg et al., 1994). People who adopt nontraditional gender roles, such as assertive, independent women and androgynous men, adjust better to divorce trauma than those who accepted traditional gender roles during their marriages (Chiriboga & Thurnher, 1980; Hansson et al., 1984).

While women appear to fare better psychologically than men after divorce, economically the consequences are disastrous for women as a group (Starrels et al., 1994; Kurtz, 1995). When a divorce involves children, mothers gain custody 90 percent of the time, usually without further legal action by fathers (Kelly, 1993). Divorce increases a woman's financial burdens. Older women, homemakers, and those reentering the labor force after a long absence are at a disadvantage in the job market at the exact time they need an adequate income to support their family.

No-fault divorce makes a bad economic situation worse for women when courts mandate an equal division of assets such as the family home and savings. No-fault divorce is increasingly linked to the rise of joint custody arrangements. While the benefits for children are still being debated, it is already clear that joint custody puts women at great financial risk. Most women do not have the economic resources to co-parent on an equal basis with their ex-husbands. As one attorney put it (Webb, 1988:245):

> Joint custody is a big lie. What's really going on is that the man will ask for joint custody so he can pay less child support. What are you supposed to do? You have less child support than you should—you can't force visitation.

Misconceptions abound about women who are "set up" for a life of leisure by their wealthy ex-husbands. Actually, alimony is awarded to only a small percentage of women and often in amounts so low that they barely match welfare or Social Security (Weitzman, 1985). The issue of what is awarded is related to the issue of what can be collected. Fewer than half of mothers actually receive child support from nonresidential fathers, and only 25 percent receive the full amount (Teachman & Paasch, 1993). In half of divorced families, by two years after the divorce there is no contact with the nonresidential parent, usually the father (Hewlett, 1987; Johnston, 1993). These fathers report feeling less competent and less satisfied in their parental role (Minton & Pasley, 1996), a factor that may help explain emotional and financial distancing from their children.

Among women of all races, marital disruption has severe economic consequences. Although young minority men are usually not well off economically, their postdivorce financial situation tends to be better than that of their ex-wives (Smock, 1994). In most cases, a man's standard of living improves after divorce, whereas a woman's deteriorates (Weitzman, 1985; Peterson, 1996). Divorce is a principal reason for the high poverty rate of single-parent women and their dependent children, a factor contributing to what we identified in Chapter 13 as the "feminization of poverty." To ease the problem, changes in divorce

The consequences of divorce and single parenting put women at higher risk for poverty than men. Failure to collect child support and decreased welfare benefits have increased the ranks of homeless women and their children, some of whom must live in their car.

law could retain the no-fault option but with recognition that men and women enter divorce with very different economic futures. Some argue that judges need to rethink the consequences of how marital property is divided (Weitzman & Dixon, 1988).

Remarriage

The United States has the world's highest divorce rate, but it also has the world's highest remarriage rate. Almost 70 percent of divorced people remarry, and close to 40 percent of all marriages are remarriages, a pattern found in both the United States and Canada (Wu & Balakrishnan, 1994; Ahlburg & DeVita, 1995). The marriage–divorce–remarriage pattern is called **serial monogamy.** Remarriages are the primary reasons for the formation of **blended families,** in which children from parents' prior relationships are brought together in a new family. This new form of kinship affects half of America's children and has a major impact on child rearing, family organization, and marital satisfaction (Coleman & Ganong, 1990; Cherlin & Furstenberg, 1994). Children already dealing with divorce must adjust to a new parent and siblings in a newly created family. They often report feelings of rejection from siblings and intense competition for parental attention and affection (Wallerstein & Blakeslee, 1989).

However, remarriages at midlife when children are older or have left the nest may be more stable (Booth & Edwards, 1992; Clarke & Wilson, 1994). Evidence also suggests that children in blended families do adjust, and compared with children in first marriage homes, have an only slightly higher risk of emotional or behavioral problems (Hetherington, 1993; Ganong & Coleman, 1994).

The remarriage rate is lower for women than for men. Almost 85 percent of men remarry, and they do so more quickly than women (Bray & Berger, 1993). Most divorced men with children are free from sole custody and economically better off than their ex-wives, allowing for greater latitude in the remarriage market. Men have an age advantage as well. There is more acceptance of the older man–younger woman pattern rather than the reverse. A ten-year age difference favoring men is common in remarriages. On the other hand, women who are poorly educated are most likely to remarry. Their remarriage chances decrease if they have dependent children since they represent a financial liability for men. Financially independent women are attractive to men for remarriage, but these women have less to gain in a remarriage, especially if they do not want to raise children (London & Wilson, 1988; Bumpass et al., 1990). Remarriage for many women appears to have at least as many costs as benefits. But the lure of marriage or remarriage for both genders remains quite strong.

EMERGING LIFESTYLES

In both global and American multicultural contexts, the family is an immensely varied social institution. Rapid social change collides with the family and provides new paths for those seeking alternatives to conventional household arrangements.

In a divorce, mothers usually have custody of children, and children often visit their fathers on weekends. If men remarry, their contact and financial support of their children decline.

Singlehood

The vast majority of both genders marry, but the percent of never-married people continues to increase, especially for women. The marriage squeeze has little to do with women's willingness to marry men who are dissimilar to them (Lichter & Landale, 1995). Strong cultural meanings of marriage and forces of attraction propelling people into marriage are more important factors (Qian & Preston, 1993; Nock, 1995). Highly educated, financially independent women are likely candidates for choosing singlehood. For every age category, the higher a woman's income, the lower the rate of marriage (McGoldrick, 1989; Wolfe, 1993).

A major shift in opinion regarding singlehood as an acceptable lifestyle is in marked contrast to earlier ideas that "failure" to marry was due to personal or social deficiencies. Many young people no longer view marriage as necessarily better than remaining single, with the result that the number of single people reporting that they are "very happy" has steadily increased (Glenn & Weaver, 1988; Acock & Hurlbert, 1993). There are no significant gender differences in terms of what is liked or disliked about being single. Both men and women enjoy its mobility, freedom, and social options, but must deal with periods of loneliness and the uncertainties of the "dating grind"

(Simenauer & Carroll, 1982; Glenn & Weaver, 1988). Contemporary singlehood represents opportunities for happiness for a significant subset of the American population who may reject marriage and any permanent and/or exclusive sexual relationship.

Cohabitation

Until recently, an unmarried couple living together was cause for condemnation, but as more and more people choose cohabitation as their preferred lifestyle, this stigma has all but disappeared. Almost half of those in their twenties and thirties have cohabited. Social support does vary, however, and as expected, younger people are more accepting than older generations. Such support may account for the dramatic increase of cohabitants and the slight decrease in the marriage rate (Bumpass et al., 1991). The number of cohabiting couples has risen steadily, from about half a million in 1970 to about 4 million today (Brown & Booth, 1997). Almost half of cohabitants are couples with children present (Spanier, 1991).

Contrary to expectations, cohabitation is not necessarily a good screening device for later marriage. Research concludes that cohabitants who marry have lower marital satisfaction, adjustment, and commitment to marriage than noncohabitants, and, perhaps more significant, have divorce rates that are equal to or higher than noncohabitants (Thompson & Colella, 1992; Brown & Booth, 1997). There are also important gender differences in cohabitation—women view it as trial marriage whereas men view it as an alternative to marriage and as a means of sexual gratification (Jackson, 1983; Macklin, 1988). Both men and women cohabitants who break up are likely to cohabit again, setting up a cycle in which one failed relationship may predispose them to another one (Stets, 1993; Wu, 1995). Living together lessens total commitment—the door to leave is always open. *Playing* house and *keeping* house are fundamentally different.

Given these findings, it may be surprising to see an ever-increasing cohabitant population. Earlier cohabitants may be at greater risk since they were the pioneers who incurred most liabilities with the least social support (Schoen, 1990). Data from the next generation of cohabitants are needed to determine overall effects related to gender roles, marital satisfaction, and divorce. Cohabitation is emerging as a normative stage in courtship between dating and marriage (Gwartney-Gibbs, 1990).

Single-Parent Families

Since 1970 the number of single-parent households has doubled, a figure that includes 60 percent of divorced couples with children (Bray & Berger, 1993;

Single parent families headed by divorced and never married women are increasing. Among African Americans, a female grandparent is often a child's guardian.

U.S. Bureau of the Census, 1999). The increase of joint-custody arrangements and sole-custody fathers has more than offset the increase of never-married women with children. The staggering prediction is that half of U.S. children, regardless of race, will live in a single-parent household before age 18 (Furstenberg & Cherlin, 1991; Hines, 1997). African American children are more likely to live with a female grandparent than are white and Latino children (O'Hare et al., 1995). There are major differences in households headed by single mothers, where most children will be living, compared with those headed by fathers.

Female-headed families are the fastest growing type of family. The odds that these families are in poverty approach one in two. Median income is almost four times lower than in husband–wife families (Costello & Stone, 1994). Over half of all poor children in the United States live in families headed by women. When race is factored in, the poverty rate for white, African American, and Latino children is 46 percent, 66 percent, and 71 percent respectively (Gimenez, 1994). Financial uncertainty heightens the physical and emotional demands on single-parent women. Compared with married couples, they rely

more on children for housework, have fewer social supports, and raise children who are also more likely to become single parents (McLanahan & Booth, 1989; Arendell, 1995). Single mothers report higher rates of depression than married mothers, especially if there is a history of early-childhood hardship (Turner & Lloyd, 1995; Davies et al., 1997). Money is the key factor in this pattern. Not only do women who are financially secure adjust better to divorce, but their children may be better off than in an intact family marked by high levels of conflict (Chollar, 1995; Winkler, 1995).

As single parents, men face a situation far different from that of women. Although about 3 percent of children live with their fathers only, joint custody arrangements have increased shared parenting. Nearly 14 percent of all single-parent households are headed by a man, a number that is expected to increase (Coltrane, 1996; U.S. Bureau of the Census, 1999). Fathers are usually better educated, occupy higher level occupations, and continue their careers after becoming single parents. Financial strength is one reason why fathers are increasingly awarded sole custody when they request it (Hanson, 1985). Like single mothers, single fathers report problems balancing work and family. For child-care and household tasks, single fathers appear to adapt well, perceive themselves as competent, share tasks with their children, and do not rely on outside help to a great extent (Schnayer & Orr, 1989; Greif et al., 1993). Fathers who are assigned the primary parenting role cannot be readily distinguished from mothers. When men "mother," they report close ties to their children and high levels of family satisfaction but must deal with gender role stereotyping that assumes they cannot be as competent parents as women (Risman, 1989; Gardner, 1995).

Egalitarian Marriages

In an **egalitarian marriage,** partners share decision making and assign family roles based on talent and choice rather than on traditional beliefs about gender. The Scandinavian countries, specifically Norway and Sweden, consistently rank the highest in all measures of human development, including gender role egalitarianism and public policies designed to translate it to the family (Eisler et al., 1995; United Nations Development Program, 1997). Parental leave for new fathers and programs to bolster women's economic status outside the home and men's child-rearing functions in the home have enhanced egalitarian marriages (Kalleberg & Rosenfeld, 1990; *Mainstreaming*, 1995). As in the United States, Scandinavian men adopt more egalitarian attitudes about the division of labor in child rearing than they actually practice, but public policy will continue to support the objective of gender equity (Haas, 1993).

Instead of ranking husband over wife, egalitarian marriage means that a partnership pattern emerges, one that is strongly associated with paid employment for wives. This pattern suggests that when wives contribute financially to the family, their decision-making powers are enhanced. Perceived imbalance in decision making lowers marital satisfaction for both husband and wife (Steil & Weltman, 1991; Amato & Booth, 1995). Egalitarian marriage fosters better communication and sharing. It may be described as a "peer marriage," which builds on a strong, empathic friendship between spouses (Schwartz, 1994). Conflict may occur, but it is not necessarily negative because it also allows for open communication (Chafetz, 1989; Burleson & Denton, 1997). Children also benefit from egalitarianism since parents share the joy and burden of child rearing more equitably.

The attitudes about gender roles in marriage are shifting toward an egalitarian model (Steil, 1995). The ultimate goal for behavior change, however, remains elusive. Over thirty years of research shows that egalitarian marriages remain compromised when

wives work full time outside the home because husbands do not share domestic roles with them on anywhere near an equal basis (Berk & Berk, 1979; Geerkin & Gove, 1983; Coltrane & Ishii-Kuntz, 1992; Spain & Bianchi, 1996). Balancing home and work for middle-class couples can be eased by hiring domestic help (Duxbury & Higgins, 1994). But most employed wives of all social classes walk into their homes to a second shift of unpaid household work after a day of paid employment (Hochschild, 1989). According to women, "helping out" at home is not the same as true task sharing, especially if their husbands' share of the domestic division of labor is taken up by child care and traditional male chores (Benin & Agostinelli, 1988; Lennon & Rosenfield, 1994). Wives' discontent about fairness decreases marital satisfaction and increases the possibility for destructive conflict outcomes (Dancer & Gilbert, 1993; Kluwer et al., 1997).

Despite the household task overload women face, the trend toward egalitarian marriages is unlikely to slow down. Marital satisfaction is enhanced when men and women are partners, when women engage in satisfying employment, and when men get involved in housework. For women, this pattern translates to better health, enhanced self-esteem, and lower rates of depression (Adelmann, 1994; Bullers, 1994). For men, it means happier marriages, better physical health, less anxiety, and even superior sex lives (Glass & Fujimoto, 1994; AtKisson, 1995). While men still embrace the provider role, they now express acceptance of women's employment as well as of their own involvement in expanded domestic and parenting roles (Willinger, 1993). Both men and women say they benefit from equal relationships (Lye & Biblarz, 1993; Steil, 1995). As society becomes more gender equitable, marriages will become more egalitarian.

AMERICAN FAMILIES IN MULTICULTURAL PERSPECTIVE

America's multicultural heritage is reflected in its families. Because this heritage is linked to minority status based on race and ethnicity, families are impacted by those disadvantages that also impact them as minorities in other parts of society. This section will highlight data (see Table 15.6) that put minority families at risk in a number of family-related social problems.

African American Families

African American families exhibit a wider variety of family and household structures and a greater degree of role sharing by wives and husbands than other

Table 15.6	Selected Family Characteristics (percent) by Race, 1998		
Race	Married Couples	Female-Headed Single-Parent Families	Families Below Poverty Level
White	80.9	14.2	8.6
Black	45.5	46.7	26.1
Hispanic origin	68.2	24.4	26.3
American Indian*	65.8	26.2	27.2
Asian and Pacific Islanders	82.0	12.0	12.0

*1990 data
Source: Adapted from Tables 51, 52, 54. U.S. Bureau of the Census, 1999.

racial groups. The key factor in the development of these patterns is traced to economic oppression rooted in discrimination. Data from a century ago reveal that African American households were less likely to be nuclear and more likely to be headed by women, a pattern that persists today (Morgan et al., 1993). Compared with European Americans, African American family life cycles are marked by fewer formal marriages, parenthood at earlier ages, higher divorce rates, and later or less likely remarriage (London, 1990; Littlejohn-Blake & Darling, 1993).

Half of African American households are made up of family members related by blood, marriage, or adoption, with about half headed by married couples (O'Hare et al., 1995). Since the other half are likely to be headed by single women, many marked by economic need, there is an advantage to accommodating household structure to meet various stressors. African American families demonstrate a strong willingness to absorb others into kin structures by creating a network of **fictive kin**, where friends who are not related by blood or marriage "become" family. Most African Americans have someone in their families they regard as fictive kin (Chatters et al., 1994). Fictive kin bring an array of exchange and support that benefits all household members. In turn, children are offered a diversity of parenting models (Dill, 1994; Jarret, 1994; Raley, 1995). Mothers as breadwinners can readily turn to fictive kin for child-care needs. Such arrangements are further strengthened by high degrees of religiosity in African American families, since fictive kin are often drawn from the church.

Overall, role flexibility has strengthened African American families in three fundamental ways. First, among all household forms, African American women traditionally assume provider roles essential to family stability and survival. A legacy of institutionalized racism and the deterioration of the economic position of African American men created many fatherless families (Staples & Johnson, 1993). Second, working-class and middle-class married couples are likely to have an egalitarian family structure in which roles are complementary and husband and wife are dual earners in stable employment (McAdoo, 1990; Staples 1997). Egalitarian arrangements are bolstered by African American women who work outside the home by choice rather than economic necessity and who do not view their roles as wife-mother and wage earner as mutually exclusive (Malson, 1983; Dugger, 1991). Third, husbands appear to be more willing than white husbands to adapt themselves and the household to the needs of their employed wives. Some data indicate more gender role convergence in African American families than in white families (Ross, 1987; Hossain & Roopnarine, 1993).

Latino/Hispanic Families

Latinos, or Hispanics, represent diverse social, cultural, and historical legacies that are readily distinguished from one another (see Chapter 12). The terms "Latino" or "Hispanic" often gloss over differences, particularly those related to immigrant status, nationality, number of generations in the United States, and economic well-being. Economic status is a key variable in viewing Hispanic American families. To review, the largest subgroups are Mexican Americans (Chicanos), Puerto Ricans, and Cuban Americans, all of whom suffer the economic consequences of minority status. Poverty is most acute for Puerto Ricans and least for Cuban Americans. Mexican Americans hover near the poverty line but have the widest variation of economic well-being. Latinos share a heritage of Spanish colonialism and through this, a solid connection to the Roman Catholic Church. Several fundamental values related to family life link these diverse groups. First, family relations are characterized by respect and honor. Second is the notion of "familism," the extension of kinship ties to relatives and very close friends outside the nuclear family who will remain intimately connected to one another throughout their lives. Third, there is a strong adherence to patriarchal

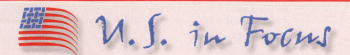

U.S. in Focus

African American Women and the Marriage Squeeze

The marriage market in America is a place where people shop for partners. Eligibility in this market is determined by strong cultural norms regarding who is "appropriate" to marry—norms that direct us toward some people and away from others. Similarity in age and race are the two most powerful predictors of marriage eligibility. Some people can be "squeezed" out of the marriage market because they find fewer eligible partners of their own race and near their own age. When considering African American women as a subgroup, the marriage squeeze is acute. Several factors explain this:

1. For both race and sex, life expectancy rates are lowest for African American males (Chapter 19). African American women outnumber men at age 18; for whites it is age 32. It is estimated that there are now eight black men for every ten African American women.

2. Education is another key variable. For every ten college-educated African American women, there are fewer than two comparably educated men. Remember that education is an indicator of social class, and in turn social class is used as a determinant of marriage eligibility. Since women tend to marry "up," the field of eligible men is further narrowed.

3. Interracial marriages, although infrequent, are increasing, but the pattern of African American men marrying white women has not changed significantly (Table 15.4). African American men who marry women of other races are also likely to be highly educated. Highly educated African American women are less likely to racially intermarry (as are highly educated white men).

These patterns significantly restrict the field of eligibles for African American women. As a result, in comparison with white women, African American women are more likely to marry men who are older, are of a lower educational level, and have been previously married. A marriage squeeze where African American women select mates of their own race, but who are otherwise significantly different than themselves, may negatively influence marital stability and happiness.

It is easy to explain the marriage squeeze for African American women simply according to unbalanced age, sex, and education ratios. Sociology, however, offers additional insights. The marriage squeeze is a byproduct of cultural beliefs determining who is "acceptable" as a marriage partner in the first place. It is not as much an objectively determined process as it is a socially constructed one. As beliefs about acceptability are altered, the norms surrounding eligibility will also be altered.

Americans have a lot of leeway in choosing marriage partners, so it is likely that some form of a marriage squeeze will always exist. The marriage squeeze may be responsible for the hard choices African American women must make in today's marriage market. But shifting cultural definitions of what is "valued" in a prospective partner can loosen the current marriage squeeze or even make it obsolete.

1. What would you predict to be the basis for a future marriage squeeze, and which groups will most likely be affected?

2. Do you think that any marriage squeeze could narrow the field of eligible partners so much that people would choose to remain single rather than marry someone so "different" from themselves? Why or why not?

African American women are finding fewer eligible men of their same race, education, and age as possible marriage partners.

Sources: Ortiz, 1994; Cready & Fossett, 1997; U.S. Bureau of the Census, 1999; Collins & Coltrane, 2001.

Latino families are very diverse. Social class, more than specific subculture, explains much of the diversity in family patterns.

gender roles in a well-defined system of mutually exclusive beliefs that separate men and women found throughout all social classes in Latino cultures. Men are associated with *machismo*, seen to include virility, sexual prowess, and the physical and ideological control of women. Women are associated with *marianismo*, seen to include spiritual and moral superiority of women over men, the glorification of motherhood, and the acceptance of a difficult marriage. Women are expected to have an infinite capacity for sacrifice in their role as mothers and to be submissive to the demands of the men in their family (Del Carmen & Virgo, 1993; Stevens, 1993). How these values are translated into the home varies according to factors such as socioeconomic status and degree of acculturation.

Most research on family relations in all Hispanic subcultures has centered on the relationship between employment and home, especially for employed women and their families. The low income of Puerto Ricans is explained by critical gender–family linkages. Almost half of Puerto Rican households are headed by women; only half of Puerto Rican women are high school graduates; and there has been declining demand in those industries in which women have traditionally been employed (Zambrana, 1994; Lichter & Landale, 1995). Families are often divided, with children raised by grandparents in Puerto Rico and husbands migrating back and forth between the island and New York City, depending on employment options. Marriages are fragile, half of all couples cohabit, and significant male dominance emotionally distances husbands and wives (Landale & Fennelly, 1992). For recent migrants, especially among middle- and working-class married couples, women strive to maintain a continuity of family life. Better educated women are more likely to value both career and family roles. Clearly defined gender roles are common, but in families with dual-earner couples, some erosion of the double standard is evident (Roopnarine & Ahmeduzzaman, 1993; Toro-Morn, 1995). Kin networks founded on familism offer support and intergenerational exchange vital to the integrity of Puerto Rican families of all social classes (Sanchez-Ayendez, 1986; Figueroa & Melendez, 1993).

Mexican American families are also tied to familism and the machismo–marianismo ideology. These factors combine to keep divorce rates low. The nuclear family is embedded in a network of kin who maintain intergenerational ties by passing on cultural traditions and serving as social and economic support (Mirande, 1988; Dietz, 1995). Ideology allows men to control the household, but male dependence on females to carry out domestic tasks gives women an important source of household power (Horowitz, 1991). The subordination of women to men in families is evident, but newer studies question the concept of the all-dominant and controlling male. Recent data document trends toward more gender equity in Mexican American households. Couples report that fathers and mothers are increasingly sharing household tasks and that joint decision making is increasing, especially for dual earners (Williams, 1990; Herrara & DelCampo, 1995). Extended family ties are also weakening (Williams, 1993). Although families may receive less child care support from older kin, there is also less chance that the children will be taught cultural norms emphasizing male dominance from their caretakers.

Of all Hispanic groups, Cuban Americans enjoy the highest standard of living. Immigrants in the 1960s were highly educated, many drawn from Cuba's professional ranks. Even though women were not likely to be in the labor force, education for middle- and upper-class women was encouraged and helped bolster the prestige of the family. The world of politics and business was reserved for men (Chilman, 1995). Later immigrants were poorer, families more fragile, and women in the workplace more common, a trend that continues. However, Cuban American families are demographically more similar to European Americans. Compared with other Latino subgroups, these families have fewer children, are economically stronger, and are more likely to be headed by a married couple (see Table 15.6 on p. 395). Unlike European Americans, Cuban American families are more likely to be extended. Caretaking regarding the elderly goes both ways. Strong cultural traditions virtually ensure that the feeble elderly will be maintained in the home, but at the same time the elderly offer major support to the family (Perez, 1994). Increasing numbers of Cuban American women in the work force is associated with child care by elderly kin. The Cuban American extended family is an excellent example of how familism functions in Latino households.

Asian American Families

Asian Americans are the fastest growing of America's racial minorities and their numbers are increasing with immigration rather than through natural increases of resident population. Asian American families also exhibit striking cultural diversity. For example, those who are classified as Pacific Islanders represent 1,200 separate language groups (Parker, 1989). Evidence does suggest, however, several interrelated patterns that are shared by Asian American families (Staples & Mirande, 1980; Gardner et al., 1985; Takaki, 1993):

1. Collectivistic kinship traditions emanating from the originating Asian cultures live on in America.
2. Marriages are routinely arranged by kin rather than left solely to the devices of the couple.
3. Extended families are normative.
4. Children are socialized to be obedient in the family and loyal to parents and elders.
5. Gender roles emphasize female subordination to all males and older females in a patriarchal family structure.
6. Married couple rates are highest and divorce rates are lowest compared with all other racial minorities—at levels similar to whites. This is especially true for Chinese, Japanese, and Filipino Americans.

The extent to which each of these patterns occurs is strongly connected to length of residence in the United States. Traditional expectations for marriage are eroding, and emerging norms emphasize choice of partners based on romantic love. While still quite low, the divorce rate and the number of female-headed households are steadily increasing among all Asian American groups. And when children become more "Americanized," problems of intergenerational conflict increase (Kitano & Daniels, 1995).

The best indicator of assimilation for racial minorities is intermarriage. The highest rates of interra-

cial marriage are between Asian and non-Asian, with Hawaii leading all other states in this regard. Most are between white men and American women of Japanese, Filipino, or Korean descent. Gender-role beliefs help explain these patterns, but in a paradoxical way. More acculturated Asian American women, particularly Koreans, report that they seek marriage to men who are more egalitarian and hold less traditional views of women (Hurh & Kim, 1984; Min, 1993). White men seek Asian American women for the opposite reason. Males may desire a stereotyped Asian female— "good at housekeeping, service oriented, willing to stay at home, and sexy" (Kitano & Daniels, 1995:188). While both groups may get what they want initially, patterns of acculturation toward egalitarian gender roles, predict more marital satisfaction among Asian American women than among white men.

Native American Families

Native Americans comprise about 0.8 percent of the U.S. population and include those asserting American Indian and Alaskan (Eskimo and Aleut) origin. About a third of Native Americans are Navaho or Cherokee (U.S. Bureau of the Census, 1999). Native Americans are very heterogeneous. In the precolonial era, there were at least 2,000 native languages (Evans, 1991). Tribal diversity remains today, but Native Americans share some key patterns related to family life.

Colonialism and accompanying Christianity altered ancient tribal patterns drastically, especially those related to gender roles in the family. Women's power and prestige varied by tribe, but historical evidence indicates that women lost status with colonialization. Many tribal units were matrilineal and matrilocal. Although gender segregation was the norm, complementarity, balance, and gynocratic (female-centered) egalitarianism also existed both in the home and outside it. Women held important political, religious, and other extra-domestic roles (Kuhlmann, 1996). With increased European contact, women were gradually stripped of these roles. An egalitarian family structure became a patriarchal one. Assimilation of native peoples was to occur under the umbrella of cultural genocide (Harjo, 1993), and altered family patterns were its first manifestation. Governmental policy is fundamentally responsible for the current economic plight of Native American populations (see Chapter 12).

About one-third of American Indian households are female headed; most of these are in poverty. The remaining two-thirds are made up mostly of married couples (Table 15.6 on p. 395). These households are

Many Native American women hold positions of power and prestige, both inside their families as well as in community and spiritual roles.

at risk for social problems related to their poverty status, such as unemployment, dropping out of high school, illiteracy, and alcoholism. However, cultural genocide did not succeed. While ancient tribal customs were altered, they were not eradicated, and they continue to reinforce family strength and stability, mostly for those living on reservations. Women retain roles offering prestige and power in both their families and communities (Joe & Miller, 1994; Woloch, 1994). Families are often extended and exist in strong kinship networks that serve as sources of intergenerational support and repositories of tribal knowledge (Yellowbird & Snipp, 1994).

Native Americans are rapidly being assimilated into majority culture, despite the resistance of Indian people to white cultural influences (Farley, 1995). Whereas cultural genocide did not succeed by force, rapid rates of intermarriage are eroding tribal integrity. In 1970 one-third of all Indians were married to non-Indians, and a 50 percent increase had occurred by a decade later. Some areas report intermar-

riage rates of 60 to 80 percent (Eschbach, 1990; O'Hare, 1992). At the same time, resurgent cultural pride has contributed to a rise in number of people claiming Native American origin. Thus it remains unclear whether Native Americans will intermarry themselves out of existence (Yellowbird & Snipp, 1994:239). The strength of kinship will be a primary determinant of that outcome.

LIFE CONNECTIONS: Family Violence in the United States

The view of the family as a safe and loving haven is in stark contrast to the dramatic increase in domestic violence that makes the family home one of America's most lethal environments. The functionalist perspective acknowledges that the social organization of family life, with its intimacy and intensity of relationships, lays the groundwork for family violence. Functionalism has difficulty explaining cross-cultural research on a number of societies where violence is rare in families (Levinson, 1989). The Semai of West Malaysia, for example, are nonviolent and physical punishment is virtually nonexistent (Robarchek & Dentan, 1979). The Manus described by Margaret Mead in the opening vignette may have cold and distant couples who quarrel, but this pattern does not result in family violence. Sweden has legally banned the use of physical punishment to discipline children, in families as well as in schools. Rather than being fined or jailed for breaking the law, offenders are sent to classes to learn more effective parenting skills.

Privacy of the family and the reluctance of the police to get involved in family disputes make it difficult to get accurate statistics on all forms of family violence and abuse. For the most common forms, research shows the following:

1. Both men and women assault one another in marriage, and mutual abuse is more common than either alone. Both men and women approve of slapping, shoving, and hitting one another under certain conditions. However, the consequences to women are more lethal. Domestic abuse is the leading cause of injury to women in the United States, and wife battering is the most common and most underreported of all crimes, including rape (Russell, 1990; Gelles & Straus, 1995).
2. One-third of all women who are murdered die at the hands of husbands or boyfriends, numbering between 2,000 and 4,000 per year. A woman's risk increases if she threatens to leave, files for divorce, or calls the police, although physical attacks will most likely continue if she stays. Half of all homeless women and children are fleeing domestic violence (Reid, 1991; Thomas-Lester, 1995).

Victims of domestic violence are often caught in a double bind: If she calls the police, she risks further attack; but if she stays or does not report it, attacks will continue.

3. For violence against children, reported cases are close to 2 million per year. Most vulnerable children are the youngest and the smallest. Between 1,300 and 2,000 children per year are killed by parents, relatives, or boyfriends of single mothers (Gelles & Straus, 1987; Ingrassia & McCormick, 1994).

4. For cases of incest, sexual abuse, and/or sexual victimization of children in families, some studies estimate that approximately one-fourth of girls and one-fifth of boys have experienced it. Father–daughter/stepdaughter and brother–sister sexual abuse are the most common (Herman, 1981; Russell, 1984; Finkelhor et al., 1990).

Family violence cuts across all demographic categories, although it is more prevalent in families with low income and unemployment and is associated with alcohol use, drug abuse, and family isolation (Smith, 1990; Straus, 1993; Gelles & Straus, 1995). The hallmark of violent families is stressful life circumstances to which all of these situations contribute. Coming from a violent family of orientation increases the risk that one will become violent in the family of procreation. A violent past can lead to a violent future (Gelles & Straus, 1995:377).

Public education on family violence has found its greatest strength in dealing with child abuse. A feminist-conflict perspective argues that wife battering has not gained as much attention because it remains subtly condoned. From this view, it is the element of power that offers the best explanation for family violence and wife battering. Violence is most common in patriarchal systems in which men hold power over the women and children in their families, a pattern that is supported by cross-cultural data (Levinson, 1989). Egalitarian families have the lowest rates of violence. The greater the inequality and the more that power resides in one person, the greater the risk of violence. For violence against women, the power is expressed sexually (Yllo, 1994; Anderson, 1997; Sheffield, 1995).

≡ SOCIETY CONNECTIONS: Gay and Lesbian Families and the Family Values Debate

When social change finally filters down to the family, it indicates that profound change is going on in society as a whole. Because the changes in family structure and function are embraced by some but feared by others, many difficult social issues surface. The sociological perspective helps clarify these issues.

Gay and Lesbian Families

To date, marriage between homosexuals is not legally recognized, although some states, most notably Vermont and Hawaii, are allowing court challenges to change the situation. If these states uphold same-sex marriages, reciprocity with other states will become an issue. The European Union is confronting the same issue, since Denmark and Holland allow certain legal benefits to heterosexual and homosexual cohabitants and reciprocity is expected between member countries (Schwartz & Rutter, 1998). Overall, however, even when a church conducts a marriage ceremony for a homosexual couple, family law works against sanctioning the relationship by usually denying custody to a homosexual parent. A small but

INTERNET ——— CONNECTIONS

Family violence continues to be a very hot topic today. The text's discussion presents a broad range of statistical data demonstrating the extent of violence among intimates in American society. *Famvi.com* (http://www.famvi.com/) offers the opportunity to examine a Web site for an organization devoted to *preventing and combating* family violence. From the opening page, try clicking on "Facts and Statistics." You will find some information here that is not presented in the text. Then, try clicking on "Comments and Questions from Readers." The candid observations there may surprise you. After you have thoroughly perused the contents of this web site, answer the following question:

1. Exercise your sociological insight by responding to the question: "Why do so many women stay in abusive situations?" Be sure to think about reasons *other than* mere economic dependency.
2. The text observes that *egalitarian* families are less likely to experience family violence. What explanations can you offer for this fact?

growing number of gay men and lesbians have gained custody, have adopted children, and live in permanent households with their homosexual partners and their children. These families face hostility and suspicion since the society holds stereotypes about homosexuality as well as idealized notions about families.

Gay men and lesbians form families that may incorporate a network of kin and non-kin relationships including friends, lovers, former lovers, co-parents, children, and adopted children. These families are organized by ideologies of love and rational choice (Weston, 1993). Notice how this structure is similar to the fictive kin and familism evident in African American and Latino families. Homosexual couples tend to be more equitable in their family arrangements than heterosexual couples. The stereotypical image of a gay relationship in which one partner is in the dominant "active" male role and the other in the subservient passive "female" role is a myth (Kitzinger, 1988; Harry, 1991; Huston & Schwartz, 1996). The egalitarian pattern tends to occur for both lesbians and gay men, although lesbians are more successful in maintaining it over the long term (Caldwell & Peplau, 1984; Kurdek, 1993a).

Gay men and lesbians have been in the forefront of a movement to redefine family structure in order to be eligible for benefits previously available only to married couples, such as health plans and parental leave. This effort has led to rulings in some states that unmarried *domestic partners* have the requisite emotional intimacy and economic interdependence that defines them as a family (Horn, 1992). Besides applying to homosexual couples, these rulings also apply to other nontraditional family forms, such as long-term heterosexual cohabitants with children. Deeply rooted ideals of kinship and beliefs that homosexuality is damaging to society shape judicial discretion in family law (Rosen, 1991).

The Family Values Debate

The issue of legal recognition of gay and lesbian families is also a feature of the "family values" movement that has gained political momentum in the last decade. The theme of the movement is that family breakdown and the support for "alternative lifestyles" are creating social havoc and neglect of children. It advocates a return to the traditional family as a solution. Led by the New Right linkage of conservative politicians and fundamentalist Christian churches, "family restorationists" often use sociological evidence to support their claims. Although diverse, they are united around the idealization of the traditional, patriarchal nuclear family (Cohen & Katzenstein, 1991). They suggest that males are disempowered in *companionate marriages*, those based on romantic love, equality, and an emphasis on balancing individual needs with family needs. Such marriages and families, they believe, undermine traditional Victorian values of self-sacrifice and family commitment. As a result, the welfare state has taken over roles the family once had. Sweden typifies this process (Popenoe, 1988, 1993, 1996).

The shortcomings of the family restorationist model center on five key points. First, how a family is defined has changed and will continue to change over time. The demand of the restorationists is for a family ideal that has never been normative. How the family is defined and which groups support the definition is a political matter (Stacey, 1996). Second is the fact that the family values movement calls for a form that is rarer today than ever, due as much to economic necessity as to feminist progress (Schwartz & Rutter, 1998:43). Data show that divorce was increasing even before women's widespread entrance into the labor force (Davis, 1984). And as documented in the link between patriarchal families and domestic violence, this family form can have dysfunctional, even lethal, consequences. Third, in examining data in four industrialized societies, including Sweden, the link between

Families are changing as society is changing and new family structures will develop as a result of this social change.

family decline and child well-being is shown to be far more complex than the across-the-board negative effects family restorationists emphasize (Cowan, 1993; Coltrane, 1997). Fourth, American couples increasingly desire gender-role egalitarianism in their marriages, in direct opposition to the patriarchal family model advocated by restorationists.

Finally, and most important, the model ignores the reality of social change. Restorationists consider traditional families in modern societies to be "in decline," regardless of the extent of change over time or between specified points in time (Houseknecht & Sastry, 1996:727). As this chapter documents, there are all kinds of "new" traditional families depending on time frame used.

With media influence and ongoing legal and political challenges to extending the rights of the married to the nonmarried, the issue of "what is a family" will be kept before the public. The focus in this chapter has been on macrosociological perspectives that suggest that families will continue to evolve new structures as they face the challenges of an increasingly diverse society. Either by choice or circumstance, families have been altered when faced with social change. The microsociological perspective of symbolic interactionism is also useful. If more inclusive definitions are used, the nuclear family has undergone change, but remains vital and functional. Most sociologists specializing in family studies would agree that the family is not doomed and is not the fundamental cause of current social problems (Johnson, 1997). They would agree with what Erma Bombeck told us at the beginning of the chapter: The family is still here—playing to a full house.

SUMMARY

1. Sociologists agree that the family is responsible for accomplishing important social functions including reproduction, regulation of sexual behavior, socialization, protection, and social placement.
2. Family structure has been altered by the processes of industrialization, urbanization, and overall modernization.
3. Functionalists argue that social stability is disrupted if families do not adequately carry out their functions. Feminists argue that viewing the patriarchal family as beneficial for social stability hampers the movement into egalitarian families. Conflict theory focuses on the family's role in preserving inequality in the broader society.

4. Marriage patterns vary considerably across the globe. Polygamy (multiple-spouse marriages), extended families, and communal families, such as the Israeli kibbutz, are examples.
5. Rather than a purely emotional process, romantic love is structured. People fall in love with those who are similar to themselves (homogamy), especially in terms of race and age.
6. Women tend to marry men who are higher in socioeconomic status. Women put a higher value on interpersonal understanding and men put a higher value on physical attractiveness in mate selection.
7. Most couples express satisfaction in their marriages. Successful marriages and families have

high levels of caring, communication, trust, loyalty, and emotional support.

8. The United States has the highest divorce rate in the world. Although the divorce rate steadily increased throughout the last century, it is leveling off.

9. Teenage marriages among couples of lower socioeconomic status are the most likely to end in divorce. Marital permanence is helped when the couple is similar in age, race, religion, attitudes, and values.

10. Divorce is a principal reason for the high poverty rate of single-parent women and their dependent children. No-fault divorce and joint custody contribute to the "feminization of poverty."

11. The remarriage rate is lower for women than for men. Men are more likely to be free from sole custody and to have an age and economic advantage in remarrying.

12. Many people are seeking alternatives to conventional household arrangements. Singlehood, cohabitation, and single-parent families are all increasing. Egalitarian marriages based on shared decision making and nontraditional beliefs about gender are also increasing.

13. America's multicultural heritage is reflected in its families. The four largest groupings are African American, Latino, Asian American, and Native American families. Their marriages and families are greatly influenced by their minority status.

14. Intimacy and intensity of relationships lay the groundwork for family violence. Family violence is associated with low income, unemployment, alcohol use, drug abuse, and family isolation.

15. Gay men and lesbians are challenging traditional views of marriage and family to receive benefits previously available only to married couples.

16. The family values movement calls for a "family restorationist" model around the ideal of the patriarchal nuclear family. Sociological critiques of the model center on its failure to account for social change.

KEY TERMS

assortive mating   384
bilateral (bilineal) descent   379
blended families   389
commune   382
egalitarian marriage   392
endogamy   379
exogamy   378
expressive role   379
extended family   379

family of orientation   378
family of procreation   378
fictive kin   393
homogamy   384
hypergamy   385
instrumental role   379
matrilineal descent   379
matrilocal residence   382

monogamy   381
nuclear family   379
patrilineal descent   379
patrilocal residence   381
polyandry   382
polygamy   381
polygyny   382
serial monogamy   389

CRITICAL THINKING QUESTIONS

1. Discuss the evidence (both pro and con) related to the following statement: "We are socialized to fall in love with only certain people, therefore the notion of romantic love is a myth."

2. Review the positive effects of egalitarian marriage for the couple, their children, and society as a whole. Given these effects, what prevents or encourages the formation of more egalitarian marriages?

3. How do family restorationists view the emerging lifestyles that compete with the traditional family? What sociological arguments can be used for or against this view, and which side has the stronger argument?

✛16✛ EDUCATION

The Joy of Teaching

Nicknamed "Bambi" by his students at Walt Whitman Intermediate School in Brooklyn for his gentle manner, social studies teacher Roman Foster has befriended his students. As head of the audiovisual section, he has given painstaking attention to the details of moviemaking, and he has earned the respect of his students—not as a disciplinarian, but as a teacher. Whitman is an inner-city school in a neighborhood rife with crime and drugs. Its students are overwhelmingly poor. Like many of the best teachers at Whitman, Foster never relies on the principal to rescue him. He solves problems himself. "You come in and tell them like it is. You do such and such and you're violating classroom rules. I don't have to raise my voice. Sure, they sometimes forget. They're kids. But I usually win them over." That such an easygoing man can instill discipline is puzzling to some. "Sometimes I feel I'm being told 'it's a bunch of dumb little black kids who don't care.' How can I tell these kids there's hope with people thinking these things about them? But that's not the kids' fault. I want them to spend the little time they have with me in a relaxed classroom, learning as much as they can." Other teachers like Foster—and there are many of them—parlay goodwill into respect; the kids listen to them. Why do they stay? They love to teach and they make a difference in the lives of the students they teach. (Adapted from Sachar, 1991)

The Menace of Teaching

The following journal entry from a high school teacher in Watts, a poverty-stricken community in South-Central Los Angeles that serves Latino and African American students, was written the second week of school.

I've met a kid, Antonio, who claims to be involved with the "Mexican Mafia," says he is selling large amounts of coke and heroin, and tells me he wants to stop but cannot because of his Mafia connections. . . . I am not invincible. This kid could attack me simply to try to prove that his story is real. . . . My other kids are mostly gems, so lovely and energetic that I move at the speed of light to give them all I have. I so love to teach. I just think I'd feel a lot better about it if I weren't afraid of being killed. (Adapted from Diver-Stamnes, 1995:85)

Challenges of Classroom Diversity

Among Chris's fifth graders are Pedro and Judith. Pedro has been raised by his grandmother and has six half-brothers, each of whom has a different mother. He comes to class one day and misses two. When he is present he falls asleep. In contrast is Judith, from a stable, two-parent family. Judith typifies students from families with economic resources and loving parents who are active in the school and who carefully monitor their childrens' education. Judith is the darling of the class.

Every class has its Judiths and Pedros. Teachers also have Chinese students to whom a pat on the head is an insult; they have Jehovah's Witnesses who don't celebrate birthdays and don't salute the flag; they have Muslims who fast from dawn to sunset every day during Ramadan and fall asleep in the afternoon. The mission of teaching is to educate everyone—and to do it without ignoring individual student differences, cultural, economic, or even physical. Many teachers get fed up with programs that ignore differences. As one teacher says, "I'm looking at the children and the heck with the programs. All classes are different. All kids are different." (Kidder, 1989; Seymour & Seymour, 1992)

Education has changed enormously. Teachers at all levels are facing far different classrooms than their predecessors did only a generation ago—classrooms that defy all stereotypes. Diversity is what's happening in classrooms across the globe. Yet reflected by the teachers quoted here, even in the most challenging classroom environments, teachers teach because they are passionate about their students.

The sociology of education focuses on how schools meet the needs of society and the needs of individual learners. Teachers are the critical link between students and society. As this chapter will show, while education is a sorting process designed to benefit society and learners, with benefits also come liabilities. A sociological perspective helps assess the benefits and liabilities associated with the process of education. Such an assessment is vital in ensuring that schools prepare students for the increasingly diverse world they will face outside the classroom.

SOCIOLOGICAL PERSPECTIVES ON EDUCATION

Sociology has made major contributions to understanding the process of education and how it affects various groups. The functionalist framework has dominated this understanding. This is because the first question functionalists ask is: What are schools expected to accomplish for society? All sociological perspectives accept certain functions of the school, but they disagree about how much to emphasize each function and how to implement the functions. Thus functionalism can serve as a springboard for evaluating other theoretical approaches.

Functionalism and the Functions of Education

The functionalist perspective provides a clear and powerful explanation demonstrating the importance of education for both society and the individual. Its focus is on how education serves as a force in social integration. At the turn of the century Émile Durkheim (1898/1956) suggested that schools are necessary to build a community and a society. When children begin formal education outside their families, they enter a society where what they do is more important than who they are. It is their first experience in a society of equals. The classroom reflects the values and norms of wider society, including ways in which its members are ranked. In the United States, like most of the world, pupils are evaluated on the basis of their achievement. These grades are the first formal indicators of what is believed to be the child's potential. Americans firmly believe that education is

the key to success and will translate to economic rewards, social prestige, and an enhanced self-concept for their children.

Although the functions of education are numerous, the four categories listed below combine many under several broad, interrelated themes. As mentioned in earlier chapters, functionalism emphasizes how society is integrated, interdependent, and maintained in a state of equilibrium. Consider how each of the following functions contributes to making a diverse society more unified and how each is linked to the other institutions.

Education as Socialization. Schools continue the socialization process that begins in the family; they introduce children to a distinct set of values, attitudes, and norms different from those learned in the family. Not only are children acquiring necessary knowledge and skills, they take on new roles and learn proper behavior in interacting with peers and teachers. Schools transmit knowledge in a social context. From the founding of the United States, the socialization function of education has emphasized that children learn academic content in a setting where they also learn critical social skills. Dick and Jane are taught computer literacy and also how to share the computer with others.

Education as Transmission of Culture. Schools are the formal channels for assuring that the fundamental values of the culture are passed to the next generation. The core cultural values emphasized in schools help prepare children for life in a democratic society where free enterprise and capitalism are dominant. They learn the values of competition, individualism, respect, self-discipline, and achievement. Globalization has added a new dimension to these values. With Japan's ascendence as one of the world's richest nations, schools are now stressing cooperation, teamwork, and group decision making. As tomorrow's workers, students need to learn how to function as "teammates" and how to play all positions to win as a team. Schools have the difficult task of simultaneously teaching children the benefits of traditional ways of thinking and acting (core values) but challenging those very traditions (emergent values). Core values are not abandoned but supplemented, and a uniquely American value system continues to evolve.

The role of education as a transmitter of culture also involves the function of assimilation, where children from many diverse cultures and subcultures are transformed to committed Americans. Because the United States is a nation of immigrants, mass education has been driven by the need to Americanize its arrivals with the heart and will to become good citizens (Graham, 1995). Schools require students to

In the United States as well as throughout much of the world, education and literacy provide the route to achievement. Barriers such as physical disability that may put children at risk in other areas of their lives may be overcome through educational success.

pledge allegiance to the flag each morning and to understand the basic elements of the U.S. Constitution and the political system flowing from it. If the transmission of culture is successful, another educational function is served—that of social control. Dick and Jane meet Ricardo and Noriko in school; together they learn to be proud of the American heritage they all share.

Education as Innovation.   Schools provide students with the attitudes and skills to adapt to a rapidly changing world. Today's curriculum reflects the need of a changing family and population structure. Boys take home economics, girls take shop, and both learn sex education. Throughout America's history, the face of the population has constantly altered, but today at an even faster rate. Estimates indicate that by 2025 half of America's population and a majority of elementary and secondary school children will be people of color (Cortes, 1991). Multiculturalism and global interdependence are facts of modern life that students must understand. Cooperative learning, group problem solving, and student-directed school projects are innovative ways children can learn about others and themselves. With a set of core values as a foundation,

children are provided with creative and beneficial tools for confronting social change and for life in a diverse society and a shrinking world.

Innovation means more than adapting *to* change. Children also learn to become agents *of* change. They mold their world according to their individual desires and talents. Ricardo, Noriko, Dick, and Jane can come together as classmates in schools that are innovative in content and structure. As we will see later, such schools emphasize multicultural education so that children learn to appreciate both their diversity and common identity. If schools carry out this function properly, social change can be empowering rather than overwhelming or fearful for children. In situations such as these, education, like other cultural elements, conditions children to their culture but also gives them directions for cultural change.

Education as Social Placement.   Education is the key institution that functions to nurture talent and achievement in children, preparing them for their future roles in society. To a great extent, all the functions of education feed into this mandate. Americans firmly believe that their children's success in life is fundamentally linked to their success in school. This process serves the dual needs of the individual and society. In school, Ricardo's ability in art and Jane's athletic prowess are discovered and developed. If education guides children to fulfill their goals and hone their talents, society will also benefit.

Education's role as an agent of social placement demonstrates that functionalism subscribes to the idea of **meritocracy.** Society rewards people on the basis of ability and achievement—on what they can do— and the school is a microcosm of society. Talent is not wasted, competence is rewarded, and students are motivated to achieve at their highest levels. As discussed in Chapter 10, *social stratification* ranks people according to a number of criteria, the most important of which is income. Schools reward students with grades for academic work and with popularity for athletic ability. Just as employed people are ranked by income, students are ranked by grades.

This function of education—and the meritocracy that is supposed to develop from it—lends itself to an emphasis on credentials or **credentialism.** In this situation an individual's qualification for a job or social status is based on the completion of some aspect of formal education. A credential may be college credit for a sociology course, a certificate for continuing education in word processing, or board certification for an MD in plastic surgery. America has become a credentialized society and its most important minimum credential is the college degree. Functionalists argue that credentials based on merit are essential for filtering people and assigning them to appropriate roles and statuses. The resulting social stratification is thus justified, according to this view.

Manifest and Latent Functions. As discussed in Chapter 1, *manifest functions* are those consequences of social life that are explicit, intended, and recognized. As such, they contribute to social integration. Less obvious, but still important for this integration, are *latent functions*, which are unintended and often remain unrecognized. Sociologists generally agree on the functions of education, but disagree as to which are manifest and which are latent. Schools are designed to serve specific social purposes, which in turn serve the needs of individual students and their families. As society changes, so does its needs. A function that was latent at one time can become manifest at another time, or vice versa. For example, schools have always provided a latent babysitting function, but this is now essential in many schools, making the babysitting function manifest rather than latent. Latchkey programs and after-school activities occupy children at school until their parents come home from work. In violent neighborhoods, school athletics for teenagers are manifestly responsible for the safety and well-being of many teens, merely by keeping them off the streets and under supervision. Such programs are vital for working parents.

Schools provide social networks where lifetime friendships are likely to form. In serving the needs of higher education and social placement, colleges also exist as marriage markets. These functions may be latent for some, but when parents pick schools precisely because they want their children to meet others for social and business reasons a manifest function operates. In Japan, college friendships are expected to evolve into long-term business relationships.

Latchkey programs and after-school activities keep children occupied at school until their parents come home from work. This babysitting function was once latent but is now essential in many schools.

Dysfunctions. Modern functionalism recognizes that when schools perform any of these duties, dysfunctions can occur that have damaging consequences. For example:

1. Education transmits culture, but what is transmitted and how it is transmitted has created tension among various groups who are scrambling for visibility in the curriculum. How much American history can be devoted to any one group without slighting another? The curriculum that is designed in part to enhance tolerance may latently contribute to intolerance.
2. Bringing masses of youngsters together as peers has contributed to a weakening of parental authority. By the middle-school years, parents find themselves competing for time and authority with their children's friends.
3. Schools led by concerned administrators and caring teachers provide an organized and predictable day for those children who come from disruptive or even violent homes. But some parents believe that inflexible school bureaucracy and teacher demands interfere too much in their family's life.

In considering the functionalist perspective and how it relates to education, remember that dysfunctional consequences are inevitable. It is impossible to do society's work without creating some negative results. As long as the functional advantages outweigh the dysfunctional disadvantages and the dysfunctions are dealt with effectively, society still benefits. The social system returns to a state of equilibrium. The American consensus on the core values instilled in schoolchildren and reinforced in the other institutions provides the foundation for this equilibrium.

Modern functionalism says of education that while the schools have problems, the educational system as a whole is doing its job. Functionalists would point to a record of increased literacy and high school graduation rates, a narrowing racial gap in dropout rates, and expanded college attendance and degree completion for both genders and all races (see Table 16.1). Unemployment is at its lowest level in two decades. Schools must be given credit for successfully transferring classroom learning to paid employment. On tests of verbal ability, social-class differences have continued to narrow, making a plausible argument that meritocracy is alive and well (Weakliem et al., 1995). Despite the dysfunctional aspects, the functions of education are being carried out effectively. This perspective paints a rather glowing portrait of American education. However, these same facts can be viewed quite differently from a conflict perspective.

Conflict Theory and Educational Inequality

Conflict theory focuses on the social placement function of education and argues that a principal function of schooling in the United States is to reproduce and reinforce inequality. Rather than assigning future roles to students based on talent and motivation, the critical factors for achievement are social class, race, and gender. Of these three, social class appears to be the best overall indicator. In a report published three decades ago, based on family background and achievement test data from over half a million students at 4,000 schools nationwide, sociologist James

Table 16.1	Educational Attainment by Race and Gender, Selected Years					
	White		Black		Hispanic*	
Year	Male	Female	Male	Female	Male	Female
Completed 4 Years of High School or More						
1965	50.2	52.2	25.8	28.4	(NA)	(NA)
1975	65.0	64.1	41.6	43.3	39.5	36.7
1985	76.0	75.1	58.4	60.8	48.5	47.4
1995	83.0	83.0	73.4	74.1	52.9	53.8
1997	82.9	83.2	73.5	76.0	54.9	54.6
Completed 4 Years of College or More						
1965	12.7	7.3	4.9	4.5	(NA)	(NA)
1975	18.4	11.0	6.7	6.2	8.3	4.6
1985	24.0	16.3	11.2	11.0	9.7	7.3
1995	27.2	21.0	13.6	12.9	10.1	8.4
1997	27.0	22.3	12.5	13.9	10.6	10.1

NA-Not Available
*Persons of Hispanic origin may be of any race.
Source: Adapted from Table 261. U.S. Bureau of the Census, 1998.

Coleman (1966) and his colleagues came to an inescapable conclusion: The single most important criterion for school achievement was socioeconomic status (SES), especially related to a child's home environment. Children with lower levels of achievement came from homes that lacked such things as an automobile, vacuum cleaner, or record player. Reading materials—books, magazines, newspapers, and encyclopedias—were largely absent from the homes of low-achieving children. Coupled with the lack of material resources was the fact that many parents failed to encourage their children for success in school, thus these children tended to have a poor self-image. Children would attribute success and failure to luck rather than motivation or ability.

Recent data continue to support Coleman's findings. As an element of SES, parental education is the most powerful predictor of a child's success in school. Such is the power of SES that when variables such as race, immigration status, and measured intelligence are held constant, upper- and middle-class children still achieve at higher overall levels than do working- and lower-class children (Entwistle & Alexander, 1992; Milligan, 1993; Nieto, 1995).

These facts cannot be dismissed by saying that when a poor child fails in school it is simply because of a home environment that discourages learning. Conflict theory argues that the schools these children attend also discourage learning. They are poorly funded, inadequately maintained, located in high crime areas and staffed by overworked and underpaid educators. They function primarily as institutions for social control and conformity rather than for achievement and innovation.

Some classical conflict theorists take this scenario a step farther. From a Marxist perspective, educational content is intentionally designed by the upper class to perpetuate their dominance as a capitalist economic elite (Bowles & Gintis, 1976). Conflict theorists of the Marxian variety argue that inequality in SES and education serves to obstruct the aspirations of lower-class children, thus reproducing the existing class structure.

Conflict theorists also emphasize the role of the **hidden curriculum** to persuade poor and working-class children to accept as inevitable their place in life as dependent, waged workers. This hidden curriculum includes all the informal, unwritten norms that schools use to keep students in line. Working-class students go to schools that stress rote learning, obedience, and little freedom of choice. Middle-class schools ensure that students follow directions but permit more student decision making. Schools catering to the elite—generally, expensive private schools—encourage creativity, divergent thinking, and independence (Anyon, 1980). Conflict theorists maintain that aspects of the hidden curriculum ensure that class position is maintained from one generation to the next.

Schooling is supposed to enhance opportunities for all to succeed, but conflict theory suggests that it actually does the opposite. The elite and a very few others are destined for success; mediocrity and failure are the destinies of most. This system remains unchallenged in part because the few nonelite who do succeed become the role models for the others: The schools are not responsible for the failure of the students, something is inherently "wrong" with the students themselves.

A conflict perspective is demonstrated by author and social critic Jonathan Kozol in his bestselling work *Savage Inequalities* (1991), which examines the massive inequality in U.S. education. Kozol contrasts several New York City public schools—those in neighborhoods of poor and heavily nonwhite residents—with others where well-educated families and few low-income students live. One school in a poor Bronx neighborhood serves 1,300 students although its capacity is 900. The principal says he is forced to take the "tenth best teachers." Students share textbooks, the school has only 26 computers, and the library has 700 books and no encyclopedias. Recess is impossible because there is no playground. Lack of space prevents the addition of a much-needed prekindergarten. Two first-grade classes share a windowless room divided by a blackboard, and four kindergartens and a sixth-grade class of Spanish-speaking children are packed into a single room, again with no windows. The school used to be a roller rink. Do the children ever comment about the building? One teacher answers, "They don't say, but they know. . . . You see it in their eyes. They understand. They all watch television and know what suburban schools are like."

In another part of the Bronx, but by no means its richest area, the public school serves 825 kindergarten through sixth grade students. The school is surrounded by large, expensive, and beautiful homes and the excellence of the school adds to the property values. The principal is enthusiastic about his teachers and staff. Classrooms are clean and well maintained. Dedicated parents and volunteers donate time, money, and school materials. The library has 8,000 volumes, and every class has at least one computer. The district cannot afford a librarian, but educated parents volunteer as library staff. Fundraisers by the parents' organization enhance resources.

Tracking: Social Class and Race. Even in the wealthier schools, two systems of education exist side

When schools cannot offer an adequate learning environment, conflict theorists argue that schools are warehouses of social control rather than sites for student achievement.

by side. Children of all races and social classes may occupy the same building but experience the learning process quite differently (Kozol, 1991). Latino and African American children, who are disproportionately poor, are far more likely to be assigned to "special" classes, including lower level nonacademic or vocationally oriented ones. This practice of grouping children according to an assessment of their ability is called **tracking.** These special classes for the lower "tracks" are overcrowded, have inadequate facilities, and are staffed by rotating teachers. The opposite is true of the higher or "gifted" tracks. The children labeled as gifted learn critical thinking and logic. According to Kozol, children tracked into low-ability classes learn to punch time cards.

With an elementary school legacy already in place, conflict theorists maintain that tracking in high school operates to separate the college and noncollege bound. Some educators justify tracking by arguing that the college bound are more ready to learn, learn more rapidly, and should not be restrained by the slower progress of other students. But critics argue that students in lower-level tracks are actually discouraged from living up to their potential. Research

shows that class and race have a great impact on tracking, *regardless of past achievement, ability, and IQ* (Schafer et al., 1994). Nonwhite and poor children more often find themselves in noncollege-bound tracks where they encounter a less rigorous and less rewarding curriculum (Braddock, 1990; Oakes & Lipton, 1996). This situation undermines self-esteem. As one student in a lower-ability track put it,

> I started losing faith in myself after the teachers kept downing me. You hear, "a guy's in the basic section, he's dumb and all this." Each year— "You're ignorant—you're stupid." (Cited in Schafer et al., 1994:198)

Conflict theorists argue that tracking is a barrier to equal opportunity. Although there are decreases in high school dropouts and increases in high school and college graduates, there remains a continuing education gap based on race (Figure 16.1). Segregation of students within schools may be the most important difference in how students are treated (Kirp, 1995). Since tracking encourages learning for some children but discourages it for others, the standard of equal opportunity in education is compromised.

Gender.   Along with social class and race, gender is another influence that, according to conflict theory, puts girls at a major disadvantage in the opportunity to compete economically. High school girls more often than boys are tracked into academic courses such as English and vocational courses such as word processing and home economics. While more girls than boys graduate from high school, more girls are also enrolled in vocational education courses. Overall, high school vocational education for girls is geared to the noncollege bound who either marry or wind up in low-paying, dead-end jobs. This pattern is especially true for working-class girls. Historically, vocational education has been reserved for the less powerful in society, whether they are women, the working poor, or other skilled laborers, a fact that conflict theorists highlight (Burge & Culver, 1990).

Conflict theorists also suggest that those women who do go on to college receive less faculty encouragement for their work and will be listened to less and interrupted more by their male classmates, thereby promoting lower expectations for achievement (Kramarae & Treichler, 1990; Chilly Collective, 1995). During college self-esteem drops for women and rises for men (American Association of University Women, 1992). This lowered self-esteem can result in lower expectations for achievement.

Men and women who graduate from college enter a gender-segregated work force. When an occupation is dominated by one gender, its pay and

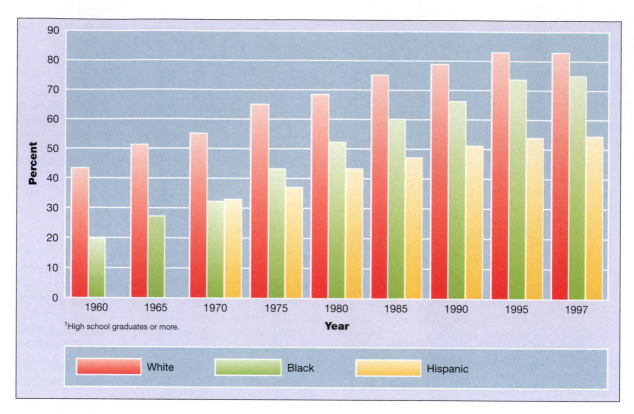

FIGURE 16.1   Percentage of Students in the United States Who Completed Four Years of High School or More, by Race and Hispanic Origin, 1960–1997 (For persons 25 years and older)

Source: Adapted from Figure 4.1, p. 158. U.S. Bureau of the Census, 1998.

prestige reflects that pattern. Gender contributes more to a wage gap than race, ethnicity, or years of schooling (Chapter 13). Conflict theorists argue that education that is "gendered" ensures that the male elite maintains its dominant economic position.

The strength of the conflict approach to education lies in the abundant evidence showing that socioeconomic status (SES) is a powerful variable that explains school achievement—a fact that holds true for the United States as well as cross-culturally. In a study of nine European nations and Japan, social class determines access to education (Ishida, 1995). In his pioneering work, Brazilian educator Paolo Freire (1970) goes even further by saying that schools provide a "pedagogy of the oppressed." He states that the oppressed are a social class unspecified by race, gender, ethnicity, language, and culture (Freire & Macedo, 1995).

However, the view that the intention of schools is to reproduce a ruling elite is not verified. Although Freire's work has stimulated over twenty-five years of international dialogue on educational philosophy, teachers do not see themselves or their schools as passive tools to maintain the class status quo. They want all students to achieve at the highest level possible.

Symbolic Interactionism: Education as Socially Constructed

Symbolic interactionism focuses on the socialization function of schools and how a child is transformed into a student. Like other roles, the student role is socially constructed. Children, teachers, and student peers actively engage in a process of mutual interaction where the roles they carry out in the school are subject to continual negotiation and definition. Recall from Chapter 5 that for symbolic interactionists, socialization is not a passive process. Unlike the behaviorist perspective, which suggests that we learn primarily by conforming to others' expectations, symbolic interactionism offers a more dynamic, reciprocal approach. Children themselves actively participate in defining their student role.

Labeling in the classroom plays a key role in the way children define themselves at school. Different expectations based on labels by teachers and other students lead to different outcomes. Ann Staton (1990) demonstrates the importance of labeling in how children are socialized throughout their school years. Through case studies, interviews, and observations in mostly public elementary and high schools,

Symbolic interactionists suggest that students learn to adapt to a classroom according to how they define and act on the expectations of their teachers and their classmates.

she finds that students develop their own culture, and they actively participate in constructing their own roles. At each stage of schooling, the following comments demonstrate the importance attached to labels in this role construction.

Kindergarten—During the first week in class, the teacher defines what it means to be in kindergarten. She characterizes her students as special and smart: "We're not the smallest in the school. How about we're the specialest?" "You're all smart. Anybody here not smart?" (p. 34)

Middle school—The child's new identity of what it means to be a seventh grader is forming: "Teachers don't always talk to you as a little kid. They treat you older." "It means that you have to act more mature 'cause we are growing up and becoming young adults." (p. 81)

High school—What does it mean to be to be a freshman? "Makes me feel much maturer." "It means to work harder and little kids will look up to me." "You feel older and more sophisticated." But students also mention being looked down upon by older students, such as "putdowns by older kids" or "getting froshed" (pushed around and threatened). (pp. 106, 109)

One consequence of tracking, according to symbolic interactionists, is that students who are labeled as having less ability may eventually give in to negative labels, such as the student quoted above who lost faith in himself. A self-fulfilling prophecy is likely. Tracking in this case is a negative label that produces such a stigma that the person's self-esteem suffers. Behavior is altered to fit this new identity. Why should this student even try to achieve when he,

along with everyone else, believes he is a failure? An educational prophecy of his low achievement is fulfilled.

But even a self-fulfilling prophecy is not a completely passive process. A student who is labeled an underachiever will resist the increased workload that a concerned teacher will insist on, but may also resist being labeled a failure. Ongoing negotiation may create a working relationship. The student may continue to behave as an "underachiever" in the teacher's estimation, but the student modifies his or her behavior through mutual interaction and ever-changing definitions of the situation. This scenario suggests that labels fluctuate and become re-created. The modification of behavior by the student illustrates the symbolic interactionist concept of the **end point fallacy**—new labels produce new behavior in an ongoing process. Behavior may be modified at one point in time but it continues to be modified in a never-ending process—there is no end point.

An understanding of the end point fallacy is important because it alerts us to potential results of labeling. If labeling has been used in a negative way, it can also be used positively. **Mainstreaming**, the integration of special-needs students into the overall classroom or school, recognizes the power of labeling. It is designed to reduce the stigma and negative outcomes of isolating children who may have learning disabilities, mild academic handicaps, or physical handicaps. Prior to mainstreaming, students with such disabilities were served primarily through special-education programs. These included "pull-out" programs where students were pulled from regular classrooms up to one hour a day to receive remedial instruction in small groups (Slavin, 1989).

Mainstreaming was not meant for children identified as mentally retarded or having severe behavioral or emotional disorders. In this sense, it is the opposite of tracking. The idea is to provide as much "normal" school life and peer interaction as a special-needs student can handle. Ideally, a three-step process occurs: Mainstreaming reduces stigma, enhances self-confidence, and generates higher expectations for achievement by both teacher and student. The process, therefore, reduces the risk of failure.

All the programs mentioned above—tracking, mainstreaming, pull-outs—either separate or integrate students who have various ability levels. Tracking, special education, and pull-out programs are designed to serve the needs of underachieving students by separating them. But empirical evidence suggests that these programs add few benefits and often limit rather than increase learning opportunities (Legters & McDill, 1994). Programs that integrate students have a slight edge in reducing stigma. But mainstreaming-type programs work only if mainstreamed students are not too disruptive. Otherwise resources are drained and teachers focus too much attention on a few children to the detriment of the others (Waddock, 1995).

Clearly, the programs that separate students from their peers have not been spectacularly successful. Their low success rate means that educators should pay attention to the power of labeling. Symbolic interactionism also recognizes that all school programs are embedded in the broader culture that includes the political arena. Some people argue that the political arena should be targeted for reform, not the way students are grouped (Hallinan et al., 1994). This argument suggests that politicians must make a real and sustained commitment to educational equality that will serve all students. The situation will not change with mere technical reform, but only when a new definition of "commitment to equality" is seriously embraced. As symbolic interactionists demonstrate, changing the label means changing the reality.

Applying Sociological Theory to Education

Of all social institutions, education perhaps best illustrates the application of sociological theory to the real world. The most effective educational programs can incorporate the strengths of each major theoretical perspective, as well as account for the impact of the other social institutions on education. Each perspective helps answer the question "What can be done to prevent the risk of student failure?" Research suggests that, at a minimum, programs including the following elements will meet with the most success (Gutherie, 1989; Farmer & Payne, 1992; Roderick, 1993). Notice how each element can be readily linked to one or more sociological theories.

1. Take a comprehensive approach. Recognize that educational disadvantages at home weaken an adolescent's attachment to school. (*Functionalism*)
2. Keep the pedagogy of classroom learning relevant to the lives of all students so they do not feel isolated and marginal and so they see an end product, such as a good job, if they succeed. Cultivate

When schools provide frequent opportunities for adolescents to see the relevance of education to their futures, such as career days, field trips to businesses, or an interview with someone at their place of work, both student interest and achievement are enhanced.

school and business partnerships. (*Functionalism and symbolic interactionism*)

3. Raise expectations for at-risk students of lower SES backgrounds. (*Conflict and symbolic interactionism*)

4. Invest in schools with the highest dropout rates, not only with money, but through staff development, summer enhancement programs, and one-to-one mentoring. Show students that they are good investments. (*Conflict and symbolic interactionism*)

Sociological theory points to multiple levels of influence in dealing with student achievement. Education touches and is touched by every other social institution:

- families provide different levels of encouragement for their children to succeed in school;
- school funding rises and falls according to interests by politicians and the health of the economy;
- religious leaders believe that moral education needs to be stronger in schools and encourage congregation members to advocate these wishes to school boards;
- the whole social system and not just small pieces of it must be part of the process to improve student learning (Waddock, 1995:217).

Not only does sociological theory offer sound support for this approach, but many of these same elements are reflected in educational reform measures. These measures will be discussed later in the chapter.

A GLOBAL VIEW OF EDUCATION

One of the best ways to ensure a country's overall well-being is to teach girls to read (Bernard, 1987:7). Indeed, the United Nations estimates that for every year beyond the fourth grade that girls go to school, family size shrinks 10 percent, child death rates drop 10 percent, and wages rise 20 percent (*Connections*, 1995:1). Education also influences rate of marriage (people marry later), patterns of work (people enter more white-collar than blue-collar jobs), health habits (people practice preventive health care), food consumption (people eat a healthier diet), and even leisure activities (people engage in recreation outside their homes and neighborhoods) (United Nations Development Program, 1998). A sociological perspective on education reveals many aspects of global interdependence. An educated population can more easily accept new technology and communicate with one another and the world more quickly and efficiently. Education creates more linkages to the "outside" world in an endless cycle of reciprocity.

Educational level has profound consequences for society. For example, one of the most important global demographic trends is that higher educational attainment is associated with lower fertility (birth) rate (Martin, 1995). This is true between countries and between women in their own countries. It is a simple correlation that masks its enormous impact, not only on the lives of individual women and their families but on the world as a whole. This means that education is inevitably an agent of social change. In the developing world, the role and content of

Education serves both a powerful socialization function and as a mirror to the society as a whole. This classroom in India reflects some gender segregation as well as less value put on a girl's education as compared to a boy's, since fewer girls attend school— even at the primary levels.

414 Chapter 16 Education

education vary according to specific cultural demands. Education serves democratic and capitalistic interests in Costa Rica and the Philippines, and it serves socialist and authoritarian interests in Cuba and Libya. Education in Nicaragua, Nigeria, and Iran has fostered swift and dramatic social and economic change (Najafizadeh & Mennerick, 1992). While some regimes often intend to keep education under their control, even in the remotest areas its influence cannot be contained. Education assures that there is no such thing as an "outside" world. Investing in education brings high returns globally.

Despite education's many benefits, and although it is no longer reserved for a culture's elite, there is a large and persistent global education gap. The largest gap is between the developed and developing world (see Table 16.2). Of the world's 1.5 billion aged 6 to 17, 428 million were not enrolled at any level in school. Most of these children are in developing countries, most are in rural areas, and most of them are girls (United Nations Development Program, 1998) (see Figure 16.2 on page 417). The illiteracy rate in China has been cut by two-thirds since 1949, so that today about 16 percent of the population is illiterate. However, 70 percent of the illiterate in China are girls. China reflects the pattern that two-thirds of the illiterate people in the world are women. In seventeen countries, 90 percent or more of the female population is illiterate (Jacobsen, 1994; *People and Development Challenges*, 1995). The highest female illiteracy rate is in South Asia (72 percent compared to 46 percent of men) and in Africa (62 percent compared to 44 percent of men) (Snyder, 1990; Conley, 1994). Although the elimination of the education gap is in the best interests of a global society, sociology reminds us that even positive social change brings both benefits and liabilities, depending on how various social groups are affected.

Although we are quick to applaud the achievements associated with education, there is another side to the coin. Consider what happens to those who are left behind when a culture shifts, first from an oral to a literate tradition, and then later when some languages are "selected" for literacy education and others are not. In an oral culture, knowledge is only what can be recalled and repeated to the next generation. In such a community of aboriginal people in the Northern Territory of Australia, for example, the transition to literacy offers both advantages and disadvantages. Literacy offers people the power to control their own destiny, but with that power comes an intrusion of "literate culture values" that are in direct conflict with traditional "oral culture values." So while the aborigines gain literacy, they may lose their culture (Eggington, 1992).

For example, in oral cultures issues are resolved quickly through face-to-face negotiation. Contracts are agreed upon and locked into personal memory. The spoken word is the final truth. In literate cultures, issues are resolved slowly through depersonalized committees that may involve many people. The spoken word is not as important as the written word. To make something valid, "Get it in writing." Those who have crossed over to literacy are usually younger, urbanized, and see people through literate-culture eyes; often they are seen by their elders as betraying traditional values (Eggington, 1992).

A parallel exists in authoritarian regimes such as Iran and Saudi Arabia, where computer technology is eagerly sought, but is associated with unwanted Western values. In China, the number of Internet users has jumped 75 percent in 1998 to 1.2 million, and it is expected to reach 10 million in five years. Most users

Table 16.2 The Global Education Gap

A. Country Income Level and Education

Income Level (GNP)	Mean Years of Education by Age 15–19	45–49
Low Income	2.4	1.7
Lower-Middle Income	5.5	2.7
Upper-Middle Income	8.9	6.9
High Income	9.4	8.0

B. Adult Literacy Rate (ALR%) and Country Income Level (Selected Countries)

Country	ALR (%)	Income Level
Niger	16	Low
Togo	43	Low
India	45	Low
China	84	Lower-Middle
Singapore	88	Upper-Middle
South Korea	96	Upper-Middle
New Zealand	99	High

Examples of Low Income Countries:
Afghanistan, Bangladesh, Haiti, India, Malawi, Niger, Peru, Sudan, Togo, Uganda

Example of Lower-Middle Income Countries:
Bahamas, Chili, China, Ecuador, Jordan, Kenya, Philippines, Thailand

Example of Upper-Middle Income Countries:
Argentina, Czech Republic, Hong Kong, Hungary, Israel, South Korea, Poland, Singapore, Taiwan, United Arab Emirates, Venezuela

Examples of High Income Countries:
Australia, Britain, Japan, Kuwait, New Zealand, Northern Europe (all countries), United States

Sources: Lockheed & Verspoor, 1991; Kennedy, 1997; United Nations Development Report, 1998.

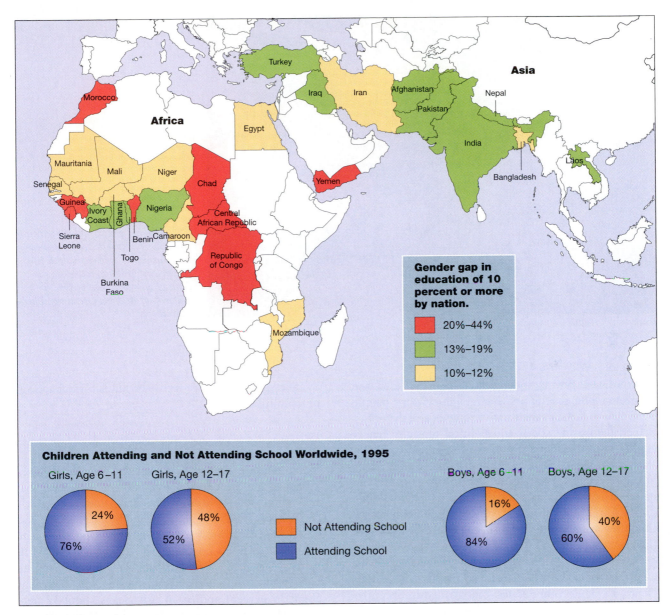

FIGURE 16.2   The Global Gender Gap in Education   The gender gap averages the difference between enrollment rates for boys and girls in primary and secondary schools. The larger the gap in percentage points, the more disadvantaged girls are relative to boys.
Source: Adapted from "Education: Gains and Gaps" in *The Washington Post*, October 24, 1998. Copyright © The Washington Post Writers Group. Reprinted by permission.

are under age 35 and represent an influential elite of students and intellectuals. China is investing millions of dollars to increase Internet access, but officials in charge of propaganda and security oppose its expansion. Police departments throughout China have people in charge of ferreting out "harmful information" on the Internet (Laris, 1998). In all societies, while Internet access and e-mail are desired, their effects cannot be completely controlled.

Literacy programs in developing countries must also deal with broader social and political issues. Adult literacy may have low priority because it conflicts with

the interests of the ruling class. Literacy would upset the balance of privilege and poverty on which some societies rest. This situation may explain the failure of literacy campaigns in parts of India (Bhola, 1987). Another consideration has to do with language choice. Literacy planners in Tanzania, where several languages are spoken, made the decision to teach literacy through the single language of Swahili in order to enhance national unity. In Ethiopia the chosen language was Amharic, the language of the dominant, educated ethnic elite. When literacy efforts stalled in Ethiopia, literacy planners shifted their strategy and

The changing demographic portrait of America is first reflected in elementary classrooms, where children from Latino backgrounds and other students of color will soon become the majority of students attending American schools.

incorporated fifteen indigenous languages into the program. The results are encouraging. More people were able to learn in their native tongue, and the policy helped defuse the social and political tensions generated by a single-language policy (Meisenhelder, 1992).

The United States is not immune to the "language of choice" issue. American Indian and Alaskan native tribal governments are concerned that if children do not learn in their native tongue at the same time they are learning English, the culture will be lost (Demmert, 1996). The same is true for native speakers of Hawaiian, a language that has decreased in usage as a result of religious and political changes (Buck, 1993). In other states, bilingual education programs that serve a large Spanish-speaking population have operated over three decades. They are designed to prepare children for the transition to speaking and writing English. Now these programs are under attack by politicians who see them as nationally divisive (Cardenas, 1995; Huddy & Sears, 1995). Supporters of bilingual education claim that students can adapt to a school's culture, even in language learning, without losing their own ethnic culture. In other words, they use the strategy of "accommodation without assimilation" (Ogbu, 1992). These issues remain unresolved. Issues related to global education are mirrored in the multicultural life of the United States.

DIVERSITY IN EDUCATION

Diversity is a thread that runs through U.S. history and serves as a force for both unity and separation. Since it is clear that U.S. schools are being reshaped

by diversity, schools are fertile grounds for debates on multiculturalism.

Multicultural Education

Demographers predict that over the next thirty years a gradual but dramatic change will occur in the racial and ethnic composition of children attending American schools (Pallas et al., 1995). The largest increase is expected to come from the Latino population (see Chapter 12). This population is expected to triple in thirty years and comprise about 25 percent of the U.S. population. African Americans will represent about 15 percent and Asian Americans about 12 percent (Marshall & Glover, 1996). The Native American population is a small but growing one. Although intermarriage rates complicate the numbers somewhat, demographers predict that thirty years from now, half the nation will be made up of people of color. As mentioned earlier, because these groups are also younger than the national average, by 2025 a majority of the nation's schools will be made up of children of color. The need for multicultural education is both obvious and urgent (Miller-Lachmann & Taylor, 1995:65).

Parents and educators agree that multicultural studies should be infused into the school curriculum. But what these studies should consist of is the subject of much debate. The debate is between groups who differ on their moral visions of the United States. Each group would like to see its own vision implemented in the school curriculum (Woolfolk, 1995). There are many definitions of multicultural

The majority of college students are now women, due mainly to a flood of "non-traditional" students—women who are returning to finish their degrees after raising a family.

education, and these in turn can serve the political agendas of various groups (McLaren, 1995; Sleeter & McLaren, 1995).

The cultural content of a school's curriculum is seen in some cases to elevate or diminish some groups at the expense of others. For example, until recently, history textbooks in secondary schools rarely acknowledged the actions of the federal government that served to conquer, subordinate, and kill Native Americans. Conflict theorists suggest that when a curriculum fails to account for the perspective of racial minorities in the historical record, the ideology of white supremacy is embedded in mainstream culture; racial differences are talked about from a white norm (Haymes, 1995). In textbooks, the contributions of Native Americans were also ignored—contributions such as planting, cooking, food storage practices, herbal remedies, and hunting techniques adopted by settlers and infused into broader American culture. Other formerly disempowered groups— African Americans, Asian Americans, women, the elderly, gay men and lesbians, to name a few—are advocating for curriculum space to highlight their history and achievements. These examples show that schools are becoming the host sites for identity politics and what has been termed "culture wars" (Miron & Lauria, 1995).

Functionalists would be sympathetic to the view that multicultural education threatens the authority of the state, which is based on cultural ideals rooted in the philosophy, literature, and art of Western civilization (Bloom, 1987; Hirsch, 1987). Remember the controversy in 1992 marking the five-hundredth anniversary of the "discovery" of America by Christo-

pher Columbus? On one side were those who believed Columbus should be depicted as a hero who overcame massive obstacles to reach the New World. On the other side were those who believed Columbus should be depicted as an inhumane conqueror who should assume historical responsibility for the subjugation and murder of indigenous people. Depending on which view of multicultural education is adopted, school children may be presented with a picture of Columbus that considers conquest and colonialism from the European perspective, from the perspective of the indigenous peoples of the Americas, or both.

Multicultural education at a minimum involves acknowledging the powerful role of culture on children—how it influences them and how their own subculture, race, ethnicity, and gender influence broader society. Multicultural education offers opportunities to examine diversity by putting *all* groups together on a level playing field (Jones & Clemson, 1996). No one group is better or worse than any other group.

With culture at the very core of the socialization function of schools, educators are moving away from the idea that a multicultural curriculum is merely about adding dark faces to the textbooks and new national holidays to the calendar (Boykin 1994:124). It is more about transforming than adding. It seeks to work against prejudice and the intolerance of differences associated with it. It prepares students to become critical agents of social change in the service of democracy (Banks & Banks, 1993; Abalos, 1996).

This goal points to the monumental and conflicting tasks of schools. They need to present "diversity within diversity." They need to avoid creating new sets of stereotypes that assume all members of a particular group share the same view of their own culture (Gonzalez, 1995). All this must be done in a limited amount of time with an already packed curriculum. Schools must also allow students from many subcultures to locate themselves in their own history while at the same time providing them the knowledge and conditions to function as part of a wider society (Aronowitz & Giroux, 1991:236). They must deal with the question of how much Americans are alike and how much they are different (Gordon & Yowell, 1994).

All theoretical perspectives in sociology strongly agree that culture does not merely mimic the past, it alters the present and transforms the future. Multicultural studies have impacted every level of education. For example, multicultural education puts "other" groups (such as people of color and females) on the same footing with dominant groups (such as whites, males, and those with European ancestry). In this way, it eliminates the idea of "other." Diversity itself is presented to students within the framework of a commitment to social justice (Estrada & McClaren, 1993:31). Because culture is transformative, sociologists suggest that even when multicultural studies represent only the narrower, additive approach to a school's curriculum, it plants the seeds for social change. Students eventually acquire the knowledge to help them realize democratic ideals and to function in an interdependent, global environment.

Desegregation and the Dilemma of Busing

Besides multicultural education, diversity is intimately linked to other racial challenges confronting America's schools. In 1896 the United States Supreme Court in *Plessy v. Ferguson* established the doctrine of "separate but equal," which protected racial segregation in public schools. A half century later, in 1954, the Supreme Court reversed the 1896 ruling in the watershed case of *Brown v. Board of Education of Topeka*, which said that segregated schools are "inherently" unequal. But making segregation illegal did not make it nonexistent. As we move into the twenty-first century, the percentage of African American children attending predominantly African American schools has increased.

More than fifty years after the *Brown* decision, the desegregation of America's schools is probably the number one educational challenge facing all segments of society, from students and parents to educators and politicians. The reality of life in a multiracial and multicultural society requires better knowledge of people whose backgrounds are different from our own, but residential segregation by race is also a fact.

While there is widespread agreement that desegregation is desirable, there is often bitter disagreement on how to accomplish it.

This power of disagreement is obvious in emotionally charged programs such as **busing,** where children of different races are transported to schools according to a certain racial parity formula. African American children are usually the ones traveling the greatest distance to school. Early court-ordered desegregation efforts of the 1970s involved crosstown busing of African American and white children within the same school districts. Current busing activities have been expanded to include busing inner-city, African American children to mostly white suburban districts and busing white children to newly created inner-city **magnet schools.** The magnet schools are attractive because they are selective and recruit better students, offer specialized programs, and provide higher quality instruction in superior facilities.

Antibusing sentiment reached its height in Boston in the fall of 1974, when the nation witnessed appalling images of racial bigotry and violence perpetrated by both whites and blacks. Opponents to forced busing saw it as a threat to their neighborhoods and lifestyles. Supporters saw it as a practical way to ensure civil rights, democratic principles, and understanding between races. If children of different races go to school together, their argument goes, they can adjust better when they meet up again in the workplace or other circumstances. Since interdependence of all the institutions is a sociological fact, antibusing fervor cannot be simply dismissed as racism in action. In Boston race, class, ethnicity, and finally, "turf" were all involved (Formisano, 1991). And in an Akron, Ohio study on a sample of white adults, opponents of busing preferred neighborhood schools and criticized the perceived costs of busing. As the researchers point out, "these do not appear to be code words for racism" (McClendon & Pestello, 1987:70).

All regions eventually were subject to court-ordered busing, and only a few experienced any form of protest, much less violent protest. A conflict perspective can help explain why. Antibusing protests were most frequent where traditional patterns of racial segregation were breaking down, that is, where African Americans were moving into formerly white neighborhoods. "Turf," as the name itself implies, was being contested. School and neighborhood desegregation involves both perceived and real threats to dominance, based on competition for scarce resources. This escalates the rate of white protest against busing, as research on school desegregation in forty-three urban areas suggests (Olzak et al., 1994). Competition is higher for those with lower levels of resources. A study of five Connecticut high schools participating in a voluntary desegregation plan found

Segregation by race is illegal in public schools, but residential patterns such as "white flight" to the suburbs have created schools that are increasing in racial segregation.

that lower levels of community wealth are associated with lower support for integration (Miller, 1990).

Busing was partly responsible for "white flight" to the suburbs and a resegregation of inner-city schools, because people with the most resources could move to the suburbs. Schools remain highly segregated because of residential segregation (Di Bona, 1988; Rivkin, 1994). Although later cross-district busing and the creation of magnet schools eased desegregation fears, competition over remaining resources is an ongoing problem. Desegregation is viewed as threat or opportunity.

How successful are desegregation programs? The evidence is mixed. Support for school integration remains strong, but support for busing to achieve it is weak. Interestingly, while white suburban opposition has decreased, city and black opposition has increased. African American parents are dismayed that their children cannot get into magnet schools due to spaces reserved for suburban whites. Others feel insulted when it is implied that their children cannot adequately learn unless in the presence of white students (Raffel, 1985; Formisano, 1991; Hardaway, 1995). This sentiment is confirmed by research showing that levels of self-esteem are virtually the same for African American and white students within all racial compositions (Inniss, 1987). African Americans in integrated schools make less progress in reading comprehension than their counterparts in segregated schools (Entwistle & Alexander, 1994). However, in integrated schools that offer supportive environments, achievement levels increase for minorities compared to those in segregated schools (Mahard & Crain, 1983; Green, 1985).

There is no consensus on a "best" method for desegregation, and there is also no one way to measure success. Voluntary plans work better than mandatory ones, especially when they serve the wishes of parents of all races. Such plans are more likely to be successful if they are linked to voluntary transfer to magnet schools that produce long-term interracial exposure. White flight is reduced, especially when parents are made part of the decision-making process (Rossell, 1990; Mickelson & Ray, 1994). Case studies of desegregation efforts in several cities with large, poor, minority populations surrounded by mostly white affluent suburbs (Dayton, Rochester, Trenton, Wilmington, and Hartford) point to civic pride, community involvement, and a positive working relationship between city and state as factors that also influence desegregation success (Stave, 1995:130). For example, business and civic leaders may offer services that enhance schools, such as internships for both African American and white students. Government-funded programs that bring parents and teachers of bused students together with parents and teachers of host schools offer opportunities for dialogue on issues that impact all the children. Race relations are viewed more positively by a strong community–school linkage.

Even with the turmoil that school desegregation continues to cause, the United States is irreversibly a multiracial society. Consistent with the value of equal opportunity, the conviction is that children should not be brought up in isolation from races other than their own (Metz, 1994). The school becomes the place for carrying out this conviction (Willie, 1991). When progress is hampered, people lose faith in the ability of the government to enforce civil rights laws

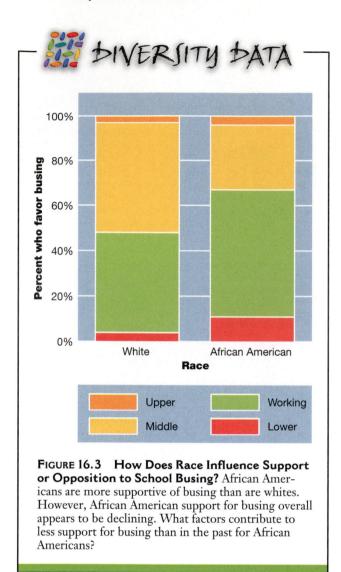

DIVERSITY DATA

FIGURE 16.3 How Does Race Influence Support or Opposition to School Busing? African Americans are more supportive of busing than are whites. However, African American support for busing overall appears to be declining. What factors contribute to less support for busing than in the past for African Americans?

(B. Anderson, 1994). In functionalist terms, social equilibrium is threatened. While debates still rage on how to accomplish integration, a wealth of research provides clear and consistent evidence that desegregated schooling has long-term benefits for African American inclusion in important areas of life. African Americans who attended desegregated schools are more likely to have friends of other races and be involved in activities and jobs that cross racial lines. Racial attitudes are also improved (Newman, 1990; Braddock et al., 1994; Dawkins & Braddock, 1994). A desegregated school is a meaningful path to a desegregated society.

LIFE CONNECTIONS: Who Goes to College?

Higher education in the United States is also experiencing enormous change as multiculturalism and global interdependence combine with continuing challenges that influence higher education.

Diversity in Higher Education

The democratization of American higher education occurred after World War II, when the GI Bill enabled veterans to enter colleges. Before that time, institutions of higher learning were reserved for primarily white, Protestant men from affluent families (S.V. Brown, 1996:71). The college population today reflects a considerably different student composition, but the academic doors are still slammed shut for most children living in poverty. Cost restricts opportunities for working and lower-middle class students, although they have a better chance to attend college than in the past.

Besides social class, college diversity has increased in terms of age, race, religion, gender, ethnicity, and number of international students. The decade between 1985 and 1995 saw almost a 60 percent increase in college enrollments for all categories of racial minorities—African American, Asian, Native American, and Latino. Their share of degrees at every level increased by about 19 percent over a twenty-year period (Carter & Wilson, 1995). This translates to a net increase of about 2 percent for minority share of all bachelor's degrees, with over half the increase among Asian Americans. Students from other countries gained 1.3 percent of all bachelors degrees, which is a higher percentage than the combined growth of Native American, African American, and Hispanic degree recipients (S.V. Brown, 1996:81). Gender composition on campus has reversed. Due mainly to the increase of part-time students, the majority of college students are women, and their numbers are expected to increase.

However, there are patterns to this diversity. As we have seen throughout the text, demographic

INTERNET ⟡ CONNECTIONS

The text discusses the issues surrounding school desegregation and the dilemma of busing. For a particularly critical and scathing point of view on *school busing*, go to: http://www.adversity.net/special/busing.htm ("School Busing 25 Years Later: Good Riddance to a Bad Idea"). After examining the contents of this Web site, answer the following questions: Do you believe that busing was a "bad idea" from its inception? Do you think that busing is a "dead issue," or does this practice hold some value in certain areas? What about "magnet schools"—what is your opinion of this strategy?

variables that now describe "diversity" are powerful determinants of behavior. For higher education, the variables of gender, race, and social class can predict the likelihood of entering college, where students go to college, what they major in, the probability that they will graduate, and how much money their degree will be worth. Think about how these demographic variables apply to your own college experience. Sociology offers explanations for these patterns.

Community Colleges

Community or two-year colleges typically channel students into two major groups. One group attends for career education in semiprofessional and technical fields, where skills must be learned but a college degree is not necessary. These students earn an "associate's degree" as well as certification in a given

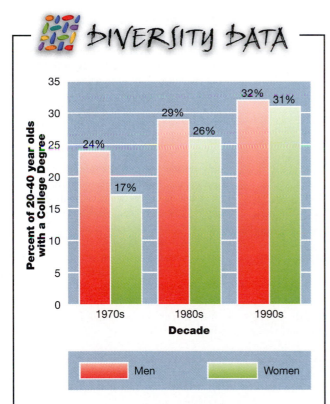

FIGURE 16.4   Percent of 20- to 40-year-olds with College Degrees, by Gender and Decade. The college graduation rate for both genders has steadily increased since the 1970s so that today about one-third of men and women are college graduates. Since women are now enrolled in college in greater numbers than men, do you think women with college degrees will eventually outnumber men?
Source: NORC. General Social Surveys, 1972–1996. Chicago: National Opinion Research Center, 1996. Reprinted by permission of NORC, Chicago, IL.

program, such as health, computer technology, paralegal studies, or mechanics. They are assured that a job is waiting for them at graduation. The other group of students at community colleges plans to transfer to four-year colleges. To the benefit of both groups, community colleges offer inexpensive courses, flexible schedules, and a variety of services to assess student interest and ability and to assist students in career choices. They serve the needs of a changing society that demands a pool of technically competent people and ongoing training and retraining programs. They also provide enrichment courses and continuing education for the community at large.

A less optimistic view of community colleges recognizes that career-education programs prepare students for jobs offering less opportunity for advancement. Because career-education students take few liberal arts courses, they are less prepared to attend four-year college programs after they have been employed for a while. Many of their community college courses are not accepted for transfer at a four-year college, so they may have to start all over again. Even for those who intend to transfer and graduate from a four-year college, the reality is that the vast majority do not. Many from this group eventually enroll in career-education programs. It is not surprising that women, racial minorities, and lower-SES students are disproportionately enrolled in community colleges and career-track programs. Although minority students have higher educational aspirations than white students, they are least likely to transfer to four-year colleges (Rendon & Hope, 1996). Community college enrollment may actually place limits on later career success (Lieberman, 1989; Monk-Turner, 1990; Rendon & Hope, 1996).

A Bachelor's Degree and a Job

For four-year colleges, the enrollment and job landscape has changed radically in the past twenty years. The predicted decline of the traditional 18- to 21-

INTERNET CONNECTIONS

The magazine *U.S. News and World Report* yearly ranks the nation's colleges on various indicators of quality. If you're curious how your own college rates, go to www.usnews.com/usnews/edu/college/corank.htm. If you were president of your college, what would you do to move up in the ratings?

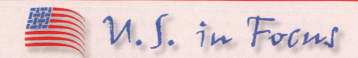

America's Violent Schools

It was Adolf Hitler's birthday. Armed with a semiautomatic rifle, two sawed-off shotguns, and dozens of homemade bombs, on April 20, 1999 two 17-year-old boys opened fire on classmates at Columbine High School, located in suburban Denver, Colorado. The massacre ended with 14 students and one teacher dead, including the two gunmen.

Violence in schools has risen dramatically. A national study of public schools reveals that during the school year 10 percent of all African American and 5 percent of all white students are wounded by deadly weapons while in school. Fighting, verbal abuse, theft, and assault are reported by students and teachers alike. Victimization rates are estimated to be as high as 20 percent for school populations. In some cities close to one-third of all students carry guns to school "for protection." The search for reasons for school violence has produced much speculation, but few definite answers. Sociologists point to three factors that offer the best leads connecting to violence in the schools.

1. The Peer Connection
The horror of the shootings in Colorado is magnified by a pattern of school violence that has surfaced in the last five years. Consider the following facts:

October, 1997: Pearl, Mississippi— A 16-year-old killed his mother and then went to his high school and opened fired, killing three and wounding seven.

December, 1997: West Paducah, Kentucky—A 14-year-old shot three students at an early morning high school prayer meeting.

March, 1998: Jonesboro, Arkansas— An 11- and a 13-year-old set off a fire alarm and killed four students and a teacher as the building was evacuated.

May, 1998: Springfield, Oregon—A 15-year-old killed his parents and shot twenty-four students at school, killing two of them.

All these shootings were done by youths who carefully planned their attacks, relied on the element of surprise, and were armed to the teeth. They were all white and middle to upper-middle class. Most important, while their grades marked them as reasonably successful students, they were later identified as relatively passive, exhibiting little empathy for others, and feeling ostracized or shamed by their peers. They may have been part of a clique made fun of by the popular kids in their schools. The common denominator is that isolation and humiliation by peers may have been the long-term triggers for the attacks. Revenge was the motive.

2. The Drug and Gang Connection
Fueling school violence is the world outside the schools. Gangs and drugs are the most important sources of violence. One in eight whites, one in three Latinos, and one in five African American students say that gangs openly operate in their schools. A Los Angeles area school district reports that among eleventh graders, 7.4 percent use marijuana daily and almost 40 percent used two or more dangerous drugs at the same time during the last six months. When families are unable to deal with these outside pressures, schools face classrooms filled with insecure and frustrated children.

3. The Media Connection
Although the media are always ripe to be blamed for violence, the link to the Denver massacre is a strong one. One of the killers was addicted to extremely violent video games such as *Doom* and *Quake*. With some games, the "gore level" can be set. The killer regularly surfed hate websites, and his own website provided information about building bombs and lethal weapons. The jury is still out on whether hours spent in a killing-machine fantasy world of video games, movies, and Internet make "a real-life version more palatable" (Chapter 5). Millions of teens who consume the popular culture of violent media do not become killers. Media attention to school shootings is clearly implicated in copycat versions, but most are not as lethal. However, the media connection cannot be dis-

---

year-old college population occurred in the 1980s and literally forced some smaller liberal arts colleges out of business. Other colleges responded with renewed effort to bring in "nontraditional" students, especially "re-entry" women, who, either by choice or circumstances such as divorce, seek alternatives to homemaker roles (Bradburn et al., 1995). The student base is additionally augmented by adults whose degrees are being paid for by their current employers. Recruitment of minority and international students has also accelerated. In this sense, multiculturalism and diver-

sity have allowed many institutions not only to survive, but to grow.

This change has been a mixed blessing. There is concern that some colleges have lowered standards to become "diverse" for reasons of economic survival, especially in terms of federal support (Hardaway, 1995; Zwerling, 1996). Social justice issues take a back seat. Another concern is that in catering to the workplace, colleges are abandoning liberal arts missions. Employers who pay for educational expenses desire skill-based programs that are readily transferred to

missed as a critical factor in school violence.

Violence is one result of the broader community problems but not the initial cause. Loss of self-esteem and adolescent insecurity cut across all classes and races and may also contribute to violence. Violence becomes an acceptable method to settle "grudges" or deal with problems facing teenagers. Using the vantage point of social structure, sociology supports several prescriptions for dealing with school violence.

In schools with a high number of students in poverty, the infusion of hope, power, opportunity, and equity into the community can help bring about positive social change. Los Angeles has implemented Operation Safe Schools (OSS), a coordinated drug-prevention effort involving parents, students as peer educators, the police, and numerous community agencies. Results are encouraging. Arrests have decreased, the student dropout rate is down, and reported drug use has declined. At the level of the school district, there are good arguments that "get-tough" responses—such as facility lock-downs, metal detectors, armed guards in the hallways, elimination of sports and after-school activities—actually fail to create safe environments. They not only interrupt learning but produce mistrust, resistance, and fear, especially since they are often applied according to race and class lines. Humanizing schools by involving the community, teaching conflict resolution, improving school spaces, and using mentoring appropriately offer more

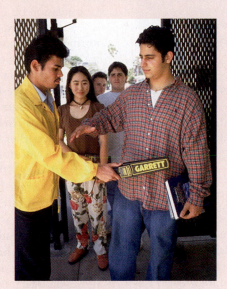

The use of guns and other weapons by American schoolchildren has prompted security measures such as daily weapons inspections of everyone entering a school building.

successful strategies. The public is supportive of such strategies. In the wake of the Colorado killings, polls showed that almost half the public believe the most effective way of preventing school shootings is to pay more attention to antisocial behavior and also identify and intervene when children are ongoing targets of peer ridicule. Only 21 percent suggest improving school-security technology as the best approach. This does not mean that "incorrigible," violence-prone students should be left unchecked or even allowed to remain in the school. It does mean, however, that a self-fulfilling prophecy is a real possibility when coercion is the accepted

method to combat violence.

At the teaching level, disrespect and student inattentiveness contribute to teacher burnout. The threat of violence keeps many from entering the profession or pushes otherwise good teachers out. Teachers also confront the daily reality of their students' lives and their increasing encounters of violence and death. Research suggests that teachers need to respond to this reality openly. From a symbolic interactionist view, the teacher shifts from the role of knowledge-giver and acknowledges the fears of the students. In this way, affirming students can become part of classroom pedagogy and used as a basis for learning.

1. Which of the three connections to school violence—peers, drugs/gangs, or media—offers the best route for intervention to curb the problem? Which sociological theory best supports your choice?
2. How much will reducing the availability of guns also reduce the threat of violence in the schools? How can this reduction occur in a society where freedom to bear arms is considered an important individual right?

Sources: Callison & Richards-Colocino, 1993; Ramirez, 1993; Palermo & Simpson, 1994; Toby, 1994; Johnson, 1995; Noguera, 1995; Bai et al., 1999; "Diary," 1999; Gibbs et al., 1999; Robbins, 1999.

the workplace. They often will pay for courses in accounting and marketing but not for courses in history and literature—but both are needed for the degree. Thus colleges have been forced into a version of the career-education dilemma faced by community colleges. The paradox is this: Career success requires a liberal arts-based education from a four-year college, but students are reluctant to major in areas that do not offer "practical" skills. The dilemma is reflected in often-heard comments during registration, such as "Why do I have to take philosophy? I'm going to be

an accountant." This orientation has led to an explosion of some majors, such as business and preprofessional studies, and a decline of others, such as literature and the humanities.

Another element of the paradox is that businesses are reluctant to hire graduates who come from programs that are too skill-based. Many of the flood of business majors vying to enter the corporate world have found themselves less competitive precisely because they did not have a strong liberal arts background. The demand for broadly educated rather

Table 16.3	Bachelor's Degrees Earned, Selected Fields	
	1990	1995
Business and Management	246,698	234,323
English Language and Literature	47,519	51,901
Liberal and General Studies	27,985	33,356
Philosophy, Religion, and Theology	12,068	12,854
Social Sciences and History	118,083	128,154

Source: Adapted from Table 325. U.S. Bureau of the Census, 1998.

than narrowly trained graduates has increased. Beyond necessary technical competence in some areas, such as computer programming, businesses provide the job-specific training that students cannot get in college anyway. If students are trained for what is relevant today, they may be shut out of the workplace tomorrow, when "relevance" changes and there is no core knowledge base to fall back on. The trend in majors has shifted, with an increase in liberal arts fields and a decline in business areas (Table 16.3).

The shift in popularity of majors is due both to marketplace realities and to the repackaging of college courses to appeal to students faced with an uncertain economic future. Recognizing this paradox, many colleges are now designing unique programs that combine ingredients of professional and liberal learning. On the applied side, curriculum requirements for a variety of majors now include an internship or volunteer work that can be highlighted as "practical experience" on a new graduate's résumé. On the liberal arts side, courses in multicultural, gender, and global studies are now required. Interdisciplinary programs, particularly between professional schools and colleges of arts and science, are gaining in popularity.

≋ SOCIETY CONNECTIONS: Student Achievement

Any complacency Americans may have had about the quality of their schools was severely jolted by a 1983 report, *A Nation at Risk*. Educational achievement in America, wrote the authors, had experienced a steep, twenty-year decline. Several measures were used to support the point: Scores on standardized tests, such as the Scholastic Aptitude Test, sharply declined. **Functional illiteracy,** the inability to do the reading, writing, or basic math necessary to carry out daily activities, dramatically increased. American children lagged far behind other nations in achievement, especially in mathematics and verbal skills. Mediocrity ruled. The United States was "at risk," because if schools produce people who cannot be competitive,

the very future of the nation is at stake (National Commission on Excellence in Education, 1983).

Standardized achievement tests have become the norm for determining quality of education and America's report card of achievement is not a positive one. Current evidence from the Scholastic Aptitude Test taken by college-bound seniors shows an overall decline in achievement since 1967 (U.S. Bureau of the Census, 1998). In overall achievement, children do better in the earlier grades, but by high school, performance in most subjects has dropped considerably (Arthur Fisher, 1992). Declines in mathematics appear to have plateaued, but verbal scores suggest a downward trend (Murray, 1993; U.S. Bureau of the Census, 1999). And even with an increase in the number of years of schooling, reading levels have stagnated and functional illiteracy has actually increased. About 21 percent of the adult population reads at the lowest level, so they would be unable, for example, to understand simple instructions on medical prescriptions (Mullis & Jenkins, 1990; U.S. Department of Education, 1993; United Nations Development Program, 1998).

Global Comparisons

Given its legacy of economic superiority and educational excellence, Americans are shocked by how public schools stack up in a global comparison. In almost all measures, achievement levels of American children are far lower than those in many other nations, including those in the developing world. In testing thousands of students throughout the world at different ages and school levels, U.S. high school seniors are typically at the lower end of the measurement scale (United Nations Development Program, 1998).

The greatest gaps are in mathematics and science (Table 16.4). Overall, Japanese and Chinese students outperform U.S. students. Asian students appear to have a mathematical edge. Math scores for Asian *American* students are higher than for Caucasian Americans, but lower than for East Asians (Chen & Stevenson, 1995). This pattern suggests the importance of cultural influences in academic performance. A major study of attitudes and achievement finds Asian American and East Asian parents believe that effort is the road to success. Americans in general believe that hard work pays off, but they also believe more strongly in limits due to natural ability (Stevenson, 1992). Therefore, American children may be discouraged from pursuing subjects their parents perceive as too difficult for them.

This rather dismal picture of student achievement in America brightens when we examine the data through sociological eyes. First, a wider range of students are now in school and staying in school longer.

Table 16.4	Ranking by Country on TIMSS* Average Scores for 13-Year-Olds			
Maths			**Science**	
1	Singapore	643	Singapore	607
2	South Korea	607	Czech Republic	574
3	Japan	603	Japan	571
4	Hong Kong	588	South Korea	565
5	Belgium (F+)	565	Bulgaria	565
6	Czech Republic	564	Netherlands	560
7	Slovakia	547	Slovenia	560
8	Switzerland	545	Austria	558
9	Netherlands	541	Hungary	554
10	Slovenia	541	England	552
11	Bulgaria	540	Belgium(F+)	550
12	Austria	539	Australia	545
13	France	538	Slovakia	544
14	Hungary	537	Russia	538
15	Russia	535	Ireland	538
16	Australia	530	Sweden	535
17	Ireland	527	United States	534
18	Canada	527	Canada	531
19	Belgium (W+)	526	Germany	531
20	Thailand	522	Norway	527
21	Israel	522	Thailand	525
22	Sweden	519	New Zealand	525
23	Germany	509	Israel	524
24	New Zealand	508	Hong Kong	522
25	England	506	Switzerland	522
26	Norway	503	Scotland	517
27	Denmark	502	Spain	517
28	United States	500	France	498
29	Scotland	498	Greece	497
30	Latvia	493	Iceland	494
31	Spain	487	Romania	486
32	Iceland	487	Latvia	485
33	Greece	484	Portugal	480
34	Romania	482	Denmark	478
35	Lithuania	477	Lithuania	476
36	Cyprus	474	Belgium (W+)	471
37	Portugal	454	Iran	470
38	Iran	428	Cyprus	463
39	Kuwait	392	Kuwait	430
40	Columbia	385	Columbia	411
41	South Africa	354	South Africa	326

*Third International Maths and Science Study International Acreage = 500
Source: World Education League, 1997:21.

adolescents and deal with the barriers that interfere with their capacity to learn. Their lives are filled with such massive deprivation that education is often a low priority. But like all Americans they have a right to an education (Powers & Jaklitsch, 1993). Comparing high school students in the 1930s with those of the 1990s means comparing 50 percent of the age group then with 95 percent of the age group now. A person defined as literate in 1990 may be redefined as illiterate by 2000 or ten years later (Kaestle, 1995:343).

Second, educational standards have not decreased but increased. Recent data show no decline in either knowledge of history or reading comprehension (National Center for Education Statistics, 1997). Both the actual number and proportion of high school students enrolled in core areas of science, math, and foreign language have also increased (Whittington, 1992; Angus & Mirel, 1995). But educational needs are rising so fast that the schools can barely keep up. The illusion, but not the reality, is one of decline because more demands are placed on the schools. It can result in real decline if the lag continues to widen the gap between what is demanded and what is produced in education. For example, computer literacy for teachers lags behind student needs. Schools may not be doing enough to keep America competitive with other industrialized nations.

Third, global comparisons must account for the proportion of students who continue school beyond a certain age. It is methodologically unsound to simply compare countries without considering the average number of years most students remain in school. In India, Bangladesh, and parts of sub-Saharan Africa, for example, illiteracy rates range from to 50 to 90 percent (United Nations Development Program, 1998). In rural areas, very few children advance beyond primary grades, especially the girls. As in an earlier United States, schools are reserved for the elite. Level of economic development in each country is probably a better indicator to compare achievement levels.

Fourth, both globally and nationally, tests need to be constructed so that they are as culturally unbiased as possible. The same questions are read by students of very different backgrounds, making it difficult to know whether test scores are due to a student's achievement or to a student's culture or subculture. Since race, class, ethnicity, religion, and gender are also culturally relevant this becomes a monumental task, especially in America's multicultural classrooms. Some believe that it is impossible to construct a completely unbiased test, so additional measures of achievement are needed. *Triangulation*, using multiple indicators and methods for data collection, adds to validity or accuracy of the results (Chapter 2).

The state of student achievement in America is complex, and it is difficult to determine whether the reported decline is empirically justified. What is clear,

Rates of school attainment, high school graduation, and college attendance have steadily increased. A more diverse student population is taking these tests today. The United States is educating more students and more difficult students to levels that a generation ago would have been available only to a favored elite. For instance, there are programs to find homeless

Examination Hell in Japan

The expression *shito goraku* guides Japanese students as they prepare for university entrance exams: "Those who sleep four hours a day will pass; those who sleep five hours will fail." Often referred to as "examination hell," the competition for entrance into the most prestigious universities in Japan is cutthroat. In Japan, the important thing is the university one graduates from; the subjects one studies are secondary. Success or failure on an entrance examination affects a student's entire future, since the prospect of finding a good job depends on the school attended. Indeed, major corporations restrict recruitment to a few select universities. Therefore, the Japanese believe that this cutthroat competition for university slots is necessary.

Japan's public schools are staunchly egalitarian and have a high commitment to mixed ability students. Students are not tracked by ability, either high or low, and individualized learning is rare. Homogeneity and sameness are valued in education, not diversity and difference. Disabled students, for example, are often rejected for high school in Japan, regardless of their scores on entrance exams. In fact, many Japanese believe diversity and catering to individual differences has hurt American education. Less than half of Japanese people see the United States' educational system as admirable. Although this view of American education may be offensive to Americans, the Japanese point out that 95 percent of Japan's students graduate from high school.

The egalitarian system of Japanese education is highly effective for the majority of students. There is a tendency to pass students to the next grade so that they can stay with their grade cohorts. But when university entrance exams determine a person's future economic life, parents are willing to spend a great deal of money for special advantages for their children. Without supplemental lessons, some students would fall behind in the competition for entrance into the best universities. To meet the need for supplemental learning, *juku* ("cram schools") have become a thriving business throughout Japan; 90 percent of urban students in Japan are in some form of juku.

By the eighth grade ambitious students are beginning to prepare seriously for high school entrance exams. Juku likely begin here. For the most motivated students, tutoring programs lasting 4 to 5 hours a day after school and 8 to 10 hours on weekends are common. High schools are ranked according to their academic standing in the community, and like the university, examinations are the main basis for admission. The best high schools better prepare students for the university exams. All Japanese high school students are affected by the competition for college admission, but only 10 percent can be said to experience the intense competition for entrance into the most prestigious universities.

A version of the cram school is called *yobiku* and exists solely for the purpose of preparing students for university entrance exams. Yobiku primarily cater to *ronin*, who in Japan's feudal times were masterless samurai, wandering warriors. Today this term refers to students who wander between schools, having graduated from one without being admitted to another. Often they have failed the entrance exam to the university of their choice once or twice. Families pay as much as $5,000 a year for a first-rate yobiku where students may stay for a year or two to try for the necessary grade. Cram schools have created an enormous financial burden for Japanese parents and a psychological burden for children. Suicide rates for Japanese adolescents, for example, are highest in April when grades are posted and the educational fate of the young test-takers is publicly acknowledged.

Japan now recognizes the national obsession of university admissions tests as a social problem. Attempts to defuse the examination war have centered on dialogues between corporations, schools, and parents. Corporations are encouraged to move away from limiting the universities from which they will hire graduates. Smaller corporations that want to attract students from the best universities are joining the dialogue. These smaller companies argue that the current university-corporation link limits overall competition and can eventually hurt Japan's economic success. It may be that Japan's economic downturn will prompt more dialogue to resolve this social problem. To date, however, examination hell is a fact of student life in Japan.

1. What fundamental social values in Japan are reflected in the rise of cram schools and an acceptance of examination hell?
2. How would functionalists and conflict theorists explain the successes and failures of Japan's egalitarian public school system and its juku counterpart?

Sources: Kenmochi, 1992; McAdams, 1993; Halloran, 1994; Keizai Koho Center, 1999.

Female illiteracy is very high in those parts of the developing world, such as India and Mali, where girls must work in the fields, where women marry early, and where wives must take care of all domestic tasks, including food production.

however, is that America cannot afford to be complacent about its schools. Perhaps the storm of controversy erupting from the reports of educational decline has provided a valuable latent function. Educational reform is now near the top of government and community agendas.

Toward Educational Reform

Both the Bush (*America 2000* program) and Clinton (*Goals 2000* program) administrations advocated ambitious educational goals to that were to be realized by the year 2000. These included the following:

1. All children should start school ready to learn.
2. The United States should have a 90 percent high school graduation rate.
3. Illiteracy should be eliminated.
4. Schools should be drug free and violence free.
5. Competence testing in core subjects should be done throughout schooling.

6. The United States should have a "world class" educational system available to everyone.
7. The United States should be second to none in science and math. (Ravitch, 1995; Corrigon, 1996).

Implementing these goals involves determining what children *should* know and *how* to provide that knowledge. Although the year 2000 is already behind us, prompted by the "Risk" report, reform efforts continue. They center on stricter discipline, better teacher training, upgrading buildings, increased homework, a longer school year, higher levels of student responsibility, and less school bureaucracy. High school graduation requirements have been expanded to include more knowledge in core areas. This is the "back to basics" curriculum embraced by many school districts with the blessing of parents. What the "basics" include, in terms of both subject area and content, remains unresolved.

While such reforms look great on paper, critics charge that they are merely technical and bureaucratic adjustments that do not address the real reasons for lack of student achievement (Grubb, 1995; Ravitch, 1995). As sociology continually reminds us, to regard social institutions such as education, family, and government as separate from one another is not only unrealistic, it is impractical. For example, when student achievement is based solely on improving the school environment, the home environment of students may be ignored. School facilities may be improved, but when a child comes to school with no breakfast, even the best teachers will find that what the child can achieve is limited. Another example is when private schools are held up as models for student discipline. But when private school students have discipline problems they are often shunted off to public schools where admission cannot be refused. Schools can be restructured to make them less bureaucratic, but higher achievement and more equity is associated with smaller high schools—and that is a matter of money and politics, not bureaucracy.

At the individual level, there are differences in a child's *readiness* to learn and her or his *opportunity* to learn. The former deals with an individual approach to learning, the latter deals with how social structure impacts it. Only one of the goals on the educational priorities' list squarely deals with this issue. The Carnegie Foundation has expanded the "readiness to learn" goal to provide an educational mandate for the nation (Boyer, 1994). But note how the list also accounts for the reality of differences in opportunity as well as linkages with other institutions. As such, it offers a sound sociological model for educational reform. The steps are:

1. *A healthy start.* To be ready to learn every child must have a healthy birth, be well nourished, and well protected in the early years of life.
2. *Empowered parents.* Since parents are the first teachers, children should live in secure homes that encourage language development.
3. *Quality preschool.* All school districts should establish programs.
4. *A responsive workplace.* Employers need family-friendly policies, such as providing access to quality day care and flexible scheduling.
5. *Television as teacher.* Expose children to educational and enriching television.
6. *Neighborhoods for learning.* Provide safe, friendly, and improved places for children to grow and explore. Facilities such as museums and libraries should be accessible.
7. *Connections across the generations.* Children need a sense of security and continuity. Schools, day-care centers, and retirement villages should be linked to bring together young and old.

Along with these goals, the Carnegie Foundation suggests programs that can help implement them. Examples are federal initiatives such as Project Head Start, a preschool program to ensure that children are armed with the necessary skills for kindergarten, and WIC (Women, Infants, and Children), a nutrition program for eligible mothers and infants. Undoubtedly, the goals are overly ambitious, but they carry forth the recurring sociological theme that schools alone cannot be completely responsible for either the rise or fall of student achievement.

The problems facing academic achievement cannot easily be put aside. But they need to be viewed in light of an increasingly diverse society where the value of quality schooling for all is passionately embraced. Schools must insure that uniform standards are maintained, and all students from all backgrounds receive the same quality of education. Schools must also nurture individual talent and desire (Kirp, 1995). Schools bring us together and also separate us. But sociologist Christopher Jencks (1988) notes that there is no one right standard of fair treatment. History points out that American education serves a political agenda considered to be in the best interests of all the groups making up a democratic society. The schools are expected to pursue this agenda—school is the one institution through which all children must pass.

SUMMARY

1. In the United States, education helps to unify a diverse society. It socializes children, helps the children of foreign-born parents to assimilate into mainstream society, and prepares the younger generation to adapt to a rapidly changing culture and economy.
2. While functionalists see the schools as nurturers of talent and ability, regardless of a child's social class, conflict theorists charge that the schools reinforce the social-class structure. Social class is, in fact, the best overall indicator of educational achievement.
3. U.S. schools mirror the communities in which they are located: Some are well staffed, well furnished, and well maintained, while others are rundown, ill equipped, and poorly staffed. Thus

students from poor communities are at a disadvantage.

4. Research shows that within American schools, students are tracked to different academic levels based more on their class, race, and gender than on their ability and past achievement.

5. According to symbolic interactionism, assigning students to lower levels, or tracks, reduces their self-esteem and their motivation to achieve. To avoid these effects, educators have adopted a policy of mainstreaming, including placing special-needs students in classrooms whenever possible.

6. A society's educational level affects its level of economic development, its marriage and birth rates, and its income and nutritional levels. Because education has such a profound effect on people's living conditions, it is a powerful agent of social change.

7. Educational diversity in America is increasing. Demographers predict that by the year 2025, slightly more than half the students in U.S. classrooms will be people of color. The realization that the racial and ethnic makeup of the nation's schools is changing has produced a shift in educational policy, away from a Western, or Eurocentric, model and toward a multicultural curriculum.

8. Busing of students was instituted to remedy inequalities in the school related to racial segrega-

tion. But it has not eliminated school segregation, and its educational results have been mixed.

9. Though the student bodies at four-year colleges and universities have become more diverse in terms of their age, race, religion, ethnicity, and nationality, most are still drawn disproportionately from the middle and upper classes. Women, racial minorities, and working and lower-class students are overrepresented at community colleges.

10. Over the last three decades, standardized test scores declined and functional illiteracy increased among American students compared to students in other countries. However, it is difficult to compare data from different countries on test scores, a wider range of students are in schools, educational standards have increased, and the tests may be culturally biased.

11. Educational reformers are seeking to improve achievement through a "back to basics" approach and standards-based competency testing.

12. Sociologists suggest that educational reform must consider that institutions are not separate. Also a child's readiness to learn is different from the opportunity to learn. Social structure impacts individual learning.

KEY TERMS

busing 418
credentialism 406
end point fallacy 411

functional illiteracy 424
hidden curriculum 408
magnet schools 418

mainstreaming 411
meritocracy 406
tracking 409

CRITICAL THINKING QUESTIONS

1. Given the fact that diversity in education is now the norm, how can education serve individual students as well as broader social needs? How can educational equity be achieved for both the individual and society?

2. From a symbolic interactionist perspective, demonstrate how the labeling process involving teachers, peers, and parents can be used as an enhancement rather than as a liability for student achievement.

3. Efforts at desegregation of the public schools in the United States have revolved around busing. What other methods can schools use to increase interracial contact and understanding? How can the success of these methods be evaluated?

4. What proposals would functionalists, conflict theorists, and symbolic interactionists offer to decrease school violence? Consider the role of institutional interdependence in these proposals.

17 RELIGION

OUTLINE

Religious Secularism

More than 90 percent of the people in the United States state a religious preference. Many who join churches, send their children to religious schools, and gladly identify themselves as religious are honest and intelligent people who take their religion seriously. Yet the religion prevailing in the United States has lost most of its authentic Christian or Jewish content. Even when thinking, feeling, or acting religiously, their thinking is not clearly related to the faith they profess. Americans may be a religious people—but they are secularly religious. (Adapted from Herberg, 1983:3)

Among the Believers

An eager gathering of Christians speaking in tongues . . . another group blocking access to a clinic that performs abortions . . . the rhythmic chanting of the crowd at rallies protesting the movie, *The Last Temptation of Christ*, or *The Satanic Verses*, whose British author, Salman Rushdie, was put under an Islamic death threat for publishing them . . . hundreds of "Moonie" couples at Madison Square Garden having their wedding vows blessed by Rev. Sun Myung Moon himself . . . the fervent worship of political leader Kim Il Sung by North Korean school children . . . a woman being beaten in Afghanistan because her veil left part of her ankles uncovered . . . Catholic priests in Latin America risking death by using scripture in the name of social justice. All these scenes evoke a sense of unease. This is the world of the fundamentalist—no matter whether Allah, Christ, or a godlike political figure is being worshipped. Fundamentalists have no doubt about their beliefs and want to clear up any doubts you may have. (Partly adapted from Swift, 1991: 99–100)

Reaching the Gate to Paradise

In 1997 near San Diego, thirty-nine people of the Heaven's Gate cult, under leader Marshall Applewhite, dressed themselves in black, ate drugged applesauce, and died in waves in an immaculately planned mass suicide. They believed angelic presences would allow an escape from their earthly bonds to be with God in the eternity of space. This was to be accomplished in a spaceship hiding behind the Hale-Bopp comet, which was making a rare appearance, to touch the souls of those who believe God sends messages in the night sky. An entire space-related theology formed the foundation of Heaven's Gate that allowed its believers to reach paradise sooner than the rest of the world. (Schodolski & Madigan, 1997)

All religions search for ways to reconcile faith with modern life, especially in societies experiencing rapid social change. These vignettes suggest ways people have accommodated their lives and faiths to modernity. The first suggests that some Americans may identify themselves as religious but that the religion they practice today is different than in the past. The second suggests that modern life, as viewed by some fervent believers, is an affront to their religion, so they may deal with the affront by cementing ties with other believers—whether on a picket line, a mass marriage, or even in a beating that may be permissable in the eyes of the state. The third suggests that people seeking answers to the riddles of modern life may join religious groups offering simple, but deadly, solutions.

Clearly there are major disagreements regarding how best to harmonize religion and modernity. People may believe that religion must adapt to social change. For others, adaptation means surrendering the faith to the forces of **secularization,** the process in which religion, challenged by science and modernization, loses its influence on society, thereby threatening its very existence. The "secularly religious" of the first vignette may represent this adaptation. The counterchallenge to secularization occurs with religious resurgence, mostly in the form of **fundamentalism,** a movement designed to revitalize faith by returning to the traditional ways the religion was practiced in the past. Traditional practices of fundamentalists are based on literal interpretation of religious doctrine. Although fundamentalists agree that "authentic" religious content *has* been lost and must be revitalized, they disagree on what this content should look like today. Can these two processes—secularization and fundamentalism—occur at the same time in the same society? This question will be addressed by examining evidence related to secularization and fundamentalism and how the political setting, especially in the way a society accommodates different religions, influences both processes. Besides seeking the hearts and minds of individuals, religions also seek the political blessings of the nation in which they exist. Finally, this chapter will show that while the tides of secularization and fundamentalism may sweep through the United States, most citizens cannot be counted as either secular or fundamentalist.

THEORETICAL PERSPECTIVES ON RELIGION

Sociologists who study religion examine the social framework through which religion operates. Different explanations for the influence of religion on society are offered by the various sociological theories. Sociologists are particularly interested in how the processes of fundamentalism and secularization are swayed by **religious pluralism,** where many religions are tolerated in a society and often compete with one another for members. We will see how each sociological theory offers insights into why religious pluralism may or may not thrive in society.

Functionalism

Émile Durkheim's brilliant scientific study of religion, *The Elementary Forms of Religious Life* (1912/1954) is regarded as the most important functionalist perspective on religion. His definition of **religion** as a "unified system of beliefs and practices relative to sacred things" is at the core of sociological thinking about religion.

This simple definition weaves together three important elements. First, religion must have beliefs and practices that are organized in some manner, usually in the form of a specific **theology,** a systematic formulation of religious doctrine. Individual expressions of spirituality do not become religion until common denominators organize them in some fashion. Second, the system of religious beliefs must be translated into behavior. Faith must be observable so that religious behavior and practices become *rituals.* Third, Durkheim argues that all known religious beliefs, no matter how simple or complex, presuppose a classification of everything in the world into two distinct,

nonoverlapping categories. One category represents religious or **sacred** things that are set apart from the everyday world, inspire awe and reverence, and are often imbued with transcendent qualities; the opposite category is the **profane,** the world of everyday objects. In this context, do not confuse the word profane with "bad." It simply means anything that is *not* sacred.

Notice that Durkheim does not use the word "supernatural" in his definition; for him religious belief is not necessarily tied to belief in divinities. To show that supernatural beings may be absent or have minor importance to the religion, he used ancient Australian *totemism,* religious beliefs that animals or plants have a special relationship with a tribal group and act as its guardians. The key to religion, then, is not the existence of god or gods, but that the sacred world is the world of religion as defined by each society. In your classroom a desk is a profane object, but if the room is used for a religious ritual at a different time, the desk becomes an altar and is therefore translated into a sacred object. There is a hierarchy of the sacred, in Durkheim's terms, "sacred things of every degree." Jerusalem is a sacred place for Jews, Christians, and Muslims, who share common religious roots. Synagogues, churches, and mosques scattered throughout the world are also sacred, but of a lesser degree than those located in Jerusalem. Hindus make pilgrimages to the sacred waters of the Ganges in Varanasi, India, more sacred than in other places where the Ganges flows. Religion is a cultural universal but its expression is infinitely varied. Each society will define what belongs to the sacred world and conduct its religious practices accordingly.

Functions of Religion

Durkheim's definition of religion is a good starting point for understanding the multiple connections between religion, society, and the individual. The reciprocal interdependence among these elements is evident when we inspect the functions of religion.

1. Religion is a significant source of social cohesion. It allows believers to establish strong bonds that form a moral community. For Durkheim, this integrative function is essential for society, providing the "social glue" necessary to bring together even a diversity of people within a specific system of religious beliefs (Miller, 1996).
2. With the establishment of a moral community, people find strength, comfort, and support from one another in times of crisis. Their social bond is reinforced by rituals that are celebrative, like weddings, or sorrowful, like funerals. Social support is also psychologically healthy.

Religion may be losing or winning in the battle against secularization. Christian revival meetings and gospel shows attract many people, but mainstream churches, especially in urban areas, are losing members.

3. By addressing "ultimate" questions that give life purpose and meaning, religion bolsters emotional well-being. Why am I alive? What is my purpose on earth? Why did my friend have to die? Religious faith can reduce the inevitable uncertainty and anxiety that arise with such questions. In this regard, science is religion's principal competitor, but historically science has been unable to provide the definitive answers people seek.

4. By addressing social as well as "private" questions, religion has a social service function. Why do evil and injustice exist in the world? What does my religion tell me about helping others? Theology can be a moral pathway. In many societies, religion provides an enormous amount of voluntary service that is beneficial to the community (Maton & Wells, 1995; Ammerman, 1997; Greeley, 1997).

5. In serving both moral and political purposes, religion has a social-control function. When government draws moral authority from religion, it legitimizes political authority. For centuries monarchs sought a religious seal of approval to "divinely sanction" their reigns. In contemporary religious states, political policies are dictated by religious interpretation; thus the government is imbued with the sacred. In these circumstances, a person who questions government authority is also questioning religious authority. The two social institutions—government and religion—come together as powerful mechanisms of social control (Turner, 1991).

6. Religion has a prophetic function that can influence social change. If a powerful religious leader emerges with a vision of an ideal reality as interpreted through a sacred text, a religiously based social movement may occur. Martin Luther King represents the prophetic function with the religious imagery in his "I Have A Dream" speech, which became a rallying cry for the civil rights movement, as did Mahatma Gandhi's message of nonviolence and Ayatollah Khomeini's "holy war" metaphor for the ideal society.

Despite the power of religion in carrying out these purposes, it can be dysfunctional when conflict between religious groups disrupts the former cohesion. According to functionalism, the social glue that binds the people in one group together in a moral community also separates it from other such communities. Consider the centuries of violence in the name of religion—from the Crusades and the witchhunts in medieval Europe to the ongoing Arab-Israeli conflict. A community may say "We are one in Christ," but there are also those who are "one" in Allah, Shiva, Buddha, or any of the contemporary religious leaders whose followers consider them divine in some manner. In a religiously pluralistic state, people can move between religious groups fairly easily and even recruit followers to begin a new church or even a new religion. Growing spiritual diversity weakens the sense of social cohesion that religion once reinforced (Berger, 1967; Demerath & Williams, 1990; Wilson, 1996). Durkheim's cohesive moral community falters when it becomes a simple matter to walk across the street into another church or synagogue.

Religion's function to transcend diversity often creates diversity. In addition, religion must compete with other institutional sources of identity, such as

In faiths around the world, such as in Eastern Europe or Southeast Asia, funerals are actually ways of celebrating a religion and serve to strengthen the social bonds of its believers.

race, social class, or nationality, which are being reactivated when formerly insulated societies become more globally interconnected. Competition between religions and between varying sources of identities may plant the seeds for secularization. For example, intermarriage rates between Protestants and Catholics have increased dramatically since the 1920s, while intermarriage rates between educational groups have decreased (Kalmijn, 1991). If education is an indicator of social class, it is replacing religion as a major factor in marriage. As the secularization hypothesis suggests, religion loses to social class a source of authority in mate selection.

Conflict Theory and Social Change

Conflict theory recognizes that religion is integral to social functioning, but focuses on its role in maintaining a stratification system that is beneficial to some and detrimental to others. The social-control function of religion is specifically targeted in this regard. In Karl Marx's (1848/1964) classic formulation, religion is the "opiate" of the people, using opiate as the symbol of the depressant drug opium to suggest apathy, lethargy, and a dulling of the senses. Religion lulls people into a *false consciousness*, Marx's term for the tendency of an oppressed class to accept the dominant ideology as expressed by the ruling class, thereby legitimizing the oppression. A divinely sanctioned monarchy, for example, perpetuates the belief that God is not only on the side of the nobility, but that God's will shuffled people into various social categories. As discussed later, Buddhist ideas about reincarnation and Confucian ideas about loyalty to rulers are other examples.

The potential for slave uprisings in the United States weakened when it was determined that slaves had souls just like white Christians and were subject to the same cycle of judgment and salvation. Chris-

tianity's notion that heavenly rewards come to those who lead humble, pious, and self-sacrificing lives bolstered in slaves an "other worldly" orientation that could deter efforts for change in this world. The religious opiate, then, works for slaves as well as other marginalized, poor, or oppressed groups. Contemporary African American churches may be so interested in uplifting their congregations' spirits that they inadvertently, and regrettably, bolster an unjust socioeconomic system (Baer & Singer, 1992). Accommodation means lack of protest, and it happens in the very place marginalized groups flock to: the church. In Marx's terms, the bourgeoisie maintains its power with no threat from the proletariat.

Conflict theory further argues that religion, by consoling those who are deprived, denies opportunities for social change necessary for greater equity. It also assumes that religion is used to serve prevailing economic or political interests. This view is accurate only if it can be determined that religion is the effect rather than the cause of social change. As will be detailed in Chapter 22, Max Weber (1905/1954) challenged this thesis with his argument that religion served as the catalyst for the growth of capitalism in early America.

According to Weber, the Protestant ethic stemmed from Calvinist beliefs in predestination—that God had already determined whether you were chosen for salvation. While your actual place as one of the "elect" could never be known, earthly signs such as material success hinted at heavenly favor. Hard work, discipline, and asceticism (austere practices involving self-denial) allowed for capital to be accumulated and then reinvested in business enterprises, whether farm or factory. For Weber, religion was not the passive recipient of economic processes. Calvinism and capitalism went hand in hand.

Finally, religion as a shaper of social change can be demonstrated in reference to religion's prophetic

Religion benefits society in many ways, such as providing volunteers for services that help the community. Churches often become recruiting centers or headquarters for programs such as Habitat for Humanity and Meals on Wheels.

function. Rather than passively accepting the world as it is, religion is used in pursuit of social justice, as in the U.S. civil rights movement or religiously based movements in other parts of the world. For example, liberation theology is a religious fundamentalism movement grounded in literal interpretations of Christian scripture promoting social justice. Advanced mainly by Catholic clergy who work directly with the poor, *liberation theology* challenges governments to redistribute wealth more equitably. Associated with radical social reform, Marxism, and challenging the powerful in the political economy, liberation theologians have been murdered for their activities (Sigmund, 1990; Smith, 1991). Although liberation theology originated in Latin America, it is gaining strength in the United States with the increase of Latino Catholic immigrants. It combines Marxism with Christianity, not in terms of the "opiate" of the people, but through support of economic equality through social change.

Rational Choice Theory

A newer contender to sociological theories of religion is rational choice theory, which applies a marketplace approach to religion, assuming that people's choice of religion will be determined by its costs and benefits to them (Iannaccone, 1991, 1992; Bruce, 1999). Rational choice theory is a good model to explain changes in membership patterns among competing religions in societies with high degrees of religious pluralism. It challenges the secularization model that religion is becoming irrelevant.

Contrary to what secularization predicts, religious pluralism actually increases religious adherence, because in many places of the world, especially the United States, there are no state-supported churches that interfere with a religious marketplace. Religion grows because of the rational choices people make to compensate for the trials and tribulations of life (Stark, 1991; Young, 1997). As in any free market economy, the religious economy must adapt to the needs of its consumers. As a result, religions become more vitalized and profits, in the form of new members, are increased.

RELIGIOUS BELIEFS AND ORGANIZATION

Religion is only one of the many different ways to structure social existence. The enormous variety of religious beliefs makes any classification scheme tenuous at best. In addition, there are criticisms that the most used schemes are rooted in Western European conceptions of religion, which do not adequately account for spirituality in the non-Western world and among indigenous peoples (Smart, 1989; Beyer, 1994). Émile Durkheim's definition of religion, with its emphasis on beliefs about the sacred, is a good tool to help categorize overall systems of religious beliefs

Rational choice theory looks at religion as a marketplace. People can shop the yellow pages in the phone book for the kind of church that appeals to them. Churches that gain the most members might be the best advertisers.

and the world religions and organizations that are grounded in them. The link between religious belief and institutionalized religion is an important one. As society becomes more complex and heterogenous, social institutions become more specialized. Spirituality, which may be identified by certain beliefs about the sacred, becomes institutionalized as religion.

Expressions of Religious Belief

Early anthropologists attempted to solve the classification problem by proposing that religious beliefs could be categorized not only by type of belief but also along evolutionary lines. Edward Tylor (1871), a founder of the anthropology of religion, argued that religion evolves through stages. The first stage is **animism,** the belief that supernatural beings or spirits capable of helping or hurting people inhabit living things (plants and animals) and inanimate objects (rocks and houses). Spirits have human emotions, so, like humans, they can be manipulated for one's own advantage or for the benefit of the community. Animist beliefs are among the earliest religious expressions, but continue today in many agriculturally based societies where various earth spirits are solicited in behalf of community needs for abundant crops, plentiful rain, or mild winters. In Durkheim's view, when spirits are beseeched for community rather than personal gains, animism plants the seeds for religion, uniting people into a moral community.

The next stage of religious evolution is characterized by **theism,** the belief in one or more independent supernatural beings (gods), who do not exist on earth and who are more powerful than people. **Polytheism** is the belief in many gods. It can be "diffuse," where all gods are equal, or "hierarchal," where gods are ranked according to degree of importance or power. Hierarchal polytheism is associated with the emergence of a separate, political state, which uses the gods to the benefit of governing powers. The ancient Roman Caesars and Egyptian pharaohs embodied god, human, and government. Contemporary Hinduism, which has both diffuse and hierarchical qualities, is an example of polytheism that has thrived for centuries. When one all-powerful, all-knowing god replaced a hierarchy of gods, polytheism was replaced by **monotheism** in Tylor's evolutionary scheme.

Tylor's categories of religious beliefs remain useful, but his evolutionary scheme is no longer reputable. Neither societies nor religions evolve along a single line of development. Also, since the evolutionary scheme ranks monotheism "higher" than any earlier form, it implies that contemporary animistic and polytheistic religions are somehow less evolved or substandard. Contemporary anthropology and sociol-

ogy would never support such a position, but as we will see, adherents of many religious faiths do not share the cultural relativist view (Chapter 3) of the social sciences that "all religions are created equal."

Some sociologists use the concept of **civil religion,** also called **secular religion,** to describe a system of values associated with sacred symbols that is integrated into the broader society and shared by the society's members, regardless of their individual religious affiliations (Bellah, 1967, 1970; Coleman, 1970). In the United States, Judeo-Christian religious symbolism is tied to a belief in a divinely sanctioned political system. Like other religions, civil religion brings intense emotional feelings that come with patriotism, nationalism, and reverence for symbols such as a nation's flag, the Declaration of Independence, national shrines like the Washington Monument and Lincoln Memorial, and the "holy days" of the Fourth of July and Thanksgiving. In the former Soviet Union, Communism as a civil religion was symbolized by Lenin's tomb, just as Mao's tomb functions in China. If civil religion were factored into Tylor's evolutionary scheme, it would be the highest, most evolved level, because patriotism does not rely on the concept of a god or the supernatural. It is a functional equivalent of religion, perhaps a "religion surrogate," because of its sacred and not its transcendent qualities.

Just as Tylor's scheme is unacceptable to contemporary social science, the very idea of civil religion with its "non-godlike" quality is offensive to many theologians and to those whose lives are conducted explicitly around their faith. For them, civil religion is implicit religion and therefore not religion at all (Marty, 1959, 1974; Bruce, 1996). While civil religion does meet Durkheim's definition of religion and can affirm common values, it is a weak competitor with any of the world's religions or most religious belief systems, because it cannot deal as effectively with ultimate questions regarding life and death. Although civil religions are more likely to be seen as part of the religious fold and accepted as such by sociologists of religion, they still come under theological suspicion because of their lack of a transcendent quality.

Types of Religious Organization

All societies structure religious beliefs in some fashion. In addition to the institutionalized religions that most belief systems eventually become, sociology identifies several types of religious organizations that help distinguish one system from another. More important, the forms that religious organizations take provide clues for understanding how religions change, develop, grow, or die.

As a formal organization, a church trains its leaders not only in theology but also in administrative functions, such as connecting the local parish to the broader church. Women now represent over half of seminary students.

A **church** is an inclusive religious body that brings together a moral community of believers in formalized worship and accommodates itself to the larger secular world. The church is an adaptive organization, an integral part of the social order that is organized similarly to other bureaucratic organizations in society. It employs professionally trained clergy who are usually ordained in seminaries representing a specific theology (Yinger, 1970; Greeley, 1972). Membership grows as people are born into the church or if the church successfully competes with other churches to attract new members. Churches are most prevalent in societies with a high degree of religious pluralism. The extensive institutional fabric of a church helps minimize tension between it and other social institutions, also competing for a peoples' time, loyalty, money, or energy.

When a church is institutionalized as a formal part of a state or nation and claims citizens as members, it is an **ecclesia,** or state religion. By definition, an ecclesia does not exist in societies with high religious pluralism, but there is considerable variation ac-

cording to degree of religious toleration and political influence in the society. The Church of Sweden is Lutheran and the Church of England is Anglican. Both are ecclesiae, both are secular states, and both allow other religious groups to worship and thrive in their societies. In contrast are the Islamic states of Iran, Saudi Arabia, and Pakistan, also ecclesia, but with low toleration of religious pluralism and governments that are organized and interpreted according to Islamic principles. Violation of religious principles is some Islamic states can result in imprisonment or beating, such as the case of the woman in the vignette.

Used in the context of religious pluralism, a **denomination** is a socially accepted and legally recognized body with bureaucratic characteristics similar to a church. Although a denomination is self-governing, it has an official relationship with a larger church. Religion and the rest of society relate to one another through denominations. They are multiple organizations of quasi-equal status that reflect an adjustment to religious pluralism (Greeley, 1972). The best examples of denominational societies in the Western world are the United States, Canada, the Netherlands, and Switzerland. Although the distinction between denomination and church is a blurry one, denominations are better devices than churches to classify the diversity encompassed in any world religion. Denominations of one religion share a common theology but different interpretations of it. They are also divided according to how strongly they embrace traditionalism and how much accommodation they make to the demands of a continually modernizing society (Johnstone, 1992). Among Christians there are Protestants, and among Protestants there are Lutherans and among Lutherans there are denominations—Lutheran Church Missouri Synod (LCMS) and Evangelical Lutheran Church in America (ELCA). According to Andrew Greeley (1972:1), "in the absence of understanding the denominations, one cannot understand American society either." The same can be said of any society where there is high religious pluralism.

Unlike church, ecclesia, or denomination—which are more inclusive and integrated into society—a **sect** is smaller, and either aloof or hostile to the secular society surrounding it. Membership is exclusive and voluntary, determined usually by a conversion experience (Demerath & Hammond, 1969; Bainbridge & Stark, 1981, 1997). Whereas church is usually an ascribed status, sect is an achieved one. Often sects break away from a church, led by dissidents who believe that the parent church is not practicing the authentic or true religion as it was originally conceived (Stark & Bainbridge, 1985). Sects must exist in religiously pluralistic societies that tolerate them, but they are likely to maintain a judgmental attitude toward nonmembers who are not part of their exclusive community of believers.

Since spiritual perfection is a goal of sects, membership standards are high—a factor that functions to keep membership low. Leaders are often charismatic, and therefore clergy may have no formal training. A high degree of spontaneity and participation of members is expected, both in worship services and to allow the organization to function. Sects often have one identifiable leader and emphasize a lack of hierarchy. Like churches, sects vary according to how many of these characteristics apply (Bruce, 1999; Aldridge, 2000). The Amish and Quakers are sects that are aloof but not necessarily hostile to the secular society, and their industriousness and piety have garnered a degree of respect from it. On the other hand, mutually hostile relations exist between the broader society and those Mormons who have formed a sect still practicing polygamy. And as sects grow in size, they inevitably take on some of the bureaucratic functions they originally disdained.

Whereas sects often begin by splintering from an established religious body, a **cult** usually organizes around a charismatic leader who provides the basis for a new, unconventional religion. Max Weber (1925/1975) defined *charisma* as an aspect of personality that sets some people apart by exceptional powers or qualities that are often viewed as supernatural or superhuman. Charismatic leaders develop a special bond of trust and love with followers that reinforces loyalty and obedience. A cult is the only type of religious organization that relies solely on charismatic authority to maintain and legitimize its mission. All other social organizations, religious or not, receive their authority by tradition, such as a monarchy, or through a rational-legal system, such as constitutional authority given to a president (Chapter 18). Weber argued that unless charisma can be "routinized" so that stable social routines evolve along a road to institutionalization, the community will not survive. Because it is so closely associated with a charismatic person who has virtually irreplaceable powers, a cult usually does not outlive its leader.

Most cults have no clearly defined structure and are associated with a great deal of tension, suspicion, and hostility with the larger society. The definition assumes that cults have a religious focus, although some do not—such as survivalists, militia-based groups, astrology followers, and those like the Heaven's Gate cult mentioned in the vignette who believe that alien beings will advance the causes of their followers on planet earth. A cult has even emerged around Elvis sightings (Weightman, 1989). Since these cults have all the characteristics of religion other than the transcendent, like a civil (secular) religion, they may be viewed as secular cults.

The media have characterized cults as brainwashing groups who prey on young people searching for alternative lifestyles and whose followers are led to their deaths through their fanatical devotion to the

The Heaven's Gate cult website was designed to recruit new members, convince others outside the cult that their beliefs were rational, and to ensure devoted cult members that their beliefs about the significance of the Hale-Bopp comet were about to come true.

cult leader. Examples are numerous: In 1978, under the leadership of charismatic messiah Jim Jones, who formed the People's Temple, over 900 Americans died of mass suicide–murder in a Guyana, South America, jungle settlement—including over 200 children whose parents gave them poisoned fruit punch. In 1993, eighty members of David Koresh's Branch Davidians, including nineteen children, burned to death in their Waco, Texas, compound when it was stormed by federal agents (Tabor & Gallagher, 1995). In preparation for the mission of world domination, followers of Shoko Asahara's Aum Supreme Truth cult, dispersed nerve gas in the Tokyo subway system afflicting over 5500 people and causing the death of twelve. Media attention to these extreme examples has reinforced stereotypes about cults.

Although it is true that cults successfully recruit from the disenchanted and those with fewer social ties, they vary considerably in terms of their religious emphasis as well as what must be surrendered to become a full-fledged member. Detrimental effects of cults are linked to the extent that members are cut off from wider society (Stark & Bainbridge, 1985; Robbins, 1988; Hatcher, 1989). Most cults do not demand such isolation because they need the ongoing financial resources from members who work in the "outside" secular world. New Age cults are good examples. *New Age* is a catch-all term for loosely organized spirituality-seeking groups with no one set of consistent beliefs who attract people who may be part of other new age groups and even conventional religions. New age groups in general are very pluralistic and are set up to meet a variety of individual needs (Bruce, 1999; Aldridge, 2000). They often gain members first as transient clients by selling a variety of services and products, such as alternative health care therapies, health foods, crystals, oils, jewelry, and books (Bruce, 1996). Also, some cults can sustain themselves without a continuing charismatic leader if they begin to develop more sectlike qualities. Examples include the Church of Scientology and the International Order of Krishna Consciousness (Hare Krishna). It remains to be seen about Reverend Sun Myung Moon's Unification church, based in Korea. Although he proclaims himself as the messiah under which all religions and nations of the world will be united, the membership and finances are large enough to continue the church after his death. The publicized mass weddings of cult members encourage early parenthood so that children are born into the church. A paid staff and highly effective administrative center, which distributes educational material worldwide, requires organizational mastery. The "Moonies" may be on the way to becoming an established sect.

There is also disagreement among sociologists about what constitutes a cult, especially how it differs from a sect (Marty, 1960; Hatcher, 1989; Melton, 1993). Gaining acceptance is the term *new religious movements*, which has been offered as a substitute (Moore & McGehee 1989; Chalfant et al., 1994). Contrary to the examples above, most cults are peaceful and safe for their members (Clark, 1993; Goldman, 1993; Kloehn, 1997). The vast majority of cults do not end with the death of their members. They simply fade away.

With the cult as a prime example, religious diversity is never conveniently classified, because there is so much overlap between categories. There is a helpful tool, however, to deal with the sociological necessity of viewing the continuity and relationships between types of religious organizations. Originating from the work of Max Weber (1919/1946), the distinction between church and sect was conceived according to *ideal types*, a typology that classifies information on a continuum between two poles (opposite categories) and serves as a tool to evaluate actual cases. Idealized or abstracted models of church and sect serve as the two opposite poles, but information can be placed according to how much or how little a religious organization represents one or the other. The same organization over time may be placed at different points on the continuum as its characteristics change. Through the use of an ideal type, we can see how religious movements grow and evolve.

For example, a denomination can represent a midpoint on a continuum between church and sect (Figure 17.1). Christianity, for example, moved from a cult to a sect to a church, to numerous denominations. Some denominations are now ecclesiae. Indeed, all contemporary world religions began as cults. On the other hand, denominations can split into sects or even cults if members feel there is too much accommodation to secular society. Since so many people around the globe already identify with one religion, it would be difficult today for another world religion to emerge from either a cult or sect. However, the way world religions are organized will shift according to pressures from social change and secularization.

WORLD RELIGIONS AND SOCIAL CHANGE

By grouping religious beliefs and religious organizations according to certain criteria, it is easier to examine the world's major religions as powerful institutionalized forces impacting social life. Remember that once a belief system or pattern of behavior is institutionalized, it is accepted by the society as legitimate, and it becomes an agent of socialization passing down the beliefs to succeeding generations. Despite any secularization trends, almost 70 percent of the world's inhabitants identify themselves with one of five major world religions (Table 17.1). Religion remains a powerful agent of socialization.

Christianity

From its origins 2,000 years ago as a Middle Eastern cult rooted in Judaism, Christianity grew around charismatic Jesus of Nazareth, himself born a Jew. Christianity is the largest of the world's religions, numbering close to 2 billion people. Christianity's phenomenal growth rate is in part due to its early focus on class and ethnic inclusiveness (Stark, 1996b). It was triggered, first, by the eleventh century split of Christianity into the Eastern Orthodox Church based in Turkey and the Roman Catholic Church, and second, by the Protestant Reformation led by Martin Luther in the sixteenth century.

Contemporary Christians separate themselves into an amazing variety of churches, denominations, and sects. They are united by the belief that Jesus is the son of God, the messiah who was crucified, resurrected from the dead, and will return as the salvation for the world. Combined with preaching a gospel based on love, a belief in one almighty god, and the virtue of leading an ethically based life, Jesus demonstrated miraculous healing powers that gradually attracted many followers. These stories are recorded in the New Testament of the Bible, the holy book of Christianity. Since adherents came mostly from the ranks of the numerous poor, discontented, and otherwise socially marginalized classes who abandoned conventional religious practices and the polytheism dictated by the Roman Empire, Jesus was perceived as a threat to the political and social order. This resulted in mass arrests and persecution of his followers, driving the cult underground and activating what Christians believe to be preordained events, Jesus' death and resurrection, on which Christian faith is founded.

After Christianity became established as an institutionalized religion, missionary work and military conquest bolstered its expansion to the Western world. As functionalists maintain, the story of Christianity shows how politics and religion join forces to return the social system to a state of equilibrium. On the other hand, conflict theory points out initially it did just the opposite: With its emphasis on inclusiveness of all people, regardless of class or ethnicity, the prevailing political and religious system was challenged.

Islam

The world's second largest and fastest growing religion is Islam, numbering a billion-plus adherents. Like Christianity, Islam has spread its message by both missionary and military means. But since Islam is an ecclesia in many nations of the developing world that have higher birthrates than in those dominated by Christianity, most growth is due to those being born into the religion. Muslims are the adherents of Islam, translated as "submission" to the will of God, or Allah. Founded in the first century, Islam is based on the teaching of Muhammad (570–632), the greatest among God's prophets that included the divinely inspired, but not divine, Jesus, as well as Abraham and Moses. Muhammad is also not deified, but was the greatest of all God's messengers whose revelations are recorded in the Qur'an (Koran), the holy book of Islam. As governed by its pillars of faith, Islam is precise in what adherents must do to lead a godly life,

Table 17.1	Religious Population of the World: 1996 (In thousands)						
	%	Africa	Asia	Latin America	North America	Europe*	Oceania
Christians	33.7	360,874	303,127	455,819	255,542	555,614	24,253
Roman Catholics	16.9	125,376	94,250	408,968	75,398	269,021	8,452
Protestants	7.0	114,726	45,326	34,816	121,361	79,534	8,257
Orthodox	3.8	25,215	13,970	460	6,390	171,665	650
Other Christians	6.1	95,557	149,581	11,575	52,393	35,394	6,894
Muslims	19.4	308,660	778,362	1,356	5,530	32,032	385
Hindus	13.7	1,986	786,991	760	1,365	1,650	323
Buddhists	5.6	38	321,985	569	920	1,563	200
Jews	0.2	165	4,257	1,084	5,836	2,432	92
Atheists	3.8	440	175,450	3,010	1,850	40,845	600
Nonreligious**	15.3	3,567	752,759	16,053	21,315	90,390	2,845
All other religions	8.3	x	x	x	x	x	x

*Includes Russia.

**Persons professing no religion, agnostics, secularists, those indifferent to all religions, freethinkers.

Source: Adapted from Table No. 1342. *Statistical Abstract of the United States.* U.S. Bureau of the Census, 1998.

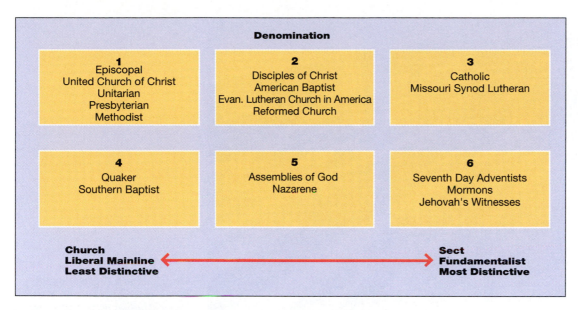

Denomination

1 Episcopal United Church of Christ Unitarian Presbyterian Methodist	**2** Disciples of Christ American Baptist Evan. Lutheran Church in America Reformed Church	**3** Catholic Missouri Synod Lutheran
4 Quaker Southern Baptist	**5** Assemblies of God Nazarene	**6** Seventh Day Adventists Mormons Jehovah's Witnesses

Church
Liberal Mainline   ⟵————————⟶   **Sect**
Least Distinctive   **Fundamentalist**
                                                                       Most Distinctive

FIGURE 17.1   Selected Denominations on a Church-Sect Typology
Source: Adapted from Iannaccone, 1994

such as praying at least five times a day, observing Ramadan, a ritual of fasting and special prayers that occurs one month per year, and making a pilgrimage to Mecca once in a lifetime.

Islam is divided into two major groups, Sunni and Shiite, who differ on beliefs about the succession of the prophets after Muhammad. These two groups generally fit the definition of denominations. Muslims are not organized into collectivities of churches, however, since formal religious structure is seen as coming between people and God. As Muhammad gained political and religious prominence, a death threat forced him to flee his birthplace of Mecca (now in Saudi Arabia), to Medina, where he founded a new government based on his revelations. Unlike Jesus, who did not witness in his earthly lifetime the profound consequences of his actions, Muhammad returned to Mecca, this time as a conqueror, and established himself as a powerful leader of a religious state. Note the continuities between the founding of Christianity and Islam, the effects of merging politics and religion, and how religion originally creates social disequilibrium until it becomes institutionalized.

Judaism

Compared to Christianity and Islam, which sprang from Jewish roots, Judaism is one of the oldest world religions, but by far the smallest. Although numbering about only 14 million adherents, it carries enormous global influence. Jewish history is recorded in the first five books of the Hebrew Bible, which Jews call the Torah (law). The Torah specifies that a Messiah will eventually bring Jews to a promised land—a state of paradise. The Torah also contains 613 commandments—including the Ten Commandments God gave to Moses on Mount Sinai—that are viewed as rabbinic law. These and other Jewish scriptures set down important beliefs and rituals, such as the promotion of community among all Jews, dedication to a synagogue or temple, doing *mitzvah* or good deeds, religious observances in families, and the belief that the human condition can be improved.

Judaism also shares with Christianity and Islam the teaching of the prophet Abraham. Judaism is traced to God's covenant with Abraham 4,000 years ago that allowed Abraham's descendants to be the chosen people, and offering them permanent, exclusive rights over what would become the land of Israel in exchange for their allegiance. The original Jewish

INTERNET ———— **CONNECTIONS**

Chartres is one of the earliest and most magnificent of Europe's Gothic cathedrals. You can't really experience it through picture, but give it a try at www1.pitt.edu/~medart/menufrance/chartres/charmain.html. What sort of religious experience do you suppose that seeing this place would have evoked in a 12th-century church-goer?

Mecca, in Saudi Arabia, is one of Islam's most holy places, where millions of Muslims make a pilgrimage as required by their faith.

land in Palestine prospered until wars with neighboring kingdoms culminated in a final confrontation with Rome that resulted in the scattering of Jews throughout the world in the first century.

Almost 2,000 years passed before an independent Jewish state was regained—years marked by intense prejudice and anti-Semitism, including the Nazi Holocaust. A persistent *Zionist* movement to recreate the Jewish state in Palestine marked the last century of struggle. While Jews celebrated Israel's founding in 1948, displaced Palestinians and their Egyptian and Syrian allies, almost all of whom are Muslim, vowed revenge, leading to four wars that ended each time with less than satisfactory peace settlements and continued outbreaks of violence. Israel's strategic location and its profoundly important religious site for Christians, Muslims, and Jews, make it a prime target for world conflict. Amidst seemingly never-ending political tension, Jews the world over must contend with the same social forces confronting other religious groups in regard to safeguarding their religious well-being.

The main Jewish denominations of Orthodox, Conservative, and Reform, as well as an emerging Reconstructionist branch, developed in response to this very confrontation—how much accommodation is necessary in one's religious life to suitably carry on other parts of one's life. As we will see later, the latter three are Jewish American adaptations to social change.

Hinduism

Dating from about 4,500 years ago, Hinduism is the oldest and third largest of the world's major religions, with over 700 million followers, most of them living in India. Unlike Christianity and Islam, Hinduism does not *proselytize*, that is, it does not gain adherents through organized efforts to convert others to the religion. High birthrates in India and a negligible number of interfaith marriages among Hindu communities throughout the world function to steadily increase their numbers. Hinduism is a polytheistic religion that has no one sacred text but uses a number of sources for guidance on morality in accordance with *dharma*, the moral responsibilities necessary for a godly life. Gods and goddesses are ranked, but there is no one supreme being who sits in judgment of every individual.

It is impossible to separate Hinduism from the caste system in which it originated (see Chapter 10). Suffice it to say that the caste system is congruent with the Hindu belief in *reincarnation*, the cycle of birth, death, and rebirth into a higher or lower caste dependent on how well an individual acts out the ideal life dictated by dharma. In each incarnation, the soul continues its journey toward *nirvana*, the point where spiritual perfection is achieved, the soul is absorbed into the universal spirit, and the reincarnation cycle ends.

Because Hinduism is based in India, one of the most ethnically diverse regions on the globe, its practices have been adapted to suit a wide variety of cultural circumstances. Shrines erected to harvest and rain gods are numerous in rural villages throughout India. The image of Ganesh, the god of prosperity who is also the "great guide," with his elephant head and human body, is emblazoned on walls near ATM machines. His figure rests on computer terminals in businesses throughout Bombay and New Delhi. Just

Tibetan Buddhism, which these monks represent, is the fastest-growing branch of Buddhism in the West. Buddhism is struggling to maintain its identity within Communist China.

as St. Christopher medals are prevalent among Christian Catholics who travel, so are Ganesh images among Hindus who travel. Hinduism emphasizes virtues often associated with one of its great personages, Mahatma Gandhi, who epitomizes the dharma of service, courage, humility, and nonviolence. Mother Theresa of Calcutta, herself a Christian, demonstrated these same virtues in her work with the poorest of India's poor. Hinduism suggests that both Ghandi and Mother Theresa led exceptional, even miraculous lives, on behalf of humanity, and thus may have ended their cycle of earthly incarnations.

Ethicalist Religions: Buddhism and Confucianism

Most ethicalist world religions originated in Asia. These religions are identified not by their belief in divine beings or manipulating supernatural forces but by their adherence to ethically based codes of behavior, culminating in the achievement of human happiness or a higher state of personal awareness or consciousness. Ethicalist religions are based on abstract ideals that provide prescriptions for moral living that not only aid individuals in their journey to higher consciousness, but also benefit those with whom they come into contact. Buddhism, which grew out of Hinduism, is the best example of an ethicalist religion and claims almost 6 percent of the globe's population as members. Buddhism was founded around 600 B.C.E. by Siddhartha Gautama, who became the "Buddha." He was a wealthy upper-caste Hindu who believed that ending human suffering

rested on ending human desire. By following a rigidly prescribed path of righteous living focusing on meditation and proper conduct, an individual could achieve enlightenment, the highest level of human consciousness. Similar to Hinduism, the soul would be released from the reincarnation cycle into eternal bliss. This spiritual quest does not need gods as mediators since godliness is the untapped potential in *all* humans.

The most secular of the ethicalist religions was founded by the Chinese philosopher Confucius (551–479 B.C.E.). Like Buddhism, Confucianism is based on a code of self-discipline and meditation designed to maintain proper relationships that enhance loyalty, respect, and morality. Reverence for ancestors is the closest Confucianism gets to the idea of worship. As a microcosm for society, proper conduct toward others is formed first in the family and then relayed to the broader community. Confucianism works toward earthly success rather than supernatural rewards. Confucianism for centuries was the philosophical foundation for Chinese as well as Korean politics (Breen, 1998). Confucianism thrived in a collectivistic society like China, which emphasizes hierarchy, harmony, and respect for authority and tradition.

In the strongly monotheistic Western world, there is often misunderstanding about ethically based religions, particularly since neither Buddha nor Confucius are elevated as gods in the religions they founded. But, as with Western religions, sociologists look not to the supernatural elements but to the consequences of religious behavior on the community of its believers.

Women and World Religions: Rediscovering the Feminine Face of God

God the Mother walks among her children, the creatures of the earth, blessing them, feeding them, teaching them to Be.
(Ruth, 1994:134)

The image of God as a woman is probably quite startling to those who identify with the major religions of the world. Interpretation of the scriptures in world religions traditionally have been androcentric—based on norms and beliefs that are male-centered. But anthropologists tell us that the religions of the world evolved from spiritual beliefs and practices that were originally female centered. When goddesses were replaced by gods or a god, spirituality became institutionalized into religion, and women lost much power and prestige. Archeological and later historical evidence now suggest the following:

1. The most ancient image of the divine is female. The first civilizations were probably *gynocentric*, with an emphasis on female and feminine interests and goddess-based religion.
2. The cult of the mother-goddess was one of the oldest, most widespread, and longest surviving religions found throughout the Paleolithic to Neolithic periods, in sites from Western Europe through to the Mediterranean civilizations and into India.
3. The goddess as creator is found in accounts from ancient Sumer, Babylon, Assyria, Greece, Egypt, and China.

4. In ancient civilizations female deities were worshipped and religious life was more of a partnership between men and women.

The roots of all world religions demonstrate evidence of more *equitable* male-female roles:

Islam—In the pre-Islamic Arab world, women had esteemed roles as soothsayers, priestesses, and queens. Islam arose in response to unique cultural needs, including Muhammad's desire to aid the poor and protect widows, orphans, and unmarried women.

Hinduism—The oldest Hindu scriptures, the Vedas (1500–500 B.C.E.) demonstrate an esteem for femininity and complementarity between spouses. Women are auspicious and vital to the well-being of the family and are celebrated by a number of prominent female deities who continue to be worshipped. Hinduism has a goddess heritage that has always allowed women to serve in temples and lead religious rituals.

Judaism—There are scriptural voices confirming God's high regard for women. In first-century documents, Eve is visioned as the mother of humanity who may have been naive, but certainly not wicked—an unselfish woman whose good character Satan abused. When Jews were scattered around the world, women had op-

portunities to climb to prestigious positions and assume leadership roles in their communities.

Christianity—Christians and Jews share the first five books of the Hebrew Bible and its images of women and men. One such image is that woman is made from the rib of a man, contrary to all subsequent natural law. But the "Adam's Rib" creation story ignores the earlier Genesis (1:27) account that God creates male and female in God's own image, a much more gender equitable image. In the New Testament many images of equity and male-female partnering exist. Mary Magdalene and the women who went to Jesus' tomb hold the credibility for Christianity itself. Jesus first appeared to them and they were told to gather the disciples. Mary Magdalene may have been the first prophet of the new religion of Christianity. And as told in the New Testament: "There is neither Jew nor Greek, there is neither slave nor free, there is neither male nor female, for you are all one in Jesus Christ" (Galatians 3:28).

In the texts of the world's religions, these positive images of women exist, but those that are in line with androcentrism are emphasized. The most common images are that women are subordinate to men and that a woman's domestic roles define her. The Chris-

Global Fundamentalism

We saw in Chapter 3 that a culture must adapt to social change, otherwise its survival chances as a culture are reduced. All religions provide guidelines for behavior, but the principle of adaptation asserts that as the world changes, guidelines must be modified accordingly. Compared to all other social institutions, religion is perhaps the most resistant to adaptation, a principle all the more evident in the rise of fundamentalism world-

wide. It relies on a view that a previous golden age existed that must be recovered. In this sense fundamentalism is more *reactionary*—a return to the past—than *conservative*—maintaining or conserving what already exists (Swift, 1991). According to fundamentalists, conservatives have already gone too far in accommodating social change. As will be explained in Chapter 24, fundamentalism is one example of a countermodernization movement that promotes ways to minimize the effects of modernization.

tian Bible has these passages: "the head of every woman is her husband" (I Corinthians 11:3); "wives be subject to your husbands" (Ephesians 5:22); "let a woman learn in silence with all submissiveness, permit no woman to teach or have authority over men" (I Timothy 2:11–12).

The Qur'an (Koran) shows a wide range of contradictory practices concerning women. Women are ideal, obedient, and gentle as well as jealous, conspiratorial, and having imperfect minds. By the third century, women were more secluded and degraded than anything known in earlier Islamic decades. Contemporary Islam defines men and women as complementary rather than equal. But men are a step above women and the protectors of women, so God gives preference and authority to men over women. A woman's job is to produce legitimate male heirs.

For Jews, interpretation of scripture is that men are to read, teach, and legislate, and women are to follow. Ancient customs prescribed daily, rigorous religious duties for men from which women were exempt since they could interfere with domestic roles. The extreme are the "Texts of Terror," parts of four books of the Torah (Old Testament), justifying rape, murder, sexual violence against female slaves and women taken as prizes of war, human sacrifice, and the widespread abuse of women and girls.

For Hindus, some scriptures criticize women for being too ambitious, energetic, and masculine, which denies their "higher" level of womanhood in serving their families. Hindu religious rituals reinforce their roles as mothers,

The goddess Dhurga serves as a powerful religious symbol for both Hindu men and women. Hinduism is the only contemporary world religion that has a long tradition and continuing practice of goddess worship.

wives, and homemakers and connections to men for their well-being. When women became "unconnected" to men by widowhood, infamous practices such as *suttee*, widow burning, occurred. A widow could feel guilty all her life because her husband died before she did.

History and religious scripture can be interpreted many different ways. The rediscovery of the goddess heritage shows that religion was not always patriarchal; men and women could be partners in a variety of ways, and women held esteemed and powerful re-

ligious roles. Female-friendly interpretations of scriptures in contemporary world religions are being emphasized. As the "hidden," positive images are uncovered, they are more likely to be advanced in the pulpit by ordained women. Women gaining leadership roles is all the more significant with sociological research showing that women have a greater degree of religious orientation than men; they attend religious services more and express a higher need for a religious dimension in their lives. Feminists of all faiths are unwilling to equate religion with oppression. They believe it is not true liberation if it means severing ties with their religious heritage. They choose to work at reform focusing on upgrading education that allows women access to the holy texts. They focus on providing a historical account of women's roles in ancient religions and reevaluating scripture accordingly, whether from the Qur'an, Torah, Bible, or Vedas.

1. How does your own religious heritage view women's roles compared to men's roles, both in religion and in other parts of life?
2. How can women who are of faiths that restrict ordination of women work for more gender role equity in their respective religions?

Sources: Davis, 1971; Ruether, 1983; Trible, 1984; Eisler, 1988, 1995; Mernissi, 1987; Gimbutas, 1989, 1991; Minai, 1991; Carmody, 1992; Engelsman, 1994; Fischer, 1994.

All world religions exhibit some fundamentalist trends. Secularization is a threat to any religion, but how that threat is actualized varies considerably (Turner, 1991). Fundamentalists would not accept functionalism's view that adaptation is required to maintain religious integrity. They would suggest the reverse: Adaptation is really compromise in disguise and leads to the surrender of religious integrity. The benign, benevolent, and ethical focus on the universal "good," evident in the overview of world religions,

contrasts sharply with the sectarian, fundamentalist side of religion that fuels tension.

There are many examples of continuing feuds between the world religions and between branches of the same religion that are activated by fundamentalism. One of the most horrifying of these occurred when Hindu India and Muslim Pakistan were separated into independent states in 1947, leaving many people trapped in regions under political control of the "other" faith. Over a million Hindus and Muslims

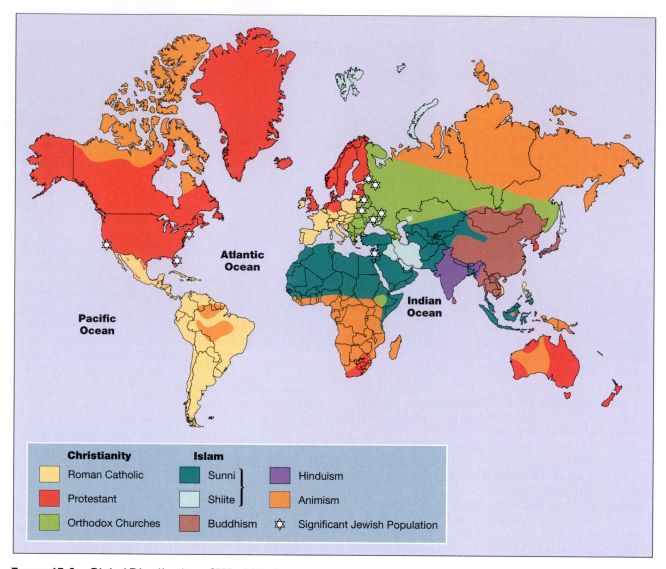

FIGURE 17.2   Global Distribution of World Religions

Source: From *Human Geography: Cultures, Connections, and Landscapes* by Edward Bergman. Copyright © 1995 by Prentice Hall, Inc. Reprinted by permission of Prentice Hall, Inc., Upper Saddle River, NJ.

slaughtered one another when they crossed lines in the flight to their new territory. Between Muslims, Turkey, Algeria, and Malaysia are striving to remain secular states in the face of fundamentalists equally determined to transform them into Islamic states. In Malaysia, Sunni and Shiite Muslims are at odds about what the potential Islamic state should look like. Between Christians, Catholics and Protestants in Northern Ireland engage in continuing, often violent, conflict over the issue of nationhood. Between Jews, a right-wing Jewish activist, who believed Israel had gone too far in compromising religious principles to meet political demands, was responsible for the assassination of Prime Minister Yitzhak Rabin.

Fundamentalism is linked to religious intolerance but not necessarily to violence in goal attainment. Just as the term "cult" is associated with negative stereotypes, so is "fundamentalism." Fundamentalists, par-

ticularly Islamic groups, are painted as reactionaries and extremists by the media and other religious organizations who see them as threats (Caplan, 1987; Esposito, 1992). Like liberation theology, fundamentalism is complex and diverse in its expression. For example, many fundamentalist groups disdain political activism, preferring instead to be left alone to pursue religious vision in settings under their control (Beckford, 1989; Lechner, 1989; Shupe & Hadden, 1989). Sects of ultraorthodox Jews in Israel and the United States reflect this pattern, even as they struggle with needs for religious commitment and the economic realities of modernization (Danzger, 1989; Fishman, 1992; Heilman, 1992).

On the other hand, fundamentalism cannot be dismissed from its more lethal expressions, because globally it is tied to both anti-Western sentiment and the growth of religious states. Western influence brings the undesirable effects of secularization, modernization, and capitalism that fundamentalism seeks to contain (Shupe & Hadden, 1989; Horowitz, 1990; Beyer, 1994). Khomeini's revolutionary brand of anti-Western Islam has appealed to young people in Malaysia who travel to Iran through trips arranged by extremist groups in both countries (Richburg, 1992). These trips are also used to recruit young people for training in terrorist acts. In the religious states of the developing world, which by definition oppose religious pluralism, fundamentalism is linked to human rights violations (see Chapter 24). Religious rights of minority groups are a specific concern (Goodstein, 1996). When revitalization efforts are politically motivated and enforced, fundamentalism is injected with the potential for violence.

BEING RELIGIOUS IN THE UNITED STATES

The United States has the highest degree of religious pluralism in the world. Secularization is kindled by pluralism. Religious toleration and the separation of church and state are hallmarks of U.S. culture, but denominations must compete with one another to attract or hold onto members. Strong cultural values of individualism and personal autonomy may reduce religious commitment (Hammond, 1992; Wuthnow, 1993). Modernization contributes to this by reinforcing faith in science rather than religion for problem solving.

Challenges to Secularization

On the other hand, the United States is second only to Ireland and Italy in levels of religious affiliation and religious belief (Lipset, 1991; Gallup, 1993). Historians tell us that 200 years ago only 10 percent of Americans were affiliated with churches and only 20 percent attended (Hudson, 1973). Today people who state a religious preference top 90 percent, 60 percent say they belong to a church, and regular church attendance is in the 30 to 40 percent range. While the 1950s witnessed the highest levels of attendance, there has been a pattern of steady increase with only slight fluctuations in decline, so when downturns occur, they tend to be short term. Overall, Americans typically demonstrate a cycle of religious attendance that shows declines in their teenage years, an increase when they marry and have children, another decline in their 40s, a modest return in middle age, and a larger return as they near old age (Jacquet, 1988; Finke & Stark, 1992; Roof & McKinney, 1997). The vast majority of Americans, close to 95 percent, identify religion as important in their lives and believe in core religious doctrines, such as the existence of God

INTERNET CONNECTIONS

In this chapter, various "challenges to secularization" are discussed. One of these challenges involves the issues surrounding *school prayer*. For example, there are many public schools throughout the country that are openly defying the federal government on this issue. Although it is "illegal" to have prayer at a public school football game, some schools are continuing this practice. In order to acquaint yourself with the school prayer controversy, go to "School Prayer Sources and Links": http://ccwf.cc.utexas.edu/~ckramer/Splinks.html. The opening page has clickable links to a number of different sites, including the official positions of the American Civil Liberties Union, the Christian Science Monitor, American Atheists, and the Christian Coalition. How do you feel about this particular issue involving secularization? Should there be a separation of church and state? Should individual schools be free to make their own policy regarding school prayer? How do you think the conflict might be rectified?

and life after death (Greeley, 1989; NORC, 1994; Niebuhr, 1999). Atheism is at an all-time low, forcing some organizations supporting atheist causes to simply cease operations. Since secularization is a long-term process, these patterns appear to refute it.

Finally, although the separation of church and state is firmly and passionately supported by Americans, religious symbolism permeates the political institution. It beckons Americans daily, from "In God We Trust" on all currency, to pledging allegiance to "one nation under God." Religious roots stemming from a Judeo-Christian foundation are entangled in U.S. government. There were state-sponsored churches in the United States that did not dissolve until the adoption of the First Amendment at the end of the eighteenth century (Handy, 1991). Americans simultaneously support separation of church and state *and* the belief that good Christians (broadly construed) are also good citizens (Williams & Demerath, 1991). One caution must be noted here. Belief in God is entrenched in the United States, but there is little support for official government endorsement of a particular brand of religion. As we will see, even in the highly publicized political activities of various religious groups, the United States continues to embrace religious pluralism.

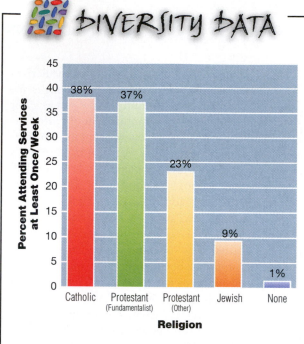

DIVERSITY DATA

FIGURE 17.3   Percent Attending Religious Services at Least Once per Week, by Religion. Catholics and Fundamentalist Protestants are much more likely to attend at least weekly religious services compared to other Protestants and Jews. Do you think Fundamentalist Protestants are more similar to Catholics or to other Protestants in religious beliefs and religious rituals? Why or why not?
Source: NORC. General Social Surveys, 1972–1996. Chicago: National Opinion Research Center, 1996. Reprinted by permission of NORC, Chicago, IL.

Measuring Religiosity

The question of whether America is undergoing secularization or religious resurgence can be answered in part by how religiosity is measured. Just as religions are varied in organizational structure, they also vary on a number of dimensions, ranging from amount and type of rituals, degree of religious expression in social justice issues, and expectations regarding religious knowledge (Glock & Stark, 1965). There is also ideal or official religion as provided by the pulpit and real, or popular, religion as exhibited by many types of cultural practices (Fig. 17.4). Sociologists tend to focus on the ideal practices, such as church attendance and religious affiliation, and may overlook important popular indicators of religious experience, such as how religious artifacts (rosaries, bibles, gospel music) are displayed and used and how non-churchgoers bring religion into their homes through rituals such as prayer at meals (Tamney, 1992; McDannell, 1995).

Documenting religious pluralism would seem to be a simpler task than measuring religiosity overall. But America's religious structure is remarkably var-

ied. The number of religious subcategories together with the rapid emergence and decline of cults and other new religious movements compounds the difficulty. Despite this diversity, America's religious salad bowl has three main ingredients—Protestant, Catholic, and Jewish—in proportions that until recently have remained pretty much stable over time. The small portion of "other religions," is enlarging somewhat, with Muslim, Hindu, and Buddhist immigrants arriving from Asia and the Middle East. But Christians, especially Catholics, are arriving from Mexico and Latin America, as well as from Christian regions of sub-Saharan Africa. In the United States, newer immigrants tend to be more religious, suggesting another argument against secularization. However, while numbers may increase in specific categories, it is unlikely that the Protestant-Catholic-Jewish proportion will be altered significantly in the near future.

LIFE CONNECTIONS: U.S. Religious Diversity

Religious pluralism is a hallmark of the United States. The three major religious groups in the United States—Protestants, Catholics, and Jews—can be described according to patterns of diversity. However, this section will show that diversity has as much to with theology as with common diversity variables such as social class and race.

There has been a great deal of controversy about using Christian prayers at events in public schools. Whereas Christianity may be the dominant religion in these schools, such practices may violate the principle of the separation of church and state.

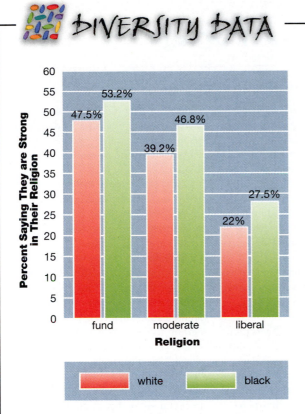

FIGURE 17.4 Percent Who Identify Themselves as Strong in Their Religious Preference, by Race and Religion. For both races and all religious preferences, African Americans and Fundamentalist Protestants report that they are strong in their religion. What is the link between race and religious preference that explains this strong religious identification?

Protestant Diversity

U.S. Protestants are so diverse they almost defy generalization. They converge under two fairly loose banners: They are Christian and they are not Catholic. One-third are Baptists, one-third are in four "mainstream" denominations and the other one-third are "other," mostly small denominations, independent churches, and those not otherwise affiliated with any specific Protestant group. This "other" one-third represents many fundamentalist churches at the core of religious resurgence in the United States. Protestantism in the United States is one of schism. Schisms promote religious pluralism (Bruce, 1990).

Social Class and Membership. Compared to other Protestants, mainstream Protestants tend to be older, have higher levels of education, earn higher incomes, come from the middle and upper class, and hold more liberal theological and political views. They have a strong sense of personal autonomy and

often come from upwardly mobile families in which religious switching occurred—from low-status to high-status denominations. Episcopalians, Presbyterians, and affiliates of the United Church of Christ are the best representatives of this profile (Gallup & Castelli, 1989; Hammond, 1992; Gallup, 1993; Waters et al., 1995).

Social class makes a difference in type of church membership. Middle-class, mainstream U.S. denominations have disproportionately lost more to other groups since the 1960s. Liberal churches gain more members from conservative churches than the reverse, but not enough to offset overall losses. However, the challenge to liberal Protestant churches is not losing out to conservatives, but losing out to a growing secular constituency (Roof & McKinney, 1997). Mainstream Protestants face the dilemma of encouraging communal ties at the same time they are eroded by increased individualism. Conservative Protestants are the winners in the membership race, with the biggest winners in churches that are both nondenominational and fundamentalist. These conservative churches also more likely to be made up of poorer people.

Theology. However, diversity is also reflected *within* the fundamentalist churches. Fundamentalism reflects two sides of Christianity—salvation of souls, the evangelical side of fundamentalism, or improving society, its political activist side (Watt, 1991; Johnstone, 1992). In the United States, pluralism combined with democracy allows any group of believers to intentionally leave their churches and begin a movement of their own. This is why there are so many different varieties of Protestant fundamentalism (Wuthnow, 1989a, 1993; Marsden, 1991; Marty & Appleby, 1992). Mainstream Protestantism attracts fewer members because of religious pluralism, but fundamentalist Protestantism has been propelled by it. Larger denominations of mainstream Protestants are theologically more tolerant than their fundamentalist siblings. Research shows that broad-based theology, designed to be accepted by everyone, cannot capture the religious hearts of different groups such as teenagers, college students, seminarians, and many African Americans. While they may have a strong identity as Christians, when asked what it means to be part of such denominations, most people simply say "nothing" (Carroll & Roof, 1993). These people more often identify with a specific congregation of close friends rather than the denomination as a whole. For fundamentalists, however, traditional sources of religious identity are easier to tap.

Another fundamentalist success story is research supporting the argument that the stricter the church, the stronger the church. Mainstream Protestant churches are more lenient—they encourage dialogue

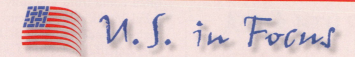

Magic and Religion in America

Leo: (July 23–August 22): Cycle is such that you land on your feet from no matter what height. Imprint style—don't follow others. You will come from behind to ultimately win the game. Aquarius, another Leo in picture.

Religiosity is strong in the United States, one of the top three countries in the world with the highest degrees of religious affiliation and belief. Yet Americans are also apparently quite comfortable with practicing rituals that might be defined as magical, superstitious, or occult. Beliefs in astrology, hexing, charms, witchcraft, water divining, and UFOs are quite strong. These beliefs contradict scientific or religious knowledge and are sometimes referred to as *nonofficial* religion. It is difficult to distinguish what falls within the categories of nonofficial and official religion. Consider the following statistics on the U.S. population:

1. One-quarter report seeing a ghost or spirit of the dead.
2. Thirteen percent have seen or been in the presence of angels.
3. Over one-third have had a mystical experience. Most believe it was religiously inspired.
4. Two-thirds have experienced déjà vu or ESP, a sense they are repeating an experience, being somewhere they have never been, or sensing things that are not immediately present.
5. Two-thirds believe that a prayer has been answered, such as using prayer for healing themselves or others.

Can these be interpreted and accepted (legitimized) according to official religion, or do they fall in the unofficial realm? Are they magical or religious?

The above example *may* be viewed positively by religion, but other practices are less likely viewed this way. Contrary to what their official religions expect them to practice or believe, Americans often, and routinely, engage in behavior that would be defined as religiously inappropriate. For example,

most of us may quickly check out our horoscope as we peruse the daily newspaper as a form of entertainment. But 25 percent of the population in the United States say they believe in astrology and often makes daily decisions based on it. Based on the horoscope above, astrology-believing Leos could be inspired to take a risk in love or finances and find another Leo or Aquarius to help out.

Other studies confirm U.S. belief in magic and superstition. New England commercial fishers who have been studied admit that they would not break certain fishing taboos. The taboos include: "don't turn a hatch cover upside down," "don't whistle on a boat," and "don't mention the word 'pig' on board." Why? Breaking a taboo risks personal safety. Breaking them brings bad luck. When on shore these fishers express disbelief about the effectiveness of their taboos, but at sea and when in danger, anxiety levels rise and they will not risk breaking them. Anxiety increases the use of magic and supersti-

and theological debate. Strict churches are more absolutist and conformist. Fundamentalist churches are often sectarian and democratic in leadership. They require high levels of commitment, participation, and energy (Kelley, 1986; Iannaccone, 1994). Theology and commitment work together to keep conservative churches strong.

Race and Ethnicity. Finally, religious identity is stronger in congregations that are homogenous in ethnicity, especially as reflected in customs, and language. Ethnic diversity, like religious pluralism, has a substantial negative effect on church adherence (Land et al., 1991). African American congregations are overrepresented in fundamentalist churches. Compared to African American mainstream denominations, they do not engage in denominational switching and have higher levels of religious participation. Religious involvement enhances feelings of psychological closeness, social support, and shared interest with other African Americans (Taylor & Chatters, 1988; Ellison, 1991; Sherkat & Ellison, 1991). As

a reflection of all these feelings, African American churches have played a dominant political role—for example, as the key sites for the civil rights movement (Lincoln & Mamiya, 1990).

Catholic Diversity

Religious homogeneity—both in theology and in the demographic composition of congregations—is more evident among Catholics than among Protestants. Nonetheless, a great deal of diversity exists. There are several branches of Catholicism worldwide that adhere to different interpretations of Jesus' teachings, but the Roman Catholic Church is by far the largest. One-third of all Americans are Roman Catholic. Half of all Europeans and almost 90 percent of Latin Americans are Roman Catholic (Eerdman, 1996).

Social Class and Race. In the twentieth century, Catholics as a group have generally moved from lower SES to middle SES categories. Today, how-

Americans express high religiosity, and they also show high degrees of superstition. They often practice "magic" in their daily lives and seek out fortunetellers.

they consider lucky, such as a four-leaf clover, rabbit's foot, or special amulet. Sports stars continue to wear the jewelry that they had on when they were on a winning streak. Studies of college students report that they wear certain jeans, shirts, or special clothing to exams to bring them luck. Most people would not walk under a ladder (probably a good idea regardless of superstition) and do not want a room on the thirteenth floor in a hotel. Indeed, hotels must also know something about superstitions and customer preferences since many do *not* have a thirteenth floor!

Every time you take a sociology exam make sure you reread this box. And knock on wood.

1. What magical and religious behaviors do you engage in routinely? Why do you engage in them and how effective are they for your purposes?
2. How can magic and religion exist comfortably alongside one another in any society that defines itself as religious?

Sources: Poggie & Pollnac, 1988; Gallup & Castelli, 1989; Womack, 1992; Kantrowitz, 1994; McGuire, 1997; Omarr, 1999.

tion. A study of professional sports and Olympic athletes shows them to be under ongoing stress and often in physical danger. Auto racers, hockey players, and football players risk severe injury every time they engage in their profession. Magical practices—whether skating three times around the ice before the game, having a teammate knock on a football helmet three times before a kickoff, or wearing blue underwear at every game—reduces their anxiety.

Superstitions are strong among Americans. While people may not say they believe in them, they routinely practice them. Ninety percent of people say they have personal items that

ever, this moderate class position is being eroded by waves of poorer Catholic immigrants mainly from Latin America. Besides Latinos, the vast majority of Catholics are non-Latino whites—African Americans make up less than 10 percent of American Catholics. However, compared to their Protestant counterparts, these African American Catholics are more likely to have higher levels of education and income. For African Americans, middle-class status is associated more with Catholicism than with Protestantism.

Religious Commitment. Although membership remains stable, U.S. Catholics represent mainstream religion. In general, they have declined in commitment to the church, as shown by less financial support, less expressed concern for the sacraments, and higher percentages who say that the church is out of date and not relevant in their lives. Like Protestants, they are becoming more individual rather than collective in their attachments to the church (Hornsby-Smith, 1987, 1991). However, among Catholics in general, there is a shift to concern for social issues and

social action (D'Antonio et al., 1989; Williams & Davidson, 1997). This may be the very thrust that injects U.S. Catholics with renewed religious commitment and energy (Deedy, 1987).

Women and Sexuality. Probably the most important issues dividing contemporary U.S. Catholics from the authority of the broader Roman Catholic church are attitudes about women in general and sexuality in particular. Combined with the growing sense of personal autonomy among U.S. Catholics, the women's issue is showing up in divisions among both religious and laypeople. For example, various orders of nuns have removed themselves from traditional patterns of Catholic hierarchy and worship; they take a distinctly female-centered view of religion, preferring to pray to "Her" rather than "Him." Other parishes stretch church authority to allow altar girls, nuns as campus ministers, and women leading "priestless parishes" in rural areas where there are shortages of male priests (Wallace, 1992, 1993). For laypeople, contrary to Vatican authority, a large majority of U.S.

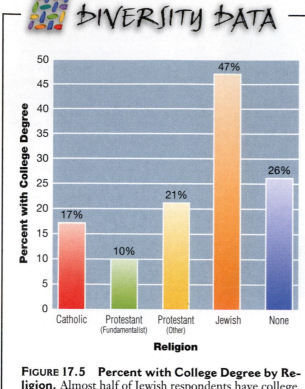

DIVERSITY DATA

FIGURE 17.5   Percent with College Degree by Religion. Almost half of Jewish respondents have college degrees, compared to an average of about 20 percent for all religions, including those who report no religion. What explains the very high educational attainment of Jewish people, especially if they are also defined as a minority group?
Source: NORC. General Social Surveys, 1972–1996. Chicago: National Opinion Research Center, 1996. Reprinted by permission of NORC, Chicago, IL.

cluding the need for ordination, was rejected by U.S. bishops—the first time in history that a letter proposed for a final vote was defeated (Filteau, 1992). Currently, the Vatican believes allegiance of Catholics can be maintained without women's ordination. Others take the view, however, that like the Protestant Reformation, it will be the very issue that irrevocably splits the church (Bohlen, 1995).

Jewish Diversity

The U.S. Jewish congregation is an ethnic congregation. Religion, ethnicity, cultural history, and anti-Semitism intertwine to make Judaism a stronger ascribed status than other religious groups. Jews represent only about 2 percent of the U.S. population, but rising intermarriage rates and low birthrates are contributing to a slight decline in numbers.

Social Class and Social Issues.   Compared to Protestants and Catholics, there are far fewer demographic differences between Jews. U.S. Jews are highly urbanized: 90 percent live in metropolitan areas, and most reside in the New York City region. They top the social class hierarchy in income and educational level; Episcopalians are second in both areas (*Gallup Report*, 1987; Dreier, 1991; U.S. Bureau of the Census, 1999). Politically, most Jews are Democrats, identify themselves as liberal, and actively lobby for causes that are central to Jewish identity, such as protecting religious freedom and support for Israel (Greeley, 1972; Roberts, 1984; Kosmin & Lachman, 1993). Jews have also been strong advocates of minority rights initiatives and were among the earliest partners with African Americans in the civil rights movement. Despite their small numbers, Jews have been very influential in U.S. politics.

Theology.   It is not demographics but interpretation of theology that best describes Jewish diversity in the United States. As mentioned earlier, Judaism is divided into several branches. Like those in Christianity, branches vary according to the degree to which theology is literally interpreted and acted on in daily life.

Orthodox Jews, for example, are sectlike and have the strictest interpretation, viewing the Torah as the word of God and absolutely binding. About 16 percent of U.S. Jews identify with its Orthodox branch (Mead, 1995). Similar to patterns among conservative Protestants, this is the branch that is attracting more members, especially among younger Jews who use orthodoxy to rediscover their heritage (Danzger, 1989; Blech, 1991). Nonetheless, diversity is also evident among Orthodox Jews. There is a split between those who want to engage more fully in activities outside the subculture and those who believe that to do so

Catholics practice birth control other than the rhythm method, support the use of condoms as well as sex education in schools, believe priests should be allowed to marry, do not believe political candidates should be judged solely on the abortion issue, believe that divorced Catholics need to be welcomed back into the church, and are receptive to women's ordination (Gallup & Castelli, 1987; Patrick H. McNamara, 1992; Williams & Davidson, 1997). Over half accept a woman's right to an abortion under certain conditions, such as rape and incest (Roper, 1993). Since so *many* Catholics have beliefs and practices that directly counter Vatican teaching, the institutionalized church is reluctant to dismiss them from church rosters. It is the issue of women in the priesthood, however, where the church does not look away. For every proclamation that reasserts the Vatican's position that women can never be ordained, a worldwide outcry centered in the United States against the position occurs. A pastoral letter that took nine years to formulate and that addressed the concerns of Catholic women, in-

As the head of the Roman Catholic Church worldwide, when the Pope celebrates a mass, such as in Victory Square in Warsaw, Poland, thousands are in attendance, including many non-Catholics.

compromises Jewish law (Heilman & Cohen, 1989). Conservative Jews are less strict, allowing for interpreting the Torah according to changes in the pressure of modern life. Some religious traditions are maintained and others are adapted to contemporary society. Reform Jews are more churchlike and are the most liberal and assimilated branch. They accept the Torah's ethical guidelines but have lenient attitudes regarding obedience to rabbinic law. A fourth denomination, the Reconstructionist branch of Judaism, is emerging. Embracing humanistic values and Judaism's historical and cultural heritage, Reconstructionists reject the traditional religious doctrines as set down in the Torah. Although its success in attracting adherents is mixed, it resembles a secular religion (Yinger, 1994; Dershowitz, 1997).

Given centuries of anti-Semitism, Jews in all denominations recognize that safety is tied to protecting religious pluralism, and that ultimately it is a political issue. The vice-presidential candidacy of Joseph Lieberman in the 2000 election is suggested as indicating both the health of religious pluralism and the decline of anti-Semitism in the United States.

≡ SOCIETY CONNECTIONS:
Challenges to Religious Pluralism

As this chapter has emphasized, the interplay of religion and political life is performed differently in democratic, religiously pluralistic states compared to authoritarian religious states. Religion and politics have always intermixed in the United States, so the rise of Christian fundamentalism in the 1980s was not an aberration (Marsden, 1991). What is different,

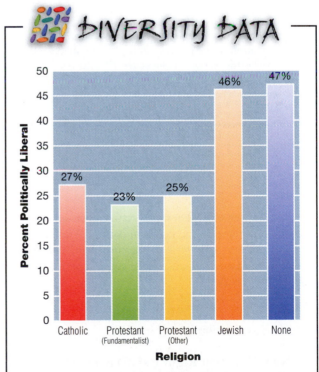

DIVERSITY DATA

FIGURE 17.6   **What Percent of People with Different Religious Preferences Identify Themselves as Liberal?** Almost half of Jews and those reporting no religion identify themselves as politically liberal, about 20 percent higher than for other religious groups. What political issues do you think separate Jews from others in all religious groups?

Source: NORC. General Social Surveys. 1972–1996. Chicago: National Opinion Research Center, 1996. Reprinted by permission of NORC, Chicago, IL.

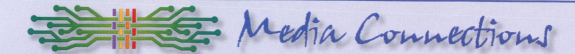

Televangelism and the Electronic Church

In Holyland, U.S.A., busloads of tourists walk through a sculpture garden depicting biblical scenes such as Noah's Ark, the Last Supper, and the Crucifixion. The gift shop sells miniature arks filled with animals as well as videos and audiotapes that help visitors relive their Holyland experience at their leisure. Thousands of tourists visit the Crystal Cathedral in Garden Grove, California, home to Rev. Robert Schuller's ministry. Christian bookstores sell the books and tapes that are first publicized on radio and television. Tourists are drawn to both places, and bookstores catering to Christians thrive through publicity via the electronic church.

The electronic church includes radio broadcasting and television ("televangelism"). Their viewers see the principal functions of religious media as the proclamation of the gospel and the drive to convert lost souls. Televangelism targets people who are already religious and who share common symbols, values, and a belief in a moral culture. The composition of the electronic church's audience has not changed appreciably over the years. The average audience for the top ten televangelist programs was about 8 million at the peak of its popularity in the 1980s. There is little evidence to suggest there has been a new surge in audience size since then.

The other group that relies heavily on religious broadcasting is the New Christian Right (NCR), which uses the electronic church for publicizing its political agenda. Pat Robertson founded the Christian Broadcasting Network to "bring us [the United States] back to traditional conceptions of morality." The New Christian Right came to rely heavily on the electronic church to couch its political appeal in religious terms, in a manner, some suggest, that combines religious and political intolerance. The height of this usage came with Pat Robertson's presidential bid in 1988 when he used his *700 Club* show to spotlight NCR's platform. The 1988 Robertson case can be used as a sociological test to assess the political strength of the electronic church.

He is a television "personality," regardless of what he says or does. However, NCR needs more than this status if it is to gain viewers of religious television for their political means. While *700 Club* viewers regularly see a mix of political and social commentary, they vary greatly on reactions to the content. Many viewers simply cannot reconcile the spiritual with the political. The electronic church's vision is too specific and its audience too religiously diverse to tap a common political denominator that brings everybody together.

Since the start of televangelism over a half century ago, televangelists have been entertainers—charismatic preachers with a tradition of showmanship that translated very well on the screen. Television preachers of all religious and political types share a common trait: They are very entre-

however, is that a number of Christian sects appear to be converging under one political banner. Fundamentalist resurgence is a global phenomenon, but U.S. Christian fundamentalism takes a unique path (Marty & Appleby, 1992).

The New Christian Right

The **New Christian Right (NCR)** is a fundamentalist political movement composed of a number of mostly Protestant conservative pressure groups with an agenda calling for returning morality to U.S. society. Secular humanism, seen as rampant in politics, is a common foe that united several Christian right-wing groups including Jerry Falwell's Moral Majority and Pat Robertson's Christian Coalition. Although supposedly wider in the scope of religions represented, the latest ally is Bill McCartney's Promise Keepers. These groups do not demand that the United States become a religious state, but only that the nation's Christian historical foundations be embraced in government policy. A specific Christian brand of morality based on the literal truth of the Bible is the blueprint for political life (Caplan, 1987). Regardless of rhetoric, this is clearly contrary to religious pluralism and the toleration it implies.

Specific items targeted in the political campaign include: support for a Constitutional amendment allowing voluntary prayer in public schools; teaching creationism in biology courses; restricting sex education; and opposing homosexual rights, the spread of pornography, abortion rights, and the Equal Rights Amendment (ERA) (Moen, 1994; Bruce et al., 1994). The last two are explicitly linked to setting back gains in gender equity.

Adherents of the New Christian Right seek to reverse the tide of gender equity, which they believe has

preneurial. The success of televangelism is measured in money: How much can their audience contribute to keep the television "ministry," as well as the organizations and preachers it supports, going? Money is not only good for the ministry but it is good for the people who contribute. Some televangelists insist that prayers will be answered and success will come when contributions are sent in.

Televangelism functions as the church for people who cannot get to a church on a regular basis. Sociologists show that the perception that the electronic church has enormous influence in gaining wider support for the Christian Right's agenda is not borne out. NCR must do more than "preach to the converted" if religious television is to be politically successful. However, when the gospel is combined with successful fund-raising techniques, televangelism appears to be financially effective. It supports its preachers (often lavishly) and publicizes its business associates. Televangelism continues because it is a profitmaking concern.

1. What kind of messages should the electronic church broadcast in order to increase audience size? Can these

Religious evangelism is often promoted through charismatic entertainers like Jimmy Swaggert. Although he was disgraced in the United States, his television ministry enjoys much popularity in Russia.

messages be successful for both mainstream and conservative Christians?
2. Demonstrate how the electronic church can be used as evidence for and against the secularization hypothesis. Which side of the hypoth-

esis is more likely to be supported by the evidence?

Sources: Hadden & Swann, 1981; Robertson, 1984; Hoover, 1988, 1990; Bruce, 1990; Hadden, 1993; Kivisto, 1994; Schultze, 1996; Buddenbaum & Stout, 1996.

eroded the divinely inspired moral order, and to return the United States to its patriarchal roots. Although the United States may have patriarchal roots, religion, particularly Christianity, does not. Preinstitutionalized religion was not only female friendly, but female centered. Women's role and status are at the nucleus of the NCR political platform. The platform opposes the Equal Rights Amendment, a proposed amendment to the U.S. Constitution stating that "equality of rights under the law shall not be denied or abridged on account of sex" (gender), and supports removing existing abortion rights (see Chapter 13).

Secularization or Religious Resurgence?

This overview of the rise of Christian fundamentalism suggests why there is not much support for the secularization hypothesis, but also why religious pluralism

is alive and well in U.S. society. The New Christian Right represents religious resurgence, but its supporters are divided between the fundamentalist and evangelical sides of the movement. Jerry Falwell attracts a more politically motivated constituency and, although he ran for president, Pat Robertson has more supporters from charismatic churches. In both ranks, there are people who are across-the-board conservatives and those who are conservative on some social issues but moderate on others (Rozzell & Wilcox, 1996; Wilcox, 1996). In trying to score political points with religious rhetoric, NCR could not please all the conservative religious constituencies. In attempting to build alliances, they gradually lost a core of dedicated followers (Bruce, 1989). Research on Protestant conservatives, for example, defies stereotypes by documenting relative liberalness on civil liberties and activism for the poor. African American Protestants who are religious conservatives are more

Several organizations, such as Jerry Falwell's Moral Majority, have lobbied to get a Christian fundamentalist agenda enacted in official government policy, such as an amendment to the U.S. Constitution for prayer in public schools.

liberal than either mainstream white Protestants and all varieties of Catholics (Hart, 1992; Miller, 1997).

Being morally conservative does not make someone politically conservative. Politicians desire endorsement from the New Christian Right, but realize it is political suicide to incorporate too many NCR

items into legislative proposals (Kivisto, 1994; Goodstein, 1998). Religious pluralism ensures that the religious right cannot muster the strength it needs to sustain an ongoing, cohesive political movement of Christian fundamentalists. The same could be said of a hypothetical religious "left," made up of secular humanists.

As for the secularization hypothesis, it has fallen on hard times. While it is apparent that religion is expressed differently than in the past, core religious beliefs continue to be embraced by Americans (Gallup & Jones, 2000). The sociology of religion has been a sociology *of the churches* (Berger, 1990). "Churchly" religiosity has declined, but religious participation has not. Televangelism reaches the homebound who may never step into a church. When measures are used to tap different dimensions, religiosity emerges unharmed. Religion has been affected by a host of major happenings, such as modernization, politics, and gender role change. When secularization occurs, the process itself prompts religious revival and innovation (Stark & Bainbridge, 1985). Sociology shows that religion has adapted and restructured, but not necessarily secularized; in the process it has added to already existing religious pluralism.

SUMMARY

1. According to Émile Durkheim, religion performs several social functions. A source of social cohesion and social control, religion promotes social service, offers believers strength and community in time of crisis, and gives meaning to life by addressing the ultimate questions of life and death.

2. Karl Marx asserted that religion maintains the stratification system and serves its prevailing economic interests. Religion is an opiate that focuses people on the "other world" rather than striving for change in this world. Max Weber argued that religion served as an incentive for the rise of capitalism and promoted social change.

3. Anthropologist Edward Tylor originally argued that religion evolved through stages, from lower to higher level forms: animism (supernatural beings and spirits that can help or hurt) to theism, belief in many gods (polytheism), to one god (monotheism). A final stage may be secular or civil religion—with sacred symbols shared by everyone in society regardless of their religion. The evolutionary view overall is no longer accepted by social scientists.

4. A church is an inclusive structure with a specific theology and professionally trained clergy.

Some societies have ecclesia, or state religions. Churches may be split into denominations, separate branches that emphasize different interpretations of the same theology. Denominations are typical in societies with high religious pluralism.

5. While churches are integrated into the larger society, sects are small, relatively informal groups, many of whose members have experienced a religious conversion. Sects often split away from established churches. Cults are small groups who begin new or unconventional religions, usually founded by a charismatic leader. Most cults have little formal organization and seldom survive beyond their leaders' lifetimes.

6. Christianity, Judaism, and Islam share common roots. Both Christianity and Islam began as monotheistic cults centered around charismatic leaders; both survived to become world religions.

7. Hinduism is the oldest of the world religions and is polytheistic. India's caste system is consistent with many Hindu beliefs, such as reincarnation and dharma (service to others).

8. Buddhism and Confucianism, which originated in Asia, are based on ethical codes intended to

promote human happiness, a higher state of consciousness and self-discipline.

9. Fundamentalism is a religious trend found in all world religions; it seeks to curb modernization and return society to a previous religious golden age. Some fundamentalists are political activists and desire a religious state. Others desire to be left alone to practice their religion with no interference. In some religious states fundamentalism is linked to human rights violations.

10. Founded on the principles of religious tolerance and the separation of church and state, the United States is the most religiously pluralistic society in the world. The vast majority of Americans are affiliated with religions and believe in God. Secularization challenges occur, such as faith in science rather than religion for problem solving.

11. Measuring religiosity and religious pluralism is complex, but these indicate less secularization and America's three main religious groups—Protestants, Catholics, and Jews—with few changes in numbers over times.

12. American religious diversity shows up both between and within religions, especially in terms of theological diversity. Protestants are divided into many denominations. Mainstream Protestants tend to be upwardly mobile and politically liberal, while fundamentalist Protestants tend to be poor and more politically conservative.

13. Like mainstream Protestants, Roman Catholics have declined in religious commitment and are more diverse than in the past. The majority of Catholics approve of birth control, are in favor of sex education in public schools, and believe divorced Catholics should be welcomed in the church. They generally believe priests can be married and women should be ordained priests. The ordination issue of women is the key one that is splitting the Vatican from U.S. Catholics overall.

14. Only about 2 percent of Americans are Jewish; most live in metropolitan areas. As a group, Jews are well educated and earn high incomes; politically liberal, they are politically influential.

15. The New Christian Right is a coalition of fundamentalist groups seeking to incorporate Christian principles into boarder life, including government policy. It generally opposes abortion rights, sex education in public schools, and the Equal Rights Amendment. It favors prayer and teaching creationism in public schools.

16. U.S. religion has adapted to social change and more religious pluralism exists, but there is not a great deal of support for the secularization hypothesis.

KEY TERMS

animism 436
church 437
civil religion 436
cult 438
denomination 437
ecclesia 437
fundamentalism 431

monotheism 436
New Christian Right (NCR) 454
polytheism 436
profane 432
religion 432
religious pluralism 432

sacred 432
sect 437
secular religion 436
secularization 431
theism 436
theology 432

CRITICAL THINKING QUESTIONS

1. What is the role of religion in socialization and how is religious socialization connected with socialization from the institutions of family and government?

2. Based on your understanding of religious pluralism in the United States, argue for or against the secularization hypothesis.

3. How do functionalists and conflict theorists explain trends toward fundamentalism and countermodernization, as well as trends toward secularization?

18 THE POLITICAL ECONOMY

EMILY's List

Fifteen years after the rebirth of the U.S. feminist movement, women had made substantial progress in many areas of public life, but elective politics remained an almost exclusively male preserve, especially at the national level. In response, twenty-five women activists met in 1985 to organize a support network that could identify promising pro-choice female Democratic candidates and help them to raise funds and conduct their campaigns.

The organization they founded was called EMILY's List, which stands for Early Money Is Like Yeast—it makes the "dough" rise. EMILY's List has grown to become the nation's largest political action committee with over 60,000 members, and it has played a central role in the recent increase in female representation to an all-time high of 13 Senators and 56 Representatives in the 107th Congress.

Advertising in the Public Schools

Without providing any opportunity for public discussion or debate, the Seattle, Washington, board of education recently decided to reduce its $5 million budget shortfall by allowing advertising in the schools. Shortly thereafter, a professor at the University of Washington launched a successful campaign to reverse this decision, charging that it allowed private economic interests to unfairly promote commercial values in the public sector and thus to divert the public schools from their primary educational mission. Is it right to expose children to advertising at school where attendance is required? What is the proper relationship between private corporations and governmental activities such as public education?

This chapter examines the **political economy.** Sociologists frequently use this term rather than speaking of the political and economic institutions as fully separate systems because of the distinctive ways that power and authority are structured at the macro level in the developed societies.

In traditional usage, politics concerns the struggle for control of the **state**, defined as the institution that maintains a monopoly over the legitimate use of force within a given territory. In contrast, the **economy** is the institution that organizes the production, distribution, and consumption of goods and services. However, the distinction between these two spheres is becoming increasingly vague.

The state is heavily involved in the economy in modern societies. It guarantees property rights, regulates economic transactions, and imposes taxes. It also provides social programs, trains people to use new technologies, owns productive assets, and even enters into partnerships with private businesses. It regulates international trade and may act militarily or diplomatically to protect its trade advantages. The debate over advertising in Seattle's public schools illustrates one aspect of the complex interconnections between government and the economy.

On the other hand, the state is strongly affected by powerful economic actors such as corporations and, to a lesser extent, unions. The supporters of EMILY's List are fully aware of the importance of money in running an effective political campaign. Our use of the concept of the political economy thus underscores the fact that these two institutions are today increasingly interrelated and interdependent.

This chapter begins with a consideration of the concepts of power and authority. Next, we examine three contrasting philosophical positions on which specific political economies may be based—liberalism, socialism, and conservatism. The chapter then briefly investigates various types of economic and political systems and reviews several interpretations of the distribution of power in modern societies. We then consider two important current trends in the political arena, democratization and the increasing involvement of minorities and women in government. The chapter concludes with a consideration of voter turnout and an examination of several ways in which globalization affects the political economy.

POWER AND AUTHORITY

Power is the most important concept in the study of the political economy. Max Weber (1947) defined it as the ability to compel others to act as the powerholder wishes, even if they attempt to resist. Power always involves interactions among at least two parties. It is also always hierarchical, in the sense that one party or group is stronger than or controls another.

Most—perhaps all—power ultimately relies on force, either physical or psychological. But no society can be organized solely on the basis of force because, given any opportunity, coerced people tend to break the rules. Naked terror is both unstable and inefficient. Consequently, powerholders try to *institutionalize* their power—that is, they try to make it more stable by convincing subordinates that it is legitimate. This is usually accomplished by means of an *ideology* (see Chapter 10).

Authority is power that is perceived by subordinates as fair and just. Whether power is legitimate depends on the social context. In a college classroom, professors assign projects and, despite groans, students generally comply with these assignments. Professors can claim expertise and thus authority over their students, although the students retain the freedom to withdraw from the course. But should instructors demand sexual favors or lack appropriate academic credentials, they lose their claim to exercise authority.

Note that there are always at least two sides in an authority relationship—the *claimant* (here, the professor) and the *subordinate* (the students). Claimants proclaim their right to control subordinates and, in varying degrees, subordinates accept these claims as fair and just. Third parties are often used to reinforce authority claims (Stinchcombe, 1968). In our classroom example, parents, college administrators, and the general public help indirectly to establish the legitimacy of professors' demands on their students.

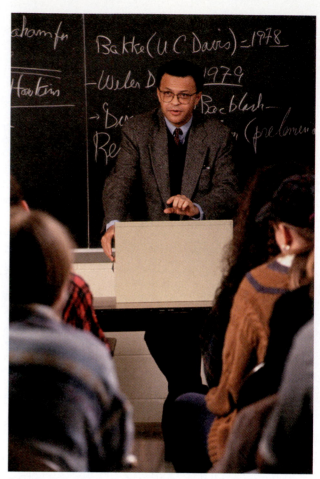

Most students accept social norms that justify the exercise of a substantial (but not unlimited) amount of power within the classroom by their professors. Max Weber refers to such legitimated power as authority.

Three Types of Power

There are three distinct types of power: decision-making power, agenda control, and systemic power (Lukes, 1974).

Decision-making power is the ability to *directly* control the behavior of others. Such resources as wealth or the threat of violence allow claimants to control subordinates, even against their will.

Agenda control is a less direct type of power, based on the ability to determine which issues will (or will not) be addressed. Agenda control has been called "non-decision making power" because it allows powerholders to prevent issues from even being considered (Bachrach & Baratz, 1970). Thus, for example, the problems of increasing income inequality or of the inevitable depletion of the world's petroleum reserves, once central to political discussion in this country, are rarely raised today.

The mass media are central in setting the political agenda in modern political economies, largely determining which issues and viewpoints will and will not be

aired. But they, in turn, are heavily influenced by the government. Nearly 80 percent of all news stories in the United States are based on press releases and interviews with government officials, which gives these officials a major say over the content of the political agenda as it is presented in the media. In many other countries, the mass media are owned by the state, giving political officials nearly complete agenda control. Similarly, large corporations maintain sizable public relations staffs that devote a great deal of their time to promoting the ideology of free-enterprise capitalism and corporate preferences concerning public policy matters.

Systemic power refers to advantages resulting from existing structural arrangements, such as the distribution of wealth. Systemic power typically results from the structural inability of subordinates to mobilize and press their claims. It also relies on claimants' ability to promote false or misleading beliefs. For example, under slavery, slaveowners promoted the idea that they were paternalistic father figures who cared for their slaves much as they did for their own children (Genovese, 1974). Slaves who accepted this

William Rehnquist holds the status of Chief Justice of the Supreme Court. His power is derived from this status, which he achieved by virtue of his outstanding formal qualifications. Sociologists classify him as a clear example of rational-legal authority.

ideology saw no need to demand their rights. Similarly, large corporations today tell employees and consumers that they are acting on their behalf when, in fact, the bottom line is corporate profit, which often comes at the expense of both groups. Table 18.1 summarizes key aspects of the three types of power.

Three Types of Authority

Max Weber (1947) described three types of authority (or legitimate power): traditional, charismatic, and rational-legal. In the real world, individual leaders often combine two or even all three of these models, but here we will discuss them separately, as ideal types.

Traditional authority is power legitimated by respect for long-established cultural patterns. The claimant's major argument is that power has always been distributed in a certain way and is therefore legitimate. In most cases, individuals who hold traditional authority do so by virtue of their ascribed statuses. Subordinates generally owe automatic and unquestioning obedience to claimants. When children ask their parents why they should obey, they are commonly told, "Because I say so!" Insofar as subordinates accept such claims without question, power is legitimate. In political systems, traditional authority is the basis of the power of kings and queens.

However, as Weber points out, industrialization and exposure to modern views tend to undermine traditional authority by encouraging subordinates to question traditional patterns. Thus, for example, in modern societies, patriarchy—the traditional dominance of men over women—persists but it is increasingly widely questioned. Most women no longer view themselves as inferior or properly subject to men, and most men agree, endorsing an egalitarian view of gender. Social change, as in this case, may encourage subordinates and claimants alike to question traditional authority, often bringing about a loss of legitimacy.

Rational-legal authority is power legitimated by legally enacted rules and regulations. It is generally associated with achieved statuses that are obtained by virtue of an individual's formal qualifications. It is especially characteristic of business and governmental bureaucracies. According to Weber, bureaucracy is a distinctive feature of modern industrial societies and is characterized by formal rules and regulations, an advanced division of labor, a hierarchy of authority, technical skills, formal training, and written rules and records (see Chapter 22).

In order to be effective, the bureaucratic rules that underlie rational-legal authority must be seen as universal, applying in every possible circumstance. They must also be clear and comprehensible to all. In

Table 18.1 Three Types of Power		
Type of Power	Definition	Example
Decision-making Power	The ability to directly control the behavior of others.	A police officer orders traffic to detour around the scene of an accident.
Agenda Control	The ability to determine which issues will or will not be addressed.	The failure by both American parties to seriously consider how to reform our current system of campaign financing.
Systemic Power	The ability to participate more or less effectively in the political system, based on one's social background or other structural factors.	The consistently greater attention given by government to issues considered important by the rich, whites, and males.

Mahatma Gandhi is one of the most outstanding charismatic leaders of the past century. He used his enormous personal appeal to forge a mass social movement that successfully challenged British colonial rule, leading to the birth of the modern Indian state in 1948.

rational-legal authority, loyalty is owed to the impersonal state, corporation, church, or university rather than to a personal ruler. Bureaucracy is the most likely of all forms of authority to persist. In fact, Weber argued that bureaucracy was becoming a restrictive "iron cage" that could not be effectively challenged, trapping and dehumanizing millions of people in modern societies. This theme will be explored in greater depth in Chapter 24.

Finally, **charismatic authority** is based on a claim to possess extraordinary or unique leadership abilities. Such claims are frequently justified by reference to the divine or transcendent. Charismatics lead independent of formal positions or offices. Political leaders such as Hitler, Gandhi, or Martin Luther King are good examples of charismatic authority, as are religious prophets and leaders like Reverend Moon or David Koresh of the Branch Davidians. Such individuals frequently find themselves in conflict with traditional and rational-legal rulers.

Charismatic authority is inherently unstable because it depends on the claimant's ability to sustain belief in her or his special qualities. Charisma requires a loyal band of "true believers" with absolute faith in their leader. Charismatic authority cannot be passed on in its pure form to the next generation of leadership, but rather must be combined with other forms of authority in a process called the **routinization of charisma**. Christianity, for example, began as a sect based on the charismatic authority of Jesus. After his death, his disciples routinized the movement by developing rational-legal authority and bureaucracy, eventually establishing the Catholic Church. Charismatic authority is present, although relatively uncommon, in both traditional and modern societies, and it has been a major force for social change throughout

history. Table 18.2 summarizes and extends this discussion of Weber's three types of authority.

THEORETICAL MODELS OF THE POLITICAL ECONOMY

Since ancient times, political philosophers have argued concerning how the ideal political economy should be structured. Three positions have dominated this debate in recent centuries: liberalism, socialism, and conservatism.

Liberalism

The core values of classical **liberalism** as developed in the seventeenth century focused on the rights of the individual, who was seen as ultimately autonomous

INTERNET CONNECTIONS

"The Protocols of the Elders of Zion," supposedly explaining how a Jewish elite plotted to control the world, was popularized by Henry Ford before he learned that the document was a forgery. Yet it is still being circulated, as you can see at site http://abbc.com/islam/english/toread/pr-zion.htm. For a discussion of the forgery, see www.adl.org/frames/front_protocols.html. Do you believe there really are secret conspiracies to rule the world, or are they pure fiction?

Table 18.2   Three Types of Authority

Type of Authority	Definition	Strengths	Weaknesses	Examples
Traditional Authority	Authority based on respect for long-established cultural patterns. Usually lodged in ascribed statuses.	Line of succession is unambiguous.	Authority holder may not be competent. Vulnerable to challenge in times of rapid social change.	Absolute monarchy. Patriarchy. Authority of parents over children.
Rational-legal Authority	Authority based on rules and regulations. Usually lodged in statuses achieved on the basis of competence.	Leaders are generally competent. Methods of replacing leaders are well established.	May become an oppressive "iron cage."	Superiors in any bureaucracy.
Charismatic Authority	Authority based on followers' perceptions of a leader's personal qualities.	Followers will do almost anything a charismatic leader asks. Leader can effectively promote sweeping social changes.	Difficulty replacing deceased or discredited leaders. Unstable charismatic leaders (e.g., Hitler) may create havoc.	Religious prophets. Gandhi. Martin Luther King.

from society and capable of reason. Philosopher Thomas Hobbes took the view that, in a "state of nature," human appetites were unlimited, giving rise to endless competition and eventually a "war of all against all." In order to prevent this state of anarchy from making life "nasty, brutish, and short," Hobbes suggested that rational actors freely accept the external authority of the state. Thus, the state exists to create political order and to protect the rights of individuals against the dangers of anarchy.

Subsequent liberal thinkers such as John Locke and Adam Smith were more skeptical about the power of the state. They argued that a limited government and a free-market economy were the best means of ensuring people's well-being. Locke believed that property ownership was the supreme natural right and that independent property holders would rationally choose to subordinate their interests to the rule of law. Adam Smith focused on the benefits of competition, maintaining that the "hidden hand" of the market provided the best assurance of peace and prosperity. The state, in his view, should limit itself to protecting individual rights, especially private property rights, and ensuring open and free-market competition.

However, classic liberalism ran up against two problems. First, it could not explain how a limited state could adequately prevent collective dangers. For example, how could a relatively weak state combat the environmental pollution that indirectly but inevitably results, given modern technologies, from market competition? A competitive market rewards short-term individual efforts but it may not adequately protect long-term collective goods such as clean air or national security.

Second, classic liberalism did not seem capable of providing an adequate solution for the tendency of competitive markets to evolve toward **monopoly,** a situation in which a single provider dominates the market and reaps windfall profits. In the late nineteenth and early twentieth centuries, industrialists in the United States—popularly known as "robber barons"—came to monopolize the railways, oil and gasoline, electricity production, and telegraphy, exploiting consumers and small businesses alike.

Solutions to such failures of the market typically require a strong state, an observation that prompted the development of **modern liberalism,** a philosophy that favors a powerful government existing alongside private property and market economics. Modern liberalism is characterized by a strong *welfare state* that lessens the harmful excesses of capitalism by providing a guaranteed minimum income, free public education, health care, and other benefits as basic citizenship rights.

Socialism

In direct contrast to capitalism, the central idea of **socialism** is that collective control of the economy by a very strong state reduces inequality and social injustice and contributes to peace and prosperity. The French philosopher Jean Jacques Rousseau argued that private property promotes greed, artificially separating the individual from the community and

Richard Nixon resigned the presidency in 1973 as a result of his involvement in efforts to cover up the Watergate burglary. The fact that this crisis did not seriously threaten the stability of the American system of government is interpreted by functionalists as evidence for the underlying legitimacy of that system.

producing poverty and vice. His solution was an extreme form of socialism called *communism*, which mandates the communal or collective ownership of all property. Instead of owning private property, under communism individuals transfer their wealth to collective control. They then receive back what they need from the community.

Twentieth-century efforts to establish socialism in the Soviet Union, Eastern Europe, and China revealed major flaws in the model. Most critically, it did not include adequate protection against the abuse of power by those controlling the state. Within a few years after the 1917 Russian Revolution, a totalitarian state had been established with virtually unlimited control over the mass media, civic organizations, and much of private life.

A second major flaw of the socialist system concerns the failure of economic planning. The Soviet system centralized control over investment and production, abolishing market competition. Without the market to guide economic decisions, surpluses of some goods existed alongside major shortages of others. Soviet housing was notoriously inadequate, and long lines at grocery stores with empty shelves were

common. Furthermore, collectivized agriculture proved a colossal failure: Three-fourths of all production came from tiny private plots that represented less than 10 percent of all agricultural land.

Conservatism

The third major model of the political economy is **conservatism,** a philosophy that emphasizes social order and sees the family, religion, and the local face-to-face community as the natural bases for that order. Early conservatives, led by the English thinker Edmund Burke, argued that gradual change was always preferable to the large-scale transformations associated with upheavals such as the French Revolution. They agreed with the classic liberals that the state was artificial and should be limited, and they agreed with the socialists that community and cooperation were critical values. However, conservatives believed that the competitive market favored by classic liberals could destroy the natural order of society by weakening the traditional bonds between people. Conservatives also opposed the socialist view that private property should be abolished, maintaining instead that property was a crucial means of reinforcing the social order.

Conservatism could not, however, respond adequately to one critical question: What if a particular political-economic system was grossly inadequate? Making many small changes over time would only reinforce a corrupt and inefficient system; yet conservatives strongly opposed revolutionary change no matter how desperately it might be needed.

Table 18.3 summarizes and extends this discussion of the three theoretical models of the political economy.

CONTEMPORARY ECONOMIC AND POLITICAL SYSTEMS

In this section we will discuss economic and political institutions separately in order to identify the principal types of each that are present in the world today.

Economic Systems

There are two basic types of economic systems, capitalism and state socialism. Mixed economies attempt to blend elements of the core types.

Capitalism.   **Capitalism** is based on the private ownership of the means of production, hired workers, and commercial markets that are today increasingly international as well as domestic. The state plays a major role in regulating the market, but its importance is ultimately secondary. That is, major eco-

Table 18.3	Theoretical Models of the Political Economy		
	View of the Proper Role of the State	View of Private Property	Representative Figures
Liberalism	A relatively weak state exists to defend the rights of the individual. Modern liberalism accepts a stronger state in order to preserve the collective good, fight monopolies, and provide welfare functions.	The right to own private property is important.	Thomas Hobbes, John Locke, Adam Smith
Socialism	A very strong state plays a dominant role in controlling the economy.	Individuals have little or no right to own productive property.	Karl Marx, Friedrich Engels
Conservatism	Role of the state is largely limited to protecting rights. Family, religion, and the local community are seen as much more important institutions than the government.	The right to own private property is paramount.	Edmund Burke

nomic players take precedence over political power-holders (Lindblom, 1977). The United States, Western Europe, Japan, and much of the developing world are capitalist. In varying degrees, the countries of Eastern Europe and the former Soviet Union have also been reorganized along capitalist lines.

State Socialism.   State socialism is a system whereby the state owns the means of production during a transitional stage between capitalism and communism. Workers are guaranteed basic food, housing, education, and health care. Markets play a secondary role at best because the state manages the economy through planning and political regulation (Lindblom, 1977; Lane, 1985). There may be small pockets of private enterprise, such as farming in formerly Communist Poland, but they are subordinate to the public sector. Workers seek jobs much as in a capitalist economy, but employment is centrally planned so that the movement of workers from job to job is regulated, in part to prevent excessive migration from the countryside to the cities.

Mixed Economies.   Mixed economies, also known as *social democracies*, combine significant state ownership and regulation of markets with some aspects of capitalism. In Sweden and much of northern Europe, strong welfare states provide education, health care, and social insurance, including generous family allowances for young children and the elderly.

The New York Stock Exchange is the nerve center of modern capitalism. The financial transactions that are conducted here influence the lives of every man, woman, and child on the planet.

Taxes are quite high—as much as 60 percent or more of the incomes of top earners—but benefits are extensive. No one is poor. State industrial policies encourage private entrepreneurs to adopt new technologies and enter new fields. The government also attempts to plan investment by regulating interest rates and co-investing in new enterprises.

How well do these various systems perform? State socialism creates more equal access to education, health care, and the like, but it also creates major inefficiencies and production bottlenecks. In the former Soviet Union, for example, the military and heavy industry were developed at the expense of consumer markets. Without market forces regulating investment and production, economic growth was overly concentrated in the sectors favored by political leaders.

The capitalist countries show stronger overall economic growth and a greater emphasis on consumer industries. At the same time, they are characterized by greater class inequality and poverty.

Social democracy combines strong state regulation and a comprehensive welfare state with capitalism. It thus may be seen as blending the more desirable characteristics of the two basic economic systems. The Nordic and northern European social democracies have greater equality than the United States and Britain but, especially in the past decade, their rates of economic growth have been lower.

Table 18.4 summarizes and extends this discussion of the major economic systems.

Political Systems

As with economic systems, there are two basic kinds of political systems or regimes: authoritarianism and democracy. By a *regime*, sociologists mean a system of government and the ideologies used to legitimate it.

Authoritarian Regimes. In **authoritarian regimes**, the people are excluded from any meaningful participation in decision making. *Monarchies* are the oldest type of authoritarian regime, allocating formal power solely on the basis of heredity.

In *dictatorships*, a "strongman" rules on the basis of personal loyalties, favors, and threats of force. Dictatorships most often arise in the least developed countries, where literacy and political mobilization among citizens are low. They are relatively weakly institutionalized because they generally lack a strong appeal to tradition or charisma (Roth, 1968). In an attempt to stabilize their regimes, dictators often claim an hereditary right to rule. In the late 1970s, for example, the longstanding dictator of Haiti, "Papa Doc" Duvalier, realized that he would soon die. To try to ensure that his son, "Baby Doc," would succeed him, he proclaimed himself emperor. But such claims rarely succeed, as "Baby Doc" found out when the Haitian military seized power and drove him from office.

In *bureaucratic-authoritarian regimes*, power is vested in a bureaucratic state dominated by the military and top government officials (O'Donnell, 1979). Because leaders use rational means of control—formal rules, a constitution—this form of government is frequently more stable than other types of authoritarian rule. A strong nationalistic ideology helps legitimate power. Elites from major institutions—the economy, education, religion—are brought into the system as consultants and advisors. A large professional military is also often important. A number of countries in the developing world, including Algeria, Myanmar, and Guatemala, fit this pattern. Bureaucratic-authoritarian regimes are relatively stable and, at least as long as economic growth continues, they are generally able to secure a measure of legitimacy.

Totalitarianism is a type of authoritarianism in which there are no formal limits on the extent to which the government can intervene in people's everyday lives. Thus, in Nazi Germany, the government routinely entered private households and seized people and goods without warrants. The state con-

Table 18.4	Types of Economic Systems		
Type of Economic System	Definition	How Involved Is the State in the Economy?	Contemporary Examples
Capitalism	Economy based on private ownership of the means of production, hired workers, and commercial markets.	Minimally.	The United States, Japan, Germany
State Socialism	State owns the means of production and guarantees certain economic rights to all citizens.	Extensively.	China, Cuba, North Korea
Mixed Economies (Social Democracies)	Significant state ownership and regulation of markets is combined with substantial elements of capitalism.	Moderately.	Sweden, Finland, the Netherlands

trolled all the mass media and all associations, from the Boy Scouts to churches and sports teams. Similarly, at the height of the Chinese "Cultural Revolution" of the late 1960s, the Red Guards publicly humiliated critics of Mao Zedong, closed down major universities, and forced educated people into the countryside to work on communal farms.

In totalitarian systems, minority groups, such as the Jews, the Roms (or Gypsies), and homosexuals in Nazi Germany, are sometimes imprisoned, sent to forced labor camps, or even executed. In Stalin's Soviet Union, the secret police had unrestricted powers of search and seizure, routinely used torture and drugs to extract confessions, and tried political enemies in kangaroo courts. People convicted of crimes against the state were sent to Siberia, imprisoned in psychiatric hospitals, or executed.

The Soviet Union held formal elections in which citizens had the right to vote "yes" or "no" to a list of candidates, but there were no competing candidates and the Communist Party preselected everyone who appeared on the ballot. Thus, totalitarian systems may appear to generate popular participation, but it is false participation in that it does not allow the citizens to control the power of the state. Totalitarian regimes are ideologically diverse, from the ultra-right and racist Nazi government to the ultra-left Communist governments of the former Soviet bloc.

Democratic Regimes.   Democratic systems are the second major type of political regime. **Democracies** routinely include citizens in government and their consent is the formal basis for the legitimacy of the state. Joseph Schumpeter (1942) distinguished between two ideal types of democracy. In a *participatory democracy*, citizens are personally involved in decision making, while in an indirect or *representative democracy*, citizens elect leaders who make decisions on their behalf.

Because of the size of modern political systems and the complexity of the decisions that they must make, participatory democracy is generally no longer a viable option. It worked well in small New England communities in the eighteenth century and in some utopian communes, but it is not feasible in modern states. Representative democracy is more practical. A healthy degree of democratic accountability is provided by competitive elections, universal adult suffrage, guaranteed rights of assembly and free speech, and the secret ballot. A representative democracy also requires an independent mass media accessible to all candidates and a voting system free of manipulation and bias (Dahl, 1958, 1982).

Table 18.5 summarizes and extends this discussion of the basic types of political systems.

Political Economies

Political sociologists have investigated the question of which types of economic and political systems are most likely to be combined. State socialism is typically associated with totalitarian regimes, although capitalist countries, such as Nazi Germany, may also be totalitarian. To date, no state socialist economy has coexisted with a full representative democracy. Yet in contemporary China, there are competing candidates and secret ballots in local elections, which help motivate officials to pay some attention to public opinion. At the national level, however, the Communist Party retains complete control.

Capitalism is compatible with a variety of political systems, but it is perhaps most often found in democracies. In fact, political scientist S. M. Lipset (1960) has argued that capitalism is a structural requisite for stable democracy. Not only is the populace in a capitalist society typically well educated and thus better able to mobilize politically, but affluence also makes economic conflicts easier to resolve because it creates a large middle class that may help find a middle ground between the extreme positions often favored by the rich and the poor.

THE DISTRIBUTION OF POLITICAL POWER

There are four basic schools of thought concerning how power is actually distributed in modern democratic capitalist states. Most modern liberals accept **pluralism,** the view that competition among elites disperses power amongst many different individuals and groups (Kariel, 1961; Dahl, 1968; Rose, 1968).

Some socialists and conservatives support some form of the **elite model,** which directly opposes pluralism by maintaining that real power is concentrated in the hands of a small and relatively cohesive group of bureaucratic elites. Socialists generally believe that this elite power should be broken up (Mills, 1956), while conservatives contend that elite domination benefits the social order (Dye, 1995).

Other socialists endorse the **ruling class model,** which maintains that the upper class dominates the political economy of the capitalist countries despite occasional challenges by the working and middle classes (Miliband, 1977; Domhoff, 1979, 1998).

Finally, some modern liberals support the **state autonomy model** that sees top government officials and professional experts as the primary powerholders (Nordlinger, 1981; Skocpol, 1985). We'll examine each of these interpretations in turn and then consider how they might be synthesized.

Table 18.5   Types of Political Systems

Type of Political System	Definition	Examples
Authoritarian Regimes	The people are excluded from any meaningful participation in decision making.	
Monarchies	Power is allocated solely on the basis of heredity.	Medieval Europe, Saudi Arabia
Dictatorships	Power is held by a single individual who did not inherit it.	Cuba, Libya, Iraq
Bureaucratic-Authoritarian Regimes	Power is held by the military and top government officials.	Nigeria, Algeria
Totalitarian Regimes	No formal limits exist on the power of the state over its citizens.	Nazi Germany, the Soviet Union
Democratic Regimes	The people are routinely included in government and their consent is the formal basis for the legitimacy of the state.	
Participatory Democracy	Each citizen is personally involved in decision making.	Traditional New England town meetings, some early feminist groups.
Representative Democracy	Citizens elect leaders who make decisions on their behalf.	The United States, the United Kingdom, Canada, France

The Pluralist Model

Pluralists claim that politics is a genuinely competitive arena. The large number of contending groups and the relative ease of mobilizing and influencing decision making ensure substantial access for all significant interests. Moreover, various types of resources—wealth, charisma, prestige—can be translated into power, and thus power may be dispersed even more widely.

Pluralists believe that the political system is structured around two key institutions: political parties and interest group organizations. *Political parties* compete for elective office, appealing to various constituencies in order to gain voter support. *Interest group organizations* are independent political associations that protect particular economic and social interests. By lobbying, filing suits, contributing to political parties, and engaging in propaganda campaigns, interest groups such as trade associations, unions, and professional societies try to influence specific governmental decisions. Examples of interest group organizations include the National Organization for Woman (NOW), EMILY's List, the National Right to Life Committee, the Sierra Club, the National Association for the Advancement of Colored People (NAACP), and the National Rifle Association (NRA).

Pluralists suggest that interest group organizations focus on "single issues" such as the legality of abortion or highway construction in particular Congressional districts. Neither business nor labor ever mobilizes as a whole, but rather there is healthy competition among a number of relatively narrow interest groups. Businesses compete with other businesses, and labor unions are theoretically as likely to forge coalitions with businesses sharing similar interests as they are to align with other unions. In this way, multiple interest groups counter one another, keeping the more extreme factions in check and preventing polarization.

Pluralists also see the overall structure of the government itself as pluralistic, with the federal system being distinct from state and local governments and often competing with these other units for power. The result is a constant "checks and balances" process, whereby no one group consistently gets its way and all interests are kept from becoming too extreme.

Finally, the plurality of group interests means that there are strong cross-cutting cleavages in modern societies. *Cross-cutting cleavages* occur when individuals find themselves pulled in different directions at the same time. One might be a Catholic and thus attracted to a pro-life position but also be a feminist and on that basis be drawn toward pro-choice policies. Cross-cutting cleavages encourage moderation and fluid political allegiances; they also help prevent polarization, which might lead to more intense and violent conflict.

The pluralist view was expressed most clearly in Robert Dahl's (1961) classic study of political power in New Haven, Connecticut. He found that a small number of wealthy families had clearly dominated the town's politics in the nineteenth century. However, this changed in the early twentieth century. Urbanization, population growth, and industrialization led to a dispersion of power that gave newly arrived immigrant groups, labor unions, and the middle class a significant say in politics. Speaking of the post–World War II New Haven political scene, Dahl concluded: "No one,

The National Rifle Association is one of America's most vocal interest group organizations. Viewing almost any effort to regulate the sale of firearms as a threat to the Second Amendment, NRA members have successfully opposed numerous efforts to strengthen gun control laws over the years.

and certainly no group of more than a few individuals, is entirely lacking in power" (1961, p. 228).

In sum, the pluralist model considers the U.S. political economy to be basically democratic and open, giving a measure of power to all competing groups. Although pluralists do not claim that power is fully equalized, they do maintain that the powerful do not consistently get their way and that the disadvantaged often are able to mobilize and have at least some of their interests addressed. Pluralists also contend that the U.S. system is relatively stable.

Critics respond that pluralism paints a misleading picture of U.S. politics. First, they note that disadvantaged groups face major obstacles in mobilizing and therefore, in practice, are often entirely excluded from the decision-making process (Gamson, 1975; McAdam, 1982; Jenkins, 1985). For example, although the civil rights movement of the 1960s was able to overturn Jim Crow laws mandating segregation, it had little success in challenging the more deeply entrenched economic and social disadvantages of African Americans (McAdam, 1982; Wilson, 1987).

Critics also point out that business and a significant portion of the upper-middle class can mobilize politically on a broader basis than other interests. Big business funds a multitude of associations that represent the general business point of view (Useem, 1984). Organized labor has the AFL-CIO, which lobbies on behalf of workers and consumers (Greenstone, 1968), but it is much weaker than the major business-oriented interest groups (Form, 1996). Similarly, the upper-middle class funds a number of public interest groups promoting environmentalism, the rights of women and consumers, and related middle-class concerns. These middle-class lobbies are also more powerful than organized labor or any other groups representing the lower or working classes (Berry, 1997).

The Elite Model

The central idea of the elite model is that power is concentrated in the hands of a single small, cohesive group holding high-level positions. Common social backgrounds and socialization experiences make this elite cohesive and capable of unified action. Most conservatives who accept this view believe that this concentration of power is functional, but socialists typically argue that it is exploitative.

C. Wright Mills (1956) was the major architect of the *power elite thesis*, which presents a highly critical interpretation of the U.S. political economy. Mills argued that, shortly after World War II, four major changes together created a U.S. "power elite":

- *The growth of the modern megacorporation.* Today, true market competition has largely been supplanted by corporate planning and the mass manipulation of consumers through advertising. The heads of these immense corporations are commonly involved in *interlocking directorates* or the practice of simultaneously holding seats on several different corporate boards of directors. This greatly increases elite coordination and cohesion, as does the "revolving door" process whereby wealthy businessmen are routinely recruited for top governmental positions.

- *The rise of the mass media.* The expansion of the media helped to create a *mass society* (after World War II) in which citizens are transformed into atomized consumers who can be readily manipulated by corporate advertising and government propaganda.

- *The growth of a huge and permanent peacetime military establishment.* At the end of WWII, the United States did not greatly reduce the size of its military as it had following every earlier war. At that time, a vast and seemingly permanent Pentagon bureaucracy with global responsibilities arose

Cesar Chavez's United Farm Workers union won several widely publicized battles against agribusiness in the 1960s and 1970s, although some of these victories have been partially reversed in the past two decades.

and seized upon the nuclear threat of the Soviet Union as a rationale for unending military expansion. Defense spending became the primary basis for stabilizing the national economy, providing a boost during recessions and enormous profits for the large corporations. Retired military leaders routinely pursued lucrative second careers with major defense firms.

- *The development of social institutions that forged an integrated national elite.* Attending Ivy League colleges and belonging to exclusive social clubs increased cohesion among the elite and helped develop an awareness of their mutual interests.

Together, these four changes created a single elite out of three once distinct groups: (1) the leaders of the largest corporations; (2) the "political directorate," who controlled the White House and the federal bureaucracy; and (3) the "new warlords" in the Pentagon. The unification of this national elite was reflected in the phrase, "the military-industrial complex," a term first introduced by President Eisenhower in 1958.

How well does the evidence support the power-elite thesis? The most systematic research on this question was conducted by Thomas Dye (1995). Dye investigated the social origins, political and economic resources, career paths, and interconnections among 5,778 corporate, political, and military elites. He found that 5,700 persons occupied 7,314 key elite positions. He also found that these elites were significantly interlocked, with well over one-third of them belonging to exclusive private clubs and attending Ivy League colleges. Although almost 80 percent held only one command position at a time, almost half had held other elite positions during their careers. Among

the "interlockers," an inner group held five or more elite positions simultaneously, integrating the corporate, governmental, and civic sectors.

Dye's work suggests that Mills was mostly correct, although he may have been wrong about the military elite, who were overwhelmingly drawn from modest class origins and educated at the military academies and who rarely assumed elite positions in the government or large corporations. He also overestimated the importance of being born into the upper class, with less than a third of the elite having upper-class parents.

Others scholars suggest that Mills may have exaggerated the power of the mass media. Lazarsfeld and Katz (1964) argued that the mass media did not atomize and manipulate consumers and voters as extensively as Mills thought. The masses were selective in their attention to the media, regularly turned to informal sources—friends and relatives—for advice, and were highly skeptical of White House press releases and corporate advertising. Thus, although the masses could not "speak back to their TVs," they were not the powerless "cheerful robots" that Mills depicted.

Some conservatives argue that elite cohesion is functionally necessary in modern complex societies (Dye, 1995). They suggest that Mills based his criticism on a romantic model of a decentralized society like nineteenth century United States, with its local markets, weak central government, and strong local communities, which does not adequately describe the modern world. Modern technology concentrates power and the complexity of modern society mandates expertise. Thus, in this view, the existence of a sophisticated elite, whose power is based on their knowledge and abilities and who are cohesive enough to make complex decisions, is imperative in modern societies.

Media Connections

Political Activism on the Web

Democratic regimes like the United States have always been characterized by a substantial amount of grassroots political activism. This has traditionally involved such mundane activities as displaying yard signs or bumper stickers, manning phone banks, or going door-to-door in support of favored candidates. Recently, however, the computer has been enlisted in the service of political advocacy, promising to alter the nature of campaigning in the future.

Six months before the 2000 Presidential election, some 6,800 private citizens had already established web sites concerning one of the major party candidates. Some of the sites directly supported either Republican George W. Bush or Democrat Al Gore. Others were parody sites, mercilessly criticizing one of the candidates. Still others were more broadly oriented, such as www.voterepublican.net, a website maintained by Eugene, Oregon, computer technician Travis Main as a means of promoting conservative Republican principles. The site includes links to related web pages, posts letters

from its readers, and sponsors online political discussions.

The established political parties are grateful for the support of activists on the web, but they express some concern over the fact that people can post political information, no matter how inaccurate, on their personal web pages without any control or regulation. The Democrats have asked the Commerce Department to consider assigning a special domain (.elect or .pol) to official web sites in order to differentiate them from the unofficial and uncontrolled web pages.

The major parties are also hustling to catch up with the grassroots activists by improving the quality of their own websites. In June 2000, the Republican National Committee sponsored a workshop called "Winning in a Web World" to help both party organizers and local activists use cyberspace more effectively. Meanwhile, the Democratic Party sponsored parody sites such as www.MillionairesForBush.com modeled after private anti-Bush web pages.

Campaigning on the web is in its infancy, and no one knows how it will

evolve, but it seems clear that computer technology has the potential to be a powerful force fighting political alienation and apathy. As Robin Orlowsky, a junior at Texas Women's College and the sponsor of a liberal website, puts it: "These sites will increase democracy in the long run. You don't have tightly scripted campaigns as the sole voice. You will have independent citizens voicing their opinions in a way they couldn't before. It's because the Internet is dirt cheap and it costs money to print campaign materials. The Internet is a great free opportunity."

1. Will online activism increase political participation in the entire populace or will it deepen the gap between the educated middle-class and the poor, who currently lag behind in access to computer technology?

2. What are some of the ways in which supporters of social movements like environmentalism or feminism might be able to make use of the web to promote their point of view?

Source: Wayne, 2000.

Finally, some observers believe that the power-elite model applies best to foreign policy, where public scrutiny is relatively weak and political secrecy is easier to justify. Citizens are more aware of their interests and better able to influence decisions regarding domestic policies.

The Ruling Class Model

Some socialists have proposed a ruling class model. G. William Domhoff (1979, 1990, 1998) argues that a cohesive upper class (as opposed to a power elite composed of people drawn from relatively diverse social backgrounds) dominates society.

The ruling class defends its power in four ways. First, elites use the *candidate-selection process* to fund candidates for high-level political office, effectively restricting competition to an acceptable field of contenders. Second, elites use the *special interest process* by which business attempts to control governmental de-

cisions. This mechanism resembles the interest-group politics of the pluralists. Third, the *ideological process* allows corporate elites and top government officials to promote popular beliefs such as "free-enterprise capitalism." Fourth is the *policy planning process*, by which corporate elites and the upper class develop long-term policy strategies to address the structural problems of the political economy.

Of the four, the policy planning process is probably the most important. It is carried out principally by a handful of business associations and research institutes that are funded and controlled by corporate elites and the upper class. Some, such as the Business Roundtable (made up of the top 100 *Fortune* manufacturing corporations) and the U.S. Chamber of Commerce, represent a wide range of business interests. They try to establish a consensus on policy options by sponsoring meetings, conferences, and private bargaining sessions. Others, such as the Brookings Institution, the Heritage Foundation, or the American

Multi-billionaire film-maker Steven Spielberg was an important contributor to Bill Clinton's presidential election campaigns. The ruling class model emphasizes that candidates must often modify their positions on important issues in order to obtain financial support from members of the upper class.

Enterprise Institute, are large policy research organizations that accept funding from private foundations and wealthy individuals to develop solutions to what they see as pressing structural problems.

For example, policies promoted in the early 1980s by the Business Roundtable, the American Enterprise Institute, and the Heritage Foundation cut corporate taxes by over half and reduced the top personal tax rate from over 65 percent to 32 percent (Peschek, 1987; Akard, 1992). Similarly, the Social Security Act of 1935 was developed by upper-class policy experts who wanted to stave off the depression and co-opt popular support for more radical measures (Jenkins & Brents, 1989; Domhoff, 1990).

Critics raise three major arguments against the ruling class model. First, they say it underestimates the autonomy of high government officials and policy experts who are, in fact, usually the central architects of major policy changes. In this view, institutional precedents and political ideologies are often more important than upper-class interests. Second, critics argue, the upper class is rarely politically unified but is instead sharply divided by industrial and firm-specific interests (Berg & Zald, 1978; Wilson, 1989). Other players, including interest groups and public opinion, are more influential than the upper class in guiding policy decisions. Finally, although decisions regarding some types of public policy—for example, defense spending—are centralized and dominated by the upper class, critics suggest that others—for example, many of those concerning education—are made in a more pluralistic fashion (Laumann & Knoke, 1987).

The State Autonomy Model

According to state autonomy theory, top government officials and policy experts play the key role in the development of policy (Skocpol, 1985; Nordlinger, 1981). Instead of being the tools of special-interest groups, as pluralists maintain, or of the upper class, as the ruling class approach would have it, government leaders develop policies largely on their own. They can do so because of the growing independence and increasing resources of the state. The state bureaucracy insulates government agencies from outside influences, making them increasingly independent.

The problem with this perspective is that it may overemphasize political power as distinct from economic and social power. This is a particularly serious weakness in analyzing the power structure of the United States, where "the business of politics is business." Hence, many critics suggest that this perspective is best combined with other theories of power (Hicks & Mishra, 1993) or that it is actually just a revised version of pluralism (Domhoff, 1996).

Table 18.6 summarizes and extends the four major models of the distribution of political power.

Toward a Synthesis

These four theories concerning the empirical distribution of political power all have some merit. Scholars are therefore currently trying to blend the insights of each into a broader theory of the political economy. For example, Alexander Hicks (Hicks & Mishra,

Table 18.6	The Distribution of Political Power		
	Who Holds Power?	Is Power Broadly or Narrowly Distributed?	Does One Group Dominate the Society?
Pluralism	A variety of competing interest groups.	Relatively broadly.	No.
The Elite Model	A small, coherent group of bureaucratic elites.	Narrowly.	Yes.
The Ruling Class Model	The upper class.	Narrowly.	Yes.
The State Autonomy Model	Top government officials and policy experts.	Fairly narrowly.	Yes, up to a point.

1993) recently proposed a "political resource" theory. He contends that in a basically pluralistic state such as the United States, political leaders are relatively weak and most policy is initiated by interest groups and business-policy organizations. On the other hand, in France or Japan, where the state is strongly institutionalized and political leaders can draw on substantial economic resources, they are more often the true architects of policy. This theory underscores two key points: We must look broadly at how different political economies are organized and we must develop an inclusive framework that incorporates the insights of all of the theories of power.

CURRENT TRENDS IN THE POLITICAL ECONOMY

In this section, we will consider two important recent trends in the political economy, the worldwide movement toward democratization and the slowly increasing involvement of minorities and women in politics.

Democratization

All around the world today, authoritarian regimes are undergoing a process of *democratization*—the transition from authoritarianism to democracy. There are two main perspectives on how this process occurs—the elite-pact thesis and the class-conflict thesis.

The *elite-pact thesis* suggests that institutional elites decide that expanding popular participation is in their own best interest (Higley & Gunther, 1992). This usually occurs at a time of political or economic crisis. The leaders of the authoritarian regime make an implicit agreement or "pact" with their opponents that guarantees the leaders a substantial amount of continued power in exchange for a measure of democratization (Linz & Stepan, 1996; Sorensen, 1998). Most recent democratizations have been elite-guided, and most have occurred in semi-industrialized countries with a substantial middle class, mass education, and market economies. Many of the nations of

Latin America have democratized over the past few decades. This tends to support Lipset's claim that stable democracy requires capitalist economic development.

On the other hand, the *class-conflict thesis* explains democratization as a consequence of political pressure resulting from working-class mobilization (Rueschemeyer et al., 1992). Throughout Western Europe, working-class social movements have pushed to expand citizenship rights and promote the growth of the welfare state. Similarly, dissent by workers (as well as intellectuals) has been critical in promoting democratization across virtually all of Eastern Europe (Misztal & Jenkins, 1995).

What are the benefits of democratization? For one thing, democracies are historically less likely to engage in wars than are authoritarian regimes. However, the most important benefit is reduced internal state repression. Using the term *democide* to refer to death at the hands of the state for political reasons, Rudolph Rummel (1995) documents that this type of political violence is closely associated with totalitarian regimes, ranging from Stalin's Russia and Hitler's Germany to Cambodia under Pol Pot, the Rwandan genocide, and the revolutionary tribunals and purges in China. Authoritarian capitalist regimes in Argentina, Chile, and Brazil during the 1970s and Nigeria in the 1980s were also guilty of democide, although of a less extreme nature. Democide has claimed almost three times as many lives in the twentieth century as has international war.

Race and Gender in the Political Economy

Throughout American history, minority groups and women have been systematically blocked from assuming positions of real power in the political economy, a generalization that remains largely valid today despite the substantial progress that has occurred in recent decades.

African Americans. While a substantial number of former slaves were elected to Congress from the South during Reconstruction (1866–1877), once local whites regained control of the region, almost all African Americans were disenfranchised by means of poll taxes, literacy tests, and other similar devices. It was not until the civil rights movement of the 1960s that African Americans regained the right to vote in the South (Morris, 1984; McKelvey, 1994).

The first important black electoral successes of the modern era took place in northern cities where white flight to the suburbs was changing the racial composition of the urban electorate. African American mayors were elected in Cleveland, Detroit, Chicago, New York, and Los Angeles, among other places. Today five of the ten largest U.S. cities are led by black mayors.

In 1963, only 103 African Americans held elective office nationwide; by 1994 over 8,000 did so. However, this figure still represented only about 3 percent of all elected officials. As of 1998, African Americans, who constitute about 12 percent of the nation's population, held just one Senate seat and 9 percent of those in the House. Two African Americans have been appointed to the Supreme Court and four were selected as members of President Clinton's original cabinet. Only three African Americans are currently widely recognized as national political leaders: former Presidential candidate Jesse Jackson, leader of the Nation of Islam Lewis Farrakhan, and retired General Colin Powell. None has ever held major elective office.

Except during the late 1960s, African American voting rates have been lower than those of whites of similar age and class level, but the participation gap has been closing in recent years (Ellison & Gay, 1989). In 1996, 51 percent of all registered African Americans voted compared with 56 percent of whites.

African Americans have been strongly identified with the Democratic Party since the New Deal era; in 1996 84 percent of the African American vote went to President Clinton. There is some concern that they have been so loyal to the Democrats that their support is sometimes taken for granted by party leaders (White, 1990).

While African Americans have made some progress in the political sphere, they hold only 3 percent of upper management slots in the nation's largest businesses (Rosenblatt, 1995) and are almost completely absent from corporate boardrooms.

Other Racial and Ethnic Minorities. Hispanic Americans are the fastest growing minority in the United States. They constitute nearly a quarter of all eligible voters in California, Texas, New Mexico, Arizona, and Florida, making them a potentially powerful voting bloc. Furthermore, recent controversies over bilingual education and "English only" laws have

Retired Gen. Colin Powell waves to delegates before speaking at the 2000 Republican National Convention. President-elect George W. Bush chose General Powell to be his secretary of state in December 2000.

intensified many Hispanics' interest in politics. Yet their turnout in recent presidential elections has been the lowest of any major ethnic group—just 27 percent in 1996. As of 1998 there were just seventeen Hispanics in the House and none in the Senate.

Like African Americans, most Hispanics find the policies of the Democratic Party appealing and give it most of their support. 72 percent backed President Clinton in 1996. However, the Cuban American population, economically better off than other Hispanics and intensely anti-communist, has generally voted Republican (Welch & Sigelman, 1993).

Most other minority groups are too small in numbers to have much political impact except in local areas where they constitute a significant percentage of the population. Asian Americans are a partial exception: Despite making up only 3 percent of the population, there are six Asian Americans in the House and two in the Senate, most from Hawaii. One Native American has been elected to the Senate, and Connecticut Senator Joseph Lieberman, an orthodox Jew, was Al Gore's running mate in the 2000 election.

Women. Feminist scholars have emphasized that politics is a highly gendered and distinctly masculine activity. Women often find it difficult to establish their credibility in the aggressive rough-and-tumble of the political arena (MacKinnon, 1983; Haney, 1996).

Like racial and ethnic minorities, women have made political progress, but it has been agonizingly slow. They were first allowed to vote in the Wyoming Territory in 1869, but they did not achieve universal suffrage until the 19th Amendment was ratified in 1920. The first woman was elected to Congress in 1917; the first female governors were elected in 1924 (both were the wives of former governors); the first female senator was elected in 1931; the first female cabinet officer was appointed in 1932; the first woman—Sandra Day O'Connor—was named to the Supreme Court in 1981; and Geraldine Ferarro was chosen as the first major-party vice presidential nominee in 1984.

No woman has ever been nominated to run for President on a major party ticket. Before 1955 a majority of Americans said that they could not support a qualified female candidate for the Presidency; as recently as 1987, 25 percent still said they would not do so (Farley, 1998). In contrast, twenty-four women served as heads of state internationally during the last century, representing nations as diverse as the United Kingdom, Israel, Norway, Turkey, Canada, Pakistan, India, and Nigeria.

Prior to the 1992 election, women held just 2 Senate seats and 29 in the House. By 2001 they occupied 13 of the 100 Senate seats and 59 of the 435 seats in the House. This meant that they made up 13 percent of the total Congress. The United States ranks fortieth out of the 116 nations with democratic systems in percentage of female representation. Sweden leads the way with 43 percent (Norris, 1997; Inter-Parliamentary Union, 1999). At the other extreme, women are still denied the right to vote in Kuwait and the United Arab Emirates.

In general, women have been more successful running for state or local offices than at the national level. Thus, between 1979 and 1998 the percentage of state legislators who were female rose from 10.3 to 21.5 (Farley, 1998). As of 1999 three states had elected female governors.

Female voting rates, once lower than those of men, are now roughly similar (Ladd, 1993). Prior to the early 1980s party preference did not very appreciably by gender, but since then college-educated women have tended to disproportionately favor the Democratic Party, a trend that has been called the *gender gap* (Ladd, 1993). In the 1998 elections, Democrats received 51 percent of women's votes and 45 percent of men's votes (Marks, 1998). Most analysts explain this pattern by the fact that national Democrats tend to emphasize health care, education, poverty, and gun control, all issues that are of special interest to women (Lake & Breglio, 1992). Interestingly, there is no gender gap between African American men and women; both strongly support liberal Democratic policies (Welch & Sigelman, 1989).

The glass ceiling is especially obvious in the corporate world, where, although reasonably well represented at the lower executive levels, no more than five percent of top managers in America's 1000 largest corporations are female (Rosenblatt, 1995) and only two of these companies have female CEOs (Townsend, 1996).

LIFE CONNECTIONS: America's Low Voter Turnout

Voting rates in the United States are much lower than they are in the other Western democracies. The 56 percent of the eligible electorate who made it to the polls in the 1996 presidential election represented a 3- to 6-point increase over the usual turnout in recent presidential contests. Participation in local and state elections is typically even lower, ranging from 40 percent to below 10 percent. Figure 18.1 illustrates the effects of age and race on voting turnout. Low turnouts raise the question of how democratic the United States really is. Why don't more Americans exercise their right to vote?

Some conservatives argue that political apathy is functional (Lipset, 1960). Nonvoters tend to be less educated, less politically informed, and more prone to extreme political views, so their failure to participate may actually stabilize the system or even reflect general satisfaction with it. Critics, however, suggest that nonvoting more often reflects the beliefs that one's vote doesn't matter and that public officials are unresponsive to the average citizen (Piven & Cloward, 1978).

Structural factors play a part in explaining low voter turnout. Laws that remove people who have moved or who have not voted in recent elections from the voting rolls contribute to low turnouts, as does the U.S. custom of holding elections on workdays when people are busy. In Europe, where three-fourths or more of the eligible voters typically go to the polls, elections are held on Sundays or on official holidays. In Italy, the state even levies fines against nonvoters.

Another structural reason why many Americans fail to vote is the fact that the United States has a two-party system. This arrangement encourages Democrats and Republicans to compete for the middle ground and to blur their distinctiveness. By emphasizing high-consensus issues like crime control or the importance of education, parties downplay their differences and thus render elections largely meaningless. In Europe, strongly ideological parties engender intense loyalties and this translates into higher voting turnouts.

Why is the United States a two-party system? The U.S. government is structured around single-member districts and winner-take-all voting. Members of Congress represent specific geographic units. Majority rule (or, more correctly, plurality rule) means that a candidate needs only one more vote than

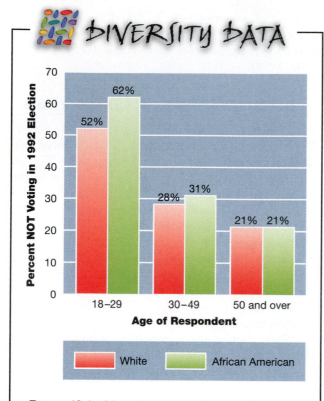

DIVERSITY DATA

FIGURE 18.1   How Do Age and Race Affect Voting Rates? In the 1992 Presidential election, older people were far more likely to vote than younger people. Young African Americans were substantially less likely to vote than young whites, whereas race had no effect on voting rates among people over 50. Why do you think youths, especially African Americans, seem to be uninterested in voting?
Source: NORC. General Social Surveys, 1972–1996. Chicago: National Opinion Research Center, 1996. Reprinted by permission of NORC, Chicago, IL.

the next closest opponent to win office. Voters rarely support third parties because doing so splits the vote and may indirectly contribute to the success of their least favored candidate. For example, in the 2000 presidential election, Ralph Nader's candidacy clearly helped George W. Bush despite the fact that most Nader voters were ideologically closer to Al Gore. This logic raises major obstacles to sustaining a successful third party challenge for the presidency, which has only occurred once in U.S. history, in the 1860 contest won by Abraham Lincoln.

In contrast to the U.S. system, most representative democracies, especially in Western Europe, allow *proportional voting*, which means that the number of candidates a party elects is proportionate to the overall number of votes that it receives. This system encourages multiple parties and it allows parties to take much clearer and stronger ideological stands on the

issues. Under these arrangements, voters typically are more interested in electoral outcomes and are more likely to vote.

Other equally persuasive explanations for Americans' low turnout in recent decades focus less on structural factors and more on sharp declines in public confidence in major institutions, including not only government but also corporations, labor unions, education, and religion (Lipset & Schneider, 1983). In the early 1960s, two-thirds of the general population expressed a high level of trust in major institutions. By the late 1970s, barely a third did so, and the percentages continued to decline slowly through the 1980s and 1990s, as is suggested by Figure 18.2. These data suggest that a very substantial and growing proportion of the U.S. electorate are alienated— they distrust the political system and consciously refuse to participate in it.

A number of factors have combined to create this crisis of confidence. They include major policy mistakes, such as the Watergate burglaries, the Vietnam War, the savings and loan scandal, the Lewinsky affair, and recent allegations that the Chinese have stolen U.S. nuclear secrets, all of which people blamed on their political leaders. The fact that President Reagan won election by portraying government as the problem rather than part of the solution is certainly relevant here. There were also incidents such as the Kennedy assassination that encouraged conspiratorial theories about politics. Some argue that the mass media, by concentrating on negative stories in order to boost their audiences, have contributed to widespread cynicism about politics and society in general (Parenti, 1986). Others note that the U.S. public has become more highly educated and knowledgeable and therefore less trusting in recent decades. In the past, high levels of confidence may have reflected ignorance and blind trust in political leaders rather than an accurate assessment of reality.

This confidence gap is a troublesome issue for U.S. democracy. Insofar as it leads to voter apathy, it raises questions about the legitimacy of the system. It strongly suggests that certain groups, including many African Americans, the poor, and other minorities, view the U.S. political system as unresponsive. At the same time, many educated middle-class people also view politics skeptically and are increasingly unlikely to vote. This cynicism and withdrawal may reflect a new type of privatism in which people withdraw from public life into their homes and personal pursuits.

Some authorities contend that the confidence gap is not a true crisis of legitimacy (Lipset & Schneider, 1983). But the gap does suggest that, should the U.S. political economy be challenged as it was, say, in the Great Depression of the 1930s—when over one-third of the work force was unemployed and when most

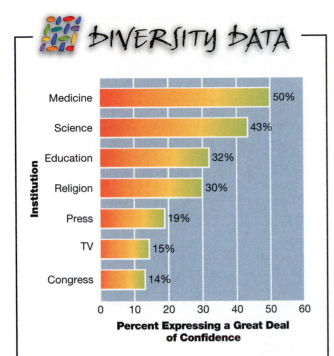

DIVERSITY DATA

FIGURE 18.2   How Much Confidence Do Americans Express in Major Institutions? Confidence levels in medicine and science are relatively high whereas fewer than one in five Americans expresses a great deal of confidence in the press, television, or Congress. There is no institution that inspires great confidence in more than half of all Americans. Why do you think Americans have become so skeptical? *Source:* NORC. General Social Surveys, 1972–1996. Chicago: National Opinion Research Center, 1996. Reprinted by permission of NORC, Chicago, IL.

people's incomes dropped significantly—the possibility of a systemic breakdown might be quite real.

SOCIETY CONNECTIONS: Globalization and the Political Economy

In this final section, we will examine three social issues that reflect the impact of globalization on the political economy. First, we will consider how local and state governments have become involved in the world economy. This will be followed by a brief discussion of political protest and terrorism. Finally, we will consider the worldwide spread of nuclear weapons.

Local Governments and the Emerging World Economy

The globalization of the economy means that the competition for international trade has come to play an increasingly important role in state and local poli-

tics. In Ohio, for example, over a third of all manufactured products are exported. Eighty percent of all sports shoes sold in the United States are now manufactured in China. A mere four decades ago, we could think of the U.S. economy as a closed system in which international trade did not play a significant role. Today, most states maintain trade offices abroad, and governors who once rarely left their home states now routinely travel the world in search of economic opportunities.

Globalization has spurred the creation of local business coalitions that actively promote economic growth, often using methods that were once considered illegitimate. For example, state and local governments have entered into partnerships with private businesses, invested directly in private firms, created export-promotion offices, encouraged universities to open their laboratories to private investors, and built industrial parks.

The new "entrepreneurial state" (Eisinger, 1988) is proactive and willing to take risks traditionally associated with private venture companies and backyard entrepreneurs. At the same time that this new vision of the state has emerged, there has also been tremendous pressure from business and conservative activists on government to reduce taxes, relax regulations, and invest public funds in ways that will benefit private enterprises.

Some fear that the competition between states for new businesses may result in weaker environmental regulation and lower wages, or that it may bankrupt city and county governments that must make new public investments despite having succumbed to pressures to roll back taxes. Others argue that the new entrepreneurial spirit in state and local government is a positive step beyond the traditional animosity between the private and public spheres and that it will generate "high tech" growth that will allow states to compete more effectively in the expanding global marketplace. Whichever view is more correct, it is clear that the economic role of local government has been transformed. Once, it supported business only indirectly; today it is an active player in building the economy of the future.

Protest and Terrorism

Citizens in democratic regimes frequently resort to nonviolent protest to express strong political opinions (Barnes & Kaase, 1979; Jennings & van Deth, 1989). Echoing the ideals of participatory democracy, *nonviolent protest* is collective action by non-elites that operates outside of routine institutional channels (Carter, 1977). Protests commonly serve two somewhat distinct purposes. They are intended to influence government officials, but they are also designed to mobilize the sympathies of third parties and so to indirectly pressure the officials (Lipsky, 1971). Thus,

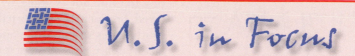

Private Information and Public Surveillance

Large corporations and modern governments have become increasingly adept at obtaining information that can be used to monitor and control people. Marketing companies collect vast quantities of data concerning individual consumer preferences for medicines, groceries, and other products and then sell this information to other firms. Does a private marketing company or a bill collection agency have the right to obtain and sell data about particular individuals? Similarly, does a government agency charged with monitoring social-program recipients have the right to scan computer tapes of these recipients' bank transactions and credit-card purchases? These and related questions are part of a major ongoing debate about the right to privacy and the increasing potential for governmental or private abuse of confidential information.

Many people—including proponents of tighter immigration control and those favoring more closely scrutinizing recipients of social insurance benefits to weed out fraudulent claims—have begun to argue for a national identity card. Civil-liberties advocates respond that such an identity card could accelerate the erosion of privacy by enhancing the ability of government agencies and private corporations alike to spy on private individuals. Making reference to the constitutional right to privacy and maintaining that individuals should have access to information concerning them so that it can be corrected, these advocates have proposed legislation to prohibit instituting a national identity card and to open computer data banks to the public.

The issue of the proper limits of privacy is a vexing one that will doubtless continue to create controversy for some time to come. It raises the question of where the proper boundary should be drawn between the private and public spheres in a modern society. Democracy rests on the right of the individual to act autonomously and make choices free of manipulation. But at the same time, the state has the legitimate right to obtain certain kinds of information concerning its citizens, such as the basic demographic data collected by the Census Bureau. How can these conflicting rights be balanced in the future? The outcome will be influenced by evolving civil-liberties law as well as by the ever-increasing ability of modern technologies to facilitate the surveillance of individuals.

1. Do you support issuing a national identity card to every citizen? What do you consider to be the advantages and drawbacks of such a proposal?
2. Do you believe that legislation is needed to limit the ability of private firms to collect and sell consumer information about particular individuals? Defend your position.

---

the civil rights movement relied on mass marches, sit-ins, freedom rides, and other protests that gained public sympathy, as well as directly pressuring elites to make concessions.

Unlike nonviolent protest, **terrorism**—the use or threat of violence as a political strategy by an individual, group, or state—attempts to disrupt the normal operation of society's institutions. Thus, for example, anti-abortion activists have bombed reproductive health clinics in order to force them to close their doors. Similarly, militant segregationists destroyed African American churches throughout the South during the civil rights era. However, the more militant and disruptive the tactic, the less effective the group usually is in mobilizing public sympathy.

Terrorism operates outside the bounds of institutional politics. Thus, in Northern Ireland, the Provisional wing of the Irish Republican Army conducted a decades-long terrorist campaign against British rule, killing and injuring thousands of people. Oppositional groups most often resort to terrorism when they lack popular support or when the government is so repressive that violence appears to be the only viable alternative. Minority groups that have been subjected to harsh repression and groups that have been forcibly colonized are especially attracted to terrorism.

Governments also sometimes use terrorism to sustain their rule. Although democracies have been known to endorse this tactic, totalitarian regimes are much more likely to do so. Revolutionary regimes like the Taliban in Afghanistan often use terrorism to consolidate their power. In the late nineteenth century, local and state governments in the United States sided with employers against labor unions, frequently using police violence to break strikes. In general, states are most prone to violence when they are relatively weak and vulnerable to challenge (Stohl & Lopez, 1987).

Nuclear Proliferation

At the end of the Cold War, the United States and the successor states to the U.S.S.R. agreed to reduce their nuclear stockpiles and to attempt to deter the spread of nuclear weapons around the globe. Many people thought that the threat of species annihilation

Global Connections

The Structural Roots of Genocide in Rwanda

In 1994, the government of Rwanda, which was controlled at the time by members of an ethnic group called the Hutu, launched a ferocious campaign to exterminate the Tutsis, who had traditionally dominated the country politically. In just four months, over half a million Tutsis and moderate Hutus who opposed the genocide were slaughtered. Then, a rebel Tutsi army based in neighboring Uganda regained political control. In the ensuing upheaval, the Tutsis killed over a quarter of a million additional Hutu. The UN subsequently established a human rights court to try officials of the former, Hutu-dominated Rwandan government for crimes against humanity.

As much as a quarter of the population was directly affected by these events—some as victims, some as perpetrators, and some as refugees who fled the violence. The attacks on the Tutsis were deliberately planned by high-level Hutu government officials who used radio broadcasts to whip up ethnic antagonism and trained entire soccer teams to ritually kill Tutsi men, women, and children. The Rwandan genocide is unique in that it involved a larger portion of the population and was conducted much more openly than any previous act of mass extermination. How can we explain this intense outpouring of collective violence?

The history and political economy of Rwanda are critical factors. During the colonial era of the late nineteenth and early twentieth centuries, the Belgian government legitimated the political power of the aristocratic Tutsis, who controlled the army and were the principal landlords. At this time, the Tutsis represented roughly 11 percent of the population. But then, when

preparing to grant Rwanda its independence, the colonial government decided to democratize the country, allowing some real power to the majority Hutus. This decision sparked a civil war, which in turn produced a refugee army of Tutsis residing in nearby Uganda. Over the next two decades, these refugees, supported by the Tutsi-dominated government of neighboring Burundi, maintained a hostile relationship with the Hutu regime in Rwanda.

Despite significant levels of intermarriage between the Hutu and the Tutsi in Rwanda, the Hutu-controlled government overtly promoted the notion that the Tutsi were subhuman and constituted a dire threat to Rwandan society. Many Hutus opposed the genocide and tried to shelter neighbors and friends from the rampaging Hutu military, but long-standing ethnic hatreds ultimately prevailed.

Moreover, international isolation and indifference reinforced the crisis. Despite incontrovertible evidence that genocide was planned or underway, most Western governments maintained that they had no strategic interests in the region and that military intervention in the internal affairs of another country was unwarranted. The Western media ignored accounts of the slaughter for almost four months, thus eliminating the possibility of reliable reporting that might have led to effective international intervention. By the time the outside world began to take the situation seriously, the invading Tutsi army had already defeated the Hutu leaders and driven them from power.

What lessons can be learned from the Rwandan genocide? First, it proved once again that people can inflict un-

speakable violence on each other. Most of the victims were killed face-to-face with pickaxes, shovels, and other hand weapons. Many of the murderers knew their victims personally.

Second, propaganda can legitimize unthinkable brutality. The Hutu government had practiced ritual killings and used hate radio and other dehumanization methods for several years in order to make the genocide appear reasonable and just.

Third, although the Hutu–Tutsi relationship was historically tense, particular decisions made by the extremist political leadership of the Hutus were critical in mobilizing the genocide. Simply referring to "ancient hatreds" and racial differences does not adequately explain the massacre.

Finally, the Rwandan genocide teaches us that foreign powers are unlikely to intervene to halt such outrages unless they feel that their own national interests are at stake. Despite the international conventions against genocide that grew out of the Holocaust, neither Western governments nor African powers stepped in before the carnage was largely ended. This is why many argue that the lack of political will is the chief obstacle to preventing genocide and lesser forms of political repression.

1. Why do you think the government of the United States refused to become involved in the Rwandan genocide, but did intervene a few years later in Kosovo?
2. Is an authoritarian or a democratic political system more likely to sponsor genocide? Explain your answer.

Sources: Hammer, 1994; Masland, 1994; Gourevich, 1995; Purvis, 1996.

INTERNET CONNECTIONS

One of the most worrisome social issues today is *terrorism*. Not that long ago, terrorism was usually viewed as an international, rather than as a domestic phenomenon. More recently, greater attention is being paid to *domestic terrorism*. Take the opportunity to have a look at excerpts from a 1997 Federal Bureau of Investigation report on the issues surrounding this topic: http://www.emergency.com/fbiter96.htm. How does the FBI explain the rise of domestic terrorism? Do you think appropriate steps are being taken by our government to avert future situations like the Unabomber and the Oklahoma City bombing incident? What suggestions do you have for improving our approach to this potentially deadly phenomenon.

INTERNET CONNECTIONS

Site www.pbs.org/wgbh/pages/frontline/shows/nukes/maps/np01.html gives a good overview of nuclear proliferation and its threat to the world's political economy. What measures would you propose to limit the spread of nuclear weapons?

had finally ended and that nuclear weapons might soon become obsolete.

These hopes have proven premature at best. Although the Soviet successor states and the United States have significantly reduced their arsenals, enough nuclear weapons still exist to destroy the world's population many times over. The international sale of plutonium and other nuclear components by financially strapped laboratories and military facilities in the former Soviet Union has created a major security worry. There is also an international

market in nuclear engineers, and critical know-how is spreading throughout the globe.

As of 2000, there were seven openly declared nuclear powers (the United States, China, France, Russia, the United Kingdom, India, and Pakistan). Several additional states are suspected of possessing nuclear weapons (Iran, Iraq, Israel) and many others have the technological ability to develop a nuclear arsenal in a fairly short period of time (Jones & McDonough, 1998, p. 11; Smith, 1997, pp. 70-71).

What are the implications of the continued proliferation of nuclear weapons? What if a quarter of the nations of the world possessed nuclear capacity? Instead of just threatening South Korean and U.S. troops, North Korea could bomb them out of existence. Long-standing disputes between India and Pakistan or between Israel and much of the Islamic world could easily escalate to the nuclear stage. Because of international alliances, a regional nuclear war could quickly spread (Posen, 1991; Blair, 1993). Rogue states with unpredictable leaders might be joined by criminal syndicates involved in smuggling that would find it useful to use nuclear weapons as bargaining tools.

The Provisional Irish Republican Army and its offshoots have engaged in a campaign of intermittent terrorism since 1969. Their immediate objective is to force the withdrawal of British troops from Northern Ireland in the hope of eventually unifying the island politically. Recent peace agreements promise some possibility of an end to the violence.

SUMMARY

1. The concept of the political economy emphasizes the fact that the economic and political institutions of modern societies are largely inseparable from one other, especially at the macro level.
2. Power is the ability to compel others to act as the powerholder wishes, even if they attempt to resist. There are three types of power: decision-making power, agenda control, and systemic power.
3. Authority is legitimate power. Max Weber identified three ideal types of authority: traditional, rational-legal, and charismatic.
4. There are three major philosophical models of the political economy: liberalism, socialism, and conservatism.
5. Most modern economic systems are capitalist, a few are state socialist, and some, termed mixed economies, are intermediate between the two polar types.
6. Political regimes may be authoritarian or democratic. Authoritarian regimes include monarchies, dictatorships, bureaucratic-authoritarian regimes, and totalitarian states. Democratic regimes may be either participatory or representative democracies.
7. There are four competing models of the actual distribution of political power in modern societies: pluralism, the power-elite model, the ruling class model, and the state autonomy model.
8. In most cases, the transition from authoritarianism to democracy is instigated by elites, although sometimes it is promoted by the lower classes.
9. Minorities and women have been systematically excluded from the top levels of the political economy, although both groups have made significant progress in recent decades.
10. Voter turnout in the United States is normally very low. In part, this may be explained by the structure of the U.S. political institution, especially the two-party system. It also reflects the low levels of confidence many Americans express in major social institutions.
11. As the world has globalized, local and state governments have begun to compete against each other to attract international businesses.
12. Citizens in democratic societies sometimes resort to nonviolent political protest to make their views known. Some oppositional groups and governments engage in terrorism, the use or threat of violence as a political strategy.
13. Nuclear proliferation is one of the most serious problems currently facing the world.

KEY TERMS

authoritarian regime　466
authority　460
capitalism　464
charismatic authority　462
conservatism　464
democracy　467
economy　459
elite model　467
liberalism　462

mixed economy　465
modern liberalism　463
monopoly　463
pluralism　467
political economy　459
power　459
rational-legal authority　461
routinization of charisma　462

ruling class model　467
socialism　463
state　459
state autonomy model　467
state socialism　465
terrorism　478
totalitarianism　466
traditional authority　461

CRITICAL THINKING QUESTIONS

1. Why do you think that rational-legal authority has largely replaced the traditional and charismatic types during the past two centuries?
2. Which of the four models of the distribution of political power do you believe most accurately describes your home community? The state in which you live? The United States as a whole? Explain how you arrived at your answers.
3. What do you believe is the best explanation for the very low voter turnout in the United States? How do you think we could best attempt a long-term and substantial reversal of this pattern?

19 ◆ HEALTH AND HEALTH CARE

OUTLINE

An Emergency Room Regular Customer

Wilma lived in a school bus with four cats and a mongrel dog, no water, and no facilities. When she came to the ER, the two nurses braced themselves for what they knew they would encounter. Layers of clothes were removed. She was covered with red splotches. Her odor was foul. Gray-white parasites crawled from her scalp. A shiny cockroach dropped to the floor. "God, Wilma, you've scratched yourself raw," one nurse exclaimed. Wilma shrugged, "Lookit sister, don't bother me with gory details. It's your job to take care of it." The nurse was furious. "You got that wrong, lady. It's not my job, it's yours. Stop expecting other people to pull you up. Go for something better than surviving." Wilma started to cry. "I got my rights . . . I'll sue you for malpractice." She muttered, "Little snipe! Treating a poor cripple like that." With conflicting emotions of anger and pity, the nurse signed her chart and walked away. (Adapted from Heron, 1994)

Organ Transplants: Rationing by Wallet

In Upper Marlboro, Maryland, William Dobbs, age 65 and retired, was bleeding internally and needed a liver transplant—a $200,000 operation. He no longer qualified for his former insurance and his Medicare coverage denied the operation. Mr. Dobbs received his transplant because, in an abrupt change of policy, Medicare decided to pay for adult liver transplants. In Rockwood, Oregon, teenager Coby Howard died of leukemia, his death coming in the midst of a campaign to raise $100,000 for a bone mar-

row treatment. A year earlier there would have been no need for the effort. But Coby became the first victim of a policy set by the Oregon legislature to stop all organ transplants for welfare recipients and instead spend the money on prenatal care. Deciding who gets organ transplants has become a formal process based on medical judgments. But there is one nonmedical characteristic almost all who get transplants share: They have a way to pay for the operation. William Dobbs had health insurance and survived. Coby Howard had no insurance and died. (Adapted from Rich, 1993:228, and Callahan, 1994:196)

Ancient Medicine in a Modern Hospital

For two weeks he was in a coma hovering on the brink of death in a San Francisco hospital. His fever hit 106°. The 28-year-old Mohawk, Richard Oakes, was a leader in a Native American movement that was pressing claims for the return of California lands. These activities triggered an attack in which he was almost beaten to death. As skeptical doctors watched, Mad Bear the Medicine Man placed an ancient and mysterious medicine in his feeding tube. Within an hour a normal temperature and pulse returned. Mad Bear was allowed to treat Richard because it was a religious rite to be administered with Indian herbs. His condition was so bad that doctors reasoned, "What harm could it do?" and they were aware that medicine men are skilled in the use of curative herbs. Mad Bear refuses to say what medicine was placed in the IV tube. The tube in a modern hospital was used to convey the secret, potent drug. In this instance there was a blending of Native American and modern healing practices. (Adapted from Kane & Kane, 1994:172)

These vignettes illustrate that health and health care exist in a sociocultural context and cannot be separated from it. The values, beliefs, and norms of society—key elements of social structure—influence the organization and delivery of health care. When patients enter the health care system, they bring their social statuses with them. Wilma, a vermin-infested street person, is a typical sight in the emergency room of large city hospitals, the only place she could go for health care. William Dobbs's life was saved by the advances of modern medicine. Coby Howard could not benefit from these same advances. The case of Richard Oakes indicates a newer trend in health care—practices that blend the traditional (indigenous) with the modern (scientific) in healing. All these people entered the health care system in the United States and had varying experiences with it. As this chapter will show, the care they and others like them receive is profoundly impacted by the structure of society in which the health care is delivered.

DEFINING AND MEASURING HEALTH AND DISEASE

The World Health Organization (WHO) defines **health** as a state of complete physical, mental, and social well-being, not merely the absence of disease or infirmity. This view of health is **holistic**—involving treatment of the "whole" person, with a focus on wellness and prevention, rather than simply on disease and cure. The "holistic health" model is fast becoming an ideal for health care delivery in the United States. But as the cases of Coby and Wilma show, the ideal of holistic health care is far from the reality when health care is compromised because people cannot afford to pay for it. Regardless of which model of health care is adopted, health care delivery itself is based on gathering accurate data.

Measurement Techniques

People who collect data on health usually work under what is referred to as a *negative health standard:* We are healthy because we are not sick, that is, we have no fever or pain and no interference in our daily activities. Although the "negative" health standard contradicts WHO's assumption that health is much more than the absence of disease, the standard is used because the "positive" standard of health is too extensive or vague (Mootz, 1986). Disease indicators involving major physical illnesses with well-defined symptoms are easier to document. These are used in combination with other demographic characteristics, such as population growth or decline, age, gender, birth and death rate, marital status, and ethnicity (Chapter 21). Therefore, data on *health* are routinely collected based on measurements of *disease*.

Various measurement techniques have been developed to determine patterns of health and well-being around the world, including the United States. The simplest measure, the **mortality rate,** is expressed as a percentage of the total number of deaths over the population size ($\times$ 1000) in a given time period, usually a year. Calculating a **morbidity rate,** the amount of disease or illness in a population, is more difficult. Although illness may have well-defined symptoms, illness itself is in part subjective. Many people do not recognize their own sickness, may recognize it but refuse to alter their behavior, or prefer to treat themselves. As a result, morbidity rates are often based on treatment, and thus the accuracy of the data is compromised.

The two most important status indicators of global health are the *infant mortality rate* (IMR) and the *life expectancy rate* (LER) at birth. IMR is the number of deaths in the first year of life for each 1,000 live births. It is a sensitive measure of overall inequality and reflects a country's success in fighting child deaths due to preventable diseases. LER at birth reflects both childhood and adult death rates. Once an individual survives childhood, the gap between the developed and developing world is narrower (Table 19.1).

Social Epidemiology

Epidemiology is the study of the causes and distribution of disease and disability in a given population. Since this study must include more than biological or physical factors, the discipline of epidemiology has expanded. *Social epidemiology* is its logical extension and includes the sociocultural and behavioral factors in disease and disability.

The word "social" before the word "epidemiology" is actually redundant. Today epidemiologists draw upon the work of many disciplines in constructing the complex web of the multiple causes of disease and disability. For all kinds of health planning, epidemiologists continually track diseases. The figures they use most are the **incidence** of disease, the number of new cases during a specified time period, and the **prevalence** of disease, the total number of cases during a specified time. Since prevalence rates are cumulative, it is essential to track them for highly contagious diseases such as influenza, tuberculosis, and measles. This practice ensures that health care facilities are prepared for the influx of patients and that the public is made aware of any preventive measures they can take. In reporting incidence and prevalence rates, global cooperation is critical.

SOCIOLOGICAL PERSPECTIVES ON HEALTH IN THE UNITED STATES

Sociological theory has contributed significantly to our understanding of health and health care. The social and cultural determinants of health are well documented. These determinants can be viewed sociologically at both the macro and micro levels. In addition, they can be readily applied to help understand the health care situation in the United States.

Table 19.1	Life Expectancy Rate at Birth (LER) and Infant Mortality Rate (IMR) of Selected Countries in Developing and Developed World			
	LER		IMR	
Year	1998	2000	1998	2000
Developing World				
Africa				
Egypt	62.1	62.7	69.2	65.7
Ethiopia	40.9	40.1	125.7	123.5
Kenya	47.6	46.5	59.4	58.8
Rwanda	41.9	40.7	113.3	112.4
Sudan	56.0	56.8	72.6	69.2
Uganda	42.6	43.5	92.9	88.5
Asia				
Afghanistan	46.8	47.8	143.6	137.5
Bangladesh	56.7	57.5	97.7	93.0
China	69.6	70.3	45.5	41.1
India	62.9	63.9	63.1	58.5
Indonesia	62.5	63.4	59.2	55.4
Pakistan	59.1	59.7	93.5	90.3
South America				
Argentina	74.5	75.0	19.0	17.8
Bolivia	60.9	62.0	63.9	60.2
Brazil	64.4	63.8	37.0	33.8
Mexico	71.6	72.4	25.8	23.4
Peru	70.0	70.8	43.4	39.4
Developed World				
Canada	79.2	79.6	5.6	5.4
France	78.5	78.8	5.7	5.6
Germany	77.0	77.3	5.2	5.1
Hong Kong	78.8	79.0	5.2	5.2
Italy	78.4	78.6	6.4	6.2
Japan	80.0	80.2	4.1	4.1
Spain	77.6	77.9	6.5	6.3
Sweden	79.2	79.4	3.9	3.9
Switzerland	78.9	79.1	4.9	4.8
United States	76.1	76.3	6.4	6.7

Source: Darnay, 1997 (Table 251); U.S. Bureau of the Census, 1998 (adapted from Tables No. 128, 134, 1345).

A Functionalist Perspective of Health

Why do people commit suicide? What happens when students call teachers to say they cannot take an exam because they are sick? Why are patients faced with a bewildering array of health care providers? As we have seen throughout the text, functionalists point out that when everyone acts in accordance with shared values and norms, the social system is in equilibrium. Patterns of behavior related to health also follow this rule. Various aspects of social structure guide people in their choices of health-related behavior. In this section three of these aspects will be viewed: suicide, the sick role, and health care delivery.

Social Structure and Suicide.   We saw in Chapters 1 and 2 that Émile Durkheim's (1897/1964) monumental work, *Suicide*, paved the way for the be-

ginnings of sociology as a science. This work may also be viewed as the first systematic study of medical sociology, because it showed that even the most intensely personal act imaginable, suicide, is rooted in social causes. Although Durkheim's original data focused on Europe, his findings are still applicable over a century later to patterns of suicide in the United States. According to Durkheim, when the usual norms of society are severely disrupted or become ineffective, and *anomie* (normlessness) prevails, the resulting stress causes some people to take their own lives. For example, refugees fleeing from violence and famine and individuals who have experienced disasters that have wiped out their communities experience mental health problems so severe that they threaten anomic suicide (Erickson, 1976; Lindsey, 1990). Social structure as these people knew it has literally disappeared.

The World Health Organization is responsible for monitoring the spread of disease worldwide. They also provide services to remote areas of the world where modern health care is unavailable.

Durkheim also explains *altruistic* suicide among those who belong to societies that strongly bind the individual to the group and hold values that emphasize group solidarity. This social structure helps explain the high rates of suicide in Japan, where individual shame reflects dishonor on the family or other important social groups, thus justifying suicide for the good of the group. Rather than creating social disruption, functionalism would explain altruistic suicide as reinforcing social cohesion. It contrasts with *egoistic* suicide, which is committed by those who are socially isolated and strongly adhere to the value of individualism. High rates of suicide among elderly widowers in the United States may point to social detachment. Coupled with role loss due to retirement, the death of their wives creates a void that is difficult to overcome.

All three types of suicide—anomic, altruistic, and egoistic—are explained by the power of social bonds, according to the functionalist perspective. This perspective is also evident in the growing research suggesting that social support is linked, both physically and mentally, to good health, as social isolation is linked to poor health (House et al., 1990; Thoits, 1995). Employment is one example of social support and correlates highly with health (Ross & Mirowsky, 1995). Functionalists emphasize that health and well-being are enhanced when the individual receives support within a society that is performing smoothly, effectively, and with little disturbance to social equilibrium.

The Sick Role.   The second area where the functionalist approach to health is evident is the concept of the sick role. As identified by the classic work of Talcott Parsons (1951, 1964), the **sick role** describes those behaviors that are socially expected of a sick person according to prevailing norms. Like other roles, it consists of privileges and obligations defined by the individual and society. Because the sick role exempts people from their normal roles and is not deliberate, it is considered to be a legitimate form of social deviance. In the United States this legitimacy is accepted as long as the person intends to get well by seeking help if necessary. Medicine exerts a strong mechanism of social control. Some teachers will exempt a student from an exam only with a written statement by a physician. Thus, how each individual performs the sick role will be strongly influenced by role partners, such as family members, nurses, and physicians.

Functionalists are interested in how social equilibrium is maintained and in the interdependence of the elements making up society. Thus, the longer a person is released from his or her typical role obligations, the greater the strain on the social system. When one college student living in a dorm contracts a highly contagious disease such as measles, there is potential for disruption of the entire campus. In turn, a measles epidemic can wreak havoc on the community of which the college is part.

The sick role works well in explaining temporary sickness according to U.S. conceptions of medicine and how illness as deviance can be brought under social control. However, it presents several problems. It does not consider how people can actively participate in their own healing, how their own actions, such as cigarette smoking, create their illness, or how they succumb to illness due to hazards over which they have no control, such as carcinogens in their workplaces.

Functionalists say that the sick role is associated with rights and responsibilities. Children are allowed to have longer sick roles, more rights, and fewer responsibilities than adults when they are sick.

Another problem with the sick role is that it fits only what today would be described as a rather narrow range of illness. **Acute disease** is characterized by sudden onset, rapid peak, and limited duration, resulting in either recovery or death. Influenza, appendicitis, and pneumonia are examples. In contrast, **chronic disease** is characterized by gradual onset, long duration, little chance for complete recovery, and often resulting in death. AIDS, Alzheimer's disease, heart disease, asthma, and some forms of cancer fall into this category. Chronic diseases have replaced acute as the major killers in most of the world, including the United States (Table 19.4). Caring for the chronically ill patient, especially if care is guided by a holistic model, impacts the entire health care delivery process. For patients with certain chronic diseases, the sick role is permanent and may exempt people from role obligations for as long as they live.

Health Care Delivery: How Effective Is It?   The third health area in which the functionalist model can be applied is in evaluating the performance of the health care delivery system in the United States. If sickness causes social disruption, it is imperative that an organized, effective health system provides the highest quality care to everyone. Functionalists would support this claim by viewing health care improvements in public health, technological advances in medicine and pharmacology leading to curing acute diseases, higher remission rates of chronic diseases, and increased life

expectancy. While functionalism would not deny the fact that the U.S. health care system is in a state of crisis and some of the population is not served well, it would suggest that drastic changes in the current health care system could be dysfunctional, creating more problems than solutions. Instead, functionalists would recommend a gradual shift from a marketplace approach that views health care as a privilege to one that views it as a right.

The functionalist perspective can be applied in some instances even to those who may not be served well in the current health care system, for example, the uninsured chronic patient. "Project Concern" is a model of care services that fits well with the functionalist perspective. It provides direct assistance to low-income, pediatric asthmatic patients; it has been successful in alleviating both the physical and psychological problems experienced by chronic patients and their families who have no health insurance (Horst, 1995). The strength of the program is tied to cost effectiveness, expansion of traditional medical social-work practices, and a coordinated approach emphasizing a health care team concept. By focusing on chronic patients who take on a sick role periodically, and the strengths of an existing system that is interdependent, coordinated, and allows for gradual change, the Project Concern model conforms to the functionalist perspective.

A Conflict Perspective of Health

Like functionalism, conflict theory provides a macro view and centers on several important aspects of social structure to explain health-related behavior. But unlike functionalism, the element of social structure conflict theorists focus on is power.

Professional Autonomy and Encroachment. One way in which conflict theory links the notion of power to health care is through the concern of professional autonomy and the control it brings. With the American Medical Association (AMA) as the key lobbying agency, the medical profession has retained absolute control and jurisdiction over health care in the United States. Established in 1847 at a time when physicians were not held in high regard, the purpose of the organization was to promote scientific medicine and public health. The AMA became medicine's accrediting body, increasing its internal cohesion in terms of recruitment, content of medical education, and licensing.

The basic principles of the AMA were established in 1934 and they remain in effect. These include the ideas that all health care and medical practice should be controlled by the medical profession, which

The Fall and Rise of Midwifery in America

In 1900 the editor of the *Journal of the American Medical Association* stated his opinion about women's ability for engaging in the medical profession: "When a critical case demands independent action and fearless judgment, man's success depends on his virile courage which the normal woman does not have or is [not] expected to have."

For a hundred years in the United States, childbirth was completely female centered. New mothers delivered their infants with the support of midwives. The norm was that mothers and midwives worked together—before, during, and after the delivery—to make certain that mothers were both emotionally and physically prepared for birth and early motherhood. They served as role models and emotional supports and helped socialize women into the status of motherhood. Midwives, both then and now, do not "deliver" babies. They teach women how to give birth. Men and women in preindustrial United States accepted the midwife's role as one that only a woman could accomplish. Men were excluded as not suitable for dealing with the demands involved in childbirth. By the early twentieth century,

midwifery was virtually eliminated in the United States. The reasons for this rather dramatic change have to do with how U.S. culture became gradually medicalized throughout the nineteenth century.

Before medicalization, childbirth was viewed as a natural event. Artificial intervention, especially with instruments, was considered dangerous. Medical training at that time also accepted the view that "nonintervention is the cornerstone of midwifery." Although the belief in the naturalness of birth was accepted, the medical establishment moved in the opposite direction, with greater reliance on intervention and the use of "aids" to control natural processes. With medicalization gradually taking hold, midwives were characterized by the new medical establishment as ignorant, meddlesome, and unscientific, as the quote by the AMA editor above suggests. The widespread belief was that a dissecting room and hospital were no places for a woman. It would harm her "delicate feelings" and "refined sensibility," and she would see things that would "taint her moral character." It is interesting that while female nurses

were absolved of these concerns, women were denied access to training to become physicians. Once childbirth became medicalized, women were seen as unsuited for independent medical roles, even with evidence showing that midwives attended deliveries that were safe for both mother and child. However, obstetrics practiced by men replaced midwifery practiced by women.

Before midwives lost their status as independent practitioners, however, they found themselves more restricted to working with poor and immigrant women who were undervalued by the male medical establishment. Doctors also believed that sensitive and delicate middle- and upper-class women, in contrast to robust farm women, had more difficult deliveries and needed greater intervention. Thus, until the AMA gained control over all medical licensing, physicians and midwives were in direct competition for patients and fees. History is repeating itself. Research today is showing that obstetricians are again resisting the private practice of nurse-midwives because they believe it will lead to renewed competition for healthy and paying clients.

---

charges on a fee-for-service basis, and that there should be no interference in the physician-patient relationship (Lasagna, 1963; Starr, 1982). The process of medicalization helped ensure that the public accepted these principles.

Once in control of the health care system, professional autonomy allows the medical profession to ward off *encroachment*, the invasion by others who would also deliver health care. Some were simply eliminated from practice, such as healers who use religion, faith, or magic in treating disease. Others who were not eliminated were severely restricted, such as midwives and chiropractors. Most were subordinated, including nurses, optometrists, pharmacists, medical technicians, psychologists, and physical therapists. By eliminating any threat in the provision of health services by potential competitors, the professional auton-

omy of medicine is secure (Gritzer, 1981; Freund & McGuire, 1999).

Conflict theory argues that physician control of health care can be sustained as long as physicians have the power and resources to successfully keep others from encroaching on their terrain. Fueled by massive increases health care cost, challenges to their dominance are now coming from many fronts. A "buyer's revolt" has led to more public scrutiny of what physicians do (Light, 1988). When cost of adequate health care rises beyond the means of more and more citizens, the public demands more control of the terms, conditions, and content of medicine as a whole.

A better educated public is also supporting allied health practitioners who believe in a team approach to healing and prevention health. Encroaching on the dominance hierarchy of medicine, nonphysician spe-

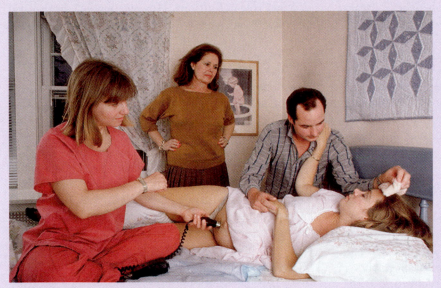

Midwifery is making a comeback in the U.S. for low risk pregnancies and for couples who desire a home birth with other close friends and family members sharing and even assisting in the birth.

Conflict theory readily explains the "then and now" situation of midwifery in the United States. This perspective suggests that the medicalization of childbirth and the social control brought with it was accepted as legitimate over time. Conflict theory also suggests that midwives lost their right to practice because they encroached on the emerging medical profession. The AMA power to license and restrict women from becoming doctors sealed midwifery's fate. Research supports these assertions. The comeback of midwifery, tentative as it is, also can be explained by conflict theory. Midwives offer an alternative ideology—translated as an alternative view of procreation—that is gaining its own power. It is fascinating that this alternative view is also an ancient one.

1. From the perspective of conflict theory, what do you think the success will be for the comeback of midwifery in America?
2. What role does the public play in determining the practice rights of midwives, and how does this role impact the AMA's position on the subject?

Sources: Little, 1982; Mumford, 1983:273; Radosh, 1986; Wertz & Wertz, 1990; Langton, 1994; Rothman & Caschetta, 1995:67–68.

However, there are indications that the "adequacy of nature" is making a comeback as the era of holistic health is ushered in. Although major restrictions on their practice roles continue, nurse-midwives are growing in number. An uneasy alliance is being forged by some obstetricians who deliver higher-risk babies and do more costly cesarean sections and nurse-midwives who are attracting those who desire a more natural birthing experience. Despite the oversupply of obstetricians, their high incomes are guaranteed even as gains are made in the professional autonomy and respectability of nurse-midwives.

Certainly there is no dispute that midwifery is an acceptable alternative to conventional obstetrics in child delivery only if there are no foreseen complications. Advances in obstetrics have saved the lives of mothers and their newborns during higher risk delivery situations.

cialists are challenging the control of medicine's technical core. For example, nurse practitioners have gradually increased their diagnostic and treatment roles and are performing tasks such as physical exams once only the prerogative of MDs. This frees physicians to do more of the specialized medicine appropriate for their training.

There are contested domains throughout the health care system. Some health professions will ascend, some will decline, and some will be maintained (Hafferty, 1995). Even hospital mergers impact standing in the health care hierarchy. Mergers and multihospital affiliations favor physicians and technical core occupations at the expense of hospital administrators (Leicht et al., 1995). Conflict theory focuses on how the medical profession can maintain its power and privilege in the face of encroachment.

Medicalization.   In the United States the social power exerted by the profession of medicine has also allowed it almost complete control over the organization and delivery of health care, the authority of other health care practitioners, and the definitions of health and illness. Taken together, this power has resulted in **medicalization,** a process that legitimizes medical control over parts of a person's life (Conrad & Schneider, 1980). Through medicalization, then, medicine in the United States becomes a major institution of social control (Zola, 1990).

Mental disorders provide good examples of the process of medicalization (see Chapter 8). Eating disorders, drug addiction, attention deficit disorder, shyness, and shoplifting are being categorized as medical problems. Even unattractiveness is a medical problem with cosmetic surgery as an extreme case of medicalization, which is encouraged in white, middle- and upper-class women in professional jobs where attractiveness is desired and financially rewarded (Sullivan, 1993). Alternative professionals to MDs, such as clinical psychologists and psychiatric social workers move to the fringes of the system (Gallagher, 1987). While medicine offers important therapeutic techniques, the conflict perspective argues that its power in defining illness, especially mental illness, only in biological terms restricts other sociocultural avenues for exploration.

Social Class and Health. Another way conflict theory links power and health is by viewing illness among the various social classes. As discussed later, there is a strong and consistent association between social class and health—lower SES people have less access to health care, less health insurance, and a higher risk of getting sick and not recovering completely. To understand how conflict theory uses social class to analyze health, consider how health is maintained. In Marxist terms, capitalism places the responsibility for health on the individual and downplays collective solutions to health problems (Navarro, 1986; Waitzkin, 1989). When you need health care, you must seek it in a monopolistic system designed to maximize profits in a seller's market. So corporations see health-related products the same way as other products that are sold for profit (Baer, 1989; Waitzkin, 1990; Moore, 1993).

Conflict theory maintains that much of our lifestyle is not under our control. Capitalist society limits the control workers have over their lives, both at work and outside of it (Navarro, 1986). Lower SES people work at jobs they can get and live in places they can afford. This may mean working and living in areas with high health risks. Daily ingestion of pollutants from work in a factory or living near a toxic waste dump are contributors to poor health among lower SES groups. And research on cancer suggests that what is attributed to a voluntary lifestyle can better be attributed to involuntary poverty (Proctor, 1994). Conflict theorists assert that adverse social conditions such as poverty are key determinants of health and illness.

Symbolic Interactionism: The Social Construction of Health

Like the other theories, symbolic interactionism begins with the idea of health as a social concept. In defining health and illness, we also define the roles we play as health professionals and patients. To some extent, the sick role concept from functionalism fits with this model. The difference is that for symbolic interactionists, the sick role is not a passive,

prescribed role, but one involving continued negotiation and role definitions. How we perceive health and respond to sickness are the results of social interaction.

For symbolic interactionism, health and illness are not simply biomedical facts—the social construction of illness involves an array of social forces, including sets of relationships and understandings that are shaped by our knowledge and experiences. Studies of people with rheumatoid arthritis, for example, find that they use many nonmedical explanations for their illness. Victims of the disease may see political, economic, psychological, or spiritual reasons as its cause. Regardless of reason, they construct a coherent analysis, which provides a way for them to deal with the ruptures that arthritis caused in their relationships and their broader social world. (Brown, 1995). Analyzing rheumatoid arthritis in their own terms allows them to regain some control over subsequent social interactions.

Labeling Health and Illness and Believing in the Labels. In explaining health, symbolic interactionism rests on three key notions. The first is labeling. People label health and illness as conditions according to their unique understanding of a situation and how social audiences react to them. These labels are social constructions that can be altered, such as the stigma associated with certain illnesses. For example, breast cancer no longer appears to be stigmatized. Following breast cancer surgery, women perceive that they have more emotional support rather than less (Bloom & Kessler, 1994). Changes in norms regarding smoking provide another example. By making the health hazards of smoking and secondhand smoke a public issue, smoking has been transformed from an acceptable to an unacceptable behavior in specific contexts, such as in theaters, in hospitals, on airplanes, and especially around children. Smoking as a right has been relabeled smoking as a privilege.

The second notion that symbolic interactionists rely on to explain health is the definition of the situation and its associated concept of self-fulfilling prophecy (Chapter 6). While medical science, for example, may be skeptical of the empirical basis for faith healing, it cannot be easily dismissed as simply a medical fluke. In such cases the self-fulfilling prophecy works to the benefit of the patient. On the other hand, patients who believe they are beyond healing and thus do not seek help are more likely to suffer the most negative effects of their illness.

Symbolic interactionism is rooted in the remarkable power of the human mind to create reality and alter it to conform to preconceived beliefs. It is interesting that science may doubt this power in healing, but in an important way symbolic interactionism is at

Health facilities in the developing world are often primitive and staffed by volunteers of NGOs. However, the services they provide are vital to the health and well-being of the people in the communities they serve.

the heart of *all* science. Medical investigations must conform to rigid guidelines based on experimental design. In a *double-blind* procedure, neither the subjects nor those conducting the research know to which experimental condition a subject is assigned. This procedure is essential to protect against the *placebo effect*, that a change will occur because of the mere suggestion that it will occur.

In medical research to test the effects of drugs, for example, both the experimental group and the control group used for comparison receive what they think is a "drug." But the control group receives a placebo. Without the safeguard of the placebo, any changes in health could be attributed to the subjects believing the drug or therapy is working. This is a clear example of the power of the definition of the situation.

Health-Related Interactions. The third idea from symbolic interactionism centers on the roles of health-related interactions. In the intimate encounters involving health and illness, such role playing is critical for both patients and physicians. Patients want to be treated as whole persons and maintain a sense of dignity and control; they feel marginalized when physicians do not respond to personal concerns (Fielding, 1995). Physicians must respect these rights but do so in an objective manner that allows them to retain control they believe is ultimately beneficial to the patient.

Patients often feel depersonalized in interactions with health providers. This depersonalization has serious consequences for health, particularly if it leads

to poor patient-provider communication (Kleinman, 1988; Haas & Shaffir, 1993). Reducing the social distance between patient and provider also reduces misunderstandings (Boulton et al., 1986; Yoels et al., 1993). When health care providers base their interactions with patients on stereotypes and cultural misconceptions, patients are put at risk. Emergency rooms in public hospitals are places where hospital staff informally evaluate patients according to their belief about how worthy the patients and how legitimate their health problems were. Wilma, the vermin-infested street person in the opening vignette, is a good example. Research shows that patients labeled as drunks are handled like baggage, ridiculed, ignored, and treated only for their drunkenness and any obvious physical injury. More than any other category of patient, drunks were consistently treated as undeserving (Roth, 1990).

Research concludes that there is a huge gap in the way physicians think about disease and the way patients experience it. Symbolic interactionism supports the idea that physicians need to listen to their patients and to learn from other disciplines about the experience of illness that is not offered within the conventional medical paradigm (Baron, 1994).

THE CHALLENGE OF INTERNATIONAL HEALTH

International health is an idea whose time has come. In 1977 the United Nations (UN) called for "the attainment by all citizens of the world by the year 2000

The AIDS Epidemic: Focus on Africa

Acquired Immunity Deficiency Syndrome (AIDS) is packed with cultural meaning. In the two decades since it erupted, it is the worst of the global epidemics. There is no vaccine to prevent it, there is no cure for it, and it costs billions of dollars to care for its victims. Providing even basic care to AIDS patients in Africa could absorb one-third to one-half of its current health care budget.

The spread of AIDS has reversed health gains made in other areas. It has emerged as a leading killer among young adults throughout the world and is spreading into what had been considered "safe" populations, such as married, heterosexual women with no history of drug use. In its path of destruction, infant mortality is rising and life expectancy is falling. Sub-Saharan Africa is a prime example. In recent years life expectancy in some areas has fallen from 62 to 47. As we move into the twenty-first century, 90 percent of people infected with HIV, the AIDS virus, are in the developing world. Given the estimates that close to 40 million people are already infected, health gains worldwide can be severely compromised.

Unquestionably, Africa is the continent most severely affected by AIDS. Sub-Saharan and Central Africa have the largest number of AIDS cases in the world. In Congo, it is estimated at 1 percent of the population. In Uganda, rates of AIDS cases range between 11 to 50 per 100,000 people in large cities and areas with high concentrations of migrant laborers. AIDS is a family disease in Africa and throughout the developing world. Tests of pregnant women in families throughout Africa reveal 25 to 30 percent as HIV positive. Men pass it to their wives who pass it to their babies. Other long-term health consequences involve the hunger and exploitation of remaining children and family members when parents die. Society also loses the strongest and most productive members of the labor force.

Cultural meanings must be accounted for in the prevention and treatment of AIDS. For example, condom use is effective for preventing AIDS, but there are many cultural barriers to their use throughout the world. In Africa and Asia, the most common route of transmission is heterosexual, with half of all new HIV infections diagnosed in women. The year 2000 saw

female AIDS victims exceeding males. Yet in these cultures, women have little power to alter sexual habits in their own families. Sexual intercourse is a husband's right, not to be vetoed by wives. By Western standards, marital rape is common. Traditional African belief systems demand large families as ways to expand a lineage; childlessness and small families may be regarded as the work of evil spirits. Polls of African women on their "desired family size" report ranges of five to nine children, and the numbers increase if a child has already died. Coupled with an AIDS epidemic in full force, the desire for large families leads to the worst possible outcome: family size larger than in most other areas of the world, increasing to millions the young Africans and their mothers who will be dying of AIDS.

From the perspective of functionalism, the global AIDS crisis reflects what sociologists call a functionalist challenge. In fighting AIDS, especially as a family disease, traditional values are compromised. There is visible strain on social order. But more social disorder will occur if AIDS is left unchecked. To control the disease, culturally appropri-

---

of a level of health that will permit them to lead a socially and economically productive life" (Basch, 1990:200). The "Health for All by the Year 2000" (HFA2000) campaign has been waged for over twenty years (Figure 19.1). The sociological perspective can help evaluate the success of this ambitious goal, both globally and in the United States.

Concern for international health began as a humanitarian issue, but with the rise of global interdependence it has become a survival issue. A college student in the U.S. Midwest or a subsistence farmer in Peru can be impacted by a cholera outbreak in North Africa, a nuclear accident in Russia, or the spread of AIDS in Thailand. Health policy is made by governments. By accepting WHO's definition of health, the governments of UN member nations also accept the idea that health is a fundamental human

right and, as stated in the preamble to WHO's constitution, health is not restricted by race, religion, political belief, economic or social condition.

Health and the Developing World

A half-hour airplane flight from Florida to Haiti represents a gap in life expectancy at birth of over nineteen years (World Health Organization, 1995). Haiti is one of the globe's poorest countries, and like much of the developing world, it is characterized by high poverty rates that translate to malnourishment, lack of disease resistance, and only a 50 percent chance that children who survive to age 5 will live to see age 40. Preventable and treatable diseases, such as measles, are far more likely to be fatal in the developing world.

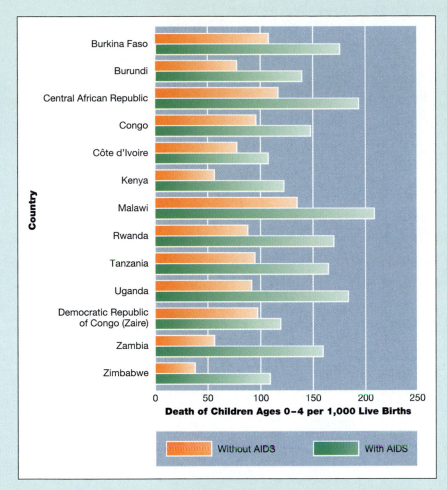

Child Mortality for AIDS in Africa, Selected Countries, Year 2010
Source: *World Population Profile: 1994.* U.S. Bureau of the Census, 1994.

ate means must be developed that alter traditional values, especially regarding family size and the roles of women.

From the perspective of symbolic interactionism, the cultural meanings associated with AIDS need to be altered to fight the disease. AIDS has been labeled a "a disease of the undeserving" because in the developed world, its first victims were gay men. IV drug users were its later victims. The "undeserving" are now in the most impoverished regions of the world and include prostitutes and other heterosexual women whose only sex partner is their spouse. Isolating AIDS victims by labeling them undeserving denies the vulnerability and responsibility of the broader population: AIDS does not respect national boundaries. The increase of AIDS in the world is a threat to everyone.

1. From the perspective of functionalism, what culturally acceptable guidelines can health workers use to prevent and treat AIDS in Africa?
2. From the perspective of symbolic interactionism, what can be done to alter the label of AIDS victims as undeserving?

Sources: Hunt, 1993; Kane, 1993; Schiller et al., 1994; Doyal, 1995; *Connections,* 1995/1996; Nelson, 1999.

Countries with higher levels of economic development also have better overall health records (Table 19.1; Figure 19.2). Countries of the developing world have shown major gains in increasing the LER, reducing the IMR and under-5 mortality rates (Figure 19.1). Between 1960 and 1996 the IMR gap between the developed and the developing world narrowed by half. But a chasm between the developed and developing world in IMR still exists, and in many regions it actually widened. In parts of the developed world only 6 out of 1,000 newborns die before age 5, but in sixteen of the least developed countries, the rate is over 200 per 1,000 children (Darnay, 1997; World Health Organization, 1998). Infant and child mortality are closely connected with maternal mortality, the death of the mother due to childbirth (Table 19.2). A study in Bangladesh found that only 12 percent of infants whose mother died in

childbirth survived two months, with only 5 percent surviving one year (Koenig et al., 1990). Overall, a person in a least developed country of the world can expect to live almost a third of a century less than one in a most developed country.

In summarizing the state of the world's health, poverty is the world's biggest killer. Data from the *World Health Report* documents the impact of poverty on health:

Poverty is the main reason why babies are not vaccinated, why clean water and sanitation are not provided, why curative drugs and other treatments are unavailable and why mothers die in childbirth. It is the underlying cause of reduced life expectancy, handicap, disability and starvation. . . . Every year in the developing world 12.2

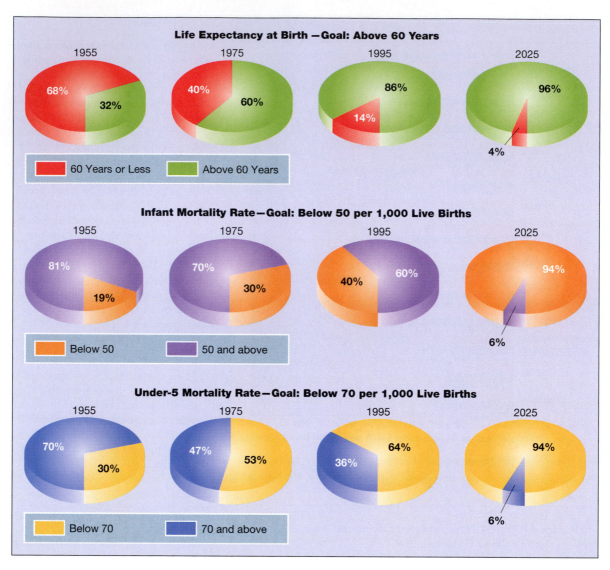

Life Expectancy at Birth —Goal: Above 60 Years

1955: 68% 60 Years or Less, 32% Above 60 Years
1975: 40% 60 Years or Less, 60% Above 60 Years
1995: 86% Above 60 Years, 14% 60 Years or Less
2025: 96% Above 60 Years, 4% 60 Years or Less

Legend: 60 Years or Less | Above 60 Years

Infant Mortality Rate—Goal: Below 50 per 1,000 Live Births

1955: 81% 50 and above, 19% Below 50
1975: 70% 50 and above, 30% Below 50
1995: 40% Below 50, 60% 50 and above
2025: 94% Below 50, 6% 50 and above

Legend: Below 50 | 50 and above

Under-5 Mortality Rate—Goal: Below 70 per 1,000 Live Births

1955: 70% 70 and above, 30% Below 70
1975: 47% 70 and above, 53% Below 70
1995: 64% Below 70, 36% 70 and above
2025: 94% Below 70, 6% 70 and above

Legend: Below 70 | 70 and above

FIGURE 19.1   Progress in Achieving HFA2000 ("Health for All by the Year 2000" campaign) for Selected Goals

Source: Adapted from *World Health Report*, World Health Organization, 1998.
http//www.who.int.whr/1998/figle.jpg

million children under 5 years die, most of them from causes which could be prevented. . . . They die largely because of world indifference, but most of all they die because they are poor. (World Health Organization, 1995)

Given this stark reality, WHO's HFA2000 campaign rests on how the world will maximize health benefits with economic resources that are becoming more limited (Abel-Smith, 1990).

Health and the Developed World

The more developed countries of Western Europe, North America, and Japan enjoy health benefits unknown to most of the world's population. These countries share the health advantages that historically have accompanied the move from agricultural to industrial economies. This process is referred to as the health transition (Gray, 1993). In the process of health transition, the rates of population growth and IMR decrease considerably, with a corresponding rise in LER. Morbidity and mortality patterns are completely altered. Acute and infectious disease caused by famine and malnourishment, pestilence, and poor sanitation are virtually eliminated as major threats to mortality, replaced by chronic and degenerative illnesses such as heart disease and cancer (Figure 19.2). Compared to the developing world, the United States is spectacularly healthy. But compared to many other developed countries, the United States lags far behind in critical health characteristics, such as IMR. Be-

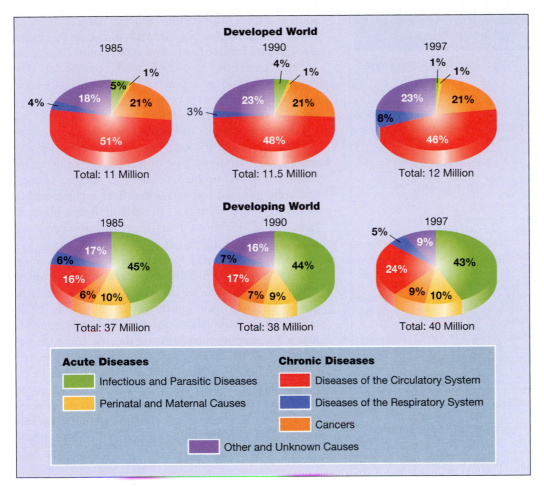

FIGURE 19.2   Main Causes of Death in the Developed and Developing World, Selected Years

Source: Adapted from *World Health Report*, World Health Organization, 1998. http://www.who.int/1998/fig6e.jpg

tween 1998 and 2000 the United States was one of the few countries in either the developed and developing world where the IMR actually *increased* (Table 19.3).

Most of the countries in the developed world have adopted policies that maximize advantages of the health transition. For example, they may change patterns of organized social response to health conditions, a process known as the *health care transition* (Frenk et al., 1991). In every country of the developed world except for the United States, this social response has been translated into some form of **national health insurance** (NHI) financed through the government, which provides health care as a right of citizenship regardless of ability to pay.

National health insurance varies widely. Despite government funding, each government determines how much of the system is private and how much is public. At one extreme is Switzerland, which simply subsidizes private health insurance. At the other end are Britain, Spain, Italy, and Sweden, which have a system of nationalized hospitals with physicians paid

directly by the government. Most other Western European countries, such as France, Germany, Belgium, and the Netherlands, fall in between (Immergut, 1992). Despite government involvement, most of these systems assure a great deal of autonomy in medical practice and allow physicians to take private

INTERNET   CONNECTIONS

We hear so much about AIDS in the United States but relatively little about the spread of the disease through less-developed parts of the world. Site www.ccisd.org/sidafrique/a_index.html describes AIDS in Africa. How are the AIDS epidemics in the United States and in Africa importantly different?

Table 19.2	Maternal Mortality Rate in Selected Countries
Country	Rate per 100,000 Births
Zambia	940
Bangladesh	710
Kenya	650
India	460
Egypt	170
Paraguay	160
South Korea	130
Philippines	100
China	95
Hong Kong	82
Costa Rica	60
Thailand	50
South Korea	26
Singapore	10
Greece	10
United States	7
Canada	6
Sweden	5

Deaths of mothers related to pregnancy and childbirth; range in years, 1994–1997
Source: Darnay, 1997; United Nations, 1998; U.S. Bureau of the Census, 1998.

patients on a fee-for-service basis. (Saltman & Von Otter, 1992; Admiraal, 1992; Broere, 1992).

But even the richest countries are concerned about health care costs, which are increasing at rates that exceed gains in national resources. Many countries are reviewing the entire structure of health care financing and organization. As the developing world creates new initiatives in achieving health for all, new directions will be offered for the developed world as well (Abel-Smith, 1990:57). Both worlds are dealing with a health care crisis. Sociological research provides data documenting that sociocultural factors are critical determinants of health.

Global Interdependence: Health and Technology

People in the developed world who can escape poverty cannot fully escape the health consequences of technology. Level of development is associated with degree of industrialization, urbanization, and technology. The most developed nations of the world especially fall prey to the very processes that allow these economic advantages.

Initially, the population of the most developed nations is vulnerable to radiation more than the population of the developing world. Both worlds are exposed to naturally occurring radioactivity from sources such as the cosmos and the natural decay of minerals and radioactive materials in the earth's crust. Background levels of radiation account for 70 percent of the radiation to which each person in the developed world is exposed. The other 30 percent comes from health care procedures, such as chest and dental x-rays (Wiesner, 1992).

Artificial sources of radiation are increasing. Radiation levels and industrial pollutants are increasing worldwide, mainly because of technology's impact on the ozone layer, problems related to nuclear energy, and contaminated soil and water. The earliest studies of the surviving victims of the atomic bomb blasts in Japan in 1945 showed an increased incidence of leukemia in the most heavily irradiated areas, followed by another peak fourteen years later (Wiesner, 1992). Those who did not die of radiation poisoning within a few months of the explosions were likely to die of cancer or some cancer-related illness. In 1979, at the Three Mile Island nuclear plant in Pennsylvania, a 52 percent meltdown of the reactor core occurred, making it the worst nuclear accident in the United States. Morbidity rates to those exposed to radiation up to twenty miles from the accident scene have been monitored ever since. Nuclear fallout is associated with a weakened immune system. Nuclear testing in the United States and other Western industrialized countries between 1945 and 1965 is now held responsible for a rise in cancer and immune deficiency diseases (Gould & Sternglass, 1994).

Table 19.3	Infant Mortality Rate, Selected Countries
Sweden	3.9
Iceland	4.3
Netherlands	4.9
Germany	5.2
Macau	5.3
Hong Kong	5.2
Austria	5.2
Australia	5.3
Canada	**5.6**
France	5.7
United Kingdom	5.7
Belgium	6.3
Spain	6.3
Taiwan	6.3
United States	**6.4**
Czech Republic	6.8
Portugal	6.9
Cuba	7.9

Range in years, 1996–1998.
Source: Darnay, 1997 (adapted from Table 90); U.S. Bureau of the Census, 1998 (adapted from Table 1345).

Poisons produced by radiation, toxic waste, and atmospheric pollution are major contributors to the dramatic increase of cancer morbidity and mortality in the developed world, but both are rapidly increasing in developing countries (Vainio et al., 1990). More than 2,500 people in Bhopal, India, died almost instantly and another 100,000 were injured when a deadly gas escaped from a faulty storage tank at a Union Carbide plant (Whitaker, 1984). As nations in the developing world are used more as sites for dumping toxic waste and for building industrial plants where labor is cheap and safety standards are low, any "advantage" to a lesser level of development will be eliminated.

The worst nuclear power accident in history occurred in 1986 at Chernobyl, in the former Soviet Union, when a reactor explosion caused the roof of the plant to cave in. Thirty-one officially recognized victims died in the accident. Those who helped with the accident and those in the exposed surrounding areas still live in fear and uncertainty about their future. Twenty percent of the farmland is also contaminated, with new areas of concentrated contamination "hot spots" still being discovered. The Russian media have labeled the mental health consequences of Chernobyl "radiophobia." People are paranoid about radiation and its effects, are infected with a mistrust of nuclear power, and are torn between what they are told officially by the government and the rumors generated unofficially (*Chugoku Newspaper*, 1992).

HEALTH IN THE UNITED STATES: LINKS TO DIVERSITY

Disease does not strike randomly. Key elements of social structure, such as social class, influence health. Another important factor that influences health is a person's unique set of social statuses within society. These elements focus on the demography of health. Demographers look at population characteristics that put some categories of people at risk for disease compared to others. Sociologists use demographic data to describe health in the United States.

The Demographics of Mortality

As we will see, mortality rates in the United States reflect what is happening globally. The most significant influence on the mortality rate has been the decline of infant deaths. A second trend has been decline of deaths due to acute diseases. Today, the leading disease causes of death are chronic, such as heart disease and cancer, and are correlated with aging and increased life expectancy (Table 19.4). This pattern reflects the benefits of medicine and better living

conditions overall. But the downside is that there are psychological and financial burdens for both patient and caregiver associated with chronic disease.

Nondisease Deaths.   A third trend is that, for the first time in history, the leading causes of death include *all three* nondisease causes—suicide, accidents, and homicide. For accidents, many environmental and public health officials now view them as the most unrecognized public health problem. Vehicle accidents, including driving while intoxicated, kill about 50,000 people per year, with about the same number dying in accidents involving work, recreation, and fire (Moeller, 1992). Nuclear disasters and toxic waste spills are also accidental but can show up as cancer deaths years later. Almost half the deaths of children are due to accidents, such as falls, drownings, and accidental shootings (National Safety Council, 1990; McGinnis & Foege, 1993).

The memorial at Chernobyl serves not only as a tribute to the victims of the worst nuclear accident in history, but also as a reminder that the planet is so interconnected that an event in one corner of the world influences the environment of the world as a whole.

Table 19.4	Leading Causes of Death in the United States in the Twentieth Century

Rank	1900
1	Pneumonia and influenza
2	Tuberculosis
3	Gastroenteritis
4	Heart diseases
5	Strokes
6	Kidney disease
7	Accidents
8	Cancers

Rank	Mid-Century
1	Heart disease
2	Cancers
3	Strokes
4	Accidents
5	Pneumonia and influenza
6	Disease of early infancy
7	Arteriosclerosis
8	Diabetes

Rank	2000 (Projected)
1	Heart diseases
2	Cancers
3	Strokes
4	Chronic obstructive pulmonary diseases
5	Accidents
6	Pneumonia and influenza
7	Diabetes
8	Human immunodeficiency virus (HIV)-AIDS
9	Suicide
10	Chronic liver disease and cirrhosis
11	Kidney disease
12	Blood poisoning
13	Homicide and legal intervention
14	Arteriosclerosis

Source: Twaddle & Hessler, 1987; Foster et al., 1997; National Center for Health Statistics, 1996; U.S. Bureau of the Census, 1998.

1993 bombing of the World Trade Center in New York City, 168 people left dead and over 400 injured in the 1995 bombing of the federal building in Oklahoma City, and 2 dead (with 100 more injured) in the Olympic Park bombing in Atlanta in 1996.

Gender. Females outlive males all over the world. In the United States, females live an average of about seven years longer than males. When race is factored in for life expectancy, both African American and white females still have a clear advantage (Figure 19.3). Males have higher mortality rates at every stage of life. Even at the prenatal stage, spontaneous abortions are more likely to occur with male fetuses. The first year of life is the most vulnerable for both genders, but infant mortality rates are higher for males. Males succumb earlier to virtually all causes of mortality, with the nondisease causes showing the greatest male-female differentials (Waldron, 1994).

Reasons for these differences are both biological and sociocultural. Females possess an additional X chromosome and protective sex hormones that are associated with a superior immune system (Doyal, 1995). When men and women are diagnosed with the same disease, such as cancer, men are more likely to die from it than women. Added to this biological ad-

The mortality rate is also increasing for deaths due to homicide, with three clear trends. The first is that most murders are committed between people who know one another, especially in the context of domestic violence (Reid, 1993). The second is that murder is intraracial, with almost 90 percent of victims slain by members of their own race (Wright et al., 1992; Bastian & Taylor, 1994). Finally, murder is urban and firearm related, most likely to be committed in poorer areas of larger cities (Canada, 1995; Uniform Crime Reports, 1997).

Epidemiologists may add terrorism, including war, as another nondisease category in determining mortality rates. While they are intentional, deaths due to terrorist activities are probably counted as accidents or homicides. These include six deaths from the

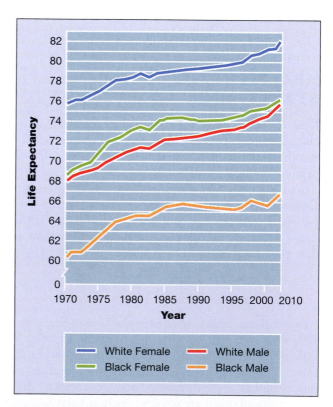

FIGURE 19.3   Life Expectancy in the United States by Gender and Race, 1970–1998 (and Projections for 2000 and 2010)
Source: National Center for Health Statistics, *Monthly Vital Statistics Report,* 1993, 41(7S):5; U.S. Bureau of the Census, 1999.

People whose lives depend on foraging for food and other resources from contaminated sources such as city dumps are susceptible to many health problems, such as diarrheal, parasitic and respiratory diseases, and skin infections. Children are the most vulnerable.

vantage is a gender-role benefit. Whereas the female gender role encourages women to seek help for health problems, the male gender role discourages men from seeking such help (see Chapter 13). For example, cancer therapies have benefited women in part because the disease is more likely to be diagnosed in earlier, more treatable stages. When men are socialized into

the belief that seeking help is a sign of weakness, they may not get needed treatment for life-threatening diseases in time.

Gender roles also put men more than women in occupations that are potentially hazardous to their health, such as police and fire protection, the military, construction, and mining. These roles may encourage men to engage in risk-taking behaviors, especially those that involve physical daring or are illegal.

It is still unclear how much of the gender differential in mortality is biological and how much is sociocultural. If women adopt the risky behaviors of men, such as cigarette smoking or dangerous sports, gender differences may decrease (Woods, 1995). To date, however, even with the movement of women into formerly male domains, the gender differentials in mortality rates have remained virtually unchanged.

SES and Race.   There is a dramatic relationship between mortality and SES, both globally and in the United States. The higher the level of occupation, education, and income, the lower the death rate. Infant mortality rates are higher for poor children in all regions of the United States (Foster et al., 1997). Since lower SES is associated with so many health-related factors such as inadequate housing and nutrition, lack of health insurance, occupational risk, and exposure to violence, it is difficult to determine specific causes for this relationship. As reflected in the IMR, we do know that SES is such a powerful indicator of mortality that the poorest Americans are comparable to those in some developing countries (see Table 19.3).

Infant mortality is also associated with racial minority status. Infant, neonatal, and postnatal deaths for African Americans are double those for whites. Economic discrimination, which places a dispropor-

Homicide in the U.S. is associated with the availability of guns and is most likely to occur among acquaintances and relatives who live in poor urban areas.

tionately high number of African Americans and other nonwhites into lower SES groups, is a contributing factor. However, persistent race differences are not simply a result of social class. Native Americans have lower neonatal death rates, indicating a possible genetic advantage, but higher postnatal rates, indicating a sociocultural (environmental) disadvantage. Both lower income Chinese Americans and higher income Japanese Americans have low infant mortality that is stable over a variety of conditions, suggesting a genetic benefit (Yu, 1982; Hayward & Heron, 1999). However, lower SES Southeast Asians have significantly higher mortality rates than whites or other Asians (AAPCHO, 1997). It is difficult to determine the effects of SES and race on overall mortality rates.

The Demographics of Morbidity

If every disease was known in the proportion to the mortality it causes, then mortality rates would be enough to determine the burden of illness on an individual, family, or community. But some chronic diseases such as epilepsy, anemia, skin conditions, arthritis, and leprosy cause substantial illness (morbidity) but little mortality. Also, since morbidity is largely subjective, measuring it is very difficult. Thus, in discussing morbidity it is important to use research that includes physical signs as well as those that are self-perceived (Fig. 19.4).

Gender. A clear and consistent pattern emerges in gender differences in mortality and morbidity. Women have higher morbidity rates but live longer than men. Men have lower morbidity rates but do not live as long as women. One of the most striking features of these data is the trend of females to report more physical and mental disorders and use health services more than males. Females have more daily and transient illnesses such as colds and headaches and a higher prevalence of nonfatal chronic conditions such as arthritis, anemia, and sinusitis. Males have lower overall acute conditions but higher prevalence of chronic conditions that are life threatening and associated with long-term disability, such as heart disease, emphysema, and atherosclerosis (Marks, 1996; U.S. Bureau of the Census, 1999).

Gender differences are apparent in morbidity related to the use of alcohol and other drugs. Alcoholism is higher among men throughout their lives. For women, the rate of alcoholism is lower, but other morbidity effects appear. Fetal Alcohol Syndrome is linked to mental retardation and low birth weight of infants (Paludi, 1992). Alcohol is also a major factor in rape and spouse abuse. The most common addiction for women is nicotine. Although there has been an overall decrease in smoking for both men and women, the percentage decline for women has been smaller,

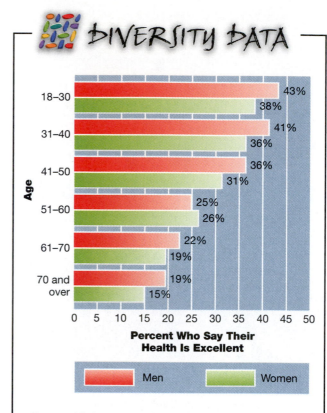

DIVERSITY DATA

FIGURE 19.4 Percent Saying Their Own Health Is Excellent, by Age and Gender. At all age levels, men report slightly higher levels of excellent health than women, an average of about 5 percent. Adults over 50 report significantly higher levels of excellent health than adults under 50. If men report excellent health, especially at older ages, why do women live longer than men?

Source: NORC. General Social Surveys, 1972–1996. Chicago: National Opinion Research Center, 1996. Reprinted by permission of NORC, Chicago, IL.

with lung cancer rates doubling for women since the 1950s (National Center for Health Statistics, 1998).

SES and Race. People of low SES have higher morbidity rates for almost every disease or illness, especially in terms of higher rates of infectious and parasitic diseases and major mental disorders (Winkelby et al., 1992; Wilkinson, 1996). This correlation has not decreased over time. SES is a vital link in understanding inequalities across diverse racial and ethnic groups in health and health care (Krieger & Fee, 1994a, 1994b).

With some notable exceptions, for example, SES appears to be more important than race in explaining overall morbidity (Fig. 19.5). African Americans have higher rates of sickle cell anemia, which appears to be genetically based. They also experience higher rates of hypertension (high blood pressure) than whites, but those with low incomes have triple the rates of those who are more affluent (Polednak, 1989). One

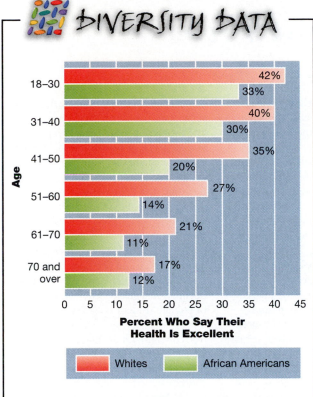

DIVERSITY DATA

FIGURE 19.5   **Percent Saying Their Own Health Is Excellent, by Age and Race.** As expected, as age increases, likelihood to report health as excellent decreases. However, at all age levels African Americans report significantly lower levels of excellent health than whites. Why do you think the race differences in reporting excellent health are the greatest between ages 41–50 and the smallest after age 70?
Source: NORC. General Social Surveys, 1972–1996. Chicago: National Opinion Research Center, 1996. Reprinted by permission of NORC, Chicago, IL.

Mental Illness

Mental illness is one of the most serious health issues facing America, yet the public has little objective information about it. The scope of the problem is reflected in prevalence estimates. Excluding mental retardation, if mental illness is defined as those who exhibit symptoms severe enough to require ongoing treatment or hospitalization, about 15 percent of Americans have some type of mental illness. If it is defined according to milder psychiatric symptoms where coping with everyday life becomes difficult due to stress, anxiety, or depression, as many as 80 percent may be affected (Barker et al., 1992; Regier, 1991; Mechanic, 1989, 1999).

For those who do seek help, treatment ranges from large numbers in outpatient community facilities or private offices of therapists to smaller numbers who are institutionalized for severe disorders and to the vast majority who receive no treatment. Mental illness has physical, psychological, and sociocultural causes. Despite the complexities, over fifty years of research provides a good overview of the social epidemiology of mental illness.

The most consistent finding is that there is an inverse relationship between mental illness and SES: the lower the SES, the higher the rate of mental illness. This holds true for treated and untreated populations and those who are institutionalized and those who are not (Hollingshead & Redlich, 1958; Srole et al., 1962; Cook & Wright, 1995).

Although empirical support for this finding remains strong, there is disagreement as to which comes first—the lower SES or the mental illness. The *drift hypothesis* suggests that SES deteriorates because of the mental illness. People who are mentally ill drift into poverty because of their inability to function adequately on a daily basis, especially remaining employed. Some research supporting the drift hypothesis shows that mental illness not only hampers upward social mobility but that often lower SES people who are mentally ill come from higher SES backgrounds (Kessler et al., 1994; Link & Dohrenwend, 1989).

In terms of gender, there appear to be no significant differences in overall *rates* of mental disorder, but there are consistent differences in *type*. Women are more likely to suffer from affective and anxiety disorders while men are more likely to suffer from personality disorders (Rothblum, 1982; Mechanic, 1989; Kessler et al., 1994).

Marriage and employment factors are linked to gender. To lower the risk of mental illness, it is better to be married, especially for men. In the United States, never-married, divorced, and single men have higher rates of mental illness when compared to women. But married women suffer more mental-health problems than married men (Steil & Turetsky,

study suggests that this is due to the greater prevalence of obesity in the lower classes in general (Syme & Berkman, 1994). Others suggest that the culprit is psychological stress resulting from discrimination, poor nutrition, and lack of medical care (Reed, 1990; Cockerham, 1995a). While the reasons for African American and white health differences are not completely clear, the compelling argument traces the differences to SES (Mutchler & Burr, 1991).

These trends are in contrast to Asian and Pacific Islanders, who are the healthiest of any racial group in the United States. And as for Native Americans, even with continuing health problems related to poverty, alcoholism, and accidents, there has been a significant improvement in their general health over the last forty years (U.S. Bureau of the Census, 1999). The evidence for a strong association between social conditions and morbidity remains, with SES as the most important indicator.

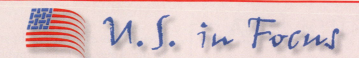

U.S. in Focus

Health and the Workplace

In the United States, people are socialized into a strong work ethic. Work is healthy. Since our physical and mental well-being is related to employment, the stress of unemployment has severe consequences for health. Unemployment has direct physiological effects, resulting in physiological problems of migraine headaches, rapid heartbeat, hypertension, and stomach problems. These conditions are intensified by poor diets, increased smoking and drinking, and a weakening of interpersonal skills.

On the other hand, work has intrinsic value that plays a valuable role in self-esteem, life satisfaction, and overall psychological well-being. The impact of work on personal identity is seen in Sigmund Freud's answer to the question of what a "normal" person should do well. His answer: "to love and to work." For Freud, normal psychological functioning emphasizes work and family. The ideal is to create an environment where work and family are not opposed to each other.

Achieving this ideal is becoming more difficult. The dual-earner household is the U.S. norm and one the majority of couples voluntarily choose. But work and family roles have different meanings for men and women. These differences in meaning, especially related to parenting, may be why the mental health advantages of multiple roles are fewer for women compared to men. Added to this are the unique stressors faced by women in the workplace, including higher levels of sexual harassment, stereotyping, and gender discrimination.

Stress in the workplace goes well beyond balancing family and work commitments. Occupational stress can be viewed as the overall illness people experience because of their work. The symptoms can be physical (headaches and fatigue), psychological (depression and anxiety), or behavioral (decreased job performance and low worker moral). Stress is associated with burnout, and depression often accompanies it. People in the helping professions and those whose work involves life-threatening situations and fast decisions, such as in hospital emergency rooms, police and fire departments, and airlines, are particularly vulnerable to occupational stress. The "occupation" of college student is also susceptible. This is seen during November and March where illness plagues students near the end of the semester, when their physical and psychological resources are exhausted.

When violence enters the workplace, stress levels may rise so high that employees cannot continue on the job

---

1987; Rosenfeld, 1989; Steil, 1995). The social support that goes along with married life might be reduced for women who have excessive multiple-role demands, such as juggling family and career. For both married men and women, however, working outside the home adds to better mental health (Thoits, 1995; Quick et al., 1992; Simon, 1995).

≋ LIFE CONNECTIONS:
Alternative Medicine in the United States

Americans are seeking out alternatives to conventional medicine in growing numbers. Three important trends have fueled this process. First, Americans are much more educated about health overall and take more responsibility for managing their health than in the past. In turn, physician dominance over patients is being challenged. Second, the United States is rapidly becoming more and more multicultural. In health care, multicultural diversity translates to patients who are seeking out practitioners who provide medical treatment consistent with their culture and belief systems. Third, a holistic health model is rapidly making its way into public consciousness about what optimal health and health care should be. Thus it is common

in the United States for people to incorporate conventional scientific medicine with other health practices that may be described as traditional, indigenous, folk, self-healing, and/or spiritual. Such practices are gaining stature among both patients and practitioners. The case of Richard Oakes in the opening vignette is an illustration.

These practices are referred to as *alternative medicine*. They are "alternatives" because medical students rarely encounter them and they are seldom used in conventional treatment in hospitals (Weitz, 2001). Therapies such as herbal remedies, megavitamins, guided imagery, massage, acupuncture, yoga, chiropractic, and faith healing are included with alternative medicine. Medical doctors who integrate alternative and conventional medicine, who refer patients to alternative healers, such as chiropractors or massage therapists, or who treat patients with both pharmaceuticals as well as herbal and vitamin products do so outside of what they were taught in medical school. These physicians often choose alternative medicine because in their practices they encounter patients whose options for help with mainstream medicine have been exhausted (Goldstein et al., 1987; Borkan et al., 1994). In addition, their personal illness experiences lead many to seek out alternatives—going against prevailing medical norms. Finally,

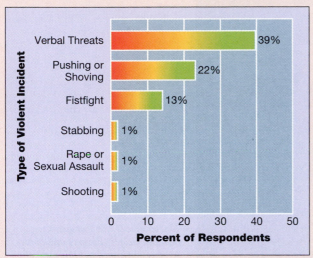

Violence in the Workplace
Source: Jacobs, 1998, p. 37.

lawyers, and by high school students vengeful against peers who ridiculed them—heightens fear of employees everywhere. When abortion clinics and government buildings are bombed, the safety of all our workplaces is called into question. The 1980s were called the stress decade in part because of work-related stress—a pattern likely to expand in the twenty-first century.

In explaining the importance of work to health, sociologists emphasize the cultural value of work. Functionalism focuses on the problems that occur when the rapid changes in the workplace create too much anomie, which hurts smooth so-cietal functioning. Conflict theory focuses on the struggle of workers at all levels to maintain their economic resources in an era of corporate downsizing and mergers. Unwanted job changes and periods of unemployment are likely for most U.S. workers in their careers. Symbolic interactionism focuses on how changing work roles are redefined and how we internalize these new labels. All three perspectives recognize that work and health and well-being are intimately connected.

1. What can employers do to create a workplace that enhances the physical and mental well-being of employees?
2. Which of the three theoretical perspectives best explains the fact that Americans find their work roles psychologically satisfying but also find them to be stressful?

Sources: Brenner, 1979; Kessler et al., 1987; Lobel, 1991; Jones & Boye, 1992; Nelson & Hitt, 1992; Quick et al., 1992; Kahn, 1993; Turner, 1995.

after the violent episode. The increased incidence of shootings—in schools and offices, carried out by disgruntled employees in post offices, by people who feel unfairly treated by judges and

these physicians, especially osteopaths, are more likely to embrace the holistic health model (Gevitz, 1998; Csordas & Kleinman, 1996).

By 1997, 83 million Americans used some form of alternative medicine, an increase of 20 million from 1990 (Grady, 1998). The majority of patients use alternative medicine mostly to prevent illnesses, at the same time they are seeing their physicians. The cost is lower than conventional therapies and the alternatives are usually not covered by health insurance. However, the people who use such therapies are generally upper income and college educated—those who do have insurance and can afford conventional treatment. Users of these therapies are also more likely to be female and have chronic health problems, a pattern found both in England and the United States (Sharma, 1996; Eisenberg et al., 1998).

The American Medical Association and the National Institute of Medicine have begun a series of research initiatives to determine the scientific basis of alternative medicine (Stabiner, 1998). For example, two of the mainstays of traditional Chinese medicine are herbal remedies and acupuncture, methods that U.S. medicine is incorporating as scientific research continues to document their efficacy. Through scientific research some alternative therapies have been reported not to work (for example, chiropractic manipulation for tension headaches and acupuncture for nerve damage caused by HIV), and some have been reported to work (such as yoga for wrist pain associated with carpal tunnel syndrome and mixtures of Chinese herbs for hard-to-treat inflammatory bowel syndrome) (Grady, 1998).

The scientific debate related to alternative therapies and conventional medicine is far from being resolved. A key aspect of the debate has to do with the concern that alternative medicine is led by unlicensed practitioners who offer fraudulent, unsafe, and untested techniques for financial gain—referred to as "quackery" in healing. The AMA funds a special unit whose goal it is to investigate quackery, fraud, and malpractice among *both* alternative healers and MDs (Young, 1992).

Holistic Health

It is apparent that beliefs about alternative medicine are altering patterns of health care practices among Americans. The data on alternative medicine clearly show the sociocultural connection to health. These data also illustrate the holistic approach to health, both in the research that is being done to find the

The poorest of the poor are often homeless people. Poverty and homelessness are linked to high rates of infectious disease and mental disorders.

threats to good health and in the way medicine is being practiced. By 1999, 600 licensed physicians belonged to the American Holistic Medical Association—numbers that are expected to increase (Weitz, 2001). Sociologists and social epidemiologists have been in the forefront of providing data to the health community, focusing on the relationship between social life and health. One result is that there is understanding among physicians and the public that a "magic pill" will not be found for the chronic diseases that plague the United States and the world. The holistic health approach does not abandon the search for cures, but recognizes that health and health care need to be considered in terms of prevention of disease and in light of the sociocultural circumstances of all patients (Armstrong, 1996). An important point to remember is that cultural beliefs, whether scientifically based or not, influence health behavior.

≡ SOCIETY CONNECTIONS: The Health Care Crisis

Health care in the United States is said to be in crisis. Of the many factors contributing to the crisis, the three most often cited are: cost (the United States spends more on health care than any other country in the world, and health care costs continue to rise, outstripping inflation), access (many Americans have no health insurance and cannot get adequate health care in public or charitable facilities), and organization (health care occurs in a complex and confusing system of providers and facilities) (see Figures 19.6 and 19.7). Sociologists clearly demonstrate that these three issues—cost, access, and organization, are interdependent.

Health care has developed in response to arising needs rather than to a rational planning process. In other words, the health care system that is evolving is a crisis-oriented one. Two factors help explain this evolution. First, the ways the crises (needs) are met are consistent with the values of U.S. society. For example, the organization of health care delivery reflects a U.S. value system that emphasizes individualism and choice in a capitalistic economy. Second, health care has moved from a model where general

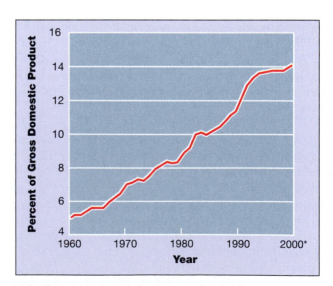

FIGURE 19.6   National Health Expenditures as a Percentage of Gross Domestic Product (GDP), 1960–2000
*projected
Source: Foster et al., 1997; U.S. Bureau of the Census, 1998.

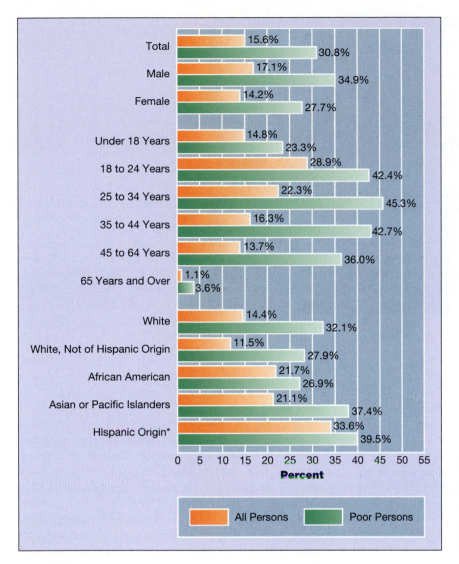

Total 15.6% / 30.8%
Male 17.1% / 34.9%
Female 14.2% / 27.7%

Under 18 Years 14.8% / 23.3%
18 to 24 Years 28.9% / 42.4%
25 to 34 Years 22.3% / 45.3%
35 to 44 Years 16.3% / 42.7%
45 to 64 Years 13.7% / 36.0%
65 Years and Over 1.1% / 3.6%

White 14.4% / 32.1%
White, Not of Hispanic Origin 11.5% / 27.9%
African American 21.7% / 26.9%
Asian or Pacific Islanders 21.1% / 37.4%
Hispanic Origin* 33.6% / 39.5%

Percent (0–55)

All Persons   Poor Persons

FIGURE 19.7 Who Lacks Health Insurance Coverage? Selected Characteristics for 1997
*Note: Persons of Hispanic origin may be of any race.
Source: Bennefield, 1997; U.S. Bureau of the Census, 1998.

practitioners (physicians) provided almost all services to one in which most practitioners are now specialists, and physicians represent only a very small minority of all health care providers. This situation is tied to the fact that health care is information and technology driven. It is impossible for any one type of health care provider to have all knowledge now deemed necessary to treat many, if not most, patients. Both of these factors have created a uniquely American health system that has profound consequences for patient care.

Cost and Access

The health care crisis is fundamentally a financial one. The technology, skill, and facilities to both treat and cure disease are available. When cure is impossible, the knowledge and compassion necessary for ongoing care are also available. Indeed, consistent with

the holistic health model, "care" rather than "cure" will be a focus of the future (Grieshaber, 1993). Although the distribution of providers is uneven, there are enough to serve the current and future health care needs of the U.S. population. As noted in the opening vignettes, the problem is that these vast resources are reserved primarily for those who can pay for them.

The percent of Americans with no health insurance has escalated. In 1996, 36.5 million people were in poverty, the largest number in thirty years, and one-third of this group had no health insurance (see Table 19.5). The working poor are only one-third as likely to receive health insurance as a benefit from their employers as the nonpoor (Seccombe & Amey, 1995). Lack of insurance is not limited to the poor, however, since 70 percent of those without health insurance are above the poverty line (Summer, 1994). People without insurance also include the chronically ill and those with preexisting medical conditions.

The health care crisis in the United States brings many diverse groups together to protest the high cost of health insurance that puts health care out of reach for many people. Groups representing women, racial minorities, and senior citizens are especially vocal—and powerful—in these protests.

Without adequate health insurance, those who need health care try to receive help from public and charitable institutions, which are overburdened, understaffed, and under the constant threat that funding cuts will curtail or eliminate their programs.

Table 19.5 Selected Health Characteristics by Race and Income in the United States		
	1990	**1995**
Not Covered by Health Insurance		
White	12.1*	14.4
Black	21.8*	21.7
Hispanic	31.3*	31.5
Poor persons	26.6*	30.8
Infant Mortality Rate		
White	7.6	6.1
Black	18.0	14.7
Maternal Mortality Rate		
White	5.4	4.2
Black	22.4	22.1
Life Expectancy Rate		
White	76.1	76.9
Black	69.1	69.7
% Reporting Health as Fair or Poor		
Family Income:		
Less than $14,000	18.6	20.4
$14,000–$24,999	10.8	12.3
$25,000–34,999	7.5	7.9
$35,000–49,000	5.3	6.2
$50,000 or more	4.0	3.0

*1989 data

Sources: Jacobs et al., 1998; National Center for Health Statistics, 1998; U.S. Bureau of the Census, 1998.

Differential access to health care is already a fact of life for many Americans. These people illustrate the problem of *allocative health care rationing,* based on lack of insurance and high cost (Conrad, 1993). Health care rationing involves budget caps, insurance protocols, and limiting treatment by type and age. Not only is the doctor-patient relationship harmed, but the most vulnerable segments of our population, such as the poor and the elderly, are prevented from receiving treatment (Conrad, 1993).

Vulnerability for such groups is heightened because health care is rendered on a **fee-for-service** basis, where the patient pays for each service provided. Even when charitable agencies provide care, patients are expected to pay some of the cost. In this way, health care is a commodity and patients are customers who pay for this commodity like any other product or service.

In reality, the cost of health care has risen so dramatically that fees cannot be paid for by patients directly. Most fees are billed to *third-party payers,* typically consisting of private insurance, provided through employers or purchased independently, and public agencies. Most patients pay some out-of-pocket expenses as co-payments for third-party coverage.

The rising cost of health care can also be traced to the development of a system in which hospitals and providers have been allowed to set their own fees and third-party payers have been expected to pay them. When combined with the medicalization trend, the fee-for-service system encourages unnecessary services because of the profit motive. Hospital services remain the largest expenditure for health care dollars (Figure 19.8). Physicians determine which patients get admitted and for how long. Any interference with this process by third-party groups is seen as an assault on the doctor-patient relationship, limiting patients

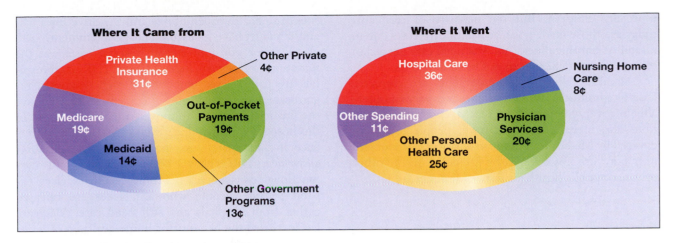

Where It Came from

- Private Health Insurance 31¢
- Other Private 4¢
- Out-of-Pocket Payments 19¢
- Medicare 19¢
- Medicaid 14¢
- Other Government Programs 13¢

Where It Went

- Hospital Care 36¢
- Nursing Home Care 8¢
- Other Spending 11¢
- Physician Services 20¢
- Other Personal Health Care 25¢

FIGURE 19.8   America's Health Care Dollar—1997

Source: Health Care Financing Review, 1996; U.S. Bureau of the Census, 1998.

in the choice of their physician, and impediment to quality care. The system thus upholds the values of individualism, choice, and profit.

The American Medical Association originally resisted the passage of any legislation that was believed to endanger physician autonomy in a fee-for-service system, including workmen's compensation and Social Security at its early stages (Starr, 1982). As it became clear that a growing segment of the population was excluded from quality health care and some excluded from *any* health care, and despite continued AMA resistance, two major pieces of federal legislation were enacted—Medicare and Medicaid. These programs have been a financial boon for health care providers.

Medicare.   Enacted in 1965 during the presidency of Lyndon B. Johnson, **Medicare** is a health insurance program funded through Social Security primarily for those age 65 and over, but with provisions for covering people of any age who have certain disabilities. Medicare is not welfare. For most elderly Americans, Part A is premium free. Part B is paid in part by premiums of enrollees. In 2000 the monthly premium for Part B was $45.50, unchanged for three years (U.S. Department of Health and Human Services, 2000). This amount is nominal given the massive expenses associated with even minor health care. But for those on limited incomes, it can become a burden when the choice is between paying rent or paying for health coverage. However, it is clear health care is a priority for the elderly in that over 98 percent take the optional Part B coverage (Green Book, 1994). Medicare pays less than half of the total health care costs of the elderly, but it dramatically increased their health coverage and is responsible for cutting the poverty rate of the elderly in half.

Medicaid.   Unlike Medicare, **Medicaid** is a joint federal and state welfare program that provides medical assistance for certain people of any age with very low income. Some welfare recipients are automatically eligible for Medicaid. For the elderly, Medicaid provides for long-term care, but only after a person "spends down" assets to get to an "acceptable" poverty level. It was designed to cover people on welfare,

Medicare provides some services, such as rehabilitation and physical therapy, that allow the elderly to remain in their homes. It is less costly and more satisfying than long term nursing home care.

especially children. But the majority of recipients today are those made poor by health care costs due to disability, chronic illness, and custodial care needed in old age (Starr, 1982; Mann & Ornstein, 1995).

Medicaid eligibility requirements are complex, costs to administer it are high, and states vary considerably in coverage. As costs increased, eligibility restrictions also increased so that fewer people today are covered by Medicaid. And the majority of the poor and near poor are not covered by Medicaid or any other private or public health insurance (Summer, 1994).

Organization

Health care in the United States is delivered through a multibillion dollar industry consisting of hospitals, a complex array of outpatient facilities, and practitioners who are relatively autonomous in how they choose to deliver their services. These practitioners include those who deliver direct patient care, such as nurses and physicians, and those who organize the care that is delivered, such as hospital and home health administrators.

The complexity of health care organization and the expansion of medical knowledge and technology propels an already existing trend toward specialization in all health professions. Medical technology has shaped how and where physicians practice and the health labor force as a whole (Aries & Kennedy, 1990). Total patient care at all stages—prevention, treatment, cure, and care—now requires the involvement of a number of specialized personnel. Optimal health care requires that such services be coordinated and that unnecessary duplication does not occur.

The organization of health care delivery into autonomous, fragmented self-regulated units often prevents this ideal. Patients are routinely shuffled from one provider to another and literally get lost in the process. Duplicate medical and lab tests cause patient discomfort and drive up costs. Specialization also prompts an oversupply of physicians in some areas, such as surgery, and an undersupply in others, such as general medicine.

The problem of health care organization directly counters the holistic health momentum in health delivery where the "whole" patient is treated. When there is too much specialization and when specialization obstructs coordination, the holistic principle is violated.

Toward Health Care Reform

Government involvement in health care, especially Medicare, has been financially lucrative for physicians, insurance companies, and hospitals. But skyrocketing health expenditures and the drive for a balanced budget have focused on cost containment.

A major effort to curtail hospital costs was the initiation of *Diagnosis Related Groups* (DRGs). Hospitals are paid a fixed amount for each diagnosis, regardless of the actual cost incurred. Hospitals have the financial incentive to move patients in and out of the hospital quickly, since they can keep the difference if they spend less than the designated DRG allowance. DRGs have both functional and dysfunctional consequences. Home health services expand because people who are sicker are released earlier from hospitals and still need care. Medicare has increased the benefits for home health in order to meet these needs. Hospitals also take advantage of the system by avoiding patients with "less profitable" DRGs.

Managed Care. Cost-cutting measures as well as the drive to make preventive health a hallmark of U.S. medicine have increased the number of **health maintenance organizations (HMOs)**. HMOs are prepaid health plans offering complete medical services where physicians and other providers are either independently contracted or salaried employees of the HMO. A variant of HMOs are *Preferred Provider Organizations* (PPOs), where employers buy discounted group health insurance packages that send employees to certain physicians and hospitals. HMOs and PPOs rely on general practitioners rather than more costly specialists, and they are expected to keep expenses low by keeping patients healthy. Physicians employed by HMOs may recognize that the MD surplus is emerging, and they may believe this form of medicine offers less competition for patients, less demanding work schedules, and less costs for the physician than starting a new private practice (Ferraro, 1994). More employers are offering employees HMO-type options where they can select from a variety of physicians at the less costly traditional fee-for-service alternative. Patients are becoming more astute consumers of health services. HMOs need to offer assurances to patients that they will not be treated impersonally by group practice providers (White, 1995; Bodenheimer, 1999).

According to the U.S. Department of Health and Human Services (1998), over one-fourth of Americans are insured through HMOs. The rise of HMOs marks a trend in health care delivery in the United States referred to as **managed care.** Managed care is designed to control health care costs by measures such as requiring authorization before a person sees an expensive specialist, undergoes expensive tests, or is hospitalized. Physicians are monitored according to the costs they incur in treating specific illnesses. But the "lower cost-healthy patient-satisfied physician" managed care model has been compromised (Table 19.6). Costs of health insurance continue to rise, and many patients who need specialized care often go unserved (Gold, 1991). Physicians complain that the doctor-patient relationship is intruded upon by too many regulations and that their HMO practices limit autonomy. Managed care typifies the current health care system in the United States. Although the fee-for-serve system remains intact, managed care has significantly altered the older model where physicians enjoyed almost complete control of their medical practices.

The Clinton Health Plan.   Despite lack of consensus on what it would like, the cost and inequity of health care prompted what appeared to be public support for a major campaign to reform it (Jacobs et al., 1993). Using the best features of HMOs as a basic model, in 1993 President Bill Clinton proposed the Health Security Act. Highlights included comprehensive benefits that could not be terminated, patient choice from health plans that included fee-for-service, HMOs, and a combination of the two, with an emphasis on prevention and primary care. Through a system of *managed competition*, where providers form health alliances, consumers would have a choice of providers and providers would have a financial incentive to form group practices (White House Domestic Policy Council, 1993; Starr, 1994).

Though it came closer to a major overhaul of health care in the United States than at any other time in history, the legislation failed. Relative to other federal expenditures, support for health reform has narrowed long-standing differences in opinion between affluent and poorer people. The public's deep ambivalence toward government reform overall appears to be a factor in this failure (Jacobs et al., 1993; Schlesinger & Lee, 1993). Although the president and Congress took lead roles in the drama, interest groups representing business, labor, the medical community, and the insurance industry played feature roles (Rovner, 1995). These groups began the fight for reform but retreated when battles did not affect them, or they devoted their energies toward defeating parts of the legislation. Regardless of which political party dominates Congress, it is certain that elements of the Clinton plan will be resurrected for a model for health care reform.

Canada's Health Care System.   Because of similar political, sociocultural, and geographical factors that shaped the nations, the Canadian system of health care has been carefully scrutinized by policymakers in the United States as a model to consider (Marmor, 1993; Iglehart, 1989). Both countries developed their health care systems in the same manner, but after World War II Canada began experimenting with government hospital insurance programs. Through federal-provincial effort, these experiments resulted in decreased costs and increased access.

Today the Canadian National Health Insurance (CNHI) program is a publicly administered one covering all legal residents and all medically necessary services provided by a physician, including hospitalization. Funding is provided from a variety of sources including federal transfers favoring poor provinces, general provincial revenues, employer payroll taxes, and insurance premiums. No one is denied coverage and special assistance is provided for those with low incomes (White, 1995). Similar to the United States, most hospitals are not government owned but profit-oriented, and physicians are reimbursed on a fee-for-service basis. A key difference is that CNHI calls for negotiated prospective budgets for hospitals and physician fees (Marmor, 1990).

How successful is the Canadian model? In controlling costs, as reflected by percent of Gross Domestic Product, Canada has been more successful than the United States (Table 19.7). Access to health care may be reflected in IMR and life expectancy rates, which are also better in Canada (Tables 19.1 and 19.3). While quality is difficult to measure, the charge that U.S. citizens would receive inferior medical care to achieve universal coverage is hard to justify given these comparisons.

Health for All.   Whether the Canadian system, a variation on the Clinton Plan, or a combination of other plans is the model, it is likely that some type of universal health insurance is necessary and will eventually be implemented. The plan will account for America's unique value system where social and economic profit are both necessary. The fact that the issue of prescription coverage for the elderly became a major presidential campaign focus in 2000 shows that politicians are taking health care very seriously. The "Health for All 2000" campaign is an initiative that applies to the United States as much as to the global community.

Table 19.6 Percentage of Consumers Saying They Are Not Satisfied with Their HMO Plan: Selected Complaints	
Complaint	Percent
Wait time for appointment	
When sick	33.0
When well	30.0
Getting specialist referrals	30.0
Panel of doctors available	25.0
Panel of hospitals available	21.0

Source: From "HMO Complaints" in *The New York Times*, February 2, 1997, p. 12Y. Copyright © 1997 by The New York Times Company. Reprinted by permission of The New York Times Company.

Table 19.7	Health Care Spending in Selected Countries in the Developed World, 1997	
Rank	Country	Percent of Gross Domestic Product
1	**United States**	**14.0**
2	Germany	10.4
3	Switzerland	10.2
4	France	9.9
5	**Canada**	**9.3**
6	Sweden	8.6
7	Netherlands	8.5
8	Australia	8.3
9	Portugal	8.2
10	Iceland	8.0
11	Austria	7.9
12	Denmark	7.7
13	Belgium	7.6
14	Italy	7.6
15	New Zealand	7.6
16	Norway	7.4
17	Spain	7.4
18	Finland	7.3
19	Japan	7.3
20	Luxembourg	7.1

Source: Adapted from Table 1349, U.S. Bureau of the Census, 1998.

INTERNET ⟶ CONNECTIONS

The debate continues about whether the United States of America should have a national health care plan. Access a search engine on the Internet (Yahoo, All-The-Web-All-The-Time, Excite, Lycos, etc.) and enter the key words *single payer health care plan.* You will discover that in many states, groups of citizens are lobbying actively for the implementation of national health care. For example, such a Web site in the state of Missouri may be found at http://mosp.missouri.org/; and in Massachusetts: http://www.masscare.org/. After you have had the opportunity to peruse these and other sites, write a brief report listing what you perceive to be the advantages and disadvantages of a national health care plan. Are you personally in favor of national health care? Why or why not?

SUMMARY

1. The World Health Organization (WHO) defines health holistically, as a state of complete physical, mental, and social well-being. Health is a fundamental human right.

2. Health is often measured in terms of a population's mortality rate (the percentage of people who die every year). Globally, the two most important indicators of health are the infant mortality rate (IMR) and the life expectancy rate at birth (LER).

3. Epidemiology is the study of the causes and distribution of disease and disability in a given population. Epidemiologists are concerned with both the incidence of disease (the number of new cases reported over time) and the prevalence of disease (the total number of cases per period).

4. Functionalists view health as contributing to social equilibrium and sickness contributing to disequilibrium. Émile Durkheim thought behaviors like suicide were caused by a lack of social support; Talcott Parsons identified the sick role as behaviors expected when a person was ill—a form of legitimate deviance. The longer the person is exempt from typical roles, the greater the strain on the social system. Functionalists agree that the health system is in crisis and health care should be a right, but that changing it should be gradual so more problems are not created.

5. Conflict theorists focus on power and social class to explain health care inequality. The professional autonomy of physicians gives them a great deal of power over definitions of disease and how health care is delivered. Compared to the middle class, lower class people have less access to health care and insurance and higher risk of sickness.

6. Symbolic interactionists see health as a social concept. The sick role is a negotiated one. Both physicians and patients label health and illness according to their own beliefs and act according to the labels. The interactions between patients and physicians are socially constructed.

7. A country's level of economic development has an enormous impact on health. Infant mortality rates are much higher, and life expectancy is much lower, in developing countries than in developed nations, due mainly to poverty and a high rate of population growth. The developed world enjoys better health overall. Except for the United States, countries in the developed world

provide national health insurance. But global interdependence and sources of risk such as radiation and pollution puts those in all countries at health risk.

8. In the United States, the leading causes of death are chronic disease and nondiseases, such as suicide, accidents, and homicide. Mortality rates are influenced by gender and race—women tend to live longer than men, and whites to live longer than African Americans. SES is the strongest influence on mortality rates—lower SES people have higher mortality rates.

9. Women have higher morbidity (sickness) rates than men, though their mortality rate is lower. Race has some influence on morbidity but SES is a stronger influence.

10. About 15 percent of Americans suffer from severe mental illness, which, like morbidity rates overall, is higher among people of lower socioeconomic status. Gender does not appear to impact rate of mental illness but there are gender differences in type. Although both married men and women have lower risk for mental illness, married women are at higher risk than married men. Employment for both genders adds to better mental health.

11. Linked to holistic health, alternative medicine, such as chiropractic, acupuncture, and guided imagery, is growing in popularity. Those who use alternative medicine tend to be middle class, educated, and using it for prevention of illness or for chronic illness, at the same time they see their physicians.

12. Though the United States spends more on health care than any other nation, millions of Americans do not have health insurance. Health care is rationed to those who are insured or who can pay for the care themselves on a fee-for-service basis.

13. Medicare is a health-insurance program funded through Social Security that primarily serves the elderly. Medicaid is a welfare program that provides medical assistance to low-income people of all ages.

14. Medical specialization, increased reliance on expensive technology, and a fragmented, uncoordinated system of competing providers are driving up health care costs in the United States.

15. To lower cost, there is a move toward managed care using health maintenance organizations (HMOs). The Clinton administration's proposal for health care reform, based on the concept of managed competition among existing providers, was defeated by coalitions of special-interest groups. Elements of the Clinton Plan and insight from Canada's health care system may be used for the next health care reform initiative.

KEY TERMS

acute disease   487

chronic disease   487

epidemiology   484

fee-for-service   506

health   484

health maintenance
   organization (HMO)   508

holistic health   484

incidence   484

managed care   508

Medicaid   507

medicalization   489

Medicare   507

morbidity rate   484

mortality rate   484

national health insurance   495

prevalence   484

sick role   486

CRITICAL THINKING QUESTIONS

1. Demonstrate how global and U.S. patterns of health are both similar and different. What characteristics of social structure explain the patterns?

2. What explains the differences in mortality and morbidity between men and women and between the races? What interventions would reduce the disadvantages created by these differences?

3. How can both patient and health care provider needs be met in the movement toward holistic health and alternative medicine?

4. Which of the three theoretical perspectives could best be applied to resolve the crisis related to cost, access, and the organization of the health care system?

5. Given the health care crisis and the desire to lower costs and provide quality care, what would be the best model of health care that could address these issues?

20 EMERGING INSTITUTIONS: MEDIA AND SPORT

OUTLINE

SOCIOLOGICAL PERSPECTIVES ON RECREATION

The Hypodermic Model
The Functions of Media and Sport
The Conflict Interpretation of Media and Sport
Symbolic Interactionism and Cultural Studies

THE MASS MEDIA

Television
Film
Popular Music

SPORT

Sport and Social Stratification
Sport and Religion
Sport and the Media

 **LIFE CONNECTIONS: THE DARK SIDE OF SPORT**

Deviance and Aggression in Sport
Racism in Sport
Sexism in Sport

SOCIETY CONNECTIONS: CENSORSHIP AND THE ELECTRONIC MEDIA

Global Media Flows

In the highest Guatemalan mountains, the stirring music is not made by the remote Qeche Indians, as visitors think; it comes from Beatles tapes. Ike and Tina Turner are heard in tiny villages in the Chinese heartland. Video nights in Katmandu clubs feature *Rambo* and *Rocky*. Burmese musicians play songs by the Doors. On a street in downtown Lhasa, Tibet, there is a karaoke bar where patrons flawlessly reproduce Michael Jackson's dance routines. In tiny Keneiba, Mali, where there is no electricity, a generator is cranked up and children gather around a VCR and an ancient black-and-white television for an exciting evening of Power Rangers and Bugs Bunny. *Robocop* and audiotapes of Madonna are smuggled into Iran by way of an electronic black market in Dubai. (V. Adams, 1996; and personal observations)

High School Football in Texas

The little city of Odessa, located on the sparsely populated plains of West Texas, recently built a new football stadium for Permian High School. It cost $5.6 million and featured

> ... a sunken artificial-surface field eighteen feet below ground level, a two-story press box with VIP seating for school board members and other dignitaries, poured concrete seating for 19,032, and a full-time caretaker who lived on the premises. (Bissinger, 1991: 42)

The school flies the team to away games on chartered airplanes, yet the English department can barely afford to supply students with textbooks. Football players routinely pass their classes whether they have learned anything or not, and the primary route to popularity for girls at Permian is to become a "Pepette." Winning is so important that the day after the team lost a big game, Permian's coach awoke to find a forest of "for sale" signs on his front lawn.

As these vignettes suggest, the mass media and sport are important parts of everyday social life. All around the globe, people are more than willing to spend a great deal of time and money in order to be entertained, whether by Michael Jackson or by the Permian High School football team.

Sociologists often analyze sport and the media as aspects of **popular culture:** commercialized art and entertainment designed to attract a mass audience. Popular culture also includes such diverse phenomena as tourism, advertising, hobbies, and fashion. We will concentrate on the media and sport in this chapter because their influence on society is especially apparent.

Popular culture may in turn be interpreted as a major component of the emerging social institution of *recreation.* Like all institutions, recreation fulfills important social needs, above all the need for leisure. Sociologists consider recreation to be an emerging institution because it has grown out of the economic institution through a process of *institutional differentiation,* much as education originally developed out of the family.

SOCIOLOGICAL PERSPECTIVES ON RECREATION

Through most of history, recreation was provided primarily in the home. In the evening, family members might play games together or work on a group project. Mother might quilt while father whittled or carved. An older child might read aloud to the others. But beginning early in the twentieth century, large-scale organized leisure activities separate from the family arose in the developed world. Today, popular culture is mass marketed, leading to the development of a variety of leisure-time options far surpassing that which was available earlier (Chandler, 1977).

While inexpensive and omnipresent in the post-industrial societies, commercial recreation is often still a luxury in the developing world. For example, only wealthier nations can afford to provide municipal services such as swimming pools, parks, and sports facilities for the majority of their citizens (Jones, 1986). In poorer countries, commercialized leisure is available, but only to a small, if rapidly growing, minority.

Prior to the industrial era, most leisure-time activities took place within the family. This pattern continues today, but it is substantially diminished. More and more contemporary recreation is commercialized and set outside of the family.

The Hypodermic Model

Most early sociological researchers accepted the **hypodermic model,** which assumes that the media have a simple, direct, one-way effect on their audience rather than one that is mediated through primary group interaction. In the 1930s, this model was applied to motion pictures. During this era, the movies were a cheap and immensely popular form of entertainment that offered a haven from the grim realities of the Depression that lurked just outside the theater doors.

Researchers noted with alarm that two of the most common themes in films of the 1930s were crime and sex; moreover, these themes were presented in ways that sometimes violated the mores of the audience (Peters, 1933). Movies were also assumed to shape people's ways of thinking about different social groups, thus arguably contributing to stereotypical attitudes. Not only were media messages often socially and morally harmful (Glover, 1985), but young people were also thought to be especially vulnerable to them (Blumer, 1933).

The hypodermic model is grounded in psychological behaviorism (see Chapter 5), which sees human action as shaped by a simple stimulus-response process. Young people were being exposed to—and directly absorbing—messages that conflicted with the (presumably) more positive viewpoints they were receiving from the family, school, and government. Parents and teachers feared that family disorganization, juvenile delinquency, and chaos in the schools could be the result. Note that these concerns, first expressed over seventy years ago, are still being raised today.

How useful is the hypodermic model for analyzing the influence of the media? Modern scholars believe that the media are generally interpreted *indirectly*. Media imagery is discussed with and interpreted by peers and family rather than simply being passively absorbed. Length of exposure, type of content, and the social characteristics of the audience are all critical factors affecting how the media influence people's attitudes and behavior.

Thus, for example, a steady diet of gangsta rap, televised professional wrestling, and films that blur the distinction between the good guys and the bad guys is likely to cultivate violence among teenagers who already live in an aggressive environment (Huesmann, 1994; Gerbner et al., 1994). On the other hand, teens who grow up in a more prosocial setting, without being exposed to delinquent peers or abusive parents, will probably not be significantly influenced by media violence.

INTERNET   CONNECTIONS

Permian High School, where Texans take their football very seriously, has a Web page at www.geocities.com/Colosseum/Loge/2631/indexj.html. Why is football a more important recreation than the debating team or chess club at most American high schools?

The Functions of Media and Sport

A good way to understand how some sociologists interpret the emerging institution of recreation is to examine the various functions that media and sport provide in society.

Providing Entertainment.   The most obvious or manifest function of both the mass media and sport is that they supply highly pleasurable entertainment to many millions of people. This entertainment allows a temporary escape from real-life activities and problems (Morley, 1989; Turow, 1990).

Creating Jobs.   The impact of sport and the media on the economy is enormous. They create millions of jobs. Actors and athletes must rely on camera operators, costume designers, technical specialists, coaches, trainers, journalists, manufacturers of athletic equipment, makeup artists, and groundskeepers.

Encouraging Sociability.   The media and sport facilitate social interaction by providing excuses to get together and furnishing topics for conversation. They promote family activities, dating, and simply mingling with friends. College students watch MTV, the WWF, *South Park*, and even the news in their dorms. Men use Super Bowl parties as friendship-enhancing rituals. Small night clubs bring like-minded music aficionados together to hear new bands.

Similarly, sports, movies, and television programs provide common ground for conversations. The Final Four or the World Series, the latest episodes of *Ally McBeal* or *The West Wing*, and films like *American Beauty*, *The Truman Show*, and *Titanic* are significant sources of U.S. commonality.

Promoting Socialization.   Although the family is the first agent of socialization that we encounter, the media, and especially television, quickly become very important in a child's life. TV often acts as an electronic babysitter. Television characters set standards of behavior for children to model, if not directly as the hypodermic model suggests, then certainly indirectly.

Similarly, sport may be an effective vehicle in socializing youth to accept a variety of social values (Coakley, 1993). In this regard, pioneering sports sociologist Harry Edwards (1973) identified what he called the "dominant American sports creed" as the widespread belief that sports promote discipline, competitiveness, physical and mental fitness, religiosity, and patriotism. Athletes are assumed to develop qualities that are important to success in life from their participation in sports, qualities such as perseverance, achievement motivation, commitment to winning, self-control, individualism, and team loyalty.

We should note that not all sports are organized exclusively around the value of competition. Sometimes participation and cooperation are more strongly emphasized, as in the Special Olympics. Athletes, especially in individual sports like track, swimming, and golf, may choose to measure their performance against some abstract standard or against their own previous best mark, rather than in simple terms of wins and losses.

Sports also directly affect people's physical health, which at the collective level may contribute to a nation's ability to defend itself militarily. Thus, during the 1950s, physical education programs in the schools were beefed up on the rationale that physically fit children would become fit adults and would help the United States respond to the Soviet challenge.

These athletes, who are taking part in the Special Olympics, are not focused on competition exclusively; in this program, participation and cooperation are also strongly emphasized.

The Social Control Function. This function is mostly performed by the media and is closely linked to socialization. In totalitarian societies, the media are under strict governmental control and are used to publicize the certainty of punishment for political deviance or lack of social conformity. But the media present and often reinforce the rules by which individuals are expected to live in all societies, whether democratic or totalitarian. Television programs like *Law and Order* that point out that offenders are likely to be apprehended and convicted are prime examples of this function.

Promoting Individual and Cultural Identity. At the individual level, interest in media celebrities or commitment to a particular team can be a significant element of one's personal identity. Sport allows people to validate their prestige claims, whether by virtue of personal athletic achievement, extensive knowledge of the history and current statistics of a favorite team, or just by wearing the "right" team jersey or basketball shoes.

Whether as a participant or a spectator, commitment to a sports team connects us to other people who feel as we do, enhancing the social bond. High schools and colleges explicitly use this fact to build solidarity among their students and alumni. Loyalty is encouraged by rituals like pep rallies, caravans to away games, and the wearing of team colors. Team logos take on a quasi-sacred quality, symbolizing the unity of the fans.

Major college and professional teams frequently provide a similar function for whole communities, states, or regions. For example, when the University of Kentucky won the NCAA basketball title in 1998, fans throughout the state tore up and down the main streets of their towns, blowing their horns and waving UK banners. The fact that few of these fans had any connection at all to the university did not seem to matter.

In the emerging global society, the media and especially sport promote social integration and patriotism for cities as well as nations. This cultural identity function is especially well illustrated by soccer, which is by far the world's favorite sport.

Nowhere is soccer more popular than in Brazil, where it functions to simultaneously divide and unify the people of this large and very heterogeneous society (Lever, 1983).

Each major Brazilian city has numerous teams that compete fiercely with each other. The teams typically draw the core of their support from different social groups. For instance, in Rio de Janeiro different teams are identified with ". . . the old rich, the modern middle class, the poor, the blacks, the Portuguese, and a number of neighborhood communities" (Lever, 1983: 146–147). At this level, team support mostly promotes social fragmentation.

But Brazilian soccer is also organized beyond the municipal level, with one team representing each city in a national championship series. During this tournament, everyone from a given city unites behind their team. This criss-crossing of loyalties helps unite the diverse populations of various cities and regions.

At an even higher level, people from all parts of Brazil passionately support their national team as it competes with other countries for the World Cup. The national team often makes allies out of bitter

Soccer is the world's most popular spectator sport. This is a small part of a huge crowd that gathered to celebrate a recent victory by the Brazilian team in World Cup competition in France. Note the representation of both men and women and of people from several different racial and ethnic groups.

opponents. Thus soccer in Brazil both reinforces internal social divisions and also helps forge a sense of national identity and collective consciousness.

The Conflict Interpretation of Media and Sport

Conflict theory suggests that the emerging institution of recreation tends to reproduce the status quo and to discourage social change. Sometimes recreation also promotes racial, gender, and age stereotypes and applauds—or at least trivializes—the antisocial behavior of media celebrities. According to the conflict perspective, the elites who control popular culture, including both media and sport, often use it to deaden critical thinking and legitimize existing power arrangements (Madrid, 1986).

For example, cross-cultural research on television in the developed world suggests that journalists often downplay the severity of national conflicts so as to pacify or reassure jittery audiences (Cohen et al., 1990). The media may thus serve what Marx would call an "opiate" function because they distract people from paying attention to—and trying to remedy—social injustice and political oppression (Hoch, 1982).

Similarly, in U.S. politics, "spin doctors" manage media campaigns so that sound bites become more important than serious political debate. Politics is reduced to "made-for-media" events (Gitlin, 1990; Donovan & Scherer, 1992; Croteau & Hoynes, 1994).

In global perspective, many conflict theorists study the impact of the Western media on the values and norms of developing societies. The enormous economic power of the Western media virtually assures that influences originate there and flow outward to the rest of the world. The potential impact is so enormous that the Western media have been banned as part of government anti-modernization campaigns in developing countries such as Afghanistan.

College Sports: A Conflict Analysis.   Conflict theorists maintain that sports generally benefit men more than women, whites more than minorities, the wealthy more than the middle and working classes, and owners and administrators more than athletes. Consider, for example, the life of a major college football or basketball player. If you add up the total number of hours devoted to conditioning, practice, travel, and actual games, even student athletes who receive full scholarships are in effect being paid little more than a minimum wage salary. Meanwhile, a successful team may produce millions of dollars of revenue and publicity for the school that sponsors it ("Top Players Produce . . . ," 1994).

Moreover, many college athletes, especially those competing in the revenue-producing sports, have trouble keeping up with their studies. As a result, these athletes have lower graduation rates than other student-athletes or the student body in general (Adler & Adler, 1991; Coakley, 1998: 453–54). It is easy to see why conflict theorists believe student athletes are being exploited.

Student athletes often accept such treatment as a necessary preparation for becoming highly paid professionals. But in most cases, this goal is unrealistic. There are, for example, some 40,000 college football players, but only about 2,300 slots in the NFL (Leonard, 1998).

At a more abstract level, big-time college and professional sports can be dehumanizing (Brohm, 1978). Athletes are often required to play despite painful injuries, to practice long after they have ceased to enjoy what they are doing, to use performance-enhancing drugs, and to regard their own bodies as little more than objects to be used in pursuit of an end (Sabo, 1995).

What Values Do Sports Really Teach?   As suggested above, most functionalists believe that the values promoted by sports are generally positive, but conflict theorists take a different position. Sports train athletes to submit without complaint to the authority of their coach, which may prepare them to become docile workers and compliant citizens.

Furthermore, because success in sports (including team sports) is often based on individual talent and effort, athletes can adopt a radically individualistic worldview, in which the unequal levels of success enjoyed by different classes, genders, and ethnic groups are explained solely by the efforts—or failings—of individuals. As Robert Lipsyte (1976) put it:

> A man must prove his faith in sports and the American way by whipping himself into shape, playing by the rules, being part of the team and putting out all the way. If his faith is strong enough, he will triumph. It's his own fault if he loses, fails, remains poor.

Although Lipsyte's comment is androcentric in that it includes only males, the same observation also applies to female athletes.

Competition is the centerpiece of the U.S. sports creed. When one individual or team wins, all the others lose. Clearly, the athlete's goal is to win. We give lip service to good sportsmanship, but most people agree with former Green Bay Packer coach Vince Lombardi, who said, "Winning is not everything; it is the only thing." Or, as another coach put it, "Show me a good loser and I'll show you a loser." This value,

Most Americans believe that successful athletes learn positive values through competition. Are the lessons the losers learn equally valuable or does athletic failure primarily destroy young people's confidence in themselves?

that winning is the only relevant goal in sport, is sometimes referred to as the *Lombardi ethic*.

What are the consequences of accepting this ethic? Does competition increase motivation? The answer is yes, under certain conditions: People who are raised in an environment that emphasizes competition, who have a competitive personality, who have some reasonable chance of success, and who participate in relatively familiar sports usually thrive on pressure to succeed. On the other hand, people who do not meet these criteria tend to find an emphasis on competition frustrating and counterproductive (Kohn, 1986). Thus, for example, Hopi Indians, who come from a strongly cooperative culture, may play high school sports, but they often disappoint their coaches because they seem to lack a "killer instinct" (Garrity, 1989).

Does the Lombardi ethic help people succeed in the real world? Success in some activities, especially sales work, requires competitiveness, but many businesses now put greater value on cooperation and teamwork. These qualities can be taught through athletics, but they are usually considered distant seconds to competitiveness.

Compare the U.S. emphasis on competition with the team orientation in Japan, a society that generally values the group over the individual (Snyder & Spreitzer, 1989). Outstanding athletes are considered deviant if they brag or try to stand out as individuals by throwing temper tantrums or complaining to the media. Most Japanese players are also more willing than their U.S. counterparts to bunt to help their teams—and less likely to try for home runs.

If, as conflict theorists maintain, big-time sports exploit and dehumanize athletes, teach them to obey authority without question, and mercilessly overemphasize competition, why do so many people persist in believing that sports are a good way to build character? One reason is because of the **halo effect.** When we see athletes perform well on the field and win, and when the media constantly associate winning with virtue, we generalize that people who are good in one area of life—in this case, sports—must be *generally* good people (Coakley, 1998).

Conflict theorists also maintain that the media and sports promote commercialism. Everything seems to come down to money: Which star or player has the biggest contract? Who receives the most money for endorsements? Corporate involvement in sports has reached unprecedented levels: Colleges routinely receive hundreds of thousands of dollars for outfitting their teams in particular brands of sports equipment. All of the major bowl games have now accepted corporate sponsorship, such as the *Sunkist* Orange Bowl. In 1999, major league baseball seriously considered allowing teams to sell advertising space on their players' uniforms.

Conflict theorists also believe that sports encourage excessive nationalism, as exemplified by the violent attacks by British "soccer hooligans" on foreign nationals during international contests (Buford, 1992). Or consider the intense euphoria when the U.S. hockey team upset the Soviet Union in the 1980 Olympics. Media coverage of such events triggers fervent nationalism that fuels ethnic and racial stereotypes at a time when global political challenges require understanding and cooperation.

Symbolic Interactionism and Cultural Studies

Symbolic interactionism is becoming an increasingly popular theoretical perspective from which to study recreational activities. Sports events and media genres such as thrillers, soap operas, and documentaries have different meanings for different people (Murdock, 1989). Symbolic interactionism is centrally concerned with the construction of these meanings and how people come to a common understanding of what various symbols represent. The negotiation process never ends; society and all its elements are continually being reconstructed.

Film critics, sportscasters, and radio station executives are cultural gatekeepers, deciding which films to review, which games to broadcast, and which music to play. They can either reinforce or weaken our social constructions. What we see as good or bad about a film, a record, or a hockey team is thus shaped by an ongoing process of social definition.

Cultural studies is a new interdisciplinary field, rooted in philosophy and the humanities and closely associated with symbolic interactionism, which studies popular culture. This discipline focus on how the meanings of cultural phenomena, including the media and sport, are constructed by individuals whose consciousness is in turn shaped by the distinctive symbolic and structural patterns of their society. Cultural studies scholars assume that no cultural product, whether a Broadway play or a World Series game, can be understood without considering the process by which it is socially constructed (McCall & Becker, 1990; Hall, 1990; Crane, 1992).

Cultural studies scholars are interested, for example, in how both participants and spectators attribute meaning to athletes. In one study, Peter Donnelly and Kevin Young (1988) interviewed rugby players and mountain climbers to learn how they went about constructing the identity of "serious athlete." Donnelly and Young found that it was a rather long-term process and involved acquiring knowledge about the sport, becoming associated with athletes whose identity was firmly established, using these people as a reference group, and reconfirming the new identity by interacting regularly with more established athletes. Similar studies have explored how athletes learn to interpret the meaning of pain (Curry, 1993) and how Little League baseball players come to understand the meaning of their sport (Fine, 1987).

Symbolic interactionists also explore how sports influence athletes' gender identities. Michael Messner (1990) interviewed a sample of men heavily involved in athletics and found that success in sports confirmed these athletes' manliness in their own eyes as well as in the eyes of others. Athletic prowess in women, however, has historically been considered unfeminine. This sexist view is gradually fading, but a recent study of women on the LPGA tour found that some still felt a distinct tension between their identities as women and as golfers (Crosset, 1995).

Finally, symbolic interactionism also offers insights into issues such as Native American names for sports teams. Some maintain that team names like the Atlanta Braves, the Kansas City Chiefs, and the Washington Redskins demean Native Americans by depicting them in offensive and stereotypical terms. Such concerns have led several universities to change their team names—for example, the Stanford Indians became the Stanford Cardinals and the St. John's

Redmen are now the Red Storm—but professional teams have resisted changing their names. Some argue that these team names and mascots are well-intentioned or even meant to honor Native Americans, but other observers find these claims less than convincing:

> . . . Just for the moment of one game, put your feet into our moccasins. Watch the red-painted faces. Watch the fanatics in the stands wearing turkey and chicken feathers in their hair. Watch the fools doing the tomahawk chop and singing that horrible chant. Then picture that section of fans as people supporting a team called the African Americans. Imagine them doing the same things to black Americans as they are doing to Native Americans. (Giago, 1998)

THE MASS MEDIA

In this section, we will consider some sociological aspects of the major commercial media—television, film, and popular music.

Television

Television has transformed the family and infiltrates all dimensions of our lives (Huston et al., 1992; Spigel, 1992). Well over 95 percent of U.S. homes have at least one television set, and it is turned on an average of seven hours each day. Figures 20.1 and 20.2 illustrate the impact of age and gender on television viewing and, for contrast, on newspaper readership.

Television is passive entertainment. It relaxes rather than excites; it puts people at ease and makes them less alert. This is not necessarily negative. Tensions that mount up over the day can be eased by watching television; in a sense, it is a form of therapy for a stress-filled lifestyle (Fowles, 1992).

On the other hand, heavy television viewing can make people feel negative and less in control of daily life events. Most adults believe television is addictive, although most deny that they are personally addicted (Smith, 1986; McIlwraith et al., 1991).

New technologies can make television a more active experience, but research suggests that most viewers continue to watch passively (Perse & Ferguson, 1997). Neither cable nor VCRs have changed television habits in any appreciable way, aside from increasing viewers' programming options, the amount of time people spend watching TV, and their satisfaction with it (Levy, 1989; Lin, 1990; Morgan & Shanahan, 1991). Most people do not use even minimally sophisticated video features such as time-shifting or simultaneous viewing and recording. Though VCR users

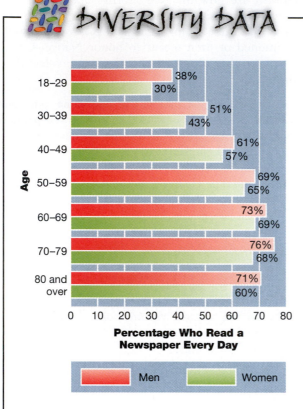

FIGURE 20.1   How Do Age and Gender Affect Newspaper Readership? Except for those over 80, older people are consistently more likely than younger ones to read a newspaper daily. For all age ranges, men are more avid newspaper readers than women. Do you think younger people are tuning out entirely, or do they get their news from other sources such as television and the Internet?
Source: NORC. General Social Surveys, 1972-1996. Chicago: National Opinion Research Center, 1996. Reprinted by permission of NORC, Chicago, IL.

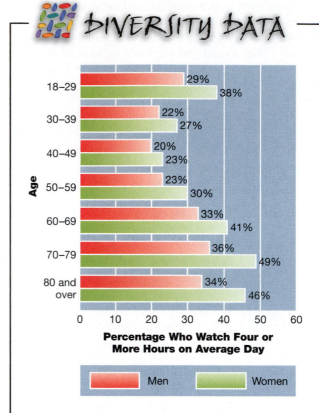

FIGURE 20.2   How Do Age and Gender Affect Television Viewing? Women are more likely than men to watch four or more hours of TV on an average day, with the largest gender gap among people who are under 30 and over 69. Viewership is heaviest among the elderly and lightest in the age range 30–59.
Source: NORC. General Social Surveys, 1972-1996. Chicago: National Opinion Research Center, 1996. Reprinted by permission of NORC, Chicago, IL.

plan their viewing more carefully, they still spend a great deal of time passively watching rented tapes and recording programs for future viewing.

New video technologies may also encourage a more solitary lifestyle: Why go to the theater when you can wait a few months and watch the film at home whenever it is convenient (Golding & Murdock, 1991; Klopfenstein, 1989)?

The remote control device is the one new TV technology that does appear to have somewhat reduced passive viewing. Many people use remotes to change channels to avoid commercials and to "channel surf," moving rapidly from station to station to sample what's on (Walker & Bellamy, 1991; Perse & Ferguson, 1997).

A number of important issues have been raised concerning the content of television programming.

Eighty percent of all programs, from cartoons to documentaries and especially prime time dramatic shows, feature some form of violence. White, middle-aged males are generally overrepresented and are usually cast as heroes who inflict more harm than they suffer. Women, minorities, and the elderly are underrepresented and portrayed disproportionately as the victims of violence. Dehumanization and physical abuse are not only common, but also often glamorized.

Since crime is rampant on television, occupations such as police officer, lawyer, and physician are overrepresented (Gerbner et al., 1986; Sparks, 1992; Burk & Shaw, 1995). On daytime television, talk shows and soap operas often feature dysfunctional families, brief sexual liaisons, and addicted or disordered people. Symbolic interactionists point out that negative portrayals of lower-class and minority characters on TV,

TV's Forgotten Minority: Hispanic Americans

Who is your favorite Hispanic TV star? This is a surprisingly difficult question to answer for the simple reason that there are virtually no Hispanics in starring roles, and only a handful in featured ones, on prime time TV. Hispanic Americans are expected to become the largest minority group in the country by 2005. Yet they are almost invisible on commercial television.

In the 1950s and 1960s, prime time TV was virtually an all-white world. The most popular shows featured suburban, middle-class white families of no specific ethnic heritage: *Father Knows Best*, *Ozzie and Harriet*, and *Leave It to Beaver*. By implication, this was the "real" United States. Hispanic characters occasionally appeared as outlaws in the Old West or lounging under sombreros in the dusty squares of Latin American towns as background, not characters, waiting for the stars to appear. The principal exception was Cuban band leader Ricky Ricardo (played by Desi Arnaz) on the *I Love Lucy Show*. Ricky's ethnicity added a comic touch: When totally exasperated by his wife Lucy's hairbrained schemes, he lapsed into Spanish and displays of stereotypical "Latin temper."

TV began to broadcast a new message about selected minorities in the early 1970s. The improbable pioneer in this trend was Archie Bunker—the narrow-minded working-class star of *All in the Family*. An equal opportunity bigot, Archie railed against virtually every minority group. Product Norman Lear's goal was to "hold up a mirror to our prejudices," using humor to raise issues that had been taboo on TV until then.

The huge success of this program led to any number of imitations and spin-offs, primarily African American family comedies. For the most part, Hispanics did not participate in the 1970s ethnic revival. As in the 1960s, there was one major exception. *Chico and the Man* paired a young, high-spirited Mexican American man (played by Latino comedian Freddy Prinze) with an aging Anglo garage owner, Ed Brown. The irrepressible Chico taught the stubborn, ill-tempered Brown to relax, enjoy himself, and be more tolerant. Sadly, the show's success ended when its star, Prinze, committed suicide in 1977.

The popularity of shows with all or mostly black characters reached new highs in 1980s with *The Cosby Show*. In some ways, the Huxtables resembled the happy prime-time families of the 1950s and 1960s. Despite high-powered careers (Cliff was a physician, Claire, a lawyer), their lives revolved around their family, whose lighthearted disagreements were always easily resolved. The show was widely criticized for presenting an idealized version of black families and ignoring serious racial issues.

In the late 1980s and early 1990s, the number of colorblind roles for African Americans crept upward—but not for Latinos. There was no Hispanic equivalent to *The Cosby Show*. To the contrary: During a decade when African Americans were being accepted (at least on TV) into the mainstream, the stereotype of the Hispanic "bandito" was revived with markedly sinister overtones. On shows like *Miami Vice*, Hispanics were frequently cast as drug lords rich and powerful enough to control entire cities and even small countries. Even on *Hill Street Blues*, *Cagney & Lacey*, and other shows that featured blacks and women in positions of authority, Hispanics lurked in the netherworld of small-time gangsters, junkies, and pimps.

A survey conducted during the 1994–1995 season found that Hispanics still were not being included in the increasingly multicultural TV image of the United States. About 2 percent of all characters on TV were Hispanic—far below the 12 percent of Americans who claim Hispanic ancestry in real life. Hispanic characters were more likely to be unskilled laborers than executives or professionals; they were twice as likely as white characters and three times as likely as black characters to be criminals.

More often than other characters, Hispanics were shown as motivated by greed, pursuing their goals through violence or deceit, and generally failing to attain whatever goals they sought. Latino characters tend to be "ghettoized" into a small number of prime-time series (many appearances on *Miami Vice* but almost none on *Baywatch*). Finally, with rare exceptions, Hispanics were portrayed as members of a single Latino ethnic group, rather than as Cubans, Mexicans, Hondurans, and so forth—as members of a variety of Spanish-speaking ethnic groups with distinct cultures and experiences in the United States.

1. Why do you think that African Americans have been much more successful than Hispanics, not only in obtaining parts on prime-time TV programs, but also in being allowed to occasionally play relatively non-stereotyped roles?
2. What are the effects on viewers of the invisibility of Hispanic Americans on television?
3. How have America's other ethnic and racial minorities—including Jews, Asian Americans, and Native Americans—been depicted on television?

Sources: Castleman & Podrazik, 1982; Lichter & Amundson, 1997.

Numerous research studies suggest that violent television programming contributes to real-life violence, either through direct modeling or as a result of a gradual desensitization to aggressive content.

especially on programs like the Jerry Springer show, may encourage viewers to see members of these groups as deviant and stigmatized (Greenberg et al., 1981; Sanders, 1990; Klein, 1996).

Film

Like other forms of popular culture, the movies have been transformed by technology and sophisticated marketing strategies. In the 1930s, Hollywood studios had complete control over the production, distribution, and exhibition of films. Despite the fact that public interest groups of the day sometimes expressed concerns about the influence of movies on young people, in most cases in this era Hollywood nurtured social stability. Movies celebrated U.S. values of hard work, individualism, and free enterprise.

Before the 1950s, most films were geared to mass audiences and families; today they increasingly target specific groups, particularly youth (Pace, 1997). Some critics maintain that Hollywood supports certain political agendas and that its films are shaped by the common backgrounds of studio heads. But the substantial profits made by films geared to very diverse audiences contradict such claims. Experimental, small budget, avant-garde films such as *The Blair Witch Project* are supported by a sizable audience niche, so innovation is not crushed in favor of more popular mass market films like *Armageddon* and *Titanic*. The film industry seeks profit wherever it can be found and cannot afford to alienate any sizable group of potential viewers (Gabler, 1988; Bayma, 1995; Powers et al., 1996; Schaefermeyer, 1997). The industry's willingness to cater to diverse tastes is reinforced by cable television and video rentals as substantial secondary markets.

Sociologists have often observed that films frequently reinforce stereotypes, especially regarding race and gender. Though stereotyping persists, significant gains have been made, especially among African Americans, who now are well represented in most facets of the movie industry, from actors like Denzel Washington, Wesley Snipes, Eddie Murphy, and Jada Pinkett to directors like Spike Lee and Bill Duke (Johansen, 1997; Wells & Hakanen, 1997).

Unfortunately, women have made less progress, and some of their earlier gains may be threatened. When the studio system was at its peak in the 1930s and 1940s, women were well represented among Hollywood's brightest stars. Some films of the World War II era presented positive images of independent women who worked at home and in defense plants. But the self-confident woman of the war years had pretty much disappeared by the 1950s, and women became increasingly one-dimensional—either good, as represented by Doris Day and Debbie Reynolds, or bad (sexually provocative), as represented by Ava Gardner, Jayne Mansfield, and Marilyn Monroe.

INTERNET ——— CONNECTIONS

See www.picpal.com/picpal/violsyn.html for the movies that have raised censorship issues. Should movies be censored, and if so, under what terms?

By the 1970s, sexual violence with women as its victims was becoming increasingly common. Many mainstream films presented women as idealized objects of desire or as threats needing to be tamed (Pribram, 1993). Today the number of romantic leading roles for women is decreasing, male studio executives still outnumber females three to one, over 70 percent of all feature film roles go to men, and female stars are often paid as little as half what leading men make (Silvas et al., 1993; Lindsey, 1997).

Hollywood executives defend themselves against charges of sexism by saying that female roles simply reflect male fantasies, and that films must appeal to a male audience in order to turn a profit. This claim may be reasonable considering that the average moviegoer is a male between the ages of 14 and 24 (Haskell, 1987; Basow, 1992; Anderson, 1994). But if Hollywood expects to keep profits high, it will need to target the growing market of financially secure women who want more positive film portrayals of women—women like TV's Murphy Brown and Ally McBeal. There are some signs that Hollywood is listening. Recent popular and critically acclaimed films featuring strong female lead performances include *Thelma and Louise*, *The Joy Luck Club*, and *Waiting to Exhale*.

Popular Music

Music is shaped by the social and organizational environment that creates it and then reshapes that very environment (Frith & Horne, 1987; Blau, 1988; Shepherd & Wicke, 1997). Music, like television and film, thus both reflects and creates social patterns.

The music industry is more change-oriented than Hollywood. Specialized musical niches cater to a wide variety of tastes. Yet, despite this diversity, the music industry recognizes that the market is driven by teens and young adults and has created an enormous product line to appeal to them (Carroll et al., 1997; Wells & Hakanen, 1997; Meeske, 1997). When rock videos entered the music scene, the competition for the teen dollar became even greater.

Popular music is often at the vanguard of social change. In the 1960s and 1970s, popular songs like "We Shall Overcome," "The Eve of Destruction," and "I Am Woman" accompanied the civil rights and women's movements (Burnett, 1997; Rose, 1997). Today, musicians like Marilyn Manson and Rage Against the Machine take conventional morality and politics to the limits, and often well beyond (Henry, 1989; Burnett, 1997).

Once a radical art form, rock music has now by-and-large become legitimate and accepted. Between the 1960s and 1990s the music of artists like the

Beatles and the Rolling Stones changed from cutting-edge innovation to massive mainstream acceptance. Heavy metal has followed a similar pattern (Weinstein, 1991). However, many of the more original rockers, such as R.E.M. and Pearl Jam, continue to maintain an uneasy relationship with the business side of the music world on which they ultimately depend (Cohen, 1991; Thornton, 1996).

SPORT

What is sport? Sociologist Jay Coakley (1998: 19) proposes this definition: **Sport** is an institutionalized, competitive activity that involves vigorous physical exertion or the use of relatively complex physical skills by individuals whose participation is motivated by both personal enjoyment and external rewards.

According to this definition, sport is a concept halfway between play and spectacle (Guttmann, 1978). Pure play, as exemplified by a group of friends tossing a frisbee around the back yard, is spontaneous, voluntary, largely without rules, and engaged in purely for its own sake. Progressing from play to sport, events are increasingly planned, formal rules emerge, and the activity becomes more relevant to the rest of the players' lives. External rewards—money, prestige, college scholarships—become a more and more important part of the athlete's reasons for participating.

What happens when sport becomes so serious that playfulness and spontaneity fade away and participation becomes, for all practical purposes, work, as in the NFL or NBA? Sociologists use the terms "spectacle" or "corporate sport" for athletics at this level, implying that these activities have become corrupted or lost some of the qualities we find most appealing about "true" sport (Hoch, 1982).

Like the media, sport is a form of popular culture that has grown increasingly significant in recent decades. Sport is often thought of as somehow less serious or important than longer established institutions like government or health care, but its pervasiveness suggests that it merits close consideration.

About 70 percent of the U.S. public is involved in sports, either as participants, as spectators, or in both roles. In 1997, major league baseball attracted 65 million fans, NCAA men's basketball drew 28 million, 37 million people attended big-time college football games, and pro basketball drew 22 million spectators (U.S. Bureau of the Census, 1999: Table 441). In the same year, roughly 60 million people swam, 26 million played golf, and 11 million played tennis. (U.S. Bureau of the Census, 1999: Table 443). Sports generate more than $60 billion in total revenue each year in the

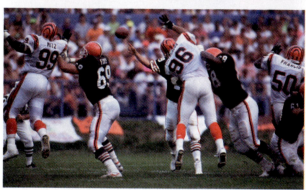

United States. The sports section is by far the most widely read part of the daily newspaper, and about 15 percent of all major network television programming is devoted to athletics (Eitzen & Sage, 1997).

Furthermore, sport is a kind of microcosm of larger society, a lens through which we can gain perspective on other aspects of social life. For example, the struggles that minorities and women fought in recent decades for full acceptance in the larger society were paralleled by similar conflicts in sport. In this regard, Jackie Robinson and Billie Jean King played equivalent roles to those of Martin Luther King and Betty Friedan.

Similarly, sport is intimately connected with other institutions. Governments use the Olympics to advance national prestige; religions use organizations like the Fellowship of Christian Athletes to build membership; events like the Super Bowl are big business in every meaning of the word; and universities rely on sports to bring them publicity and alumni donations.

If you doubt the cultural significance of sport, consider how often you hear the following sports terms used in nonathletic contexts: ground rules, low

blow, foul play, jump the gun, the bush leagues, game plan, cheap shot, touch bases, go to bat, or out of bounds.

Since sport is closely integrated with so many aspects of life in modern society, it is fertile soil for sociology. In the following sections, we will look at the role sport plays in three areas of social life: social stratification, religion, and the media.

Sport and Social Stratification

Sociologists have studied various issues concerning sport and social stratification, but two seem especially interesting. First, what is the connection between class and choice of sport? Second, does participating in sports promote upward social mobility?

Most studies show that wealthy men and women are more oriented toward sports participation and that the lower classes are more inclined to be spectators. As participants, the higher classes favor individual sports whereas the lower classes prefer team games (Loy, 1972). More specifically, the wealthy are especially likely to enjoy golf, tennis, yachting, skiing,

Modern commercial sports clearly reflect the reality of social stratification. Corporations and wealthy individuals relax in air-conditioned luxury suites, such as this one at the Toronto Skydome, while less affluent fans swelter in General Admission.

and polo. These sports require expensive equipment and extensive instruction, and they are often played at country clubs that the children of the elite frequent. Thorstein Veblen (1934) saw elite sports participation of this sort as a classic example of **conspicuous consumption,** activity undertaken to validate the social status of the upper class by demonstrating that they could afford to throw money away on nonessentials.

Less affluent people tend to go bowling or play basketball, baseball, and volleyball, none of which is expensive to learn or play. People toward the bottom of the class ladder often favor physically aggressive sports like wrestling, boxing, and demolition derbies. Perhaps this is because their life experiences leave them more frustrated and thus more in need of a safety valve to release their tensions (Zelman, 1976).

As for the major spectator sports, people from all classes enjoy football, basketball, baseball, and hockey, but note that sports arenas are sharply segregated on the basis of class. The corporate rich relax in "sky boxes" while the middle classes occupy the bulk of the seats. Most members of the working class can no longer afford to attend major league sports unless they come on bargain night or sit in general admission. And as for the poor, well, they can always watch the game on TV.

Does sports participation aid social mobility? Most studies show that both male and female high

Sports fans frequently engage in rituals such as cheering and painting their faces in team colors in hopes of spurring their team on to victory. Sociologists note that such actions have a religious quality to them.

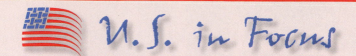

Little League and Moral Socialization

Nowhere is the socialization function of sport more evident than in Little League baseball, which was created specifically to provide young boys (and, since the early 1970s, young girls as well) with values and principles that would guide them throughout life. Coaches view "building character" as equally or even more important than teaching athletic skills. But what values does Little League really teach? Gary Fine's study, *With the Boys* (1987), identified four main themes: personal effort, sportsmanship, teamwork, and winning and losing.

Personal effort. The saying, "It's not whether you win or lose that counts, but how you play the game," may be a cliche, but adults want children to internalize this principle. Coaches take Little League seriously. They want their players to do the same, but assume the youngsters will "horse around" if given the chance. Horsing around has its place, coaches tell their teams, but once a practice or game begins they expect the players to "hustle."

Coaches usually attribute wins and losses to effort. Criticizing the team or an individual for lack of hustle has the positive effect of suggesting that they can win next time. On the other hand, players tend to credit effort for wins, but to blame losses on external factors such as a bad call by the umpire, cheating by the other team, or lack of hustle by a teammate. A good coach treats such scapegoating as poor sportsmanship.

Sportsmanship. Sportsmanship has been defined as the Golden Rule ("Do unto others . . .") applied to athletics. Little League coaches tend to be more specific. One interpreted sportsmanship as not griping when you lose, not complaining when the umpire makes a bad call against you, and not riding the other team. In practice, the definition of good versus bad sportsmanship is often more subtle. For example, "rattling" another team is okay but harassing them is not. Players who are good sports—who control anger, frustration, and disappointment—are seen as mature; players who exhibit bad sportsmanship are viewed as needing minor correction more than stern discipline.

Teamwork. Little League is often the first time that children participate in a collective effort outside their family, and one that adults take very seriously. Playing baseball depends on collaboration, and coaches consider teamwork as one of the most important lessons they can instill. Whereas effort is a personal responsibility, teamwork is a social one. In many cases, however, the presence or absence of teamwork is

---

school athletes have somewhat better grade averages than nonathletes. In part this is because they must keep their marks up in order to stay eligible. But they also tend to have higher educational aspirations and ultimately to do a little better in life (Otto & Alwin, 1977; Sabo et al., 1993). Perhaps sports really do build character. It may also be that the friendships that result from being on a team provide networking opportunities. The visibility of star athletes may also help them in their search for good jobs.

Many college athletes, especially in the major sports, are first-generation college students. This factor alone explains why they often do better than their parents. However, these athletes are generally less likely to graduate than minor-sport competitors or nonathletes, partly because they tend as a group to be less well prepared academically and also because the rigors of big-time sports may leave them with little time or energy to apply themselves properly to their studies.

A handful of the best college athletes make it into the professional ranks, but the vast majority do not. Even those who do become pros usually have short careers—averaging less than five years—and only a few superstars earn astronomical salaries. Some pro athletes, especially in football and boxing, suffer serious physical damage by the time they retire, and many lack the nonathletic skills that would allow them to make a good living after they leave sports. Finally, as we will discuss shortly, opportunities for African Americans, especially in coaching and administrative roles, remain relatively limited, and there are still very few lucrative positions in professional sports open to women.

Sport and Religion

Sport and religion have long been associated. Many traditional cultures viewed athletic rituals as a way to honor the gods. For example, the original Olympic games were dedicated to Zeus. In fact, when the Olympics were suppressed late in the fourth century, it was because they were seen by the church as a pagan survival (Brasch, 1970). Similarly, before the industrial era, Christians and especially Calvinist Protestants often considered sport a sinful celebration of the body and a waste of time that could better be spent working or in church (Brailsford, 1991).

a subjective evaluation, based more on the outcome than on behavior during the game. Winning teams are praised for exhibiting teamwork; losing teams are criticized for not working together.

Winning and losing. A major goal of Little League is to teach youths how to deal with victory and defeat. In the midst of an important game, other lessons may take a back seat to the all-important goal of winning. How players behave after a win or loss is the true test. In post-game reviews coaches may touch on ways the team can improve, but their main goal is to establish a consensus on what the outcome meant. The reasons why one team wins and the other loses are rarely clear-cut. Especially at this young age, winning depends in large part on luck. A coach or parent may tell a disheartened player that an embarrassing strike out or a dropped ball was just bad luck. But to say that the entire game was a fluke would be demoralizing. If winning or losing is a matter of luck, why bother trying?

When a team loses, the coaches focus on players' state of mind. If a coach senses that the team is "down" and needs moral support, he or she may compliment individuals for playing well even though they lost; if the coach feels the players are overconfident or under-motivated, they may be lectured for doing a sloppy job. Players who accept the coach's explanations are praised for being grown-up, while those who resist his or her interpretations are branded as self-centered, rebellious, or poor sports.

This description of socialization via Little League suggests that, from a symbolic interactionist perspective, many adults see sports as a moral enterprise, in which wins and losses reflect the character of participants. This view reflects the "just world" hypothesis: the belief that winners must be doing something right and, conversely, losers must be doing something wrong. In reality, identifying the "true" cause of success or failure in any endeavor is problematic. But human beings need to see events as meaningful. Americans, in

particular, like to believe that they control their own destiny and feel that it's important for young people to develop a sense of being in control. A major part of socialization entails interacting with children in ways that lead them to internalize culturally constructed meanings. In this way, Little League prepares young people for the "major leagues" of adult social life.

1. Have the values Little League baseball promotes been modified to reflect the increasing numbers of young women who are participating in sports or do they remain implicitly androcentric, that is, more oriented toward boys than girls?

2. If you have participated in organized youth sports, do you feel that they effectively promote the values discussed in this box? Are there additional values, perhaps less positive ones, that they also teach?

Source: Excerpted from *With the Boys* by Gary Fine. Copyright © 1987 by Gary Fine. Reprinted by permission of the University of Chicago Press.

This view began to change in the United States during the nineteenth century when a movement called *muscular Christianity* arose, in part as a result of concerns among the upper and middle classes about the enormous numbers of immigrants flooding into the larger cities (Guttmann, 1988). This movement sponsored softball and bowling leagues and established the YMCA as a way to keep workers busy, distract them from crime and radical politics, and remove boys from the "feminine" influences of the home. All of this was done in the name of vigorous physical activity combined with robust spirituality.

The tradition of using sports as a way to build religious commitment continues today in the activities of evangelistic groups. For example, the Fellowship of Christian Athletes, founded in 1954, is active in thousands of high schools and colleges. Athletes in Action, a similar organization, sends teams of young Christians out to play exhibition games and testify at halftime to their faith (Mathiesen, 1990). Religiously affiliated universities—most notably Notre Dame and Brigham Young—have also found that intercollegiate

athletics programs can build loyalty to both their institutions and their faiths.

Just as religions sometimes use sports for their own purposes, athletes and teams often use religious rituals in hope of enhancing their performance. At church-affiliated institutions, formal prayers often precede games; in more secular settings, many athletes pray individually. We have all seen basketball players make the sign of the cross before attempting a free throw.

At another level, sports often serve as a kind of secular religion for their followers, providing many of the functions of religion, even though they do not include a transcendent element (Prebish, 1993) (see Chapter 17). The ability of sport to perform this role stems from its social integration function. In a religiously heterogeneous society, loyalty to a sports team may be one of the few factors that gives people a sense of commonality and shared fate.

Along the same lines, sport provides many rituals—pep rallies, awards ceremonies, the games themselves—that bring people together in large numbers to celebrate their shared loyalties. Team logos and colors take on a kind of sacred quality, affirming each fan's loyalty to the team. The most dedicated supporters find that sport, like any other religion, makes their lives more meaningful.

Sport provides its "believers" with sacred days (Super Bowl Sunday), holy writings (statistics books), and shrines (halls of fame). Fans engage in sacred ritual cheers and sometimes make pilgrimages to watch their teams play away from home. Athletes are expected to purify themselves for the contest, if no longer by abstaining from sex, as once was common, at least by keeping regular hours and avoiding drugs and gambling. Players who violate such rules risk being cast out of their sport.

Sport and the Media

In commercialized popular culture, sport and the media have a symbiotic relationship, each contributing directly to the growth of the other. Sports coverage attracts newspaper and magazine readers and television viewers, while media publicity promotes the popularity of sports (Wenner, 1989; Lever & Wheeler, 1993).

Newspapers began regular coverage of sports in the 1890s; today sports take up about half of the space devoted to all hard news combined. Moreover, the sports section of the paper attracts about five times as many readers as any other feature (Stevens, 1987). The newsstands are filled with sports magazines; *Sports Illustrated*, with a weekly circulation of 3 million, enjoys the nation's fifth-largest readership.

Radio airs over half a million hours of sports coverage each year (Eitzen & Sage, 1997: 224). But television is the real thousand-pound gorilla in the world of sports media. The major networks broadcast about 2,000 hours of sports programming annually. Even this figure is dwarfed by the 24-hour-per-day coverage of the several all-sports cable networks, most prominently ESPN, which was founded in 1980.

Although sport and the media are symbiotic, sports need the media more then the media need sports. The revenue that the media have made available to sport has radically transformed big-time athletics. The broadcast rights for the 2000 Winter Olympics cost $705 million. In 1995, each NFL team received over $40 million from television, about 65 percent of all team revenues. The per-team figures for major league baseball and NBA basketball in that year were $12 million and $23 million, respectively. A single 30-second commercial during the Super Bowl—which will reach about 125 million viewers—costs well over a million dollars (Eitzen & Sage, 1997).

How have these economic realities changed sports? In almost every way imaginable (Klatell &

Marcus, 1988; Zimbalist, 1992). Consider the following examples:

- The flow of media dollars has played a crucial role, along with the establishment of free agency, in increasing player salaries. In 1970, the average annual wage in the NFL was $23,000; in the NBA it was $40,000; and in major league baseball, $29,300. In 1997 the equivalent figures, not adjusted for inflation, were $800,000, $2.2 million, and $1.37 million (Coakley, 1998).

- The number of franchises has expanded. Baseball, for example, has grown from sixteen teams to thirty. More teams mean more televised games and more money. For the same reason, the number of teams eligible for post-season play has increased in all major sports.

- Television has largely killed off minor league sports, especially baseball. Why watch second-rate players when you can turn on the TV and see Mark McGwire, Alex Rodriguez, and Randy Johnson? In turn, college sports have become de facto minor leagues, which has accelerated the commercialization of college game.

- Numerous rule changes have been made, not because they necessarily enhance the game, but because they meet the needs of television. Many of these changes—such as the shot clock and the three-point shot in basketball—make games more exciting, especially to less-knowledgeable fans. Sudden-death tie breakers in football and tennis keep games predictable in length and thus allow them to fit better into broadcast schedules. In the NFL, official time outs at the end of each quarter and the two-minute warning exist solely to allow more time for commercials.

- Athletes have become far more flamboyant, diminishing, in some people's eyes, the dignity of sports. While the pros have always attracted characters—Ty Cobb, Babe Ruth, and Wilt Chamberlain certainly had their personality quirks—before television their excesses were generally covered up by the print media. Today the unblinking eye of the TV camera focuses on bizarre sports personalities like Dennis Rodman, Mike Tyson, and Don King.

≣ LIFE CONNECTIONS: The Dark Side of Sport

Unquestionably, the media and sport pervade our lives. But despite the positive functions—and just plain good times—they provide, they also have a dark side, sometimes promoting violence, racism, and sexism. The relationship between the media and violence was discussed in Chapter 5; the connection between the media and sexism is covered in depth in Chapters 5 and 13; and the Media and Technology box (page 530) on "TV's Forgotten Minority: Hispanic Americans" concerns the treatment of minorities in the media. Accordingly, this section will focus on deviance, violence, racism, and sexism in sport.

Deviance and Aggression in Sport

Earlier in this century, some social scientists thought that watching sports served as a catharsis, a release of emotional energy, especially violent and aggressive urges. The noted animal behaviorist Konrad Lorenz (1963) recommended expanding international athletic competition as an alternative to warfare. However, while some forms of vigorous exercise can reduce aggressiveness in some instances among participants, there is no evidence that watching violent sports has a comparable effect on spectators. In fact, androcentric but instructive research shows that men watching football games tend to become more aggressive, which is not true of male spectators of nonviolent sports like gymnastics (Berkowitz, 1993).

Most sociologists today believe that violence is learned, not innate, and that this learning usually occurs when an individual observes other people being rewarded for their aggressive behavior. This is true for both watching and playing sports. Sport is the only institution other than the military that routinely condones violence. Young athletes who have internalized the Lombardi ethic are often pressured to use violence in pursuit of victory, whether in the form of late hits in football, high-sticking in hockey, or deliberate fouls in basketball.

Not surprisingly, the result is frequently injury. Boxing is the most extreme case: Some 500 fighters died between 1950 and 1995 from ring-related problems. About one out of five NFL players misses at least one game each year due to injury; two-thirds of retired pro football players believe the game shortened their life expectancies (Huizenga, 1994). An average of eight high school football players die annually. And most observers believe that the problem is getting worse, in part because of the constant emphasis on violence in the media.

Worse, players sometimes take their aggressiveness with them off the field. Recent studies document that male college athletes are considerably more likely than nonathletes to be involved in sexual assault; one researcher in Maryland found athletes were 5.5 times more likely than other students to admit having committed date rape (Melnick, 1992; Crosset et al., 1995).

Some sociologists note that sports are an important means of male gender-role socialization. The roles that male athletes learn generally emphasize toughness, denial of empathy, and dominance. This construction of masculinity is clearly compatible with sexual assault (Nelson, 1994).

Deviance among athletes is by no means limited to violence. Over the past two decades we have become increasingly aware of the widespread use of illegal, performance-enhancing drugs in sports (Donohoe & Johnson, 1986). Such practices are not new; through history athletes have used everything from caffeine to nitroglycerine to strychnine to amphetamines to improve their performance. But the advent of anabolic steroids, extensive media coverage of their use, and today's extremely strong antidrug attitudes make the problem more serious in many people's minds.

There is no accurate way to estimate how many athletes abuse steroids. Research suggests that between 6 and 10 percent of male high school students take them, as do 29 percent of college football players, 16 percent of female track and field athletes, and 75 percent of NFL players (Lucas, 1994). As usage rises—and is more widely publicized—pressure to take performance-enhancing drugs escalates. The result, despite increased drug testing, may well be a continuing growth in the use of steroids and in the incidence of their harmful side effects (Voy, 1991).

Racism in Sport

Before World War II, American sports were almost completely segregated, with the exception of boxing, where Jack Johnson and Joe Louis had been heavyweight champions. But when the Brooklyn Dodgers brought Jackie Robinson up to the majors in April, 1947, the barriers to black participation began to crumble (Tygiel, 1983). By 1957, 12 percent of all major league baseball players were African Americans, the same percentage that blacks made up at that time (and now) in the society as a whole. The NBA reached that milestone one year later and the NFL did so in 1960. Over the next fifteen years, almost all formal resistance to black participation at both the amateur and the professional levels ended: Today African Americans make up 77 percent of the NBA, 65 percent of the NFL, and 18 percent of major league baseball players. Hispanic-American participation remains limited, although the representation of Latin Americans in professional baseball has increased sharply in recent years.

These data reflect real progress. Sports were desegregated earlier than other sectors of U.S. life for several reasons (Edwards, 1973). The competitive nature of sport meant that there would be strong support for nondiscrimination if minorities could help their teams win. Crucially, performance in sports can be precisely and objectively measured, so bias is less of a factor than is the case in more subjective situations. Furthermore, success on the field does not require that athletes be friends. And, finally, the success of a minority athlete is not likely to lead to his or her promotion over whites, a significant way in which sport differs from most other careers.

Many people cite the success of minorities in sports as evidence that U.S. society is no longer discriminatory, but the truth is more complex. For one thing, **stacking** continues in college and professional football and baseball. In this practice, minorities are disproportionately assigned to "noncentral" positions that are low in outcome control and leadership responsibility (Loy & McElvogue, 1970).

For example, in 1994, just 7 percent of NFL quarterbacks were African Americans compared with 92 percent of the running backs; in baseball, 3 percent of the catchers, 7 percent of the pitchers, but 51 percent of the outfielders were black (Lapchick & Benedict, 1994). On the positive side, stacking is no longer apparent in basketball and real progress has been made in selected sports—eight African American quarterbacks were starting in the NFL at one point in the 2000 season. Interestingly, stacking is by no means an exclusively American phenomenon: cross-cultural research shows that English-speaking Canadian hockey players, African and West Indian soccer players in Britain, and aborigines in Australian rugby are all underrepresented in central positions in their sports (Maguire, 1988; Lavoie, 1989; Hallinan, 1991).

Noncentral sports positions are believed to require speed, aggressiveness, and good "instincts," whereas central roles call for intelligence and coolness under pressure (Williams & Youssef, 1975). Stacking apparently occurs because white coaches and owners do not believe that minorities have the mental abilities necessary for central positions. This prejudiced attitude thus relegates minorities to physically demanding positions that generally result in shorter careers.

Stacking also contributes to the underrepresentation of African Americans and other minorities in coaching and administrative positions because most successful candidates for these jobs played central positions when they were athletes. In 1994 there were only four African American head coaches in major league baseball and two in the NFL. In 1995, just 6 percent of big-time college football coaches—but 51 percent of the players—were African Americans. A 1990 survey of the 63 top NCAA Division I sports programs found that only 12.5 percent of 3,083 key administrative jobs were held by minorities—and that only two of the programs were headed by minorities (Eitzen & Sage, 1997: 274). Finally, despite obvious but occasional exceptions like Michael Jordan and Tiger Woods, most minority athletes have only limited opportunities to earn money through endorsements.

Research also shows that marginal white players are more likely to be successful in college and professional sports than marginal minorities. A generation ago, Aaron Rosenblatt (1967) found that African Americans had a mean major league batting average 21.2 points higher than whites. More recent studies also find that mediocrity is more acceptable for whites than for African Americans (Kooistra et al., 1993).

Because of these hard realities, many prominent black Americans have urged African American youth to think carefully before setting their sights on a career in professional sports (Asch, 1977). Despite the presence of many successful minority athletes as role models, the hard fact is that there simply are not very many opportunities at the top. There are twelve times as many African American lawyers and doctors as there are black major league athletes (Coakley, 1998).

Source: Adam@home © 2000 by Universal Press Syndicate. Reprinted with permission.

As traditional gender roles have weakened, female athletes have started participating in sports such as boxing from which they were historically excluded.

Sexism in Sport

Like racial and ethnic minorities, women have also made impressive gains in sport in recent decades. Nevertheless, they too often experience less than fully equal treatment (Boutilier & San Giovanni, 1993; Hargreaves, 1994).

Women rarely participated in organized sports in the United States until the later nineteenth century. At this time, substantial numbers became involved in croquet, roller skating, golf, bowling, and bicycling (Mangan & Park, 1987). Also during these years, many women's colleges began programs in swimming, basketball, and field hockey. Unfortunately, most of these pioneering efforts had ended by the 1920s, done in by college administrators and female physical education teachers who thought athletic competition was incompatible with traditional gender-role expectations. These opponents of female participation argued, incorrectly, that vigorous athletic activity led to problems in childbearing, damaged the uterus and breasts, developed unsightly muscles, and caused nervous breakdowns (Sargent, 1912).

Between the 1920s and the early 1970s, opportunities for women in athletics, especially at the high school and college levels, were very limited. But all this began to change when the Educational Amendments Act of 1972 was passed over the strong opposition of the NCAA. Title IX of the act mandates that

no person in the United States shall, on the basis of sex, be excluded from participation in, be denied the benefits of, or be subjected to discrimi-

nation under any education program or activity receiving federal financial assistance.

Title IX requires that schools provide substantially equal athletic opportunities to both genders. While some of the details of what the Act mandates are still being clarified in the courts, Title IX has dramatically altered women's sports. In 1971, 3,667,000 high school boys participated in organized sports programs compared with just 294,000 girls. Today the figures are 3,536,000 boys and 2,240,000 girls; 39 percent of high school athletes are female (Eitzen & Sage, 1997: 292).

Changes also occurred at the college level. Before Title IX, about 15 percent of college athletes were female, and female sports in coeducational colleges rarely received more than 2 or 3 percent of the total athletic budget. By the mid-1990s, women made up a third of varsity athletes, and they received 36 percent of all scholarship aid (Tarkan, 1995). The continuing disparity results primarily from the emphasis large schools place on the revenue-producing sports of football and men's basketball.

As female sports participation increased, stereotypes about female athletes, which historically discouraged many women from sports, began to fade. Opponents of gender equality have traditionally maintained that athletics and femininity are incompatible, implying that women who excel at sports run the risk of being labeled lesbians. These stereotypes were applied to all female athletes, but especially to those who played traditionally male sports like baseball and basketball. Women who swam, played tennis

Women's Basketball: Before and After Title IX

Between the 1920s and the 1970s, competitive team sport in the United States was essentially an all-male domain. Women were not totally banned, but rather were limited to those sports considered "appropriate" for them. At private clubs, middle- and upper-class women engaged in such "feminine" recreational activities as tennis and golf, croquet and archery, swimming, horseback riding, and ice skating. In the 1920s, women's fencing, track and field, and a few gymnastic events were added to the Olympics. Individual athletes such as Sonja Henie (ice skating), Helen Wills (tennis), Gertrude Ederle (swimming), and Babe Didrikson Zaharias (golf) became national heroines.

However, women's athletics were not only separate from men's sports in high schools and colleges, they were also clearly inferior to them. While boys prepared for varsity competition, with the ultimate goal of winning championships for their school, girls were confined to the calisthenics and to girls' games—basketball, volleyball, field hockey, track and field—played by girls' rules.

The history of women's basketball nicely illustrates the changing gender gap in sports. After the sport was invented in 1891, it quickly became popular among college women, who loved the freedom of movement and vigorous competition. Ironically, however, female physical educators led the drive to portray basketball as a threat to women. Serious competition, they argued, could foster such unfeminine qualities as roughness, determination, tenacity, and goal orientation, qualities that would make young women unattractive to the opposite sex. These women feared that sports might interfere with girls' future happiness as homemakers. Senda Berenson, director of physical education at Smith College, argued that

women must be protected from the "evils" of male sports (Rader, 1990).

In the 1890s Berenson developed a modified set of rules to make women's basketball "less stressful." There were six rather than five players on a side. The court was divided into three backcourt and three frontcourt sectors. Players were prohibited from moving out of their sector, dribbling, snatching the ball from an opponent's hands, or even talking during play. These rules resulted in a "stand-and-pass" game as boring to players as to spectators. Girls continued to play basketball by "boys' rules" at many high schools and colleges well into the 1920s. But opposition to competitive team sports for women was growing.

In 1923, the Women's Division of the National Amateur Athletic Foundation (NAAF) adopted a platform against varsity competition. Representing their school, college, or university in public athletic competitions was seen as a male prerogative. The only appropriate role for women at coed schools was a supportive one, on the cheerleading squad. Women athletes, the NAAF declared, must be "protected from exploitation for the enjoyment of spectators, the athletic reputation, or the commercial advantage of any school or organization. . . ." Women's colleges were viewed as extensions of the family where young women received additional training in the social graces. Intercollegiate games would require students to leave their protective campuses and perform before audiences of both sexes, risking their modesty and reputations. In keeping with the feminine role, women's athletics should be noncompetitive and inclusive: "a sport for every girl, and every girl in a game" (Rader, 1990, p. 232).

The NAAF endorsed four alternatives to interscholastic and intercollegiate competition. One was intramural

competition among students at the same school or college (with no outside spectators). In "telegraphic meets," colleges didn't play face-to-face but rather, the results of intramural competitions were telegraphed to "competing" schools. On "play days," women from several schools got together but competition was minimized by the random assignment of girls from different schools to one-day-only teams. The primary emphasis was on social interaction, not competition. On "sports days," teams from different schools or colleges competed, but the focus was on recreation. Which teams won or lost was not even reported, and schools whose teams played too aggressively or too well risked not being invited back. In general, girls' games offered limited opportunities for participants to develop their athletic potential to the fullest and generated little enthusiasm among female students.

In the 1970s, as part of a rising tide of feminism, players and coaches across the country began rebelling against such restrictions. In basketball, women's high school and college teams threw out "girls' rules" and switched to a five-player, full-court game. Title IX gave this grassroots movement legal backing. But change has been slow and uneven. In the 1980s, women tennis and track stars began to attract national attention. But not until the mid- to late-1990s were women's team sports granted full professional status, with the creation of the Women's National Basketball Association (WNBA).

1. What are the messages about the meaning of being female that were communicated by girls' rules basketball?
2. Are there continuing inequalities between men's and women's sports? If so, why have they persisted?

Source: Rader, 1990.

INTERNET CONNECTIONS

Take a look at "Women in Sports: A Level Playing Field": http://www.advancingwomen.com/womsports.html. The contents will provide you with a detailed history of women's quest for equality in sports, including a graphic look at Title IX legislation and its impact on the issues involved. After you have examined this Web site, answer the following questions: Whether you are male or female, do you think the changes that have taken place in women's sports over the past several decades have made a difference in terms of women's overall quest for social equality? Why or why not? What are your reactions to women's participating in "traditionally male" athletic competitions, such as tackle football, boxing, and collegiate-style wrestling?

or golf, or figure-skated faced considerably less hostility (Harris, 1980).

Earlier research suggested that these stereotypes created significant gender-role problems for many female athletes, but more recent studies demonstrate that the problem is less serious today (Blinde & Taub, 1993). Still, many female athletes wear makeup and jewelry during games and tie their long hair back with pink ribbons, which symbolic interactionists would interpret as efforts to reaffirm their feminine identity.

Female participation in non-school-based sports has also increased greatly in the past twenty-five years. Today, over a million girls are playing in youth soccer leagues. For years, Little League baseball firmly resisted gender integration, but some 200,000 girls now play on Little League teams (Eitzen & Sage, 1997).

It would seem logical that this sharp increase in female participation in competitive sports would have led to equal opportunities for women as coaches and administrators. But this isn't necessarily the case. In the early days of Title IX, women's intercollegiate athletics were managed by an essentially all-women's organization called the Association for Intercollegiate Athletics for Women (AIAW). However, the NCAA moved into women's sports in 1981, and within a year the AIAW had collapsed. Since then, women's sports have moved much closer to the highly competitive male model. More significantly, the percentage of female coaches has declined.

In the early 1970s, virtually all collegiate women's teams were coached by women; by 1990, the figure had fallen to just 48 percent. It is now beginning to edge slowly upward, but female coaches still typically earn only about half the salaries received by their male counterparts. Similarly, in 1972 over 90 percent of women's sports programs were administered by women; in 1994 only 21 percent still were (Acosta & Carpenter, 1994). Women currently make up just 37 percent of the delegates to the governing body of the NCAA.

Overall, it is clear that attitudes and norms about race and gender constantly intrude into sport. And this intrusion is insidious. It actually works against what sport is designed to do: to allow any athlete to achieve to the height of his or her ability. Continued racism and sexism in sports demonstrates that the playing field is not yet fully level.

SOCIETY CONNECTIONS: Censorship and the Electronic Media

Despite First Amendment guarantees of freedom of speech, the United States has a long tradition of censoring unpopular ideas and graphic content in the mass media (Garry, 1993). While the courts have generally been reluctant, especially in recent decades, to significantly restrict the written word, freedom of speech has been far more problematic in the movies and other popular arts (Sanders, 1994). In 1915, the Supreme Court ruled that film was a business, not an art form, and accordingly was not constitutionally protected speech. This judgment was not reversed until 1952 (Heins, 1993).

Advocates of censorship generally focus on graphic sexual content and, in recent years, on violence. They use the hypodermic model of media influence, arguing that media sexuality and violence directly encourage such behavior and desensitize children to antisocial acts (Callahan & Appleyard, 1997). Their opponents do not necessarily deny such effects, but they believe that restricting freedom of speech poses a more serious problem (Maines, 1993; Zuckerman, 1995).

In practice, the government has rarely directly acted as a censor, because the motion picture, television, and popular music industries voluntarily developed their own rating systems. In 1922, an organization of Hollywood producers and directors first published a code of standards for what could and could not be shown on screen (Plagenz, 1997). But in the later 1950s, the industry began to relax its puritanical standards, and films became markedly more explicit. This immediately led to renewed demands for outright censorship. Hollywood responded in

1968 by establishing the G-PG-R-X rating system. Then, in 1984, the PG-13 rating was introduced after criticism of violent content in *Indiana Jones and the Temple of Doom*. In 1990 the NC-17 designation was developed to allow audiences to differentiate between serious films with strong erotic or violent content and outright pornography (Heins, 1993).

Similar voluntary rating systems have been introduced in both popular music and television. In 1985, the music industry started applying a "parental advisory" sticker to potentially offensive releases, mostly rap and heavy metal, and in the mid-1990s, television introduced a detailed rating system (Minnow & LeMay, 1995).

Voluntarily imposed ratings have been very popular with parents and appear to be firmly established. Critics, however, point out that these schemes amount to a kind of pre-censorship because most theaters will not book NC-17 films, some music stores hesitate to stock albums with parental advisory labels, and networks resist airing TV programs with MA (mature) ratings. Under these circumstances, artists and writers—creators of popular culture—feel strong commercial pressure to avoid controversial sexual material and violence. Furthermore, content warnings may actually be counterproductive, attracting some adolescents precisely because they are "forbidden fruit."

The latest development in the censorship wars is the *v-chip*, a device that allows parents to block the reception of programs they don't want their children to watch. In 1996, Congress mandated that all new sets include v-chip technology. Some applaud this legislation as a victory in the battle against televised violence, but others see it as a high-tech variation of existing rating systems and another step toward restricting freedom of speech through pre-censorship (Zoglin, 1996; Thierer & Chapman, 1997).

SUMMARY

1. Popular culture, including sport and the media, is an important component of the emerging institution of recreation.

2. Early studies of the media often used the hypodermic model, which incorrectly suggests that the media's effects on their audiences are direct rather than mediated.

3. The media and sport serve various functions, including providing employment, entertainment, and information; encouraging sociability; contributing to socialization; reinforcing social control; and promoting individual and cultural identity.

4. Conflict theorists believe that the media perpetuate stereotypes and defend the interests of the powerful. They also argue that sport exploits and dehumanizes athletes, overemphasizes winning, stresses commercialism, and encourages excessive nationalism.

5. Symbolic interactionists and cultural studies theorists focus on how the meaning of popular culture is constructed. Applied to sport, this approach draws attention to issues such as the development of gender roles and the use of Native American team names and mascots.

6. Watching television is a passive experience. New technologies have the potential to make it more active, but they are not being widely used for this purpose.

7. Minorities have made considerable progress in Hollywood but women may be losing ground in film.

8. Popular music is youth oriented, often linked with movements for social change, and has become increasingly mainstream.

9. Sport is an intermediate category between play and spectacle. It is enormously popular in the United States and in many ways may be regarded as a microcosm of our society.

10. People in different classes participate in and watch different sports. Most research suggests that sport participation is loosely linked with upward social mobility.

11. Religions often use sport to attract support. Conversely, sport can be seen as a functional equivalent of religion with its own sacred rituals, heroes, and shrines.

12. The media and sport enjoy an unequal symbiotic relationship in which sport depends more on the media than the media do on sport.

13. Sport frequently promotes aggressive and violent behavior. It also encourages such forms of deviance as the use of illicit performance-enhancing drugs.

14. African Americans have made considerable progress in gaining equal treatment in sports, although subtle forms of discrimination such as stacking still exist.

15. Opportunities in sport for women have also expanded greatly as gender stereotypes have begun to fade. However, neither minorities nor women have greatly increased their involvement in coaching or sports administration.

16. Government rarely censors the media in the United States because the popular culture industries have developed voluntary rating systems.

KEY TERMS

cultural studies   519
conspicuous consumption   525
halo effect   518

hypodermic model   514
popular culture   513

sport   523
stacking   530

CRITICAL THINKING QUESTIONS

1. Sport and the media have been strongly criticized by conflict theorists, who claim that they negatively affect society. On the other hand, functionalists believe popular culture contributes positively to social life. Select a particular type of popular culture, indicate whether you feel its influence on society is basically positive or negative, and support your view.

2. On the whole, do you think that popular culture mainly reflects the culture in which it develops? Or does it significantly shape that culture? Defend your position.

3. Are current rating systems for films, TV programs, and popular music useful? Should government actively censor the media?

POPULATION, URBANIZATION, AND THE ENVIRONMENT

OUTLINE

How Many People Can the Earth Support?

As a species we are in the midst of a major biophysical transformation of the Earth. In 1700, only five cities had populations of one-half million people. By 1900, the number rose to 43, and 16 of these had populations of over 1 million. In 2000 there are 400 cities that exceed 1 million people, and many of these are megacities of 10 million people plus. The good news is that we will not grow forever. The bad news is that there are 6 billion of us already, a number the planet is already straining to support. World population may reach 9 billion during our lifetimes. So how many people can the earth support?

The answer may depend on whether you are an environmental pessimist or a technological optimist. The environmental pessimist points out that the planet's natural resources are being consumed faster than they are replenished or recycled, and future generations will be harmed. The technological optimist believes that new technology can produce an equivalent or superior option and future generations will be better off. Taxpayers seem to care only about how much it costs to protect the environment. Technology has managed to come up with solutions to many human dilemmas, but there is no guarantee that ingenuity will continue to work. What if technology is too little and too late? (Adapted from Cohen, 1993; Weiskel, 1997; McKibben, 1998)

Back to Saigon

Vietnam is a country in transition, but in transition to its own past, to subordination, and to poverty. Ho Chi Minh City, formerly called Saigon, is the center of the transformation. Ho Chi Minh City, for all the hope of economic development, is reverting to its former identity. While not yet as bad as in Bangkok or Jakarta, traffic is a serious problem. Bicycles still dominate, but on Sunday nights a sea of motorbikes converge on the city center. There is no attempt being made to build adequate mass transit and no infrastructure to deal with the increase of private transport. Drainage is poor; garbage collection is unreliable. A declining health system faces more health problems from the sicknesses of overcrowding, respiratory diseases, and lung and eye infections as dust, grit, carbon dioxide, and industrial pollution fill the air. In air-conditioned malls people can forget briefly that they are in Saigon and imagine they are anywhere in the world—anywhere but where they must stay and make their lives. (Adapted from Seabrook, 1996:146,163–64)

Women as the First Environment

The Akwesasne Mohawk reservation has been singled out as the most polluted among 63 Native communities in Canada's Great Lake Basin. On the U.S. side of the border, things aren't much better. A General Motors plant may be the biggest PCB dump site yet uncovered. PCB is the chemical known to cause brain, liver, and skin disorders in humans. The Mohawk reservation is downstream from the General Motors site, and PCBs have made it a hotbed of contamination. Katsi Cook, a Mohawk woman and midwife, promotes breastfeeding among her people. "Women are the first environment," she explains. "We accumulate toxic chemicals dumped into the waters that are stored in our bodyfat and excreted through breastmilk, our sacred link to our babies." Katsi and a group of women banded together to form the Akwesasne Mothers' Milk Project to understand the scope of the challenge they face and to seek scientific help. They are organizers and investigators—not merely research objects—of an ongoing breastmilk study. Their agenda is not only to document the connection between women and the environment, but to clean up the environment. (Adapted from LaDuke, 1998)

INTERNET ━━━◆━━━ CONNECTIONS

For some pictures of Ho Chi Minh City, visit site http://members.aol.com/alphavilla/saigonpano/index.html. How do the pictures correspond to the description of the city in your text?

One of the principal objectives of sociology is to document the importance of social connectedness on human social behavior. These vignettes demonstrate not simply connectedness, but the profound consequences of *inter*connectedness and the impossibility of separating humans from any of their environments—social, psychological, and physical. The unifying theme of this chapter is technology. It is both a cause and an effect of trends related to population, urbanization, and environmental change. Perhaps more than any other topics in this book, these represent the nature of our interdependent world. A U.S. taxpayer, an urban dweller in Vietnam, and a Canadian Mohawk woman have much in common. They (and we) are all sheltered in the same global environment.

POPULATION: DEMOGRAPHIC INTERDEPENDENCE

In order to approach the topic of population, we need to understand some basic elements of **demography,** the scientific study of population that focuses on its size, distribution, and composition, and how birth, death, and migration rates influence each element. Demography is one-dimensional in time, picturing all countries on a single continuum of change (Kirk, 1986). It provides snapshots of populations as they change from traditional to modern, from developing to developed, from rural to urban. Demography tells us *how* change occurs, but sociology examines the demographic portraits to explain *why*.

Studying Population: Demographic Tools

Studies of population depend on gathering accurate statistics. The statistics frequently used by demographers are gathered from a **census,** when a population is fully counted and measured according to key demographic characteristics. Birth and death rates are two of the most important statistics provided by census data. Along with census data, a number of organizations continually gather information on a range of variables that are demographically important. For example, the Centers for Disease Control in Atlanta and the World Health Organization in Geneva monitor infectious diseases, when and where they are occurring and who is infected. Demographers assess the overall impact of death rates from diseases on population growth or decline.

Determining the world's population today and tomorrow ultimately depends on knowing three facts: how many people are born (the birthrate), how long they live (the life expectancy rate), and when they will die (the mortality rate). When age is added to each of these variables, a more useful demographic portrait emerges. The most common measure of birth is the **crude birthrate,** the annual number of births per 1,000 population. Chapter 19 explained that the infant mortality rate (IMR)—how many infants die before they reach their first birthday—is a good measure of the overall health and well-being of a society. The focus in this chapter is on a specific birthrate measure, the **fertility rate**, which is actual reproductive behavior determined by annual number of live births per 1,000 to women of childbearing age. It differs from the *fecundity rate*, which is the biological potential for bearing children. The fecundity rate appears to be influenced by factors such as health technology, nutrition, and the environment. Demography demonstrates that what were previously believed to be biological limits of childbearing now have been expanded.

Another useful demographic indicator of population change is the **migration rate,** the movement of people in and out of various areas, specifically tracked according to political boundaries. It is very important when charting the global urbanization that has moved millions of people out of rural areas in the developing world. For the developed world, urbanization still occurs, but it is primarily the movement of people from central cities into suburbs. Migration can proceed only so far. Migration does not affect world population. Since we cannot migrate from the planet Earth, we now need to determine resources to meet the needs of the planet's population and at the same time ensure that the planet remains capable of supporting human life. Demography and sociology join forces in this quest.

Understanding Development: The Demographic Transition

Demographers report that for centuries the typical global population pattern showed high levels of both fertility and mortality, so overall population growth was minimal. Two centuries ago in Europe that pattern began to change. The extraordinary rate of growth of the human population in the last half century is traced directly to the influences of that period (around 1750). By now your sociological imagination will surely allow you to predict that the fundamental influence was the Industrial Revolution. England was the world's first country to experience the revolution and was socially, economically, politically, and demographically transformed in the process. Europe and then North America followed suit, so that by the early nineteenth century the Industrial Revolution was in full swing in the Western world. Remember that development is associated with progress, modernization, and an overall improvement in the life chances and lifestyle of all people impacted by it. Industrialization is its most important element.

One model that helps explain the effect of industrialization on population is called the **demographic transition,** a three-stage model that describes the change from high fertility and mortality rates to lower ones (Figure 21.1). In the first stage, the rate of population growth is slow because, although fertility rates are high, so are mortality rates—thus they offset one another. In the second stage, fertility rates remain high but mortality rates decrease, so there is a rapid growth in population. By the third stage population falls to replacement levels or even lower, because both fertility and mortality rates decrease. The demographic transition is linked to two other significant results worldwide—a lower IMR (Infant Mortality Rate) and an increase in life expectancy (Chapter 19).

These changes occur in the wake of industrialization, which introduces improvements in health, nutrition, and sanitation (Duden, 1992). Thus a decline in fertility can still increase population at an astounding rate.

A good example of the long-range result of the demographic transition is a **population pyramid,** a figure that provides the age-and-sex structure of a population at a given point in time (Figure 21.2). With the demographic transition, population growth becomes stabilized and the pyramid begins to resemble a vertical rectangle. Individuals not only survive infancy, the most precarious time of life, but people survive well into old age. As explained in Chapter 14, this pattern of global graying is associated with major social and economic consequences related to health policy, patterns of caregiving, changes in family structure and labor-force participation. Global graying also suggests that a combination of physical, social, and psychological life-enhancing qualities are now available for a sizable proportion of the world's population. The demographic transition predicts that the Stage 3 world will be healthier and life enhancing. That is the good news.

But the bad news is that fertility rates in many parts of the world have not declined fast enough to stem population growth, which may be threatening the very existence of our increasingly fragile planet. Some estimates suggest that if the population continues to grow at the current rate, it will double in forty years (Figures 21.3 and 21.4). The increase of close to

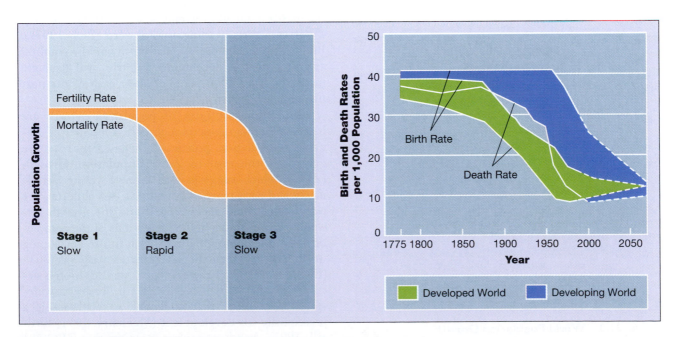

FIGURE 21.1   **Model of the Demographic Transition: Developed and Developing World**
Sources: Gray, 1993; *World Development Report,* 1982, 1997.

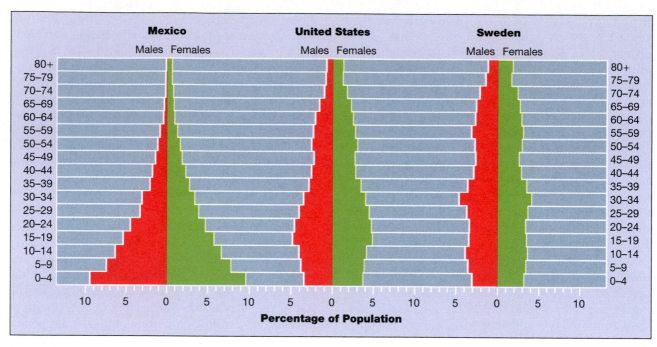

FIGURE 21.2 **Populations Pyramids of the United States, Mexico, and Sweden**
Source: United Nations, 1997.

1 billion people in the 1990s alone is the greatest increase in a single decade in history (Westoff, 1995; Weiskel, 1997).

Demographers project that the percentage of the global population living in the developing world will be close to 90 percent by 2030, with most of these people living in megacities in Asia and Latin America,

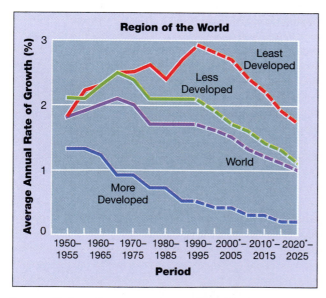

FIGURE 21.3 **World Population Growth**
*projected
Sources: Gray, 1993; United Nations, 1997;
http://www.who.imt/1998/clocke.jpg.

such as Mexico City, São Paulo, Calcutta, and Manila (Table 21.1). To understand the population surge of the developing world, it is important to distinguish between the *rate* of population growth and actual *numbers* of people. In many developing countries population growth rates have diminished after peaking in 1970 at about 2.5 percent. If the demographic transition continues in the developing world, the effect on the global population would be a growth rate of only 1 percent, then heading toward zero (Piel, 1997b). But as implied by the population pyramids, youthful age structures in developing countries will generate increases of a billion people during each of the next two decades (Merrick, 1994).

Projections of rates of population growth are based on demographic modeling in a number of scenarios. Population policies in many countries are guided by the goal of **Zero Population Growth (ZPG)**, which suggests that if most young people marry and each married couple has two children, the population would replace itself and the growth *rate* would remain static. Some projections of the completion of the demographic transition in the developing world see replacement level by as early as 2035 (El-Badry, 1991). If the demographic transition is accurate, birthrates will inevitably fall. There is widespread agreement that a decline in birthrate is a prerequisite for development (McHenry, 1991; Birdsall, 1994). Another scenario suggests that ZPG can be reached if the world's economy can expand fourfold and if its resources are shared so that the poorest

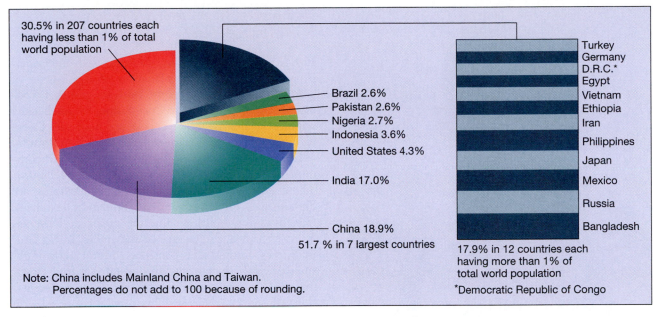

30.5% in 207 countries each having less than 1% of total world population

Brazil 2.6%
Pakistan 2.6%
Nigeria 2.7%
Indonesia 3.6%
United States 4.3%

India 17.0%

China 18.9%
51.7 % in 7 largest countries

Turkey
Germany
D.R.C.*
Egypt
Vietnam
Ethiopia
Iran
Philippines
Japan
Mexico
Russia
Bangladesh

17.9% in 12 countries each having more than 1% of total world population
*Democratic Republic of Congo

Note: China includes Mainland China and Taiwan.
Percentages do not add to 100 because of rounding.

FIGURE 21.4   Distribution of the World's Population in 2020 (Projected)
Source: Jacobs et al., 1996:4.

20 percent of the world's population are brought out of poverty (Piel, 1997b).

Another problem of determining population growth in the developing world is that the demographic transition itself is modeled on the Western version of the Industrial Revolution, which may not proceed the same way in the contemporary developing world. Rapid population growth in the developing world intensifies urban and environmental threats, and it can set back or even defeat development efforts. As the opening vignette stated, as a species we are confronting limited planetary resources. According to this argument, the world's resources and ecosystem simply cannot sustain continued growth (Calne, 1994).

Thomas Malthus is considered to be one of the first demographers. In 1798, he wrote *An Essay on the Principles of Population*, one of the most influential demographic studies of all time. Using England and Europe as a model, he argued that while populations increase faster than agriculture's ability to feed them, it is inevitable that a population will outstrip its ability to survive. When labor is sold for the purposes of production, the process includes three steps:

Table 21.1 The World's Largest* Cities, Selected Years					
1970		**1985**		**2000**	
1. New York	(16.29)	Tokyo/Yokohama	(18.82)	Mexico City	(26)
2. Tokyo/Yokohama	(14.91)	Mexico City	(17.30)	São Paulo	(25)
3. Shanghai	(11.41)	São Paulo	(15.88)	Tokyo/Yokohama	(24)
4. London	(10.59)	New York	(15.64)	New York	(20)
5. Mexico City	(9.12)	Shanghai	(11.96)	Calcutta	(16.52)
6. Buenos Aires	(8.55)	Calcutta	(10.95)	Bombay	(16.00)
7. Los Angeles	(8.43)	Buenos Aires	(10.88)	Shanghai	(14.30)
8. Paris	(8.34)	Rio de Janeiro	(10.37)	Seoul	(13.77)
9. Peking	(8.29)	London	(10.36)	Teheran	(13.58)
10. Osaka/Kobe	(7.61)	Seoul	(10.28)	Rio de Janeiro	(13.26)
Developed world cities	(6)		(3)		(2)
Developing world cities	(4)		(7)		(8)

*Population in millions
Source: Table adapted from "The Age of the City" by Sukae Raunoyama in *Humanising the City: Social Context of Urban Life at the Turn of the Millennium,* ed. by Anthony P. Cohen and Katsuyoshi Fuku. Copyright © 1993. Reprinted by permission of Edinburgh University Press.

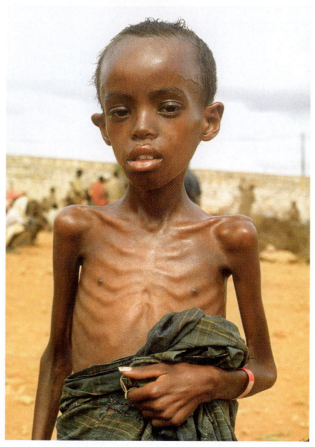

According to Malthus, starvation occurs when a population grows so fast that it outstrips the food supply. However, famine and starvation are more likely caused by factors such as war and the unequal distribution of available food.

1. A rise in population leads to a rise in food prices through increased demand.
2. A rise in food prices means the same amount of money buys less food. Real wages fall as more labor comes onto the market.
3. As real wages fall, mortality increases through starvation, malnutrition, and disease. (Gray, 1993)

In the battle of people against food, it is the people who lose.

According to Malthus, the laws of nature dominate human desires. He argued that one such law is the "passion between the sexes," which is so powerful and unalterable that population, unless checked, will double itself every twenty-five years. The checks he notes are famine and epidemics that will result in human misery and death. Thus Malthus's position appears to be compatible with the argument that the earth cannot sustain itself indefinitely with uncontrolled population growth. This chapter will shed light on Malthus's grim prediction from two centuries ago and how sociology can provide clues in determining if he was right.

Explaining Population Trends: Sociological Theory

In one very important way, Malthus and functionalism share a common explanation of the impact of population growth on society. Both suggest that if social disequilibrium is produced due to unchecked population growth, other checks are necessary to return the system to a state of balance or equilibrium. Malthus called them *positive checks*, and included common diseases, epidemics, wars, plague, and famine. These are unavoidable results, so death rates are higher than birthrates and a population stabilizes. "Positive" for Malthus did not mean desirable as much as it meant necessary or inevitable. In his later writings, Malthus did consider "moral restraints," such as delaying marriage and abstaining from "promiscuous intercourse, unnatural passions and violations of the marriage bed" as preventive checks on population. According to Malthus, the culprits responsible for economic crisis leading to social instability and the resulting dismal positive checks include dependent, lower-class people whose unbridled passions lead to uncontrollable population increase. As for preventive checks, Malthus was realistic about his own gender and believed that moral restraints among men were not particularly prevalent (Leisinger & Schmitt, 1994:47).

Émile Durkheim (1893/1964), a founder of functionalism, asserted that society was doomed unless it could adapt to more people competing for fewer resources. But unlike Malthus, Durkheim saw this situation as a way to stimulate development, especially in transition to industrialization. Population problems would create the incentive to make more productive use of land, which in turn would increase the division of labor. The division of labor becomes more and more specialized to accommodate arising social needs, particularly during periods of rapid social change. Farmers become specialists in certain crops. Ranchers specialize in beef cattle or dairy production. They sell their produce to other specialists who package, market, and sell to consumers. The complex division of labor is responsible for the interdependency that makes modern society not only orderly, but possible. In Durkheim's evolutionary view of human progress, the potential liabilities associated with population growth and density become social assets.

Contemporary functionalism is also concerned about the possible disruption of social order with rapid population growth, but it looks not to inevitable Malthusian natural laws or evolution to return the social system to equilibrium but rather to creative and versatile human social behavior. Adaptability is the functionalist key that opens the door to understanding how societies cope with population changes. Humans are capable of self-regulation, including altering marriage patterns and birth-control techniques. Even before modern contraceptives, breastfeeding—which can reduce the likelihood of frequent pregnancies—was a common technique. The functionalist perspective would support the view that poor people the world over are not helpless captives of sexual passion, incapable of regulating their own fertility, with or without the aid of contraceptives (Eberstadt, 1995: 28). And in the direst circumstances, humans have resorted to infanticide or gerontocide of the feeble, the infirm, or the nonproductive. In each case adaptability of human social behavior restores social equilibrium.

As we have seen throughout the text, there is ample disagreement between conflict theory and functionalism in explaining social trends. But when considering the Malthusian claim that population pressures inevitably cause food shortages, there is surprising consensus. Like Durkheim, Karl Marx (1867/1975) believed that population growth can aid social progress. Durkheim and Marx also shared a view that a minimum population density was necessary for the birth of the great cites that would be the homes for social progress (Holton, 1986). For industrial development and urbanization to be kindled, there must be an adequate population base for production.

At this point Marx and Durkheim diverge. For Marx, the offender behind human misery tied to lack of food is capitalism, which dictates how food and all other resources are distributed. Capitalism creates an incentive to maintain workers (proletariat) who will produce more than they will receive in consumption. Since capitalism depends on an unequal distribution of resources, the root of the problem is found there and not in population numbers. The smaller number of wealthy consume at the expense of the greater number of poor who are dependent on the jobs the wealthy provide. Neither population growth nor the shortage of food creates food problems; it is created by the shortage of jobs. Capitalism offers little or no incentive to expand jobs to meet all but the minimal needs of workers. Marx believed that population growth can serve economic development, but that it is impossible under capitalism (Leeds, 1994).

The Marxian perspective in contemporary conflict theory has been borne out in one very important way: Rich nations and richer people in all nations possess and consume most of the wealth. A persistent feature of the developing world is that, from colonial times through to the present, their economies have been oriented to export and not to meeting the needs of the larger population that produce the exported goods. Conflict theory focuses on the continued dependency of the poor nations on the rich nations, even generations after the end of colonialism.

The contemporary variant of this approach is *dependency theory* (see Chapter 9). It also provides an important framework for social change, which we will revisit in Chapter 24. Evidence suggests that much of the developing world has a population that is growing faster than the output of goods and services necessary to sustain genuine development (Duden, 1992; Webster, 1990). It is not so much population pressure but food maldistribution that causes hunger (Erb, 1990; *Hunger*, 1990). Unless the developing world can catch up in industrial and agricultural expansion, population increases can only make matters worse.

The "catch-up" process can be described as one of *cultural lag*. Technological development has favorably impacted death rates, but the process has happened so quickly that fertility rates have not been balanced in correspondence. Cultural lag can also explain why so many developing countries remain snared in the middle of the demographic transition.

Both the functionalist and conflict perspectives provide clues to understanding the relationship between population growth and economic development, especially in terms of adequacy of food supply. But the "people versus food" hypothesis that results in starvation is the most dire of all possible outcomes of population pressure. It should come as no surprise that numerous options exist prior to that fate, with migration the most likely one. For rural people, migration due to famine or war is far less frequent than their movement *away* from subsistence farming. With the substitution of cash crops and the trend toward agribusiness, the land can no longer support many rural families, a trend that was echoed earlier in the century in the United States. The resultant loss of jobs requires migration for many. For others, migration is voluntary, as they hear the call of the city with its promises of cash wages. Development through industrialization heralds jobs. It also heralds the growth of cities.

URBANIZATION

Cities are increasingly becoming the home to humanity with 90 percent of future global population growth expected to be clustered there (World Resources Institute, 1996). Crowded conditions, noise and air pollution, large pockets of poverty, and limited but expensive residential space are the byproducts of urban life throughout the world. These urban byproducts may be negative, but people continue to choose urban life over an imagined rural life offering space, tranquility, and serenity.

Simply stated, the word **urban** means a place of settlement, often called a city, that is populated more densely than rural areas. **Urbanization** is the process

The Birth and Growth of Cities

Jericho, in modern Jordan, is honored as perhaps the world's first "true" city. With a population of about 600, Jericho was one of the first urban settlements that arose in the Middle East between 8,000 and 10,000 years ago. By today's standards Jericho was minuscule, but because its 600 people lived close to one another and had a reliable source of food that could support those not engaged in agriculture, Jericho qualifies as a city. Most important, the intersection of the lives of city dwellers created a lifestyle distinctly different from their rural counterparts. Free from the demands of producing their own food, city residents could experiment with new social and economic forms. The city spawned craftspeople, shopkeepers, and religious and political leaders who provided specialized services. The birth of civilization could occur only through the birth of cities. As sociology explains, when people come together in sustained interaction, their individual lives and their social surroundings are changed forever.

Tiny Jericho may have been the first city, but ongoing urban growth began about 5,500 years ago in areas near the confluence of major rivers and oceans—the Tigris and Euphrates in Mesopotamia, the Nile River of North Africa, and the Indus and Yellow Rivers of Asia, and the ports along the West African and Chinese coastlines. The first "modern" cities can be traced here. Cities of 30,000 inhabitants were typical, with Athens peaking at 100,000 and Rome estimated at 1 million by the first century B.C.E. (Before Common Era). Archeological and historical records of life in these and other cities such as Shanghai and Constantinople (now Istanbul, Turkey) are extensive and provide mixed, often contradictory images. These cities are praised for their sacredness, beauty, or technological achievements, but condemned for their vice, moral decay, and as sites of corruption, crime, and pestilence. Consider the biblical images of Jerusalem and Sodom and Gomorrah in this regard.

After the sack of Rome in the sixth century C.E., urban life deteriorated throughout Europe. Between 1347 and 1350 bubonic plague reduced Europe's population by about one-third, with most deaths occurring in cities. Larger cities in Asia were also vulnerable to periodic pillaging by warlords, which kept city expansion at a minimum. Until the seventeenth century in Europe, most cities were market towns with populations of no more than 3,000. Whereas food surplus and trade allowed the first cities to develop, other mechanisms were necessary for them to flourish. These came with industrialization and irrevocably altered our concept of city and with it our ideas and ideals about social life. For almost two hundred years, industrialization and urbanization have been inseparable, a trend that will surely continue.

Industrialization spawns specialization, another requirement for urban growth. And since urbanization is *always* a matter of degree, it cannot be defined easily by numbers or density. Urbanization is better understood as a complex interaction of different types of specialized functions. The most important specializations are neighborhoods (localities), technology, and institutions. Think about how a neighborhood depends on technology, such as highways, computers, and telephones, to link it with other localities. Urban residents also organize their lives around a host of institutions, which have evolved to meet specialized needs. A journey to Manhattan on a Saturday evening by a family living thirty miles away in Upper Saddle River, New Jersey, may find them enjoying Moroccan food, after watching "Titanic" on Broadway and visiting the Museum of Modern Art. Within a few city blocks of the intersection of Times Square and Broadway in New York City, a dazzling array of entertainment and dining offerings is available to meet every conceivable taste. It is not numbers that explain how cities grow and develop, but the interdependence of functions. Ten thousand years ago Jericho was the world's largest city with 600 people. With population estimates ranging between 24 and 26 million, Tokyo, São Paulo, and Mexico City are competing for that distinction today. Throughout their histories, the residents of these cities led interdependent lives. With a world economy fueling global urbanization, the trend toward increasing interdependence will certainly continue.

1. Identify the cities in your state, region, or country that have expanded the most. What accounts for that expansion?
2. How is your life organized around neighborhood, technology, and institutions? Which of these three influences your activities the most?

Sources: Fischer, 1984; Holton, 1986; Palen, 1992; Leeds, 1994.

of city population growth. The greater the number of people living in an area, the more urban it is. Urban, then, is a matter of degree (Leeds, 1994). The problem with these simple definitions is that the distinction between rural and urban is reduced to merely a matter of numbers. Sociology demonstrates how the size of the community in which people reside has a significant impact on their lives.

Global Urbanization

About half the world's population lives in urban areas, but the developed world is twice as urbanized (80 percent) as the developing world (40 percent). Europe is about 84 percent urbanized, a level slightly higher than in the United States (81 percent) (Fudge, 1996; U.S. Bureau of the Census, 1999). Urban growth in the United States as well as in most European cites has been from urban to suburban. In the developed world, the retreat from the cities has been led by the affluent. In the developing world, urban growth has been led by the poor, once clustered in rural areas. Although in-migration accounts for less overall increase (40 percent) than natural increases in the urban population (60 percent), the combination of the two factors produces staggering numbers of urbanites (Preston, 1988). The majority of people in the Northern hemisphere already inhabit urban areas, but the urban trend is on the fast track in Asia and Africa, and on the fastest track in Latin America, where 75 percent of the population is already urbanized (Ducci, 1996; De Olivera & Roberts, 1996). Not only do cities in poor countries now exceed cities of the industrialized world in total numbers, but the urban population of the developing world is double in comparison. With migration from villages accelerating the growth, by 2015 their numbers will have grown another 2 billion. Over half of the world's population and half of the population of developing nations will be in cities (Piel, 1997a) (see Figure 21.5). Consider such demographic changes in light of the following facts:

1. Fifty cities in the developing world have populations over 4 million. Eight of the ten cities of the world with populations of 11 million plus are in the developing world. (Tsunoyama, 1993; Gugler, 1996a)
2. In most large cities of the developing world, at least one-quarter of the population lives in absolute poverty. (Oberai, 1991)
3. Of the countries with the fastest growing urban population (urban growth rate), the top twenty cities are in Africa. (Devas & Rakodi, 1993a)
4. China has the largest urban population in the world, but India continues to have the largest absolute increase in urban population of any country in the world—and India is still over 70 percent rural! (Devas & Rakodi, 1993a; Seabrook, 1996)
5. The two largest cities in the developing world are in Central and South America—Mexico City and São Paulo, Brazil, with populations bordering 25 million. (Devas & Rakodi, 1993a).

The tidal wave of rural migrants is swamping cities throughout Asia, Africa, and South America. Urban migration is partly explained by poor subsistence farmers selling off small parcels of land for low prices to agribusinesses. Many rural people are robbed of their livelihood. However, the residents of the world's cities, including those in developing countries, have enjoyed a much higher standard of living than their rural counterparts. The economic lure of the cities offers hope to those who are quitting a desperate life on the soil for a marginally less desperate life as a squatter in an urban slum. In the Malthusian view, cities such as Calcutta, Manila, Mexico City, and Nairobi cannot indefinitely support a burgeoning population of the very poor. The city becomes a "miseropolis" (McGurn, 1997). Disease and famine eventually follow the flood of new migrants into cities, which do not have the resources to accommodate them.

Cities of the developing world offer opportunities to rural migrants for jobs and education, better housing, and health care. Traditionally, a superior quality of life has been associated with urban residency (Ahmed, 1996). But will a population explosion of rural migrants and long-term urban poor transform the once-prosperous cities into vast wastelands of urban squalor? Sociology is keenly interested in determining the consequences of the emerging powerful "megacities" for the world's economy and specifically for its urban residents.

Global cities are centers of population growth, political action, and economic activities that are becoming the dominant force in national and world economies (Sassen, 1996; Yeung, 1996, 1997). In most developing countries, one city dominates the national scene and has the highest concentration of its nation's urban population. Jakarta, Indonesia, for example, is the site of the country's rural-urban migration on a magnitude so vast that in three decades the number of migrants increased 114 percent, while the total population increased by 183 percent (Hugo, 1996a). In the global economy, such cities are becoming more linked with one another, nationally and internationally (Mehta, 1996). Because urban regions have large numbers of potential consumers, they can generate high levels of growth from within (Ziegler, 1997). Global cities serve as engines of economic growth and prosperity for their urban residents from this view.

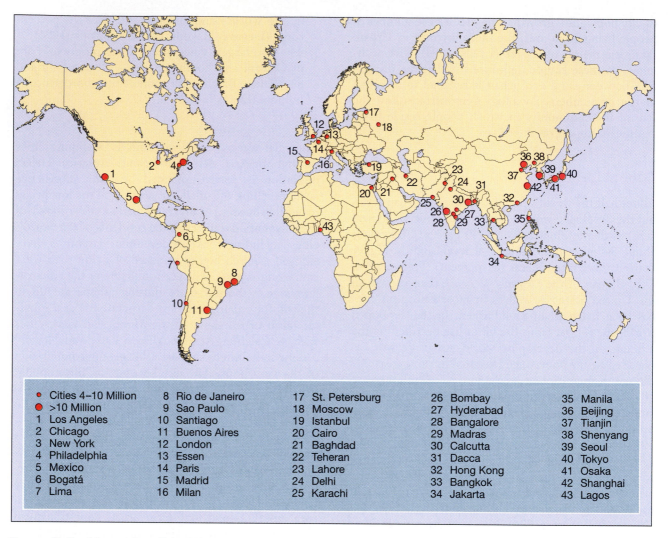

FIGURE 21.5   Megacities of the World

Source: Figure 1.1 from "Regional Trajectories in the Urban Transformation: Convergences and Divergences" by Josef Gugler in *The Urban Transformation of the Developing World* ed. by Josef Gugler. Copyright © 1996 by Oxford University Press. Reprinted by permission of Oxford University Press.

Urban patterns and processes also vary according to a nation's position in the world economy. Dependency theory suggests that if a nation is strangled by economic reliance on other nations, only a small elite will benefit from global linkages. Economic restructuring that is ushered in with development is bringing few benefits to the urban poor (Gilbert, 1994; Smith, 1996). A variation of this argument—called *urban bias*—is that class conflict is not between foreign or national interests or even between labor and capital but between urban and rural. The rural sector contains most of the world's poverty but the urban sector gets most of the world's wealth. As centers of power, cities maintain economic dominance over rural areas. As expressed by a peasant from Kenya,

> I thought I should go to the capital to look for work. Why? Because when money is borrowed from foreign lands, it goes to build Nairobi . . . all

our labour goes to fatten Nairobi and the big towns. (Gugler, 1996b:211)

Regardless of whether it is the rural poor or the rural *and* urban poor who lose most, both views suggest that only a small urban elite benefit from the increased growth and economic dominance of global cities.

In sociological terms, these two views reappear as the basic functionalist and conflict approaches to urban processes. Yet these approaches offer important points of convergence. The reality is that urban growth, fueled by rural in-migration, will continue and that democratic governments cannot forcibly cut it off. If governments seek to minimize migration of rural people to urban areas, they must do so within an acceptable democratic and human rights framework (Habitat II, 1996). China is the only country in the

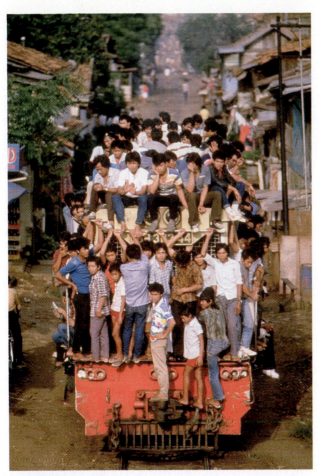

Jakarta, Indonesia dominates the entire nation, not only because of its massive population, but because of its vital importance to the nation's economy. Jakarta provides most jobs for the nation as a whole, and urban dwellers get to these jobs by whatever means available.

developing world to manage urban growth effectively—but China is not a democratic country.

The issue today is how to guide and manage growth, and city planners have addressed this issue in earnest. Large cities must be flexible and responsive to changes that come with rapid growth. Both functionalism and conflict theory would concede that public and private sectors together must serve the needs of the poor as well as improve urban productivity. City planners strike bargains with private landowners to achieve public objectives. In São Paulo, Brazil, and Bombay, India, for example, government-sponsored housing for low-income families is allowed to be constructed at greater height and density, thereby allowing private developers to realize greater profits (Mattingly, 1993). Likewise, Manila has constructed Fort Bonifacio, an urban renewal project that affirms the notion of public-private interdependence. If Manila's economic boom is to continue, developers cannot build a luxury high-rise and "leave the surrounding area to fate" (McGurn, 1997). Both Manila

and Bangkok have been experimenting with programs that bring in local groups at the very beginning of urban development projects (Berner & Korff, 1995; Perkins et al., 1996). These programs suggest that strategic planning and construction must go hand in hand with community-based development and participation of residents who will be directly impacted by the projects.

Evidence suggests that industrialized cities in the West have reversed their economic and environmental fortunes with long-term infusion of public funds acting as "pump-priming" for private investment (Robson, 1993). The gains may be smaller, but similar strategies are meeting with success in some cities of the developing world as well (Devas & Rakodi, 1993b). The challenge of the twenty-first century is to maintain a public-private balance that serves the needs of the globe's urban citizens.

Urbanization in the United States

Because urbanization is a matter of degree, the demarcation between urban and rural is a gradual one. The United States has witnessed an almost complete reversal of its population from rural to urban. Two hundred years ago, 90 percent of the population lived in rural areas. The U.S. Bureau of the Census (1999) tells us that today the United States is 80 percent urbanized, up by 3 percent from just a decade ago. Two predictions about continued urban expansion are implied: (1) It may have reached its environmental limits—limits dictated by water, desert, mountains, or other uninhabitable locations; and/or (2) remaining (arable) land suitable for agriculture will continue to shrink. To survive the Malthusian endpoint, therefore, the United States must be more technologically efficient in food production or must import more food. Regardless of which option occurs, urban expansion at this point means cities literally bumping into one another.

Keeping up with urban growth also means that terminology used to designate it must be continually modified. A **metropolitan area** is a central city and surrounding smaller cities that function as an integrated economy. These smaller surrounding urban areas outside the political boundaries of the central city are **suburbs,** which are often municipalities in themselves. A **megalopolis** is a system of several metropolitan areas and their surrounding suburbs that expand until they overlap. Although these terms provide images of urban growth, they are too vague for demographers, politicians concerned about numbers of voters, and city planners interested in providing services. More precise definitions use population numbers. The Census Bureau designates a **Metropolitan**

Statistical Area (MSA) as a central city of at least 50,000 people and its adjacent urbanized areas. When the largest MSAs are grouped together, they become **Consolidated Metropolitan Statistical Areas (CMSAs)** and form the megalopolis mentioned above. As Table 21.2 indicates, MSAs and CMSAs have multiplied as the United States has urbanized. For sociology, the population numbers are important because they signify that the population of the United States is increasingly becoming interdependent, hence more specialized in function.

Suburbanization

With the shortcomings of the ecological approach apparent by the 1960s, explanations for evolving urban patterns, especially decentralization, focused on the combined roles of politics and economics. When considering the impact of historical circumstances such as World War II and the postwar population explosion, the economic-political explanation for decentralization is a reasonable one. These factors provided the right mix for the most important population trend of the twentieth century: the suburbanization of America. Half the urban population is suburbanized. Sub-

urbanization is responsible for the urbanites' enhanced quality of life, but it has come at the expense of the cities around which suburbs have grown.

Class and Race in Suburbia. Like many neighborhoods in central cities, but larger and politically separate, suburbs cater to different segments of the population. Upper- and middle-class residents live in expensive homes with manicured lawns and a minivan in the driveway and commute to white-collar jobs in the city or, increasingly, to outer-belt headquarters. The working classes are located closer to the first outer rims of cities. Social class homogeneity is still normative within suburbs, but suburbs today exhibit much more diversity.

When minority status is factored in, the suburbanization of racial and ethnic groups is beginning to catch up with whites. Asians are the fastest growing racial group in the suburbs, followed by Latinos and African Americans. In a study of eleven metropolitan suburban regions, residential location is similar for whites, Asians, and Latinos. Asians and whites live in places of equivalent social standing. Latinos live in poorer suburbs than whites. However, suburban African Americans live in poorer areas even after ac-

Table 21.2 Largest Consolidated Metropolitan Statistical Areas and Fastest Growing Metropolitan Statistical Areas in the United States

Largest CMSAs in 1996 Rank	CMSA	Approximate Population in Millions
1	New York	20
2	Los Angeles	15.5
3	Chicago	8.6
4	Washington	7.2
5	San Francisco	6.7
6	Philadelphia	6.0
7	Boston	5.6
8	Detroit	5.3
9	Dallas	4.6
10	Houston	4.4

Fastest Growing MSAs, 1990–1996 Rank	MSA	Percent Increase
1	Las Vegas, Nevada	40.9
2	Laredo, Texas	32.7
3	McAllen-Edinburg-Mission, Texas	29.2
4	Boise, Idaho	25.9
5	Naples, Florida	23.7
6	Fayetteville-Springdale-Rogers, Arkansas	23.7
7	Austin-San Marcos, Texas	23.1
8	Phoenix-Mesa, Arizona	22.7
9	Provo-Orem, Utah	21.3
10	Brownsville-Harlingen-San Benito, Texas	21.1

Source: U.S. Census Bureau: 1996 Metropolitan Area Estimates (CB97–212), Washington, DC: U.S. Department of Commerce.

counting for differences in income, education, and home ownership (Logan & Alba, 1995). In urbanized areas generally, upper-income blacks are no more likely to live near whites than are lower-income blacks. This suggests that there are reduced spatial payoffs for black social mobility (Farley, 1991; Fainstein, 1995). Racial segregation and biased housing markets against African Americans combine to explain this trend (Phelan & Schneider, 1996). In measures of racial segregation alone, the outer city suburbs contain the new ghettos.

The stereotyped image of the suburbs as isolated areas of white affluence is far from reality (Baumgartner, 1988). Pockets of poverty exist throughout suburbia, and some suburbs are uniformly poor. Numbers of suburban homeless are increasing. As the most normative form of U.S. residence, suburbia is inhabited by people of all ages and all household types, rather than just the suburban pioneers of young families with young children (Gans, 1991). The oldest suburbs closest to the city rim are also likely to be both low income and stagnant (Palen, 1994). Except for density and more single-family residences, the suburbs increasingly resemble larger cities in the scope of the social problems they are encountering.

Suburban Political Autonomy.   If suburbs are becoming more heterogeneous in terms of race, ethnicity, and income, they still contrast sharply on all these dimensions. Though suburbs today are confronting similar problems originally faced by the central cities, they remain the most desired residential form in the United States. Seeking to maximize access and representation, the number of separate suburban municipalities has skyrocketed. Suburbs control a whole series of municipal services, such as schools, police and fire protection, trash collection, and recreational facilities. Besides tax increases, the price for control includes a confusing and often conflicting array of services. For example, homes have been allowed to burn to the ground because of lack of agreements about providing water or fire protection to those outside the municipal boundaries. But by the same token, the existence of suburbs independent from the core city is also a myth. In a megalopolis, where suburbs meet other suburbs, it is impossible to separate the two. As we will see later, the impact of suburbanization on the central cities of the United States is the pivotal factor in explaining urban decay.

Sociological Explanations for Urban Trends

Sociologists offer a great deal toward understanding patterns of urbanization. Industrialization not only helped create the discipline of sociology, but also the

important early subfield of urban sociology (Chapter 1).

Urban Ecology.   At the turn of the century, using Chicago as his laboratory, sociologist Robert Park (1916, 1926) began to explore patterns of urbanization, which led to the development of **urban ecology,** a field interested in determining the relationships between urban populations and their physical and spatial environments. This ecological approach suggests that population density in urban areas increases competition for scarce land, resulting in distinctive spatial patterns found in most cities Park declared that typical patterns of urban growth occurred in industrial nations (Park et al., 1925). Using Chicago as a prototype, he developed the *concentric zone model* of urban growth. This model described the organization of industrial cities according to manufacturing, occupational, and residential areas that radiated out from a central business district (CBD). Zones were interdependent but distinct by function. The homes of the wealthy would not be located next door to a manufacturing plant. The result was a distribution of population according to land use.

The automobile dramatically changed land use patterns, and there were numerous modifications of the original concentric zone model to explain the changes. The two most notable are the *sector concept* (Hoyt, 1939, 1943) and the *multiple nuclei model* (Harris & Ullman, 1945), both of which are based on the evolution of cities from a central business district (CBD). With Minneapolis and San Francisco as examples, the sector model suggests that urban growth occurs according to transportation lines. Housing and businesses follow highways and railroads, for instance, and extend in wedges outward from the CBD. With Boston as an example, the multiple nuclei model suggests that many discrete centers (nuclei) develop according to some specialized activity, such as finance or heavy industry.

Subsequent ecological models attempted to keep up with the fast-paced process of urbanization, but fewer and fewer patterns that fit the spatial ideas contained in the models emerged, such as the dramatic shift of the population to the suburbs.

Symbols and Urbanization.   Besides urban ecology, early research showed that sentiment is associated with land use. Over a half century ago, Bostonians sought to preserve Beacon Hill, the Boston Common, and colonial cemeteries scattered through the central business district that thwarted business expansion. The value of the land had more to do with sentiment than with economics (Firey, 1945). Boston has retained this characteristic ever since. Central Park in New York City and Forest Park in St.

Neighborhoods of the Globe

People living in cities often conjure up images of rural life as more simple, virtuous, and wholesome. Indeed, such images dominated the texts of both Western and Eastern cultures, from ancient to modern times. Yet research consistently shows that although people define the "good" life in the countryside, they still prefer to live in cities—even when they have a choice. There is a strong rural bias, but there is a stronger urban preference. Sociologists suggest that this preference is linked to the fact that cities *can* provide what residents of small towns also have: a sense of community. Cities are homes to *communities*, made up of residents who share common values, interact on a face-to-face basis, and have a strong sense of identification with their residential neighborhood. Urbanization may have transformed the world, but urban dwellers are part of smaller, viable communities within cities.

The notion of community-within-city is demonstrated in research in some of the world's most poverty-stricken cities. Squatters in a Lima, refugees in Peshawar, Pakistan, and Cairo's cemetery dwellers live precarious, but socially integrated lives. Quality of life in a community made up of cardboard and cloth-covered homes is based only on delicate networks of informal support from neighbors and kin. A study of Tondo, one of Manila's poorest districts, for example, suggests that poverty itself increases contact, help, and identification among neighbors, all fostered by a common lifestyle. Social isolation and alienation are not caused by life in these neighborhoods but when communities—as poor as they are—are torn apart, especially through compulsory eviction.

By recognizing that even the poorest cities on the planet have self-contained viable communities, local governments find it easier to mobilize the urban population for development projects. Programs bring together urban planners and residents to build community *empowerment* through high levels of resident participation. An already established sense of community is a catalyst leading to better outcomes for community development. Neighborhood councils in Nigeria and Columbia engage residents in self-help strategies to upgrade housing and integrate economic activities to serve community needs. Urban planners working in Bangladesh, Calcutta, Dakar, Senegal, and São Paulo, Brazil, build on ethnic community traditions to establish and maintain social harmony and stability. South Africa has embarked on an ambitious program to determine how best to serve tight-knit communities of the old apartheid townships by designing and planning housing and businesses that suit the social and economic needs of their neighborhoods.

In the United States, the idea that neighborhoods with strong, primary ties endure despite urban change took sociological root in the 1960s with an important study of a poor ethnic neighborhood in Boston's West End. This study showed that vital social linkages persisted, even when the community was severely affected by changes that compromised its physical and economic integrity, such as deterioration of schools and churches and loss of small businesses. Residents existed in an "urban village," seeing their neighborhood as a low-rent district—*not* as a slum. Later research on cities throughout the United States shows that neigh-

borhoods have special meaning to residents, especially when they function as networks of informal social support and as havens from the stress of contemporary life.

Communities are not the relics of a bygone, preindustrial age. Perhaps because social change is happening so fast, and in light of the urban transformation of the developing world, people develop community bonds rather quickly. When faced with a potentially alienating urban environment, city dwellers all over the world—including its poorest parts—mark their neighborhoods with distinctive, self-chosen ways of life. Older sociological views of the world's urban poor as rampant with social pathologies that paralyze them both socially and economically are being replaced. Compared to rural living, urban living is certainly different, but not necessarily alienating. Newer research shows that urbanites throughout the globe, whether in Copenhagen, Cairo, or Calcutta, cope with the urban monolith by domesticating it through community-building.

1. What do you prefer as a permanent residence—a small town or an urban area? How is this preference affected by where you grew up as well as by your images of rural and city life?

2. How does your residence, college, neighborhood, town, or city reflect the idea of community?

Sources: Gans, 1962, 1967; Freudenberg, 1986; Hollnsteiner-Racelis, 1988; Lomnitz, 1988; Chavis & Wandersman, 1990; Mabogunje, 1990; Awotona, 1995; Etzioni, 1995; Rainero, 1996; Laquian, 1996; Teitz, 1997.

Louis, large green spaces surrounded by million-dollar real estate, are a few of the numerous examples of the sentiment-symbol relationship found in urban areas around the globe (Anderson & Loughlin, 1986; Boyer, 1993). Contemporary research continues to document that symbolism is as important to images of the city as is its economic aspects (Herzog & Gale, 1996; Keith & Pile, 1996).

New Urban Sociology. Because urban ecology could not adequately account for the new patterns or other social problems that emerged with urbanization, other models were needed. The *new urban sociology* focuses on social inequality and conflict. Cities are analyzed by capital production, politics, ideology, and consumption patterns that produce advantages for some groups and disadvantages for others. There is a clear emphasis on the political economy as a driving force of urbanization (Fine & Leopold, 1993; Smith, 1995). Whereas earlier sociologists saw urban patterns motivated mostly by individual desires, the newer approach suggests that municipal regulations combined with economic incentives also influence patterns. For example, moving to the suburbs might be to reduce fear of crime but also because of affordable housing with tax incentives. Businesses may be enticed to suburban locations for the same reasons (Gottdiener, 1999). The new model has a strong conflict theoretical perspective that fits well with the view that cities are physically and economically located in a hierarchy and are shaped by that location.

Symbolic interactionism is also an important component of the new urban sociology. Symbolic interactionists suggest that people construct a symbolic world that is especially meaningful to them in carrying out their work and living activities. A key part of this symbolic world involves the "built" environment that surrounds them, such as their cities, suburbs, and neighborhoods. Located within each of these built environments are a variety of subcultures, including those based on ethnicity, religion, race, gender, or age (Gottdiener, 1999). People locate and identify themselves according to these subcultural sites. For example, they celebrate ethnic heritage in festivals featuring their food, crafts, and distinctive dress, inviting other urbanites to join in the celebrations. Such festivals help urban dwellers to adjust to, and symbolically construct urban life. Perhaps like the sentiment associated with the Boston Commons fifty years ago, the symbolic aspect of space and the built environment are as important as their functional uses.

Urbanism as a Way of Life

For both the older and newer varieties of urban sociology, the impact of urban life on its residents has been an ongoing research focus. Much of this work is founded on Louis Wirth's (1938) classic essay, "Urbanism as a Way of Life." Wirth popularized a view of city life in which population density and social heterogeneity paved the way for a social structure based on impersonal, transitory, secondary relationships. According to Wirth (1938:55), in the city "our physical contacts are close, but our social contacts are distant."

Anthropologist Robert Redfield's (1941, 1947) work in peasant villages in Mexico support Wirth's images. Redfield built an "ideal" type of a folk society

Some urban sociologists suggest that cities may provide sources of entertainment and diversion for their dwellers, but the payment for it is isolation or detachment from others. This view has less support today.

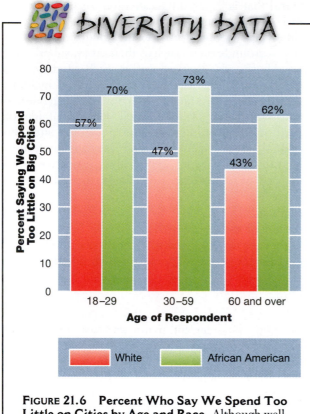

DIVERSITY DATA

FIGURE 21.6   Percent Who Say We Spend Too Little on Cities by Age and Race. Although well over half of respondents in all age groups say we are spending too little to solve problems of big cities, Africans Americans are on average 20 percent more likely to say this than whites. How can knowledge about race and age patterns of those living in big cities explain this finding?

Source: NORC. General Social Surveys, 1972–1996, Chicago: National Opinion Research Center, 1996. Reprinted by permission of NORC, Chicago, IL.

describing it as one that is small, economically self-sufficient and highly integrated. Continuous face-to-face interaction produces a strong sense of community. In cities, secondary groups replace primary group ties indicative of rural life.

A functionalist interpretation of both Wirth and Redfield maintains that secondary groups serve city dwellers well. With loss of primary contacts, people must find other outlets to meet social needs, so they come together in formal and voluntary associations. These are adaptations to the onslaught of stressful urban living used as psychological protection. Although these groups meet social needs, the city dweller pays a price. The city is comprised of a mosaic of little "selves," which touch but do not interpenetrate. Thus the fragmented self is a distinctive feature of urban life (Cohen, 1993). The result is an efficient, rational, and sophisticated city dweller but one who is

also anonymous, isolated, and interpersonally detached from other residents. Urban anomie (normlessness) and alienation are also results. If cities break down interpersonally, they will break down socially.

Although written over a half century ago, Wirth's essay is one of the most cited in all of sociology. How has his account stood the empirical test of time? In U.S. cities as well as globally, Wirth was correct in asserting that urbanization has a profound impact on all social life. But how that impact is actualized varies according to several factors. For example, common stressors in the rapidly growing cities of South Asia are noise, air pollution, and crowding, which interact to produce perceptions for some city dwellers that they have less control over their lives. In India and Bangladesh, when people were informed of the effects of air pollution and crowding, they actually felt worse than if they had not been given any information at all (Ruback et al., 1997)!

However, the most important impact on urban residents is an economic one. Urban decline is linked to a shredding of social ties in those areas hit hardest by job loss. Virtually every central city in the United States continues to experience a steady decrease in manufacturing, leading to unemployment and worsening poverty of the inner-city. Referred to as the *spatial mismatch hypothesis*, an already weakened social fabric declines further as people who can afford to do so move out of deteriorating neighborhoods (Wilson, 1987; Kain, 1992). The people who remain are the poorest and the most psychologically vulnerable to the stresses of urban life.

Undeniably, large pockets of extreme poverty exist throughout cities, some of which are associated with fragile or absent social bonds. However, poverty does not always produce urban social breakdown. The evidence is clear that a sense of community can exist among those who dwell in deteriorating homes, located on littered streets, in crime ridden urban areas. Lurking within the slums are vital neighborhoods bound together by a sense of identification, urgency, and social need.

ENVIRONMENT: ECOLOGICAL INTERDEPENDENCE

The two most important direct causes of environmental destruction are population growth and industrial expansion (Szell, 1994; Nitta & Yoda, 1995). Because both industry and population are concentrated in cities, urbanization is the indirect or mediating cause. Astounding economic growth magnifies already existing problems of the urban environment. Since 1950, the global economy has rapidly expanded almost sixfold, and more in the last seven years than the entire 10,000 years that began with the advent of agriculture (Brown et al., 2000). Such dramatic growth poses a serious threat to the earth's ecosystem. Even telecommunications, often viewed as a clean and benign industry, takes an environmental sacrifice, particularly as it generates new demands for travel (Hecq et al., 1993; Marvin, 1997).

The technology that allowed for last century's unprecedented economic growth is taking a toll on natural resources: Global consumption of wood has doubled, paper use has increased six times, with fossil fuels up nearly fivefold (Figure 21.7). Grain consumption has tripled and fish consumption has increased fivefold. The resulting environmental stress includes shrinking forests and wetlands, eroding soil, pollution of international waters, collapsing fisheries, vanishing plant and animal species, and rising temperatures. Half the world's population lives on coastlines, rivers, and estuaries. This half includes rural people who rely on waterways for their livelihoods—fishing, transportation, communication, and irrigation for farmlands—and are the most vulnerable when waterways become polluted. Based on UN population predictions, by 2050 one in five people is likely to live in a country with severe shortages of fresh water serious enough to threaten health and economic well-being (Brown et al., 1998).

The change that has generated the most attention to the environment worldwide is the global temperature rise. Referred to as **global warming** or the "greenhouse effect," temperature increases are linked to burning fossil fuels, to industrial and agricultural waste, and other emissions such as the fluorocarbons in refrigeration and air conditioning. These emissions are associated with ozone-layer depletion and the speed up of global warming (Commoner, 1993; Dowie, 1996). In addition, the effect of rising temperatures on human health is documented in increased rates of skin cancer and the reemergence of diseases such as cholera and viral fevers, traced to alterations in land use that come with urbanization and development (Tickell, 1996).

The interdependent nature of global warming can be linked to other climatic changes. Recall the monumental global impact a few years ago of *El Niño*, the nickname for an ocean/atmosphere system normally occurring off the Peruvian Coast about every five to seven years. El Niño changes the temperature of much of the Pacific, causing the air above it to be heated or cooled in response. From 1991 to 1998 three El Niño events have occurred. The effects eventually showed up as torrential rain in the Pacific and drought in Africa and Latin America. It was also responsible for landslides in California and deadly tornadoes in Florida (Suplee, 1997; Lush, 1998). Prolonged drought and flooding ravaged crops throughout the developing world, causing food shortages and malnutrition in some areas and famine and starvation in others. In 1997, thousands of miles of primary rain forests in Indonesia, Malaysia, and New

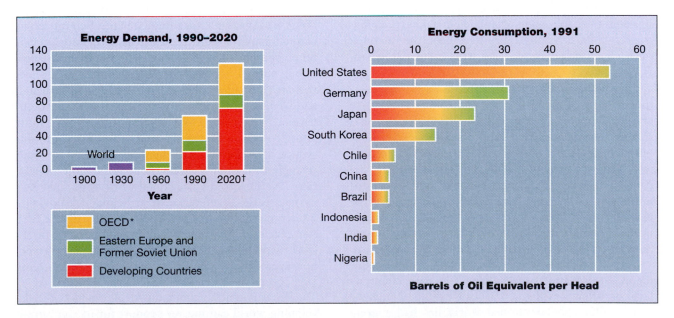

FIGURE 21.7   **Energy Demand and Energy Consumption by Regions of the World**
*OECD (Organization for Economic Cooperation): Member nations include U.S., Western European countries, Iceland, Poland, Czech Republic, Turkey, Japan, and South Korea.
†projected
Sources: Economist, 1994; United Nations, 1997.

Evidence shows that people are becoming more conscious of the environment and that recycling is now a way of life for many, especially when children are socialized at school and at home in these efforts.

Guinea, already thinned out by massive logging, easily caught fire following prolonged drought (*Washington Post*, 1997). El Niño may have been the final link on a causal chain originating with industrial expansion.

If industry is the offender, it follows that environmental control must be tied to reducing its negative effects. However, the demographic transition suggests that development requires industrial expansion. Economic benefits to families will in turn reduce fertility rates. The underlying problem is that industrial expansion has created environmental havoc. And for much of the developing world still in Stage 2 of the demographic transition, fertility rates are not declining as fast as mortality rates. The result is massive population increases that further strain the ecosystem.

Research consistently documents that environmental degradation varies according to a country's level of affluence (Hugo, 1996b; Keyfitz, 1996; Keohane, 1996). The developed world has had a great deal of success in cleaning up more localized environmental damages because their economies have the resources and requisite political momentum to use public monies for environmental purposes. In the

United States, there is widespread bipartisan support for increased attention to environmental causes, especially those related to curbing global warming. Spending for environmental improvement and working on international agreements to deal with global ecological threats ranks high at the polls for voter concern (Mathews, 1996; *Monday Developments*, 1997). The concern and the spending are justified in light of the fact that technologically advanced countries remain significant contributors to global environmental burdens (Urbanization, 1996). (Figure 21.8.)

The Game of Ecopolitics

Countries in the developing world are unquestionably aware of their environmental plight: Industrial pollutants must be cleaned up, but not at the expense of economic expansion. Environmental degradation and development initiatives intertwine (Pedersen, 1996). World leaders play out "greenhouse politics," and as conflict theorists suggest, the division between rich and poor countries determines which cards are being played. As the division grows, reversing practices and policies threatening to the environment are hindered as well (Leisinger, 1995).

In 1997, 160 nations signed the "Kyoto Protocol," which identified what industrialized and developing nations can do to reduce the gases implicated in global warming. Targeted reductions are based in part on the economic profiles of each country, so that targets for poorer countries are less stringent. Developing nations argue that since wealthier countries account for about 60 percent of heat-trapping carbon monoxide emissions, they need to shoulder the economic burden in reducing them. Morality enters into the environmental arena as well. Leaders in Tanzania and Malawi, who represent the caucus of developing nations in environmental talks, state that they cannot afford to devote a large share of precious resources to reduce emissions when there is an ongoing daily struggle to feed and clothe their burgeoning populations. Nations of the developed world raise their own fairness issue in reference to principles of ecological interconnectedness. These nations cite figures that the developing world already has 80 percent of the world's population, and it will soon exceed greenhouse gas emissions of the developed world (Sims, 1997; Stevens, 1997a, 1997b).

What is unique about this debate is that the developing world can muster support for its side simply through the undeniable fact of ecological interdependence. From a sociological perspective, conflict theory takes center stage in explaining the issue. Many of today's global ecological problems stem from the very

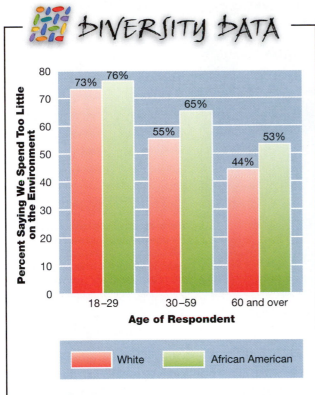

DIVERSITY DATA

FIGURE 21.8   Percent Who Say We Spend Too Little on Environment by Age and Race. Although over half of respondents say we spend too little, white and African Americans under 30 are significantly more likely than those over 30 to state this. Why do you think that younger people might want more spent on the environment?
Source: NORC. General Social Surveys, 1972–1996. Chicago: National Opinion Research. Reprinted by permission of NORC, Chicago, IL.

nature of modernization and how modernization itself has polarized the world into two classes of nations, one rich and the other poor. Environmental conflict cannot be reduced to climate control or other ecological problems without considering the politics that mediate the process (Salih, 1992). The game of ecopolitics means that wealthy nations, accustomed to being autonomous players, can no longer act autonomously in our ecologically interconnected world. Not only are unilateral approaches outdated, they are now environmentally dangerous (Finger, 1992; Vaahtoranta, 1992).

Strategies for Environmental Success

To protect the ecosystem, the rich and poor nations have reached several important compromises. They represent at least some cautious optimism concerning the world's ecological problems. First, through UN

efforts, the Global Environment Facility (GEF) was initiated in 1990. GEF is a pilot program that provides funds to developing countries to work on environmental problems including global warming, pollution of international waters, and the depletion of the ozone layer (GEF, 1995). Although to date GEF's contribution in actually alleviating these problems has been modest, it continues to receive worldwide support from a diverse array of stakeholders, including nongovernmental organizations (NGOs) that often have conflicting priorities among themselves as well as with politicians in their own nations. The hope is that future GEF contributions for environmental protection will eclipse past shortcomings (Fairman, 1996).

Second, some achievements have occurred with a program known as the "debt-for-nature" swap. Such agreements reward developing countries for adopting conservation measures to safeguard their rain forests and biodiversity by writing off a portion of their foreign debts (Jakobeit, 1996:127). The program has been most successful in Costa Rica, a country already committed to conservation in principle but also in the throes of deforestation. Yet Costa Rica could achieve only a fraction of its conservation program from this funding source. Other parts of Latin America and Jamaica joined the process but could not gather enough additional funding to make it very effective. While hardly a success story at this point, the debt-for-nature swap demonstrates another creative approach to conservation in public-private (government-NGO) partnership. Environmental aid from private sources will never be adequate enough to solve massive environmental problems, such as saving the rain forest or the ozone layer. But they will help donor agencies gain the political savvy they need to attract more substantial financial resources from within their own NGO communities and especially from public sources (Connolly, 1996:327).

Third, technology can increase agricultural production, yet not at the expense of either the producers themselves or the environment. The story of the "green revolution" illustrates the cost-benefit analysis. In the mid-twentieth century the **green revolution** was the term given to the industrial and technological innovations used to produce high-yield crops that would solve the world's food supply problem. With technology as a basis, worldwide grain harvests, for example, have achieved outstanding results. Technology is now being developed to selectively breed crops not only to increase yield, but to boost nutritional content. Results such as these are spectacular but they come at a grave ecological and social cost (Schnaiberg & Gould, 1994). To reap the benefits, abundant water is necessary and irrigation systems must be expanded or built. In many areas of the world chemical fertiliz-

Another strategy calling attention to the environment is to focus international attention on problems such as the depletion of the ozone layer. NGOs such as Greenpeace conduct organized protests in cities across the world and are at the vanguard of the worldwide environmental movement.

ers, pesticide, and genetically engineered seed, used more haphazardly and without proper checks, transformed renewable soil fertility and plant life into a nonrenewable resource (Shiva, 1992). Many producers also suffered. Poor farmers could obtain the new technology only by borrowing money. Any crop failure then had a doubly severe impact—not only loss of self-sufficiency but loss of land due to loan default (Webster, 1990).

Because of stricter environmental regulations, the green revolution has achieved substantial success in the developed world. But the idea that technology can manipulate nature to continually expand its limits has been ultimately dysfunctional. Productivity was raised in the short run, but long-term results were just the opposite—agrosystems became artificial, unstable, and prone to rapid degradation (Stutz, 1993). On the positive side, however, there are hints that a second

INTERNET CONNECTIONS

The Natural Resources Defense Council is one of the nation's major environmental organizations. Its Web site, www.nrdc.org/nrdc, is loaded with information on environmental issues, including "backgrounders" on particular problems and "experts" to whom you can address specific questions. Pick an environmental problem that especially interests you and see what the NRDC has to say about it.

"green revolution" is making global headway, but this time with earlier lessons to guide it. The action agenda the second time around includes using environmentally friendly and appropriate technology to revitalize small farms. For urban ecosystems, improvements in recycling and the economical use of water can save resources and also be a self-funding mechanism for employment (Sachs, 1994).

In Kenya, a program of technological improvements coupled with management innovations has enabled rural incomes to grow substantially and at the same time improved environmental conservation. Most important, this case demonstrates that technology can be used in environmental recovery. And in countering Malthus, the program shows economic growth rates outpacing population growth (Tiffen & Mortimore, 1994). A combined approach incorporating nonpolluting energy sources, forest management, and new technology in line with traditional cultural practices can safeguard Africa's environment (Niang, 1990). There is optimism that the world's food supply can continue to expand (Smil, 1987). If technology is culturally and ecologically appropriate, the second green revolution may stand a better chance of success in the developing world.

Sustainable Development

Population and environmental problems are interwoven with urbanization. The major thrust in dealing with these issues that accounts for their interdependence is sustainable development (World Commission on Environment and Development, 1987). **Sustainable development** (SD) requires interna-

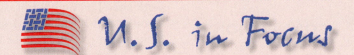

Autocentric America and Urban Sprawl

The first conquest of the American West occurred when land-hungry pioneers began settling the regions west of the Mississippi 150 years ago. By the twentieth century, these settlements emerged as major metropolitan centers, such as Kansas City, Denver, Phoenix, and Los Angeles. These cities have continued to expand ever since. The critical ingredient in the expansion was the affordable automobile and an entire transportation system designed around it. With the automobile, suburbanization was born and fed and grows ever stronger. Although cities have more work and resident activities *per acre*, most jobs and retail sales are now in the suburbs. As metropolitan areas continue to expand, suburbs are swallowed up by other suburbs encroaching on their outer rims, forming new megalopolises. The result is *suburban* sprawl, a pattern becoming so typical that it is referred to as the "Second Conquest of the American West." By living in single-family residences close to highways, supermarkets, and recreational facilities, an "autocentric" existence is necessary.

The first suburbs were often referred to as dormitory or bedroom communities, because people slept there but still relied on their cars to get to the central city that served most other aspects of their lives, from their jobs to their recreational activities. After World War II, suburbs began to develop their own services to accommodate residents, with less and less reliance on the city. Suburban municipalities politically incorporated and developed their own school districts, hospitals, shopping, and recreational areas that made them semi-autonomous. The dream of home ownership was in the reach of thousands of World War II veterans who could use their veteran status to purchase affordable housing. Tax incentives enticed businesses to the suburbs, so jobs followed.

Suburbanites could now have an independent existence from the core cities that spawned them.

But the attempt to escape from the congestion of city life brings with it much of what people thought they were escaping from. Research on Orange County, California, shows that the perceived quality of life and sense of community of suburban residents decreases over time because of urbanization, especially in larger, higher density, and more ethnically diverse suburbs. California is the symbol of suburban sprawl. It is oriented to an autocentric drive-in culture, and this pattern is repeating itself on the edges of virtually every metropolitan area throughout America. As Kenneth Jackson (1985:281) explains in his historical analysis of U.S. suburbs:

No longer forced outside by the heat and humidity, no longer attracted by the corner drugstore, and no longer within walking distance of relatives, suburbanites often choose to remain in the family room. When they do venture out, it is often through a garage into an air-conditioned automobile. Streets are no longer places to promenade, but passageways for high-powered machines.

Not only can we eat and pay for gas from our cars, we can buy groceries, get married, go to church, and even attend a funeral. When teens venture from the family room TV, they don't walk anywhere, they cruise in their cars.

Suburban sprawl does not appear to be slowing down. Not only do suburbs swallow everything in their forward march to rural areas, they do so at the expense of the environment (more pollution and more gasoline) and at the expense of the central cities (loss of housing, jobs, and a tax-base) they leave behind. Detroit and Washington, D.C., are examples of the victims of the march to the once greener pastures of

suburbia. However, at least one model seems to offer hope in controlling the march to suburbia. Two decades ago Portland, Oregon limited suburban sprawl by creating an "urban growth boundary" (UGB) over the city's surrounding farmland. UGB zones are regulated as to what can be built and how far development can extend. Developers are required to provide housing for low-income people when homes for the middle class and affluent are built. Older urban zones are reclaimed and revitalized before development is extended outward. Environmental impact studies are required before any development takes place. The UGB model appears to meet the interests of farmers, environmentalists, businesses, and suburban residents. Portland looks inward rather than outward in terms of development.

Although Portland is as autocentric as most other U.S. cities, its efforts to curtail suburban sprawl are impressive. Whether its UGB model can be successful in other cities is uncertain. What is certain, however, is that suburbia is still inextricably connected to its original urban centers. Unless the suburbanization can be curtailed, or at least controlled, it will be to the detriment of both urban and suburban centers. Interdependence is the inescapable fact of urban life.

1. Using the UGB model of Portland as a guide, suggest other models that could deal with suburban growth that would also benefit residents of the older urban centers.
2. How would functionalists and conflict theorists explain the suburbanization of America? What suggestions would each offer to deal with the problems that result?

Sources: Fischer, 1984; Jackson, 1985; Baldassare & Wilson, 1995; Gersh, 1996; Wilson & Baldassare, 1996; *Economist*, 1998.

INTERNET ━━◆━━ CONNECTIONS

The *U.S. in Focus* insert in Chapter 21 is entitled "Autocentric America and Urban Sprawl." Some American communities are making a consolidated effort to combat urban sprawl, including Durham, North Carolina. Take a look at the "C.A.U.S.E (Citizens Against Urban Sprawl Everywhere)" Web site: http://www.stopthe-sprawl.org/cause.htm. What suggestions do these concerned residents of Durham have for dealing with the problem of urban sprawl? Do you live in a community where this phenomenon is a problem, or do you know someone who lives in such a community? Even if you have no practical or indirect experience with urban sprawl, *imagine* that where you live has this problem. What do you think your reactions would be? What would you want to do about it?

tional cooperation in finding humane ways for the human species to live on the planet indefinitely without risking the future of either the planet or its inhabitants. Ideally, population growth can be slowed, hunger can be alleviated, and the cities of the world can be environmentally friendly. This is a tall order. There are powerful forces working both for and against sustainable development. Sociological functionalism focuses on the cooperative efforts that will restrict some uses of our environmental systems in order to protect them. Conflict theory suggests that SD will be limited by powerful economic interests until competing interests muster enough resources to effectively challenge them. Symbolic interactionism focuses on how people envision the process, culturally construct definitions around it, and then operate on those definitions. All three perspectives would accept the ecological principle that human and nonhuman species interact, change, and evolve with their environments (Clayton & Radcliffe, 1996).

≡ LIFE CONNECTIONS: The U.S. City: Decline or Renaissance?

The most descriptive measure of urban decline is population loss—first in a central city and then in its municipal boundaries. The economic consequences of population loss in the flight to the suburbs has been profound in terms of jobs, housing, and education.

Many industries have followed their employees to the suburbs, enticed by favorable taxes and retention of employees who are more satisfied with a suburban

work site. The number of central-city jobs lost when manufacturing plants and small businesses close is higher than the service jobs that replace them. Cities then must raise taxes on the remaining businesses to maintain the same level of services. A self-fulfilling prophecy results because lowered services decrease satisfaction with the city, in turn causing more businesses to flee. Over two-thirds of suburbanites live and work there. Except for the recreational offerings of professional sports or cultural institutions such as art museums, fewer than one-third even need the central business district at all (Gans, 1991:67).

The same scenario applies to housing. Major housing abandonment by the urban middle class leaves vacant large tracts of residentially zoned land. But quality, affordable housing for the urban poor concentrated in the central city is unavailable. With middle-class suburban flight, inner city neighborhoods have either vacant homes or a spillover of the poor who eventually occupy them. Strict housing-quality codes for the middle class can initially be used to legally exclude the poor from high growth areas. But when the neighborhood changes, codes are relaxed to keep houses occupied. Low-income households cannot afford to maintain the initial condition of the house. Thus, as the housing deteriorates, reverberations are felt throughout the neighborhood, causing an overall decline of SES in the metropolitan area (Bradbury et al., 1982).

Given the job and housing situation, the education consequence of population loss due to suburbanization is predictable. The tax base for public education is further eroded so better teachers cannot be attracted by either higher pay or good working conditions. The remaining middle class send their children to private schools. Property values are directly linked to school quality. Think about your own locality and notice how the prices of similar homes vary on a street that is divided according to municipality. Much of the price disparity can be explained by the quality of the school district in which the home is located. As Chapter 16 explained, although successful strategies have helped curtail the deterioration of urban America's public schools, a solid and predictable tax-paying population is necessary to fuel any urban revival.

Alarmed by the rapid decline of cities, and in partnership with the federal government, various forms of urban revival or renewal began in earnest in the 1970s. Two major forms emerged: enticing the more affluent back into the city and upgrading housing for the poor. The first form is **gentrification**, a process of renovating specific working-class or poor neighborhoods to attract new affluent residents. As the most visible form of urban renewal, gentrification upgrades an entire neighborhood, particularly as small businesses, such as dry cleaners, pubs, restau-

The tragedy of inadequate, poorly maintained and unsafe public housing in inner-city America was symbolized by the infamous Pruett-Igoe apartments in St. Louis. With no practical solution offered to make the housing project inhabitable again, the city chose to bomb it away.

rants, and specialty stores, emerge to cater to newcomers. Most important, gentrification reestablishes a middle-class tax base.

The second form of urban renewal is related to the first. People can qualify for low-rate federal loans to upgrade homes and businesses near gentrified neighborhoods. However, homeowners in these neighborhoods must now correct longstanding housing-code violations or risk being evicted. For many people, eviction to poorer-quality homes or public housing is typical. Overall, public housing projects have been disastrous for their residents. The failure of metropolitan governments to provide adequate and safe housing for their citizens is exemplified in the infamous Pruett-Igoe public housing project in St. Louis. Rampant with crime and drugs, Pruett-Igoe was literally bombed out of existence. Twenty-five years later the land remains as a huge, littered, vacant lot.

The development of a megalopolis blurs the city-suburb distinction, and this very blurring gives hope to America's cities. Just as powerful social and demographic forces spurred decentralization, others will counter it. First, population has slowed among all classes and races and ZPG has been reached. Second, with 80 percent of the U.S. population living in cities already, urbanization can go only so far. As Malthus predicted a limit to food, there is also a predictable limit to expansion. Third, the cost of the land that remains is enormous. Technological answers offer few permanent fixes. Fourth, there is an endpoint to gasoline consumption, as Americans learned during the fuel crisis in the 1970s. U.S. dependence on foreign oil is unlikely to change in the foreseeable future. Without gasoline, car-dependent suburbia can come to a virtual standstill.

Finally, if a central city continues to decline, the effect will inevitably be felt in the suburbs. All socio-

logical theories underscore the fact of urban interdependence. The rise of megalopolises indicates that urban-suburban interconnections are so tangled that even affluent suburbs can face economic disaster if the industries they grew around falter.

SOCIETY CONNECTIONS:
Population Control

Acceptable methods of environmentally sustainable development may be easier to find than acceptable methods of limiting population growth. Although intensely personal, sexuality and reproduction are highly political. As noted by a participant of a reproductive health conference held in Africa, "government, parents, and religious leaders are all literally in bed with us" (Berer, 1993:1). It is also very clear that the population explosion in the developing world is making poor people poorer, the hungry hungrier, and an already fragile environment too weak to support its increasing number of inhabitants (Robert S. McNamara, 1992). Attaining development goals depends on stabilizing population as well as climate (McHenry, 1991; Brown, 1996). Global reductions in mortality and increases in life expectancy are causes for celebrating the progress of humanity, and no one would seriously consider reversing these trends. Slowing the rate of population growth ultimately depends on a decline in fertility. Although this objective has worldwide support, how it is carried out has divided nations and different groups within nations.

The Status of Women

The most contentious issue in international debates about population involves the role and status of women. In 1994 the United Nations International

Programs to upgrade housing and neighborhoods in inner cities have been most successful when community groups are in partnership with agencies such as the local police and schools.

Conference on Population and Development convened in Cairo to debate future population policy for the globe. The conference agreed that population management should be a top government priority, especially in the context of sustainable development. The humanitarian effort of reproductive health-related services was also a key feature (Cohen & Richards, 1994). But the most important component was targeting the status of women as fundamental to the success of any population policy. Of all factors associated with falling birthrates, the one that consistently demonstrates the highest correlation is improvement in the lives of women (UNICEF, 1991; Pope, 1999). The fourth UN Conference on Women,

held in 1995 in Beijing, again reinforced the idea that women's emancipation was a key to solving problems related to population, environment, and economic development (Johnson & Turnbull, 1995). The strongest advocates for family planning now are women from developing nations.

Family planning is the deceptively simple notion that couples have the right and means to decide how many children they will have. Effective contraception is the number one cause for declining fertility throughout the world. The condom is the most widely used method, followed by birth-control pills. Surgical sterilization of women occurs more often than vasectomies for men. Abstinence is the least used

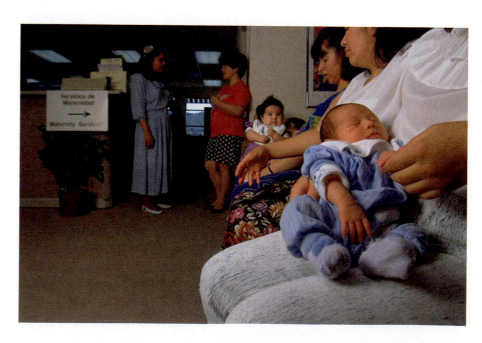

Family planning and effective contraception are desired by couples throughout the world. But in many places cultural traditions restrict access to family planning.

method of contraception. When abortion is a legal option, it is highest in countries where other birth-control options are limited, a trend most likely in the poorer countries of the world. Evidence consistently suggests that countries adopting family-planning strategies with safe and effective birth control have lower rates of abortion (Dixon-Mueller, 1993; Freedman & Isaacs, 1993; Sen et al., 1994).

The global concern for high population growth masks the fact that through effective birth control, developing countries nearing the end of the demographic transition, such as South Korea, Taiwan, and Thailand, have attained fertility rates at or near replacement levels (Greenspan, 1994). The percentage of couples in the developing world who use family planning increased from 10 to 50 percent in the last three decades. For the first time in history, if family-planning efforts can be maintained, most of the world could see an absolute decline in population growth by the middle of the next century (El-Badry, 1991; Holmes, 1996). However, an unmet need for family planning still exists for the vast majority of the developing world.

The *unmet need hypothesis* suggests that effective birth control, particularly in developing countries, is wanted but either unavailable or culturally unacceptable (Figure 21.9). The cultural factor is critically linked to the status of women. As a major test of the unmet need hypothesis, over 100 million married women of childbearing age say they want to postpone or end childbearing but are not currently using contraceptives (Population Action International, 1997). With declines in infant mortality, couples now desire fewer children, and women desire fewer than men (Ashford, 1995; Bankole & Westoff, 1995). Women are bound by laws and customs that restrict education and job opportunities associated with decision making in their families.

Combining conflict theory with symbolic interactionism is useful in explaining these patterns. There are powerful cultural definitions of sexual expression and women's roles in family life. Men and women accept the idea that a woman's foremost role is childbearer, taking precedence over her role as wife. Fertility rates may be lowered when alternative definitions of women's roles are embraced by both genders. Women also need the empowerment that leads to increased autonomy in decision making. Research suggests that the most effective strategies for women to implement their reproductive preferences are those that support organizing peer groups and mobilizing community resources and public services, particularly health services (Dixon-Mueller, 1993; Mahmud & Johnston, 1994).

There is a strong case that the focus of population policy should move beyond simply attaining demographic goals to guaranteeing that couples have full reproductive rights (Johnson & Nurick, 1995).

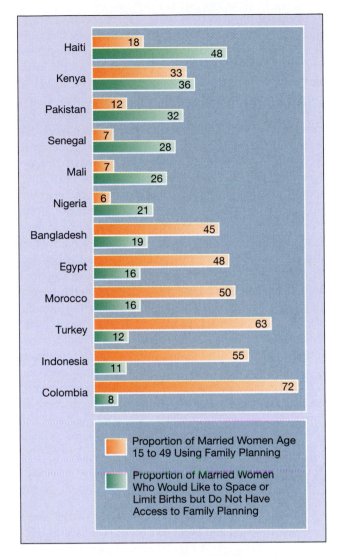

FIGURE 21.9 Unmet Needs for Birth Control, Selected Countries in the Developing World
Source: Population Action International, 1997.

Such a policy would also work against the abuses of both forced pregnancy, a frequent outcome in Latin America and Africa, and forced abortions, a common outcome in China. Population programs that deny condom usage because it is culturally offensive and then offer female sterilization as the only legitimate option to childbearing risk reproductive health as well as abridging human rights (Fathalla, 1994; Mason, 1994). Policies designed to meet the unmet need for contraception must balance cultural sensitivity with women's rights.

Malthus Revisited

Malthus has haunted us throughout our exploration of population, urbanization, and the environment. How does Malthus stand the test of time?

Population growth is no longer viewed as an unequivocal benefit to development because it is no longer favorable to economic production. The industrial revolution in the West commenced over a long period of time and was able to economically absorb a growing population. Population growth was apace with food production and the demand for workers. By comparison, the contemporary developing world is industrializing so rapidly that, as we saw, agricultural production and the environment in which it is produced are at risk. The inability of the planet to feed itself, Malthus would say, is just around the corner. He would also view the unmet need hypothesis as an indication that people cannot control their sexual passions. In later editions of his essay he did suggest that altering marriage patterns (positive checks) affect the fertility rate. Overall, however, for Malthus population is destined to increase until checked by famine.

What Malthus failed to recognize is the monumental role of social processes in explaining both population growth and food production. From a sociological view, Malthus was wrong. Despite unmet needs for contraception, poor couples are not unregulated in their sexual passions. Spacing births by breast feeding may not be the most reliable birth-control

mechanism, but it has been used by couples for centuries (UNICEF, 1991). The presumed population pressure of the potato famine in Ireland in the 1800s played a less important role than the colonial status of Ireland that required export of potatoes to England (Ross, 1986).

Malthus also did not predict the green revolution. Technology linked with social and economic development has transformed the productive potential of many nations and relaxed some constraints imposed by the physical environment (Clayton & Radcliffe, 1996:76). It is often overlooked that farmers in drought areas have evolved sophisticated strategies to cope with environmental risks. In Mali, a land tenure system allows farmers reciprocal access to resources both between and within ecosystems in times of environmental stress when their own systems are not productive enough (Moorehead, 1992). Sociology takes exception to Malthus's predictions. The discipline emphasizes the flexibility of culture and the enormous variability of human inventiveness. In the common struggle for the survival of humanity, population growth is expected to stabilize. This goal should be accomplished in conjunction with environmentally acceptable approaches to sustainable development.

SUMMARY

1. Demography is the scientific study of the size, distribution, and composition of population over time. To account for changes in population, demographers study the fertility rate—the annual number of births to women of childbearing age—as well as birth, death, and migration rates, among others.

2. In Europe and North America, the Industrial Revolution caused a profound drop in fertility and mortality rates and a corresponding increase in life expectancy, referred to as the demographic transition. The demographic transition in the developing world today is slower since fertility rates remain high but mortality rates have fallen.

3. In his famous essay on population, Thomas Malthus in 1789 predicted that population growth would eventually outstrip agricultural production, causing widespread famine and death. Malthus was pessimistic about people's ability to change their reproductive behavior in response to diminishing resources.

4. Émile Durkheim saw population growth as a stimulus for industrial development, in turn increasing the division of labor and the specialization that goes with it. Durkheim stressed human

resourcefulness and adaptability to increased population.

5. Karl Marx stressed suggested that population growth also could aid progress but that the unequal distribution of resources and food under capitalism is the cause for human misery. Contemporary conflict theorists emphasize the maldistribution of resources and the economic dependency of poor nations on rich nations.

6. Urbanization is the process of city population growth. About half the world's population lives in urban areas. While the developing world is primarily rural, cites in Asia, Africa, and Latin America are the globe's fastest growing, due to migration from impoverished rural areas. Globally, urban centers of population growth and economic activity are increasingly interconnected.

7. The United States is 80 percent urban and metropolitan areas are expanding until they overlap, forming a megalopolis. But the most important population trend in the United States in the last half century is suburbanization. Suburbs are increasingly diverse in both class and race. Suburbs have political autonomy and may control

their own services, such as fire and police protection, but they are not independent from the core city they grew around.

8. The earliest sociological explanation for city growth was urban ecology—the relationship between population and physical space. Ecological models could not keep pace with urban trends such as decentralization and suburbanization. This led to the new urban sociology, focusing on the political economy (conflict theory) and urban symbolism (symbolic interactionism) to explain urban patterns.

9. According to Louis Wirth and Robert Redfield, compared to intimate rural communities, cities tend to foster impersonal and distant social relations. In functionalist terms, though city dwellers seek a sense of community in formal and voluntary associations, their urban residence puts them at risk for normlessness and alienation. Job loss and economic problems may cause breakdowns in the social fabric of cities, but residents of many neighborhoods maintain a strong sense of community.

10. Though industrialization benefits people economically, it has also degraded the environment globally. Global warming is one outcome. Developing countries, with their limited resources and rapidly growing populations, face a difficult trade-off between economic development and environmental protection. The green revolution created more food through technology but the technology also damaged the environment.

11. Sustainable development accounts for the interdependence of population, urbanization, and the environment—the goal is continuing economic development that also protects the environment.

12. In the United States, half the urban population now lives in suburbs. The trend is threatening the viability of cities through loss of jobs and taxes, undermining housing and education in the process. Urban renewal focus on gentrification to attract middle class residents and upgrading homes in low-rent areas.

13. Improving the status of women is the single most effective way to slow global population growth. Better educated women and a couple's access to culturally acceptable forms of family planning and contraception are associated with smaller families.

14. From a sociological viewpoint, Malthus was incorrect because he did not account for the major role of social processes in explaining population growth and food production.

KEY TERMS

census   538
Consolidated Metropolitan
   Statistical Area
   (CMSA)   548
crude birthrate   538
demographic transition   539
demography   538
fertility rate   538

gentrification   558
global cities   545
global warming   553
green revolution   555
megalopolis   547
metropolitan area   547
Metropolitan Statistical Area
   (MSA)   547

migration rate   538
population pyramid   539
suburbs   547
sustainable development   556
urban   543
urban ecology   549
urbanization   543
Zero Population Growth
   (ZPG)   540

CRITICAL THINKING QUESTIONS

1. Demonstrate how the idea of interdependence shapes population, urbanization, and the environment. What role does technology play in each of these areas?

2. How do functionalism and conflict theory explain the trend that the poor are migrating to the cities of the developing world but the middle class and affluent are migrating out of cities to the suburbs of the developed world?

3. How can the process of sustainable global development work to the benefit of the poor, who are often displaced by the process?

4. From a symbolic interactionist view, what culturally appropriate methods can be suggested for couples' "unmet need" for contraception?

FORMAL ORGANIZATIONS AND THE SOCIOLOGY OF WORK

Voices from the Workplace

Studs Terkel is a journalist who has made a career out of interviewing ordinary people about sociologically oriented topics. In one of his best-known books, *Working*, Terkel presents a fascinating variety of first-hand observations about the world of work. Here are excerpts from three of his interviews:

Phil Stallings, spot welder on the Ford Assembly line:

I stand in one spot, about [a] two or three foot area, all night. The only time a person stops is when the line stops. We do about 32 jobs per car, per unit. 48 units an hour, 8 hours a day. 32 times 48 times 8. Figure it out. That's how many times I push that button . . . It doesn't stop. It just goes and goes and goes. I bet there's men who have lived and died out there, never seen the end of that line. (Terkel, 1985: 221-222)

Sharon Atkins, receptionist for a large business:

You're just there to filter people and filter telephone calls. You're there just to handle equipment. You're treated like a piece of equipment, like the telephone. You come in at nine, you open the door, you look at the piece of machinery, you plug in the headpiece. That's how my day begins. You tremble when you hear the first ring. After that, it's sort of downhill. (Terkel, 1985: 57-58)

Ray Wax, stockbroker:

It's up at 6:30. I read the *New York Times* and the *Wall Street Journal* before eight. I read the Dow Jones ticker tape between 8 and 10. At 3:30, when the market closes, I work until 4:30 or 5. I put in a great deal of technical work. I listen to news reports avidly. I try to determine what's happening. I'm totally immersed in what I'm doing. (Terkel, 1985: 441)

The Dilbert Principle

Sociologists sometimes investigate social issues by studying popular culture—films, television shows, music, and even comic strips. The strip that best captures the feel of the present era may well be "Dilbert" (Scott Adams, 1996; Levy, 1996). Created by Scott Adams, a former middle manager at Pacific Bell, "Dilbert" is currently distributed to about 1,100 newspapers, "Dilbert" books often top the bestseller lists, a weekly "Dilbert" television program debuted early in 1999, and the Dilbert Zone website receives 1.5 million hits every day.

The comic strip is a nightmarish parody of the bureaucratic work environment. Dilbert and his fellow employees toil away at meaningless tasks, isolated from each other by the walls of their tiny cubicles, supervised by a totally incompetent boss and required to attend endless meetings that serve no identifiable purpose. Their ability to accomplish anything at work is constantly subverted by clueless management consultants, inane mission statements, absurd management fads, and the ever-present threat of downsizing. The underlying premise of this insane universe is the Dilbert Principle: ". . . the most ineffective workers are systematically moved to the place where they can do the least damage: management." (Adams, 1996: 14)

Source: DILBERT reprinted by permission of United Features Syndicate, Inc.

This chapter examines two interrelated topics that together help to explain the work experiences of Phil Stallings, Sharon Atkins, Ray Wax, and Dilbert. First, we will consider the growth and character of formal organizations, which have come to dominate not only work but also many other spheres of public life, including education, medicine, politics, and religion. Then we will look at the workplace with a particular emphasis on how bureaucratic organizations have transformed the human experience of work in industrial and postindustrial societies.

FORMAL ORGANIZATIONS AND BUREAUCRACIES

A **formal organization** is a special type of secondary group (see Chapter 4) designed to allow a relatively large number of people to accomplish complex goals (Haas & Drabek, 1973; Hall, 1996). Formal organizations are characterized by clearly stated operating principles, special mechanisms to coordinate the activities of their members, clear lines of authority and communication, identifiable leaders, and unambiguous boundaries. Examples of formal organizations abound in today's world: your college or university, the federal government, Microsoft, CBS.

The study of formal organizations is important because there are so many of them and because they have become very large—the federal government directly employs over 5 million people. Indeed, we live in an age of formal organizations (Perrow, 1991; Volti, 1995). They shape how we think and how we act toward each other in an increasingly wide variety of contexts (Ritzer, 1996). If we wish to influence others, we do so more and more by joining formal organizations.

Types of Formal Organizations

Formal organizations may be classified according to the means they use to encourage their members to conform to their role expectations. An organization may force obedience, it may reward it, or it may promote conformity by engaging its members' moral commitment (Etzioni, 1975). In real life the three types are often mixed, but it is instructive to consider each separately.

A *coercive organization*—a prison, for example—secures obedience through force and the threat of punishment. Most total institutions (see Chapter 5), such as mental hospitals, are largely coercive. When there is a military draft, the army is, in part, a coercive organization. But force is a relatively ineffective strategy because a great deal of time and energy must be devoted to social control over unwilling participants.

Businesses and other *utilitarian organizations* reward their employees with money and other valued goods and privileges. This is generally a less costly way to obtain compliance. Today's military heavily relies on this approach. It offers new recruits incentives such as job training and money for a college education. Utilitarian organizations are more efficient than coercive ones, but the minute the money runs out, compliance becomes problematic.

A third strategy maximizes involvement with virtually no social control costs. *Voluntary associations* use

INTERNET CONNECTIONS

You'll find a month of Dilbert comic strips at http://umweb1.unitedmedia.com/comics/dilbert/archive/. Which one best applies to your school?

normative power—that is, they secure almost limitless obedience by pursuing goals to which their members are personally committed. Examples include the American Association of Retired Persons, the Presbyterian Church, the United Auto Workers, the Republican Party, the Sierra Club, self-help groups like Alcoholics Anonymous (Wuthnow, 1994), and in patriotic times, the military.

The United States has long been characterized by a very high level of membership in voluntary associations. There are perhaps 200,000 such groups in the United States today (Krysan & D'Antonio, 1992). A sizable majority of citizens participate in at least one voluntary association, and about 25 percent belong to three or more (Curtis et al., 1992). In part, this extensive associational involvement reflects the long-term historical decline in the size and strength of the family in modern urban societies (see Chapter 15). Many functions of extended families—such as providing sociability, mutual aid, and some forms of advanced socialization—are now increasingly sought in voluntary associations instead.

Class, Gender, and Voluntary Associations. What sort of people are most likely to participate in voluntary associations? One striking finding involves class: People from higher socioeconomic backgrounds are considerably more likely to hold multiple organizational memberships (Gilbert & Kahl, 1993). These people have both the money and the time to be joiners. In turn, belonging to clubs and other such groups constitutes an important element of their cultural capital. Working-class people often are involved in unions, churches, and sports-related organizations, but their overall level of participation tends to be relatively lower.

Both men and women participate actively in voluntary associations. About half of all such groups are more or less all female, while 20 percent are all male (Odendahl, 1990). Women's associations have been extremely important in U.S. history—consider, for example, the suffrage and abolitionist movements. Unfortunately, however, the contributions of predominantly female voluntary associations have historically been devalued due to widespread sexism.

Bureaucracy

Most contemporary formal organizations take the form of **bureaucracies.** A bureaucracy is an organization designed to accomplish routine tasks by large numbers of people as efficiently as possible. This emphasis on efficiency runs counter to most people's understanding of the nature of bureaucracy, but if bureaucracies were not reasonably efficient, they

would not have come to dominate the modern world as they have.

Bureaucracies are not new; as early as 4000 B.C.E., governments in China, Egypt, and Mesopotamia were organized along bureaucratic lines (Wallace, 1983). However, before the industrial revolution few organizations could have been accurately described as bureaucracies, whereas over the past two centuries bureaucratic structures have expanded tremendously and out-competed all other types of organizations (Volti, 1995).

Max Weber analyzed bureaucratic organization as part of his effort to understand the origins of modern society (Weber, 1947) (see Chapter 24). His analysis of bureaucracy takes the form of an **ideal type,** a description that emphasizes, and even exaggerates, a phenomenon's most distinctive or characteristic qualities. Ideal type models are meant to identify the core or essence of a phenomenon; they are not necessarily entirely accurate descriptions of empirical reality (Udy, 1959; Hall, 1963; Blau & Meyer, 1987). Thus, the following six points drawn from Weber describe what a bureaucracy is supposed to be like, although real-life organizations may be more or less bureaucratic, depending on how closely they resemble the model.

- *An extensive division of labor.* Each participant in the organization is expected to accomplish a relatively narrow, specialized set of tasks and bureaucratic roles fit together in order to effectively promote the achievement of the organization's goals. For example, each employee of a university has a different specialized task to perform, from the academic dean, to the chairperson of the sociology department, to the reference librarian, to a worker in the snack bar.
- *Explicit written rules and regulations.* If there is ever any question about an individual's role or responsibilities, all he or she has to do is look it up. Thus, faculty, staff, and students are all given handbooks that explain the rules by which their university operates.
- *Written records.* A written record not only makes it possible to prove that the rules have been followed, but it also provides a precedent in case a similar issue arises in the future.
- *A hierarchy of authority.* Bureaucratic statuses are ranked, and everyone in the organization has both a boss and subordinates, except for those at the top and at the extreme bottom. Power is vested in the bureaucratic role itself (Weber called it an *office*), not in the person currently playing the role.
- *Hiring and promotion on the basis of objective qualifications.* Like all bureaucracies, universities are

Careers in the Twenty-First Century

As the twenty-first century dawns, the job prospects for college graduates look bright. Many students enjoy the luxury of choosing among several good job offers months before commencement day. But tomorrow's career paths may be quite different from those experienced by previous generations.

Between the 1960s and the early 1990s, the route to success was relatively straightforward. Ambitious men—and increasingly, women—took positions as executive trainees at major corporations, worked hard, made the right connections, gradually moved into middle or upper management, and, ideally, retired with comfortable pensions. No longer. In 1997 alone, U.S. corporations laid off 103,000 employees. Jobs in sales and services multiplied, while positions in management declined. Most new jobs are with small companies (499 employees or less), not large corporations.

What can new graduates expect? Here is how some members of the class of 1997 started out (Meredith, 1997). William D. Lucy (Missouri State University, marketing major) turned down two other offers to accept a job at Enterprise Rent-a-Car, where his duties include working behind the counter, picking up customers at their homes and offices, and even washing cars—hardly tasks that require a college degree. Why did he choose Enterprise? Because of the company's entrepreneurial spirit. The chief executive describes Enterprise as "a confederation of small businesses" (Meredith, 1997, p. 10). All new hires start at the bottom for salaries of $22,000 to $30,000. If they demonstrate responsibility and initiative, they can expect promotions within their first year or two, with raises tied to their branch's performance.

Rachel D. Gunderson (University of Wisconsin, journalism major) chose a job as a merchandise analyst at the Target discount-store chain. Two months into the job, she is in charge of potting soil. More importantly, she is learning how to analyze flow charts, place electronic orders, and keep Target's 750 stores supplied with twenty different types of dirt. Whatever the product, successful trainees can expect to become full-fledged buyers, at salaries ranging from $40,000 to $70,000, in four to five years.

Malane Rogers (University of Arkansas, industrial engineering) works for Andersen Consulting, a giant temporary firm offering much higher starting salaries ($31,000 to $45,000) and more challenging work than the old secretarial/clerical "temp" agencies. Ms Rogers' current assignment is to find data on Texas Instruments' huge mainframe computers and produce easy-to-read reports for company executives. Many Fortune 500 corporations depend on Andersen to fill the gaps created when they lay off full-time employees.

More than likely, today's college graduates will change jobs at least once during their twenties, joining the ranks of what *Newsweek* magazine called the "New Nomads" (McGinn & McCormick, 1999). Company loyalty is no longer a prerequisite for promotions and raises; on the contrary, mass layoffs in the 1990s showed that "steady jobs" have become the exception, not the rule. New jobs (such as webmaster, wireless engineer, and desktop publisher) appear almost every year, and employers are competing for workers with technological, sales, and human or public relations experience. Today's workers have more choices, and hence more independence, than past generations enjoyed. Increasingly, U.S. workers are using their current jobs to develop expertise they can transfer from one company or one industry to another, in some cases job-hopping around the world. In one survey, more than one in four workers had been at their current job less than twelve months.

The number of self-employed free agents, working as everything from personal trainer to urban planner, has also grown—in part because it costs a company less to hire outside contractors for specific projects than to take on full-time employees; in part because workers prefer the freedom and flexibility of being their own bosses. Even within companies, employees are redesigning their jobs and launching their own ventures under the corporate umbrella. For example, after working at several different jobs, Neil Teplica settled down in real estate and became one of his company's most valued employees. At age 35, Teplica requested (and was granted) flex time, began traveling to remote places, and started an offbeat travel website called "What's Going On." The following year, he and his flex-time partner began negotiating a deal with America OnLine (Marin & Gegax, 1997:74).

One possible scenario is that twenty-first century workers will spend their twenties as "nomads," become dedicated company men and women in their thirties, and choose self-employment in their forties and fifties, when most people's skills peak. This new flexibility may exact a cost, however. In addition to becoming an expert in a particular area, tomorrow's worker will also need to develop skills in advertising (to sell him- or herself to different employers), finance (to arrange start-up costs for a new venture and manage his or her own retirement plan), and technology (to keep up to date). Self-confidence, self-reliance, and a high tolerance for ambiguity and risk will be important.

1. On the whole, do you regard the changes discussed in this article as positive or negative? Explain your view.
2. Do you think the changing character of the U.S. workplace will make it easier or harder for people to combine work with family involvement?

Sources: Marin & Gegax, 1997; Meredith, 1997; McGinn & McCormick, 1999.

expected to be *meritocracies*, hiring and promoting solely on the basis of specialized skills and knowledge. For example, a university hires faculty members only if they have the appropriate degrees and a good record of teaching and research.

- *Impartial, universalistic treatment.* Bias and favoritism are to be avoided. Every student, administrator, and faculty member is to be treated like everyone else occupying a similar position. The desire not to violate this principle explains why many organizations have anti-nepotism rules, which prohibit hiring close relatives of current employees. It also explains why professors may refuse to allow their children to enroll in their classes.

The final two principles of Weber's ideal type model are sometimes violated in the real world. This does not mean the model is inaccurate, but rather that these real-life organizations are less than fully bureaucratic. It also means that they are more likely to fail over the long run as they compete with organizations that reflect the model more precisely.

All of these characteristics ultimately serve a single purpose: to make the organization as efficient—or, in Weber's terms, as rational—as possible. By **rationality**, Weber means consciously using the most effective means to pursue a chosen end. He believed the modern world was undergoing a continual process of **rationalization**, in which efficiency was becoming more and more characteristic of all spheres of life. Thus, for example, a relentlessly rational bureaucracy like Blockbuster is driving out less efficient video stores that hire friends of the owners despite the fact that they are not very good workers or that stock mostly films the owners like but that might not be rented very often.

Weber was not optimistic about the long-term consequences of rationalization. Efficiency is important, but so is spontaneity. Highly rationalized social systems can be oppressive and dehumanizing. Weber believed that we were at risk of being trapped in an "iron cage" of bureaucratic rationality. As he put it, "It is horrible to think that the world would one day be filled with nothing but these little cogs, little men clinging to little jobs and striving for better ones" (Bendix, 1962). Highly rationalized social systems stamp out the personal, traditional, emotional, whimsical aspects of life; in Weber's terms, they "disenchant" the world. But, from within the iron cage, it is hard to develop a convincing argument that we should spend more time smelling the roses and less time fixated on the bottom line. These issues will be discussed further in Chapter 24.

Informal Life Within the Bureaucracy. The oppressive quality of bureaucratic rationality helps explain why all real-life organizations are characterized by an informal structure as well as a formal one. Informal relationships inevitably grow up between the particular people who occupy bureaucratic statuses (Perrow, 1986). Weber's model does not take into account "bureaucracy's other face" (Page, 1946), but he was certainly aware of its existence (Blau & Meyer, 1987).

A number of symbolic interactionist studies of bureaucratic functioning have demonstrated the importance of *informal structure*. Whether we research the military (Little, 1970), the IRS (Blau, 1963), medicine (Strauss et al., 1985), or retail sales (Benson, 1986), we invariably discover that informal norms emerge among the participants. These norms complement, modify, and in some cases oppose the organization's official guidelines. In other words, a bureaucracy's formal structure matters, but so do the people who staff it (Blumer, 1969a).

Sometimes the informal structure promotes the accomplishment of the organization's goals. If the formal guidelines are too rigid or do not fit the present circumstances, workers may develop new rules that cut through the red tape (Scott, 1981). Informal communication networks—grapevines—disseminate information through the organization more rapidly and broadly than routine channels. And bonding through informal interaction with co-workers improves worker morale, which can, in turn, increase productivity (Barnard, 1938; Perrow, 1986).

On the other hand, informal norms may arise that hinder an organization's ability to achieve its goals. This most often occurs among lower-ranking participants in large, rigid industrial bureaucracies. For example, researchers investigating a Western Electric plant near Chicago found that workers informally rejected the production quotas set by management, replaced them with their own lower quotas, and sarcastically labeled workers who strove to meet management's norms as "speed kings" or "rate busters." People who reported slacking fellow workers to the bosses were called "squealers" and ostracized (Roethlisberger & Dickson, 1939).

From a functionalist perspective, such informal norms reduce the organization's productivity. The conflict perspective, however, sees informal structure as a way workers attempt to protect themselves from victimization by their employers (Burawoy, 1980).

The main point is that to understand a bureaucracy we must consider both its formal and informal structure. The actual character of an organization is always a sort of *negotiated order*: The formal structure is modified through compromises with the preferences of the people staffing it (Strauss et al., 1964).

Dysfunctions of Bureaucracy. Bureaucracies accomplish certain kinds of tasks extremely well,

The logic of bureaucracy dictates that authority should be distributed in a hierarchical fashion with a small number of people at the top holding most of the power. From the interactionist perspective, the authority of these individuals is symbolized and validated by "perks" such as large private offices.

especially when the job is fairly simple and routine or when it is only rarely necessary to deviate from standard procedures. But the fact that bureaucracies are highly rational and efficient does not make them equally suitable for all purposes, nor does it mean that they do not generate certain problems. In fact, bureaucracies are prone to a number of major dysfunctions unless precautions are taken against them.

1. *Communication Problems.* Communication generally flows readily down the bureaucratic hierarchy, but underlings may hesitate to report a problem to their superiors, especially if it makes them look bad or will require them to do extra work. As a result, unless special steps (like suggestion boxes) are taken to encourage lower-level participants to communicate freely, decisions may be made on the basis of faulty information with negative consequences for bureaucratic functioning (Blau & Meyer, 1987).

2. *Trained Incapacity.* The elaborate division of labor in a bureaucracy can lead to a kind of tunnel vision that keeps individuals from responding effectively to new situations. When a new problem arises, bureaucrats sometimes keep their heads down and avoid making adaptive decisions. "It's not my responsibility," they cry. Thorstein Veblen (1933) referred to this problem as **trained incapacity.**

Robert Merton (1968) put the problem slightly differently: In some cases, people who work in large formal organizations develop a general mind-set, called the *bureaucratic personality*, that makes them rigid and inflexible. This image of the blinkered bureaucrat has been popular for decades. Most recent research, however, tends to refute Merton's claim. Al-

though bureaucrats may well display trained incapacity *in their official roles*, as individuals they have often been found to be creative, flexible and adaptive, and inclined to tolerate nonconformity (Kohn, 1978; Foster, 1990).

3. *Bureaucratic Ritualism.* In a closely related dysfunction, bureaucrats can become so committed to obeying the official guidelines that the rules, in effect, become the organization's ends, even when such behavior ultimately blocks attainment of the group's real goals. This is the familiar problem of "red tape" or **bureaucratic ritualism** (Merton, 1968). In other words, the operation was a success—we followed the prescribed procedures—but the patient died (Coleman, 1990). It is possible to avoid bureaucratic ritualism, but it requires that someone high up in the hierarchy regularly reviews whether the rules are relevant and determines if they are being applied appropriately.

4. *Goal Displacement.* Another way bureaucracies can lose sight of their original goals is through **goal displacement:** Under some circumstances, an organization may devote most of its attention to survival rather than to achieving its ends. As Weber (1978) noted, bureaucracies are very hard to destroy.

Goal displacement is likely to occur when the public strongly opposes a bureaucracy. For example, small socialist parties in the United States were forced to focus on survival to the exclusion of other activities during the conservative 1980s.

Goal displacement can also occur when the organization succeeds in achieving its main objective. When this happens, it usually selects a new goal, a process called *goal succession*. The classic example is

In the first half of the twentieth century, most American grocery stores were small, locally owned operations offering only a limited variety of goods. Stores like this were unable to compete with modern, bureaucratically structured chain supermarkets featuring lower prices and a much wider choice of goods.

the March of Dimes, which was established to raise money for polio research. But when the Salk vaccine was developed and polio was essentially eradicated in the late 1950s, the organization did not simply fold its tents and fade away (Sills, 1957). Too many people derived their livelihood, status, and identity from membership in it (see Selznick, 1957), so a new goal was chosen—the battle against birth defects. Not surprisingly, this objective is not likely to be achieved in the near future!

5. *Parkinson's Law.* This dysfunction and the next one, like the "Dilbert Principle," were originally proposed in jest, but in fact they accurately reflect some underlying realities of organizational life. **Parkinson's Law** states that work in a bureaucracy expands to fill the time available for its completion (Parkinson, 1962). Because employees know that they must look busy in order to keep their jobs, they create busy work and may even hire assistants—who must, in turn, be supervised—to complete the busy work. The result is an overgrown, bloated bureaucracy that could accomplish its goals with far fewer employees.

6. *The Peter Principle.* Bureaucrats who do entry-level jobs well are normally rewarded by being promoted up the hierarchy, often into administrative positions (Peter & Hull, 1969). Thus, teachers become principals and floor nurses become head nurses. If they continue to do well in their new jobs, they are promoted again. But the skills that ensure success at one level do not necessarily guarantee good performance in higher-level jobs. Sooner or later most people find themselves in positions in which they do not succeed. This is the **Peter Principle**—that bureaucrats are promoted until they reach their "level of incompetence."

Bureaucracies hesitate to fire or demote dedicated, long-term employees, so the workers tend to stay at this level, creating a logjam of deadwood toward the top of the hierarchy. Meanwhile, their work is being done by subordinates who have not yet reached their own level of incompetence or who lack the formal credentials for advancement. One solution to the Peter Principle is to create well-paid and prestigious upper-level positions (like "master teachers") that require the same skills that workers have demonstrated in lower-level roles.

7. *Oligarchy.* Finally, there is substantial evidence that, even if their members are personally committed to running the organization democratically, bureaucracies often succumb to what political scientist Robert Michels (1876–1936) called the **iron law of oligarchy:** They fall under the control of a small number of top leaders (Michels, 1962). In fact, Michels went so far as to say that "who says organization says oligarchy."

Why does this occur? It is inefficient for organizations to spread power among too many people, especially if decisions must be made quickly, so a group of leaders always emerges. Even if these people try to avoid becoming an elite, through their leadership experience they inevitably acquire skills and knowledge not available to the rank and file.

Furthermore, most members are too busy to get involved in the daily life of the organization, so they willingly leave most of the decisions to the emerging leadership. Eventually these leaders start benefiting from their position of power, and they become a largely unaccountable oligarchy (Tolson, 1995).

Michels thought that the rise of a leadership elite was inevitable, and considerable research shows that, indeed, it is very common (Lipset et al., 1956; Fox & Arquitt, 1985; Cnaan, 1991). However, the histories of some modern groups, especially those associated with the feminist movement, demonstrate that

The impersonal treatment provided by bureaucracies such as this unemployment security office reduces the possibility of bias but it often makes clients feel as if they are being stifled by the "red tape" of bureaucratic ritualism.

oligarchy can be avoided, or at least minimized. Leadership positions must be rotated regularly and power deliberately dispersed across the bureaucracy (Olsen, 1978; Staggenborg, 1988; Fisher, 1994). The downside is that such organizations have difficulty making decisions quickly.

Refining Weber's Model

As the preceding discussion makes clear, bureaucracies have their problems. Ever since the onset of the industrial era, people have tried to modify Weber's model in order to respond to its limitations. We will review five such efforts in the chronological order in which they arose.

Scientific Management. Scientific management was an early effort to improve bureaucratic function-

INTERNET ——— CONNECTIONS

The former Soviet Union was one of the world's most bureaucratic nations, its workings directed by ubiquitous Communist Party officials. Visit http://library-newark.rutgers.edu/pubadmin/russianposters/ for an exhibit called "Red Tape from Red Square," featuring Russian cartoons and posters satirizing the ever-present bureaucracy. Could these illustrations apply as well to U.S. society?

ing on the factory floor by accentuating some of the defining characteristics of Weber's model. Initially developed by Frederick Winslow Taylor (1856–1915), and hence sometimes called Taylorism, scientific management relied heavily on time-and-motion studies, which broke down the physical process of working on the assembly line into its most minute details and then restructured the process in order to maximize efficiency (Miller & Form, 1964).

Taylorism essentially viewed the industrial worker as little more than a machine. Employees, it was assumed, could not think for themselves; they needed to be told exactly how to do their jobs. Work was thus *deskilled*. In addition, scientific management assumed that laborers were motivated strictly by economics, so they had to be closely supervised and paid on a piecework basis, earning a set sum for each item they turned out. Taylorism took no notice at all of the informal relationships that developed between workers.

Scientific management did increase productivity, and it made it easier to replace workers—outcomes that pleased management. But it also rendered employees powerless and widened the gap between labor and management (Zuboff, 1988; Westrum, 1991). Most workers hated Taylorism (Braverman, 1974). A new management strategy that was more in touch with workers' human needs emerged early in the twentieth century (Perrow, 1986).

The Human Relations Approach. By the 1920s, industrial sociologists were becoming aware of the importance of the informal norms that develop on the factory floor (Mayo, 1933). They began to advocate a

Employee picnics—like this one at IBM—are an important component of the human relations approach to bureaucratic management. Company-sponsored social events bring workers together and strengthen their interpersonal bonds. However, critics point out that the human relations school fails to empower workers in their ongoing struggle with management over salaries and working conditions.

new approach to management designed to promote positive human relations between workers. This perspective was grounded in the assumption that if the human needs of bureaucratic employees were met, morale would increase, workers would be more likely to accept the company's goals as their own, and productivity would go up (Argyris, 1960; Auster, 1996). Thus, the human relations approach was characterized, first, by marginally closer and more supportive relationships between bosses and workers and, second, by deliberate efforts to promote primary interaction and teamwork among workers through mechanisms such as company sports leagues.

This philosophy seemed to represent a considerable advance over Taylorism; at least workers were being treated like people, not machines. But conflict theorists were quick to point out that the human relations approach could be interpreted as little more than manipulative window dressing. Workers were still largely powerless in their relationship with the bosses; the new style partially obscured—but did not change—this reality (Burris, 1989). Like scientific management, the human relations approach is a low-trust system. Not until the later 1960s did a high-trust system emerge that actually empowered the workers.

Collectives.   The collective is not a modification of Weber's model so much as a repudiation of it. Instead of an elaborate division of labor, collective workers are nonspecialized. Instead of a top-down hierarchy, collectives feature participatory democracy; they may have spokespersons, but there are no bosses. Human relations within the collective are, ideally, warm and personal. There are few written rules. Objective merit

is not completely ignored, but it is only one of several factors taken into account in personnel decisions (Rothschild & Whitt, 1986).

Collective work organizations have existed in the United States since the early nineteenth century, especially in the form of communes. But the model gained popularity in the 1960s when thousands of "alternative institutions"—food co-ops, free medical and legal clinics, alternative schools—were founded, some of which endure to this day.

Collective organizations sacrifice the efficiency and profitability of the traditional bureaucracy in order to escape the dehumanization of the "iron cage." They are enormously satisfying places to work, although the amount of time necessary to reach fully democratic decisions can be frustrating. But they tend to be small—with an average of about six workers—and generally cannot compete effectively with bureaucracies. Accordingly, the collective was never considered as a serious model for major U.S. formal organizations. However, some of its qualities are incorporated in two refinements of bureaucracy—the Japanese and the humanized models—that have become popular over the past three decades. These two models assume that workers, who are typically much better educated today than they were in the days of Taylor, are capable of making good decisions and are happier and more productive when they are allowed to do so. We turn now to these two new approaches.

The Japanese Model.   Japan's dramatic rise as a world economic leader in the 1970s led many U.S. organizational theorists to consider adopting some of the distinctive features of Japanese bureaucracies

Most modern approaches to workplace management stress the importance of constructing small, cohesive, temporary teams of workers who bring a variety of different skills to bear on the project at hand.

(Cole, 1989; Lincoln & Kalleberg, 1990; Florida & Kenney, 1991). In particular, five aspects of Japanese corporate life attracted attention (Vogel, 1979; Ouchi, 1982; Lindsey, 1998):

Collective Hiring and Promotion. In the classic model, Japanese firms hire a group of management trainees and promote them on the basis of seniority; individual merit, except in extreme cases, only becomes relevant later in one's career. This practice promotes a team orientation.

Holistic Training. Instead of being narrowly specialized, Japanese managers are moved from department to department during their careers. In this way, they develop a general understanding of how the organization as a whole functions (Sengoku, 1985).

Decentralized Decision Making. Although much less democratic than the collective model, Japanese firms encourage input from all their workers. This is meant to increase morale and commitment to the organization (White & Trevor, 1982).

Lifetime Employment. Japanese managers rarely look to advance their careers by moving from one company to another, as is standard in this country (Samuels, 1991). Promotion is generally from within, and downsizing—at least until recently—was rare: Top executives sometimes took pay cuts rather than fire their employees (Taira & Levine, 1996).

Total Involvement. In order to build employee loyalty, Japanese firms are paternalistically involved in their workers' lives. Businesses sponsor collective recreational activities and encourage on-the-job rituals such as mass calisthenics, the singing of company songs, and the wearing of company uniforms. Workers and managers are encouraged to think of each other as part of a huge extended family (Dore, 1990). Naturally, this tends to minimize "we/they" thinking and support for unions.

Can the United States and other Western nations adopt this model of bureaucracy? Probably not wholesale (Florida & Kenney, 1991). The United States is a much more individualistic society than Japan; many elements of the Japanese model strike us as overly constraining. Company songs and volleyball teams have little appeal here. Management and union leaders are often unwilling to give up even a little of their power (Grenier, 1988), while many workers think being involved in decision making will have no effect other than increasing their workload.

U.S. enthusiasm for the Japanese model has also waned as the health of Japanese economy has begun to falter (Besser, 1993). Complaints have been raised by workers that, despite the façade of democracy, upper management still makes all the major decisions. On the other hand, many executives feel that collective promotion by seniority rather than individual promotion by merit is wasteful. Furthermore, with Japanese labor costs rising and productivity falling below the U.S. rate, some Japanese managers are even questioning their basic model. Layoffs are up, fewer workers are being offered lifetime tenure, and merit pay is becoming more frequent (Hamada, 1992).

The Flexible and Humane Bureaucracy. Over the past several decades, many observers have concluded that the traditional model of bureaucracy is inappropriate for the modern workplace. It was designed to organize minimally motivated and often ill-educated workers to produce highly standardized material goods. But today most employees are intelligent, highly skilled workers who deal with people rather than things and do work that requires constant case-by-case adjustment. In other words, a model of formal organization that worked well for the Model T assembly line is inappropriate for a computer research-and-development company in California's Silicon Valley (Vaill, 1989; Reich, 1991; Peters, 1992). Something new is needed.

There are many different approaches to the problem. Some talk about humanizing bureaucracy (Kanter, 1977, 1983), self-managed work teams (Yeatts, 1991), "ad-hocracies" (Bennis & Slater, 1968), flexible organizations, or the horizontal model (Byrne, 1993). Most of these images of twenty-first century organizations share certain common themes:

Temporary Work Teams. Workers do not stay permanently in a single organizational structure.

Instead, a diverse group of specialists is assigned to work together for a while and complete a certain task. Then the team is dissolved and its members are reassigned to other groups working on other projects. Within the team, interaction is intense and often resembles that in a primary group more than that in a secondary one.

Collective Responsibility.   Although the performance of individuals is assessed, the primary emphasis is placed on the effectiveness of the team.

Minimal Hierarchy.   Highly skilled workers neither need to be nor enjoy being ordered around—one of the core themes of "Dilbert." A humanized bureaucracy emphasizes colleagueship and resembles a network more than a pyramid. Decision making within the work team is, to a considerable extent, democratic.

Fewer Rules.   It is assumed that workers are able to cope with many situations on their own, so there is less need for detailed guidelines.

Social Inclusiveness.   The U.S. labor force is becoming increasingly diverse. Modern organizations go out of their way to encourage full participation by women and minorities. Ability is valued over ascription.

More Opportunities for Advancement.   Humanized organizations try to develop the abilities of all their members. Dead-end jobs are minimized, and training programs to enhance workers' skills are emphasized.

All these factors build loyalty to the work team and, by extension, to the employer. Absenteeism declines. Research shows that humanized and flexible organizations are, as a rule, happier, more productive, and more profitable (Peters & Waterman, 1982; Kanter, 1983; Shonk, 1992; Drucker, 1993).

Unfortunately, businesses in the United States often hesitate to accept new organizational models, especially when they substantially empower workers (Baron et al., 1988; Cole, 1989). So not only has adoption of the new model been relatively slow, but employees have also sometimes discovered that work relations in flexible organizations are less egalitarian than they had initially hoped would be the case.

THE CHANGING CHARACTER OF WORK

We turn next to the sociology of work. We will begin by introducing some key terminology and discussing some important changes that have taken place in the workplace in recent decades.

Sectors of the Economy and Labor Markets

Sociologists identify three distinct sectors of the economy of modern societies as well as two different labor markets.

The Three Sectors of the Economy.   Sociologists divide work into three broad categories or sectors. The *primary sector* includes jobs in which material goods are obtained directly from nature, for example farming, mining, and fishing. Manufacturing industries make up the *secondary sector*, and services constitute the *tertiary sector*. The category of service jobs is extremely broad, including such diverse occupations as teachers, physicians, fast food workers, typists, ministers, housekeepers, business executives, police officers, and child care workers.

The federal government has identified roughly 500 distinct occupations and some 21,000 occupational specialties within these three general categories (U.S. Department of Labor, 1995). The distribution of people in these various jobs has changed radically over the past century.

As Figure 22.1 demonstrates, the primary sector has declined sharply (Drucker, 1994). In the early nineteenth century, about 80 percent of all workers worked in primary sector jobs, mainly as farmers. At that time, the typical farmer could feed only about five people. In 1900, about half the labor force was still in the primary sector. Today that figure has declined to less than 3 percent. This change is the result of two principal factors: growing opportunities in other sectors and technological changes that enable each farmer to feed seventy or eighty people. Today the family farm is vanishing rapidly and everywhere being replaced by corporate agribusiness.

Secondary sector manufacturing jobs peaked around midcentury at about 40 percent of the labor force. They have been declining ever since as the United States moves from an industrial to a post-industrial society. Today the secondary sector makes up less than 20 percent of all jobs, a figure that is projected to drop as low as 10 percent by 2020 (Lee, 1990; Rifkin, 1995).

The tertiary sector has expanded rapidly during the twentieth century, accounting for about 30 percent of all jobs in 1900, about half in 1955, and roughly 75 percent today. The United States added 29.4 million service jobs in the 1980s alone, and about 90 percent of all new jobs are now located in that sector (McKenzie, 1989; Crispell, 1990; Plunkert, 1990).

The Two Labor Markets.   Regardless of the sector in which a job is located, it may be further classified as part of either the primary or the secondary labor market. **Primary labor market** jobs are, simply

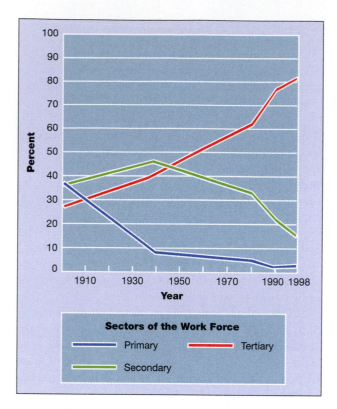

FIGURE 22.1 Three Sectors of the American Work Force, 1900–1998

Source: Statistical Abstract, various years and 1999, Tables 675 & 678.

put, good jobs. They offer at least a living wage, often provide interesting work experiences, may lead to better positions in the future, and provide fringe benefits such as health insurance, paid vacations, and retirement plans (Bailey & Waldinger, 1991). Most primary labor market jobs are white-collar service jobs or unionized, highly skilled blue-collar positions. They are disproportionately held by white males (Coverdill, 1988). About one-third of the service jobs currently being created in the United States are in the primary labor market.

On the other hand, jobs in the **secondary labor market** are bad jobs, jobs that do not offer the advantages of primary labor market jobs. Examples include seasonal farm work, unskilled industrial labor, and service jobs such as janitorial work and jobs in the fast food business. They are primarily filled by women, immigrants, and minorities (Perman & Stevens, 1989). These are the kinds of jobs you are in college to avoid. Fully two-thirds of all new service jobs are in the secondary labor market. These positions are sometimes derisively referred to as "McJobs" because employment at fast food franchises like McDonald's is one of the most rapidly expanding and quintessential types of all secondary labor market jobs.

Change in the Primary Labor Market: Professionalization

One of the most important developments in the primary labor market in recent decades has been a sharp increase in the number of professional jobs (Brint, 1994). In everyday usage, a professional is simply someone who is paid for his or her work—for example, a professional (as opposed to an amateur) athlete. But sociologists use the term differently, defining a **profession** as a prestigious white-collar occupation that displays the following characteristics (Parsons, 1954; Goode, 1960; Ritzer, 1977; Friedson, 1986):

- A rigorous education covering both theory and practice. Thus aspiring doctors must learn anatomy and biochemistry as well as the practical skills needed to heal patients. In addition, professionals are expected to keep up to date with the literature in their field (Leventman, 1981).

- A professional association that controls entry into and expulsion from the field. The American Medical Association and the Bar Association are examples of such groups. Professional associations defend the claim that only one's fellow professionals have enough knowledge to make decisions concerning an individual's right to engage in a given occupation. In other words, a profession follows a *norm of autonomy*. The professional association also usually accredits educational programs in its field and publishes a code of ethics.

- A *norm of authority*, that states that professionals have the right, at least up to a point, to tell their clients what services they need (Hodson & Sullivan, 1995). Customers at a grocery store buy whatever they want; a doctor's patients expect, at least up to a point, to be told what needs to be done to keep them healthy.

- A *norm of altruism*, which states that professionals are at least partly motivated by the desire to do good rather than being exclusively driven by financial considerations (Greenwood, 1962).

In recent decades, as clients have become increasingly empowered, many people have begun to challenge the autonomy and authority of professionals and to doubt their altruistic motivation. But the traditional professions, including medicine, law, academics, and the ministry, have been reasonably successful in defending their status.

Meanwhile, people in a number of other occupations, seeking to increase their prestige and autonomy, have undertaken a process of **professionalization,** which mainly involves increasing in the amount of education needed to enter the field and establishing a professional association (Collins, 1979; Abbott, 1988;

Halpern, 1992). Dentists and certified public accountants have largely completed this process, while social workers, teachers, and nurses are in the midst of it.

Two factors help explain the rather slow progress of professionalization in teaching, social work, and nursing. First, most people in these fields are female, and sexist attitudes make it relatively difficult for women to validate their claim to professional status. In addition, these workers are increasingly found in bureaucracies where they must acknowledge the authority of nonprofessionals such as hospital administrators and school boards who are above them in the organizational hierarchy—obviously a direct challenge to the norm of professional autonomy.

Under these circumstances, some occupations are actually undergoing *deprofessionalization*, a process whereby their work is being partially deskilled. Pharmacists, who used to counsel clients and prepare medicines, now do little more in some cases than count pills (Ritzer & Walczak, 1988; Hodson & Sullivan, 1995).

Even some higher professionals have discovered that work in a bureaucracy can be constraining (Perrow, 1986; Powell, 1985). For instance, physicians who work for HMOs find that organizational rules often limit their ability to do everything for their patients that their professional socialization tells them ought to be done. The movement of more and more professionals into bureaucracies threatens to reduce the prestige of many fields, including both medicine and the law.

Problems in the Secondary Labor Market

Real wages—that is, wages adjusted for inflation—have been declining in the United States for several decades, especially among lower skilled workers (Borjas, 1995). Only employees with postgraduate degrees gained economic ground between 1973 and 1993 (Bluestone, 1995), and people at the low end of the pay scale were hit the hardest (Duncan, 1996). Most Americans are working longer hours today just to avoid falling farther behind (Rifkin, 1995).

Among the hardest hit are people who work for minimum wage, about 6 percent of the total labor force. One-third of minimum wage earners work full-time, and 63 percent of them are female. Because the minimum wage is not indexed to the inflation rate and because the government has tended to resist raising it, the real value of the minimum wage has been eroding for decades. In the 1960s, a full-time minimum wage worker earned 105 percent of a poverty line income for a family of four; by 1992, that figure had dropped to 79 percent (Quigley, 1995; Greenstein, 1996). The minimum wage was raised from $4.25 to $5.15 in 1997, but this increase still left many full-time workers in poverty.

Two factors are especially important in explaining this wage stagnation toward the bottom: the globalization of the economy and the decline of the union movement (Mishel, 1995).

Globalization. Globalization has had several effects (Zippay, 1991). Most obviously, U.S. workers lose work when jobs are exported to nations where wages are far lower than they are here, primarily in Latin America and Asia. Between 1987 and 1994 over 5 million U.S. jobs, most of them in manufacturing, were relocated abroad (Aronowitz & DiFazio, 1994). Most of these displaced workers end up taking service jobs in the secondary labor market with lower pay and fewer benefits (Kletzer, 1991). Globalization also helps explain why those workers who do retain their jobs find their real earnings slipping: In a global economy, Americans compete against laborers in places like Indonesia, where factory wages may be as low as $1.35 a day. Naturally, this means that U.S. wages tend to decline (Barnet & Cavanaugh, 1994).

The Declining Strength of Unions. Well into the twentieth century, the union movement met heavy and often violent opposition from both capitalists and government. Thousands of men and women were beaten, imprisoned, and even killed for demanding an eight-hour work day or minimal workplace safety standards (Dulles & Dubofsky, 1984). But by the mid 1930s unions had finally secured the right to bargain collectively for their members (McCammon, 1993). Over the next several decades, they achieved not only an eight-hour work day but also health insurance, pension plans, sick leave, unemployment benefits, and paid vacations (Shostak, 1990).

At the end of World War II, about one-third of all nonfarm workers were unionized, with the largest representation in heavy "smokestack" industries in the North and Midwest. In absolute numbers, unions peaked at about 25 million members in the early 1970s. Research consistently shows that union members earn more than nonmembers (Wiatrowski, 1994) and that they are more productive as well (Mishel & Voos, 1992; Galenson, 1996). Furthermore, when unions are strong, there is a spillover effect: Businesses pay their nonunion workers well in hopes of keeping them from organizing (Amott, 1993). Unions do have their problems, including a history of hostility to women, minorities, and immigrants (Schutt, 1987; Olzak, 1989; Asher & Stephenson, 1990)—but they have clearly bettered the lives of most U.S. workers.

Since the 1970s, however, the union movement has declined and power has shifted dramatically back to management (Harrison, 1994). Figure 22.2 illustrates historic trends in union membership. Today slightly over 16 million people are union members, and less

The law, medicine, and the ministry were among the first occupations to professionalize. Like all professionals, lawyers are trained in the theory as well as practice of their craft, are governed by a powerful professional association, enjoy considerable authority over their clients, and are expected to obey the norm of altruism.

than 14 percent of the nonfarm labor force is organized. Unions are seeing some of their hard-won victories slipping away, as benefits and wages are routinely reduced (Hathaway, 1993). Strikes have become far less common now that the government has thrown its support to the permanent hiring of nonunion replacement workers (Galenson, 1996). The union movement is much stronger in Europe. Ninety percent of Swedish workers, 50 percent of those in Britain, and 40 percent of German workers are union members, but unions are gradually losing power abroad as well as in the United States (Western, 1993).

There are several reasons for this downward trend. First, many highly unionized industrial jobs have disappeared with the shift to a service economy and the relocation of millions of jobs abroad. Also, anti-union conservatives have controlled either the executive or the legislative branches of the federal government (or both) since 1980. Finally, the union movement has been damaged in recent years by a series of well-publicized scandals.

Can unions regain enough power to stop or even reverse the erosion of pay and benefits? Will workers' anger over shrinking real wages overcome the unions' negative image? Perhaps—but nothing seems likely to reverse the globalization of jobs or the decline of the manufacturing sector. Many unions are now trying to organize the public sector—40 percent of government workers are now unionized—and to increase the number of lower-skill service workers and women who are union members. In another line of attack, unions are expanding internationally in order to increase the wages of foreign workers, and thus, indirectly, to do the same for Americans (Cavanagh & Broad, 1996). However, these are difficult goals, and the short-run outlook for unions is clouded.

The Contingency Work Force

Another important trend in modern societies is the growth of the **contingency work force,** workers who are not permanent, full-time employees of a single firm (Pfeffer & Baron, 1988; Peters, 1992; Castro, 1993). This type of employment is expanding rapidly: The contingency work force grew 250 percent between 1985 and 1995, years when the overall number of employees increased by less than 20 percent. The contingency work force has historically been made up primarily of low-skill workers, but in recent years large numbers of highly skilled knowledge workers have also taken these jobs. Over one-third of all workers are now in the contingency work force, and further increases appear inevitable (Moore, 1994). In fact, early in the twenty-first century, a *majority* of all employees are expected to fall into one of the following three categories (Morrow, 1993; Larson, 1996):

- *Temporary workers* generally are employed by employee-leasing firms like Manpower, Incorporated (Castro, 1993). Most "temps" work at low-skill service jobs.
- *Part-time workers* are also increasing rapidly (Howell, 1994). For example, 80 percent of K-Mart's 250,000 employees work less than 30 hours per week. About 75 percent of all part-timers are female, and up to 90 percent say that they would prefer to work full-time (Collins, 1994).
- *Independent contractors* are hired in a process called outsourcing or subcontracting by firms that previously would have given the work to regular employees. These workers are also called consultants and freelancers (Lozano, 1989). Unlike part-

Over the past several decades, many hundreds of American-owned factories have been relocated to nations in the developing world such as Mexico, where wages are low, unions are weak or nonexistent, and environmental regulations are rarely enforced.

timers, they are full-time workers; unlike temps, they tend to be highly skilled. White-collar unions view outsourcing as a major threat, especially when "downsized" former employees are hired back as independent contractors at lower salaries and with no fringe benefits. Downsizing will be discussed further later in this chapter.

Contingency work does provide certain advantages, especially to women and students who cannot or prefer not to take conventional full-time jobs because of household or academic responsibilities. But the primary beneficiary is the corporation. It obtains a docile, nonunionized labor force at low wages and without having to provide health insurance, vacations, or other fringe benefits (Henson, 1996).

Independent contractors are sometimes paid well enough to purchase their own health insurance and set up their own pensions, but this is not true for most part-timers or temps. This explains why 82 percent of all independent contractors but only 39 percent of other types of contingency workers like their present job arrangement (U.S. Department of Labor, 1995). Contingency employment also weakens employees' ability to protest job discrimination or dangerous working conditions. More generally, contingency work virtually

eliminates job security and weakens the already fragile social contract between workers and employers.

Telecommuting

Before the industrial revolution, most manufacturing took place in the home in a system called *cottage industry*. The introduction of the factory in the eighteenth century led to a radical separation between work and home, a change that definitively shaped people's lives for two centuries. However, the invention of fax machines and the Internet has now made it increasingly possible for people to work at home in what Alvin Toffler (1980) calls the electronic cottage and others refer to as **telecommuting** (Halal, 1992; Churbuck & Young, 1992). As of 1997, an estimated 7 million people telecommuted (Tanaka, 1997).

Many home workers are self-employed, but others work for large firms. For example, over 10 percent of AT&T's work force telecommutes (Boroughs, 1995). The production of this text was greatly facilitated by telecommuting: It was written by two sociologists, one working at a college in Kentucky and the other writing at her home in St. Louis. Our developmental editor works out of her home in New Jersey,

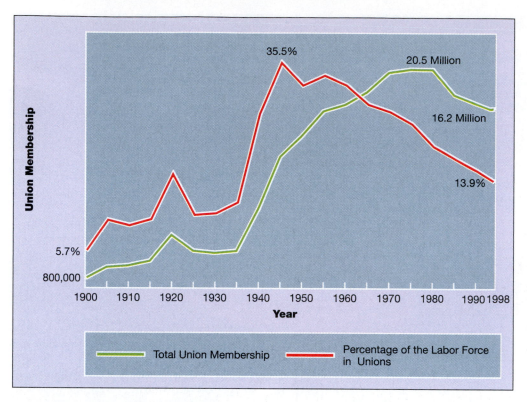

FIGURE 22.2   Union Membership Trends, 1900–1998
Sources: Larry J. Griffin, Philip J. O'Connell, and Holly J. McCammon, 1989, "National Variation in the Context of Struggle." *Canadian Review of Sociology and Anthropology* 26,1 (February):pp. 37–68. Reprinted by permission of Larry J. Griffin. 1999 U.S. Statistical Abstract, Table 718.

and the project is coordinated by editors located at Prentice Hall's main office, also in New Jersey.

Telecommuting has many advantages (Volti, 1995). It allows workers more autonomy than they would have in a conventional work setting and eliminates wasted time driving to and from work every day. It lets people work full time yet also be constantly available for their children. It allows workers who live in remote areas to hold jobs that previously were available only to city dwellers. And it has given options to the physically handicapped that they did not have previously (Nelson, 1995). The primary drawback of the electronic cottage is isolation: Many telecommuters miss the human contact with co-workers that is part of the conventional workplace.

SOCIOLOGICAL THEORY AND THE EXPERIENCE OF WORK

Many people think of work as just a way to obtain a paycheck, but it's really much more important than that. We typically spend more time working than engaged in any other activity. People who work together—construction workers and police officers for example—often form tightly bonded occupational subcultures with very distinct norms and values (Riemer, 1979; Pavalko, 1988).

In addition, work is a critical element in shaping people's identities in modern societies; when we meet someone, we almost always inquire, "What do you do for a living?" (Friedland & Robertson, 1990). Work is usually a master status (see Chapter 4), which is why people who work in less prestigious jobs sometimes euphemize or upgrade their occupational titles: "Sanitary engineer" and "security specialist" convey a much more positive image than sewer worker and bouncer!

Because work is so important in people's lives, it has been a major focus of sociological theory. In this section, we will introduce two classic theoretical contributions to the sociology of work, one dealing with the origins of the work ethic and the other exploring why workers in bureaucracies sometimes lack strong motivation to work. We will also briefly discuss a related topic, contemporary empirical research into job satisfaction.

The Protestant Ethic

In 1905 Max Weber published one of the most important sociological studies ever written, an investigation into the origins of what is commonly called the *work ethic*. This book was called *The Protestant Ethic and the Spirit of Capitalism*, and it sparked one of the most intense debates in the history of ideas.

Weber's inquiry was part of his ongoing effort to show that ideas can be important causes of social change. This position contrasts with Marx's contention that new structural arrangements—especially altered economic relationships between members of society—provide the best explanation for social change.

More specifically, Weber was interested in the birth of a type of capitalism that arose in Europe during the Reformation and that, he believed, was significantly different from earlier varieties of capitalism that had existed for millennia. *Rational capitalism*, as it may be called, is capitalism that reflects the spirit of rationalization. That is, the relentless and unending accumulation of money—using the most efficient means possible—is viewed as an end in itself, rather than as simply a means of obtaining valued goods and services.

Weber noted that capitalism of this sort had emerged primarily in the Protestant areas of northern Europe, and that Protestants seemed to be more actively involved in capitalism than were their Catholic neighbors. Marx would have said that Protestantism, an idea, grew in response to capitalism, a new structural factor. But Weber found evidence that certain aspects of Protestantism predated and thus led to rational capitalism.

In the sixteenth century, both Protestantism and Catholicism overtly taught that the pursuit of profit—while not entirely immoral—was at best ethically questionable. However, a series of religious developments at the beginning of the Reformation lent covert support to the emerging entrepreneurial spirit.

First of all, Martin Luther taught that God gave each person a particular role to play or *calling* on Earth. Whether you were a minister, a mother, a blacksmith, or a business owner, God expected you to work hard at your calling; this was a way to glorify Him.

Luther also introduced the notion that people have a direct and unmediated relationship with God. This meant that salvation could neither be obtained nor guaranteed by the church; whether you went to heaven was entirely up to you and God.

In the next generation, John Calvin (1509–1564) took Luther's ideas a crucial step further with the idea of *predestination*. Predestination meant that God had decided before a person was born whether that individual would be saved. Nothing we can do on Earth can change our predestined fate—or even let us know whether we are saved.

As one might expect from his authorship of such aphorisms as "A penny saved is a penny earned," or "Up, sluggard, and waste not life; in the grave will be sleeping enough," Benjamin Franklin was a strong proponent of a secularized version of the Protestant work ethic.

Given these beliefs, all we can do is work hard at our calling and live a modest life, shunning, as Calvin urged, worldly pleasures. But, in practice, the uncertainty of not knowing one's fate or even being able to influence it was unbearable. Gradually, people became convinced that surely God would cause the elect to succeed in their callings as a sign of His favor. Naturally, people who thought this way worked very hard to convince themselves and others that they were indeed saved.

Because they were such hard workers, Calvinist business owners tended to become wealthy. Moreover, they plowed their profits back into their businesses—after giving a share to the church—so that they become more and more prosperous. Note that, by this logic, one could never be too rich because one could never be entirely sure that he or she was among the elect. Any slowdown in the accumulation of profit cast into doubt one's future after death. So rational capitalism, unlike earlier forms, implied an entirely unlimited quest for economic success.

Over the centuries, this motivational pattern became disconnected from its religious justification; what remained was intense socialization to achieve economic success. In the nineteenth century, Calvinistic Protes-

The Rewards of "Dirty Work": Garbage Collectors

"Dirty work" is stigmatized in all societies. As sociologist Everett Hughes once pointed out, in order for some members of society to be clean and pure, someone else must take care of unclean, often taboo work, such as handling dead bodies and filth. In India and Japan, such jobs were (and to some extent still are) relegated to the Dalits (or Untouchables) and the Eta, respectively. Both groups were regarded as ritually impure. Our society does not have formal taboos against dirty work, but some jobs are rated near the bottom of the scale of occupational prestige and are viewed as not quite respectable, certainly not something to brag about. Garbage collection is a good example.

Why would anyone choose to become a garbage collector? Stewart Perry (1978) asked this question of sanitation workers for the Sunset Scavenger Business in San Francisco. For a job that requires little training or education, the pay is relatively good. But pay was not what drew men to the job.

One attraction of becoming a garbage collector was variety. The job involves many different activities, including driving the truck, hauling cans, operating the blade, solving problems with customers, and so on. Collecting garbage also means being outdoors and moving around. Several of the men Perry met had worked at higher paying, higher prestige office jobs for a while, but they chose to return to sanitation routes. "Staying in one place all day? Naw!" (Perry, p. 80). On another level, variety meant the unexpected: Every day brought something different. They talked about witnessing a robbery, calling in a fire alarm and getting residents out of the building before the fire truck arrived, and about the time that the FBI

requested that they save all the rubbish from a house under surveillance.

The garbage itself was full of surprises. Almost every day the men found something of interest, whether a good book, a child's toy or a fixable radio. Almost inevitably, garbage men became collectors. As one informant suggested, no matter what you want, eventually you'll find it. His own collection included a brass rail from a bar and a rubber life raft; similarly, in the course of his research, Perry acquired a rare seventeenth-century book of sermons and a sheepskin rug.

Garbage men got to know the neighborhoods in which they worked intimately. Watching children grow up, couples marry or separate, or one house or block deteriorating while another was being renovated, had the appeal of an ongoing story, not unlike a soap opera on TV. They witnessed not just public performances, but also what Erving Goffman called the "backstage" of life. The respectable facades in affluent neighborhoods cannot hide the alcoholism a garbage man detects from cans full of empty liquor bottles or the sexual longings symbolized by bundles of pornographic magazines.

A second attraction of garbage collection was a sense of camaraderie among workers. The friendships people make on the job are a major source of satisfaction in any occupation. Many Sunset workers came from the same (Italian) ethnic background and in some cases from the same neighborhood. Often their fathers, uncles, and other relatives, as well as old family friends, had also worked for the company. All of the men hoped that their own sons would go to college and make something better of themselves. But at least thirty were following in their father's

footsteps—indeed, working for no pay until they had proved themselves and were offered a job. These intergenerational family ties and friendships made the company a familiar and welcome place—and a stronghold of tradition for members of ethnic communities that were beginning to break apart.

Third, the garbage collectors liked working at their own pace, scheduling their own breaks, deciding when to do their paperwork—in short, being their own bosses. Freedom from constant supervision did not mean that they did as little work at the slowest rate possible. To the contrary, they worked as fast as they could manage.

Equally important—and in this Sunset may be unusual—the men owned shares in the business. Being a shareholder meant, first, having a permanent job. If company profits declined, workers would have to accept lower wages, but they could not be laid off. Shareholder dividends, distributed around Christmas, were welcome but usually modest (about $600). Most important was pride of ownership and the feeling that they were more than just workers.

Collecting garbage may be "dirty work" in many peoples' eyes, but these men were proud of what they did for a living.

1. What are some of the qualities that can make a job "dirty" in Americans' eyes? What does this tell us about this society's values?
2. Can you think of some other jobs that most people regard as "dirty work"? Do some of them, like scavenger, have hidden appeals?

Sources: Hughes, 1962; Perry, 1978.

Although the American union movement has been gradually losing support as the number of jobs in heavy "smokestack" industries has declined over the past three decades, unionization continues to be workers' most effective means of protecting their hard-earned wages and benefits.

tants still enjoyed an economic edge. But today many Catholics and others have clearly accepted a secularized version of the work ethic and are as highly motivated—or more so—than their Protestant neighbors.

Are Americans still committed to the Protestant ethic? Certainly Ray Wax, the stockbroker we met at the beginning of this chapter, seems highly motivated. However, many observers believe that the work ethic is weakening in contemporary United States. They see it being replaced by a more hedonistic philosophy that stresses personal growth and fulfillment more than economic success (Schor, 1991). On the other hand, substantial research suggests the presence of a strong work ethic in Japan and parts of Southeast Asia, which bodes well for those nations' continued economic growth (Levy, 1992). Interestingly, the origins of the Japanese work ethic have been traced to non-Christian religious developments in the eighteenth and nineteenth centuries (Bellah, 1957).

Alienation and Job Satisfaction

Karl Marx, who originated the concept, considered alienation to be a structural phenomenon, a quality inherent in certain relations of production (Ollman,

1971; McClellan, 1977). Alienation is much more than simply disliking your job. In Marx's view, **alienation** arises whenever people are controlled by social institutions that seem to be beyond their ability to influence. It may arise in many settings. Governments, workplaces, schools, and religions are all ultimately human creations, Marx argued, but they often grow so large and their power over us becomes so coercive that we forget that we created them and that we can, at least collectively and in theory, change them (Seeman, 1972).

Specifically regarding work, Marx stressed that under certain structural conditions, workers feel alienated or estranged from the productive process, from the products of their labor, from their fellow workers, and ultimately from themselves. Alienated workers feel *powerless* on the job, and they may consider their work *meaningless* because they do not see how their efforts contribute to the final outcome or product (Blauner, 1964).

Marx believed alienation resulted from capitalism (Young, 1975) and some observers suggest that it is widespread in the U.S. workplace (Terkel, 1985; Erickson & Vallas, 1990; Geyer & Heinz, 1992). However, the high levels of alienation that were present in the

The first member of any minority group to enter a given work setting is likely to be treated as a token. Pioneering women, African Americans, Latinos, gays, or members of any other different or devalued category often face similar problems in the workplace.

former Soviet Union strongly suggest that the principal cause of alienation is bureaucracy, not capitalism.

Consider the assembly line, perhaps the ultimate expression of Weber's rational bureaucracy (Thompson, 1983). As the account at the beginning of this chapter by Phil Stallings suggested, assembly line workers must keep pace with the line, which dictates even minor details of the work process. In Weber's words, the worker is reduced to ". . . a small cog in a ceaselessly moving mechanism that prescribes to him [sic.] an endlessly fixed routine . . ." (Weber, 1978: 988). Not only are the employees utterly lacking in autonomy, but their work is also largely meaningless because they do such a small part of the whole task that they do not see their place in the larger scheme of things (Schooler & Naoi, 1988). Because their jobs have been deskilled, they take little if any pride in what they do (Braverman, 1974; Feldberg & Glenn, 1982). They are also isolated from their co-workers by noise and by having to stay at their work station whenever the line is running.

Marx believed that a need for self-expression through work was an inherent part of human nature, so an alienated person could not be a fully authentic human being. Alienation has been found to be related to such problems as alcoholism, drug abuse, mental and physical illness, family violence, and political extremism. But today many Americans seem to deliberately seek out alienating work situations that ask little of them except mindless obedience. These workers seem content to endure five days of tedium so that they can come to life on the weekend. Critics of Marx say that the existence of these people refutes his basic assumption concerning human nature. His defenders respond that a fundamentally flawed system, bureaucratic capitalism, creates warped and flawed individuals.

Can any of the approaches to modifying bureaucracy discussed earlier in this chapter reduce alienation? Taylorism clearly intensifies the problem by reducing worker autonomy to a minimum. To the extent that the human relations approach is superficial window dressing, it has a similar effect. However, the other three models, and especially collectives and humanized systems, hold some promise as antidotes to alienation. Each substantially empowers the worker, calls for a less rigid division of labor, and genuinely encourages the development of primary relationships within the workplace. If these models are adopted in the emerging postindustrial service economy, work alienation may well decline.

Job Satisfaction. Few modern researchers make use of the structural concept of alienation; they tend instead to investigate the self-reported social-psychological condition termed "job satisfaction." In contrast to the findings of studies of alienation discussed previously, sociologists using survey research techniques generally find a fairly high level of satisfaction among workers. According to the 1993 General Social Survey, whose respondents are selected randomly from all adults, 42 percent of all Americans reported that they were "very satisfied" with their jobs, and another 40 percent were "moderately satisfied." Only 5 percent were unsatisfied (NORC, 1994). Most studies show that roughly 70 percent of all adults say that they would continue working if they won the lottery, and between 80 and 90 percent of all white-collar professionals—but only 24 percent of blue collar workers—would choose the same job if they could relive their lives (Tausky, 1984). Figures 22.3 and 22.4 illustrate the effects of age, educational level, income, and gender on job satisfaction.

These findings concerning job satisfaction can be read two ways. Perhaps Americans really are, for the most part, happy with their work, or maybe few of us are willing to admit to dissatisfaction because, given widespread classism (see Chapter 10), being in a bad job can only mean that an individual is personally inadequate. It is quite possible that workers who are structurally alienated could nevertheless report a fairly high level of job satisfaction.

In general, older workers say they are more content with their jobs than younger ones, which may be because older people typically have better jobs, or it may suggest that people lower their expectations after working for a few years. White-collar workers are more satisfied than blue-collar workers, and union members are particularly dissatisfied, probably because unions raise people's expectations (Schwochau, 1987).

Women and minorities are particularly likely to work in alienating settings (Loscocco & Spitze, 1990). Sharon Atkins' job as a receptionist, discussed at the beginning of this chapter, provides a good example. However, despite being in objectively less desirable jobs, on the average, women express higher levels of job satisfaction than men—clearly a result of internalized lower expectations (Weaver & Matthews, 1990). This observation suggests that we need to consider the important issue of how women experience the modern workplace.

≋ LIFE CONNECTIONS: Women in the Workplace

Women have entered the paid labor force in large numbers in recent decades (see Chapter 13). In 1960, about 38 percent of all working-age women were in

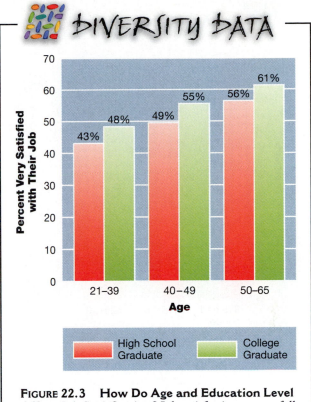

DIVERSITY DATA

FIGURE 22.3 How Do Age and Education Level Affect Job Satisfaction? Job satisfaction among full-time workers rises steadily with age and with level of educational attainment. Are older workers more satisfied because they are in better jobs or because they have learned to reduce their expectations?
Source: NORC. General Social Surveys, 1972–1996. Chicago: National Opinion Research Center, 1996. Reprinted by permission of NORC, Chicago, IL.

the labor force; today over 60 percent are. Women accounted for fully two-thirds of the increase in the American labor force between 1982 and 1995. Consequently, employers are being forced to rethink the character of the workplace environment.

Historically, most women were hired for gender-typed, "pink-collar" jobs. These jobs were poorly paid, offered little chance of career advancement, and reinforced sexist stereotypes (Lowe, 1987). The traditional secretary, for example, worked under the direct supervision of a man to whom she provided a variety of services, often including tasks like making coffee and picking up dry cleaning, which would never have been expected of a male worker (Millman & Kanter, 1975).

Much of this is changing. Today, women's problems are less likely to result from a company's formal policies than from its informal norms or, as they are sometimes called, its **organizational culture** (Reed & Hughes, 1992; Pheysey, 1993; Trice & Beyer, 1993). Women often find the organizational culture of a firm hostile or at best nonsupportive (Reskin &

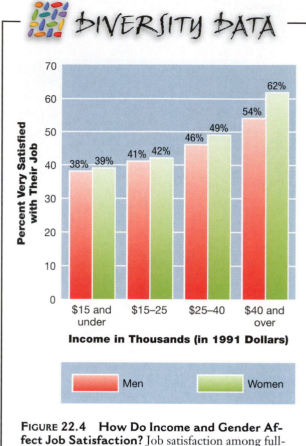

DIVERSITY DATA

FIGURE 22.4   How Do Income and Gender Affect Job Satisfaction? Job satisfaction among full-time workers rises steadily as annual income goes up. However, women are more satisfied than men at all income levels despite the fact that they generally earn less money then men do. How would you explain this seeming incongruity?

Source: NORC. General Social Surveys, 1972–1996. Chicago: National Opinion Research Center, 1996. Reprinted by permission of NORC, Chicago, IL.

types of women: the mother, the sex object, the mascot, or the stern "iron maiden" (Millman & Kanter, 1975). Because she is so visible, she is likely to be under extreme pressure to do well. She may feel that she must work twice as hard as anyone else (Kanter & Stein, 1979). She is often lonely, excluded from the personal as well as the career advantages of the informal office network (Benokraitis & Feagin, 1986). She may be unable to find a senior executive who will mentor her.

Some observers have suggested that women could soften and humanize the masculine organizational culture (Hennig & Jardin, 1977). Research indicates that, as a result of gender-role socialization, most women prefer an interpersonal style that emphasizes collaboration and helping co-workers. Women are more likely than men to ask questions and share information, and they are more responsive to the human needs of those around them (Helgesen, 1990; Tannen, 1994; Morgen, 1994). Perhaps the current increase in the number of women in management will eventually make corporate organizational culture more humane, although it seems equally possible that women will simply learn to play the game by men's rules.

≡ SOCIETY CONNECTIONS: Unemployment and Electronic Surveillance

We have already discussed a number of social issues that have arisen in the workplace including declining real wages, alienation, and the special problems faced by working women. In this final section we will consider two additional concerns, unemployment and electronic surveillance.

Unemployment and Downsizing

There are several different types of unemployment. Some are temporary and thus of relatively less concern to sociologists. These include the seasonal unemployment of some farm workers and the cyclical unemployment caused by periodic swings of the business cycle. Of greater interest is **structural unemployment,** which results from a mismatch between the skills of the work force and the current needs of the economy (McEachern, 1994). For example, because computers are rapidly replacing typewriters in the modern world, typewriter repair workers cannot find work.

The official unemployment rates that are reported on the nightly news do not accurately portray the size or character of the unemployed population. These figures were developed primarily so that employers can determine how many people are actively looking for work, not how serious the unemployment problem really is. As a result, they exclude several groups of people, including (a) **discouraged workers,**

Padovic, 1994). The traditional corporate organizational culture is distinctly masculine, stressing toughness, competition, and aggression (Hearn et al., 1989). Women are sometimes devalued because they are seen as weak (Baron & Newman, 1990; Mills & Tancred, 1992; Kemp, 1994). Employers often falsely assume that they do not take their jobs as seriously as they take their family lives. Thus, women may be hired, but eventually they are likely to bump up against the "glass ceiling" (see Chapter 12).

Rosabeth Moss Kanter (1977, 1983) has written a classic analysis of the problems that typically face the first few women (or minorities) who are hired to work in executive positions in the corporate world—an environment that is still overwhelmingly male and white. These women are often treated as *tokens* (Epstein, 1970). The first female hired is likely to be seen more as a woman than as a fellow worker. She may feel pressured to adopt one of a small number of rigidly defined office roles, each of which is derived from male stereo-

Workers at McDonald's and other fast food franchises rarely if ever have to exercise initiative or make decisions; everything is spelled out for them in the company's rulebook. This low level of autonomy helps explain why jobs like these are often highly alienating.

who have given up looking for jobs, (b) part-time workers who would prefer full-time employment, and (c) the **underemployed,** who are working but at jobs that do not make full use of their skills (Carnoy & Levin, 1985). In 1994, the government changed the way the unemployment rate is computed, which will increase the usefulness of this statistic.

The official unemployment rate has been very low in recent years; in early 1999 it was just over 4 percent. If we add in discouraged workers, the figure increases to about 7 percent—or roughly 8 million people. This low figure should not necessarily be interpreted as evidence that most workers feel secure in their current positions. In fact, unemployment rates are often low when jobs are scarce, because people stay where they are. Rates may be higher when there are plenty of jobs, because people may feel more free to quit their current job while looking for a better one.

Even when official rates are low, unemployment touches many people. At least two-thirds of all workers will experience involuntary unemployment at some time in their lives (Kates et al., 1990). During a recession year, as much as one-fifth of the labor force may be out of work at least briefly.

Table 22.1 illustrates how official unemployment rates vary by age, gender, education, and race. In gen-

eral, joblessness is higher among young people, men, and the poorly educated. Young lower-class high school dropouts routinely experience unemployment at rates of 25 percent or more (Kasarda, 1990). Minorities, particularly African Americans, have long suffered especially high rates, generally at least twice those of the general population (Pavalko, 1988). In some inner-city neighborhoods, true unemployment rates for teenagers regularly exceed 50 percent.

Traditionally, unemployment has been a more serious problem among blue-collar workers than in the white-collar work force, but since about 1980, major corporations have been firing or *downsizing* substantial numbers of executives. Between 1980 and 1995, roughly 24.8 million manual workers and 18.7 million white-collar employees lost their jobs. During this period the Fortune 500 companies alone downsized about 5 million people (Uchitelle & Kleinfeld, 1996).

Most of these highly skilled workers never expected to lose their positions; for this reason, they may actually be more distressed than their blue-collar counterparts. Losing a job has consequences far beyond going without a paycheck. Work provides us with a predictable temporal structure for organizing our daily lives (Fryer & McKenna, 1987). It gives us

Table 22.1	Social Characteristics of Officially Unemployed Workers, 1998
Percent Unemployed	
Overall	4.5%
Age	
16 to 19	14.6%
20 to 24	7.9
25 to 44	3.8
45 to 64	2.7
65 and up	3.2
Sex	
Male	4.4%
Female	4.6
Race	
White	3.9%
Black	8.9
Hispanic	7.2
Educational Attainment	
Not High School Graduate	8.5%
High School Graduate, No College	4.8
College, No Degree	3.6
College Graduate	1.8
Percent of Unemployed without Work for:	
Fewer Than 5 Weeks	42.2%
5–10 Weeks	22.1
11–14 Weeks	9.3
15–26 Weeks	12.3
27 Weeks or More	14.1

Source: 1999 Statistical Abstract, Tables 680 & 684.

opportunities to use our innate abilities and learned skills. It provides some of our most valued interactions with other people. Unemployment diminishes self-esteem, isolates fired workers from their former co-workers, and can even threaten an individual's core identity (Kessler et al., 1989). It is related to a host of pathologies, including domestic abuse, alcoholism, drug use, divorce, and suicide (Hamilton et al., 1990; Catalano et al., 1993; Turner, 1995).

Consider this comment by a man named Don, who lost an academic position at age 41 and found it extremely difficult to obtain a comparable job:

> I know that it takes a very weak man to lose his way when he has a beautiful wife and four healthy children living under his roof, no debt, over $3000 left in the bank, and he's not in a war or facing anything even close to real peril, but I was so lost. . . . There were too many people, too many talented and driven people, waiting at every slot for a way in. (Snyder, 1997)

Most downsized executives and professionals do eventually find work, but usually in less prestigious firms and at a lower salary (Rosen, 1987; Moore, 1990). After receiving ninety-six rejection letters from colleges and universities, Don worked as a greenskeeper, a construction laborer, a house painter, and a cottage caretaker (Matthews, 1997). Many downsized white-collar workers ultimately join the contingency work force as consultants and independent contractors (Harrison, 1994).

Electronic Surveillance

Before the industrial revolution, individuals who left home to work were controlled by the direct, face-to-face supervision of their superiors. The expansion of bureaucracy changed the character of workplace social control. With each worker responsible for a narrowly defined part of the productive process and occupying a definite place in a hierarchy of authority, supervision became less personal but more intensive (Goldman & Van Houten, 1977; Heydebrand, 1977; Perrow, 1986). It is exactly these qualities that make the assembly line so alienating.

Management's ability to control workers has been further expanded by computer technology (Giddens, 1990). Computerized surveillance allows superiors to monitor phone calls and e-mail and to assess worker productivity literally on a minute-to-minute basis (Sewell & Wilkinson, 1992; Rule & Brantley, 1992).

According to sociologist Gary Marx, we are at risk of becoming a "surveillance society." Computerized methods of collecting and storing information and supervising work threaten our last vestiges of personal and workplace privacy (Marx, 1985a, 1985b). Marx and others are calling for new legislation to limit the expansion of technological control before we slip into computerized totalitarianism (Marx, 1988; Flaherty, 1989).

INTERNET ━━◆━━ CONNECTIONS

The *Society Connections* feature in this chapter deals with **electronic surveillance,** which has become an increasingly controversial issue over the past decade in American society. The American Civil Liberties Union (ACLU) maintains a Web site dealing with the issues surrounding electronic surveillance in the workplace: "Privacy in America: Electronic Monitoring": http://www.aclu.org/library/pbr2.html. Reading the contents of this site will provide you with an excellent overview. After you have evaluated this material, write a brief report on the major issues involved. Do you believe there is sufficient justification for employers to electronically monitor their employees? If employees were informed beforehand, would this make a difference in how you feel?

SUMMARY

1. Formal organizations have come to dominate many aspects of life in modern societies.
2. There are three basic types of formal organizations: coercive and utilitarian organizations and voluntary associations.
3. A bureaucracy is a special type of formal organization designed to allow large numbers of people to efficiently accomplish routine tasks. Max Weber developed a well-known six-point ideal type model of bureaucracy.
4. Weber saw modern society as moving toward ever greater levels of bureaucratic rationality.
5. Real-life bureaucratic functioning is strongly influenced by the internal structures that develop among bureaucratic employees and is frequently impeded by various bureaucratic dysfunctions.
6. Scientific management and the human relations school were early efforts to respond to the inefficiencies of bureaucracies. More recent reform efforts include the antibureaucratic collective model, the Japanese model, and the emerging "humanized" model.
7. Sociologists have identified three sectors of the economy—primary, secondary, and tertiary—and two labor markets, primary and secondary.
8. In recent decades, the number of jobs that are organized as professions has increased substantially.
9. The real wages of many U.S. workers, especially those in the secondary labor market, have been declining due to globalization and the weakening of the union movement.
10. The contingency work force—temporary workers, part-time workers, and independent contractors—has been expanding rapidly.
11. Computers and fax machines allow increasing numbers of workers to earn a living without leaving their homes, an innovation known as telecommuting.
12. Max Weber believed that the strong work ethic associated with rational capitalism was an unintended consequence of doctrinal changes introduced during the Protestant reformation.
13. Many U.S. workers experience high levels of what Marx called alienation, a feeling of powerlessness that comes from not being able to control or even influence one's working conditions.
14. Levels of job satisfaction vary sharply among different types of workers.
15. Women have entered the workplace in unprecedented numbers in recent years. While real progress has been made, many female workers continue to confront hostile organizational cultures, tokenism, and dead-end jobs.
16. Structural unemployment is a major problem for both blue-collar workers and downsized executives.
17. Electronic surveillance is becoming increasingly common in the workplace.

KEY TERMS

alienation 583
bureaucracy 567
bureaucratic ritualism 570
contingency work force 578
discouraged workers 586
formal organization 566
goal displacement 570
ideal type 567

iron law of oligarchy 571
organizational culture 585
Parkinson's Law 571
Peter Principle 571
primary labor market 575
profession 576
professionalization 576

rationality 569
rationalization 569
secondary labor market 576
structural unemployment 586
telecommuting 579
trained incapacity 570
underemployment 587

CRITICAL THINKING QUESTIONS

1. Is it possible for workers to find personal fulfillment in a conventional bureaucratic organization? Which of the proposals to modify bureaucratic structure strike you as most promising? Why?
2. Do you believe that the U.S. work ethic—the commitment to hard work as a value—is declining? If so, why has this happened, and how might it be strengthened?
3. How has work changed since your parents entered the work force? What further changes do you expect to see during the next few decades? On the whole, do you think these changes will be positive or negative?

23 COLLECTIVE BEHAVIOR AND SOCIAL MOVEMENTS

The Los Angeles Riot of 1992

South Central Los Angeles—a severely disadvantaged, heavily minority community—exploded into violence on April 29, 1992. Tension had been escalating since March 3rd. On that date, an amateur photographer had videotaped four white police officers savagely beating a young African American man named Rodney King who had been pulled over for a minor traffic violation. The spark that actually set off the riot was the failure of a jury in suburban Simi Valley—a jury without a single black member—to convict any of the officers.

Something just snapped. As rioters ran through the streets looting and burning, images flashed across television screens all across the country. In one of the most startling, a white man named Reginald Denney was pulled from his truck and beaten by a group of angry African American men.

Before order was fully restored six days later, over 50 people had died, thousands more were injured, 5,000 adults had been arrested, and property damage ran over a billion dollars. (Dentler, 1992; Webster Commission, 1992; Murty et al., 1994)

Protest in Beijing

Three years earlier, an equally powerful image held the attention of viewers around the world: the almost unbelievable scene of an heroic lone protestor in Beijing's Tienanmen Square facing down a government tank. On June 4, 1989, hundreds of members of the student-led Chinese movement for democracy were killed, beaten, and arrested by the authorities.

Today, their movement operates largely underground, but its goal is the same now as it was in 1989: to replace the totalitarian Chinese government with a democratic political system. (Russo, 1994)

Virtual Pets

In 1997, the most popular children's pet wasn't a cat or a dog or an iguana. It wasn't even alive. In May of that year, the same Japanese company that created the Power Rangers introduced the tamagotchi, an egg-shaped electronic "virtual pet" that beeped if it needed to be fed or cleaned or if it wanted to be played with. If its needs were not met, it "died" (although it could be revived by pushing a "reset" button).

In the next few months, toy stores found it impossible to keep tamagotchis—like Cabbage Patch dolls and Tickle Me Elmo before them—in stock. Then, quite suddenly, sales plummeted. The demanding little creatures found themselves relegated to bargain bins and dusty toychests, while merchants and customers alike waited for the next fad to come down the chute. (Kantrowitz, 1997)

COLLECTIVE BEHAVIOR

You may well wonder what a riot, a political movement, and the short-lived popularity of a silly electronic toy have in common. Sociologists would see each as an example of **collective behavior,** relatively spontaneous, short-lived, unconventional, and unorganized activity by large numbers of people, that occurs when norms are unclear or rapidly changing.

Most of the types of social action we have discussed in this text are relatively highly *institutionalized.* That is, the norms that guide the behavior are relatively firmly established in people's minds. Going to school, voting, taking a date to the movies, or working for a large company are routine, stable, highly predictable activities. Everyone knows pretty much what to expect in these sorts of situations.

But sometimes the norms are less well established and people are largely left to their own devices in deciding how to act. There are no clear scripts to guide us when a fire breaks out in a theater or when mobs roam the streets, breaking store windows and looting. Under such circumstances, we must improvise, and the usual result is collective behavior of one type or another (Turner & Killian, 1993; Goode, 1992; Marx & McAdam, 1994).

INTERNET ⎯ CONNECTIONS

This chapter opens with a brief discussion of the Los Angeles riots of 1992. As pointed out in the text, the riots were set off by the failure of an all-white jury in suburban Simi Valley to convict any of the officers involved in the beating of a young African American named Rodney King. Since the King incident, a great deal of controversy has ensued regarding the conduct of these police officers and whether their actions were in any way justified, and, if not, what triggered the brutality. On the Internet, go to http://www.process.org/Process_Books/Hate/Rking.html. There, you will find an actual transcript of computer transmissions between squad cars and the Watch Commander's office at the Los Angeles Police Department's Foothills Division on the morning that Rodney King was severely injured in the process of a routine traffic stop. After evaluating the transcript, do you believe that the officers involved were justified in their actions, or are you suspicious that these officers are guilty of excessive force and police brutality? What do you think should be done to prevent future incidents like the one involving Rodney King?

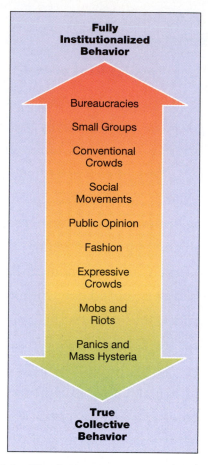

FIGURE 23.1   The Collective Behavior Continuum

Explaining Collective Behavior

As Figure 23.1 suggests, the various forms of collective behavior may be arranged along a continuum from greater to lesser institutionalization. The most spontaneous, least structured types—rumors, panic, and mass hysteria—are located toward the bottom. Mobs, riots, fads, and crazes occupy the middle range, while fashion and social and political protest movements are at the top because they display some marked similarities with fully institutionalized behavior.

This chapter begins with a look at the simpler, less-structured forms of collective behavior and at the major theories that have been developed to explain them. Then we examine social movements, which many regard as the most complex and enduring type of collective behavior. We conclude with a look at the training of social movement activists and a quick overview of some current trends in social movement development.

Explaining Collective Behavior

Under what circumstances do people riot, spread rumors, or take up fads and crazes? Social scientists have proposed several major theories to explain these sorts of behavior including contagion theory, convergence theory, value-added theory, and emergent-norm theory.

Contagion Theory. Early theories of collective behavior primarily addressed mobs and riots. They emphasized psychological factors, especially the irrationality of the crowd and suggested that the contagious excitement generated by being caught up in a mob or riot led to a collective or herd mentality. The normal restraints of civilization were swept aside and participants, encouraged by the anonymity of the crowd, acted much like unreasoning animals (LeBon, 1960). Feeling invincible, members of a crowd occasionally committed atrocities that appalled them when they returned to their senses.

The metaphor of *contagion* was obviously chosen to convey the view that collective behavior is like a kind of mental illness. Another theory, developed more recently by symbolic interactionist Herbert Blumer, takes a somewhat similar view (1969a). Though Blumer recognized that crowd members retained most if not all of their reasoning ability, he was still greatly impressed by the emotional character of collective behavior. His theory stressed the processes of *milling* and *circular reaction*, in which participants were visualized as wandering through the crowd, gradually intensifying their own emotionality by feeding off the nonverbal cues of others.

Today, sociologists consider contagion theory, especially LeBon's formulation, to be seriously biased. Its adherents were primarily upper- and middle-class individuals who felt personally threatened by collective behavior. While crowds can indeed sway the emotions, research suggests that their members are by no means as irrational as contagion theory claims (McPhail, 1991).

Convergence Theory.   Unlike contagion theory, which explained the apparent similarity among the members of crowds as a consequence of overpowering internal pressures to conform, convergence theory argues that only certain kinds of people will be attracted by the opportunity to participate in a given episode of collective behavior. Thus, if everyone at an environmental rally seems to share the same views, this is not a result of the operation of a crowd mentality, but rather a consequence of the fact that only people who share certain values will take part in such a demonstration (Milgram & Toch, 1968).

Convergence theory has the virtue of viewing crowd members as relatively rational, but it does not explain why many people who share the crowd's viewpoint do not join in (McPhail, 1971).

Value-Added Theory.   In the early 1960s, functionalist Neil Smelser (1963) published a very influential theory of collective behavior. Smelser identified six preconditions that must be met before any episode of collective behavior can begin. Each condition must be in place before the next one can become relevant in the development of a riot, panic, fad, or social movement. We may illustrate this theory by using it to analyze the 1992 Los Angeles riot.

First, the society must be *structurally conducive* to collective behavior. That is, it must be organized in a way that allows or permits such activity. The fact that the citizens of South Central Los Angeles were free to assemble and protest was a key factor promoting conduciveness. The fact that they could communicate easily with one another because most of them spoke the same language was another reason why the riot could occur.

Smelser's second factor is *structural strain*: The target population becomes discontented because of what are seen as unjust social conditions. Structural strain disturbs the smooth, predictable functioning of the social system. The Rodney King incident did not occur in a vacuum; it was merely the latest expression of anger over the way minorities have been treated in this country.

Third, a *generalized belief* must emerge to explain what is wrong—why people are feeling strain—and what can be done to relieve the pressure. The generalized belief that developed in South Central after the King incident held that police brutality, poverty, and the general lack of opportunities available to members of the community were the inevitable consequences of white racism.

Next, a *precipitating incident* must occur, some event that sums up the whole situation in microcosm and galvanizes the populace into action. This was accomplished by media reports of the "not guilty" verdict in the trial of the four white police officers who had beaten Rodney King.

Although the 1992 Los Angeles riots were sparked by anger over a jury's failure to convict white officers accused of beating a black man, looters came from a variety of ethnic and racial backgrounds. Total property losses from the riots exceeded one billion dollars.

Smelser's fifth point, *mobilization for action*, simply refers to the actual onset of the episode. In this case, people began rioting and looting.

Finally, the role of the agents of formal *social control* becomes relevant. The response of the police and national guard can cool tensions or, as was the case in South Central, it may further inflame passions and intensify and prolong the collective behavior episode.

Emergent-Norm Theory. Emergent-norm theory proposes yet another way of explaining crowd functioning, one grounded in the symbolic interactionist perspective (Turner & Killian, 1993). This theory is based on the observation that collective behavior arises when expectations regarding how to act are relatively vague. Under these circumstances, crowd members may propose various courses of action, sometimes verbally and sometimes by example. Some of these suggestions will be ignored, while others will be readily accepted, becoming new shared norms (Weller & Quarantelli, 1973). Thus crowd norms develop or emerge from ongoing interaction. Those who do not agree with these norms are free to leave; those who accept them stay, which leads the entire group to display the unity of purpose that both contagion and convergence theorists find important (McPhail & Wohlstein, 1983).

A good example of emergent-norm theory in action occurred a few years ago at a protest staged at the British embassy in Dublin. At one point, an obviously inebriated participant started to throw stones at the building, but no one copied him and the speaker urged him to stop, which he did. A few minutes later, another crowd member suggested that the group move to the American embassy to protest U.S. support for the British presence in Northern Ireland. Several other people shouted their support for this plan, and in the end the whole group walked over to the American embassy.

Note that emergent-norm theory views collective behavior participants as quite rational (Berk, 1974). For example, in the Los Angeles riots, emergent norms encouraged the looters to target stores owned by Korean immigrants, who were widely believed to be exploiting the community, whereas shops owned by blacks were less likely to be attacked (Quarantelli & Dynes, 1970).

Forms of Collective Behavior

Sociologists generally refer to the people engaged in collective behavior as a collectivity rather than a group in order to emphasize the weakness of the bonds connecting them. Formally speaking, a *collectivity* is a substantial number of people who interact on the basis of loosely defined norms. Unlike groups, collectivities generate little solidarity or group loyalty, usually last only a short while, have no clear boundaries, recognize few leaders, and display only a limited division of labor.

There are two distinct types of collectivities. In *localized collectivities*, the participants are in each other's immediate physical presence. In *dispersed collectivities*, the participants are not in the same place at the same time (Turner & Killian, 1993).

Localized Collectivities. The two principal varieties of collective behavior that take place on a face-to-face basis are crowds—including mobs, riots, and demonstrations—and panics.

Crowds. **Crowds** are temporary gatherings of people who influence each other in some way and share a focus of attention (Snow et al., 1981). Crowd behavior generally displays some of the qualities emphasized by contagion theorists. Because individuals blend into a crowd, they are relatively anonymous. This fact often increases their willingness to violate conventional norms: They know they probably will not be held accountable for their behavior. The permissive atmosphere of the crowd and the physical presence of large numbers of other people generate a sense of urgency. Faced with a relatively unscripted situation, crowd members tend to become suggestible and emotionally aroused (Turner & Killian, 1993). The dominant emotion in a crowd may be joy, anger, fear, or some combination of the three (Lofland, 1985).

The best known typology of crowd behavior was developed by Herbert Blumer (1969). He identified four basic types of crowds: casual, conventional, expressive, and acting. However, since crowds are inherently volatile, it is important to remember that one type can easily change into another.

The **casual crowd** is the simplest form of collective behavior. It consists of a number of people who gather to watch some event such as a movie star signing autographs, a street performer, or an automobile accident. Casual crowds are little more than aggregates (see Chapter 4), with few emergent norms and little if any structure or leadership (Wright, 1978).

Conventional crowds grow out of relatively structured gatherings such as parades, sports events, and funerals. These activities attract audiences that usually act in line with well-established, institutionalized norms. Occasionally, however, spectators display a certain amount of emotional and nonstandard behavior, under which circumstances they may be seen as engaging in a borderline type of collective behavior.

Most people find the experience of being caught up in a highly emotional crowd simultaneously fright-

Some members of protest crowds appear far more passionate than others, but most share the same basic point of view. Contagion theory suggests that this unanimity develops out of the crowd experience itself, whereas convergence theory argues that people with similar outlooks will be drawn to a given demonstration.

ening and exhilarating. On occasion, we deliberately seek out collective behavior experiences because they are an enjoyable way to release our emotions (Rose, 1982). These gatherings may be called **expressive crowds.** Sometimes—as with the crowds of students who gather annually during spring break at South Padre Island, Texas, or the revelers at Mardi Gras in New Orleans—the dominant emotion is joy. In other cases, the most apparent emotion is grief, as in the outpourings of sorrow that erupt in the crowds that gather after the unexpected death of a greatly loved public figure. In either case, the expressive crowd directs its attention inward, focusing primarily on the feelings of its participants.

When the dominant emotion in a crowd is anger, and its attention is focused outward, we speak of an **acting crowd**—a mob or a riot. A **mob** is a highly emotional crowd that pursues a specific target, attacks it, and then fades away. Mobs frequently arise in revolutionary situations. Think of the anti-tax mobs in Boston during the American revolution or the previously mentioned anti-British demonstration in Dublin (Tilly, 1992).

Lynch mobs occupy a singular place in U.S. history. They are identified with vigilante justice on the frontier and, in particular, with white attacks on African Americans. Between 1880 and 1930, about 5,000 African American men were hung by lynch mobs in the South, in many cases under suspicion—often unfounded—of having expressed sexual interest in white women (Franklin, 1967; Raper, 1970). In the West, Mexican and Asian men were the most likely victims of lynch mobs (Mirande, 1987).

Unlike a mob, a **riot** is an acting crowd that directs its hostility toward a wide and shifting range of targets, moving from one to the next in a relatively unpredictable manner. Also unlike mobs, riots may continue for days, with the participants dispersing and regrouping in response to the actions of the police and national guard. The Los Angeles riots lasted six days.

When Americans think of riots, they are likely to think first of our nation's long history of race riots. In the twentieth century, major racially motivated riots took place in Chicago in 1919, in the Watts district of Los Angeles in 1965, in dozens of cities—most notably Detroit and Newark—in the later 1960s, in Miami in 1980, and in Los Angeles again in 1992. Before the 1960s, American race riots usually consisted of white mobs attacking black neighborhoods. More recent riots have been more likely to involve African Americans and other minority groups destroying property, looting, and fighting with the police in their own communities (Spilerman, 1976; Porter & Dunn, 1984).

Many people assume that rioters come from the dregs of society, the "criminal class"—a view sometimes called the "riff-raff theory." However, research shows that a surprisingly broad cross-section of the community typically participates in large-scale race riots (National Advisory Commission on Civil Disorders, 1968; McPhail, 1991).

Most Americans are quick to condemn rioters, but many individuals in riot-prone communities take a different stance. They point out that civil disturbances are sometimes the only way to direct the attention of the larger society to the plight of poor minorities. Symbolic interactionists note in particular that what outsiders call "riots" and regard as nothing more than criminal behavior are often defined as

Neil Smelser's value-added theory points out that the actions of social control agents have a major effect on whether a riot is quickly extinguished or continues for days.

"insurrections" or even "rebellions" by those who participate in them (Jacobs, 1996).

By no means are all riots about race. For example, in 1886 the Chicago police attacked a large crowd of labor sympathizers in what came to be called the Haymarket riot, killing eleven. Police riots also took place in 1963 in Birmingham, Alabama, when the authorities brutally victimized civil rights demonstrators, and in Chicago in 1968 during the national Democratic Party convention.

Riots are also common in prisons, occurring most recently in 1971 at Attica in New York and in 1980 at the New Mexico State Penitentiary (New York State Special Commission on Attica, 1972; Useem, 1985). Finally, some serious riots occur at sporting events, most notably at British soccer matches and in Chicago after the end of several recent National Basketball Association championship series (Roadburg, 1980). Such riots generally reflect a complex mixture of anger and joy.

A fifth type, the **protest crowd,** was recently added to the four types originally identified by Blumer (McPhail & Wohlstein, 1983). Protest crowds are deliberately assembled by the leaders of social movements to demonstrate their public support.

Good examples of protest crowds include the 1963 civil rights rally in Washington, D.C., where over 250,000 people heard Martin Luther King give his immortal "I have a dream" speech; the large demonstrations against the Vietnam War held in the late 1960s; or the Million Man March on Washington sponsored by Lewis Fahrakahn in October 1995.

Panics. A **panic** is a type of localized collective behavior in which a large number of people respond to a real or imaginary threat with a desperate, uncoordinated, seemingly irrational flight to secure safety— often placing themselves in more danger than they would have otherwise faced. The classic panic results from someone yelling "fire" in a crowded building; in a mad rush to find an exit, smaller and weaker people are trampled underfoot. This kind of panic occurred in 1903 at the Iroquois Theater in Chicago (602 dead); in 1942 at the Coconut Grove nightclub in Boston (491 dead); in 1980 at the Beverly Hills Supper Club in Southgate, Kentucky (164 dead); and in Mecca, a religious site in Saudi Arabia, in 1990 (1,426 dead).

Panic is a relatively rare type of collective behavior. It can occur only under rather special circum-

The hundreds of thousands of people who celebrate Mardi Gras in the streets of New Orleans' French Quarter make up what Blumer calls an expressive crowd. Most of them participate, not to achieve some larger goal, but simply to enjoy the emotional experience of being part of a large group of revelers.

stances. Escape must be possible, but not certain; there must be a sense that only some people will be able to get out. If there is no chance to escape—and people know this—there will be no panic (Smelser, 1963). In addition, the lines of communication from the front of the crowd—near the exit—to the rear must break down (Brown & Goldin, 1973). Even under these circumstances, panic may not occur (Schultz, 1964). Thus, for example, until very close to the end, many passengers and crew members of the "Titanic" continued to help load people into lifeboats, obeying the "women and children first" norm.

While panics appear mindless, sociologists emphasize that, given the amount of information available, rushing toward an exit may well appear to be the most rational course of action at the time (Quarantelli, 1957).

Besides the classic model, there are several other types of panic, but all are variations on the same basic theme. Sometimes people are not trying to escape, but rather to gain entry. This was the case at a 1979 concert by the rock group The Who at Cincinnati's Riverfront Stadium, when 11 people died as the crowd pushed forward in a frantic crush for the best

In May of 1985, over 35 people were killed at a European Cup soccer match in Brussels when frantic attempts by spectators to flee a riot that had erupted in the stands caused the collapse of a section of the stadium.

nonreserved seats; at a soccer match in 1989 in Sheffield, England, when 95 people were killed; and at a basketball game in 1991 at the City College of New York when 9 died.

Dispersed Collectivities. In a dispersed collectivity, numerous individuals or small groups who are not in each other's direct physical presence react in an emotional and relatively unconventional way to a common stimulus (Lofland, 1981). In most cases, the media are centrally involved in this process (Goode, 1992). There are five major types of dispersed collective behavior: rumors; mass hysteria; disaster behavior; fashions, fads, and crazes; and public opinion.

Rumors. A **rumor** is unverified information passed informally from person to person (Rosnow & Fine, 1976). Rumors arise in ambiguous situations when people desperately want accurate information but none is available (Shibutani, 1966; Berk, 1974). People are particularly likely to believe rumors if they are very anxious and if the bearer is regarded as generally credible. Rumors are hard to stop; people often continue to believe them even after more accurate information has become available (Tannen, 1990).

Sociologists analyze rumors somewhat more positively than most people do. Rather than emphasizing their inaccuracies, sociologists see them as a kind of collective effort to solve problems and interpret reality in order to reduce anxiety (Rosnow, 1991). They frequently help people adapt to social change (Rosnow & Fine, 1976; Kapferer, 1992).

Only occasionally are rumors deliberately manipulative. However, distortions routinely arise as they are passed along. They generally become shorter, and one central theme emerges as the heart of the rumor; social psychologists call these processes *leveling* and *sharpening*. They are also modified or *assimilated* in line with the interests of those who are conveying them (Allport & Postman, 1947).

Rumor is not only a type of collective behavior in itself, it also plays an important role in the genesis and development of mobs, riots, panics, fads, and disaster behavior. Furthermore, modern means of communication, especially the Internet, have substantially increased the speed whereby a rumor may spread.

There are two special types of rumors: gossip and urban legends. **Gossip** consists of rumors about other peoples' personal affairs (Cooley, 1962). It is more likely than other types of rumor to be passed on to bolster the teller's status. Gossip may concern one's friends or the rich and (in)famous.

Urban legends are rumors that recount ironic and usually grisly events that supposedly happened to "a friend of a friend" (Brunvand, 1980). For example,

there is the tale about a drug-addicted babysitter who stuffed a baby instead of a turkey and cooked it in the microwave. In the urban legend called "Kentucky fried rat," an incompetent fry cook serves a customer a rat that accidentally fell into the fryer at a fast food restaurant.

Most urban legends are modern cautionary tales that play off anxieties about the rapid pace of change in modern society. The basic moral is always the same: The world is a dangerous place and the old ways are the best. If women just stayed home and prepared family dinners, nobody would have to risk eating out at a restaurant or entrusting their children to incompetent sitters.

Sometimes the media pick up urban legends and disseminate them. Examples include the false claims that large numbers of children are abducted by Satanists and sacrificed in their rituals (Richardson et al., 1991), and that deranged people are putting razor blades in the apples they pass out at Halloween. When rumors like these are reported in the media, they can spark episodes of mass hysteria.

Mass Hysteria. **Mass hysteria** is similar to panic in that it is an intense, fearful, and seemingly irrational reaction to a perceived, but often misunderstood or imaginary threat. However, it is longer lasting than panic and takes place in at least partially dispersed collectivities. One of the best-known cases of mass hysteria was the terror felt by many thousands of people across the country in response to the Orson Welles broadcast of "The War of the Worlds" on Halloween eve, 1938 (Cantril, 1940). Two other examples:

- In 1954 in Seattle, hundreds of motorists became concerned over tiny pits that seemed to be appearing on the windshields of their cars. No empirical cause was ever identified; some people attributed the damage to atomic bomb tests. In reality, people were merely noticing the minor damage that occurs to all cars from small airborne particles of gravel. They had suddenly started looking *at* their windshields, not *through* them (Medalia & Larson, 1958).
- In 1962 a textile mill in the South was temporarily closed down after dozens of workers reported a mysterious illness that they believed was caused by an insect bite. The plant was fumigated, but no insect was ever found (Kerckhoff & Back, 1968).

What is going on here? Sometimes people who are under intense strain that they can neither control nor reduce find a collective outlet for their tensions in an outbreak of mass hysteria. In these examples, the

While initial responses to disasters like earthquakes and floods are sometimes emotional and nonadaptive, within a few hours the survivors usually pitch in to help restore order to their community.

source of the strain was, respectively, fear of the Cold War and nuclear weapons, and a rumor about layoffs at the factory. The hysteria does not address the real sources of people's fears, but it does partially relieve their tension.

Disaster Behavior. When hurricanes, earthquakes, tidal waves, or other natural or humanly created disasters strike communities, most everyday institutionalized behavior patterns are no longer effective or even possible. Accordingly, people must improvise, developing new norms in order to cope with the devastation.

Sometimes, when the scope of the disaster is overwhelming, the result is widespread demoralization and anomie (Erickson, 1976). But contrary to the conventional wisdom, the usual reaction is much more adaptive. New patterns of organization and community leadership emerge rapidly, often so quickly that much of the aid that pours in from the outside is unneeded (Quarantelli, 1978).

Fashion, Fads, and Crazes. The term **fashion** refers to periodic changes in the popularity of styles of hair, clothes, automobiles, architecture, music, sports, language, and even pets. Fashions change relatively gradually and show considerable historical continuity (Lofland, 1985). Fashion is a relatively institutionalized form of collective behavior, often heavily influenced by manufacturers in search of profits (Klapp, 1972).

This type of collective behavior is largely limited to modern societies where change is valued, people are sufficiently affluent to follow the latest trends, and the mass media disseminate information about which styles are currently popular (Lofland, 1973). Keeping up with fashion is an important way in which people in modern societies can establish a claim to a distinctive—but not too distinctive—personal identity (Simmel, 1971).

The rich are usually the trendsetters. Over time, modified versions of fashions embraced by the elite trickle down to the masses—at which point, of course, the upper classes have inevitably moved on to a different style (Davis, 1992). Occasionally, however, styles move up rather than down the class ladder, as when middle- and upper-class youth began wearing proletarian fashions like blue jeans and work shirts. Such a show of pseudo-egalitarianism seems especially appropriate in a society like ours that preaches the value of equality but does not actually allow as much upward mobility as we would like to believe.

Fads are shorter-lived than fashions, adopted briefly and enthusiastically and then quickly abandoned (Johnson, 1985). They usually have a playful quality. Fads tend to appeal especially to the young and clearly are used to validate personal status with one's peers (Turner & Killian, 1993). They are extensively publicized by the media and spread through friendship networks (Aguirre et al., 1988). Fads are usually regarded with amusement or disdain by outsiders. Unlike fashions, they have little historical continuity and have few if any lasting consequences.

There are four distinct types of fads (Lofland, 1993):

- *Object fads*—hula hoops, Rubik cubes, Cabbage Patch dolls, pogs, tamagotchis, Beanie Babies, Air Jordans, Pokemon cards.

Adolescents are often attracted to clothing and hairstyle fads. They provide a convenient way of proclaiming a distinct identity that a person shares with a few friends but that differentiates that person sharply from everyone else. In the early 1980s, punk styles were popular; today, body piercing plays a similar role.

- *Idea fads*—astrology, UFOs, the occult.
- *Activity fads*—body piercing, bungee jumping, streaking, tattooing, mosh pits.
- *Personality fads*—Elvis, Davy Crockett, Princess Di, Micahel Jordan.

A **craze** is simply a relatively long-lasting fad with significant economic or cultural implications (Lofland, 1981). The classic example is "tulipmania," an extreme passion for tulips that swept over Holland in 1634, appreciably distorting the Dutch economic structure. More recent examples include Beatlemania, Star Trek, video games, and the exercise and fitness craze.

Publics.   The public is the least coordinated type of dispersed collective behavior. A **public** is a large number of people, not necessarily in direct contact with each other, who are interested in a particular controversial issue (Lang & Lang, 1961; Turner & Killian, 1993). Thus every major area of popular con-

cern—welfare, abortion, national defense, affirmative action, education—creates a separate and distinct public.

In everyday usage, the phrase *public opinion* usually refers to a "snapshot" based on survey research of the opinions of a large number of people at a given point in time. In contrast, collective behavior researchers conceptualize a public as an enduring collectivity of people who maintain interest in a particular issue over an extended period of time.

When a public becomes organized enough to actively convey its point of view to decision makers, then it has become either an interest group or a social movement (Greenberg & Page, 1996).

SOCIAL MOVEMENTS

Social movements are everywhere in modern societies. Among the most visible as we move into the new millennium are environmentalism, the pro-choice and pro-life movements, feminism, the movement for the rights of the disabled, movements for and against tougher gun control, the white supremacist movement, the animal rights movement, the gay liberation movement, and the numerous movements supporting the rights of racial and ethnic minority groups.

A **social movement** is a relatively large and organized group of people working for or opposing social change and using at least some unconventional or uninstitutionalized methods (Wilson, 1973; Marx & McAdam, 1994). The wealthy and powerful can generally use their positions and influential personal networks to bring about the changes they favor. But the vast majority of the population, lacking access to established channels of power, find social movements the most practical way to promote change (Piven & Cloward, 1977; Adams, 1991; Tarrow, 1994).

Until about thirty years ago, social movements were almost always analyzed as a type of collective behavior, perhaps because the fervor of some participants impressed many early sociologists as threat-

INTERNET — CONNECTIONS

The internet has become an effective medium for rumor transmission. Many recent Web-lies are listed at site http://www.Colorado.EdU/English/legends.1999/. Pick one that you think is the most ridiculous and another that you think seems believable.

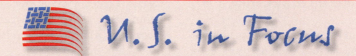

"Up in Smoke": The Cigar Craze

By the mid-1990s, the opponents of tobacco use seemed to be winning their struggle. All across the country, smoking had been banned in public places. Tobacco companies faced class-action suits for knowingly marketing an addictive product that cost people millions of dollars every year in health care. Rates of smoking were declining slowly but steadily among adults. It seemed that smoking was no longer seen as sophisticated, sexy, or "hip." But then came the cigar craze.

According to legend, the craze was initiated by the manager of the elegant Ritz Carlton Hotel in Boston. After dinner with a colleague in the hotel's restaurant, the manager lit up a cigar. His friend was shocked and the manager stubbed out the offending cigar, but he noticed a look of envy in the eyes of other male diners. Later that year, the Ritz held its first black tie "cigar smoker"—today an annual, $500-per-person event with hundreds of names on the waiting list.

When elite men began buying cigars, prices climbed. Sensing a trend, the publisher of a highly successful magazine, *The Wine Spectator*, launched *Cigar Aficionado*; the subject was different, but the format, the presentation, and the audience were nearly identical. Soon "Generation X" yuppies and would-be yuppies were signing up for "smokers," filling wood-paneled, leather-chaired cigar bars, and even building cigar rooms into their homes. One of the keys to the cigar's attraction is that it is a relatively inexpensive status symbol—beyond the reach of the working class, but far cheaper than BMWs, hand-tailored suits, or other similar symbols of true elite status.

In our fast-paced society, establishing and projecting one's identity is often problematic. Before the current craze, cigars conjured up images of stogie-chomping union bosses or Cuban leader Fidel Castro, who is rarely photographed without a cigar. The cigar craze symbolized rebellion against the current obsession with health and fitness and an assertion of masculinity in a period of increasing androgyny (though women soon joined the trend). It was a symbolic redefinition of a formerly working-class custom.

Will the cigar craze last? Just as sociologists identify predictable stages in social movements, so marketing experts see predictable stages in fashions and crazes. In the "pre-cool stage," trends appear on society's fringes. In the "cool stage," large numbers of people join in. In the "post-cool stage," corporate America capitalizes on the craze with brand name accessories and increased production. In the final "non-cool stage," a trend loses status, filters down to the working class, and then burns out entirely.

1. Why do you think cigar smoking appeals to trendy women as well as men?
2. In addition to smoking cigars, are there other ways in which affluent young people can "act out" against social pressures for conformity without imperiling their privileged status?
3. Contrast how contagion theory, value-added theory, and emergent norm theory might analyze the cigar craze.

Sources: Davis, 1992; Hamilton, 1997.

ening and somewhat irrational. There are, however, some major differences between collective behavior and social movements.

Compared to the elementary forms of collective behavior, social movements are longer lasting, better organized, more goal oriented, and have far more significant effects on the society in which they arise. These characteristics have led modern scholars to question whether social movements should be lumped together in the same conceptual category as riots, rumor, and fads (McAdam et al., 1988).

Most social movements include a number of distinct formal organizations, referred to as social movement organizations or *SMOs*—each of which works in its own way in support of the basic goals of the entire movement (Goode, 1992). Thus, for example, SMOs within the general environmental movement include the Audubon Society, the Sierra Club, Earth First!, and Greenpeace. Typically SMOs specialize; some concentrate on direct political action while others try to influence legislation; each may appeal to a different element of the larger population (Maheu, 1995). Though SMOs sometimes compete with one another, they usually complement one another's activities (Cable & Cable, 1995).

The overall level of social movement activity in a society fluctuates. Sometimes there are many movements competing for attention while at other times relatively few are active (Zald, 1992; Tilly, 1993). These cycles have been referred to as "waves of protest" (Tarrow, 1994). The period between 1960 and 1975 witnessed a dramatic profusion of social movement activity. As anyone can testify who lived through these years, there was an almost palpable sense of change in the air (Zald & McCarthy, 1987; Koopmans, 1993).

Waves of protest sometimes arise from major social dislocations caused by factors such as wars, economic recessions, major technological innovations, or unusual demographic events such as the Baby Boom. The activism of the 1960s and early 1970s was also aided by the affluence of the era, which allowed young social movement supporters to work for change rather than worry about making a living.

The various movements that arise during an era of protest also tend to reinforce one another. Supporters of the civil rights, feminist, student, anti-war, and environmental movements learned from one another's mistakes and were buoyed by one another's successes, a phenomenon called *social movement spillover* (Meyer & Whittier, 1994).

Sociologists study the development of social movements at three levels. They ask why individual people join movements—the micro level of analysis; how organizational factors influence movement development—the intermediate level; and how larger social and political factors affect movement growth—the macro level.

Why Do People Join Social Movements?

Like contagion theory, early micro-level explanations of social movement membership saw participants as less than fully rational. However, more modern approaches disagree, generally interpreting movement participation as the most effective way that relatively powerless people can promote their collective goals. In this section, we will review four major theories of movement participation, beginning with the oldest.

Mass Society Theory. Strongly influenced by their abhorrence of the atrocities committed in Europe by supporters of the Nazi movement, theorists in the mass-society school largely discounted the reasons that supporters themselves gave for joining movements—which tended to emphasize the importance of the changes they were trying to bring about. Instead, they focused on members' personal inadequacies (Hoffer, 1951; Kornhauser, 1959; Feuer, 1969). Participants were depicted as frustrated, socially isolated individuals in modern mass societies who felt insignificant and powerless. They joined movements in order to lose themselves in ill-considered ventures to remake the world.

Subsequent research has seriously challenged the basic assumptions of the mass-society approach. Most activists—in the civil rights movement (Morris, 1984; McAdam, 1988), in other 1960s movements, or even

Nazis (Lipset, 1963; Oberschall, 1973)—are not social atoms; they are well integrated into functioning social networks (McAdam & Paulsen, 1994).

Relative Deprivation Theory. Theorists next focused on the discontent that activists themselves claimed to be their primary reason for joining social movements. Attention was focused on the notion of **relative deprivation,** a conscious feeling of a negative discrepancy between legitimate expectations and perceived actualities (Morrison, 1971; Wilson, 1973). Relative deprivation theory argues that people compare their situation with the situations of members of relevant reference groups and conclude that change is necessary (Gurr, 1970).

This theory explains the fact that movements tend to arise, not when conditions are at their worst, but rather when things seem to be getting better. During times of absolute deprivation, most people just concentrate on survival; when life starts improving and expectations rise, they are more likely to develop a sense of relative deprivation and join social movements. This school of thought is also compatible with research that shows most movement supporters come from the middle ranks of society, not from the most downtrodden groups (McAdam, 1988; Fendrich & Lovoy, 1988).

One well-known deprivation theory was developed by James Davies (1962). He describes a pattern called the *J-curve* (see Figure 23.2): For quite some time, social conditions appear to be improving in line with people's rising expectations; but then, although their hopes continue to escalate, people see their lives suddenly becoming worse. Davies suggests that J-curve relative deprivation preceded several major revolutions, including the French Revolution of 1789 and the 1917 Bolshevik Revolution in Russia.

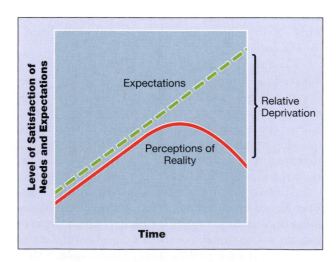

FIGURE 23.2   J-Curve Relative Deprivation

Relative-deprivation theory is an advance over mass-society theory in that it takes activists' discontent seriously. However, critics point out that there is always a certain amount of relative deprivation present in society, yet movements do not always arise. Thus, deprivation alone cannot fully explain movement growth (Wilson & Orum, 1976; Gurney & Tierney, 1982; Johnson & Klandermans, 1995).

Furthermore, the concept of relative deprivation has been attacked as circular. Theorists argue that movements arise because of relative deprivation, but often the only way they can demonstrate the existence of that deprivation is by pointing to the emergence of social movements (Jenkins & Perrow, 1977).

Recruitment Through Networks. Beginning in the 1980s, some social movement theorists began to emphasize the importance of preexisting networks in the recruitment of members (Marwell et al., 1988; Cable, 1992). This "micro-mobilization" perspective effectively turns mass-society theory on its head by stressing that activists maintain extensive relationships with like-minded others.

In support of this view, research has repeatedly shown that people often join social movements because their friends or relatives are members (Snow et al., 1980); sometimes entire families have a tradition of activism. Furthermore, the most successful movements are often those whose members maintain a dense network of interpersonal connections, a network that helps the movement obtain the various resources it needs (Opp & Gern, 1993; Marx & McAdam, 1994). Relative deprivation and ideological commitment are certainly important, but they often arise or at least reach their peak only after members have been recruited into a social movement by their friends and been socialized to fully accept the movement's worldview (McAdam et al., 1988; Hirsh, 1990).

Frame Alignment. The newest theoretical perspective to address the issue of why people join movements takes a symbolic interactionist approach. The frame-alignment approach emphasizes the process by which movements shape or "frame" their definition of the situation in order to attempt to recruit new members. (Snow et al., 1986; Snow & Benford, 1988). The "collective action frame" that a movement constructs has three elements: an "injustice component" designed essentially to promote relative deprivation; an "agency component," meant to convince potential recruits that the movement really can make a difference; and an "identity component," which enhances commitment by building a strong collective identity with the movement and its goals (Gamson, 1992).

The collective-action frame must be reasonably congruent with the interests, understandings, and values held by the target population. It must also extend the perspectives of prospective members by increasing their outrage and building their commitment to the movement (W. Gamson, 1991; Jasper & Poulsen, 1995). The process of frame alignment is similar to the establishment of what Marx called class consciousness (see Chapter 10).

Resource-Mobilization Theory

Resource-mobilization theory has been the dominant school of thought regarding social-movement development for most of the past two decades (Klandermans, 1994). These theorists are not so much concerned with why individuals join movements as they are with analyzing SMOs as formal organizations (see Chapter 22) and isolating the structural factors that explain which movements succeed and which fail (Oberschall, 1973; McCarthy & Zald, 1977; Jenkins, 1983).

Resource-mobilization theorists thus argue that movement outcomes are principally determined, not by their ideas, but by how effectively SMOs acquire and use key resources (Walsh, 1981; Gamson, 1990). Far from seeing movements as irrational, resource-mobilization theorists interpret them as frequently embodying high levels of what Weber termed bureaucratic rationality (see Chapter 22) (Jenkins & Perrow, 1977; Tilly, 1978; Opp, 1989).

Some SMO resources are quite concrete: money, fax machines, telephones, computers. Others are more abstract but no less important; chief among these is talented leadership. In the earliest phases of social-movement development, leadership is often based on charisma. But once a coherent organizational structure emerges, administrators often become more important than agitators or prophets (Wilson, 1973). During periods of intense movement activity, leaders may switch from one movement to another—for example, from the civil-rights movement to the anti-war and feminist causes—bringing their organizational skills with them.

Supporters are another crucial category of movement resource (Freeman, 1979). Recruited mostly from the personal networks of current members, followers not only serve as demonstrators but also provide crucial financial and other material assistance.

Sometimes SMO supporters are drawn from population elements that hope to benefit directly from the success of the movement. Others are "conscience constituents," such as whites who supported the civil-rights struggle or men who endorse feminism (McCarthy & Zald, 1973). Outsiders often provide the

Contemporary social movement activists are well aware that access to the mass media is a critical organizational resource. Many demonstrations are held primarily so that they will be reported on the evening news.

largest share of movement financing (Oberschall, 1973; McCarthy & Zald, 1977).

Access to the mass media is a particularly crucial organizational resource (Molotch, 1979; Zald, 1992). In fact, social movements and the media have a symbiotic relationship: Movement activities are often compelling news items, and media coverage is an important means of recruiting and consciousness-raising for activist groups (Gamson & Wolfsfeld, 1993).

However, the relationship between movements and the mass media is always edgy. By definition, movements promote a definition of reality that is somewhat different from the one that most people accept, whereas the media normally attempt to position themselves to attract the largest possible audience. As a result, activists constantly criticize the media for sensationalizing issues and for missing what they consider the real issues (Gitlin, 1980).

Resource mobilization is not without its critics. The principal complaint is that, not unlike the mass-society approach, the resource-mobilization school tends to ignore the grievances that spur relative deprivation and the ideas that the movement promotes (Klandermans, 1984; Zygmunt, 1986; Buechler, 1993; Scott, 1995), except to the extent that they help recruit new members (Benford, 1993).

The Political-Process Approach

The political-process approach is a relatively recent, historically based type of social-movement theory. It focuses on the changing relationship over time between movements and the macrolevel political and economic systems of the societies in which they emerge (Tilly, 1978; Quadagno, 1992; Tarrow, 1994). This highly sophisticated school of thought examines systemic factors that either encourage or discourage movement activism and success. It also assesses the impact of movements on the larger society. Two of the clearest findings of this school are that movements emerge more readily in democratic societies (Jenkins & Perrow, 1977) and that weak governments are especially vulnerable to pressure from activists.

Except for the discredited mass-society approach, each of the micro, organizational, and macro theories helps us understand the dynamics of movement development. None is adequate by itself, but taken as a whole this body of sociological theorizing answers most of the important questions about social movements (Kowalewski & Porter, 1992; Marx & McAdam, 1994).

INTERNET ━━◆━━ **CONNECTIONS**

In December 1997, Julie Butterfly climbed 180 feet up an ancient redwood tree, which she named Luna, to protest the logging of these old giants. If she's still in the tree, and you want to add your support, you can reach Julie through her Web site, www.lunatree.org. What would it take for you to make so extreme a gesture of protest?

MOVEMENT TYPES AND CAREERS

Among the many empirical issues that interest sociologists of social movements, two have attracted particular attention. First, can we reduce the bewildering variety of social movements into a small number of distinct types? And, second, is there a sequence of stages or a career process through which most movements pass?

Varieties of Social Movements

Social movements may be classified on the basis of several different criteria:

- Some aim for relatively modest changes, while others advocate broad, sweeping transformations (Turner & Killian, 1993).
- Some advocate changes that are *progressive* or generally in line with the direction in which society is moving, while others work to reverse current trends (Turner & Killian, 1993).
- Some seek immediate change, while others are content to work for more gradual improvement (Blumer, 1974).
- Some target individuals for change, while others focus on larger systems or whole societies (Aberle, 1966).

The first two issues are especially important. We will use them as the basis for our discussion of three types of social movements: reformist, revolutionary, and reactionary.

Reformist Movements. Reformist movements aim for relatively small-scale or limited progressive change. They do not try to substantially alter society's basic political, economic, or stratification systems, or to reverse the general direction in which society is currently moving. Examples include the civil-rights movement, the nineteenth century movement for female suffrage, most environmental groups, the movement protesting the war in Vietnam, and the pro-choice movement.

In other words, reformist movements work within the system. While they may use moderately unconventional tactics like sit-ins and mass demonstrations, they almost always avoid violence. They at least grudgingly accept the current political and legal institutions and accordingly devote most of their energies to trying to change laws and governmental policies. They are especially common in democratic societies where citizens have the right to work peacefully for change.

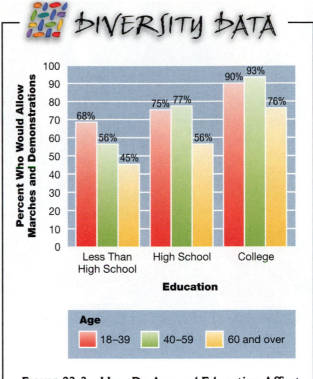

FIGURE 23.3 How Do Age and Education Affect Acceptance of Anti-Government Demonstrations? Regardless of age, people with higher levels of education are more likely to accept the legitimacy of public protest. However, individuals between 40 and 59 with at least a high school education are actually more supportive of protest than those in their twenties and thirties. This is the generation that was in school during the great wave of movement activism of the 1960s and 1970s. How might the attitudes of this age group affect social movements today?
Source: NORC. General Social Surveys, 1972–1996. Chicago: National Opinion Research Center, 1996. Reprinted by permission of NORC, Chicago, IL.

Those who oppose the goals of reformist movements usually try to depict them as more extreme than they really are. For example, most SMOs in the contemporary gay rights movement advocate relatively modest reforms, such as including sexual preference in anti-discrimination statutes and increasing funding for AIDS research. But opponents of gay rights commonly paint these groups in sinister terms, arguing that the gay movement is a serious threat to "family values" and "Christian morality." Sometimes opponents of a movement are aided in their efforts by the existence of small, highly visible extreme groups within most broadly reformist movements. Regarding gay rights, for example, opponents point to ACT-UP as evidence that the whole movement is extremist.

Reformist movements use unconventional but nonviolent tactics like mass demonstrations. These Arab students at the American University of Beirut have chosen to protest American attacks on Iraq peacefully rather than engage in rioting or acts of terrorism.

Revolutionary Movements. Some social movements seek broad and sweeping progressive changes, including major alterations in society's economic and political institutions and system of stratification (Hopper, 1950). These movements typically arise when efforts to bring about reform have failed or proven inadequate, or in authoritarian societies where virtually any attempt to implement social change is considered subversive by the government. By definition, these movements work outside of the established institutional structure.

Such groups are commonly called **revolutionary movements,** although this term is somewhat deceptive. Sometimes efforts to topple one group of political leaders and replace them with other individuals, but not alter the basic structure of society, are termed "revolutions." But such events are not really revolutions in the sense we are using this word. Such uprisings—for example, the American revolution of 1776—may be termed *political revolutions,* reserving the term *social revolution* for more sweeping changes such as occurred in the French Revolution of 1789, the Iranian Revolution of 1979, and the Russian Revolutions of 1917 and 1989 (Skocpol, 1979). Other examples of revolutionary movements include the Black Panthers of the late 1960s, radical environmental groups that use sabotage in pursuit of their goals, and communist revolutionary movements. Revolutionary movements often employ extreme and violent tactics, but not always: The recent dramatic social changes in Russia and South Africa were accomplished with a minimum of bloodshed (Boswell, 1989).

Sometimes people seek fundamental change not by directly challenging the existing system, but by withdrawing from it and creating their own alternate societies. Such efforts are called *utopian movements* (Alexander & Gill, 1984; Berger, 1988). Utopians usually form communes such as the nineteenth century Oneida Colony or the Shaker settlements. Others retain some connections with the larger society but also create their own institutions. Examples include the free schools and people's clinics that counterculture members founded in the 1970s and that still exist in some parts of the country (Rothschild-Whitt, 1979). Utopian movements whose ideology is religious rather than secular have a much stronger record of survival. Their sacred belief systems seem to be more effective in sustaining commitment in the face of a hostile or at least indifferent society (Kanter, 1973).

Reactionary Movements. Some social movements seek to reverse the general direction of social change and return to an earlier and, in their view, better time. Though their conception of the way things used to be is often distorted or wholly mythic, it nevertheless serves to rally the support of people who are uncomfortable with the present and fear the future. These groups, whether seeking large-scale or modest change, are called **reactionary movements.** Examples include the Ku Klux Klan, the militia movement, the Christian Right, the anti-feminist Eagle Forum, and the pro-life movement.

Reactionary movements often arise when the actual or impending success of a progressive movement

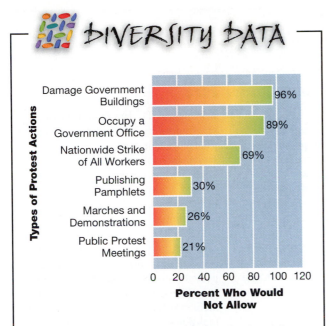

DIVERSITY DATA

FIGURE 23.4   Percent Who Would NOT Allow These Protest Actions Against Government
Large majorities of Americans reject violent or disruptive protest tactics. However, between one-fifth and one-third of the general public also would not allow dissenters to express their anti-government feelings in writing or at public meetings despite the fact that such activities are clearly protected by the First Amendment. What are the potential consequences of the fact that so many people are prepared to deny others their right to freedom of speech?
Source: NORC. General Social Surveys, 1972–1996. Chicago: National Opinion Research Center, 1996. Reprinted by permission of NORC, Chicago, IL.

alarms people with a vested interest in the status quo. Such groups are termed **countermovements** (Mottl, 1980; Lo, 1982; Lyman, 1995). For example, the early successes of the civil rights movement revived the Klan and led to the creation of White Citizens' Councils all across the Deep South.

Many sociologists expect to see reactionary movements gain strength around the world as the ongoing globalization of the economy forces more and more traditional peoples into increasingly direct contact with the modern world. Consider the dramatic success of traditional Islamic "fundamentalist" movements in Iran and Afghanistan. This may be only the first wave of opposition to the broad social and cultural trends that are transforming lives and nations worldwide.

Movement Careers

A number of theorists have proposed models of the developmental stages through which social movements pass (Zald & Ash, 1966; Blumer, 1969a; Mauss,

1975; Spector & Kitsuse, 1977; Tilly, 1978). Each theory uses somewhat different terminology, but most identify four general career phases: incipience, coalescence, bureaucratization, and decline.

Incipience.   In its earliest phase, a social movement is not an organized group but rather a general mood of discontent or relative deprivation among some segments of society. Incipient movements often arise during the societal disruption caused by events such as war, economic crisis, migration, major technological change, or similar upheavals.

During this stage one or more individuals arise who give voice and definition to the widespread but poorly understood sense of unease felt by significant numbers of people. They are agitators and prophets, initially operating without any substantial organizational base.

In the words of C. Wright Mills (see Chapter 1), these early leaders teach people to reinterpret their "personal troubles" as "public issues." For example, before the birth of the modern feminist movement, Betty Friedan wrote a widely read book called *The Feminine Mystique* (1963), in which she used the phrase "the problem that has no name" to identify the discontent felt in the 1950s by educated women who were expected to happily abandon their career plans in order to be wives and mothers.

Coalescence.   After public consciousness has been raised, the next step is to actually build a movement. The women's rights component of modern feminism was organized largely around preexisting networks of socially and politically active women, many of whom had participated in John Kennedy's 1961 Presidential Commission on the Status of Women (Chafetz & Dworkin, 1986). During coalescence, then, a formal organization is established, concerns are focused, leaders are selected, and tactics are chosen. Alliances are often built with other like-minded movements. The group begins to actively pursue its goals, in the process attracting attention from the media. While early media coverage is likely to be skeptical and distorted, it does spread public awareness of the new movement, which often attracts supporters and key organizational resources.

Bureaucratization.   If the movement succeeds in attracting followers and appears to be making progress toward achieving its goals, it tends to experience strong pressures to become more highly structured. Its internal division of labor becomes more elaborate, the staff grows, and leaders gradually become administrators. As the movement gains in stature and becomes increasingly respectable, its tactics usually become less confrontational. This causes some of

The Pro-Life Movement Under Fire

The anti-abortion or right-to-life movement is a classic example of a countermovement, one that seeks to reverse current patterns of social change. The history of this group also provides insights into the life cycle of social movements.

The 1960s were an era of social upheaval in the United States. Throughout this period, the number of women (especially married women and mothers) entering the workforce grew steadily. To many Americans, "women's liberation" symbolized everything that had gone wrong in the 1960s. Feminists, they argued, threatened to undermine the traditional religious and family values that had made the United States strong. The Supreme Court decision in *Roe v. Wade* (1974), which held that a woman has the right to decide whether to terminate a pregnancy during the first six months, marked a turning point. Hailed as a victory by supporters of women's rights, the ruling galvanized the opposition.

In the 1970s and the 1980s, abortion became a symbolic marker between Americans who were alarmed by social change, sought to maintain traditional gender roles, and viewed motherhood as a sacred calling, and those who welcomed change, sought gender equality, and viewed motherhood as only one of many roles a woman might (or might not) choose. The right-to-life movement united groups that had traditionally been suspicious of one another—urban Catholics and rural Southern Protestants, as well as white (and some black) working-class Americans. The movement also played a key role in the emergence of the "New Right." To a large degree, a candidate's stand on abortion became a political litmus test. The pro-life movement gained numbers and influence, culminating in the election of conservative abortion foe Republican Ronald Reagan

as president in 1980.

Through the 1970s and 1980s, the anti-abortion movement pursued its goal—the repeal of *Roe v. Wade*—primarily through conventional politics and peaceful protest. Gradually, the Supreme Court, Congress, and state legislatures placed more and more restrictions on abortion, including mandatory waiting periods of several hours or days, the requirement that teenagers obtain parental consent, and a ban on so-called "partial birth" abortions.

In the late 1980s, the pro-life movement became more confrontational and militant. This often occurs when a movement has achieved some, but only partial, success. Out of frustration, some SMOs begin to employ unconventional tactics. Much as the nonviolent civil rights movement gave rise to the militant Black Panthers, the pro-life movement spawned "Operation Rescue." Members of this group began by staging prayer vigils outside women's health clinics but soon escalated to establishing blockades around clinics, using posters portraying aborted near-term fetuses to frighten clinic workers and patients, picketing the homes of physicians who performed abortions, mailing gruesome films to patients, telephoning threats to abortion providers, and the like. These tactics have been quite effective. Many doctors have stopped performing abortions and in rural and conservative areas, a woman who is legally entitled to an abortion may no longer be able to obtain one (Rubin, 1995). But another effect was to mobilize the pro-choice movement to stage counterdemonstrations, arrange clinic escorts, and lobby Congress to pass laws against blockading clinics.

Beginning with the murder of Dr. David Gunn in March 1993, some hardcore anti-abortion activists turned

to violence. To date there have been seven murders (three of doctors) and numerous sniper attacks, physical assaults, and stalkings. Dozens of clinics have been bombed, set on fire, or vandalized. Hundreds of phoned and faxed threats have been reported. In some communities, activists have circulated "WANTED" posters with the photographs, names, and addresses of abortionists. Lists of abortion providers are posted on websites like the "Nuremberg Files"; the name of Dr. Barnett Slepian was crossed off one such list the night he was murdered outside his home by a sniper. Some groups, such as Pro-Life Virginia and the American Coalition of Life Activists, openly promote violence and charge the government with repression of their right to free speech. The majority of those who oppose abortion are appalled by these violent tactics, with the result that the pro-life movement has become increasingly fragmented. If terrorism is the "weapon of the weak," these violent assaults may suggest that the anti-abortion movement has lost momentum and support. Nevertheless, extremist rhetoric does create an atmosphere of permissiveness in which individuals may take justice into their own hands.

1. How would the various theories of movement development analyze the pro-life crusade? In particular, consider the relative deprivation, frame alignment, resource mobilization, and value-added perspectives.
2. In what ways has the violent fringe of the pro-life movement harmed the larger movement? In what ways has it helped?
3. Is there any way in which the two sides of the abortion debate can find common ground?

Sources: Chafe, 1991; Rubin, 1995; Gegax & Clemetson, 1998.

Rachel Carson published Silent Spring *in 1962, almost a full decade before the coalescence of the environmental movement. In it she presented the first widely read account of the problems of pollution and environmental degradation that have now become familiar to virtually all Americans.*

the more extreme and enthusiastic members to criticize it for becoming part of "the establishment." For example, as the National Organization for Women (NOW) began to bureaucratize, some of its early members charged that by designating formal leaders and adopting a bureaucratic structure it had "sold out" (Carden, 1974; Staggenborg, 1988).

Decline. Although social movements are much longer lived than the elementary forms of collective behavior, they are ultimately always temporary. Whether they succeed or fail in their efforts to promote or resist change, all eventually end (Miller, 1985).

A movement may be considered successful if the major changes it seeks are implemented and/or if its leaders come to be recognized as legitimate spokespersons for their cause (Gamson, 1990; Rochon & Mazmanian, 1993). Under these circum-

stances, the movement tends to become an *interest group*—part of the political institution—and by definition no longer a social movement (von Eschen et al., 1976; Piven & Cloward, 1977). Such was the fate of NOW, the NAACP, and the U.S. labor movement.

In some cases, political leaders pursue a policy of *co-optation*, adopting watered-down versions of the changes advocated by a reformist movement and offering movement leaders rewarding positions within the power structure (Meyer, 1993). A few true believers may keep the group alive, but, deprived of the issues that originally motivated its members, the co-opted movement becomes impotent.

Other movements experience *goal displacement*: So much attention is devoted to simply keeping the group alive that it largely loses track of the changes it was originally created to advocate (see Chapter 22). This is especially likely to occur when progress has been slow and it has been hard to maintain the participants' enthusiasm (Zald & Ash, 1966; McCarthy & Zald, 1973; Oegema & Klandermans, 1994).

Perhaps the most common single cause of movement decline is *fragmentation* (Frey et al., 1992). Disagreements about goals or strategies can easily split a movement, as can overt or covert power struggles (Ryan, 1989). Fragmentation is especially likely after the loss of a charismatic leader, as occurred after the death of Elijah Muhammad, the founder of the Nation of Islam.

Finally, a social movement may decline as a result of *repression* (Opp & Roehl, 1990; Della Porta, 1995). Repression by the authorities is a common fate of revolutionary movements. This was the case with the International Workers of the World, a Marxist labor movement of the 1930s, and the Black Panthers of the late 1960s, many of whose key leaders were killed by the police (Marine, 1969). However, repression is a risky tactic because it can easily create martyrs. It is much safer to *ridicule* a movement into insignificance, a control strategy that is almost impossible to fight effectively. This was the strategy used to discredit and eventually destroy most of the more extreme SMOs in the 1970s women's liberation movement.

LIFE CONNECTIONS: Training Movement Activists

As resource mobilization theory emphasizes, dedicated supporters are among the most important resources on which social movements depend. Because the struggle to bring about social change is often a long one, it is critical that a core of activists be available to lead the movement and provide continuity as less committed supporters come and go. For this reason, many movements have gone out of their way to provide some sort of relatively structured training experience for their adherents.

Social movement training programs serve a number of functions. They provide participants with a detailed and coherent exposition of the movement's understanding of the social problem it is attempting to remediate. In theoretical terms, the participants' sense of relative deprivation is heightened and they are provided with an appropriate conceptual frame. Participants are also taught a variety of specific tactics as well as the broader philosophy (such as nonviolence) that informs the movement's choice of how to pursue its goals. The trainees also form strong interpersonal bonds with their fellow activists that help them to endure the rejection and abuse that so often accompany movement participation.

Until recently, most social movements provided their own specialized training programs. For example, the Northern student volunteers who participated in the Freedom Summer voter registration and freedom school projects in Mississippi trained in two week-long sessions held in June 1964 on the campus of the Western College for Women in Oxford, Ohio (Belfrage, 1965; McAdam, 1988). These workshops, sponsored by the National Council of Churches, included large morale-building and general orientation meetings, smaller section meetings for activists interested in particular issues, and groups of five to ten people who would actually be working together in Mississippi. The latter groups were especially intense and included role-playing sessions and lessons on how to protect yourself if attacked.

In the decades since the great wave of activism of the 1960s and 1970s, many movements have become more professional, a trend that will be discussed in greater depth in the next section of this chapter. One aspect of this professionalization process has been the development of broadly based training programs run by veteran activists and designed to serve the needs of people interested in protesting a variety of different issues.

Perhaps the best-known of the groups providing activist training is the Ruckus Society, founded in 1995 by John Sellers, who was at the time a 27-year-old veteran of the environmental group Greenpeace (Crenson, 2000; "Direct Action Figure," 2000; www.ruckus.org). Ruckus is a nonprofit, tax-exempt organization based in Berkeley, California. Its slogan is "Actions speak louder than words." The group has trained hundreds of activists interested in labor, human rights, and environmental issues in the techniques of nonviolent direct action, especially civil disobedience.

The primary vehicle by which Ruckus trains movement participants is the week long "Action Camp." Held in rural areas around the country, the camps emphasize the history, philosophy, and techniques of nonviolent protest and feature extensive role playing. Among the specific units of instruction:

- *Scouting.* Maps and photos, dealing with the authorities, intro to security, dealing with barriers, evasion.
- *Action Planning and Coordination.*
- *Climbing.* Basic ropework, belaying, rapelling, etc.
- *Electronics.* Radios, scanners, frequency analyzers, computers, and databases.
- *Blockades.* Tree sits, vehicle blockades, water blockades, bridge actions.
- *Media Training.* Crafting leads and soundbites, pitching the story, spin control, and message delivery.
- *Banner Workshop.*
- *Political Theater.* (www.ruckus.org/workshops.html)

Ruckus is distinctive in comparison to earlier training programs in several ways. It is far more sophisticated than the 1960s' groups were in its understanding of how to manipulate the media and in its computer savvy. It is oriented toward left-wing activism in general rather than toward any specific issue. And its style is more contemporary; as its founders put it, "There's a different dynamic. It's not the pony-tailed, gray-haired guys who remember the sixties" (Crenson, 2000). "We plot and scheme and conspire to save the planet. We have a blast" ("Direct Action Figure," 2000). Ruckus played a major role in training activists for the Seattle World Trade Organization demonstrations discussed in Chapter 1 and for street protests at the 2000 Republican and Democratic National Conventions. Its leaders are happily looking forward to a long and contentious future.

☰ SOCIETY CONNECTIONS: Current Trends in Movement Development

Starting in the late 1970s, sociologists began to notice a trend away from movements that arose spontaneously at the grassroots level and toward the increasing professionalization of movement activity. More recently, a new type of movement has begun to emerge all around the world, less oriented to economics and more concerned with cultural and lifestyle issues.

Professional Social Movements

Most of the major social movements that arose during the great wave of activism of the 1960s and 1970s were amateur efforts, staffed by people whose main qualifications for leadership were speaking ability and

Patricia Ireland, the head of the National Organization for Women, is an outstanding contemporary example of professional social movement leadership.

often improves the movement's effectiveness. Movement coalitions can be formed more easily when leaders know each other and share a common understanding of their role (Staggenborg, 1988).

And yet something has been lost when movements are headed by people whose desire to run a well-organized campaign may seem stronger than their passion for the cause. Professional managers, with at least one eye firmly fixed on the financial bottom line, may push a movement away from even moderately radical goals or tactics in order to avoid alienating wealthy potential donors. In professional movements, most members do little more than pay dues, read newsletters, and show up for the occasional rally (Kleidman, 1994). But where is the passion? How can professional movements maintain the "white-hot" commitment that seems so essential? At a minimum, social movements need to nurture a few small, relatively radical SMOs. Not only are such groups a critical source of enthusiasm and new ideas, but they also allow more conventional SMOs to present their goals as reasonable and moderate compared to the programs advocated by their "loony" compatriots.

New Social Movements

Perhaps partly in response to the professionalization trend, a new type of grassroots movement has begun to appear, called—logically enough—**new social movements** (Melucci, 1980, 1989; Touraine, 1981; McAdam et al., 1988; Larana et al., 1994; Kriesi et al., 1995; Scott, 1995). Most are concerned with issues such as protecting the environment, opposing nuclear power, changing the social definitions of gays and women, and securing animal rights. These are the chief characteristics of the new social movements:

ideological fervor. The inexperience of these leaders often severely handicapped the movements' efforts to achieve their goals.

Over time, many of these leaders began to gain expertise in organizational management. Frequently, as a result of social-movement spillover, individuals moved from one group to another, gaining valuable experience. The result was the emergence of what have been called *professional social movements* (McCarthy & Zald, 1973, 1977). Today, groups as diverse as the Sierra Club, NOW, and the NAACP are managed by full-time professionals who are highly skilled in fund-raising, obtaining positive publicity from the media, and organizing well-structured and carefully controlled public demonstrations.

In some ways, professionalization is positive. Professional movements present an image of respectability, which helps them solicit funds from foundations, the government, and well-heeled supporters (McCrea & Markle, 1989). Leadership by careerists also provides long-term organizational continuity, which

- They are ideologically inclusive, resisting the impulse to carve out narrow areas of concern. Movements like ecological feminism, the struggle against environmental racism, or women's peace groups stress the interconnectedness between various seemingly distinct causes (Merchant, 1983; Epstein, 1991; Bullard & Wright, 1992; Mies & Shiva, 1993). Many activists therefore participate in several new social movements at the same time.
- Unlike most earlier progressive movements, which frequently drew explicitly on the Marxist view that capitalism was the primary impediment to the changes they were seeking, most new social movements do not emphasize coherent anti-capitalism. In fact, these movements are more likely to consider the government irrelevant to their

concerns than they are to identify it as either an enemy or a potential ally.

- While most individual new social movement groups are small and localized, they are linked together in global networks. This is especially appropriate because most of the causes in which these movements are interested clearly transcend national boundaries.
- New social movements are nonbureaucratic and highly participatory. In many cases, they are as much about providing a fulfilling and liberating lifestyle as they are concerned with actually promoting social change (Gamson & Wolfsfeld, 1993). Like the 1970s feminist movement, they deliberately bridge the gap between the personal and the political. Their members join, in large part, to obtain a sense of autonomy and self-determination.
- New social movements are strongly oriented toward emotionality and tend to be suspicious of authority, science, and rationality, orientations

that they share with the New Age counterculture (Scott, 1990; Garner, 1996). They often deliberately seek confrontation, sometimes simply for the sake of confrontation.
- Like many other recent social movements, the new social movements attract mostly middle-class members—usually well-educated professionals and other knowledge workers.

In a sense, these two trends—the professionalization of much movement activity and the emergence of the deliberately nonprofessional new social movements—represent two sides of the same coin. Both may be seen as attempts to promote a new wave of social change by redefining the nature of the social movement. If the first decade of the new millennium sees a rebirth of large-scale activism, will it be spurred by professional movements, new social movements, or some synthesis of the two? We will know soon enough.

SUMMARY

1. Collective behavior arises in situations in which institutionalized norms appear inadequate because they are unclear or rapidly changing. It tends to be relatively short-lived, spontaneous, and unorganized.
2. Contagion theory emphasizes the emotional dimensions of collective behavior. Convergence theory explains the similarity of crowd participants as a consequence of the fact that only certain types of people choose to participate in any particular episode of collective behavior.
3. Neil Smelser's value-added theory identifies six factors that must be present if collective behavior is to occur: structural conduciveness, structural strain, a generalized belief, a precipitating incident, mobilization for action, and social control.
4. Emergent-norm theory suggests that definitions of appropriate behavior gradually develop out of ongoing crowd interaction.
5. Crowds and panics are the major types of localized collectivities. There are five varieties of crowds: casual, conventional, expressive, acting, and protest.
6. The major forms of dispersed collectivities include rumors; mass hysteria; disaster behavior; fashion, fads, and crazes; and publics.
7. Social movements are collective efforts to promote or resist change that use at least some rela-

tively uninstitutionalized methods. They have traditionally been analyzed as a type of collective behavior.
8. The formal organizations that promote the goals of social movements are known as SMOs. The level of movement activity in a society fluctuates over time.
9. Mass-society theory, now generally discredited, suggests people join social movements to compensate for their own personal inadequacies.
10. Relative-deprivation theory explains movement membership as a consequence of people feeling a negative discrepancy between their present situation and the circumstances to which they feel they are entitled.
11. Modern explanations of movement membership focus on recruitment through interpersonal networks and on the process of frame alignment.
12. Resource-mobilization theory analyzes the origin and development of social movements in terms of their ability to obtain and make effective use of such resources as leadership, supporters, and access to the mass media.
13. Political process theory is a macrolevel approach that studies the relationship between social movement development and the political and economic structure of the society where the movement arises.
14. Reformist social movements work for relatively

small-scale changes, whereas revolutionary movements seek to change a society's fundamental economic, political, and stratification systems. Reactionary social movements try to reverse the direction in which change is currently moving.

15. Many social movements pass through a four-stage career or life cycle pattern of incipience, coalescence, bureaucratization, and decline.

16. Social movements commonly sponsor structured training programs for their members.

17. Movements are becoming increasingly professionalized. But sociologists have also noticed the emergence of a new type of movement that is ideologically inclusive, global in scope, highly participatory, and emotional.

KEY TERMS

acting crowd   595
casual crowd   594
collective behavior   591
conventional crowd   594
countermovement   607
craze   600
crowd   594
expressive crowd   595
fads   599

fashion   599
gossip   598
mass hysteria   598
mob   595
new social movement   611
panic   596
protest crowd   596
public   600

reactionary movement   606
reformist movement   605
relative deprivation   602
revolutionary movement   606
riot   595
rumor   598
social movement   600
urban legend   598

CRITICAL THINKING QUESTIONS

1. In explaining participation in collective behavior and social movements, some theories emphasize the members' personal qualities, whereas others stress such external factors as the availability of resources and problems in the larger society. Which approach do you find more useful? Why do you think different people might prefer one type of theory over the other?

2. Are minority riots better understood as political protests or as deviant behavior? What factors might influence a person's answer to this question?

3. Is the dividing line between reformist and revolutionary movements clear cut? How would you classify such modern movements as feminism, environmentalism, gun control, and gay rights? Can the members of your class reach a consensus regarding these movements?

4. Why do you think there is less social movement activity today than there was in the late 1960s? Do you expect to see a new wave of movement activity in the early twenty-first century? Why?

SOCIAL CHANGE AND DEVELOPMENT

24

OUTLINE

Walking the Edge
of the Censor's Sword

At a shopping center in Teheran, Iranian boutiques display sleeveless black dresses and white miniskirts even though publicly wearing such garments has been outlawed since the 1979 revolution. Meanwhile, a voice on a loudspeaker reminds women to keep their veils properly in place. Outside a crowded pizza parlor in wealthy north Teheran, young women in full Islamic dress name their favorite bands: Metallica, Pink Floyd, and Guns 'N' Roses. They get videos of these groups from illicit satellite dishes hidden under mattresses or concealed by clothes hung permanently out to dry. As one woman states, "We do everything in hiding, but in the open we have to be very careful." As these occurrences suggest, despite the government's best efforts to maintain the fervor of the revolution, a liberalizing current is now coursing through Iranian life. (Shadid, 1996:10)

Economies of Exclusion

A new world economic order is arising. It is most easily seen, not in the high rises of Tokyo or Manhattan, or in the desolate poverty of Zaire or Somalia, but rather in places like Bangkok, Tijuana, Rio de Janeiro, and Nairobi—cities where dramatic economic growth coexists with massive social problems. Here products and services are provided for a growing global middle class. Upward economic mobility is in the air, but without fundamental changes in the structure of this new world order, the best that most workers in these cities can do is to catch a quick glimpse of air-conditioned affluence from the streets. (Sernau, 1997:49)

An Interview with the Founder
of the Grameen Bank of Bangladesh

Muhammad Yunas is the founder of the Grameen Bank in Bangladesh. This institution provides small loans to groups of people who wish to start household-based agricultural or manufacturing enterprises in order to pull themselves up from poverty. In a recent interview, he admitted that he ". . . was not trained to understand self-help. Like all economics students, I believed that people should prepare themselves for the job market. If you fail to get a job, you register yourself for charity. But I could not hold on to these beliefs when I faced the real life of the poor in Bangladesh. For the most part, the job market did not mean much, and for survival they turned to economic activities on their own. The economic institutions they turned to did not notice their struggle. Through no fault of their own, and unable to come up with even a dollar for working capital, they were rejected by the formal systems. Yet each individual is very important. . . . We need to build enabling environments to discover the limits of our potential. Humans are not born to suffer the misery of hunger and poverty. They suffer now because we turn our minds away from the issue." (Adapted from Countdown 2005: 2)

Each of these brief accounts focuses on a different aspect of social change and economic development around the globe. As was emphasized in Chapter 1, explaining social change has been a central concern of sociology throughout its existence as a distinct discipline. In this final chapter, we will review and expand upon a number of change-related themes that were introduced earlier in the text.

We begin with an overview of the major concepts and perspectives that sociologists use to analyze change and with a discussion of the sources of social change. Next, the chapter will review the theories of change developed by Durkheim, Marx, and Weber and show how each has been modified to interpret ongoing social change in the contemporary developed world. The chapter concludes with a look at a few of the critical issues that confront the less- developed societies in our increasingly globalized world.

WHAT IS SOCIAL CHANGE?

Social change is a very broad concept, referring to alterations over time in social structure, culture, and behavior patterns (Moore, 1967:3). As the three

INTERNET CONNECTIONS

The Grameen Bank of Bangladesh is sited at www.grameen-info.org/index.html. The Bank grew by making loans to poor women for small, home-based business enterprises. Do you think it should or should not make loans to poor men, too?

vignettes that open this chapter imply, social change is universal (Rogers & Shoemaker, 1971). It occurs at all levels, from whole societies to microlevel social interactions. Sometimes it is predictable, often it is not. It may be gradual or abrupt, but the unmistakable global trend is toward an ever more rapid pace of change.

Change takes place in both social structure and culture, and each influences the other. Cultural change may involve *discoveries*—uncovering aspects of reality that were previously unknown, such as the existence of dinosaurs—or *inventions*—recombinations of existing material or nonmaterial culture elements in order to create something new, like the automobile or the idea of a university (see Chapter 3) (White, 1949). Change can arise within a culture, or it can enter from outside through a process of *diffusion* (Linton, 1936); anthropologists believe that the vast majority of all change in any given society originates somewhere else. However, cultural elements almost never diffuse into a new setting without some modification (Lauer, 1991).

A number of factors determine whether a new idea or technology will be accepted (Etzkowitz, 1992). In general, changes are more likely to be adopted: (a) if they originate from cutting edge sources—from Silicon Valley rather than from Pakistan; (b) if they respond to a strongly felt need among the public, which is why the metric system has not been widely accepted whereas VCRs have been; (c) if they are material rather than nonmaterial, as predicted by culture lag theory (see Chapter 3); and (d) if they are broadly compatible with people's existing values, which is why the highly effective French abortion pill RU-486 was not available in the United States until 2000 and continues to meet strong resistance in regions of the country where the pro-life movement is strong.

The spread of a new idea or invention—the personal computer is a good example—usually follows a curvilinear pattern. A few pioneers, generally people with strong connections to relatively broad social networks, gradually pick up on the new development. Then, the bulk of the population adopts it, often quite rapidly. Finally, a relatively small number of stragglers grudgingly jump on the bandwagon (Coleman et al., 1957).

The communications media play an important role in spreading awareness of innovations because they can accomplish this more rapidly than is possible through word of mouth. Thus, the printing press, radios, telephones, televisions—and, today, the Internet—have all contributed to the escalating pace of social change (Zaret, 1996).

Resistance to change in developing societies is often strong because of *cultural inertia*, a deep preference for traditional ways of living and thinking. Cultural inertia is often based in religious institutions. The medieval Catholic church, for example, vehemently opposed the scientific worldview of Galileo (Manchester, 1993). Since that time, conservative religions have fought hard against such changes as the abolition of slavery, female suffrage, the teaching of evolution, civil rights, the end of apartheid in South Africa, the right to abortion, and the acceptance of homosexuality as an alternate lifestyle.

Opponents of change may be described as **vested interests,** a term coined by the American sociologist Thorstein Veblen (1964) to refer to individuals and groups whose advantages are threatened by impending social change. The Luddites, for example, were textile workers in the early years of the Industrial Revolution who deliberately sabotaged the new machines that threatened their livelihood (Sale, 1996). People today who are uncomfortable with computers are sometimes called neo-Luddites (Bauerlein, 1996).

Other examples of vested interests abound: the American Medical Association resists national health care, the National Rifle Association opposes gun control legislation, the tobacco industry fights restrictions on smoking, and the Pentagon and defense industries lobby against post-Cold War cutbacks in military spending.

SOURCES OF SOCIAL CHANGE

Sociologists have identified numerous sources of social change, including the natural environment, demographic change, new ideas, innovations in technology, the government, competition and war, elite-initiated change, and social movements. Let's look at each of these sources more closely.

The Natural Environment

Human social and cultural patterns are constantly shifting to adapt to changes in the physical environment. Sometimes the changes are sudden, as when earthquakes and floods disrupt everyday social life

Fifty-Five Years of Social Change

Consider some of the changes that have taken place in the United States in the fifty-five years since the end of the Second World War:

- In 1945, the South was still segregated by law: African Americans were required to attend separate (and inferior) schools, drink from "colored" water fountains, and sit in the back of the bus. Interracial dating was unthinkable. Throughout the country, legally enforceable restrictive covenants ensured that homes in desirable neighborhoods would not be resold to blacks, Hispanics, Asians, Jews, and sometimes even to Catholics. Most women were housewives; efforts by women to enter prestigious, traditionally male professions were strongly resisted; and the demand for equal pay for equal work was widely regarded as radical.
- The divorce rate was less than half of what it is now, and divorcing couples faced significant legal barriers as well as strong social disapproval. Sex was not discussed in polite company, and homosexuality was such a taboo subject that a schoolteacher who even mentioned it could expect to be fired. Many young people remained virgins throughout their adolescence.
- The vast majority of the public trusted the government. Nobody except a few scientists thought about the environment. The Berlin Wall was brand new and the collapse of communism was unimaginable. Official crime rates were a quarter to a third of what they are now, and only a small group of people at the bottom of the social ladder used illicit drugs. Few college students knew anyone who had ever used marijuana, much less harder drugs.
- Television was in its infancy. There were no microwave ovens, no stereos, no rock 'n' roll, no rap. Most movies were filmed in black and white. There were no interstate highways, no indoor shopping malls, no HMOs, and very few fast food franchises. Pizza was just being introduced. Cars had no seat belts and no air bags. Trips to the moon, industrial robots, computers, and fax machines were found only in the pages of science-fiction novels.

And now, the obvious question: How will society change in the *next* fifty-five years? It's impossible to predict exactly what will happen in the future, but we can be confident that many aspects of life today will appear just as old-fashioned in 2055 as America in 1945 seems to us now.

1. What aspects of social life do you expect NOT to undergo substantial change prior to the middle of the twenty-first century? Explain your choices.

(Erickson, 1976). Even more significant are gradual but long-lasting changes in climate like the slow expansion of the Sahara Desert, the loss of topsoil on the western plains that resulted in the Dust Bowl of the 1930s, or the worldwide coastal flooding that will occur if global warming melts the polar ice caps (Lamb, 1982; Peterson, 1994).

Demographic Change

Alterations in the size, composition, and distribution of the human population have led to a variety of social changes. The rapid growth of the world's population after industrialization had far-reaching effects (see Chapter 21). On the other hand, rapid declines in the population of indigenous peoples, due mainly to diseases introduced by colonialists, have had catastrophic effects on their ability to maintain their cultures.

Changes in the composition of the population are also important. When the huge Baby Boom generation reached young adulthood in the 1960s, the crime rate soared (see Chapter 9). Today, their children, the "Baby Boom Echo," are crowding the schools (Crispell, 1995). Early in the twenty-first century, graying Boomers will probably force changes in Social Security and in the health care delivery system, as discussed in Chapters 14 and 19 (Riley, 1985; Roush, 1996).

Immigration and high minority birth rates are also having profound effects on U.S. society. Soon racial and ethnic minorities will collectively constitute a numerical majority of the population, ushering in an era that many sociologists believe will mandate a deeper commitment to multiculturalism than has been present in this country up until now (see Chapter 12).

New Ideas

New ways of thought change how people see the world, and they call for structural and cultural adjustments (Kuhn, 1970). The development of the scientific method (Chapter 2), of revolutionary Marxism (Chapter 10), of the Protestant work ethic (Chapter

Vested interests oppose social changes because they fear their consequences. Here Phillip Morris CEO William Campbell testifies before a congressional hearing in an unsuccessful effort to prevent further governmental regulation of the tobacco industry.

22), and of rational bureaucracy (also Chapter 22) are good examples.

New Technologies

Technologies are tools and the skills needed to manufacture and use them. They are the artificial means by which humans extend their ability to manipulate the environment (Volti, 1995; Teich, 1993). Technological change is especially significant because, like population (see Chapter 21), it has the potential to grow geometrically. Each major new development further expands the culture base, providing more elements that can be recombined to yield ever more rapid change in the future (Freeman, 1974).

Consider the humble microwave oven. It has led to many unexpected, or latent, social changes. Microwaves reduce the amount of time it takes to cook meals, thus freeing more women to enter the work force. They make it easier to prepare single-portion meals, which makes it simpler to live alone, which, in turn, makes divorce marginally less unattractive. Microwaves also allow family members to eat whenever it is convenient, which has weakened the tradition of family meals and, arguably, somewhat weakened the family. We could make similar observations about virtually any major new technology, including the electric light bulb, the automobile, television, computers, new reproductive technologies, and genetic engineering (Peterson, 1994).

Technological developments are an important source of social change. The ongoing shift from traditional mail to e-mail has greatly increased the pace of communications worldwide. Sociologists are currently investigating other consequences of the computer revolution.

At the same time, however, we must avoid *technological determinism*, the view that technology is the only important source of social change. New technologies are important, but each society decides how (and if) it will use them (Lauer, 1991).

Government

The rise of modern nation-states with strong governments has directly contributed to social change. Strong, centralized political leadership can mobilize large-scale efforts to alter the character of a society. In the United States, for example, the government has significantly contributed to major changes in civil rights and environmentalism. Furthermore, patriotism helps people to accept the dislocations that often accompany large-scale change, convincing them that their suffering is necessary "for the good of the nation" (Greenfield, 1992).

Competition and War

High levels of competition—whether to develop a new technology or to succeed in business—often inspire innovation (Hage & Aiken, 1970). Good examples include the invention of the automobile, the airplane, and the computer, or the effort to unravel the mysteries of the DNA molecule. In each case, several individuals or teams were competing with each other to perfect the new technology, and in each case the rivalry clearly speeded up the process.

War can also be viewed as a spur to significant innovations, from new medicines, including sulfa and penicillin, to nuclear power (Janowitz, 1978; Nisbet, 1988; Chirot, 1994).

Institutionalized Social Change

In the past, most social change just happened, but in the modern era more and more of it is deliberately planned. Sometimes, as previously noted, this planning is done by government. But today, especially in the developed world, every major organization—from universities to corporations—has created specialized research and development branches to plan for the future. In other words, we have institutionalized social change.

Social Movements

While institutional elites plan for change from above, as we saw in Chapter 23, the less powerful are simultaneously organizing social movements and pushing for change from below. Sometimes, as in the case of the civil rights movement, these popular efforts gain the grudging support of government. At other times, as with the anti-war and pro-life movements, they work against the government. And sometimes they aim for revolutionary change in the government itself, as did the movements that led to both of the Russian revolutions in the twentieth century (Skocpol, 1979).

THEORETICAL PERSPECTIVES ON SOCIAL CHANGE

Four general theoretical perspectives on social change —cyclical, evolutionary, functional, and conflict— have emerged from the writings of sociologists and other scholars. These four theories attempt to describe the broad patterns by which all societies develop; they exist on the borderline between social science and philosophy.

Cyclical Theory

Before the industrial era, most people thought about societal change by means of an analogy with the seasons or with the human life cycle. This view denies that social change is directional; instead, societies rise and fall in a series of trendless cycles (Moore, 1974). The primary causes of social change are believed by cyclic theorists to be **immanent,** or located within each society, just as the genetic "blueprint" for a mature oak tree lies deep within every acorn (Hughes, 1962).

Historians have been especially attracted to a cyclic view; most notably in Edward Gibbons's six-volume *The Decline and Fall of The Roman Empire*, published between 1776 and 1788. More recently, Oswald Spengler's nonscholarly *The Decline and Fall of the West* (1928) drew striking parallels between the late Roman Empire and early twentieth-century Europe.

The English historian Arnold Toynbee (1889–1975) also believed that civilizations rose and fell, but he was less pessimistic than Spengler (Toynbee, 1946). Toynbee maintained that societies must meet an endless series of external and internal challenges. If these challenges are either too easily overcome or too severe, the society will collapse. But so long as "creative elites" can respond effectively to the challenges their society faces, it will endure.

Paul Kennedy, a contemporary historian, also views the course of social change as cyclical. He argues that great civilizations decline when they devote so many resources to the military that their domestic economies weaken. This, he believes, is a problem that the United States may now be facing (Kennedy, 1988).

Before the modern era, less than 5 percent of humanity lived in cities. Urban areas grew enormously as a result of the industrial revolution, and today up to 75 percent of the population in the developed nations are city dwellers. Some sociologists believe that urban areas may shrink in postindustrial societies because many people can now work using computers and fax machines, freeing them to live wherever they wish.

The best-known sociologist whose work reflects a cyclical view is Pitirim Sorokin (1889–1968). Sorokin wrote that societies alternate between *sensate eras,* in which ultimate truth is believed to be discoverable through scientific research; and *ideational periods,* during which people seek truth through the transcendent (Sorokin, 1941). Every aspect of culture—from government to family to art—reflects the underlying character of the era, either sensate or ideational. Sorokin posited that, after centuries, the possibilities of one cultural pattern become exhausted and society inevitably shifts either to the other type or, occasionally, to a short-lived *idealistic era,* when both possibilities blend smoothly together. He thought that contemporary civilization was in an "overripe" sensate phase, almost ready to shift to another pattern, probably ideational, with faith replacing reason and science.

Critique. Cyclic theory is appealing because some things really do appear to change in cycles, from hemlines to the stock market (Caplow, 1991). But in other cases, especially where the adoption of new technologies such as television or computers is involved, there does appear to be a direction to change. Furthermore, cyclic theory is more descriptive than analytic; it really doesn't tell us *why* societies change. It may be that cyclic theory was more applicable in the past than it is in the rapidly changing modern era (Wilkinson, 1987).

Evolutionary Theory

In contrast to the cyclical approach, evolutionary theory maintains that social change is indeed moving in a direction. Specifically, the general trend of history is toward greater complexity and increased *institutional differentiation,* toward the development of more and more specialized institutional arrangements (Dietz et al., 1990). Thus, for example, education began as one of the family's many functions, but later it shifted to a separate institutional setting—initially the one-room, all-grade schoolhouse, but now the large, immensely complex, highly specialized, modern multiversity.

Evolutionary thought does share one key assumption with cyclic theory: Both see change as largely immanent. For evolutionists, all societies have a natural internal dynamic that impels them to become ever more adaptive in order to successfully compete with other societies for survival. Thus, the classic evolutionary theorists believed that change is normally progress.

It should be evident that this approach is grounded in Charles Darwin's theory of biological evolution. Darwin had an immense influence on nineteenth-century social thought, especially that of the English sociologist Herbert Spencer (Spencer, 1860; Nisbet, 1969). Spencer and his followers thought that all societies would ultimately follow the same evolutionary path—or set sequence of stages—and would all end up looking very much like nineteenth-century Europe. This approach to change is called **unilinear** (one line) **evolutionary theory.**

Auguste Comte, the "father of sociology," also espoused unilinear evolutionary theory. He saw all societies progressing from a theological stage to a metaphysical stage and, ultimately, to a positive or scientific stage (Comte, 1858). As we discussed in Chapter 4, Émile Durkheim (1933) saw a historical movement from societies bonded by *mechanical solidarity* toward societies held together by *organic solidar-*

Unilinear evolutionary theory was extremely popular during the colonial era of the later nineteenth century. This perspective supported the view that European societies were more "advanced" than those of India and other countries in Asia and Africa, and implied that it was only proper that Europeans should dominate these societies both politically and economically.

ity. Similarly, Ferdinand Tönnies (1963) proposed that societies evolve from *Gemeinschaft* to *Gesellschaft.*

Critique.   Unilinear evolutionary theory, especially in its earlier versions, was severely criticized for at least three reasons. First, it simply does not fit the facts: Not all traditional societies are organized in the same way, and when they do change, they do not all pass through the same stages.

Second, the underlying evolutionary assumption that all change is ultimately progress is obviously based on a value judgment, one that became increasingly difficult to maintain in the face of the world wars and societal upheavals that characterized the twentieth century (Smart, 1990; Harper, 1993).

Finally, unilinear evolutionary theory was all too easily used to defend colonialism. If every culture is eventually going to be like the "advanced" European societies, then it seemed only natural and right that people in "backward" parts of the world should be brought under Europeans' "benevolent" political and economic control. Kipling called this "improvement" of colonized peoples "the white man's burden." And if, in the process, Europeans became wealthy using the labor power and natural resources of their colonies, what could be wrong with that? This logic helps explain the great popularity of evolutionary theory in the nineteenth century. Recognizing the harm that resulted from colonial exploitation later contributed to a widespread rejection of unilinear thought (Nisbet, 1969).

Some modern sociologists, most notably Neil Smelser (1973) and Gerhard and Jean Lenski (Nolan & Lenski, 1999) (see Chapter 4), have modified evo-

lutionary thinking. They have retained the idea that as societies grow, they tend to become more complex, institutionally differentiated, and adaptive, but they reject the notion that change is necessarily progress and recognize that societies may change at different paces and in quite different ways (Sahlins & Service, 1960). This approach, which is currently quite popular, is called **multilinear evolutionary theory.** However, some critics point out that a few societies have become less—rather than more—complex and differentiated (Alexander & Colomy, 1990).

Functional Theory

As we saw in Chapter 1, classic functionalist theory argues that stability, not change, is the natural order of things. As formulated by Talcott Parsons (1951), functionalism assumes that the origins of change always lie outside a social system, and that most, if not all, social change amounts to efforts to restore the equilibrium that has been disrupted by external forces. Thus, for example, the feminist movement has directly contributed to massive increases in the number of mothers who work outside of the home over the past three decades. This change has thrown the social system out of balance because there were initially few child-care options available to these working mothers. In response, there has been a substantial (though still inadequate) growth of the day-care industry, which has begun to restore equilibrium to the system. As this example suggests, functionalists tend to see most change as slow and adaptive. If the pressure for social change is too great, the system simply collapses.

Critique. Classic functionalism has been severely faulted for its implicit assumption that change is abnormal, which does not fit most people's experience. Furthermore, many critics believe that it cannot adequately explain abrupt or revolutionary change. In response, Parsons's later work acknowledges several inherent causes of change, including imperfect integration between the parts of a social system—for example, the current mismatch between the number of people who are graduating from college in the United States and the (smaller) number of available jobs that actually require college skills. Parsons also blends the key assumption of evolutionary theory into his reworked functionalism, arguing that the tendency of all social systems to become more complex and differentiated means that the equilibrium point changes over time. It is a moving equilibrium, not a static one (Parsons, 1966).

Conflict Theory

Conflict theory refutes the functionalist claim that social change is secondary or abnormal. Quite the opposite: Since society is based on the struggle of various competing interest groups for scarce goods and services, social life is constantly changing as one party and then another achieves dominance (Wuthnow, 1989a). The source of change may be either external or immanent, although classic Marxist thought stresses the latter, referring to internal pressures for change as *contradictions*. For example, as technology expands, capitalists must increase the level of education received by their workers so that they can keep up to date, yet the more education they receive, the more likely they are to achieve class consciousness and rise in revolution.

Critique. Conflict theory accounts for the universality of social change and is well prepared to explain revolutionary and discontinuous change. On the other hand, it fails to acknowledge that change sometimes proceeds gradually and without much apparent conflict (March, 1981).

THE GREAT TRANSFORMATION

The term **modernization** refers to the sum total of the structural and cultural changes that accompanied the industrial revolution. More specifically, the shift to inanimate sources of energy in Europe and North America led to the following major social transformations (Smelser, 1973):

- An unprecedented increase in the human population resulting from sharp declines in mortality. (Chapter 21)
- A shift in population from the countryside to the cities, with a consequent dramatic growth of urban areas. (Chapter 21)
- The emergence of science and education as major social institutions. (Chapter 16)
- A great increase in the size and power of the government. (Chapter 18)
- A change from the extended to the nuclear family and a general reduction in the importance of the family. (Chapter 15)
- Substantial secularization and a general decline in the significance of religion in most people's lives. (Chapter 17)
- The spread of rational bureaucracy into almost all aspects of social life. (Chapter 22)
- The growth of a large middle class and some reduction in the misery of the poor. (Chapters 10 and 11)
- A movement away from the importance of ascribed status and toward greater emphasis on equal rights, leading to considerably reduced discrimination against ethnic and racial minorities, women, and other disadvantaged groups. (Chapters 12–14)

These social changes have, in turn, altered individual behavior patterns, creating a personal orientation termed **modernity.** Modern people, unlike people living in traditional, preindustrial societies, are more open to new experiences; tend to reject traditional patterns of authority, valuing science and rationality in their stead; are much more future oriented and less fatalistic; strongly desire upward social mobility; and accept a much more diverse set of beliefs (Inkeles, 1973; Berger, 1977).

Today, at the same time that the developing nations are modernizing, the developed societies are moving out of the industrial era and into a new phase. In **postindustrial society,** manufacturing is largely replaced by knowledge-based service industries. Workers devote most of their time to producing information rather than material objects (Touraine, 1974; Bell, 1976). The computer replaces the steam engine and the assembly line. This transition is occurring even more rapidly than the shift from farming to manufacturing did, and there is every reason to believe that it will cause—like the industrial revolution before it—a host of social problems.

The difficulty of moving into the postindustrial era has stimulated the rise of a school of thought called **post-modernism.** Post-modernist thinkers reject many of the basic ideas of modernity. Specifically, they deny the idea that science and rationality are viable means of discovering truth. They also reject the notion that current patterns of social change represent any kind of progress (Bernstein, 1992; Borgmann, 1992). In its most extreme form, postmodernism denies that there is any objective meaning in written communications beyond that which the observer reads into them. At this point, post-modernism has probably produced more questions than answers, but its popularity hints at the intellectual turmoil caused by the transition to postindustrial society.

An important part of the sociologist's task in the twenty-first century will be to study the social problems that arise in the developed world as a result of the transition into postindustrial society. However, this does not mean that the problems that led to the birth of the discipline in the early industrial era—problems such as poverty, discrimination, alienation, and anomie—are no longer relevant. They continue to confront us today, although in somewhat different forms.

SOCIAL CHANGE IN THE DEVELOPED WORLD

Each of the three nineteenth-century theorists who are generally regarded as sociology's most important founders—Émile Durkheim, Karl Marx, and Max Weber—analyzed modernization and interpreted different aspects of this process as problematic.

Durkheim observed that, as industrialization proceeded, people played increasingly differentiated roles in the expanding economy. In the past, when almost everyone farmed, people all accepted pretty much the same values, or, in Durkheim's terms, they shared a *collective conscience*. This collective conscience both produced and reflected the mechanical solidarity that in turn provided moral guidance and held society together. Today, however, people commonly hold very different values. While economic interdependence provides a certain amount of unity (organic solidarity), the weakening of the collective conscience leads, in Durkheim's view, to widespread uncertainty about how to think and behave, a condition he called *anomie*. Anomie leads in turn to a host of social problems, including crime, drug abuse, broken families, and suicide (see Chapter 8).

For *Marx*, the growth of industrial society sharpened and clarified class conflict, ultimately leaving only two major classes struggling with each other, the bourgeoisie and the proletariat. Over time, he believed that the proletariat would be ground further and further down until eventually its members achieved class consciousness and revolted. The primary problem of the industrial era, in Marx's opinion, was class oppression (see Chapter 10).

Weber saw industrial society as both cause and consequence of a process of *rationalization*, the systematic examination of all aspects of social life in order to identify the most technically efficient means of accomplishing chosen ends. The problem was that this relentless rationalization process seemed to have become an "iron cage" that sacrificed everything spontaneous and humanistic to bottom-line efficiency (see Chapter 22).

Updating Durkheim

Undeniably, anomie continues to plague modern society (Dahrendorf, 1981). Social conservatives continually decry the weakening of traditional values like patriotism, family, and Christianity. Though we were probably never as strongly committed to these ideals as traditionalists would like to believe, it is very clear that as we have become a more diverse people, fewer shared values hold us together than did so in the past.

Durkheim was correct in observing that organic solidarity provides a measure of functional integration, but life in modern society lacks the passionate unity that comes from a strong core of shared sacred values. Traditional life stifles individualism, but many people today feel that we have lost our sense of moral community, and this is too great a price to pay for the freedom and privacy of the modern city (Selznick, 1992).

Robert Putnam identifies the problem as a decline in **social capital,** by which he means the ". . . features of social organization such as networks, norms, and social trust that facilitate coordination and cooperation for mutual benefit" (Putnam, 1995:67). He sees signs of this decline everywhere, from plummeting levels of trust in government and low voter turnout to reduced membership in unions, PTAs, churches, and other voluntary associations. This is of particular concern because affluence and education, which usually accompany civic involvement, have been rising at the same time that participation has declined.

Perhaps, however, the picture isn't as grim as Putnam suggests. A recent survey conducted for the American Association of Retired Persons (AARP) showed fairly high levels of civic involvement despite rampant cynicism about politics, especially at the national level (Guterbock & Fries, 1997). The average citizen was found to have 4.2 memberships in voluntary associations; only one in seven had none. The study found by far the highest levels of anomie and the lowest civic involvement among adults aged 25 and younger. Whether this will change once the "Generation Xers" settle down remains to be seen.

Is it possible for a modern society to reverse the trend toward individualism? Can we rebuild moral community? Are there really any overarching values uniting nearly all Americans? The governments of Iran and Afghanistan are currently struggling to rebuild their societies on a rigid set of traditional Islamic values. The problems they are experiencing in attempting to achieve this goal, in nations far less individualistic than ours, suggest how difficult such a project would be in a fully modern society.

Perhaps the best we can hope for is what Durkheim envisioned: the restoration of some measure of moral unity to groups of relatively similar people, while the society as a whole remains morally fragmented but held together functionally through organic solidarity. If there are few shared values among all Americans, maybe there are some values shared by environmentalists or Hispanics or Star Trek fans. Sociologists have speculated that the Internet may help pull together people who do not live near one another but who share common interests (Griswold, 1994; Hornsby, 1998).

Recently, the well-known sociologist Amitai Etzioni (1988, 1993) helped establish the *communitarian movement*. The communitarians recognize that we cannot simply return to the *Gemeinschaft* of preindustrial days, but they are actively engaged in searching for ways to reduce the anomic disconnectedness of modern life. In particular, communitarians argue that we must balance our demand for individual rights with a stronger commitment to our collective responsibilities. This is yet another example of the activist tradition that has been part of sociology since the days of Comte and Marx.

Modern conflict theorists have substantially broadened Marx's notion of class conflict. They recognize that many different groups of people—for example, the gay activists staging this demonstration—are continually struggling with other groups for power, prestige, and material advantage.

Updating Marx

A number of major historical changes have compelled twentieth-century sociologists to substantially rethink Marx's work. Marx did not foresee (a) that the bourgeoisie would globalize the capitalist system, thereby further maximizing their profit by exploiting the labor and natural resources of the developing world; (b) that the process of collective bargaining would improve the proletariat's living conditions enough to greatly retard the development of class consciousness among them; or (c) that a huge new middle class of salaried white-collar workers would arise who are structurally proletariat but who have accepted the worldview of the bourgeoisie.

Probably the most useful updating of the conflict tradition comes from the work of Ralf Dahrendorf, a German sociologist who has taught in the United States and is now at Oxford University in England (and is a member of the British House of Lords)

(Dahrendorf, 1959, 1973). Dahrendorf writes that although class conflict was the most visible form of intergroup struggle in Marx's day, today many other groups of people—including racial and ethnic minorities, women, consumers, gays, the elderly, children, college students, the obese, and the physically disabled—recognize their oppression and are now struggling to obtain prestige, material advantages, and power.

Dahrendorf's key insight is that Marxist class conflict is simply one example of a much more general type of conflict over what he terms *authority relations*. He argues as follows:

1. In any social system with a formally legitimated system of authority, there will always be two fundamentally opposed groups of people: those who have the authority to give orders, to reward conformity to these orders, and to punish disobedience; and those who must follow these orders lest

they be punished. Conflict is always dichotomous, whether it involves classes or any other type of group.

2. The true interest of the dominant group is always to preserve the present situation, and the true interest of subordinate groups is always to change the status quo.

Much of Dahrendorf's work explores the conditions under which subordinate groups—those that lack authority—come to recognize their true interests. He also investigates the factors that shape the intensity, violence, and consequences of the ensuing conflict. But it is his concept of authority relations that is crucial because it demonstrates that Marx's theory is not outdated. In fact, modified Marxist theory contributes tremendously to understanding the dynamics of all sorts of intergroup conflicts in today's highly diverse society.

Dahrendorf's analysis is, in a sense, pessimistic, because, unlike Marx, he does not foresee any end to social conflict. There will always be groups of people who have authority and others who do not. Few people like to take orders. But conflict is not necessarily negative; it can produce badly needed change, as the struggles of the civil rights and feminist movements show. Dahrendorf's vision of the future is not tranquil, but it does envision a society where oppressed people will continue to fight, often successfully, to improve their lives.

Updating Weber

Max Weber doubted that society could escape the iron cage of rationalization, and the history of the twentieth century suggests that his skepticism was well grounded. It is true that assembly-line workers are increasingly robots rather than human beings, and there is a trend, especially in the knowledge-oriented sectors of the emerging postindustrial economy, toward the flexible bureaucracies that were discussed in Chapter 22. Nevertheless, bureaucratic rationality continues to define more and more sectors of modern life.

George Ritzer convincingly argues that modern societies are in the grip of an even more relentless rationalization process than Weber observed (Ritzer, 1996). Ritzer calls this trend **McDonaldization,** "the process by which the principles of the fast-food restaurant are coming to dominate more and more sectors of American society as well as of the rest of the world" (Ritzer, 1996:1). Whether we look at banks, schools, recreation, the health care system, the media, or even funerals, four basic principles of McDonaldization seem to be ever present.

First, McDonaldization mandates *efficiency*. In fast-food restaurants, the process of preparing food and moving the customers along is as streamlined as possible: The menu is simplified, and customers are put to work filling their own soda cups and busing their own tables, all in the name of greater efficiency. To take just one of many possible parallel examples, in the modern university the registration process is highly formalized, and multiple-choice tests are increasingly computer generated and computer graded.

McDonaldization also maximizes *calculability*. Every component of each menu item is precisely measured, and great emphasis is put on how quickly food is delivered to the customers. Similarly, quantity is stressed over quality: It's a Big Mac, not a Great Mac. In higher education, students often choose schools based on their numerical rankings, and schools accept students largely on the basis of their class rank and test scores. Students evaluate their teachers on quantitative scales, and faculty seeking tenure must publish a large number of research articles.

Third, McDonaldization emphasizes *predictability*. Every Big Mac is exactly like every other Big Mac. No surprises. Regarding the university, each semester is organized in a highly predictable fashion with the same progression of registration, midterms, and final examinations.

Finally, McDonaldization maximizes *institutional control* over workers and customers. As anyone who has ever worked at a fast-food restaurant knows, almost every aspect of the job is guided by nonhuman technology, from fryers that cook potatoes automatically to computerized cash registers. Human choice is minimized. Consumers are subtly encouraged to eat their food and clear out. In the university, a relatively rigid curriculum, detailed syllabi, and fixed time periods all help control the educational process.

Ritzer does not deny that people like many aspects of McDonaldization. It does produce high profits, and it fits well in a culture that values efficiency, but it also has an irrational side. To Ritzer, ". . . irrationality means that rational systems are unreasonable systems that deny the humanity, the human reason, of the people who work within them or are served by them. In other words, rational systems are dehumanizing" (1996:121). In the fast food restaurant, workers can only use a few of their skills, and customers are reduced to managed automatons. Relationships between customers and workers are dehumanized because they are reduced to prepackaged impersonal scripts—"Would you like fries with that?"

Can McDonaldization be reversed? Like Weber before him, Ritzer is doubtful. He encourages people to create less rationalized niches in order to live a less dehumanized life, but the plain fact is that most people today like McDonaldized efficiency, calculability, and predictability, and perhaps even control.

SOCIAL CHANGE IN THE DEVELOPING WORLD

In the remainder of this chapter, we will examine several important aspects of social change in the nations of the **developing world.** These nations—often referred to as *less developed countries* (LDCs)—are characterized by per capita incomes at or below the poverty level, agricultural economies predominantly based on the export of raw materials, serious overpopulation problems, and high levels of illiteracy and unemployment.

We will begin with a consideration of the relationship between foreign aid, economic development, and democracy, after which we will discuss the emergence of the global economy, briefly note the importance of the informal sector in the economies of the LDCs, and contrast the pace of development in the Pacific Rim and in sub-Saharan Africa. The chapter concludes with an overview of the logic of microenterprise and a discussion of the emerging global consensus on human rights.

Foreign Aid, Capitalism, and Democracy

Most of the countries that gained their independence shortly after World War II—such as Nigeria, Kenya, and India—had relatively weak economies. To obtain the capital they needed for economic development, they could turn to the wealthy nations of North America and Europe or to the Communist bloc. Most preferred the former option, in part because the socialist nations were themselves struggling with development issues and also because the Soviets offered more military aid than direct economic assistance (Arnold, 1988).

Foreign aid has been part of American foreign policy almost from the time of this nation's founding, although the United States currently devotes less of its gross national product to this purpose than any other major developed country (see Figs. 24.1, 24.2). Most international development aid goes to agriculture, housing, health, and education.

As conceived by the United States and its allies after World War II, foreign aid had both political and humanitarian goals. In simple humanitarian terms, Western assistance has allowed millions of people worldwide to survive. On the political side, foreign aid helped assure that the new nations of the developing world remained sympathetic to the aims of the West. Even after the Soviet system disintegrated, Western foreign aid continued to have a strong ideological motive—to spread democracy and capitalism to the less-developed countries.

The *United States Agency for International Development* (USAID) is the major economic assistance pro-

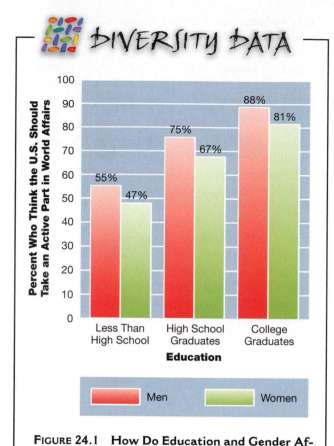

FIGURE 24.1 How Do Education and Gender Affect Attitudes Concerning Whether the United States Should Take an Active Part in World Affairs? As educational attainment rises, both men and women become less isolationist; however, at each educational level, men are more supportive of international involvement than women. How might traditional gender role socialization affect people's views on this issue?

Source: NORC. General Social Surveys, 1972-1996. Chicago: National Opinion Research Center, 1996. Reprinted by permission of NORC, Chicago, IL.

gram run by the U.S. government. Its stated purpose is to promote political, social, and economic stability in developing countries through economic growth, ideally by means of programs that involve minimal state intervention and control. USAID also puts a high priority on trying to cushion the short-term effects of reform on the most vulnerable groups of people (IDCA, 1991). However, the agency often finds that its humanitarian goal of reducing poverty conflicts, in practice, with its ideological goals of spreading capitalism and democracy.

Nongovernmental organizations (NGOs) are also heavily involved in the economic development of the LDCs. As the name implies, NGOs are not part of any governmental agency. They are privately funded nonprofit groups concerned with development, economic relief, and advocacy for the poor. An

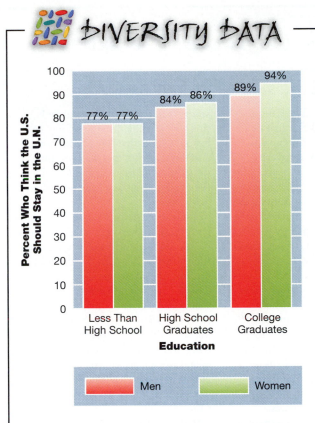

FIGURE 24.2   How Do Education and Gender Affect Support for U.S. Participation in the United Nations? Most Americans believe that we should stay in the U.N., with somewhat greater support for this position among the better educated. Gender has little influence on opinions except among the college educated, where women are somewhat more supportive of the U.N. than are men. How would you explain these findings?

Source: NORC. General Social Surveys, 1972-1996. Chicago: National Opinion Research Center, 1996. Reprinted by permission of NORC, Chicago, IL.

"Less government" is a hot slogan today worldwide. In the LDCs, however, government cannot simply wither away, if only because too many people depend on its safety net for physical survival. However, calls persist for the "heavy hand of government" to be reduced in the developing world. If this trend continues, government may become little more than the "guardian of the entitlements of citizenship and facilitator of economic growth" (Dahrendorf, 1987:120–21).

As government involvement in the economies of the LDCs declines, new players increasingly control the destinies of millions of people. Especially important in this context are the **multinational corporations (MNCs),** also called transnational corporations. Multinationals are large private business enterprises operating simultaneously in several countries. Their overall economic impact today is as great as that of many sizable nation-states. One possible effect of the emergence of the multinationals in an increasingly laissez-faire worldwide market system is that democracy may be compromised if corporate needs come before those of the people as a whole (Strange, 1996; Lempert, 1997).

Research generally suggests that democracy and economic development are correlated (Goulet, 1989; Eisler et al., 1995; United Nations Development Program, 1997) (see Chapter 18). The argument that authoritarian governments can reverse economic chaos in LDCs is not convincing. When the government of an LDC is relatively accountable to its citizens and committed to implementing social change through "people-centered policies," economic development and socioeconomic equality are generally enhanced (Lindenberg, 1993; Wickrama & Mulford, 1996). Thus, for example, Kerala—a state in India with a strong tradition of participatory democracy, a relatively egalitarian distribution of income, a low fertility rate, and a history of providing more funding for primary and secondary education than other Indian states—has an excellent record of economic development (Franke, 1989; Repetto, 1995).

However, the connection between democracy and capitalism is not without problems. First, when the market is left to run without significant government regulation, development may be more of a burden than a boon for the poor. Second, as suggested by the current economic turmoil in Russia and Eastern Europe, progress toward democracy will likely be slow and painful if the change to a market economy is difficult (Shahidullah, 1997:130). Third, it is important to recognize that capitalism is becoming more diverse and that it often takes a different form in the LDCs than in the developed world (Stallings & Streek, 1995; Moore, 1997). Capitalism thrives today in some developing nations characterized by high degrees of political repression, such as Saudi Arabia, the Gulf States, and, increasingly, China.

estimated half million of these organizations exist around the globe. The Global Connections box entitled "The NGO Explosion" explores the dramatic worldwide growth of NGOs in recent decades.

NGOs are particularly effective in looking after the interests of the poor and allowing them to weather the turmoil connected with the early stages of economic development (Lee, 1994; Meisler, 1995). However, NGOs must accept the underlying reality that governmental agencies like USAID expect to have a substantial voice in how their aid is dispersed. Western governments generally expect that aid recipients must be working toward a free-market capitalistic economy and a democratic political system even though these arrangements may disadvantage the poor.

The proper role of government in economic development in the LDCs is far from determined (Ellemann-Jensen, 1987; Iglesias, 1987; DeMar, 1992).

Global Connections

The NGO Explosion

Nongovernmental organizations (NGOs) began in the 1970s, grew to adolescence in the 1980s, and came of age in the 1990s. It is easier to say what an NGO is not than to identify what it is. Obviously, it is not a government, though NGOs work in partnership with governments. It is not a business, though many NGOs raise money with help from commercial enterprises. Most NGOs are involved with humanitarian issues, from refugee resettlement to famine relief, literacy campaigns, and agricultural programs.

NGOs symbolize globalization. Their rapidly growing numbers and influence in the development arena have captured the attention of world leaders, politicians, and multinational corporations. All routinely seek NGO expertise when development assistance programs are started or when new companies enter an LDC in search of cheap labor. NGOs have the resources needed to obtain maximum advantages for their constituents. Profit may rule the global economy, but NGOs monitor the profit-making process to ensure that the poor can gain some benefit from it.

At the Fourth UN Conference on Women in Beijing in 1995, more than 3,000 NGOs were represented, ten times as many as were present at the 1985 conference in Nairobi. Some observers believe that the rise of NGOs may be as significant for the late twentieth century as the rise of nation-states

was for the nineteenth. The Clinton administration pledged that half of all USAID funds would be channeled through NGOs instead of governments. Since aid dollars are scarce, this means that governments must now work with grassroots organizations or risk losing development funds entirely.

With a membership of over 150 development, relief, and refugee assistance groups, InterAction is kind of a "super NGO" that partners with NGOs worldwide. Well-known members of InterAction include the End Hunger Network, Oxfam America, the American Red Cross, World Vision, the Children's Survival Fund, and the United Way International. Tens of millions of Americans and people worldwide contribute to these agencies and their international affiliates.

The controversy over the marketing of baby formula in the developing world provides a classic example of how NGOs function. In the 1970s, Nestle's formula was sold to new mothers in LDCs as a modern way to feed their infants. However, unlike mothers in the developed world, these women often had no access to pure water or to the technology required to sterilize bottles and nipples. When their babies were born, the mothers were initially given free or low-cost formula. Later, when they had to pay for it themselves, many could not afford the cost, so the formula was diluted and the babies got less nutrition. Because these new mothers

started their newborns on formula, their breast milk dried up. They had become dependent on a product they could not afford, that was not nutritionally sound as used, and for which they had no substitute. Result: Many babies died.

Health care professionals working with these women expressed outrage to Nestle and to government leaders in the countries in which Nestle's did business. Nothing was done until IN-FACT (the Infant Formula Action Committee) became involved. IN-FACT was an umbrella NGO including over 100 private organizations based in 65 different countries. By means of an international boycott of Nestle products, INFACT was able to force Nestle to end its marketing campaign. In 1981, as a direct result of IN-FACT agitation, the World Health Organization adopted a code of conduct regarding the marketing of infant formula.

1. What NGOs are present in your community? Have they been involved in issues related to development, either in the United States or internationally?
2. How would a conflict theorist explain the rise of the NGOs?

Sources: Posner, 1994; Alliance for a Global Community, 1996; Lindsey, 1997; Lopez et al., 1997; *Monday Developments*, 1998.

In practice, many LDCs have adopted **state capitalism**—a model whereby public funds are extensively used to promote economic development, but the system remains responsive to market conditions. Turkey, Peru, and Tanzania are good examples of state capitalism (Berberoglu, 1992). South Korea and Taiwan have enjoyed high economic growth under fairly rigid, state-controlled, export-oriented economic policies and, along with Singapore, Mexico, and Brazil, have experienced rapid growth despite one-party or military rule (McMichael, 1996; Suh, 1996; Huang & Marshall, 1997).

Even the United States exhibits a quasi-state capitalist orientation because the government sometimes contracts with private firms to operate formerly state-run agencies. The postal service has long reflected such an arrangement, but today some prisons, hospitals, and even public schools are also moving in this direction.

The Global Economy

Earlier models of international economic interdependence have been replaced by the concept of a **global economy,** the multitude of exchanges uniting consumers and producers around the world. "Global" is a broader concept than "international"—the global economy does not only link nations, but also regions, cities, and even neighborhoods (McMichael, 1996). The theories of global stratification that were introduced in Chapter 10 are centrally concerned with the emergence and character of the global economy.

International economic interdependence has been present in some form for centuries, but the emerging global economy is vastly different from earlier models in several ways. The global marketplace is no longer dominated by one or two nations—economic power is more widely distributed; there has been a massive increase in international trade; and both production and sales have been internationalized (Tietmeyer, 1987). The extent to which financial markets have become internationalized was demonstrated by the extensive repercussions of the global stock market crash of 1987 (Chuppe et al., 1992), and the same can be said regarding the Asian financial crisis a decade later.

As the global economy has emerged, the number of poor in the world has increased. One-fourth of the world's population still lives in absolute poverty and over 1 billion people eke out a marginal existence on less than $1 a day. The vast majority of the world's poor are concentrated in rural areas. At the same time, overall quality of life indicators, such as access to basic education and health care, have improved

in the LDCs (IFAD, 1994; Overseas Development Council, 1998). Employment opportunities have also dramatically increased for workers in the developing world, especially in the clothing industry. Jobs are currently moving from the developed to the developing world at a dramatic rate (see Figure 24.3).

The Informal Sector.   Many of the world's poor labor long and hard but either do not earn any pay or the pay they do receive is undocumented in official economic figures. These people work in the **informal sector,** the economic activities of people such as subsistence farmers and urban laborers who work in small-scale home-based production. Other informal-sector jobs include street vending, prostitution, and domestic work. Most informal-sector work worldwide is performed by women (Rogers, 1980; Buono, 1996). Individuals who lack the training and education needed to find work in the global economy's formal sector eke out a living through informal-sector activities. This sector also benefits poor consumers, who often can obtain what they need by bartering and exchanging services.

Informal-sector economic activities are usually ignored in calculating a nation's GDP, but they do contribute significantly to the economies of the LDCs. More than half of the developing world's labor force is self-employed, and most of these people work in the informal sector (DeSoto, 1989; Chickering &

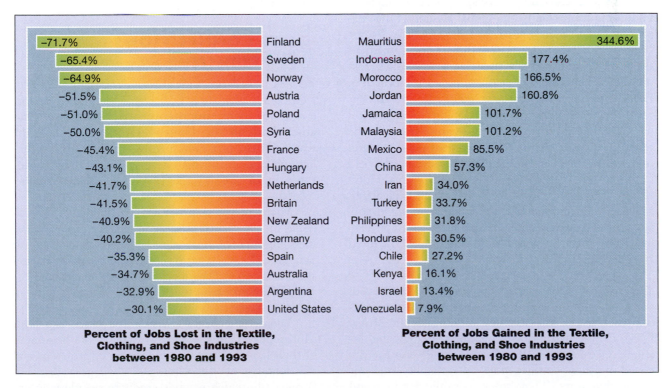

FIGURE 24.3   Job Drift from Developed to Developing World
Source: Chart from "What on Earth?" from *The Washington Post*, December 28, 1996. Copyright © 1996 by The Washington Post Writers Group. Reprinted by permission.

The new millennium is being called the Pacific Century because of Asia's increasingly important technological and manufacturing role in the global economy. The computer industry has thrived in Malaysia because of the ability of skilled but cheap labor and low overhead costs.

Salahdine, 1991; El Amouri Institute, 1993; *Connections*, 1997).

The development of the global economy has had varying effects on different regions of the world. Southern and eastern Asia—the nations of the Pacific Rim—have generally thrived, while much of Africa lags far behind.

The Pacific Century.   Because of Asia's increasingly important role in the global economy, the current era has been hailed by some as the Pacific Century. On most indicators of life chances, many of the LDCs that have been the most successful in closing the global human-development gap are located in East Asia. Japan's spectacular economic growth has fueled the economies of its developing neighbors and has contributed heavily to the growth of trans-Pacific trade. As a result, Asia's LDCs are in a good position to decrease their dependency on the developed world in the coming decades. Taiwan, South Korea, Hong Kong, and Singapore lead the pack. Thailand, Malaysia, and Indonesia are rapidly becoming important manufacturing centers. India has reduced poverty by 25 percent in two decades (Kennedy, 1993; United Nations Development Program, 1997).

The African Contrast.   The dramatic progress of the Asian economies contrasts sharply with the situation in most of the nations in sub-Saharan Africa. Here, many quality-of-life measures are actually declining (see Chapter 19). Most of these countries are mired in ethnic conflict, political instability, and ongoing civil wars. They suffer periodic famines and some house permanent refugee populations that strain their resources. Most aid received by African nations must be devoted to desperately needed short-term relief, which necessarily puts long-term economic development on hold.

Along with differences in their political economies, population factors also help explain the differing levels of economic success of East Asia and sub-Saharan Africa: Asia has been much more successful in curbing population growth than Africa (see Chapter 21).

LIFE CONNECTIONS: Microenterprise

Because most large-scale economic development projects do not adequately address the plight of the poorest of the poor, **microenterprise programs** have arisen both in the United States and around the world. These programs involve small-scale income-earning manufacturing or agricultural activities located in or around the household (Samarasinghe, 1993).

Microenterprise programs are funded by *microcredit* or microenterprise lending. In this arrangement, groups of borrowers receive small loans at commercial interest rates to help them start or expand small businesses. Members of the group assume responsibility for each other's loans: If one fails, they all fail.

Microcredit began twenty-five years ago with Muhammad Yunus, whom we met at the beginning of this chapter. Yunas is an economics professor and the founder of the Grameen ("village") Bank of Bangladesh, which extends credit to people who are too poor to qualify for loans from conventional banks. The first microcredit loan came out of his pocket. He lent $26 to a group of 42 people who used the cash to buy materials for a day's work weaving chairs and making pots. At the end of the first day, they sold their wares and bought more materials. Soon they were able to repay the loan (Micro-Loans, 1997). The Grameen program proved astonishingly successful. Ninety-seven percent of the participants repaid their loans at a 20 percent interest rate.

From a sociological perspective, the success of microcredit enterprises may be explained by four principal factors. First, this approach acknowledges the importance of informal-sector economic activities. The microenterprise definition of productive work includes unpaid economic activity. Thus, borrowers can use their weaving or agricultural skills as collateral, skills that traditional lenders would consider irrelevant.

Second, microcredit enterprises allow the poor to participate in making the decisions that directly affect their lives. Money flows "up" to the larger society from the poor. This is the opposite of the traditional "trickle down" approach, which assumes that money provided to manufacturers or other formal-sector institutions will create jobs for the poor.

Third, microcredit plans obtain most of their funding from NGOs that work directly with the poor rather than from the government. This minimizes bureaucratic entanglement, is more time effective, and reduces overhead costs.

Finally, microcredit works better for the very poor because the very poor are often women. Muhammad Yunus noticed very early on that women usually used the profits from their microenterprise activities to feed their children and build up their businesses, whereas men more often bought electronics and personal consumer goods. A growing body of re-

search suggests that when women have disposable income, it is typically spent on family needs, including nutrition, health care, and education (Overholt et al., 1991; Jabbra & Jabbra, 1992; Okine, 1993).

Because the social benefits were much greater when money was loaned to women, the Grameen Bank decided to concentrate on them. Most of the 2 million Grameen borrowers in Bangladesh are female, and their success with microcredit enterprise has been repeated throughout the world (El Amouri Institute, 1993; Samarasinghe, 1993; *USAID Developments*, 1997a).

Microcredit programs have also been effective in helping the poor in the United States. Successful peer-lending programs are operating in Baltimore and Washington, D.C. The Grameen Bank has been asked to train bank officials in Chicago and Little Rock in microcredit lending. Microcredit programs have also been initiated in Seattle, Boston, and Alaska (McDonnell et al., 1993; *USAID Developments*, 1997a; Mann, 1998).

In 1997, a microcredit summit with participants from 100 countries was held in Washington, DC. NGOs and donor nations pledged to expand

INTERNET CONNECTIONS

Go to the "Human Rights Explained" section of the *Human Rights and Equal Opportunity Commission* Web site: http://www.hreoc.gov.au/hr_explained/index.html. Read the contents of this opening page. Then, click on "Human Rights and You." Take the human rights poll. Then, click on "The Global View of Human Rights" and read the contents. After you have participated in these exercises, answer the following questions: What is your personal stance on human rights issues? Do you think that American society should pay more attention to human rights worldwide? If so, what more should be done to ensure these rights? If not, why not?

Table 24.1   The Universal Declaration of Human Rights

1. All humans are born free and equal in dignity and rights.
2. Everyone is entitled to all rights and freedoms set forth in this Declaration without distinction of any kind, such as race, color, sex, language, religion, political or other opinion, national or social origin.
3. Everyone has a right to life, liberty, and security.
4. No one shall be held in slavery or servitude.
5. No one shall be subject to torture or to cruel, inhuman, or degrading treatment or punishment.
6. All are equal before the law and entitled to equal protection of the law.
7. Everyone has the right to seek and to enjoy in other countries asylum from persecution.
8. Everyone has the right to a nationality.
9. Everyone has the right to freedom of peaceful assembly and association.
10. Everyone has the right to work and to just conditions of work.
11. Everyone has the right to a standard of living adequate for health and well-being.
12. Everyone has the right to education.
13. Everyone has duties to the community in which the full development of one's personality is possible.

Abridged from the Declaration proclaimed by the General Assembly of the United Nations on December 10, 1948.
Source: Reoch, 1994

Social Change and Countermodernization

When modernization collides with tradition, support for rediscovering and revitalizing older cultural patterns often increases. Western values promoting achievement, individualism, secularism, rationalism, and scientific empiricism undermine traditional forms of social organization in the developing world. Increasing global interdependence thus often has two conflicting consequences: the spread of Western culture and the widespread rejection of this culture by some segments of the population. Efforts by "fundamentalists" to create (or re-create) traditional religious states are among the more familiar expressions of this rejection.

Countermodernization is a social trend generated by the very processes of modernization itself. Countermodern movements resist certain aspects of modernization and also promote ways to neutralize their effects. They have been especially important in recent years in Afghanistan and Iran.

Afghanistan has been divided for centuries along tribal, ethnic, sectarian, and regional lines. However, despite this diversity, Islamic authorities or "mullahs" have long played an influential role in virtually all aspects of Afghan social life.

All through the long battle against the Soviet-backed government that was imposed on Afghanistan in 1978, it was evident that the temporary alliance uniting diverse population elements would shatter once the Soviets were expelled. The issue that became central at this time concerned the proper relationship between Islam and Western culture. What form should economic development take—Western or Islamic?

In 1996 the Islamic Taliban movement gained control of most of the country and imposed a very strict version of Islamic "fundamentalism" on virtually all aspects of everyday life. The Taliban banned photographs, television, music, movies, and most games. Men were required to wear beards and women to don the *burqa*, a veiling garment many had given up in favor of Western clothing, or at least scarves and skirts that revealed only parts of their faces or ankles.

Under the Taliban, countermodernization took the form of *Islamization*, a movement that seeks a return to traditional Islam as a remedy for a society that is seen as corrupted by Western values. In Islamization, religion and state are inseparable and all laws governing public and private life are derived from religion. Millions of Muslims in South Asia and parts of the Middle East and North Africa have enthusiastically embraced this movement.

Before the Taliban takeover of Afghanistan, the best-known example of Islamization was the 1979 Iranian revolution that overthrew the Shah and propelled the Ayatollah Khomeini to power. Islamization targets women as particularly likely to have been corrupted by the West. They are virtually forced to return to their traditional domestic roles. Religious principle is invoked to deny women reproductive choice, educational opportunities, and even paid employment. In Iran and Afghanistan, women have been executed for adultery and prostitution, often defined as simply being seen with a man to whom they are not related, and they have been beaten to death for wearing clothing that does not sufficiently cover their entire bodies.

The Taliban's rule has not only put thousands of women and their families in peril, but it has also had serious economic repercussions. Women have been banned from the workforce, and schools for girls and hospitals serving women have closed, lest women come into contact with men to whom they are not related. Denied the right to work, an estimated 30,000 war widows in the capital of Kabul alone have been forced to beg in the streets in order to survive. Women have died after being refused admittance to hospitals because there were no female nurses or doctors

small lending programs from $8 million to $100 million by 2005 (*Connections*, 1997; Baker, 1997; Bennet, 1997; *Countdown 2005*, 1997; *USAID Developments*, 1997b).

SOCIETY CONNECTIONS: The New Consensus on Human Rights

In 1993 the UN convened the World Conference of Human Rights, bringing together 171 nations and scores of NGOs. It was the largest gathering of its kind in history. Human rights are seen as inherent to human beings in any culture. They include not only civil and political rights but also economic, social, and cultural rights. However, even as attendees signed the Declaration of Human Rights (see Table 24.1), difficult issues related to development and cultural interference remained unresolved.

Most Western delegates maintained that economic and social development cannot proceed without political freedom to participate in the process, including the right to dissent. But some governments argued that restrictions on political freedom are necessary to jumpstart their economies. Other delegates maintained that the very idea of universal human

Human rights have been advanced by groups such as Amnesty International, which publicizes cases where rights have been violated, usually for political reasons. Organized protests bring international support to safeguard victims who are denied rights because they are of the "wrong" political party, race, ethnicity, tribe, religion, or gender.

to care for them. An estimated 40 percent of Kabul's doctors are women. Some have been allowed to return to work, but only to examine women and only if the doctors agree to wear full Islamic dress.

The government has been unable to guarantee the safety of Afghan women. Many have been beaten, robbed, and kidnapped by roving bands of pro-Taliban male vigilantes who insist that women be completely veiled. Some NGOs have tried to improve the situation through quiet diplomacy with the Taliban, but many important programs have nevertheless ground to a halt.

When a significant portion of a population is forcibly excluded from the labor force, economic crisis follows close behind. The excesses of

the Afghan and Iranian leaders have also led to international economic sanctions, which have further weakened their nations' economies. Additional research is needed to confirm that "fundamentalist" Islamic rule is invariably associated with economic decline and deterioration in education and health. However, every model of development predicts the eventual demise of this sort of extreme countermodernization movement.

Under the present circumstances, there is no possibility of a sustained women's movement in Afghanistan or Iran. However, a progressive Muslim feminist movement is gaining strength worldwide. This movement interprets the Koran, the holy book of Islam, in a way that improves rather than weakens the rights of women. It gained worldwide attention at the Beijing international women's conference.

1. How should the developed nations respond to the violations of human rights that are occurring in Afghanistan and Iran? Do we have the right to demand that repression be ended?
2. Are there equivalents to countermodernization movements in the United States? What are they? Why have they arisen?

Sources: Tehranian, 1980; Horowitz, 1982; Usman, 1985; Canfield, 1986; Zakaria, 1986; Brydon & Chant, 1989; Jabbra & Jabbra, 1992; Lyon, 1996; Rasekh, 1998.

rights conflicts with some cultural practices and customs, especially those related to religion and the role of women. Still others wanted to separate civil rights, which are relatively easy on which to agree, from economic rights. The division between the developing and the developed world became evident when some delegates charged that the Declaration itself was nothing more than an effort to impose Western "bourgeois" rights on the entire world (Reoch, 1994).

The LDCs present a strong case that the West shaped the Declaration of Human Rights in line with its own economic interests. Major NGOs working directly with the LDCs are increasingly supportive of

this side of the debate. Some social scientists also endorse the LDC position since it is consistent with the ideal of cultural relativism (see Chapter 3).

On the other hand, the developed world can point to data that show that development is generally more successful in democracies and that a favorable economic environment is a necessary condition for social equity. In addition, science—essential for economic development—requires a free and open atmosphere, and democracy is the best means of providing such an environment. Powerful international financial institutions generally support this side of the argument.

Religous fundamentalists in nations such as Pakistan and Afghanistan desire to create religious states that are not contaminated by Western influences that they believe compromise religious integrity.

Sociologists find the emphasis of the Declaration on the rights of minorities particularly encouraging. These rights include developing their own culture, speaking their own language, and practicing their own religion. Minorities may include women, the disabled, the aged, and gays and lesbians. However, can ethnic diversity and minority rights be adequately accommodated by states with ethnically or religiously aligned governments? As the recent civil wars in the Congo, Rwanda, Somalia, Sierra Leone, Cambodia, and Bosnia have so vividly demonstrated, such governments all too commonly discriminate against minorities (Lippman, 1997; Pomfret, 1997).

The demand for human rights is supported by the democratizing influence of the media. Television has forever etched on the global community the German people's jubilation when the Berlin Wall fell and the world's despair over the tragedy of Tienanmen Square. The emergence of a worldwide electronic network of NGOs that monitors government policy also supports the struggle for human rights.

Despite the ongoing debates, the die appears to be cast in support of human rights. Many activists, politicians, and ordinary citizens insist that economic development proceed only within a human rights framework (Broadbent, 1992). And, as sociology tells us over and over again, increased global interdependence cannot help but positively contribute to translating the concept of universal human rights from ideal to reality.

SUMMARY

1. Social change is a feature of all societies. However, its pace has increased dramatically over the past few centuries. Cultural change may take the form of invention, discovery, or diffusion. Resistance to change is motivated by cultural inertia and promoted by the actions of vested interests.

2. Major sources of social change include the natural environment, demographic change, new ideas and technologies, government, competition and war, deliberate planning, and social movements.

3. Cyclical theory sees societies as moving through long-term, directionless phases of growth and decay. Evolutionary theory suggests that societies

tend to change in the direction of greater complexity and increased institutional differentiation.

4. Classic functional theory interpreted most social change as an effort to restore systemic equilibrium. Conflict theory sees change as a natural consequence of struggles between competing groups for scarce resources.

5. Over the past two hundred years, large parts of the world have undergone modernization. The fully developed nations are now moving into a postindustrial phase.

6. Sociologists working in the Durkheimian tradition regard the rise of anomie and the consequent weakening of the social bond as a major problem of contemporary developed societies. The communitarian movement is an effort to respond to this challenge.

7. Post-Marxist conflict theorists like Dahrendorf have redefined the problem of class struggle in terms of the broader concept of authority relations.

8. George Ritzer, working in the Weberian tradition, sees McDonaldization as an extension of bureaucratic rationality.

9. Foreign aid is provided to the developing world both out of humanitarian motives and as a stimulus to the growth of democracy and free-enterprise capitalism. NGOs and MNCs are important players in the process of international economic development.

10. Much of the economic activity of the developing nations is located in the informal sector.

11. The nations of the Pacific Rim have been especially successful in the emerging global economy while most of those in sub-Saharan Africa are lagging far behind.

12. Microenterprise programs help people, especially women, in the developing world establish small businesses, particularly in the informal sector.

13. Recent international conferences have led to an emerging worldwide consensus concerning the importance of basic human rights.

KEY TERMS

countermodernization   632
developing world   626
global economy   628
immanent change   619
informal sector   629
McDonaldization   625
microenterprise programs   630
modernity   622

modernization   622
multilinear evolutionary theory   621
multinational corporations (MNCs)   627
nongovernmental organizations (NGOs)   626
postindustrial society   622

post-modernism   622
social capital   623
social change   617
state capitalism   628
technology   618
unilinear evolutionary theory   620
vested interests   616

CRITICAL THINKING QUESTIONS

1. Americans have traditionally found evolutionary and functional theories of change more appealing than the cyclical and conflict approaches. What distinctive aspects of U.S. history and culture might help to explain this observation?

2. Which set of problems poses the most serious threat to developed societies—those identified by modern theorists working in the tradition of Durkheim, in the tradition of Marx, or in the tradition of Weber? Explain your reasoning.

3. How can the link between democracy and development be strengthened in LDCs that do not have capitalist systems? What role can NGOs play in this process?

4. How would the various theories of social change explain countermodernization? What predictions would each theory make regarding the likelihood that countermodernization efforts will be successful?

GLOSSARY

absolute poverty   Poverty defined as an inability to satisfy basic needs for food, shelter, and clothing.

achieved status   Statuses that we acquire over time as a result of our own actions.

acting crowd   A type of crowd that directs its members' hostile emotions toward some external target.

activity theory   Theory explaining that successful aging is linked to middle-aged norms, so roles should be continued, substituted, and expanded.

acute disease   Characterized by sudden onset, rapid peak, and limited duration resulting in either recovery or death.

adaptation   The process enabling a culture to maintain equilibrium despite fluctuations in the culture.

adversarial principle   A legal tradition whereby guilt or innocence is determined by a contest between the prosecution and the defense.

affirmative action   Employment policy that takes either voluntary or involuntary action to increase, maintain, or change the number, rank, or position of certain categories of employees, usually defined by their race or gender.

age grades   Sets of behavioral expectations that are linked to chronological and biological age that change as we get older.

ageism   Devaluation and negative stereotyping of the elderly.

agents of socialization   The people, groups, and social institutions that provide the critical information needed for children to become fully functioning members of society.

age stratification theory   Explains how society uses age strata or categories to make distinctions about people.

aggregate   A collection of people who are physically at the same place at the same time but do not interact in any meaningful way.

aging-out   A process by which crime rates decline sharply once individuals reach their mid-30s.

alienation   Marx's term for a situation in which people are controlled by social institutions that seem beyond their ability to influence.

androcentrism   Male-centered norms that operate throughout all social institutions and become the standard to which all people adhere.

animism   The belief that supernatural beings or spirits inhabit living things and inanimate objects.

anticipatory socialization   A process whereby people practice what they want to achieve.

applied sociology   The view that sociologists should put their knowledge and skills to work in the real world.

ascribed status   Statuses into which we are born and that we cannot change, or that we acquire involuntarily over the life course.

assimilation   The process by which minorities shed their differences and blend in with the dominant group.

assortive mating   A pattern in which coupling occurs based on similarity rather than chance.

authoritarian leader   A leader who makes the major decisions for a group.

authoritarian regime   A type of political system that excludes the people from any meaningful participation in decision making.

authority   Power that is widely perceived by subordinates as legitimate.

bilateral (bilineal) descent   Most common in Western societies, a system that uses both mother and father to trace family lines.

birth cohort   All the people born at a given point in time who age together and experience events in history as a group.

bisexual   The category for people with shifting sexual orientations; they are sexually responsive to either gender.

blended families   Also called reconstituted families, families in which children from parents' prior relationships are brought together in a new family.

bourgeoisie   Marx's term for the class that owns the means of production.

bureaucracy   A formal organization designed to allow large numbers of people to accomplish routine tasks in the most efficient possible way.

bureaucratic ritualism   The tendency in bureaucracies to focus more on the rules than on the goal.

busing   The transporting of children of different races to schools according to a racial parity formula to achieve school desegregation.

capitalism   An economic system based on the private ownership of the means of production.

caste system   A system of stratification made up of several sharply distinct ascribed groups or castes. Caste systems allow little or no social mobility.

casual crowd   A simple type of crowd lacking significant emergent norms, structure, or leadership.

category   Individuals who share a social status but do not interact.

census   When a population is fully counted according to key demographic characteristics.

charismatic authority   Weber's term for power legitimated by an individual's claim to possess extraordinary or unique personal qualities.

chivalry hypothesis   The view that females have been treated less harshly by the criminal justice system in deference to their gender.

chronic disease   Characterized by gradual onset, long duration, and little chance for complete recovery, often resulting in death.

church   Inclusive religious body that brings together a moral community of believers in formal worship and accommodates itself to the larger secular world.

civil law   A tradition of imposing law on a society from above.

civil religion   Also called secular religion, a system of values associated with sacred symbols integrated into broader society and shared by members of that society regardless of their own religious affiliations.

class consciousness   Marx's term for an awareness of the implications of your class position.

classism   An ideology that legitimates economic inequality.

collective behavior Relatively spontaneous, short-lived, unconventional, and unorganized activity by large numbers of people arising in situations where norms are unclear or rapidly changing.

colonialism A system whereby high-income nations take political, economic, and cultural control of less developed societies.

common law A tradition of developing law over time through the accumulation of numerous cases.

commune A collective household where people, who may or may not be related, share roles typically associated with families.

comparable worth The idea that male and female jobs should be assessed according to skill level, effort, and responsibility; used mainly to upgrade women in primarily female jobs.

conservatism A political philosophy that emphasizes order and opposes most social change.

Consolidated Metropolitan Statistical Area (CMSA) When the largest Metropolitan Statistical Areas are grouped together to form one or more megalopolises.

conspicuous consumption Veblen's term for a means of validating social status, especially in the upper class, by wasting money or other resources on nonessentials.

contact hypothesis The theory that certain types of intergroup interaction can reduce prejudice.

content analysis A technique that systematically codes and quantifies the content of documents, such as magazines, newspapers, and archival sources.

contingency work force Workers who are not permanent, full-time employees of a single firm.

continuity theory Suggests that previously developed personality characteristics continue into old age and serve as guidelines for adjusting to aging.

control group The subject group in an experiment that is not exposed to the independent variable.

control variable The variable held constant to help clarify the relationship between the independent and dependent variable.

conventional crowd A type of crowd that develops when an audience expresses some sort of institutionalized emotionality.

corporate crime Criminal acts committed by businesses against employees, customers, or the public.

correlation A condition in which two variables are associated in a patterned way so that a change in one corresponds to a change in another; also called covariation.

counterculture A subculture with values and norms in opposition to the dominant culture.

countermodernization A movement in society that either resists certain aspects of modernization or promotes ways to neutralize their effects.

countermovement A social movement that arises to oppose the goals of another movement.

craze A relatively long-lasting fad with significant economic or cultural implications.

credentialism An emphasis on credentials; qualifications for a job or social status based on the completion of some aspect of formal education.

crime A violation of a formal statute enacted by a legitimate government.

crowd A temporary gathering of people who influence each other in some way and share a focus of attention.

crude birthrate The annual number of births per 1000 population.

cult Most often organized around a charismatic leader who provides the basis for a new, unconventional religion, usually with no clearly defined structure; associated with tension, suspicion, and hostility from the larger society.

cultural capital Bourdieu's term for the subcultural patterns into which members of high-ranking strata are socialized.

cultural integration The process in which cultural elements are closely connected and mutually interdependent.

cultural lag The gap between the time an artifact is introduced and the time it is integrated into a culture's value system.

cultural relativism The principle that all cultures have intrinsic worth and each must be evaluated and understood by its own standards.

cultural studies An interdisciplinary field that focuses on how the meanings of cultural phenomena are constructed by individuals whose consciousness is in turn shaped by the distinctive symbolic and structural patterns of their society.

cultural universals Common features found in all societies.

culture A human society's total way of life; it is learned and shared and includes values, customs, material objects, and symbols.

culture of poverty Subcultural values among the poor, especially the inability to defer gratification, that supposedly make it difficult for them to escape poverty.

culture shock Experiences of alienation, depression, or loneliness when entering a culture vastly different from one's own.

Davis-Moore thesis The view that structured social inequality is functional for society because it ensures that key statuses will be held by highly capable people.

debunking Looking beyond obvious explanations for social behavior and seeking out less obvious and deeper explanations.

decriminalization A policy whereby previously illegal goods or services are legally allowed to adults under certain conditions.

deficiency theory An approach to stratification that explains social inequality as the consequence of individual variations in ability.

degradation ceremony A public ritual whose purpose is to attach a stigma.

deindustrialization The transformation of an economy from a manufacturing to a service base.

democracy A political system in which the people have a significant voice in the government and in which their formal consent is the basis for the legitimacy of the state.

democratic leader A leader who encourages group discussion and input.

demographic transition A three-stage model describing the change from high fertility and mortality to lower ones.

demography Scientific study of population that focuses on size, distribution, and composition and how birth, death, and migration influence each.

denomination Socially accepted and legally recognized religious body that is self-governing, where local congregations have an official relationship with a larger church.

dependent variable The variable presumed to be changed or caused by the independent variable.

developing world Countries characterized by poverty level incomes, agricultural economies, overpopulation, illiteracy, and unemployment. Often used synonymously with the term "less developed countries" (LDCs).

deviance Behavior, beliefs, or conditions that are considered by relatively powerful segments of society to be serious violations of important norms.

diffusion   The borrowing of cultural elements from one society to another.

direct institutional discrimination   Openly discriminatory practices by institutions.

discouraged workers   Unemployed workers who have stopped looking for a job.

discrimination   Treating individuals unequally and unjustly on the basis of their category memberships.

disengagement theory   Theory explaining that successful aging is linked to a gradual, beneficial, and mutual role withdrawal between the elderly and society.

dramaturgical approach   Analyzing social interaction as if it is a play acted on a stage.

dysfunction   Anything that keeps social systems from operating smoothly and efficiently (Merton).

ecclesia   When a church is institutionalized as a formal part of a state and claims citizens as members.

ecological fallacy   Uncritically applying group-level findings to particular individuals.

economy   The institution that organizes the production, distribution, and consumption of material goods and services.

egalitarian marriage   A form of marriage in which partners share decision making and assign roles based on talent and choice rather than on traditional gender beliefs.

ego   Freud's term for the part of the personality that mediates between biological drives and the culture that would deny them.

elite model   The view that real political power is concentrated in the hands of a small and cohesive group of top bureaucrats.

empirical evidence   Information that can be apprehended directly through observation and sensory experience.

end point fallacy   The symbolic interactionist assertion that new labels produce new behavior in an ongoing process.

endogamy   A cultural norm in which people marry within certain groups.

epidemiology   The study of the causes and distribution of disease, and disability in a given population.

equilibrium   The tendency of social systems to resist change.

ethnic group   A category of people who are seen by themselves and others as sharing a distinct subculture.

ethnocentrism   The tendency to evaluate one's own culture as superior to others.

ethnography   A description of the customs, beliefs, and values of a culture by a researcher typically spending a prolonged period living with members of the culture.

ethnomethodology   The study of how people socially construct their everyday world and give meaning to their experiences and interactions.

exogamy   A cultural norm in which people marry outside a particular group.

experimental group   The subject group in an experiment that is exposed to the independent variable.

expressive crowd   A type of crowd whose main function is to provide an opportunity for emotional release among its members.

expressive leader   A leader who is principally concerned with maintaining group morale.

expressive role   In traditional families, the nurturing role usually assigned to the wife-mother.

extended family   A family that consists of parents, dependent children, and other relatives, usually of at least three generations, living in the same household.

fads   Short-lived but intense periods of enthusiasm for new elements in a culture.

false consciousness   Marx's term for anything that retards the growth of class consciousness.

family of orientation   The family we grow up in and the vehicle for primary socialization.

family of procreation   The family we establish at marriage.

fashion   Periodic fluctuations in the popularity of styles of such things as clothes, hair styles, or automobiles.

fee-for-service   Health care where the patient pays for each service provided.

feminism   An inclusive worldwide movement to end sexism and sexist oppression by empowering women.

feminization of poverty   An increase in the percentage of women who are in the poverty population.

fertility rate   Actual reproductive behavior determined by annual number of births per 1000 to women of childbearing age. A more sensitive measure than the crude birthrate.

fictive kin   People who are not related by blood or marriage but are accepted as family members, a pattern common in African American families.

field research   Research design aimed at collecting data directly in natural settings on what people say and do.

folkways   Informal norms that suggest customary ways of behaving.

formal organization   A large secondary group designed to accomplish specific tasks by means of an elaborate internal division of labor.

formal social control   Efforts to discourage deviance made by people whose jobs require them to punish nonconformity and reward obedience.

functional illiteracy   The inability to do the reading, writing, or basic math necessary to carry out daily activities.

fundamentalism   A movement designed to revitalize faith by returning to the traditional ways the religion was practiced in the past.

Gemeinschaft   Tönnies's term for a society based on natural will relationships.

gender   Those social, cultural, and psychological characteristics linked to male and female that define people as masculine and feminine.

gender identity   The awareness that the two sexes behave differently and that two gender roles are proper.

gender roles   Expected attitudes and behaviors a society associates with each sex.

gender schema theory   The theory that suggests that once a child learns cultural definitions of gender, they become the key structures around which all other information is organized.

gender socialization   The process by which individuals learn the cultural behavior of feminine or masculine that is associated with the biological sex of female or male.

gender typing   Stereotypes based on gender that become a normative expectation when the majority of an occupation is made up of one gender.

general deterrence   Punishing an offender in order to keep others from committing crimes.

generalized other   The ability to understand broader cultural norms and judge what a typical person might think or do.

genocide   The extermination of all or most of the members of a minority group.

gentrification   A process of renovating specific working-class or poor neighborhoods to attract new, more affluent residents.

gerontocracy   Cultures in which the elderly, primarily the oldest males, hold the most powerful positions.

gerontology   The scientific study of aging with an emphasis on the elderly population.

Gesellschaft   Tönnies's term for a society constructed primarily on the basis of rational will relationships.

glass ceiling   Argument that women fail to rise to senior level positions because they encounter invisible and artificial barriers constructed by male management.

global cities   Centers of population growth, political actions, and economic activities that are becoming the dominant force in national and world economies.

global economy   The multitude of commodity exchanges that unite consumers and producers around the world.

global stratification   The division of the nations of the world into richer and poorer categories.

global warming   Also called the greenhouse effect, associated with temperature increases linked to burning fossil fuels and industrial and agricultural waste.

goal displacement   The tendency for bureaucracies to focus more on organizational survival than on achieving their primary goals.

gossip   Rumors about other people's personal affairs.

green revolution   The industrial and technological innovations used to produce high yield crops that would help solve the world's food supply problems.

groupthink   A tendency for highly cohesive groups to make poor decisions because of conformity pressures.

halo effect   The tendency to assume that a single characteristic of an individual may be broadened into a general evaluation of that person; thus an athlete who is good at sports may come to be seen as a generally good person.

Hawthorne effect   A phenomenon in which research subjects are influenced by the knowledge that they are in an experiment or study, thus contaminating the results of the study.

health   Defined by the World Health Organization, a state of complete physical, mental, and social well-being, not merely the absence of disease or infirmity.

health maintenance organization (HMO)   A prepaid health plan where health providers are contracted or salaried employees.

hermaphrodites   Children born with both male and female sexual organs or ambiguous genitals.

heterosexual   The category for people who have sexual preferences for those of the other gender.

hidden curriculum   All the informal, unwritten norms and rules that keep students in line.

holistic health   Treating the whole person, with a focus on wellness and prevention.

homogamy   The likelihood of becoming attracted to and marrying someone similar to yourself.

homophobia   Negative attitudes and overall intolerance against homosexuals and homosexuality.

homosexual   The category for people who have sexual preference and erotic attraction for people of their own gender.

horizontal mobility   Social mobility that occurs when an individual moves from one status to another, both of which occupy roughly similar levels in a stratification hierarchy.

human rights   Those rights inherent to human beings, including dignity, personal integrity, inviolability of body and mind, and civil and political rights.

hypergamy   The pattern in which women tend to marry men of higher social and economic status than themselves.

hypodermic model   A theory that assumes the media have a simple, one-way, direct effect on their audiences.

hypothesis   An expectation or prediction derived from a theory; the probable outcome of the research question.

I   Mead's term for that aspect of self that is spontaneous, creative, and impulsive.

id   Freud's term for an individual's biological drives and impulses that strive for gratification.

ideal type   Weber's term for a description of a phenomenon that emphasizes and even exaggerates its most distinctive and characteristic qualities.

ideology   A belief that legitimates patterns of structured social inequality.

immanent change   Change whose causes are internal to the society or other social group in question.

impression management   Information and cues we provide to others to present ourselves in a favorable light.

incidence   The number of new cases of a disease during a specified time period.

income   Salaries, rents, interest, and dividends received from stocks and bonds.

independent variable   The variable presumed to cause change in the dependent variable.

index crimes   Eight street crimes given special attention in the FBI's *Uniform Crime Reports*.

indirect institutional discrimination   Policies that appear to be neutral or colorblind but, in practice, discriminate against minority groups.

individual discrimination   Intentional discrimination by particular individuals.

informal sector   The economic activities of people such as subsistence farmers and urban laborers who work in small-scale home-based production.

informal social control   Efforts to discourage deviance made by friends and family.

informed consent   A condition in which potential subjects have enough knowledge about the research to determine whether they choose to participate.

in-group   A group to which individuals belong and toward which they feel pride and loyalty.

inquisitorial principle   A legal tradition whereby guilt or innocence is determined by a judge without an adversarial contest between defense and prosecution.

instrumental leader   A leader who is principally concerned with accomplishing a group's task.

instrumental role   In traditional families, the breadwinning role usually assigned to the husband-father.

intergenerational social mobility   Social mobility measured by comparing an individual's class position with that of his or her parents or grandparents.

intragenerational social mobility   Social mobility that occurs during an individual's lifetime.

iron law of oligarchy   Michels's theory that all organizations eventually fall under the control of a small group of top leaders.

Kuznets curve   A graphic representation of the relationship between economic development and economic inequality at the societal level.

labeling theory   A perspective that investigates the effects on deviants of being publicly identified as such.

laissez-faire leader   A leader who is highly nondirective.

language   A shared symbol system of rules and meanings that govern the production and interpretation of speech.

latent functions   The unintended and often nonobvious functions of some social phenomenon (Merton).

laws   Formal norms codified and enforced by the legal power of the state.

liberalism   A political philosophy that advocates a relatively weak state existing primarily to defend the rights of the individual, especially property rights.

life course   The perspective that considers the roles people play over a lifetime and the ages associated with these roles.

looking-glass self   Cooley's term for the idea that we use other people as a mirror to gain an image of ourselves.

macrosociology   The study of large-scale social phenomena.

magnet schools   Selective, high quality innercity schools created in the wake of busing; suburban white students are recruited for these schools.

mainstreaming   The integration of special-needs students into the overall classroom or school.

managed care   Designed to control health care costs by measures such as requiring authorization for hospitalization and expensive treatment.

manifest functions   The obvious and intended functions of some social phenomenon (Merton).

mass hysteria   An intense, fearful, and seemingly irrational reaction to a perceived but often misunderstood or imaginary threat that occurs in at least partially dispersed collectivities.

master status   A status that is exceptionally powerful in determining an individual's identity.

material culture   The tangible and concrete artifacts, physical objects, and items found in a society.

matrilineal descent   A system in which the family name is traced through the mother's line and daughters and female kin usually inherit property.

matrilocal residence   A pattern in which a couple moves into the wife's house at marriage.

McDonaldization   Ritzer's term for the process by which bureaucratic principles come to shape more and more of social life.

me   Mead's term for the socialized self; the one that makes us concerned about how others judge us.

means-tested   Refers to government programs that are only provided to persons falling below a particular income level.

mechanical solidarity   Durkheim's term for internal cohesion that results from people being very much like each other.

Medicaid   Joint federal and state welfare program, assisting welfare and low income persons of any age to get medical care.

medicalization   A process that legitimizes medical control over parts of a person's life or in society as a whole.

medicalization of deviance   Reconceptualizing the character of a deviant from "evil" to "sick."

Medicare   Health insurance funded through Social Security for those 65 and over and covering some persons of any age with certain disabilities.

megalopolis   A system of several metropolitan areas and their surrounding suburbs that expand until they overlap.

meritocracy   A system in which individuals are hired and promoted solely on the basis of their specialized skills and knowledge.

metropolitan area   A central city with surrounding smaller cities that function as an integrated economy.

Metropolitan Statistical Area (MSA)   A central city of at least 5000 people and its adjacent urbanized areas.

microenterprise programs   Small scale income-earning manufacturing or agricultural activities located in or near the household.

microsociology   The study of the details of interaction between people, mostly in small-group settings.

migration rate   The movement of people in and out of various areas.

minority group   A category of people who lack power and experience prejudice and discrimination.

mixed economy   An economic system that combines elements of capitalism and socialism; also called a social democracy.

mob   An acting crowd that directs its hostility toward a specific target.

modern liberalism   A political philosophy that combines a strong welfare state with private property and market economics.

modernity   The personal orientations characteristic of people living in a modernized society.

modernization   The sum total of the structural and cultural changes which accompanied the industrial revolution.

monogamy   Marriage to one spouse at a time.

monopoly   A situation in which a single provider dominates a market.

monotheism   Belief in one all powerful and all knowing god.

morbidity rate   The amount of disease or illness in a population over a given time period.

mores   Norms that carry a strong sense of social importance and necessity.

mortality rate   The total number of deaths expressed as a percentage of the population in a given time period, usually a year.

multiculturalism   The concept that different cultural groups exist side by side within the same culture and the belief that the heritage of each should be understood and respected.

multilinear evolutionary theory   A variety of evolutionary thought in which different societies are seen as changing at different paces and in different directions.

multinational corporations (MNCs)   Private business enterprises operating in several countries that have a powerful economic impact worldwide. Also called transnational corporations.

national health insurance   Health coverage provided as a right of citizenship in a country regardless of ability to pay.

negative sanction   A punishment intended to discourage deviance.

neocolonialism   A system whereby previously colonial societies continue to be economically and culturally dominated by their former colonial masters or by multinational corporations.

network   A broad web of social ties that radiates out from a given individual.

New Christian Right (NCR)   A fundamentalist political movement composed of mostly Protestant conservative pressure groups with an agenda for returning morality to U.S. society.

new social movement   An ideologically inclusive, globally linked social movement that emphasizes participation, identity, and emotionality.

nongovernmental organizations (NGOs)   A wide variety of privately funded nonprofit groups, most of which are concerned with development, economic relief, and advocacy for the poor.

nonmaterial culture   The intangible and abstract components of a society, including values, beliefs, and traditions.

nonverbal communication   The ways people communicate without words, including body movements, facial expressions, personal space, and touching.

norms Rules of conduct that guide people's behavior in specific situations.

nuclear family A family that consists of wife, husband, and their dependent children who live apart from other relatives in their own residence.

objective approach Operationalizing the variable of class by assigning individuals to class positions on the basis of indicators such as income or occupation.

occupational crime Criminal acts committed by employees against their employers.

operational definition Guideline that specifies how a concept will be empirically measured.

organic solidarity Durkheim's term for internal cohesion that results from economic interdependency.

organizational culture The informal norms found within a formal organization.

organized crime Crime conducted by relatively large-scale and highly structured syndicates that routinely use corruption and violence to maximize their profits.

out-group A group to which individuals do not belong and toward that they feel disdain and possibly hostility.

panic A type of localized collective behavior in which a large number of people respond to a real or imaginary threat with a desperate, uncoordinated, seemingly irrational flight to secure safety.

Parkinson's Law Theory that work in a bureaucracy expands to fill the time available for its completion.

participant observation A fieldwork technique in which the researcher witnesses or engages firsthand in the activities of the group or culture under study.

patriarchal (patriarchy) Male-dominated social structures leading to the oppression of women.

patrilineal descent A system in which the family name is traced through the father's line and sons and male kin usually inherit property.

patrilocal residence A pattern in which a couple moves into the husband's house at marriage.

peer groups Groups made up of people who are the same age and generally share the same interests and positions.

personality The distinctive complex of attitudes, beliefs, behaviors, and values that makes up an individual.

Peter Principle Theory that bureaucrats are promoted until they reach their level of incompetence, where they then stay.

plea bargaining A system by which defendants agree to plead guilty to a lesser charge rather than proceed to a formal trial.

pluralism A situation in which minority and dominant groups retain their cultural identity yet do not experience discrimination and participate in common economic and political institutions. (Ch. 12)

pluralism The view that competition among elites tends to disperse political power broadly among different individuals and groups. (Ch. 18)

political economy A concept that describes how power and authority are structured in modern societies; it acknowledges the extensive interdependency of the economic and political institutions.

polyandry A rare form of plural marriage allowing a woman to marry more than one man at a time, usually brothers.

polygamy Marriage to more than one spouse at a time.

polygyny The most common form of plural marriage, allowing a man to marry more than one woman at a time.

polytheism Belief in many gods; can either be diffuse where all gods are equal or hierarchal where gods are ranked in importance or power.

popular culture Commercialized art and entertainment designed to attract a mass audience.

population The entire group of people who are the focus of a body of research and to whom the results will be generalized.

population pyramid A visual representation of the age and sex structure of a population at a given point in time.

positive sanction A reward intended to encourage conformity.

positivism An approach to understanding human behavior through the scientific method.

post-modernism An intellectual movement that emphasizes that the meaning of writings, art, or other "texts" is largely or entirely read into the "text" by the observer.

postindustrial society A society in which manufacturing is largely replaced by knowledge-based service activities.

power The ability to compel others to act as the powerholder wishes, even if they attempt to resist.

prejudice A negative attitude toward an entire category of people.

prevalence The total number of cases of a disease during a specified time period.

primary aging The physical and biological changes that accompany the aging process.

primary deviance Any deviant act that is not followed by labeling.

primary group Cooley's term for small groups characterized by warm, informal, and long-lasting interaction.

primary labor market Jobs that provide decent wages, interesting work, benefits, and a possibility of career advancement.

primary socialization Occurring mostly during the early years of life, the stage when language is learned and the first sense of self is gained.

profane Durkheim's term for the world of everyday objects; anything that is not sacred.

profession A prestigious white-collar occupation governed by a professional association.

professionalization The process by which occupations become increasingly professional.

proletariat Marx's term for the class that must sell its labor to the bourgeoisie in order to survive.

protest crowd A type of crowd assembled by the leaders of a social movement to demonstrate its popular support.

public A large number of people who are interested in a particular controversial issue.

pure sociology The view that sociologists should limit their activities to researching the facts and developing theories to explain them.

qualitative analysis Nonnumerical analysis of data to discover underlying meanings, explore relationships, and build theory.

quantitative analysis Data that can be readily translated into numbers.

race A category of people who are believed to be physically distinct from others.

racism The ideology that maintains one race is inherently superior to another.

random sample Also called a probability sample; one in which the researcher can calculate the likelihood that any subject in the population will be included in the sample.

rational choice theory Assumes that people's decisions are made on the basis of a determination of the costs and benefits of each alternative.

rational-legal authority Power legitimated by legally enacted rules and regulations, especially in a bureaucracy (Weber).

rationality Weber's term for consciously using the most effective means in order to pursue a chosen end.

rationalization The process by which human activities become more and more oriented toward the deliberate selection of the most efficient way to accomplish any particular task (Weber).

reactionary movement A social movement that seeks to reverse the general direction of social life.

reference group People to whom we look in order to evaluate our own behavior.

reformist movement A social movement that aims for relatively small-scale progressive change.

relative deprivation A conscious feeling of a negative discrepancy between legitimate aspirations and perceived actualities.

relative poverty Poverty defined as an inability to afford goods and services that most people take for granted in a given society.

reliability An issue in measurement quality asking whether you would get the same results if you repeated the measurement; consistency of measurement.

religion A unified system of beliefs and practices relative to the sacred.

religious law A legal tradition in which the source of law is believed to be divine.

religious pluralism A system that exists when many religions are tolerated, often in competition with one another for members.

reputational approach Operationalizing the variable of class by asking well-informed members of a community to locate other people's positions in the stratification system.

research design An organized plan for collecting data that is guided by the research question and hypothesis.

resocialization The process people go through to remedy patterns of behavior that society finds destructive or to alter behavior to make it fit with other personal or social goals.

revolutionary movement A social movement that aims for broad and sweeping progressive change.

riot An acting crowd that directs its hostility toward a wide and shifting array of targets.

rites of passage Formal events, such as a retirement dinner, that mark important life transitions.

role Cultural norms that define the behaviors expected of an individual occupying a particular status.

role conflict Difficulty performing one role associated with one status because of incompatibility with another role associated with a different status.

role set All of the roles associated with a single status.

role strain Difficulty performing all the elements of the role set connected to a single social status.

role-taking Imagining what it is like to be in other people's shoes in order to increase empathy and social connectedness.

routinization of charisma The transformation from charismatic to either traditional or rational-legal authority (Weber).

ruling class model The view that political power is concentrated in the hands of big business and the upper class.

rumor Unverified information, passed informally from person to person.

sacred Durkheim's term for things set apart from the everyday world that inspire awe and reverence.

sample A subset or part of a larger population that is being studied.

sanction A penalty for norm violation as well as approval or disapproval for norm adherence.

sandwich generation Care givers to the elderly, primarily women, who are caught between caring for two generations—their children and their elderly parents—at the same time.

Sapir-Whorf hypothesis The idea that language determines thought; also called linguistic relativity.

scapegoat A person who is unfairly blamed for other people's problems.

schema Cognitive structures used to understand the world and process new information.

scientific method A systematic procedure for acquiring knowledge that relies on empirical evidence.

secondary aging Aging due to the lifetime of stresses our bodies are subjected to, which include disease, emotional trauma, and age prejudice.

secondary analysis Research in which data already available and created for other purposes are accessed and reanalyzed.

secondary deviance A period of time following labeling during which deviants reorganize their lives around their stigma.

secondary group A group that is formal, emotionally cool, and often temporary.

secondary labor market Jobs that pay poorly, are boring, and provide few benefits and little opportunity for advancement.

sect A smaller religious body, with exclusive or voluntary membership, which is aloof or hostile to the secular society surrounding it.

secular religion *See* civil religion.

secularization The process in which religion, challenged by science and modernization, loses its influence on society.

segregation The physical and social separation of dominant and minority groups.

self The unique sense of identity that distinguishes each individual from all other individuals.

self-fulfilling prophecy Expectations about others lead them to behave in ways that confirm the expectations.

separatism A policy of voluntary structural and cultural isolation from the dominant group.

serial monogamy A pattern of marriage–divorce–remarriage.

sex Those biological characteristics distinguishing male and female.

sexism The belief that one category, female, is inferior to the other category, male.

sexual dimorphism The separation of the sexes into two distinct groups.

sexual harassment Unwelcome sexual advances, requests for sexual favors, and other verbal or physical conduct of a sexual nature.

sexual orientation A person's preference for sexual partners; generally divided into two broad categories, heterosexuality and homosexuality.

sexual scripts Shared beliefs about what society considers acceptable sexual thoughts, feelings, and behavior for each gender.

sexuality A type of social interaction where we perceive, experience, and express ourselves as sexual beings.

sick role Behaviors that are socially expected of a sick person according to prevailing norms.

significant others People whose approval and affection we desire who are therefore most important to the development of our self-concept.

social capital Features of social organization that facilitate coordination and cooperation for mutual benefit.

social change Alterations over time in social structure, culture, and behavior patterns.

social class A category of people who share a common position in a vertical hierarchy of differential social reward.

social construction of reality Our perception of reality as shaped by the subjective meanings we bring to any experience or social interaction.

social control The measures taken by members of a society that are intended to ensure conformity to norms.

social Darwinism Opposition to aid to the poor on the grounds that such assistance interferes with natural selection.

social democracy *See* mixed economy.

social group Two or more people who regularly interact and feel some sense of solidarity or common identity.

social institution A predictable, established way to provide for one of society's basic needs.

social interaction How people behave toward one another when they meet.

social marginality The condition of being partially excluded from the mainstream of society.

social mobility A change in an individual's or group's position in a stratification hierarchy.

social movement A relatively large and organized group of people working for or opposing social change and using of at least some unconventional or uninstitutionalized means.

social stratification The division of a large group or society into ranked categories of people.

social structure The relatively stable patterns of social interaction that characterize human social life.

socialism A political philosophy that advocates collective control over the economy in order to reduce inequality and social injustice.

socialization The lifelong process by which we learn our culture, develop our sense of self, and become functioning members of society.

society A sizable number of people who interact, share a culture, and usually live in a single geographic territory.

sociobiology The science that uses evolutionary theory and genetic inheritance to examine the biological roots of social behavior.

socioeconomic status (SES) An objective measure of class position based on income, occupation, and education.

sociology The systematic and scientific study of human social behavior.

specific deterrence Punishing an offender in order to keep that individual from committing further crimes.

sport Institutionalized, competitive activities that involve vigorous physical exertion or relatively complex physical skills motivated by both personal enjoyment and external rewards.

spurious relationship An observed relationship that is not a true one because it is caused by another variable.

stacking Disproportionately assigning minorities to noncentral sports positions that are low in leadership responsibility and outcome control.

state The institution that maintains a monopoly over the legitimate use of force within a given territorial area.

state autonomy model The view that political power is concentrated in the hands of top government officials and professional experts.

state capitalism A model in which governmental enterprises are financed with public funds but are responsive to market conditions.

state socialism A political system in which the state owns the means of production; seen as a transitional stage between capitalism and communism.

status Social positions that people occupy.

status groups Weber's term for strata based on different lifestyles.

status inconsistency A situation in which an individual occupies several ranked statuses, some of which are evaluated more positively than others.

status set All the statuses that a given individual occupies.

stereotype A broad generalization about a category of people that is applied globally.

stigma A powerfully negative public identity.

strata Segments of a large population that receive different amounts of valued resources by virtue of their position in a ranked system of structural inequality.

structural mobility Social mobility that results principally from changes in the range of occupations that are available in a society.

structural unemployment Unemployment resulting from a mismatch between the skills of the work force and the current needs of the economy.

structured social inequality The advantages and disadvantages enjoyed by members of different social categories that are built into the ongoing operation of society.

subculture Segments of a culture that share characteristics that distinguish it from the broader culture.

subjective approach Operationalizing the variable of class by directly asking people to identify their own class position.

suburbs Smaller surrounding urban areas usually outside the political boundary of a central city.

superego Freud's term for all the norms, values, and morals that are learned through socialization; similar to conscience.

survey research Most frequently used research design in sociology typically using questionnaires and interviews for data collection.

sustainable development Humane ways for the human species to live on the Earth indefinitely without compromising the future of either the planet or its inhabitants; involves international cooperation.

symbol Something that stands for or represents something else.

technology Tools and the body of knowledge pertaining to their use that help accomplish social tasks.

telecommuting Working at home by means of technology such as fax machines and the Internet.

terrorism The use or threat of violence as a political strategy.

tertiary deviance Efforts by organized groups of deviants to secure acceptance.

theism Belief in one or more independent supernatural beings (gods) who do not exist on earth and who are more powerful than people.

theology A systematic formulation of religious doctrine.

theoretical perspective A general orientation within sociology that guides research and theory construction.

theory An explanation of the relationship between specific facts.

Thomas Theorem The idea that what people define as real is real in its consequences.

total institutions Places of residence and work that exert complete control over the people they contain.

totalitarianism A type of authoritarian regime that has unlimited power to intervene in people's everyday lives.

tracking The practice of grouping children according to an assessment of their ability.

traditional authority   Weber's term for authority legitimated by long-established cultural patterns.

trained incapacity   The bureaucratic tendency to respond to new situations ineffectively.

underemployment   Working at a job that does not make full use of your skills and qualifications.

unilinear evolutionary theory   A variety of evolutionary thinking that sees all societies as progressing through a set sequence of stages and ultimately closely resembling each other.

unobtrusive measures   Methods of data collection in which the researcher does not interact with what or who is being studied.

urban   Pertaining to a place of settlement, often called a city, that is populated more densely than rural areas.

urban ecology   A field of urban sociology that studies the relationships between urban populations and their physical and spatial environments.

urban legend   Rumors that recount ironic and usually grisly events that supposedly happen to "a friend of a friend."

urbanization   The process of city population growth.

validity   An issue in measurement quality asking whether you are measuring what you think you are measuring.

values   Beliefs about ideal goals and behavior that serve as standards for social life.

variable   A characteristic or trait that can be measured.

vertical mobility   Social mobility up or down a stratification hierarchy.

vested interests   Veblen's term for individuals or groups whose advantages are threatened by impending social change.

victim blaming   Considering individuals responsible for negative conditions that are in fact primarily the result of larger structural factors beyond their control.

victimless crime   Crimes created when the criminal law is used to prohibit the exchange of strongly desired goods and services between willing adults.

victimology   A subfield of criminology devoted to the study of the victims of crime.

wealth   Net accumulated assets including homes, land, automobiles, jewelry, factories, and stocks and bonds.

white-collar crime   Criminal acts committed by high-status people in the course of their occupations.

Zero Population Growth (ZPG)   Also called replacement level; occurs when the population growth rate is static, or zero, because each couple has two children to replace them.

REFERENCES

AAASHRAN. 1998. "Progress in the elimination of female genital mutilation." Alerts by the American Association for the Advancement of Science, distributed electronically by the Human Rights Action Network: January 6.

AAPCHO. 1997. *Taking Action: Improving Access to Health Care for Asian Pacific Islanders.* Oakland, CA: Association of Asian Pacific Community Health Organizations.

Abadinsky, Howard. 1990. *Organized Crime,* 3rd ed. Chicago: Nelson-Hall.

Abalos, David T. 1996. *Strategies of Transformation Toward a Multicultural Society: Fulfilling the Story of Democracy.* Westport, CT: Praeger.

Abbott, Andrew. 1988. *The System of Professions.* Chicago: University of Chicago Press.

Abel, G.G., D.H. Barlow, E. Blanchard, & D. Guild. 1977. "The components of rapist's sexual arousal." *Archives of General Psychiatry* 34: 895–903.

Abel-Smith, 1990. "The economics of health care." In Thomas A. Lambo & Stacey B. Day (eds.), *Issues in Contemporary International Health.* New York: Plenum: pp. 55–71.

Abercrombie, Nicholas, Stephen Hill, & Bryan S. Turner (eds.), 1990. *Dominant Ideologies.* Cambridge, MA: Unwin Hyman.

Aberle, David. 1966. *The Peyote Religion Among the Navajo.* Chicago: Aldine.

Aberle, David. 1982. *The Peyote Religion Among the Navajo.* Chicago: University of Chicago Press.

Aberle, David F., A. K. Cohen, A. K. David, M. J. Leng, Jr., & F. N. Sutton. 1950. "The functional prerequisites of a society." *Ethics* 60: 100–110.

Acker, Sandra, 1994. *Gendered Education: Sociological Reflections on Women, Teaching and Feminism.* Buckingham, UK: Open University Press.

Acock, A. C., & J. S. Hurlbert. 1993. "Social networks, marital status, and well-being." *Social Networks* 15: 309–34.

Acosta, R. Vivian, & Linda J. Carpenter. 1994. "Women in intercollegiate sport: A longitudinal study." Brooklyn, NY: Brooklyn College Department of Physical Education.

Adams, Mike S., James D. Johnson, & T. David Evans. 1998. "Racial Differences in Informal Labeling Effects," *Deviant Behavior* 19: 157–171.

Adams, Scott. 1996. *The Dilbert Principle.* New York: HarperCollins.

Adams, Tom. 1991. *Grass Roots: How Ordinary People Are Changing America.* New York: Citadel.

Adams, Vincanne. 1996. "Karaoke as modern Lhasa, Tibet: Western encounters with cultural politics." *Cultural Anthropology* 11(4): 510–46.

Aday, David P. Jr. 1989. *Social Control at the Margins: Toward a General Understanding of Deviance.* Belmont, CA: Wadsworth.

Addams, Jane. 1981. *Twenty Years at Hull House.* New York: Signet. Originally published in 1910.

Adelmann, Pamela. 1994. "Multiple roles and physical health among older adults." *Research on Aging* 16(2): 142–66.

Ades, Alberto F., & Edward L. Glaeser. 1995. "Trade and circuses: Explaining urban giants." *The Quarterly Journal of Economics* 110: 195–227.

Adler, Jerry. 1991. "Drums, sweat and tears." *Newsweek* (June 24): 48–51.

Adler, Patricia A. 1996. "Preadolescent clique stratification and the hierarchy of identity." *Sociological Inquiry* 66(2): 111–42.

Adler, Patricia A., & Peter Adler. 1991. *Backboards & Blackboards: College Athletes & Role Engulfment.* New York: Columbia University Press.

Adler, Patricia A., & Peter Adler. 1995. "Dynamics of inclusion and exclusion in preadolescent cliques." *Social Psychology Quarterly* 58: 145–62.

Admiraal, Peter H. 1992. "Competition in health care." In H. E. G. M. Hermans, A. F. Casparie, & J. H. P. Paelinck (eds.), *Health Care in Europe After 1992.* Aldershot, Hants, UK: Darthmouth: 49–51.

Adorno, Theodor W., Else Frenkel-Brunwick, D. J. Levinson, & R. N. Sanford. 1950. *The Authoritarian Personality.* New York: Harper & Row.

Adriance, M. 1985. "Opting for the poor: A social-historical analysis of the changing Brazilian Catholic church." *Sociological Analysis* 46: 131–146.

Afshar, Haleh. 1991. "Women and development: Myth and realities—some introductory notes." In Haleh Afshar (ed.), *Women, Development, and Survival in the Third World.* Essex, UK: Longman.

Aganbegyan, A. 1989. *Peristroika 1989.* New York: Scribner.

Agassi, Judith Buber. 1989. "Theories of gender equality: Lessons from the Israeli kibbutz." *Gender & Society* 3(2): 160–86.

Age Concern. 1992. *Dependence: The Ultimate Fear.* London: Age Concern.

Ageton, Suzanne, & Delbert Elliott. 1973. *The Effect of Legal Processing on Self-Concept.* Boulder, CO: Institute of Behavioral Science.

Agnew, Robert, & David Petersen. 1989. "Leisure and delinquency." *Social Problems,* 36: 322–50.

Aguirre, B. E., E. L. Quarantelli, & J. L. Mendoza. 1988. "The collective behavior of fads." *American Sociological Review* 53: 569–84.

Ahlburg, Dennis A., & Carol J. DeVita. 1995. "New realities of the American family." In Mark Robert Rank & Edward L. Kain (eds.), *Diversity and Change in Families: Patterns, Prospects, and Policies.* Upper Saddle River, NJ: Prentice Hall.

Ahmad, Leila. 1986. "Women and the advent of Islam." *Signs* 11: 665–91.

Ahmad, Zubeida, & Martha Loutfi. 1985. *Women Workers in Rural Development.* Geneva: International Labour Organization.

Ahmed, Ghyasuddin. 1996. "Metropolis 2000: A forum on urban issues." *SAIS Review* 16: 181–85.

Akard, Patrick. 1992. "Corporate mobilization and political power." *American Sociological Review* 57: 597–615.

Akers, Ronald L. 1992. *Drugs, Alcohol, and Society.* Belmont, CA: Wadsworth.

Akers, Ronald L. 1997. *Criminological Theories,* 2nd ed. Los Angeles: Roxbury.

Alba, R. D. 1992. "Ethnicity." In E. F. Borgotta & M. L. Borgotta, (eds.), *Encyclopedia of Sociology,* Vol. 1. New York: Macmillan: 575–584.

Albanese, Jay. 1989. *Organized Crime in America,* 2nd ed. Cincinnati: Anderson.

Aldag, R. J., & S. R. Fuller. 1993. "Beyond fiasco: A reappraisal of the group-think phenomenon and a new model of group decision processes." *Psychological Bulletin* 113: 533–522.

Aldous, Joan, 1991. "Symposium review: Families by the book." *Contemporary Sociology* 20: 660–62.

Aldrich, Nelson W. Jr. 1988. *Old Money: The Mythology of America's Upper Class.* New York: Vintage.

Aldridge, Alan. 2000. *Religion in the Contemporary World: A Sociological Introduction.* Cambridge, UK: Polity.

Alexander, Edward. 1994. "Multiculturalists and anti-semitism." *Society* 31: 58–64.

Alexander, Jeffrey C. 1998. *Neofunctionalism and After.* Malden, MA: Blackwell.

Alexander, Jeffrey, & Paul Colomy. 1990. "Neofunctionalism." In George Ritzer, (ed.), *Frontiers of Social Theory: The New Synthesis.* New York: Columbia University Press: 33–67.

Alexander, Paul. 1986. "Labor expropriation and fertility: Population growth in nineteenth century Java." In W. Penn Handwerker (ed.), *Culture and Reproduction: An Anthropological Critique of Demographic Transition Theory.* Boulder, CO: Westview: 249–62.

Alexander, Peter, & Roger Gill, eds. 1984. *Utopias.* London: Duckworth.

Alfred, Randall. 1976. "The Church of Satan." In Charles Glock & Robert Bellah (eds.), *The New Religious Consciousness.* Berkeley, CA: University of California: 180–202.

Allen, Brandt. 1978. "Racism and research: The case of the Tuskegee syphilis study." *Hastings Center Magazine.* Hastings-on-Hudson, NY: Institute of Society, Ethics, and the Sciences.

Allen, Henry Southworth. 1994. *Going too far enough: American culture at century's end.* Washington, DC: Smithsonian Institution.

Allen, Michael P. 1987. *The Founding Fortunes.* New York: Dutton.

Allen, Paula Gunn. 1995. "When women throw down bundles: Strong women make strong nations." In Sheila Ruth (ed.), *Issues in Feminism: An Introduction of Women's Studies.* Mountain View, CA: Mayfield.

Allen, Paula Gunn. 1998. "When women throw down bundles: Strong women make strong nations." In Sheila Ruth (ed.), *Issues in Feminism: An Introduction of Women's Studies.* Mountain View, CA: Mayfield.

Allen, Walter R., & Joseph D. Jewell. 1995. "African-American education since *An American Dilemma.*" *Daedalus* 174/1: 77–100.

Allgeier, Elizabeth Rice, & Albert R. Allgeier. 2000. *Sexual Interactions.* Boston: Houghton Mifflin.

Alliance for a Global Community. 1996. "The NGO explosion." Insert in *Connections* 3/2. Published by *Interaction.*

Allison, Julie, & Lawrence Wrightman. 1993. *Rape: The Misunderstood Crime.* Newbury Park, CA: Sage.

Allison, Scott T., & Caryn E. Herlocker. 1994. "Constructing impressions in demographically diverse organizational settings: A group categorization analysis. *American Behavioral Scientist* 37(5): 637–52.

Allport, Gordon. 1958. *The Nature of Prejudice.* New York: Doubleday.

Allport, Gordon W., & Leo Postman. 1947. *The Psychology of Rumor.* New York: Holt.

Almquist, Elizabeth M. 1987. "Labor market gender inequality in minority groups." *Gender & Society* 1: 400–14.

Almquist, Elizabeth M. 1995. "The experiences of minority women in the United States: Intersections of race, gender, and class." In Jo Freeman (ed.), *Women: A Feminist Perspective.* Mountain View, CA: Mayfield.

Altenbaugh, Richard J. 1993. "Families, children, schools, and the workplace." In Stanley William Rothstein (ed.), *Handbook of Schooling in Urban America*. Westport, CT: Greenwood: 19–42.

Alter, Jonathan. 1996. "Washington washes its hands." *Newsweek* (August 12): 42–44.

Alter, Jonathan. 2000. "The death penalty on trial." *Newsweek* (June 12): 24–34.

Alter, Jonathan, & Mark Miller. 2000. "A life or death gamble." *Newsweek* (May 29): 22–27.

Amato, Paul R. 1993. "Children's adjustment to divorce: Theories, hypotheses, and empirical support." *Journal of Marriage and the Family* 55: 23–38.

Amato, Paul R. 1996. "Explaining the intergenerational transmission of divorce." *Journal of Marriage and the Family* 58(3): 628–40.

Amato, Paul R., & Alan Booth. 1995. "Changes in gender role attitudes and perceived marital quality." *American Sociological Review* 60(1): 58–66.

American Association of University Women. 1992. *The AAUW Report: How Schools Shortchange Girls*. Prepared by the Wellesley College Center for Research on Women. Washington, DC: AAUW Educational Foundation.

American Association of University Women. 1993. *Hostile Pathways: The AAUW Survey on Sexual Harassment in America's Schools*. Washington, DC: American Association of University Women.

American Demographics. 1985. "Entrepreneurial eighties." 7: 11.

American Psychological Association, 1985. *Developing a National Agenda to Address Women's Health Needs*. Washington, D.C.: APA.

American Psychological Association. 1985. *Developing a National Agenda to Address Women's Mental Health Needs*. Washington, DC: American Psychological Association.

American Psychological Association. 1993. *Violence and Youth: Psychology's Response*. Washington, DC: American Psycological Association.

American Sociological Association. 1997. *Code of Ethics of the American Sociological Association*. Washington, DC: American Sociological Association.

Amin, Samir. 1974. *Accumulation on a World Scale*. New York: Monthly Review.

Ammerman, Nancy Tatom. 1990. *Baptist Battles: Social Change and Religious Conflict in the Southern Baptist Convention*. New Brunswick, NJ: Rutgers University.

Ammerman, Nancy Tatom. 1993. *Southern Baptists Observed: Multiple Perspectives on a Changing Denomination* (edited collection). Knoxville, TN: University of Tennessee Press.

Ammerman, Nancy Tatom. 1997. "Organized religion in a voluntaristic society." *Sociology of Religion* 58: 203–15.

Amott, Teresa. 1993. *Caught In the Crisis: Women and the U.S. Economy Today*. New York: Monthly Review Press.

Anderson, Beverley. 1994. "Permissive social and educational inequality 40 years after Brown." *Journal of Negro Education* 63(3): 443–450.

Anderson, Catherine, & Caroline Loughlin. 1986. *Forest Park*. Columbia, MO: Junior League of St. Louis and University of Missouri.

Anderson, Elijah. 1990. *Streetwise: Race, Class and Change in an Urban Community*. Chicago: University of Chicago.

Anderson, Elijah. 1995. "The black male in public." In Spencer E. Cahill (ed.), *Inside Social Life: Readings in Sociological Psychology and Microsociology*. Los Angeles: Roxbury.

Anderson, John. 1994. "Held hostage in Hollywood: Female stars buy into bad roles, big time." *St. Louis Post-Dispatch* (December 4): 3C.

Anderson, Kristin L. 1997. "Gender, status, and domestic violence: An integration of feminist and family violence approaches." *Journal of Marriage and the Family* 59(3): 655–69.

Anderson, L. S., Theodore G. Chiricos, & Gordon P. Waldo. 1977. "Formal and informal sanctions: A comparison of deterrent effects." *Social Problems* 25: 103–14.

Anderson, Margaret L., & Patricia Hill Collins. 1995. "Shifting the center and reconstructing knowledge." In Margaret L. Anderson & Patricia Hill Collins (eds.), *Race, Class and Gender: An Anthology*. Belmont, CA: Wadsworth.

Anderson, Margaret L., & Patricia H. Collins (eds.). 1998. *Race, Class, and Gender*, 3rd ed. Belmont, CA: Wadsworth.

Anderson, Ronald, Meei-Shia Chen, Lu Anne Aday, & Llewellyn Cornelius. 1987. "Health status and medical care utilization." *Health Affairs* 6(1): 136–56.

Andrews, D. A., & J. Stephen Warmith. 1989. "Personality & crime: knowledge & construction in criminology." *Justice Quarterly* 6: 289–310.

Andrews, D. A., & James Bonta. 1994. *The Psychology of Criminal Conduct*. Cincinnati: Anderson.

Angier, Natalie. 1997. "Laughter: Rhythmic bursts of social glue." In Mark H. Davis (ed.), *Annual Editions: Social Psychology 97/98*. Guilford, CT: Dushkin/Brown & Benchmark: 127–29.

Angus, David, & Jeffrey Mirel. 1995. "Rhetoric and reality: The high school curriculum." In Diane Ravitch & Maris A. Vinovskis (eds.), *Learning From the Past: What History Teaches Us About School Reform*. Baltimore, MD: Johns Hopkins University: 295–328.

Annez, Patricia, & Alfred Friendly. 1996. "Cities in the developing world: Agenda for action following Habitat II." *Finance and Development* 33: 12–14.

Annin, Peter, & Tom Morganthau. 1997. "The verdict: Death." *Newsweek* (June 23): 40–42.

Ansolabehere, S., R. Behr, & S. Iyengar. 1991. "Mass media and elections: An overview." *American Politics Quarterly* 19: 109–39.

Ansolabehere, S., R. Behr, & S. Iyengar. 1993. *The Media Game: American Politics in the Television Age*. New York: Macmillan.

Anson, Ofra, Arieh Levenson, & Dan Y. Booneh. 1990. "Gender and health on the kibbutz." *Sex Roles* 22(3–4): 213–236.

Antilla, Susan. 1995. "Young white men only, please: Women accuse a broker of blatant discrimination." *The New York Times* April 26: C1,D7.

Anyon, Jean. 1980. "Social class and the hidden curriculum of work." *Journal of Education* 162: 67–92.

Anzaldua, Gloria E. 1995. "The strength of my rebellion." In Sheila Ruth (ed.), *Issues in Feminism: An Introduction to Women's Studies*. Mountain View, CA: Mayfield.

Applebome, Peter. 1998. "No room for childhood in a world of little adults." *New York Times* (May 10): 4–1, 4–3.

Apt, Nana Araba. 1992. "Family support to elderly people in Ghana." In Hal Kendig, Akiko Hashimoto, & Larry C. Coppare (eds.), *Family Support for the Elderly: The International Experience*. New York: Oxford University Press.

Aptheker, Herbert. 1990. "W. E. B. Du Bois: Struggle, not despair," *Clinical Sociology Review* 8: 58–65.

Arbuckle, Alan. 1996. "Seniors take to technology." *Marketing* 101 (July 22): 15.

Archer, D., B. Iritani, D. D. Kimes, & M. Barrios. 1983. "Faceisms: Five studies of sex differences in facial prominence." *Journal of Personality and Social Psychology* 45: 725–35.

Archer, Dane, & Rosemary Gartner. 1984. *Violence and Crime in Cross-National Perspective*. New Haven, CT: Yale University Press.

Archer, Melanie, & Judith R. Blau. 1994. "Class formation in 19th century America." *Annual Review of Sociology* 19: 17–41.

Arenberg, David & Elizabeth A. Robertson-Tchabo (eds.). 1980. "Age differences and age changes in cognitive development." In R. L. Sprott (ed.), *Age, Learning Ability and Intelligence*. New York: Van Nostrand Reinhold.

Arendell, Terry. 1995. *Fathers and Divorce*. Thousand Oaks, CA: Sage.

Argyle, M. 1988. *Bodily Communication*. London: Methuen.

Argyris, Chris. 1960. *Understanding Organizational Behavior*. Homewood, IL: Dorsey.

Aries, Nancy, & Louanne Kennedy. 1990. "The health labor force: The effects of change." In Peter Conrad & Rochelle Kern (eds.), *Sociology of Health and Illness: Critical Perspectives*. New York: St. Martin's Press.

Aries, Philippe. 1962. *Centuries of Childhood*. New York: Random House.

"Arizona sheriff thrives on jails' mean reputation." 1996. *Evansville Courier* (February 19).

Arliss, Laurie P. 1991. *Gender Communication*. Upper Saddle River, NJ: Prentice Hall.

Armas, Genaro C. 2000. "Millions Still Poor, But Report Is the Best in 21 Years," *Evansville Courier & Press* (September 27).

Armstrong, David. 1996. "The problem of the whole-person in holistic medicine." In Basiro Davey, Alastair Gray, & Clive Seale (eds.), *Health and Disease: A Reader*. Buckingham, UK: Open University: 45–49.

Armstrong, Elizabeth. 1995. *Mental Health Issues in Primary Care: A Practical Guide*. London: Macmillan.

Arnold, Guy. 1988. *The Third World Handbook*. London: Cassell Educational.

Aronowitz, S., & W. DiFazio. 1994. *The Jobless Future*. Minneapolis: University of Minnesota Press.

Aronowitz, Stanley. 1993. *Roll Over Beethoven: The Return of Cultural Strife*. Hanover, NH: Wesleyan University Press.

Aronowitz, Stanley, & Henry A. Giroux. 1991. "Textual authority, culture, and the politics of literacy." In Michael W. Apple & Linda K. Christian-Smith (eds.), *The Politics of the Textbook*. New York: Routledge: 213–41.

Aronson, Elliot. 1996. *The Social Animal*. New York: W. H. Freeman.

Arrighi, Giovanni. 1994. *The Long 20th Century*. New York: Verso.

Arthur, Paul. 1984. *Government and Politics of Northern Ireland*, 2nd ed. London: Longman.

Arvanites, Thomas. 1992. "Increasing imprisonment: A function of crime or socioeconomic factors?" *American Journal of Criminal Justice* 17: 19–38.

Asch, Arthur. 1977. "Send your children to the libraries," *The New York Times* (February 6): S–2.

Asch, Solomon. 1952. "Effects of group pressure upon the modification and distortion of judgements." In Guy Swanson, Theodore M. Newcomb, & Eugene L. Hartley, (eds.), *Readings In Social Psychology*. New York: Holt, Rinehart & Winston.

Ascha, Ghassan. 1995. "The 'Mothers of the Believers': Stereotypes of the Prophet Muhammad's wives." In Ria Kloppenborg & Wouter J. Hanegraaff (eds.), *Female Stereotypes in Religious Traditions*. Leiden, Netherlands: Brill.

Asher, Marty. 1994. *The Disappearance of Childhood*. New York: Vintage.

Asher, Robert, & Charles Stephenson, (eds.), 1990. *Labor Divided*. Albany, NY: State University of New York Press.

Ashford, Lori S. 1995. *Population Bulletin*. (Report reviewing world population conditions and policy issues). Population Reference Bureau.

Asia-Pacific Population and Policy. 1994. "After the demographic transition: Policy responses to low fertility in four Asian countries." East-West Center Program on Population No. 30: 1–4.

Asimov, Isaac. 1988. *Prelude to Foundation*. New York: Bantam.

Associated Press. 1999. "Verdict upsets backers of assisted suicide." *St. Louis Post-Dispatch* (March 28): A15.

Astin, Alexander W., William S. Korn, & Ellyne R. Berz. 1989. *The American Freshman: National Norms for Fall 1989*. Los Angeles: Higher Education Research Institute, University of California.

Atchley, Robert C. 1989. "A continuity theory of normal aging." *The Gerontologist* 29: 183–90.

Atchley, Robert C. 1994. *Social Forces and Aging*. Belmont, CA: Wadsworth.

Atchley, Robert C. 2000. *Social Forces and Aging*. Belmont, CA: Wadsworth.

Atchley, Robert C., & Sheila J. Miller. 1983. "Types of elderly couples." In Timothy H. Brubaker (ed.), *Family Relationships in Later Life*. Beverly Hills, CA: Sage.

Atkins, G. Lawrence. 1992. "Making it last: Economic resources of the oldest old." In Richard M. Suzman, David P. Willis & Kenneth G. Manton (eds.), *The Oldest Old*. New York: Oxford University Press.

Atkinson, Anthony B., Lee Rainwater, & Timothy M. Smeeding. 1995. *Income Distribution in OECD Countries*. Paris: Organization for Economic Cooperation & Development.

AtKisson, Alan. 1995. "What makes love last." In Kathleen R. Gilbert (ed.), *Marriage and the Family 95/96 (Annual Editions)*. Guilford, CT: Dushkin/Brown & Benchmark.

Atlink, Sietske. 1995. Stolen Lives: *Trading Women into Sex and Slavery*. London: Scarlet Press.

Atwater, Lynn. 1982. *The Extramarital Connection: Sex, Intimacy, Identity*. New York: Irvington.

Auerbach, Elsa. 1992. "The challenge of the English only movement." *College English* 54(7): 843–51.

Auletta, Ken. 1982. *The Underclass*. New York: Random House.

Auster, Carol J. 1996. *The Sociology of Work: Concepts & Cases*. Thousand Oaks, CA: Pine Forge.

Austin, James, & John Irwin. 1989. *Who Goes to Prison?* San Francisco: National Council on Crime & Delinquency.

Awotona, Adenrele. 1995. "Focus: Integration and urbanisation of existing townships in South Africa." *Urbanisation*, Newsletter of the Overseas Development Administration 1: 4–5.

Axinn, William G., & Arland Thornton. 1993. "Mothers, children, and cohabitation: The intergenerational effects of attitudes and behaviors." *American Sociological Review* 58(2): 233–46.

Ayres, B. Drummond, Jr. 1996. "U.S. judge blocks voters' initiative on job preference." *The New York Times* (Nov. 28): A1+.

Babb, Florence E. 1990. "Women and work in Latin America." *Latin American Research Review* 25(2): 236–47.

Babbie, Earl. 1994. *What Is Society?* Thousand Oaks, CA: Pine Forge.

Babbie, Earl. 1997. *The Practice of Social Research*. Belmont, CA: Wadsworth.

Bachman, Ronet. 1992. *Death and Violence on the Reservation*. New York: Auburn House.

Bachrach, Peter, & Morton Baratz. 1970. *Power and Poverty*. New York: Oxford University Press.

Bacon, Elizabeth E. 1980. *Central Asians Under Russian Rule: A Study In Cultural Change*. Ithaca, NY: Cornell University Press.

Badinter, Elisabeth. 1995. *XY: On Masculine Identity*. New York: Columbia University.

Baer, Hans A. 1989. "The American diminutive medical system as a reflection of social relations in the larger society." *Social Science and Medicine* 28: 1103–12.

Baer, Hans A., & Merrill Singer. 1992. *African-American Religion in the Twentieth Century: Varieties of Protest and Accommodation*. Knoxville, TN: University of Tennessee.

Bagguley, Paul, & Kirk Mann. 1992. "Idle thieving bastards? Scholarly representation of the 'underclass.'" *Work, Employment and Society* (6/1): 113–126.

Bai, Matt, Sharon Begley, Scott Johnson, & Steven Levy. 1999. "Death at Columbine High." *Newsweek*: 22–39.

Bailey, Frankie, & Donna Hale (eds.). 1998. *Popular Culture, Crime and Justice*. Belmont, CA: West/Wadsworth.

Bailey, Thomas, & Roger Waldinger. 1991. "Primary, secondary & enclave labor markets," *American Sociological Review* 56: 432–445.

Bainbridge, William S., & Rodney Stark. 1981. "American-born sects: Initial findings." *Journal for the Scientific Study of Religion* 20: 130–49.

Bainbridge, William S., & Rodney Stark. 1997. "Sectarian tension." In Thomas E. Dowdy & Patrick H. McNamara, (eds.), *Religion: North American Style*. New Brunswick, NJ: Rutgers University Press: 86–103.

Bakanic, Von. 1995. "I'm not prejudiced, but . . . A deeper look at racial attitudes." *Sociological Inquiry* (65/1): 67–86.

Baker, High D. R. 1979. *Chinese Family and Kinship*. New York: Columbia University.

Baker, Peter. 1997. "Saying her views haven't changed, First Lady takes on 'micro' agenda." *Washington Post* (January 31): A6.

Baker, Susan. 1994. "Gender, ethnicity, and homelessness." *American Behavioral Scientist* 37(4): 476–504.

Baker, Wayne E., & Robert R. Faulkner. 1993. "The social organization of conspiracy: Illegal networks in the electrical equipment industry," *American Sociological Review* 58: 837–60.

Bakshian, Douglas. 1996. "Taliban woman doctor." *Voice of America* October 8. Electronically distributed by the Human Rights Information Network (HURINet).

Baldassare, Mark, & Georjeanna Wilson. 1995. "More trouble in paradise: Urbanization and the decline in suburban quality-of-life ratings." *Urban Affairs Review* 30: 690–708.

Baldus, D. C., C. Pulaski, & G. Woodworth. 1990. *Equal Justice and the Death Penalty: A Legal and Empirical Analysis*. Boston: Northeastern University Press.

Baldwin, Bruce A. 1988. *Beyond the Cornucopia Kids: How to Raise Healthy Achieving Children*. Wilmington, NC: Direction Dynamics.

Baldwin, Bruce A. 1995. "The family circle." In Kathleen R. Gilbert (ed.), *Marriage and Family 95/96* (Annual Editions). Guilford, CT: Dushkin/Brown & Benchmark.

Bales, Robert F. 1950. *Interaction Process Analysis*. Reading, MA: Addison-Wesley.

Bales, Robert F. 1951. "Channels of communication in small groups." *American Sociological Review* 16: 461–468.

Bales, Robert F. 1953. "The equilibrium problem in small groups." In Talcott Parsons, Robert F. Bales & Edward A. Shils (eds.), *Working Papers in the Theory of Action*. Glencoe: Free Press.

Balkwell, James W. 1990. "Ethnic inequality and the rate of homicide." *Social Forces* 69: 53–70.

Baltzell, E. Digby. 1990. "Upperclass and elites." *Society* 27 (January/February): 72–75.

Bandura, Albert. 1973. *Aggression: A Social Learning Analysis*. Upper Saddle River, NJ: Prentice Hall.

Bandura, Albert, & Richard H. Walters. 1963. *Social Learning and Personality Development*. New York: Holt, Rinehart & Winston.

Bane, Mary Jo, & David T. Ellwood. 1989. "One-fifth of the nation's children: Why are they poor?" *Science* 245: 1047–1053.

Bane, Mary Jo, & David T. Ellwood. 1994. *Welfare Realities: From Rhetoric to Reform*. Cambridge, MA: Harvard University Press.

Banfield, Edward C. 1974. *The Unheavenly City Revisited*. Boston: Little, Brown.

Bankole, Akinrinola, & Charles F. Westoff. 1995. *Childbearing Attitudes and Intentions*. Demographic and Health Surveys Comparative Studies No. 17. Calverton, MD: Macro International.

Banks, J., & C. A. Banks (eds.). 1993. *Multicultural Education: Issues and Perspectives*. Boston: Allyn & Bacon.

Barash, David P. 1982. *Sociobiology and Behavior*. New York: Elsevier.

Barbato, Carole A. & Jerry D. Feezel. 1987. "The language of aging in different age groups." *The Gerontologist* 27(4): 527–31.

Bardwell, J. R., S. W. Cochran, & S. Walker. 1986. "Relationship of parental education, race and gender to sex-role stereotyping in five-year-old kindergartners." *Sex Roles* 15: 275–81.

Barer, Barbara M. 1994. "Men and women aging differently." *International Journal of Aging and Human Development* 38(1): 29–40.

Barker, P. R., G. Manderscheid, & I. G. Gendershot. 1992. "Serious mental illness and disability in the adult household population in the United States, 1989." In R. W. Manderscheid & M. A. Sonnenschein, (eds.), *Mental Health, United States, 1992*. Washington, DC: Center for Mental Health Services & National Institute of Mental Health.

Barlett, Donald L., & James B. Steele. 1994. *America: Who Really Pays the Taxes?* New York: Simon & Schuster.

Barnard, Chester. 1938. *The Functions of the Executive*. Cambridge, MA: Harvard University Press.

Barner, Robert. 1996. "Seven changes that will challenge managers—and workers." *Futurist* 30 (March–April): 14–18.

Barnes, Gordon E., Leonard Greenwood, & Reena Sommer. 1991. "Courtship violence in a Canadian sample of male college students." *Family Relations* 40: 37–44.

Barnes, Samuel, & Max Kaase. 1979. *Political Action*. London: Sage.

Barnet, Richard J. 1993. "The end of jobs." *Harpers* 287/1720: 47–52.

Barnet, Richard J., & John Cavanagh. 1994. *Global Dreams: Imperial Institutions and the New World Order*. New York: Simon & Schuster.

Baron, James N., & Andrew E. Newman. 1990. "For what it's worth." *American Sociological Review* 55: 155–75.

Baron, James N., P. D. Jennings, & Frank R. Dobbin. 1988. "Mission control? The development of personnel systems in U.S. industry." *American Journal of Sociology* 53: 497–514.

Baron, Richard. 1994. "I can't hear you while I'm listening." In William Kornblum & Carolyn D. Smith (eds.), *The Healing Experience: Readings on the Social Context of Health Care*. Upper Saddle River, NJ: Prentice Hall: 23–33.

Barrett, Richard A. 1991. *Culture and Conduct: An Excursion in Anthropology*. Belmont, CA: Wadsworth.

Barringer, H. R., R. W. Gardner, & M. J. Levin. 1993. *Asians and Pacific Islanders in the United States*. New York: Russell Sage.

Barrow, Georgia & P. A. Smith. 1986. *Aging, Ageism and Society*. St. Paul, MN: West.

Barry, Kathleen. 1979. *Female Sexual Slavery*. New York: Basic Books.

Barry, Kathleen. 1995. *The Prostitution of Sexuality: The Global Exploitation of Women*. New York: New York University.

Bartlett, Donald L., & James B. Steele. 1994. *America: Who Really Pays the Taxes?* New York: Simon & Schuster.

Bartos, Omar. 1995. "Growth of Russian organized crime poses serious threat." *CJ International* 11: 8–9.

Basch, Paul E. 1990. *Textbook of International Health*. New York: Oxford University Press.

Basow, Susan A. 1992. *Gender Stereotypes: Traditions and Alternatives*. Belmont, CA: Wadsworth.

Bassuk, E.L. 1991. "Homeless families." *Scientific American* (December): 66–74.

Bastian, Lisa D., & Bruce M. Taylor. 1994. "Young black male victims." *Bureau of Justice Statistics Crime Data Brief, National Crime Victimization Survey*. NCJ47004 (December). Washington, DC: Bureau of Justice Statistics.

Bauerlein, Monika. 1996. "The Luddites are back." *Utne Reader* (March–April): 24, 26.

Baumann, Zygmunt. 1991. *Modernity and the Holocaust*. Ithaca, NY: Cornell University Press.

Baumgartner, M. P. 1988. *The Moral Order of a Suburb*. New York: Oxford University Press.

Bayles, Michael D. 1991. "A note on the death penalty as the best bet." *Criminal Justice Ethics* 10: 7–10.

Bayma, Todd. 1995. "Art world culture and institutional choices: The case of experimental film." *Sociological Quarterly* 36(1): 79–95.

Beach, Stephen W. 1977. "Religion and political change in Northern Ireland." *Sociological Analysis* (38/1): 37–48.

Beals, Alan R. 1980. *Gopalpur: A South Indian Village*. New York: Holt, Rinehart and Winston.

Bean, Frank D., & Marta Tienda. 1987. *The Hispanic Population of the United States*. New York: Russell Sage.

Becker, Gary S. 1994. "Working women's staunchest allies: Supply and demand." In Susan F. Feiner (ed.), *Race & Gender in the American Economy: Views from Across the Spectrum*. Upper Saddle River, NJ: Prentice Hall.

Becker, Howard S. 1963. *Outsiders*. New York: Free Press.

Beckford, James A. 1989. *Religion and Advanced Industrial Society*. London: Unwin Hyman.

Beeghley, Leonard. 1983. *Living Poorly in America*. New York: Praeger.

Beeghley, Leonard. 1989. *The Structure of Social Stratification in the United States*. Boston: Allyn & Bacon.

Beeghley, Leonard. 2000. *The Structure of Social Stratification in the United States*, 4th ed. Boston: Allyn & Bacon.

Beggs, John J. 1995. "The institutional environment: Implications for race and gender inequality in the U.S. labor market." *American Sociological Review* 60: 612–33.

Belfrage, Sally. 1965. *Freedom Summer*. Greenwich, CT: Fawcett.

Belknap, Joanne. 1996. *The Invisible Woman: Gender, Crime and Justice*. Belmont, CA: Wadsworth.

Bell, Alan P., & Martin S. Weinberg. 1978. *Homosexualities: A Study of Diversity Among Men and Women*. New York: Simon & Schuster.

Bell, Daniel. 1953. "Crime as an American way of life." *Antioch Review* 13: 131–54.

Bell, Daniel. 1976. *The Coming of Post-Industrial Society: A Venture in Social Forecasting*. New York: Basic Books.

Bell, Derrick. 1992. *Race, Racism and American Law*. Boston: Little, Brown.

Bell, Wendell. 1981. "Neocolonialism." In *Encyclopedia of Sociology*. Guilford, CT: Dushkin: 193.

Bellah, Robert. 1957. *Tokagawa Religion*. Glencoe, IL: Free Press.

Bellah, Robert N. 1967. "Civil religion in America." *Daedalus* 96: 1–21.

Bellah, Robert N. 1970. *Beyond Belief*. New York: Harper.

Bellah, Robert, Richard Madsen, William M. Sullivan, Ann Swidler, & Steven M. Tipton. 1985. *Habits of the Heart*. New York: Harper & Row.

Bellas, Marcia L. 1993. "Faculty salaries: Still a cost of being female." *Social Science Quarterly* 74(1): 62–75.

Bellinger, David C., & Jean Berko Gleason. 1982. "Sex differences in parental directives to young children." *Sex Roles* 8: 1123–39.

Belsky, Jay, & John Kelly. 1995. "His and hers transition." In Mark Robert Rank & Edward L. Kain (eds.), *Diversity and Change in Families: Patterns, Prospects and Policies*. Upper Saddle River, NJ: Prentice Hall.

Belz, H. 1991. *Equality Transformed: A Quarter Century of Affirmative Action*. New Brunswick, NJ: Rutgers University Press.

Bem, Sandra Lipsitz. 1981. "Gender schema theory: A cognitive account of sex-typing." *Psychological Review* 88: 354–64.

Bem, Sandra Lipsitz. 1983. "Gender schema theory and its implications for child development: Raising gender-aschematic children in a gender-schematic society." *Signs* 8: 598–616.

Bem, Sandra Lipsitz. 1996. "Transforming the debate on sexual inequality: From biological difference in institutionalized androcentrism." In Joan C. Chrisler, Carla Golden, & Patricia D. Rozee (eds.). *Lectures on the Psychology of Women*. New York: McGraw-Hill.

Bendix, Richard. 1962. *Max Weber: An Intellectual Portrait*. Garden City, NY: Anchor.

Bendroth, Margaret Lamberts. 1996. "Fundamentalism and the media, 1930–1990." In Daniel A. Stout & Judith M. Buddenbaum, eds., *Religion and Mass Media: Audiences and Adaptations*. Thousand Oaks, CA: Sage: 74–84.

Benford, Robert D. 1993. "Frame disputes within the nuclear disarmament movement." *Social Forces* 71: 677–701.

Bengston, Vern L., & J. F. Robertson (eds.). 1985. *Grandparenthood*. Beverly Hills, CA: Sage.

Bengston, Vern L., Carolyn Rosenthal, & Linda Burton. 1990. "Families and aging: Diversity and heterogeneity." In Robert H. Binstock & Linda K. George (eds.), *Handbook of Aging and the Social Sciences*. New York: Academic Press.

Bengston, Vern L., Margaret N. Reedy, & Chad Gordon. 1985. "Aging and self conceptions: Personality processes and social contexts." In James E. Birren & K. Warner Schaie (eds.), *Handbook of the Psychology of Aging*. New York: Van Nostrand Reinhold.

Benin, Mary Holland, & Joan Agostinelli. 1988. "Husbands' and wives' satisfaction with the division of labor." *Journal of Marriage and the Family* 50: 349–61.

Benin, Mary Holland, & Verna M. Keith. 1995. "The social support of employed African American and Anglo mothers." *Journal of Family Issues* 16(3): 275–97.

Benjamin, Bernard, & Chris Wallis. 1963. "The mortality of widowers." *Lancet* 2 (August): 76–89.

Benjamin, Jessica. 1988. *The Bonds of Love: Psychoanalysis, Feminism and the Problem of Domination*. New York: Pantheon.

Bennefield, Robert. 1997. *Health Insurance Coverage: 1996*. Washington, DC: U.S. Bureau of the Census.

Bennet, James. 1997. "First Lady re-emerges, with an aid plan for tiny businesses." *New York Times*, (January 31): A1.

Bennis, Warren G., & Philip E. Slater. 1968. *The Temporary Society*. New York: Harper & Row.

Benokraitis, Nijole V. 1996. *Marriages and Families: Changes, Choices, and Constraints*. Upper Saddle River, NJ: Prentice Hall.

Benokraitis, Nijole V. 1999. *Marriages and Families: Changes, Choices, and Constraints*. Upper Saddle River, NJ: Prentice Hall.

Benokraitis, Nijole V., & Joe R. Feagin. 1986. *Modern Sexism*. Upper Saddle River, NJ: Prentice Hall.

Benson, S. P. 1986. *Counter Cultures*. Urbana, IL: University of Illinois Press.

Bentham, Jeremy. 1967. *A Fragment on Government and an Introduction to the Principle of Morals & Legislation*. Oxford, England: Basil Blackwell.

Bentov, Marilyn, Dori Smith, Diana Siegal, Paula Doress, & Eve Nichols. 1987. "Age and well-being." In Paula Brown Doress & Diana Laskin Siegal (eds.), *Ourselves Growing Older: Women Aging with Knowledge and Power*. New York: Simon and Schuster/Touchstone Books.

Berberoglu, Berch. 1992. *The Political Economy of Development: Development Theory and Prospects for Change in the Third World*. Albany, NY: State University of New York Press.

Berer, Marge. 1993. "Reproductive health: Towards a definition." In *Reproductive Health Policy & Programs: Reflections on the African Experience*. A Conference Report, Harare, July. Washington, DC: Henry J. Kaiser Foundation.

Berg, Ivar, & Mayer Zald. 1978. "Business and society." *Annual Review of Sociology* 4: 115–43.

Berger, Asa, & Aaron Wildavsky. 1994. "Who laughs at what?" *Society* 31(6): 82–86.

Berger, Bennett M. 1988. "Utopia and its environment," *Society* (Jan/Feb): 37–41.

Berger, Brigette, & Peter L. Berger. 1991. "The family and modern society." In Mark Hutter (ed.), *The Family Experience: A Reader in Cultural Diversity*. New York: Macmillan.

Berger, Joseph, Robert Z. Norman, James W. Balkwell, & Roy F. Smith. 1992. "Status inconsistency in task situations: A test of four status processing principles." *American Sociological Review* 57: 843–55.

Berger, Peter L. 1963. *Invitation to Sociology: A Humanistic Perspective*. Garden City, NY: Anchor.

Berger, Peter L., & Thomas Luckmann. 1966. *The Social Construction of Reality*. New York: Doubleday.

Berger, Peter. 1967. *The Sacred Canopy: Elements of a Sociological Theory of Religion*. New York: Doubleday.

Berger, Peter. 1977. *Facing up to Modernity: Excursions in Society, Politics and Religion*. New York: Basic Books.

Berger, Peter. 1986. *The Capitalist Revolution: 50 Propositions About Prosperity, Equality and Liberty*. New York: Basic.

Berger, Peter. 1990. *A Rumor of Angels: Modern Society and the Rediscovery of the Supernatural* (expanded edition). New York: Anchor/Doubleday.

Berk, Richard A. 1974. *Collective Behavior*. Dubuque, IA: Brown.

Berk, Richard A., & Sarah F. Berk. 1979. *Labor and Leisure at Home: Content and Organization of the Household Day*. Beverly Hills, CA: Sage.

Berkowitz, Leonard. 1993. *Aggression: Its Causes, Consequences & Control*. New York: McGraw-Hill.

Berlin, B., & P. Kay. 1969. *Basic Color Terms*. Berkeley, CA: University of California.

Berman, Peter, Carl Kendall, & Karabi Bhattacharyya. 1994. "The household production of health: Integrating social science perspectives on micro-level health determinants." *Social Science and Medicine* 38(2): 205–15.

Bernard, Jesse. 1981. *The Female World*. New York: Free Press.

Bernard, Jesse. 1987. *The Female World from a Global Perspective*. Bloomington, IN: Indiana University Press.

Bernardi, Bernardo. 1985. *Age Class Systems: Social Institutions and Polities Based on Age*. Cambridge, UK: Cambridge University.

Berndt, Thomas J., & Keunho Keefe. 1995. "Friends' influence on adolescents' adjustment to school." *Child Development* 66(5): 1312–29.

Berner, Erhard, & Rudiger Korff. 1995. "Globalization and local resistance: The creation of localities in Manila and Bangkok." *International Journal of Urban and Regional Research* 19: 208–22.

Bernstein, Richard J. 1992. *The New Constellation: The Ethical-Political Horizons of Modernity/Postmodernity*. Cambridge, MA: MIT Press.

Berreman, Gerald D. 1987. "Caste in India and the United States." In Celia S. Heller, (ed.), *Structured Social Inequality: A Reader in Comparative Social Stratification*, 2nd ed. New York: Macmillan: 81–88.

Berrick, Jill D. 1995. *Faces of Poverty*. New York: Oxford University Press.

Berry, Jeffrey. 1997. *The Interest Group Society*, 3rd ed. New York: Longman.

Berry, R. E., & F. L. Williams. 1987. "Assessing the relationship between quality of life and marital and income satisfaction: A path analytic approach." *Journal of Marriage and the Family* 49: 107–16.

Besser, Terry L. 1993. "A critical approach to the study of Japanese management." *Humanity and Society* (16/2): 176–95.

Best, Raphaela. 1983. *We've Got All the Scars: What Boys and Girls Learn in Elementary School*. Bloomington, IN: Indiana University Press.

Betz, N. E., & L. F. Fitzgerald. 1987. *The Career Psychology of Women*. Orlando, FL: Academic Press.

Beyer, Peter. 1994. *Religion and Globalization*. London: Sage.

Bhola, H. S. 1987. "Adult literacy for development in India: An analysis of policy and performance." In R.F. Arnove & J. Graff (eds.), *National Literacy Campaigns: Historical and Comparative Perspectives*. New York: Plenum.

Biblarz, Timothy, Vern L. Bengtson & Alexander Bacur. 1996. "Social Mobility Across Generations," *Journal of Marriage and the Family* 58: 188–200.

Biderman, Albert D., & James P. Lynch. 1991. *Understanding Crime Incidence Statistics: Why the UCR Diverges from the NCS*. New York: Springer-Verlag.

Biesele, M., & N. Howell. 1981. "The old people give you life: Aging among the !Kung hunter-gathers." In P. T. Amoss & S. H. 1977. "Formal and Informal Sanctions: A Comparison of Deterrent Effects." *Social Problems* 25: 103–14.

Billson, Janet. 1994. "Bringing new knowledge into the development program." American Sociological Association, *Footnotes* 22 (December): 6–7.

Billson, Janet Mancini. 1991. "The progressive verification method: Toward a feminist methodology for studying women cross-culturally." *Women's Studies International Forum* 14(3): 201–8.

Binder, Amy. 1993. "Constructing racial rhetoric: Media depictions of harm in heavy metal and rap music." *American Sociological Review* 58(6): 753–67.

Birdsall, Nancy, & Charles C. Griffin. 1988. "Fertility and poverty in developing countries." *Journal of Policy Modeling* 10(1): 29–56.

Birdsall, Nancy. 1994. "Government, population, and poverty: A win-win tale." In Robert Cassen et al. (eds.), *Population and Development: Old Debates, New Conclusions*. New Brunswick, NJ: Transaction: 253–74.

Birren, James E. & K. Warner Schaie (eds.). 1990. *Handbook of the Psychology of Aging*. San Diego: Academic Press.

Bischoping, Katherine. 1993. "Gender differences in conversation topics." *Sex Roles* 28(1–2): 1–18.

Bishop, Jerry E. 1988. "Study discovers biochemical difference between some alcoholics, non-alcoholics." *Wall Street Journal* (October 24): A1,A10.

Bissinger, H. G. 1991. *Friday Night Lights*. New York: Harper & Row.

Black, Jan Knippers. 1991. "Dowry abuse: No happily ever after for Indian brides." *Contemporary Review* 258: 237–39.

Blackwell, J. E. 1982. "Persistence & change in intergroup relations: The crisis upon us." *Social Problems* 29: 325–346.

Blackwood, Evelyn. 1984. "Sexuality and gender in certain Native American tribes: The case of cross-gender females." *Signs* 10(2): 27–42.

Blair, Bruce. 1993. *The Logic of Accidental Nuclear War*. Washington, DC: Brookings Institution.

Blair, Cornelia, Mark A. Siegel, & Jacquelyn (eds.). 1997. *Growing Up in America*. Wylie, TX: Information Plus.

Blakely, Edward J., & Mary Gail Snyder. 1998. *Fortress America*. Washington, DC: Brookings Institute.

Blanchard, R., B. W. Steiner, & L. H. Clemmensen. 1985. "Gender dysphoria, gender reorientation, and the management of transsexualism." *Journal of Consulting and Clinical Psychology* 53(3): 295–304.

Blasi, Gary. 1994. "And we are not seen: Ideological and political barriers to understanding homelessness." *American Behavioral Scientist* 37(4): 563–86.

Blau, Francine D., & Marianne A. Ferber. 1992. *The Economics of Women, Men and Work*. Upper Saddle River, NJ: Prentice Hall.

Blau, Judith R. 1988. "Music as social circumstance." *Social Forces* 66: 885–904.

Blau, Peter & Otis Dudley Duncan. 1967. *The American Occupational Structure*. New York: Wiley.

Blau, Peter M., & Marshall W. Meyer. 1987. *Bureaucracy in Modern Society*, 3rd ed. New York: Random House.

Blau, Peter. 1963. *The Dynamics of Bureaucracy*. Chicago: University of Chicago Press.

Blauer, Ettagale. 1994. "Mystique of the Maasai." In Elvio Angeloni, (ed.), *Anthropology 93/94*. Guilford, CT: Dushkin.

Blauner, Bob. 1989. *Black Lives, White Lives: Three Decades of Race Relations in America*. Berkeley: University of California Press.

Blauner, Robert. 1964. *Alienation and Freedom*. Chicago: University of Chicago Press.

Blauner, Robert. 1972. *Racial Oppression in America*. New York: Harper & Row.

Blech, Benjamin. 1991. *Understanding Judaism: The Basics of Creed and Deed*. Northdale, NJ: Aronson.

Blinde, E. M., & D. E. Taub. 1993. "Sports participation & women's personal empowerment." *Journal of Sport and Social Issues* (17/1): 47–60.

Bliss, Sheperd. 1990. "Overcoming toxic masculinity." *Changes* (September–October): 36–39.

Bloch, Maurice. 1994. "Language, anthropology, and cognitive science." In Robert Borofsky, (ed.), *Assessing Cultural Anthropology*. New York: McGraw-Hill.

Block, Alan A. 1983. *East Side—West Side: Organizing Crime in New York, 1930–1959*. New Brunswick, NJ: Rutgers University Press.

Block, Alan A. 1991. *Perspectives on Organizing Crime*. Amsterdam: Kluwer.

Block, Alan A., & William J. Chambliss. 1981. *Organizing Crime*. New York: Elsevier.

Block, R. 1994. "The tragedy of Rwanda." *New York Review of Books* 41: 3–8.

Bloom, Allen. 1987. *The Closing of the American Mind*. New York: Simon & Schuster.

Bloom, Joan R., & Larry Kessler. 1994. "Emotional support following cancer: A test of the stigma and social activity hypotheses." *Journal of Health and Social Behavior* 35(2): 118–33.

Bloom, Steven. 1988. "A transsexual's life." In Bryan Strong & Christine DeVault, *Human Sexuality*. St. Paul, MN: West: 119–122.

Bluestone, Barry. 1995. *The Polarization of American Society*. New York: Twentieth Century Fund.

Blumberg, Paul. 1989. *Inequality in an Age of Decline*. New York: Oxford University Press.

Blumer, Herbert G. 1969. *Symbolic Interactionism: Perspective and Method*. Upper Saddle River, NJ: Prentice Hall.

Blumer, Herbert. 1933. *The Movies and Conduct*. New York: Macmillan.

Blumer, Herbert. 1969. "Collective behavior." In Alfred M. Lee, (ed.), *Principles of Sociology*, 3rd ed. New York: Barnes & Noble: 65–121.

Blumer, Herbert. 1974. "Social movements." In R. Serge Denisoff, (ed.), *The Sociology of Dissent*. New York: Harcourt Brace Jovanovich: 74–90.

Blumler, J., & C. Spicer. 1990. "Prospects for creativity in the new television marketplace." *Journal of Communication* 40(4): 78–101.

Bly, Robert. 1990. *Iron John: A Book about Men*. Reading, MA: Addison-Wesley.

Bobo, Lawrence, & James R. Kluegel. 1991. "Modern American prejudice." Presented at the annual meeting of the American Sociological Association.

Bobo, Lawrence. 1991. "Social responsibility, individuality and redistributive policies." *Sociological Forum* 6: 71–92.

Bodenheimer, Thomas. 1999. "The American health care system: Physicians and the changing medical marketplace." *New England Journal of Medicine* 340(7): 584–88.

Bodley, John H. 1994. *Cultural Anthropology: Tribes, States and the Global System*. Mountain View, CA: Mayfield.

Bohlen, C. 1995. "Catholics defying an infallible church." *The New York Times* (November 26): E3.

Bohm, Robert M., (ed.), 1991. *The Death Penalty in America: Current Research*. Cincinnati: Anderson.

Bohmer, Carol, & Andrea Parrot. 1993. *Sexual Assault on Campus: The Problem and the Solution*. New York: Lexington.

Boissonnat, Jean. 1987. "World underdevelopment." *Sociological Quarterly* 32(3): 321–42.

Bolstein, Richard. 1991. "Comparison of the likelihood to vote among pre-election poll respondents and nonrespondents." *Public Opinion Quarterly* (Winter): 648–50.

Bombeck, Erma. 1987. *The Ties That Bind . . . and Gag*. New York: Fawcett Crest.

Bonacich, Edna. 1972. "A theory of ethnic antagonism: The split labor market." *American Sociological Review* 37: 547–49.

Bonacich, Edna. 1976. "Advanced capitalism & black/white relations in the U.S." *American Sociological Review* 41: 34–51.

Bonnes, Mirilia, Marino Bonaiuto, & Anna Paola Ercolani. 1991. "Crowding and residential satisfaction in the urban environment: A contextual approach." *Environment and Behavior* 23: 531–52.

Boone, Louis E. et al.. 1988. "The road to the top," *American Demographics* 10.

Boonsue, Kornvipa. 1992. *Women's Development Models and Gender Analysis: A Review*. Bangkok: Asian Institute of Technology.

Booth, Alan, & John N. Edwards. 1992. "Starting over: Why remarriages are more unstable." *Journal of Marriage and the Family* 13: 179–94.

Borgmann, Albert. 1992. *Crossing the Postmodern Divide*. Chicago: University of Chicago Press.

Borjas, George J. 1995. "The internationalization of the U.S. labor market and the wage structure." *Federal Reserve Bank of NY Economic Review* (1/1): 3–9.

Borkan, Jeffrey, Jon O. Neher, Ofra Anson, & Bret Smoker. 1994. "Referrals for alternative therapies." *Journal of Family Practice* 39: 545–50.

Bornscheier, Volker, Christopher Chase-Dunn, & Richard Rubinson. 1978. "Cross-national evidence of the effects of foreign investment & aid on economic growth & inequality: A survey of findings & a reanalysis." *American Journal of Sociology* 84: 651–83.

Boroughs, Don L. 1995. "Telecommuting picks up speed." *U.S. News & World Report* (July 17): 42.

Borstelmann, L. J. 1983. "Children before psychology: Ideas about children from antiquity to the late 1800s." In W. Kessen (ed.) *Handbook of Child Psychology: Vol. 1. History, Theory and Methods.* New York: Wiley: 1–40.

Bose, C. E., & Peter H. Rossi. 1983. "Gender and jobs." *American Sociological Review* 48: 316–330.

Boserup, Ester. 1970. *Women's Role in Economic Development.* London: Elgar.

Boswell, Terry (ed.). 1989. *Revolution in the World System.* New York: Greenwood.

Boudreau, F. A. 1986. "Education." In F. A. Boudreau, R. S. Sennott, & M. Wilson (eds.), *Sex Roles and Social Patterns.* New York: Praeger.

Bouffard, Jeffrey, M. Lyn Exum, & Raymond Paternoster. 2000. "Whither the beast? The role of emotions in a rational choice theory of crime." In Sally S. Simpson (ed.), *Of Crime and Criminality.* Thousand Oaks, CA: Pine Forge: 159–178.

Boulding, Elise. 1976. *The Underside of History.* Boulder, CO: Westview.

Boulton, Mary, David Tuckett, Coral Olson, & Anthony Williams. 1986. *Sociology of Health and Illness* 8: 325–50.

Bouma, Gary D. 1993. *The Research Process.* Melbourne, AS: Oxford University.

Bourdeau, Pierre, Jean-Claude Chamboredom, & Jean-Claude Passeron. 1991. *The Craft of Sociology.* New York: de Gruyter.

Bourdieu, Pierre. 1984. *Distinction: A Social Critique of the Judgement of Taste.* Cambridge, MA: Harvard University Press.

Bourdieu, Pierre. 1987. *Choses Dites.* Paris: Edition de Minuit.

Boutilier, M. A., & L. San Giovanni. 1993. *The Sporting Woman.* Champaign, IL: Human Kinetics Press.

Bowles, Samuel, & Herbert Gintis. 1976. *Schooling in Capitalist America: Educational Reform and the Contradictions of Economic Life.* New York: Basic Books.

Bowles, Samuel. 1977. "Unequal education and the reproduction of the social division of labor." In Jerome Karabel & A. H. Halsey, (eds.), *Power and Ideology in Education.* New York: Oxford University Press: 137–153.

Boyer, Ernest L. 1994. "Ready to learn: A mandate for the nation." In Daniel J. Curran & Claire M. Renzetti (eds.), *Contemporary Societies: Problems and Prospects.* Upper Saddle River, NJ: Prentice Hall: 443–51.

Boyer, M. Christine. 1993. "The city of illusion: New York's public places." In Paul L. Knox (ed.), *The Restless Urban Landscape.* Upper Saddle River, NJ: Prentice Hall: 111–26.

Boykin, A. Wade. 1994. "Harvesting talent and culture: African-American children and educational reform." In Robert J. Rossi (ed.), *Schools and Students at Risk: Context and Framework for Positive Change.* New York: Teacher's College Press, Columbia University: 116–38.

Bradburn, Ellen M., Phyllis Moen, & Donna Dempster-McClain. 1995. "Women's return to school following the transition to motherhood." *Social Forces* 73(4): 1517–51.

Bradbury, Katharine L., Anthony Downs, & Kenneth A. Small. 1982. *Urban Decline and the Future of American Cities.* Washington, DC: Brookings Institution.

Braddock, Jomills Henry, II, Marvin P. Dawkins, & William Trent. 1994. "Why desegregate? The effect of school desegregation on adult occupational desegregation of African Americans, whites and Hispanics." *International Journal of Contemporary Sociology* 31(7): 273–83.

Braddock, Jomills Henry, II. 1990. *Tracking: Implications for Student Race-Ethnic Subgroups.* Baltimore, MD: Johns Hopkins University, Center for Research for the Effective Schooling of Disadvantaged Children.

Bradshaw, York. 1988. "Reassessing economic dependency and uneven development: The Kenyan experience." *American Sociological Review* 53: 693–708.

Brailsford, Dennis. 1991. *Sport, Time and Society.* New York: Routledge.

Braithwaite, John. 1981. "The myth of social class and criminality, reconsidered." *American Sociological Review.* 46: 36–58.

Braithwaite, John. 1985. "White-collar crime." *Annual Review of Sociology* 11: 1–25.

Brasch, Rudolph. 1970. *How Did Sports Begin?* New York: David McKay.

Braverman, H. 1974. *Labor and Monopoly Capital.* New York: Monthly Review Press.

Bray, James H., & Sandra H. Berger. 1993. "Nonresidential parent-child relationships following divorce and remarriage." In Charlene E. Depner & James H. Bray (eds.), *Nonresidential Parenting: New Vistas in Family Living.* Newbury Park, CA: Sage.

Bray, Rosemary. 1992. "So how did I get here?" *The New York Times Magazine* (November 8).

Breakaway. 1995. "Mass wedding in India aims to evade dowry tradition." *St. Louis Post-Dispatch* (April 9): 12D.

Brecher, Jeremy, & Tim Costello. 1994. *Global Village or Global Pillage? Economic Reconstruction from the Bottom Up.* Boston: South End.

Breen, Michael. 1998. *The Koreans: Who They Are, What They Want, Where Their Future Lies.* New York: St. Martin's.

Brehm, Sharon S., and Saul M. Kassin. 1996. *Social Psychology.* Boston: Houghton Mifflin.

Brenner, M. Harvey. 1973. *Mental Illness and the Economy.* Cambridge, MA: Harvard University Press.

Brenner, M. Harvey. 1979. "Mortality and the national economy." *Lancet* 2(8,142): 568–73.

Breuilly, Elizabeth, JoAnne O'Brien, & Martin Palmer (eds.), 1997. *Religions of the World: The Illustrated Guide to Origins, Beliefs, Traditions and Festivals.* New York: Facts on File.

Bridger, Susan. 1992. "Soviet rural women: Employment and family life." In Beatrice Farnsworth & Lynne Viola (eds.), *Russian Peasant Women.* New York: Oxford University.

Bridges, George F., & Robert D. Crutchfield. 1988. "Law, social standing and imprisonment." *Social Forces* 66: 699–724.

Bridges, J. S. 1989. "Sex differences in occupational values." *Sex Roles* 20: 205–211.

Brinn, Janet, Kathey Kraemer, & Joel S. Warm. 1984. "Sex-role preferences in four age levels." *Sex Roles* 11: 90–99.

Brint, Steven. 1994. *In an Age of Experts: The Changing Role of Professionals in Politics and Public Life.* Princeton, NJ: Princeton University Press.

Broadbent, Edward. 1992. "Foreign policy, development, and democracy." In Kenneth E. Bauzon, (ed.), *Development and Democratization in the Third World: Myths, Hopes, and Realities.* Washington, DC: Crane Russak: 99–107.

Brock, Dan W. 1992. "Voluntary active euthanasia." *Hastings Center Report* March/April: 10–22.

Brodeur, Paul. 1985. *Outrageous Misconduct: The Asbestos Industry on Trial.* New York: Pantheon.

Broere, F. P. 1992. "Competition and the new structure of the health care system in the Netherlands." In H. E. G. M. Hermans, A. F. Casparie, & J. H. P. Paelinck (eds.), *Health Care in Europe After 1992.* Aldershot, Hants, UK: Dartmouth.

Brohm, Jean-Marie. 1978. *Sport: A Prison of Measured Time.* London: Inks Links.

Brooke, James. 1990. "Brazil's new chief gives radical plan to halt inflation." *The New York Times* (March 17): 1, 45.

Brooke, James. 1994. "Women in Colombia move to job forefront: Aggressively pursuing new freedom." *The New York Times* July 15: A6.

Brooks, Virginia R. 1982. "Sex differences in student dominance behavior in female and male professor's classrooms." *Sex Roles* 8: 683–90.

Brooks-Gunn, Jeanne. 1986. "The relationship of maternal beliefs about sex typing to maternal and young children's behavior." *Sex Roles* 14: 21–35.

Broude, G.C., & S.J. Greene. 1967. "Cross-cultural codes on twenty sexual attitudes and practices." *Ethnology* 15: 409–429.

Brown, Arnold S. 1990. *The Social Processes of Aging and Old Age.* Upper Saddle River, NJ: Prentice Hall.

Brown, Coramae R. 1993. *Unequal Justice: A Question of Color.* Bloomington: University of Indiana Press.

Brown, David. 1997. "Tracing a way to more nutritious harvests." *Washington Post* August 18: A3.

Brown, Dee. 1991. *Wonderous Times on the Frontier.* Little Rock, AR: August House.

Brown, John. 1983. "Neighborhood policing in West Berlin." *Police Studies* (5/4): 29–32.

Brown, Lee. 1990. "Neighborhood-oriented policing." *American Journal of Police* 9: 197–207.

Brown, Lester. 1994. *Vital Signs 1994: The Trends That Are Shaping Our Future.* New York: Norton.

Brown, Lester R. 1996. "We can build a sustainable economy." *Futurist* (July/August): 8–11.

Brown, Lester R., Christopher Flavin, & Hilary French. 1998. *State of the World 1998: A Worldwatch Institute Report on Progress Toward a Sustainable Society.* Worldwatch Institute.

Brown, Lester R., Christopher Flavin, Hilary French, et al. 2000. *State of the World: A Worldwatch Institute Report on Progress toward a Sustainable Society.* New York: Norton.

Brown, Michael, & Amy Goldin. 1973. *Collective Behavior.* Pacific Palisades, CA: Goodyear.

Brown, Phil. 1995. "Naming and framing: The social construction of diagnosis and illness." *Journal of Health and Social Behavior* Extra Issue, 1995: 34–52.

Brown, Roger. 1973. *A First Language: The Early Stages.* Cambridge, MA: Harvard University.

Brown, Shirley Vining. 1996. "Responding to the new demographics in higher education." In Laura I. Rendon & Richard O. Hope (eds.), *Educating a New Majority: Transforming America's Educational System for Diversity.* San Francisco: Jossey-Bass: 71–96.

Brown, Susan L., & Alan Booth, 1997. "Cohabitation versus marriage: A comparison of relationship quality." *Journal of Marriage and the Family* 58(3): 668–78.

Browne, A., & S.S. Bassuk. 1997. "Intimate violence in the lives of homeless and poorly housed women." *American Journal of Orthopsychiatry* 67: 261–278.

Browne, Angela. 1987. *When Battered Women Kill.* New York: Macmillan.

Bruce, Steve. 1989. *The Rise and Fall of the New Christian Right: Conservative Protestant Politics in America 1978–1988.*

Bruce, Steve. 1990. *A House Divided: Protestantism, Schism, and Secularization.* London & New York: Routledge.

Bruce, Steve. 1996. *Religion in the Modern World: From Cathedrals to Cults.* New York: Oxford University Press.

Bruce, Steve. 1999. *Choice and Religion*. New York: Oxford University.

Bruce, Steve, Peter Kivisto, & William H. Swatos, eds. 1994. *The Rapture of Politics: The Christian Right as the United States Approaches the Year 2000*. New Brunswick, NJ: Transaction.

Bruess, Carol J., & Judy C. Pearson. 1996. "Gendered Patterns in Family Communication." In Julia T. Wood, (ed.), *Gendered Relationships*. Mountain View, CA: Mayfield.

Brunvand, Jan Harold. 1980. "Urban legends: Folklore for today." *Psychology Today* 14.

Brush, Lisa D. 1990. "Violent acts and injurious outcomes in married couples: Methodological issues in the National Survey of Families and Households." *Gender & Society* 4(1): 56–67.

Bryant, Jennings (ed.). 1990. *Television and the American Family*. Hillsdale, NJ: Lawrence Erlbaum.

Brydon, Lynn, & Sylvia Chant. 1989. *Women in the Third World: Gender Issues in Rural and Urban Areas*. Hants, UK: Edward Elgar.

Bryjak, George J., & Michael P. Soroka. 1994. *Sociology: Cultural Diversity in a Changing World*, 2nd ed. Boston: Allyn & Bacon.

Buck, Elizabeth. 1993. *Paradise Remade: The Politics of Culture and History in Hawaii*. Philadelphia: Temple University.

Buckley, Walter. 1967. *Sociology and Modern Systems Theory*. Upper Saddle River, NJ: Prentice Hall.

Buddenbaum, Judith M., & Daniel A. Stout. 1996."Religion and mass media use: A review of the mass communication and sociology literature." In D. A. Stout & J. M. Buddenbaum, (eds.), *Religion and Mass Media: Audience and Adaptations*. Thousand Oaks, CA: Sage: 12–34.

Buechler, Steven M. 1993. "Beyond resource mobilization? Emerging trends in social movement theory." *The Sociological Quarterly* 34: 217–235.

Buehler, Cheryl. 1995. "Divorce law in the United States." *Marriage and Family Review* 21(3–4): 99–120.

Buford, Bill. 1992. *Among the Thugs*. New York: Norton.

Bullard, Robert B., & Beverly H. Wright. 1992. "The quest for environmental equity." In Riley E. Dunlap & Angela T. Mertig, (eds.), *American Environmentalism*. New York: Taylor & Francis: 39–49.

Bullers, Susan. 1994. "Women's roles and health: The mediating effect of perceived control." *Women and Health* 22(2): 11–30.

Bullough, Vern, & Bonnie Bullough. 1987. *Women and Prostitution: A Social History*. Buffalo, NY: Prometheus.

Bumpass, Larry L., James A. Sweet, & Andrew Cherlin. 1991. "The role of cohabitation in declining rates of marriage." *Journal of Marriage and the Family* 53: 913–27.

Bumpass, Larry, James Sweet, & Teresa Castro-Martin. 1990. "Changing patterns of remarriage." *Journal of Marriage and the Family* 52: 747–56.

Buono, Richard A. Dello. 1996. "Nicaraguan women in the formal and informal economy." In Paula J. Dubeck & Kathryn Borman, (eds.), *Women and Work: A Handbook*. New York: Garland: 495–99.

Burawoy, Michael. 1980. *Manufacturing Consent*. Chicago: University of Chicago Press.

Burch, Beverly. 1993. "Heterosexuality, bisexuality, and lesbianism: Rethinking psychoanalytic views of women's sexual object choice." *Psychoanalytic Review* 80(1): 82–99.

Burge, Penny L., & Steven M. Culver. 1990. "Sexism, legislative power and vocational education." In Susan L. Gabriel & Isaiah Smithson (eds.), *Gender in the Classroom: Power and Pedagogy*. Urbana, IL: University of Illinois Press.

Burk, Martha, & Kirsten Shaw. 1995. "How the entertainment industry demeans, degrades and dehumanizes women." In Sheila Ruth (ed.), *Issues in Feminism: An Introduction to Women's Studies*. Mountain View, CA: Mayfield.

Burleson, Brant R., & Wayne H. Denton, 1997. "The relationship between communication skill and marital satisfaction: Some moderating effects." *Journal of Marriage and the Family* 59(4): 884–902.

Burnett, Robert. 1997. "The popular music industry in transition." In Alan Wells & Ernest A. Hakanen, (eds.), *Mass Media and Society*. Greenwich, CT: Ablex: 183–205.

Burns, Gene. 1992. *The Frontiers of Catholicism: The Politics of Ideology in a Liberal World*. Berkeley, CA: University of California Press.

Burris, Beverly H. 1989. "Technocratic organization and control." *Organization Studies* (10/1): 1–22.

Burstein, Paul. 1991. "Reverse discrimination cases in the federal courts." *Sociological Quarterly* (32/4): 511–28.

Burstyn, Linda. 1996. "Asylum in America: Does fear of female mutilation qualify?" *Washington Post* March 17: C5.

Burt, Martha R. 1992. *Over the Edge*. New York: Russell Sage.

Burtless, Gary (ed.) 1990. *A Future of Lousy Jobs? The Changing Structure of U.S. Wages*. Washington, DC: Brookings Institute.

Burton, C. Emery. 1992. *The Poverty Debate: Politics and the Poor in America*. Westport, CT: Praeger.

Burton, N. W., C. Lewis, & N. Robertson. 1988. "Sex differences in SAT scores." *College Board Report* No. 88–9.

Buss, David M., & Michael Barnes. 1986. "Preferences in human mate selection." *Journal of Personality and Social Psychology* 50: 559–70.

Buss, Terry F., & Stevens F. Redburn. 1983. *Mass Unemployment: Plant Closings and Community Mental Health*. Beverly Hills, CA: Sage.

Butler, D., & F. L. Geis. 1990. "Nonverbal affect responses to male & female leaders." *Journal of Personality & Social Psychology* 58: 48–59.

Butsch, Ricard. 1992. "Class and gender in four decades of television comedy." *Critical Studies in Mass Communication* 9: 387–99.

Butsch, Richard. 2000. "Ralph, Fred, Archie, and Homer: Why television keeps recreating the white, male working-class buffoon." In Tracey E. Ore (ed.), *The Social Construction of Difference and Inequality: Race, Class, Gender, and Sexuality*. Mountain View, CA: Mayfield: 361–70.

Byrne, Donn, & Kathryn Kelly. 1981. *An Introduction to Personality*. Upper Saddle River, NJ: Prentice Hall.

Byrne, John A. 1993. "The horizontal corporation." *Business Week* (December 20): 76–81.

Cable, Sherry. 1992. "Women's social movement involvement." *Sociological Quarterly* (33/1): 35–50.

Cable, Sherry, & Charles Cable. 1995. *Environmental Problems, Grassroots Solutions*. New York: St. Martin's Press.

Cagatay, Nilufer, Caren Grown, & Aida Santiago. 1989. "The Nairobi women's conference: Toward a global feminism." In Laurel Richardson & Verta Taylor (eds.), *Feminist Frontiers II: Rethinking Sex, Gender, and Society*. New York: Random House.

Cage, Mary C. 1993. "Graduation rates of American Indians and blacks improve, lag behind others." *Chronicle of Higher Education* (May 26): A29.

Cahill, Robert. 1987. "Children and civility: Ceremonial deviance and the acquisition of ritual competence." *Social Psychology Quarterly* 50: 312–21.

Cahill, Spencer E. (ed.). 1995a. *Inside Social Life: Readings in Social Psychology and Microsociology*. Los Angeles: Roxbury.

Cahill, Spencer E., (ed.). 1995b. "Erving Goffman." Chapter 12 in Joel M. Charon, *Symbolic Interaction: An Introduction, An Interpretation, An Integration*. Upper Saddle River, NJ: Prentice Hall: 186–201.

Calasanti, T. M. 1988. "Participation in a dual economy and adjustment to retirement." *International Journal of Aging and Human Development*. 26: 13–27.

Calasanti, T. M. 1993. "Bringing in diversity: Toward an inclusive theory of retirement." *Journal of Aging Studies* 7: 133–50.

Calasanti, T. M. 1996. "Incorporating diversity: Meaning, levels of research, and implications for theory." *The Gerontologist* 36: 147–56.

Calavita, K., & H. N. Pontell. 1991. "Other people's money revisited: Collective embezzlement in the Savings and Loan and Insurance industries." *Social Problems* 38: 94–112.

Caldera, Y. M., A. C. Huston, & M. O'Brien. 1989. "Social interactions and play patterns of parents and toddlers with feminine, masculine and neutral toys." *Child Development* 60: 70–76.

Caldwell, M. A., & L. Anne Peplau. 1984. "The balance of power in lesbian relationships." *Sex Roles* 10: 587–99.

Calhoun, C., & H. Hiller. 1988. "Coping with insidious injuries: The case of Johns-Manville Corporation and asbestos exposure." *Social Problems* 35/2: 162–81.

Callahan, Charles M., & Frederick P. Rivara. 1992. "Urban high school youth and handguns." *Journal of the American Medical Association* 267(June 10): 3038–42.

Callahan, Daniel. 1994. "From explosion to implosion: Transforming healthcare." In William Kornblum & Carolyn D. Smith (cds.), *The Healing Experience: Readings on the Social Context of Health Care*. Englewood Cliffs, NJ: Prentice Hall: 195–208.

Callahan, Sidney, & Bryan Appleyard. 1997. "Violence in the media should be censored." In Byron L. Stay (ed.), *Censorship*. San Diego: Greenhaven: 154–59.

Callender, Charles, & Lee Kochems, 1983. "The North American berdache." *Current Anthropology* 24(4): 443–70.

Callison, William L., & Nancy Richards-Colocino. 1993. "Crime, violence, gangs, and drug abuse: What urban schools can do about them." In Stanley William Rothstein (ed.), *Handbook of Schooling in Urban America*. Westport, CT: Greenwood: 340–63.

Calne, Sir Roy. 1994. *Too Many People: A Radical Solution to the Population Explosion and a Survey of What Has Led to It*. London: Calder.

Campbell, Angus. 1981. *The Sense of Well-Being in America: Recent Patterns and Trends*. New York: McGraw-Hill.

Canada, Geoffrey. 1995. *Fist, Stick, Gun: A Personal History of Violence in America*. Boston: Beacon.

Canfield, Robert L. 1986. "Ethnic, regional, and sectarian alignments in Afghanistan." In A. Banuzizi & M. Weiner, (eds.), *The State, Religion, and Ethnic Politics: Afghanistan, Iran, and Pakistan*. Syracuse, NY: Syracuse University Press: 75–103.

Canham-Clyne, John. 1994. "Both sides are not enough: The restricted debate over health care reform." *International Journal of Health Services* 24(3): 415–19.

Cann, A., & S. Palmer. 1986. "Children's assumptions about the generalizability of sex-typed abilities." *Sex Roles* 15: 551–57.

Canner, Glenn B., Stuart A. Gabriel, & J. Michael Woolley. 1991. "Race default risk & mortgage lending." *Southern Economic Journal* 58: 249–61.

Cannon, Angie. 1999. "DWB: Driving while black." *U.S. News and World Report*. (March 15).

Cantor, David, & Kenneth C. Land. 1985. "Unemployment and crime rates in the post-World War II United States: A theoretical and empirical analysis." *American Sociological Review* 50: 317–22.

Cantor, Marjorie H., Mark Brennan, & Anthony Sainz. 1994. "The importance of ethnicity in the social support systems of older New Yorkers: A longitudinal perspective (1970–1990)." *Journal of Gerontological Social Work* 22(3–4): 95–128.

Cantor, Muriel G. 1987. "Popular culture and the portrayal of women: Content and control." In Beth B. Hess & Myra Marx Ferree (eds.), *Analyzing Gender: A Handbook of Social Science Research*. Newbury Park, CA: Sage.

Cantril, Hadley. 1940. *The Invasion from Mars: A Study in the Psychology of Panic*. Princeton, NJ: Princeton University Press.

Caplan, Lionel. 1987. "Introduction: Popular conceptions of fundamentalism." In L. Caplan, (ed.), *Studies in Religious Fundamentalism*. Albany, NY: State University of New York Press: 1–24.

Caplan, Nathan, Marcella H. Choy, & John K. Whitmore. 1992. "Indochinese refugee families and academic achievement." *Scientific American* 266: 36–42.

Caplan, Paula J., & Jeremy B. Caplan. 1994. *Thinking Critically About Research on Sex and Gender*. New York: Harper Collins College Publications.

Caplow, Theodore et al. 1983. *All Faithful People*. Minneapolis: University of Minnesota Press.

Caplow, Theodore. 1991. *American Social Trends*. New York: Harcourt Brace Jovanovich.

Carden, Maren L. 1974. *The New Feminist Movement*. New York: Russell Sage.

Cardenas, Jose A. 1995. *Multicultural Education: A Generation of Advocacy*. Boston: Simon & Schuster.

Cardoso, Fernando H., & Enzo Faletto. 1979. *Dependency and Development in Latin America*. Berkeley: University of California Press.

Careers in Sociology, 4th ed. 1995. Washington, DC: American Sociological Association.

Carlin, V. & R. Mansberg. 1984. *If I Live to Be 100: Congregate Housing for Later Life*. West Nyack, NY: Parker.

Carlson, Norman A. 1976. "Corrections in the U.S. today." *The American Criminal Law Review* (13/4): 615–47.

Carlson, Susan M. 1992. "Trends in race/sex occupational inequality." *Social Problems* 39: 268–290.

Carmichael, Stokeley, & Charles V. Hamilton. 1967. *Black Power: The Politics of Liberation in American Education*. New York: Random House.

Carmody, Denise Lardner. 1989. *Women and World Religions*. Upper Saddle River, NJ: Prentice Hall.

Carmody, Denise Lardner. 1992. *Mythological Women: Contemporary Reflections on Ancient Religious Stories*. New York: Crossroad.

Carnoy, Martin, & Henry M. Levin. 1985. *Schooling and Work In the Democratic State*. Stanford, CA: Stanford University Press.

Caro, Francis G., Scott A. Bass, & Yung-Ping Chen. 1993. "Introduction: Achieving a Productive Aging Society." In Scott A. Bass, Francis G. Caro & Yung-Ping Chen (eds.), *Achieving a Productive Aging Society*. Westport, CT: Auburn House.

Carroll, Jackson W., & Wade Clark Roof, (eds.), 1993. *Beyond Establishment: Protestant Identity in a Post-Protestant Age*. Louisville, KY: Westminster/John Knox Press.

Carroll, John L., K. D. Volk, & Janet S. Hyde. 1985. "Differences between males and females in motives for engaging in sexual intercourse." *Archives of Sexual Behavior* 14: 131–39.

Carroll, Michael P. 1996. *Veiled Threats: The Logic of Popular Catholicism in Italy*. Baltimore MD: Johns Hopkins University Press.

Carroll, Raymond L., Michael L. Silbergleid, Christopher M. Beachum, Stephen D. Perry, Patrick J. Pluscht, & Mark J. Pescatore. 1997. "Meanings of radio to teenagers in a niche-programming era." In Alan Wells & Ernest A. Hakanen, (eds.), *Mass Media and Society*. Greenwich, CT: Ablex: 163–81.

Carson, R., J. Butcher, & J. Coleman. 1988. *Abnormal Psychology and Modern Life*. Glenvie, IL: Scott Foresman.

Carter, April. 1977. *Direct Action Democracy*. New York: Harper.

Carter, D. Bruce, & Laura A. McCloskey. 1983. "Peers and the maintenance of sex-typed behavior: The development of children's conceptions of cross-gender behavior in their peers." *Social Cognition* 2(4): 294–314.

Carter, D. J., & R. Wilson. 1995. *Minorities in Higher Education*. Washington, DC: American Council on Education.

Carter, Stephen L. 1991. *Reflections of an Affirmative Action Baby*. New York: Basic.

Casalego, Federico. 1996. "Cyberspace: A New Territory for Interaction in a Magic Time." *Societes* 51 (Febuary): 39–48.

Casey, M. B., E. Pezaris, & R. L. Nuttall. 1992. "Spatial ability as a predictor of math achievement: The importance of sex and handedness patterns." *Neuropsychologia* 30: 35–45.

Cashion, Barbara G. 1982. "Female-headed families: Effects on children and clinical implications." *Journal of Marital and Family Therapy* (April): 77–85.

Casper, Lynne M, Sara S. McLanahan, & Irwin Garfinkel. 1994. "The gender-poverty gap: What can we learn from other countries?" *American Sociological Review* 59.

Caspi, A. & Daryl J. Bem. 1990. "Personality continuity and change across the life course." In L. Pervin (ed.), *Handbook of Personality: Theory and Research*. New York: Guilford Press.

Cassem, N. 1988. "The person confronting death." In A. Nicholi (ed.), *The New Harvard Guide to Psychiatry*. Cambridge, MA: Belknap.

Cassidy, J. 1995. "Who killed the middle class?" *New Yorker* (October 16): 113–124.

Cassidy, M. L., & G. R. Lee. 1989. "The study of polyandry: A critique and synthesis." *Journal of Comparative Family Studies* 20(1): 1–11.

Castells, M. 1977. *The Urban Question: A Marxist Approach*. London: Edward Arnold.

Castleman, Harry, & Walter Podrazik. 1982. *Watching TV: Four Decades of American Television*. New York: McGraw-Hill.

Castles, Stephen. 1986. "The guest-worker in Western Europe—an obituary." *International Migration Review* (20/4): 761–78.

Castro, Janice. 1993. "Disposable workers," *Time* (131/14): 43–47.

Castro-Martin, Teresa, & Larry L. Bumpass. 1989. "Recent trends in marital disruption." *Demography* 26: 37–51.

Catalano, Ralph, David Dooley, Georjeanna Wilson, & Richard Hough. 1993. "Job loss and alcohol abuse." *Journal of Health and Social Behavior* 34: 215–25.

Cavalli-Sforza, Luca, Paolo Menozzi, & Alberto Piazza. 1994. *The History and Geography of Human Genes*. Princeton, NJ: Princeton University Press.

Cavanagh, J., & R. Broad. 1996. "Global reach: Workers fight the multinationals," *The Nation* (March 18): 21–24.

Cavanaugh, John C. 1993. *Adult Development and Aging*. Pacific Grove, CA: Brooks/Cole.

Cavender, Gray. 1995. "Alternative theories." In Joseph F. Sheley, (ed.), *Criminology: A Contemporary Handbook*, 2nd ed. Belmont, CA: Wadsworth: 349–71.

CBS. 1993. "The year of the woman." A *60 Minutes* Television Report. January 24.

Centers for Disease Control. 1997. *Teen Sex Down, New Study Shows*. (January). Washington, DC: Health and Human Services.

Cernovich, Stephen A. 1978. "Value orientations and delinquency involvement," *Criminology* 15: 443–458.

Cerulo, Karen A., Janet M. Ruane, & Mary Chayko. 1992. "Technological ties that bind: Media-generated primary groups." *Communication Research* 19: 109–129.

Chafe, W.H. 1991. *The Paradox of Change: American Women in the Twentieth Century*. New York: Oxford University Press.

Chafetz, Janet S., & Anthony G. Dworkin. 1986. *Female Revolt*. Totowa, NJ: Rowman & Allenheld.

Chafetz, Janet Saltzman. 1989. "Marital intimacy and conflict: The irony of spousal equality." In Jo Freeman (ed.), *Women: A Feminist Perspective*. Mountain View, CA: Mayfield.

Chalfant, H. Paul, Robert E. Beckley, & C. Eddie Palmer. 1994. *Religion in Contemporary Society*. Itasca, IL: Peacock.

Chambliss, William J. 1969. *Crime and The Legal Process*. New York: McGraw-Hill.

Chambliss, William J. 1973. "The Saints and the Roughnecks." *Society* (2/1): 24–31.

Chambliss, William J. 1988. *On the Take: From Petty Crooks to Presidents*. Bloomington: University of Indiana Press.

Chambliss, William J. 1994. "Policing the ghetto underclass: The politics of law and law enforcement." *Social Problems* 41: 177–94.

Chan, C. 1992. "Cultural considerations in counseling Asian American lesbians and gay men." In S. Dworkin & F. Guiterres (ed.), *Counseling Gay Men and Lesbians: Journey to the End of the Rainbow*. Alexandria, VA: American Association of Counseling and Development.

Chan, S. 1991. *Asian-Americans*. Boston: Twayne.

Chandler, Alfred D., Jr. 1977. *The Visible Hand: The Managerial Revolution in American Business*. Cambridge, MA: Harvard University Press.

Charles, Maria. 1992. "Cross-national variation in occupational sex segregation." *American Sociological Review* 57(4): 483–502.

Charmaz, Kathy. 1980. *The Social Reality of Death: Death in Contemporary America*. Reading, MA: Addison-Wesley.

Charmaz, Kathy. 1991. *Good Days, Bad Days: The Self in Chronic Illness & Time*. New Brunswick, NJ: Rutgers University Press.

Charon, Joel M. 1995. *Symbolic Interaction: An Introduction, An Interpretation, An Integration*. Upper Saddle River, NJ: Prentice Hall.

Charon, Mona. 1997. "Women in the military not a good idea." *St. Louis Post Dispatch* : 7B.

Chase-Dunn, Christopher. 1990. *Global Formation: Structures of the World Economy*. Cambridge, MA: Basil Blackwell.

Chasin, B.H. 1997. *Inequality and Violence in the United States: Casualties of Capitalism*. New York: Humanities Press.

Chatters, Linda M., Robert Joseph Taylor, & Rukmalie Jayakody. 1994. "Fictive kinship relations in black extended families." *Journal of Comparative Family Studies* 25(3) (autumn): 297–312.

Chavis, David M., & Abraham Wandersman. 1990. "Sense of community in the urban environment: A catalyst for participation and community development." *American Journal of Community Psychology* 18: 55–81.

Chen, Chuansheng, & Harold W. Stevenson. 1995. "Motivation and mathematics achievement: A comparative study of Asian-American, Caucasian-American, and East Asian high school students." *Child Development* 66(4): 1215–34.

Cherlin, Andrew J. & Frank F., Furstenberg. 1994. "Stepfamilies in the United States: A reconsideration." *Annual Review of Sociology* 20: 359–381.

Cherlin, Andrew J. 1992. *Marriage, Divorce, Remarriage*. Cambridge, MA: Harvard University.

Cherlin, Andrew J. 1992. *Marriage, Divorce, Remarriage*. Cambridge, MA: Harvard University.

Chesney-Lind, Meda, & Randall G. Shelden. 1998. *Girls, Delinquency, and Juvenile Justice*, 2nd ed. Belmont, CA: Wadsworth.

Cheung, Yuet-Wah & Agnes M. C. Ng. 1988. "Social factors in adolescent deviant behavior in Hong Kong." *International Journal of Comparative and Applied Criminal Justice* (12): 27–44.

Chi, Chunhuei. 1994. "Integrating traditional medicine into modern health care systems: Examining the role of Chinese medicine in Taiwan." *Social Science and Medicine* 39(3): 307–21.

Chickering, Lawrence A., & Mohamed Salahdine. 1991. *The Silent Revolution*. New York: Harper & Row.

Child, J. 1994. *Management in China During the Age of Reform*. Cambridge, UK: Cambridge University.

Child, J., & L. Markoczy. 1993. "Host country managerial behavior and learning in Chinese and Hungarian joint ventures." *Journal of Management Studies* 30: 611–31.

Childe, V. Gordon. 1951. *Social Evolution*. Cleveland: World.

Chilly Collective (eds.). 1995. *Breaking Anonymity: The Chilly Climate for Women Faculty*. Waterloo, Ontario: Wilfrid Laurier University.

Chilman, Catherine Street. 1995. "Hispanic families in the United States: Research perspectives." In Mark Robert Rank & Edward T. Kain (eds.), *Diversity and Change in Families: Patterns, Prospects, and Policies*. Upper Saddle River, NJ: Prentice Hall.

Chin, Ko-Lin. 1990. *Chinese Subculture and Criminality: Nontraditional Crime Groups in America*. Westport, CT: Greenwood.

Chino, A., & D. Funabiki. 1984. "A Cross-validation on sex differences in the expression of depression," *Sex Roles* 11: 175–187.

Chipman, S. F., & V. G. Thomas. 1985. "Women's participation in mathematics: Outlining the problem." In S. F. Chipman, L. R. Brush, & D. M. Wilson (eds.), *Women and Mathematics: Balancing the Equation*. Hillsdale, NJ: Lawrence Erlbaum.

Chipman, S. F., L. R. Brush, & D. M. Wilson (eds.). 1985. *Women and Mathematics: Balancing the Equation*. Hillsdale, NJ: Lawrence Erlbaum.

Chiriboga, D. A., & M. Thurnher. 1980. "Marital lifestyles and adjustments to separation." *Journal of Divorce* 3: 379–90.

Chirot, Daniel. 1994. *How Societies Change*. Thousand Oaks, CA: Pine Forge.

Chodak, Simon. 1973. *Societal Development: Five Approaches with Conclusions from Comparative Analysis*. New York: Oxford University Press.

Chollar, Susan. 1995. "Happy families: Who says they all have to be alike?" In Kathleen R. Gilbert (ed.), *Marriage and the Family 95/96* (Annual Editions). Guilford, CT: Dushkin/Brown & Benchmark.

Christ, Carol. 1997. *Laughter of Aphrodite: Reflections on a Journey to the Goddess*. San Francisco: Harper & Row.

Christen, Yves. 1991. *Sex Differences: Modern Biology and the Unisex Fallacy*. Translated by Nicholas Davidson, New Brunswick, NJ: Transaction.

Christian Century. 1997. "Standing in the mall." October 22: 934–36.

Christie, Sandra, & Linda L. Lindsey. 1997. "Gender and the workplace." Chapter 9 in Linda Lindsey, *Gender Roles: A Sociological Perspective*. Upper Saddle River, NJ: Prentice Hall.

Chugoku Newspaper. 1992. Exposure: Victims of Radiation Speak Out. Translated by Kirsten McIvor. Tokyo: Kodansha International.

Chuppe, Terry M., High R. Haworth, & Kumoli Ramakrishnan. 1992. "Current developments in global banking and securities markets." In Cheryl R. Lehman & Russell M. Moore, (eds.), *Multinational Culture: Social Aspects of a Global Economy*. Westport, CT: Greenwood: 61–72.

Churbuck, David C., & Jeffrey S. Young. 1992. "The virtual workplace." *Forbes* (November 23): 184–90.

Churchill, Ward. 1994. *Indians Are Us?* Monroe, ME: Common Courage Press.

Clark, Candace. 1995. "Emotions and micropolitics of relationships." In Spencer E. Cahill (ed.), *Inside Social Life: Readings in Sociological Psychology and Microsociology*. Los Angeles: Roxbury.

Clark, Charles S. 1993. "Cults in America." *CQ Researcher* 3(May 7): 385–408.

Clark, Charles S. 1997. "The new immigrants." *CQ Researcher* (January 24): 49–72.

Clarke, A. H. 1984. "Perceptions of crime and fear of victimization among elderly people." *Aging and Society* 4: 327–42.

Clarke, S. C., & B. F. Wilson. 1994. "The relative stability of remarriages: A cohort approach using vital statistics." *Family Relations* 43(3): 305–10.

Clayton, Anthony M. H., & Nicholas J. Radcliffe. 1996. *Sustainability: A Systems Approach*. London: Earthscan.

Cleaver, Joan. 1999. "Surfing for seniors: Where to find them, how to reach them in cyberspace." *Marketing News* 33 (July 19): 1.

Clemetson, Lynette. 2000. "Color my world." *Newsweek* (May 8): 70–74.

Clinard, Marshall B. 1990. *Corporate Corruption: The Abuse of Power*. New York: Praeger.

Clinard, Marshall B., & P. C. Yeager. 1980. *Corporate Crime*. New York: Free Press.

Clinard, Marshall B., & Richard Quinney. 1973. *Criminal Behavior Systems: A Typology*. New York: Holt Rinehart and Winston.

Cnaan, Ram A. 1991. "Neighborhood-representing organizations: How democratic are they?" *Social Science Review* (December): 614–34.

Coakley, Jay J. 1998. *Sport in Society: Issues & Controversies*, 6th ed. Boston: Irwin/McGraw.

Coakley, Jay. 1993. "Socialization & sport." In R. N. Singer, M. Murphey, & L. K. Tennant, (eds.), *Handbook on Research In Sport Psychology*. New York: Macmillan: 571–86.

Coates, Jennifer. 1988. "Gossip revisited: Language in all-female groups." In Jennifer Coates & Deborah Cameron (eds.), *Women in Their Speech Communities: New Perspectives on Language and Sex*. Harlow, Essex, UK: Longman.

Cobb, Ron. 1997. "The king and I." *St. Louis Post-Dispatch* (June 1): 8T.

Cockerham, William C. 1991. *This Aging Society*. Upper Saddle River, NJ: Prentice Hall.

Cockerham, William C. 1995a. *Medical Sociology*. Upper Saddle River, NJ: Prentice Hall.

Cockerham, William C. 1995b. *The Global Society*. New York: McGraw-Hill.

Coder, John, Lee Rainwater, & Timothy Smeeding. 1989. "Inequality among children and elderly in ten modern nations." *American Economic Review* 79/2: 320–324.

Cohen, Akiba A., Hanna Adoni, & Charles R. Bantz. 1990. *Social Conflict and Television News*. Newbury Park, CA: Sage.

Cohen, Albert. 1965. "The sociology of the deviant act: Anomie theory & beyond." *American Sociological Review* 30: 5–14.

Cohen, Anthony. 1993. "The future of the self." In Anthony Cohen & Katsuyoshi Fukui (eds.), *Humanising the City? Social Contexts of Urban Life at the Turn of the Millennium*. Edinburgh, UK: Edinburgh University: 201–21.

Cohen, J. I. 1990. "Health policy, management and economics." In Thomas A. Lambo & Stacey B. Day (eds.), *Issues in Contemporary International Health*. New York: Plenum: 13–33.

Cohen, Joel E. 1995. *How Many People Can the Earth Support?* New York: W.W. Norton.

Cohen, S. 1985. *Visions of Social Control*. Cambridge, MA: Polity.

Cohen, Sara. 1991. *Rock Culture on Liverpool: Popular Music in the Making*. Oxford, UK: Clarendon.

Cohen, Susan A., & Cory L. Richards. 1994. "The Cairo consensus: Development and women." *International Family Planning Perspectives*. 20(4): 150–55.

Cohen, Susan, & Mary Fainsod Katzenstein. 1991. "The war over the family is not over the family." In Mark Hutter (ed.), *The Family Experience: A Reader in Cultural Diversity*. New York: Macmillan.

Colapinto, John. 2000. *As Nature Made Him: The Boy Who Was Raised as a Girl*. New York: HarperCollins.

Colarusso, Calvin A. 1994. *Fulfillment in Adulthood: Paths to the Pinnacle of Life*. New York: Plenum.

Cole, David. 1994. "Five myths about immigration." *The Nation* 259 (October 17): 410–12.

Cole, Robert E. 1989. *Strategies for Learning*. Berkeley, CA: University of California Press.

Coleman, James S. 1990b. "Rational organization," *Rationality and Society* 2: 94–105.

Coleman, James S. et al. 1966. *Equality of Educational Opportunity*. Washington, DC: US. Government Printing Office.

Coleman, James S., Elihu Katz, & Herbert Menzel. 1957. "The diffusion of innovation among physicians." *Sociometry* 20: 253–69.

Coleman, James W. & Donald R. Cressey. 1999. *Social Problems*, 7th ed. New York: Longman.

Coleman, John A. 1970. "Civil religion." *Sociological Analysis* 31(2): 76.

Coleman, John, & Debi Rocker. 1998. *Teenage Sexuality: Health, Risk and Education*. Amsterdam: Harwood.

Coleman, Marilyn, & Lawrence H. Ganong. 1990. "Remarriage and step-family research in the 1980s: Increased interest in an old family form." *Journal of Marriage and the Family* 52: 925–40.

Collins, Patricia H. 1990. *Black Feminist Thought*. Cambridge, MA: Unwin & Hyman.

Collins, Patricia Hill. 1996. "Toward a new vision: Race, class and gender as categories of analysis and connection." In Karen E. Rosenblum & Toni-Michelle Travies (eds.), *The Meaning of Difference: American Constructions of Race, Sex and Gender, Social Class and Sexual Orientation*. New York: McGraw-Hill.

Collins, Randall, & Michael Makowsky. 1998. *The Discovery of Society*, 6th ed. New York: McGraw-Hill.

Collins, Randall, & Scott Coltrane. 1995. *Sociology of Marriage and the Family: Gender, Love, and Property*. Chicago: Nelson-Hall.

Collins, Randall, & Scott Coltrane. 2001. *Sociology of Marriage and the Family: Gender, Love, and Property*. Chicago: Nelson-Hall.

Collins, Randall. 1975. *Conflict Sociology: Toward an Explanatory Science*. New York: Academic Press.

Collins, Randall. 1979. *The Credential Society*. New York: Academic Press.

Collins, Randall. 1988. "Women & Men in the Class Structure," *Journal of Family Issues* 9: 27–50.

Collins, Randall. 1989. "Sociology: Proscience or antiscience." *American Sociological Review* 54: 124–139.

Collins, Sara. 1994. "The new migrant workers." *U.S. News & World Report* 117 (July 4): 553–55.

Coltrane, Scott, & Masako Ishii-Kuntz. 1992. "Men's housework: A life course perspective." *Journal of Marriage and the Family* 54: 43–47.

Coltrane, Scott. 1995. *Family Man: Fatherhood, Housework, and Gender Equity*. New York: Oxford University.

Coltrane, Scott. 1996. *Family Man: Fatherhood, Housework, and Gender Equity*. New York: Oxford University.

Coltrane, Scott. 1997. "Scientific heal-truths and postmodern parody in the family values debate." *Contemporary Sociology* 26(1): 7–10.

Commission on Civil Rights. 1981. *Affirmative Action in the 1980s: Dismantling the Process of Discrimination*. Washington, DC: GPO.

Committee on Small Business. 1988. *New Economic Realities: The Rise of Women Entrepreneurs*. Washington, DC: U.S. Government Printing Office.

Commoner, Barry. 1993. "Population, development, and the environment: Trends and key issues in the developed countries." *International Journal of Health Services* 23(3): 519–39.

Comstock, George, & Haejung Paik. 1991. *Television and the American Child*. San Diego, CA: Academic Press.

Comte, Auguste. 1858. *The Positive Philosophy*. New York: Calvin Blanchard.

Condon, Jane. 1985. *A Half Step Behind: Japanese Women of the 80s*. New York: Dodd, Mead.

Condry, J.C. 1989. *The Psychology of Television*. Hillsdale, NJ: Lawrence Erlbaum.

Conger, Rand D., et al. 1990. "Linking economic hardship to marital quality and instability." *Journal of Marriage and the Family* 52: 642–66.

Conley, Shanti, (ed.), 1994. *Closing the Gender Gap: Educating Girls*. Washington, DC: Population Action International.

Connections. 1995. "Girls = gains." 1(8): 1. Published by Alliance for a Global Community.

Connections. 1995/1996. "The gathering storm: HIV/AIDS in the developing world." 2(3): 1. Published by Alliance for a Global Community.

Connections. 1997. "Credit where it's due: For world's poor, small loans have big payoff." *Interaction* 3(2).

Connell, Robert. 1993. "Cool guys, swots and wimps: The interplay of masculinity and education." In Lawrence Angus (ed.), *Education, Inequality and Social Identity*. London: Falmer: 91–103.

Connolly, Barbara. 1996. "Increments for the earth: The politics of environmental aid." In Robert O. Keohane & Marc A. Levy (eds.), *Institutions for Environmental Aid: Pitfalls and Promises*. Cambridge, MA: Massachusetts Institute of Technology Press: 327–65.

Conrad, John P. 1983. "Deterrence, the death penalty, and the data." In Ernest van den Haag & John P. Conrad, (eds.), *The Death Penalty: A Debate*. New York: Plenum.

Conrad, Peter, & Joseph W. Schneider. 1980. *Deviance and Medicalization: From Badness to Sickness*. St. Louis: Mosby.

Conrad, Peter, & Joseph W. Schneider. 1990. "Professionalization, Monopoly and the Structure of Medical Practice." In Peter Conrad & Rochelle Kern (eds.), *The Sociology of Health and Illness: Critical Perspectives*. New York: St. Martin's.

Conrad, Peter, & Rochelle Kern (eds.). 1990. *The Sociology of Health and Illness*. New York: St. Martin's.

Conrad, Peter. 1993. "Rationing health care: A sociological reflection." *Research in the Sociology of Health Care* 10: 3–22.

Conway, M. M. 1991. *Political Participation in the United States*, 2nd ed. Washington, DC: Congressional Quarterly.

Cook, Alicia Skinner, & Kevin Ann Oltjenbruns. 1989. *Dying and Grieving: Lifespan and Family Perspectives*. New York: Holt, Rinehart and Winston.

Cook, Judith A., & Eric R. Wright. 1995. "Medical sociology and the study of severe mental illness: Reflections on past accomplishments and directions for future research." *Journal of Health and Social Behavior* (Extra Issue). 1995: 95–114.

Cooley, Charles Horton. 1902/1983. *Human Nature and the Social Order*. New Brunswick, NJ: Transaction.

Cooley, Charles Horton. 1909. *Social Organization*. New York: Scribner's.

Cooley, Charles Horton. 1962. *Social Organization*. New York: Schocken. Originally published in 1909.

Coontz, Stephanie. 1992. *The Way We Never Were: American Families and the Nostalgia Trap*. New York: Basic Books.

Coontz, Stephanie. 1997. *The Way We Really Are: Coming to Terms with America's Changing Families*. New York: BasicBooks.

Cooper, Harris M. 1989. *Integrating Research: A Guide for Literature Reviews*. Applied Social Research Methods Series, Vol.2. Newbury Park, CA: Sage.

Cooper, P. 1989. "Children's literature: The extent of sexism." In C. Lont & S. Friedly (eds.), *Beyond Boundaries: Sex and Gender Diversity in Education*. Fairfax, VA: George Mason University.

Corcoran, Mary, Greg J. Duncan, Gerand Gurin, & Patricia Gurin. 1985. "Myth and reality: The causes and persistence of poverty." *Journal of Policy Analysis and Management* 4/4: 516–536.

Cornelius, Wayne A. 1996. "Economics, culture and the politics of restricting immigration." *Chronicle of Higher Education* 43 (November): B4–B5.

Cornish, Derek, & Ronald Clarke, (eds.). 1986. *The Reasoning Criminal: Rational Choice Perspectives On Offending*. New York: Springer Verlag.

Cornwell, Gretchen T., David J. Eggebeen, & Laurie L. Meschke. 1996. "The changing family context of early adolescence." *Journal of Early Adolescence* 16(2): 141–56.

Corrigon, Don. 1996. "Webster welcomes a president—president: Say no to crime, guns, drugs." *Webster-Kirkwood Times* (May 24–30): 1,10.

Corsaro, W. A., & D. Eder. 1990. "Children's peer cultures." In W. R. Scott (ed.), *Annual Review of Sociology*. Palo Alto, CA: Annual Reviews.

Cortes, C. E. 1991. "Pluribus and unum: The quest for community amid diversity." *Change* 25 (September/October): 9–13. 30: 1,10.

Cose, Elis. 2000. "Our new look: The colors of race." *Newsweek*. (January 1): 28–30.

Coser, Lewis A. 1977. *Masters of Sociological Thought: Ideas in Historical and Cultural Context*. New York: Harcourt, Brace, Jovanovich.

Coser, Lewis. 1956. *The Functions of Social Conflict*. New York: Free Press.

Coser, Rose L. 1991. *In Defense of Modernity: Role Complexity & Internal Autonomy*. Stanford, CA: Stanford University Press.

Costa, Pail T. & Robert R. McCrea. 1989. "Personality continuity and the changes and the changes of adult life." In M. Storandt & G. Vandenbos (eds.), *The Adult Years: Continuity and Change*. Washington, DC: American Psychological Association.

Costello, Cynthia, & Anne J. Stone (eds.). 1994. *The American Woman 1994–95: Where We Stand*. New York: W. W. Norton.

Council on International Educational Exchange. 1988. *Educating for Global Competence*. New York: The Council.

Countdown 2005. 1997. "USAID takes initiative." Newsletter of the Microcredit Summit Campaign. 1(2): 10–11.

Coverdill, James E. 1988. "The dual economy and sex differences in earnings." *Social Forces* 66: 970–93.

Coverman, Shelley W. 1989. "Women's work is never done: The division of household labor." In Jo Freeman (ed.), *Women: A Feminist Perspective*. Mountain View, CA: Mayfield.

Covey, Herbert C., & Scott Menard. 1988. "Trends in elderly criminal victimization from 1973 to 1984." *Research on Aging* 10(3): 329–41.

Cowan, Philip A. 1993. "The sky IS falling, but Poponoe's analysis won't help us do anything about it." *Journal of Marriage and the Family* 55: 525–26.

Coward, Raymond T., Horne Claydell, & Jeffrey W. Dwyer. 1992. "Demographic perspectives on gender and family caregiving." In Jeffrey W. Dwyer & Raymond T. Coward (eds.), *Gender, Families and Elder Care*. Newbury Park: CA: Sage.

Cowell, A. 1996. "Old Catholic church offers new Catholic ways." *The New York Times* (May 28): A4.

Cowgill, Donald O. 1974. "Aging and modernization: A revision of theory." In Jaber F. Gubrium (ed.), *Late Life: Communities and Environmental Policy*.

Cowgill, Donald O. 1986. *Aging Around the World*. Belmont, CA: Wadsworth.

Cowley, Goeffrey. 1988. "Science and the cigarette." *Newsweek* (April 11): 67.

Cox, Frank D. 1999. *Human Intimacy: Marriage, the Family, and Its Meaning*. Belmont, CA: Wadsworth.

Cox, Harold G. 1990. "Roles for aged individuals in post-industrial societies." *International Journal of Aging and Human Development* 30(1): 55–62.

Cox, Harold G. 1996. *Later Life: The Realities of Aging*. Upper Saddle River, NJ: Prentice Hall.

Cox, Harold G. 2000. *Later Life: The Realities of Aging*. Upper Saddle River, NJ: Prentice-Hall.

Cox, Oliver. 1948. *Caste, Class and Race*. Detroit: Wayne State University Press.

Coyula, Mario. 1996. "Metropolis 2000: A forum on urban issues." *SAIS Review* 16: 185–88.

Crandall, C.S. 1995. "Do parents discriminate against their heavyweight daughters?" *Personality & Social Psychology Bulletin* 21: 724–735.

Crandon, Libbet. 1983. "Between shamans, doctors, and demons: Illness curing and cultural identity midst culture change." In John H. Morgan (ed.), *Third World Medicine and Cultural Change*. Lanham, MD: University Press of America: 69–84.

Crane, Diana. 1992. *The Production of Culture: Media and the Urban Arts*. Newbury Park, CA: Sage.

Crane, Jonathan. 1991. "The epidemic theory of ghettoes and neighborhood effects on dropping out and teenage childbearing." *American Journal of Sociology* 96: 1226–59.

Crank, John. 1997. *Understanding Police Culture*. Cincinnati: Anderson.

Crapo, Richley H. 1993. *Cultural Anthropology: Understanding Ourselves & Others*. Guilford, CT: Dushkin.

Cready, Cynthia M., & Mark A. Fossett. 1997. "Mate availability and African American family structure in the U.S. nonmetropolitan South." *Journal of Marriage and the Family* 59(1): 192–203.

Crenson, Matt. 2000. "Social activism class in session." *Owensboro (Ky) Messenger-Inquirer* (April 9): 5.

Cresswell, J. L., C. Grifford, & D. Huffman. 1988. "Implications of right/left brain research for mathematics educators." *School Science and Mathematics* 88(2): 119–31.

Crispell, Diane. 1990. "Workers in 2000." *American Demographics* (March): 36–40.

Crispell, Diane. 1995. "Generations to 2025." *American Demographics* 17 (January): 4ff.

Critchlow, Donald T., & Ellis W. Hawley, (eds.). 1989. *Poverty and Public Policy in Modern America*. Chicago: Dorsey.

Crites, Laura L. 1987. "Wife abuse: The judicial record." In Laura L. Crites & Winifred L. Hepperle (eds.), *Women, the Courts and Equality*. Beverly Hills, CA: Sage.

Cronin, E. David, 1969. *Black Moses: The Story of Marcus Garvey*. Madison: University of Wisconsin Press.

Crosbie, Paul V., (ed.). 1975. *Interaction in Small Groups*. New York: Macmillan.

Crosby, Alfred W. 1986. *Biological Imperialism: The Biological Expansion of Europe, 900–1900*. Cambridge, UK: Cambridge University.

Crosby, Faye J. 1982. *Relative Depression and Working Women*. Oxford, UK: Oxford University.

Cross, William E., Jr. 1991. *Shades of Black*. Philadelphia: Temple University.

Crossen, C. 1990. "Getting down to business." *Wall Street Journal* (February 9): R30.

Crosset, Todd W. 1995. *Outsiders in the Clubhouse: The World of Women's Professional Golf*. Albany, NY: State University of New York Press.

Crosset, Todd W., Jeffrey R. Benedict, & Mark A. McDonald. 1995. "Male student-athletes reported for assault," *Journal of Sport & Social Issues* 19: 126–140.

Crossette, Barbara. 1995. "U.N. documents inequities for women as world forum nears." *The New York Times* (August 18).

Crossette, Barbara. 1996. "Muslim women's movement is gaining strength." *New York Times International* (May 12).

Croteau, David, & William Hoynes. 1994. *By Invitation Only: How the Media Limit Political Debate*. Monroe, ME: Common Courage Press.

Crouter, Ann C., Beth A. Manke, & Susan M. McHale. 1995. "The family context of gender intensification in early adolescence." *Child Development* 66(2): 317–29.

Cruz, Yolands. 1996. "A twofer's lament." In Harold A. Widdison (ed.), *Social Problems 96/97* (Annual Editions). Guilford, CT: Dushkin/Brown & Benchmark.

Csordas, Thomas J. 1997. *Language, Charisma, and Creativity: The Ritual Life of a Religious Movement*. Berkeley, CA: University of California.

Csordas, Thomas J., & Arthur Kleinman. 1996. "The therapeutic process." In C.F. Sargent & T.M Johnson (eds.), *Medical Anthropology: Contemporary Theory and Method*. Westport, CT: Praeger.

Cullen, Francis, & Karen Gilbert. 1982. *Reaffirming Rehabilitation*. Cincinnati, OH: Anderson.

Culp, R. E., A. S. Cook, & P. C. Housley. 1983. "A comparison of observed and reported adult-infant interactions: Effects of perceived sex." *Sex Roles* 9: 475–79.

Cumming, Elaine, & William E. Henry. 1961. *Growing Old: The Process of Disengagement*. New York: Basic Books.

Cumming, Elaine. 1963. "Further thoughts on the theory of disengagement." *UNESCO International Social Science Bulletin* 15: 377–93.

Cummings, Scott, & Del Taebel. 1978. "The economic socialization of children: A Neo-Marxist analysis." *Social Problems* 26: 198–210.

Currie, Elliott. 1989. "Confronting crime: Looking toward the 21st century." *Justice Quarterly* 6: 5–25.

Curry, G. David & Scott H. Decker. 1988. *Confronting Gangs: Crime & Community*. Los Angeles: Roxbury: 65–67.

Curry, Tim. 1993. "A little pain never hurt anyone." *Symbolic Interaction* (16/3): 273–90.

Curry, Z. D., & J. Shroyer. 1989. "Alternative housing designed for the rural elderly." *The Southwestern* 5: 47–60.

Curtis, J. E., E. G. Grabb, & D. Baer. 1992. "Voluntary association membership in 15 countries." *American Sociological Review* 57: 139–52.

Cutright, Phillips. 1995. "Neighborhood social structure and the lives of black and white children." *Sociological Focus* 27(3): 243–55.

Cuzzort, R.P., & Edith W. King. 1995. *Twentieth-Century Social Thought*. New York: Harcourt Brace.

D'Antonio, William V., James D. Davidson, Dean R. Hoge, & Ruth A. Wallace. 1989. *American Catholic Laity in a Changing Church*. Kansas City: Sheed & Ward.

D'Antonio, William V., James D. Davidson, Dean R. Hoge, & Ruth A. Wallace. 1996. *Laity American and Catholic: Transforming the Church*. Kansas City, MO: Sheed & Ward.

Dahl, Robert. 1958. "A critique of the ruling elite model." *American Political Science Review* 52: 463–69.

Dahl, Robert. 1961. *Who Governs?* New Haven, CT: Yale University Press.

Dahl, Robert. 1968. *Pluralist Democracy in the United States*. Chicago: Rand McNally.

Dahl, Robert. 1982. *Dilemmas of Pluralist Democracy*. New Haven, CT: Yale University Press.

Dahrendorf, Ralf. 1959. *Class & Class Conflict in Industrial Society*. Stanford, CA: Stanford University Press.

Dahrendorf, Ralf. 1973. "Toward a theory of social conflict." In Amitai Etzioni & Eva Etzioni-Halevy, (eds.), *Social Change—Sources, Patterns & Consequences*. New York: Basic Books: 100–13.

Dahrendorf, Ralf. 1981. *Life Chances*. Chicago: University of Chicago Press.

Dahrendorf, Ralf. 1987. "Changing perceptions of the role of government." In *Interdependence and Co-operation in Tomorrow's World: A Symposium Marking the Twenty-Fifth Anniversary of the Organisation for Economic Co-operation and Development*. Paris: OECD: 110–22.

Dail, Paula W. 1988. "Prime-time television portrayal of older adults in the context of family life." *The Gerontologist* 28(5): 700–706.

Dalton, George. 1967. *Tribal and Peasant Economies*. Garden City, NY: Natural History Press.

Dancer, L. Suzanne, & Lucia Albino Gilbert. 1993. "Spouses' family work participation and its relation to wives' occupation level." *Sex Roles* 28(3–4): 127–45.

Daniels, Arlene K. 1988. *Invisible Careers*. Chicago: University of Chicago Press.

Daniels, Cynthia. 1993. "There's no place like home." In Alison M. Jaggar & Paula S. Rothenberg (eds.), *Feminist Frameworks: Alternative Theoretical Accounts of the Relations Between Women and Men*. New York: McGraw-Hill.

Dannefer, Dale, & Russell K. Schutt. 1982. "Race and juvenile processing in court and police agencies." *American Journal of Sociology* 87: 1113–132.

Danzger, M. Herbert. 1989. *Returning to Tradition: The Contemporary Revival of Orthodox Judaism*. New Haven: Yale University Press.

Darby, John. 1995. *Northern Ireland: Managing Difference*. London: Minority Rights Group International.

Darnay, Arsen J. (ed.). 1998. *Statistical Record of Health and Medicine*. Detroit: Gale.

Darnay, Arsen J. 1994. *Statistical Record of Older Americans*. Detroit: Gale Research.

Darnay, Brigitte T. (ed.). 1997. *Gale Country & World Rankings Reporter*. Detroit: Gale.

Darnton, Nina. 1985. "Woman and stress on the job and at home." *New York Times* (August 8): C-1.

Date-Bah, Eugenia. 1997. "Introduction." In Eugenia Date-Bah (ed.), *Promoting Gender Equality at Work*. London: Zed: 1–23.

Dauber, S. 1986. "Sex differences on the SAT-M, SAT-V, TWSE and ACT among college-bound high school students." Paper presented at the American Education Research Association, Washington, DC.

Davidson, O. G. 1993. *Under Fire: The NRA and the Battle For Gun Control*. New York: Henry Holt.

Davidson, T. Kenneth, & Nelwyn B. Moore. 1994. "Masturbation and premarital sexual intercourse among college women: Making choice for sexual fulfillment. *Journal of Sex and Marital Therapy* 20(3): 178–99.

Davies, Bronwyn. 1989. *Frogs and Snails and Feminist Tales: Preschool Children and Gender*. Sydney: Allen & Unwin.

Davies, Christie. 1990. *Ethnic Humor Around the World: A Comparative Analysis*. Bloomington, IN: Indiana University.

Davies, James C. 1962. "Toward a theory of revolution." *American Sociological Review* 27/1: 5–19.

Davies, Lorraine, William R. Avison, & Donna D. McAlpine. 1997. "Significant life experiences and depression among single and married mothers." *Journal of Marriage and the Family* 59(2): 294–308.

Davis, D. M. 1990. "Portrayals of women in prime-time network television: Some demographic characteristics." *Sex Roles* 23(5–6): 325–32.

Davis, Elizabeth Gould. 1971. *The First Sex*. New York: Penguin.

Davis, F. James. 1991. *Who Is Black? One Nation's Definition*. University Park, PA: Penn State University.

Davis, Fred. 1992. *Fashion, Culture and Identity*. Chicago: University of Chicago Press.

Davis, Kingsley, & Wilbert E. Moore. 1945. "Some principles of stratification." *American Sociological Review* 10: 242–49.

Davis, Kingsley. 1947. "Final note on a case of extreme isolation." *American Journal of Sociology* 52: 432–37.

Davis, Kingsley. 1984. "Wives and work: The sex role revolution and its consequences." *Population and Development Review* 10(3): 397–417.

Davis, Murray S. 1993. *What's So Funny? The Comic Conception of Culture and Society*. Chicago: University of Chicago.

Davis, Nancy J. & Robert V. Robinson. 1998. "Do Wives Matter? Class Identities of Wives and Husbands in the United States, 1974–1994," *Social Forces* 76: 1063–1086.

Davis, Nancy J. 1992. "Teaching About inequality: Student resistance, paralysis, and rage." *Teaching Sociology* 20 (July): 232–238.

Davis, R., & J. Davis. 1986. *TV's Image of the Elderly*. Lexington, MA: Lexington Books.

Davis, Theodore J. 1995. "The Occupational Mobility of Black Males Revisited," *Social Science Journal* 32: 121–136.

Davis-Friedmann, Deborah. 1991. *Long Lives: Chinese Elderly and the Communist Revolution*. Stanford, CA: Stanford University Press.

Dawkins, Marvin P., & Jomills Henry Braddock, II. 1994. "The continuing significance of desegregation: School racial composition and African American inclusion in American society." *Journal of Negro Education* 63(3): 394–405.

Day, Stacey B., & Thomas A. Lambro. 1990. "Introduction: International health and health for all." In Thomas A. Lambo & Stacey B. Day (eds.). *Issues in Contemporary International Health*. New York: Plenum: 285–300.

De Lange, Janice. 1995. "Gender and communication in social work education: A cross-cultural perspective." *Journal of Social Work Education* 31(1): 75–81.

De Lehr, Esther Contreras. 1992. "Aging and family support in Mexico." In Hal Kendig, Akido Hasimoto, & Larry C. Coppard (eds.), *Family Support for the Elderly: The International Experience*. New York: Oxford University Press.

De Olivera, Orlandina, & Bryan Roberts. 1996. "Urban development and social inequality in Latin America." In Josef Gugler (ed.), *The Urban Transformation of the Developing World*. Oxford, UK: Oxford University: 253–314.

DeBuono, Barbara A., Stephen H. Zinner, Maxim Daamen, & William M. McCormack. 1990. "Sexual behavior of college women in 1975, 1986, and 1989." *New England Journal of Medicine* 322: 821–25.

DeCurtis, Anthony. 2000. "Eminem's hate rhymes." *Rolling Stone* 846 (August 3): 17–18, 21.

Dedman, Bill. 1999. "DNA tests are freeing scores of prison inmates." *New York Times* (April 19): A12.

Deedy, J. 1987. *American Catholicism: Now Where?* New York: Plenum.

Deegan, Mary Jo. 1988. "W.E.B. DuBois and the women of Hull House, 1895–1899." *American Sociologist* (Winter): 301–311.

Deegan, Mary Jo. 1988. "W. E. B. DuBois & the women of Hull House, 1895–1899." *American Sociologist* (Winter): 301–311.

Deegan, Mary Jo. 1991. *Women In Sociology: A Bio-Bibliographical Sourcebook.* New York: Greenwood.

Degher, Douglas, & Gerald Hughes. 1991. "The identity change process: A field study of obesity." *Deviant Behavior* 12: 385–402.

Del Carmen, Rebecca, & Gabrielle N. Virgo. 1993. "Marital disruption and nonresidential parenting: A multicultural perspective." In Charlene E. Depner & James H. Bray (eds.), *Non-residential Parenting: New Vistas in Family Living.* Newbury Park, CA: Sage.

Delaney, Kevin K. 1992. *Strategic Bankruptcy.* Berkeley: University of California Press.

Delattre, Edwin J. 1990. "New faces of organized crime." *American Enterprise* 1: 38–45.

Della Piana, L. 1995. "Categories count." *Poverty and Race* 4: 11–12.

Della Porta, Donatella. 1995. *Social Movements, Political Violence and the State.* New York: Cambridge University Press.

DeMar, Margaretta. 1992. "The 'new' internationalization: Implications for development and welfare in the Third World." In Cheryl R. Lehman & Russell M. Moore, (eds.), *Multinational Culture: Social Impacts of a Global Economy:* Westport, CT: Greenwood: 11–32.

DeMaris, Alfred, & K. Vaninadha Rao. 1992. "Premarital cohabitation and subsequent marital stability in the United States: A reassessment." *Journal of Marriage and the Family* 54: 178–90.

Demerath, Nicholas J. III, & Phillip E. Hammond. 1969. *Religion in Social Context.* New York: Random House.

Demerath, Nicholas J. III. 1990. "Religion and power in the American experience." In T. Robbins & D. Anthony (eds.), *In Gods We Trust: New Patterns of Religious Pluralism in America.* New Brunswick, NJ: Transaction: 427–48.

Demerath, Nicholas J., & Rhys H. Williams. 1990. "Religion and power in the American experience." In T. Robbins & D. Anthony (eds.), *In Gods We Trust: New Patterns of Religious Pluralism in America.* New Brunswick, NJ: Transaction: 427–48.

Demmert, William G., Jr. 1996. "Indian nations at risk: An educational strategy for action." In Laura I. Rendon & Richard O. Hope (eds.), *Educating a New Majority: Transforming America's Educational System for Diversity.* San Francisco: Jossey-Bass: 231½–64.

Demo, David, & Alan Acock,. 1991. "The impact of divorce on children." In Alan Booth (ed.), *Contemporary Families: Looking Forward, Looking Back.* Minneapolis: National Council on Family Relations: 161–191.

Dennis, W. 1966. "Cognitive productivity between the ages of 20 and 80 years." *Journal of Gerontology* 21: 1–8.

Dentan, R. K. 1968. *The Semai: A Nonviolent People of Malaya.* New York: Holt, Rinehart & Winston.

Dentler, R. A. 1992. "The Los Angeles riots of spring, 1992." *Sociological Practice Review* 3: 229–44.

Denzin, Norman. 1992. *Symbolic Interactionism and Cultural Studies: The Politics of Interpretation.* Cambridge, MA: Blackwell.

Denzin, Norman. 1993. "Sexuality and gender: An interactionist/poststructural reading." In Paula England (ed.), *Theory on Gender/Feminism on Theory.* New York: Aldine DeGruyter.

DeParle, J. 1998. "In booming economy, poor still struggle to pay the rent." *New York Times* (June 16).

DeParle, Jason. 1992. "Why marginal changes don't rescue the welfare system." *The New York Times* (March 1): E3.

DePaulo, B. M. 1992. Nonverbal behavior and self-presentation." *Psychological Bulletin* 3: 203–43.

DePaulo, B. M., C. S. LeMay, & J. Epstein. 1991. "Effects of importance of success on effectiveness in deceiving." *Personality and Social Psychology Bulletin* 1: 14–24.

Dershowitz, Alan. 1997. *The Vanishing American Jew.* Boston: Little, Brown.

DeSoto, Hernando. 1989. *The Other Path.* New York: Harper & Row.

DeSpelder, Lynne, & Albert Lee Strickland. 1996. *The Last Dance: Encountering Death and Dying.* Mountain View, CA: Mayfield.

Deutscher, Irwin. 1966. "Words and deeds: Social science and social policy." *Social Problems* 13: 233–54.

Deutscher, Irwin. 1973. *What We Say/What We Do: Sentiments and Acts.* Glenview, IL: Scott, Foresman.

Devas, Nick, & Carole Rakodi. 1993a. "The urban challenge." In Nick Devas & Carole Rakodi (eds.), *Managing Fast Growing Cities: New Approaches to Urban Planning and Management in the Developing World.* Essex, UK: Longman: 1–39.

Devas, Nick, & Carole Rakodi. 1993b. "Conclusions: Assessing the new approaches." In Nick Devas & Carole Rakodi (eds.), *Managing Fast Growing Cities: New Approaches to Urban Planning and Management in the Developing World.* Essex, UK: Longman: 265–96.

Devine, Don. 1972. *Political Culture of the United States: The Influence of Member Values on Regime Maintenance.* Boston: Little, Brown.

Devine, Francis E. 1982. "Cesare Beccaria and the theoretical foundations of modern penal jurisprudence." *New England Journal on Prison Law* 7: 8–21.

Devine, Joel A., Mark Plunkett, & James D. Wright. 1992. "The chronicity of poverty." *Social Forces* 70: 787–812.

Di Bona, Joseph. 1988. "The resegregation of schools in small towns and rural areas of North Carolina." *Journal of Negro Education* 57(1): 43–50.

Di Leonardo, Michaela (ed.). 1991. *Gender at the Crossroads of Knowledge: Feminist Anthropology in the Postmodern Era.* Berkeley: University of California Press.

Diamond, Milton. 1993. "Homosexuality and bisexuality in different populations." *Archives of Sexual Behavior* 22: 291–310.

Diamond, Timothy. 1992. *Making Gray Gold: Narratives of Nursing Home Care.* Chicago: University of Chicago.

Diary. 1999. "Diary shows that gunmen sought revenge." *St. Louis Post-Dispatch.* (April 25): A1, A8.

Dietz, Thomas, Tom R. Burns, & Frederick Buttel. 1990. "Evolutionary thinking in sociology: An examination of current thinking." *Sociological Forum* 5.

Dietz, Tracy L. 1995. "Patterns of intergenerational assistance within the Mexican American family: Is the family taking care of the older generation's needs?" *Journal of Family Issues* 16(3): 344–56.

Dill, Bonnie Thornton, 1994. "Fictive kin, paper sons, and compadrazgo: Women of color and the struggle for family survival." In Maxine Baca Zinn & Bonnie Thornton Dill (eds.), *Women of Color in U.S. Society.* Philadelphia: Temple University.

Dill, Bonnie Thorton. 1999. "Fictive kin, paper sons, and compadrazgo: Women of color and the struggle for family survival." In Stephanie Coontz (ed.), *American Families: A Multicultural Reader.* New York: Routledge: 2–29.

Dino, Geri A., Mark A. Barnett, & Jeffrey A. Howard. 1984. "Children's expectations of sex differences in parent's responses to sons and daughters encountering interpersonal problems." *Sex Roles* 11: 709–15.

Dion, K. L., E. Berscheid, & Elaine Walster (Hatfield). 1972. "What is beautiful is good." *Journal of Personality and Social Psychology* 24: 285–90.

"Direct Action Figure," 2000. *Mother Jones* (September/October): 23.

"Disabled." 1991. "Disabled student rejected for high school in Japan." *St. Louis Post-Dispatch* (August 4): 11D.

Diver-Stamnes, Ann C. 1995. *Lives in the Balance: Youth, Poverty, and Education in Watts.* Albany, NY: State University of New York Press.

Dixon-Mueller, Ruth. 1985. *Women's Work in Third World Agriculture.* Geneva: International Labour Organization.

Dixon-Mueller, Ruth. 1993. *Population Policies & Women's Rights.* Westport, CT: Praeger.

Dizard, Jan E., & Howard Gadlin. 1990. *The Minimal Family.* Amherst: University of Massachusetts.

Doane, Ashley W. Jr. 1993. "Bringing the majority back in." Presented at the annual meeting of the Society for the Study of Social Problems.

Doezema, Jo. 1998. "Forced to choose: Beyond the voluntary v. forced prostitution dichotomy." In Kamala Kempadoo & Jo Doezema (eds.), *Global Sex Workers: Rights, Resistance, and Redefinition.* New York: Routledge: 34–50.

Dohrenwend, Bruce P., & Barbara Snell Dohrenwend. 1974. "Social and cultural influences on psychopathology." *Annual review of Psychology* 25: 417–52.

Dolan, B. 1991. "Cross-cultural aspects of anorexia nervosa and bulimia: A review." *International Journal of Eating Disorders* 10: 67–79.

Dolbeare, Cushing. 1995. *Out of Reach: Why Everyday People Can't Find Affordable Housing.* Washington, DC: Low Income Housing Information Service.

Dollard, John, Neal E. Miller, Leonard W. Doob, O. H. Mowrer, & Robert R. Sears. 1939. *Frustration and Aggression.* New Haven, CT: Yale University Press.

Domhoff, G. William. 1974. *The Bohemian Grove & Other Retreats: A Study in Ruling-Class Cohesiveness.* New York: Harper & Row.

Domhoff, G. William. 1979. *The Powers That Be.* New York: Random House.

Domhoff, G. William. 1990. *The Power Elite and The State: How Policy Is Made In America.* Hawthorne, NY: Aldine de Gruyter.

Domhoff, G. William. 1996. *State Autonomy or Class Dominance?* New York: Aldine DeGruyter.

Domhoff, G. William. 1998. *Who Rules America?*, 3rd ed. Mountain View, CA: Mayfield.

Donath, J.S. 1997. "Identity Deception in the Virtual Community." In P. Kollock & M. Smith (eds.), *Communities in Cyberspace.* Berkeley: University of California.

Donnelly, Peter, & Kevin Young. 1988. "The construction and confirmation of identity in sport subcultures." In *Sociology of Sport Journal* (5/3): 223–40.

Donohoe, T., & N. Johnson. 1986. *Foul Play: Drug Abuse in Sport.* New York: Basil Blackwell.

Donovan, Robert J., & Ray Scherer. 1992. *Unsilent Revolution: Television News and American Public Life, 1948–1991.* New York: Cambridge University Press.

Donziger, Steven R., (ed.) 1996. *The Real War on Crime: The Report of the National Criminal Justice Commission.* New York: Harper Perennial.

Doob, Christopher B. 1999. *Racism: An American Cauldron*, 3rd ed. New York: Longman.

Dore, R. 1990. "Support and be supported." *Government and Opposition* 25: 438–45.

Doress, Paula Brown, & Diana Laskin Siegal (eds.). 1987. *Ourselves Growing Older: Women Aging with Knowledge and Power*. New York: Simon and Schuster/Touchstone Books.

Doress-Worters, Paula B. 1994. "Adding elder care to women's multiple roles: A critical review of the caregiver stress and multiple roles literatures." *Sex Roles* 31(9–10): 597–616.

Douglas, Marie C. 1993. "The Mutter-Kind-Heim at Frankfurt am Main." *International Journal of Comparative & Applied Criminal Justice* (17/1): 181–87.

Dovidio, J. F., J. A. Piliavin, S. L. Gaertner, D. A. Schroeder, & R. D. Clark. 1991. "The arousal: Cost-reward model and the process of intervention: A review of the evidence." In M. S. Clark (ed.), *Prosocial Behavior*. Newbury Park, CA: Sage.

Dowie, Mark. 1996. "A sky full of holes: Why the ozone layer is torn worse than ever." *Nation* July 8: 11–12, 14–16.

Downes, David. 1992. "The case for going Dutch: The lessons of post-war penal policy." *The Political Quarterly* (63/1): 12–24.

Downie, Mark. 1977. "Pinto madness." *Mother Jones* 2.

Downs, A. C., & S. K. Harrison. 1985. "Embarrassing age spots or just plain ugly? Physical attractiveness stereotyping as an instrument of sexism on American television commercials." *Sex Roles* 13(1–2): 9–19.

Doyal, Lesley. 1995. *What Makes Women Sick*. New Brunswick, NJ: Rutgers University.

Doyle, James A. 1995. *The Male Experience*. Dubuque, IA: Brown & Benchmark.

Doyle, James A., & Michele A. Paludi. 1995. *Sex and Gender: The Human Experience*. Dubuque, IA: Brown & Benchmark.

Drakakis-Smith, David. 1996. "Third World cities: Sustainable urban development." *Urban Studies* 33: 673–701.

Dreier, Peter. 1991. "Judaism." In Richard Lachmann, (ed.), *The Encyclopedic Dictionary of Sociology*. Guilford, CT: Dushkin.

Dressel, Paula L. 1994. "Gender, race and class: Beyond the feminization of poverty in later life." In Eleanor Palo Stoller & Rose Campbell Gibson (eds.), *Worlds of Difference: Inequality in the Aging Experience*. Thousand Oaks, CA: Pine Forge.

Dresser, N. 1994. "Even smiling can have a serious side." *Los Angeles Times* (May 9): 1,5.

Drucker, Peter F. 1993. *Post-Capitalist Society*. New York: HarperCollins.

Drucker, Peter F. 1994. "The age of social transformation." *Atlantic Monthly* 274/5: 53ff.

Drucker, Peter. 1969. *The Age of Discontinuity*. New York: Harper & Row.

Du Bois, W. E. B. 1899. *The Philadelphia Negro: A Social Study*. Philadelphia: University of Pennsylvania Press.

Du Bois, W. E. B. 1903. *The Souls of Black Folk*. New York: Dover.

Du Bois, W. E. B. 1968. *The Autobiography of W. E. B. Du Bois*. New York: International.

DuBois, W.E.B. 1899. *The Philadelphia Negro: A Social Study*: Philadelphia: University of Pennsylvania Press.

DuBois, W.E.B. 1903. *The Souls of Black Folk*. New York: Dover.

DuBois, W.E.B. 1968. *The Autobiography of W.E.B. DuBois*. New York: International.

Ducci, Maria Elena. 1996. "Metropolis 2000: A forum on urban issues." *SAIS Review* 16: 175–81.

Duchin, Faye. 1996. "Population change, lifestyle, and technology: How much difference do they make?" *Population and Development Review* 22: 321–30.

Duck, Steve, & P. H. Wright. 1993. "Re-examining gender differences in same-gender friendships." *Sex Roles* 32(5–6): 375–91.

Duden, Barbara. 1992. "Population." In Wolfgang Sachs (ed.), *The Development Dictionary: A Guide to Knowledge as Power*. London: Zed: 146–57.

Dudley, William, (ed.). 1998. *Native Americans: Opposing Viewpoints*. San Diego: Greenhaven.

Dugger, Karen. 1991. "Social location and gender-role attitudes: A comparison of black and white women." In Judith Lorber & S. A. Ferrell (eds.), *The Social Construction of Gender Gap*. Newbury Park, CA: Sage.

Duke, Benjamin. 1986. *Lessons for Industrial America: The Japanese School*. Westport, CT: Praeger.

Duke, J. T. 1976. *Conflict & Power in Social Life*. Provo, UT: Brigham Young University Press.

Dulles, Foster R., & Melvyn Dubofsky. 1984. *Labor in America*, 4th ed. Arlington Heights, IL: Harlan Davidson.

Duncan, Greg. 1996. "Slow motion: Earnings mobility of young workers in the 1970s and 1980s." paper presented at the annual meeting of the Midwest Sociological Society.

Duncan, Greg J., Timothy Smeeding, & Willard Rogers. 1992. "The incredible shrinking middle class." *American Demographics* 14/4: 34–39.

Dunn, Dana. 1997. "Introduction to the study of women and work." In Dana Dunn (ed.), *Workplace/Women's Place*. Los Angeles: Roxbury: 1–18.

Dunn, Linda. 1991. "Research alert! Qualitative research may be hazardous to your health!" *Qualitative Health Research* 1: 388–92.

duPreez, Peter. 1994. *Genocide: The Psychology of Mass Murder*. New York: Marion Boyers.

Durkheim, Emile. 1893/1964. *The Division of Labor in Society*. New York: Free Press.

Durkheim, Emile. 1897/1964. *Suicide*. Glencoe, IL: Free Press.

Durkheim, Emile. 1898/1956. *Education and Sociology* (Sherwood D. Fox, trans.). Glencoe, IL: Free Press. 1964. *The Division of Labor in Society* (George Simpson, trans.), New York: Free Press.

Durkheim, Emile. 1912/1954. *The Elementary Forms of Religious Life*. Glencoe, IL: Free Press.

Durkheim, Emile. 1933. *The Division of Labor in Society*. New York: Free Press. Originally published in 1893.

Durkheim, Emile. 1966. *Suicide*. New York: Free Press.

Dussart, Francoise. 1993. "First impressions: Diary of a French anthropologist in New York City." In Philip R. DeVita & James D. Armstrong (eds.), *Distant Mirrors: America as a Foreign Culture*. Belmont, CA: Wadsworth: 66–76.

Dussart, Francoise. 1993. "First impressions: Diary of a French anthroologist in New York City." In Phillip R. DeVita & James D. Armstrong (eds.), *Distant Mirrors: America as a Foreign Culture*. Belmont, CA: Wadsworth: 66–76.

Dutton, Diana. 1986. "Social class, health and illness." In L. Aiken & David Mechanic (eds.), *Applications of Social Science to Clinical Medicine and Health Policy*. New Brunswick, NJ: Rutgers University Press.

Duxbury, Linda, & Christopher Higgins. 1994. "Interference between work and family: A status report on dual-career and dual-earner mothers and fathers." *Employee Assistance Quarterly* 9(3–4): 55–80.

Duxbury, Linda, Christopher Higgins, & Catherine Lee. 1994. "Work-family conflict: A comparison by gender, family type, and perceived control." *Journal of Family Issues* 15(5) (September): 449–466.

Dworkin, Andrea. 1989. "Gynocide: Chinese footbinding." In Laurel Richardson & Verta Taylor (eds.), *Feminist Frontiers II*. New York: Random House: 15–24.

Dye, Thomas. 1995. *Who's Running America? The Clinton Years*, 6th ed. Upper Saddle River, NJ: Prentice-Hall.

Dziech, Billie Wright, & Linda Weiner. 1993. "The lecherous professor: Portrait of an artist." In Laurel Richardson and Verta Taylor (eds.), *Feminist Frontiers III*. New York: McGraw-Hill.

Eagly, A. H. 1993. "Gender & social influence." *American Psychologist* 38: 971–981.

Eagly, A. H., & B. T. Johnson. 1990. "Gender & leadership style." *Psychological Bulletin* 108: 233–256.

Eagly, A. H., & S. J. Karau. 1991. "Gender & the emergence of leaders." *Journal of Personality & Social Psychology* 60: 687–710.

Eagly, A. H., R. D. Ashmore, M. G. Makhijani, & L. C. Longo. 1991. "What is beautiful is good, but ...: A meta-analytic review of research on the physical attractiveness stereotype." *Psychological Bulletin* 110: 109–28.

Eaton, William M. 1980. "A formal theory of selection for schizophrenia," *American Journal of Sociology* 86: 149–158.

Eberstadt, Nicholas. 1995. "What is population policy?" *Society* 32(4): 26–29.

Eccles, Jacquelynne S., Janis E. Jacobs, & Rena D. Harold. 1990. "Gender role stereotypes, expectancy effects and parents' socialization of gender differences." *Journal of Social Issues* 46(2): 183–201.

Echikson, William. 1992. "Europe's new face of fear." *World Monitor* (November): 30–35.

Economist. 1994. "Energy: The new prize." June 18: 1–6.

Economist. 1998. "America's cities: They can yet be resurrected." January 10: 17–19.

Eder, Donna, & David A. Kinney. 1995. "The effect of middle school extracurricular activities on adolescent's popularity and peer status." *Youth and Society* 26(3): 298–324.

Edgerton, Robert B. 1992. *Sick Societies: Challenging the Myth of Primitive Harmony*. New York: Free Press.

Edin, Kathryn. 1991. "Surviving the welfare system: How AFDC recipients make ends meet in Chicago." *Social Problems* 38: 462–470.

Edmonds, P. 1993. "After war: Parade to shelters." *USA Today* (June 1): A-4.

Edmondson, Brad. 1997. "The wired bunch." *American Demographics* (49/6): 10–15.

Edmunds, Holly. 1996. *AMA Complete Guide to Marketing Research for Small Business*. Lincolnwood, IL: National Textbook Company.

Edwards, Harry. 1973. *Sociology of Sport*. Homewood, IL: Dorsey.

Edwards, Richard. 1985. *Contested Terrain: The Transformation of the Workplace in the 20th Century*. New York: Basic.

Eerdman, William B. (ed.). 1996. *Eerdmans' Handbook to the World's Religions*. Grand Rapids, MI: William B. Eerdmans Publishing.

Eggebeen, David J., & Daniel T. Lichter. 1991. "Race, family structure and changing poverty among women." *American Sociological Review* 56: 801–817.

Eggington, William. 1992. "From oral to literate culture: An Australian Aboriginal experience." In Fraida Dubin & Natalie A. Kuhlman, (eds.), *Cross-Cultural Literacy: Global Perspectives on Reading and Writing*. Upper Saddle River, NJ: Prentice Hall.

Egolf, Brenda, Judith Lasker, Stewart Wolf, & Louise Potvin. 1993. "The Roseto Effect." *American Journal of Public Health* 82: 1089–1092.

Ehrenreich, Barbara, & Annette Fuentes. 1981. "Life on the global assembly line." *Ms* 9 (January): 53–59,71.

Ehrenreich, Barbara. 1983. *The Hearts of Men: American Dreams and the Flight from Commitment.* Garden City, NY: Doubleday (Anchor).

Ehrenreich, Barbara. 1998. "The silenced majority: Why the average working person has disappeared from American media and culture." In Margaret L. Anderson & Patricia Hill Collins (eds.), *Race, Class and Gender: An Anthology.* Belmont, CA: Wadsworth: 147–49.

Ehrlich, Howard J. 1973. *The Social Psychology of Prejudice.* New York: Wiley Interscience.

Einhorn, Barbara. 1997. "The impact of the transition from centrally planned market-based economies on women's employment in East Central Europe." In Eugenia Date-Bah (ed.), *Promoting Gender Equality at Work.* London: Zed: 59–84.

Eisenberg, David M., Roger B. Davis, Susan L. Ettner, Scott Appel, Sonja Wilkey, Maria Von Rompay, & Ronald Kessler. 1998. "Trends in alternative medicine use in the United States, 1990–1997: Results of a follow-up national survey." *Journal of the American Medical Association* 280: 1569–75.

Eisenstadt, S. N. 1973. *Tradition, Change and Modernity.* New York: Wiley.

Eisinger, Peter. 1988. *The Rise of the Entrepreneurial State.* Madison: University of Wisconsin Press.

Eisler, Diane, & David Loye. 1990. *The Partnership Way.* New York: Harper-SanFrancisco.

Eisler, Diane, David Loye, & Kari Norgaard. 1995. *Women, Men, and the Global Quality of Life. A Report of the Gender Equity and Quality of Life Project of the Center for Partnership Studies.* Pacific Grove, CA: Center for Partnership Studies.

Eisler, Diane. 1988. *The Chalice and the Blade: Our History, Our Future.* San Francisco: Harper San Francisco.

Eisler, Diane. 1995. *Sacred Pleasure: Sex, Myth, and the Politics of the Body.* San Francisco: HarperSan Francisco.

Eitzen, D. Stanley, & George H. Sage. 1997. *Sociology of North American Sport,* 6th ed. Madison, WI: Brown & Benchmark.

Eitzen, D. Stanley, & M. Baca Zinn. 1992. *Social Problems,* 5th ed. Boston: Allyn & Bacon.

Ekerdt, David J. 1987. "Why the notion persists that retirement harms health." *The Gerontologist* 27(4): 454–56.

Ekerdt, David J. 1998. "The busy ethic: Moral continuity between work and retirement." In Harold C. Cox (ed.), *Aging: Annual Editions, 98/99.* Guilford, CT: Dushkin/McGraw-Hill: 128–133.

Ekman, Paul & M. O'Sullivan. 1991. "Facial expression: Methods, means and moods." In Robert S. Feldman & B. Rime (eds.), *Fundamentals of Nonverbal Behavior.* Cambridge, UK: Cambridge University.

Ekman, Paul, Wallace V. Friesen & M. O'Sullivan. 1988. "Smiles when lying." *Journal of Personality and Social Psychology* 54: 414–20.

Ekman, Paul, Wallace V. Friesen, & S. Ancoli. 1980. "Facial signs of emotional experience." *Journal of Personality and Social Psychology* 39: 1125–34.

El Amouri Institute. 1993. "Women's role in the informal sector in Tunisia." In Joycelin Massiah, (ed.), *Women in Developing Economies: Making Visible the Invisible.* Oxford, UK: Berg: 135–66.

el Saadawi, Nawal. 1980. *The Hidden Faces of Eve: Women in the Arab World.* London: Zed.

El-Badry, M. A. 1991. "The growth of world population: Past, present and future." In *Consequences of Rapid Population Growth in Developing Countries.* Proceedings of the United Nations National Institute of Demographic Studies. Expert Group Meeting. New York: Taylor & Francis: 15–40.

Ellemann-Jensen, R. 1987. "Government in transition." In *Interdependence and Co-operation in Tomorrow's World. A Symposium Marking the Twenty-Fifth Anniversary of the Organisation for Economic Co-operation and Development.* Paris: OECD: 157–70.

Elliot, Michael. 2000. "The new radicals." *Newsweek* (December 13).

Elliott, Marta, & Lauren J. Krivo. 1991. "Structural determinants of homelessness in the United States." *Social Problems* 38: 113–131.

Elliott, Michael. 1993. "Global Mafia." *Newsweek* (December 13): 22–29.

Elliott, Michael. 1994. "Crime and punishment." *Newsweek* April 18: 18–22.

Ellis, Lee, & Anthony Walsh. 2000. *Criminology: A Global Perspective.* Boston: Allyn & Bacon.

Ellis, Lee, & Harry Hoffman, (eds.). 1990. *Crime in Biological, Social and Moral Contexts.* New York: Praeger.

Ellison, Christopher G. 1991. "Identification and separatism: Religious involvement and racial orientation among Black Americans." *The Sociological Quarterly* 32(3): 477–78.

Ellison, Christopher G., & Darren E. Sherkat. 1990. "Patterns of religious mobility among black Americans." *Sociological Quarterly* 31: 551–68.

Ellison, Christopher G., & David A. Gay. 1989. "Black political participation revisited." *Social Science Quarterly* 70: 101–119.

Ember, Carol R., & Melvin Ember. 1996. *Cultural Anthropology.* Upper Saddle River, NJ: Prentice Hall.

Emimbeyer, Mustafa, & Jeff Goodwin. 1994. "Network analysis, culture, & the problem of agency." *American Journal of Sociology* 99: 1411–1454.

Emmanuel, Arghiri. 1972. *Unequal Exchange: A Study of the Imperialism of Trade.* New York: Monthly Review.

Engelsman, Joan Chamberlain. 1994. *The Feminine Dimension of the Divine.* Wilmette, IL: Chiron.

Engelter, George H. 1988. "The impact of older voters on the 1988 elections." *Aging Network News* 4(11): 1,6.

England, Paula, & Irene Browne. 1992. "Trends in women's economic status." *Sociological Perspectives* 35(1): 17–51.

Engles, Friedrich. 1942 (original 1884). *The Origin of the Family, Private Property, and the State.* New York: International.

Entessar, Nader. 1988. "Criminal law and the legal system in revolutionary Iran." *Boston College Third World Journal,* 8(1): 91–102.

Entwistle, Doris R., & Karl L. Alexander. 1992. "Summer setback: Race, poverty, school composition, and mathematics achievement in the first two years of school." *American Sociological Review* 57: 72–84.

Entwistle, Doris R., & Karl L. Alexander. 1994. "Winter setback: The racial composition of schools and learning to read." *American Sociological Review* 59(3): 446–60.

Epstein, Barbara. 1991. *Political Protest and Cultural Revolution.* Berkeley, CA: University of California Press.

Epstein, Cynthia F. 1970. *Women's Place: Options and Limits on Professional Careers.* Berkeley: University of California Press.

Epstein, Jonathan S. (ed.). 1994. *Adolescents and Their Music.* Hamden, CT: Garland.

Erb, Gene. 1990. *A Plague of Hunger.* Ames, IA: Iowa State University.

Erben, Rosemarie. 1995. "Special AIDS threat to women." *World Health.* Special Issue on Women and Health (September): 26–28.

Erickson, F. 1984. "School literacy, reasoning, and civility: An anthropologist's perspective." *Review of Educational Research* 54: 525–46.

Erickson, Kai T. 1962. "Notes on the sociology of deviance." *Social Problems* 9: 307–14.

Erickson, Kai T. 1966. *Wayward Puritans: A Study in the Sociology of Deviance.* New York: Wiley.

Erickson, Kai, & Steven B. Vallas, (eds.). 1990. *The Nature of Work: Sociological Perspectives.* New Haven, CT: Yale University Press.

Erickson, Kai. 1976. *Everything in Its Path.* New York: Simon & Schuster.

Erickson, Rebecca J., & Ginna M. Babcock. 1995. "Men and family law: From patriarchy to partnership." *Marriage and Family Review* 21(3–4): 3 1–54.

Erikson, Erik. 1963. *Childhood and Society.* New York: Norton.

Erikson, Robert, & John H. Goldthorpe. 1992. *The Constant Flux: A Study of Class Mobility in Industrial Societies.* Oxford, England: Clarendon Press.

Eron, Leonard D., L. R. Brice, P. Fischer, & R. Mermelstein. 1983. "Age trends in the development of aggression, sex typing, and related television habits." *Developmental Psychology* 19(1): 71–77.

Eschbach, Karl. 1990. "The enduring and vanishing American Indian: Population growth and intermarriage in 1990." *Ethnic and Racial Studies* 18: 89–108.

Eshleman, J. Ross. 1997. *The Family: An Introduction.* Boston: Allyn & Bacon.

Eshleman, J. Ross. 2000. *The Family.* Boston: Allyn & Bacon.

Eshleman, J. Ross. 2000. *The Family: An Introduction.* 9th ed. Boston: Allyn & Bacon.

Esposito, John L. 1992. *The Islamic Threat: Myth or Reality?* New York: Oxford University Press.

Esterberg, Kristin, Phyllis Moen, & Donna Demster McClain. 1994. "Transition to divorce: A life course approach to women's marital duration and dissolution." *Sociological Quarterly* 35(2): 289–307.

Estrada, Kelly, & Peter L. McLaren. 1993. "A dialogue on multiculturalism and democratic culture." *Educational Researcher* 22(3): 27–33.

Etaugh, Claire, & Marsha B. Liss. 1992. "Home, school, and playroom: Training grounds for adult gender roles." *Sex Roles* 26: 129–47.

Etaugh, Claire, & T. Duits. 1990. "Development of gender discrimination: Role of stereotypic and counterstereotypic gender cues." *Sex Roles* 23(5–6): 215–22.

Etzioni, Amitai. 1964. *Modern Organizations.* Upper Saddle River, NJ: Prentice Hall.

Etzioni, Amitai. 1975. *A Comparative Analysis of Complex Organization,* revised ed. New York: Free Press.

Etzioni, Amitai. 1988. *The Moral Dimension.* New York: Free Press.

Etzioni, Amitai. 1993. *The Spirit of Community.* New York: Crown.

Etzioni, Amitai. 1995. "The attack on community: The grooved debate." *Society* 32(5): 12–17.

Etzkowitz, Henry. 1992. "Inventions." In Edgar Borgatta & Marie L. Borgatta, (eds.), *Encyclopedia of Sociology.* New York: Macmillan: 1001–5.

Euthanasia, 1993. "Euthanasia: What is the 'good death'?" In *Dying, Death and Bereavement.* Guilford, CT: Dushkin: 106–108.

Evans, Debra. 1993. *Beauty and the Best.* Colorado Springs, CO: Focus on the Family Publishing.

Evans, Denis E. et al. 1992. "The impact of Alzheimer's disease in the United States population. In Richard M. Suzman, David P. Willis, & Kenneth G. Manton (eds.), *The Oldest Old.* New York: Oxford University Press.

Evans, Peter. 1979. *Dependent Development: The Alliance of Multinational, State and Local Capital in Brazil.* Princeton, NJ: Princeton University Press.

Evans, Sara. 1991. "The first American women." In Linda K. Kerber & Jane Sherron De Hart (eds.), *Women's America: Refocusing the Past.* New York: Oxford University.

Evans-Pritchard, E. E. 1940. *The Nuer.* New York: Oxford University Press.

Exter, Thomas. 1987. "How many Hispanics?" *American Demographics* (May): 36–39.

Ezorsky, G. 1991. *Affirmative Action.* Ithaca, NY: Cornell University Press.

Fagan, Jeffrey, Ellen Slaughter, & Eliot Hartstone. 1987. "Blind justice? The impact of race on the juvenile justice process." *Crime & Delinquency* 33(2): 224–58.

Fagot, Beverly I. 1984. "The child's expectancies of differences in adult male and female interactions." *Sex Roles* 11: 593–600.

Fagot, Beverly I. 1985. "Beyond the reinforcement principle: Another step toward understanding sex role development." *Developmental Psychology* 21: 1097–104.

Fagot, Beverly I. 1994. "Peer relations and the development of competence in boys and girls." In Campbell Leaper (ed.), *Childhood Gender Segregation: Causes and Consequences*. San Francisco: Jossey-Bass.

Fainstein, Norman. 1995. "Black ghettoization and social mobility." In Michael Peter Smith & Joe R. Feagin (eds.), *The Bubbling Cauldron: Race, Ethnicity, and the Urban Crisis*. Minneapolis: University of Minnesota Press: 123–39.

Fairchild, Erika. 1993. *Comparative Criminal Justice Systems*. Belmont, CA: Wadsworth.

Fairman, David. 1996. "The Global Environment Facility: Haunted by the shadow of the future." In Robert O. Keohane & Mary A. Levy (eds.), *Institutions for Environmental Aid: Pitfalls and Promise*. Cambridge, MA: Massachusetts Institute of Technology Press: 55–87.

Faist, Thomas, & Hartmut Haubermann. 1996. "Immigration, social citizenship and housing in Germany." *International Journal of Urban & Regional Geography* (March): 83–98.

Faludi, Susan. 1991. *Blacklash: The Undeclared War Against American Women*. New York: Crown.

Fang, Yuan, Wang Chuanbin, & Song Yuhua. 1992. "Support of the elderly in China." In Hal Kendig, Akiko Hashimoto, & Larry C. Coppard (eds.), *Family Support for the Elderly: The International Experience*. New York: Oxford University Press.

Farber, Bernard. 1964. *Family Organization and Interaction*. San Francisco: Chandler.

Faris, Robert E. & H. W. Dunham. 1939. *Mental Disorders in Urban Areas*. Chicago: University of Chicago Press.

Faris, Robert E. L. 1979. *Chicago Sociology: 1920–1932*. Chicago: University of Chicago Press.

Farley, John E. 1998. *Sociology*, 4th ed. Upper Saddle River, NJ: Prentice Hall.

Farley, John. 1995. *Minority-Majority Relations*. Upper Saddle River, NJ: Prentice Hall.

Farley, Reynolds, & Walter Allen. 1987. *The Color Line and the Quality of Life in America*. New York: Russell Sage Foundation.

Farley, Reynolds. 1988. "After the starting line: Blacks and women in an uphill race." *Demography* 25: 477–95.

Farley, Reynolds. 1991. "Residential segregation of social and economic groups among blacks, 1970–1980." In Christopher Jencks, Farley Reynolds, & Walter Allen. 1987. *The Color Line and the Quality of Life in America*. New York: Russell Sage Foundation.

Farmer, James A., & Yolanda Payne. 1992. *Dropping Out: Issues and Answers*. Springfield, IL: Charles C Thomas.

Farone, Stephen et al. 1993. "Intellectual performance and school failure in children with attention deficit hyperactivity disorder and in their siblings." *Journal of Abnormal Psychology* 102: 616–23.

Fathalla, Mahmoud F. 1994. "Fertility control technology: A woman-centered approach to research." In Gita Sen, Andrienne Germain, & Lincoln C. Chen (eds.), *Population Policies Reconsidered: Health, Empowerment and Human Rights*. Harvard Series on Population and International Health. Boston: Harvard University Press: 223–34.

Fattah, Ezzat A. 1981. "Is capital punishment a unique deterrent?" *Journal of Criminology* 23: 291–311.

Fay, B. 1987. *Critical Social Science: Liberation & Its Limits*. Ithaca, NY: Cornell University Press.

Fay, R.E., C. Turner, A. Klassen, & J.H. Gagnon. 1989. "Prevalence and patterns of same-gender sexual contact among men." *Science* 246: 338–48.

Feagin, Joe R., & Clairece B. Feagin. 1999. *Racial and Ethnic Relations*, 6th ed. Upper Saddle River, NJ: Prentice-Hall.

Feagin, Joe, & Clairece B. Feagin. 1996. *Racial and Ethnic Relations*, 5th ed. Upper Saddle River, NJ: Prentice-Hall.

Featherman, Robert L. & Robert M. Hauser. 1978. *Opportunity and Change*. New York: Academic Press.

Federal Glass Ceiling Commission, 1997. "The glass ceiling." In Dana Dunn (ed.), *Workplace/Women's Place: An Anthology*. Los Angeles: Roxbury: 226–33.

Fei, X. 1985. *A Probe into Sociology*. Tianjin, China: People's Publishing House.

Feingold, A. 1992. "Good-looking people are not what we think." *Psychological Bulletin* 11: 304–41.

Feinman, Clarice. 1994. *Women in the Criminal Justice System*. Westport, CT: Praeger.

Feldberg, Roslyn, & Evelyn N. Glenn. 1982. "Technology and work degradation." In Joan Rothschild, (ed.), *Women, Technology and Innovation*. New York: Pergamon.

Feldman, Robert S. 1995. *Social Psychology*. Boston: Allyn and Bacon.

Feminist Majority Report. 1998. "Gender apartheid worsens in Afghanistan" (9/3). Distributed electronically by the Human Rights Action Network: January 6.

Fendrich, James M., & Kenneth L. Lovoy. 1988. "Back to the future." *American Sociological Review* 53: 780–84.

Fennema, Elizabeth, & Julia Sherman. 1977. "Sex related differences in mathematics achievement: Spatial visualization and affective factors." *American Educational Research Journal* 14: 51–71.

Ferguson, M. 1983. *Forever Feminine: Women's Magazines and the Cult of Femininity*. Exeter, NH: Heinemann Educational Books.

Ferguson, T., & J. S. Dunphy. 1992. *Answers to the Mommy Track*. Far Hills, NJ: New Horizon.

Fermlee, Diana H. 1995. "Causes and consequences of women's employment discontinuity, 1967–1973." *Work and Occupations* 22(2): 167–87.

Ferraro, Gerald. 1992. "The human relations area files: A cultural data bank for international management." In Cheryl R. Lehman & Russell M. Moore (eds.), *Multinational Culture: Social Impacts of a Global Economy*. Westport, CT: Greenwood: 129–39.

Ferraro, Kenneth F. 1994. "Physician resistance to innovations: The case of contract medicine." *Sociological Focus* 26(2): 109–31.

Ferraro, Kenneth F. 1995. *Fear of Crime: Interpreting Victimization Risk*. Albany: SUNY Press.

Ferraro, Kenneth. 1985. "The effect of widowhood on the health status of older persons." *International Journal of Aging and Human Development* 21: 9–25.

Festinger, Leon, Henry W. Riecken, & Stanley Schacter. 1956. *When Prophecy Fails*. Minneapolis: University of Minnesota.

Feuer, Lewis. 1969. *The Conflict of Generations*. New York: Basic.

Feuerbach, Eileen J., & Carol J. Erdwins. 1994. "Women's retirement: The influence of work history." *Journal of Women and Aging* 6(3): 69–85.

Fiechter, Georges-Andre. 1975. *Brazil Since 1964: Modernization Under a Military Regime*. New York: Wiley.

Fiedler, Fred E. 1967. *A Theory of Leadership Effectiveness*. New York: McGraw-Hill.

Fiedler, Fred E. 1981. "Leadership effectiveness." *American Behavioral Scientist* 24: 619–632.

Fielding, Stephen L. 1995. "Changing medical practice and medical malpractice claims." *Social Problems* 42(1): 38–55.

Figart, Deborah M. 1995. Book review of Elaine Sorensen's *Comparable Worth: Is It a Worthy Policy?* In *Gender & Society* 9(6): 779–81.

Figueroa, Janis Barry, & Edwin Melendez. 1993. "The importance of family members in the labor supply of Puerto Rican, black, and white single mothers." *Social Science Quarterly* 74(4): 867–83.

Fijnaut, Cyrille. 1990. "Organized crime: A comparison between the USA and Western Europe." *British Journal of Criminology* 30: 321–40.

Filteau, Jerry. 1992. "Bishops reject proposed pastoral letter on women." *St. Louis Review* 51 (November 20): 1, 10.

Fine, Ben, & Ellen Leopold. 1993. *The World of Consumption*. London: Routledge.

Fine, Gary A. 1987. *With the Boys: Little League Baseball and Preadolescent Culture*. Chicago: University of Chicago Press.

Fine, Michelle, & Adrienne Asch. 1988. *Women with Disabilities: Essays in Psychology, Culture & Politics*. Philadelphia: Temple University Press.

Fingarette, Herbert. 1990. "Alcoholism: The mythical disease." In William Feigelman (ed.), *Readings on Social Problems: Probing the Extent, Causes and Remedies of America's Social Problem*. Fort Worth, TX: Holt, Rinehart and Winston.

Finger, Anne. 1997. "Forbidden fruit." In Estelle Disch (ed.), *Reconstructing Gender: A Multicultural Anthology*. Mountain View, CA: Mayfield: 256–59.

Finger, Mathias. 1992. "New horizons for peace research: The global environment." In Jyrki Kakonen (ed.), *Perspectives on Environmental Conflict and International Relations*. London: Printer: 4–43.

Fingerhut, Lois A. 1993. "Firearm mortality among children, youth and young adults 1–34 years of age, trends and current status: United States, 1985–1990." *Advance Data* 231 (March 23): 1–20.

Finke, Roger, & Rodney Stark. 1992. *The Churching of America, 1776–1990: Winners and Losers in Our Religious Economy*. New Brunswick, NJ: Rutgers University.

Finke, Roger, & Rodney Stark. 1997. "The churching of America." In Thomas E. Dowdy & Patrick H. McNamara, (eds.), *Religion: North American Style*. New Brunswick, NJ: Rutgers University Press: 43–49.

Finkel, Norman J., Stephen T. Maloney, Monique Z. Valbuena, & Jennifer Groscup. 1996. "Recidivism, proportionalism, and individualized punishment." *American Behavioral Scientist* 39(4): 474–87.

Finkelhor, David, et al. 1990. "Sexual abuse in a national survey of adult men and women." *Child Abuse and Neglect* 14(1): 19–28.

Finley, Colleen, & Eric Corty. 1995. "Rape on campus: The prevalence of sexual assault while enrolled in college." *Journal of College Student Development* 34: 113–17.

Firebaugh, Glenn, & Frank D. Beck. 1994. "Does economic growth benefit the masses? Growth, dependence and welfare in the third world." *American Sociological Review* (59/5): 631–53.

Firebaugh, Glenn, & Kenneth E. Davis. 1988. "Trends in antiblack prejudice, 1972–1984." *American Sociological Review* 94/2: 251–72.

Firebaugh, Glenn. 1992. "Growth effects of foreign & domestic investments." *American Journal of Sociology* (98/1): 105–30.

Firey, Walter. 1945. "Sentiment and symbolism as ecological variables." *American Sociological Review* 10: 140–48.

Fischer, Claude S. 1982. *To Dwell Among Friends: Personal Networks in Town & City*. Chicago: University of Chicago Press.

Fischer, Claude S. 1984. *The Urban Experience*. San Diego: Harcourt Brace Jovanovich.

Fischer, David. 1978. *Growing Old in America*. New York: Oxford University Press.

Fischer, Irmgard. 1994. "'Go and suffer oppression' said God's messenger to Hagar." In Elisabeth Schussler Fiorenza & M. Shawn Copeland, (eds.), *Violence Against Women*. London: Stichtin Concillium/SCM Press.

Fishbein, Harold D. 1996. *Peer Prejudice and Discrimination*. Boulder, CO: Westview.

Fisher, Anne B. 1992. "The new debate over the very rich." *Fortune* (June 29): 42–54.

Fisher, Arthur. 1992. "Science + math + F: Crisis in education." *Popular Science* August: 58.

Fisher, Elizabeth. 1979. *Woman's Creation: Sexual Evolution & the Shaping of Society*. New York: Anchor.

Fisher, Jo. 1993. *Out of the Shadows: Women, Resistance and Politics in South America*. London: Latin American Bureau.

Fisher, Julie. 1994. "Is the iron law of oligarchy rusting away in the Third World?" *World Development* (22/2): 55ff.

Fishman, Aryei. 1992. *Judaism and Modernization on the Religious Kibbutz*. Cambridge, UK: Cambridge University Press.

Flaherty, David. 1989. *Protecting Privacy in Surveillance Societies*. Chapel Hill, NC: University of North Carolina Press.

Flannagan, Dorothy, Lynne Baker-Ward, & Loranel Graham. 1995. "Talk about preschool: Patterns of topic discussion and elaboration related to gender and ethnicity." *Sex Roles* 32(1–2): 1–15.

Fleming, Joyce Dudney. 1974. "The state of the apes." *Psychology Today* 7: 31–38.

Florida, Richard, & Martin Kenney. 1991. "Transplanted organizations." *American Sociological Review* 56: 381–98.

Flowers, R. Barri. 1998. *The Prostitution of Women and Girls*. Jefferson, NC: McFarland.

Foner, Nancy. 1984. *Ages in Conflict: A Cross-cultural Perspective on Inequality Between Young and Old*. New York: Columbia University Press.

Fong, Rowena, & David Y. Wu. 1996. "Socialization issues for Chinese American children and families." *Social Work in Education* 18(2): 71–83.

Forden, Carie. 1981. "The influence of sex-role expectations on the perception of touch." *Sex Roles* 7: 889–94.

Forer, L. G. 1984. *Money & Justice*. New York: Norton.

Form, William. 1996. *Segmented Labor, Fractured Politics*. New York: Plenum.

Formisano, Ronald P. 1991. *Boston Against Busing: Race, Class and Ethnicity in the 1960s and 1970s*. Chapel Hill, NC: University of North Carolina Press.

Foster, Carol D., Mark A. Siegel, & Alison Landes (eds.). 1997. *Health: A Concern for Every American*. Wylie, TX: Information Plus.

Foster, John L. 1990. "Bureaucratic rigidity revisited." *Social Science Quarterly* 71: 223–38.

Fosu, Augustin K. 1997. "Occupational Gains of Black Women Since the 1964 Civil Rights Act," *American Economic Review* 87: 311–15.

Foucault, M. 1965. *Madness and Civilization*. NY: Vintage.

Foucault, Michael. 1990. The uses of pleasure, Volume II of Robert Hurley (trans.), *The History of Sexuality*. New York: Vintage.

Fouts, Roger S., D. H. Fouts, & D. Schoenfeld. 1984. "Cultural transmission of a human language in a chimpanzee mother–infant relation." *Sign Language Studies* 42: 1–17.

Fowles, Jib. 1992. *Why Viewers Watch: A Reappraisal of Television's Effects*. Newbury Park, CA: Sage.

Fox, Elaine, & George R. Arquitt. 1985. "The VFW and the 'Iron Law of Oligarchy.'" In James M. Henslin, (ed.), *Down to Earth Sociology*, 4th ed. New York: Free Press: 147–55.

Fox, Lynn H. 1981. *The Problem of Women and Mathematics*. New York: Ford Foundation.

Fox, Mary F. 1995. "Women and higher education: Gender differences in the status of students and scholars." In Jo Freeman (ed.), *Women: A Feminist Perspective*. Mountain View, CA: Mayfield.

Fox, Renee C. 1990. "The medicalization and demedicalization of society." In Peter Conrad & Rochelle Kern (eds.), *The Sociology of Health and Illness: Critical Perspectives*. New York: St. Martin's.

Frank, Andre Gunder. 1966. "The development of underdevelopment." *Monthly Review*, September.

Frank, Andre Gunder. 1967. *Capitalism and Underdevelopment in Latin America*. New York: Monthly Review.

Frank, Andre Gunder. 1980. *Crisis in the Third World*. New York: Holmes & Meier.

Frank, Nancy, & Michael Lynch. 1992. *Corporate Crime, Corporate Violence*. Albany, NY: Harrow & Heston.

Franke, Richard W. 1989. *Kerala: Radical Reform as Development in an Indian State*. San Francisco: Institute for Food and Development Policy.

Frankfort-Nachmias, Chava, & David Nachmias. 1996. *Research Methods in the Social Sciences*. New York: St. Martin's.

Franklin, Clyde W. 1994. "Men's studies, the men's movement, and the study of black masculinities: Further demystification of masculinities in America." In Richard G. Majors & Jacob U. Gordon (eds.), *The American Black Male: His Present Status and His Future*. Chicago: Nelson-Hall.

Franklin, John Hope. 1967. *From Slavery to Freedom: A History of Negro Americans*, 3rd ed. New York: Vintage.

Franzwa, Hellen H. 1974a. "Pronatalism in women's magazine faction." In Ellen Peck & Judith Senderowitz (eds.), *Pronatalism: The Myth of Mom and Apple Pie*. New York: N.Y. Crowell.

Franzwa, Hellen H. 1974b. "Working women in fact and fiction." *Journal of Communication* 24(2): 104–9.

Frayser, Suzanne. 1985. *Varieties of Sexual Experience: An Anthropological Perspective of Human Sexuality*. New Haven, CT: Human Relations Area Files.

Freddi, G., & J. W. Bjorkman. 1989. *Controlling Medical Professionals: The Comparative Politics of Health Governance*. Newbury Park, CA: Sage.

Frederickson, George M. 1981. *White Supremacy: A Comparative Study in American and South African History*. New York: Oxford University Press.

Free, Marvin D., Jr. 1994. "Religiosity, religious conservatism, bonds to school and juvenile delinquency among three categories of drug users." *Deviant Behavior* 15: 151–170.

Freedman, Lynn P., & Stephen L. Isaacs. 1993. "Human rights and reproductive choice." *Studies in Family Planning* (January/February): 18–30.

Freedman, Rita. 1995. "Myth America grows up." In Sheila Ruth, *Issues in Feminism: An Introduction to Women's Studies*. Mountain View, CA: Mayfield.

Freeman, David M. 1974. *Technology and Society*. Chicago: Rand McNally.

Freeman, Jo. 1979. "The origins of the women's liberation movement." *American Journal of Sociology* 78: 792–811.

Freeman, Jo. 1995. "The revolution for women in law and public policy." In Jo Freeman (ed.), *Women: A Feminist Perspective*. Mountain View, CA: Mayfield: 365–404.

Freeman, Richard. 1994. *Working Under Different Rules*. New York: Russell Sage.

Freidman, L. 1989. "Mathematics and the gender gap: A metaanalysis of recent studies on sex differences in mathematical tasks." *Review of Educational Research* 59: 185–213.

Freire, Paulo & Donaldo Macedo. 1995. "A dialogue: culture, language, and race." *Harvard Educational Review* 65(3): 377–402.

Freire, Paulo. 1970. *Pedagogy of the Oppressed*. New York: Seabury.

Freivogel, William H. 1993. "Acceptable behavior: Sexual harassment message is swift and clear—Don't do it." *St. Louis Post-Dispatch* (November 14): 1B,7B.

Freize, I. H., J. E. Olson, & J. Russell. 1991. "Attractiveness and income for men and women in management." *Applied Social Psychology* 21: 1039–57.

Frenk, J., J. L. Bobadilla, & C. Stern. 1991. "Elements of the theory of the health transition." *Health Transition Review* 1(1): 21–38.

Freud, Sigmund. 1961. *Civilization and Its Discontents*. New York: W. W. Norton.

Freud, Sigmund. 1962. *Three Contributions to the Theory of Sex*. New York: E. P. Dutton.

Freud, Sigmund. 1963. "Introductory lectures on psychoanalysis." In J. Strachley (ed. and trans.), *The Standard Edition of the Complete Psychological Works of Sigmund Freud*. London: Hogarth.

Freudenberg, William R. 1986. "The density of acquaintanceship: An overlooked variable in community research?" *American Journal of Sociology* 92: 27–63.

Freudenhein, M. 1993. "Many patients unhappy with H.M.O.'s." *New York Time*, August 18: A14.

Freund, Peter E. S., & Meredith B. McGuire. 1991. *Health, Illness and the Social Body: A Critical Sociology*. Upper Saddle River, NJ: Prentice Hall.

Freund, Peter E.S. & Meredith B. McGuire. 1999. *Health, Illness and the Social Body: A Critical Sociology*. Englewood Cliffs, NJ: Prentice Hall.

Frey, R. Scott, Thomas Dietz, & Linda Kalof. 1992. "Characteristics of successful American protest groups." *American Journal of Sociology* 98: 368–87.

Frey, William H., & Jonathan Tilove. 1995. "Immigrants in, native whites out." *New York Times Magazine* (August 20): 44–45.

Friedan, Betty. 1963. *The Feminine Mystique*. New York: W. W. Norton.

Friedan, Betty. 1993. *The Fountain of Age*. New York: Simon & Schuster.

Friedland, Roger, & A. F. Robertson, (eds.). 1990. *Beyond the Marketplace*. New York: Aldine de Gruyter.

Friedman, Isaac A. 1995. "Student behavior patterns contributing to teacher burnout." *Journal of Educational Research* 88(5): 281–89.

Friedman, Lawrence M. & Robert V. Percival. 1981. *The Roots of Justice*. Chapel Hill: University of No. Carolina Press.

Friedrichs, David. 1996. *Trusted Criminals*. Belmont, CA: Wadsworth.

Friedson, Eliot. 1986. *Professional Powers*. Chicago: University of Chicago Press.

Frith, Simon, & Howard Horne. 1987. *Art into Pop*. New York: Methuen.

Fryer, David, & Stephen McKenna. 1987. "The laying off of hands—unemployment and the experience of time." In Stephen Fineman, (ed.), *Unemployment: Personal & Social Consequences*. London: Tavistock.

Fryxell, Gerald E., & Linda D. Lerner. 1989. "Contrasting corporate profiles: Women and minority representation in top management positions." *Journal of Business Ethics* 8: 341–52.

Fuchs, Victor R. 1988. *Women's Quest for Economic Equality*. Cambridge, MA: Harvard University Press.

Fudge, Colin. 1996. "Metropolis 2000: A forum on urban issues." SAIS Review 16: 170–73.

Fukuyama, Francis. 1993. "The end of history?" *National Interest* (summer): 3–18.

Furnham, Adrian, & Nadine Bitar. 1993. "The stereotyped portrayal of men and women in British television advertisements." *Sex Roles* 29(3–4): 297–310.

Furstenberg, Frank F. Jr., & Andrew J. Cherlin. 1991. *Divided Families*. Cambridge, MA: Harvard University.

Fussell, Paul. 1992. *Class: A Guide Through the American Status System*. New York: Touchstone.

Gabler, Neal. 1988. *An Empire of Their Own: How the Jews Invented Hollywood*. New York: Crown.

Gabriel, Trip. 1996. "Computers help unite campuses, but also drive some students apart." *New York Times* (November 11).

Gadberry, James H., & Richard A. Dodder. 1993. "Educational homogamy in interracial marriage: An update." *Journal of Social Behavior and Personality* 8(6)(special issue): 155–63.

Gaes, Gerald G., & William J. McGuire. 1985. "Prison violence: The contribution of crowding versus other determinants of prison assault rates." *Journal of Research In Crime and Delinquency* 22: 41–65.

Gagnon, John H. 1990. The explicit and implicit of the scripting perspective in sex research." *Annual Review of Sex Research* 1: 1–43.

Gagnon, John H., & William Simon. 1973. *Sexual Conduct: The Social Sources of Human Sexuality*. Chicago: Aldine.

Gaines, Donna. 1991. *Teenage Wasteland: Suburbia's Dead End Kids*. New York: Pantheon.

Galanter, Marc. 1974. "Why the 'haves' come out ahead: Speculations on the limits of legal change." *Law and Society Review* 9: 95–160.

Galenson, Walter. 1996. *The American Labor Movement, 1955–1995*. Westport, CT: Greenwood.

Gallagher, Bernard J. 1987. *The Sociology of Mental Illness*. Englewood Cliffs, NJ: Prentice-Hall.

Gallup Report. 1987. "Religion in America." No. 259(April): 24–27.

Gallup, George H., Jr. 1990. *Gallup Poll Monthly*. September.

Gallup, George H., Jr. 1993. *Religion in America, 1992–93*. Princeton, NJ: Princeton Religion Research Center.

Gallup, George H., Jr., & Timothy K. Jones. 2000. *The Next American Spirituality: Finding God in the Twenty-First Century*. Colorado Springs, CO: Cook Communications Ministries.

Gallup, George, & Jim Castelli. 1987. *The American Catholic People: Their Beliefs, Practices, and Values*. Garden City, NY: Doubleday.

Gallup, George, & Jim Castelli. 1989. *The People's Religion: American Faith in the 90s*. New York: Macmillan.

Gallup, George. 1997. *Homosexuality*. Survey from the Gallup Organization. Roper Center for Public Opinion Research. Storrs, CT: University of Connecticut.

Gallup, Gordon G. 1977. "Self-recognition in primates: A comparative approach to the bidirectional properties of consciousness." *American Psychologist* 32: 328–38.

Galster, George C. 1990. "Racial discrimination in housing markets during the 1980s." *Journal of Planning Education and Research* 9: 165–75.

Gamson, Joshua. 1991. "Silence, death & the invisible enemy: AIDS activism & social movement 'Newness.'" In Michael Burawoy et al., (eds.), *Ethnography Unbound*. Berkeley, CA: University of California Press.

Gamson, William A. 1990. *The Strategy of Social Protest*, 2nd ed. Belmont, CA: Wadsworth.

Gamson, William A. 1991. "Commitment and agency in social movements." *Sociological Forum* 6: 27–50.

Gamson, William A. 1992. *Talking Politics*. Cambridge, England: Cambridge University Press.

Gamson, William A., & Gadi Wolfsfeld. 1993. "Movements and media as interacting systems." *The Annals* 528: 114–25.

Gandy, O. H., & P. W. Matabane. 1989. "Television and social perceptions among African-Americans and Hispanics." In M. K. Asante & W. B. Gudykunst (eds.), *Handbook of International and Intercultural Communication*. Newbury Park, CA: Sage.

Ganong, Lawrence H., & Marilyn Coleman. 1992. "Gender differences in self and future partner expectations." *Journal of Family Issues* 13: 55–64.

Ganong, Lawrence H., & Marilyn Coleman. 1994. *Remarried Family Relationships* Thousand Oaks, CA: Sage.

Gans, Herbert J. 1962. *The Urban Villagers*. New York: Free Press.

Gans, Herbert J. 1967. *The Levittowners*. New York: Random House.

Gans, Herbert J. 1991. *People, Plans, and Policies: Essays on Poverty, Racism, and other National Urban Problems*. New York: Columbia University Press.

Gans, Herbert J., (ed.). 1990. *Sociology In America*. Newbury Park, CA: Sage.

Garbarino, Merwyn S., & Robert F. Sasso. 1994. *Native American Heritage*, 3rd ed. Prospect Heights, IL: Waveland.

Garber, M. 1995. *Vice Versa*. New York: Simon & Schuster.

Garcia, A. M. 1991. "The development of Chicana feminist discourse." In Judith Lorber & S. A. Farrell (eds.), *The Social Construction of Gender Gap*. Newbury Park, CA: Sage.

Garcia, Alejandro. 1988. "An examination of the economic support systems of elderly Hispanic." In Marta Sotomayer & Herman Curiel (eds.), *Hispanic Elderly: A Cultural Signature*. Edinburg, TX: Pan American University Press.

Gardner, Beatrix T., & Allen R. Gardner. 1969. "Teaching sign language to a chimpanzee." *Science* 16: 664–72.

Gardner, Beatrix T., & Allen R. Gardner. 1985. "Signs of intelligence in cross-fostered chimpanzees." *Philosophical Transactions of the Royal Society of London* B308: 150–76.

Gardner, Marilyn. 1995. "Of super dads, and absent ones." In Kathleen R. Gilbert (ed.), *Marriage and the Family 95/96* (Annual Editions). Guilford, CT: Dushkin/Brown & Benchmark.

Gardner, Robert W., Bryant Robey, & Peter C. Smith. 1985. "Asian Americans: Growth, change and diversity." *Population Bulletin* 40(4): 1–43. Washington, DC: Population Reference Bureau.

Garfinkel, Harold. 1956. "Conditions of successful degradation ceremonies." *American Journal of Sociology* (61/2): 420–24.

Garfinkel, Harold. 1967. *Studies in Ethnomethology*. Englewood Cliffs, NJ: Prentice Hall.

Garfinkel, Harold. 1997. "A conception of and experiments with 'trust' as a condition of concerted stable actions." In Jodi O'Brien & Peter Kollock (eds.), *The Production of Reality: Essays and Readings in Social Interaction*. Thousand Oaks, CA: Pine Forge: 396–407.

Garfinkel, Perry. 1985. *In a Man's World: Father, Son, Brother, Friend and Other Roles Men Play*. New York: New American Library.

Garner, Roberta Ash. 1996. *Contemporary Movements & Ideologies*. New York: McGraw-Hill.

Garrity, J. 1989. "A clash of cultures on the Hopi reservation." *Sports Illustrated* (71/21): 10–17.

Garry, Patrick. 1993. *An American Paradox: Censorship in a Nation of Free Speech*. Westport, CT: Praeger.

Gatchel, Robert J., Andrew Baum, & David S. Krantz. 1989. *An Introduction to Health Psychology*. New York: Random House.

Gates, David. 1990. "The rap attitude." *Newsweek* (March 19): 56–63.

Gavora, Jessica. 1995. "Winners and losers in gender equity game." *St. Louis Post-Dispatch*, (December 10): 3B.

Geerkin, Michael, & Walter Gove. 1983. *At Home and at Work: The Family's Allocation of Labor*. Beverly Hills, CA: Sage.

GEF. 1995. Global Environmental Facility. *Bulletin and Quarterly Operational Summary*. No. 14.

Gegax, T. Trent, & Lynette Clemetson. 1998. The abortion wars come home." *Newsweek* (November 9): 34–35.

Gehlmann, Shella C. 1992. "Individual differences in employee stress as related to office environment and individual personality factors." In James Campbell Quick, Lawrence R. Murphy & Joseph J. Hurrell, Jr. (eds.), *Stress and Well-Being at Work: Assessments and Interventions for Occupational Mental Health*. Washington, DC: American Psychological Association: 225–34.

Gehry, Frank B., J. Hateley, & Susan Rose. 1994. "The politics of empowerment: A paradigm shift in thought and action for feminists." *American Behavioral Scientist* 37(8): 1122–37.

Geis, Florence L. 1993. "Self-fulfilling prophecies: A social psychological view of gender." In Anne E. Beall & Robert J. Sternberg (eds.), *The Psychology of Gender*. New York: Guilford.

Gelles, Richard J. 1995. "Profiling violent families." In Mark Robert Rank & Edward L. Kain (eds.), *Diversity and Change in Families: Patterns, Prospects, and Policies*. Upper Saddle River, NJ: Prentice Hall.

Gelles, Richard J. 1995a. *Contemporary Families: A Sociological View*. Thousand Oaks, CA: Sage.

Gelles, Richard J., & J.W. Harop. 1991. "The risk of abusive valance among children with nongenetic caretakers." *Family Relations* . 40: 78–83.

Gelles, Richard J., & Murray A. Straus. 1987. "Is violence toward children increasing? A comparison of 1975–1985 national survey rates . *Journal of Interpersonal Violence* 2: 212–22.

Gelles, Richard J., & Murray A. Straus. 1995. "Profiling violent families." In Mark Robert Rank & Edward L. Kain (eds.), *Diversity & Change in Families: Patterns, Prospects, and Policies*. Englewood Cliffs, NJ: Prentice Hall.

Gender Equality in Norway. 1994. *The National Report to the Fourth UN Conference on Women in Beijing, 1995*. Oslo: Royal Ministry of Foreign Affairs.

Genovese, Eugene G. 1974. *Roll, Jordan, Roll! The World the Slaves Made*. New York: Vintage.

George, L. K., & L. P. Gwyther. 1986. "Caregiver well-being: A multidimensional examination of family caregivers of demented adults." *Gerontologist* 26(3): 253–59.

Geraghty, Christine. 1993. "Women and soap opera." In Stevi Jackson et al. (eds.), *Women's Studies Essential Readings*. New York: New York University Press.

Gerami, Shahin. 1996. *Women and Fundamentalism: Islam and Christianity*. New York: Garland Publishing, Inc.

Gerbner, George, L. Cross, Nancy Signorielli, & M. Morgan. 1980. "Aging with television: Images of television drama and conceptions of social reality." *Journal of Communication* 30(1): 37–47.

Gerbner, George, L. Cross, M. Morgan, & N. Signorielli. 1986. "Living with television: The dynamics of the cultivation process." In J. Bryant & D. Zillmann, (eds.), *Perspectives on Media Effects*. Hillsdale, NJ: Lawrence Erlbaum.

Gerbner, George. 1990. *Violence Profile*. Philadelphia: Annenberg School of Communications.

Gerbner, George. 1993a. "Violence on television." *Challenging Media Images of Women* 5(2): 1, 4, 7–9.

Gerbner, George. 1993b. "Learning productive aging as a social role: The lessons of television." In Scott A. Bass, Francis G. Caro, & Yung-Ping Chen (eds.), *Achieving a Productive Aging Society*. Westport, CT: Auburn House.

Gerbner, George. 1994. "The politics of media violence: Some reflections." In C. Hamelink & O. Linne (eds.), *Mass Communication Research: On Problems and Policies*. Norwood, NJ: Ablex.

Gerlach, Michael. 1992. *Alliance Capitalism*. Berkeley: University of California Press.

Germani, Gino. 1981. *The Sociology of Modernization: Studies on its Historical and Theoretical Aspects with Special Regard to the Latin American Case*. New Brunswick, NJ: Transaction Books.

Gersh, Jeff. 1996. "Subdivide and conquer: Concrete, condos, and the second conquest of the American West." *Amicus Journal* 18: 14–20.

Gerth, Hans H., & C. Wright Mills, (eds.). 1958. *From Max Weber: Essays In Sociology*. New York: Galaxy.

Gesler, Wilbert M. 1991. *The Cultural Geography of Health Care*. Pittsburgh, PA: University of Pittsburgh Press.

Gest, Ted, & Patricia M. Schersel. 1985. "Stealing $200 billion 'the respectable way.' " *US News and World Report* (May 20): 83–85.

Gevitz, Norman. 1998. "Osteopathic medicine: From deviance to difference." In Norman Gevitz (ed.), *Other Healers: Unorthodox Medicine in America*. Baltimore, MD: Johns Hopkins University.

Geyer, Felix, & Walter R. Heinz, (eds.). 1992. *Alienation, Society and the Individual*. New Brunswick, NJ: Transaction.

Giacalone, Robert A., & Jon W. Beard. 1994. "Impression management, diversity, and international management." *American Behavioral Scientist* 37(5): 621–36.

Giago, Tom. 1998. "Indian-named mascots: An assault on self-esteem." In Susan Lobo and Steve Talbot, (eds.), *Native American Voices: A Reader*. New York: Longman: 204–6.

Gibbs, Jack P. 1975. *Crime, Punishment and Deterrence*. New York: Elsevier.

Gibbs, Jack P. 1987. "An incorrigible positivist." *Criminology* 12: 2–3.

Gibbs, Jack P. 1989. *Control: Sociology's Central Notion*. Urbana: University of Illinois Press.

Gibbs, Jack. 1966. "Conceptions of deviant behavior: The old and the new," *Pacific Sociological Review* 9: 11–13.

Gibbs, Nancy, John Cloud, Amy Dickenson, Adam Cohen, Lance Morrow, & Richard Corliss, 1999. "Special report: The Littleton massacre." *Time* May 3: 20–50.

Gibson, Margaret A., & John V. Ogbu. 1991. *Minority Status and Schooling*. New York: Garland.

Gibson, Mary Jo. 1992. "Public health and social policy." In Hal Kendig, Akiko Hashimoto, & Larry C. Coppard (eds.), *Family Support for the Elderly: The International Experience*. New York: Oxford University Press.

Giddens, Anthony. 1990. *The Consequences of Modernity*. Cambridge, England: Polity Press.

Giele, Janet Zollinger. 1988. "Changing sex roles and changing families." In J. Gipson Wells (ed.), *Current Issues in Marriage and the Family*. New York: Macmillan.

Gigliotti, Richard J., & Heather K. Huff. 1995. "Role related conflicts, strains and stresses of older-adult college students." *Sociological Focus* (28/3): 329–342.

Gilbert, Alan. 1986. "Self-help housing and state intervention: Illustrated reflections on the petty commodity production debate." In David Drakakis-Smith (ed.), *Urbanisation in the Developing World*. London: Croom Helm: 175–94.

Gilbert, Alan. 1994. Third World cities: Poverty, employment, gender roles and the environment during a time of restructuring." *Urban Studies* 31: 605–33.

Gilbert, Dennis, & Joseph A. Kahl. 1993. *The American Class Structure: A New Synthesis*, 4th ed. Belmont, CA: Wadsworth.

Gilford, Rosalie. 1984. "Contrasts in marital satisfaction throughout old age: An exchange theory analysis." *Journal of Gerontology* 39(3): 325–33.

Gill, Stephen, & David Law. 1988. *Global Political Economy: Perspectives, Problems & Policies*. Baltimore: Johns Hopkins University Press.

Gilligan, Carol A. 1982. *In a Different Voice*. Cambridge, MA: Harvard University.

Gimbutas, Marija. 1989. *The Language of the Goddess: Unearthing the Hidden Symbols of Western Civilization*. San Francisco: Harper & Row.

Gimbutas, Marija. 1991 *The Civilization of the Goddess: The World of Old Europe*. San Francisco: Harper & Row.

Gimenez, Martha E. 1994. "The feminization of poverty: Myth or reality." In Elizabeth Fee & Nancy Krieger (eds.), *Women's Health, Politics, and Power: Essays on Sex/Gender, Medicine, and Public Health*. Amityville, NY: Baywood.

Gitlin, Todd. 1980. *The Whole World Is Watching*. Berkeley, CA: University of California Press.

Gitlin, Todd. 1990. "Blips, bites, and savvy talk." In Nicholas Mills, (ed.), *Culture in an Age of Money: The Legacy of the 1980s in America*. Chicago: Ivan R. Dee.

Glascock, Anthony P., & S. Feinman. 1986. "Toward a comparative framework: Propositions concerning the treatment of the aged in non-industrial societies." In C. L. Fry & Jennie Keith (eds.), *New Methods for Old Age Research*. South Hadley, MA: Bergin and Garvey.

Glaser, Nathan. 1976. *Affirmative Discrimination*. New York: Basic.

Glaser, William A. 1993. "University health insurance that really works: Foreign lessons for the United States." *Journal of Health Politics, Policy and Law* 18(3): 695–722.

Glaser, William A. 1994. "Doctors and public authority: The trend toward collaboration." *Journal of Health Politics, Policy and Law* 19(4): 705–27.

Glasgow, D. 1981. *The Black Underclass*. New York: Vintage.

Glass, Jennifer, & Tetsushi Fujimoto. 1994. "Housework, paid work and depression among husbands and wives." *Journal of Health and Social Behavior* 35(2): 179–191.

Glazer, Ilsa M. 1995. "A cloak of many colors: Jewish feminism and feminist Jews." In Jo Freeman (ed.), *Woman: A Feminist Perspective*. Mountain View, CA: Mayfield: 632–40.

Glazer, Nathan. 1997. *We Are All Multiculturalists Now*. Cambridge, MA: Harvard.

Glenn, Evelyn N., & Roslyn L. Feldberg. 1995. "Clerical work: The female occupation." In Jo Freeman (ed.), *Women: A Feminist Perspective*. Mountain View, CA: Mayfield: 262–86.

Glenn, Norval D. 1997. "A reconsideration of the effect of no-fault divorce on divorce rates." *Journal of Marriage and the Family* 59(4): 1023–30.

Glenn, Norval D., & Charles N. Weaver. 1988. "The changing relationship of marital status to reported happiness." *Journal of Marriage and the Family* 50 (May): 317–24.

Glenn, Norval D., & Michael Supancic. 1984. "The social and demographic correlates of divorce and separation in the United States: An update and reconsideration." *Journal of Marriage and the Family* 46: 563–75.

Global Environmental Facility. 1995. *Bulletin and Quarterly Operational Summary*. No. 14.

Glock, Charles Y., & Rodney Stark. 1965. *Religion and Society in Tension*. Chicago: Rand McNally.

Glouchevitch, Philip. 1992. *Juggernaut: The German Way of Business*. New York: Simon & Schuster.

Glover, David. 1985. "The sociology of the mass media." In Michael Haralambos, ed., *Sociology: New Directions*. Lancashire, UK: Causeway Press: 371–442.

Goffman, Erving. 1959. *The Presentation of Self in Everyday Life*. Garden City, NY: Doubleday (Anchor).

Goffman, Erving. 1959b. "The moral career of the mental patient." *Psychiatry* (22): 125–31.

Goffman, Erving. 1961a. *Asylums: Essays on the Social Situation of Mental Patients and Other Inmates*. Garden City, NY: Anchor Books.

Goffman, Erving. 1961b. *Encounters*. Indianapolis: Bobbs-Merrill.

Goffman, Erving. 1963a. *Behavior in Public Places*. New York: Free Press.

Goffman, Erving. 1963b. *Stigma: Notes on the Management of Spoiled Identity*. Upper Saddle River, NJ: Prentice Hall.

Goffman, Erving. 1967. *Interaction Ritual*. Garden City, NY: Doubleday.

Goffman, Erving. 1974. *Frame Analysis*. New York: Harper & Row.

Golant, Stephen. 1996. "Problems in conventional dwellings and neighborhoods." In Jill Quadagno & Debra Street (eds.), *Aging for the Twenty-First Century: Readings in Social Gerontology*. New York: St. Martin's: 207–35.

Gold, Marsha. 1991. "HMOs and managed care." Health Affairs 10: 189–206.

Golden, S. 1992. *The Women Outside*. Berkeley: University of California Press.

Golding, Peter, & Graham Murdock. 1991. "Culture, communications, and political economy." In James Curran & Michael Gurevitch (eds.), *Mass Media and Society*. London: Edward Arnold: 15–32.

Goldman, Ari L. 1993. "Religious notes." *The New York Times* (April 24): 11.

Goldman, H.H., R.G. Frank & T.G. McGuire. 1994. "Mental Health Care," in E. Ginzberg, ed., *Critical Issues In US Health Care Reform*. Boulder, CO: Westview.

Goldman, N., C. Westoff, & C. Hammerslough. 1984. "Demography of the marriage market in the United States." *Population Index* 50 (spring): 5–25.

Goldman, P., & D. R. Van Houten. 1977. "Managerial strategies and the worker: A marxist analysis of bureaucracy." *Sociological Quarterly* 18: 108–25.

Goldman, Steven L., Roger N. Nagel, & Kenneth Preiss. 1995. *Agile Competitors and Virtual Organizations: Strategies for Enriching the Customer*. New York: Van Nostrand Reinhold.

Goldsborough, Reid. 2000. "Bridging the digital divide." *Tech Directions* 59(10): 13.

Goldstein, Michael S., Dennis Jaffe, Carol Sutherland, & Josie Wilson. 1987. "Holistic physicians: Implications for the study of the medical profession." *Journal of Health and Social Behavior* 28(2): 103–19.

Goldstein, Stanley E., & Arthur Blank. 1988. "The elderly: Abuse or abusers?" In Benjamin Schlesinger & Rachel Schlesinger (eds.), *Abuse of the Elderly: Issues and Annotated Bibliography*. Toronto: University of Toronto Press.

Gonzalez, Norma. 1995. "Processual approaches to multicultural education." *Journal of Applied Behavioral Science* 31(2): 233–44.

Goodall, Richard. 1995. *The Comfort of Sin: Prostitutes and Prostitution in the 1990s*. Kent, UK: Renaissance Books.

Goode, Erich. 1989. *Drugs in American Society*. NY: McGraw-Hill.

Goode, Erich. 1992. *Collective Behavior*. Fort Worth, TX: Harcourt Brace Jovanovich.

Goode, Erich. 1997. *Deviant Behavior*, 5th ed. Upper Saddle River, NJ: Prentice Hall.

Goode, William J. 1960. "A theory of role strain." *American Sociological Review* 25: 483–496.

Goode, William J. 1963. *World Revolution and Family Patterns*. New York: Free Press.

Goode, William J. 1982. *The Family*. Upper Saddle River, NJ: Prentice Hall.

Goode, William J. 1984. "Idealization of the recent past: The United States." In Arlene S. Skolnick & Jerome H. Skolnick (eds.), *Family in Transition*. Boston: Little, Brown.

Goode, William J. 1993. *World Changes in Divorce Patterns*. New Haven, CT: Yale University.

Goodgame, Dan. 1993. "Welfare for the well-off." *Time* 141 (February 22): 36–38.

Goodman, Ellen. 1994. "Women's tales of torture ..." *Washington Post* (March 19).

Goodrich, Norma Lorre. 1991. *Priestesses*. New York: HarperCollins.

Goodstein, Laurie. 1996. "U.S. panel will monitor religious rights overseas." *Washington Post* (November 13).

Goodstein, Laurie. 1998. "Religious right, frustrated, trying new tactic on G.O.P." *The New York Times* (March 23): A1, A12.

Goodwin, Beverly J. 1996. "The impact of popular culture on images of African American women." In Joan C. Chrisler, Carla Golden, & Patricia D. Rozee (eds.), *Lectures on the Psychology of Women*. New York: McGraw-Hill.

Gordon, David. 1973. "Capitalism, class and crime in America." *Crime & Delinquency* 19: 163–86.

Gordon, Edmund W., & Constance Yowell. 1994. "Cultural dissonance as a risk factor in the development of students." In Robert J. Rossi (ed.), *Schools and Students at Risk: Context and Framework for Positive Change*. New York: Teacher's College Press, Columbia University: 51–69.

Gordon, Milton M. 1964. *Assimilation in American Life*. New York: Oxford University Press.

Gordon, Milton M. 1978. *Human Nature, Class and Ethnicity*. New York: Oxford University Press.

Gore, M. S. 1992. "Family support to elderly people: The Indian situation." In Hal Kendig, Akiko Hashimoto, & Larry C. Coppard (eds.), *Family Support for the Elderly: The International Experience*. New York: Oxford University Press.

Gorey, K.M., & D.R. Leslie. 1997. "The prevalence of child sexual abuse: Integrative review for potential response and measurement biases." *Child Abuse and Neglect* 21: 391–98.

Gortmaker, S.L., A. Must, J.M. Perrin, A.M. Sobel, & W.H. Dietz. 1993. "Social and economic consequences of overweight in adolescence and young adulthood," *New England Journal of Medicine* 329: 1008–1012.

Gottdiener, Mark. 1999. *The New Urban Sociology*. New York: McGraw-Hill.

Gottfredson, Michael, & Don Gottfredson. 1988. *Decision Making in Criminal Justice: Toward the Rational Exercise of Discretion*, 2nd. ed. New York: Plenum.

Gottfredson, Michael, & Travis Hirschi. 1990. *A General Theory of Crime*. Stanford, CA: Stanford University Press.

Gould, Jay M., & Ernest J. Sternglass. 1994. "Nuclear fallout, low birthweight and immune deficiency." *International Journal of Health Services* 24(2): 311–35.

Goulet, Denis. 1989. "Participation in development: New avenues." *World Development* 17(2): 165–78.

Gourevitch, Phillip. 1995. "After the genocide." *New Yorker* (Dec 18): 78–94.

Gove, Walter R. & Jeanette Tudor. 1973. "Adult sex roles and mental illness," *American Journal of Sociology* 78: 812–835.

Gove, Walter R. 1980. *The Labeling of Deviance*, 2nd ed. Beverly Hills, CA: Sage.

Gove, Walter R., Carolyn Briggs Style, & Michael Highes. 1990. "The effect of marriage on the well-being of adults." *Journal of Family Issues* 11: 4–35.

Gowdy, John M. 1994. "Progress and environmental sustainability." *Environmental Ethics* 16(1): 41–55.

Grady, Denise. 1998. "To aid doctors, A.M.A. Journal devotes entire issue to alternative medicine." *New York Times* November 11: A23.

Graff, H. 1987. *The Legacies of Literacy: Continuities and Contradictions in Western Culture and Society*. Bloomington, IN: Indiana University.

Graham, Patricia Albjerg. 1995. "Assimilation, adjustment, and access: An antiquarian view of American education." In Diane Ravitch & Maris A. Vinovskis (eds.), *Learning from the Past: What History Teaches Us about School Reform*. Baltimore, MD: Johns Hopkins University: 4–24.

Gramsci, A. 1971. *Selections From Prison Notebooks*. London: Routledge & Kegan Paul.

Gramsci, Antonio. 1959. *The Modern Prince and Other Writings*. New York: International Publishers.

Granovetter, Mark. 1973. "The strength of weak ties." *American Journal of Sociology* 78: 1360–1380.

Granovetter, Mark. 1995. *Getting a Job: A Study of Contacts and Careers*, 2nd ed. Chicago: University of Chicago Press.

Grant, Linda. 1993. *Sexing the Millennium: A Political History of the Sexual Revolution*. London: Harper Collins.

Grasmick, Harold, Charles Tittle, Robert Bursik, & Bruce Arneklev. 1993. "Testing the core empirical indications of Gottfredson and Hirschi's general theory of crime." *Journal of Research in Crime and Delinquency* (30): 5–29.

Gratton, Brian, & Carole Haber. 1996. Three phases in the history of American grandparenting: Authority, burden, and companion." *Generations* (spring): 7–12.

Gray, Alastair. 1993. *World Health and Disease*. Buckingham, UK: Open University Press.

Gray, Francine du Plessix. 1990. *Soviet Women: Walking the Tightrope*. New York: Doubleday.

Gray, Susan. 1990. "Exposure to pornography and aggression toward women: The case of the angry male." In William Feigelman (ed.), *Readings on Social Problems: Probing the Extent, Causes, and Remedies of America's Social Problems*. Fort Worth, TX: Holt, Rinehart & Winston.

Gray, Wayne, & John Scholz. 1993. "Does regulatory enforcement work?" *Law & Society Review* 27: 1771–191.

Greeley, Andrew M. 1972. *The Denominational Society: A Sociological Approach to Religion in America*. Glenview, IL: Scott, Foresman.

Greeley, Andrew M. 1989. *Religious Change in America*. Cambridge, MA: Harvard University Press.

Greeley, Andrew M. 1997. "Coleman revisited: Religious structures as a source of social capital." *American Behavioral Scientist* 40: 587–94.

Green Book. 1994. *Green Book Background Material and Data on Programs within the Jurisdiction of the Committee on Ways and Means*. Washington, DC: Government Printing Office.

Green, R. L. (ed.). 1985. *Metropolitan Desegregation*. New York: Plenum.

Greenberg, Bradley S., Robert Abelman, & Kimberley Neuendorf. 1981. "Sex on the soap operas: Afternoon delight." *Journal of Communication* 31: 83–89.

Greenberg, David F., & Ronald C. Kessler. 1982. "The effects of arrests on crime: A multivariate panel analysis." *Social Forces* 60: 771–90.

Greenberg, David, (ed.). 1981. *Crime and Capitalism*. Palo Alto, CA: Mayfield.

Greenberg, Edward S., & Benjamin I. Page. 1996. *The Struggle for Democracy*, 2nd ed. New York: Addison-Wesley.

Greenberg, Vivian E. 1994. *Children of a Certain Age: Adults and Their Aging Parents*. New York: Lexington Books.

Greene, B. 1994. "Ethnic-minority lesbians and gay men: Mental health and treatment issues." *Journal of Consulting and Clinical Psychology* 62: 243–51.

Greenfield, Liah. 1992. *Nationalism: Five Roads to Modernity*. Cambridge, MA: Harvard University Press.

Greenhouse, Linda. 1995. "Justices, 5 to 4, cast doubts on U.S. programs that give preferences based on race." *The New York Times* (June 13): A1+.

Greenspan, Allison. 1994. "After the demographic transition: Policy responses to low fertility in four Asian countries." *Asia-Pacific Population and Policy*. East-West Center Program on Population 30 (September).

Greenstein, R. 1996. *Raising Families with a Full-Time Worker Out of Poverty*. Washington: Center on Budget and Policy Priorities.

Greenstein, Robert, & Scott Barancik. 1990. *Drifting Apart: New Findings on Growing Income Disparities Between the Rich, the Poor, and the Middle Class*. Washington, DC: Center on Budget and Policy Priorities.

Greenstone, David. 1968. *Labor in American Politics*. Chicago: University of Chicago Press.

Greenwood, Ernest. 1962. "Attributes of a profession." In *Man, Work and Society: A Reader in the Sociology of Occupations*, Sigmund Nosow, & William H. Form (eds.). New York: Basic Books: 206–18.

Gregg, G. 1985. "Women entrepreneurs: The second generation." *Across The Board* 22: 10–18.

Gregory, Ann. 1990. "Are women different and why are women thought to be different? Theoretical and methodological perspectives." *Journal of Business Ethics* 9: 257–66.

Greif, Geoffrey L., Alfred Demaris, & Jane C. Hood. 1993. "Balancing work and single fatherhood." In Jane C. Hood (ed.), *Men, Work, and Family*. Newbury Park, CA: Sage.

Greif, Geoffrey, L. 1985a. "Children and housework in the single father family." *Family Relations* 34: 353–57.

Greif, Geoffrey, L. 1985b. *Single Fathers*. Lexington, MA: D.C. Heath.

Grella, Christine E. 1990. "Irreconcilable differences: Women defining class after divorce and downward mobility." *Gender & Society* 4(1): 41–55.

Grenier, Guillermo. 1988. *Inhuman Relations: Quality Circles and Anti-Unionism in American Industry*. Philadelphia: Temple University Press.

Grieshaber, Larry. 1993. "Managing the emerging organization." *Health Management Quarterly* 15(4): 25–28.

Grimes, Michael D. 1991. *Class in 20th Century American Sociology*. New York: Praeger.

Grimm, D. E. 1987. "Toward a theory of gender: Transsexualism, gender, sexuality and relationships." *American Behavioral Scientist* 31: 66–85.

Griswold, Wendy. 1994. *Cultures and Societies in a Changing World*. Thousand Oaks, CA: Pine Forge.

Gritzer, Glenn. 1981. "Occupational specialization in medicine: Knowledge and market explanations." *Culture, Medicine and Psychiatry* 11: 207–27.

Groce, Stephen B., & Margaret Cooper. 1990. "Just me and the boys? Women in local-level rock and roll." *Gender & Society* 2(4): 220–28.

Grossman, Herbert, & Suzanne H. Grossman. 1994. *Gender Issues in Education*. Boston: Allyn & Bacon.

Grossman, Tracy Barr. 1986. *Mothers and Children Facing Divorce*. Ann Arbor, MI: UMI Research.

Grubb, W. Norton. 1995. "The old problem of 'new students': Purpose, content, and pedagogy." In Erwin Flaxman & Harry Passow (eds.), "Changing Populations Changing Schools." *Ninety-Fourth Yearbook of the National Society for the Study of Education, Part II*. Chicago: NSSE: 4–29.

Gruenbaum, Ellen. 1997. "The movement against clitorectomy and infibulation in Sudan: Public health policy and the women's movement. In Caroline B. Brettell & Carolyn F. Sargent, (eds.), *Gender in Cross-Cultural Perspective*. Upper Saddle River, NJ: Prentice Hall: 441–53.

Grusky, David, & Robert M. Hauser. 1984. "Comparative social mobility revisited: Models of convergence and divergence in 16 countries." *American Sociological Review* 49: 19–38.

Guest, Robert. 1992. "A tale of two sisters." *Far Eastern Economic Review* 155: 28–29.

Gugler, Josef. 1996a. "Regional trajectories in the urban transformation: Convergences and divergences." In Josef Gugler (ed.), *The Urban Transformation of the Developing World*. Oxford, UK: Oxford University: 1–14.

Gugler, Josef. 1996b. "Urbanization in Africa south of the Sahara: New identities in conflict." In Josef Gugler (ed.), *The Urban Transformation of the Developing World*. Oxford, UK: Oxford University: 211–51.

Gurian, M. 1992. *The Prince and the King*. Los Angeles: Tarcher/Putnam.

Gurley, John G. 1984. "Marx's contributions and their relevance today." *American Economic Review* 74: 110–15.

Gurney, Joan M., & Kathleen T. Tierney. 1982. "Relative deprivation and social movements." *Sociological Quarterly* 23: 33–47.

Gurr, Ted R. 1970. *Why Men Rebel*. Princeton, NJ: Princeton University Press.

Guterbock, Thomas M., & John C. Fries. 1997. *Maintaining America's Social Fabric*. Washington, DC: AARP.

Gutherie, Larry F. 1989. *What Schools Can Do for Students at Risk*. San Francisco: Far West Laboratory for Educational Research and Development.

Guttmann, Allen. 1978. *From Ritual to Record*. New York: Columbia University Press.

Gwartney-Gibbs, Patricia A. 1990. "The institutionalization of premarital cohabitation: Estimates from marriage license applications, 1970 and 1980." In Christopher Carlson (ed.), *Perspectives on the Family: History, Class and Feminism*. Belmont, CA: Wadsworth.

Haas, J. E., & T. E. Drabek. 1973. *Complex Organizations: A Sociological Perspective*. New York: Macmillan.

Haas, Jack, & William Shaffir. 1993. "The cloak of competence." In James M. Henslin (ed.), *Down to Earth Sociology: Introductory Readings*. New York: The Free Press.

Haas, Linda. 1993. "Nurturing fathers and working mothers: Changing gender roles in Sweden." In Jane C. Hood (ed.), *Men, Work, and Family*. Newbury Park, CA: Sage.

Habib, Jack, Gerdt Sundstrom, & Karen Windmiller. 1993. "Understanding the pattern of support for the elderly: A comparison between Israel and Sweden." *Journal of Aging and Social Police* 5(1–2): 187–206.

Habitat II. 1996. "The Istanbul Declaration on human settlements." *Population and Development Review* 22: 591–94.

Hacker, Andrew. 1992. *Two Nations: Black and White, Separate, Hostile, Unequal*. New York: Ballantine.

Hacker, Holly K. 2000. "Gaps between race and achievement pose thorny problems for educators." *St. Louis Post-Dispatch* (June 4): B1,B5.

Hackler, T. 1980. "Health maintenance organizations." *Mainliner* (December): 85–86.

Hadden, Jeffrey K. 1993. "The rise and fall of American televangelism." *Annals of the American Academy of Political and Social Science* 527(May): 113–14.

Hadden, Jeffrey K., & Charles E. Swann. 1981. *Prime-Time Preachers: The Rising Power of Televangelism*. Reading, MA: Addison-Wesley.

Haeberle, Steven H. 1999. "Gay and lesbian rights: Emerging trends in public opinion and voting behavior." In Ellen D.B. Riggle & Barry L. Tadlock (eds.), *Gays and Lesbians in the Democratic Process*. New York: Columbia University: 146–69.

Hafferty, Frederic W. 1995. "Global perspectives on health care." In E. B. Gallagher & J. Subedi (eds.), *Lessons from Some Cross-National Case Studies*. Upper Saddle River, NJ: Prentice Hall.

Hafner, Katie. 1994. "Making Sense of the Internet." *Newsweek* (October 24): 46–48.

Hagan, John, A. R. Gillis, & John Simpson. 1985. "The class structure of gender and delinquency: Toward a power-control theory of common delinquent behavior." *American Journal of Sociology* 90 (May): 1151–178.

Hagan, John, Ross MacMillan, & Blair Wheaton. 1996. "New kid in town: Social capital and the life course effects of family migration on children." *American Sociological Review* 61(3): 368–85.

Hage, Jerald, & Michael Aiken. 1970. *Social Change in Complex Organizations*. New York: Random House.

Hagen, Monys A. 1993. "Women and economics." In Jodi Wetzel, Margo Linn Espenlaub, Monys A. Hagen, Annette Bennington McElhiney, & Carmen Braun Williams (eds.), *Women's Studies Thinking Women*. Dubuque, IA: Kendall/Hunt.

Hahn, Robert A. 1985. "Between two worlds: Physicians as patients." *Medical Anthropology Quarterly* 1(3): 256–82.

Halal, William E. 1992. "The information technology revolution." *The Futurist* 26 (July–August): 10–15.

Halberstadt, A. G., & M. B. Saitta. 1987. "Gender, nonverbal behavior and perceived dominance: A test of the theory." *Journal of Personality and Social Psychology* 53: 257–72.

Hall, Christine C., & Matthew J. Crum. 1994. "Women and 'bodyisms' in television beer commercials." *Sex Roles* 31(5–6): 329–37.

Hall, Edward T. 1959. *The Silent Language*. Greenwich, CT: Fawcett.

Hall, Edward T. 1966. *The Hidden Dimension*. Garden City, NY: Doubleday.

Hall, John R. 1990. "Social interaction, culture, and historical studies." In Howard S. Becker & Michal M. McCall, (eds.), *Symbolic Interaction and Cultural Studies*. Chicago: University of Chicago Press: 16–45.

Hall, Richard H. 1963. "The concept of bureaucracy: An empirical assessment." *American Journal of Sociology* 69: 32–40.

Hall, Richard H. 1996. *Organizations: Structures, Processes and Outcomes*, 6th ed. Upper Saddle River, NJ: Prentice Hall.

Hallinan, Christopher. 1991. "Aborigines and positional segregation in the Australian Rugby League." *International Review for the Sociology of Sport* 26: 69–81.

Hallinan, Maureen T., Jeannie Oakes et al., 1994. "Tracking: From theory to practice." *Sociology of Education* 67(2): 79–84.

Halloran, Fumiko Mori. 1994. "Flunking the grade: Americans seek educational diversity and get ignorance." *Japan Update* (January): 10–11.

Halper, Jan. 1988. *Quiet Desperation: The Truth About Successful Men*. New York: Warner.

Halperin, R. H. 1987. "Age in cross-cultural perspective: An evolutionary approach. In P. Silverman (ed.), *The Elderly as Modern Pioneers*. Bloomington, IN: University of Indiana Press.

Halpern, Sydney A. 1992. "Dynamics of professional control, internal coalitions and crossprofessional boundaries." *American Journal of Sociology* 97: 994–1021.

Ham, R. J. 1980. "Alternatives to institutionalization." *American Family Physical* 22: 100.

Hamada, T. 1992. "Under the silk banner." In T. S. Lebra, (ed.), *Japanese Social Organization*. Honolulu: University of Honolulu Press.

Hamilton, Jendall. 1997. "Blowing smoke." *Newsweek* (July 21): 54–61.

Hamilton, Mykol C. 1988. "Using masculine generics: Does generic 'he' increase male bias in the user's imagery?" *Sex Roles* 19(11–12): 785–99.

Hamilton, V. Lee, Clifford L. Broman, William S. Hoffman, & Deborah S. Renner. 1990. "Hard times & vulnerable people." *Journal of Health and Social Behavior* 31: 123–40.

Hammer, Joshua. 1994. "Death Watch." *Newsweek* (August 8): 14–17.

Hammer, Joshua. 1998. "Shunned at Berkeley." *Newsweek* (October): 70–71.

Hammond, Phillip E. 1992. *Religion and Personal Autonomy: The Third Disestablishment in America*. Columbia, SC: University of South Carolina Press.

Handel, Warren H. 1993. *Contemporary Sociological Theory*. Englewood Cliffs, NJ: Prentice Hall.

Handlin, Oscar. 1992. "The newcomers." In Paula Rotherberg, (ed.), *Race, Class & Gender in the United States*. New York: St. Martin's.

Handy, Robert T. 1991. *Undermined Establishment: Church-State Relations in America, 1880–1920*. Princeton: Princeton University Press.

Haney, Lynne. 1996. "Homeboys, babies, men in suits." *American Sociological Review* 61: 759–778.

Hansen, Christine H., & Ronald D. Hansen. 1988. "How rock music videos can change what is seen when boy meets girl: Priming sterotypic appraisal of social interaction." *Sex Roles* 19: 287–316.

Hansmann, Henry B., & John M. Quigley. 1982. "Population heterogeneity and the sociogenesis of homicide." *Social Forces* 61: 206–24.

Hanson, Shirley M. H. 1985. "Single custodial fathers." In Shirley M. H. Hanson & Frederick W. Bozett (eds.), *Dimensions of Fatherhood*. Beverly Hills, CA: Sage.

Hansson, Robert O., Marieta F. Knoft, Anna E. Downs, Paula R. Monroe, Susan E. Stegman, & Donna S. Wadley. 1984. "Femininity, masculinity and adjustment of divorce among women." *Psychology of Women Quarterly* 8(3): 248–49.

Hardaway, Robert M. 1995. *America Goes to School: Law, Reform, and Crisis in Public Education*. Westport, CT: Praeger.

Hare, A.P., H.H. Blumberg, M.F. Davis, & V. Kent. 1994. *Small Group Research: A Handbook*. Norwood, NJ: Ablex.

Hare-Mustin, Rachel T. 1992. "China's marriage law: A model for family responsibilities and relationships." *Family Process* 21: 477–81.

Hargreaves, J. 1994. *Sporting Females: Critical Issues in the History and Sociology of Women's Sports*. London: Routledge.

Harjo, Suzan Shown. 1993. "The American Indian experience." In Harriette Pipes McAdoo (ed.), *Family Ethnicity: Strength in Diversity*. Newbury Park, CA: Sage.

Harkey, J. D., L. Miles & W. A. Rushing. 1976. "The relationship between social class and functional status," *Journal of Health and Social Behavior* 17: 194–204.

Harlow, Carolyn W. 1991. *Female Victims of Violent Crime*. Washington, DC: Bureau of Justice Statistics.

Harlow, Harry F. 1958. "The nature of love." *American Psychologist*. 13: 673–85.

Harlow, Harry, & Margaret Kuenne Harlow. 1970. "The young monkeys." In P. Kramer (ed.), *Readings in Developmental Psychology Today*. Del Mar, CA: CRM Books.

Harper, C. L. 1993. *Exploring Social Change*, 2nd ed. Upper Saddle River, NJ: Prentice Hall.

Harragan, Betty Lehan. 1977. *Games Mother Never Taught You*. New York: Rawson.

Harrell, Steven. 1981. "Growing old in rural Taiwan." In P. Amoss & S. Harrell (eds.), *Other Ways of Growing Old*. Palo Alto, CA: Standford University Press.

Harries, Keith D. 1990. *Serious Violence: Patterns of Homicide and Assault in America*. Springfield, IL: Charles C Thomas.

Harrington, Michael. 1977. *The Vast Majority: A Journey to the World's Poor*. New York: Simon & Schuster.

Harris, Adella J., & Jonathon F. Feinberg. 1977. "Television and aging: Is what you see, what you get? *Journal of Gerontology*. 17: 464–66.

Harris, Chauncy D., & Edward L. Ullman. 1945. "The nature of cities." *Annals of the American Academy of Political and Social Science* 242: 7–17.

Harris, Diana K. 1990. *Sociology of Aging*. New York: Harper and Row.

Harris, Dorothy V. 1980. "Femininity & athleticism: Conflict or consonance?" In Donald F. Sabo & Ross Runfola, (eds.), *Jock: Sports & Male Identity*. Upper Saddle River, NJ: Prentice Hall.

Harris, Helen. 1995. "Rethinking Polynesian heterosexual relationships." In William Jankowiak (ed.), *Romantic Passion*. New York: Columbia University Press: 96–127.

Harris, Ian, Joes B. Torres, & Dale Allender. 1994. "The responses of African American men to dominant norms of masculinity within the United States." *Sex Roles* 31(11–12): 703–19.

Harris, Kathleen M. 1993. "Work and welfare among single mothers in poverty." *American Journal of Sociology* 99/2: 317–352.

Harris, Louis & Associates. 1975. *The Myth and Reality of Aging in America*. Washington, DC: The National Council on Aging. 1981. *Aging in the Eighties: America in Transition*. Washington, DC: The National Council on Aging.

Harris, Marvin. 1974. *Cows, Pigs, Wars and Witches: The Riddles of Culture*. New York: Random House.

Harris, Marvin. 1977. *Cannibals & Kings: The Origins of Cultures*. New York: Random House.

Harris, Marvin. 1979. *Cultural Materialism: The Struggle for a Science of Culture*. New York: Random House.

Harris, Marvin. 1981. *America Now: The Anthropology of a Changing Culture*. New York: Simon & Schuster.

Harris, Marvin. 1994. "Cultural materialism is alive and well and won't go away until something better comes along." In Robert Borofsky, (ed.), *Assessing Cultural Anthropology*. New York: McGraw-Hill.

Harris, Nigel. 1987. *The End of the Third World: Newly Industrializing Countries and the Decline of an Ideology*. Harmondsworth, England: Penguin.

Harris, R., A. Ellicott, & D. Holmes. 1986. "The timing of psychosocial transitions and changes in women's lives: An examination of women aged 45 to 60." *Journal of Personality and Social Psychology* 51: 409–16.

Harris, Rosemary. 1972. *Prejudice and Tolerance in Ulster*. Totowa, NJ: Rowman & Littlefield.

Harrison, B. 1994. *Lean and Mean: The Changing Landscape of Corporate Power in the Age of Flexibility*. New York: Basic Books.

Harrison, B., & B. Bluestone. 1988. *The Great U-Turn: Corporate Restructuring and the Polarizing of America*. New York: Basic.

Harrison, Lawrence E. 1992. *Who Prospers? How Cultural Values Shape Economic and Political Success*. New York: Basic.

Harrison, Paul. 1993. *Inside the Third World: The Anatomy of Poverty*, 3rd ed. London: Penguin.

Harriss, John (ed.). 1991. *The Family: A Social History of the Twentieth Century*. New York: Oxford University.

Harry, Joseph. 1991. "Gay male and lesbian relationships." In Leonard Carrgan (ed.), *Marriages and Families: Coping with Change*. Upper Saddle River, NJ: Prentice Hall.

Hart, Daniel, & Suzanne Fegley. 1995. "Prosocial behavior and caring in adolescence: Relations to self-understanding and social judgment." *Child Development* 66(5): 1346–59.

Hart, Elizabeth et al. 1994. "Developmental change in attention-deficit hyperactivity disorder in boys." *Journal of Consulting & Clinical Psychology* 62: 472–91.

Hart, Paul. 1991. "Groupthink, risk-taking & recklessness." *Politics & the Individual* (1/1): 67–90.

Hart, Stephen. 1992. *What Does the Lord Require? How American Christians Think About Economic Justice*. New York: Oxford University Press.

Hartley, Eugene. 1946. *Problems in Prejudice*. New York: King's Crown Press.

Harvey, David L. 1993. *Potter Addition: Poverty, Family, and Kinship in a Heartland Community*. New York: Aldine de Gruyter.

Hashimoto, Akiko, & Hal L. Kendig. 1992. "Aging in international perspective." In Hal Kendig, Akiko Hashimoto, & Larry C. Coppard (eds.), *Family Support for the Elderly: The International Experience*. New York: Oxford University Press.

Haskell, Molly. 1987. *From Reverence to Rape: The Treatment of Women in the Movies*. New York: Holt, Rinehart and Winston.

Hatcher, Chris. 1989. "Cults, society and government." In Rebecca Moore & Fielding McGehee III, (eds.), *New Religious Movements, Mass Suicide, and Peoples Temples: Scholarly Perspectives on a Tragedy*. Lewiston, NY: Edwin Mellen: 179–98.

Hatfield, Elaine, & Susan Sprecher. 1986. "Measuring passionate love in intimate relationships." *Journal of Adolescence* 9: 383–410.

Hathaway, Dale A. 1993. *Can Workers Have a Voice? The Politics of Deindustrialization in Pittsburgh*. University Park, PA: Penn State University Press.

Havemann, J. 1997. "N.J. allows gays to adopt jointly." *Washington Post* (December 18): A1, A24.

Havinghurst, Robert J. 1963. "Successful aging." In R. Williams, C. Tibbitts, & W. Donahue (eds.), *Processes of Aging*. New York: Atherton.

Havinghurst, Robert J., Bernice L. Neugarten, & Shelton S. Tobin. 1968. "Disengagement and patterns of aging." In Bernice L. Neugarten (ed.), *Middle Age and Aging*. Chicago: University of Chicago Press.

Hawkins, David. 1990. "The roots of literacy." *Daedalus* 19(2): 1–14.

Hawkins, K., & J. M. Thomas, (eds.). 1984. *Enforcing Regulation*. Boston: Kluwer-Nijhoff.

Hawley, Amos. 1950. *Human Ecology: A Theory of Community Structure*. New York: Ronald Press.

Hayes, Bernadette C., & Audrey Vandenheuvel. 1994. "Attitudes toward mandatory retirement: An international comparison." *International Journal of Aging and Human Development*. 39(3): 209–31.

Haymes, Stephen Nathan. 1995. "White culture and the politics of racial difference: Implications for multiculturalism." In Christine E. Sleeter & Peter L. McClaren (eds.), *Multicultural Education, Critical Pedagogy, and the Politics of Difference*. Albany, NY: State University of New York: 105–27.

Hayslip, Bert Jr., & Paul E. Panek. 1993. *Adult Development and Aging*. New York: HarperCollins.

Hayward, Mark D., & Melonie Heron. 1999. "Racial inequality in active life among adult Americans." *Demography* 36: 77–91.

Health Care Financing Review. 1996. "The nation's health dollar." 18(1). Health Care Financing Administration, Office of the Actuary.

Hearn, Jeff, Deborah L. Sheppard, Petra T. Sherriff & Gibson Burrell, eds. 1989. *The Sexuality of Organizations*. Newbury Park, CA: Sage.

Heaton, Tim B., & Cardell K. Jacobson. 1994. "Race differences in changing family demographics in the 1980s." *Journal of Family Issues* 15(2): 290–308.

Heckathorn, Douglas D. 1990. "Collective sanctions and compliance norms: A formal theory of group-mediated social control." *American Sociological Review* 55: 366–84.

Hecq, Walter, Youri Borisov, & Claire Debever. 1994. "An empirical hybrid model for the assessment of daily concentrations in an urban environment." *Journal of Environmental Management* 42: 181–96.

Heidensohn, Frances. 1991. "Women and crime in Europe." In Frances Heidensohn and M. Farrell, (eds.), *Crime In Europe*. London: Routledge: 55–83.

Heilman, Samuel C. 1992. *Defenders of the Faith: Inside Ultra-orthodox Jewry*. New York: Schocken.

Heilman, Samuel C., & Steven M. Cohen. 1989. *Cosmopolitans and Parochials: Modern Orthodox Jews in America*. Chicago: University of Chicago Press.

Heimer, Karen. 1997. "Socioeconomic status, subcultural definitions & violent delinquency." *Social Forces* 75: 799–833.

Heins, Marjorie. 1993. *Sex, Sin, and Blasphemy: A Guide to America's Censorship Wars*. New York: New Press.

Heintz, K. 1987. "An examination of sex occupational role presentations of female characters in children's picture books." *Women's Studies in Communication* 11: 67–78.

Helgesen, Sally. 1990. *The Female Advantage: Women's Ways of Leadership*. New York: Doubleday.

Henderson, Carter. 1998. "Today's affluent oldsters: Marketers see gold in gray." *The Futurist* (November): 19–23.

Henderson, George. 1989. *A Practitioner's Guide to Understanding Indigenous and Foreign Cultures: An Analysis of Relationships Between Ethnicity, Social Class and Therapeutic Intervention Strategies with Third World People from Other Countries*. Springfield, IL: Charles C. Thomas.

Hendin, Herbert. 1995. *Suicide in America*. New York: W. W. Norton.

Henley, B. 1977. *Body Politics*. Upper Saddle River, NJ: Prentice Hall.

Hennig, Margaret, & Anne Jardin. 1977. *The Managerial Woman*. Garden City, NY: Doubleday.

Hennon, Charles. 1983. "Divorce and the elderly: A neglected area of research." In T. Brubaker (ed.), *Family Relationships in Later Life*. Beverly Hills, CA: Sage.

Henry J. Kaiser Family Foundation, 1993. *Reproductive Health Policy & Programs: Reflections on the African Experience*. A Conference Report, Harare, July.

Henry, Tricia. 1989. *Break All Rules! Punk Rock and the Making of a Style*. Ann Arbor, MI: UMI Research Press.

Henson, Kevin. 1996. *The Temp*. Philadelphia: Temple University Press.

Herberg, Will. 1983. *Protestant-Catholic-Jew: An Essay in American Religious Sociology*. Chicago: University of Chicago Press.

Herbert, Ulrich. 1995. "Immigration, integration, foreignness." *International Labor & Working Class History* (Fall): 91–93.

Herman, Dianne. 1989. "The rape culture." In Jo Freeman (ed.), *Women: A Feminist Perspective*. Mountain View, CA: Mayfield.

Herman, Edward S., & Noam Chomsky. 1988. *Manufacturing Consent: The Political Economy of the Mass Media*. New York: Pantheon.

Herman, Judith L. 1981. *Father-Daughter Incest*. Cambridge, MA: Harvard University.

Hernandex, Francisco. 1996. "Just something you did as a man." In Karen E. Rosenblum & Toni-Michelle C. Travis (eds.), *The Meaning of Difference: American Constructions of Race, Sex and Gender, Social Class and Sexual Orientation*. New York: McGraw-Hill.

Heron, Echo. 1994. "Emergency room nurse." In William Kornblum & Carolyn D. Smith (eds.), *The Healing Experience: Readings on the Social Context of Health Care*. Upper Saddle River, NJ: Prentice Hall: 64–73.

Herrera, Ruth S., & Robert L. DelCampo. 1995. "Beyond the superwoman syndrome: Work satisfaction and family functioning among working-class, Mexican American women." *Hispanic Journal of Behavioral Sciences* 17(1): 49–60.

Herrnstein, Richard J., & Charles Murray. 1994. *The Bell Curve: Intelligence and Class Structure in American Life*. New York: Free Press.

Hertzog, C. K., & K. Warner Schaie. 1988. "Stability and change in adult intelligence." *Psychology and Aging*. 3: 122–30.

Herzog, Thomas R., & Theresa A. Gale. 1996. "Preference for urban buildings as a function of age and nature context." *Environment and Behavior* 28: 44–72.

Hess, Beth B., & Beth J. Soldo. 1985. "Husband and wife networks." In W. J. Sauer & R. T. Coward (eds.), *Social Support Networks and the Care of Elderly: Theory, Research and Practice*. New York: Springer.

Heston, L. L., & J. A. White. 1991. *The Vanishing Mind*. New York: Freeman.

Hetherington, E. M. 1993. "An overview of the Virginia Longitudinal Study of Divorce and Remarriage with a focus on adolescents." *Journal of Family Psychology* 7: 39–56.

Hetherington, E., & P. Baltes. 1988. "Child psychology and life-span development." In E. Hetherington, R. Lerner, & M. Perlmutter (eds.), *Child Development in Life-Span Perspective*. Hillsdale, NJ: Erlbaum.

Hetherly, Marian. 1997. "PK publicity and production: Between the lines and behind the scenes." *Humanist* (September/October): 14–18.

Hewitt, John P. 1997. *Self and Society: A Symbolic Interactionist Social Psychology*. Boston: Allyn & Bacon.

Hewlett, Sylvia Ann. 1987. "When a husband walks out." *Parade Magazine* (June 7): 4–5.

Heyck, Denis L. 1994. *Barrios and Borderlands: Cultures of Latinos and Latinas in the United States*. New York: Routledge.

Heydebrand, W. 1977. "Organizational contradictions in public bureaucracies: Toward a Marxian theory of organizations." *Sociological Quarterly* 18: 83–107.

Hicks, Alexander, & Joya Mishra. 1993. "Political resources and the growth of welfare in affluent democracies, 1960–1982." *American Journal of Sociology* 99: 668–710.

Higginbotham, Elizabeth. 2000. "Race, gender and professional work for black women." Women's History Month Lecture at Maryville University-St. Louis, March 29.

Higginbotham, Evelyn Brooks. 1997. "Black professional women: Job ceilings and employment sectors." In Dana Dunn (ed.), *Workplace/Women's Place: An Anthology*. Los Angeles: Roxbury: 234–46.

Higley, John, & Richard Gunther (eds.). 1992. *Elites and Democratic Consolidation in Latin America and Southern Europe*. New York: Cambridge University Press.

Hill, G. H., & S. S. Hill. 1985. *Blacks on Television*. Metuchen, NJ: Scarecrow.

Hills, S. L. 1987. *Corporate Violence: Injury and Death for Profit*. Totowa, NJ: Rowman & Littlefield.

Himes, Christine L. 1994. "Parental caregiving by adult women." *Research on Aging* 16(2): 191–211.

Hines, Alice M. 1997. "Divorce-related transitions, adolescent development, and the role of the parent-child relationship: A review of the literature." *Journal of Marriage and the Family* 59(2): 375–88.

Hirsch, E. D., Jr. 1987. *Cultural Literacy: What Every American Needs to Know*. Boston: Houghton Mifflin.

Hirsch, K. 1990. "Fraternities of fear." *MS* 1(2): 52–56.

Hirschi, Travis, & Michael Gottfredson. 1983. "Age and the explanation of crime." *American Journal of Sociology*, 89: 552–84.

Hirschi, Travis. 1969. *Causes of Delinquency*. Berkeley: University of California Press.

Hirschman, Charles. 1983. "America's melting pot reconsidered." *Annual Review of Sociology* 9: 397–423.

Hirsh, Eric L. 1990. "Sacrifice for the cause." *American Sociological Review* 55: 243–54.

Hisrich, Robert D., & Candida G. Brush. 1984. "The woman entrepreneur: Management skills and business problems." *Journal of Small Business Management* 22: 30–37.

Hoch, Paul. 1982. *Rip Off the Big Game*. New York: Doubleday.

Hochschild, Arlie. 1989. *The Second Shift: Working Parents and the Revolution at Home*. New York: Viking.

Hockstader, Lee. 1995. "For women, new Russia is far from liberating." *Washington Post* (September 1): A25, A31.

Hodson, Randy, & Robert L. Kaufman. 1982. "Economic dualism: A critical review." *American Sociological Review* 47: 727–39.

Hodson, Randy, & Teresa A. Sullivan. 1995. *The Social Organization of Work*, 2nd ed. Belmont, CA: Wadsworth.

Hoebel, E. Adamson. 1978. *The Cheyennes*. Fort Worth, TX: Holt Rinehart Winston.

Hoecker-Drysdale, Susan. 1992. *Harriet Martineau: First Woman Sociologist*. New York: Berg.

Hoffer, Eric. 1951. *The True Believer*. New York: Harper & Row.

Hofferth, Sandra L. 1985. "Updating children's life course." *Journal of Marriage and the Family* 47: 93–115.

Hoffman, Charles D., & Edward C. Teyber. 1985. "Naturalistic observations of sex differences in adult involvement with girls and boys of different ages." *Merrill-Palmer Quarterly* 31(1): 93–97.

Hoffnung, Michelle. 1995. "Motherhood: Contemporary conflict for women." In Jo Freeman (ed.) *Women: A Feminist Perspective*. Mountain View, CA: Mayfield: 162–181.

Hogan, Dennis. 1985. "The demography of life-span transitions: Temporal and gender comparisons." In Alice S. Rossi (ed.), *Gender and the Life Course*. New York: Aldine.

Holland, Dorothy, & Margaret A. Eisenhart. 1990. *Educated in Romance: Women, Achievement and College Culture*. Chicago: University of Chicago.

Hollingshead, August B., & Frederick C. Redlich. 1958. *Social Class and Mental Illness: A Community Study*. New York: Wiley.

Hollnsteiner-Racelis, Mary. 1988. "Becoming an urbanite: The neighbourhood as a learning environment." In Josef Gugler (ed.), *The Urbanization of the Third World*. Oxford, UK: Oxford University: 230–41.

Holloway, R. 1994. "Trends in women's health: A global view. *Scientific American* (August): 76–83.

Holmes, Steven A. 1996. "U.S. aid to world birth-control efforts face cuts." *New York Times International* (September 12).

Holton, R. J. 1986. *Cities, Capitalism and Civilization*. London: Allen & Unwin.

Homans, George C. 1950. *The Human Group*. New York: Harcourt Brace.

Homans, George C. 1951. *The Western Electric Researches*. Indianapolis, IN: Bobbs-Merrill.

Hondagneu-Sotelo, Pierrette. 1994. "Regulating the unregulated? Domestic workers' social networks." *Social Problems* 41: 50–64.

Hood, Thomas C. 1995. "The practical consequences of sociology's pursuit of 'justice for all'." *Social Forces* 74(1): 1–14.

Hook, Donald. 1989. *Death in the Balance*. Lexington, MA: Heath.

hooks, bell. 1992. "Feminism: A transformational politic." In Paula S. Rothenberg (ed.), *Race, Class and Gender in the United States: An Integrated Study*. New York: St. Martin's.

Hoover, Stewart M. 1988. *Mass Media Religion: The Social Sources of the Electronic Church*. Newbury Park, CA: Sage.

Hoover, Stewart M. 1990. "Ten myths about religious broadcasting." In Robert Abelman & Sewart M. Hoover, eds., *Religious Television: Controversies and Conclusions*. Norwood, NJ: Ablex: 23–39.

Hooyman, Nancy R., & H. Asuman Kiyak. 1996. *Social Gerontology*. Boston: Allyn & Bacon.

Hopper, D. Ian. 2000. "Welfare Rolls Keep Shrinking," *Evansville Courier-Press* (August 23).

Hopper, Rex D. 1950. "The revolutionary process: A frame of reference for the study of revolutionary movements." *Social Forces* 25: 270–79.

Horgan, John. 1991. "Death with dignity: The Dutch explore the limits of a patient's right to die." *Scientific American* (March): 17,21.

Horn, Patricia. 1992. "To love and to cherish: Gays and lesbians lead the way in redefining the family." In Michael S. Kimmel & Michael A. Messner (eds.), *Men's Lives*. New York: Macmillan.

Horner, Constance. 1996. "Reclaiming the vision: What should we do after affirmative action?" IN Harold A. Widdison (ed.), *Social Problems 96/97*. Guilford, CT: Dushkin/Brown & Benchmark.

Hornsby, Anne M. 1998. "Surfing the net for community." In Peter Kvisto (ed.), *Illuminating Social Life*. Thousand Oaks, CA. Pine Forge: 63–106.

Hornsby-Smith, Michael P. 1987. *Roman Catholics in England: Studies in Social Structure Since the Second World War*. Cambridge, UK: Cambridge University.

Hornsby-Smith, Michael P. 1991. *Roman Catholic Beliefs in England: Customary Catholicism and Transformations of Religious Authority*. Cambridge, UK: Cambridge University Press.

Horowitz, Irving L. 1982. "The new fundamentalism." *Society* (November–December): 40–47.

Horowitz, Irving Louis. 1990. "The limits of modernity." In Thomas Robbins & Dick Anthony, (eds.), *In Gods We Trust: New Patterns of Religious Pluralism in America*. New Brunswick, NJ: Transaction: 63–76.

Horowitz, Ruth. 1991. "The expanded family and family honor." In Mark Hutter (ed.), *The Family Experience: A Reader in Cultural Diversity*. New York: Macmillan.

Horst, Marilyn L. 1995. "Model for management of services to low income pediatric asthma patients." *Social Work in Health Care* 21(1): 129–36.

Hoschschild, Jennifer. 1995. *Facing Up to the American Dream: Race, Class and the Soul of the Nation*. Princeton, NJ: Princeton University Press.

Hosenball, Mark. 1999. "It is not the act of a few bad apples." *Newsweek* (May 17).

Hossain, Ziarat, & Jaipaul L. Roopnarine. 1993. "Division of household labor and child care in dual-earner African-American families with infants." *Sex Roles* 39: 571–83.

Hostetler, John A. 1980. *Amish Society*, 3rd ed. Baltimore: Johns Hopkins University Press.

Hostetler, John A., & Gertrude E. Huntington. 1971. *Children in Amish Society*. New York: Holt, Rinehart & Winston.

House, James S., Karl R. Landis, & Debra Umberson. 1990. "Social Relationships and Health." In Peter Conrad & Rochelle Kern (eds.), *The Sociology of Health and Illness: Critical Perspectives*. New York: St. Martin's.

Houseknecht, Sharon K., & Jaya Sastry. 1996. "Family 'decline' and child well-being: A comparative assessment." *Journal of Marriage and the Family* 58(3): 726–39.

Houssain, Hameeda. 1995. "Introduction." In Hameeda Houssain & Salma Sobhan, (eds.), *Sanglap: Attack on Fundamentals*. Dhaka, Bangladesh: Ain O Salish Nendra.

Hout, Michael. 1988. "More Universalism, Less Structural Mobility," *American Journal of Sociology* 93: 1358–1400.

Howell, David. 1994. "The skills myth." *The American Prospect* 18: 81–90.

Howell, J. 1982. *UK Aid to Co-Operatives in Developing Countries, 1977–1981: An Evaluation*. London: Overseas Development Administration.

Howes, C. 1988. "Peer interaction of young children." *Monographs of the Society for Research in Child Development*. 53: 1 (Serial No. 217).

Hoxie, Frederick E., & Peter Iverson, (eds.). 1998. *Indians in American History: An Introduction*, 2nd ed. Wheeling, IL: Harlan Davidson.

Hoyenga, Katharine Blick, & Kermit T. Hoyenga. 1993. *Gender-Related Differences: Origins and Outcomes*. Boston: Allyn & Bacon.

Hoyert, Donna L., & Marsha Mallick Seltzer. 1992. "Factors related to the well-being and life activities of family caregivers." *Family Relations* 41: 74–81.

Hoyt, Homer. 1939. *The Structure and Growth of American Neighborhoods in Residential Cities*. Washington, DC: Federal Housing Authority.

Hoyt, Homer. 1943. "The structure and growth of American cities in the post-war era." *American Journal of Sociology* 48: 475–92.

Hrdy, Sarah Blaffer. 1986. "Empathy, polyandry and the myth of the coy female." In Ruth Bleier (ed.), *Feminist Approaches to Science*. New York: Pergamon.

Hsieh, Chin-Chi, & M. D. Pugh. 1993. "Poverty, income inequality, and violent crime." *Criminal Justice Review* 18: 182–199.

Hsu, Francis L. K. 1981. *Americans and Chinese: Passage to Difference*. Honolulu: University of Hawaii.

Huang, Chien Ju, & Harvey Marshall. 1997. "The effects of state strength on economic growth in the Third World: A critical perspective on World-System Theory." In Joseph E. Behar & Alfred G. Cuzan, (eds.), *At the Crossroads of Development: Transnational Challenges to Developed and Developing Societies*. Leiden, Netherlands: E.J. Brill: 19–37.

Hubbard, Ruth. 1994. "Race and sex as biological categories." In Ethel Tobach & Betty Rosoff (eds.), *Challenging Racism and Sexism: Alternatives to Genetic Explanations*. New York: Feminist Press at City University of New York.

Huber, Joan, & William H. Form. 1973. *Income & Ideology*. New York: Free Press.

Huber, Joan. 1995. "Centennial essay: Institutional perspectives on sociology." *American Journal of Sociology* 101: 194–216.

Huddy, Leonie, & David O. Sears. 1995. "Opposition to bilingual education: prejudice or the defense of realistic interests?" *Social Psychology Quarterly* 58(2): 133–43.

Hudson, Winthrop S. 1973. *Religion in America*. New York: Charles Scribner's Sons.

Huesmann, L. Rowell, (ed.). 1994. *Aggressive Behavior: Current Perspectives*. New York: Plenum.

Hughes, Everett. 1945. "Dilemmas and contradictions of status." *American Journal of Sociology* 50: 353–359.

Hughes, Everett, 1962. "Good people and dirty work." *Social Problems* 10: 3–11.

Hughes, Fergus P. 1991. *Children, Play, and Development*. Boston: Allyn & Bacon.

Hughes, H. Stewart. 1962. *Oswald Spengler: A Critical Estimate*. New York: Scribner's.

Hugo, Graeme. 1996a. "Urbanization in Indonesia: City and countryside linked." In Josef Gugler (ed.), *The Urban Transformation of the Developing World*. Oxford, UK: Oxford University: 133–93.

Hugo, Graeme. 1996b. "Environmental concerns and international migration." *International Migration Review* 30(1), (113): 105–31.

Huizenga, Rob. 1994. *You're OK, It's Just a Bruise*. New York: St. Martin's Press.

Huizinga, David, & Delbert S. Elliott. 1987. "Juvenile offenders: Prevalence, offender incidence and arrest rates by race." *Crime & Delinquency* 33(2): 206–23.

Hulme, Davis & Mark M. Turner. 1990. *Sociology and Development: Theories, Policies, and Practices*. New York: St. Martin's.

Humphreys, Laud. 1970. *Tearoom Trade: Impersonal Sex in Public Places*. Chicago: Aldine.

Hunger. 1990. *A Report on the State of World Hunger*. Washington, DC: Bread for the World Institute on Hunger & Development.

Hunt, Charles W. 1993. "The social epidemiology of AIDS in Africa: Migrant labor and sexually transmitted disease." In Peter Conrad & Eugene Gallagher (eds.), *Health and Health Care in Developing Countries: Sociological Perspectives*. Philadelphia: Temple University: 1–37.

Hunt, M. 1974. *Sexual Behavior in the 1970s*. Chicago: Playboy.

Hunter, Andrea G., & James Earl Davis. 1994. "Hidden voices of black men: The meaning, structure and complexity of manhood." *Journal of Black Studies* 25(1): 20–40.

Hurh, Won Moo, & Kwang Chung Kim. 1984. *Korean Immigrants in American: A Structural Analysis of Ethnic Confinement and Adhesive Adaptation*. Rutherford, NJ: Farleigh Dickenson University.

Hurst, Charles E. 1992. *Social Inequality: Forms, Causes and Consequences*. Boston: Allyn & Bacon.

Huston, A. C., E. Donnerstein, H. Fairchild, N. D. Feshbach, P. A. Katz, & J. P. Murray. 1992. *Big World, Small Screen: The Role of Television in American Society*. Lincoln, NE: University of Nebraska Press.

Huston, Michelle, & Pepper Schwartz. 1996. "Gendered dynamics in the romantic relationships of lesbians and gay men." In Julie T. Wood (ed.), *Gendered Relationships*. Mountain View, CA: Mayfield.

Hyde, Janet Shibley. 1981. "How large are cognitive gender differences? A meta-analysis using w and d." *American Psychologist* 36: 892–901.

Hyde, Janet Shibley. 1984. "Children's understanding of sexist language." *Developmental Psychology* 20: 697–706.

Hyde, Janet Shibley. 1996. *Half the Human Experience: The Psychology of Women*. Lexington, MA: D.C. Heath.

Hyman, Herbert H. 1942. "The psychology of status." *Archives of Psychology* 38.

Hyman, Herbert H., & Charles R. Wright. 1971. "Trends in voluntary association memberships of American adults." *American Sociological Review* 36: 191–206.

Iannaccone, Laurence R. 1991. "The consequences of religious market structure." *Rationality and Society* 3: 156–77.

Iannaccone, Laurence R. 1992. "Religious markets and the economics of religion." *Social Compass* 39(1): 123–31.

Iannaccone, Laurence R. 1994. "Why strict churches are strong." *American Journal of Sociology* 99(5): 1180–1211.

Ianni, Frank. 1974. *Black Mafia: Ethnic Succession in Organized Crime*. New York: Simon & Schuster.

IDCA. 1991. *Development Issues, 1991: U.S. Actions Affecting Developing Countries*. Washington, DC: U.S. International Development Cooperation Agency.

IFAD. 1994. "The poverty process." International Fund for Agricultural Development. In *Human Rights: The New Consensus*. London: Regency Press in association with the United Nations High Commissioner for Refugees: 117–18.

Iglehart, John K. 1989. "Health policy report: The United States looks at Canadian health care." *New England Journal of Medicine* (December) 12: 1767–72.

Iglesias, Enrique. 1987. "The impact of OECD economic policies on LDCs: A comment." In *Interdependence and Co-operation in Tomorrow's World. A Symposium Marking the Twenty-Fifth Anniversary of the Organisation for Economic Co-operation and Development*. Paris: OECD: 107–8.

Iiyama, P., & Harry H. L. Kitano. 1982. "Asian Americans and the media." In G. Berry & C. Mitchell-Kerman (eds.), *Television and the Socialization of the Minority Child*. New York: Academic Press.

Immergut, Ellen M. 1992. *Health Politics: Interests and Institutions in Western Europe*. Cambridge, UK: Cambridge University Press.

In P.S. Kirkbride (ed.), *Human Resource Management in Europe: Perspectives for the Nineties*. London: Routledge.

Inciardi, James A. 1992. *The War on Drugs II*. Mountain View, CA: Mayfield.

Inciardi, James, (ed.). 1980. *Radical Criminology: The Coming Crisis*. Beverly Hills: Sage.

Inglehart, Ronald. 1996. *Modernization and Postmodernization: Cultural, Economic, and Political Change in Forty-three Societies*. Princeton, NJ: Princeton University Press.

Ingrassia, M., & J. McCormick. 1994. "Why leave children with bad parents?" *Newsweek* (April 25): 52–58.

Inkeles, Alex. 1973. "Making man modern." In Amitai Etzioni & Eva Etzioni-Halvey, (eds.), *Social Change—Sources, Patterns and Consequences*. New York: Basic Books: 342–61.

Inkeles, Alex. 1983. *Exploring Individual Modernity*. New York: Columbia University Press.

Inman, Chris. 1996. "Friendships among men: Closeness in the doing." In Julia T. Wood, (ed.), *Gendered Relationships*. Mountain View, CA: Mayfield.

Inniss, Leslie Baham. 1987. "School racial composition and adolescent self-concepts." *Sociological Viewpoints* 8: 1–30.

Inter-Parliamentary Union. 1999. "Women in national parliaments as of 30 September, 1999." Geneva, Switzerland: IPU (www.ipu.org/wmn-e/classif.htm).

Intons-Peterson, Margaret Jean. 1988. *Children's Concepts of Gender*. Norwood, NJ: Ablex.

Irwin, John, & James Austin. 1994. *It Is About Time: America's Imprisonment Binge*. Belmont, CA: Wadsworth.

ISEI. 1986. *The Life of a Senior High School Student*. Tokyo: International Society for Educational Information.

Ishida, Hiroshi. 1995. "Class origin, class destination, and education: A cross-national study of ten industrial nations." *American Journal of Sociology* 101(1): 145–93.

Izraeli, Dafna N. 1994. "Money matters: Spousal incomes and family/work relations among physician couples in India." *Sociological Quarterly* 35(1): 69–84.

Jabbra, Nancy W., & Joseph G. Jabbra, (eds.). 1992. *Women and Development in the Middle East and North Africa* Leiden, Netherlands: E.J. Brill: 1–10.

Jackman, Jennifer. 1995. "1995 women's equality poll released." *Feminist Majority Report* 7(2): 1,12–13.

Jackman, Robert, & Mary Jackman. 1983. *Class Awareness in the United States*. Berkeley: University of California Press.

Jackson, Kenneth T. 1985. *Crabgrass Frontier: The Suburbanization of the United States*. New York: Oxford University Press.

Jackson, L. 1983. "On living together unmarried." *Journal of Social Issues* 4(1): 35–59.

Jackson, L. A., J. E. Hunter, & C. N. Hodge. 1995. "Physical attractiveness and intellectual competence: A meta-analytic review." *Social Psychology Quarterly* 58: 108–22.

Jackson, S. E. et al. (eds.). 1992. *Diversity in the Workplace: Human Resources Initiatives*. New York: Guilford.

Jacobs, Charles, & Mohamad Athie. 1994. "Bought and sold." *The New York Times* (July 13): A–11.

Jacobs, D. 1989. "Inequality and economic crime." *Sociology and Social Research*, (66/1): 12–28.

Jacobs, G. 1990. "Aging and politics." In R. H. Binstock & L. George (eds.), *Handbook of Aging and the Social Sciences*. New York: Academic Press.

Jacobs, James B. 1989. *Drunk Driving*. Chicago: University of Chicago Press.

Jacobs, Jane. 1970. *The Economy of Cities*. New York: Vintage.

Jacobs, Jerry A., & Ronnie J. Steinberg. 1990. "Compensating differentials and the male-female wage gap: Evidence from the New York State Comparable Worth Study." *Social Forces* 69: 439–68.

Jacobs, Lawrence R. 1998. "Health reform impasse: The politics of American ambivalence toward government." *Journal of Health Politics, Policy and Law* 18(3): 629–55.

Jacobs, Lawrence R., Robert Y. Shapiro, & Eli C. Schulman. 1993. "Trends: Medical care in the United States—An update. *The Public Opinion Quarterly* 57(3): 394–427.

Jacobs, Nancy R., Mark A. Siegel, & Jacquelyn Quiram (eds.). 1998. *Profile of the Nation: An American Portrait*. Wylie, TX: Information Plus.

Jacobs, Nancy R., Mark A. Siegel, & Jacquelyn Quiram. 1996. *Profile of the Nation: An American Portrait*. Wylie, TX: Information Plus.

Jacobs, Ronald N. 1996. "Civil society and crisis: Culture, discourse & the Rodney King beating." *American Journal of Sociology*.

Jacobsen, Joyce P. 1994. *The Economics of Gender*. Cambridge, MA: Blackwell.

Jacobson, David. 1995. "Incomplete institution or culture shock: Institutional and processual models of stepfamily instability." *Journal of Divorce and Remarriage* 24(1–2): 3–18.

Jacobson, Matthew F. 1998. *Whiteness of a Different Color*. Cambridge, MA: Harvard.

Jacquet, Constant H., Jr., (ed.) 1988. *Yearbook of American and Canadian Churches*. Nashville, TN: Abingdon.

Jakobeit, Cord. 1996. "Nonstate actors leading the way: Debt-for-nature swaps." In Robert O. Keohane & Mary A. Levy (eds.), *Institutions for Environmental Aid: Pitfalls and Promise*. Cambridge, MA: Massachusetts Institute of Technology Press: 127–66.

Jamieson, Lynn. 1994. "Theories of family development and the experience of being brought up." In Michael Drake (ed.), *Time, Family and Community: Perspectives on Family and Community History*. Oxford, UK: Open University Press.

Janis, Irving. 1972. *Victims of Groupthink*. Boston: Houghton-Mifflin.

Janofsky, M. 1998. "Shortage of housing for poor grows in U.S." *New York Times* (April 28).

Janowitz, Morris. 1978. *The Last Half Century: Societal Change and Politics in America*. Chicago: University of Chicago Press.

Janus, Samuel, & Cynthia Janus. 1993. *The Janus Report on Sexual Behavior*. New York: Wiley.

Jarret, Robin L. 1994. "Living poor: Family life among single parent African-American women." *Social Problems* 41: 30–49.

Jasper, James M., & Jane D. Poulsen. 1995. "Recruiting strangers and friends." *Social Problems* 42/4: 493–512.

Jaynes, F. D., & R. M. Williams, Jr. 1989. *A Common Destiny: Blacks & American Society*. Washington, DC: National Academy Press.

Jeffreys-Fox, Bruce. 1977. *"How Realistic Are Television's Portrayals of the Elderly?"* University Park, PA: The Annenberg School of Communication.

Jelin, Elizabeth. 1991. *Family, Household and Gender Relations in Latin America* (edited volume). London: Kegan Paul.

Jencks, C. 1994. *The Homeless*. Cambridge, MA: Harvard University Press.

Jencks, Christopher et al.. 1972. *Inequality: A Reassessment of the Effect of Family and Schooling in America*. New York: Basic.

Jencks, Christopher, & Paul E. Peterson. (eds.). 1991. *The Urban Underclass*. Washington, DC: Brookings Institute.

Jencks, Christopher. 1988. "Whom must we treat equally for educational opportunity to be equal?" *Ethics* 98: 518–33.

Jendrek, Margaret Platt. 1996. "Grandparents who parent their grandchildren: Effects on lifestyle." In Jill Quadagno & Debra Street (eds.), *Aging for the Twenty-First Century*. New York: St. Martin's: 286–305.

Jenkins, J. Craig 1983. "Resource mobilization theory and the study of social movements." *Annual Review of Sociology*: 527–53.

Jenkins, J. Craig, & Barbara Brents. 1989. "Social protest, hegemonic competition and social reform: The political origins of the American welfare state." *American Sociological Review*, 54: 891–909.

Jenkins, J. Craig, & Charles Perrow. 1977. "Insurgency of the powerless." *American Sociological Review* 42/2: 249–68.

Jenkins, J. Craig. 1985. *The Politics of Insurgency*. New York: Columbia University Press.

Jenkins, R. 1994a. "Rethinking ethnicity: Identity categorization and power." *Ethnic & Racial Studies* 17: 197–223.

Jenkins, Ron. 1994b. *Subversive Laughter: The Liberating Power of Comedy*. New York: Free Press.

Jenkins, Virginia, & Martha Perkins. 1991. "Portrayals of persons in television commercials." *Psychology* 28: 30–37.

Jenness, V. 1993. *Making it Work: The Prostitute Rights Movement in Perspective*. New York: Aldine de Gruyter.

Jenness, Valerie. 1990. "From sex as sin to sex as work: COYOTE and the reorganization of prostitution as a social problem." *Social Problems* 37: 103–20.

Jennings, M. Kent, & Jan W. van Deth, (ed.). 1989. *Continuities in Political Action*. New York: Aldine DeGruyter.

Jensen, Arthur R. 1969. "How much can we boost IQ and scholastic achievement?" *Harvard Educational Review* 39: 1–123.

Jiang, Lin. 1995. "Changing kinship structure and its implications for old-age support in urban and rural China." *Population Studies* 49(1): 127–45.

Joe, Jennie R., & Dorothy Lonewolf Miller. 1994. "Cultural survival and contemporary American Indian women in the city." In Maxine Baca Zinn & Bonnie Thornton Dill (eds.), *Women's History*. New York: Routledge.

Johansen, Bruce E. 1997. "Race, ethnicity and the media." In Alan Wells & Ernest A. Hakanen, (eds.), *Mass Media and Society*. Greenwich, CT: Ablex: 513–25.

Johnson, Colleen L. 1994. "Differential expectations and realities: Race, socioeconomic status and health of the oldest-old." *International Journal of Aging and Human Development* 38(1): 13–27.

Johnson, Fern L. 1996. "Friendships among women: Closeness in dialogue." In Julia T. Wood (ed.), *Gendered Relationships*. Mountain View, CA: Mayfield.

Johnson, Hank, & Bert Klandermans, (eds.), 1995. *Social Movements and Culture*. Minneapolis: University of Minnesota Press.

Johnson, J. Alleyne. 1995. "Life after death: Pedagogy in an urban classroom." *Harvard Educational Review* 65(2): 213–30.

Johnson, Jeanette H., & Wendy Turnbull. 1995. "The women's conference: Where aspirations and realities met." *International Family Planning Perspectives* 21(4): 155–59.

Johnson, Miriam. 1997. "Review of six prominent sociology of the family textbooks in teaching, research and reference section." *Contemporary Sociology* 26(3): 395–99.

Johnson, Richard A. 1985. *American Fads*. New York: Beech Tree.

Johnson, Robert. 1990. *Death Work: A Study of the Modern Execution Process*. Pacific Grove, CA: Brooks/Cole.

Johnson, Roberta Ann. 1993. "Affirmative action as a woman's issue." In Lois Lovelace Duke (ed.), *Women in Politics: Outsiders or Insiders?* Upper Saddle River, NJ: Prentice Hall.

Johnson, Victoria, & Robert Nurick. 1995. "Behind the headlines: The ethics of the population and environment debate." *International Affairs* 71: 547–65.

Johnston, Janet. 1993. "Children of divorces who refuse visitation." In Charlene E. Depner & James H. Bray (eds.), *Nonresidential Parenting: New Vistas in Family Living*. Newbury Park, CA: Sage.

Johnston, W. B., & A. H. Packer. 1987. *Workforce 2000: Work and Workers for the 21st Century*. Indianapolis, IN: Hudson Institute.

Johnstone, Ronald L. 1992. *Religion in Society: A Sociology of Religion*. Upper Saddle River, NJ: Prentice Hall.

Johnstone, Ronald L. 1997. *Religion in Society*, 5th ed. Englewood Cliffs, NJ: Prentice Hall.

Jones, James H. 1993. *Bad Blood: The Tuskegee Syphilis Experiment*. New York: Free Press.

Jones, John W., & Michael W. Boye. 1992. "Job stress and employee counterproductivity." In James Campbell Quick, Lawrence R. Murphy, & Joseph J. Hurrell, Jr., (eds.), *Stress and Well-Being at Work: Assessments and Interventions for Occupational Mental Health*. Washington, DC: American Psychological Association: 239–51.

Jones, Rodney & Mark McDonough. 1998. *Tracking Nuclear Proliferation*. Washington, DC: Carnegie Endowment for International Peace.

Jones, Stephen G. 1986. *Workers at Play: A Social and Economic History of Leisure, 1918–1939*. London: Routledge & Kegan Paul.

Jones, Vinetta C., & Rochelle Clemson. 1996. "Promoting effective teaching for diversity." In Laura I. Rendon & Richard O. Hope (eds.), *Educating a New Majority: Transforming America's Educational System for Diversity*. San Francisco: Jossey-Bass: 159–67.

Jopke, Christian. 1996. "Multiculturalism and immigration." *Theory and Society* (25/4): 449–500.

Jordan, Ellen, & Angela Cowan. 1995. "Warrior narratives in the kindergarten classroom: Renegotiating the social contract?" *Gender & Society* 9(6): 727–43.

Jordon, Mary. 1996. "College dorms reflect trend of self-segregation." In The Washington Post Writer's Group, (ed.), *Ourselves & Others*, 2nd ed. Boston: Allyn & Bacon: 85–87.

Jorgensen, D. O., & C. Lange. 1975. "Graffiti content as an index of political interest." *Perceptual and Motor Skills* 40: 616–18.

Jorgensen, Stephen R. 1986. *Marriage and the Family*. New York: Macmillan.

Jorgensen, Stephen R. 1993. "Adolescent pregnancy and parenting." In Thomas P. Gullota, Gerald R. Adams, & Raymond Montemayer (eds.), *Adolescent Sexuality*. Newbury Park, CA: Sage.

Jughes, Everett. 1962. "Good people and dirty work." *Social Problems* 10: 3–11.

Kaestle, Carl F. 1995. "Literate America: High-level adult literacy as a national goal." In Diane Ravitch & Maris A. Vinovskis (eds.), *Learning from the Past: What History Teaches Us About School Reform*. Baltimore, MD: Johns Hopkins University: pp. 330–54.

Kahl, Joseph A. 1988. *Three Latin American Sociologists.* New Brunswick, NJ: Transaction.

Kahn, Arthur D. 1997. *The Many Faces of Gay: Activitists Who Are Changing the Nation.* Westport, CT: Praeger.

Kahn, Jeffrey P. 1993. "Workplace mental health problems: Management, assessment and treatment." In Jeffrey P. Kahn (ed.), *Mental Health in the Workplace: A Practical Psychiatric Guide.* New York: Van Nostrand Reinhold: 3–25.

Kain, J. F. 1992. "The spatial mismatch hypothesis: Three decades later." *Housing Policy Debate* 3: 371–460.

Kalick, S. Michael. 1988. "Physical attractiveness as a status cue." *Journal of Experimental Social Psychology* 24: 469–489.

Kalish, Susan. 1995. "Interracial births increase as U.S. ponders racial definitions." *Population Today* (23/4): 1–2.

Kalleberg, Arne L., & Rachel A. Rosenfeld. 1990. "Work in the family and in the labor market: A cross-national, reciprocal analysis." *Journal of Marriage and the Family* 52: 331–46.

Kalmijn, Matthijs. 1991. "Shifting boundaries: Trends in religious and educational homogamy." *American Sociological Review* 56(6): 786–800.

Kalmijn, Matthijs. 1993. "Trends in black-white intermarriage." *Social Forces* 72(1): 119–46.

Kalof, Linda. 1993. "Dilemmas of femininity: Gender and the social construction of sexual imagery." *Sociological Quarterly* 34(4): 639–51.

Kameda, T., & S. Sugimori. 1999. "Psychological Entrapment in Group Decision Making." *Journal of Personality & Social Psychology* 65: 282–292.

Kamerman, Jack B. 1988. *Death in the Midst of Life: Social and Cultural Influences on Death, Grief and Mourning.* Upper Saddle River, NJ: Prentice Hall.

Kammeyer, K. C. W. et al. 1990. *Sociology: Experiencing Changing Societies.* Boston: Allyn & Bacon.

Kandal, Terry R. 1988. *The Woman in Classical Sociological Theory.* Miami: Florida International University Press.

Kandel, Denise, & Mark Davies. 1991. "Friendship networks, intimacy and illicit drug use in young adults." *Criminology* (29): 441–67.

Kandiyoti, Deniz. 1985. *Women in Rural Production Systems: Problems and Policies.* Paris: UNESCO.

Kane, Robert L., & Rosalie A. Kane. 1994. "Satisfaction guaranteed." In William Fornblum & Carolyn D. Smith (eds.), *The Leading Experience: Readings on the Social Context of Health Care.* Upper Saddle River, NJ: Prentice Hall: 171–76.

Kane, Stephanie. 1993. "National discourse and the dynamics of risk: Ethnography and AIDS intervention." *Human Organization* 52(2): 224–28.

Kanne, Bernice. 1995. "Guy stuff: A new man is regular Joe." *St. Louis Post-Dispatch* (October 29): 7E.

Kanter, Rosabeth Moss. 1973. *Communes: Creating and Managing the Collective Life.* New York: Harper & Row.

Kanter, Rosabeth M. 1977. *Men and Women of the Corporation.* New York: Basic Books.

Kanter, Rosabeth Moss, & Barry A. Stein. 1979. "The gender pioneers: Women in an industrial sales force." In Rosabeth Moss Kanter, & Barry A. Stein, (eds.), *Life in Organizations.* New York: Basic Books: 134–60.

Kanter, Rosabeth Moss. 1983. *The Change Masters.* New York: Simon & Schuster.

Kantor, G. K., & Murray A. Straus. 1987. "The 'drunken bum' theory of wife beating." *Social Problems* 34(3): 213–30.

Kantrowitz, Barbara. 1994. "In search of the sacred." *Newsweek* (November 28): 53–55.

Kantrowitz, Barbara. 1997. "A new pet rock for the digital generation." *Newsweek.* (June 9): 62.

Kapferer, Jean-Noel. 1992. "How rumors are born." *Society* 29: 53–60.

Kaplan, Howard B. 1989. "Health, disease and the social structure." In H. Freeman & S. Levine (eds.), *Handbook of Medical Sociology.* Upper Saddle River, NJ: Prentice Hall.

Kappler, Victor E., Mark Blumberg, & Gary W. Potter. 1996. *The Mythology of Crime & Criminal Justice.* Prospect Heights, IL: Waveland.

Kariel, Henry. 1961. *The Decline of American Pluralism.* Stanford, CA: Stanford University Press.

Karman, Andrew. 1995. *Crime Victims*, 3rd. ed. Belmont, CA: Wadsworth.

Karmen, Andrew. 1996. *Crime Victims*, 3rd ed. Belmont, CA: Wadsworth.

Karmen, Andrew. 2000. *Crime Victims*, 4th ed. Belmont, CA: Wadsworth.

Karp, David A., Gregory P. Stone, & William C. Yoels. 1991. *Being Urban: A Sociology of City Life.* New York: Praeger.

Karsten, Siegfried G. 1995. "Health care: Private good versus public good." *The American Journal of Economics and Sociology* 54(2): 129–44.

Kasarda, John D. (ed.). 1990. *Jobs, Earnings and Employment Growth Patterns in the United States.* Boston: Kluwer.

Kasarda, John D. 1989. "Urban industrial transition and the underclass." *The Annals* 501: 26–47.

Kastenbaum, R. 1985. "Dying and death: A life-span approach." In James E. Birren & K. Warner Schaie (eds.), *The Handbook of the Psychology of Aging.* New York: Van Nostrand.

Kates, Nick K., Barrie S. Grieff, & Duane Q. Hagen. 1990. *The Psychosocial Impact of Job Loss.* Washington: American Psychiatric Press.

Katz, J.N. 1995. *The Invention of Heterosexuality.* New York: Dutton.

Katz, Michael B. 1989. *The Undeserving Poor: From the War On Poverty to the War on Welfare.* New York: Pantheon.

Katz, Michael B. 1995. *Improving Poor People.* Princeton, NJ: Princeton University Press.

Katzman, M. A., & S. C. Wooley (eds.). 1994. *Feminist Perspectives on Eating Disorders.* New York: Guilford.

Kaufman, Debra R. 1995. "Professional women: How real are the recent gains?" In Jo Freeman (ed.), *Women: A Feminist Perspective.* Mountain View, CA: Mayfield.

Kaus, Mickey. 1997. "The GOP's welfare gut check." *Newsweek* (June 30): 38.

Kausler, A. 1991. *Experimental Psychology and Human Aging.* New York: Springer-Verlag.

Kay, P., & W. Kempton. 1984. "What is the Sapir-Whorf hypothesis?" *American Anthropologist* 86: 65–79.

Kayser-Jones, J. S. 1981. *Old, Alone and Neglected: Care of the Aged in Scotland and the United States.* Berkeley, CA: University of California Press.

Kean, Rita C., Sally Van Zandt, & Wendy Maupin. 1993. "Successful aging: The older entrepreneur." *Journal of Women and Aging* 5(1): 25–42.

Kearl, M. C. 1989. *Endings: A Sociology of Death and Dying.* New York: Oxford University Press.

Keefe, Keunho, & Thomas J. Berndt. 1996. "Relations of friendship quality to self-esteem in early adolescence." *Journal of Early Adolescence* 16(1): 110–29.

Kegan, R. 1982. *The Evolving Self: Problem and Process in Human Development.* Cambridge, MA: Harvard University.

Keillor, Garrison. 1994. "It's good old monogamy that's really sexy." *Time* (October 17): 71.

Keith, Jennie, Christine L. Fry, Anthony P. Glascock, Charlotte Ikels, Jeanette Dickerson-Putman, Henry C. Harpending, & Patricia Draper. 1994. *The Aging Experience: Diversity and Commonality Across Cultures.* Thousand Oaks, CA: Sage.

Keith, Jennie. 1990. "Age in social and cultural context: Anthropological perspectives." In Robert H. Binstock & Linda K. George (eds.), *Handbook of Aging and the Social Sciences.*" New York: Academic Press.

Keith, Jennie. 1992. "Care-taking in cultural context: Anthropological queries." In Hal Kendig, Akiko Hashimoto, & Larry C. Coppard (eds.), *Family Support for the Elderly: The International Experience.* New York: Oxford University Press.

Keith, M., & S. Pile. 1996. "Imaging the city." *Environment and Planning* 28: 381–86.

Keizai Koho Center. 1999. *Japan 1999: An International Comparison.* Tokyo: Keizai Koho Center (Japan Institute for Social and Economic Affairs).

Keller, Bill. 1993. "Misfits of peace: Is this the end of the bushmen?" *New York Times* (May 10): A4.

Keller, Helen. 1917. *The Story of My Life.* Garden City, NY: Doubleday.

Keller, Robert, & Edward Sbarboro. 1994. *Prisons in Crisis.* Albany, NY: Harrow & Heston.

Kelley, D. 1986. *Why Conservative Churches are Growing: A Study in the Sociology of Religion.* Macon, GA: Mercer University Press.

Kelley, Jonathan & M. D. R. Evans. 1995. "Class and class conflict in six western nations." *American Sociological Review* 60: 157–78.

Kelley, Jonathan, & M. D. R. Evans. 1993. "The legitimization of inequality: Occupational earnings in nine nations." *American Journal of Sociology* 99.

Kelly, Joan B. 1993. "Developing and implementing post-divorce parenting plans: Does the forum make a difference?" In *Americans: Emerging Minorities.* Upper Saddle River, NJ: Prentice Hall.

Kelly, Rita Mae. 1997. "Sex-role spillover: Personal, familial, and organizational roles." In *Workplace/Women's Place: An Anthology.* Los Angeles: Roxbury: 150–60.

Kemp, Alice A. 1994. *Women's Work: Degraded and Devalued.* Upper Saddle River, NJ: Prentice Hall.

Kemp, Alice Abel. 1995. "Poverty and welfare for women." In Jo Freeman (ed.), *Women: A Feminist Perspective.* Mountain View, CA: Mayfield.

Kemper, Susan. 1984. "When to speak like a lady." *Sex Roles* 10(5–6): 435–43.

Kempf, Kimberly L. (ed.), 1990. *Measurement Issues in Criminology.* New York: Springer-Verlag.

Kendig, Hal L., Aliko Hashimoto, & Larry C. Coppard (eds.). 1992. *Family Support for the Elderly: The International Experience.* New York: Oxford University Press.

Kenmochi, Takashi. 1992. "Defusing the examination war: How can companies and parents relieve pressure on students?" *Japan Update* (December): 12–15.

Kennedy, Leslie W., & Vincent F. Sacco. 1998. *Crime Victims In Context.* Los Angeles: Roxbury.

Kennedy, Paul M. 1988. *The Rise & Fall Of the Great Powers.* New York: Random House.

Kennedy, Paul. 1993. *Preparing for the Twenty-First Century.* New York: Random House.

Kennedy, Paul. 1997. "Preparing for the 21st century: Winners and losers." In Robert M. Jackson (ed.), *Global Issues 97/98.* Guilford, CT: Dushkin/McGraw-Hill: 8–24.

Kent, Susan. 1989. "And justice for all: The development of political Ccentralization among newly sedentary foragers." *American Anthropologist* 91(3): 703–12.

Keohane, Robert O. 1996. "Analyzing the effectiveness of international environmental institutions." In Robert O. Keohane & Marc A. Levy (eds.), *Institutions for Environmental Aid: Pitfalls and Promises.* Cambridge, MA: Massachusetts Institute of Technology: 3–27.

Kerbo, Harold R. 1991. *Social Stratification and Inequality,* 2nd ed. New York: McGraw-Hill.

Kerbo, Harold R. G., John A. McKinstry. 1998. *Modern Japan.* New York: McGraw-Hill.

Kerckhoff, Alan C., & Kurt W. Back. 1968. *The June Bug: A Study of Hysterical Contagion.* New York: Appleton-Century-Crofts.

Kesner, I. F. 1988. "Director's characteristics and committee membership: An investigation of type, occupation, tenures, and gender." *Academy of Management Journal* 131: 66–84.

Kessler, Ronald C., J. Blake Turner, & James S. House. 1989. "Unemployment, reemployment and emotional functions in a community sample." *American Sociological Review* 54: 648–57.

Kessler, Ronald C., James House, & Blake Turner. 1987. "Unemployment and health in a community sample." *Journal of Health and Social Behavior* 28: 51–59.

Kessler, Ronald C., Katherine A. McGonagle, Shanyang Zhao, Christopher B. Nelson, Michael Hughes, Susan Eshleman, Hans-Ulrich Wittchen, & Kenneth S. Kendler. 1994. "Lifetime and 12-month prevalence of DSM-III-R psychiatric disorders in the United States: Results from the national comorbidity study." *Archives of General Psychiatry* 51: 8–19.

Kessler, Suzanne J., & Wendy McKenna. 1978. *Gender: An Ethnomethodological Approach.* New York: John Wiley.

Kettl, Donald F. 1991. "The savings and loan bailout: The mismatch between the headlines and the issues." *PS* 24/3: 441–47.

Keyfitz, Nathan. 1996. "Population growth, development and the environment." *Population Studies* 50(3): 335–59.

Kidder, Tracy. 1989. *Among Schoolchildren.* Boston: Houghton Mifflin.

Kimble, Charles E., & J. I. Musgrove. 1988. "Dominance in arguing in mixed-sex dyads: Visual dominance patterns, talking time and speech loudness." *Journal of Research in Personality* 22: 1–16.

Kimble, Charles E., J. C. Yoshikawa, & H. D. Zehr. 1981. "Vocal and verbal assertiveness in same-sex and mixed-sex groups." *Journal of Personality and Social Psychology* 40: 1047–54.

Kimbrell, Andrew. 1993. "A manifesto for men." In Virginia Cyrus (ed.), *Experiencing Race, Class, and Gender in the United States.* Mountain View, CA: Mayfield.

Kimmel, Michael S. 1994. "Masculinity as homophobia: Fear, shame and silence in the construction of gender identity." In H. Brod & M. Kaufman (eds.), *Theorizing Masculinities.* Thousand Oaks, CA: Sage.

Kimmel, Michael. 1997. "Promise Keepers: Patriarchy's second coming as masculine renewal." *Tikkun* (March): 46–50.

Kimsa, G., & E. Leeuwen. 1993. "Dutch euthanasia: Background, practice, and present justifications." *Cambridge Quarterly of Healthcare Ethics* 2: 19–35.

Kincaid, Stephen B., & Robert A. Caldwell. 1995. "Marital separation: Causes, coping, and consequences." *Journal of Divorce and Remarriage* 22(3–4): 109–128.

King, Colbert I. 1997. "Calcutta can be found all over the world." *Washington Post* (September 13).

King, L. A. 1993. "Emotional expression, ambivalence over expression, and marital satisfaction." *Journal of Personal and Social Relationships* 10: 601–7.

Kinney, Eleanor D., & Suzanne K. Steinmetz. 1994. "Notes from the insurance underground: How the chronically ill cope." *Journal of Health Politics, Policy and Law* 19(3): 633–42.

Kinsey, Alfred E., Wardell B. Pomeroy, & Clyde E. Martin, & H. Gephard. 1953. *Sexual Behavior of the Human Female.* Philadelphia: Saunders.

Kinsey, Alfred E., Wardell B. Pomeroy, & Clyde E. Martin. 1948. *Sexual Behavior in the Human Male.* Philadelphia: Saunders.

Kinsman, Gary. 1992. "Men loving men: The challenge of gay liberation." In Michael S. Kimmel & Michael A. Messner (eds.), *Men's Lives.* New York: Macmillan.

Kirk, Dudley. 1986. "Foreword." In W. Penn Handwerker (ed.), *Culture and Reproduction: An Anthropological Critique of Demographic Transition Theory.* Boulder, CO: Westview.

Kirk, Gwyn, & Margo Okazawa-Rey. 1998. *Women's Lives: Multicultural Perspectives.* Mountain View, CA: Mayfield.

Kirp, David L. 1995. "Changing conceptions of educational equity." In Diane Ravitch & Maris A. Vinovskis (eds.), *Learning from the Past: What History Teaches Us About School Reform.* Baltimore, MD: Johns Hopkins University Press: 98–112.

Kitano, H. 1980. *Race Relations.* Upper Saddle River, NJ: Prentice-Hall.

Kitano, Harry H. L., & Roger Daniels. 1995. *Asian Americans: Emerging Minorities.* Englewood Cliffs, NJ: Prentice Hall.

Kitano, Harry H.L., & Roger Daniels. 1988. *Asian Americans.* Englewood Cliffs, NJ: Prentice-Hall.

Kite, Mary E., & Bernard Whitley. 1996. "Sex differences in attitudes toward homosexual persons, behaviors, and civil rights: A meta-analysis." *Personality and Social Psychology Bulletin* 22: 336–53.

Kitschelt, Herbert P. 1986. "Political opportunity structures and political protest." *British Journal of Political Science* 16: 57–85.

Kitsuse, John I. 1980. "Coming out all over: Deviants and the politics of social problems." *Social Problems* (28/1): 1–13.

Kitzinger, Celia. 1988. *The Social Construction of Lesbianism.* Newbury Park, CA: Sage.

Kivisto, Peter. 1994. "The rise or fall of the Christian right: Conflicting reports from the frontlines." *Sociology of Religion* 55(3): 223–37.

Klagsbrun, Francis. 1995. "Marriages that last." In Mark Robert Rank & Edward L. Kain (eds.), *Diversity and Change in Families: Patterns, Prospects, and Policies.* Upper Saddle River, NJ: Prentice Hall.

Klandermans, Bert. 1984. "Mobilization & participation." *American Sociological Review* 49: 583–600.

Klandermans, Bert. 1994. "Targeting the critical mass." *Social Psychological Quarterly* 57: 360–67.

Klapp, Orris E. 1972. *Currents of Unrest.* New York: Holt.

Klatell, David A., & Norman Marcus. 1988. *Sports For Sale: Television, Money and the Fans.* New York: Oxford University Press.

Klee, Kenneth. 2000. "The siege of Seattle." *Newsweek* (December 13).

Kleidman, Robert. 1994. "Volunteer activism & professionalism in social movement organizations." *Social Problems* 41: 257–76.

Klein, Dorie. 1995. "The etiology of female crime: A review of the literature." In Barbara R. Price & Natalie J. Sokoloff, (eds.), *The Criminal Justice System and Women,* 2nd ed. New York: McGraw-Hill: 30–46.

Klein, Lloyd. 1996. "Close encounters of the media kind: Class conflict on daytime talk shows." Paper presented at the annual meeting of the American Sociological Association, San Francisco, August.

Klein, Stephen P., Susan Turner, & Joan Petersilia. 1988. *Racial Equity in Sentencing.* Santa Monica: Rand.

Kleinberg, Seymour. 1992. "The new masculinity of gay men and beyond." In Michael S. Kimmel & Michael A. Messner (eds.), *Men's Lives.* New York: Macmillian.

Kleinke, C. L. 1986. "Gaze and eye contact: A research review." *Psychological Bulletin* 16: 740–45.

Kleinman, Arthur. 1988. *The Illness Narratives: Suffering, Healing and the Human Condition.* New York: Basic Books.

Kleinman, Sherryl, & Martha A. Copp. 1993. *Emotions and Fieldwork.* Qualitative Research Methods Series 28. Newbury Park, CA: Sage.

Klenke, Karin. 1996. *Women & Leadership.* New York: Springer.

Klepper, Steven, & Daniel Nagin. 1989a. "Tax compliance and perceptions of risk detection & criminal prosecution." *Law and Society Review* 23: 209–240.

Klepper, Steven, & Daniel Nagin. 1989b. "The deterrent effect of perceived certainty and severity of punishment revisited." *Criminology* 27: 721–46.

Kletzer, L. G. 1991. "Job displacement, 1979–1986." *Monthly Labor Review* 114: 17–25.

Klir, George J. 1972. *Trends in General Systems Theory.* New York: John Wiley & Sons.

Kloehn, Steve. 1997. "Most alternative sects are safe, experts say." *Chicago Tribune* (March 28): 1: 7.

Klopfenstein, Bruce C. 1989. "The diffusion of the VCR in the United States." In Mark R. Levy, (ed.), *The VCR Age: Home Video and Mass Communication.* Newbury Park, CA: Sage: 21–39.

Klopfenstein, Bruce C. 1997. "New technology and the future of media." In Alan Wells Ernest A. Hakanen, (eds.), *Mass Media and Society.* Greenwich, CT: Ablex: 19–49.

Kluegel, James R. 1990. "Trends in whites' explanations of the black-white gap in socioeconomic status, 1977–1989." *American Sociological Review* 55: 512–25.

Kluegel, James R., & Elliot R. Smith. 1986. *Beliefs About Inequality: Americans' Views of What Is and What Ought to Be.* Hawthorne, NY: Aldine de Gruyter.

Kluwer, Esther S., Jose A. M. Heesink, & Evert Van De Vliert. 1997. *Journal of Marriage and the Family* 59(3): 635–53.

Knoke, David. 1990. *Political Networks.* New York: Cambridge University Press.

Kobrin, Solomon. 1959. "The Chicago Area Project—25 year assessment." *The Annals* 322: 20–29.

Koenig, Michael A., James F. Phillips, Oona M. Campbell, & Stan D'Souza. 1990. "Birth intervals and childhood mortality in rural Bangladesh." *Demography* 27(2): 251–65.

Kogos, Jennifer L., & John Snarey. 1995. "Parental divorce and the moral development of adolescents." *Journal of Divorce and Remarriage* 23(3–4): 177–86.

Kohlberg, Lawrence. 1966. "A cognitive-developmental analysis of children's sex-role concepts and attitudes." In Eleanor E. Maccoby (ed.), *The Development of Sex Differences.* Stanford, CA: Stanford University.

Kohlberg, Lawrence. 1969. "Stage and sequence: The cognitive developmental approach to socialization." In David A. Goslin (ed.), *Handbook of Socialization Theory and Research.* Chicago: Rand McNally.

Kohlberg, Lawrence. 1969. *Stages in the Development of Moral Thought and Action.* New York: Holt Rinehart & Winston.

Kohlberg, Lawrence. 1981. *The Psychology of Moral Development: The Nature and Validity of Moral Stages.* New York: Harper & Row.

Kohn, A. 1986. *No Contest: The Case Against Competition.* Boston: Houghton Mifflin.

Kohn, Melvin. 1978. "The benefits of bureaucracy." *Human Nature* (August): 60–66.

Kohn, Melvin L. 1977. *Class and Conformity: A Study in Values,* 2nd ed. Homewood, IL: Dorsey.

Kolaric, Giselle C., & Nancy L. Galambos. 1995. "Face-to-face interactions in unacquainted female–male sdolescent dyads: How do girls and boys behave?" *Journal of Early Adolescence* 15(3): 363–82.

Kolata, G. 1987. "Alcoholism: Genetic links grow clearer." *New York Times* (November, 10): C1, C2.

Kolenda, Pauline. 1985. *Caste in Contemporary India*. Prospect Heights, IL: Waveland.

Komarovsky, Marra. 1987. "College men: Gender roles in transition." In Carol Lasser (ed.), *Educating Men and Women Together: Education in a Changing World*. Upper Saddle River, NJ: Prentice Hall.

Kooistra, Paul, John S. Mahoney, & Lisha Bridges. 1993. "The unequal opportunity for equal ability hypothesis: Racism in the NFL?" *Sociology of Sport Journal* 10: 241–55.

Koopmans, Ruud. 1993. "The dynamics of protest waves." *American Sociological Review* 58: 637–58.

Kornblum, William & Carolyn D. Smith. (eds.), 1994. *The Healing Experience: Readings on the Social Context of Health Care*. Upper Saddle River, NJ: Prentice Hall.

Kornhauser, William. 1959. *The Politics of Mass Society*. New York: Free Press.

Kosmin, Barry A., & Seymour P. Lachman. 1993. *One Nation Under God*. New York: Harmony Books.

Koss, Mary P., L. Goodman, L. Fitzgerald, N. Russo, G. Keita, & A. Browne. 1994. *No Safe Haven: Male Violence Against Women at Home, at Work, and in the Community*. Washington, DC: American Psychological Association.

Kotkin, Joel. 1993. *Tribes: How Race, Religion & Identity Determine Success in the New Global Economy*. New York: Random House.

Kottak, Conrad Phillip. 1987. *Cultural Anthropology*. New York: Random House.

Kouba, Leonard & Judith Muasher. 1985. "Female circumcision in Africa: An overview." *African Studies Review* 28(1): 95–110.

Kowalewski, David, & Karen L. Porter. 1992. "Ecoprotest: Alienation, deprivation or resources." *Social Science Quarterly* 73/3: 523–34.

Kozol, Jonathan. 1991. *Savage Inequalities: Children in America's Schools*. New York: Crown.

Kramarae, Cheris, & Paula A. Treichler. 1990. "Power relationships in the classroom." In Susan L. Garbirel & Isaiah Smithson (eds.), *Gender in the Classroom: Power and Pedagogy*. Urbana, IL: University of Illinois Press.

Kramer, Jane. 1993. "Letter from Europe: Neo-Nazis: A chaos in the head." *New Yorker* (June 14): 52–70.

Kratcoski, Peter C., & Lucille D. Kratcoski. 1996. *Juvenile Delinquency*, 4th ed. Upper Saddle River, NJ: Prentice Hall.

Kraus, Stephen J. 1995. "Attitudes and the prediction of behavior: A meta-analysis of the empirical literature." *Personality and Social Psychology Bulletin* 21: 58–75.

Kreisi, Hanspeter, et al. 1995. *New Social Movements in Western Europe*. Minneapolis: University of Minnesota Press.

Krieger, Nancy, & Elizabeth Fee. 1994a. "Man-made medicine and women's health: The biopolitics of sex/gender and race/ethnicity." *International Journal of Health Services* 24(2): 265–83.

Krieger, Nancy, & Elizabeth Fee. 1994b. "Social class: The missing link in U.S. health data." *International Journal of Health Services* 24(1): 25–44.

Krisberg, Barry et al. 1987. "The incarceration of minority youth." *Crime and Delinquency* 33(2): 173–205.

Kristof, Nicholas D. 1993. "Via satellite, information revolution stirs China." *New York Times* (April 11).

Kroger, Jane. 1996. *Identity in Adolescence: The Balance Between Self and Other*. London: Routledge.

Krugman, Paul R. 1992. "The right, the rich, and the facts: Deconstructing the income distribution debate." *The American Prospect* 11: 20–31.

Krymkowski, Daniel H., & Tadeusz K. Krauze. 1992. "Occupational mobility in the year 2000." *Social Forces* 71: 145–157.

Krysan, Maria, & William V. D'Antonio. 1992. "Voluntary associations." In Edgar F. Borgatta, & Marie L. Borgatta, (eds.), *Encyclopedia of Sociology*. New York: Macmillan: 2231–34.

Kubler-Ross, Elisabeth. 1969. *On Death and Dying*. New York: Macmillan.

Kuebli, Janet, & Robyn Fivish. 1992. "Gender differences in parent–child conversations about past emotions." *Sex Roles* 27(11–12): 683–98.

Kuhlmann, Annette. 1996. "Indian country in the 1990s: Changing roles of American Indian women." Paper presented at the Midwest Sociological Society, Chicago, April.

Kuhn, Thomas. 1970. *The Structure of Scientific Revolutions*, 2nd ed. Chicago: University of Chicago Press.

Kuisel, Richard. 1993. *Seducing the French: The Dilemma of Americanization*. Berkeley: University of California.

Kumar, Krishnan. 1995. *From Post-Industrial to Post-Modern Society: New Theories of the Contemporary World*. Oxford, UK: Blackwell.

Kumin, Judith. 1998. "An uncertain direction: European countries are increasingly coordinating their asylum procedures, but will refugees be more...or less...welcome in the future?" *Refugees* 2(1113): 5–9.

Kuper, Leo, & M. G. Smith. 1969. *Plural Societies*. Chicago: Aldine.

Kurdek, L. A. 1993a. "The allocation of household labor in gay, lesbian, and heterosexual married couples." *Journal of Social Issues* 49: 127–39.

Kurdek, L. A. 1993b. "Predicting marital dissolution: A five year prospective longitudinal study of newlywed couples." *Journal of Personality and Social Psychology* 64(2): 221–42.

Kurtz, Demie. 1995. *For Richer, For Poorer: Mothers Confront Divorce*. New York: Routledge.

Kurz, Karin, & Walter Muller. 1987. "Class mobility in the industrial world." *Annual Review of Sociology* 13: 417–442.

Kusterer, Ken. 1993. "Women-oriented NGOs in Latin America: Democratization's decisive wave." In Gay Young, Vidyamali Samarasinghe, & Ken Kusterer (eds.), *Women at the Center: Development Issues and Practices for the 1990s*. West Hartford, CT: Kumarian: 182–92.

Kutner, B., C. Wilkins, & P. Yarrow. 1952. "Verbal attitudes and overt behavior involving racial prejudice." *Journal of Abnormal and Social Psychology* 47: 649–52.

Kuypers, J. A., & Vern L. Bengston. 1973. "Competence and social breakdown: A social psychological view of aging." *Human Development* 16(2): 37–49.

Kuznets, Simon. 1955. "Economic growth and income inequality." *The American Economic Review* 45: 1–28.

La Dou, Joseph. 1991. "Deadly migration: Hazardous industries' flight to the Third World." *Technology Review* 94/5: 46–53.

Lackey, P. N. 1989. "Adults' attitudes about assignments of household chores to male and female children." *Sex Roles* 20: 271–81.

Ladd, Everett C. 1993. "The 1992 vote for President Clinton." *Political Science Quarterly* 108: 1–28.

LaDuke, Winona. 1998. "Breastmilk, PCBs and motherhood." In Gwyn & Margo Okazawa-Rey (eds.), *Women's Lives: Multicultural Perspectives*. Mountain View, CA: Mayfield: 415–17.

LaFramboise, Teresa D., Anneliese M. Heyle, & Emily J. Ozer. 1990. "Changing and diverse roles of women in American Indian culture." *Sex Roles* 22(7–8): 455–76.

Lake, C.C., & V.J. Breglio. 1992. "Different voices, different views: The politics of gender." in P. Reis & A.J. Stone (eds.), *The American Woman, 1992–1993*. New York: W.W. Norton: 178–201.

Lake, Celinda C., & Vincent J. Breglio. 1992. "Different voices, different views: The politics of gender." In Paula Ries & Anne J. Stone (eds.), *The American Woman, 1992–93: A Status Report*. New York: W. W. Norton.

Lakoff, Robin. 1975. *Language and Women's Place*. New York: Colophon.

Lakoff, Robin. 1991. "You are what you say." In Evelyn Ashton-Jones & Gary A. Olson, (eds.), *The Gender Reader*. Boston: Allyn & Bacon.

Lamb, H. H. 1982. *Climate History and the Modern World*. London: Methuen.

Lambrecht, Rank L. 1985. "Human behavior and health in developing Africa." In Christine I. Zeichner (ed.), *Modern and Traditional Health Care in Developing Societies: Conflict and Cooperation*. Lanham, MD: University Press of America.

Lame Deer, John, & Richard Erdoes. 1972. *Lame Deer, Seeker of Visions*. New York: Simon & Schuster.

Lamont, Michelle, & Marcel Fournier. 1992. *Cultivating Differences: Symbolic Boundaries & the Making of Inequality*. Chicago: University of Chicago Press.

Lamont, Michelle. 1992. *Money, Morals and Manners: The Culture of the French and American Upper-Middle Class*. Chicago: University of Chicago Press.

Lamont, Michelle. 1997. "Money, morals, and manners." In David M. Newman (ed.), *Sociology: Exploring the Architecture of Daily Life—Readings*. Thousand Oaks, CA: Pine Forge: 224–240.

Lancaster, William. 1997. *The Rwala Bedouin Today*. Prospect Heights, IL: Waveland.

Land, Kenneth C., Glenn Deane, & Judith R. Blau. 1991. "Religious pluralism and church membership: A spatial diffusion model." *American Sociological Review* 56(2): 237–49.

Land, Kenneth C., Patricia L. McCall, & Lawrence E. Cohen. 1990. "Structural covariates of homicide rates: Are there any invariances across time and social space?" *American Journal of Sociology*, 95: 922–63.

Landale, Nancy S., & Katherine Fennelly. 1992. "Informal unions among mainland Puerto Ricans: Cohabitation or an alternative to legal marriage?" *Journal of Marriage and the Family* 54: 269–80.

Landry, Bart. 1988. *The New Black Middle Class*. Berkeley: University of California Press.

Lane, David. 1985. *State and Politics in the USSR*. Oxford, UK: Blackwell.

Lane, Jan-Erik. 1990. "Data archives as an instrument for comparative research." In Else Oyen (ed.), *Comparative Methodology: Theory and Practice in International Social Research*. London: Sage.

Lang, Eric. 1992. "Role conflict." In Edgar F. Borgatta & Marie L. Borgatta, eds., *Encyclopedia of Sociology*. New York: Macmillan: 1676–1679.

Lang, Kurt, & Gladys E. Lang. 1961. *Collective Dynamics*. New York: Thomas Y. Crowell.

Langan, Patrick A. 1991. "America's soaring prison population." *Science* (251): 1568–573.

Langer, E. J. 1985. "Playing the middle against both ends: The usefulness of older adult cognitive activity in childhood and old age." In S. Yussen (ed.), *The Growth of Reflection in Children*. New York: Academic Press.

Langlois J.H., J.M. Ritter, R.J. Casey, & D.B. Sawin. 1995. "Infant attractiveness predicts maternal behaviors and attitudes." *Developmental Psychology* 31: 464–72.

Langlois, J. H., & L. Musselman. 1995. "Myths and mysteries of beauty." In D. R. Calhoun (ed.), *1996 Yearbook of Science and the Future*. Chicago: Encyclopedia Britannica.

Langois, J. H., & A. C. Downs. 1979. "Peer relations as a function of physical attractiveness: The eye of the beholder or behavioral reality?" *Child Development* 50: 409–18.

Langston, D. 1992. "Tired of playing monopoly?" In M. L. Anderson, & P. H. Collins, (eds.), *Race, Class and Gender: An Anthology*. Belmont, CA: Wadsworth.

Langton, Phyllis A. 1994. "Obstetricians resistance to independent private practice by nurse-midwives in Washington, D.C. hospitals." *Women and Health* 22(1): 27–48.

Lannoy, Richard. 1971. *The Speaking Tree*. New York: Oxford University Press.

Lannoy, Richard. 1975. *The Speaking Tree: A Study of Indian Culture and Society*. New York: Oxford University Press.

Lapchick, Richard E., & Jeffrey R. Benedict. 1994. *1994 Racial Report Card*. Boston: Center For the Study of Sport in Society.

Lapham, Lewis H. 1988. *Money & Class in America: Notes and Observations on our Civil Religion*. New York: Weidenfield and Nicolson.

LaPierre, Richard. 1934. "Attitudes versus actions." *Social Forces* 13: 230–37.

Lappe, Frances M., Joseph Collins, & David Kinley. 1981. *Aid As Obstacle: 20 Questions About Our Foreign Policy and the Hungry*. San Francisco: Institute for Food and Development Policy.

Laquian, Aprodicio A. 1996. "The multi-ethnic and multicultural city: An Asian perspective." *International Social Science Journal* 48: 43–54.

Larana, E., H. Johnson, & J. R. Gusfield, (eds.) 1994. *New Social Movements: From Ideology to Identity*. Philadelphia: Temple University Press.

Larick, Roy. 1986. "Age grading and ethnicity in the style of Loikop (Samburu) Spears." *World Archaeology* 18(2): 269–83.

Laris, Michael. 1998. "Internet police on the prowl in China." *Washington Post* (October 24): A12.

Larmer, Brook. 1992. "Dead end kids." *Newsweek* (May 25): 38–40.

LaRose, H., J. Tracy, & S. J. McKelvie. 1993. "Effects of gender on the physical attractiveness stereotype." *Journal of Psychology* 127: 677–80.

Larson, C. J. 1995. "Theory & applied sociology." *Journal of Applied Sociology* 12(9): 13–29.

Larson, Jan. 1996. "Temps are here to stay." *American Demographics* (February): 26–31.

Lasagna, Louis. 1963. *The Doctors' Dilemmas*. New York: Crowell-Collier.

Lasch, Christopher. 1979. *Haven in a Heartless World*. New York: Basic Books.

Laslett, Barbara. 1990. "Unfeeling knowledge: Emotion & objectivity in the history of sociology." *Sociological Forum* 5: 413–434.

Laslett, Peter. 1972. *Household and Family in Past Time*. New York: Cambridge University.

Laslett, Peter. 1979. *The World We Have Lost*. London: Methuen.

Lauer, Jeanette C., & Robert H. Lauer. 1986. *'Til Death Do Us Part: How Couples Stay Together*. New York: Haworth.

Lauer, Robert H. 1991. *Perspectives on Social Change*, 4th ed. Boston: Allyn & Bacon.

Lauer, Robert H., & Jeanette C. Lauer. 1991. *Marriage and Family: The Quest for Intimacy*. Dubuque, IA: William C. Brown.

Lauer, Robert H., Jeanette C. Lauer, & Sarah T. Kerr. 1990. "The long-term marriage: Perceptions of stability and satisfaction." *International Journal of Aging and Human Development* 31(3): 189–95.

Laumann, Edward O., John H. Gagnon, Robert T. Michael, & Stuart, Michaels. 1994. *The Social Organization of Sexuality: Sexual Practices in the United States*. Chicago: University of Chicago.

Laumann, Edward, & David Knoke. 1987. *The Organizational State*. Madison: University of Wisconsin Press.

Lavoie, Marc. 1989. "Stacking, performance differentials and salary discrimination in professional ice hockey." *Sociology of Sport Journal* 6: 17–35.

Laws, Judith L., & Pepper Schwartz. 1977. *Sexual Scripts: The Social Construction of Female Sexuality*. Hinsdale, IL: Dryden.

Lawson, A. 1988. *Adultery: An Analysis of Love and Betrayal*. New York: Basic Books.

Lawton, M. Powell, Miriam Moss, & E. Moles. 1984. "The supra-personal neighborhood context of older people: Age heterogeneity and well-being." *Environment and Behavior* 16: 86–109.

Lazarsfeld, P. F., & J. G. Reitz. 1989. "History of applied sociology." *Sociological Practice* 7: 42–52.

Lazarsfeld, Paul, & Elihu Katz. 1964. *Personal Influence*. Glencoe, IL: Free Press.

Lazier-Smith, L. 1989. "A new generation of images of women." In P. J. Creedon (ed.), *Women in Mass Communication*. Newbury Park, CA: Sage.

Leahy, Robert L., & Stephen R. Shirk. 1984. "The development of classificatory skills and sex-trait stereotypes in children." *Sex Roles* 10(3–4): 281–92.

Leaper, Campbell. 1994. "Exploring the consequences of gender segregation on social relationships." In Campbell Leaper (ed.), *Childhood Gender Segregation: Causes and Consequences*. San Francisco: Jossey-Bass.

LeBon, Gustave. 1960. *The Crowd: A Study of the Popular Mind*. New York: Viking. Originally published in 1896.

Lechner, Frank L. 1989. "Fundamentalism revisited." *Society* (January/February): 51–9.

LeChner, Frank L. 1993. "Global fundamentalism." In William H. Swatos, Jr. (ed.), *A Future for Religion? New Paradigms for Social Analysis*. Newbury Park, CA: Sage: 19–36.

Lee, Barrett A. 1992. "Homelessness." In Edgar F. Borgatta & Marie L. Borgatta (eds.), *Encyclopedia of Sociology*, Vol. 2. New York: Macmillan: 843–847.

Lee, Gary R., & Les B. Whitbeck. 1993. "Economic systems and rates of polygyny." In Lorne Tepperman & Susannah J. Wilson (eds.), *Next of Kin: An International Reader on Changing Families*. Upper Saddle River, NJ: Prentice Hall.

Lee, S. M. 1993. "Racial classifications in the U.S. census, 1890–1990." *Ethnic and Racial Studies* 16: 75–94.

Lee, Shu-ching. 1953. "China's traditional family: Its characteristics and disintegration." *American Sociological Review* 18: 272–80.

Lee, Tony. 1990. "Here comes the pink slip." *American Demographics* (March): 46–49.

Lee, Yok Shiu. 1994. "Community-based urban environmental management: Local NGOs as catalysts." *Regional Development Dialogue* 15(2): 158–76.

Leeds, Anthony. 1994. "City and countryside in anthropology." In Roger Sanjek (ed.), *Cities, Classes, and the Social Order: Anthony Leeds*. Ithaca, NY: Cornell University: 51–69.

Leeft-Pellegrini, Helena M. 1980. "Conversational dominance as function of gender and expertise." In Howard Giles, W. Peter Robinson, & Philip M. Smith (eds.), *Language: Social Psychological Perspectives*. New York: Pergamon.

Leeuwen, Mary Stewart. 1997. "Mixed messages on the mall." *Christian Century* (October 22): 932–34.

Lefkowitz, Margaret B. 1972. "The women's magazine short story heroine in 1957 and 1967." In Constantine Safilios-Rothschild (ed.), *Toward a Sociology of Women*. Lexington, MA: Xerox.

Legters, Nettie, & Edward L. McDill. 1994. "Rising to the challenge: Emerging strategies for educating youth at risk." In Robert J. Rossi (ed.), *Schools and Students at Risk: Context and Framework for Positive Change*. New York: Teacher's College Press, Columbia University Press: 23–47.

Lehmann, Arthur C. 1989. "Eyes of the Ngangas: Ethnomedicine and power in Central African Republic." In Arthur C. Lehmann & James E. Meyers, (eds.), *Magic, Witchcraft, and Religion: An Anthropological Study of the Supernatural*. Mountain View, CA: Mayfield.

Lehne, Gregory K. 1992. "Homophobia among men: Supporting and defining the male role." In Michael S. Kimmel & Michael A. Messner (eds.), *Men's Lives*. New York: Macmillian.

Leicht, Kevin T., Mary L. Fennell, & Kristine M. Witkowski. 1995. "The effects of hospital characteristics and radical organizational change on the relative standing of health care professions." *Journal of Health and Social Behavior* 36(2): 151–67.

Leigh, B. C. 1989. "Reasons for having and avoiding sex: Gender, sexual orientation, and relationship to sexual behavior." *Journal of Sex Research* 26: 199–209.

Leisinger, Klaus M., 1995. "Sustainable development: A common challenge for north and south." *The International Journal of Sociology and Social* 15(8–10): 27–64.

Leisinger, Klaus, & Karin Schmitt. 1994. *All Our People: Population Policy with a Human Face*. Washington, DC: Island Press.

Leland, John. 1993. "Criminal Records." *Newsweek* (November 29): 60–64.

Lemann, Nicholas. 1991. *The Promised Land: The Great Black Migration and How It Changed America*. New York: Vintage.

Lemert, Charles A. 1994. "A classic from the other side of the veil: Du Bois' Souls of Black Folks." *Sociological Quarterly* (35/3): 383–396.

Lemert, Charles. 1997. *Social Things: An Introduction to the Sociological Life*. Lanham, MD: Rowman & Littlefield.

Lemert, Edwin M. 1951. *Social Pathology*. New York: McGraw-Hill.

Lempert, David. 1997. "Development and constitutional democracy: A set of principles for 'perfecting the market.'" In Joseph E. Behar & Alfred G. Cuzan, eds., *At the Crossroads of Development: Transnational Challenges to Developed and Developing Societies*. Leiden, Netherlands: E.J. Brill: 149–71.

Lengermann, Patricia M., & Jill Niebrugge-Brantley. 1998. *The Women Founders: Sociology & Social Theory, 1830–1930*. New York: McGraw-Hill.

Lengermann, Patricia M., & Jill Niebrugge-Brantley. 2000. "Contemporary feminist theory." In George Ritzer, *Modern Sociological Theory*. New York: McGraw-Hill: 307–355.

Lennon, Mary Clare, & Sarah Rosenfield. 1994. "Relative fairness and the division of housework: The importance of options." *American Journal of Sociology* 100(2): 506–31.

Lenski, Gerhard. 1954. "Status crystallization: A nonvertical dimension of social status." *American Sociological Review* 19: 405–13.

Lenski, Gerhard. 1956. "Social participation and status crystallization." *American Sociological Review* 21: 458–64.

Lenski, Gerhard. 1966. *Power and Privilege: A Theory of Social Stratification*. New York: McGraw-Hill.

Leo, John. 1997. "Men behaving well." *U.S. News and World Report* (November 3): 16.

Leonard, Wilbert M. II. 1998. *A Sociological Perspective of Sport*. Boston: Allyn & Bacon.

LePage, Robert, & Andree Tabouret-Keller. 1985. *Acts of Identity: Creole-Based Approaches to Language and Ethnicity*. Cambridge, UK: Cambridge University.

Lerman, H. 1996. *Pigeonholing Women's Misery*. New York: Basic.

Lerner, Max, ed. 1948. *The Portable Veblen*. New York: Penguin.

Lerner, R. M. 1985. "Adolescent maturational changes and psychosocial development: A dynamic interactional process." *Journal of Youth and Adolescence* 14: 355–72.

Leslie, Connie. 1995. "You can't high-jump if the bar is set too low." *Newsweek* (November 6): 82–83.

Letich, Larry. 1991. "Do you know who your friends are? Why most men over 30 don't have friends and what they can do about it." *Utne Reader* (May-June): 85–87.

Leventman, Paula G. 1981. *Professionals out of Work*. New York: Free Press.

Lever, Janet, & S. Wheeler. 1993. "Mass media and the experience of sport," *Communication Research* (20/1): 125–43.

Lever, Janet. 1978. "Sex differences in the complexity of children's play and games." *American Sociological Review* 43(4): 471–83.

Lever, Janet. 1983. *Soccer Madness*. Chicago: University of Chicago Press.

Levin, Jack, & William C. Levin. 1980. *Ageism*. Belmont, CA: Wadsworth.

Levin, Jack, & William Levin. 1982. *The Functions of Discrimination and Prejudice*, 2nd ed. New York: Harper & Row.

Levine J.M., & R.L. Moreland. 1998. "Small groups." In D.T. Gilbert at al. (eds.), *Handbook of Social Psychology*. New York: Random House: 415–469.

Levine, Donald. 1991. "Simmel & Parsons reconsidered." *American Journal of Sociology* 96: 1097–1116.

Levine, Martin P. 1998. *Gay Macho: The Life and Death of the Homosexual Clone*. New York: New York University.

Levine, Robert. 1987. "Waiting is a power game." *Psychology Today*, (April): 24–33.

Levinson, Daniel. 1978. *The Seasons of a Man's Life*. New York: Knopf.

Levinson, Daniel. 1986. "A conception of adult development." *American Psychologist* 41: 3–13.

Levinson, David. 1989. *Family Violence in Cross-Cultural Perspective*. Newbury Park, CA: Sage.

Levitan, Sar A. & Isaac Shapiro. 1987. *Working But Poor*. Baltimore: Johns Hopkins.

Levy, Frank. 1988. *Dollars & Dreams: The Changing American Income Distribution*. New York: W. W. Norton.

Levy, Marion J. Jr. 1992. "Confucianism and modernization." *Society* (24/4): 15–18.

Levy, Mark R., ed. 1989. *The VCR Age: Home Video and Mass Communication*. Newbury Park, CA: Sage.

Levy, Steven. 1996. "Working in Dilbert's world." *Newsweek* (August 12): 52–57.

Lewis, David L. 1993. *The Biography of a Race: 1868–1919*, New York: Holt.

Lewis, Gregory B., & Marc A. Rogers. 1999. "Does the public support equal employment rights for gays and lesbians? In Ellen D.B. Riggle & Barry L. Tadlock (eds.), *Gays and Lesbians in the Democratic Process*. New York: Columbia University: 118–45.

Lewis, J. D., & R. Smith. 1980. *American Sociology and Pragmatism*. Chicago: University of Chicago Press.

Lewis, Lisa A. 1990. *Gender Politics and MTV: Voicing the Difference*. Philadelphia: Temple University.

Lewis, M. 1978. *The Culture of Inequality*. New York: New American Library.

Lewis, Oscar. 1966. "The culture of poverty." *Scientific American 115* (October): *19–25*.

Lewontin, R. C. 1994. "Women versus the biologists." *New York Review* (April 7): 31–35.

Liazos, Alexander. 1972. "The poverty of the sociology of deviance: Nuts, sluts and perverts." *Social Problems* (20/1): 103–20.

Lichtenberger, B., & G. Naulleau. 1993. "Cultural conflicts and synergies in the management of French-German joint ventures." In P. S. Kirkbride (ed.), *Human Resource Management in Europe: Perspectives for the Nineties*. London: Routledge.

Lichter, Daniel T., & David J. Eggebeen. 1993. "Rich kids, poor kids: Changing income inequality among American children." *Social Forces* 73: 761–780.

Lichter, Daniel T., & Nancy C. Landale, 1995. "Parental work, family structure, and poverty among Latino children." *Journal of Marriage and the Family* 57: 346–54.

Lichter, Daniel T., Robert N. Anderson, & Mark D. Hayward. 1995. "Marriage markets and marital choice." *Journal of Family Issues* 16(4): 412–31.

Lichter, S. Robert, & Daniel R. Amundson. 1997. "Distorted reality: Hispanic characters in TV entertainment." In Clara Rodriquez E. *Latin Looks*. Boulder, CO: Westview Press: 57–72.

Lichter, S. Robert, & Daniel R. Amundson. 2000. "Distorted reality: Hispanic characters in tv entertainment." In Clara Rodriguez (ed.), *Latin Looks*. Boulder, CO: Westview: 57–92.

Lieberman, Janet. 1989. "A plan for high school/community college collaboration." *College Board Review* Fall: 14–19.

Lieberson, Stanley. 1992. "Einstein, Renoir, & Greely: Some thoughts about evidence in sociology." *American Sociological Review* 57: 1–15.

Liebow, Elliot. 1967. *Tally's Corner: A Study of Negro Streetcorner Men*. Boston: Little, Brown.

Liebow, Elliott. 1995. *Tell Them Who I Am: The Lives of Homeless Women*. New York: Penguin.

Lief, H. I., & L. Hubschman. 1993. "Orgasm in the post-operative transsexual." *Archives of Sexual Behavior* 22: 145–55.

"Life after welfare is not exactly a bed of roses," *Evansville Courier-Press* (from the Associate Press) (May 12).

Lifton, Robert J. 1979. *The Broken Connection*. New York: Simon & Schuster.

Lifton, Robert J. 1992. Foreword to Chugoku Newspaper's *Exposure: Victims of Radiation Speak Out*. Tokyo: Kodansha International.

Light, Donald W. 1988. "Towards a new sociology of medical education." *Journal of Health and Social Behavior* 29: 307–22. 1993. "Countervailing power: The changing character of the medical profession in the United States." In Frederic W. Hafferty & John B. McKinlay (eds.), *The Changing Medical Profession: An International Perspective*. New York: Oxford University Press.

Light, Ivan H., & Edna Bonacich. 1988. *Immigrant Entrepreneurs: Koreans in Los Angeles, 1965–1982*. Berkeley: University of California Press.

Lin, C. A. 1990. "Audience activity and VCR use." In J. R. Dobrow (ed.), *Social and Cultural Aspects of VCR Use*. Hillsdale, NJ: Lawrence Erlbaum: 75–92.

Lin, Nan, & Wen Xie. 1988. "Occupational prestige in urban China." *American Journal of Sociology* 93/4: 793–832.

Lin, Nan, W. M. Ensler, & J. C. Vaughn. 1981. "Social resources & strength of ties." *American Sociological Review* 46: 393–405.

Lincoln, C. Eric, & Lawrence H. Mamiya. 1990. *The Black Church in the African American Experience*. Durham, NC: Duke University Press.

Lincoln, James R., & Arne L. Kalleberg. 1990. *Culture Control and Commitment*. Cambridge, MA: Cambridge University Press.

Lindblom, Charles. 1977. *Politics and Markets*. New York: Basic.

Linden, Eugene. 1994. "Lost Tribes, Lost Knowledge." In Elvio Angeloni, (ed.), *Anthropology 93/94*. Guilford, CT: Dushkin.

Lindenberg, Marc M. 1993. *The Human Development Race: Improving the Quality of Life in Developing Countries*. San Francisco: Institute for Contemporary Studies.

Lindermalm, G., D. Korlin, & N. Uddenberg. 1986. "Long-term followup of sex change in 134 male to female transsexuals." *Archives of Sexual Behavior* 15: 187–210.

Lindsey, Linda L. 1974. *Speech Behavior, Communicative Interference and Interracial Contact*. PhD Dissertation, Case Western Reserve University. Cleveland, Ohio.

Lindsey, Linda L. 1978. "Sex roles and modernization: On the persistence of tradition." Paper presented at the IX World Congress of Sociology, Uppsala, Sweden.

Lindsey, Linda L. 1979. "Marketing research and sociological analysis." Paper presented at the Midwest Sociological Society. Milwaukee, April.

Lindsey, Linda L. 1982. "Pharmacy and Health Care in India." *American Pharmacy* NS22: 14–17.

Lindsey, Linda L. 1983. "Health care in India: An analysis of the existing models." In John H. Morgan (ed.), *Third World Medicine and Social Change: A Reader in Social Science and Medicine*. Lanham, MD: University Press of America: 111–23.

Lindsey, Linda L. 1985. "Health care and countermodernization in India." Paper presented at the North Central Sociological Association, Louisville, KY.

Lindsey, Linda L. 1988. "The health status of women in Pakistan: The impact of islamization." Paper presented at the Midwest Sociological Society, Minneapolis, MN.

Lindsey, Linda L. 1990. "The health status of Afghan refugees: Focus on women." *Women in Development Forum*. Women in Development Publication Series (August), Michigan State University.

Lindsey, Linda L. 1992. "Gender and the workplace: Some lessons from Japan." Paper presented at the Midwest Sociological Society, Kansas City.

Lindsey, Linda L. 1995. "Religious fundamentalism and the civil rights of Third World women." Paper presented at the NGO Forum of the United Nations Conference on Women, Beijing. (August).

Lindsey, Linda L. 1995a. "Living arrangements for the elderly: Alternatives to institutionalization." In Jeffrey C. Delafuente & Ronald B. Stewart (eds.), *Therapeutics in the Elderly*. Cincinnati, OH: Harvey Whitney: 70–83.

Lindsey, Linda L. 1996a. "Full-time homemaker as unpaid laborer." In Paula J. Dubeck & Kathryn Borman (eds.), *Women and Work: A Handbook*. New York: Garland.

Lindsey, Linda L. 1996b. "Women and agriculture in the developing world." In Paula J. Dubeck & Kathryn Borman (eds.), *Women and Work: A Handbook*. New York: Garland: 435–37.

Lindsey, Linda L. 1997. *Gender Roles: A Sociological Perspective*, 3rd ed. Upper Saddle River, NJ: Prentice Hall.

Lindsey, Linda L. 1998. "Gender issues in Japanese style management: Implications for American corporations." Paper presented at the Asian Studies Development Program National Conference. Baltimore. (March).

Lindsey, Linda L. 1999. "Chinese minority women and empowerment." Paper presented at the Midwest Sociological Society, Minneapolis. (April).

Lindsey, Linda L. 2000. "Living arrangements for the elderly: Alternatives to institutionalization." In Jeffrey C. Delafuente & Ronald B. Steward (eds.), *Therapeutics in the Elderly*. Cincinnati: Harvey Whitney Books.

Link, B. G., F. T. Cullen, J. Frank, & J. F. Wozniak. 1987. "The social rejection of former mental patients." *American Journal of Sociology* (54/3).

Link, B.G., E. Susser, A. Stueve, J. Phelan, R.E. Moore, & E. Struening. 1994. "Lifetime and five-year prevalence of homelessness in the United States." *American Journal of Public Health*: 1907–1912.

Link, Bruce G., & Bruce P. Dohrenwend. 1989. "The epidemiology of mental disorders. In Howard E. Freeman & Sol Levine (eds.), *Handbook of Medical Sociology*. Englewood Cliffs, NJ: Prentice Hall: 102–27.

Linton, Ralph. 1936. *The Study of Man*. New York: Appleton-Century-Crofts.

Linz, Juan, & Alfred Stepan, (eds.(. 1996. *Problems of Democratic Transition and Consolidation*. Baltimore, MD: Johns Hopkins University Press.

Lipovetsky, Gilles. 1994. *The Empire of Fashion.* Princeton, NJ: Princeton University Press.

Lippman, Thomas W. 1997. "U.S. plans modest aid for Congo despite some concerns, officials tell panel." *Washington Post* (July 9): A18.

Lips, Hilary M. 1995. "Gender role socialization: Lessons in femininity." In Jo Freeman (ed.), *Women: A Feminist Perspective.* Mountain View, CA: Mayfield.

Lips, Hilary M. 1997. *Sex and Gender: An Introduction.* Mountain View, CA: Mayfield.

Lipset, S.M. 1960. *Political Man: The Social Bases of Politics.* Garden City, NY: Doubleday.

Lipset, S. M. 1963. *Political Man: The Social Bases of Politics.* Garden City, New York: Anchor.

Lipset, S. M., Martin Trow, & James S. Coleman. 1956. *Union Democracy.* New York: Free Press.

Lipset, Seymour M. 1959. "Democracy and working-class authoritarianism." *American Sociological Review* 24: 482–502.

Lipset, Seymour M. 1982. "Social mobility in industrial societies." *Public Opinion* 5 (June/July): 41–44.

Lipset, Seymour Martin, & Reinhard Bendix. 1959. *Social Mobility in Industrial Society.* Berkeley: University of California Press.

Lipset, Seymour Martin, & William Schneider. 1983. *The Confidence Gap.* New York: Free Press.

Lipset, Seymour Martin. 1991. "Comments on Luckmann." In Pierre Bourdieu & James S. Coleman, (eds.), *Social Theory in a Changing Society.* Boulder, CO: Westview.

Lipset, Seymour Martin. 1994. "The social requisites of democracy revisited." *American Sociological Review* 59: 1–22.

Lipsky, Michael. 1971. *Protest in the City.* Chicago: Rand McNally.

Lipsyte, Robert. 1976. *Sportsworld.* New York: Quadrangle.

Lipton, Michael. 1979. *Why Poor People Stay Poor: Urban Bias in World Development.* Cambridge, MA: Harvard University Press.

Lipton, Michael. 1988. "Why poor people stay poor: Urban bias in world development." In Josef Gugler (ed.), *The Urbanization of the Third World.* Oxford, UK: Oxford University: 40–51.

Little, Marilyn. 1982. "Conflict and negotiation in a new role: The family nurse practitioner." *Research in the Sociology of Health* 2: 31–59.

Little, Roger W. 1970. "Buddy Relations and Combat Performance," in O. S. Grusky & G. A. Miller, eds., *The Sociology of Organizations.* NY: Free Press.

Littlejohn-Blake, Sheila M., & Carol Anderson Darling. 1993. "Understanding the strengths of African American families." *Journal of Black Studies* 23(4): 460–71.

Lively, Kit, Yi Shun Lai, Lisa Levinson, & Dylan Rivera. 1995. "Academics assess effect of new ban on racial preferences." *Chronicle of Higher Education* (August 1): A1.

Lo, Clarence Y. H. 1982. "Countermovements & conservative movements in the contemporary US." *Annual Review of Sociology* 8: 107–34.

Lobel, S. A. 1991. "Allocation of investment in work and family roles: Alternative theories and implications for research." *Academy of Management Review* 16: 507–21.

Locher, P., G. Unger, P. Sociedade, & J. Wahl. 1993. "At first glance: Accessibility of the physical attractiveness stereotype." *Sex Roles* 28: 729–43.

Lockheed, Marlaine E., & A. M. Verspoor et al. 1991. *Improving Primary Education in Developing Countries.* New York: Oxford University.

Lockwood, Victoria. 1997. "The impact of development on women: The interplay of material conditions and gender ideology." In Caroline B. Brettell & Carolyn F. Sargent (eds.), *Gender in Cross-Cultural Perspective.* Upper Saddle River, NJ: Prentice Hall: 504–18.

Loden, Marilyn. 1985. *Feminine Leadership or How to Succeed in Business Without Being One of the Boys.* New York: New York Times Books.

Lofland, John. 1985. *Protest.* New Brunswick, NJ: Transaction.

Lofland, John F. 1981. "Collective behavior: The elementary forms." In N. Rosenberg & R. H. Turner, (eds.), *Social Psychology: Sociological Perspectives.* New York: Basic.

Lofland, Lyn. 1973. *A World of Strangers.* New York: Basic.

Logan, John R., & Harvey Molotch. 1987. *Urban Fortunes: The Political Economy of Place.* Berkeley, CA: University of California.

Logan, John R., & Richard D. Alba. 1995. "Who lives in affluent suburbs? Racial differences in eleven metropolitan regions." *Sociological Focus* 28(4): 353–64.

Lombroso-Ferreo, G. 1972. *Lombroso's Criminal Man.* Montclair, NJ: Patterson Smith.

Lomnitz, Larissa. 1988. "The social and economic organization of a Mexican shanty town." In Josef Gugler (ed.), *The Urbanization of the Third World.* Oxford, UK: Oxford University: 242–63.

London, K. A. 1990. "Cohabitation, marriage, marital dissolution and remarriage: United States, 1988." *Advance Data from Vital and Health Statistics,* No. 194. Hyattsville, MD: National Center for Health Statistics.

London, Kathryn A., & Barbara Foley Wilson. 1988. "Divorce." *American Demographics* 10(10): 23–6.

Longino, Charles F., & Cary S. Kart. 1982. "Explicating activity theory: A formal replication." *Journal of Gerontology* 37: 713–22.

Lopata, Helena Znaniecke. 1973. *Widowhood in an American City.* Cambridge, MA: Schenkman.

Lopez, George A., Jackie G. Smith, & Ron Pagnucco. 1997. "The global tide." In Robert M. Jackson, (ed.), *Global Issues 97/98.* Guilford, CT: Dushkin: 31–37.

Lorber, Judith. 1994. *Paradoxes of Gender.* New Haven, CT: Yale.

Lorenz, Konrad. 1963. *On Aggression.* New York: Harcourt Brace & World.

Loscocco, Karyn A., & Glenna Spitze. 1990. "Working conditions, social support and the well-being of female and male factory workers." *Journal of Health & Social Behavior* 31: 313–27.

Loscocco, Karyn A., & Joyce Robinson. 1991. "Barriers to women's small-business success in the United States." *Gender & Society* 6: 511–32.

Lott, Bernice, & Diane Maluso. 1993. "The social learning of gender." In Anne E. Beall & Robert J. Sternberg (eds.), *The Psychology of Gender.* New York: Guilford.

Lott, Bernice. 1994. *Women's Lives: Themes and Variations in Gender Learning.* Pacific Grove, CA: Brooks/Cole.

Lottes, Ilsa L. 1993. "Nontraditional gender roles and the sexual experiences of heterosexual college students." *Sex Roles* 29(9–10): 645–69.

Louie, Miriam Ching Yoon, & Nguyen Louie. 1998. "The conversation begins." In Gwyn Kirk & Margo Okazawa-Rey (eds.), *Women's Lives: Multicultural Perspectives.* Mountain View, CA: Mayfield: 145–51.

Love, Alice A. 1999. "Study Finds Gap In Wages Increases," *Owensboro (Ky) Messenger-Inquirer* (August 30).

Lowe, Graham S. 1987. *Women in the Administrative Revolution: The Feminization of Clerical Work.* Toronto: University of Toronto Press.

Lowery, E.H. 1993. *Freedom and Community.* Albany: State University of New York.

Loy, John W. Jr. 1972. "Social origins and occupational mobility patterns of a selected sample of American athletes." *International Review of Sport Sociology* 7: 5–12.

Loy, John W. Jr., & Joseph F. McElvogue. 1970. "Racial segregation in American sport." *International Review of Sport Sociology* 5: 5–24.

Lozano, Beverly. 1989. *The Invisible Work Force.* New York: Free Press.

Lucal, Betsy. 1994. "Class stratification in introductory textbooks: Relational or distributional models?" *Teaching Sociology* 22: 139–150.

Lucas, Scott E. 1994. *Steroids.* Hillside, NJ: Enslow.

Luker, Kristin. 1978. *Taking Chances: Abortion and the Decision Not to Contracept.* Berkeley and Los Angeles: University of California.

Luker, Kristin. 1984. *Abortion and the Politics of Motherhood.* Berkeley: University of California.

Lukes, Steven. 1974. *Power.* London: Macmillan.

Lundstrum, B., I. Pauley, & J. Walinder. 1984. "Outcome of sex reassignment surgery." *Acta Psychiatrica Scandinavica* 70: 289–94.

Lunneborg, Patricia. 1998. "Abortion: A positive alternative." In Sheila Ruth (ed.), *Issues in Feminism.* Mountain View, CA: Mayfield: 296–301.

Lurie, Alison. 1981. *The Language of Clothes.* New York: Vintage.

Lush, Tamara. 1998. "El Nino winter has misery to spare." *USA Today* (February 24): 3A.

Lustbader, Wendy. 1997. "On bringing older people into the computer age." *Generations* 21: 30–1.

Lye, Diane N., & Timothy J. Biblarz. 1993. "The effects of attitudes toward family life and gender roles on marital satisfaction." *Journal of Family Issues* 14(2): 157–88.

Lyman, Stanford M., ed. 1995. *Social Movements: Critiques, Concepts, Case Studies.* NY: New York University Press.

Lynch, John W., George A. Kaplan & Sarah J. Shema. 1997. "Cumulative Impact of Sustained Economic Hardship on Physical, Cognitive, Psychological, and Social Functioning," *New England Journal of Medicine* (337/26): 1889–1895.

Lynch, Michael, & W. Byron Groves. 1989. *A Primer in Radical Criminology,* 2nd ed. Albany, NY: Harrow & Heston.

Lynch, Michael. 1994. "Rediscovering criminology: Lessons from the Marxist tradition." In Donald McQuarie & Patrick McGuire (eds.), *Marxist Sociology: Surveys of Contemporary Theory and Research.* New York: General Hall.

Lynn, David B. 1969. *Parental and Sex Roles Identification: A Theoretical Formulation.* Berkeley, CA: McCutchan.

Lynxwiler, John & David Gay. 1994. "Reconsidering race differences in abortion attitudes." *Social Science Quarterly* 75(1): 67–84.

Lyon, Alistair. 1996. "Taliban force women into strict islamic mold." Excerpted article electronically distributed by the Human Rights Information Network (HURINet). October 3.

Lyotard, Jean F. 1993. *The Post-Modern Explained.* Minneapolis: University of Minnesota Press.

Lyson, T. A., & G. D. Squires. 1993. "The 'lost generation' of sociologists." *ASA Footnotes* 21: 4–5.

Mabogunje, Akin L. 1990. "The organization of urban communities in Nigeria." *International Social Science Journal* 42(3): 355–66.

Maccoby, Eleanor Emmons. 1994. "Commentary: Gender segregation in childhood." In Campbell Leaper (ed.), *Childhood Gender Segregation: Causes and Consequences.* San Francisco: Jossey-Bass.

Macedo, Donaldo. 1995. "Literacy for stupidification: The pedagogy of the big lies." In Christine E. Sleeter & Peter L. McClaren (eds.), *Multicultural Education, Critical Pedagogy, and the Politics of Difference.* Albany, NY: State University of New York: 71–104.

Macionis, John J. 1999. *Sociology*, 7th ed. Upper Saddle River, NJ: Prentice Hall.

Mack, Raymond W., & Calvin P. Bradford. 1979. *Transforming America: Patterns of Social Change*, 2nd ed. New York: Random House.

MacKinnon, Catherine. 1983. "Feminism, Marxism, method, and the state: An agenda for theory." *Signs* 7: 635–658.

MacKinnon, Catherine. 1989. *Toward a Feminist Theory of the State*. Cambridge, MA: Harvard University.

MacKinnon, Neil J., & Tom Langford. 1994. "The meaning of occupational scores." *The Sociological Quarterly* 35/2: 215–245.

Macklin, Eleanor D. 1988. "Cohabitation in the United States." In J. Gipson Wells (ed.), *Current Issues in Marriage and the Family*. New York: Macmillan.

MacLeod, Jay. 1987. *Ain't No Makin' It*. Boulder, CO: Westview.

MacLeod, S. M., & H. N. McCullough. 1994. "Social science education as a component of medical training." *Social Science and Medicine* 39(9): 1367–73.

MacRae, C. Neil, Charles Stangor, & Miles Hewstone. 1999. 1996. *Stereotypes & Stereotyping*. New York: Guilford.

Madrid, Javier Esteinou. 1986. "Means of communication and construction of hegemony." In Rita Atwood & Emile G. McAnany (eds.), *Communication and Latin American Society: Trends in Critical Research, 1960–1985*. Madison, WI: University of Wisconsin Press: 112–124.

Maguire, Brendan. 1988. "The applied dimension of radical criminology." *Sociological Spectrum* 8/2: 133–51.

Maguire, Joe A. 1988. "Race & position assignment in English soccer." *Sociology of Sport Journal* 5: 257–69.

Maguire, Kathleen, Ann L. Pastore, & Timothy Flanagan. 1992. *Sourcebook of Criminal Justice Statistics*. Washington, DC: Dept. of Justice.

Maguire, P. 1984. "Women in development: An alternative analysis." Boston: Center for International Education, University of Massachusetts.

Mahard, Rita E., & Robert L. Crain. 1983. "Research on minority achievement in desegregated schools." In Christine H. Rossell & Willis D. Hawley (eds.), *The Consequences of School Desegregation*. Philadelphia: Temple University Press.

Maheu, Louis, (ed.), 1995. *Social Movements & Social Classes*. Newbury Park, CA: Sage.

Mahmoody, Betty. 1991. *Not Without My Daughter*. New York: St. Martin's.

Mahmud, Simeen, & Anne M. Johnston. 1994. "Women's status, empowerment, and reproductive outcomes." In Gita Sen, Andrienne Germain & Lincoln C. Chen (eds.), *Population Policies Reconsidered: Health, Empowerment, and Rights*. Harvard Series on Population and International Health. Boston: Harvard University: 151–59.

Maine, Deborah, Lynn Freedman, Farida Shaheed, & Schuyler Frautschi. 1994. "Risk, reproduction, and rights: The uses of reproductive health data." In Robert Cassen et al. (eds.) *Population and Development: Old Debates, New Conclusions*. New Brunswick, NJ: Transaction: 203–27.

Maines, Patrick D. 1993. "Whatever happened to free speech?" *American Journalism Review* (November).

Mainstreaming. 1995. *Mainstreaming of Gender Equality in Norway: Introducing the Gender Perspective into Norwegian Public Administration*. Oslo: Royal Ministry of Children and Family Affairs.

Malson, Michelene Ridley. 1983. "Black women's sex roles: The social context for a new ideology." *Journal of School Issues* 39(3): 101–13.

Manchester, William. 1993. *A World Lit Only by Fire*. Boston: Little, Brown.

Mandel, Michael, & Paul Magnusson. 1993. "The economics of crime." *Business Week* (December 13): 72–85.

Mandel, Ruth B., & Debra L. Dodson. 1992. "Do women officeholders make a difference?" In Paula Ries & Anne J. Stone (eds.), *The American Woman, 1992–93: A Status Report*. New York: W.W. Norton.

Mangan, J. A., & Roberta J. Park (eds.). 1987. *From "Fair Sex" to Feminism: Sport and the Socialization of Women in the Industrial and Post-Industrial Eras*. Totowa, NJ: Cass.

Mann, Judy. 1996. "Beijing comes home." *Washington Post* (March 8): E3.

Mann, Judy. 1998. "Aid for women who mean business." *Washington Post* (March 6).

Mann, Kenneth. 1985. *Defending White-Collar Criminals: A Portrait of Attorneys At Work*. New Haven, CT: Yale University Press.

Mann, Thomas E., & Norman J. Ornstein (eds.). 1995. *Intensive Care: How Congress Shapes Health Policy*. Washington, DC: American Enterprise Institute and The Brookings Institution.

Manton, Kenneth G., & Beth J. Soldo. 1992. "Disability and mortality among the oldest old: Implications for current and future health and long-term-care service needs." In Richard M. Suzman, David P. Willis & Kenneth J. Manton (eds.), *The Oldest Old*. New York: Oxford University Press.

Mantsios, G. 1995. "Media magic: Making class invisible." In Paula S. Rothenberg, (ed.), *Race, Class and Gender in the United States*. New York: St. Martin's.

March, James G. 1981. "Footnotes to organizational change." *Administrative Science Quarterly* 26.

Marcus, Robert E., & Phyllis D. Betzer. 1996. "Attachment and antisocial behavior in early adolescence." *Journal of Early Adolescence* 16(2): 229–48.

Marden, Charles E., Gladys Meyer, & Madeline H. Engle. 1992. *Minorities in American Society*, 6th ed. New York: HarperCollins.

Mare, Robert D., & Christopher Winship. 1991. "Socioeconomic change and the decline of marriage for blacks and whites." In Christopher Jencks & Paul E. Peterson (eds.), *The Urban Underclass*. Washington, DC: Brookings Institution: 175–202.

Maret, Elizabeth, & Barbara Finlay. 1984. "The distribution of household labor among women in dual-earner families." *Journal of Marriage and the Family* 46: 357–64.

Marger, Martin. 1998. *Social Inequality: Patterns and Processes*. Mountain View, CA: Mayfield.

Marger, Martin N. 1993. "The mass media as a power institution." in Marvin E. Olsen & Martin N. Marger (eds.), *Power in Modern Societies*. Boulder, CO: Westview: 238–249.

Marger, Martin N. 2000. *Racial and Ethnic Relations*, 5th ed. Belmont, CA: Wadsworth.

Margolin, Leslie. 1992. "Deviance on record." *Social Problems* 39: 58–70.

Marin, Geraldo, & Barbara Vanoss Marin. 1991. *Research with Hispanic Populations*. Newbury Park, CA: Sage.

Marin, Rick, & T. Trent Gegax. 1997. "'Sell in,' bliss out." *Newsweek* (December 8): 72–74.

Marine, Gene. 1969. *The Black Panthers*. New York: Signet.

Marini, Margaret Mooney. 1989. "Sex differences in earnings in the United States." In W. R. Scoot & J. Blake (eds.), *Annual Review of Sociology*, vol. 15. Palo Alto, CA: Annual Review.

Mark, N. 1998. "Beyond individual differences: Social differentiation from first principles." *American Sociological Review* 63: 309–330.

Markides, Kyriakos S., & Charles H. Mindel. 1987. *Aging and Ethnicity*. Newbury Park, CA: Sage.

Markides, Kyriakos S., R. S. Boldt, & L. A. Ray. 1986. "Sources of helping and intergenerational solidarity: A three generations study of Mexican-Americans." *Journal of Gerontology* 41: 506–11.

Markle, Gerald E. & Ronald J. Troyer. 1990. "Smoke gets in your eyes: Cigarette smoking as deviant behavior." In William Feigelman (ed.), *Readings on Social Problems: Probing the Extent, Causes, and Remedies of America's Social Problems*. Fort Worth, TX: Holt, Rinehart and Winston: 82–94.

Markos, A. 1983. "The effect of culture, local traditions, and religious beliefs on the health behavior in different African countries and tribes." In P. Oberender, H. J. Diesfeld, & W. Gitter (eds.), *Health and Development in Africa*. Frankfort: Verlag Peter Lang.

Marks, Alexandria. 1998. "Key swing vote in 1998: Women." *Christian Science Monitor* (July 14): 3.

Marks, Jonathan. 1994. "Black, white, other." *Natural History* 8: 32–35.

Marks, Nadine. 1996. "Socioeconomic status, gender, and health at midlife." *Research in the Sociology of Health Care* 13(a): 135–52.

Marks, Stephen R. 1994. "Intimacy in the public realm: The case of co-workers." *Social Forces* 72: 843–858.

Marmor, Theodore R. 1990. "Canada's path, America's choices: Lessons from the Canadian experience with national health insurance." In Peter Conrad & Rochelle Kern (eds.), *The Sociology of Health and Illness: Critical Perspectives*. New York: St. Martin's: 463–73.

Marmor, Theodore R. 1993. "Health care reform in the United States: Patterns of fact and fiction in the use of Canadian experience." *American Review of Canadian Studies* 23(1): 47–64.

Marquis, Stewart. 1968. "Ecosystems, societies, and cities." *American Behavioral Scientist* 11: 11–15.

Marriot, M. 1998. "Internet unleashing a dialogue on race," *New York Times* (March 8).

Marsden, George M. 1991. *Understanding Fundamentalism and Evangelicalism*. Grand Rapids, MI: William B. Eerdmans.

Marsden, Peter V. 1987. "Core discussion networks of Americans." *American Sociological Review* 52: 122–131.

Marsden, Peter V. 1992. "Social network theory." In Edgar F. Borgatta & Marie L. Borgatta, (eds.), *Encyclopedia of Sociology*, vol 4. New York: Macmillan: 1887–1894.

Marsden, Peter V., & Nan Lin. 1982. *Social Structure & Network Analysis*. Beverly Hills, CA: Sage.

Marshall, Donald S. 1971. "Too much sex in Mangaia." *Psychology Today* (4/9): 43 ff.

Marshall, Ray, & Robert W. Glover. 1996. "Education, the economy and tomorrow's workforce." In Laura I. Rendon & Richard O. Hope (eds.), *Educating a New Majority: Transforming America's Educational System for Diversity*. San Francisco: Jossey-Bass: p35–70.

Marsiglio, William, & Constance L. Shehand. 1993. "Adolescent males' abortion attitudes: Data from a national survey." *Family Planning Perspectives* 25(4): 162–69.

Marsiglio, William. 1993. "Attitudes toward homosexual activities and gays as friends: A national survey of 15–19 year old males." *Journal of Sex Research* 30(1): 12–17.

Martin, Carol Lynn, & Jane K. Little. 1990. "The relation of gender understanding to children's sex-type preferences and gender stereotypes." *Child Development* 61: 1427–39.

Martin, Douglas. 1997. "Eager to bit the hands that would feed them." *The New York Times* (June 1): 4–1, 4–6.

Martin, Emily. 1988. "Gender and ideological differences in representations of life and death." In James L. Watson & Evelyn S. Rawski (eds.), *Death Ritual in Late Imperial and Modern China*. Berkely, CA: University of California.

Martin, J. 1990. "Language and control: Fighting with words." In C. Walton & William Eggington, (eds.), *Language: Maintenance, Power and Education in Australian Aboriginal Contexts*. AS: Northern Territory University.

Martin, Patricia Yancey, & Robert A. Hummer. 1993. "Fraternities and rape on campus." In Laurel Richardson and Verta Taylor (eds.), *Feminist Frontiers III*. New York: McGraw-Hill.

Martin, Susan Erlich. 1995. "Sexual harassment: The link joining gender stratification, sexuality and women's economic status." In Jo Freeman (ed.), *Women: A Feminist Perspective*. Mountain View, CA: Mayfield.

Martin, Teresa Castro. 1995. "Women's education and fertility: Results from 26 demographic and health surveys." *Studies in Family Planning* 26(4): 187–202.

Martin, Teresa, & Larry Bumpass. 1989. "Recent trends in marital disruption." *Demography* 26: 37–51.

Martinson, Robert. 1974. "What works? Questions and answers about prison reform." *Public Interest* 35: 22–54.

Marty, Martin E. 1959. *The New Shape of American Religion*. New York: Harper & Row.

Marty, Martin E. 1960. "Sects and cults." *Annals of the American Academy of Political and Social Science* 332: 125–34.

Marty, Martin E. 1974. "Two kinds of civil religion." In Russell E. Richey & Donald G. Jones, (eds.), *Civil Religion in America*. New York: Harper & Row: 139–57.

Marty, Martin E., & R. Scott Appleby. 1992. *The Glory and the Power: The Fundamentalist Challenge to the Modern World*. Boston: Beacon Press.

Marvin, Simon. 1997. "Environmental flows: Telecommunications and the dematerialisation of cities." *Futures* 29: 47–65.

Marwell, Gerald, Pamela Oliver, & Ralph Prahl. 1988. "Social networks & collective action." *American Journal of Sociology* 94: 502–34.

Marx, Anthony W. 1998. *Making Race and Nation: A Comparison of South Africa, the United States, and Brazil*. Cambridge: Cambridge University.

Marx, Gary T., & Douglas McAdam. 1994. *Collective Behavior and Social Movements*. Upper Saddle River, NJ: Prentice Hall.

Marx, Gary. 1985a. "The surveillance society." *The Futurist* 19 (June): 21–26.

Marx, Gary. 1985b. "I'll be watching you: Reflections on the new surveillance." *Dissent* 32 (Winter): 26–34.

Marx, Gary. 1988. *Undercover: Police Surveillance in America*. Berkeley: University of California Press.

Marx, Karl. 1848/1964. *Karl Marx: Early Writings*. (T. B. Bottomore, ed.). New York: McGraw-Hill.

Marx, Karl. 1867/1975. *Capital: A Critique of Political Economy*. New York: International.

Masland, T. 1994. "Will it be peace or punishment?" *Newsweek* (August 1): 3.

Mason, Karen Openheim. 1994. "Do population programs violate women's human rights?" *AsiaPacific Issues* No. 15: August.

Massey, D. S. & N. A. Denton. 1993. *American Apartheid: Segregation and the Making of the Underclass*. Cambridge, MA: Harvard University Press.

Master, Brooke. 1994. "Staying the science course." *Washington Post Education Review* (April 3): 8,10.

Masters, William H., & Virginia Johnson. 1966. *Human Sexual Response*. Boston: Little, Brown.

Masters, William H., & Virginia Johnson. 1970. *Human Sexual Inadequacy*. Boston: Little, Brown.

Mastrofski, Stephen D., & R. Richard Ritti. 1996. "Police training and the effects of organization on drunk driving enforcement." *Justice Quarterly* 13: 291–320.

Matarese, Susan M., & Paul G. Salmon. 1993. "Heirs to the promised land: The children of Oneida." In Lorne Tepperman & Susannah J. Wilson (eds.), *Next of Kin: An International Reader on Changing Families*. Upper Saddle River, NJ: Prentice Hall: 157–61.

Mathews, Jay. 1992. "Undercover bias busters." *Newsweek* (November 23): 88.

Mathews, Jessica. 1996. "Earth first at the polls." *Washington Post* (November 11).

Mathiesen, James A. 1990. "Reviving 'muscular christianity': Gil Dodds & the institutionalization of sports evangelism." *Sociological Focus*: 23: 233–49.

Maton, Kenneth I., & Elizabeth A. Wells. 1995. "Religion as a community resource for well-being: Prevention, healing, and empowerment pathways." *Journal of Social Issues* 51: 177–93.

Matsueda, Ross L. 1992. "Reflected appraisals, parental labeling and delinquency," *American Journal of Sociology* 97: 1577–1611.

Matsueda, Ross, & Karen Heimer. 1987. "Race, family structure and delinquency: A test of differential association and social control theories." *American Sociological Review* 52: 826–40.

Matsumoto, David. 1994. *Cultural Influences on Research Methods and Statistics*. Pacific Grove, CA: Brooks/Cole.

Matthews, Anne. 1997. "Without a parachute." *New York Times Book Reviews* (May 18).

Mattingly, Michael. 1993. "Urban management intervention in land markets." In Nick Devas & Carole Rakodi (eds.), *Managing Fast Growing Cities: New Approaches to Urban Planning and Management in the Developing World*. Essex, UK: Longman: 102–31.

Matza, David. 1969. *Becoming Deviant*. Upper Saddle River, NJ: Prentice Hall, 1969.

Mauer, Marc. 1994. "A generation behind bars: Black males and the criminal justice system." In Richard G. Majors & Jacob U. Gordon, (eds.), *The American Black Male: His Present Status and His Future*. Chicago: Nelson-Hall.

Mauss, Armand L. 1975. *Social Problems as Social Movements*. Philadelphia: Lippincott.

Mayer, Susan. 1997. *What Money Can't Buy*. Cambridge, MA: Harvard University Press.

Mayo, Elton. 1933. *The Human Problems of an Industrial Civilization*. New York: Macmillan.

Mazur, Allan. 1993. "Signs of status in bridal portraits." *Sociological Forum* 8: 273–84.

McAdam, Doug, & Ronnelle Paulsen. 1994. "Specifying the relationship between social ties and activism." *American Journal of Sociology* 99: 640–67.

McAdam, Doug, John D. McCarthy, & Mayer N. Zald. 1988. "Social movements." In Neil J. Smelser (ed.), *Handbook of Sociology*. Newbury Park, CA: Sage: 695–737.

McAdam, Doug. 1982. *Political Process and the Development of Black Insurgency*. Chicago: University of Chicago Press.

McAdam, Doug. 1988. *Freedom Summer*. New York: Oxford University Press.

McAdams, Richard P. 1993. *Lessons from Abroad: How Other Countries Educate Their Children*. Lancaster, PA: Technomic.

McAdoo, Harriette Pipes. 1990. "A portrait of African-American families in the United States." In S. E. Rix (ed.), *The American Woman, 1990–19: A Status Report*. New York: W. W. Norton.

McCall, Michal M., & Howard S. Becker. 1990. "Introduction." In Howard S. Becker & M. M. McCall, (eds.) *Symbolic Interaction and Cultural Studies*. Chicago: University of Chicago Press: 1–15.

McCammon, Holly J. 1993. "From Repressive Intervention to Integrative Prevention: The US State's Legal Management of Labor Militance, 1881–1978," *Social Forces* 71: 569–601.

McCandless, B., & R. Coop. 1979. *Adolescents: Behavior and Development*. New York: Holt, Rinehart and Winston.

McCarthy, John D., & Mayer N. Zald. 1973. *The Trend of Social Movements in America*. Morristown, NJ: General Learning Press.

McCarthy, John D., & Mayer N. Zald. 1977. "Resource mobilization & social movements: A partial theory." *American Journal of Sociology* 82: 1212–41.

McCauley, C. 1989. "The nature of social influence in groupthink: Compliance & internalization." *Journal of Personality & Social Psychology* 57: 250–260.

McClaren, Angus. 1999. *Twentieth-Century Sexuality: A History*. Oxford, UK: Blackwell.

McClearn, G. & T. Foch. 1985. "Behavioral genetics." In James E. Birren & K. Warner Schaie (eds.), *Handbook of the Psychology of Aging*. New York: Van Nostrand Reinhold.

McClellan, David (ed.). 1977. *Karl Marx: Selected Writings*. New York: Oxford University Press.

McClendon, McKee J., & Fred P. Pestello. 1987. "White opposition: To busing or desegregation?" *Social Science Quarterly* 63(1): 70–87.

McCord, John, & Richard E. Tremblay (eds.). 1992. *Preventing Antisocial Behavior: Interventions from Birth Through Adolescence*. New York: Guilford.

McCord, William, & Arline McCord. 1986. *Paths to Progress: Bread and Freedom in Developing Societies*. New York: Norton.

McCorkle, Richard. 1993. "Research note: Punish and rehabilitate?" *Crime & Delinquency* 39: 240–252.

McCormick, John. 1998. "The wrongly condemned." *Newsweek* (November 9): 64.

McCormick, John. 1999. "Coming two days shy of martyrdom." *Newsweek* (February 15): 35.

McCrae, Robert R., & Paul T. Costa, Jr. 1982. "Aging the life course, and models of personality." In T. M. Field et al. (eds.), *Review of Human Development* New York: Wiley: 602–13.

McCrea, Frances B., & Gerald E. Markle. 1989. *Minutes to Midnight: Nuclear Weapons Protest in America*. Newbury Park, CA: Sage.

McCreery, John L. 1993. "Women's property rights and dowry in China and South Asia." In Caroline B. Brettell & Carolyn F. Sargent (eds.), *Gender in Cross-Cultural Perspective*. Upper Saddle River, NJ: Prentice Hall.

McDannell, Colleen. 1995. *Material Christianity: Religion and Popular Culture in America*. New Haven, CT: Yale University Press.

McDonnell, Nancy S., Tsitsi V. Himunyanga-Phiri, & Annie Tembo. 1993. "Widening economic opportunities for women: Removing barriers one brick at a time." In Gay Young, Vidyamali Samarasinghe, & Ken Kusterer (eds.), *Women at the Center: Development Issues and Practices for the 1990s*. West Hartford, CT: Kumarian: 17–29.

McEachern, William. 1994. *Economics: A Contemporary Introduction*. Cincinnati: South-Western.

McFeatters, Ann. 1999. "Gap Between Rich and Poor Around World Grows Wider," *Evansville Courier & Press* (May 25).

McGinn, Daniel, & John McCormick. 1999. "Your next job." *Newsweek* (February 1): 43–45.

McGinnis, J. Michael, & William H. Foege. 1993. "Actual causes of death in the United States." *Journal of the American Medical Association* 270: 2207–12.

McGoldrick, Monica. 1989. "Women and the family life cycle." In Betty Carter & Monica McGoldrick (eds.), *The Changing Family Life Cycle: A Framework for Family Therapy*, 29–68.

McGovern, A. F. 1988. *Liberation Theology and Its Critics*. Maryknoll, NY: Orbis.

McGrew, Kathryn B. 1991. *Daughters' Decisionmaking About the Nature and Level of Their Participation in the Long-Term Care of Their Dependent Elderly Mothers: A Qualitative Study*. Oxford, OH: Scripps Gerontology Center.

McGroarty, Mary. 1996. "Language attitudes, motivation, and standards." In Sandra Lee McKay & Nancy H. Hornberger, (eds.), *Sociolinguistics and Language Teaching*. Cambridge, UK: Cambridge University.

McGuire, Meredith B. 1997. *Religion: The Social Context*. Belmont, CA: Wadsworth.

McGurn, William. 1997. "City limits." *Far Eastern Economic Review* 160: 34–37.

McHenry, John. 1991. *Socioeconomic Development and Fertility Decline: Columbia, Costa Rica, Sri Lanka and Tunisia*. New York: United Nations.

McIlwraith, Robert, Robin Smith Jacobvitz, Robert Kubey, & Alison Alexander. 1991. "Television addiction: Theories and data behind the ubiquitous metaphor." *American Behavioral Scientist* 35(2): 104–21.

McKelvey, Charles. 1994. *The African-American Movement*. Dix Hills, NJ: General Hall.

McKenzie, Richard B. 1989. "How big is the displaced worker problem?" *Society* 26 (March/April): 43–48.

McKibben, Bill. 1998. "A special moment in history." *Atlantic Monthly* (May): 55–76.

McKormick, John, & Evan Thomas. 1997. One family's journey from welfare to work." *Newsweek* (May 26): 28–32.

McLanahan, Sara, & Karen Booth. 1989. "Mother-only families: Problems, prospects and politics." *Journal of Marriage and the Family* 51: 557–80.

McLaren, Peter L. 1995. "White terror and oppositional agency: Towards a critical multiculturalism." In Christine E. Sleeter & Peter L. McLaren (eds.), *Multicultural Education, Critical Pedagogy and the Politics of Difference*. Albany, NY: State University of New York Press: 33–70.

McLoughlin, Merrill. 1988. "Men versus women: The new debate over sex differences." *U.S. News and World Report* (August 8): 48,51–56.

McMichael, Philip. 1996. *Development and Social Change: A Global Perspective*. Thousand Oaks, CA: Pine Forge.

McMillan, Julie R., A. Kay Clifton, Diane McGrath, & Wanda S. Gale. 1977. "Women's language: Uncertainty or interpersonal sensitivity and emotionality?" *Sex Roles* 3: 345–59.

McNamara, Patrick H. 1992. *Conscience First, Tradition Second: A Study of Young American Catholics*. Albany, NY: State University of New York Press.

McNamara, Robert S. 1992. "The population explosion." *The Futurist* 26: 9–13.

McPhail, Clark, & Ronald T. Wohlstein. 1983. "Individual & collective behaviors within gatherings, demonstrations & riots." *Annual Review of Sociology* 9: 579–600.

McPhail, Clark. 1971. "Civil disorder participation: A critical examination of recent research." *American Sociological Review* 36: 1058–73.

McPhail, Clark. 1991. *The Myth of the Madding Crowd*. New York: deGruyter.

McWilliam, Carol L., Judith Belle Brown, Janet L. Carmichael, & Jocelyn M. Lehman. 1994. "A new perspective on threatened autonomy in elderly persons: The disempowering process." *Social Science and Medicine* 38(2): 327–38.

Mead, George Herbert. 1934. *Mind, Self, and Society*. Chicago: University of Chicago.

Mead, Lawrence M. 1992. *The New Politics of Poverty: The Nonworking Poor in America*. New York: Basic.

Mead, Margaret. 1935. *Sex and Temperament in Three Primitive Societies*. New York: William Morrow.

Mead, Margaret. 1942. *And Keep Your Powder Dry: An Anthropologist Looks at America*. New York: Morrow.

Mead, Margaret. 1953. *Growing Up in New Guinea*. New York: Mentor.

Meade, M. 1993. *Men and the Water of Life: Initiation and the Tempering of Men*. San Francisco: HarperSanFrancisco.

Mechanic, David. 1986. *From Advocacy to Allocation: The Evolving American Health Care System*. New York: The Free Press.

Mechanic, David. 1989. *Mental Health and Social Policy*. Englewood Cliffs, NJ: Prentice-Hall.

Mechanic, David. 1999. *Mental Health and Social Policy: The Emergence of Managed Care*. Boston: Allyn & Bacon.

Medalia, Nehum Z., & Otto N. Larson. 1958. "Diffusion and belief in a collective delusion." *American Sociological Review* 23: 221–32.

Meeske, Milan D. 1997. "Specialization & competition in radio." In Alan Wells & Ernest A. Hakanen, (eds.), *Mass Media and Society*. Greenwich, CT: Ablex: 149–62.

Mehmet, Ozay. 1995. *Westernizing the Third World: The Eurocentricity of Economic Development Theories*. London: Routledge.

Mehta, Dinesh. 1996. "Metropolis 2000: A forum on urban issues." *SAIS Review* 16: 188–90.

Meisenhelder, Susan. 1992. "Literacy and national development: The case of Botswana." In Fraida Dubin & Natalie A. Kuhlman (eds.), *Cross-cultural Literacy: Global Perspectives on Reading and Writing*. Englewood Cliffs, NJ: Regents/Prentice Hall: 1–18.

Meisler, Stanley. 1995. "Thinking locally spreads globally." *Los Angeles Times* (June 13): 1, 4.

Melnick, Merrill. 1992. "Male athletes & sexual assault," *Journal of Physical Education, Recreation and Dance* 63 (May–June): 32–35.

Melton, J. Gordon. 1993. "Another look at new religions." *Annals of the American Academy of Political and Social Science* 527: 97–112.

Melton, Willie, & Linda L. Lindsey. 1987. "Instrumental and expressive values in mate selection among college students revisited: Feminism, love and economic necessity." Paper presented at the Midwest Sociological Society, Chicago, April.

Melucci, Alberto. 1980. "The new social movements: A theoretical approach." *Social Science Information* 19/2: 199–226.

Melucci, Alberto. 1989. *Nomads of the Present: Social Movements and Individual Needs in Contemporary Society*. London: Hutchinson Radius.

Menard, Scott. 1995. "A developmental test of Mertonian anomie theory." *Journal of Research in Crime & Delinquency* 32: 136–74.

Mendenhall, Mark E., & Carolyn Wiley. 1994. "Strangers in a strange land: The relationship between expatriate adjustment and impression management." *American Behavioral Scientist* 37(5): 605–20.

Merchant, Carolyn. 1983. *The Death of Nature: Women, Ecology and the Scientific Revolution*. New York: Harper & Row.

Meredith, Robyn. 1997. "For this we sent you to college?" *The New York Times* (June 8): F1, 11–12.

Mernissi, Fatima. 1987. *Beyond the Veil: Male-Female Dynamics in Modern Muslim Society*. Bloomington, IN: Indiana University Press.

Merrick, Thomas W. 1994. "Population dynamics in developing countries." In Robert Cassen et al. (eds.), *Population and Development: Old Debates, New Conclusions*. New Brunswick, NJ: Transaction: 79–105.

Merton, Robert K. 1938. "Social structure and anomie." *American Sociological Review* (3): 672–82.

Merton, Robert K. 1948. "Discrimination & the American creed." In Robert MacIver (ed.), *Discrimination and National Welfare*. New York: Institute for Religious & Social Studies.

Merton, Robert K. 1967. "Manifest & latent functions." In *On Theoretical Sociology*. New York: Free Press: 73–137.

Merton, Robert K. 1968. *Social Theory & Social Structure*, 2nd ed. New York: Free Press.

Merton, Robert K., & Alice S. Kitt. 1950. "Contributions to the theory of reference group behavior." In Robert K. Merton & Paul L. Lazarsfeld, (eds.), *Continuities in Social Research*. New York: Free Press: 40–105.

Messenger, John. 1971. *Inis Beag*. Prospect Heights, IL: Waveland.

Messeri, Peter, Merril Silverstein, & Eugene Litwak. 1993. "Choosing optimal support groups." *Journal of Health & Social Behavior* 34: 122–137.

Messner, Michael. 1990. "Boyhood, organized sports & the construction of masculinities." *Journal of Contemporary Ethnography* (18/4): 416–44.

Messner, Steven, & Richard Rosenfeld. 1994. *Crime and the American Dream*. Belmont, CA: Wadsworth.

Metcalf, Fred (ed.). 1993. *The Penguin Dictionary of Jokes, Wisecracks, Quips and Quotes*. London: Viking.

Methvin, Eugene H. 1997. "Mugged by reality." *Policy Review* (July/August).

Metz, Mary Haywood. 1994. "Desegregation as necessity and challenge." *Journal of Negro Education* 63(1): 64–76.

Metzger, J. T. 1996. "The theory and practice of equity planning: An annotated bibliography." *Journal of Planning Literature* 11: 112–26.

Meyer, David S. 1993. "Institutionalizing dissent." *Sociological Forum* 8: 157–80.

Meyer, David S., & Nancy Whittier. 1994. "Social movement spillover." *Social Problems* 41: 277–98.

Meyer, Madonna Harrington, Debra Street, & Jill Quadagno. 1994. "The impact of family status on income security and health care in old age: A comparison of Western nations." *The International Journal of Sociology and Social Policy* 14(1–2): 53–83.

Meyer, Madonna Harrington. 1996. "Family status and poverty among older women: The gendered distribution of retirement income in the United States." In Jill Quadagno & Debra Street (eds.), *Aging in the Twenty-First Century*. New York: St. Martin's: 464–79.

Meyers, George C. 1992. "Demographic aging and family support for older persons." In Hal Kendig, Akiko Hashimoto, & Larry C. Coppard (eds.), *Family Support for the Elderly: The International Experience*. New York: Oxford University.

Meyrowitz, Joshua. 1984. "The adultlike child & the childlike adult: Socialization in an electronic age." *Daedalus* 113: 19–48.

Mezey, Susan Gluck. 1998. "Law and equality." In Sheila Ruth (ed.). *Issues in Feminism: An Introduction to Women's Studies*. Mountain View, CA: Mayfield: 406–17.

Michael, Robert T. 1995. "Measuring poverty: A new approach." *Focus* 12/1: 2–13.

Michael, Robert T., John H. Gagnon, Edward O. Laumann, & Gina Kolata. 1994. *Sex in America: A Definitive Study*. Boston: Little, Brown.

Michaels, Marguerite. 1993. "Rio's dead end kids." *Time* (August 9): 35, 37.

Michalowski, Ray. 1985. *Order, Law and Crime*. New York: Random House.

Michels, Robert. 1962. *Political Parties*. New York: Dover.

Michelson, W. 1977. *Environmental Choice, Human Behavior, and Residential Satisfaction*. New York: Oxford University.

Mickelson, Roslyn Arlin, & Carol Axtell Ray. 1994. "Fear of falling from grace: The middle class, downward mobility, and school desegregation." *Research in Sociology of Education and Socialization* 10: 207–38.

Micozzi, Marc. 1996. "Medicine for a small planet." *World Health* 49: 8–9.

Micro-Loans. 1997. "Micro-loans for the very poor." *New York Times* (February 16).

Miedzian, Myriam. 1991. *Boys Will Be Boys: Breaking the Link Between Masculinity and Violence*. New York: Doubleday.

Mies, Maria, & Vendana Shiva. 1993. *Ecofeminism*. Highlands, NJ: Zed.

Miethe, Terance, & Charles A. Moore. 1986. "Racial differences in criminal processing." *Sociological Quarterly* 27: 217–237.

Milanovic, Dragan. 1996. "Postmodern criminology: Mapping the terrain." *Justice Quarterly* 13: 567–610.

Miles, Robert. 1989. *Racism*. London: Tavistock/Routledge.

Milgram, Stanley. 1963. "Behavioral study of obedience." *Journal of Abnormal and Social Psychology* 67: 371–78.

Milgram, Stanley. 1967. "The small world problem." *Psychology Today* 1: 61–67.

Milgram, Stanley. 1974. *Obedience to Authority*. New York: Harper and Row.

Milgram, Stanley, & Hans Toch. 1968. "Collective behavior." In G. Lindzey & E. Aronson (eds.), *The Handbook of Social Psychology*, Vol. 4, 2nd ed. Reading, MA: Addison-Wesley.

Miliband, Ralph. 1977. *Marxism and Politics*. New York: Oxford University Press.

Miller, B., & T. Heaton. 1991. "Age at first intercourse and the timing of marriage and child birth." *Journal of Marriage and the Family* 53: 719–732.

Miller, Barbara D. 1993. "Female infanticide and child neglect in rural north India." In Caroline B. Brettell & Carolyn F. Sargent (eds.), *Gender in Cross-Cultural Perspective*. Upper Saddle River, NJ: Prentice Hall.

Miller, Brent C., Cynthia R. Christopherson, & Pamela K. King, & Tim B. Heaton. 1991. "Age at first marriage and the timing of marriage and childbirth." *Journal of Marriage and the Family* 53 (August): 719–32.

Miller, Brent C., Cynthia R. Christopherson, & Pamela K. King. 1993. "Sexual behavior in adolescence." In Thomas P. Gullota, Gerald R. Adams, & Raymond Montemayor (eds.), *Adolescent Sexuality*. Newbury Park, CA: Sage.

Miller, Cynthia L. 1987. "Qualitative differences among gender stereotyped toys: Implications for cognitive and social development in girls and boys." *Sex Roles* 16(9–10): 473–87.

Miller, D. C., & W. H. Form. 1964. *Industrial Sociology*, 2nd ed. New York: Harper.

Miller, David L. 1985. *Introduction to Collective Behavior*. Belmont, CA: Wadsworth.

Miller, Donald E. 1997. *Reinventing American Protestantism: Christianity in the New Millennium*. Berkeley, CA: University of California Press.

Miller, Francesca. 1991. *Latin American Women and the Search for Social Justice*. Hanover, NH: University Press of New England.

Miller, Frederick D. 1983. "The end of SDS & the emergence of weathermen." In Jo Freeman (ed.), *Social Movements of the Sixties & Seventies*. New York: Longman.

Miller, G. R. & J. B. Stiff. 1992. "Applied issues in studying deceptive communication." In Robert S. Feldman (ed.), *Applications of Nonverbal Theories and Research*. Hillsdale, NJ: Erlbaum.

Miller, Randi I. 1990. "Beyond contact theory: The impact of community affluence on integration efforts in five suburban high schools." *Youth and Society* 77(1): 17–34.

Miller, W. Watts. 1996. *Durkheim, Morals, and Modernity*. London: University College of London (UCL).

Miller, Walter. 1958. "Lower-class culture as a generating milieu of gang delinquency." *Journal of Social Issues* (14): 5–19.

Miller-Lachmann, Lyn, & Lorraine T. Taylor. 1995. *Schools for All: Educating Children in a Diverse Society*. Albany, NY: Delmar.

Millett, Kate. 1995. "Sexual politics." In Stevi Jackson et al. (eds.), *Women's Studies Essential Readings*. New York: New York University.

Milligan, Charles. 1993. "Education, society, and the school dropout." In Stanley William Rothstein (ed.), *Handbook of Schooling in Urban America*. Westport, CT: Greenwood: 317–31.

Millman, Marcia, & Rosabeth Moss Kanter. 1975. *Another Voice*. New York: Doubleday.

Mills, Albert J., & Peta Tancred (eds.). 1992. *Gendering Organizational Analysis*. Newbury Park, CA: Sage.

Mills, C. Wright. 1956. *The Power Elite*. New York: Oxford University Press.

Mills, C. Wright. 1959. *The Sociological Imagination*. New York: Oxford University Press.

Milovanovic, Dragan. 1996. "Postmodern criminology: Mapping the terrain." *Justice Quarterly* 13: 567–610.

Milton S. Eisenhower Foundation. 1993. *Investing in Children and Youth: Reconstructing Our Cities*. Washington, DC: Milton S. Eisenhower Foundation.

Milton, Katharine. 1994. "Civilization and its discontents." In Elvio Angeloni, (ed.), *Anthropology 93/94*. Guilford, CT: Dushkin.

Min, P. G. 1993. "Korean immigrants' marital patterns and marital adjustments." In Harriet Pipes McAdoo (ed.), *Family Ethnicity: Strength in Diversity*. Newbury Park, CA: Sage.

Minai, Naila. 1991. "Women in early Islam." In Carol J. Verburg (ed.), *Ourselves Among Others: Cross-Cultural Readings for Writers*. Boston: Bedford Books.

Mincer, Jillian. 1994. "Boys get called on." *The New York Times Education Life* January 9: 27–29.

Mind of a killer. 1990. "The Dobson-Bundy interview." In James M. Henslin (ed.), *Social Problems Today: Coping with the Challenges of a Changing Society*. Englewood Cliffs, NJ: Prentice Hall: 148–54.

Miner, Horace. 1956. "Body ritual among the Nacirema." *American Anthropologist* 58(3): 503–507.

Mingione, Enzo, & Enrico Pugliese. 1994. "Rural subsistence, migration, urbanization and the new global food regime." In Bonanno, Alessandro, et al. (eds.), *From Columbus to ConAgra: The Globalization of Agriculture and Food*. Lawrence, KS: University Press of Kansas: 52–68.

Minkler, Meredith, & Kathleen M. Roe. 1991. *Preliminary Findings from the Grandmother Caregiver Study of Oakland California*. Berkeley, CA: University of California.

Minnow, Newton N., & Craig L. LeMay. 1995. *Abandoned in the Wasteland: Children, Televison & the First Amendment*. New York: Hill & Wang.

Minton, Carmelle, & Kay Pasley. 1996. "Fathers' parenting role identity and father involvement: A comparison of nondivorced and divorced, nonresident fathers." *Journal of Family Issues* 17(1) (January): 26–45.

Mirande, Alfredo. 1979. "Machismo: A reinterpretation of male dominance in the Chicano family." *Family Coordinator* 28: 473–79.

Mirande, Alfredo. 1987. *Gringo Justice*. South Bend, IN: University of Notre Dame Press.

Mirande, Alfredo. 1988. "Chicano fathers: Traditional perceptions and current realities." In P. Bronstein & C. P. Cowan (eds.), *Fatherhood Today: Men's Changing Role in the Family*. New York: Wiley.

Miron, Louis F., & Mickey Lauria. 1995. "Identity politics and student resistance to inner-city public schooling." *Youth and Society* 27(1): 29–54.

Mirowsky, John, & Catherine Ross. 1989. *The Social Causes of Psychological Distress*. Hawthorne, NY: Aldine.

Mirowsky, John. 1995. "Age and the sense of control." *Social Psychological Quarterly* 58(1): 31–43.

Mirrors: America as a Foreign Culture, 2nd ed. Belmont, CA: West/Wadsworth: 43–49.

Mischel, W. A. 1966. "A social learning view of sex differences in behavior." In Eleanor E. Maccoby (ed.), *The Development of Sex Differences*. Stanford, CA: Stanford University.

Mishel, Lawrence, & Paula B. Voos (eds.). 1992. *Unions and Economic Competitiveness*. Armonk, NJ: M. E. Sharpe.

Mishel, Lawrence. 1995. "Rising tides, sinking wages." *The American Prospect* 23 (Fall): 60–64.

Misztal, Bronislaw, & J. Craig Jenkins. 1995. "Starting from scratch is not always the same: The politics of protest and the post-communist transitions in Poland and Hungary." In J. Craig Jenkins & Bert Klandermans (eds.), *The Politics of Social Movements*. Minneapolis: University of Minnesota Press: 324–64.

Mitchell, G. Duncan. 1968. *A Hundred Years of Sociology*. Chicago: Aldine.

Miwa, Yoshiro. 1996. *Firms and Industrial Organization in Japan*. New York: New York University.

Miyazawa, Setuso. 1992. *Policing in Japan*. Albany: SUNY Press.

Moeller, David W. 1992. *Environmental Health*. Cambridge, MA: Harvard University Press.

Moen, Matthew C. 1994. "From revolution to evolution: The changing nature of the Christian right." *Sociology of Religion* 3: 345–57.

Moen, Phyllis, Julie Robison, & Donna Dempster-McClain. 1995. "Caregiving and women's well-being: A life course approach." *Journal of Health and Social Behavior* 36(3): 259–73.

Moffatt, Michael. 1989. *Coming of Age in New Jersey: College and American Culture*. New Brunswick, NJ: Rutgers University.

Mohr, John, & Paul DiMaggio. 1995. "The intergenerational transmission of cultural capital." *Research in Social Stratification and Mobility* 14: 167–99.

Mokhiber, Russell. 1988. *Corporate Crime and Violence*. San Francisco: Sierra Club.

Molotch, Harvey. 1979. "Media and movements." In Meyer N. Zald & John D. McCarthy (eds.), *The Dynamics of Social Movements*. Cambridge, MA: Winthrop.

Monday Developments. 1997. "World Wildlife Fund survey shows widespread American support to cut emission, curb global warming." 15(21): 7. Newsletter of the American Council for Voluntary International Action (InterAction).

Monday Developments. 1997a. "El Nino threatens parts of Africa and Latin America." 15(17): 3.

Monday Developments. 1997b. "World Wildlife Fund survey shows widespread American support to cut emission, curb global warming." 15(21): 7. Newsletter of the American Council for Voluntary International Action (InterAction).

Monday Developments. 1998. "New global connections mailing offers 98 ways to get connected." Newsletter of InterAction 16(2): 5.

Money, John, & Anke A. Ehrhardt. 1972. *Man and Woman, Boy and Girl*. Baltimore, MD: Johns Hopkins University.

Money, John, & P. Tucker. 1975. *Sexual Signatures*. Boston: Little, Brown.

Monk-Turner, Elizabeth. 1985. "Sex differences in type of first college entered and occupational status: Changes over time." *Social Science Journal* 22: 89–97.

Monk-Turner, Elizabeth. 1990. "The occupational achievements of community and four-year college entrants." *American Sociological Review* 55: 719–25.

Monroe, R. R. 1978. *Brain Dysfunction in Aggressive Criminals*. Lexington, MA: D.C. Heath.

Montagu, M. F. Ashley. 1964. *The Concept of Race*. New York: Free Press.

Montgomery, James D. 1992. "Job search & network composition." *American Sociological Review* 57: 586–596.

Montgomery, Lori. 1996. "Study backs crime prevention efforts." *Owensboro (KY) Messenger-Inquirer* (June 20).

Moore, Dorothy P. 1990. "An examination of present research on the female entrepreneur: Suggested research strategies for the 1990's." *Journal of Business Ethics* 9: 275–81.

Moore, Elizabeth, & Michael Mills. 1990. "The neglected victims and unexamined costs of white-collar crime." *Crime and Delinquency* 36/3: 408–18.

Moore, Gwen. 1991. "Structural determinants of men's and women's personal networks." *American Sociological Review* (55/5): 726–735.

Moore, Henrietta. 1988. *Feminism and Anthropology*. Minneapolis: University of Minnesota Press.

Moore, K., C. Nord, & J. Petersen. 1989. "Nonvoluntary sexual activity among adolescents." *Family Planning Perspectives* 21: 110–14.

Moore, Mick. 1997. "Societies, polities and capitalists in developing countries: A literature review." *Journal of Development Studies* 33: 287–363.

Moore, R. 1994. "Permanently temporary: The new employment relationship in US society." In D. J. Curran, & C. M. Renzetti (eds.), *Contemporary Societies*. Upper Saddle River, NJ: Prentice Hall: 37–48.

Moore, Rebecca, & Fielding McGehee III. (eds.). 1989. *New Religious Movements, Mass Suicide, and Peoples Temple: Scholarly Perspectives on a Tragedy*. Lewiston, NY: Edwin Mellen.

Moore, Susan, & Jennifer Boldero. 1991. "Psychosocial development and friendship functions in adolescence." *Sex Roles* 25(9–10): 521–36.

Moore, Thomas J. 1993. *Lifespan: Who Lives Longer and Why*. New York: Simon & Schuster.

Moore, Thomas S. 1990. "The nature and unequal incidence of job displacement costs." *Social Problems* 37: 230–42.

Moore, Wilbert E. 1967. *Order & Change: Essays in Comparative Sociology*. New York: Wiley.

Moore, Wilbert E. 1974. *Social Change*, 2nd ed. Upper Saddle River, NJ: Prentice-Hall.

Moore, Wilbert E. 1979. *World Modernization: The Limits of Convergence*. New York: Elsevier.

Moorehead, Richard. 1992. "Land tenure and environmental conflict: The case of the Inland Niger Delta, Mali." In Jyrki Käkönen (ed.), *Perspectives on Environmental Conflict and International Relations* London: Pinter: 96–115.

Mootz, M. 1986. "Health indicators." *Social Science and Medicine* 22: 255–63.

Moran, Theodore. 1978. "Multinational corporations and dependency." *International Organization* 32: 79–100.

Morgan, Babette. 1994. "To Lynn Martin, breaking glass ceilings is good business." *St. Louis Post-Dispatch* (December 4): E1, E8.

Morgan, Michael, & James Shanahan. 1991. "Do VCRs change the TV picture?" *American Behavioral Scientist* 35(2): 122–35.

Morgan, Robin (ed.). 1984. *Sisterhood Is Global: The International Women's Movement Anthology* (preface). New York: Anchor/Doubleday.

Morgan, S. Philip, Antonio McDaniel, Andrew T. Miller, & Samuel H. Preston. 1993. "Racial differences in household and family structure at the turn of the century." *American Journal of Sociology* 98(4): 799–828.

Morganthau, Tom, & Ginny Carroll. 1996. "The backlash wars." *Newsweek* (April 1): 54–55.

Morganthau, Tom. 1988. "The housing crunch." *Newsweek* 111 (January 4): 18–20.

Morganthau, Tom. 1995. "The lull before the storm." *Newsweek* (December 4): 40–42.

Morgen, Sandra. 1994. "Personalizing personnel decisions in feminist organizational theory and practice." *Human Relations* 47: 665–84.

Morley, David. 1989. "Changing paradigms in audience studies." In Ellen Seiter, Hans Borchers, Gabriele Kreutzner & Eva-Maria Warth (eds.), *Remote Control: Television, Audiences, and Cultural Power*. London: Routledge.

Morris, Aldon D. 1984. *The Origins of the Civil Rights Movement*. New York: Free Press.

Morris, Martina, Annette D. Bernhardt, & Mark S. Handcock. 1994. "Economic inequality: New methods for new trends." *American Sociological Review* 59: 205–219.

Morrison, A. M., R. P. White, F. Van Velsor, & the Center for Creative Change. 1992. *Breaking the Glass Ceiling: Can Women Reach the Top of America's Largest Corporations?* Reading, MA: Addison-Wesley.

Morrison, Denton E. 1971. "Some notes toward theory on relative deprivation, social movements and social change." *American Behavioral Scientist* 14/5: 675–90.

Morrow, Lance. 1992. "Japan in the Mind of America." *Time* (February 10): 16–20.

Morrow, Lance. 1993. "The temping of America." *Time* 131/19: 40–41.

Mortenson, Thomas G. 1992. "College participation rates by family income." *Postsecondary Education Opportunity* (April): 1–4.

Mosca, Gaetano. (1939/1986). *The Ruling Class*. New York: McGraw-Hill.

Mottl, Tahi L. 1980. "The analysis of countermovements." *Social Problems* 27: 620–35.

Mucha, Janusz L. 1993. "An outsider's view of American culture." In Philip R. DeVita & James D. Armstrong (eds.), *Distant Mirrors: America as a Foreign Culture*. Belmont, CA: Wadsworth: 43–49.

Mucha, Janusz L. 1998. "An outsider's view of American culture." In Philip R. DeVita & James D. Armstrong (eds.), *Distant*

Mufwene, Salikoko S. 1998. "Forms of address: How their social functions may vary." In Philip R. DeVita & James D. Armstrong (eds.), *Distant Mirrors: America as a Foreign Culture*. Belmont, CA: West/Wadsworth: 55–59.

Muir, Donal E. 1991. "'White' fraternity and sorority attitudes toward 'blacks' on a Deep-South campus." *Sociological Spectrum* 11/1: 93–103.

Mulac, A., J. M. Wiemann, S. J. Widenmann, & T. W. Gibson. 1988. "Male/female language differences and effects in same-sex and mixed-sex dyads: The gender-linked language effect." *Communication Monographs* 55: 315–35.

Mulcahy, Aogan. 1995. "'Headhunter' or real cop? Identity in the world of internal affairs officers." *Journal of Contemporary Ethnography* 24: 99–130.

Mullis, Ina V. S., & Lynn B. Jenkins. 1990. *The Reading Report Card, 1971–88: Trends from the Nation's Report Card*. Princeton, NJ: Educational Testing Service.

Mumford, Emily. 1983. *Medical Sociology: Patients, Providers and Policies*. New York: Random House.

Mundorf, Norbert, & Winifred Brownell. 1990. "Media preferences of older and younger adults." *The Gerontologist* 30(5): 685–91.

Muraskin, Roslyn. 1993. "Abortion: Is it abortion or compulsory childbearing?" In Roslyn Muraskin & Ted Alleman (eds.), *It's a Crime: Women and Justice*. Upper Saddle River, NJ: Prentice Hall.

Murdock, George Peter. 1945. "The common denominator of cultures." In Ralph Linton (ed.), *The Science of Man in World Crisis*. New York: Columbia University.

Murdock, George Peter. 1965. *Social Structure*. New York: Free Press.

Murdock, Graham. 1989. "Cultural studies: Missing links." *Critical Studies in Mass Communication* 6(4): 436–40.

Murphy, Robert F. 1994. "The dialectics of deeds and words." In Robert Borofsky (ed.), *Assessing Cultural Anthropology*. New York: McGraw-Hill.

Murray, C. 1993. "Bad lessons." *New York Times* (January 8): A25.

Murray, Christopher J. L., Richard G. A. Feachem, Margaret A. Phillips, & Carla Willis. 1992. "Adult morbidity: Limited data and methodological uncertainty." In Richard Feachem, Tord Kjellstrom, Christopher Murray, Mead Over & Margaret Phillips (eds.), *The Health of Adults in the Developing World*. New York: Oxford University Press.

Murstein, Bernard I. 1986. *Paths to Marriage*. Beverly Hills, CA: Sage.

Murstein, Bernard I. 1991. "Dating: Attracting and meeting." In John N. Edwards & David H. Demo (eds.), *Marriage and Family in Transition*. Boston: Allyn & Bacon.

Murty, Komanduri S., Julian B. Roebuck, & Gloria R. Armstrong. 1994. "The black community's reaction to the 1992 Los Angeles riot." *Deviant Behavior* 15: 85–104.

Musto, David F. 1987. *The American Disease: Origins of Narcotic Control*, expanded edition. New York: Oxford University Press.

Mutchler, Jan E., & Jeffrey A. Burr. 1991. "Racial differences in health and health care service utilization in later life: The effect of socioeconomic status." *Journal of Health and Social Behavior* 32: 342–56.

Myers, David G. 1996. *Social Psychology*. New York: McGraw-Hill.

Myers, George C. 1992. "Demographic aging and family support for older persons." In Hal Kendig, Akiko Hashimoto, & Larry C. Coppard (eds.), *Family Support for the Elderly: The International Experience*. New York: Oxford University Press.

Myers, George C., Barbara Boyle Torrey, & Kevin G. Kinsella. 1992. "The paradox of the oldest old in the United States: An international comparison." In Richard M. Suzman, David P. Willis, & Kenneth G. Manton (eds.), *The Oldest Old*. New York: Oxford University Press.

Myles, John, & Adnan Turgeon. 1994. "Comparative studies in class structure." *Annual Review of Sociology* 20: 103–124.

Myrdal, Gunnar. 1962. *Challenge to Affluence*. New York: Pantheon.

Nader, Laura. 1994. "Comparative consciousness." In Robert Borofsky (ed.), *Assessing Cultural Anthropology*. New York: McGraw-Hill.

Nader, Ralph, & Mark Green. 1972. "Crime in the suites." *New Republic* (April 29): 17–19.

Naffine, Ngaire. 1996. *Feminism and Criminology*. Philadelphia: Temple University Press.

Nafziger. 1984. *The Economics of Developing Countries*. Belmont, CA: Wadsworth.

Nagel, Joann. 1994. "Constructing ethnicity." *Social Problems* 41: 152–76.

Nagin, Daniel, & Raymond Paternoster. 1993. "Enduring individual differences and rational choice theories of crime." *Law and Society Review* 27: 467–89.

Najafizadeh, Mehrangiz, & Lewis A. Mennerick. 1992. "Sociology of education or sociology of ethnocentrism? The portrayal of education in U.S. introductory sociology textbooks." *Teaching Sociology* 20/3: 215–21.

Nakao, Keiko & Judith Treas. 1994. "Updating Occupational Prestige and Socioeconomic Scores," in Peter V. Marsden, ed., *Sociological Methodology*. Washington, DC: American Sociological Association: 1–72.

Nanda, Serena. 1990. *Neither Man Nor Woman: The Hijras of India*. Belmont, CA: Wadsworth.

Nardi, Peter M. 2000. "Changing gay and lesbian images in the media." In Tracey E. Ore (ed.), *The Social Construction of Difference: Race, Class, Gender, and Sexuality*. Mountain View, CA: Mayfield: 384–96.

Nas, Peter J. M. (ed.). 1993. *Urban Symbolism*. Leiden, Netherlands: E. J. Brill.

Nasar, Sylvia. 1992. "Fed gives new evidence of 80s gain by richest." *The New York Times* (April 21).

Nash, Gary. 1995. "American history reconsidered: Asking new questions about the past." In Diane Ravitch & Maris A. Vinovskis (eds.), *Learning from the Past: What History Teaches Us About School Reform*. Baltimore, MD: Johns Hopkins University Press: 135–63.

"Nation of jailbirds: One in 150 Americans locked up." 1999. *Evansville Courier & Press* (March 15): 1A.

National Advisory Commission on Civil Disorders. 1968. *Report of the National Advisory Commission on Civil Disorders*. New York: Bantam.

National Center for Health Statistics. 1993. *Health, United States, 1992*. Washington, DC: U.S. Government Printing Office.

National Center for Health Statistics. 1997. *Health Statistics, United States, 1996*. Hyattsville, MD: Public Health Service.

National Center for Health Statistics. 1998. *Health, United States, 1997*. Washington, DC: U.S. Government Printing Office.

National Center for Health Statistics. 1999. "Highlights of trends in pregnancies and pregnancy rates by outcome: Estimates for the United States, 1976–1996. *National Vital Statistics Reports* 47: 1–10.

National Center on Women and Family Law. 1987. *Arrest in Domestic Violence Cases: A State by State Summary*. New York: National Center on Women and Family Law.

National Commission on Excellence in Education. 1983. *A Nation at Risk: The Imperative for Educational Reform*. Washington, DC: National Commission on Excellence in Education.

National Institute of Mental Health. 1982. *Television and Behavior: Ten Years of Scientific Progress and Implications for the Eighties. Volume I: Summary Report*. Rockville, MD: National Institute of Mental Health.

National Law Center on Homelessness and Poverty. 1996. *Mean Sweeps*. Washington, DC: Author.

National Opinion Research Center. 1994. *General Social Surveys, 1972–1994: Cumulative Codebook*. Chicago: NORC.

National Safety Council. 1990. *Accident Facts*. Chicago: National Safety Council.

Navarro, Vicente. 1986. *Crisis, Health and Medicine: A Social Critique*. New York: Tavistock.

Navarro, Vicente. 1991. "Class & Race: Life & Death Situations," *Monthly Review* 43 (September): 1–13.

Neal, Arthur G., H. Theodore Groat, & Jerry W. Wicks. 1989. "Attitudes about having children: A study of 600 couples in the early years of marriage." *Journal of Marriage and the Family* 51: 313–27.

Nee, Victor, Jimy M. Sanders, & Scott Sernau. 1994. "Job transitions in an immigrant metropolis." *American Sociological Review* 59: 849–72.

Nelkin, Dorothy, David P. Willis, & Scott V. Parris (eds.). 1991. *A Disease of Society: Cultural and Institutional Responses to AIDS*. Cambridge, UK: Cambridge University Press.

Nelson, Debra L., & James Campbell Quick. 1985. "Professional women: Are stress and disease inevitable?" *Academy of Management Journal* 10: 206–18.

Nelson, Debra L., & Michael A. Hitt. 1992. "Employed women and stress: Implications for enhancing women's mental health in the workplace." In James Campbell Quick, Lawrence R. Murphy & Joseph J. Hurrell, Jr. (eds.), *Stress and Well-Being at Work: Assessments and Interventions for Occupational Mental Health*. Washington, DC: American Psychological Association: 164–77.

Nelson, Jack. 1995. "The Internet, the virtual community, and those with disabilities." *Disability Studies Quarterly* 15: 15–20.

Nelson, Mariah B. 1994. *The Stronger Women Get, The More Men Love Football: Sexism & the American Culture of Sports*. New York: Harcourt Brace.

Nelson, Toni. 1999. "Violence against women." In Kurt Finsterbusch (ed.), *Social Problems 99/00*. Guilford, CT: Dushkin/McGraw-Hill: 109–12.

Nemeroff, Carol J., Alana Brinkman, & Claudia K. Woodward. 1994. "Medical contagion and AIDS risk: Perception in a college population." *AIDS Education and Prevention* 6(3): 249–65.

Nemeth, Mary. 1998. "Amazing greys." In Harold Cox (ed.). *Annual Aging: Annual Editions, 98/99*. Guilford, CT: Dushkin/McGraw-Hill: 90–97.

Nettler, Gwynn. 1984. *Explaining Crime*, 3rd. ed. New York: McGraw-Hill.

Neugarten, Bernice L., Robert J. Havinghurst, & Sheldon S. Tobin. 1968. "Personality patterns and aging." In Bernice L. Neugarten (ed.), *Middle Age and Aging*. Chicago: University of Chicago Press: 173–77.

Neugarten, Bernice L., & Karol K. Weinstein. 1964. "The changing American grandparents." *Journal of Marriage and the Family* 26: 199–204.

Neuman, Shoshana. 1991. "Occupational sex segregation in the kibbutz: Principles and practice." *Kyklos* 44: 203–19.

Newdorf, David. 1991. "Bailout agencies like to do it in secret." *Washington Journalism Review* 13/4: 15–16.

Newfield, Jack, & Paul Dubrul. 1979. "The political economy of organized crime." In Jerome H. Skolnick, and Elliott Currie (eds.). *Crisis in American Institutions*, 4th ed. Boston: Little Brown: 414–27.

Newman, Joseph W. 1990. *America's Teachers*. New York: Longman.

Newman, Katherine S. 1988. *Falling From Grace: The Experience of Downward Mobility in the American Middle Class*. New York: Vintage.

Newman, Katherine. 1993. *Declining Fortunes: The Withering of the American Dream*. New York: Basic.

Newman, William M. 1973. *American Pluralism: A Study of Minority Groups and Social Theory*. New York: Harper & Row.

New York State Special Commission on Attica. 1972. *Attica: The Official Report On the New York State Special Commission on Attica*. New York: Bantam.

Niang, Cheikh Ibrahima. 1990. "From ecological crises in the West to the energy problem in Africa." *International Social Science Journal* 42 (2)124: 225–39.

Nichols, E. K. 1989. *Mobilizing Against AIDS: Revised and Enlarged Edition*. Cambridge, MA: Harvard University Press.

Nichols, Roger L. (ed.). 1992. *The American Indian: Past and Present*, 4th ed. New York: McGraw-Hill.

Niebuhr, H. Richard. 1957. *The Social Sources of Denominationalism*. New York: Meridian Books.

Niebuhr, Richard. 1999. "Alternative religions as a growing industry." *New York Times* (December 25): C1.

Nielsen Media Research. 1994. *Report on Television*. New York: A. G. Nielsen.

Nieto, Sonia. 1995. "From brown heroes and holidays to assimilationist agendas: Reconsidering the critiques of multicultural education." In Christine E. Sleeter & Peter L. McClaren (eds.), *Multicultural Education, Critical Pedagogy and the Politics of Difference*. Albany, NY: State University of New York: 191–220.

Nigro, Georgie W., Dina E. Hill, & Martha E. Gelbein. 1988. "Changes in the facial prominence of women and men over the last decade." *Psychology of Women Quarterly* 12: 225–35.

Nisbet, Robert A. 1969. *Social Change & History*. New York: Oxford University Press.

Nisbet, Robert A. 1988. *The Present Age*. New York: Harper & Row.

Nisbet, Robert A., & Robert G. Perrin. 1977. *The Social Bond*, 2nd ed. New York: Knopf.

Nitta, Yoshitaka, & Susumu Yoda. 1995. "Challenging the human crisis: 'The trilemma.'" *Technological Forecasting and Social Change* 49(2): 175–94.

Noble, Barbara Presley. 1994. "Putting women on the agenda." *New York Times* May 1: 21.

Nochimson, Martha. 1992. *No End to Her: Soap Opera and the Female Subject*. Berkeley, CA: University of California Press.

Nock, Steven L. 1995. "Spousal preferences of never-married, divorced and cohabiting Americans." *Journal of Divorce and Remarriage* 23(3–4): 91–108.

Noel, D. L. 1991. "A theory of the origin of ethnic stratification." In N. R. Yetman (ed.), *Majority & Minority*. Boston: Allyn & Bacon: 113–125.

Noelker, Linda S., & Aloen Townsend. 1987. "Perceived caregiving effectiveness." In T. H. Brubaker (ed.), *Aging, Health and Family*. Newbury Park, CA: Sage.

Noeller, Patricia. 1980. "Marital misunderstanding: A study of couples' nonverbal communication." *Journal of Personality and Social Psychology* 39: 1135–48.

Noguera, Pedro A. 1995. "Preventing and producing violence: A critical analysis of responses to school violence." *Harvard Educational Review* 65(2): 189–212.

Nolan, Patrick, & Gerhard E. Lenski. 1999. *Human Societies: An Introduction to Macrosociology*, 8th ed. New York: McGraw-Hill.

Noley, G. 1990. "The foster child of American education." In G. E. Thomas (ed.), *Race Relations in the 1980s & 1990s*. New York: Hemisphere: 239–48.

NORC (National Opinion Research Center. 1994. *General Social Surveys, 1972–1994: Cumulative Codebook*. Storrs, CT: Roper.

NORC. 1996. *General Social Survey, 1996*. Chicago: NORC.

NORC. 1999. *General Social Surveys, 1976–1998*. Chicago: National Opinion Research Center.

Nordlinger, Eric A. 1981. *On the Autonomy of the Democratic State*. Cambridge, MA: Harvard University Press.

Normandeau, Andre. 1993. "Community policing in Canada: A review of some recent studies." *American Journal of Police* (12/1): 57–73.

Norrick, Neal R. 1993. *Conversational Joking: Humor in Everyday Talk*. Bloomington, IN: Indiana University.

Norris, J. E. 1994. "Effects of marital disruption on older adults: Widowhood. In L. Ploufe (ed.), *Writings in Gerontology: Late Life Marital Disruptions*. Ottawa: National Advisory Council on Aging.

Norris, Mary E. 1992. "The impact of development on women: A specific-factors analysis." *Journal of Development Economics* 38(1): 183–201.

Norris, Pippa. 1997. *Women, Media and Politics*. New York: Oxford University Press.

Novosad, Nancy. 1996. "God squad." *Progressive* August: 25–27.

Nowak, Stefan. 1989. "Comparative studies and social theory." In Melvin L. Kohn (ed.), *Cross-National Research in Sociology*. Newbury Park, CA: Sage.

Nussbaum, Martha C. & Amartya Sen. 1993. "Introduction." In Martha Nussbaum & Amartya Sen (eds.), *The Quality of Life: A Study Prepared for the World Institute for Development Economics Research* Oxford, UK: Clarendon.

O'Brien, Joanne, & Martin Palmer. 1993. *The State of Religion Atlas*. New York: Simon & Schuster.

O'Brien, Jody, & Peter Kollock (eds.). 1997. *The Production of Reality: Essays and Readings on Social Interaction*. Thousand Oaks, CA: Pine Forge.

O'Bryant, S. L., & D. Nocera. 1985. "Psychological significance of 'home' to older widows." *Psychology of Women Quarterly* 9: 403–12.

O'Connor, Pat. 1992. *Friendships between Women: A Critical Review*. New York: Guilford.

O'Dea, Thomas. 1966. *The Sociology of Religion*. Upper Saddle River, NJ: Prentice Hall.

O'Donnell, Guillermo A. 1979. *Modernization and Bureaucratic-Authoritarianism*. Berkeley: Institute for International Studies, University of California.

O'Hare, William P. 1992. "America's minorities: The demographics of diversity." *Population Bulletin* 47(4). Washington, DC: Population Reference Bureau.

O'Hare, William P., & Judy C. Felt. 1991. "Asian-Americans: America's fastest growing minority group." *Population Trends and Public Policy*.

O'Hare, William P., Kevin M. Pollard, Taynia L. Mann, & Mary M. Kent. 1995. "African-Americans in the 1990s." In Mark Robert Rank & Edward L. Kain (eds.), *Diversity and Change in Families: Patterns, Prospects, and Policies*. Upper Saddle River, NJ: Prentice Hall.

O'Kane, James M. 1992. *The Crooked Ladder: Gangsters, Ethnicity and the American Dream*. New Brunswick, NJ: Transaction.

O'Keefe, G. J., & K. Reid-Nash. 1985. "Fear of crime and crime prevention competence among the elderly." Paper presented at the American Psychological Association, Los Angeles.

O'Kelly, C. G., & L. S. Carney. 1986. *Women & Men in Society: Cross-Cultural Perspectives on Gender Stratification*. Belmont, CA: Wadsworth.

O'Malley, Padraig. 1990. *Northern Ireland: Questions of Nuance*. Belfast: Blackstaff Press.

O'Rand, Angela. 1996. "The precious and the precocious: Understanding cumulative disadvantage over the life course." *The Gerontologist* 36: 230–38.

Oakes, Jeannie, & Martin Lipton. 1996. "Developing alternatives to tracking and grading." In Laura I. Rendon & Richard O. Hope (eds.), *Educating a New Majority: Transforming America's Educational System for Diversity*. San Francisco: Jossey-Bass: 168–200.

Oberai, A. S. 1991. "Urban population growth, employment and poverty in developing countries: A conceptual framework for policy analysis." In *Consequences of rapid population growth in developing countries*. Proceedings of the United Nations National Institute of Demographic Studies Expert Group Meeting. New York: Taylor & Francis: 191–218.

Oberschall, Anthony. 1973. *Social Conflict and Social Movements*. Englewood Cliffs, NJ: Prentice Hall.

Occiogrosso, Peter. 1996. *The Joy of Sects: A Spirited Guide to the World's Religious Traditions*. New York: Doubleday.

Odendahl, Teresa. 1990. *Charity Begins At Home*. New York: Basic Books.

Oegema, Dirk, & Bert Klandermans. 1994. "Why social movement sympathizers don't participate." *American Sociological Review* 59: 703–22.

Office of Technology Assessment. 1990. "The changing health care system." In Peter Conrad & Rochelle Kern (eds.), *Sociology of Health and Illness: Critical Perspectives*.

Ogbu, J. U. 1992. "Understanding cultural diversity and learning." *Educational Researcher* 21(8): 5–14.

Ogburn, William F. 1938. "The changing family." *Family* 19: 139–43.

Ogburn, William F. 1964. *On Culture and Social Change*. Chicago: University of Chicago.

Ojeda, Amparo B. 1993. "Growing up American: Doing the right thing." In Philip R. DeVita & James D. Armstrong (eds.), *Distant Mirrors: America as a Foreign Culture*. Belmont, CA: Wadsworth: 54–59.

Ojeda, Amparo B. 1993. "Growing up American: Doing the right thing." In Phillip R. DeVita & James D. Armstrong (eds.), *Distant Mirrors: America as a Foreign Culture*. Belmont, CA: Wadsworth: 54–59.

Okine, Vicky. 1993. "The survival strategies of poor families in Ghana and the role of women therein." In Joycelin Massiah (ed.), *Women in Developing Economies: Making Visible the Invisible*. Oxford, UK: Berg: 167–94.

Okubayashi, B. 1993. "Japanese style of management." *Annals of the School of Business Administration*, Kobe University.

Oliver, M.B., & Janet S. Hyde. 1993. "Gender differences in sexuality: A meta-analysis." *Psychological Bulletin* 114: 29–51.

Oliver, Melvin L., & Thomas M. Shapiro. 1990. "Wealth of a nation." *American Journal of Economics and Sociology* 49/2: 129–151.

Oliver, Melvin, & Tom Shapiro. 1995. *Black Wealth, White Wealth*. New York: Routledge.

Ollman, Bertell. 1971. *Alienation*. Cambridge, England: Cambridge University Press.

Olmstead, Michael S., & A. Paul Hare. 1978. *The Small Group*, 2nd ed. New York: Random House.

Olmstead, R. E., S. M. Guy, P. M. O'Malley, & P. M. Bentler. 1991. "Longitudinal assessment of the relationship between self-esteem, fatalism, loneliness, and substance abuse." *Journal of Social Behavior and Personality* 6: 749–70.

Olsen, Mancur E. 1978. *The Process of Social Organization: Power in Social Systems*, 2nd ed. New York: Holt, Rinehart & Winston.

Olson, David H., Hamilton I. McCubbin, et al. 1983. *Families: What Makes Them Work*. Beverly Hills, CA: Sage.

Olzak, Susan, & Joann Nagel (eds.). 1986. *Competitive Ethnic Relations*. San Diego: Academic Press.

Olzak, Susan, Suzanne Shanahan, & Elizabeth West. 1994. "School desegregation, interracial exposure, and antibusing activity in contemporary urban America." *American Journal of Sociology* 100(1): 196–241.

Olzak, Susan. 1989. "Labor unrest, immigration and ethnic conflict in urban America." *American Journal of Sociology* 94: 1303–33.

Omarr, Sydney. 1999. Horoscope. *St. Louis Post-Dispatch* (March 28): F8.

Omi, Michael, & Howard Winant. 1994. *Racial Formation in the United States*, 2nd ed. New York: Routledge.

Omran, A. R. 1971. "The epidemiologic transition: A theory of the epidemiology of population change." *Milbank Memorial Fund Quarterly* 49: 509–38.

Omran, A. R. 1982. "Epidemiological transition 1: Theory. In J. A. Ross (ed.), *International Encyclopedia of Population*. New York: The Free Press: 172–75.

Ong, Paul M. 1989. *The Widening Divide*. Los Angeles: UCLA Asian-American Studies Center.

Opp, Karl-Dieter, & Christine Gern. 1993. "Dissident groups, personal networks and spontaneous cooperation." *American Sociological Review* 58: 659–80.

Opp, Karl-Dieter, & Wolfgang Roehl. 1990. "Repression, micromobilization and political protest." *Social Forces* 69: 521–47.

Opp, Karl-Dieter. 1989. *The Rationality of Political Protest*. Boulder, CO: Westview.

Oppermann, Martin. 1998. *Sex Tourism and Prostitution: Aspects of Leisure, Recreation, and Work*. Elmsford, NY: Cognizant Communications.

Orbuch, Terri L., James S. House, Richard P. Mero, & Pamela S. Webster. 1996. "Marital quality over the life course." *Social Psychology Quarterly* 59(2): 162–71.

Orenstein, Peggy. 1994. *School Girls: Young Women, Self-Esteem, and the Confidence Gap*. New York: Doubleday.

Orenstein, Peggy. 1997. "Shortchanging girls: Gender socialization in schools." In Dana Dunn (ed.), *Workplace/Women's Place: An Anthology*. Los Angeles: Roxbury: 43–52.

Organization for Economic Cooperation & Development. 1997. *Annual Report*. Paris: OECD.

Orshansky, Mollie. 1969. "How poverty is measured." *Monthly Labor Review* 92/2: 37–41.

Ortiz, Vilma. 1994. "Women of Color: A Demographic Overview." In Maxine Baca Zinn & Bonnie Thornton Dill (eds.), *Women of Color in U.S. Society*. Philadelphia: Temple University.

Orum, Anthony M. 1998. "The urban imagination of sociologists: The centrality of place." *Sociological Quarterly* 39(1): 1–10.

Ossowski, Stanislaw. 1983. "Marx's concept of class." In T. Bottomore & P. Goode (eds.), *Readings in Marxist Sociology*. New York: Oxford University Press: 99–102.

Ostrander, Susan A. 1984. *Women of the Upper Class*. Philadelphia: Temple University Press.

Ostrander, Susan. 1980. "Upper-class women: Class consciousness as conduct and meaning." In G. William Domhoff, ed., *Power Structure Research*. Beverly Hills: Sage.

Oswalt, Wendell H., & Sharlotte Neely. 1999. *This Land Was Theirs*, 6th ed. Mountain View, CA: Mayfield.

Otto, F., & D. Alwin. 1977. "Athletics, aspirations and attainments," *Sociology of Education* 42: 102–13.

Ouchi, William G. 1982. *Theory Z: How American Business Can Meet the Japanese Challenge*. New York: Avon.

Overholt, Catherine A., Kathleen Cloud, Mary B. Anderson, & James E. Austin. 1991. "Gender analysis framework." In Aruna Rao, M. B. Anderson, & C. A. Overholt (eds.), *Gender Analysis in Development Planning: A Case Book*. West Hartford, CT: Kumarian: 9–20.

Overseas Development Council. 1998. *Perspectives on Aid and Development*. Washington, DC: ODC.

Owomero, Basil. 1988. "Crime in Tanzania: Contradictions of a socialist experiment," *International Journal of Comparative and Applied Criminal Justice* 12: 177–89.

Pace, Geoffrey L. 1997. "The origins of mass media in the United States." In Alan Wells & Ernest A. Hakanen (eds.), *Mass Media and Society*. Greenwich, CT: Ablex: 9–18.

Page, Charles H. 1946. "Bureaucracy's other face," *Social Forces* 25 (October): 89–94.

Page, Joseph A. 1995. *The Brazilians*. Reading, MA: Addison-Wesley.

Palazzolo, Charles S. 1981. *Small Groups: An Introduction*. New York: Van Nostrand.

Palen, John J. 1992. *The Urban World*. New York: McGraw-Hill.

Palen, John J. 1994. *The Suburbs*. New York: McGraw-Hill.

Palermo, George B., & Douglas Simpson. 1994. "At the roots of violence: The progressive decline and dissolution of the family." *International Journal of Offender Therapy and Comparative Criminology* 38(2): 105–16.

Paley, Vivian Gussin. 1984. *Boys and Girls: Superheroes in the Doll Corner*. Chicago: University of Chicago.

Pallas, Aaron M., Gary Natriello, & Edward L. McDill. 1995. "Changing Students/Changing Needs." In Erwin Flaxman & Harry Passow (eds.), *Changing Populations Changing Schools. Ninety-fourth Yearbook of the National Society for the Study of Education, Part II*. Chicago: NSSE: 30–58.

Palmore, Erdman B. 1990. *Ageism: Negative and Positive*. New York: Springer.

Paludi, Michele A. 1996. *Sexual Harassment on College Campuses: Abusing the Ivory Power*. Albany, NY: State University of New York.

Paludi, Michele A., & Richard B. Barickman. 1991. *Academic and Workplace Sexual Harassment: A Workplace Manual.* Albany, NY: State University of New York.

Paludi, Michele. 1992. *The Psychology of Women.* Dubuque, IA: WCB Brown & Benchmark.

Pampel, Fred C., & Melissa Hardy. 1994. "Changes in income inequality in old age." *Research in Social Stratification and Mobility* 13: 239–63.

Parade Magazine. 1991. "Sexual harassment: Gender gap on Capitol Hill." November 17: 10.

Parade Magazine. 1995. "Worse news about family values." December 31: 12.

Parenti, Michael. 1978. *Power and the Powerless,* 2nd ed. New York: St. Martin's.

Parenti, Michael. 1986. *Inventing Reality: The Politics of the Mass Media.* New York: St. Martin's Press.

Parenti, Michael. 1995. *Democracy for the Few,* 6th ed. New York: St. Martin's Press.

Park, Robert Ezra, Ernest Burgess, & Roderick McKenzie (eds.). 1925. *The City.* Chicago: University of Chicago Press.

Park, Robert Ezra. 1916. "The city: Suggestions for the investigation of human behavior in an urban environment." *American Journal of Sociology* 20: 577–612.

Park, Robert Ezra. 1926. "Succession, an ecological concept." *American Sociological Review* 1: 171–79.

Parker, J. G., & S. R. Asher. 1987. "Peer relations and later personal adjustment: Are low-accepted children at risk?" *Psychological Bulletin* 102: 357–89.

Parker, John, & Harold C. Grasmick. 1979. "Linking actual and perceived certainty of punishment: An exploratory study of an untested proposition in deterrence theory." *Criminology* 17: 366–79.

Parker, Linda S. 1989. *Native American Estate.* Honolulu: University of Hawaii.

Parker, Robert N. 1995. "Violent crime." In Joseph F. Sheley (ed.). *Criminology: A Contemporary Handbook,* 2nd ed. Belmont, CA: Wadsworth: 169–85.

Parkinson, C. N. 1962. *Parkinson's Law,* 2nd ed. Boston: Houghton Mifflin.

Parks, Malcolm R. 1996. "Making friends in cyberspace." *Journal of Communication* 46: 80–96.

Parlee, Mary Brown. 1989. "Conversational politics." In Laurel Richardson & Verta Taylor (eds.), *Feminist Frontiers II: Rethinking Sex, Gender and Society.* New York: Random House.

Parrillo, Vincent N. 2000. *Strangers to These Shores,* 6th ed. Boston: Allyn & Bacon.

Parsons, Talcott, & Robert F. Bales. 1955. *Family, Socialization and Interaction Process.* Glencoe, IL: Free Press.

Parsons, Talcott. 1951. *The Social System.* Glencoe, IL: Free Press.

Parsons, Talcott. 1954. "The professions & social structure." In *Essays in Sociological Theory,* revised ed. New York: Free Press: 34–49.

Parsons, Talcott. 1964. "Definitions of health and illness in light of American values and social structure." In Talcott Parsons (ed.), *Social Structure and Personality.* New York: The Free Press.

Parsons, Talcott. 1966. *Societies: Evolutionary & Comparative Perspectives.* Upper Saddle River, NJ: Prentice Hall.

Passas, N., & R. Agnew. 1997. *The Future of Anomie Theory.* Boston: Northeastern University Press.

Passuth, Patricia M., & Vern L. Bengston. 1988. "Sociological theories of aging: Current perspectives and future directions." In James Birren & Vern Bengston (eds.), *Emergent Theories of Aging.* New York: Springer: 333–55.

Pastalan, L. A. 1982. "Research in environment and aging: An alternative to theory." In M. Powell Lawton, P. G. Windley, & T. O. Byerts (eds.), *Aging and the Environment: Theoretical Approaches.* New York: Springer.

Paternoster, Raymond, Linda Saltzman, Gordon Waldo, & Theodore Chiricos. 1983. "Perceived risk and social control: Do sanctions really deter? *Law and Society Review* (17/3).

Paternoster, Raymond. 1989. "Absolute and restrictive deterrence in a panel of youth." *Social Problems* 36: 289–309.

Paternoster, Raymond. 1991. *Capital Punishment in America.* New York: Lexington.

Patterson, F. 1978. "Conversations with a gorilla." *National Geographic* 154(4): 438–65.

Patterson, G. R., B. D. DeBaryshe, & E. Ramsey. 1989. "A developmental perspective on antisocial behavior," *American Psychologist* (44).

Patterson, James T. 1994. *America's Struggle with Poverty, 1990–1994.* Cambridge, MA: Harvard University Press.

Patterson, Orlando. 1982. *Slavery and Social Death: A Comparative Study.* Cambridge, MA: Harvard University Press.

Pauly, Ira, & Milton Edgerton. 1986. "The gender-identity movement: A growing surgical-psychiatric liaison." *Archives of Sexual Behavior* 15(4): 315–27.

Pavalko, Ronald M. 1988. *Sociology of Occupations and Professions,* 2nd ed. Itasca, IL: Peacock.

Paz, J. J. 1993. "Support of Hispanic elderly." In Harriet Pipes McAdoo (ed.), *Family Ethnicity: Strength in Diversity.* Newbury Park, CA: Sage.

Peacock, Walter G., Greg A. Hoover, & Charles D. Killian. 1988. "Divergence and convergence in international development: A decomposition analysis of inequality in the world system." *American Sociological Review* 53: 838–52.

Pearce, Diana. 1978. "The feminization of poverty: Women, work and welfare." *Urban and Social Change Review* 11: 28–36.

Pearce, Frank, & Steve Tombs. 1997. "Hazards, law & class: Contextualizing the regulation of corporate crime." *Social and Legal Studies* 6: 79: 107.

Pearson, Ethel Specter. 1999. *The Sexual Century.* New Haven, CT: Yale University.

Pedersen, Duncan. 1996. "Disease ecology at a crossroads: Man-made environments, human rights and perpetual development utopias." *Social Science and Medicine* 43(5): 745–58.

Peirce, Date. 1990. "A feminist theoretical perspective on the socialization of teenage girls through *Seventeen* magazine." *Sex Roles* 23(9–10): 491–500.

Penha-Lopes, V. 1993. "Make room for daddy: Patterns of family involvement among contemporary African American men." In C.K. Jacobson (ed.), *American Families: Issues in Race and Ethnicity.* New York: Garland: 179–99.

People and Development Challenges. 1995. "Special report: China." 2(3): 5–18. International Planned Parenthood Federation.

People Weekly. 1999. "Web feat: Work of B. Fox." 52 (November 8): 86.

Pepinsky, Harold E., & Richard Quinney (eds.). 1993. *Criminology as Peacemaking.* Bloomington, IN: Indiana University Press.

Peplau, Letitia Anne & S. L. Gordon. 1983. "The intimate relationships of lesbians and gay men." In E. R. Allgeier & N. B. McCormick (eds.), *Changing Boundaries: Gender Roles and Sexual Behavior.* Palo Alto, CA: Mayfield: 226–44.

Pepper, Claude D. 1983. "Frauds against the elderly." In J. I. Kosberg (ed.), *Abuse and Maltreatment of the Elderly.* Littleton, MA: John Wright.

Peretti, P. O., & T. M. Sydney. 1995. "Parental toy stereotyping and its effect on child toy preference." *Social Behavior and Personality* 12: 213–16.

Perez, L. 1994. "Cuban families in the United States." In R. L. Taylor (ed.), *Minority Families in the United States: A Multicultural Perspective.* Upper Saddle River, NJ: Prentice Hall.

Perkins, Douglas D., Barbara B. Brown, & Ralph B. Taylor. 1996. "The ecology of empowerment: Predicting participation in community organizations." *Journal of Social Issues* 52: 85–110.

Perkins, H. Wesley, & Debra K. DeMeis. 1996. "Gender and family effects on the 'second shift' domestic activity of college-educated young adults." *Gender & Society* 10(1): 78–93.

Perkins, Kathleen. 1993a. "Recycling poverty: From the workplace to retirement." *Journal of Women and Aging* 5(1): 5–23.

Perkins, Kathleen. 1993b. "Working-class women and retirement." *Journal of Gerontological Social Work* 20(3–4): 129–46.

Perlman, J. E. 1976. *The Myth of Marginality: Urban Poverty and Politics in Rio de Janeiro.* Berkeley: University of California Press.

Perman, Lauri, & Beth Stevens. 1989. "Industrial segregation and the gender distribution of fringe benefits." *Gender & Society* 3: 388–404.

Perrine, Daniel M. 1994. "The view from platform zero: How Holland handles its drug problem." *America* 171: (October 15) 9–12.

Perrow, Charles. 1986. *Complex Organizations: A Critical Essay,* 3rd ed. New York: Random House.

Perrow, Charles. 1991. "A society of organizations." *Theory and Society* (20/6): 725–62.

Perry, Joellen. 2000. "Retirees stay wired to kids—and to one another." *U.S. News & World Report* 128 (June): 80.

Perry, Stewart A. 1978. *San Francisco Scavengers: Dirty Work & the Pride of Ownership.* Berkeley: U of California Press.

Perse, Elizabeth M., & Douglas A. Ferguson. 1997. "The impact of the newer television technologies on television satisfaction." In Alan Wells & Ernest A. Hakanen (eds.), *Mass Media and Society.* Greenwich, CT: Ablex: 317–36.

Peschek, Joseph. 1987. *Policy-Planning Organizations.* Philadelphia: Temple University Press.

Peter, Lawrence J., & Raymond Hull. 1969. *The Peter Principle.* New York: Morrow.

Peters, Charles C. 1933. *Motion Pictures and Standards of Morality.* New York: Macmillan.

Peters, Michael. 1991. "Sex handedness, mathematical ability and biological causation." *Canadian Journal of Psychology* 45(3): 415–19.

Peters, Thomas J., & Robert H. Waterman, Jr. 1982. *In Search of Excellence.* New York: Warner.

Peters, Tom J. 1992. *Liberation Management.* New York: Knopf.

Peterson del Mar, David. 1996. *What Trouble I Have Seen: A History of Violence Against Wives.* Cambridge, MA: Harvard University.

Peterson, John L. 1994. *The Road to 2015: Profiles of the Future.* Corte Madera, CA: Waite Group.

Peterson, Richard R. 1996. "A re-evaluation of the economic consequences of divorce." *American Sociological Review* 61(3)(June): 528–36.

Peterson, Ruth D., & William C. Bailey. 1991. "Felony murder and capital punishment: An examination of the deterrence question." *Criminology* 29: 367–95.

Pettey, Gary R. 1990. "Bible, ballots and beatific vision: The cycle of religious activism." In Robert Abelman & Stewart M. Hoover (eds.), *Religious Television: Controversies and Conclusions.* Norwood, NJ: Ablex: 197–205.

Petty, R., & H. Mirels. 1981. "Intimacy and scarcity of self-disclosure: Effects on interpersonal sttraction for males and females." *Personality and Social Psychology Bulletin* 7: 490–503.

Pfeffer, Jeffrey, & James N. Baron. 1988. "Taking the workers back out." *Research In Organizational Behavior* 10: 257–303.

Pharr, Suzanne. "A match made in heaven." *Progressive* (August): 28–29.

Phelan, J., B.G. Link, R.E. Moore, & A. Stueve. 1997. "The stigma of homelessness." *Social Psychology Quarterly* 60: 323–337.

Phelan, Thomas J., & Mark Schneider. 1996. "Race, ethnicity and class in American suburbs." *Urban Affairs Review* 31: 659–80.

Pheysey, Diana. 1993. *Organizational Cultures: Types and Transformations*. London: Routledge.

Phillips, David P. 1980. "The deterrent effect of capital punishment: New evidence on an old controversy." *American Journal of Sociology* 86: 139–48.

Phillips, G. M., & J. T. Wood (eds.). 1984. *Emergent Issues in Human Decision Making*. Carbondale: Southern Illinois University Press.

Phillips, Kevin. 1991. *The Politics of Rich and Poor*. New York: Simon & Schuster.

Piaget, Jean, & Barbel Inhelder. 1969. *The Psychology of the Child*. New York: Basic Books.

Piaget, Jean. 1950. *The Psychology of Intelligence*. Boston: Routledge & Kegan Paul.

Piel, Gerard. 1997a. "The urbanization of poverty worldwide." *Challenge* 40: 58–68.

Piel, Gerard. 1997b. "Worldwide development or population explosion: Our choice." In Robert M. Jackson (ed.), *Global Issues 97/98*. Annual Editions. Guilford, CT: Dushkin/McGraw-Hill: 43–52.

Pierce, K. 1993. "Socialization of teenage girls through teen-magazine fiction: The making of a new woman or an old lady?" *Sex Roles* 29: 59–68.

Piliavin, Irving, Rosemary Gartner, Craig Thornton, & Ross L. Matsueda. 1986. "Crime deterrence and rational choice." *American Sociological Review* 51: 101–19.

Pinkney, Alphonso. 2000. *Black Americans*, 5th ed. Upper Saddle River, NJ: Prentice-Hall.

Pirenne, Henri. 1937. *Economic & Social History of Medieval Europe*. New York: Harcourt, Brace & World.

Piven, Frances Fox, & Richard A. Cloward. 1977. *Poor People's Movements: Why They Succeed, How They Fail*. New York: Random House.

Piven, Frances, & Richard Cloward. 1978. *Why Americans Don't Vote*. New York: Pantheon.

Plagenz, George R. 1997. "Censorship of the entertainment media may be necessary." In Byron L. Stay (ed.), *Censorship*. San Diego: Greenhaven: 148–150.

Plotkin, Mark. 1993. *Tales of a Shaman's Apprentice*. New York: Viking.

Plummer, David. 1999. *One of the Boys: Masculinity, Homophobia, and Modern Manhood*. Binghamton, NY: Harrington Park.

Plunkert, Lois M. 1990. "The 1980s: A decade of job growth and industry shifts." *Monthly Labor Review* (September): 3–15.

Podesta, Anthony T., & James S. Kurtzke. 1990. "Conflict between the electronic church and state: The Religious Right's crusade against pluralism." In Robert Abelman & Stewart M. Hoover (eds.), *Religious Television: Controversies and Conclusions*. Norwood, NJ: Ablex: 207–26.

Podrouzek, W., & D. Furrow. 1988. "Preschoolers' use of eye contact while speaking: The influence of sex, age and conversation pattern." *Psycholinguistic Research* 17: 89–98.

Poggie, John J. Jr., & Richard B. Pollnac. 1988. "Danger and rituals of avoidance among New England fisherman." *MAST: Maritime Anthropological Studies* 1: 67–88.

Poire, B. A., J. K. Burgoon, & R. Parrott. 1992. "Status and privacy restoring communication in the workplace." *Journal of Applied Communication Research* 4: 419–36.

Polakow, Valerie. 1993. *Lives on the Edge: Single Mothers and Their Children in the Other America*. Chicago: University of Chicago Press.

Polednak, Anthony P. 1989. *Racial and Ethnic Differences in Disease*. New York: Oxford University Press.

Pollack, Andrew. 1996. "A cyberspace front in a multicultural war." *New York Times* (August 7): D1, 4.

Pollard, Kevin M. 1992. *African-Americans in the 1990s*. Washington, DC: Population Reference Bureau.

Pollock, Joycelyn M. 1999. *Criminal Women*. Cincinnati: Anderson.

"Polygamy in Utah." 1998. *Honolulu Star Bulletin* (August 4): A-12.

Pomer, Marshall I. 1986. "Labor market structure, intergenerational mobility and discrimination." *American Sociological Review* 51/5: 650–659.

Pomfret, John. 1997. "In Congo, revenge became rebellion: Tutsi-led campaign against Hutus turned sights on Mobutu." *Washington Post* (July 6): A1, A17.

Pontell, Henry A. 1984. *A Capacity to Punish*. Bloomington, IN: Indiana University Press.

Pope, Carl. 1999. Solving the population problem: The key is to improve the lives of women." *Sierra* (September/October): 14–15.

Popenoe, David. 1988. *Disturbing the Nest: Family Change and Decline in Modern Societies*. New York: Aldine DeGruyer.

Popenoe, David. 1993. "American family decline, 1960–1990: A review and appraisal." *Journal of Marriage and the Family* 55: 527–42.

Popenoe, David. 1996. *Life Without Father: Compelling New Evidence that Fatherhood and Marriage Are Indispensable for the Good of Children and Society*. New York: Free Press.

Poplin, Dennis. 1979. *Communities*, 2nd ed. New York: Macmillan.

Poppema, Suzanne. 1999. "The future of Roe v. Wade: Medical." In Patricia Ojea & Barbara Quigley (eds.), *Women's Studies: Annual Editions, 99–00*. Guilford, CT: Dushkin/McGraw-Hill: 117–18.

Poppen, Paul J. 1995. "Gender and patterns of sexual risk taking in college students." *Sex Roles* 32(7–8): 545–55.

Population Action International. 1997. *Contraceptive Choice: Worldwide Access to Family Planning*. Washington, DC: Population Action International.

Porter, B., & M. Dunn. 1984. *The Miami Riot of 1970: Crossing the Bounds*. Lexington, MA: Lexington.

Portes, Alejandro, & Ruben G. Rumbaut. 1990. *Immigrant America*. Berkeley: University of California Press.

Posen, Barry. 1991. *Inadvertent Escalation*. Ithaca, NY: Cornell University Press.

Posner, Michael. 1994. "Human rights defenders." In Richard Reoch (ed.), *Human Rights: The New Consensus*. London: Regency Press: 91–96.

Powell, Michael J. 1985. "Developments in the regulation of lawyers." *Social Forces* (64/2): 281–305.

Powers, Jane L., & Barbara Jaklitsch. 1993. "Reaching the hard to reach: Educating homeless adolescents in urban settings." *Education and Urban Society* 25(4): 394–409.

Powers, Stephen, David J. Rothman, & Stanley Rothman. 1996. *Hollywood's America: Social and Political Themes in Motion Pictures*. Boulder, CO: Westview.

Powers, Susan. 1992. "Sexual harassment: Civil rights act increases liability." *HR Focus* 2: 12.

Pratt, C. C., & V. L. Schmall. 1989. "College students attitudes toward elderly and sexual behavior: Implications for family life education." *Family Relations* 38: 137–41.

Prebish, Charles S. (ed.). 1993. *Religion and Sport: The Meeting of Sacred and Profane*. Westport, CT: Greenwood.

President's Commission for the Study of Ethical Problems in Medicine and Biomedical and Behavioral Research. 1981. *Defining Death: A Report on the Medical, Legal and Ethical Issues in the Determination of Death*. Washington, DC: Government Printing Office.

Preston, Samuel H. 1988. "Urban growth in developing counties: A demographic reappraisal." In Josef Gugler (ed.), *The Urbanization of the Third World*. Oxford, UK: Oxford University: 11–31.

Pribram, E. Deidre. 1993. "Female spectators." In Stevi Jackson et al. (eds.), *Women's Studies Essential Readings*. New York: New York University Press.

Proctor, Robert N. 1994. "The politics of cancer." *Dissent* 41(2): 215–22.

Puddington, Arch. 1994. "Black anti-semitism and how it grows." *Commentary* (April).

Puddington, Arch. 1995. "What to do about affirmative action." *Commentary* (June).

Puddington, Arch. 1996. "What to do about affirmative action." In Harold A. Widdison (ed.), *Social Problems 96/97* (Annual Editions). Guilford, CT: Dushkin/Brown & Benchmark.

Purcell, Piper, & Lara Stewart. 1990. "Dick and Jane in 1989." *Sex Roles* 22(3–4): 177–85.

Purvis, Andrew. 1996. "A contagion of genocide." *Time* (July 8): 38–39.

Putnam, Robert D. 1995. "Bowling alone: America's declining social capital." *Journal of Democracy* (6/1): 65–78.

Qian, Zhenchao, & Samuel H. Preston. 1993. "Changes in American marriage, 1972 to 1987: Availability and forces of attraction by age and education." *American Sociological Review* 58(4): 482–95.

Quadagno, Jill. 1992. "Social movements and state transformation." *American Sociological Review* 57: 616–34.

Quadagno, Jill. 1999. *Aging and the Life Course: An Introduction to Social Gerontology*. Boston: McGraw-Hill College.

Quarantelli, Enrico L. (ed.). 1978. *Disasters: Theory & Research*. Beverly Hills, CA: Sage.

Quarantelli, Enrico L. 1957. "The behavior of panic participants." *Sociology & Social Research* 41: 187–94.

Quarantelli, Enrico L., & Russell R. Dynes. 1970. "Property norms & looting." *Phylon* 31: 168–82.

Queen, Stuart A., Robert W. Habenstein, & Jill Sobel Quadagno. 1985. *The Family in Various Cultures*. New York: Harper & Row.

Queenan, Joe. 1989. "The many paths to riches." *Forbes* (October 23): 148–149.

Quick, James Campbell, Lawrence R. Murphy & Joseph J. Hurrell, Jr. (eds.). 1992. *Stress and Well-Being at Work: Assessments and Interventions for Occupational Mental Health*. Washington, DC: American Psychological Association.

Quigley, William. 1995. "The minimum wage and the working poor." *America* (June 3): 6–7.

Quinn, Joseph F., & Richard V. Burkhauser. 1990. "Work and retirement." In Robert H. Binstock & Linda K. George (eds.), *Handbook of Aging and the Social Sciences*. New York: Academic Press.

Quinn, R. P., B. A. Gutek, & J. T. Walsh. 1980. "Telephone interviewing: A reappraisal and a field experiment." *Basic and Applied Social Psychology* 1: 127–53.

Quinney, Richard. 1970. *The Social Reality of Crime*. Boston: Little, Brown.

Quinney, Richard. 1971. *Criminology*. Boston: Little Brown.

Quinney, Richard. 1972. "The ideology of law." *Issues in Criminology* (7/1).

Quinney, Richard. 1977. *Class, State and Crime*. New York: David McKay.

Radelet, Michael L., & Hugo A. Bedau. 1992. *In Spite of Innocence: Erroneous Convictions in Capital Cases.* Boston: Northeastern University Press.

Rader, Benjamin G. 1990. *American Sports*, 2nd ed. Upper Saddle River, NJ: Prentice-Hall.

Rader, Dotson. 1999. "Life is easier if you can share the burdens." *Parade Magazine* (February 19).

Radosh, Polly F. 1986. "Midwives in the United States: Past and present." *Population Research and Policy Review* 5: 129–45.

Radway, J. B. 1984. *Reading and Romance: Women, Patriarchy and Popular Literature.* Chapel Hill, NC: University of North Carolina.

Raffel, Jeffrey A. 1985. "The impact of metropolitan school desegregation on public opinion: A longitudinal analysis." *Urban Affairs Quarterly* 71(7): 745–65.

Ragan, P., & W. Davis. 1982. "The diversity of older voters. In Beth Hess (ed.), *Growing Old in America.* New Brunswick, NJ: Transaction Books.

Rainero, Liliana. 1996. "Environment and urban life: An Argentinean woman's view." *Women & Environments* 39–40 (summer): 14–16.

Raley, R. Kelly. 1995. "Black-white differences in kin contact and exchange among never married adults." *Journal of Family Issues* 16(1): 77–103.

Rambo, A. Terry. 1997. "The fallacy of global sustainable development." *Asia Pacific Issues* 30: March.

Ramirez, W. R. 1993. *The State of Hispanic Education.* Washington, DC: ASPI-RA.

Ramos, Francisco Martins. 1998. "My American glasses." In Philip R. DeVita & James D. Armstrong (eds.), *Distant Mirrors: America as a Foreign Culture.* Belmont, CA: West/Wadsworth: 9–160.

Rank, Mark R. 1989. "Fertility among women on welfare." *American Sociological Review* 54: 296–304.

Ransford, H. Edward, & Bartolomeo J. Palisi. 1992. "Has there been a resurgence of racist attitudes in the general population?" *Sociological Spectrum* 12: 231–55.

Ranson, Gillian, & William Joseph Reeves. 1996. "Gender earnings, and proportions of women: Lessons from a high-tech occupation." *Gender & Society* 10(2): 168–84.

Rao, Aruna, Mary B. Anderson, & Catherine A. Overholt (eds.). 1991. *Gender Analysis in Development Planning.* West Hartford, CT: Kumarian.

Raper, Arthur F. 1970. *The Tragedy of Lynching.* New York: Dover.

Rapp, Rayna. 1991. "Family and class in contemporary America." In Elizabeth Jelin (ed.), *Family, Household and Gender Relations in Latin America.* London: Kegan Paul.

Rapp, Stan, & Thomas L. Collins. 1994. *Beyond MaxiMarketing: The New Power of Daring and Caring.* New York: McGraw-Hill.

Rappaport, Roy A. 1994. "Humanity's evolution and anthropology's future." In Robert Borofsky (ed.), *Assessing Cultural Anthropology.* New York: McGraw-Hill.

Rasekh, Zohra. 1998. "Women's health and human rights in Afghanistan." *Journal of the American Medical Association* (280/5): 449–55.

Raskin Murray A., & Elaine R. Peskind. 1992. "Alzheimer's disease and other dementing disorders." In James E. Birren, R. Bruce Sloane, & Gene D. Cohen (eds.), *Handbook of Mental Health and Aging.* New York: Academic Press.

Rathus, Spencer A., Jeffrey S. Nevid, & Lois Fichner-Rathus. 1997. *Human Sexuality in a World of Diversity.* Boston: Allyn & Bacon.

Rau, William, & Dennis W. Roncek. 1987. "Industrialization and world inequality: The transformation of the division of labor in the world." *American Sociological Review* 52: 359–67.

Rauhala, A. 1987. "Religion is key for anti-abortionists, study finds." *Toronto Globe and Mail*: A1, A5.

Ravitch, Diane. 1995. "The search for order and the rejection of conformity: Standards in American education." In Diane Ravitch & Maris A. Vinovskis (eds.), *Learning from the Past: What History Teaches Us about School Reform.* Baltimore, MD: Johns Hopkins University Press: 168–90.

Ray, Melvin, & William Downs. 1986. "An empirical test of labeling theory using longitudinal data," *Journal of Research in Crime and Delinquency* (23): 169–94.

Reckless, Walter. 1969. *The Crime Problem.* New York: Appleton-Century-Crofts.

Redfield, Robert. 1941. *The Folk Culture of Yucatan.* Chicago: University of Chicago Press.

Redfield, Robert. 1947. The folk society. *American Journal of Sociology* 52: 293–308.

Reed, Michael, & Michael Hughes (eds.). 1992. *Rethinking Organization: New Directions in Organization Theory and Analysis.* Newbury Park, CA: Sage.

Reed, Wornie. 1990. "Racism and health: The case of black infant mortality." In Peter Conrad & Rochelle Kern (eds.), *Sociology of Health and Illness: Critical Perspectives.* New York: St. Martin's: 34–44.

Reeves, B., & M. M. Miller. 1978. "A multidimensional measure of children's identification with television characters." *Journal of Broadcasting* 22(1): 71–86.

Reeves, Joy B., & Ray L. Darville. 1994. "Social contact patterns and satisfaction with retirement of women in dual-career/earner families." *International Journal of Aging and Human Development* 39(2): 163–75.

Refugees. 1998. Special Issue on Asylum. No. 111 (spring).

Regev, Martha J. 1995. "Producing artistic value: The case of rock music." *Sociological Quarterly* 35(1): 85–102.

Regier, D. 1991. *Psychiatric Disorders in America: The Epidemiological Catchment Areas Study.* New York: Free Press.

Regier, D., W. Narrow, D. Rae, R. Manderscheid, B. Locke, & F. Goodwin. 1993. "The de facto U.S. mental health and addictive disorders service system: Epidemiological catchment area prospective one-year prevalence rates of disorders and services." *Archives of General Psychiatry* 50: 85–94.

Reich, Robert B. 1991. *The Work of Nations: Preparing Ourselves for Twenty-First Century Capitalism.* New York: Knopf.

Reichel, Phillip L. 1994. *Comparative Criminal Justice Systems: A Topical Approach.* Upper Saddle River, NJ: Prentice Hall.

Reid, S. T. 1991. *Crime and Criminology.* Fort Worth, TX: Holt, Rinehart & Winston.

Reid, Susan Titus. 1993. *Criminal Justice.* New York: Macmillan.

Reiman, Jeffrey. 1995. *The Rich Get Richer and the Poor Get Prison*, 4th ed. Boston: Allyn & Bacon.

Reinarman, Craig & Harry G. Levine. 1989. "The crack attack." in J. Best, ed., *Images of Issues: Typifying Contemporary Social Problems.* New York: Aldine deGruyter: 115–38.

Reinharz, Shulamit. 1991. "Feminist research principles." In Dale Spender & Cheris Kramerae (eds.), *Knowledge Explosion: Disciplines and Debates.* New York: Pergamon.

Reinharz, Shulamit. 1992. *Feminist Methods in Social Research.* New York: Oxford University.

Reiss, Ira L. 1986. *Journey into Sexuality: An Exploratory Voyage.* Englewood Cliffs, NJ: Prentice Hall.

Reitzes, Donald C., Elizabeth J. Mutran, & Maria E. Fernandez. 1996. "Does retirement hurt well-being? Factors influencing self-esteem and depression among retirees and workers." *The Gerontologist* (October): 649–56.

Rendon, Laura I., & Richard O. Hope. 1996. "An educational system in crisis." In Laura I. Rendon & Richard O. Hope (eds.), *Educating a New Majority: Transforming America's Educational System for Diversity.* San Francisco: Josey-Bass: 1–32.

Renzetti, Claire M., & Daniel J. Curran. 1992. *Women, Men and Society.* Boston: Allyn & Bacon.

Reoch, Richard. 1994. "Human rights: The new consensus." In *Human Rights: The New Consensus.* London: Regency Press in association with the United Nations High Commissioner for Refugees.

Repetti, Rena L., & Daniel J. Curran. 1992. "Women and depression: Exploring the adult role explanation." *Journal of Social and Clinical Psychology* 2(1): 57–70.

Repetto, Robert. 1995. *The "Second India" Revisited.* Washington, DC: World Resources Institute.

Resick, P. A. 1983. "Sex role stereotypes and violence against women." In V. Franks & E. Rothblum (eds.), *The Stereotyping of Women: Its Effects on Mental Health.* New York: Springer.

Reskin, Barbara F. 1988. "Bringing the man back in: Sex differentiation and the devaluation of women's work." *Gender & Society* 2(1): 58–81.

Reskin, Barbara, & Irene Padovic. 1994. *Women and Men at Work.* Thousand Oaks, CA: Pine Forge.

"Reverse discrimination of whites is rare, labor study reports." *The New York Times* (March 31): A23.

Reynolds, Larry T. 1992. "A retrospective on 'race': The career of a concept." *Sociological Focus* 25(1): 1–14.

Reynolds, Paul Davidson. 1982. *Ethics and Social Science Research.* Upper Saddle River, NJ: Prentice Hall.

Rheingold, H., & K. Cook. 1975. "The content of boys' and girls' rooms as an index of parent behavior." *Child Development* 46: 459–63.

Rhinegold, H. 1994. *The Virtual Community.* New York: Harper.

Rhoads, Steven E. 1993. *Incomparable Worth: Pay Equity Meets the Market.* New York: Cambridge University.

Rhode, Deborah L. 1993. "Gender equality and employment policy." In Sherri Matteo (ed.), *American Women in the Nineties: Today's Critical Issues.* Boston: Northeastern University.

Rhyne, D. 1981. "Bases of marital satisfaction among men and women." *Journal of Marriage and the Family* 43: 941–54.

Rich, Spencer. 1993. "Organ transplants: Rationing by wallet? Uninsured are unlikely recipients, raising questions of fairness." In The Washington Post Writers Group (eds.). *Society in Crisis: The Washington Post Social Problems Companion.* Boston: Allyn & Bacon: 228–31.

Richardson, D.C., & G. Hammock. 1991. "The role of alcohol in acquaintance rape." In A. Parrot & L. Bechhofer (eds.), *Acquaintance Rape: The Hidden Crime.* New York: John Wiley.

Richardson, James T., Joel Best, & David G. Bromley, 1991. "Satanism as a social problem." In James T. Richardson, Joel Best, & David G. Bromley (eds.), *The Satanism Scare.* New York: Aldine deGruyter: 3–17.

Richardson, Laurel. 1988. *The Dynamics of Sex and Gender: A Sociological Perspective.* New York: Harper and Row.

Richburg, Keith B. 1992. "Islamic resurgence in Malaysia: Singapore, Indonesia worried about leader's control." In *Ourselves and Others: The Washington Post Sociology Companion.* Boston: Allyn & Bacon: 237–39.

Ridgeway, Cecelia. 1991. "The social construction of status value." *Social Forces* 70/24: 367–386.

Riemer, Jeffrey W. 1979. *Hard Hats: The Work World of Construction Workers.* Beverly Hills, CA: Sage.

Rifkin, Jeremy. 1995. *The End of Work.* New York: Putnam.

Riger, Stephanie. 1993. "Gender dilemmas in sexual harassment: Policies and procedures." In Sherri Matteo (ed.), *American Women in the Nineties: Today's Critical Issues*. Boston: Northeastern University.

Riggle, Ellen D.B., & Barry L. Tadlock. 1999. "Gays and lesbians in the democratic process" Past, present and future." In Ellen Riggle and Barry Tadlock (eds.). *Gays and Lesbians in the Democratic Process*. New York: Columbia University: 1–21.

Riley, Matilda W. 1985. "Aging & social change." In Matilda W. Riley (ed.), *Aging and Society: A Sociology of Age Stratification*, Vol 3. New York: Russell Sage.

Riley, Matilda White, & K. Bond. 1983. "Beyond ageism: Postponing the onset of disability." In Matilda White Riley, B. B. Hess, & K. Bond (eds.), *Aging and Society: Selected Reviews of Recent Research*. Hillsdale. NJ: Erlbaum.

Riley, Matilda White, Anne Foner, & Joan Waring. 1988. "Sociology of age." In Neil Smelser (ed.), *Handbook of Sociology*. Beverly Hills, CA: Sage.

Riley, Matilda White. 1971. "Social gerontology and the age stratification of society." *The Gerontologist* 11: 79–81.

Riley, Matilda White. 1985. "Age strata in social systems." In Robert H. Binstock & Ethel Shanas (eds.), *Handbook of Aging and the Social Sciences*. New York: Van Nostrand Reinhold.

Riley, Matilda White. 1987. "On the significance of age in sociology." *American Sociological Review* 52: 1–14.

Riordan, Catherine A., Tamara Gross, & Cathlin C. Maloney. 1994. "Self-monitoring, gender, and the personal consequences of impression management." *American Behavioral Scientist* 37(5): 715–25.

Risman, Barbara J. 1987. "Intimate relationships from a microstructural perspective: Men who mother." *Gender & Society* 1(1): 6–32.

Risman, Barbara J. 1989. "Can men mother? Life as a single father." In Barbara J. Risman & Pepper Schwartz (eds.), *Gender in Intimate Relationships* 17(1–2): 29–43.

Ritzer, George A., & David Walcazk. 1988. "Rationalization and the deprofessionalization of physicians," *Social Forces* 67/1: 1–22.

Ritzer, George. 1977. *Working: Conflict & Change*, 2nd. ed. Upper Saddle River, NJ: Prentice Hall.

Ritzer, George. 1994. *Sociological Beginnings*. New York: McGraw-Hill.

Ritzer, George. 1996. *The McDonaldization of Society*, revised ed. Thousand Oaks, CA: Pine Forge.

Ritzman, Rosemary L., & Donald Tomaskovic-Devey. 1992. "Life chances and support for equality and equity as normative and counternormative distribution rules." *Social Forces* 70: 745–763.

Rivkin, Steven G. 1994. "Residential segregation and school integration." *Sociology of Education* 67(4): 279–97.

Rivlin, A. M., & J. M. Wiener. 1988. *Caring for the Disabled Elderly: Who Will Pay?* Washington, DC: The Brookings Institution.

Roadburg, Allan. 1980. "Factors precipitating fan violence." *British Journal of Sociology* 31: 265–76.

Robarchek, C. A., & R. K. Dentan. 1979. "Conflict, emotion, and abreaction: Resolution and conflict among the Semai Senoi." *Ethos* 7: 104–23.

Robbins, Kevin. 1999. "Two school shootings have chilling similarities." *St. Louis Post-Dispatch*. (April 15): A1, A8.

Robbins, T. 1988. *Cults, Converts, and Charisma: The Sociology of New Religious Movements*. London: Sage.

Roberto, L. G. 1983. "Issues in diagnosis and treatment of transsexualism." *Archives of Sexual Behavior* 12: 445–73.

Roberts, George W. 1994. "Brother to brother: African American modes of relating among men." *Journal of Black Studies* 24(4): 379–90.

Roberts, Julian V. 1996. "Public opinion, criminal record, and the sentencing process." *American Behavioral Scientist* 39(4): 488–99.

Roberts, Keith A. 1984. *Religion in Sociological Perspective*. Homewood, IL: Dorsey.

Roberts, Robert E. L., & Vern L. Bengston. 1996. "Affective ties to parents in early adulthood and self-esteem across twenty years." *Social Psychology Quarterly* 59(1): 96–106.

Roberts, Sam. 1993. *Who We Are*. New York: Times Books.

Robertson, Pat. 1984. "700 Club." May 13. Christian Broadcast Network telecast (CBN).

Robertson, Roland. 1988. "The sociological significance of culture: Some general considerations." *Theory, Culture and Society* 5 (February): 3–23.

Robertson, Roland. 1992. *Globalization: Social Theory and Global Culture*. Newbury Park, CA: Sage.

Robinson, R. V., & J. Kelly. 1979. "Class as conceived by Marx and Dahrendorf." *American Sociological Review* 44: 38–58.

Robson, Brian. 1993. "The twenty-first century city: A British perspective." In Anthony P. Cohen & Katsuyoshi Fukui (eds.), *Humanising the City? Social Contexts of Urban Life at the Turn of the Millennium*. Edinburgh, UK: Edinburgh University: 36–51.

Rochon, Thomas R., & Daniel A. Mazmanian. 1993. "Social movements & the policy process." *The Annals* 528: 75–88.

Rock, J. 1985. "Symbolic interactionism." In A. Kuper & J. Kuper (eds.), *The Social Science Encyclopedia*. London: Routledge & Kegan Paul.

Roderick, Melissa. 1993. *The Path to Dropping Out: Evidence for Intervention*. Westport, CT: Auburn House.

Rodgers, Joseph Lee, Paul A. Nakonezny, & Robert D. Shull. 1997. "The effect of no-fault divorce legislation on divorce rates." *Journal of Marriage and the Family* 59(4): 1026–30.

Roethlisberger, F. J., & William J. Dickson. 1939. *Management and the Worker*. Cambridge, MA: Harvard University Press.

Rogers, Barbara. 1980. *The Domestication of Women: Discrimination in Developing Societies*. London: Tavistock.

Rogers, E. M., & E. F. Shoemaker. 1971. *Communication of Innovations: A Cross-Cultural Approach*, 2nd ed. New York: Free Press.

Rollins, B. C., & K. L. Cannon. 1974. "Marital satisfaction over the life cycle: A reevaluation." *Journal of Marriage and the Family* 36: 271–82.

Rollins, B. C., & K. L. Cannon, & H. Feldman. 1970. "Marital satisfaction over the family life cycle." *Journal of Marriage and the Family* 32(February): 20–28.

Rollins, Judith. 1985. *Between Women: Domestics and Their Employers*. Philadelphia: Temple University.

Rong, Xue L., & Linda Grant. 1992. "Ethnicity, generation and school attainment of Asians, Hispanics and non-Hispanic whites." *Sociological Quarterly* 33: 625–36.

Roof, Wade C. 1979. "Socioeconomic differentials among white socioreligious groups in the United States," *Social Forces* 58: 280–289.

Roof, Wade Clark, & William McKinney. 1997. "American mainline religion: Its changing shape and future." In Thomas E. Dowdy & Patrick H. McNamara (eds.), *Religion: North American Style*. New Brunswick, NJ: Rutgers University Press: 66–80.

Roof, Wade Clark, Jackson W. Carroll, & David A. Roozen (eds.). 1995. *The Post-War Generation and Establishment Religion: Cross-Cultural Perspectives*. Boulder, CO: Westview Press.

Roopnarine, Jaipaul L., & Mohammad Ahmeduzzaman. 1993. "Puerto Rican father involvement with their preschool-age children." *Hispanic Journal of Behavioral Sciences* 15(1): 96–107.

Root, Maria P.P. (ed.). 1992. *Racially Mixed People in America*. Newbury Park, CA: Sage.

Ropers, Richard H. 1991. *Persistent Poverty: The American Dream Turned Nightmare*. New York: Plenum.

Roscoe, Will. 1992. *The Zuni Man-Woman*. Albuquerque, NM: University of New Mexico.

Rose, Arnold. 1951. *The Roots of Racism*. Paris: UNESCO.

Rose, Arnold. 1968. *The Power Structure*. New York: Oxford University Press.

Rose, Jerry D. 1982. *Outbreaks: The Sociology of Collective Behavior*. New York: Free Press.

Rose, Peter I. 1990. *They and We: Racial and Ethnic Relations in the United States*. 4th ed. New York: McGraw-Hill.

Rose, Richard. 1971. *Governing Without Consensus*. London: Faber & Faber.

Rose, Tricia. 1994. *Black Noise*. Hanover, NH: Wesleyan University Press.

Rose, Tricia. 1997. "Orality and technology: Rap music and Afro-American cultural resistance." In Alan Wells & Ernest A. Hakanen (eds.), *Mass Media and Society*. Greenwich, CT: Ablex: 207–16.

Rosen, David M. 1991. "What is a family? Nature, culture, and the law." *Marriage and Family Review* 17(1–2): 29–43.

Rosen, Ellen I. 1987. *Bitter Choices: Blue Collar Women in and out of Work*. Chicago: University of Chicago Press.

Rosenblatt, Aaron. 1967. "Negroes in baseball: The failure of success." *Transaction* 4: 53.

Rosenblatt, Robert A. 1995. "Glass ceiling still too hard to crack, U.S. panel finds." *Los Angeles Times* (March 16): 1A.

Rosenblatt, Roger. 1992. *Life Itself: Abortion in the American Mind*. New York: Random House.

Rosener, Judy B. 1990. "Ways women lead." *Harvard Business Review* 68: 119–25.

Rosener, Judy B. 1991. "The valued ways men and women lead." *Human Resources* 36(6): 147, 149.

Rosener, Judy B. 1995. *America's Competitive Secret: Utilizing Women as a Management Strategy*. New York: Oxford University Press.

Rosenfeld, Paul, Robert A. Giacalone, & Catherine A. Riordan. 1994. "Impression management theory and diversity: Lessons for organizational behavior." *American Behavioral Scientist* 37(5): 601–4.

Rosenfeld, Sarah. 1989. "The effects of women's employment: Personal control and sex differences in mental health," *Journal of Health & Social Behavior* (36/3): 77–91.

Rosenhan, David L. 1973. "On being sane in insane places," *Science* 179: 250–258.

Rosenthal, Jack. 1997. "The age boom." *The New York Times Magazine* (March 9): 39–43.

Rosenthal, Robert, & Lenore Jacobson. 1968. *Pygmalion in the Classroom: Teacher Expectations and Pupils' Intellectual Development*. New York: Holt, Rinehart and Winston.

Rosenthal, Robert. 1995. "Critiquing Pygmalion: A 25-year perspective." *Current Directions in Psychological Science* 4: 171–72.

Rosnow, Ralph L. 1991. "Inside rumor: A personal journey." *American Psychologist* 46: 484–96.

Rosnow, Ralph L., & Gary A. Fine. 1976. *Rumor and Gossip: The Social Psychology of Hearsay*. New York: Elsevier.

Ross, Catherine E. 1987. "The division of labor at home." *Social Forces* 65: 816–33.

Ross, Catherine E., & John Mirowsky. 1995. "Does employment affect health?" *Journal of Health and Social Behavior* 36(3): 230–43.

Ross, Catherine, John Mirowsky, & Karen Goldsteen. 1991. "The impact of the family on health." In Alan Booth (ed.), *Contemporary Families: Looking Forward, Looking Back*. Minneapolis: National Council on Family Relations.

Ross, Eric B. 1986. "Potatoes, population, and the Irish Famine: The political economy of demographic change." In W. Penn Handwerker (ed.), *Culture and Reproduction: An Anthropological Critique of Demographic Transition Theory*. Boulder, CO: Westview: 196–220.

Rossell, Christine H. 1990. "The carrot or the stick for school desegregation policy?" *Urban Affairs Quarterly* 25(3): 474–99.

Rosser, Sue V. 1992. *Biology and Feminism: A Dynamic Interaction*. New York: Twayne.

Rosser, Sue V. 1994. "Gender bias in clinical research: The difference it makes." In Alice J. Dan (ed.), *Reframing Women's Health: Multidisciplinary Research and Practice*. Thousand Oaks, CA: Sage.

Rossi, Alice. 1984. "Gender and parenthood: An evolutionary perspective." *American Sociological Review* 49: 1–19.

Rossi, Peter H., James D. Wright, Gene A Fisher, & Georgianna Willis. 1987. "The urban homeless: Estimating composition and size." *Science* 235 (March 13): 1136–1140.

Rossides, Daniel W. 1990. *Comparative Societies: Social Types and Their Interrelationships*. Upper Saddle River, NJ: Prentice Hall.

Rostow, Walt W. 1978. *The World Economy: History and Prospect*. Austin: University of Texas Press.

Rostow, Walt W. 1990. *The Stages of Economic Growth: A Non-Communist Manifesto*, 3rd ed. New York: Cambridge University Press.

Roszak, Theodore. 1969. *The Making of a Counter-Culture: Reflections on the Technocratic Society and Its Youthful Opposition*. New York: Doubleday.

Roth, Gunther. 1968. "Personal rulership, patrimonialism and empire-building." *World Politics*. 20: 124–206.

Roth, Julius A. 1963. *Timetables*. Indianapolis, IN: Bobbs-Merrill.

Roth, Julius. 1990. "Some contingencies of the moral evaluation and control of patients." In Peter Conrad & Rochelle Kern (eds.), *The Sociology of Health and Illness; Critical Perspectives*. New York: St. Martin's.

Rothblum, E. D. 1982. "Women's socialization and the prevalence of depression: The feminine mistake. *Woman & Therapy* 1: 5–13.

Rothchild, John. 1995. "Wealth: Static wages except for the rich," *Time* (January 30): 60–61.

Rothschild-Whitt, Joyce. 1979. "The collectivist organization." *American Sociological Review* 44: 509–27

Rothenberg, Paula S. (ed.). 1998. *Race, Class, and Gender in the United States*, 4th ed. New York: St. Martin's Press.

Rothman, Barbara Katz, & Mary Beth Caschetta. 1995. "Treating health: Women and medicine." In Jo Freeman (ed.), *Women: A Feminist Perspective*. Mountain View, CA: Mayfield: 65–78.

Rothman, Barbara Katz. 1994. "Midwifery as feminist praxis." In William Kornblum & Carolyn D. Smith (eds.), *The Healing Experience: Readings in the Social Context of Health Care*. Upper Saddle River, NJ: Prentice Hall: 1320–38.

Rothschild, Joyce, & J. Allen Whitt. 1986. *The Cooperative Workplace*. Cambridge, England: Cambridge University Press.

Rothstein, Stanley William. 1993. "A short history of urban education." In Stanley William Rothstein (ed.), *Handbook of Schooling in Urban America*. Westport, CT: Greenwood.

Rothstein, Stanley William. 1996. *Schools and Society: New Perspectives in American Education*. Upper Saddle River, NJ: Prentice Hall: 1–17.

Roush, Wade. 1996. "Demography: Live long & prosper." *Science* 273: 42.

Rovner, Julie. 1995. "Congress and health care reform 1993–94." In Thomas E. Mann & Norman J. Ornstein (eds.), *Intensive Care: How Congress Shapes Health Policy*. Washington, DC: American Enterprise Institute and The Brookings Institution.

Rowe, David, D. Wayne Osgood & W. Alan Nicewander. 1990. "A latent trait approach to unifying criminal careers." *Criminology* (28): 237–70.

Rowe, David. 1995. *Popular Cultures: Rock Music, Sport and the Politics of Pleasure*. London: Sage.

Rowly, Anthony. 1990. "Unmentioned underclass." *Far Eastern Economic Review* 150: 36–37.

Royal Dutch Society, 1994. *Administration and Compounding of Euthanasic Agents*. Royal Dutch Society for the Advancement of Pharmacy. The Hague: Netherlands.

Rozzell, Mark J., & Clyde Wilcox (eds.). 1996. *God at the Grassroots, 1996: The Christian Right in the American Elections*. Lanham, MD: Rowman and Littlefield.

Ruback, R. Barry, Janek Pandey, & Hamida Akhtar Begum. 1997. "Urban stressors in South Asia: Impact on male and female pedestrians in Delhi and Dhaka." *Journal of Cross-Cultural Psychology* 28: 23–43.

Rubenstine, Carin. 1983. "The modern art of courtly love." *Psychology Today* 19: 40–49.

Rubin, Beth A. 1986. "Class struggle American style: Unions, strikes & wages." *American Sociological Review* 51/5: 618–31.

Rubin, L. 1980. "The empty nest: Beginning or end?" In L. Bond & J. Rosen (eds.), *Competence and Coping During Adulthood*. Hanover, NH: University Press of New England.

Rubin, Lillian B. 1976. *Worlds of Pain: Life in the Working-Class Family*. New York: Basic.

Rubin, Lillian B. 1983. *Intimate Strangers: Men and Women Together*. New York: Harper Colophon.

Rubin, Lillian. 1994. *Families on the Fault Line*. New York: HarperCollins.

Rubin, Rita, with Susan Headden. 1995. Physicians under fire." *U.S. News & World Report* (January 16).

Rubin, Zick. 1983. "Are working wives hazardous to their husband's mental health?" *Psychology Today* 17: 70–72.

Rueschemeyer, Dietrich, Evelyne H. Stephens, & John D. Stephens. 1992. *Capitalist Development and Democracy*. Chicago: University of Chicago Press.

Ruether, Rosemary. 1983. *Sexism and God-Talk: Toward a Feminist Theology*. Boston: Bascon.

Ruggiero, J. A., & L. C. Weston. 1985. "Work options for women in women's magazines: The medium is the message." *Sex Roles* 12: 535–47.

Ruggles, Patricia. 1989. "Short and long-term poverty in the United States." Washington, DC: Urban Institute.

Ruggles, Patricia. 1990. "The poverty line: Too low for the 1990s." *The New York Times* (April 23): A31.

Rule, James, & Peter Brantley. 1992. "Computerized surveillance in the workplace: Forms & delusions." *Sociological Forum* (7/3): 405–23.

Rummel, Rudolph. 1995. *Democide*. New Brunswick, NJ: Transaction.

Runciman, W. G. 1990. "How many classes are there in contemporary British society?" *Sociology* 24: 377–96.

Rushwan, Hamid. 1995. "Female circumcision." *World Health*. Special Issue on Women and Health. (September): 16–17.

Russell, Cheryl. 1995. "Overworked? Overwhelmed?" *American Demographics* 17/3: 8.

Russell, Cheryl. 1998. "The haves and the want-nots." *American Demographics* 20(4): 10–12.

Russell, Diana E.H. 1984. "The prevalence and seriousness of incestuous abuse: Step-fathers vs biological fathers." *Child Abuse and Neglect* 8: 15–22.

Russell, Diana E.H. 1990. *Rape in Marriage*. Bloomington, IN: Indiana University.

Russo, Brian. 1994. "Tienanmen Square: A personal chronicle from China." In John J. Macionis & Nijole V. Benokraitis (eds.), *Seeing Ourselves*, 4th ed. Upper Saddle River, NJ: 467–73.

Russo, Nancy Felipe, & Jody D. Horn. 1995. "Unwanted pregnancy and its resolution: Options, implications." In Jo Freeman (ed.), *Women: A Feminist Perspective*. Mountain View, CA: Mayfield: 47–64.

Russo, Nancy Felipe, Jody D. Horn, & R. Schwartz. 1992. "U.S. abortion in context: Selected characteristics and motivations of women seeking abortions." *Journal of Social Issues* 48(3): 183–202.

Ruth, Sheila. 1994. *Take Back the Light: A Feminist Reclamation of Spirituality and Religion*. Lanham, MD: Littlefield Adams.

Ruth, Sheila. 1995. *Issues in Feminism: An Introduction to Women's Studies*. Mountain View, CA: Mayfield.

Ruth, Sheila. 1998. *Issues in Feminism: An Introduction to Women's Studies*, 2nd ed. Mountain View, CA: Mayfield.

Ryan, Barbara. 1989. "Ideological purity & feminism." *Gender & Society* 3: 239–57.

Ryan, William. 1971. *Blaming the Victim*. New York: Pantheon.

Rydell, C. Peter, & Susan S. Everingham. 1994. *Controlling Cocaine: Supply and Demand*. Santa Monica, CA: RAND.

Sabo, Don, M. J. Melnick, & B. E. Vanfossen. 1993. "High school athletic participation & postsecondary educational and occupational mobility." *Sociology Of Sport Journal* (10/1): 44–56.

Sabo, Don. 1995. "Pigskin, patriarchy & pain." In Paula S. Rothenberg (ed.), *Race, Class & Gender in the United States: An Integrated Study*, 3rd ed. New York: St. Martin's Press: 227–30.

Sachar, Emily. 1991. *Shut Up and Let the Lady Teach: A Teacher's Year in a Public School*. New York: Poseidon Press.

Sachs, Ignacy. 1994. "Population, development and employment." *International Social Science Journal* 46 (3) (141): 343–59.

Sachs-Jeantet, Celine. 1996. "Interview: Rome, sustainable city." *International Social Science Journal* 48: 103–6.

Sack, Kevin. 1992. "Welfare experiment showing signs of success." *The New York Times* (June 11).

Sadker, Myra, & David Sadker. 1990. "Confronting sexism in the college classroom." In Susan L. Gabriel & Isaiah Smithson (eds.), *Gender in the Classroom: Power and Pedagogy*. Urbana, IL: University of Illinois.

Sadker, Myra, & David Sadker. 1994. *Failing at Fairness: How America's Schools Cheat Girls*. New York: Charles Scribner's.

Saegert, S., & G. H. Winkler. 1990. "Environmental psychology." *Annual Review of Psychology* 41: 441–77.

Sahlins, Marshall D. 1960. "The origin of society." *Scientific American* (September): 76–87.

Sahlins, Marshall D. 1972. *Stone Age Economics*. Chicago: Aldine.

Sahlins, Marshall D., & Elman R. Service. 1960. *Evolution and Culture*. Ann Arbor: University of Michigan Press.

Sahlins, Marshall, 1976. *Culture and Practical Reason*. Chicago: University of Chicago.

Sahlins, Marshall. 1994. "Goodbye to tristes tropes: Ethnography in the context of modern world history." In Robert Borofsky (ed.), *Assessing Cultural Anthropology*. New York: McGraw-Hill.

Saitoti, Tepilit Ole. 1994. "The initiation of a Maasai warrior." In Elvio Angeloni (ed.), *Anthropology 93/94*. Guilford, CT: Dushkin.

Sale, Kirkpatrick. 1996. *Rebels Against the Future*. Reading, MA: Addison-Wesley.

Salih, M. A. Mohamed. 1992. "Environmental conflict in Africa arid lands: Cases from the Sudan and Nigeria." In Jyrki Kakonen (ed.), *Perspectives on Environmental Conflict and International Relations*. London: Pinter: 116–35.

Salkind, Neil J. 2000. *Exploring Research*, 4th ed. Upper Saddle River, NJ: Prentice Hall.

Saltman, Richard B., & Casten Von Otter. 1992. *Planned Markets and Public Competition: Strategic Reform in Northern European Health Systems*. Buckingham, UK: Open University Press.

Saltzberg, Elayne, & Joan C. Chrisler. 1995. "Beauty is the beast: The psychological effects of the pursuit of the perfect female body." In Jo Freeman (ed.), *Women: A Feminist Perspective*. Mountain View, CA: Mayfield: 306–15.

Saluter, A. F. 1992. "Marital status and living arrangements." *Current Population Reports, Population Characteristics* (Series P–20, No. 461). March. Washington, DC: U.S. Government Printing Office.

Samarasinghe, Vidyamali. 1993. "The last frontier or a new beginning? Women's microenterprises in Sri Lanka." In Gay Young, Vidyamali Samarasinghe, & Ken Kusterer (eds.), *Women at the Center: Development Issues and Practices for the 1990s*. West Hartford, CT: Kumarian: 30–44.

Sampson, Robert & John Laub. 1993. *Crime in the Making*. Cambridge, MA: Harvard UP.

Sampson, Robert J. 1986. "Effects of socioeconomic context on official reaction to juvenile delinquency." *American Sociological Review* (51, 6): 876–85.

Sampson, Robert J. 1987. "Urban black violence: The effect of male joblessness and family disruption." *American Journal of Sociology* 93: 348–82.

Samuels, R. J. 1991. "Reinventing security: Japan since Meiji." *Daedalus* 120: 47–68.

Samuelson, Paul A., & William D. Nordhaus. 1989. *Economics*, 13th ed. New York: McGraw-Hill.

Samuelson, Robert J. 1997. "The culture of poverty." *Newsweek* (May 5): 49.

Sanasarian, Eliz. 1992. "The politics of gender and development in the Islamic Republic of Iran." In Joseph G. Jabbra & Nancy W. Jabbra (eds.), *Women and Development in the Middle East and North Africa*. Leiden, Netherlands: E.J. Brill: 56–68.

Sanchez-Ayendez, Melba. 1986. "Puerto Rican elderly women: Shared meanings and informal supportive networks." In Johnnetta Cole (ed.), *All-American Women: Lines that Divide, Ties that Bind*. New York: Free Press.

Sanders, Barry. 1994. *A Is for Ox: Violence, Electronic Media, and the Silencing of the Written Word*. New York: Pantheon.

Sanders, Clinton R. (ed.). 1990. *Marginal Conventions: Popular Culture, Mass Media and Social Deviance*. Bowling Green, OH: Bowling Green University Press.

Sanders, Thomas G. 1987. "Brazilian street children." *USFI Reports* numbers 17–18.

Sandler, Bernice R. 1987. "The classroom climate: A chilly one for women." In Carol Lasser (ed.), *Educating Men and Women Together: Coeducation in a Changing World*. Chicago: University of Illinois.

Sandqvist, K. 1987. *Fathers and Family Work in Two Cultures*. Stockholm: Almqvist and Wiksell.

Santiago-Irizarry, Vilma. 1996. "Culture as cure." *Cultural Anthropology* 11(1): 3–24.

Sapir, Edward. 1949. *Language: An Introduction to the Study of Speech*. New York: Harcourt, Brace & World.

Sargent, Dudley A. 1912. "Are athletics making girls masculine?" *Ladies Home Journal* 29: 72.

Sasaki, Naoto. 1990. *Management and Industrial Structure in Japan*. Oxford, UK: Pergamon.

Sassen, Saskia. 1996. "Rebuilding the global city: Economy, ethnicity and space." In Anthony D. King (ed.,) *Re-Presenting the City: Ethnicity, Capital and Culture in the Twenty-First Century Metropolis*. London: Macmillan: 23–42.

Sauerwein, Kristina. 1996. "Survey of students: Sexual harassment an issue for many." *St. Louis Post-Dispatch Metro Post*. (January 17): 2W.

Saunders, D. G. 1989. "Who hits first and who hurts most? Evidence for the greater victimization of women in intimate relationships." Paper presented at the American Society of Criminology meetings, Reno, NV.

Savant, Marilyn Vos. 1999. "Ask Marilyn." *Parade Magazine* (February 12): 8.

Savelsberg, Joachim J. 1994. "Knowledge, domination and criminal punishment." *American Journal of Sociology* 99: 911–43.

Sawhill, Isabel V. 1988. "Poverty in the United States: Why is it so persistent? *Journal of Economic Literature*. 26/3: 1072–1119.

Schaefer, Richard T. 1998. *Racial and Ethnic Groups*, 7th ed. New York: Longman.

Schaefer, Richard T. 2000. *Racial and Ethnic Groups*, 8th ed. Upper Saddle River, NJ: Prentice-Hall.

Schaefermeyer, Mark J. 1997. "Video criticism." In Alan Wells & Ernest A. Hakanen (eds.), *Mass Media and Society*. Greenwich, CT: Ablex: 303–16.

Schafer, Walter E., Carol Olexa, & Kenneth Polk. 1994. "Programmed for social class: Tracking in high school." In John W. Heeren & Marylee Mason (eds.), *Sociology: Windows on Society*. Los Angeles: Roxbury: 196–201.

Schaie, K. Warner (ed.). 1983. *Longitudinal Studies of Adult Psychological Development*. New York: Guilford Press.

Schaie, K. Warner (ed.). 1990. "Intellectual development in adulthood." In James E. Birren, & K. Warner Schaie (eds.), *Handbook of the Psychology of Aging*. San Diego: Academic Press.

Scharlach, Andrew W., & Karen I. Fredrikson. 1994. "Elder care versus adult care: Does care recipient age make a difference?" *Research on Aging* 16(1): 43–68.

Schatzman, Leonard, & Anselm Strauss. 1972. "Social class and modes of communication." In Saul D. Feldman & Gerald W. Thiebar (eds.), *Life Styles: Diversity in American Society*. Boston: Little, Brown: 48–60.

Scheff, Thomas J. 1963. "The role of the mentally ill and the dynamics of mental disorder," *Sociometry* 26: 436–453.

Scheff, Thomas J. 1984. *Being Mentally Ill: A Sociological Theory*, 2nd ed. New York: Aldine.

Schellenberg, Kathryn (ed.). 1996. *Computers and Society*, 6th ed. Guilford, CT: Dushkin.

Schiller, Nina Glick, Stephen Crystal, & Denver Lewellen. 1994. "Risky business: The cultural construction of AIDS risk groups." *Social Science and Medicine* 38(10): 1337–46.

Schlafly, Phyllis. 1981. *Testimony: Sex Discrimination in the Workplace*. Washington, DC: U.S. Government Printing Office.

Schlegel, Alice, & Rohn Eloul. 1988. "Marriage transactions: Labor, property, status." *American Anthropologist* 90: 291–309.

Schlesinger, Mark, & Tae-Ku Lee. 1993. "Is health care different? Popular support of federal health and social policies." *Journal of Health Politics, Policy and Law* 18(3): 551–628.

Schmeck, Harold. 1985. "Quinlan case: It became a symbol of ethical problems inherent in new medical technology." *The New York Times*. (June 13): 24.

Schnaiberg, Allan, & Kenneth Alan Gould. 1994. *Environment and Society: The Enduring Conflict*. New York: St. Martin's.

Schnayer, Reuben, & R. Robert Orr. 1989. "A comparison of children living in single mother and single father families." *Journal of Divorce* 12: 171–84.

Schneider, Linda, & Arnold Silverman. 2000. *Global Sociology: Introducing Five Contemporary Societies*. New York: McGraw-Hill.

Schodolski, Vincent J., & Charles M. Madigan. 1997. "The deadly riddle of Heaven's Gate: How they perished." *Chicago Tribune* (March 28): 1–1, 1–6.

Schoen, Robert. 1990. "First unions and the stability of first marriages." *Journal of Marriage and the Family* 54: 281–84.

Schooler, Carmi, & Atushi Naoi. 1988. "The psychological effects of traditional and economically peripheral job settings in Japan." *American Journal of Sociology* 94: 335–55.

Schor, Juliet B. 1991. *The Overworked American: The Unexpected Decline of Leisure*. New York: Basic.

Schrag, Peter. 1996. "Backing off Bakke: The new assault on affirmative action." *The Nation* 262 (April 22): 11–14.

Schulhofer, Stephen J. 1984. "Is plea bargaining inevitable?" *Harvard Law Review* 97: 1006–7.

Schultz, Duane P. 1964. *Panic Behavior*. New York: Random House.

Schultze, Quentin J. 1996. "Evangelicals' uneasy alliance with the media." In Daniel A. Stout & Judith M. Buddenbaum (eds.), *Religion and Mass Media: Audiences and Adaptations*. Thousand Oaks, CA: Sage: 61–73.

Schumpeter, Joseph. 1942. *Capitalism, Socialism and Democracy*. New York: Harper.

Schur, Edwin. 1971. *Labeling Deviant Behavior*. New York: Harper & Row.

Schur, Edwin. 1973. *Radical Non-Intervention*. Upper Saddle River, NJ: Prentice-Hall.

Schur, Edwin. 1980. *The Politics of Deviance*. Upper Saddle River, NJ: Prentice-Hall.

Schur, Edwin M. 1984 *Labeling Women Deviant*. New York: Random House.

Schur, Edwin M. 1979. *Interpreting Deviance: A Sociological Introduction*. New York: Harper and Row.

Schutt, Russell K. 1987. "Craft unions & minorities." *Social Problems* 34: 388–400.

Schwartz, Barry. 1975. *Queuing and Waiting: Studies in the Social Organization of Access and Delay*. Chicago: University of Chicago Press.

Schwartz, Elaine G. 1995. "Crossing borders/shifting paradigms: Multiculturalism and children's literature." *Harvard Educational Review* 65(4): 634–50.

Schwartz, Felice N. 1989. "Management women and the new facts of life." *Harvard Business Review* 67: 65–76.

Schwartz, Felice N. 1994. "Women as a business imperative." In Susan E. Feiner (ed.), *Race & Gender in the American Economy: Views from Across the Spectrum*. Upper Saddle River, NJ: Prentice Hall.

Schwartz, Howard D. 1987. "Irrationality as a feature of health care in the United States. " In Howard D. Schwartz (ed.), *Dominant Issues in Medical Sociology*. New York: Random House.

Schwartz, John E., & Thomas J. Volgy. 1993. "Above the poverty line—but poor." *The Nation* (February 15): 191–192.

Schwartz, Pepper, & Virginia Rutter. 1998. *The Gender of Sexuality*. Thousand Oaks, CA: Pine Forge.

Schwartz, Pepper. 1994. *Peer Marriage: How Love Between Equals Really Works*. New York: Free Press.

Schwartz, Pepper. 1994b. "Peer marriage: What does it take to create a truly egalitarian relationship?" *The Family Therapy Networker* October: 57–61,92.

Schwartz, R. D., & J. H. Skolnick. 1962. "Two studies of legal stigma." *Social Problems* (10): 133–38.

Schweitzer, Marjorie M. 1983. "The elders: Cultural dimensions of aging in two American Indian communities." In Jay Sololovsky (ed.), *Growing Old in Different Societies: Cross-Cultural Perspectives*. Belmont, CA: Wadsworth.

Schwochau, Susan. 1987. "Union effects on job attitudes." *Industrial and Labor Relations Review* 40: 209–24.

Scott, Alan. 1990. *Ideology and the New Social Movements*. London: Routledge.

Scott, Catherine V. 1995. *Gender and Development: Rethinking Modernization and Dependency Theory*. Boulder, CO: Lynne Rienner.

Scott, W. Richard. 1981. *Organizations: Rational, Natural and Open Systems*. Upper Saddle River, NJ: Prentice Hall.

Seabrook, Jeremy. 1996. *In the Cities of the South: Scenes from a Developing World*. London: Verso.

Seal, David Wyatt, Gina Agostinbelli, & Charlotte A. Hannett. 1994. "Extradyadic romantic involvement: Moderating effects of sociosexuality and gender." *Sex Roles* 31(1–2): 1–22.

Seale, Clive, & Julia Addington-Hall. 1995. "Euthanasia: The role of good care." *Social Science and Medicine* 40(5): 581–87.

Seccombe, K., & G. Lee. 1986. "Gender differences in retirement satisfaction and its antecedents." *Research on Aging* 8: 426–40.

Seccombe, Karen, & Cheryl Amey. 1995. "Playing by the rules and losing: Health insurance and the working poor." *Journal of Health and Social Behavior* 36(2): 168–81.

Seeman, Melvin, Teresa Seeman, & Marnie Sayles. 1985. "Social networks & health status." *Social Psychology Quarterly* (48/3): 237–248.

Seeman, Melvin. 1972. "The signals of '68: Alienation in pre-crisis France." *American Sociological Review* (37/3): 385–402.

Segal, Jonathan A. 1991. "Women on the verge . . . of equality." *Human Resources* 36(6): 117–18, 120, 123.

Seidler, John, & Katherine Meyer. 1989. *Conflict and Change in the Catholic Church*. New Brunswick, NJ: Rutgers University Press.

Seidler, Victor J. 1992. "Men, feminism, and power." In Larry May & Robert Strikwerda (eds.), *Rethinking Masculinity: Philosophical Explorations in Light of Feminism*. Lanham, MD: Rowman & Littlefield.

Seidman, Steven. 1992. "An investigation of sex-role sterotyping in music videos." *Journal of Broadcasting and Electronic Media* 36: 209–16.

Sell, R.L., J.A. Wells, & D. Wypij. 1995. "The prevalence of homosexual behavior and attraction in the United States, the United Kingdom and France: Results of national populaton-based samples. *Archives of Sexual Behavior*: 235–48.

Selnow, Gary W. 1985. "Sex differences in uses and perceptions of profanity." *Sex Roles* 12(3–4): 303–12.

Selznick, Philip. 1957. *Leadership in Organizations*. Evanston, IL: Row, Peterson.

Selznick, Philip. 1992. *The Moral Commonwealth*. Berkeley: University of California Press.

Sen, Gita, Adrienne Germain, & Lincoln C. Chen (eds.). 1994. *Population Policies Reconsidered: Health, Empowerment, and Rights*. Boston: Harvard University.

Sengoku, Tamatsu. 1985. *Willing Workers*. Westport, CT: Quorum.

Sennett, Richard, & Jonathan Cobb. 1973. *The Hidden Injuries of Class*. New York: Vintage.

Serbin, Lisa A., Kimberly K. Powlishta, & Judith Gulko. 1993. "The development of sex typing in middle childhood." *Monographs of the Society for Research in Child Development* 58(2), Serial No. 232: 1–74.

Sered, Susan Starr. 1994. *Priestess, Mother, Sacred Sister: Religions Dominated by Women*. New York: Oxford University Press.

Sernau, Scott. 1997. "Economies of exclusion: Economic change and the global underclass." In Joseph E. Behar & Alfred G. Cuzan, (eds.), *At the Crossroads of Development: Transnational Challenges to Developed and Developing Societies*. Leiden, Netherlands: E.J. Brill: 38–51.

Service, Elman R. 1966. *The Hunters*. Upper Saddle River, NJ: Prentice Hall.

Sewell, Graham, & Barry Wilkinson. 1992. "Someone to watch over me." *Sociology* 26: 271–89.

Seymour, Daniel, & Terry Seymour. 1992. *America's Best Classrooms: How Award-Winning Teachers Are Shaping Our Children's Future*. Princeton, NJ: Peterson's Guides.

Shadid, Anthony. 1996. "Islam veils economic crisis: Iran walks edge of censor's sword." *Japan Times*. (September 8).

Shahidullah, Shahid M. 1997. "The Third World after the Cold War: Global imperatives and local peculiarities." In Joseph E. Behar & Alfred G. Cuzan (eds.), *At the Crossroads of Development: Transnational Challenges to Developed and Developing Societies*. Leiden, Netherlands: E.J. Brill: 119–35.

Shakin, M., D. Shakin, & S. H. Sternglanz. 1985. "Infant clothing: Sex labeling for strangers." *Sex Roles* 12: 955–64.

Shakur, Sanyika. 1993. *Monster: The Autobiography of an L.A. Gang Member*. New York: Penguin.

Shanklin, R. 1993. *Anthropology and Race*. Belmont, CA: Wadsworth.

Shannon, Thomas R. 1989. *World System Perspective*. Boulder, CO: Westview.

Shapiro, Isaac, & Robert Greenstein. 1991. *Selective Prosperity*. Washington, DC: Center on Budget and Policy Priorities.

Sharma, Ursula M. 1996. "Using alternative therapies: Marginal medicine and central concerns." In Basiro Davey, Alastair Gray, & Clive Seale (eds.), *Health and Disease: A Reader*. Buckingham, UK: Open University: 38–44.

Shawcross, William. 1979. *Sideshow: Kissinger, Nixon and the Destruction of Cambodia*. New York: Pocket Books.

Sheehy, Gail. 1976. *Passages: Predictable Crises of Adult Life*. New York: Dutton.

Sheehy, Gail. 1995. *New Passages: Mapping Your Life Across Time*. New York: Random House.

Sheffield, Carole E. 1995. "Sexual terrorism." In Jo Freeman (ed.), *Women: A Feminist Perspective*. Mountain View, CA: Mayfield.

Shehan, Constance L., & Karen Seccombe. 1996. "The changing circumstances of children's lives." *Journal of Family Issues* 17(4): 435–40.

Shelton, Beth Anne, & Daphne John. 1993. "Does marital status make a difference? Housework among married and cohabiting men and women." *Journal of Family Issues* 14(3): 401–20.

Shelton, Beth Anne, & Juanita Firestone. 1989. "Household labor time and the gender gap in earnings." *Gender & Society* 3(1): 105–12.

Shepherd, John, & Peter Wicke. 1997. *Music and Cultural Theory*. Cambridge, UK: Polity Press.

Sherkat, Darren E., & Christopher G. Ellison. 1991. "The politics of black religious change: Disaffiliation from black mainline denominations. *Social Forces* 70: 431–54.

Sherman, B. L., & J. R. Dominick. 1986. "Violence and sex in music videos: TV and Rock 'n' role." *Journal of Communication* 36: 94–106.

Sherman, Lawrence W., & Douglas A. Smith. 1992. "Crime, punishment and stake in conformity." *American Sociological Review* 57/5: 680–690.

Sherman, Lawrence W., & Richard A. Berk. 1984. "The specific deterrent effects of arrest for domestic violence." *American Sociological Review* 49: 261–72.

Shibley, Mark A. 1996. *Resurgent Evangelicalism in the United States: Mapping Cultural Change since 1970*. Columbia: University of South Carolina Press.

Shibutani, Tamotsu. 1966. *Improvised News: A Study of Rumor*. Indianapolis: Bobbs-Merrill.

Shiva, Vandana. 1992. "Resources." In Wolfgang Sachs (ed.), *The Development Dictionary: A Guide to Knowledge as Power*. London: Zed: 206–218.

Shizun, Gui. 1986. *Population Sociology*. Shandong, China: People's Publishing House.

Shock, N. W. 1977. "Biological theories of aging." In James E. Birren & K. Warner Schaie (eds.), *Handbook of the Psychology of Aging*. New York: Van Nostrand Reinhold.

Shonk, James H. 1992. *Team-Based Organization*. Homewood, IL: Irwin.

Shore, R. J., & Bert Hayslip, Jr. 1992. "Custodial grandparenting: Implications for children's development." In A. Gottfried & A. Gottfried (eds.), *Redefining Families: Implications for Children's Development*. New York: Plenum.

Shorris, Earl. 1992. *Latinos: A Biography of the People*. New York: Norton.

Short, James. 1960. "Differential association as a hypothesis." *Social Problems* (8): 14–24.

Shostak, Arthur. 1990. *Robust Unionism*. Ithaca, NY: Industrial and Labor Relations Press.

Shostak, Marjorie. 1994. "Memories of a !Kung girlhood." In Elvio Angeloni (ed.), *Anthropology 93/94*. Guilford, CT: Dushkin.

SHRM, 1996. *Workplace Violence*. Alexandria, VA: Society for Human Resource Management.

Shupe, Anton, & Jeffrey K. Hadden. 1989. "Is there such a thing as global fundamentalism?" In A. Shupe & J. K. Hadden (eds.), *Secularization and Fundamentalism Reconsidered: Religion and the Political Order, Vol 3*. New York: Paragon: 109–22.

SIDA, 1995. *Gender Equality in Development Cooperation: Taking the Next Step*. Stockholm: Swedish International Development Cooperation Agency.

Sidel, Ruth. 1996. *Keeping Women and Children Last*. New York: Penguin.

Siegel, Larry. 1995. *Criminology*, 5th ed. Minneapolis: West.

Siegel, Larry J. 2000. *Criminology*, 7th ed. Belmont, CA: Wadsworth.

Sigelman, Lee, & Susan Welch. 1993. "The contact hypothesis revisited." *Social Forces* 71: 781–95.

Sigmund, Paul E. 1990. *Liberation Theology at the Crossroads: Democracy or Revolution?* New York: Oxford University Press.

Signorielli, Nancy. 1989. "Television and conceptions about sex-roles: Maintaining conventionality and the status quo." *Sex Roles* 21(5–6): 337–56.

Signorielli, Nancy. 1990. "Television's mean and dangerous world: A continuation of the cultural indicators perspective." In Nancy Signorielli & M. Morgan (eds.), *Cultivation Analysis: New Directions in Media Effects Research*. Newbury Park, CA: Sage.

Signorielli, Nancy. 1991. *A Sourcebook on Children and Television*. New York: Greenwood.

Silbert, M.H., & A.M. Pines. 1984. "Pornography and sexual abuse of women." *Sex Roles* 10: 857–68.

Sills, David L. 1957. *The Volunteers*. Glencoe, IL: Free Press.

Silvas, Sharon, Barbara Jenkins, & Polly Grant. 1993. "The overvoice: Images of women in the media." In Jodi Wentzel et al., (eds.), *Women's Studies Thinking Women*. Dubuque, IA: Kendall/Hunt.

Silver, Harry, & Frances Goldscheider. 1994. "Flexible work and housework: Work and family constraints on women's domestic labor." *Social Forces* 72(4): 1103–9.

Silverstein, Merril, & Vern L. Bengston. 1991. "Do close parent–child relations reduce the mortality risk of older parents?" *Journal of Health and Social Behavior* 32: 82–95.

Simenauer, J., & D. Carroll. 1982. *Singles: The New Americans*. New York: Simon & Schuster.

Simmel, Georg. 1950. *The Sociology of Georg Simmel*, ed. and trans. by Kurt H. Wolff. Glencoe, IL: Free Press.

Simmel, Georg. 1971. "Fashion." In Donald N. Levine (ed.), *Georg Simmel: On Individuality & Social Forms*. Chicago: University of Chicago Press. Originally published in 1904.

Simmons, Melanie. 1999. "Theorizing prostitution: The question of agency." In *Sex Work and Sex Workers* (Sexuality & Culture, Volume 2). New Brunswick, NJ: Transaction.

Simon, A. 1998. "The relationship between stereotypes of and attitudes toward lesbians and gays." In G.M. Herek (ed.), *Stigma and Sexual Orientation: Understanding Prejudice Against Lesbians, Gay Men, and Bisexuals*. Thousand Oaks, CA: Sage: 62–81.

Simon, D. R., & D. Stanley Eitzen. 1986. *Elite Deviance*. Boston: Allyn & Bacon.

Simon, Robin W. 1995. "Gender, multiple roles, role meaning and mental health," *Journal of Health and Social Behavior* (36/2): 182–194.

Simons, M. 1993. "Dutch parliament approves law permitting euthanasia." *New York Times*, (February 10).

Simons, R. C., & C. C. Hughes. (eds.). 1985. *The Culture-Bound Syndromes: Folk Illnesses of Psychiatric Anthropological Interest*. Boston: D. Reidel.

Simons, Ronald L., & Phyllis A. Gray. 1989. "Perceived blocked opportunity as an explanation of delinquency among lower-class black males." *Journal of Research in Crime and Delinquency* (26): 90–101.

Simonton, Dean K. 1990a. "Creativity and wisdom in aging. In James E. Birren & Warner Schaie (eds.), *Handbook of the Psychology of Aging*. San Diego: Academic Press.

Simonton, Dean K. 1990b. "Creativity in later years: Optimistic prospects for achievement." *The Gerontologist* 30(5): 626–31.

Simpson, George E., & Milton J. Yinger. 1985. *Racial and Cultural Minorities*, 5th. ed. New York: Plenum.

Simpson, Ida Harper, David Stark, & Robert A. Jackson. 1988. "Class identification processes of married working men & women." *American Sociological Review* 53: 284–93.

Simpson, Richard L. 1956. "A modification of the functional theory of social stratification." *Social Forces* 35: 132–37.

Sims, Calvin. 1997. "Poor nations reject role on warming." *The New York Times* (December 13).

Singh, Ajit. 1992. "The lost decade: The economic crisis of the Third World in the 1980s: How the north caused the south's crisis." *Contention* 2: 58–80.

Sjoberg, Gideon, & Roger Nett. 1997. *A Methodology for Social Research*. Prospect Heights, IL: Waveland.

Skinner, Denise A. 1984. "Dual-career family stress and coping." In Patricia Voydanoff (ed.), *Work and Families*. Palo Alto, CA: Mayfield.

Sklar, Holly. 1999. "U.S. Boom Just Letting Workers Keep Pace with Costs," *Owensboro (KY) Messenger-Inquirer* (Oct 10).

Sklar, Leslie. 1995. *Sociology of the Global System*, 2nd. ed. Baltimore: Johns Hopkins University Press.

Skocpol, Theda. 1979. *States and Social Revolutions: A Comparative Analysis of France, Russia and China*. New York: Cambridge University Press.

Skocpol, Theda. 1985. "Bringing the state back in: Strategies of analysis in current research." In Peter Evans, Dietrich Rueschemeyer, & Theda Skocpol, (eds.) *Bringing the State Back In*. New York: Cambridge University Press: 3–37.

Slater, Robert. 1995. *The Psychology of Growing Old: Looking Forward*. Buckingham, UK: Open University Press.

Slavin, Robert E. 1989. "Students at risk of school failure: The problem and its dimensions." In Robert E. Slavin, N. L. Karweit, & N. A. Madden (eds.), *Effective Programs for Students at Risk*. Boston: Allyn & Bacon.

Sleeter, Christine E. 1995. "Curriculum controversies in multicultural education." In Erwin Flaxman & Harry Passow (eds.), *Changing Populations Changing Schools. Ninety-fourth Yearbook of the National Society for the Study of Education, Part II*. Chicago: NSSE: 162–85.

Sleeter, Christine E., & Peter McLaren (eds.). 1995. *Multicultural Education, Critical Pedagogy, and the Politics of Difference*. Albany, NY: State University of New York Press.

Sloan, Ethyl. 1985. *Biology of Women*. New York: John Creiley.

Smart, Barry. 1990. "On the disorder of things." *Sociology* (24/3): 397–416.

Smart, Ninian. 1989. *The World Religions*. Upper Saddle River, NJ: Prentice Hall.

Smedley, Audrey. 1999. *Race in North America*. Boulder, CO: Westview.

Smeeding, Timothy M., Michael O'Higgins, & Lee Rainwater (eds.). 1990. *Poverty, Inequality and Income Distribution in Comparative Perspective*. Washington, DC: Urban Institute Press.

Smeeding, Timothy, B. B. Torrey, & M. Rein. 1988. "Patterns of income and poverty." In Timothy Smeeding, J. L. Palmer, & B. B. Torrey (eds.), *The Vulnerable* Washington, DC: Urban Institute Press.

Smelser, Neil J. 1973. "Toward a theory of modernization." In Amitai Etzioni & Eva Etzioni-Halvey (eds.), *Social Change—Sources, Patterns and Consequences*. New York: Basic: 268–84.

Smelser, Neil J. 1988. "Social structure." In Neil J. Smelser (ed.), *Handbook of Sociology*. Newbury Park, CA: Sage: 103–129.

Smelser, Neil. 1963. *Theory of Collective Behavior*. Glencoe, IL: Free Press.

Smil, Vaclav. 1987. *Energy, Food, Environment: Realities, Myths, Options*. New York: Clarendon.

Smith, C. E. 1991. *Courts and the Poor*. Chicago: Norton.

Smith, Christian. 1991. *The Emergence of Liberation Theology: Radical Religion and Social Movement Theory*. Chicago: University of Chicago.

Smith, Dan. 1997. *The State of War and Peace Atlas*. Baltimore, MD: Penguin.

Smith, David A. 1995. "The new urban sociology meets the old: Rereading some classical human ecology." *Urban Affairs Review* 30(3): 432–57.

Smith, David A. 1996. *Third World Cities in Global Perspective: The Political Economy of Uneven Urbanization*. Boulder, CO: Westview.

Smith, Dorothy. 1992. *The Everyday World as Problematic*. Boston: Northeastern University Press.

Smith, Douglas A. 1987. "The neighborhood context of police behavior." In A. J. Reiss, & M. Tonry (eds.), *Communities and Cities*. Chicago: University of Chicago Press.

Smith, Douglas A., & Patrick R. Gartin. 1989. "Specifying specific deterrence: The influence of arrest on future criminal activity." *American Sociological Review* 54: 94–105.

Smith, Douglas, Christy Visher, & G. Roger Jajoura. 1991. "Dimensions of delinquency." *Journal of Research in Crime and Delinquency* (28): 6–32.

Smith, Douglas, Christy Visher, & Laura Davidson. 1984. "Equity and discretionary justice." *Journal of Criminal Law and Criminology* 75: 234–49.

Smith, E. R., & James R. Kleugel. 1984. "Beliefs and attitudes about women's opportunities." *Social Psychology Quarterly*: 47: 81–95.

Smith, Herman W. 1991. *Strategies of Social Research*. Orlando, FL: Holt, Rinehart and Winston.

Smith, J. P., & F. R. Welch. 1986. *Closing the Gap: Forty Years of Economic Progress for Blacks*. Santa Monica, CA: Rand.

Smith, Jane E., V. Ann Waldorf, & David L. Trembath. 1990. "Single white male looking for thin, very attractive . . ." *Sex Roles* 23(11–12): 675–85.

Smith, Michael D. 1990. "Sociodemographic risk factors in wife abuse: Results from a survey on Toronto women." *Canadian Journal of Sociology* 15: 39–58.

Smith, R. 1986. "Television addiction." In J. Bryant & D. Anderson (eds.), *Perspectives on Media Effects*. Hillsdale, NJ: Lawrence Erlbaum: 109–28.

Smith, Robert B. 1993. "Health care reform now." *Society* 30(3): 56–65.

Smith, Russell. 1994. "Invisible women: Hollywood puts on blinders when it comes to lesbians." *St. Louis Post-Dispatch*. (July 17): 3C,6C.

Smith, Vern E., & Daniel Pedersen. 1997. South toward home." *Newsweek* (July 14): 36–38.

Smith, W. J. 1985. *Dying in the Human Life Cycle: Psychological, Biomedical and Social Perspectives*. New York: Holt, Rinehart & Winston.

Smock, Pamela J. 1994. "Gender and the short-run economic consequences of marital disruption." *Social Forces* 73(1): 243–62.

Smolak, Linda. 1993. *Adult Development*. Upper Saddle River, NJ: Prentice Hall.

Smolowe, J. 1993. "Giving the cold shoulder." *Time* (December 6).

Smolowe, J. 1995. "One drug, two sentences." *Time*, (June 19): 45.

Snell, T. L. 1996. *Capital Punishment*. 1995. Washington, DC: U.S. Department of Justice, Office of Justice Programs.

Snipes, Jeffrey B., & Edward R. Maguire. 1995. "Country music, suicide, and spuriousness." *Social Forces* 74(1): 327–29.

Snow, David A., & Robert D. Benford. 1988. "Ideology, frame resonance and participant mobilization." *International Social Movement Research* 1: 197–217.

Snow, David A., E. Burke Rochford, Jr., Steven K. Worden, & Robert D. Benford. 1986. "Frame alignment processes, micromobilization and movement participation," *American Sociological Review* 51: 464–81.

Snow, David A., Louis A. Zurcher Jr., & Robert Peters. 1981. "Victory celebrations as theater." *Symbolic Interaction* 4/1.

Snow, David A., Louis A. Zurcher, Jr., & Sheldon Ekland-Olson. 1980. "Social networks and social movements." *American Sociological Review* 80: 787–801.

Snow, David, & Leon Anderson. 1993. *Down on Their Luck*. Berkeley: University of California Press.

Snyder, Don J. 1997. *The Cliff Walk*. Boston: Little, Brown.

Snyder, Eldon E., & Elmer A. Spreitzer. 1989. "Baseball in Japan." In D. Stanley Eitzen (ed.), *Sport in Contemporary Society*, 3rd ed. New York: St. Martin's Press.

Snyder, Margaret. 1990. "Women: The key to ending hunger." *The Hunger Project Papers* 8 (August): 1–32.

Snyder, Mark, Elizabeth Decker Tanke, & Ellen Berscheid. 1996. "Social perception and interpersonal behavior: On the self-fulfilling nature of social stereotypes." In Sharon S. Brehm & Saul M. Kassin (eds.), *Readings in Social Psychology: The Art and Science of Research*. Boston: Houghton Mifflin.

Snyder, Mark. 1997. "When belief creates reality: The self-fulfilling impact of first impressions on social interaction prophecy." In Jodi O'Brien & Peter Kollock (eds.), *The Production of Reality: Essays and Readings on Social Interaction*. Thousand Oaks, CA: Pine Forge, pp. 438–42.

So, Alvin Y. 1990. *Social Change and Development: Modernization, Dependency and World System Theories*. Newbury Park, CA: Sage.

Soares, Luiz. 1996. "Introduction." In *UNESCO Conference on Multiculturalism, Globalization and Identity*. Rio de Janeiro.

Solano, Cecilia H., & Mina Dunnam. 1985. "Two's company: Self-disclosure & reciprocity in triads versus dyads." *Sociology & Social Research* 75: 182–188.

Solomon, Charlene. 1991. "Sexual harassment after the Thomas hearings." *Personnel Journal* 70: 32–37.

Solomon, Jolie. 1996. "Breaking the silence." *Newsweek 179*, (May 20): 20. (179): 250–58.

Solon, Gary. 1992. "Intergenerational income mobility in the United States." *American Economic Review* (June).

Sommers-Flanagan, R., J. Sommers-Flanagan, & B. Davis. 1993. "What's happening on music television? A gender role content analysis." *Sex Roles* 28(11–12): 745–53.

Son, In S., Suzanne W. Model, & Gene A. Fisher. 1989. "Polarization and progress in the black community: Earnings and status gains for young black males in the era of affirmative action." *Sociological Forum* 4: 309–27.

Sorensen, Elaine. 1994. *Comparable Worth: Is It a Worthy Policy?* Princeton, NJ: Princeton University Press.

Sorenson, Georg. 1998. *Democracy and Democratization*, 2nd ed. Boulder, CO: Westview.

Sorokin, Pitirim A. 1941. *Social and Cultural Dynamics.* New York: American.

Sorokin, Pitirim A. 1959. (Original edition, 1927.) *Social and Cultural Mobility.* New York: Free Press.

Sotomayor, Marta, & Suzanne Randolph. 1988. "A preliminary review of caregiving issues among Hispanic elderly." In Marta Sotomayor & Herman Curiel (eds.), *Hispanic Elderly: A Cultural Signature.* Edinburg, TX: Pan American University Press.

Sowell, Thomas. 1972. *Black Education: Myths and Tragedies.* New York: McKay.

Sowell, Thomas. 1981. *Ethnic America.* New York: Basic Books.

Sowell, Thomas. 1990. *Preferential Policies.* New York: Morrow.

Spain, Daphne, & Suzanne M. Bianchi. 1996. *Balancing Act: Motherhood, Marriage, and Employment Among American Women.* New York: Russell Sage Foundation.

Spalter-Roth, Roberta, & Sunhwa Lee. 2000. "Profile of ASA Membership." *Footnotes* (March).

Spanier, Graham B. 1991. "Cohabitation: Recent changes in the United States." In John N. Edwards & David H. Demo (eds.), *Marriage and Family in Transition.* Boston: Allyn & Bacon.

Sparks, Allister. 1990. *The Mind of South Africa.* New York: Knopf.

Sparks, Richard. 1980. "A critique of Marxist criminology." In Norval Morris & Michael Tonry (eds.), *Crime and Justice*, Vol. 2. Chicago: University of Chicago Press: 159–208.

Sparks, Richard. 1992. *Television and the Drama of Crime: Moral Tales and the Place of Crime in Public Life.* Buckingham, UK: Open University Press.

Spates, J., & John Macionis. 1987. *Sociology of Cities.* New York: St. Martin's.

Spector, Malcolm, & John Kitsuse. 1977. *Constructing Social Problems.* Menlo Park, CA: Cummings.

Spencer, Herbert. 1860. *The Social Organism.* London: Greenwood.

Spencer, Paul. 1988. *The Maasai of Matapato: A Study of Rituals of Rebellion.* Bloomington, IN: University of Indiana.

Spender, Dale. 1989. *The Writing or the Sex: Or Why You Don't Have to Read Women's Writing to Know It's No Good.* New York: Teacher's College Press.

Spengler, Oswald. 1928. *The Decline and Fall of the West.* New York: Alfred A. Knopf.

Spickard, Paul R. 1991. *Mixed Blood: Intermarriage and Ethnic Identity In Twentieth-Century America.* Madison: University of Wisconsin Press.

Spigel, Lynn. 1992. *Make Room for TV: Television and the Family Ideal in Postwar America.* Chicago: University of Chicago Press.

Spilerman, S. 1976. "Structural characteristics of cities and the severity of racial disorders." *American Sociological Review* 41: 771–93.

Spitze, Glenna. 1986. "The division of task responsibility in U.S. households: Longitudinal adjustments to change." *Social Forces* 64 (March): 689–701.

Squyres, Suzanne, Nancy R. Jacobs, & Jacquelyn F. Quiram (eds.). *Minorities: A Changing Role in American Society.* Wylie, TX: Information Plus.

Srole, Leo et al. 1962. *Mental Health in the Metropolis.* New York: McGraw-Hill.

Srole, Leo, Thomas S. Langer, Stanley T. Michael, Marvin K. Opler & Thomas A. C. Rennie. 1962. *Mental Health in the Metropolis: The Midtown Manhattan Study.* New York: McGraw-Hill.

Stabiner, Karen. 1998. "With alternative medicine, profits are big, rules are few." *The New York Times* (June 21): WH25.

Stacey, Judith. 1996. *In the Name of the Family: Rethinking Family Values in the Postmodern Age.* Boston: Beacon Press.

Stack, Carol B. 1975. *All Our Kin: Strategies for Survival in a Black Community.* New York: Harper & Row.

Stack, Carol. 1996. *Call to Home: African-American Reclaim the Rural South.* New York: Basic Books.

Stack, S. 1990. "Execution publicity and homicide in South Carolina: A research note." *Sociological Quarterly* (31/4): 559–611.

Stack, Steven, & James Gundlach. 1995. "Country music and suicide: Individual, indirect, and interaction effects: A reply to Snipes and Maguire." *Social Forces* 74(1): 331–35.

Staggenborg, Suzanne. 1988. "The consequences of professionalization and formalization in the pro-choice movement." *American Sociological Review* 53: 586–606.

Stahl, Abraham. 1993. "Changing attitudes toward the old in Oriental families in Israel." *International Journal of Aging and Human Development* 37(4): 261–69.

Stalans, Loretta J., & Arthur J. Lurigio. 1996. "Editors' introduction: Public opinion about the creation, enforcement, and punishment of criminal offenses." *American Behavioral Scientist* 39(4): 369–78.

Stallings, Barbara, & S. Streek. 1995. "Capitalism in conflict?" In Barbara Stallings (ed.), *Global Change, Regional Responses: The New International Context of Development.* New York: Cambridge University Press.

Staples, Brent. 1997. "Just walk on by: A black man ponders his power to alter public space." In Estelle Disch (ed.). *Reconstructing Gender: A Multicultural Anthology.* Mountain View, CA: Mayfield: 165–68.

Staples, Robert, & Alfredo Mirande. 1980. "Racial and cultural variations among American families: A decennial review of the literature on minority families." *Journal of Marriage and the Family* 33: 119–35.

Staples, Robert, & Leanor Boulin Johnson. 1993. *Black Families at the Crossroads: Challenges and Prospects.* San Francisco: Jossey-Bass.

Stark, Rodney, & William S. Bainbridge. 1985. *The Future of Religion: Secularization, Revival and Cult Formation.* Berkeley & Los Angeles: University of California Press.

Stark, Rodney. 1991. "Normal revelations: A rational choice model of 'mystical experiences'." In David G. Bromley (ed.), *Religion and the Social Order*, Volume I. Greenwich, CT: JAI Press.

Stark, Rodney. 1996a. *Sociology*, 6th ed. Belmont, CA: Wadsworth: 255–56.

Stark, Rodney. 1996b. *The Rise of Christianity: A Sociologist Reconsiders History.* Princeton, NJ: Princeton University Press.

Starr, Paul. 1982. *The Social Transformation of American Medicine.* New York: Basic Books.

Starr, Paul. 1994. *The Logic of Health Care Reform.* New York: Penguin.

Starrels, Marjorie E. 1994. "Gender differences in parent-child relations." *Journal of Family Issues* 15(4): 590–607.

Starrels, Marjorie E., Sally Bould, & Leon J. Nicholas. 1994. "The feminization of poverty in the United States: Gender, race, ethnicity and family factors." *Journal of Family Issues* 15(1): 148–85.

Staton, Ann Q. 1990. *Communication and Student Socialization.* Norwood, NJ: Ablex.

Stave, Sondra Astor. 1995. *Achieving Racial Balance: Case Studies of Contemporary School Desegregation.* Westport, CT: Greenwood.

Steele, Shelby. 1990. "A negative vote on affirmative action." *The New York Times Magazine* (May 13): 46–49+.

Steering Committee of the Physician's Health Study Research Group. 1989. "Final report of the aspirin component of the ongoing physician's health study." *New England Journal of Medicine* 321(3): 129–35.

Steffensmeier, Darrell, & Cathy Streifel. 1991. "Age, gender and crime across three historical periods: 1935, 1960 and 1985." *Social Forces* (69/3): 869–94.

Steffensmeier, Darrell, & M. D. Harer. 1991. "Did crime rise or fall during the Reagan presidency? *Journal of Crime and Delinquency.* 28: 330–59.

Steil, Janice M. 1995. "Supermoms and second shifts: Marital inequality in the 1990s." In Jo Freeman (ed.), *Women: A Feminist Perspective.* Mountain View, CA: Mayfield: 149–161.

Steil, Janice, & Beth Turetsky. 1987. "Is equal better? The relationship between marital equality and psychological symptomology." In S. Oskamp (ed.), *Family Processes and Problems: Social Psychological Aspects.* Beverly Hills, CA: Sage.

Steil, Janice M., & Karen Weltman. 1991. "Marital inequality: The importance of resources, personal attributes, and social norms on career valuing and the allocation of domestic responsibilities." *Sex Roles* 24(3–4): 161–79.

Steinem, Gloria. 1995. "Sex, lies and advertising." In Jo Freeman (ed.), *Women: A Feminist Perspective.* Mountain View, CA: Mayfield.

Steinmetz, Suzanne K. 1988. *Duty Bound: Elder Abuse and Family Care.* Newbury Park, CA: Sage Publications.

Steinmetz, Suzanne K., & Deborah J. Amsden. 1983. "Dependent elders, family stress and abuse." In Timothy Brubaker (ed.), *Family Relationships in Later Life.* Beverly Hills, CA: Sage.

Sternberg, Robert J. 1988. *The Triangle of Love.* New York: Basic Books.

Stets, Jan. 1993. "The link between past and present intimate relationships." *Journal of Family Issues* 14(2): 236–60.

Stetson, Dorothy McBride. 1991. *Women's Rights in the U.S.A.: Policy Debates and Gender Roles.* Pacific Grove, CA: Brooks/Cole.

Stevens, Evelyn P. 1993. "Marianismo: The other face of machismo in Latin America." In Anne Minas (ed.), *Gender Basics: Feminist Perspectives on Women and Men.* Belmont, CA: Wadsworth.

Stevens, John. 1987. "The rise of the sports page." *Gannett Center Journal* 1: 1–11.

Stevens, William. 1997a. "Battle stage is set: Clinton proposal on global warming defines issues for rich and poor alike." *New York Times* (October 23).

Stevens, William. 1997b. "Greenhouse gas issue: Haggling over fairness." *The New York Times* (November 30).

Stevenson, Harold W. 1992. "Learning from Asian Schools." *Scientific American* (December): 70–76.

Stewart, A. T. Q. 1977. *The Narrow Ground: Patterns of Ulster History.* Belfast: Pretani Press.

Stewart, L. P., A. D. Stewart, S. A. Friedley, & P. J. Cooper. 1990. *Communication Between the Sexes: Sex Differences and Sex Role Stereotypes.* Scottsdale, AZ: Gorsuch Scarisbrick.

Stiff, J. B., G. R. Miller, C. Sleight, P. I. Mongeau, R. Gardelck, & R. Rogan. 1989. "Explanations for visual cue primacy in judgments of honesty and deceit." *Journal of Personality and Social Psychology* 156: 555–64.

Stinchcombe, Arthur. 1968. *Constructing Social Theories*. Chicago: University of Chicago Press.

Stinnett, Nick, Linda M. Carter, & James E. Montgomery. 1972. "Older persons' perceptions of their marriage." *Journal of Marriage and the Family* 34: 665–70.

Stipek, Deborah J., & J. Heidi Gralinski. 1991. "Gender Differences in children's achievement-related beliefs and emotional responses to success and failure in mathematics." *Journal of Educational Psychology* 83: 361–71.

Stogdill, R. M. 1974. *Handbook of Leadership*. New York: Free Press.

Stohl, Michael, & George Lopez (eds.). 1987. *The State as Terrorist*. Westport, CT: Greenwood.

Stone, Merlin. 1979. *When God Was a Woman*. San Diego: Harcourt Brace Jovanovich.

Stoneman, Z., G. H. Brody, & C. MacKinnon. 1986. "Same-sex and cross-sex siblings: Activity choices, roles, behavior and gender stereotypes." *Sex Roles* 15: 495–511.

Stott, M. 1981. *Ageing for Beginners*. Oxford, UK: Blackwell.

Strange, Susan. 1996. *The Retreat of the State: The Diffusion of Power in the World Economy*. Cambridge, UK: Cambridge University Press.

Straus, Murray A. 1980. "A sociological perspective on the causes of family violence." In M. Green (ed.), *Violence in the Family*. Boulder, CO: Westview.

Straus, Murray A. 1993. "Identifying offenders in criminal justice research on domestic assault." *American Behavioral Scientist* 36(5): 587–600.

Strauss, A., S. Fagerhaugh, B. Suczek, & C. Weiner. 1985. *The Social Organization of Medical Work*. Chicago: University of Chicago Press.

Strauss, Anselm, Leonard Schatzman, Rue Bucher, Danuta Ehrlich, & Melvin Sabslim. 1964. *Psychiatric Ideologies and Institutions*. New York: Free Press.

Strauss, Anselm. 1977. *Negotiations: Varieties, Contexts, Processes & Social Order*. San Francisco: Jossey-Bass.

Strauss, Claudia, & Naomi Quinn. 1994. "A cognitive/cultural anthropology." In Robert Borofsky (ed.), *Assessing Cultural Anthropology*. New York: McGraw-Hill.

Street, Penny. 1997. "Scenario workshops: A participatory approach to sustainable urban living?" *Futures* 29: 139–58.

Strikwerda, Robert A., & Larry May. 1992. "Male friendship and intimacy." In Larry May & Robert Stikwerda (eds.), *Rethinking Masculinity: Philosophical Explorations in Light of Feminism*. Lanham, MD: Rowman and Littlefield.

Stryker, Sheldon. 1990. "Symbolic interactionism: Themes & variations." In M. Rosenberg & R. H. Turner (eds.), *Social Psychology: Sociological Perspectives*. New Brunswick, NJ: Transaction.

Stuart, Peggy. 1992. "What does the glass ceiling cost you?" *Personnel Journal* 171(11): 70–9.

Stutz, Bruce. 1993. "The landscape of hunger." *Audubon* (March/April): 54–63.

Sudol, Frank, & Allen Dresdner. 1995. "The sustainable city." *American City & County* 110 (March 31): 6–7.

Suh, Moon-Gi. 1996. "The structural relationship between economic growth and distribution of wealth in South Korea." Paper presented at annual meeting of the American Sociological Association, New York, August.

Sullivan, Deborah A. 1993. "Cosmetic surgery: Market dynamics and medicalization." *Research in the Sociology of Health Care*. 10: 97–115.

Sullivan, Thomas J. 1992. *Applied Sociology: Research & Critical Thinking*. New York: Macmillan.

Summer, Laura. 1994. "The escalating number of uninsured in the United States." *International Journal of Health Services*. 24(3): 409–13.

Sumner, W. G. 1883. *What Social Classes Owe to Each Other*. New York: Harper & Brothers.

Sumner, William Graham. 1960. *Folkways*. New York: New American Library. Originally published in 1906.

Sun, L. H. 1990. "China seeks ways to protect elderly: Support agreements replacing traditional respect for the elderly." *Washington Post* (October 23): A1, A18.

Sung, Betty Lee. 1994. "Bicultural conflict." In Elvio Angeloni (ed.), *Anthropology 93/94*. Guilford, CT: Dushkin.

Suplee, Curt. 1997. "El Nino: Preparing for the worst." *Washington Post* (September 21).

Suppe, Frederick (ed.). 1974. *The Structure of Scientific Theories*. Urbana: University of Illinois Press.

Surette, Ray, 1998. *Media, Crime, and Criminal Justice*, 2nd ed. Belmont, CA: West/Wadsworth.

Sussman, Marvin D. 1985. "The family life of old people." In Robert H. Binstock & Ethel Shanas (eds.), *Handbook of Aging in the Social Sciences*. New York: Van Nostrand Reinhold.

Sutherland, Edwin H. 1940. "White-collar criminality." *American Sociological Review* (5): 1–12.

Sutherland, Edwin H. 1978. *Criminology*, 10th ed. New York: Harper & Row: 8–34.

Sutherland, Edwin, & Donald Cressey. 1970. *Criminology*, Philadelphia: J. P. Lippincott.

Sutherland, Edwin. 1949. *White-Collar Crime*. New York: Dryden.

Suzman, Richard M., Tamara Harris, Evan C. Hadley, Mary Grace Kovar, & Richard Weindruch. 1992. "The robust oldest old: Optimistic perspectives for increasing healthy life expectancy." In Richard M. Suzman, David P. Willis & Kenneth G. Manton (eds.), *The Oldest Old*. New York: Oxford University Press.

Swedin, Goran. 1995. "Modern Swedish fatherhood: Challenges which offer great opportunities." In *Men on Men: Eight Swedish Men's Personal Views on Equality, Masculinity and Parenthood*. Stockholm: Equality Affairs Division of the Ministry of Health and Social Affairs.

Swift, Richard. 1991. "Among the believers." *Utne Reader* 45 (May/June): 99–104.

Swomley, John. 1998. "Promises we *don't* want kept." In Alsion D. Spalding (ed.), *Taking Sides: Clashing Views on Controversial Issues in Gender Studies*. Guilford, CT: Dushkin/McGraw-Hill: 50–53.

SWS Network News. 1997. "Members speak out—Sociologists differ about family textbooks' messages." *Newsletter of Sociologists for Women in Society* 14(4): 7–9.

Syme, S. Leonard, & Lisa F. Berkman. 1990. "Social class: Susceptibility and illness." In Peter Conrad & Rochelle Kern (eds.), *Sociology of Health and Illness: Critical Perspectives*. New York: St. Martin's: 28–34.

Syme, S. Leonard, & Lisa F. Berkman. 1994. "Social class: Susceptibility and illness." In Peter Conrad & Rochelle Kern (eds.), *Sociology of Health and Illness: Critical Perspectives*. New York: St. Martin's: 28–34.

Symons, Donald. 1979. *The Evolution of Human Sexuality*. New York: Oxford University.

Szasz, Thomas S. 1961. *The Myth of Mental Illness*. New York: Harper & Row.

Szasz, Thomas. 1994. "Mental illness is still a myth," *Society* (31/4): 34–39.

Szasz, Thomas. 1994. *Cruel Compassion: Psychiatric Control of Society's Unwanted*. New York: Wiley.

Szell, Gyorgy. 1994. "Technology, production, consumption and the environment." *International Social Science Journal* 46(2)(140): 213–25.

Tabor, James D., & Eugene V. Gallagher. 1995. *Why Waco? Cults and the Battle for Religious Freedom in America*. Berkeley, CA: University of California.

Taira, Koji, & Solomon B. Levine. 1996. "Employment flexibility and joblessness in low-growth, restructured Japan." *The Annals* 544: 140–53.

Tajfel, Henri. 1982. "Social psychology of intergroup relations." In *Annual Review of Psychology*. Palo Alto, CA: Annual Reviews: 1–39.

Takaki, Ronald. 1993. *A Different Mirror: A History of Multicultural America*. Boston: Little, Brown.

Tamney, Joseph B. 1992. *The Resilience of Christianity in the Modern World*. Albany: State University of New York Press.

Tanaka, Jennifer. 1997. "There's no place like home, unless it's the office." *Newsweek* (July 7): 14.

Tannen, Deborah. 1990. *You Just Don't Understand: Women and Men in Conversation*. New York: William Morrow.

Tannen, Deborah. 1994. *Gender and Discourse*. New York: Oxford University.

Tannen, Deborah. 1994. *Talking From 9 to 5*. New York: William Morrow.

Tarkan, Laurie. 1995. "Unequal opportunity." *Women's Sport & Fitness* (September): 25–27.

Tarrow, Sidney G. 1994. *Power In Movement: Social Movements, Collective Action and Politics*. New York: Cambridge University Press.

Tartakov, Carlie, & Gary Tartakov. 1994. "Interracial or crosscultural?" In Walton R. Johnson & D. Michael Warren (eds.), *Inside the Mixed Marriage: Accounts of Changing Attitudes, Patterns, and Perceptions of Cross-Cultural and Interracial Marriages*. Lanham, MD: University Press of America.

Tartre, L. A. 1990. "Spatial skills, gender and mathematics." In Elizabeth Fennema & G. C. Leder (eds.), *Mathematics and Gender*. New York: Teachers College Press.

Tausky, Curt. 1984. *Work and Society*. Itasca, IL: Peacock.

Tavris, Carol. 1996. "The mismeasure of woman." In Karen E. Rosenblum & Carol Travis (eds.), *The Meaning of Difference: American Constructions of Race, Sex, Gender, Social Class, and Sexual Orientation*. New York: McGraw-Hill.

Taylor, Charles. 1995. *Multiculturalism and the Politics of Recognition*. Princeton, NJ: Princeton University Press.

Taylor, Robert Joseph, & Linda M. Chatters. 1988. "Church members as a source of informal social support." *Review of Religious Research* 30: 193–203.

Teachman, Jay D., & Kathleen Paasch. 1993. "The economics of parenting apart." In Charlene E. Depner & James H. Bray (eds.), *Nonresidential Parenting: New Vistas in Family Living*. Newbury Park, CA: Sage.

Teays, Wendy. 1991. "The burning bride: The dowry problem in India." *Journal of Feminist Studies in Religion* 7 (Fall): 29–52.

Tehranian, Majid. 1980. "The curse of modernity: The dialectics of modernization and communication." *International Social Science Journal* 32(2): 257–63.

Teich, Albert H. (ed.). 1993. *Technology and the Future*, 6th ed. New York: St. Martin's Press.

Teitz, Michael B. 1997. "American planning in the 1990s: Part II, the dilemma of the cities." *Urban Studies* 34(5–6): 775–95.

Tennenbaum, David. 1977. "Research studies of personality & criminality." *Journal of Criminal Justice* 5: 1–19.

Terkel, Studs. 1985. *Working*. New York: Penguin.

Terrelonge, Pauline. 1995. "Feminist consciousness and black women." In Jo Freeman (ed.), *Women: A Feminist Perspective*. Mountain View, CA: Mayfield.

Tessler, Richard C. & Deborah L. Dennis. 1992. "Mental illness among homeless adults," *Research in Community and Mental Health* 7: 3–53.

The New York Times. 1997. "HMO complaints." 2(February): 12Y.

"The widening gap between CEO pay and what others make," 1993. *Business Week* (April 26): 56–57.

Thierer, Adam, & Stephen Chapman. 1997. "The V-chip will result in censorship." In Byron L. Stay (ed.), *Censorship*. San Diego: Greenhaven: 171–75.

Thoits, Peggy A. 1986. "Multiple identities: Examining gender and marital status differences in distress." *American Sociological Review* 51: 259–72.

Thoits, Peggy A. 1995. "Stress, coping and social support processes: Where are we? What next?" *Journal of health and Social Behavior* Extra Issue, 1995: 53–79.

Thomas, Volker. 1996. "Facts and figures: Foreigners in Germany." In *Foreigners in Our Midst*. Bonn: Inter Nationes: 13–15.

Thomas, W. I. 1923. *The Unadjusted Girl*. New York: Harper & Row.

Thomas, W. I., & D. S. Thomas. 1928. *The Child in America*. New York: Knopf.

Thomas-Lester, Avis. 1995. "Domestic violence." *Washington Post* (January 17): C5.

Thompson, Elizabeth, & Ugom Colella. 1992. "Cohabitation and marital stability: Quality or commitment." *Journal of Marriage and the Family* 54: 259–67.

Thompson, Hunter S. 1966. *Hell's Angels*. New York: Ballantine.

Thompson, William E. 1983. "Hanging tongues: A sociological encounter with the assembly line." *Qualitative Sociology* 6: 215–37.

Thorkelson, Anne E. 1985. "Women under the Law: Has equity been achieved?" In Alice G. Sargent (ed.), *Beyond Sex Roles*. St. Paul, MN: West.

Thornberry, Terence. 1987. "Toward an interactional theory of delinquency." *Criminology* (25): 863–91.

Thornberry, Terence P., & Margaret Farnsworth. 1982. "Social correlates of criminal involvement." *American Sociological Review*. 47: 505–18.

Thornberry, Terence P., & R. L. Christenson. 1984. "Unemployment and criminal involvement: An investigation of reciprocal causal structures." *American Sociological Review* 49: 398–411.

Thornborrow, Nancy M., & Marianne B. Sheldon. 1995. "Women in the labor force." In Jo Freeman (ed.), *Women: A Feminist Perspective*. Mounain View, CA: Mayfield.

Thorne, Barrie. 1993. *Gender Play: Girls and Boys in School*. New Brunswick, NJ: Rutgers University.

Thorne, Barrie. 1997. "Girls and boys together ... but mostly apart: Gender arrangements in elementary schools." In Laurel Richardson, Verta Taylor, & Nancy Whittier (eds.), *Feminist Frontiers IV*. New York: McGraw-Hill: 176–87.

Thornton, Arland, & Deborah Freedman. 1986. "Changing attitudes toward marriage and single life." In Ollie Pocs & Robert H. Walsh (eds.), *Marriage and Family* (Annual Editions). Guilford, CT: Dushkin.

Thornton, Arland. 1988. "Cohabitation and marriage in the 1980s." *Demography* 25: 497–508.

Thornton, J. 1984. "Family violence emerges from the shadows." *U.S. News & World Report* (January 23): 66.

Thornton, Sarah. 1996. *Music, Media, and Subcultural Capital*. Hanover, NH: Wesleyan University Press.

Thurow, Lester C. 1987. "A surge in inequality." *Scientific American* 256/5: 30–37.

Tickell, Crispin. 1996. "Rising temperatures place cities at risk." *Forum for Applied Research and Public Policy* 11: 134–36.

Tietmeyer, Hans. 1987. *Interdependence and Co-operation in Tomorrow's World. A Symposium Marking the Twenty-Fifth Anniversary of the OECD*. Paris: Organisation for Economic Co-operation and Development: 89–94.

Tiffen, Mary, & Michael Mortimore. 1994. "Malthus controverted: The role of capital and technology in growth and environment recovery in Kenya." *World Development* 22: 991–1010.

Tilly, Charles. 1978. *From Mobilization to Revolution*. Reading, MA: Addison-Wesley.

Tilly, Charles. 1992. *Coercion, Capital and European States, AD 990–1992*. Cambridge, MA: Basil Blackwell.

Tilly, Charles. 1993. *European Revolutions, 1492–1992*. Oxford, England: Blackwell.

Tilly, Charles. 1994. "Stratification and inequality." In Peter N. Stearns (ed.), *Encyclopedia of Social History*. New York: Garland.

Tittle, Charles R., & Robert F. Meier. 1990. "Specifying the SES/delinquency relationship." *Criminology* 28: 271–99.

Tittle, Charles R., W. J. Villemez, & D. A. Smith. 1978. "The myth of social class and criminality: An empirical assessment of the empirical evidence." *American Sociological Review* 43: 643–56.

Tittle, Charles. 1975. "Labeling and crime: An empirical evaluation." In Walter Gove (ed.), *The Labeling of Deviance*. New York: John Wiley: 79–100.

Tjosvold, D., I. R. Andrews, & J. T. Struthers. 1992. "Leadership influence." *Journal of Social Psychology* 132: 39–50.

Toby, Jackson. 1979. "The new criminology is the old sentimentality." *Criminology* (16): 513–26.

Toby, Jackson. 1994. "Everyday school violence: How disorder fuels it." *American Educator* 17: 4.

Toffler, Alvin. 1980. *The Third Wave*. New York: Bantam.

Tolson, Jay. 1995. "The trouble with elites." *The Wilson Quarterly* (19/1): 6–8.

Tönnies, Ferdinand. 1963. *Community and Society*. New York: Harper & Row. Originally published in 1887.

"Top players produce up to $1 million in revenue for their universities." 1994. *Chronicle of Higher Education* (April 13): A33–34.

Topping, Donald M. 1992. "Literacy and cultural erosion in the Pacific Islands." In Fraida Dubin & Natalie A. Kuhlman (eds.), *Cross-Cultural Literacy: Global Perspectives on Reading and Writing*. Upper Saddle River, NJ: Regents/Prentice Hall.

Tordoff, William. 1992. "The impact of ideology on development," *Journal of International Development* 4/1: 41–53.

Tornstam, Lars. 1992. "Formal and informal support to the elderly in Sweden." In Hal Kendig, Akiko Hashimoto, & Larry C. Coppard (eds.), *Family Support for the Elderly: The International Experience*. New York: Oxford University Press.

Toro-Morn, Maura I. 1995. "Gender, class, family, and migration: Puerto Rican women in Chicago." *Gender & Society* 9(6): 712–26.

Torry, S. 1997. "ABA leader criticizes admissions policies." *Washington Post* (August 5): A7.

Touraine, Alain. 1974. *The Post-Industrial Society*. London: Wildwood.

Touraine, Alain. 1981. *The Voice & the Eye*. Cambridge, England: Cambridge University Press.

Townsend, Bickley. 1996. "Room at the top for women." *American Demographics* (18/7): 28–37.

Toynbee, Arnold J. 1946. *A Study of History*. New York: Oxford University Press.

Trebach, Arnold. 1989. "Why not decriminalize?" *New Perspectives Quarterly* (6/2): 40–45.

Triandis, Harry C. 1994. *Culture and Social Behavior*. New York: McGraw-Hill.

Tribe, Laurence H. 1992. *Abortion: The Clash of Absolutes*. New York: W. W. Norton.

Trible, Phyllis. 1984. *The Texts of Terror*. Philadelphia: Fortress.

Trice, Harrison M., & Janice M. Beyer. 1993. *The Cultures of Work Organizations*. Upper Saddle River, NJ: Prentice Hall.

Troeltsch, Ernst. 1931. *The Social Teaching of the Christian Churches*. New York: Macmillan.

Troiden, Richard R. 1988. *Gay and Lesbian Identity: A Sociological Analysis*. Dix Hills, NY: General Hall.

Trounstine, Philip J., & Terry Christensen. 1982. *Movers and Shakers: The Study of Community Power*. New York: St. Martin's Press.

Trujillo, C. (ed.). 1991. *Chicana Lesbians: The Girls Our Mothers Warned Us About*. Berkeley, CA: Third Woman Press.

Tsunoyama, Sakae. 1993. "The age of the city." In Anthony P. Cohen & Katsuyoshi Fukui (eds.), *Humanising the City? Social Contexts of Urban Life at the Turn of the Millennium*. Edinburgh, UK: Edinburgh University: 19–35.

Tumin, Melvin M. 1953. "Some principles of stratification: A critical analysis." *American Sociological Review* 18: 387–393.

Tumin, Melvin M. 1963. "On inequality." *American Sociological Review* 28: 19–26.

Tumin, Melvin M. 1985. *Social Stratification: The Forms and Functions of Inequality*, 2nd ed. Upper Saddle River, NJ: Prentice Hall.

Tumin, Melvin. 1964. "The functionalist approach to social problems." *Social Problems* 12: 379–388.

Tunnell, Kenneth D. 1992. *Choosing Crime: The Criminal Calculus of Property Offenders*. Chicago: Nelson-Hall.

Turk, Austin. 1977. "Class, conflict and criminology." *Sociological Focus* 10: 209–20.

Turkle, Sherry. 1995. *Life on the Screen: Identity in the Age of the Internet*. New York: Simon & Schuster.

Turner, Bryan S. 1991. *Religion and Social Theory*. London: Sage.

Turner, Bryan. 1986. *Equality*. London: Tavistock.

Turner, C. F., & E. Martin (eds.). 1984. *Surveying Subjective Phenomena* (Vol. 1). New York: Russell Sage Foundation.

Turner, J. Blake. 1995. "Economic context and the health effects of unemployment." *Journal of health and Social Behavior* 36(3): 213–301.

Turner, Jonathan H., & A. Maryanski. 1979. *Functionalism*. Menlo Park, CA: Benjamin/Cummings.

Turner, R. J., & D. Lloyd. 1995. "Lifetime traumas and mental health: The significance of cumulative adversity." *Journal of Health and Social Behavior* 36: 360–76.

Turner, R. Jay & Franco Marino. 1994. "Social support and social structure: A descriptive epidemology," *Journal of Health and Social Behavior* (35/3): 193–212.

Turner, R. Jay & M.O. Wagonfeld. 1967. "Occupational mobility and schizophrenia," *American Sociological Review* 32: 104–113.

Turner, Ralph H., & Lewis M. Killian. 1993. *Collective Behavior*, 4th ed. Upper Saddle River, NJ: Prentice Hall.

Turner, Ralph. 1962. "Role taking: Process versus conformity." In Arnold Rose (ed.), *Human Behavior & Social Processes*. Boston: Houghton Mifflin.

Turner, Stephen P., & Jonathan H. Turner. 1990. *The Impossible Science: An Institutional Analysis of American Sociology*. Newbury Park, CA: Sage.

Turner, Terence. 1993. "The role of indigenous peoples in the environmental crisis: The example of the Kayapo of the Brazilian Amazon." *Perspectives in Biology and Medicine*, 36(3): 526–45.

Turow, Joseph. 1990. "A mass communications perspective on entertainment industries." In James Curran & Michael Gurevitch (eds.), *Mass Media and Society*. London: Edward Arnold: 160–77.

Twaddle, Andrew C., & Richard M. Hessler. 1987. *A Sociology of Health*. New York: Macmillan.

Twain, Mark. 1875/1946. *The Adventures of Tom Sawyer*. New York: Grosset & Dunlap. (Originally published in 1875)

Tygiel, Jules. 1983. *Baseball's Great Experiment: Jackie Robinson and His Legacy*. New York: Oxford University Press.

Tyler, Stephen A. 1973. *India: An Anthropological Perspective*. Prospect Heights, IL: Waveland.

Tylor, Edward Burnett. 1871. *Primitive Culture: Researches into the Development of Mythology, Philosophy, Religion, Language, Art and Custom*. London: John Murray.

Tyson, A. S. 1994. "Asian-Americans spurn image as a model minority." *Christian Science Monitor* (August 26).

U.S. Bureau of the Census. 1995. *Statistical Abstract of the United States*. Washington, DC: Department of Commerce.

U.S. Bureau of the Census. 1998. *Statistical Abstract of the United States*. Washington, DC: U.S. Department of Commerce.

U.S. Bureau of the Census. 1999. *Statistical Abstract of the United States*. Washington, DC: U.S. Department of Commerce.

U.S. Conference of Mayors. 1996. *A Status Report on Hunger and Homelessness in America's Cities: 1996*. Washington, DC: Author.

U.S. Department of Education. 1993. *The Condition of Education*. National Center for Educational Statistics, Office of Educational Research Law Improvement. Washington, DC: U.S. Government Printing Office.

U.S. Department of Health and Human Services. 2000. http: \\www.os.dhhs. gov\news\press

U.S. Department of Justice. 1986. "*Attorney General's Commission on Pornography: Final Report*. Washington, DC: Government Printing Office.

U.S. Department of Justice. 1993. *Sourcebook of Criminal Justice Statistics*. Washington, DC: U.S. Government Printing Office.

U.S. Department of Labor. 1991. *Working Women: A Chartbook*, Bulletin 2385. Washington, DC: U.S. Government Printing Office.

U.S. Department of Labor. 1995. *Report on the American Workforce*. Washington: GPO.

U.S. Public Health Service. 1985. *Women's Health: Report of the Public Health Service Task Force on Women's Health Issues, Vol. 1*. 100(1): 73–106. Hyattsville, MD: National Center for Health Statistics.

U.S. Senate Special Committee on Aging. 1991. *Aging America: Trends and Projections*. Department of Health and Human Services No. (FCoA) 91–28001. Washington, DC: U.S. Government Printing Office.

Uchitelle, L., & N. R. Kleinfeld. 1996. "On the battlefields of business, millions of casualties." *New York Times* (March 3): 1ff.

Udy, Stanley H. Jr. 1959. "Bureaucracy and 'rationality' in Weber's organizational theory: An empirical study." *American Sociological Review* 24: 791–95.

Uhlenberg, Peter. 1988. "Aging and the social significance of cohorts." In James E. Birren & Vern L. Bengston (eds.), *Emergent Theories of Aging*. New York: Springer.

UNHCR. 1998. *The State of the World's Refugees*. Geneva: United Nations High Commissioner for Refugees.

UNICEF, 1991. *The State of the World's Children 1991*. United Nations Children's Fund. London: Oxford University Press.

Uniform Crime Reports. 1993. *Crime in the United States*. Washington, DC: U.S. Government Printing Office.

Uniform Crime Reports. 1997. *Crime in the United States* (Annual). Federal Bureau of Investigation. Washington, DC: U.S. Government Printing Office.

United Nations Development Program. 1995. *Human Development Report, 1995*. New York: Oxford University.

United Nations Development Program. 1997. *Human Development Report, 1997*. New York: Oxford University.

United Nations Development Program. 1998. *Human Development Report, 1998*. New York: Oxford University.

United Nations Development Programme. 1999. *Human Development Report: 1999*. New York: Oxford University Press.

United Nations. 1998. *Demographic Yearbook*. Department of Economic and Social Development. New York: United Nations.

Updike, John. 1979. *Problems and Other Stories*. New York: Alfred Knopf.

Urbanization. 1996. "Urbanization: The challenge for the next century." *Finance and Development* 33: 50.

USAID Developments. 1997a. "Focus on lessons without borders." 4(1): 1–5.

USAID Developments. 1997b. "Hillary Clinton praises USAID's microenterprise initiative." 3(4): 3.

Useem, Bert. 1985. "Disorganization and the New Mexico prison riot." *American Sociological Review* 50: 677–88.

Useem, Michael. 1984. *The Inner Circle*. New York: Oxford University Press.

Usman, Sushil. 1985. "Countermodernization in the Third World countries: Theoretical issues and policy implications." Paper presented at the meeting of the North Central Sociological Association, Louisville, April.

Vaahtoranta, Tapani. 1992. "The control of atmospheric pollution: In there an East-West conflict? In Jyrki Kakonen (ed.), *Perspectives on Environmental Conflict and International Relations*. London: Pinter: 44–54.

Vacon, R. 1990. "Rethinking the war on drugs." *Hartford Courant* (May 27): 1.

Vaill, Peter. 1989. *Managing as a Performing Art*. San Francisco: Jossey-Bass.

Vainio, H., D. M. Parkin, & L. Tomatis. 1990. "International cancer care." In Thomas A. Lambo & Stacey B. Day (eds.), *Issues in Contemporary International Health*. New York: Plenum.

Valenzuela, Angela. 1993. "Liberal gender role attitudes and academic achievement among Mexican-origin adolescents in two Houston inner-city Catholic schools." *Hispanic Journal of Behavioral Sciences* 15(3): 310–23.

Vallas, Steven P. 1987. "The labor process as a source of class consciousness: A critical examination." *Sociological Forum* 2: 237–256.

van den Berge, Pierre L. 1973. *Age and Sex In Human Societies*. Belmont, CA: Wadsworth.

Van Den Haag, Ernest. 1985. "Could successful rehabilitation reduce the crime rate?" *Journal of Criminal Law and Criminology* 73: 1022–35.

Vanneman, Reeve, & Lynn W. Cannon. 1987. *The American Perception of Class*. Philadelphia: Temple University Press.

Vannoy-Hiller, Dana, & William W. Philiber. 1989. *Equal Partners: Successful Women in Marriage*. Newbury Park, CA: Sage.

Vayda, Andrew P. 1994. "Actions, variations, and change: The emerging anti-essentialist view in anthropology." In Robert Borofsky (ed.), *Assessing Cultural Anthropology*. New York: McGraw-Hill.

Veblen, Thorstein. 1933. *The Engineers and the Price System*. New York: Viking.

Veblen, Thorstein. 1934. *The Theory of the Leisure Class*. New York: Modern Library.

Veblen, Thorstein. 1964. *The Vested Interests & the Common Man*. New York: Augustus M. Kelley. Originally published in 1919.

Veneziano, Carol, & Louis Veneziano. 1992. "The relationship between deterrence & moral reasoning." *Criminal Justice Review* 17: 209–16.

Verbrugge, Lois M. 1985. "Gender and health: An update of hypotheses and evidence." *Journal of Health and Social Behavior* 26: 156–82.

Verbrugge, Lois M., & Deborah L. Wingard. 1991. "Sex differentials in health and mortality." In Laura Kramer (ed.), *The Sociology of Gender: A Text-Reader*. New York: St. Martin's.

Verry, Stewart A. 1978. *San Francisco Scavengers: Dirty Work and the Pride of Ownership*. Berkeley: University of California Press.

Vincent, R. C., D. K. Davis, & L. A. Borouszkowski. 1987. "Sexism on MTV: The portrayal of women in rock videos." *Journalism Quarterly* 64(4): 750–55.

Vinick, Barbara H. 1979. "Remarriage." In R. H. Jacobs & Barbara H. Vinick (eds.), *Re-Engagement in Later Life*. Stamford, CT: Greylock.

Vinovskis, Maris A. 1995. *Education, Society, and Economic Opportunity: A Historical Perspective on Persistent Issues*. New Haven CT: Yale University Press.

Viss, D. C., & Shawn M. Burn. 1992. "Divergent perceptions of lesbians: A comparison of lesbian self-perceptions and heterosexual perceptions." *Journal of Social Psychology* 132: 169–78.

Vogel, Ezra F. 1979. *Japan as Number One: Lessons for America*. New York: Harper & Row.

Vogel, Ezra F. 1991. *The Four Little Dragons: The Spread of Industrialization In East Asia*. Cambridge, MA: Harvard University Press.

Volti, Rudi. 1988. *Society and Technology Change*. New York: St. Martin's Press.

Volti, Rudi. 1995. *Society and Technological Change*, 3rd ed. New York: St. Martin's.

von Eschen, Donald, Jerome Kirk, & Maurice Pinard. 1976. "The disintegration of the Negro non-violent movement." In Robert H. Lauer (ed.), *Social Movements & Social Change*. Carbondale, IL: SIUP: 203–36.

Von Hirsch, Andrew. 1976. *Doing Justice*. New York: Hill & Wang.

Voy, R. 1991. *Drugs, Sport & Politics*. Champaign, IL: Leisure Press.

Wacquant, Loic. 1994. "The new urban color line." In Craig Calhoun (ed.), *Social Theory and the Politics of Identity*. Cambridge, England: Blackwell, 231–276.

Waddock, Sandra A. 1995. *Not by Schools Alone: Sharing Responsibility for America's Educational Reform*. Westport, CT: Praeger.

Wagley, Charles, & Marvin Harris. 1958. *Minorities in the New World*. New York: Columbia University Press.

Waitzkin, Howard. 1989. "Marxist perspectives in social medicine." *Social Science and Medicine* 28(11): 1099–101.

Waitzkin, Howard. 1990. "A Marxian interpretation of the growth and development of coronary care technology." In Peter Conrad & Rochelle Kern (eds.), *The Sociology of Health and Illness: Critical Perspectives*. New York: St. Martin's.

Wal, G., & R. Dillman. 1994. "Euthanasia in the Netherlands." *British Medical Journal* 308: 1346–49.

Waldman, S., & R. Thomas. 1990. "Bonfire of the S&L's: How did it happen?" *Newsweek*, May 21: 20–25, 27–28.

Waldron, Ingrid. 1983. "Sex differentials in human mortality: The role of genetic factors." *Social Science and Medicine* 17(6): 321–33.

Waldron, Ingrid. 1990. "What do we know about causes of sex differences in mortality?" In Peter Conrad & Rochelle Kern (eds.), *Sociology of Health and Medicine: Critical Perspectives*. New York: St. Martin's: 45–57.

Waldron, Ingrid. 1994. "What do we know about causes of sex differences in mortality?" In Peter Conrad & Rochelle Kern (eds.), *Sociology of Health and Medicine: Critical Perspectives*. New York: St. Martin's: 42–55.

Walker, Allan & Carol Walker. 1995. "Poverty," in Adam Kupfer & Jessica Kupfer, eds., *The Social Science Encyclopedia*, 2nd ed. London: Routledge: 655–657.

Walker, J. R., & R. V. Bellamy, Jr. 1991. "Gratifications of grazing: An exploratory study of remote control use." *Journalism Quarterly* 68: 422–31.

Walker, Karen. 1994. "Men, women and friendship: What they say, what they do." *Gender & Society* 8(2): 246–65.

Walker, Kathryn, & Margaret Woods. 1976. *Time Use: A Measure of Household Production of Family Goods and Services.* Washington, DC: American Home Economics Association.

Walker, Samuel. 1985. *Sense and Nonsense About Crime.* Monterey, CA: Brooks Cole.

Walker, Samuel. 1994. *Sense and Nonsense About Crime and Drugs: A Policy Guide*, 3rd ed. Belmont, CA: Wadsworth.

Wallace, Ronald L. 1983. *Those Who Have Vanished: An Introduction to Prehistory.* Homewood, IL: Dorsey.

Wallace, Ruth A. (ed.). 1989. *Feminism and Sociological Theory.* Newbury Park, CA: Sage.

Wallace, Ruth A., & Alison Wolf. 1999. *Contemporary Sociological Theory*, 5th ed. Upper Saddle River, NJ: Prentice Hall.

Wallace, Ruth. 1992. *They Call Her Pastor.* Albany, NY: State University of New York.

Wallace, Ruth. 1993. "The social construction of a new leadership role: Catholic women pastors." *Sociology of Religion* (54(1): 31–42.

Wallerstein, Immanuel. 1974. *Capitalist Agriculture and the Origins of the World Economy in the 16th Century.* New York: Academic Press.

Wallerstein, Immanuel. 1979. *The Capitalist World Economy.* Cambridge, England: Cambridge University Press.

Wallerstein, Immanuel. 1990. *The Modern World System II.* New York: Academic Press.

Wallerstein, Immanuel. 1991. *Geopolitics and Geoculture: Essays on the Changing World System.* Cambridge, MA: Cambridge University Press.

Wallerstein, Judith S. 1984. "Children of divorce: Preliminary report of a ten-year follow-up of young children." *American Journal of Orthopsychiatry* 54: 444–58.

Wallerstein, Judith S., & Sandra Blakeslee. 1989. *Second Chances: Men, Women, and Children a Decade After Divorce.* New York: Ticknor & Fields.

Walsh, Edward J. 1981. "Resource mobilization and citizen protest in communities around Three Mile Island." *Social Problems* 29: 1–21.

Walsh, Sharon. 1995. "Still looking for a path to the top." *Washington Post* (May 28): H6.

Walster, Hatfield, Elaine Walster, G. W. Pilivin, & L. Schmidt. 1973. "Playing hard to get: Understanding an elusive phenomenon." *Journal of Personality and Social Psychology* 26: 113–21.

Walters, Glenn & Thomas White. 1989. "Heredity and crime—bad genes or bad research?" *Criminology* (27): 455–86.

Walton, John. 1987. "Theory and research on industrialization." *Annual Review of Sociology* 13: 89–103.

Walzer, Susan. 1994. "The role of gender in determining abortion attitudes." *Social Science Quarterly* 75(3): 687–93.

Ward, Martha C. 1999. *A World Full of Women.* Boston: Allyn & Bacon.

Ward, Russell A. 1984. *The Aging Experience: An Introduction to Social Gerontology.* New York: Harper and Row.

Wardwell, Walter. 1994. "Alternative medicine in the United States." *Social Science and Medicine* 38(8): 1061–68.

Waring, Marilyn. 1988. *If Women Counted: A New Feminist Economics.* San Francisco: HarperSanFrancisco.

Warner, Judith. 1993. "The assassination of Dr. Gunn: Scare tactics turn deadly." *Ms* 3 (May–June): 86–87.

Warner, W. Lloyd, & Paul S. Hunt. 1941. *The Social Life of a Modern Community.* New Haven, CT: Yale University Press.

Warner, W. Lloyd, Paul S. Hunt, Marsha Meeker, & Kenneth Eels. 1949. *Social Class in America.* New York: Harper.

Warr, Mark. 1995. "America's perceptions of crime and punishment." In Joseph F. Sheley (ed.), *Criminology: A Contemporary Handbook*, 2nd ed. Belmont, CA: Wadsworth: 15–31.

Washington Post. 1997. "Shrinking forests." October 11.

Washington Post. 1998. "Education: Gains and gaps." From *What on Earth: A Weekly Look at Trends, People and Events Around the World.* October 24.

Wasilchide, John V. 1992. *Amish Social Life: A Portrait of Plain Living.* New York: Crescent Books.

Waskul, Dennis. 1997. "Selfhood in the age of computer-mediated interaction." Paper presented at the annual meeting of the Southwest Social Science Association.

Wasserman, Stanley, & Katherine Faust. 1994. *Social Network Analysis: Methods & Applications.* New York: Cambridge University Press.

Waters, M. S., W. C. Heath, & J. K. Watson. 1995. "A positive model of the determination of religious affiliation." *Social Science Quarterly* 76: 105–23.

Watson, J. Mark. 1988. "Outlaw motorcyclists." In James M. Henslin (ed.), *Down to Earth Sociology*, 5th ed. New York: Free Press: 203–13.

Watson, Mary N., Thomas C. Cesario, Susan Ziemba, & Pamela McGovern. 1993. "Elder abuse in long-term care environments: A pilot study using information from long-term care ombudsman reports in one California county." *Journal of Elder Abuse and Neglect* 5(4): 95–111.

Watson, O. M. 1970. *Proxemic Behavior: A Cross-Cultural Study.* The Hague: Mouton.

Watson, O. M., & T. D. Graves. 1966. "Quantitative research in proxemic behavior." *American Anthropologist* 68: 971–85.

Watson, R. 1992. "Ethnic cleansing." *Newsweek* (Aug 17): 16–20.

Watson, Ruby S., & Patricia Buckley Ebrey. 1991. *Marriage and Inequality in Chinese Society.* Berkeley, CA: University of California.

Watson, W. E., L. K. Michaelson, & W. Sharp. 1991. "Member competence, group interaction & group decision making." *Journal of Applied Psychology* 76: 803–809.

Watson, Wilber H. 1990. "Family care, economics and health." In Zev Harel, Edward A. McKinney & Michael Williams (eds.), *Black Aged: Understanding Diversity and Service Needs.* Newbury Park, CA: Sage.

Watt, David Harrington. 1991. *A Transforming Faith: Explorations of Twentieth-Century American Evangelicalism.* New Brunswick, NJ: Rutgers University Press.

Wayne, Leslie. 2000. "On Web, voters re-invent grass-roots activism." *New York Times* (May 21): 30.

Weakliem, David, Julia McQuillan, & Tracy Schauer. 1995. "Toward meritocracy? Changing social-class differences in intellectual ability." *Sociology of Education* 68(4): 271–86.

Weaver, Charles N. & Michael D. Matthews. 1990. "Work Satisfaction of Females With Full-Time Employment & Full-Time Housekeeping: 15 Years Later," *Psychological Reports* 66: 1248–1250.

Webb, Eugene J., Donald T. Campbell, Richard D. Schwartz, & Lee Sechrest. 1966. *Unobtrusive Measures: Nonreactive Research in the Social Sciences.* Chicago: Rand McNally.

Webb, Marilyn. 1988. "The debate over joint custody." In J. Gipson Wells (ed.), *Current Issues in Marriage and the Family.* New York: Macmillan.

Weber, Max. 1905/1954. *The Protestant Ethic and the Spirit of Capitalism.* (Talcott Parsons, trans.). New York: Charles Scribner's Sons.

Weber, Max. 1905/1977. *The Protestant Ethic and the Spirit of Capitalism* (trans. Talcott Parsons). New York: Scribner.

Weber, Max. 1919/1946. *From Max Weber: Essays in Sociology.* (trans. and eds. Hans Gerth & C. Wright Mills). New York: Oxford University Press.

Weber, Max. 1925/1975. *The Theory of Social and Economic Organization.* (trans. A. M. Henderson & Talcott Parsons. New York: Oxford University Press.

Weber, Max. 1947. *From Max Weber.* Hans Gerth & C. Wright Mills, (eds.) New York: Oxford University Press.

Weber, Max. 1978. *Economy and Society.* Berkeley, University of California Press.

Webster Commission. 1992. *The City in Crisis.* Los Angeles: Institute of Government and Public Affairs, UCLA.

Webster, Andrew. 1990. *Introduction to the Sociology of Development*, 2nd. ed. Atlantic Highlands, NJ: Humanities Press.

Weicher, John C. 1989. "Wealth and poverty among the elderly." In Marion Erin Lewin & Sean Sullivan (eds.), *The Care of Tomorrow's Elderly.* Washington, DC: American Enterprise Institute for Public Policy Research.

Weightman, Judith M. 1989. "The People's Temple as a continuation and an interruption of religious marginality in America." In Rebecca Moore & Fielding McGehee III (eds.), *New Religious Movements, Mass Suicide, and People's Temple.* Lewiston, NY: Edwin Mellen: 5–21.

Weinberg, M. S. et al. 1994. *Dual Attraction.* New York: Oxford University.

Weinberg, M.S., C.J. Williams, & D.W. Pryor. 1994. *Dual Attraction: Understanding Bisexuality.* New York: Oxford University.

Weinstein, Deena. 1991. *Heavy Metal: A Cultural Sociology.* New York: Lexington.

Weisberger, Adam. 1992. "Marginality and its directions." *Sociological Forum* 7: 425–46.

Weisburd, David, Stanton Wheeler, Elin Waring, & Nancy Bode. 1991. *Crimes of the Middle Class: White-Collar Defendants in the Courts.* New Haven, CT: Yale University Press.

Weiskel, Timothy C. 1997. "Can humanity survive unrestricted population growth?" In Robert M. Jackson (ed.), *Global Issues 97/98.* Annual Editions. Guilford, CT: Dushkin/McGraw-Hill: 40–42.

Weitz, Rose. 2001. *The Sociology of Health, Illness and Health Care.* Belmont, CA: Wasdworth.

Weitzman, Lenore J. 1984. "Sex-role socialization: A focus on women." In Jo Freeman (ed.), *Women: A Feminist Perspective.* Palo Alto, CA: Mayfield.

Weitzman, Lenore J. 1985. *The Divorce Revolution: The Unexpected Social and Economic Consequences for Women and Children in America.* New York: Free Press.

Weitzman, Leonore J., & Ruth B. Dixon. 1988. "The transformation of legal marriage through no-fault divorce." In J. Gipson Wells (ed.), *Current Issues in Marriage and the Family.* New York: Macmillan.

Wekesser, Carol (ed.). 1995. *Violence in the Media.* San Diego: Greenhaven Press.

Welch, Michael R., David C. Leege, & James C. Cavendish. 1995. "Attitudes toward abortion among U.S. Catholics: Another case of symbolic politics?" *Social Science Quarterly* 76(1): 142–97.

Welch, Susan, & Lee Sigelman. 1989. "A black gender gap?" *Social Science Quarterly* 70: 120–133.

Welch, Susan, & Lee Sigelman. 1993. "The politics of Hispanic Americans." *Social Science Quarterly* 74: 76–94.

"Welfare mistrust." 1996. *USA Today*, (July 2).

Weller, Jack M., & Enrico L. Quarantelli. 1973. "Neglected characteristics of collective behavior," *American Journal of Sociology* 79/3: 665–85.

Wellford, Charles. 1975. "Labeling theory and criminology: An assessment." *Social Problems* 22: 335–47.

Wellman, Barry, Janet Salaff, et al. 1996. "Computer networks as social networks." *Annual Review of Sociology* 22: 213–238.

Wells, Alan, & Ernest A. Hakanen (eds.). 1997. *Mass Media and Society*. Greenwich, CT: Ablex.

Wells, H. G. 1969. *The Time Machine*. Chicago: Children's Press. Originally published in 1895.

Wendt, Ann C., & William M. Slonaker, 1994. "Discrimination reflects on you." In Susan F. Feiner (ed.), *Race and Gender in the American Economy: Views from Across the Spectrum*. Upper Saddle River, NJ: Prentice Hall.

Wenger, G. Clare. 1992. "The major English speaking countries." In Richard M. Suzman, David P. Willis, & Kenneth G. Manton (eds.), *The Oldest Old*. New York: Oxford University Press.

Wenner, Lawrence A. (ed.) 1989. *Media, Sports and Society*. Newbury Park, CA: Sage.

Wertz, Richard W., & Dorothy C. Wertz. 1990. "Notes on the decline of midwives and the rise of medical obstetricians." In Peter Conrad & Rochelle Kern (eds.), *The Sociology of Health and Illness: Critical Perspectives*. New York: St. Martin's.

Weslowski, Wlodzimierz. 1966. "Some notes on the functional theory of stratification." In Reinhard Bendix, and Seymour M. Lipset (eds.), *Class Status and Power: Social Stratification in Comparative Perspective*, 2nd ed. New York: Free Press: 28–38.

West, Candace, & Don H. Zimmerman. 1983. "Small insults: A study of interruptions in cross-sex conversations between unaquainted persons." In Barrie Thorne, Cheris Kramarae, & Nancy Henley (eds.), *Language, Gender & Society*. Rowley, MA: Newbury House.

West, Candace, & Sarah Fenstermaker, 1995. "Doing difference." *Gender and Society* 9(1): 8–27.

West, D. J., & David P. Farrington. 1977. *The Delinquent Way of Life*. London: Heinemann.

Westermann, Ted D., & James W. Burfeind. 1991. *Crime and Justice in Two Societies: Japan and the U.S.* Pacific Grove, CA: Brooks/Cole.

Western, Bruce. 1993. "Postwar unionization in 18 advanced capitalist countries." *American Sociological Review* 58: 266–82.

Westoff, Charles F. 1995. "International population policy." *Society* 32(4): 11–15.

Weston, Kath. 1993. "Is 'straight' to 'gay' as 'family' is to 'no family'?" In Anne Minas (ed.), *Gender Basics: Feminist Perspectives on Women and Men*. Belmont, CA: Wadsworth.

Weston, Kath. 1998. *Long Slow Burn: Sexuality and Social Science*. New York: Routledge.

Westphal, David. 1999. "Uninsured ranks up by One Million," *Evansville Courier & Press* (October 4).

Westrum, Ron. 1991. *Technologies and Societies*. Belmont, CA: Wadsworth.

Whalen, William. 1964. *The Latter-Day Saints In the Modern-Day World*. New York: Day.

Wharton, Carol S. 1994. "Finding time for the 'second shift': The impact of flexible work schedules on women's double days." *Sociological Quarterly* 36(2): 189–205.

Wheeler, Stanton, Kenneth Mann, & Austin Sarat. 1988. *Sitting in Judgement: The Sentencing of White-Collar Criminals*. New Haven, CT: Yale University Press.

Wheelock, Anne. 1992. *Crossing the Tracks*. New York: New Press.

Whelan, Carolyn. 1998. "A computer for grandma: Seniors with time and money could be the next big market." *Electronic News* 44 (July 27): 44–5.

Whitaker, Catherine J. 1987. *Elderly Victims*. Bureau of Justice Special Report. Washington, DC: U.S. Government Printing Office.

Whitaker, Mark. 1984. "It was like breathing fire . . ." *Newsweek* (December 17): 26–32.

Whitbourne, Susan K. 1985. *The Aging Body: Physiological Changes and Psychological Consequences*. New York: Springer-Verlag.

White House Domestic Policy Council. 1993. *The President's Report to the American Public*. New York: Simon & Schuster. Health Security: The official text: NY-Touchstone).

White, Jack E. 1997. "I'm just who I am." *Time* (May 5): 32–36.

White, John. 1990. *Black Leadership in America*, 2nd ed. London: Longman.

White, Joseph. 1995. *Competing Solutions: American Health Care Proposals and International Experience*. Washington, DC: The Brookings Institution.

White, Leslie A. 1949. *The Science of Culture: A Study of Man and Civilization*. New York: Grove.

White, Lynn. 1991. "Determinants of divorce: A review of research in the eighties." In Alan Booth (ed.), *Contemporary Families: Looking Forward, Looking Back*. Minneapolis: National Council on Family Relations.

White, Michael, & Malcolm Trevor. 1982. *Under Japanese Management*. New York: Gower.

White, Philip G., & James Gillett. 1994. "Reading the muscular body: A critical decoding of advertising in *Flex* magazine. *Sociology of Sport Journal* 11(1): 18–39.

White, Ralph K., & Ronald O. Lippitt. 1960. *Autocracy & Democracy*. New York: Harper & Bros.

White, Richard W. 1992. *Rude Awakening: What the Homeless Crisis Tells Us*. San Francisco: ICS.

Whiteman, David. 1994. "The poor aren't poorer." *US News & World Report* (July 25): 33–38.

Whittington, Dale. 1992. "What have our 17-years-olds known in the past?" *American Education Research Journal* (winter): 776–78.

Whorf, Benjamin Lee. 1956. *Language, Thought and Reality: Selected Writings of Benjamin Lee Whorf* (J. B. Carroll, ed.). New York: Wiley.

Whyte, William Foote. 1943/1981. *Street Corner Society: Social Structure of an Italian Slum*. Chicago: University of Chicago.

Whyte, William H. 1957. *The Organization Man*. Garden City, New York: Anchor.

Wiatrowski, William J. 1994. "Employee benefits for union and nonunion workers." *Monthly Labor Review* 117: 34–38.

Wicker, Allan W. 1969. "Attitudes versus actions: The relationship between verbal and overt behavioral responses to attitude objects." *Journal of Social Issues* 25(4): 41–78.

Wickrama, K. A. S., & Charles L. Mulford. 1996. "Political democracy, economic development, disarticulation and social well-being in developing countries." *Sociological Quarterly* 37(3): 375–90.

Wickrama, K. A. S., Frederick O. Lorenz, & Rand D. Conger. 1997. "Marital quality and physical illness: A latent growth curve analysis." *Journal of Marriage and the Family* 59(1): 143–55.

Wiesner, Diane. 1992. *Your World, Our Health: The Impact of Environmental Degradation on Human Wellbeing*. Dorset, UK: Prism Press.

Wilbanks, William. 1987. *The Myth of a Racist Criminal Justice System*. Monterey, CA: Brooks/Cole.

Wilcox, Clyde. 1996. *Onward Christian Soldiers: The Religious Right in American Politics*. Boulder, CO: Westview.

Wiles, Charles. 1991. "A comparison of role portrayal of men and women in magazine advertising in the USA and Sweden." *International Journal of Advertising* 10: 259–67.

Wilkes, R. E., & H. Valencia. 1989. "Hispanics and blacks in television commercials." *Journal of Advertising* 18: 19–25.

Wilkie, Janet Riblett. 1993. "Changes in U.S. men's attitudes toward the family provider role, 1972–1989." *Gender & Society* 9(2): 261–79.

Wilkins, Roger. 1995. "The case for affirmative action: Racism has its privileges." *The Nation* (March 27).

Wilkinson, Barry. 1988. "Social engineering in Singapore." *Journal of Contemporary Asia* (18): 165–88.

Wilkinson, David. 1987. "Central civilization." *Comparative Civilization Review* 17: 31–59.

Wilkinson, Ray. 1998. "Human rights, human wrongs." *Refugees* No. 111 (spring): 6–10, 12.

Wilkinson, Richard G. 1996. *Unhealthy Societies: The Afflictions of Inequality*. London: Routledge.

Williams, Andrea S., & James D. Davidson. 1997. "Catholic conceptions of faith: A generational analysis." In Thomas E. Dowdy & Patrick H. McNamara (eds.), *Religion: North American Style*. New Brunswick, NJ: Rutgers University Press: 124–36.

Williams, Carmen Braun. 1993. "The psychology of women." In Jodi Wetzel, Margo Linn Espenlaub, Monys A. Hagen, Annette Bennington McElhiney, & Carmen Braun Williams (eds.), *Women's Studies Thinking Women*. Dubuque, IA: Kendall/Hunt.

Williams, Christine L. 1992. "The glass escalator: Hidden advantages for men in the 'female' professions." *Social Problems* 39(3): 253–67.

Williams, Juanita A., & Arthur Jacoby. 1989. "The effects of premarital heterosexual and homosexual experience on dating and marriage desirability." *Journal of Marriage and the Family* 51: 489–97.

Williams, Kirk, & Susan Drake. 1980. "Social structure, crime and criminalization." *Sociological Quarterly* 21 (Autumn): 563–75.

Williams, Linda S. 1984. "The classic rape: When do victims report? *Social Problems* 31: 459–67.

Williams, Norma. 1990. *The Mexican American Family: Tradition and Change*. Dix Hills, NY: General Hall.

Williams, Norma. 1993. "Elderly Mexican American men: Work and family patterns." In Jane C. Hood (ed.), *Men, Work, and Family*. Newbury Park, CA: Sage.

Williams, R., & Y. Youssef. 1975. "Division of labor in college football along racial lines." *International Journal of Sports Psychology* 6: 3–13.

Williams, Rhys H. & N. J. Demerath III. 1991. "Religion and political process in an American city." *American Sociological Review* 56(4): 417–31.

Williams, Robin M., Jr. 1951. *American Society: A Sociological Interpretation*. New York: Alfred Knopf.

Williams, Walter L. 1986. *The Spirit and the Flesh: Sexual Diversity in American Indian Culture*. Boston: Beacon Press.

Williams, Walter L. 1996. "The berdache tradition." In Karen E. Rosenblum & Toni-Michelle C. Travis (eds.), *The Meaning of Difference: American Constructions of Race, Sex and Gender, Social Class and Sexual Orientation*. New York: McGraw-Hill.

Willie, Charles V. 1991. "Controlled choice: An alternative desegregation plan for minorities who feel betrayed." *Education and Urban Society* 23(2): 200–207.

Willing, Richard. 1999. "Assisted-suicide supporters lament sentence as harsh." *USA Today* (April 14): 1A, 21A.

Willinger, Beth. 1993. "Resistance and change: College men's attitudes toward family and work in the 1980s." In Jane C. Hood (ed.), *Men, Work and Family*. Newbury Park, CA: Sage.

Wilson, Anna V. (ed.), 1993. *Homicide: The Victim/Offender Connection*. Cincinnati: Anderson.

Wilson, Bryan R. 1990. *The Social Dimensions of Sectarianism: Sects and New Religious Movements in Contemporary Society*. New York: Oxford University.

Wilson, Bryan R. 1996. "Religious toleration, pluralism and privatization." In Pal Repstad (ed.), *Religion and Modernity: Modes of Co-existence*. Oslo: Scandinavian University Press: 11–34.

Wilson, Edward O. 1975. *Sociobiology: The New Synthesis*. Princeton, NJ: Princeton University.

Wilson, Francis, & Mamphela Ramphele. 1989. *Uprooting Poverty: The South African Challenge*. New York: Norton.

Wilson, Georgeanna, & Mark Baldassare. 1996. "Overall sense of community in a suburban region: the effects of localism, privacy, and urbanization." *Environment and Behavior* 28: 27–43.

Wilson, Graham. 1989. *Business and Politics* Chatham, NJ: Chatham House.

Wilson, James Q. 1983. *Thinking About Crime*, revised edition. New York: Vintage.

Wilson, James Q., & George Kelling. 1982. Broken windows: The police and neighborhood safety." *Atlantic Monthly* March): 29–38.

Wilson, James Q., & Richard Herrnstein. 1985. *Crime and Human Nature: The Definitive Study of the Causes of Crime*. New York: Simon & Schuster.

Wilson, John. 1973. *Introduction to Social Movements*. New York: Basic.

Wilson, Kenneth L., & Anthony M. Orum. 1976. "Mobilizing people for collective action." *Journal of Political and Military Sociology* 4: 187–202.

Wilson, P. J. 1977. "The problem with simple folk." *Natural History* (December): 26–32.

Wilson, Stan Le Roy. 1995. *Mass Media/Mass Culture: An Introduction*. New York: McGraw-Hill.

Wilson, William Julius. 1987. *The Truly Disadvantaged: The Inner City, the Underclass and Public Policy*. Chicago: University of Chicago Press.

Wilson, William Julius. 1989. "The underclass: Issues, perspectives and public policy." *The Annals* 501: 182–192.

Wilson, William Julius. 1990. "Race-neutral programs and the democratic coalition." *The American Prospect* 1: 75–81.

Wilson, William Julius. 1991. "Studying inner-city social dislocations." *American Sociological Review* 56: 1–14.

Wilson, William Julius. 1996. *When Work Disappears*. New York: Random House.

Wimberley, Dale E. 1990. "Investment dependence and alternative explanations of Third World mortality: A cross-national study." *American Sociological Review* 55(1): 75–91.

Winch, Robert. 1971. *The Modern Family*. New York: Holt.

Wink, P., & R. Helson. 1993. "Personality change in women and their partners." *Journal of Personality and Social Psychology* 65: 597–606.

Winkelby, Marilyn A., Darius E. Jatulis, Erica Frank, & Stephen P. Fortmann. 1992. "Socioeconomic status and health: How education, income and occupation contribute to risk factors for cardiovascular disease." *American Journal of Public Health* 82: 816–20.

Winkler, Anne E. 1993. "The living arrangements of single mothers with dependent children: An added perspective." *The American Journal of Economics and Sociology* 52(1): 1–18.

Winkler, Anne E. 1995. "The living arrangements of single mothers with dependent children: An added perspective." *American Journal of Economics and Sociology* 52: 1–18.

Winnick, Louis. 1990. "America's 'model minority.'" *Commentary* 90 (August): 22–29.

Wirth, Louis. 1938. "Urbanism as a way of life." *American Journal of Sociology*. 44(1): 1–24.

Wirth, Louis. 1945. "The problem of minority groups." In Ralph Linton (ed.), *The Science of Man In the World Crisis*. New York: Columbia University Press: 347–72.

Wittfogel, Karl. 1957. *Oriental Despotism: A Comparative Study of Total Power*. New Haven, CT: Yale University Press.

Wolf, Eric R. 1983. *Europe & the People Without a History*. Berkeley: University of California Press.

Wolf, Margery. 1972. *Women and the Family in Rural Taiwan*. Stanford, CA: Stanford University.

Wolf, Naomi. 1991. *The Beauty Myth: How Images of Beauty Are Used Against Women*. New York: William Morrow.

Wolfe, Leanna. 1993. *Women Who May Never Marry*. Atlanta, GA: Longstreet.

Wolff, Edward N. 1995. *Top Heavy: A Study of the Increasing Inequality of Wealth in America*. New York: Twentieth Century Fund.

Wolfgang, Marvin E., & Marc Reidel. 1973. "Race, judicial discretion, and the death penalty." *The Annals* 407: 119–133.

Wolfgang, Marvin E., & Frances Ferracuti. 1981. *The Subculture of Violence*. Beverly Hills: Sage.

Wolfgang, Marvin F., Terence P. Thornberry, & Robert M. Figlio. 1987. *From Boy to Man, From Delinquency to Crime*. Chicago: University of Chicago Press.

Woloch, Nancy. 1994. *Women and the American Experience*. New York: McGraw-Hill.

Wolpert, Stanley. 1991. *India*. Berkeley: University of California Press.

Womack, Mari. 1992. "Why athletes need ritual: A study of magic among professional athletes." In Shirl J. Hoffman (ed.), *Sport and Religion*. Champaign, IL: Human Kinetics Books.

Women's Equality Poll, 1995. *Feminist Majority Report* 7(2): 1,12–13.

Woo, Deborah. 1985. "The socioeconomic status of Asian-American women in the labor force." *Sociological Perspectives* 28: 307–28.

Wood, Charles, & Jose de Carvalho. 1988. *The Demography of Inequality in Brazil*. Cambridge, England: Cambridge University Press.

Wood, Julia T. 1994. *Gendered Lives: Communication, Gender and Culture*. Belmont, CA: Wadsworth.

Wood, Lawrence D. 1996. "Alone among its peers." In Robert Heiner (ed.), *Criminology: A Cross-Cultural Perspective*. St. Paul: West: 197–212.

Woods, Nancy Fugate. 1995. "Women and their health." In C.I. Fogel & F.G. Woods (eds.), *Women's Health Care: A Comprehensive Handbook*. Thousand Oaks, CA: Sage: 1–22.

Woolfolk, Alan. 1995. "A house divided? Diagnosing the American kulturkampf." *Qualitative Sociology* 18(4): 487–93.

Worell, Judith. 1996. "Feminist identity in a gendered world." In Joan C. Chrisler, Carla Golden, & Patricia D. Rozee (eds.), *Lectures on the Psychology of Women*. New York: McGraw-Hill.

Work Week. 1996. "A special news report about life on the job—and trends taking place there." *Wall Street Journal* (June 4): A1.

World Bank. 1995. *World Development Report 1995*. London: Oxford University Press.

World Commission on Environment and Development. 1987. *Our Common Future (Brundtland Report)*. New York: Oxford University.

World Education League. 1997. "Who's top?" *The Economist* (March 29): 21–23.

World Health Organization. 1995. *The World Health Report 1995: Bridging the Gaps*. Geneva: World Health Organization.

World Health Organization. 1998. *The World Health Report, 1998: Global Health Situation and Trends, 1955–2025*. Geneva: World Health Organization.

World Resources Institute. 1996. *World Resources 1996–97*. Oxford, UK: Oxford University.

Worrell, Judith. 1996. "Feminist identity in a gendered world." In Joan C. Chrisler, Carla Golden, & Patricia D. Rozee (eds.), *Lectures on the Psychology of Women*. New York: McGraw-Hill.

Worsley, Peter. 1984. *The Three Worlds*. Chicago: University of Chicago Press.

Worsnop, R. 1996. "Helping the homeless." *CQ Researcher* (January 26).

Wright, Erik Olin. 1979. *Class, Crisis and the State*. London: Verso.

Wright, Eric Olin. 1985. *Classes*. London: Verso.

Wright, Eric Olin. 1989. *The Debate on Classes*. New York: Verso.

Wright, Eric R. 1995. "Personal networks and anomie." *Sociological Focus* (28/3): 261–282.

Wright, Eric Olin, & Bill Martin. 1987. "The transformation of the American class structure, 1960–1980." *American Journal of Sociology* 93/1: 1–29.

Wright, Erik Olin, David Hachen, Cynthia Castello, & Joey Spoogne. 1982. "The American class structure." *American Sociological Review* 47: 709–726.

Wright, J. D., P. H. Rossi, & K. Daly. 1983. *Under the Gun: Weapons, Crime and Violence in America*. Chicago: Aldine.

Wright, James D., Joseph F. Sheley, & M. Dwayne Smith. 1992. "Kids, guns, and killing fields." *Society* 30 (December).

Wright, Lawrence. 1994. "One drop of blood." *New Yorker* (July 25).

Wright, Sam. 1978. *Crowds and Riots*. Beverly Hills, CA: Sage.

Wrong, Dennis H. 1959. "The functional theory of stratification: Some neglected considerations." *American Sociological Review* 24: 772–82.

Wrong, Dennis H. 1961. "The over-socialized conception of man in modern sociology." *American Sociological Review* 26: 185–193.

Wu, Zheng, & T. R. Balakrishnan. 1994. "Cohabitation after marital disruption in Canada." *Journal of Marriage and the Family* 56: 723–34.

Wu, Zheng. 1995. "Premarital cohabitation and postmarital cohabiting union formation." *Journal of Family Issues* 16(2): 212–32.

Wuthnow, Robert, Virginia A. Hodgkinson et al., eds. 1990. *Faith and Philanthropy in America: Exploring the Role of Religion in America's Voluntary Sector*. San Francisco: Jossey-Bass.

Wuthnow, Robert. 1988. *The Restructuring of American Religion: Society and Faith Since World War II*. Princeton: Princeton University Press.

Wuthnow, Robert. 1989. *Communities of Discourse: Ideology and Social Structure in the Reformation*. Cambridge, MA: Harvard University Press.

Wuthnow, Robert. 1989. *The Struggle for America's Soul: Evangelicals, Liberals, and Secularism*. Grand Rapids, MI: William B, Eerdmans.

Wuthnow, Robert. 1993. *Christianity in the Twenty-First Century: Reflections on the Challenges Ahead*. New York: Oxford University Press.

Wuthnow, Robert. 1994. *Sharing the Journey: Support Groups and America's New Quest for Community*. New York: Free Press.

www.ruckus.org.

Wysocki, Bernard Jr. 1988. "Stressful system: In Japan, they even have cram schools for the cram schools." *Wall Street Journal* (January 13): 1.

Xu, Wu, & Ann Leffler. 1992. "Gender and race effects on occupational prestige, segregation, and earnings." *Gender and Society* 6: 376–92.

Yanagishita, Machiko, & Landis MacKellar. 1995. "Homicide in the United States: Who's at risk?" *Population Today.* (23/2): 1–2.

Yang, Alan S. 1997. "Attitudes toward homosexuality." *Public Opinion Quarterly* 61: 477–507.

Yeatts, Dale E. 1991. "Self-managed work teams: Innovation in progress." *Business & Economic Quarterly* (Fall/Winter): 2–6.

Yellen, John E. 1994. "The transformation of the Kalahari !Kung." In Elvio Angeloni (ed.), *Anthropology 93/94.* Guilford, CT: Dushkin.

Yellowbird, Michael, & C. Matthew Snipp. 1994. "American Indian families." In Ronald L. Taylor (ed.), *Minority Families in the United States: A Multicultural Perspective.* Upper Saddle River, NJ: Prentice Hall.

Yeung, Yue-man. 1996. "An Asian perspective on the global city." *International Social Science Journal* 48: 25–31.

Yeung, Yue-man. 1997. "Geography in the age of mega-cities." *International Social Science Journal* 49: 91–104.

Yinger, J. Milton. 1957. *Religion, Society and the Individual.* New York: Macmillan.

Yinger, J. Milton. 1970. *The Scientific Study of Religion.* New York: Macmillan.

Yinger, J. Milton. 1985. "Assimilation in the United States: The Mexican Americans." In W. Connor (ed.), *Mexican Americans in Comparative Perspective.* Washington, DC: Urban Institute Press: 30–55.

Yinger, Milton. 1994. Ethnicity: Source of Strength? Source of Conflict? Albany, NY: State University of New York.

Yllo, Kersti. 1993. "Through a feminist lens: Gender, power, and violence." In Richard J. Gelles & D. R. Loseke (eds.), *Current Controversies on Family Violence.* Newbury Park, CA: Sage.

Yllo, Kersti. 1994. "The status of women, marital equality and violence against wives: A contextual analysis." *Journal of Family Issues* 5: 307–20.

Yoder, Janice D. 1999. *Women and Gender: Transforming Psychology.* Upper Saddle River, NJ: Prentice Hall.

Yoels, William C., Jeffrey Michael Clair, Ferris J. Ritchey, & Richard M. Allman. 1993. "Role-taking accuracy in medical encounters: A test of two theories." *Sociological Focus* 26(3): 183–201.

Young, Gay, Vidyamali Samarasinghe, & Ken Kusterer (eds.). 1993. *Women at the Center: Development Issues and Practices for the 1990s.* West Hartford, CT: Kumarian.

Young, James Harvey. 1992. *American Health Quackery.* Princeton, NJ: Princeton University.

Young, Lawrence A. (ed.). 1997. *Rational Choice Theory and Religion: Summary and Assessment.* New York: Routledge.

Young, T. R. 1975. "Karl Marx and alienation." *Humboldt Journal of Social Relations* (2/2): 26–33.

Yu, E. 1982. "The low mortality rate of Chinese infants: Some plausible explanatory factors." *Social Science and Medicine* 16: 253–65.

Zablocki, B. 1980. *Alienation and Charisma: A Study of Contemporary American Communes.* New York: Free Press.

Zakaria, Fouad. 1986. "The standpoint of contemporary Muslim fundamentalists." In Nahid Toubia (ed.), *Women of the Arab World: The Coming Challenge.* London: Zed.

Zald, Mayer N. 1992. "Looking backward to look forward." In Aldon D. Morris & Carol M. Mueller (eds.), *Frontiers in Social Movement Theory.* New Haven, CT: Yale University Press: 326–48.

Zald, Mayer N., & John D. McCarthy (eds.). 1987. *Social Movements in an Organizational Society.* New Brunswick, NJ: Transaction.

Zald, Mayer N., & Roberta Ash. 1966. "Social movement organizations: Growth, decay and change." *Social Forces* 44: 327–41.

Zambrana, Ruth E. 1994. "Puerto Rican families and social well-being." In Maxine Baca Zinn & Bonnie Thornton Dill (eds.), *Women of Color in U.S. Society.* Philadelphia: Temple University.

Zamir, Shamoon. 1995. *Dark Voices: W. E. B. DuBois & American Thought, 1888–1903.* Chicago: University of Chicago Press.

Zaret, David. 1996. "Petitions and the 'Invention' of public opinion in the English revolution." *American Journal of Sociology* 101: 1487–1555.

Zarit, S. H. 1980. *Aging and Mental Disorders: Psychological Approaches to Assessment and Treatment.* New York: Free Press.

Zedlewski, Sheila R., Roberta O. Barnes, Martha R. Burt, Timothy D. McBride, & Jack A. Meyer. 1990. *The Needs of the Elderly in the 21st Century.* Washington, DC: Urban Institute Press.

Zelizer, Viviana A. 1991. "From baby farms to Baby M." In Mark Hutter (ed.), *The Family Experience: A Reader in Cultural Diversity.* New York: Macmillan.

Zelman, Walter A. 1976. "The sports people play." *Parks & Recreation* 11: 27–38.

Zenie-Ziegler, Wedad. 1988. *In Search of Shadows: Conversations with Egyptian Women.* London: Zed.

Zhang, Xiaouri 1996. "Traditional medicine and WHO." *World Health* 49: 4–5.

Ziegler, Dominic. 1997. "City life." *Economist.* 342: 17–18.

Zimbalist, Andrew. 1992. *Baseball and Billions.* New York: Basic Books.

Zimbardo, Philip G. 1972. "Pathology of imprisonment." *Society* 9: 4–8.

Zippay, A. 1991. *From Middle Income to Poor: Downward Mobility Among Displaced Steelworkers.* New York: Praeger.

Zoglin, Richard. 1996. "Chips ahoy!" *Time* (February 19).

Zola, Irving Kenneth. 1990. "Medicine as an institution of social control." In Peter Conrad & Rochelle Kern (eds.), *The Sociology of Health and Illness: Critical Perspectives.* New York: St. Martin's: 398–408.

Zuboff, Shoshana. 1982. "New worlds of computer mediated work." *Harvard Business Review* (60/5): 142–52.

Zuboff, Shoshana. 1988. *In the Age of the Smart Machine.* New York: Basic.

Zuckerman, Diana M., & Donald H. Sayre. 1982. "Cultural sex-role expectations and children's sex-role concepts." *Sex Roles* 8: 853–62.

Zuckerman, M., & S. C. Kieffer. 1994. "Race differences in face-ism: Does facial prominence imply dominance?" *Journal of Personality and Social Psychology* 66: 86–92.

Zuckerman, Mortimer B. 1995. "Forest Gump vs. Ice-T," *U.S. News & World Report* (July 24).

Zweigenhaft, Richard L., & G. William Domhoff. 1991. *Blacks in the White Establishment? A Study of Race and Class in America.* New Haven, CT: Yale University Press.

Zwerling, L. Steven. 1996. "Expanding external support for at-risk students." In Laura I. Rendon & Richard O. Hope (eds.), *Educating a New Majority: Transforming America's Educational System for Diversity.* San Francisco: Jossey-Bass: pp. 372–389.

Zygmunt, Joseph E. 1986. "Collective behavior as a phase of societal life." *Research in Social Movements, Conflict and Change* 9: 25–46.

PHOTO CREDITS

Market, 389; Bob Daemmrich/Stock Boston, 390; Michael Newman/PhotoEdit, 391; Jack Star/PhotoDisc, Inc., 394; Bachmann/PhotoEdit, 395; Parsons, Jack/Omni-Photo Communications, Inc., 397; (c) 1991 Donna Ferrato/Domestic Abuse Awareness Project (NYC), 398; Chris Maynard/Liaison Agency, Inc., 400 (left); Laura Dwight/PhotoEdit, 400 (right).

Chapter 16 Peter Vander Mark/Stock Boston, 402; Corbis/Laura Dwight, 405; Will Faller, 406; John Giordano/Saba/Corbis/SABA Press Photos, Inc., 409; Corbis/Bob Rowan, Progressive Image, 411; Will Hart, 412; Dr. Linda Lindsey, 413; David Rentas/*New York Post*, 416; Barbara Stitzer/PhotoEdit, 417; Mancuso, Michael/Omni-Photo Communications, Inc., 419; Michael Newman/PhotoEdit, 423; Dr. Linda Lindsey, 427 (left and right).

Chapter 17 Corbis/Francoise de Mulder, 430; Corbis/Annie Griffiths Belt, 433; Corbis/David Turnley, 434 (left); Corbis/Bettmann, 434 (right); Mark C. Burnett/Photo Researchers, Inc., 435; First United Methodist Church of Webster Groves, 436; Corbis/Dave Bartruff, 437; Internet/AP/Wide World Photos, 438; Corbis/AFP, 442; Corbis/Brian Vikander, 443; Corbis/Sergio Dorantes, 445; AP/Wide World Photos, 448; Corbis/Phil Schermeister, 451; Corbis/Bettmann, 453; Corbis/Philip Gould, 455; Corbis/Wally McNamee, 456.

Chapter 18 Corbis/Steve Chenn, 458; Corbis/Bob Krist, 460; Corbis/Wally McNamee, 461; Corbis/Bettmann, 462; AP/Wide World Photos, 464; Corbis/Ed Eckstein, 465; David Woo/Liaison Agency, Inc., 469; Mark Richards/PhotoEdit, 470; Corbis/AFP, 472; Elise Amendola/AP/Wide World Photos, 474; Alondra_Reporteros_Asociados/Hulton Getty, 480.

Chapter 19 Doug Menuez/PhotoDisc, Inc., 482; Chang Hongen/World Health Organization, 486; CORBIS/Alison Wright, 491; CORBIS/Peter Turnley, 497; Corbis/Philip James Corwin, 487; J.T. Miller/The Stock Market, 489; AP/Wide World Photos, 499 (top); Dana Fisher/AP/Wide World Photos, 499 (bottom); Robert Harbison, 504; Paul Conklin/PhotoEdit, 506; Corbis Digital Stock, 507.

Chapter 20 Jamie Squire/Allsport Photography (USA), Inc., 512; Corbis/James Marshall, 514; Jose Carrillo/PhotoEdit, 515; Corbis/Owen Franken, 516; Lawrence M. Sawyer/PhotoDisc, Inc., 518; Peter Byron/Photo Researchers, Inc., 522; Corbis, 524 (top left), CORBIS/S. Carmona, 524 (bottom left); Corbis/Kevin R. Morris, 524 (right); Corbis/Bob Krist, 525 (top); Dr. Stephen Beach, 525 (bottom); Corbis/Michael Brennan, 531.

Chapter 21 Porterfield/Chickering/Photo Researchers, Inc., 536; Andy Holbrooke/Corbis/Stock Market, 542; Chuck O'Rear/Woodfin Camp & Associates, 547; Leland Bobbe/Stone, 551; Corbis/SABA Press Photos, Inc., 556; David Young-Wolff/PhotoEdit, 554; Saint Louis Post-Dispatch, 559; Lynchburg Police Department, 560 (top); Mark Richards/PhotoEdit, 560 (bottom).

Chapter 22 Walter Hodges/Stone , 564; Corbis/Nathan Benn, 570; Corbis/Layne Kennedy, 571 (left); Corbis/ Macduff Everton, 571 (right); Mark Cardwell/Reuters/ Corbis, 572; Cobris/Michael S. Yamashita, 573; Doug Menuez/PhotoDisc, Inc., 574; PhotoDisc, Inc., 578; Corbis/Sergio Dorantes, 579; The Metropolitan Museum of Art, 581; Corbis/Lee Snider, 583; Seitz, Blair/Photo Researchers, Inc., 584; Tony Freeman/PhotoEdit, 587.

Chapter 23 Chris Pizzello/AP/Wide World Photos, 590; Corbis/Peter Turnley, 593; Corbis/Bettmann, 595; Richard Baillie/AP/Wide World Photos, 596; Jim Pickerell/Stock Boston, 597 (top); Nick Didlick/Reuters/Corbis, 597 (bottom); Corbis/AFP, 599; Tomi/PhotoDisc., 600; Keiser/AP/Wide World Photos, 604; Corbis/AFP, 606; Erich Hartmann/Magnum Photos, Inc., 609; Corbis/Wally McNamee, 611.

Chapter 24 Philippe Maille-Explorer/Photo Researchers, Inc., 614; Mike Theiler/Reuters/Corbis, 618 (top); Corbis/Henry Diltz, 618 (bottom left); Corbis, 618 (bottom right); Dario Lopez-Mills/AP/Wide World Photos, 620; Liaison Agency, Inc., 621; A. Tannenbaum-Sygma, 624; Corbis/Charles O'Rear, 630; Corbis/AFP, 633; Dr. Linda Lindsey, 634.

NAME INDEX

SUBJECT INDEX

Goal displacement, 570, 609
Goals 2000 program, 427
Goal succession, 570
God, belief in existence of, 62
Goodall, Jane, 69
Grameen Bank of Bangladesh, 615
Grandparenting, 368
Gray Panthers, 374
Green revolution, 555
Group dynamics, 93–97
  conformity, 96
  decision making, 96–97
  leadership, 94–96
  size, 93–94
Groupthink, 97
Guest workers in Germany, 316

Hawthorne effect, 42
Health and health care, 482–511
  alternative medicine in U.S., 502–504
    holistic health, 503–504
  health and disease, defining and measuring, 484
    social epidemiology, 484
    techniques, 484
  health care crisis, 504–510
    cost and access, 505–508
    organization, 508
    reform, 508–510
  health in U.S.: links to diversity, 497–502
    demographics of morbidity, 500–501
    demographics of mortality, 497–500
    mental illness, 501–502
  international health, challenge of, 491–497
    developed world, 494–496
    developing world, 492–494
    global interdependence, 496–497
  sociological perspectives, 484–491
    conflict, 487–490
    functionalist, 485–487
    symbolic interactionism, 490–491
Health care crisis, 504–510
  cost and access, 505–508
    Medicaid, 507–508
    Medicare, 507
  organization, 508
  reform, 508–510
    Canada's health care system, 509
    Clinton health plan, 509
    Health for All, 509–510
    managed care, 508–509
Health for All 2000, 509–510
Health maintenance organizations (HMOs), 508
Heaven's Gate cult, 431
Hermaphrodites, 164–165
Heterosexual, 166
Hidden curriculum, 130, 408
Hijras, 168
Hinduism, 442–443
Hispanic Americans, 311–312
  families in multicultural perspective, 393–396
  TV's forgotten minority, 521
Holistic, 484
Holocaust, 302
Homogamy, 384
Homophobia, 170
Homosexual, 166
Horatio Alger myth, 240
Human capital model, 335
Human relations approach, 572–573
Human rights, 81
  new consensus on, 632–634
Humor
  cultural differences in, 68–69
Hypergamy, 385
Hypodermic model, 514
Hypothesis, 33

I and me concepts, 114
Ideal type, 567
Ideological hegemony, 240
Ideology, 11
Immanent, 619
Immigration, 306–308
Impression management, 144–145

Incidence, 484
Index crimes, 213
Industrial Revolution, 13
Infant mortality rate (IMR), 484, 538
Informal sector, 629
Informal social control, 190
Informed consent and need to know, 55–56
Inquisitorial principle, 223
Insanity defense, 134–136
Institutional sexism, 158
Institutions, 98
Instrumental role, 379
Internalization of norms, 190
International health, challenge of, 491–497
  developed world, 494–496
  developing world, 491–494
  global interdependence: health and technology, 496–497
Internet
  globalization and social inequality, 107–108
Intimate distance, 66–67
Iron law of oligarchy, 571
Islam, 440–441
Isolation, cases of, 111

Japan
  crime rates in, 215–216
  examination hell in, 426
  gender inequality in, 3
  minorities in, 315
Japanese model, 573–574
Japanese Style Management (JSM), 337
J-curve, 602
Job satisfaction, 585
Judaism, 441–442
  Jewish diversity, 452–453
    social class and social issues, 452
    theology, 452–453

Kibbutz, 382
Kuznets curve, 244

Labeling theory, 202–205
Labor market
  primary, 302
  secondary, 302
  split, 302
Language, 64–69
  and gender, 67–68
  of laughter, 68–69
  nonverbal communication, 66–67
  and thought, 65–66
Latent functions, 20
Laws, 63
Leaders, types of, 94–95
  authoritarian, 94–95
  democratic, 95
  expressive, 94
  instrumental, 94
  laissez-faire, 95
Leakage, 149
Leakey, Louis, 69
Legal protection/continued discrimination, 304
Liberalism, 462–463
  modern, 463
Liberation theology, 435
Libido, 116
Life course, critical review of, 128–129
Life expectancy rate (LER), 484
Little League and moral socialization, 526–527
Living arrangements and aging, 365–367
  institutionalization, 367
  range of housing alternatives, 366–367
Lombardi ethic, 518
Long-term care facilities (LTCFs), 367
Looking-glass self, 113

Machismo, 170
Macrosociological perspective, 18
Mafia or Cosa Nostra, 218–219
Magazines and advertising
  gendered messages in, 339–341
Magnet schools, 418
Mainstreaming, 411

Managed care, 508–509
Managed competition, 509
Manifest functions, 20
Marriage forms and residence patterns, global
  perspective of, 381–382
Marriage relationship in later life, 367–368
  remarriage, 368
Marxist exploitation theory, 302
Mass hysteria, 598–599
Mass society theory, 602
Master status, 87, 297
Material culture, 60
Mate selection, 384–386
  age and race, 384–385
  gender, 385–386
  marriage squeeze, 385, 394
Matrilineal descent, 379
Matrilocal residence, 382
McDonaldization, 625
Means-tested welfare efforts, 286
  antidestitution programs, 286
  antipoverty programs, 286
Measurement (in research process), 35–36
Measures commonly used in research, 39
Mechanical solidarity, 99
Media
  as agent of socialization, 131–132
Media and sport, 512–535
  censorship and electronic media, 533–534
  mass media, 519–523
    film, 522–523
    popular music, 523
    television, 519–522
  recreation, sociological perspectives on, 513–519
    conflict interpretation of media and sport, 517–518
    functions of media and sport, 513–519
    hypodermic model, 514–517
    symbolic interactionism and cultural studies, 518–519
  sport, 523–528
    dark side of, 528–533
    and the media, 528
    and religion, 526–528
    and social stratification, 524–526
Medicaid, 507–508
Medicalization of deviance, 207
Medical model, 206
Medicare, 507
Megalopolis, 547
Melting pot model, 304
Men's images in media, 340
  advertising, 340
  television, 340
Mental illness, 501–502
  as deviant behavior, 205–207
Meritocracy, 406
Metropolitan area, 547
Metropolitan Statistical Area (MSA), 548
Microenterprise programs, 630–632
Microsociological perspective, 18
Migration rate, 538
Milgram, Stanley, 31–32
Minority-dominant group relations, 302–306
  assimilation, 304–305
  expulsion and population transfer, 303
  genocide, 302–303
  legal protection/continued discrimination, 304
  minority responses, 305–306
  open subjugation, 303–304
  pluralism, 305
Minority groups, 295–297
Misogyny, 341
Mixed economies, 465–466
Modernity, 622
Modernization, 622
Modernization theory, 258
Monogamy, 381
Monotheism, 436
Morbidity
  demographics of, 500–501
    gender, 500
    SES and race, 500–501

Rape, myths of, table, 179
Rational choice theory, 196
  and religion, 435
Rationality, 569
Rationalization, 569
Recidivism, 134
Relative deprivation theory, 602–603
Relative poverty, 277
Reliability, 36
Religion, 430–457
  being religious in the United States, 447–448
    challenges to secularization, 447
    measuring religiosity, 448
  challenges to religious pluralism, 453–456
    New Christian Right, 454–455
    secularization or religious resurgence, 455–456
  religious beliefs and organization, 435–439
    expressions of religious belief, 436
    types of religious organization, 436–439
  religious diversity, 448–453
    Catholic, 450–452
    Jewish, 452–453
    Protestant, 449–450
  sport and, 526–528
  theoretical perspectives, 432–435
    conflict theory and social change, 434–435
    functionalism, 432
    functions of religion, 432–434
    rational choice theory, 435
  world religions and social change, 439–447
    Christianity, 440
    ethicalist religions: Buddhism and Confucianism, 443
    global fundamentalism, 444–447
    Hinduism, 442–443
    Islam, 440–441
    Judaism, 441–442
Religious institutions, 132
Religious law, 213
Religious organization, types of, 436–439
Religious pluralism, 432
Remarriage, 389
Repression, 609
Repression-medicalization-acceptance cycle, 207–208
Reputational approach (to identifying class), 268–269
Research design, choice of, 36–38
Research process, 30–57
  ethics of research, 53–56
    informed consent and need to know, 55–56
    losing self-identity, 53–54
    observing very private behavior, 54–55
    Tuskegee experiment, 55
  research design, 39–52
    experimental design, 40–42
    field research, 49–52
    secondary research, 47–49
    surveys, 43–47
  and the science of sociology, 32–33
  steps in, 33–39
    analyzing and interpreting data, 38–39
    choosing a research design, 36–38
    collecting data, 38
    evaluating results, 39
    formulating the problem, 34–35
    measurement, 35–36
Residual deviance, 206
Resocialization, 134
Resource-mobilization theory, 603–604
Response rate, 45
Retirement, 364–365
Retrospective reinterpretation, 203
Ridicule, 609
Rites of passage, 125
Rock 'n' roll, sex, drugs, and deviance, 186–187
Roe v. Wade, 345
Role, 89–90
  conflict, 89
  distance, 90
  embracement, 90
  engulfment, 204
  expectations, 89

making, 89
performance, 89
set, 89
strain, 89
-taking, 114
Roman Catholic Church, 13
Routinization of charisma, 462
Ruling class model, 467, 471–472
  candidate-selection process, 471
  ideological process, 471
  policy planning process, 471
  special interest process, 471
Rumors, 598
  gossip, 598
  urban legends, 598
Rwanda, genocide in, 479

Sacred, 432
Sample, 37
Sanctions, 63
Sapir-Whorf hypothesis, 65
Scapegoats, 300
Schema, 118
Scientific management, 572
Scientific method, 32
Secondary aging, 350–351
Secondary deviance, 203
Secondary labor market, 576
  problems in, 577–578
    globalization, 577
    unions, declining strength of, 577–578
Secondary research, 47–49
  content analysis, 48–49
  documentary methods, assessing, 49
  unobtrusive measures, 49
Second World, 256
Sect, 437
Sector concept, 549
Sectors of the economy, 575
Secularization, 431
Secular religion, 436
Segregation, 304
Self, 113
Self-fulfilling prophecy, 145, 197
Self-labeling, 203
Seniorcitizen.com, 370
Senior power, 373–374
Separatism, 306
Serial monogamy, 389
Sex, 164
Sexism, 322
  in sport, 531–533
Sex reassignment surgery (SRS), 165, 166–167
Sexual dimorphism
Sexual harassment, 157–158
Sexuality, 160–183
  attitudes and behaviors, 172–176
    gendered sexuality, 173–176
    in later life, 176
  in diverse world, 162–164
  in later life, 176
  macrolevel perspectives, 176–177
    conflict theory, 177
    functionalism, 177
  sex and the college student, 177–180
    exploring sex, 178
    nonconsensual sex, 178–180
  sex for profit, 180–182
    pornography, 180–181
    prostitution, 181–182
  sexual orientation, 165–172
    continuum of, 167–168
    definitions, problems with, 166
    discrimination and diversity, 169–172
    global patterns, 168–169
    transsexuals, 169
  as socially constructed, 164–165
    defining sex, gender, sexual orientation, 164
    gender identity, 164–165
Sexual orientation, 164, 165–172, 322
Sexual scripts, 165
Shamans, 101
Significant others, 114
Singlehood, 390

Single-parent families, 390–392
Slavery, 244, 303
Social breakdown syndrome, 362
Social capital, 623
Social change, 12–13
Social change and development, 614–635
  definition of, 615–616
  great transformation, 622–623
  human rights, new consensus on, 632–634
  microenterprise, 630–632
  social change in the developed world, 623–625
    updating Durkheim, 623–624
    updating Marx, 624–625
    updating Weber, 625
  social change in the developing world, 626–630
    foreign aid, capitalism, and democracy, 626–628
    global economy, 628–630
  sources of social change, 616–619
    competition and war, 619
    demographic change, 617
    government, 619
    institutionalized social change, 619
    natural environment, 616–617
    new ideas, 617–618
    new technologies, 618–619
    social movements, 619
  theoretical perspectives on social change, 619–622
    conflict theory, 622
    cyclical theory, 619–620
    evolutionary theory, 620–621
    functional theory, 621–622
Social class, 239
Social class in modern societies, 266–291
  differences between classes, 283–286
    life chances, 283–284
    lifestyles, 284–286
  measuring class, 267–269
    dual earner households, 269
    objective approach, 269
    reputational approach, 268–269
    subjective approach, 268
    occupational prestige, 271–272
  poverty, 277–280
    explaining, 278–280
    identity of poor, 278
    number of poor, 277
  property, 269–271
  social mobility, 280–283
  U.S. class system, 272–277
    lower-middle class, 274
    "underclass," 276–277
    upper class, 273–274
    upper-middle class, 274
    working class, 274–275
    working poor, 275–276
  welfare, 286–290
Social construction of reality, 140
Social control, 189–190
Social Darwinism, 16, 247–248
Social groups, 90
  in-groups and out-groups, 92
  primary and secondary, 91–92
  reference, 93
Social identity, 113
Social institutions, 11
Social institutions, gendered, 329–337
  education, 330–333
    elementary school, 331–332
    higher education, 333
    high school, 332–333
    kindergarten, 331
    Title IX, 333
  family life, 329–330
  workplace, 333–337
    management styles: partnership alternative, 337
    wage gap, 334–336
    women in business, 336–337
Social integration, 7
Social interaction, 138–159
  constructing social class on U.S. television, 152
    class as socially constructed, 154–156